Regulation of Lawyers: Statutes and Standards

2003 Edition

Regulation of Lawyers: Statutes and Standards

2003 Edition

Stephen Gillers
Vice Dean and Professor of Law
New York University

Roy D. Simon
Professor of Law
Hofstra University

1185 Avenue of the Americas, New York, NY 10036
www.aspenpublishers.com

Permissions
Aspen Publishers
1185 Avenue of the Americas
New York, NY 10036

Printed in the United States of America

ISBN 0-7355-2879-9

Summary of Contents

Acknowledgments vii
Introduction to the Regulation of Lawyers xi

Model Codes and Standards 1

ABA Model Rules of Professional Conduct 3
Restatement of the Law Governing Lawyers 497
ABA Model Code of Professional Responsibility 557
ABA Standards for Criminal Justice: The Prosecution Function; The Defense Function 591
ABA Code of Judicial Conduct (1990) 621

Attorney-Client Privilege and Work Product Provisions 663

Federal Rules of Evidence 666
Federal Rules of Civil Procedure 668
New York Civil Practice Law and Rules 670
Arizona Revised Statutes 672
California Evidence Code 673
California Code of Civil Procedure 678

Federal Statutes and Regulations 681

Federal Provisions on Conflicts, Confidentiality, and Crimes 683
Statutes on Disqualification and Discipline of Federal Judges 709

California Materials 719

California Rules of Professional Conduct 721
Selected California Statutes 767

District of Columbia Materials **821**

District of Columbia Rules of Professional Conduct 823

New York Materials **937**

New York Code of Professional Responsibility 939
Selected Provisions of the New York Judiciary Law 1029

Special Section: Some Legal Ethics Issues in the Enron Investigation **1047**

Acknowledgments

The authors appreciate the time and effort of the following people who helped the authors keep this book accurate and up-to-date: Jeanne Gray, Director of the ABA Center for Professional Responsibility; Joanne Pitulla, formerly Assistant Ethics Counsel to the ABA Standing Committee on Ethics and Professional Responsibility; George Kuhlman, Ethics Counsel, and Eileen Libby, Associate Ethics Counsel to the ABA Standing Committee on Ethics and Professional Responsibility; ABA Staff Counsel Susan Hillenbrand; Bruce Green, a professor at Fordham Law School who served as Reporter for the ABA Commission on Multijurisdictional Practice, and John Holtaway, the Staff Counsel for that Commission; Carol Weiss and David Brent, both of whom held various positions at the ABA Center for Professional Responsibility; Donna Spilis, Staff Director of the ABA Commission on Lawyer Assistance Programs; Nancy Coleman, Director of the ABA Commission on Legal Problems of the Elderly; Barrie Althoff of the Washington State Bar Association; Tom Smith, Staff Counsel to the ABA Section on Criminal Justice; Randall Difuntorum, Larry Doyle, Ann Wassam, and Mengesha Wondaferow of the California State Bar; Chief Justice E. Norman Veasey of the Delaware Supreme Court and his secretary Carol Miller; Becky Stretch, Special Counsel to the ABA Ethics 2000 Commission; Michael Albano and Arthur Balbirer, past presidents of the American Academy of Matrimonial Lawyers, and Lorraine West, its Executive Director; David Isbell of Covington & Burling in Washington, D.C.; Charles Wolfram, Professor Emeritus at Cornell Law School and Chief Reporter for the ALI's Restatement of the Law Governing Lawyers; Michael Greenwald, Elena Capella, and Todd Feldman of the American Law Institute; William P. Smith III, General Counsel to the State Bar of Georgia; Rex Perschbacher and Richard Wydick, professors at University of California-Davis School of Law; Diane L. Karpman, a member of the California Bar, Richard Zitrin, a past Chair of the California State Bar's Committee on Professional Responsibility and Conduct; Dennis Rendleman, General Counsel to the Illinois State Bar Association; Gene Whetzel, General Counsel, and Albert Bell, former

General Counsel, to the Ohio Bar Association; Greg Finnerty of the Ohio Bar Association's Government Affairs Office; Alice Moseley, Assistant Executive Director of the North Carolina State Bar; Cynthia Kuhn of the District of Columbia Bar; John Howe, Sam Phillips, and Sara Rittman of Missouri's Office of Chief Disciplinary Counsel; Tony Boggs of the Florida Bar; William Hornsby, Staff Counsel to the ABA Commission on Responsibility in Client Development (formerly the ABA Commission on Lawyer Advertising); Alec Schwartz, Staff Director of the ABA Standing Committee on Specialization, and Jeremy Perlin, Staff Counsel to the Committee; Robert Bloom, who works at the Supreme Judicial Court of Massachusetts; George Reimer of the Oregon Bar; John Rabiej, Chief of the Rules Committee Support Office of the Administrative Office of the United States Courts; Margaret Downie of the Arizona State Bar's Discipline Department; Tom Byerly, Counsel to the Michigan State Bar; attorney Keefe Brooks, former Chair of the Michigan State Bar's Committee on Professional and Judicial Ethics; Todd Sidor of the New Jersey State Bar; John Tonelli, Staff Counsel to the New Jersey Supreme Court's Committee on Paralegal Education and Training; Lucian Pera of Armstrong Allen in Memphis, Tennessee; Robert Weldon, General Counsel of the Washington State Bar Association; Kathleen Mulligan Baxter, Counsel to the New York State Bar Association's Committee on Professional Ethics; Michael Colodner, Counsel to New York's Chief Administrative Judge, the Hon. Jonathan Lippman; Jim McCauley, Ethics Counsel to the Virginia State Bar; Louise Lamoreaux, Ethics Coordinator for the Pennsylvania Bar Association; Frances Kahn Zemans and Cynthia Gray of the American Judicature Society; John A. Jostad, Chair of the Ethics Committee of the Colorado Bar Association; Marcy Glenn of Holland & Hart in Denver, Colorado; Jessica Reynolds of the office of Assemblyman Paul Horcher in California; Marge Dover, Executive Director of the National Association of Legal Assistants, Inc.; Peter Jarvis of Stoel Rives Boley Jones & Grey in Portland, Oregon; staff members Steve Kaczkowski and Jonathan Hewett of the State Bar of Georgia; and many others who provided us with helpful information about changes in the standards and statutes governing lawyers.

The authors also thank the editors of the ABA/BNA Lawyer's Manual on Professional Conduct, whose biweekly Current Reports are indispensible to keeping up with state and national developments in the legal profession.

Stephen Gillers thanks his Secretary, Shirley Gray, and Roy Simon thanks his Secretary, Joanne Masci, for their indispensible work in managing the manuscript for this book. Professor Simon also thanks his excellent Research Assistants Charles-Christophe Carter, Chad Ayoub, Tim Cameron, and Robert Johnston, and proofreaders Ji Choi, Minni Bhatia, Jody Brockman, Teresa Caffrey, Christine Raffa, Michelle Walton, and Rachel Anello, all of whom are students at the Hofstra University School of Law. Professor Gillers would like to thank the following students at

New York University School of Law: Seth G. Blaylock, Shannon L. Goff, Brett S. Phillips, and Jonathan Slonim.

The authors deeply appreciate the exceptional work done by our Project Manager: Paul Sobel, Developmental Editor: Eric Holt, Assistant Developmental Editor: Kathy Yoon, and Copy Editor: Barbara Rappaport at Aspen Publishers.

The authors also thank the following copyright holders for their permission to reprint the materials in this book. The copyright holders reserve all rights to the following materials.

The American Bar Association, for permission to reprint the ABA Model Rules of Professional Conduct, the ABA Model Code of Professional Responsibility, excerpts from the Ethics 2000 Commission's Reports and numerous other items, all of which are separately acknowledged where the materials first appear. Copies of ABA materials are available from ABA Member Services, Order Fulfillment, 750 North Lake Shore Drive, Chicago, Illinois 60611.

The American Law Institute, for permission to reprint the black letter sections from the Restatement (Third) of the Law Governing Lawyers, copyright © 2000.

The American Trial Lawyer's Association, for permission to reprint its 1988 Code of Conduct and its 1986 Victim's Bill of Rights.

The Federal Bar Association, for permission to reprint excerpts from the Model Rules of Professional Conduct for Federal Lawyers © 1990.

The American Academy of Matrimonial Lawyers (AAML), for permission to reprint excerpts from the Bounds of Advocacy.

The Roscoe Pound Foundation (formerly the Roscoe Pound-American Trial Lawyers Foundation), for permission to reprint excerpts from the 1982 Revised Draft of the American Lawyer's Code of Conduct.

TRIAL magazine, for permission to reprint excerpts from the Preface to the American Lawyer's Code of Conduct. (The Preface originally appeared in TRIAL magazine.)

The National Association of Legal Assistants, Inc., 1601 South Main St., Suite 300, Tulsa, OK 74119, for permission to reprint excerpts from the NALA's Model Standards and Guidelines for Utilization of Legal Assistants.

Introduction to the Regulation of Lawyers

This book contains rules regulating the behavior of lawyers and judges. These rules come from many sources: statutes, administrative regulations, rules of evidence and procedure, and, most prominently, ethical codes. These rules continue to grow and change.

What's New Since Our Last Edition?

This edition of Regulation of Lawyers: Statutes and Standards represents the most comprehensive revision of this book since the first edition in 1989. In our chapter on the ABA Model Rules of Professional Conduct, which comprises nearly half the book, it is no exaggeration to say that nearly every page has been changed. What accounts for the tremendous change? This section of our introduction answers that question and highlights some pending developments that could lead to more changes in the future.

NATIONAL DEVELOPMENTS

American Bar Association Developments

The American Bar Association is the largest professional organization in the world, with more than 400,000 members, and it devotes significant resources to the study and improvement of the rules governing lawyers and judges. Several major developments have occurred during the past year.

ABA Model Rules of Professional Conduct: In February 2002, capping a five-year process of review and debate, the ABA comprehensively amended the ABA Model Rules of Professional Conduct. These changes, which affected nearly every rule, were based on the work of the ABA Ethics 2000 Commission, a select 13-member commission appointed in 1997 to review the Model Rules in light of advances in technology, globalization, and the new RESTATEMENT OF THE LAW GOVERNING LAWYERS (published in 2000 after more than a decade of work). The changes include three brand new rules — Rule 1.18 (Duties to Prospective Clients), Rule 2.4 (Lawyer Serving as Third-Party Neutral), and Rule 6.5 (Nonprofit and Court-Annexed Limited Legal Services Programs). The ABA also deleted Rule 2.2 (Intermediary), and amended scores of other Rules and Comments.

In addition, in August 2002 the ABA added a new subparagraph (b)(4) to Rule 7.2 (Advertising), and substantially amended Rule 5.5 (Unauthorized Practice of Law; Multijurisdictional Practice of Law) and Rule 8.5 (Disciplinary Authority; Choice of Law). The ABA also amended the Comments to these three Rules, and the Comment to Rule 7.5 (Firm Names and Letterheads).

The ABA also voted down three of the Ethics 2000 Commission's most controversial proposals — a proposed amendment to Rule 1.5 (Fees) that would have required written fee agreements in many more situations; a proposed amendment to Rule 1.6 (Confidentiality of Information) that would have permitted a lawyer in certain circumstances to disclose a client's fraud or intention to commit fraud; and a proposed amendment to Rule 1.10 (Imputation of Conflicts of Interest: General Rule) that would have permitted timely screening to avoid disqualification based on a lateral attorney's conflicts.

In our Editors' Introduction to the ABA Model Rules of Professional Conduct, we describe the ABA's historical role in lawyer regulation, the development of the ABA Model Rules of Professional Conduct, and the specific changes in this year's rules. We also reprint the Model Rules in legislative style, with additions since last year underscored and deletions since last year stricken through. The Legislative History following each Model Rule provides additional details about the changes, including the proposed changes that the ABA rejected.

Looking ahead, at its February 2003 Mid-Year Meeting the ABA will consider amendments to Model Rule 1.4 (Communication) and Rule 7.1 (Advertising) that would require lawyers who do not carry legal malpractice insurance to disclose that fact to current and prospective clients. The proposed amendments have been drafted by the ABA Standing Committee on Client Protection, which is chaired by Linda Shely, Ethics Counsel to the Arizona Bar. Alaska, Ohio, and South Dakota already require lawyers to advise their clients if they do not maintain a specified minimum amount of malpractice coverage, and Virginia requires lawyers to certify annually whether they do or do not carry malpractice insurance.

Only Oregon currently requires lawyers to carry malpractice insurance as a condition of practicing law.

For a vast treasury of information on the ABA Model Rules of Professional Conduct, including extensive materials from the Ethics 2000 Commission, visit the web site of the ABA Center for Professional Responsibility at www.abanet.org/cpr.

ABA Commission on Multijurisdictional Practice: In July 2000, the president of the American Bar Association created the Commission on Multijurisdictional Practice (the MJP Commission) to study the practice of law by lawyers in jurisdictions where they are not admitted. The MJP Commission's chairperson was attorney Wayne Positan of Roseland, New Jersey, and its Reporter was Professor Bruce Green of Fordham University School of Law. The commission held public hearings around the country, solicited comments from the bench and bar, and issued an Interim Report in November 2001. After reviewing comments on the interim report and holding more public hearings, the MJP Commission issued a Final Report in May 2002. The Final Report contained nine specific recommendations, including: proposed amendments to ABA Model Rule 5.5 (Unauthorized Practice of Law; Multijurisdictional Practice of Law) and to Rule 8.5 (Disciplinary Authority; Choice of Law); a Model Rule on pro hac vice admission; a Model Rule on admission by motion; and amendments to Rules 6 and 22 of the ABA Model Rules for Lawyer Disciplinary Enforcement. At its August 2002 annual meeting, the ABA overwhelmingly approved every one of the MJP Commission's nine recommendations nearly verbatim. The only significant modification was the addition of two new sentences at the end of Comment 1 to Rule 8.5. We reprint substantial excerpts from the Final Report of the Commission on Multijurisdictional Practice in the Legislative History and Related Materials following Rule 5.5 and in the Legislative History following Rule 8.5.

ABA Commission on Billable Hours: In August 2001, ABA President Robert Hirshon appointed the Commission on Billable Hours to address the growing concern among lawyers and judges that increased billable hour demands are compromising the health and well-being of lawyers and the communities in which lawyers live. The commission, co-chaired by attorney Jeffrey Liss of Piper, Marbury, and Anastasia Kelly, senior vice president and general counsel for Sears Roebuck, is addressing the unintended consequences of the billable hours system, including its adverse effects on pro bono practice, ethics, mentoring, and professional development, and is exploring alternative methods of billing for legal services. In August 2002, the commission issued a report, which is available (together with other useful materials on billable hours) at www.abanet.org/careercounsel/billable.html. We reprint excerpts from the preface to that report in the Related Materials section following Rule 1.5 (Fees).

ABA Task Force on Corporate Responsibility: In March 2002, ABA President Robert Hirshon appointed a Presidential Task Force on

Corporate Responsibility to study issues arising out of events at Enron and other large corporations involving false or misleading financial statements and alleged misconduct by executive officers. The task force's chairperson is attorney James H. Cheek, III, of Nashville, Tennessee, and its Reporter is Professor Lawrence Hamermesh of Widener University School of Law. In July 2002, the task force issued its preliminary report recommending amendments to ABA Model Rules 1.2, 1.6, 1.13, 1.16, and 4.1.

The task force's central proposal is an amendment to Rule 1.13 (Organization as Client) that would: require lawyers to pursue remedial measures whether misconduct relates to the representation or is merely learned through the representation; require lawyers to communicate with higher corporate authorities where other efforts fail to prevent or rectify the problem; and make clear that disclosing confidential client information to higher authorities within a corporation does not violate Rule 1.6. The task force also recommends amending Rule 1.6 (Confidentiality of Information) to permit lawyers to disclose corporate misconduct that has resulted or is reasonably certain to result in substantial injury to the financial interests or property of another, and to *require* such disclosure when necessary to prevent felonies or other serious crimes, including violations of the federal securities laws. (This proposal goes even further than an Ethics 2000 Commission proposal that the ABA House of Delegates rejected in August 2001.) The task force also recommends expanding Rules 1.2(d), 1.13, and 4.1 beyond actual knowledge to reach circumstances in which the lawyer "reasonably should know" of a crime or fraud. Other sections of the preliminary report suggest ways of improving corporate governance and ways of improving communication between a corporation's inside and outside counsel. The task force plans to hold public hearings on its proposals and bring the proposals to the ABA House of Delegates for a vote at the ABA's February 2003 Mid-Year Meeting. The full preliminary report is available online on the task force's home page at www.abanet.org/buslaw.

ABA Task Force on the Model Definition of the Practice of Law: At the ABA's August 2002 Annual Meeting, the ABA House of Delegates created a seven-member Task Force on the Model Definition of the Practice of Law. The task force will work in conjunction with the ABA Standing Committee on Client Protection to develop a model definition of the practice of law. The Chairperson of the task force is Lish Whitson, a trial lawyer at Lish Whitson PLLC in Washington State. In September 2002, the task force posted a preliminary draft definition of the practice of law at www.abanet.org/cpr. Comments on the draft definition were due by December 20, 2002. The task force also scheduled a half-day public hearing during the ABA's Midyear Meeting in Seattle in February 2003, and plans to report to the ABA Board of Governors by August 2003.

Ethical Guidelines for Settlement Negotiations: In August 2002, the ABA Section on Litigation issued a comprehensive set of ethical guidelines for settlement negotiations. The guidelines cover (a) settlement negotiations generally, (b) issues relating to lawyers and their clients, and (c) issues relating to a lawyer's negotiations with opposing parties. The guidelines are available in full at www.abanet.org/litigation/ethics.

Federal Statutes and Regulations

Because the regulation of lawyers is mainly a matter of state law, we usually have little or nothing to report about changes in federal statutes and regulations directly regulating lawyers. This year is a major exception.

Sarbanes-Oxley Act: On July 30, 2002, President Bush signed the Sarbanes-Oxley Act of 2002, Pub. L. No. 107-204. (The Senate version was called the "Public Company Accounting Reform and Investor Protection Act of 2002.") Section 307 of that act, titled "Rules of Professional Responsibility for Attorneys," requires the Securities and Exchange Commission (SEC), within 180 days from promulgation of the act (i.e., by about January 25, 2003), to issue "rules, in the public interest and for the protection of investors, setting forth minimum standards of professional conduct for attorneys appearing and practicing before the commission in any way in the representation of issuers . . . ." Section 307 then mandates that the commission include a rule:

> (1) requiring an attorney to report evidence of a material violation of securities law or breach of fiduciary duty or similar violation by the company or any agent thereof, to the chief legal counsel or the chief executive officer of the company (or the equivalent thereof); and
>
> (2) if the counsel or officer does not appropriately respond to the evidence (adopting, as necessary, appropriate remedial measures or sanctions with respect to the violation), requiring the attorney to report the evidence to the audit committee of the board of directors of the issuer or to another committee of the board of directors comprised solely of directors not employed directly or indirectly by the issuer, or to the board of directors.

The new rule will thus impose far more severe obligations on lawyers than ABA Model Rule 1.13 (Organization as Client). It is not yet known what other rules the SEC might adopt to govern attorneys who practice before it. We discuss the rule mandated by §307 in more detail in the Related Materials section following Rule 1.13.

The Sarbanes-Oxley Act also amended certain federal criminal statutes relating to client perjury and client fraud. Specifically, the act added a new offense, codified at 18 U.S.C. §1512(c), that makes it a crime to "corruptly" alter, destroy, mutilate, or conceal a document with the intent to make it unavailable in an official proceeding, or otherwise obstruct any official proceeding. The act also added a new 18 U.S.C. §1519, which makes it a crime to alter, destroy, mutilate, conceal, falsify, or make a false entry in any document with the intent to obstruct a federal investigation or bankruptcy case, "or in relation to or contemplation of any such matter or case." Violations of §1512(c) and §1519 are punishable by a fine and/or up to 20 years in prison. We reprint both new provisions in our chapter on Federal Provisions on Conflicts, Confidentiality, and Crimes.

Gramm-Leach-Bliley Act Developments: In 1999, Congress passed the Gramm-Leach-Bliley Financial Modernization Act, Pub. L. No. 106-102. The main purposes of the act were to limit instances in which a "financial institution" may disclose nonpublic personal information about a consumer to unaffiliated third parties and to require a "financial institution" to disclose its privacy and information-sharing practices to all of its customers. A "financial institution" includes (among other things) any institution that engages in activities such as "[p]roviding financial, investment, or economic advisory services. . . ." In 2001, the ABA passed a resolution stating that lawyers should not be subject to the notification provisions of the Gramm-Leach-Bliley Act. The ABA also wrote a letter to the chairman of the Federal Trade Commission (FTC), which enforces the Gramm-Leach-Bliley Act, expressing "grave concerns" about applying the act to attorneys and arguing that the rules of professional conduct governing lawyers were more than adequate to protect consumers. On April 8, 2002, the FTC wrote a letter to the ABA president taking the position that the FTC had no authority to exempt attorneys from the reach of the Gramm-Leach-Bliley Act. On April 29, 2002, the New York State Bar Association filed suit against the FTC seeking declaratory relief from application of the act to attorneys. The complaint is available at www.nysba.org (put "Gramm-Leach" in the Search box at the upper right corner to find the complaint). The ABA filed a similar suit against the FTC in September 2002. The suits were still pending when we went to press.

Monitoring Conversations Between Attorneys and Prisoners: On October 31, 2002, effective immediately, the United States Bureau of Prisons issued an interim rule, 28 C.F.R. §501.3(d), that permits the federal government to monitor conversations between prisoners and their attorneys under certain circumstances. We set out the full text of the regulation in the Related Materials section following ABA Model Rule 1.6.

United States Supreme Court Cases

The Supreme Court issued three opinions during its October 2001 Term that are directly relevant to regulations governing the conduct of lawyers and judges. In Mickens v. Taylor, 122 S. Ct. 1237 (2002), the Court addressed a criminal defense lawyer's successive conflict. The petitioner had been convicted of murder. He sought to overturn his conviction because (as he later learned) his lawyer had represented the murder victim on an unrelated criminal matter until a week before the court appointed the lawyer to defend the murder charge. The Court held that these facts did not require "automatic reversal." Rather, to demonstrate a

Sixth Amendment violation where the trial court failed to inquire into a potential conflict of interest about which it knew or reasonably should have known, the defendant had to establish that the conflict of interest adversely affected counsel's performance. We discuss this case at greater length in the Related Materials section following ABA Model Rule 1.9 (Duties to Former Clients).

In Republican Party of Minnesota v. White, 122 S. Ct. 2528 (2002), the Court struck down a provision of the Minnesota Code of Judicial Conduct barring judicial candidates from stating their views on disputed legal or political issues. By a 5-4 vote, the Court held that the restriction violated the First Amendment. We discuss this case at greater length in the Editors' Introduction to the ABA Model Code of Judicial Conduct, on which the Minnesota provision was based.

In Alabama v. Shelton, 122 S. Ct. 1764 (2002), also a 5-4 ruling, the Court held that under the Sixth Amendment, judges may not impose suspended sentences on indigent defendants, even in misdemeanor cases, if the state has not provided defense counsel at trial (unless the defendant knowingly and intelligently waived the right to counsel). The trial court in *Shelton* warned the defendant that proceeding pro se was risky but never offered him counsel at state expense. Shelton was convicted of misdemeanor assault and sentenced to a 30-day jail term, which the trial court immediately suspended, placing Shelton on two years' unsupervised probation instead. The Supreme Court invalidated the suspended sentence but remanded to the Alabama courts for a determination as to whether the probation by itself was valid under state law despite the invalid suspended sentence. (We do not discuss this case elsewhere in the book.)

Looking ahead, the Supreme Court has granted certiorari in Washington Legal Foundation v. Legal Foundation of Washington, 122 S. Ct. 2355 (2002). The case will review a Ninth Circuit en banc opinion holding that Washington State's mandatory rules governing Interest on Lawyers' Trust Accounts (IOLTA) do not amount to an unconstitutional taking of clients' property. Oral arguments are set for January 2003. Since every state in the country has some form of IOLTA program, the case will have a broad impact on state regulation of lawyer trust accounts. We say more about this case and its context in the Related Materials section following ABA Model Rule 1.15 (Safekeeping Property), in an entry titled "IOLTA Programs."

Federal Rules of Civil Procedure

In April of 2002, the United States Supreme Court transmitted to Congress a proposed new Rule 7.1 (Disclosure Statement) intended to assist judges in complying with the financial disclosure provisions and anti-bias provisions of the Code of Judicial Conduct. Specifically, the new rule would require a nongovernmental corporate party to disclose any parent corporation and any publicly held corporation that owns 10 percent of its stock, or state that no such corporation exists. (Similar changes have been proposed to the Appellate, Bankruptcy, and Criminal Rules.) Unless both houses of Congress reject, modify, or delay the effective date of the new rule, it will take effect on December 1, 2002.

The Advisory Committee on Civil Rules is discussing significant amendments to the class action rule, Rule 23. The amendments would affect many aspects of class action litigation, including the selection of class counsel and the settlement of class actions, both of which raise complex professional responsibility issues. In September 2002, the Judicial Conference of the United States unanimously approved the proposed amendments, which were then transmitted to the United States Supreme Court. If the Supreme Court approves the amendments and if Congress does not reject, modify, or delay them, the amended version of Rule 23 will take effect on December 1, 2003.

For additional information about proposed or pending changes to the Federal Rules of Civil Procedure (as well as other federal rules), visit the official web site of the U.S. Courts at www.uscourts.gov or contact John Rabiej, Chief of the Rules Committee Support Office, at (202) 273-1820.

DEVELOPMENTS IN THE STATES

Many states were in a waiting mode during the past year, watching to see how the ABA responded to the Ethics 2000 Commission proposals. Accordingly, there were fewer amendments than usual to state rules of professional conduct over the last year. This section highlights a few major developments and describes some developments that will take shape in the year ahead.

Broad Trends: Before discussing particular states, we want to call attention to two broad trends that sweep across many states. First, many states are studying multidisciplinary practice (MDP), multijurisdictional practice (MJP), and the unauthorized practice of law (UPL). This trend stems largely from the work of the ABA Commission on Multidisciplinary Practice from 1998 to 2000 and the work of the ABA Commission on Multijurisdictional Practice from 2000 to 2002, both of which included discussions of the unauthorized practice of law. For a wealth of information about state activity regarding MDP, visit www.abanet.org/cpr (click on "Commission on Multidisciplinary Practice," then scroll down to "Summary of State MDP Activity" and click on "Updated chart"). For extensive state-by-state information regarding MJP, check out www.abanet.org/cpr (click on "Commission on Multijurisdictional Practice," then choose "Written Comments/Position Papers," then scroll down to "Other organizations," which includes many state bars). For comprehensive information about UPL, visit www.crossingthebar.com.

Second, many states are beginning a comprehensive re-evaluation of their rules of professional conduct in light of the February 2002 amendments to the ABA Model Rules (based on work of the ABA Ethics 2000 Commission), the August 2000 publication of the Restatement of the Law Governing Lawyers, and developments in technology, globalization, and law practice in general.

For updated information about developments in particular states, visit the web sites given below after each state or link to state resources through a national web site about legal ethics such as www.law.cornell.edu/ethics/listing.html or www.legalethics.com. Now here is news about legal ethics developments in a few individual states.

California (www.calbar.ca.gov): In June 2002, the California State Bar formally recommended that the California Supreme Court amend the Discussion following Rule 3-310 of the California Rules of Professional Conduct (Avoiding the Representation of Adverse Interests), which is California's main provision governing conflicts of interest. (The text of Rule 3-310 would not change.) The proposal would add a new paragraph to the Discussion to clarify conflicts for insurance defense lawyers. The California Supreme Court was still considering this proposal when this book went to press in September 2002.

In May 2002, the California Supreme Court rejected proposed amendments to Rule 3-600 (Organization as Client) that would have clarified the circumstances under which public agency attorneys may disclose client confidences to report corruption or wrongdoing by government officials. In August 2002, the Legislature enacted a law on the same subject, but Governor Davis vetoed it in late September.

In addition, since our last edition California committees have issued lengthy reports on both multidisciplinary practice and multijurisdictional practice. These reports are available online. Also, in February 2002 California appointed a Commission for the Revision of the Rules of Professional Conduct and directed the Commission to review the California Rules of Professional Conduct comprehensively and recommend amendments. The revision effort will be a long-term project that may last five years or more. Finally, California's Board of Legal Specialization has recommended three major substantive changes to the rules governing California's Legal Specialization program.

On the legislative side in California, it was another busy year. The legislature enacted and Governor Davis signed new laws affecting legal services to senior citizens, pro bono services by law firms receiving state contracts for legal services, loan repayment by law graduates who take public interest legal jobs, and remedies against unscrupulous "immigration consultants" and other nonlawyers. The legislature also amended the statute governing paralegals and stiffened the penalties for the unauthorized practice of law. Governor Davis vetoed only two bills relating to the practice of law — a bill that would have created the Office of Immigrant

Assistance in the office of the attorney general to provide education and outreach services to California's resident immigrant community and the bill that would have defined the circumstances under which attorneys for public agencies could "blow the whistle" on wrongdoing by government officials.

We discuss these and other California developments in detail in the Editors' Introductions to the California Rules of Professional Conduct and to our Selected California Statutes later in this book.

Colorado (www.cobar.org): In May 2002, the Colorado Supreme Court adopted a new provision of Rule 1.5 to govern advance fees. We reprint the new rule in our Selected State Variations section following Rule 1.5. In addition, Colorado is seriously considering a new "temporary lawyer" rule that would permit almost unrestricted temporary practice in Colorado by lawyers who are in good standing in all other states where they are admitted as long as the out-of-state lawyers do not (a) establish domicile in Colorado, (b) open an office in Colorado, or (c) hold themselves out to the public as licensed to practice in Colorado. The Colorado Bar Association and the Denver Bar Association jointly submitted the proposed rule to the Colorado Supreme Court in 2001. The supreme court suggested some changes to the proposed rule, and the Bar committees responded to the court. Further revisions were in progress when we went to press in September of 2002.

District of Columbia (www.dcbar.org): The District of Columbia has not amended any of its Rules of Professional Conduct since our last edition, but in May 2002 the District of Columbia Bar Board of Governors voted to forward to the D.C. Court of Appeals (the District's highest court) the final report and recommendations of the D.C. Bar's Special Committee on Multidisciplinary Practice. That report, which was issued in October 2001, recommends significant amendments to D.C. Rule 1.7 (Conflict of Interest: General Rule) and to D.C. Rule 5.4 (Professional Independence of a Lawyer). The amendments would permit lawyers to enter partnerships with nonlawyers and to share legal fees with nonlawyers under certain conditions. We quote the proposed amendments in full in our Editors' Introduction to the District of Columbia Rules of Professional Conduct.

The D.C. Bar has appointed an MJP committee, which met for the first time in March 2002. Also, the D.C. Bar's Rules Committee recently began reviewing the work of the ABA Ethics 2000 Commission to determine whether to incorporate some of the ABA's new rules into the District's rules.

Illinois (www.isba.org): The Illinois State Bar Association is considering a proposal to amend Rule 5.5 of the Illinois Rules of Professional Conduct to expand the range of permissible multijurisdictional practice by lawyers. The proposal takes a so-called safe harbor approach that contains several unique features. Simultaneously, Illinois continues to consider amendments to toughen its UPL statute, 705 ILCS §205/1, as it applies to nonlawyers. The amendments were written by the State Bar's Task Force on the Unauthorized Practice of Law and approved in December 2001 by the State Bar's Assembly. When we went to press in September of 2002, the State Bar was lobbying for their adoption.

New York (www.nysba.org and www.courts.state.ny.us): In December 2001 New York made relatively minor amendments to DR 1-107 (Contractual Relationships Between Lawyers and Nonlegal Professionals), one of New York's unique rules governing relationships between lawyers and nonlawyers. Looking ahead, New York's Committee on Standards of Attorney Conduct is beginning to look into the advantages and disadvantages of converting New York's Code of Professional Responsibility to a Model Rules format, and perhaps adopting more language from the ABA Model Rules.

In March 2002, New York's courts adopted a new 22 N.Y.C.R.R. Part 1215 (Written Letter of Engagement) mandating that lawyers set forth, either in a signed retainer agreement or in a written letter of engagement, (a) the scope of an engagement; (b) the firm's fees, expenses, and billing practices; and (c) the client's right to fee arbitration. The letter of engagement or signed retainer is required at the outset of every new engagement where fees are expected to be $3,000 or more unless the client has previously paid for legal services of the "same general kind" or some other exemption applies. (The new rule was slightly amended in April 2002.) We set forth the full text of the letter of engagement rule and the amendments to DR 1-107 in our chapter on the New York Code of Professional Responsibility.

In addition, a new 22 N.Y.C.R.R. Part 137 (Fee Dispute Resolution Program) took effect as scheduled on January 1, 2002. The new rules require a lawyer to offer a client fee arbitration in civil matters whenever clients dispute between $1,000 and $50,000 of legal fees, unless one of the specified exemptions applies. The new rules are available online at www.courts.ny.us.

In legislative developments, on August 20, 2002, Governor Pataki signed into law an amendment to §4503 of the CPLR to narrow and clarify the common law "fiduciary exception" to the attorney-client privilege. We reprint the amended version of §4503 below in our chapter on Attorney-Client Privilege and Work Product provisions. In addition, in May 2002, Governor Pataki signed a new law prohibiting a matrimonial attorney from foreclosing on "the primary residence of a litigant in a matrimonial action pursuant to a mortgage or security interest given by such litigant to his or her attorney to secure payment of legal fees in connection with such matrimonial action." We say more about this new law in the Editors' Introduction to our chapter on Selected Provisions of the New York Judiciary Law.

In New York State Bar Association developments, the State Bar established an entity to provide financial assistance to attorneys who are seeking a career in public service. The entity will help public interest lawyers pay off their law school debt. The State Bar also generally approved the report and recommendations of its Special Committee on Multi-Jurisdictional Practice. The committee opposed a national lawyer licensing plan, supported a model "admission on motion" rule similar to New York's existing rule, and urged that lawyers who open law offices in states where they are not admitted should be required to pay registration fees and comply with local continuing legal education (CLE) rules. Finally, the State Bar approved the report of the Special Committee on Judicial Campaign Conduct, which is working with local bar associations to establish local judicial campaign conduct committees to "help ensure that campaigns for judicial office are consistent with the dignity and integrity of the legal profession."

Ohio (www.osba.org and www.sconet.state.oh.us/rules): On April 1, 2002, new rules governing Ohio's IOLTA program took effect. Among other things, these long and complex new rules require each attorney, law firm, legal professional association, *or ancillary business related to the practice of law in which the attorney is the principal* to establish and maintain an IOLTA or IOTA account for the deposit of client funds held in a common escrow or trust account.

Oregon (www.orbar.org): Oregon, Idaho, and Washington State have entered into a compact providing that any lawyer who is licensed and in good standing in any of the three states may obtain admission in either or both of the other two states without taking the bar exam. This is similar to reciprocity among states that allow admission on motion, but Oregon, Idaho, and Washington State allow admission on motion immediately. The compact does not require lawyers to practice for any specified length of time before becoming eligible for admission on motion.

Separately, effective January 31, 2002, Oregon adopted a new and unique DR 1-102(D) to govern lawyers who supervise covert activity or advise clients about covert activity. The rule resolves a dispute precipitated by the Oregon Supreme Court's decision in In re Gatti, 8 P.3d 966 (Or. 2000). We reprint the new rule and additional background about it in our Selected State Variations section following ABA Model Rule 8.4.

Tennessee (www.tba.org): On August 27, 2002, the Tennessee Supreme Court formally approved comprehensive new Tennessee Rules of Professional Conduct based on the pre-2002 ABA Model Rules of Professional Conduct — though Tennessee has made many significant changes to the ABA Model Rules. The new rules will take effect on March 1, 2003. (The state's current rules are based on the old ABA Model Code of Professional Responsibility.) The new rules, which represent more than seven years of work by the Tennessee Bar Association's Standing Committee on Ethics and Professional Responsibility, are posted on the Tennessee Bar's web site.

Legal Ethics Research Sites

Much of the information discussed above was obtained by using some of the truly remarkable free online research sources that are now available regarding lawyer regulation. Among the most useful of these sites are the following:

www.abanet.org/cpr: This web site, which is maintained by the ABA Center for Professional Responsibility, collects and posts vital information from the ABA Ethics 2000 Commission, the ABA Commission on Multijurisdictional Practice, the ABA Commission on Multidisciplinary Practice, and other ABA sources. It also provides the full text of the ABA Model Rules of Professional Conduct, and links to dozens of other ethics resources.

www.law.cornell.edu: This web site, which is maintained by Cornell Law School, is the best single legal ethics resource on the web. It contains Cornell's American Legal Ethics Library, which links to resources from every state. In addition, Cornell has commissioned lengthy narratives about the legal ethics rules in more than a dozen states, including all of the largest states.

www.legalethics.com: This privately maintained web site concentrates on the ethics of electronic communications, and posts important new developments in that area on its home page. The site also links to resources from every state and to many other useful sources.

www.crossingthebar.com: This privately maintained web site, which "aspires to be the source of information and commentary on the Internet on the multijurisdictional practice of law by lawyers," collects information about the unauthorized practice of law, bar admission, and related topics.

www.findlaw.com: This massive web site offers a searchable database containing state and federal statutes, rules, regulations, and judicial opinions. The listing of "Legal Subjects" includes "Ethics & Professional Responsibility Law."

Areas Deserving Special Attention

Several areas of variation between the ABA Model Rules of Professional Conduct and state ethics rules deserve special attention. These areas include confidentiality, corporate representation, and lawyer advertising and solicitation. Model Rules 1.6, 1.9(c), 3.3, and 4.1 prominently address the issue of confidentiality. Rule 1.13 addresses the responsibilities of a lawyer whose client is an organization. Rules 7.1, 7.2, 7.3, and 7.4 are concerned with various methods for marketing legal services.

Other areas in which we see significant variation among jurisdictions or between drafts of the Model Rules and the Model Rules as adopted include conflicts of interest (Rules 1.7, 1.8, 1.9, 1.10, and 1.11); fairness to opposing parties and counsel (Rule 3.4); relationships between lawyers and nonlawyers (Rule 5.4); and pro bono service (Rule 6.1).

Two dominant concerns underlie the provisions containing these variations. The first concern is the proper scope of the lawyer's loyalty to current and former clients, including the scope of the lawyer's duty to protect client confidences. Competing demands on this loyalty come from the justice system, third persons, other clients, and the lawyer's personal or financial interests.

The second concern is competition, from within and from outside the profession, in marketing and profiting from legal services. One question is whether non-lawyers should be permitted to invest in or share profits from organizations that sell legal services for a profit. This question brings up competition between lawyers and persons or entities outside the legal profession. Another question is what limits should be placed on the ways in which lawyers compete with other lawyers. This question addresses issues of lawyer advertising and solicitation.

Another issue that engaged the ABA in the early 1990s was whether lawyers should be permitted to own "ancillary" non-law businesses (such as title insurance companies, investment advisors, and real estate developers) that serve both clients and non-clients. By a slim vote, the ABA said "no" when it originally adopted Rule 5.7 in 1991. But only a year later, again by a slim margin, the ABA repealed Rule 5.7. In 1994, the ABA adopted a redrafted, permissive version of Rule 5.7 that says "yes" to lawyer ownership of ancillary non-law businesses if lawyers satisfy certain conditions.

Some Special Features of Our Book

The areas of special concern that we have just identified generated great controversy within the legal profession prior to their adoption by the ABA, and they have generated the most frequent and pronounced variations among the states. But other provisions of the ABA Model Rules have sparked serious debate during the drafting phase and have resulted in major disagreements among the states. Every ABA Model Rule has its own history, and the various United States jurisdictions have put many twists on each ABA Model Rule. Moreover, the ABA continually studies and monitors the rules to determine whether more amendments are needed, and various committees, commissions, and task forces within and without the ABA frequently propose amendments or new rules. In addition, many sources other than the ABA Model Rules directly or indirectly regulate or influence the conduct of lawyers.

To capture the history, complexity, context, and variety of the ABA Model Rules, we have developed many special features for this book. Here are the most important of these special features:

- ***Editors' Introductions.*** At the beginning of each set of materials in this book, we have written an Editors' Introduction that provides an overview of the materials in the chapter and alerts readers to any significant changes since our last edition and any pending or anticipated proposals for significant change. We urge students to read each of these introductions.
- ***Editors' Notes.*** To provide background or to highlight changes to particular items, we have written Editors' Notes throughout the book.
- ***Legislative-Style Text.*** To alert readers to exactly what has changed since our last edition, we have reprinted the ABA Model Rules of Professional Conduct, the California Rules of Professional Conduct, and the New York Code of Professional Responsibility in legislative style (with additions underscored and deletions stricken through). This will be especially helpful in understanding the comprehensive changes to the ABA Model Rules of Professional Conduct. (We realize that legislative-style text is harder to read than plain text, but we think the gain in understanding outweighs the problems in readability.)
- ***Cross-References in Other Rules.*** The meaning and impact of a given ABA Model Rule is often illuminated by how the rule is cross-referenced — and how often — elsewhere in the Model Rules. For the ABA Model Rules, therefore, we have compiled a complete list of Cross-References in Other Rules after each Model Rule. This list quotes every other place in the Rules and Comments where the rule in question is mentioned.
- ***Canon and Code Antecedents.*** The ABA has been drafting rules of ethics for the legal profession for nearly 100 years. The earlier efforts (the 1908 Canons of Professional Ethics and the 1969 Code of Professional Responsibility) look very different, but they often reveal common and enduring themes. After each ABA Model Rule, therefore, we unlock this history by quoting in full the most closely related provisions from the ABA Canons of Professional Ethics, and by citing the most closely related provisions of the old Model Code of Professional Responsibility. (The Disciplinary Rules of the Model Code are reprinted in full later in this volume.)
- ***Legislative History.*** Alternative ways that a given Model Rule might have been drafted are difficult to imagine in the abstract, but they become visible and concrete when we examine earlier drafts of the same rule and read ABA committee reports supporting and explaining specific amendments. We have therefore sifted through the four major drafts circulated by the Kutak Commission (which drafted the original ABA Model Rules between 1977 and 1983), and in our Legislative History following each Model Rule we have excerpted the portions of each draft

that differ significantly from the rule as originally adopted. Our Legislative History also notes every amendment and proposed amendment to each Model Rule since the 1983 adoption and reprints excerpts from the ABA committee report submitted in support of proposed amendments. In addition, to help understand the enormous changes that occurred in 2002, we state after each Model Rule whether the Ethics 2000 Commission's proposals were accepted without change, accepted with minor changes, or rejected. For most rejected proposals, including the Ethics 2000 Commission's controversial proposals to amend the rules regarding fee agreements, confidentiality, and imputed conflicts of interest (Rules 1.5, 1.6, and 1.10), we reprint the rejected language and the Reporter's Explanation for the proposed change.

- ***Selected State Variations.*** The ABA Model Rules are not binding on the states in any way, so each state is free to accept, reject, or modify each individual ABA Model Rule. The states have taken advantage of this freedom by adopting rules that reflect local conditions, politics, and values. Because the states differ sharply from the ABA and from each other, we have compiled state variations on the Model Rules that differ in important ways from each ABA Model Rule. These variations are by no means comprehensive or exhaustive. Rather, they merely illustrate some possible alternative approaches to a particular issue. (We compare some of these variations to the ABA Model Rules after the 2002 amendments, but in other instances we compare them to the ABA Model Rules as they stood before the 2002 changes.) We have drawn these variations from dozens of jurisdictions, large and small, but we have systematically compared the ABA Model Rules to the ethics rules in the following 15 jurisdictions: Arizona, California, the District of Columbia, Florida, Georgia, Illinois, Massachusetts, Michigan, Missouri, New Jersey, New York, North Carolina, Pennsylvania, Texas, and Virginia. In addition, in separate chapters later in this volume, we have reprinted in full the legal ethics rules of California, the District of Columbia, and New York. This wide variety of samples from different jurisdictions should dispel any notion that the ABA Model Rules of Professional Conduct are "the rules" of professional conduct. The ABA Model Rules have been and continue to be highly influential, but the ABA is only one voice among many on the subject of legal ethics.
- ***Related Materials.*** Just as the ABA Model Rules of Professional Conduct are only one voice among many, so the rules of legal ethics adopted by the states are just one source of regulation and guidance within the legal profession. Many other authorities — some binding and some merely advisory — influence or mandate the conduct of lawyers. Among these other sources are state and federal statutes, common law doctrines, federal regulations, the

United States Constitution, ABA ethics opinions, ABA entities that regularly deal with particular types of issues (e.g., the ABA Commission on Lawyer Assistance Programs), United States Supreme Court cases, and competing codes and guidelines drafted by other groups to guide lawyers in general (e.g., the Restatement of the Law Governing Lawyers and the American Lawyers' Code of Conduct), to guide lawyers in particular fields of law (e.g., the Bounds of Advocacy for domestic relations lawyers), or to guide lawyers in particular positions (e.g., the Federal Bar Association's Model Rules of Professional Conduct for Federal Lawyers). In particular, the Related Materials cite the most comparable provisions of the Restatement of the Law Governing Lawyers and the most relevant ABA ethics opinions.

At the end of the ABA Model Rules, we include an index updated to reflect all amendments through August 2002. We have based this index on the index prepared by the ABA Center for Professional Responsibility, but we have added some of our own enhancements as well.

Finally, judges are subject to special regulations beyond those that govern practicing lawyers. Some of these are in statutory law, such as §455 of Title 28 of the United States Code. Others are in codes of judicial conduct. We include these sources as well.

We always appreciate news about developments and proposals in the states and in bar organizations. Please contact us by e-mail at roy.simon@hofstra.edu and stephen.gillers@nyu.edu.

Stephen Gillers
Roy D. Simon

September 2002

Model Codes and Standards

ABA Model Rules of Professional Conduct*
As amended through August 2002

Editors' Introduction. The ABA Model Rules of Professional Conduct are the primary influence on the rules of professional conduct governing lawyers in the United States. Forty-four states and the District of Columbia have adopted the Model Rules numbering system and most of the language suggested by the Model Rules. (The exceptions are California and Maine, which have adopted their own unique rules, and Iowa, Nebraska, New York, Ohio, and Oregon, which have retained versions of the old ABA Model Code of Professional Responsibility.

Students should immediately realize two important points. First, the ABA Model Rules are not binding on any jurisdiction; they are merely a model for each individual state to consider. The courts of each state adopt the state's rules of professional conduct, and the American Bar Association — a voluntary, private organization with no government affiliation — has no power to discipline lawyers and no control over state courts beyond the power of persuasion.

Second, even though 45 jurisdictions have adopted some version of the ABA Model Rules, no state has adopted all of the ABA Model Rules. In fact, no two states have adopted exactly the same ethics rules. Most states have adopted most of the ABA Model Rules nearly verbatim with respect to many issues, but the states still differ sharply from the ABA — and from each other — with respect to difficult issues such as confidentiality, conflicts of interest, advertising, relationships between lawyers and nonlawyers, and pro bono service. Thus, the ABA Model Rules serve as a starting point for discussing the rules of legal ethics, but they are not binding authority. For this reason, our book includes Selected State Variations sections after each Model Rule to illustrate various approaches the states have taken to particular issues.

Nevertheless, the ABA Model Rules reflect a broad consensus among the states and within the legal profession as a whole about the areas in which rules are needed to govern lawyer conduct, and how those rules should be organized and formatted. If you were to look at the table of contents of the rules of professional conduct in all 45 jurisdictions that have adopted the ABA Model Rules, you would find that the order, titles, and numbering systems of the rules are remarkably similar. Few states have added new rules (i.e., rules on subjects that the ABA Model Rules do not address), and few states have omitted more than one or two of the ABA Model Rules. Moreover, nearly all of the 45 Model Rules jurisdictions have adopted the format of the ABA Model Rules — a black letter rule followed by an official Comment explaining and elaborating on the black letter rule. (A few states have decided not to adopt the Comments to the Model Rules.)

The ABA Model Rules of Professional Conduct represent the third generation in the ABA's long tradition of drafting model ethics rules for the legal profession. In 1908, the ABA adopted the ABA Canons of Professional Ethics, a broadly worded set of guidelines that were adopted by most states with few variations. These Canons governed the profession for more than 60 years.

In 1969, after five years of study by a special committee (the Wright Committee), the ABA adopted the ABA Model Code of Professional Responsibility. The Code used a three-part structure: axiomatic one-line Canons that stated broad basic principles and themes, aspirational Ethical Considerations (ECs) for each Canon, and mandatory Disciplinary Rules (DRs) organized by Canon. The Model Code quickly replaced the Canons of Ethics in nearly every state, again with few variations.

The Code's shortcomings soon became apparent. In 1977, only seven years after adopting the Model Code, the ABA appointed another special commission (commonly called the Kutak Commission) to recommend revisions to the rules. The Kutak Commission's chairperson was the late Robert Kutak of Omaha, and its Reporter was Professor Geoffrey Hazard, Jr., then of Yale Law School. The Kutak Commission soon decided that the Model Code should be completely rewritten and reorganized. Between 1979 and 1982, the Kutak Commission circulated four major drafts of its proposed Model Rules of Professional Conduct — the 1979 Unofficial Pre-Circulation Draft, the 1980 Discussion Draft, the 1981 Draft, and the 1982 Draft. After significantly revising some of the proposed rules, the ABA House of Delegates formally adopted the Model Rules in 1983. The rules abandoned the Model Code's confusing three-part formula in favor of a Restatement-style formula — each black letter Rule is followed by its own explanatory Comment.

The ABA Model Rules of Professional Conduct have undergone many changes since their original adoption in 1983. The ABA began amending one or two Model Rules or Comments nearly every year starting in 1987, but by the late 1990s the ABA believed that a more systematic approach was required. Changes to the Rules were needed to account for the rapid development of technology, the globalization of the profession, and the extensive debate over the Restatement of the Law Governing Lawyers (which was written between 1986 and 2000). In 1997, therefore, the ABA appointed a new select body, the Ethics 2000 Commission, whose Mission Statement charged it with conducting "a comprehensive study and evaluation of the ethical and professionalism precepts of the legal profession" and "examining and evaluating the ABA Model Rules of Professional Conduct. . . ." The chairperson of the Ethics 2000 Commission was the Honorable E. Norman Veasey, Chief Justice of the State of Delaware. The Commission's Reporters were Professor Nancy Moore of Boston University School of Law (who served as Chief Reporter), Professor Carl Pierce of the University of Tennessee, and Professor Thomas Morgan of the George Washington University Law School.

From 1997 to 2001, the Ethics 2000 Commission held public hearings around the country and solicited public comments on various drafts of proposed amendments to the Model Rules. In June 2001, the Ethics 2000 Commission issued its final report, which proposed adding three new Rules, eliminating Rule 2.2, and making at least some changes to most Rules and Comments. The ABA House of Delegates debated the proposed changes at its August 2001 and February 2002 meetings and ultimately adopted nearly all of the changes proposed by the Ethics 2000 Commission. The result is a comprehensively revised set of Model Rules, including a new Rule 1.18 (Duties to Prospective Clients), a new Rule 2.4 (Lawyer Serving as Third-Party Neutral), a new Rule 6.5 (Nonprofit and Court-Annexed Limited Legal Services Programs), a deleted Rule 2.2 (Intermediary), occasional new subparagraphs, and scores of significant amendments within the existing framework.

The ABA also rejected three of the Ethics 2000 Commission's most controversial proposals. With respect to Rule 1.5 (Fees), the ABA voted against a proposal to require lawyers to put all fee agreements in writing unless the lawyer is charging a "regularly represented client" on the same basis as before or the reasonably foreseeable costs and fees in a given matter are $500 or less. With respect to Rule 1.6 (Confidentiality of Information), the ABA voted against a proposal to permit a lawyer to reveal information "to prevent, mitigate or rectify substantial injury to the financial interests or property of another that is reasonably certain to result or has resulted from the client's commission of a crime or fraud in furtherance of which the client has used the lawyer's services." (The Ethics 2000 Commission then withdrew a related proposal to permit lawyers to reveal information necessary to mitigate or rectify a client's past financial frauds or crimes in which the lawyer's services had been used.) With respect to Rule 1.10 (Imputation of Conflicts of Interest: General Rule), the ABA rejected a proposal to permit timely screening and written notice to avoid disqualification based on a conflict with a lateral attorney's former client.

The changes to the Model Rules did not stop with the Ethics 2000 Commission. Based on proposals by the ABA Commission on Multijurisdictional Practice, which was appointed in 2000 to study the practice of law by lawyers in jurisdictions where they are not admitted, the ABA House of Delegates amended both Rule 5.5 (Unauthorized Practice of Law; Multijurisdictional Practice of Law) and Rule 8.5 (Disciplinary Authority;

Choice of Law) at its August 2002 Annual Meeting. If adopted by the states, the amendments to Rule 5.5 are likely to have a far-reaching impact on the practice of law in the United States.

Finally, based on a proposal by the ABA's Standing Committee on Ethics and Professional Responsibility, the ABA also amended Rule 7.2 (Advertising) at its August 2002 Annual Meeting by adding a new subparagraph (b)(4), which permits lawyers to enter into nonexclusive reciprocal referral arrangements, either with other lawyers or with nonlawyer professionals, provided the client is informed of the arrangement. The amendment was accompanied by a new paragraph to the Comment to Rule 7.2 that explains the reciprocal referral provision, and by an amendment to the Comment to Rule 7.5 (Firm Names and Letterheads) branding it "misleading" to use the name of a nonlawyer in a law firm's name.

The version of the ABA Model Rules of Professional Conduct reprinted below reflects all amendments through August 2002. To capture the complexity, history, and variety of these Rules, to illustrate state approaches to the issues, and to put the Rules in context, we have used a seven-part format to present each Rule:

(1) The black letter ABA Model Rule of Professional Conduct, printed in legislative style to show the 2002 amendments (additions are underscored, while deletions are stricken through);

(2) The official ABA Comment, also printed in legislative style to show the 2002 amendments;

(3) Cross-References in Other Rules, compiled especially for this book to show each place in the Rules and Comments where a particular Rule is mentioned in the Model Rules as amended through August of 2002;

(4) Canon and Code Antecedents, compiled especially for this book so that readers can trace the ABA's historical treatment of related issues;

(5) Legislative History of the Model Rule, which we compiled especially for this book to describe the four Kutak Commission's drafts, the frequent amendments and proposed amendments to particular Rules between 1987 and 2001, and the Ethics 2000 Commission's proposals and how each one fared in the House of Delegates in 2001 and 2002;

(6) Selected State Variations, which we compiled especially for this book to show some of the ways in which states have diverged from the ABA Model Rule — some of these variations are expressly compared to the ABA Model Rules as adopted, but many are compared to the ABA Model Rules as they stood before the 2002 changes; and

(7) Related Materials, which we compiled especially for this book to show such things as cross-references to equivalent sections of the Restatement of the Law Governing Lawyers (which is reprinted later in this volume), descriptions of ABA entities that regularly deal with particular types of issues, and references to statutes, Supreme Court cases, and other items that shed light on a particular Rule.

Finally, at the end of the ABA Model Rules, we include an index updated to reflect all amendments through August 2002.

For extensive materials regarding the work of the Ethics 2000 Commission, including the Commission's full reports, summaries of House of Delegates action, biographies of the Commission members, written testimony from eight public hearings on the Commission's proposals, minutes of the Commission's meetings, and other valuable items, as well as for updated information about the ABA Model Rules, visit the web site of the ABA Center for Professional Responsibility at *www.abanet.org/cpr.*

Contents

Preamble: A Lawyer's Responsibilities
Scope

Article 1. Client-Lawyer Relationship

Rule

<u>1.0</u> Terminology
1.1 Competence
1.2 Scope of Representation <u>and Allocation of Authority Between Client and Lawyer</u>
1.3 Diligence
1.4 Communication
1.5 Fees
1.6 Confidentiality of Information
1.7 Conflict of Interest: ~~General Rule~~ <u>Current Clients</u>
1.8 Conflict of Interest: ~~Prohibited Transactions~~ <u>Current Clients: Specific Rules</u>
1.9 ~~Conflict of Interest:~~ <u>Duties to</u> Former ~~Client~~ <u>Clients</u>
1.10 ~~Imputed Disqualification~~ <u>Imputation of Conflicts of Interest</u>: General Rule
1.11 ~~Successive~~ <u>Special Conflicts of Interest for Former and Current</u> Government <u>Officers</u> and ~~Private Employment~~ <u>Employees</u>
1.12 Former Judge ~~or~~<u>,</u> Arbitrator<u>, Mediator or Other Third-Party Neutral</u>
1.13 Organization as Client
1.14 Client ~~Under a Disability~~ <u>with Diminished Capacity</u>
1.15 Safekeeping Property
1.16 Declining or Terminating Representation
1.17 Sale of Law Practice
<u>1.18 Duties to Prospective Client</u>

Article 2. Counselor

Rule

2.1 Advisor
~~2.2 Intermediary~~
2.3 Evaluation for Use by Third Persons
<u>2.4 Lawyer Serving as Third-Party Neutral</u>

Article 3. Advocate

Rule

3.1 Meritorious Claims and Contentions

3.2 Expediting Litigation
3.3 Candor Toward the Tribunal
3.4 Fairness to Opposing Party and Counsel
3.5 Impartiality and Decorum of the Tribunal
3.6 Trial Publicity
3.7 Lawyer as Witness
3.8 Special Responsibilities of a Prosecutor
3.9 Advocate in Nonadjudicative Proceedings

Article 4. Transactions with Persons Other Than Clients

Rule
4.1 Truthfulness in Statements to Others
4.2 Communication with Person Represented by Counsel
4.3 Dealing with Unrepresented Person
4.4 Respect for Rights of Third Persons

Article 5. Law Firms and Associations

Rule
5.1 Responsibilities of ~~a Partner or~~ Partners, Managers, and Supervisory Lawyers
5.2 Responsibilities of a Subordinate Lawyer
5.3 Responsibilities Regarding Nonlawyer Assistants
5.4 Professional Independence of a Lawyer
5.5 Unauthorized Practice of Law; Multijurisdictional Practice of Law
5.6 Restrictions on Right to Practice
5.7 Responsibilities Regarding Law-Related Services

Article 6. Public Service

Rule
6.1 Voluntary Pro Bono Publico Service
6.2 Accepting Appointments
6.3 Membership in Legal Services Organization
6.4 Law Reform Activities Affecting Client Interests
6.5 Nonprofit and Court-Annexed Limited Legal Services Programs

Article 7. Information About Legal Services

Rule
7.1 Communications Concerning a Lawyer's Services
7.2 Advertising
7.3 Direct Contact with Prospective Clients
7.4 Communication of Fields of Practice and Specialization
7.5 Firm Names and Letterheads
7.6 Political Contributions to Obtain Government Legal Engagements or Appointments by Judges

Article 8. Maintaining the Integrity of the Profession

Rule
8.1 Bar Admission and Disciplinary Matters
8.2 Judicial and Legal Officials
8.3 Reporting Professional Misconduct
8.4 Misconduct
8.5 Disciplinary Authority; Choice of Law

Index to the Model Rules

PREAMBLE: A LAWYER'S RESPONSIBILITIES

[1] A lawyer, as a member of the legal profession, is a representative of clients, an officer of the legal system and a public citizen having special responsibility for the quality of justice.

[2] As a representative of clients, a lawyer performs various functions. As advisor, a lawyer provides a client with an informed understanding of the client's legal rights and obligations and explains their practical implications. As advocate, a lawyer zealously asserts the client's position under the rules of the adversary system. As negotiator, a lawyer seeks a result advantageous to the client but consistent with requirements of honest dealings with others. ~~As intermediary between clients, a lawyer seeks to reconcile their divergent interests as an advisor and, to a limited extent, as a spokesperson for each client. A~~ As an evaluator, a lawyer acts ~~as evaluator~~ by examining a client's legal affairs and reporting about them to the client or to others.

[3] In addition to these representational functions, a lawyer may serve as a third-party neutral, a nonrepresentational role helping the parties to resolve a dispute or other matter. Some of these Rules apply directly to lawyers who are or have served as third-party neutrals. See, e.g., Rules 1.12 and 2.4. In addition, there are Rules that apply to lawyers who are not active in the practice of law or to practicing lawyers even when they are acting in a nonprofessional capacity. For example, a lawyer who commits fraud in the conduct of a business is subject to discipline for engaging in conduct involving dishonesty, fraud, deceit or misrepresentation. See Rule 8.4.

~~[3]~~ [4] In all professional functions a lawyer should be competent, prompt and diligent. A lawyer should maintain communication with a client concerning the representation. A lawyer should keep in confidence information relating to representation of a client except so far as disclosure is required or permitted by the Rules of Professional Conduct or other law.

~~[4]~~ [5] A lawyer's conduct should conform to the requirements of the law, both in professional service to clients and in the lawyer's business and personal affairs. A lawyer should use the law's procedures only for legitimate purposes and not to harass or intimidate others. A lawyer should demonstrate respect for the legal system and for those who serve it, including judges, other lawyers and public officials. While it is a lawyer's duty, when necessary, to challenge the rectitude of official action, it is also a lawyer's duty to uphold legal process.

~~[5]~~ [6] As a public citizen, a lawyer should seek improvement of the law, access to the legal system, the administration of justice and the quality of service rendered by the legal profession. As a member of a learned profession, a lawyer should cultivate knowledge of the law beyond its use for clients, employ that knowledge in reform of the law and work to strengthen legal education. In addition, a lawyer should further the public's understanding of and confidence in the rule of law and the justice system because legal institutions in a constitutional democracy depend on popular participation and support to maintain their authority. A lawyer should be mindful of deficiencies in the administration of justice and of the fact that the poor, and sometimes persons who are not poor, cannot afford adequate legal assistance~~, and~~. Therefore, all lawyers should ~~therefore~~ devote professional time and resources and use civic influence ~~in their behalf~~ to ensure equal access to our system of justice for all those who because of economic or social barriers cannot afford or secure adequate legal counsel. A lawyer should aid the legal profession in pursuing these objectives and should help the bar regulate itself in the public interest.

~~[6]~~ [7] Many of a lawyer's professional responsibilities are prescribed in the Rules of Professional Conduct, as well as substantive and procedural law. However, a lawyer is also guided by personal conscience and the approbation of professional peers. A lawyer should strive to attain the highest level of skill, to improve the law and the legal profession and to exemplify the legal profession's ideals of public service.

~~[7]~~ [8] A lawyer's responsibilities as a representative of clients, an officer of the legal system and a public citizen are usually harmonious. Thus, when an opposing party is well represented, a lawyer can be a zealous advocate on behalf of a client and at the same time assume that justice is being done. So also, a lawyer can be sure that preserving client confidences ordinarily serves the public interest because people are more likely to seek legal advice, and thereby heed their legal obligations, when they know their communications will be private.

~~[8]~~ [9] In the nature of law practice, however, conflicting responsibilities are encountered. Virtually all difficult ethical problems arise from conflict between a lawyer's responsibilities to clients, to the legal system and to the lawyer's own interest in remaining an ~~upright~~ ethical person while earning a satisfactory living. The Rules of Professional Conduct often prescribe terms for resolving such conflicts. Within the framework of these Rules, however, many difficult issues of professional discretion can arise. Such issues must be resolved through the exercise of sensitive professional and moral judgment guided by the basic principles underlying the Rules. These principles include the lawyer's obligation zealously to protect and pursue a client's legitimate interests, within the bounds of the law, while maintaining a professional, courteous and civil attitude toward all persons involved in the legal system.

~~[9]~~ [10] The legal profession is largely self-governing. Although other professions also have been granted powers of self-government, the legal profession is unique in this respect because of the close relationship between the profession and the processes of government and law enforcement. This connection is manifested in the fact that ultimate authority over the legal profession is vested largely in the courts.

~~[10]~~ [11] To the extent that lawyers meet the obligations of their professional calling, the occasion for government regulation is obviated. Self-regulation also helps maintain the legal profession's independence from government domination. An independent legal profession is an important force in preserving government under law, for abuse of legal authority is more readily challenged by a profession whose members are not dependent on government for the right to practice.

~~[11]~~ [12] The legal profession's relative autonomy carries with it special responsibilities of self-government. The profession has a responsibility to assure that its regulations are conceived in the public interest and not in furtherance of parochial or self-interested concerns of the bar. Every lawyer is responsible for observance of the Rules of Professional Conduct. A lawyer should also aid in securing their observance by other lawyers. Neglect of these responsibilities compromises the independence of the profession and the public interest which it serves.

~~[12]~~ [13] Lawyers play a vital role in the preservation of society. The fulfillment of this role requires an understanding by lawyers of their relationship to our legal system. The Rules of Professional Conduct, when properly applied, serve to define that relationship.

SCOPE

~~[13]~~ [14] The Rules of Professional Conduct are rules of reason. They should be interpreted with reference to the purposes of legal representation and of the law itself. Some of the Rules are imperatives, cast in the terms "shall" or "shall not." These define proper conduct for purposes of professional discipline. Others, generally cast in the term "may," are permissive and define areas under the Rules in which the lawyer has ~~professional~~ discretion to exercise professional judgment. No disciplinary action should be taken when the lawyer chooses not to act or acts within the bounds of such discretion. Other Rules define the nature of relationships between the lawyer and others. The Rules are thus partly obligatory and disciplinary and partly constitutive and descriptive in that they define a lawyer's professional role. Many of the Comments use the term "should." Comments do not add obligations to the Rules but provide guidance for practicing in compliance with the Rules.

~~[14]~~ [15] The Rules presuppose a larger legal context shaping the lawyer's role. That context includes court rules and statutes relating to matters of licensure, laws defining specific obligations of lawyers and substantive and procedural law in general. The Comments are sometimes used to alert lawyers to their responsibilities under such other law.

[16] Compliance with the Rules, as with all law in an open society, depends primarily upon understanding and voluntary compliance, secondarily upon reinforcement by peer and public opinion and finally, when necessary, upon enforcement through disciplinary proceedings. The Rules do not, however, exhaust the moral and ethical considerations that should inform a lawyer, for no worthwhile human activity can be completely defined by legal rules. The Rules simply provide a framework for the ethical practice of law.

~~[15]~~ [17] Furthermore, for purposes of determining the lawyer's authority and responsibility, principles of substantive law external to these Rules determine whether a client-lawyer relationship exists. Most of the duties flowing from the client-lawyer relationship attach only after the client has requested the lawyer to render legal services and the lawyer has agreed to do so. But there are some duties, such as that of confidentiality under Rule 1.6, that ~~may~~ attach when the lawyer agrees to consider whether a client-lawyer relationship shall be established. See Rule 1.18. Whether a client-lawyer relationship exists for any specific purpose can depend on the circumstances and may be a question of fact.

~~[16]~~ [18] Under various legal provisions, including constitutional, statutory and common law, the responsibilities of government lawyers may include authority concerning legal matters that ordinarily reposes in the client in private client-lawyer relationships. For example, a lawyer for a government agency may have authority on behalf of the government to decide upon settlement or whether to appeal from an adverse judgment. Such authority in various respects is generally vested in the attorney general and the state's attorney in state government, and their federal counterparts, and the same may be true of other government law officers. Also, lawyers under the supervision of these officers may be authorized to represent several government agencies in intragovernmental legal controversies in circumstances where a private lawyer could not represent multiple private clients. ~~They also may have authority to represent the "public interest" in circumstances where a private lawyer would not be authorized to do so.~~ These Rules do not abrogate any such authority.

~~[17]~~ [19] Failure to comply with an obligation or prohibition imposed by a Rule is a basis for invoking the disciplinary process. The Rules presuppose that disciplinary assessment of a lawyer's conduct will be made on the basis of the facts and circumstances as they existed at the time of the conduct in question and in recognition of the fact that a lawyer often has to act upon uncertain or incomplete evidence of the situation. Moreover, the Rules presuppose that whether or not discipline should be imposed for a violation, and the severity of a sanction, depend on all the circumstances, such as the willfulness and seriousness of the violation, extenuating factors and whether there have been previous violations.

~~[18]~~ [20] Violation of a Rule should not itself give rise to a cause of action against a lawyer nor should it create any presumption in such a case that a legal duty has been breached. In addition, violation of a Rule does not necessarily warrant any other nondisciplinary remedy, such as disqualification of a lawyer in pending litigation. The Rules are designed to provide guidance to lawyers and to provide a structure for regulating conduct through disciplinary agencies. They are not designed to be a basis for civil liability. Furthermore, the purpose of the Rules can be subverted when they are invoked by opposing parties as procedural weapons. The fact that a Rule is a just basis for a lawyer's self-assessment, or for sanctioning a lawyer under the administration of a disciplinary authority, does not imply that an antagonist in a collateral proceeding or transaction has standing to seek enforcement of the Rule. ~~Accordingly, nothing in the Rules should be deemed to augment any substantive legal duty of lawyers or the extra-disciplinary consequences of violating such a duty.~~ Nevertheless, since the Rules do establish standards of conduct by lawyers, a lawyer's violation of a Rule may be evidence of breach of the applicable standard of conduct.

~~[19] Moreover, these Rules are not intended to govern or affect judicial application of either the attorney-client or work product privilege. Those privileges were developed to promote compliance with law and fairness in litigation. In reliance on the attorney-client privilege, clients are entitled to expect that communications within the scope of the privilege will be protected against compelled disclosure. The attorney-client privilege is that of the client and not of the lawyer. The fact that in exceptional situations the lawyer under the rules has a limited discretion to disclose a client confidence does not vitiate the proposition that, as a general matter, the client has a reasonable expectation that information relating to the client will not be voluntarily disclosed and that disclosure of such information may be judicially compelled only in accordance with recognized exceptions to the attorney-client and work product privileges.~~

~~[20] The lawyer's exercise of discretion not to disclose information under Rule 1.6 should not be subject to reexamination. Permitting such reexamination would be incompatible with the general policy of promoting compliance with law through assurances that communications will be protected against disclosure.~~

[21] The Comment accompanying each Rule explains and illustrates the meaning and purpose of the Rule. The Preamble and this note on Scope provide general orientation. The Comments are intended as guides to interpretation, but the text of each Rule is authoritative. ~~Research notes were prepared to compare counterparts in the ABA Model Code of Professional Responsibility (adopted 1969, as amended) and to provide~~

~~selected references to other authorities. The notes have not been adopted, do not constitute part of the Model Rules, and are not intended to affect the application or interpretation of the Rules and Comments.~~

Canon and Code Antecedents

ABA Canons of Professional Ethics:* The Preamble to the ABA Canons provided as follows:

> In America, where the stability of Courts and of all departments of government rests upon the approval of the people, it is peculiarly essential that the system for establishing and dispensing Justice be developed to a high point of efficiency and so maintained that the public shall have absolute confidence in the integrity and impartiality of its administration. The future of the Republic, to a great extent, depends upon our maintenance of Justice pure and unsullied. It cannot be so maintained unless the conduct and the motives of the members of our profession are such as to merit the approval of all just men.
>
> No code or set of rules can be framed, which will particularize all the duties of the lawyer in the varying phases of litigation or in all the relations of professional life. The following canons of ethics are adopted by the American Bar Association as a general guide, yet the enumeration of particular duties should not be construed as a denial of the existence of others equally imperative, though not specifically mentioned.

ABA Model Code of Professional Responsibility: Compare Preamble and Preliminary Statement (reprinted later in this volume).

Cross-References in Other Rules

Scope ¶21: "The Comment accompanying each Rule explains and illustrates the meaning and purpose of the Rule. The **Preamble** and this note on Scope provide general orientation. The Comments are intended as guides to interpretation, but the text of each Rule is authoritative."

Rule 1.6, Comment 3: "A lawyer may not disclose such information except as authorized or required by the Rules of Professional Conduct or other law. See also **Scope.**"

Rule 1.7, Comment 3: "As to whether a client-lawyer relationship exists or, having once been established, is continuing, see Comment to Rule 1.3 and **Scope**."

Rule 1.13, Comment 6: "Defining precisely the identity of the client and prescribing the resulting obligations of such lawyers may be more difficult in the government context and is a matter beyond the scope of these Rules. See **Scope** [18]. . . . In addition, duties of lawyers employed by the government or lawyers in military service may be defined by statutes and regulation. This Rule does not limit that authority. See **Scope**."

Legislative History of Preamble and Scope

1980 Discussion Draft contained the following Preface:

> The decade past has witnessed an extraordinary concern with professional responsibility. Barely ten years ago, the American Bar Association adopted its Model Code of Professional Responsibility, the product of a committee chaired by Edward L. Wright. . . . [I]n every sphere one finds searching inquiry into the meaning of professionally responsible conduct.
>
> That inquiry has led to reconsideration of the Model Code, the creation of the Commission on Evaluation of Professional Standards, and, finally, the development of this document — the Discussion Draft of the Model Rules of Professional Conduct.
>
> In reconsidering the concepts of professional standards, the Commission soon realized that more than a series of amendments or a general restatement of the Model Code of Professional Responsibility was in order. The Commission determined that a comprehensive reformulation was required. We have built on the Code's foundation, but we make no apology for having pushed beyond it. . . .

2002 Amendments: At its February 2002 Mid-Year Meeting, the ABA House of Delegates adopted without change the ABA Ethics 2000 Commission proposal to amend the Preamble and Scope of the Model Rules of Professional Conduct.

Selected State Variations

District of Columbia: See District of Columbia Rules of Professional Conduct below.

Georgia: In the rules effective January 1, 2001, Georgia eliminates paragraph 7 of the Preamble, the second sentence of paragraph 19 of the Scope note, and all of paragraph 20 of the Scope note.

Illinois entirely omits the Scope section and omits various portions of the Preamble.

Massachusetts: Scope, quoting case precedent, provides that "if a plaintiff can demonstrate that a disciplinary rule was intended to protect one in his position, a violation of that rule may be some evidence of the attorney's negligence."

Michigan: Rule 1.0(b) provides:

> Failure to comply with an obligation or prohibition imposed by a rule is a basis for invoking the disciplinary process. The rules do not, however, give rise to a cause of action for enforcement of a rule or for damages caused by failure to comply with an obligation or prohibition imposed by a rule. In a civil or criminal action, the admissibility of the Rules of Professional Conduct is governed by the Michigan Rules of Evidence and other provisions of law.

New Jersey omits both the Preamble and Scope from its rules.

Pennsylvania adds the following sentence to its Scope section: "The Rules omit some provisions that appear in the ABA Model Rules of Professional Conduct. The omissions should not be interpreted as condoning behavior proscribed by the omitted provision."

Related Materials

American Academy of Matrimonial Lawyers: The American Academy of Matrimonial Lawyers (AAML) is an organization of approximately 1,600 members who have "devoted their professional lives to representing husbands, wives, and other family members in the throes or aftermath of marital dissolution." In 1991, the AAML published a set of ethical standards entitled Bounds of Advocacy directed specifically at matrimonial lawyers. The Reporter was Professor Robert Aronson of the University of Washington School of Law. Excerpts from the Bounds of Advocacy are reprinted, with the kind permission of the AAML, in our Related Materials sections throughout the Model Rules. The following excerpts from the Preliminary Statement to the Bounds of Advocacy explain the project's purpose and scope.

Preliminary Statement to the Bounds of Advocacy

The primary purpose of the Standards of Conduct is to provide guidance to matrimonial lawyers confronting moral and ethical problems; that is, to establish bounds of advocacy. Existing codes often do not provide adequate guidance to the matrimonial lawyer. First, their emphasis on zealous representation of individual clients in criminal and some civil cases is not always appropriate in family law matters. Second, the existing codes delineate the minimum level necessary to avoid professional discipline, rather than describe optimum ethical behavior toward which attorneys should strive. Third, the rules are often vague and provide contradictory guidelines in some of the most difficult family law situations. The Standards of Conduct are an effort to provide clear, specific guidance in areas most important to matrimonial lawyers.

In many ways, matrimonial practice is unique. Family disputes occur in a volatile and emotional atmosphere. It is difficult for matrimonial lawyers to represent the interests of their clients without addressing the interests of other family members. Unlike most other concluded disputes in which the parties may harbor substantial animosity without practical effect, the parties to matrimonial disputes may be required to interact for years to come. In addition, many matrimonial lawyers believe themselves obligated to consider the best interests of children, regardless of which family member they represent. A survey of Academy Fellows indicated that the harm to children in an acrimonious family dispute was seen as the most significant problem for which there is insufficient guidance in existing ethical codes.

Canon 7 of the ABA Code of Professional Responsibility (CPR) provided: "A Lawyer Should Represent a Client Zealously Within the Bounds of the Law." Ethical Consideration 7-1 indicates that "bounds of the law" include "Disciplinary Rules and enforceable professional regulations." Many courts, bar disciplinary committees and individual lawyers interpreted the CPR to require an attorney to do everything, short of violating the law, to achieve the client's goals. Attorneys of this persuasion were therefore obligated to carry out even those client directives which the attorney found harsh, ethically distasteful or unnecessarily harmful to opposing parties, counsel or other persons, such as children.

Partly in response to the overzealous representation occasioned by the CPR and overly narrow interpretations of "bounds of the law," the ABA Rules of Professional Conduct (RPC) eliminated the zealous representation language. . . .

. . . While reaffirming the attorney's obligation of competent and zealous representation, the Standards promote greater professionalism, trust, fair dealing and concern for opposing parties and counsel, third persons and the public. In addition, they encourage efforts to reduce costs, delay and emotional trauma and urge interaction between parties and attorneys on a more reasoned, cooperative level. . . .

American Lawyer's Code of Conduct: In 1982, the Roscoe Pound-American Trial Lawyer's Foundation circulated a revised draft of a proposed code of legal ethics entitled the American Lawyer's Code of Conduct (ALCC). The ALCC was intended to influence the ABA's Model Rules of Professional Conduct, drafts of which were then being circulated for public comment by the Kutak Commission. The ALCC differs from the ABA Model Rules on many issues, especially confidentiality. The overall tone of the differences is reflected in the Preface and Preamble to the ALCC, which harshly criticized the Kutak Commission's 1982 Draft of the ABA Model Rules. The Preface and the Preamble state:

*Preface to American Lawyer's Code of Conduct**

The Kutak Commission sees lawyers as ombudsmen, who serve the system as much as they serve clients. This is a collectivist, bureaucratic concept. It is the sort of thinking you get from a commission made up of lawyers who work for institutional clients, in institutional firms, and who have lost sight of the lawyer's basic function. Lawyers are not licensed to write prospectuses for giant corporations, or to haggle with federal agencies over regulations and operating rights. We are licensed to represent people in court, which often means people in trouble with the law, and with the government. We are the citizens' champions against official tyranny.

Preamble to American Lawyer's Code of Conduct

The legal system that gives context and meaning to basic American rights is the adversary system. It is the adversary system which assures each of us a "champion against a hostile world," and which thereby helps to preserve and enhance our dignity as individuals.

Recognizing that the American attorney functions in an adversary system, and that such a system expresses fundamental American values, helps us to appreciate the emptiness of some cliches of lawyers' ethics. . . . In the context of the adversary system, it is clear that the lawyer for a private party is and should be an officer of a court only in the sense of serving a court as a zealous, partisan advocate of one side of the case before it, and in the sense of having been licensed by a court to play that very role.

Rule 1.0 Terminology

Editors' Note. The ABA Model Rules of Professional Conduct have always contained a "Terminology" section, but in February 2002 the ABA House of Delegates approved the Ethics 2000 Commission's proposal to designate the "Terminology" section as Rule 1.0 and to add Comments regarding some terms.

*The American Lawyer's Code of Conduct is copyright © 1982 by the Roscoe Pound Foundation; the excerpts here and elsewhere in this chapter are reprinted with its permission. The Preface to the ALCC, which first appeared in the July 1982 issue of TRIAL magazine, is copyright © 1982 by TRIAL magazine and is reprinted with the permission of the Association of Trial Lawyers of America.

(a) "Belief" or "believes" denotes that the person involved actually supposed the fact in question to be true. A person's belief may be inferred from circumstances.

~~"Consult" or "consultation" denotes communication of information reasonably sufficient to permit the client to appreciate the significance of the matter in question.~~

(b) "Confirmed in writing," when used in reference to the informed consent of a person, denotes informed consent that is given in writing by the person or a writing that a lawyer promptly transmits to the person confirming an oral informed consent. See paragraph (e) for the definition of "informed consent." If it is not feasible to obtain or transmit the writing at the time the person gives informed consent, then the lawyer must obtain or transmit it within a reasonable time thereafter.

(c) "Firm" or "law firm" denotes a lawyer or lawyers in a ~~private firm,~~ law partnership, professional corporation, sole proprietorship or other association authorized to practice law; or lawyers employed in a legal services organization or the legal department of a corporation or other organization ~~and lawyers employed in a legal services organization. See Comment, Rule 1.10~~.

(d) "Fraud" or "fraudulent" denotes conduct ~~having~~ that is fraudulent under the substantive or procedural law of the applicable jurisdiction and has a purpose to deceive ~~and not merely negligent misrepresentation or failure to apprise another of relevant information~~.

(e) "Informed consent" denotes the agreement by a person to a proposed course of conduct after the lawyer has communicated adequate information and explanation about the material risks of and reasonably available alternatives to the proposed course of conduct.

(f) "Knowingly," "known," or "knows" denotes actual knowledge of the fact in question. A person's knowledge may be inferred from circumstances.

(g) "Partner" denotes a member of a partnership ~~and~~, a shareholder in a law firm organized as a professional corporation, or a member of an association authorized to practice law.

(h) "Reasonable" or "reasonably" when used in relation to conduct by a lawyer denotes the conduct of a reasonably prudent and competent lawyer.

(i) "Reasonable belief" or "reasonably believes" when used in reference to a lawyer denotes that the lawyer believes the matter in question and that the circumstances are such that the belief is reasonable.

(j) "Reasonably should know" when used in reference to a lawyer denotes that a lawyer of reasonable prudence and competence would ascertain the matter in question.

(k) "Screened" denotes the isolation of a lawyer from any participation in a matter through the timely imposition of procedures within a firm that are reasonably adequate under the circumstances to protect in-

formation that the isolated lawyer is obligated to protect under these Rules or other law.

(l) "Substantial" when used in reference to degree or extent denotes a material matter of clear and weighty importance.

(m) "Tribunal" denotes a court, an arbitrator in a binding arbitration proceeding or a legislative body, administrative agency or other body acting in an adjudicative capacity. A legislative body, administrative agency or other body acts in an adjudicative capacity when a neutral official, after the presentation of evidence or legal argument by a party or parties, will render a binding legal judgment directly affecting a party's interests in a particular matter.

(n) "Writing" or "written" denotes a tangible or electronic record of a communication or representation, including handwriting, typewriting, printing, photostating, photography, audio or videorecording and e-mail. A "signed" writing includes an electronic sound, symbol or process attached to or logically associated with a writing and executed or adopted by a person with the intent to sign the writing.

COMMENT

Confirmed in Writing

[1] If it is not feasible to obtain or transmit a written confirmation at the time the client gives informed consent, then the lawyer must obtain or transmit it within a reasonable time thereafter. If a lawyer has obtained a client's informed consent, the lawyer may act in reliance on that consent so long as it is confirmed in writing within a reasonable time thereafter.

Firm

[2] Whether two or more lawyers constitute a firm within paragraph (c) can depend on the specific facts. For example, two practitioners who share office space and occasionally consult or assist each other ordinarily would not be regarded as constituting a firm. However, if they present themselves to the public in a way that suggests that they are a firm or conduct themselves as a firm, they should be regarded as a firm for purposes of the Rules. The terms of any formal agreement between associated lawyers are relevant in determining whether they are a firm, as is the fact that they have mutual access to information concerning the clients they serve. Furthermore, it is relevant in doubtful cases to consider the underlying purpose of the Rule that is involved. A group of lawyers could be regarded as a firm for purposes of the Rule that the same lawyer should not represent opposing parties in litigation, while it might not be so regarded for purposes of the Rule that information acquired by one lawyer is attributed to another.

[3] With respect to the law department of an organization, including the government, there is ordinarily no question that the members of the department constitute a firm within the meaning of the Rules of Professional Conduct. There

can be uncertainty, however, as to the identity of the client. For example, it may not be clear whether the law department of a corporation represents a subsidiary or an affiliated corporation, as well as the corporation by which the members of the department are directly employed. A similar question can arise concerning an unincorporated association and its local affiliates.

[4] Similar questions can also arise with respect to lawyers in legal aid and legal services organizations. Depending upon the structure of the organization, the entire organization or different components of it may constitute a firm or firms for purposes of these Rules.

Fraud

[5] When used in these Rules, the terms "fraud" or "fraudulent" refer to conduct that is characterized as such under the substantive or procedural law of the applicable jurisdiction and has a purpose to deceive. This does not include merely negligent misrepresentation or negligent failure to apprise another of relevant information. For purposes of these Rules, it is not necessary that anyone has suffered damages or relied on the misrepresentation or failure to inform.

Informed Consent

[6] Many of the Rules of Professional Conduct require the lawyer to obtain the informed consent of a client or other person (e.g., a former client or, under certain circumstances, a prospective client) before accepting or continuing representation or pursuing a course of conduct. See, e.g, Rules 1.2(c), 1.6(a) and 1.7(b). The communication necessary to obtain such consent will vary according to the Rule involved and the circumstances giving rise to the need to obtain informed consent. The lawyer must make reasonable efforts to ensure that the client or other person possesses information reasonably adequate to make an informed decision. Ordinarily, this will require communication that includes a disclosure of the facts and circumstances giving rise to the situation, any explanation reasonably necessary to inform the client or other person of the material advantages and disadvantages of the proposed course of conduct and a discussion of the client's or other person's options and alternatives. In some circumstances it may be appropriate for a lawyer to advise a client or other person to seek the advice of other counsel. A lawyer need not inform a client or other person of facts or implications already known to the client or other person; nevertheless, a lawyer who does not personally inform the client or other person assumes the risk that the client or other person is inadequately informed and the consent is invalid. In determining whether the information and explanation provided are reasonably adequate, relevant factors include whether the client or other person is experienced in legal matters generally and in making decisions of the type involved, and whether the client or other person is independently represented by other counsel in giving the consent. Normally, such persons need less information and explanation than others, and generally a client or other person who is independently represented by other counsel in giving the consent should be assumed to have given informed consent.

[7] Obtaining informed consent will usually require an affirmative response by the client or other person. In general, a lawyer may not assume consent from a client's or other person's silence. Consent may be inferred, however, from the conduct of a client or other person who has reasonably adequate information about the matter. A number of Rules require that a person's consent be confirmed in writing. See Rules 1.7(b) and 1.9(a). For a definition of "writing" and "confirmed in writing," see paragraphs (n) and (b). Other Rules require that a client's consent be obtained in a writing signed by the client. See, e.g., Rules 1.8(a) and (g). For a definition of "signed," see paragraph (n).

Screened

[8] This definition applies to situations where screening of a personally disqualified lawyer is permitted to remove imputation of a conflict of interest under Rules 1.11, 1.12 or 1.18.

[9] The purpose of screening is to assure the affected parties that confidential information known by the personally disqualified lawyer remains protected. The personally disqualified lawyer should acknowledge the obligation not to communicate with any of the other lawyers in the firm with respect to the matter. Similarly, other lawyers in the firm who are working on the matter should be informed that the screening is in place and that they may not communicate with the personally disqualified lawyer with respect to the matter. Additional screening measures that are appropriate for the particular matter will depend on the circumstances. To implement, reinforce and remind all affected lawyers of the presence of the screening, it may be appropriate for the firm to undertake such procedures as a written undertaking by the screened lawyer to avoid any communication with other firm personnel and any contact with any firm files or other materials relating to the matter, written notice and instructions to all other firm personnel forbidding any communication with the screened lawyer relating to the matter, denial of access by the screened lawyer to firm files or other materials relating to the matter and periodic reminders of the screen to the screened lawyer and all other firm personnel.

[10] In order to be effective, screening measures must be implemented as soon as practical after a lawyer or law firm knows or reasonably should know that there is a need for screening.

Cross-References in Other Rules

Rule 1.4(a): "A lawyer shall promptly inform the client of any decision or circumstance with respect to which the client's informed consent, as defined in **Rule 1.0(e)**, is required by these Rules."

Rule 1.4, Comment 5: "In certain circumstances . . . the client must give informed consent, as defined in **Rule 1.0(e)**."

Rule 1.6, Comment 2: "See **Rule 1.0(e)** for the definition of informed consent."

Rule 1.7, Comment 1: "For definitions of 'informed consent' and 'confirmed in writing,' see **Rule 1.0(e) and (b)**."

Rule 1.7, Comment 17: "[M]ediation is not a proceeding before a 'tribunal' under **Rule 1.0(m)**."

Rule 1.7, Comment 18: "Informed consent requires that each affected client be aware of the relevant circumstances and of the material and reasonably foreseeable ways that the conflict could have adverse effects on the interests of that client. See **Rule 1.0(e)** (informed consent)."

Rule 1.7, Comment 20: "Paragraph (b) requires the lawyer to obtain the informed consent of the client, confirmed in writing. . . . See **Rule 1.0(b)**. See also **Rule 1.0(n)**. If it is not feasible to obtain or transmit the writing at the time the client gives informed consent, then the lawyer must obtain or transmit it within a reasonable time thereafter. See **Rule 1.0(b)**."

Rule 1.8, Comment 2: For a definition of informed consent see **Rule 1.0(e)**.

Rule 1.8, Comment 13: See **Rule 1.0(e)** for a definition of informed consent.

Rule 1.9, Comment 9: "The provisions of this Rule are for the protection of former clients and can be waived if the client gives informed consent, which consent must be confirmed in writing under paragraphs (a) and (b). See **Rule 1.0(e)**."

Rule 1.10, Comment 1: "For purposes of the Rules of Professional Conduct, the term 'firm' denotes lawyers in a law partnership, professional corporation, sole proprietorship or other association authorized to practice law; or lawyers employed in a legal services organization or the legal department of a corporation or other organization. See **Rule 1.0(c)**. Whether two or more lawyers constitute a firm within this definition can depend on the specific facts. . . . See **Rule 1.0**, Comments [2]-[4]."

Rule 1.10, Comment 4: Paragraph (a) does not "prohibit representation if the lawyer is prohibited from acting because of events before the person became a lawyer. . . . Such persons, however, ordinarily must be screened from any personal participation in the matter to avoid communication to others in the firm of confidential information that both the nonlawyers and the firm have a legal duty to protect. See **Rules 1.0(k)** and 5.3."

Rule 1.10, Comment 6: "For a definition of informed consent, see **Rule 1.0(e)**."

Rule 1.11, Comment 1: "See **Rule 1.0(e)** for the definition of informed consent."

Rule 1.11, Comment 6: "Paragraphs (b) and (c) contemplate a screening arrangement. See **Rule 1.0(k)** (requirements for screening procedures)."

Rule 1.12, Comment 2: "This Rule forbids such representation unless all of the parties to the proceedings give their informed consent, confirmed in writing. See **Rule 1.0(e) and (b)**."

Rule 1.12, Comment 4: "Requirements for screening procedures are stated in **Rule 1.0(k)**."

Rule 1.17, Comment 11: A lawyer selling a law practice has an "obligation to avoid disqualifying conflicts, and to secure the client's informed consent for those conflicts that can be agreed to (see Rule 1.7 regarding conflicts and **Rule 1.0(e)** for the definition of informed consent)."

Rule 1.18, Comment 5: "See **Rule 1.0(e)** for the definition of informed consent."

Rule 1.18, Comment 7: "[I]mputation may be avoided if the conditions of paragraph (d)(2) are met and all disqualified lawyers are timely screened and written notice is promptly given to the prospective client. See **Rule 1.0(k)** (requirements for screening procedures)."

Rule 2.3, Comment 5: "Where, however, it is reasonably likely that providing the evaluation will affect the client's interests materially and adversely, the lawyer must first obtain the client's consent after the client has been adequately informed concerning the important possible effects on the client's interests. See Rules 1.6(a) and **1.0(e)**."

Rule 2.4, Comment 5: "When the dispute-resolution process takes place before a tribunal, as in binding arbitration (see **Rule 1.0(m)**), the lawyer's duty of candor is governed by Rule 3.3."

Rule 3.3, Comment 1: "See **Rule 1.0(m)** for the definition of tribunal."

Rule 3.3, Comment 8: "A lawyer's knowledge that evidence is false, however, can be inferred from the circumstances. See **Rule 1.0(f)**."

Rule 3.5, Comment 5: "The duty to refrain from disruptive conduct applies to any proceeding of a tribunal, including a deposition. See **Rule 1.0(m)**."

Rule 3.7, Comment 6: "See **Rule 1.0(b)** for the definition of 'confirmed in writing' and **Rule 1.0(e)** for the definition of 'informed consent.'"

Rule 4.2, Comment 8: "The prohibition on communications with a represented person only applies in circumstances where the lawyer knows that the person is in fact represented in the matter to be discussed. This means that the lawyer has actual knowledge of the fact of the representation; but such actual knowledge may be inferred from the circumstances. See **Rule 1.0(f)**."

Rule 5.1, Comment 1: "Paragraph (a) applies to lawyers who have managerial authority over the professional work of a firm. See **Rule 1.0(c)**."

Legislative History of Terminology

2002 Amendments: At its February 2002 Mid-Year Meeting, the ABA House of Delegates adopted, with only minor changes, the ABA Ethics 2000 Commission proposals to amend the Terminology section, to add a Comment to the Terminology section, and to designate the Terminology section as "Rule 1.0."

Selected State Variations

District of Columbia: See District of Columbia Rules of Professional Conduct below.

Illinois retains the Model Code definitions of "confidence" and "secret" and adds the following terminology:

> "Contingent fee agreement" denotes an agreement for the provision of legal services by a lawyer under which the amount of the lawyer's compensation is contingent in whole or in part upon the successful completion of the subject matter of the agreement, regardless of whether the fee is established by formula or is a fixed amount.
>
> "Disclose" or "disclosure" denotes communication of information reasonably sufficient to permit the client to appreciate the significance of the matter in question.
>
> "Person" denotes natural persons, partnerships, business corporations, not-for-profit corporations, public and quasi-public corporations, municipal corporations, State and Federal governmental bodies and agencies, or any other type of lawfully existing entity.

Massachusetts: Rule 9.1(i) defines "Qualified legal assistance organization." Amended Comment 3 to Rule 9.1 provides: "The final category of qualified legal assistance organization requires that the organization 'receives no profit from the rendition of legal services.' That condition refers to the entire legal services operation of the organization; it does not prohibit the receipt of a court-awarded fee that would result in a 'profit' from that particular lawsuit."

Missouri: In 1994, reflecting the surging popularity of limited liability companies across the country, Missouri expanded its definition of "partner" to include "a member of a law firm organized as a limited liability company."

New Jersey has no separate Terminology section. However, New Jersey Rule 1.6(d) states:

> Reasonable belief for purposes of RPC 1.6 is the belief or conclusion of a reasonable lawyer that is based upon information that has some foundation in fact and constitutes prima facie evidence of the matters referred to in subsection (b) or (c).

New York defines "fraud" as follows:

> "Fraud" does not include conduct, although characterized as fraudulent by statute or administrative rule, which lacks an element of scienter, deceit, intent to mislead, or knowing failure to correct misrepresentations which can be reasonably expected to induce detrimental reliance by another.

New York also defines "domestic relations matter," and defines "tribunal" to include "all courts, arbitrators and other adjudicatory bodies."

Pennsylvania defines "partner" to denote "an equity owner in a law firm, whether in the capacity of a partner in a partnership, a shareholder in a professional corporation, a member in a limited liability company, a beneficiary of a business trust, or otherwise."

Texas adds or modifies the following definitions:

> "Adjudicatory Official" denotes a person who serves on a Tribunal.
>
> "Adjudicatory Proceeding" denotes the consideration of a matter by a Tribunal.
>
> "Competent" or "Competence" denotes possession or the ability to timely acquire the legal knowledge, skill, and training reasonably necessary for the representation of the client.
>
> "Consult" or "Consultation" denotes communication of information and advice reasonably sufficient to permit the client to appreciate the significance of the matter in question.
>
> "Firm" or "Law firm" denotes a lawyer or lawyers in a private firm; or a lawyer or lawyers employed in the legal department of a corporation, legal services organization, or other organization, or in a unit of government.
>
> "Fitness" denotes those qualities of physical, mental and psychological health that enable a person to discharge a lawyer's responsibilities to clients in conformity with the Texas Rules of Professional Conduct. Normally a lack of fitness is indicated most clearly by a persistent inability to discharge, or unreliability in carrying out, significant obligations.
>
> "Should know" when used in reference to a lawyer denotes that a reasonable lawyer under the same or similar circumstances would know the matter in question.
>
> "Substantial" when used in reference to degree or extent denotes a matter of meaningful significance or involvement.
>
> "Tribunal" denotes any governmental body or official or any other person engaged in a process of resolving a particular dispute or controversy. "Tribunal" includes such institutions as courts and administrative agencies when engaging in adjudicatory

or licensing activities as defined by applicable law or rules of practice or procedure, as well as judges, magistrates, special masters, referees, arbitrators, mediators, hearing officers and comparable persons empowered to resolve or to recommend a resolution of a particular matter; but it does not include jurors, prospective jurors, legislative bodies or their committees, members or staffs, nor does it include other governmental bodies when acting in a legislative or rule-making capacity.

Virginia: The Terminology section adds: "'Should' when used in reference to a lawyer's action denotes an aspirational rather than a mandatory standard."

Related Materials

Model Rules of Professional Conduct for Federal Lawyers* add the following definitions:

> "Federal Agency" means: (1) An Executive agency, including an Executive department, military department, Government corporation, Government controlled corporation, and an independent establishment; (2) The Congress, committees of Congress, members of Congress who employ lawyers, and Congressional agencies; (3) The courts of the United States and agencies of the Judiciary; (4) The Governments of the territories and possessions of the United States; or (5) The Government of the District of Columbia.
>
> "Federal lawyer" means a Government lawyer or a Non-Government lawyer, as hereinafter defined.
>
> "Government lawyer" means a Government employee who holds a position as an attorney with a Federal Agency or serves as a judge advocate in one of the Armed Forces, but only while performing official duties. The term includes a lawyer in private practice who has contracted with or been specially retained by a Federal Agency to represent the Agency or another person while engaged in the performance of the contractual obligation.
>
> "Non-Government lawyer" means an individual who is a member of the bar of a Federal court or the highest court of a State or Territory, who represents persons before a Federal Agency. When a Government lawyer is engaged in the private practice of law or pro bono representation not related to the Government lawyer's official duties, the lawyer is considered a Non-Government lawyer.
>
> "Supervisory lawyer" means a Federal lawyer within an office or organization with authority over or responsibility for the direction, coordination, evaluation, or assignment of responsibilities and work of subordinate lawyers, contract legal representation, nonlawyer assistants (e.g., paralegals), and clerical personnel.

ARTICLE 1. CLIENT-LAWYER RELATIONSHIP

Rule 1.1 Competence

A lawyer shall provide competent representation to a client. Competent representation requires the legal knowledge, skill, thoroughness and preparation reasonably necessary for the representation.

*This and all other excerpts from the Model Rules of Professional Conduct for Federal Lawyers, copyright © 1990 Federal Bar Association, 1815 H Street, NW, Washington, D.C. 20006-3697, have been directly quoted here with the permission of the Federal Bar Association.

COMMENT

Legal Knowledge and Skill

[1] In determining whether a lawyer employs the requisite knowledge and skill in a particular matter, relevant factors include the relative complexity and specialized nature of the matter, the lawyer's general experience, the lawyer's training and experience in the field in question, the preparation and study the lawyer is able to give the matter and whether it is feasible to refer the matter to, or associate or consult with, a lawyer of established competence in the field in question. In many instances, the required proficiency is that of a general practitioner. Expertise in a particular field of law may be required in some circumstances.

[2] A lawyer need not necessarily have special training or prior experience to handle legal problems of a type with which the lawyer is unfamiliar. A newly admitted lawyer can be as competent as a practitioner with long experience. Some important legal skills, such as the analysis of precedent, the evaluation of evidence and legal drafting, are required in all legal problems. Perhaps the most fundamental legal skill consists of determining what kind of legal problems a situation may involve, a skill that necessarily transcends any particular specialized knowledge. A lawyer can provide adequate representation in a wholly novel field through necessary study. Competent representation can also be provided through the association of a lawyer of established competence in the field in question.

[3] In an emergency a lawyer may give advice or assistance in a matter in which the lawyer does not have the skill ordinarily required where referral to or consultation or association with another lawyer would be impractical. Even in an emergency, however, assistance should be limited to that reasonably necessary in the circumstances, for ill considered action under emergency conditions can jeopardize the client's interest.

[4] A lawyer may accept representation where the requisite level of competence can be achieved by reasonable preparation. This applies as well to a lawyer who is appointed as counsel for an unrepresented person. See also Rule 6.2.

Thoroughness and Preparation

[5] Competent handling of a particular matter includes inquiry into and analysis of the factual and legal elements of the problem, and use of methods and procedures meeting the standards of competent practitioners. It also includes adequate preparation. The required attention and preparation are determined in part by what is at stake; major litigation and complex transactions ordinarily require more ~~elaborate~~ extensive treatment than matters of lesser complexity and consequence. An agree-

ment between the lawyer and the client regarding the scope of the representation may limit the matters for which the lawyer is responsible. See Rule 1.2(c).

Maintaining Competence

[6] To maintain the requisite knowledge and skill, a lawyer should keep abreast of changes in the law and its practice, engage in continuing study and education and comply with all continuing legal education requirements to which the lawyer is subject. ~~If a system of peer review has been established, the lawyer should consider making use of it in appropriate circumstance.~~

Canon and Code Antecedents

ABA Canons of Professional Ethics: No comparable Canon.

ABA Model Code of Professional Responsibility: Compare DR 6-101 (reprinted later in this volume).

Cross-References in Other Rules

Rule 1.2, Comment 7: Limited representation "is a factor to be considered when determining the legal knowledge, skill, thoroughness and preparation reasonably necessary for the representation (see **Rule 1.1**)."

Rule 1.2, Comment 8: "All agreements concerning a lawyer's representation of a client must accord with the Rules of Professional Conduct and other law (see **Rules 1.1**, 1.8 and 5.6)."

Rule 1.5, Comment 7: "A lawyer should only refer a matter to a lawyer whom the referring lawyer reasonably believes is competent to handle the matter (see **Rule 1.1**)."

Rule 1.6, Comment 15: "A lawyer must act competently to safeguard information relating to the representation of a client against inadvertent or unauthorized disclosure by the lawyer or other persons who are participating in the representation of the client or who are subject to the lawyer's supervision (see **Rules 1.1**, 5.1 and 5.3)."

Rule 1.7, Comment 15: In the case of a conflict of interest, "representation is prohibited if in the circumstances the lawyer cannot reasonably conclude that the lawyer will be able to provide competent and diligent representation (see **Rules 1.1** and 1.3)."

Rule 1.17, Comment 11: A lawyer selling a law practice has an "obligation to exercise competence in identifying a purchaser qualified to assume the practice and the purchaser's obligation to undertake the representation competently (see **Rule 1.1**)."

Rule 1.18, Comment 9: "For the duty of competence of a lawyer who gives assistance on the merits of a matter to a prospective client, see **Rule 1.1**."

Rule 6.2, Comment 2: A lawyer has good cause to decline appointment by a court to represent a person "if the lawyer could not handle the matter competently, see **Rule 1.1**. . . ."

Legislative History of Model Rule 1.1

1979 Unofficial Pre-Circulation Draft:

> . . . (b) A lawyer acts incompetently in a particular matter, if:
> (i) He or she fails to use the knowledge, skill, preparation, and judgment that a reasonably competent lawyer would use in the circumstances; and
> (ii) The result of the lawyer's act or failure to act is substantial expense, delay, harm, or risk of harm to a client or other person for whose benefit the advice or assistance is provided.

1980 Discussion Draft: "A lawyer shall undertake representation only in matters in which the lawyer can act with adequate competence. . . ."

1981 Draft defined competence to include "efficiency."

1982 Draft was adopted.

2002 Amendments: At its February 2002 Mid-Year Meeting, the ABA House of Delegates adopted without change the ABA Ethics 2000 Commission proposal to amend the Comment to Rule 1.1. (The Ethics 2000 Commission did not propose any changes to the text of Rule 1.1.)

Selected State Variations

Alabama: The Alabama Legal Services Liability Act prohibits plaintiffs from using the rules of professional conduct or expert testimony about them in a legal malpractice or like action. The Act provides, in §6-5-578(b), as follows:

> Neither evidence of a charge of a violation of the rules of professional conduct against a legal service provider nor evidence of any action taken in response to such charge shall be admissible in a legal services liability action and the fact that a legal service provider violated any provision of the rules of professional conduct shall not give rise to an independent cause of action or otherwise be used in support of recovery in a legal services liability action.

Alaska: Rule 1.1 adds language from the ABA Comment to the Rule, allowing the lawyer, in emergency situations, to give advice or assistance in a matter in which the lawyer does not have the skill ordinarily required.

California: See Rule 3-110 (Failing to Act Competently).

District of Columbia: See District of Columbia Rules of Professional Conduct below.

Georgia: In the rules effective January 1, 2001, Georgia adopts ABA Model Rule 1.1 nearly verbatim, but adds the following sentence before ABA Comment 1: "Competent representation as used in this Rule means that a lawyer shall not handle a matter which the lawyer knows or should know to be beyond the lawyer's level of competence without associating another lawyer who the original lawyer reasonably believes to be competent to handle the matter in question." Georgia also adds the following new paragraph 1A to the Comment to Rule 1.1:

> [1A] The purpose of these rules is not to give rise to a cause of action nor to create a presumption that a legal duty has been breached. These Rules are designed to provide guidance to lawyers and to provide a structure for regulating conduct through disciplinary agencies. They are not designed to be a basis for civil liability.

Illinois adds the following subparagraphs to Rule 1.1:

> (b) A lawyer shall not represent a client in a legal matter in which the lawyer knows or reasonably should know that the lawyer is not competent to provide representation, without the association of another lawyer who is competent to provide such representation.
>
> (c) After accepting employment on behalf of a client, a lawyer shall not thereafter delegate to another lawyer not in the lawyer's firm the responsibility for performing or completing that employment, without the client's consent.

Louisiana adds Rule 1.1(b), which provides: "A lawyer is required to comply with the minimum requirements of continuing legal education as prescribed by Louisiana Supreme Court rule."

Michigan retains some language from DR 6-101 of the ABA Model Code in its Rule 1.1.

New Hampshire substitutes for Rule 1.1:

> (a) A lawyer shall provide competent representation to a client.
>
> (b) Legal competence requires at a minimum:
>
> (1) specific knowledge about the fields of law in which the lawyer practices;
>
> (2) performance of the techniques of practice with skill;
>
> (3) identification of areas beyond the lawyer's competence and bringing those areas to the client's attention;
>
> (4) proper preparation; and
>
> (5) attention to details and schedules necessary to assure that the matter undertaken is completed with no avoidable harm to the client's interest.
>
> (c) In the performance of client service, a lawyer shall at a minimum:
>
> (1) gather sufficient facts regarding the client's problem from the client, and from other relevant sources;
>
> (2) formulate the material issues raised, determine applicable law and identify alternative legal responses;
>
> (3) develop a strategy, in collaboration with the client, for solving the legal problems of the client; and
>
> (4) undertake actions on the client's behalf in a timely and effective manner including, where appropriate, associating with another lawyer who possesses the skill and knowledge required to assure competent representation.

New Jersey: Rule 1.1 provides that a lawyer shall not:

> (a) Handle or neglect a matter entrusted to the lawyer in such manner that the lawyer's conduct constitutes gross negligence.
>
> (b) Exhibit a pattern of negligence or neglect in the lawyer's handling of legal matters generally.

Regarding the standard of care in legal malpractice cases, in 1995 the New Jersey Legislature enacted an Affidavit of Merit Bill, N.J. Stat. Ann. 2A:53A-26, which requires the plaintiff in a legal malpractice action, within sixty days after a defendant answers the suit, to "provide each defendant with an affidavit of an appropriate licensed person that there exists a reasonable probability that the care, skill or knowledge exercised or exhibited in the . . . work that is the subject of the complaint, fell outside acceptable professional or occupational standards. . . ." A plaintiff's failure to provide the affidavit of merit (or a statement in lieu thereof) "shall be deemed a failure to state a cause of action."

New York: Compare ABA Model Rule 1.1 to New York's DR 6-101.

Pennsylvania omits the word "reasonably" in its version of Rule 1.1.

Texas: Rule 1.01 provides:

> (a) A lawyer shall not accept or continue employment in a legal matter which the lawyer knows or should know is beyond the lawyer's competence, unless:
>
> (1) another lawyer who is competent to handle the matter is, with the prior informed consent of the client, associated in the matter; or
>
> (2) the advice or assistance of the lawyer is reasonably required in an emergency and the lawyer limits the advice and assistance to that which is reasonably necessary in the circumstances.
>
> (b) In representing a client, a lawyer shall not:
>
> (1) neglect a legal matter entrusted to the lawyer; or
>
> (2) frequently fail to carry out completely the obligations that the lawyer owes to a client or clients.
>
> (c) As used in this Rule, "neglect" signifies inattentiveness involving a conscious disregard for the responsibilities owed to a client or clients.

Related Materials

ABA Model Rule for Minimum Continuing Legal Education (MCLE): In 1988, to give states guidance on implementing MCLE programs, the ABA adopted a Model Rule for MCLE. It is reprinted in the ABA/BNA Lawyers' Manual on Professional Conduct.

ABA Standards for Imposing Lawyer Sanctions:*

> 4.51. Disbarment is generally appropriate when a lawyer's course of conduct demonstrates that the lawyer does not understand the most fundamental legal doctrines or procedures, and the lawyer's conduct causes injury or potential injury to a client.
>
> 4.52. Suspension is generally appropriate when a lawyer engages in an area of practice in which the lawyer knows he or she is not competent, and causes injury or potential injury to a client.

ABA Standards for the Operation of a Telephone Hotline: At its August 2001 Annual Meeting, the ABA adopted new "Standards for the Operation of a Telephone Hotline Providing Legal Advice and Information." The Standards are intended to provide operational direction to those who provide legal services in whole or in part through a telephone hotline. The Standards contain rules and extensive comments covering such topics as "Confidentiality and Expectations of Privacy," "Third Party Callers," "Prompt Service," "Managing Backlogs," "Referrals to Non-Legal Resources," "Identifying Callers," and "Emergency Matters."

American Academy of Matrimonial Lawyers: The "Bounds of Advocacy" drafted by the American Academy of Matrimonial Lawyers contains the following provisions and commentary:

*This and all subsequent ABA Standards for Imposing Lawyer Sanctions are copyright © 1986 by the American Bar Association. All rights reserved. Reprinted with permission of the American Bar Association.

1.3. An attorney should not advise a client about a matter concerning which the attorney is not sufficiently competent.

Comment to Rule 1.3

No attorney has complete command of every field of the law or every issue that may be encountered in a family law matter. Clients, however, often ask matrimonial lawyers to provide psychological or investment counseling or to provide advice on issues of real estate and corporate law. A matrimonial lawyer should recommend that such a client consult more knowledgeable lawyers or other professionals when in the best interest of the client.

IRS Regulations: In the regulations governing practice before the Internal Revenue Service, 31 C.F.R. §10.52(b) provides that a practitioner "may be disbarred or suspended from practice before the Internal Revenue Service for . . . (b) [r]ecklessly or through gross incompetence . . . violating §10.33 or §10.34 of this part."

Mandatory Continuing Legal Education: About two-thirds of the states have adopted mandatory continuing legal education ("MCLE") programs, requiring lawyers to take a minimum number of hours of CLE each year. About half of these states require that a portion of the MCLE hours be devoted to "ethics" or "professionalism." (One state, Pennsylvania, mandates CLE *only* in the subjects of ethics and professionalism.) Many states adopted their MCLE programs after the ABA passed a resolution in 1986 supporting the idea of continuing legal education for all active lawyers.

One of the most recent states to adopt MCLE is New York, which began requiring CLE for newly admitted lawyers beginning in 1997 and for veteran lawyers beginning in 1998. In the District of Columbia, however, lawyers voted overwhelmingly against two MCLE proposals in a December 1995 advisory referendum. Only one state, Michigan, has repealed an MCLE program. In 1994, after trying MCLE for a few years, the Michigan Supreme Court dropped the program as "ineffective."

Restatement of the Law Governing Lawyers: See Restatement §§16, 17, 29, 48–50, 52 and 53–55 in our chapter on the Restatement later in this volume.

Sixth Amendment: The Sixth Amendment to the United States Constitution guarantees criminal defendants "the assistance of counsel" for their defense. This phrase has consistently been interpreted to guarantee the *effective* assistance of counsel, which means that lawyers for criminal defendants must perform at a certain minimum level of competence to satisfy the Sixth Amendment guarantee of effective assistance. If a convicted defendant believes that his lawyer was ineffective, the defendant can challenge the conviction. In Strickland v. Washington, 466 U.S. 668 (1984), the Supreme Court said that whether a lawyer was "ineffective" depended on "whether, in light of all the circumstances, the identified acts or omissions were outside the wide range of professionally competent assistance." Model Rule 1.1, which requires a lawyer to be "competent," may help to determine the range of professionally "competent" assistance.

Rule 1.2 Scope of Representation and Allocation of Authority Between Client and Lawyer

(a) ~~A~~ Subject to paragraphs (c) and (d), a lawyer shall abide by a client's decisions concerning the objectives of representation, subject to

paragraphs (c), (d) and (e), and, as required by Rule 1.4, shall consult with the client as to the means by which they are to be pursued. A lawyer may take such action on behalf of the client as is impliedly authorized to carry out the representation. A lawyer shall abide by a client's decision whether to ~~accept an offer of settlement of~~ settle a matter. In a criminal case, the lawyer shall abide by the client's decision, after consultation with the lawyer, as to a plea to be entered, whether to waive jury trial and whether the client will testify.

(b) A lawyer's representation of a client, including representation by appointment, does not constitute an endorsement of the client's political, economic, social or moral views or activities.

(c) A lawyer may limit the ~~objectives~~ scope of the representation if the limitation is reasonable under the circumstances and the client ~~consents after consultation~~ gives informed consent.

(d) A lawyer shall not counsel a client to engage, or assist a client, in conduct that the lawyer knows is criminal or fraudulent, but a lawyer may discuss the legal consequences of any proposed course of conduct with a client and may counsel or assist a client to make a good faith effort to determine the validity, scope, meaning or application of the law.

~~(e) When a lawyer knows that a client expects assistance not permitted by the rules of professional conduct or other law, the lawyer shall consult with the client regarding the relevant limitations on the lawyer's conduct.~~

COMMENT

~~Scope of Representation~~ Allocation of Authority between Client and Lawyer

[1] ~~Both lawyer and client have authority and responsibility in the objectives and means of representation. The~~ Paragraph (a) confers upon the client ~~has~~ the ultimate authority to determine the purposes to be served by legal representation, within the limits imposed by law and the lawyer's professional obligations. ~~Within those limits, a client also has a right to consult with the lawyer about the means to be used in pursuing those objectives. At the same time, a lawyer is not required to pursue objectives or employ means simply because a client may wish that the lawyer do so. A clear distinction between objectives and means sometimes cannot be drawn, and in many cases the client-lawyer relationship partakes of a joint undertaking. In questions of means the lawyer should assume responsibility for technical and legal tactical issues, but should defer to the client regarding such questions as the expense to be incurred and concern for third persons who might be adversely affected. Law defining the lawyer's scope of authority in litigation varies among jurisdictions.~~ The decisions specified in paragraph (a), such as whether to settle a civil mat-

ter, must also be made by the client. See Rule 1.4(a)(1) for the lawyer's duty to communicate with the client about such decisions. With respect to the means by which the client's objectives are to be pursued, the lawyer shall consult with the client as required by Rule 1.4(a)(2) and may take such action as is impliedly authorized to carry out the representation.

[2] On occasion, however, a lawyer and a client may disagree about the means to be used to accomplish the client's objectives. Clients normally defer to the special knowledge and skill of their lawyer with respect to the means to be used to accomplish their objectives, particularly with respect to technical, legal and tactical matters. Conversely, lawyers usually defer to the client regarding such questions as the expense to be incurred and concern for third persons who might be adversely affected. Because of the varied nature of the matters about which a lawyer and client might disagree and because the actions in question may implicate the interests of a tribunal or other persons, this Rule does not prescribe how such disagreements are to be resolved. Other law, however, may be applicable and should be consulted by the lawyer. The lawyer should also consult with the client and seek a mutually acceptable resolution of the disagreement. If such efforts are unavailing and the lawyer has a fundamental disagreement with the client, the lawyer may withdraw from the representation. See Rule 1.16(b)(4). Conversely, the client may resolve the disagreement by discharging the lawyer. See Rule 1.16(a)(3).

[3] At the outset of a representation, the client may authorize the lawyer to take specific action on the client's behalf without further consultation. Absent a material change in circumstances and subject to Rule 1.4, a lawyer may rely on such an advance authorization. The client may, however, revoke such authority at any time.

~~[2]~~ [4] In a case in which the client appears to be suffering ~~mental disability~~ diminished capacity, the lawyer's duty to abide by the client's decisions is to be guided by reference to Rule 1.14.

Independence from Client's Views or Activities

~~[3]~~ [5] Legal representation should not be denied to people who are unable to afford legal services, or whose cause is controversial or the subject of popular disapproval. By the same token, representing a client does not constitute approval of the client's views or activities.

~~Services Limited in Objectives or Means~~ Agreements Limiting Scope of Representation

~~[4]~~ [6] The ~~objectives or~~ scope of services to be provided by a lawyer may be limited by agreement with the client or by the terms under which the lawyer's services are made available to the client. ~~For example, a~~

retainer may be for a specifically defined purpose. Representation pro-~~vided through a legal aid agency may be subject to limitations on the types of cases the agency handles.~~ When a lawyer has been retained by an insurer to represent an insured, for example, the representation may be limited to matters related to the insurance coverage. ~~The~~ A limited representation may be appropriate because the client has limited objectives for the representation. In addition, the terms upon which representation is undertaken may exclude specific ~~objectives or~~ means that might otherwise be used to accomplish the client's objectives. Such limitations may exclude ~~objectives or means~~ actions that the client thinks are too costly or that the lawyer regards as repugnant or imprudent.

[7] Although this Rule affords the lawyer and client substantial latitude to limit the representation, the limitation must be reasonable under the circumstances. If, for example, a client's objective is limited to securing general information about the law the client needs in order to handle a common and typically uncomplicated legal problem, the lawyer and client may agree that the lawyer's services will be limited to a brief telephone consultation. Such a limitation, however, would not be reasonable if the time allotted was not sufficient to yield advice upon which the client could rely. Although an agreement for a limited representation does not exempt a lawyer from the duty to provide competent representation, the limitation is a factor to be considered when determining the legal knowledge, skill, thoroughness and preparation reasonably necessary for the representation. See Rule 1.1.

~~[5]~~ [8] ~~An agreement~~ All agreements concerning ~~the scope of~~ a lawyer's representation of a client must accord with the Rules of Professional Conduct and other law. ~~Thus, the client may not be asked to agree to representation so limited in scope as to violate Rule 1.1, or to surrender the right to terminate the lawyer's services or the right to settle litigation that the lawyer might wish to continue.~~ See, e.g., Rules 1.1, 1.8 and 5.6.

Criminal, Fraudulent and Prohibited Transactions

~~[6]~~ [9] ~~A~~ Paragraph (d) prohibits a lawyer from knowingly counseling or assisting a client to commit a crime or fraud. This prohibition, however, does not preclude the lawyer ~~is required to give~~ from giving an honest opinion about the actual consequences that appear likely to result from a client's conduct. ~~The~~ Nor does the fact that a client uses advice in a course of action that is criminal or fraudulent ~~does not,~~ of itself~~,~~ make a lawyer a party to the course of action. ~~However, a lawyer may not knowingly assist a client in criminal or fraudulent conduct.~~ There is a critical distinction between presenting an analysis of legal aspects of questionable conduct and recommending the means by which a crime or fraud might be committed with impunity.

~~[7]~~ [10] When the client's course of action has already begun and is continuing, the lawyer's responsibility is especially delicate. ~~The lawyer is not permitted to reveal the client's wrongdoing, except where permitted by Rule 1.6. However, the~~ The lawyer is required to avoid ~~furthering the purpose~~ assisting the client, for example, by drafting or delivering documents that the lawyer knows are fraudulent or by suggesting how ~~it~~ the wrongdoing might be concealed. A lawyer may not continue assisting a client in conduct that the lawyer originally ~~supposes is~~ supposed was legally proper but then discovers is criminal or fraudulent. ~~Withdrawal~~ The lawyer must, therefore, withdraw from the representation~~, therefore, may be required~~ of the client in the matter. See Rule 1.16(a). In some cases, withdrawal alone might be insufficient. It may be necessary for the lawyer to give notice of the fact of withdrawal and to disaffirm any opinion, document, affirmation or the like. See Rule 4.1.

~~[8]~~ [11] Where the client is a fiduciary, the lawyer may be charged with special obligations in dealings with a beneficiary.

~~[9]~~ [12] Paragraph (d) applies whether or not the defrauded party is a party to the transaction. Hence, a lawyer ~~should~~ must not participate in a ~~sham~~ transaction~~; for example, a transaction~~ to effectuate criminal or fraudulent ~~escape~~ avoidance of tax liability. Paragraph (d) does not preclude undertaking a criminal defense incident to a general retainer for legal services to a lawful enterprise. The last clause of paragraph (d) recognizes that determining the validity or interpretation of a statute or regulation may require a course of action involving disobedience of the statute or regulation or of the interpretation placed upon it by governmental authorities.

[13] If a lawyer comes to know or reasonably should know that a client expects assistance not permitted by the Rules of Professional Conduct or other law or if the lawyer intends to act contrary to the client's instructions, the lawyer must consult with the client regarding the limitations on the lawyer's conduct. See Rule 1.4(a)(5).

Canon and Code Antecedents

ABA Canons of Professional Ethics: Canons 16, 24, and 32 provided as follows:

16. Restraining Clients from Improprieties

A lawyer should use his best efforts to restrain and to prevent his clients from doing those things which the lawyer himself ought not to do, particularly with reference to their conduct towards Courts, judicial officers, jurors, witnesses and suitors. If a client persists in such wrongdoing the lawyer should terminate their relation.

24. Right of Lawyer to Control the Incidents of the Trial

As to incidental matters pending the trial, not affecting the merits of the cause, or working substantial prejudice to the rights of the client, such as forcing the opposite lawyer to trial when he is under affliction or bereavement; forcing the trial on a particular day to the injury of the opposite lawyer when no harm will result from a trial at a different time; agreeing to an extension of time for signing a bill of exceptions, cross interrogatories and the like, the lawyer must be allowed to judge. In such matters no client has a right to demand that his counsel shall be illiberal, or that he do anything therein repugnant to his own sense of honor and propriety.

32. The Lawyer's Duty in Its Last Analysis

No client, corporate or individual, however powerful, nor any cause, civil or political, however important, is entitled to receive nor should any lawyer render any service or advice involving disloyalty to the law whose ministers we are, or disrespect of the judicial office, which we are bound to uphold, or corruption of any person or persons exercising a public office or private trust, or deception or betrayal of the public. When rendering any such improper service or advice, the lawyer invites and merits stern and just condemnation. Correspondingly, he advances the honor of his profession and the best interests of his client when he renders service or gives advice tending to impress upon the client and his undertaking exact compliance with the strictest principles of moral law. He must also observe and advise his client to observe the statute law, though until a statute shall have been construed and interpreted by competent adjudication, he is free and is entitled to advise as to its validity and as to what he conscientiously believes to be its just meaning and extent. But above all a lawyer will find his highest honor in a deserved reputation for fidelity to private trust and to public duty, as an honest man and as a patriotic and loyal citizen.

ABA Model Code of Professional Responsibility: Compare DR 2-110(C)(1)(c), DR 7-101(A)(1), DR 7-101(B)(1), DR 7-102(A)(6)-(7), DR 7-106, and DR 9-101(C) (reprinted later in this volume).

Cross-References in Other Rules

Rule 1.0, Comment 6: "Many of the Rules of Professional Conduct require the lawyer to obtain the informed consent of a client or other person before accepting or continuing representation or pursuing a course of conduct (see **Rules 1.2(c)**, 1.6(a) and 1.7(b))."

Rule 1.1, Comment 5: "An agreement between the lawyer and the client regarding the scope of the representation may limit the matters for which the lawyer is responsible. See **Rule 1.2(c)**."

Rule 1.3, Comment 1: "A lawyer may have authority to exercise professional discretion in determining the means by which a matter should be pursued. See **Rule 1.2**."

Rule 1.3, Comment 4: "Whether the lawyer is obligated to prosecute the appeal for the client depends on the scope of the representation the lawyer has agreed to provide to the client. See **Rule 1.2**."

Rule 1.4, Comment 2: "If these Rules require that a particular decision about the representation be made by the client, paragraph (a)(1) requires that the lawyer promptly consult with and secure the client's consent prior to taking action unless prior discussions with the client have resolved what action the client wants the lawyer to take. See **Rule 1.2(a)**."

Rule 1.6, Comment 13: Some Rules require "disclosure of information relating to a client's representation to accomplish the purposes specified in paragraphs (b)(1) through (b)(4)," only if such disclosure would be permitted by paragraph (b). See **Rules 1.2(d)**, 4.1(b), 8.1 and 8.3.

Rule 1.7, Comment 32: "Any limitations on the scope of the representation made necessary as a result of the common representation should be fully explained to the clients at the outset of the representation. See **Rule 1.2(c)**."

Rule 1.8, Comment 5: It is prohibited to partake in the "disadvantageous use of client information unless the client gives informed consent, except as permitted or required by these Rules. See **Rules 1.2(d)**, 1.6, 1.9(c), 3.3, 4.1(b), 8.1 and 8.3."

Rule 1.8, Comment 13: "**Rule 1.2(a)** protects each client's right to have the final say in deciding whether to accept or reject an offer of settlement and in deciding whether to enter a guilty or nolo contendere plea in a criminal case."

Rule 1.8, Comment 14: "An agreement in accordance with **Rule 1.2** that defines the scope of the representation," is not prohibited.

Rule 1.13, Comment 5: "If the lawyer's services are being used by an organization to further a crime or fraud by the organization, **Rule 1.2(d)** can be applicable."

Rule 1.14, Comment 4: "If the lawyer represents the guardian as distinct from the ward, and is aware that the guardian is acting adversely to the ward's interest, the lawyer may have an obligation to prevent or rectify the guardian's misconduct. See **Rule 1.2(d)**."

Rule 1.16, Comment 1: "Ordinarily, a representation in a matter is completed when the agreed-upon assistance has been concluded. See **Rules 1.2(c)** and 6.5. See also Rule 1.3, Comment [4]."

Rule 2.3, Comment 1: "An evaluation may be performed at the client's direction or when impliedly authorized in order to carry out the representation. See **Rule 1.2**."

Rule 3.3, Comment 3: "The obligation prescribed in **Rule 1.2(d)** not to counsel a client to commit or assist the client in committing a fraud applies in litigation. Regarding compliance with **Rule 1.2(d)**, see the Comment to that Rule."

Rule 3.3, Comment 11: The alternative to disclosing a client's deception to the court or to the other party "is that the lawyer cooperate in deceiving the court, thereby subverting the truth-finding process which the adversary system is designed to implement. See **Rule 1.2(d)**."

Rule 4.1, Comment 3: "Under **Rule 1.2(d)**, a lawyer is prohibited from counseling or assisting a client in conduct that the lawyer knows is criminal or fraudulent. Paragraph (b) states a specific application of the principle set forth in **Rule 1.2(d)**. . . ."

Rule 4.4, Comment 3: "Where a lawyer is not required by applicable law to do so, the decision to voluntarily return such a document is a matter of professional judgment ordinarily reserved to the lawyer. See **Rules 1.2** and 1.4."

Rule 6.4, Comment 1: "Lawyers involved in organizations seeking law reform generally do not have a client-lawyer relationship with the organization. . . . See also **Rule 1.2(b)**."

Rule 6.5, Comment 2: "A lawyer who provides short-term limited legal services pursuant to this Rule must secure the client's informed consent to the limited scope of the representation. See **Rule 1.2(c)**."

Rule 8.4, Comment 4: "The provisions of **Rule 1.2(d)** concerning a good faith challenge to the validity, scope, meaning or application of the law apply to challenges of legal regulation of the practice of law."

Legislative History of Model Rule 1.2

1980 Discussion Draft (then called Rule 1.3):

(a) A lawyer shall accept a client's decisions concerning the objectives of the representation and the means by which they are to be pursued except as stated in paragraphs (b) and (c).

(b) A lawyer shall not pursue a course of action on behalf of a client in violation of law or the rules of professional conduct.

(c) The lawyer may decline to pursue a lawful course of action . . . and, if the client insists upon such course of action, the lawyer may withdraw from representation subject to the provisions of Rule 1.16.

The 1980 Draft also contained the following separate rules (then called Rules 2.3 and 2.4):

Advice Concerning Wrongful Conduct

(a) A lawyer shall not give advice which the lawyer can reasonably foresee will:

(1) Be used by the client to further an illegal course of conduct except as part of a good faith effort to determine the validity, scope, meaning, or application of the law; or

(2) Aid the client in contriving false testimony or making a legally wrongful misrepresentation.

(b) A lawyer may decline to give advice that might assist the client in any conduct that would violate the law or . . . that the lawyer considers repugnant.

Duty to Offer Advice

A lawyer who knows that a client contemplates a course of action which has a substantial likelihood of serious legal consequences shall warn the client of the legal implications of the conduct, unless a client has expressly or by implication asked not to receive such advice.

The 1980 Draft also contained the following rule (then called Rule 4.1) similar to the adopted version of Rule 1.2(a):

Disclosures to a Client

A lawyer conducting negotiations for a client shall:

(a) inform the client of facts relevant to the matter and of communications from another party that may significantly affect resolution of the matter;

(b) in connection with an offer, take reasonable steps to assure that the judgment of the client rather than that of the lawyer determines whether the offer will be accepted.

1981 Draft of Rule 1.2(d) prohibited a lawyer from counseling or assisting a client "in the preparation of a written instrument containing terms the lawyer knows or reasonably should know are legally prohibited. . . ."

1982 Draft of Rule 1.2 was the same as adopted, except that Rule 1.2(d) also prohibited a lawyer from counseling or assisting "in the preparation of a written instrument containing terms the lawyer knows are expressly prohibited by law. . . ."

2002 Amendments: At its February 2002 Mid-Year Meeting, the ABA House of Delegates adopted with only minor changes the ABA Ethics 2000 Commission proposal to amend Rule 1.2 and its Comment.

Selected State Variations

Alaska: Rule 1.2(a) adds: "In a criminal case the lawyer shall abide by the client's decision . . . whether to take an appeal."

California: See Rule 3-210 (Advising the Violation of Law) and B & P Code 6068(c). In addition, §283 of the California Code of Civil Procedure gives a lawyer express statutory authority to bind a client in certain situations.

Colorado: In 1999, Colorado amended Rule 1.2(a) and (c) and the Comment to Rule 1.2 to encourage "limited representation" of pro se clients. As amended, Rule 1.2(c) provides that a lawyer may limit the "scope or" objectives, "or both," of the representation if the client consents after consultation, and that a lawyer "may provide limited representation to pro se parties . . . ." The amended Comment states, in pertinent part:

> . . . When a lawyer is providing limited representation to a pro se party . . . the consultation with the client shall include an explanation of the risks and benefits of such limited representation. A lawyer must provide meaningful legal advice consistent with the limited scope of the lawyer's representation, but a lawyer's advice may be based upon the pro se party's representation of the facts and the scope of representation agreed upon by the lawyer and the pro se party.
>
> A lawyer remains liable for the consequences of any negligent legal advice. Nothing in this rule is intended to expand or restrict, in any manner, the laws governing civil liability of lawyers.

Colorado simultaneously amended the Comments to Rules 4.2 and 4.3 so that a pro se party who is receiving "limited representation" is considered "unrepresented" for purposes of Rules 4.2 and 4.3. In addition, Colorado amended its Rules of Civil Procedure regarding sanctions and service of papers. See our Selected State Variations following Rules 3.1, 4.2, and 4.3 for more details.

District of Columbia: D.C. Rule 1.2(d) differs significantly from the ABA Model Rule — see District of Columbia Rules of Professional Conduct below.

Florida adds the words "or reasonably should know" in Rule 1.2(d) and (e). In addition, Florida's Statement of Client's Rights, which must be provided to every contingent fee client (see Florida Rule 1.5(D)), provides that "[y]ou, the client, have the right to make the final decision regarding settlement of a case. . . ."

Georgia: In the rules effective January 1, 2001, Georgia adopts ABA Model Rule 1.2 and its Comment essentially verbatim, but Georgia's Comment adds that "the language of particular rules" also varies among jurisdictions, and cautions that a lawyer "should be mindful of the nuances and differences of the law and rules of each location in which he or she practices." Georgia also adds to Comment 5 that an agreement concerning the scope of representation "should be in writing."

Illinois includes language from DR 7-102(A)-(B) as paragraphs (f)-(h), and adds the following new paragraph (based on DR 7-105) as Rule 1.2(e): "A lawyer shall not present, participate in presenting, or threaten to present criminal charges or professional disciplinary actions to obtain an advantage in a civil matter."

Louisiana replaces the ABA Model Rules version of paragraphs (a) and (b) with the following Rule 1.2(a): "Both lawyer and client have authority and responsibility in the objectives and means of representation. The client has ultimate authority to determine the purposes to be served by legal representation within the limits imposed by law and the lawyer's professional obligations."

Maryland adds "when appropriate" before the words "shall consult" in Rule 1.2(a).

Massachusetts: Rule 1.2(a) provides that a lawyer "does not violate this rule . . . by acceding to reasonable requests of opposing counsel which do not prejudice the rights of his or her client, by being punctual in fulfilling all professional commitments, by avoiding offensive tactics, or by treating with courtesy and consideration all persons involved in the legal process."

Michigan deletes Rule 1.2(b) and adds the following sentence to Rule 1.2(a): "In representing a client, a lawyer may, where permissible, exercise professional judgment to waive or fail to assert a right or position of the client." Where the official ABA Comment to Rule 1.2, paragraph 6, refers to "criminal or fraudulent conduct," the Michigan Comment refers to "illegal or fraudulent conduct." Michigan places the substance of Rule 1.2(b) in the Comment to Rule 1.2.

Minnesota relegates all of Rule 1.2(b) to the Comment.

New Jersey: In Rule 1.2(d), New Jersey forbids a lawyer to assist a client "in the preparation of a written instrument containing terms the lawyer knows are expressly prohibited by the law."

New York: Compare ABA Model Rule 1.2(a) to New York EC's 7-7 and 7-8 and DR 7-101(A)(1). Compare Rule 1.2(b) to New York's EC 2-27 (last sentence). Compare Rule 1.2(c) to New York's DR 7-101(B)(1). Compare Rule 1.2(d) to New York's DR 7-102(A) and DR 7-106(A).

North Carolina: Rule 1.2(a) adds language taken verbatim from DR 7-101(A)(1) and DR 7-101(B)(1) of the old ABA Model Code of Professional Responsibility.

Texas omits ABA Model Rule 1.2(b).

Virginia: Paragraph (b) of Model Rule 1.1 has been moved to Comment [3]. Comment [1] requires lawyers to "advise the client about the advantages, disadvantages and availability of dispute resolution processes that might be appropriate in pursuing" the client's objectives.

Related Materials

Aiding and Abetting: In many jurisdictions, a lawyer's violation of Rule 1.2(d) would also violate criminal laws prohibiting anyone from aiding or abetting the commission of a crime.

American Academy of Matrimonial Lawyers: The "Bounds of Advocacy" drafted by the American Academy of Matrimonial Lawyers contains the following provisions and commentary:

> 2.13. An attorney should never encourage a client to hide or dissipate assets.
>
> Comment to Rule 2.13
>
> . . . Whether the client proposes opening up an out-of-state bank account or having a family member hold sums of cash for the purpose of concealment, the advice to the client must be the same: "Don't do it." Hiding assets is a fraud upon the client's spouse and likely to result in a fraud upon the court. However, advice to protect, rather than hide, assets is appropriate. The client must also be advised not to

conceal data about his property, fail to furnish relevant documents, insist on placing unrealistic values on properties in, or omit assets from, sworn financial statements.

On the other hand, "[t]here is a critical distinction between presenting an analysis of legal aspects of questionable conduct and recommending the means by which a crime or fraud might be committed with impunity." It may sometimes be difficult to determine whether a client's questions concerning legal aspects of predivorce planning are asked to facilitate an improper purpose. Although the attorney should initially give the client the benefit of any doubt, later discovery of improper conduct mandates that the attorney cease such assistance and may require withdrawal from representation.

2.27. An attorney should refuse to assist in vindictive conduct toward a spouse or third person and should not do anything to increase the emotional level of the dispute.

Comment to Rule 2.27

. . . The matrimonial lawyer should make every effort to lower the emotional level of the interaction between the parties and their counsel. Some dissension and bad feelings can be avoided by a frank discussion with the client at the outset of how the attorney handles cases, including what the attorney will and will not do regarding vindictive conduct or actions likely to adversely affect the children's interests. Although not essential, a letter to the client confirming the understanding, before specific issues or requests arise, is advisable. To the extent that the client is unwilling to accept any limitations on objectives or means, the attorney should decline the representation.

If such a discussion did not occur, or the client despite a prior understanding asks the attorney to engage in conduct the attorney believes to be imprudent or repugnant, the attorney should attempt to convince the client to work toward family harmony or the interests of the children. Conduct in the interests of the children or family will almost always be in the client's long term best interests.

American Lawyer's Code of Conduct: Rules 3.3 and 3.4 provide:

3.3. A lawyer shall not advise a client about the law when the lawyer knows that the client is requesting the advice for an unlawful purpose likely to cause death or serious physical injury to another person.

3.4. A lawyer shall not knowingly encourage a client to engage in illegal conduct, except in a good faith effort to test the validity or scope of the law.

Medicaid Fraud Legislation: As part of the Balanced Budget Act of 1997, Congress enacted the so-called "Granny's Lawyer Goes to Jail" law, 42 U.S.C. §1320a-7b(a)(6), which provides in part:

Whoever . . . (6) for a fee knowingly and willfully counsels or assists an individual to dispose of assets (including by any transfer in trust) in order for the individual to become eligible for medical assistance . . . shall . . . (ii) . . . be guilty of a misdemeanor and upon conviction thereof fined not more than $10,000 or imprisoned for not more than one year, or both.

In 1997, the New York State Bar Association filed a suit challenging the law on grounds that it violated both the First Amendment and the Due Process Clause of the Fifth Amendment. On March 11, 1998, Attorney General Janet Reno sent a letter to Congress stating that the United States Department of Justice would not defend the constitutionality of the law or bring any criminal prosecutions under it because the counseling prohibition in the statute "plainly is unconstitutional under the First Amendment and cannot survive judicial scrutiny." The letter further stated that because "professional advisors such as attorneys would be prohibited from providing truthful, non-misleadng advice to their clients about lawful behavior, we are unable to identify a government interest that would justify this restriction on protected speech." On April 7, 1998, a federal district court in New York granted a preliminary injunction enjoining enforcement of the law. See New York State Bar Association v. Reno, 999 F. Supp. 710 (N.D.N.Y. 1998). But in Magee v. United States, 93 F. Supp. 2d 161 (D.R.I. 2000), the court rejected a challenge to the same law, even though the United States did not dispute that the law was "plainly unconstitutional." The Rhode Island court dismissed the suit for lack of any justiciable "case or controversy" because Attorney General Reno's 1998 letter to Congress made clear that the United States would not enforce the law.

Restatement of the Law Governing Lawyers: See Restatement §§16, 21–23, 26, 51, 67, 82, 93, 94, and 120 in our chapter on the Restatement later in this volume.

Rule 1.3 Diligence

A lawyer shall act with reasonable diligence and promptness in representing a client.

COMMENT

[1] A lawyer should pursue a matter on behalf of a client despite opposition, obstruction or personal inconvenience to the lawyer, and ~~may~~ take whatever lawful and ethical measures are required to vindicate a client's cause or endeavor. A lawyer ~~should~~ must also act with commitment and dedication to the interests of the client and with zeal in advocacy upon the client's behalf. ~~However, a~~ A lawyer is not bound, however, to press for every advantage that might be realized for a client. ~~A~~ For example, a lawyer ~~has~~ may have authority to exercise professional discretion in determining the means by which a matter should be pursued. See Rule 1.2. ~~A lawyer's work load should be controlled so that each matter can be handled adequately.~~ The lawyer's duty to act with reasonable diligence does not require the use of offensive tactics or preclude the treating of all persons involved in the legal process with courtesy and respect.

[2] A lawyer's work load must be controlled so that each matter can be handled competently.

~~[2]~~ [3] Perhaps no professional shortcoming is more widely resented than procrastination. A client's interests often can be adversely affected by the passage of time or the change of conditions; in extreme instances, as when a lawyer overlooks a statute of limitations, the client's legal position may be destroyed. Even when the client's interests are not affected in substance, however, unreasonable delay can cause a client needless anxiety and undermine confidence in the lawyer's trustworthiness. A lawyer's duty to act with reasonable promptness, however, does not preclude the lawyer from agreeing to a reasonable request for a postponement that will not prejudice the lawyer's client.

~~[3]~~ [4] Unless the relationship is terminated as provided in Rule 1.16, a lawyer should carry through to conclusion all matters undertaken for a client. If a lawyer's employment is limited to a specific matter, the relationship terminates when the matter has been resolved. If a lawyer has served a client over a substantial period in a variety of matters, the client sometimes may assume that the lawyer will continue to serve on a continuing basis unless the lawyer gives notice of withdrawal. Doubt about whether a client-lawyer relationship still exists should be clarified by the lawyer, preferably in writing, so that the client will not mistakenly suppose the lawyer is looking after the client's affairs when the lawyer has ceased to do so. For example, if a lawyer has handled a judicial or administrative proceeding that produced a result adverse to the client ~~but has not been specifically instructed concerning pursuit of an~~ and the lawyer and the client have not agreed that the lawyer will handle the matter on appeal, the lawyer ~~should advise~~ must consult with the client ~~of~~ about the possibility of appeal before relinquishing responsibility for the matter. See Rule 1.4(a)(2). Whether the lawyer is obligated to prosecute the appeal for the client depends on the scope of the representation the lawyer has agreed to provide to the client. See Rule 1.2.

[5] To prevent neglect of client matters in the event of a sole practitioner's death or disability, the duty of diligence may require that each sole practitioner prepare a plan, in conformity with applicable rules, that designates another competent lawyer to review client files, notify each client of the lawyer's death or disability, and determine whether there is a need for immediate protective action. Cf. Rule 28 of the American Bar Association Model Rules for Lawyer Disciplinary Enforcement (providing for court appointment of a lawyer to inventory files and take other protective action in absence of a plan providing for another lawyer to protect the interests of the clients of a deceased or disabled lawyer).

Canon and Code Antecedents

ABA Canons of Professional Ethics: Canon 21 provided as follows:

21. Punctuality and Expedition

It is the duty of the lawyer not only to his client, but also to the Courts and to the public to be punctual in attendance, and to be concise and direct in the trial and disposition of causes.

ABA Model Code of Professional Responsibility: Compare DR 6-101, DR 7-101(A), and DR 7-101(A)(3) (reprinted later in this volume).

Cross-References in Other Rules

Rule 1.7, Comment 3: "As to whether a client-lawyer relationship exists or, having once been established, is continuing, see Comment to **Rule 1.3** and Scope."

Rule 1.7, Comment 15: In the case of a conflict of interest, "representation is prohibited if in the circumstances the lawyer cannot reasonably conclude that the lawyer will be able to provide competent and diligent representation (see Rules 1.1 and **1.3**)."

Rule 1.16, Comment 1: "Ordinarily, a representation in a matter is completed when the agreed-upon assistance has been concluded. See Rules 1.2(c) and 6.5. See also **Rule 1.3**, Comment [4]."

Legislative History of Model Rule 1.3

1980 Discussion Draft:

> A lawyer shall attend promptly to matters undertaken for a client and give them adequate attention until completed or until the lawyer has properly withdrawn from representing the client.

1981 and 1982 Drafts were the same as adopted.

2002 Amendments: At its February 2002 Mid-Year Meeting, the ABA House of Delegates adopted without change the ABA Ethics 2000 Commission proposal to amend the Comment to Rule 1.3. (The Ethics 2000 Commission did not propose any changes to the text of Rule 1.3.)

Selected State Variations

California: See Rule 3-110(B) (Failing to Act Competently).

Colorado: Rule 1.3 adds a second sentence, taken from DR 6-101 of the old Code: "A lawyer shall not neglect a legal matter entrusted to that lawyer."

District of Columbia: D.C. adds Rules 1.3(b) and (c) — see District of Columbia Rules of Professional Conduct below.

Georgia: In the rules effective January 1, 2001, Georgia adopts ABA Model Rule 1.3 and its Comment essentially verbatim, but adds the following sentence to Rule 1.3: "Reasonable diligence as used in this Rule means that a lawyer shall not without just cause to the detriment of the client in effect wilfully abandon or wilfully disregard a legal matter entrusted to the lawyer."

Massachusetts: Rule 1.3 adds the following sentence: "The lawyer should represent a client zealously within the bounds of the law."

New Hampshire adds Rule 1.3(b), which provides:

> Performance by a lawyer is prompt and diligent when:
>
> (1) it is carried out in the manner and within the time parameters established by the agreement between the client and the lawyer; however, the lawyer may not rely upon the terms of an agreement to excuse performance which is not prompt and diligent in light of changes in circumstances, known to the lawyer, which require adjustments to the agreed upon schedule of performance.
>
> (2) in all other matters of representation, it is carried out with no avoidable harm to the client's interest nor to the lawyer-client relationship.

New York: Compare ABA Model Rule 1.3 to New York's DR 6-101(A)(3) and DR 7-101(A).

Texas omits Rule 1.3.

Virginia adds the following subparagraphs (b) and (c) to Rule 1.3, using language based on DR 7-101(A)(2) and (A)(3) of the ABA Model Code of Professional Responsibility:

> (b) A lawyer shall not intentionally fail to carry out a contract of employment entered into with a client for professional services, but may withdraw as permitted under Rule 1.16.
>
> (c) A lawyer shall not intentionally prejudice or damage a client during the course of the professional relationship, except as required or permitted under Rule 1.6 and Rule 3.3.

Related Materials

ABA Standards for Imposing Lawyer Discipline:

> 4.41. Disbarment is generally appropriate when:
>
> (a) a lawyer abandons the practice and causes serious or potentially serious injury to a client; or
>
> (b) a lawyer knowingly fails to perform services for a client and causes serious or potentially serious injury to a client; or
>
> (c) a lawyer engages in a pattern of neglect with respect to client matters and causes serious or potentially serious injury to a client.
>
> 4.42. Suspension is generally appropriate when:
>
> (a) a lawyer knowingly fails to perform services for a client and causes injury or potential injury to a client; or
>
> (b) a lawyer engages in a pattern of neglect and causes injury or potential injury to a client.

IRS Regulations: In the regulations governing practice before the Internal Revenue Service, 31 C.F.R. §10.22 requires each attorney to "exercise due diligence" in preparing and filing tax returns, documents, affidavits, and other papers relating to Internal Revenue Service matters and in "determining the correctness of oral or written representations made" to the Department of the Treasury or in any matter administered by the Internal Revenue Service.

Restatement of the Law Governing Lawyers: See Restatement §16 in our chapter on the Restatement later in this volume.

Rule 1.4 Communication

(a) A lawyer shall ~~keep a client reasonably informed about the status of a matter and promptly comply with reasonable requests for information.~~:

(1) promptly inform the client of any decision or circumstance with respect to which the client's informed consent, as defined in Rule 1.0(e), is required by these Rules;

(2) reasonably consult with the client about the means by which the client's objectives are to be accomplished;

(3) keep the client reasonably informed about the status of the matter;

(4) promptly comply with reasonable requests for information; and

(5) consult with the client about any relevant limitation on the lawyer's conduct when the lawyer knows that the client expects assistance not permitted by the Rules of Professional Conduct or other law.

(b) A lawyer shall explain a matter to the extent reasonably necessary to permit the client to make informed decisions regarding the representation.

COMMENT

[1] Reasonable communication between the lawyer and the client is necessary for the client effectively to participate in the representation.

Communicating with Client

[2] If these Rules require that a particular decision about the representation be made by the client, paragraph (a)(1) requires that the lawyer promptly consult with and secure the client's consent prior to taking action unless prior discussions with the client have resolved what action the client wants the lawyer to take. For example, a lawyer who receives from opposing counsel an offer of settlement in a civil controversy or a proffered plea bargain in a criminal case must promptly inform the client of its substance unless the client has previously indicated that the proposal will be acceptable or unacceptable or has authorized the lawyer to accept or to reject the offer. See Rule 1.2(a).

[3] Paragraph (a)(2) requires the lawyer to reasonably consult with the client about the means to be used to accomplish the client's objectives. In some situations — depending on both the importance of the action under consideration and the feasibility of consulting with the client — this duty will require consultation prior to taking action. In other circumstances, such as during a trial when an immediate decision must be made, the exigency of the situation may require the lawyer to act without prior consultation. In such cases the lawyer must nonetheless act reasonably to inform the client of actions the lawyer has taken on the client's behalf. Additionally, paragraph (a)(3) requires that the lawyer keep the client reasonably informed about the status of the matter, such as significant developments affecting the timing or the substance of the representation.

[4] A lawyer's regular communication with clients will minimize the occasions on which a client will need to request information concerning

the representation. When a client makes a reasonable request for information, however, paragraph (a)(4) requires prompt compliance with the request, or if a prompt response is not feasible, that the lawyer, or a member of the lawyer's staff, acknowledge receipt of the request and advise the client when a response may be expected. Client telephone calls should be promptly returned or acknowledged.

Explaining Matters

~~[1]~~ [5] The client should have sufficient information to participate intelligently in decisions concerning the objectives of the representation and the means by which they are to be pursued, to the extent the client is willing and able to do so. ~~For example, a lawyer negotiating on behalf of a client should provide the client with facts relevant to the matter, inform the client of communications from another party and take other reasonable steps that permit the client to make a decision regarding a serious offer from another party. A lawyer who receives from opposing counsel an offer of settlement in a civil controversy or a proffered plea bargain in a criminal case should promptly inform the client of its substance unless prior discussions with the client have left it clear that the proposal will be unacceptable. See Rule 1.2(a). Even when a client delegates authority to the lawyer, the client should be kept advised of the status of the matter. [2]~~ Adequacy of communication depends in part on the kind of advice or assistance that is involved. For example, ~~in negotiations where~~ when there is time to explain a proposal made in a negotiation, the lawyer should review all important provisions with the client before proceeding to an agreement. In litigation a lawyer should explain the general strategy and prospects of success and ordinarily should consult the client on tactics that ~~might~~ are likely to result in significant expense or to injure or coerce others. On the other hand, a lawyer ordinarily ~~cannot~~ will not be expected to describe trial or negotiation strategy in detail. The guiding principle is that the lawyer should fulfill reasonable client expectations for information consistent with the duty to act in the client's best interests, and the client's overall requirements as to the character of representation. In certain circumstances, such as when a lawyer asks a client to consent to a representation affected by a conflict of interest, the client must give informed consent, as defined in Rule 1.0(e).

~~[3]~~ [6] Ordinarily, the information to be provided is that appropriate for a client who is a comprehending and responsible adult. However, fully informing the client according to this standard may be impracticable, for example, where the client is a child or suffers from ~~mental disability~~ diminished capacity. See Rule 1.14. When the client is an organization or group, it is often impossible or inappropriate to inform every one of its members about its legal affairs; ordinarily, the lawyer should address communications to the appropriate officials of the organization. See Rule 1.13.

Where many routine matters are involved, a system of limited or occasional reporting may be arranged with the client. ~~Practical exigency may also require a lawyer to act for a client without prior consultation.~~

Withholding Information

~~[4]~~ [7] In some circumstances, a lawyer may be justified in delaying transmission of information when the client would be likely to react imprudently to an immediate communication. Thus, a lawyer might withhold a psychiatric diagnosis of a client when the examining psychiatrist indicates that disclosure would harm the client. A lawyer may not withhold information to serve the lawyer's own interest or convenience or the interests or convenience of another person. Rules or court orders governing litigation may provide that information supplied to a lawyer may not be disclosed to the client. Rule 3.4(c) directs compliance with such rules or orders.

Canon and Code Antecedents

ABA Canons of Professional Ethics: Canon 8 provided as follows:

8. Advising Upon the Merits of a Client's Cause

A lawyer should endeavor to obtain full knowledge of his client's cause before advising thereon, and he is bound to give a candid opinion of the merits and probable result of pending or contemplated litigation. The miscarriages to which justice is subject, by reason of surprises and disappointments in evidence and witnesses, and through mistakes of juries and errors of Courts, even though only occasional, admonish lawyers to beware of bold and confident assurances to clients, especially where the employment may depend upon such assurance. Whenever the controversy will admit of fair adjustment, the client should be advised to avoid or to end the litigation.

ABA Model Code of Professional Responsibility: Compare DR 6-101(A)(3) and DR 9-102(B)(1) (reprinted later in this volume).

Cross-References in Other Rules

Rule 1.2 (a): "Subject to paragraphs (c) and (d), a lawyer shall abide by a client's decisions concerning the objectives of representation and, as required by **Rule 1.4**, shall consult with the client as to the means by which they are to be pursued."

Rule 1.2, Comment 1: "The decisions specified in paragraph (a) . . . must also be made by the client. See **Rule 1.4(a)(1)** for the lawyer's duty to communicate with the client about such decisions. With respect to the means by which the client's objectives are to be pursued, the lawyer shall consult with the client as required by **Rule 1.4(a)(2)**. . . ."

Rule 1.2, Comment 3: "Absent a material change in circumstances and subject to **Rule 1.4**, a lawyer may rely on such an advance authorization."

Rule 1.2, Comment 13: "If a lawyer comes to know or reasonably should know that a client expects assistance not permitted by the Rules of Professional Conduct or other law or if the lawyer intends to act contrary to the client's instructions, the lawyer must consult with the client regarding the limitations on the lawyer's conduct. See **Rule 1.4(a)(5)**."

Rule 1.3, Comment 4: "Doubt about whether a client-lawyer relationship still exists should be clarified by the lawyer, preferably in writing, so that the client will not mistakenly suppose the lawyer is looking after the client's affairs when the lawyer has ceased to do so. See **Rule 1.4(a)(2)**."

Rule 1.6, Comment 10: "When disclosure of information relating to the representation appears to be required by other law, the lawyer must discuss the matter with the client to the extent required by **Rule 1.4**."

Rule 1.6, Comment 11: "In the event of an adverse ruling, the lawyer must consult with the client about the possibility of appeal to the extent required by **Rule 1.4**."

Rule 1.7, Comment 31: "As to the duty of confidentiality, continued common representation will almost certainly be inadequate if one client asks the lawyer not to disclose to the other client information relevant to the common representation. This is so because the lawyer has an equal duty of loyalty to each client, and each client has the right to be informed of anything bearing on the representation that might affect that client's interests and the right to expect that the lawyer will use that information to that client's benefit. See **Rule 1.4**."

Rule 2.1, Comment 5: "When a lawyer knows that a client proposes a course of action that is likely to result in substantial adverse legal consequences to the client, the lawyer's duty to the client under **Rule 1.4** may require that the lawyer offer advice if the client's course of action is related to the representation. Similarly, when a matter is likely to involve litigation, it may be necessary under **Rule 1.4** to inform the client of forms of dispute resolution that might constitute reasonable alternatives to litigation."

Rule 4.4, Comment 3: "Where a lawyer is not required by applicable law to do so, the decision to voluntarily return such a document is a matter of professional judgment ordinarily reserved to the lawyer. See Rules 1.2 and **1.4**."

Rule 5.5, Comment 20: "[A] lawyer who practices law in this jurisdiction pursuant to paragraphs (c) or (d) may have to inform the client that the lawyer is not licensed to practice law in this jurisdiction. For example, that may be required when the representation occurs primarily in this jurisdiction and requires knowledge of the law of this jurisdiction. See **Rule 1.4(b)**."

Legislative History of Model Rule 1.4

1979 Unofficial Pre-Circulation Draft (then Rule 1.3):

(a) A lawyer shall keep a client informed about a matter in which the lawyer's services are being rendered. Informing the client includes:

(1) Periodically advising the client of the status and progress of the matter;

(2) Explaining the legal and practical aspects of the matter and foreseeable effects of alternative courses of action; and . . .

(c) A lawyer may withhold information to which a client is otherwise entitled only when doing so is necessary to protect the client's interest or some superior interest.

1980 Discussion Draft prohibited a lawyer from withholding information to which a client was entitled "except when doing so is clearly necessary to protect the client's interest or to comply with the requirements of law or the rules of professional conduct."

1981 Draft provided:

(b) A lawyer shall explain the legal and practical aspects of a matter and alternative courses of action to the extent reasonably necessary to permit the client to make informed decisions regarding the representation.

1982 Draft was adopted.

2002 Amendments: At its February 2002 Mid-Year Meeting, the ABA House of Delegates adopted without change the ABA Ethics 2000 Commission proposal to amend Rule 1.4 and its Comment.

Selected State Variations

California: Compare Rule 3-500 (Communication), Rule 3-510 (Communication of Settlement Offer), and B & P Code §6068(m) (regarding communication generally).

District of Columbia: D.C. adds Rule 1.4(c) — see District of Columbia Rules of Professional Conduct below.

Florida: Rule 4-1.5(f)(4)(C) requires every lawyer entering into a contingent fee agreement to provide the client with a Statement of Client's Rights for Contingency Fees that contains the following paragraph:

10. . . . Your lawyer must notify you of all offers of settlement before and after the trial. Offers during the trial must be immediately communicated and you should consult with your lawyer regarding whether to accept a settlement. However, you must make the final decision to accept or reject a settlement.

Georgia: In the rules effective January 1, 2001, Georgia adopts ABA Model Rule 1.4 and its Comment essentially verbatim, but adds a new paragraph 1B to the Comment providing that "[t]he timeliness of a lawyer's communication must be judged by all of the controlling factors. 'Prompt' communication with the client does not equate to 'instant' communication with the client and is sufficient if reasonable under the relevant circumstances."

Louisiana Rule 1.4(b) provides: "The lawyer shall give the client sufficient information to participate intelligently in decisions concerning the object of the representation and the means by which they are to be pursued, to the extent the client is willing and able to do so."

Massachusetts: The Comment to Rule 1.4 states: "There will be circumstances in which a lawyer should advise a client concerning the advantages and disadvantages of available dispute resolution options. . . ."

Michigan adds to Rule 1.4(a): "A lawyer shall notify the client promptly of all settlement offers, mediation evaluations, and proposed plea bargains."

New Hampshire adds Rule 1.4(c), which provides: "A client is reasonably informed when information relevant to the protection of the client's interest is provided at an appropriate time and in an appropriate manner."

New York: Compare ABA Model Rule 1.4(a) to New York's EC 9-2, DR 6-101(A)(3), and DR 9-102(C)(1) and (4). Compare Rule 1.4(b) to EC 7-8.

Pennsylvania omits the word "reasonably" from Rules 1.4(a) and (b).

Rhode Island: In 1998, Rhode Island adopted an innovative new subparagraph to Rule 1.4 that provides as follows:

> (a) When a lawyer has not regularly represented a client and has reason to believe that the client does not fully understand the nature of the attorney-client relationship and the expectations and obligations arising out of that relationship, the lawyer shall take reasonable steps to inform the client of the nature of the attorney-client relationship before the representation is undertaken. Such disclosure should include what the lawyer expects of the client and what the client can expect from the lawyer. . . .

At the same time, Rhode Island adopted (as Appendix 2 to the state ethics rules) a new Client's Statement of Rights and Responsibilities, which discusses attorney fees and other fundamental aspects of the attorney-client relationship. A lawyer may satisfy the disclosure requirements of Rule 1.4 by providing the client with a copy of the Statement of Client's Rights and Responsibilities, but is not obligated to do so if the lawyer takes other reasonable steps to ensure the client's understanding of the attorney-client relationship.

Virginia: Rule 1.4(c) requires a lawyer to "inform the client of facts pertinent to the matter and of communications from another party that may significantly affect settlement or resolution of the matter."

Related Materials

ABA Formal Ethics Opinions: See ABA Formal Ethics Op. 92-366 (1992).

ABA Standards for Imposing Lawyer Sanctions:

> 4.61. Disbarment is generally appropriate when a lawyer knowingly deceives a client with the intent to benefit the lawyer or another, and causes serious injury or potentially serious injury to a client.
>
> 4.62. Suspension is generally appropriate when a lawyer knowingly deceives a client, and causes injury or potential injury to the client.

American Academy of Matrimonial Lawyers: The "Bounds of Advocacy" drafted by the American Academy of Matrimonial Lawyers contains the following provision and commentary:

> 2.6 An attorney should keep the client informed of developments in the representation and promptly respond to letters and telephone calls.

Comment to Rule 2.6

> The duty of keeping the client reasonably informed and promptly complying with reasonable requests for information, includes the attorney or a staff member responding to telephone calls, normally by the end of the next business day. The client should be informed at the outset, however, that communications with the attorney

are chargeable. In addition, the attorney should routinely: send the client a copy of all pleadings and correspondence, except in unusual circumstances; provide the client with frequent statements of costs and fees (see Standards 2.1-2.5); provide notice before incurring any major costs; provide notice of any calendar changes, scheduled court appearances, and discovery proceedings; communicate all settlement offers, no matter how trivial or facetious; advise of major changes in the law affecting the proceedings; and provide periodic status reports on progress in the case and major changes in case strategy.

Frequent communication with the client on important matters (1) empowers the client, (2) satisfies the client's need for information about the progress of the case, (3) helps to build a positive attorney-client relationship, and (4) helps the client understand the amount and nature of the work the attorney is performing, thereby reducing concern that nothing is happening and that the attorney is not earning her fees. While the attorney should understand that a pending divorce is usually the single most important matter in the life of the client, the client should understand that a successful lawyer has many clients, all of whom believe their case to be the most important.

Financial Institutions: Despite Rule 1.4, attorneys for banks and other financial institutions may be prohibited by federal law from disclosing certain information to their clients. In 1989, as a reaction to the savings and loan crisis, Congress passed 12 U.S.C. §3420(b), the first federal statute ever to impose an absolute ban on disclosures of certain grand jury subpoenas to "any person named" in the subpoenas. As amended Oct. 26, 2001, §3420(b) provides (with emphasis added):

> No officer, director, partner, employee, or shareholder of, or agent or *attorney* for, a financial institution shall, directly or indirectly, notify any person named in a grand jury subpoena served on such institution in connection with an investigation relating to a possible —
>
> (A) crime against any financial institution or supervisory agency . . . ; or
>
> (B) conspiracy to commit such crime,
>
> about the existence or contents of such subpoena, or information that has been furnished to the grand jury in response to such subpoena.

Violation of §3420(b) with intent to obstruct grand jury proceedings is punishable by up to five years in prison and/or a $250,000 fine, and violations without any obstructionist intent are punishable by up to one year in jail and/or a $100,000 fine. See Norman A. Bloch, Gagging Bankers: Grand Jury Nondisclosure Statutes and the First Amendment, 107 Banking L.J. 441 (1990).

Restatement of the Law Governing Lawyers: See Restatement §20 in our chapter on the Restatement later in this volume.

Rule 1.5 Fees

> **Editors' Note.** At its August 2001 Annual Meeting, the ABA House of Delegates rejected certain parts of the Ethics 2000 Commission's proposal to amend Rule 1.5. The rejected provisions are reprinted after the heading "2002 Amendments" in the Legislative History below.

(a) A ~~lawyer's fee~~ lawyer shall ~~be reasonable~~ not make an agreement for, charge, or collect an unreasonable fee or an unreasonable

amount for expenses. The factors to be considered in determining the reasonableness of a fee include the following:

(1) the time and labor required, the novelty and difficulty of the questions involved, and the skill requisite to perform the legal service properly;

(2) the likelihood, if apparent to the client, that the acceptance of the particular employment will preclude other employment by the lawyer;

(3) the fee customarily charged in the locality for similar legal services;

(4) the amount involved and the results obtained;

(5) the time limitations imposed by the client or by the circumstances;

(6) the nature and length of the professional relationship with the client;

(7) the experience, reputation, and ability of the lawyer or lawyers performing the services; and

(8) whether the fee is fixed or contingent.

(b) ~~When the lawyer has not regularly represented the client,~~ The scope of the representation and the basis or rate of the fee and expenses for which the client will be responsible shall be communicated to the client, preferably in writing, before or within a reasonable time after commencing the representation, except when the lawyer will charge a regularly represented client on the same basis or rate. Any changes in the basis or rate of the fee or expenses shall also be communicated to the client.

(c) A fee may be contingent on the outcome of the matter for which the service is rendered, except in a matter in which a contingent fee is prohibited by paragraph (d) or other law. A contingent fee agreement shall be in a writing signed by the client and shall state the method by which the fee is to be determined, including the percentage or percentages that shall accrue to the lawyer in the event of settlement, trial or appeal; litigation and other expenses to be deducted from the recovery; and whether such expenses are to be deducted before or after the contingent fee is calculated. The agreement must clearly notify the client of any expenses for which the client will be liable whether or not the client is the prevailing party. Upon conclusion of a contingent fee matter, the lawyer shall provide the client with a written statement stating the outcome of the matter and, if there is a recovery, showing the remittance to the client and the method of its determination.

(d) A lawyer shall not enter into an arrangement for, charge, or collect:

(1) any fee in a domestic relations matter, the payment or amount of which is contingent upon the securing of a divorce or upon the amount of alimony or support, or property settlement in lieu thereof; or

(2) a contingent fee for representing a defendant in a criminal case.

(e) A division of a fee between lawyers who are not in the same firm may be made only if:

(1) the division is in proportion to the services performed by each lawyer or~~, by written agreement with the client,~~ each lawyer assumes joint responsibility for the representation;

(2) the client ~~is advised of and does not object to the participation of all the lawyers involved~~ agrees to the arrangement, including the share each lawyer will receive, and the agreement is confirmed in writing; and

(3) the total fee is reasonable.

COMMENT

Reasonableness of Fee and Expenses

[1] Paragraph (a) requires that lawyers charge fees that are reasonable under the circumstances. The factors specified in (1) through (8) are not exclusive. Nor will each factor be relevant in each instance. Paragraph (a) also requires that expenses for which the client will be charged must be reasonable. A lawyer may seek reimbursement for the cost of services performed in-house, such as copying, or for other expenses incurred in-house, such as telephone charges, either by charging a reasonable amount to which the client has agreed in advance or by charging an amount that reasonably reflects the cost incurred by the lawyer.

Basis or Rate of Fee

~~[1]~~ [2] When the lawyer has regularly represented a client, they ordinarily will have evolved an understanding concerning the basis or rate of the fee and the expenses for which the client will be responsible. In a new client-lawyer relationship, however, an understanding as to ~~the fee~~ fees and expenses ~~should~~ must be promptly established. ~~It is not necessary to recite all the factors that underlie the basis of the fee, but only those that are directly involved in its computation. It is sufficient, for example, to state that the basic rate is an hourly charge or a fixed amount or an estimated amount, or to identify the factors that may be taken into account in finally fixing the fee. When developments occur during the representation that render an earlier estimate substantially inaccurate, a revised estimate should be provided to the client.~~ Generally, it is desirable to furnish the client with at least a simple memorandum or copy of the lawyer's customary fee arrangements that states the general nature of the legal services to be provided, the basis, rate or total amount of the fee and whether and to what extent the client will be responsible for any costs, expenses or disbursements in the course of the representation. A written statement concerning the ~~fee~~ terms of the engagement reduces the possibility of misunderstanding. ~~Furnishing the client with a simple memorandum or a copy of the lawyer's customary fee schedule is sufficient if the basis or rate of the fee is set forth.~~

[3] Contingent fees, like any other fees, are subject to the reasonableness standard of paragraph (a) of this Rule. In determining whether a particular contingent fee is reasonable, or whether it is reasonable to charge any form of contingent fee, a lawyer must consider the factors that are relevant under the circumstances. Applicable law may impose limitations on contingent fees, such as a ceiling on the percentage allowable, or may require a lawyer to offer clients an alternative basis for the fee. Applicable law also may apply to situations other than a contingent fee, for example, government regulations regarding fees in certain tax matters.

Terms of Payment

~~[2]~~ [4] A lawyer may require advance payment of a fee, but is obliged to return any unearned portion. See Rule 1.16(d). A lawyer may accept property in payment for services, such as an ownership interest in an enterprise, providing this does not involve acquisition of a proprietary interest in the cause of action or subject matter of the litigation contrary to Rule 1.8~~(j)~~(i). However, a fee paid in property instead of money may be subject to ~~special scrutiny because it involves questions concerning both the value of the services and the lawyer's special knowledge of the value of the property~~ the requirements of Rule 1.8(a) because such fees often have the essential qualities of a business transaction with the client.

~~[3]~~ [5] An agreement may not be made whose terms might induce the lawyer improperly to curtail services for the client or perform them in a way contrary to the client's interest. For example, a lawyer should not enter into an agreement whereby services are to be provided only up to a stated amount when it is foreseeable that more extensive services probably will be required, unless the situation is adequately explained to the client. Otherwise, the client might have to bargain for further assistance in the midst of a proceeding or transaction. However, it is proper to define the extent of services in light of the client's ability to pay. A lawyer should not exploit a fee arrangement based primarily on hourly charges by using wasteful procedures. ~~When there is doubt whether a contingent fee is consistent with the client's best interest, the lawyer should offer the client alternative bases for the fee and explain their implications. Applicable law may impose limitations on contingent fees, such as a ceiling on the percentage.~~

Prohibited Contingent Fees

[6] Paragraph (d) prohibits a lawyer from charging a contingent fee in a domestic relations matter when payment is contingent upon the securing of a divorce or upon the amount of alimony or support or property settlement to be obtained. This provision does not preclude a contract for a contingent fee for legal representation in connection with the recovery of post-judgment balances due under support, alimony or other financial orders because such contracts do not implicate the same policy concerns.

Division of Fee

~~[4]~~ [7] A division of fee is a single billing to a client covering the fee of two or more lawyers who are not in the same firm. A division of fee facilitates association of more than one lawyer in a matter in which neither alone could serve the client as well, and most often is used when the fee is contingent and the division is between a referring lawyer and a trial specialist. Paragraph (e) permits the lawyers to divide a fee ~~on~~ either on the basis of the proportion of services they render or ~~by agreement between the participating lawyers~~ if ~~all assume~~ each lawyer assumes responsibility for the representation as a whole. ~~and~~ In addition, the client ~~is advised and does not object. It does not require disclosure to the client of~~ must agree to the arrangement, including the share that each lawyer is to receive, and the agreement must be confirmed in writing. Contingent fee agreements must be in a writing signed by the client and must otherwise comply with paragraph (c) of this Rule. Joint responsibility for the representation entails ~~the obligations stated in Rule 5.1 for purposes of the matter involved~~ financial and ethical responsibility for the representation as if the lawyers were associated in a partnership. A lawyer should only refer a matter to a lawyer whom the referring lawyer reasonably believes is competent to handle the matter. See Rule 1.1.

[8] Paragraph (e) does not prohibit or regulate division of fees to be received in the future for work done when lawyers were previously associated in a law firm.

Disputes over Fees

~~[5]~~ [9] If a procedure has been established for resolution of fee disputes, such as an arbitration or mediation procedure established by the bar, the lawyer must comply with the procedure when it is mandatory, and, even when it is voluntary, the lawyer should conscientiously consider submitting to it. Law may prescribe a procedure for determining a lawyer's fee, for example, in representation of an executor or administrator, a class or a person entitled to a reasonable fee as part of the measure of damages. The lawyer entitled to such a fee and a lawyer representing another party concerned with the fee should comply with the prescribed procedure.

Canon and Code Antecedents

ABA Canons of Professional Ethics: Canons 12, 13, 14, and 42 provided as follows:

12. Fixing the Amount of the Fee

In fixing fees, lawyers should avoid charges which overestimate their advice and services, as well as those which undervalue them. A client's ability to pay cannot justify a charge in excess of the value of the service, though his poverty may require a less charge, or even none at all. The reasonable requests of brother lawyers, and of their widows and orphans without ample means, should receive special and kindly consideration.

In determining the amount of the fee, it is proper to consider: (1) the time and labor required, the novelty and difficulty of the questions involved and the skill requisite properly to conduct the cause; (2) whether the acceptance of employment in the particular case will preclude the lawyer's appearance for others in cases likely to arise out of the transaction, and in which there is a reasonable expectation that otherwise he would be employed, or will involve the loss of other employment while employed in the particular case or antagonisms with other clients; (3) the customary charges of the Bar for similar services; (4) the amount involved in the controversy and the benefits resulting to the client from the services; (5) the contingency or the certainty of the compensation; and (6) the character of the employment, whether casual or for an established and constant client. No one of these considerations in itself is controlling. They are mere guides in ascertaining the real value of the service.

In determining the customary charges of the Bar for similar services, it is proper for a lawyer to consider a schedule of minimum fees adopted by a Bar Association, but no lawyer should permit himself to be controlled thereby or to follow it as his sole guide in determining the amount of his fee.

In fixing fees it should never be forgotten that the profession is a branch of the administration of justice and not a mere money-getting trade.

13. Contingent Fees

A contract for a contingent fee, where sanctioned by law, should be reasonable under all the circumstances of the case, including the risk and uncertainty of the compensation, but should always be subject to the supervision of a court, as to its reasonableness.

14. Suing a Client for a Fee

Controversies with clients concerning compensation are to be avoided by the lawyer so far as shall be compatible with his self-respect and with his right to receive reasonable recompense for his services; and lawsuits with clients should be resorted to only to prevent injustice, imposition or fraud.

42. Expenses of Litigation

A lawyer may not properly agree with a client that the lawyer shall pay or bear the expenses of litigation; he may in good faith advance expenses as a matter of convenience, but subject to reimbursement.

ABA Model Code of Professional Responsibility: Compare DR 2-106(A), DR 2-106(B), DR 2-106(C), and DR 2-107(A) (reprinted later in this volume).

Cross-References in Other Rules

Rule 1.8, Comment 1: Rule 1.8 "does not apply to ordinary fee arrangements between client and lawyer, which are governed by **Rule 1.5**."

Rule 1.8, Comment 9: Rule 1.8(d) "does not prohibit a lawyer representing a client in a transaction concerning literary property from agreeing that the lawyer's fee shall consist of a share in ownership in the property, if the arrangement conforms to **Rule 1.5**."

Rule 1.8, Comment 16: Rule 1.8(i) "states the traditional general rule that lawyers are prohibited from acquiring a proprietary interest in litigation. . . . The Rule is subject to specific exceptions . . . Contracts for contingent fees in civil cases are governed by **Rule 1.5**."

Rule 1.17, Comment 5: "If an area of practice is sold and the lawyer remains in the active practice of law, the lawyer must cease accepting any matters in the area of practice that has been sold, either as counsel or co-counsel or by assuming joint responsibility for a matter in connection with the division of a fee with another lawyer as would otherwise be permitted by **Rule 1.5(e)**."

Rule 7.2, Comment 8: "Except as provided in **Rule 1.5(e)**, a lawyer who receives referrals from a lawyer or nonlawyer professional must not pay anything solely for the referral. . . ."

Legislative History of Model Rule 1.5

1979 Unofficial Pre-Circulation Draft (then Rule 1.4):

(b) A fee agreement shall . . .

(2) State with reasonable definiteness, expressly or by implication, the nature and extent of the services to be provided; and . . .

(c) A fee agreement shall be expressed or confirmed in writing before the lawyer has rendered substantial services in the matter, except:

(1) Where an agreement as to the fee is implied by the fact that the lawyer's services are of the same general kind as previously rendered to and paid for by the client;

(2) For services rendered in an emergency where a written agreement or confirmation is impracticable. . . .

1980 Discussion Draft (then Rule 1.6):

(b) The basis or rate of a lawyer's fee shall be put in writing before the lawyer has rendered substantial services in the matter, except when:

(1) An agreement as to the fee is implied by the fact that the lawyer's services are of the same general kind as previously rendered to and paid for by the client; or

(2) The services are rendered in an emergency where a writing is impracticable.

(c) The form of a fee and the terms of a fee agreement shall involve no inducement for the lawyer to perform the services in a manner inconsistent with the best interests of the client. . . .

(e) A division of fee between lawyers who are not in the same firm may be made only if:

(1) The division is in proportion to the services performed by each lawyer, or both lawyers expressly assume responsibility as if they were partners;

(2) The terms of the division are disclosed to the client. . . .

1981 Draft of Rule 1.5(b) continued to require that the "basis or rate of a lawyer's fee shall be communicated to the client in writing before the lawyer renders substantial services in a matter. . . ."

1982 Draft was substantially the same as adopted.

2002 Amendments: At its August 2001 Annual Meeting, the ABA House had Delegates adopted the ABA Ethics 2000 Commission's proposed amendments to Rules 1.5(a), (c), and (e) without change — no changes were proposed to Rule 1.5(d) — but the House of Delegates rejected the Commission's proposal to delete the word "preferably" before the words "in writing" in Rule 1.5(b). In addition, the House substituted the words "to the client" for the words "in writing" at the end of the new requirement in Rule 1.5(b) requiring lawyers to communicate any changes in the basis or rate of the fee or expenses. Finally, the House rejected a proposed final sentence in Rule 1.5(b) that would have qualified the proposed "in writing" requirement by stating: "This paragraph does not apply in any matter in which it is reasonably foreseeable that the total cost to a client, including attorney fees, will be [$500] or less." (The brackets around "$500" indicated that each state could choose its own threshold amount.) The August 2001 votes were confirmed at the ABA's February 2002 Mid-Year Meeting.

Selected State Variations

Alaska: Rule 1.5(b) adds: "In a case involving litigation, the lawyer shall notify the client in the written fee agreement of any costs, fees or expenses for which the client may be liable if the client is not the prevailing party." In addition, Alaska adds Rule 1.5(f), which provides that a lawyer "should be zealous in his or her efforts to avoid controversies over fees with clients and should attempt to resolve amicably any differences on the subject."

Arizona: Rule 1.5(d), comment permits an attorney to charge a contingent fee for the enforcement of child support or spousal maintenance orders, but the length of time that the contingency fee will apply to future payments must be spelled out and the agreement must be fair and equitable to the client.

Arkansas: Rule 1.5(d)(1) adds that in a domestic relations matter, "after a final order or decree is entered an attorney may enter into a contingent fee contract for collection of payments which are due pursuant to such decree or order."

California: See Rule 4-200 (Fees for Legal Services), B & P Code 6147-6149 (governing contingency fee contracts and other fee arrangements), and B & P Code 6200-6206 (establishing system and procedures for arbitrating fee disputes). California Public Contract Code §10353.5(a)(6) requires lawyers contracting to provide legal services to a state agency to "submit to legal bill audits and law firm audits if requested by the state agency." The audits may be conducted by employees or designees of the state agency or by any legal cost control providers retained by the state agency for that purpose.

Colorado: Effective July 1, 2000, Rule 1.5(b) eliminates the word "preferably" before "in writing," thus requiring a lawyer who has not regularly represented a client to communicate the basis or rate of the fee "in writing, before or within a reasonable time after commencing the representation." Rule 1.5(c) adds: "A contingent fee shall meet all the requirements of Chapter 23.3 of the Colorado Rules of Civil Procedure, 'Rules Governing Contingent Fees.'" Rule 23.3 itself contains seven separate rules, including Rule 4(a), which requires an attorney to disclose the following six things in writing before entering into a contingent fee agreement: "(1) The nature of other types of fee arrangements; (2) The nature of specially awarded attorney fees; (3) The nature of expenses and the estimated amount of expenses to handle the matter to conclusion; (4) The potential for an award of costs and attorneys' fees to the opposing party; (5) What is meant by 'associated counsel'; and (6) What is meant by 'subrogation' and the effect of any subrogation interest or lien." In addition, Rule 6 in Colo. R. Civ. P. 23.3 provides: "No contingent fee agreement shall be enforceable by the involved attorney unless there has been substantial compliance with all of the provisions of this rule." Rule 7 in Colo. R. Civ. P. 23.3 sets out various suggested disclosures for clients to sign, including this one:

> I have been informed and understand that there are several types of attorney fee arrangements: (1) time based, (2) fixed or (3) contingent. "Time based" means a fee that is determined by the amount of time involved such as so much per hour, day or week. "Fixed" means a fee that is based on an agreed amount regardless of the time or effort involved or the result obtained. "Contingent" means a certain agreed percentage or amount that is payable only upon attaining a recovery regardless of the time or effort involved. I understand I have the right to choose the type of attorney fee arrangement.

Colorado also adds a section (e) prohibiting referral fees. Rules 1.5(f) and (g), which took effect on July 1, 2002, provide as follows:

> (f) Fees are not earned until the lawyer confers a benefit on the client or performs a legal service for the client. Advances of unearned fees are the property of the client and shall be deposited in the lawyer's trust account pursuant to Rule 1.15(f)(1) until earned. If advances of unearned fees are in the form of property other than funds, then the lawyer shall hold such property separate from the lawyer's own property pursuant to Rule 1.15(a).
>
> (g) Nonrefundable fees and nonrefundable retainers are prohibited. Any agreement that purports to restrict a client's right to terminate the representation, or that unreasonably restricts a client's right to obtain a refund of unearned or unreasonable fees, is prohibited.

For information about the history of these rules, see the Colorado entry in the Selected State Variations after Rule 1.15 below.

Connecticut: Rule 1.5(a)(2) replaces the word "apparent" with the phrase "made known." Rule 1.5(b) provides that when the lawyer has not regularly represented a client:

> the basis or rate of the fee, whether and to what extent the client will be responsible for any court costs and expenses of litigation, and the scope of the matter to be undertaken shall be communicated to the client, in writing, before or within a reasonable time after commencing the representation. . . .

In addition, Connecticut's version of the fee sharing rule deletes ABA Model Rule 1.5(e)(1), and adds that the client must be advised of "the compensation sharing agreement and" of the participation of all lawyers involved.

District of Columbia: D.C. Rule 1.5(b), (d), and (e) differ significantly from the ABA Model Rule, and D.C. adds Rule 1.5(f) — see District of Columbia Rules of Professional Conduct below.

Florida: In 2000, Florida significantly amended its elaborate rules governing attorney fees. Florida's Rule 4-1.5(a) prohibits any fee "generated by employment that was obtained through advertising or solicitation not in compliance with the Rules Regulating The Florida Bar" or that is "clearly excessive." A clearly excessive fee includes (1) a fee that exceeds a reasonable fee by so much that it constitutes "clear overreaching or an unconscionable demand," or (2) a fee sought or secured "by means of intentional misrepresentation or fraud upon the client, a nonclient party, or any court, as to either entitlement to, or amount of, the fee." Florida also caps the percentage amount of any contingent fee.

Regarding fee sharing between lawyers in different firms, Rule 4-1.5(f)(2) requires that each participating lawyer "shall sign the contract with the client and shall agree to assume joint legal responsibility to the client for the performance of the services in question as if each were partners of the other lawyer or law firm involved." Florida also tightly controls the terms on which lawyers in different firms may share fees. Rule 4-1.5(f)(4)(D) provides that the lawyer assuming "primary responsibility for the legal services" must receive "a minimum of 75 percent of the total fee," and the lawyer assuming "secondary responsibility" can receive "a maximum of 25 percent of the total fee. Any fee in excess of 25 percent shall be presumed to be clearly excessive." But if two or more lawyers expect to "accept substantially equal active participation in the providing of legal services," then they may seek court authorization to divide the fee however they propose "based upon a sworn petition signed by all counsel that shall disclose in detail those services to be performed."

Florida Rule 4-1.5(g) provides that if lawyers in different firms share fees on a basis not in proportion to the amount of work done, then each lawyer must not only agree to assume "joint legal responsibility for the representation" but must also agree "to be available for consultation with the client."

Finally, in December 1990 the Florida Supreme Court gave itself the power to order any lawyer found guilty of violating the fee rules "to forfeit the fee or any part thereof," either by returning the excessive part of any fee to the client or by forfeiting all or part of an otherwise improper fee to the Florida Bar Clients' Security Fund. See Florida Rule 3-5.1(i).

Georgia: In the rules effective January 1, 2001, Georgia adopted the pre-2002 version of ABA Model Rule 1.5 essentially verbatim, but added to Rule 1.5(c) that a lawyer must include in the written statement at the conclusion of a contingent fee matter the amount of the attorney fee and "(D) if the attorney's fee is divided with another lawyer who is not a partner in or an associate of the lawyer's firm or law office, the amount of fee received by each and the manner in which the division is determined." Georgia also added to Rule 1.5(e)(2) that the client must be "advised of the share that each lawyer is to receive" when lawyers in different firms share a fee.

Georgia's court rules, beginning at Rule 6-101, include an elaborate fee arbitration program that handles fee disputes (1) between attorneys and their clients, (2) between lawyers arguing over fees when a lawyer withdraws from a partnership or when a partnership dissolves, or (3) between lawyers arguing over how to divide fees earned from joint services. Any lawyer or client requesting arbitration must agree to be bound by the result of the arbitration even if the other party does not. (This rule discourages people from filing frivolous complaints or invoking the arbitration process simply to obtain an "advisory opinion.") If the respondent does agree to be bound, the resulting arbitration award is enforceable under Georgia's general arbitration laws.

If a respondent lawyer refuses to be bound by the arbitration, and if bar counsel's investigation has determined that the client's claim appears to warrant a hearing, an ex parte arbitration hearing will be held. If the outcome of this hearing is in the client's favor, the State Bar will provide a lawyer at no cost to the client to represent the client in any subsequent litigation to adjust the fee in accordance with the arbitration award. According to the State Bar, this is intended to "relieve the client of the burden of paying a second lawyer to recover fees determined to have been excessively charged by the first lawyer." For more information, see the Georgia State Bar's web site at www.gabar.org (click on "Handbook," then on "Part VI — Fee Arbitration."

Idaho: Rule 1.5(d)(1) allows contingent fees in "proceedings to enforce or satisfy a judgment for property distribution or past due alimony or child support." Idaho also adds Rule 1.5(f), which provides as follows:

> (f) Upon reasonable request by the client, a lawyer shall provide, without charge, an accounting for fees and costs claimed or previously collected. Such an accounting shall include at least the following information:
>
> (1) Itemization of all hourly charges, costs, interest assessments, and past due balances.
>
> (2) For hourly rate charges, a description of the services performed and a notation of the person who performed those services. The description shall be of sufficient detail to generally apprise the client of the nature of the work performed.

Illinois provides that "the prohibition set forth in Rule 1.5(d)(1) shall not extend to representation in matters subsequent to final judgments in such cases."

Illinois adds a new subparagraph providing:

> (e) Notwithstanding Rule 1.5(c), a contingent fee agreement regarding the collection of commercial accounts or of insurance company subrogation claims may be made in accordance with the customs and practice in the locality for such legal services.

Illinois also adds the following new subparagraphs:

> (g) A division of fees [between lawyers not in the same firm] shall be made in proportion to the services performed and responsibility assumed by each lawyer, except where the primary service performed by one lawyer is the referral of the client to another lawyer and
>
> (1) the receiving lawyer discloses that the referring lawyer has received or will receive economic benefit from the referral and the extent and basis of such economic benefit, and
>
> (2) the referring lawyer agrees to assume the same legal responsibility for the performance of the services in question as would a partner of the receiving lawyer.
>
> (h) The total fee of the lawyers shall be reasonable.

(i) For purposes of Rule 1.5 "economic benefit" shall include:

(1) the amount of participation in the fee received with regard to the particular matter;

(2) any other form of remuneration passing to the referring lawyer from the receiving lawyer, whether or not with regard to the particular matter; and

(3) an established practice of referrals to and from or from and to the receiving lawyer and the referring lawyer.

(j) Notwithstanding Rule 1.5(f), a payment may be made to a lawyer formerly in the firm, pursuant to a separation or retirement agreement.

Kansas: Rule 1.5(c) adds that a court's determination that a fee is not reasonable "shall not be presumptive evidence of a violation that requires discipline of the attorney." Rule 1.5(e) adds:

> Upon application by the client, all fee contracts shall be subject to review and approval by the appropriate court having jurisdiction of the matter and the court shall have the authority to determine whether the contract is reasonable. If the court finds the contract is not reasonable, it shall set and allow a reasonable fee.

Maryland adds that a fee cannot be contingent upon a client's "securing custody of a child." Maryland also prohibits fees contingent "upon the amount of an award pursuant to Section 8-201-213 of Family Law Article Annotated Code of Maryland."

Massachusetts: Rule 1.5(c) does not require a contingent fee to be in writing if it concerns "the collection of commercial accounts" or "insurance company subrogation claims." The rule requires greater detail in the written contingent fee agreements required in all other cases. Rule 1.5(e) permits fee division with client consent but does not require the referring lawyer to perform any services or take joint responsibility for the matter. The client's consent need not be in writing.

Michigan: Rule 1.5(d) forbids contingent fees in "a domestic relations matter" without qualification. In 1998, Michigan adopted the requirement of ABA Model Rule 1.5(c) that a contingent fee agreement "shall be in writing . . . ." Michigan's Rule 8.121 further regulates contingent fees by setting a maximum allowable fee of "one-third of the amount recovered" in personal injury and wrongful death claims and providing that receiving, retaining, or sharing a contingent fee greater than one third in such a case "shall be deemed to be the charging of a 'clearly excessive fee' in violation of" Rule 1.5(a). Michigan omits ABA Model Rule 1.5(e)(1).

Minnesota adds to Rule 1.5(e)(2) that the client must be "advised of the share that each lawyer is to receive."

Montana adds the following item to the list of factors to be considered in determining whether a fee is reasonable: "[I]n contingent fee cases, the risk of no recovery, and the market value of the lawyer's services at the time and place involved."

New Jersey requires a fee agreement to be in writing if the lawyer has not regularly represented the client. In addition, New Jersey has adopted various court rules that tightly control contingent fees, especially in tort cases. Supreme Court Rule 1:21-7, for example, provides as follows:

> (c) In any matter where a client's claim for damages is based upon the alleged tortious conduct of another, including products liability claims, and the client is not

a subrogee, an attorney shall not contract for, charge, or collect a contingent fee in excess of the following limits:

(1) 33⅓% on the first $250,000 recovered;

(2) 25% on the next $250,000 recovered;

(3) 20% on the next $500,000 recovered; and

(4) on all amounts recovered in excess of the above by application for reasonable fee in accordance with the provisions of paragraph (f) hereof; and

(5) where the amount recovered is for the benefit of a client who was an infant or incompetent when the contingent fee arrangement was made, the foregoing limits shall apply, except that the fee on any amount recovered by settlement without trial shall not exceed 25%.

New Jersey also controls fees in matrimonial cases. Supreme Court Rule 1:21-7A provides: "All agreements for legal services by an attorney or attorneys in connection with family actions shall be in writing signed by the attorney and client."

New York: Compare ABA Model Rule 1.5(a) to New York's DR 2-106(A) and (B). Compare Rule 1.5(b) to New York's EC 2-19, DR 2-106(E) and (F), and 22 N.Y.C.R.R. Part 1215 ("Written Letter of Engagement"). Compare Rule 1.5(c) to New York's DR 2-106(D). Compare Rule 1.5(d) to New York's DR 2-106(C). Compare Rule 1.5(e) to New York's DR 2-107.

In medical, dental, and podiatric malpractice litigation, §474-a of the New York Judiciary Law imposes a strict sliding scale limit on contingent fees (ranging from 30 percent of the first $250,000 recovered to only 10 percent of any recovery over $1,250,000). In most other personal injury and property damage cases, New York's court rules allow attorneys on contingent fees to choose either a flat 33⅓ percent or a sliding scale (ranging from 50 percent of the first $1,000 recovered down to 25 percent of any recovery over $25,000), see e.g., 22 N.Y.C.R.R. §691.20(e). Fees exceeding these limits are "unreasonable and unconscionable" and violate the Code of Professional Responsibility unless a court raises the limits because of "extraordinary circumstances." In domestic relations matters, special court rules prohibit nonrefundable fees, restrict an attorney's right to obtain security for fees, require all retainer agreements to contain certain specified information, and mandate fee arbitration at the election of the client, see 22 N.Y.C.R.R. Part 1400. In addition, in domestic relations actions only, 22 N.Y.C.R.R. §§202.16(c) and (k)(3) require lawyers to file retainer agreements with the court and to provide certain information by affidavit with any application for counsel fees.

Effective January 1, 2002, new rules found at 22 N.Y.C.R.R. Part 137 require all New York attorneys to offer fee arbitration to clients in all civil matters, and to submit to fee arbitration if a client in a civil matter requests it. Under §137.1(b), the fee arbitration program does not apply to (1) criminal matters; (2) fee disputes involving less than $1000 or more than $50,000 (unless an arbitral body and the parties all consent); (3) "claims involving substantial legal questions, including professional malpractice or misconduct"; (4) claims for relief other than adjusting a legal fee; (5) disputes over a legal fee set by a court; (6) disputes where no legal services have been rendered for more than two years; (7) disputes with out-of-state attorneys who either have no office in New York or did not render any material portion of the services in New York; and (8) disputes where the person requesting arbitration is neither the client nor the client's legal representative. Part 137 will replace the old domestic relations fee arbitration rules found at 22 N.Y.C.R.R. Part 136, which have been in effect since the mid-1990s.

Moreover, effective March 4, 2002 (and slightly amended on April 3, 2002), the New York courts adopted a new 22 N.Y.C.R.R. Part 1215 that requires written letters of engagement in many matters. It provides as follows:

Part 1215 Written Letter of Engagement

§1215.1 Requirements

(a) Effective March 4, 2002, an attorney who undertakes to represent a client and enters into an arrangement for, charges or collects any fee from a client shall provide to the client a written letter of engagement before commencing the representation, or within a reasonable time thereafter (i) if otherwise impracticable or (ii) if the scope of services to be provided cannot be determined at the time of the commencement of representation. For purposes of this rule, where an entity (such as an insurance carrier) engages an attorney to represent a third party, the term "client" shall mean the entity that engages the attorney. Where there is a significant change in the scope of services or the fee to be charged, an updated letter of engagement shall be provided to the client.

(b) The letter of engagement shall address the following matters:

(1) Explanation of the scope of the legal services to be provided;

(2) Explanation of attorney's fees to be charged, expenses and billing practices; and, where applicable, shall provide that the client may have a right to arbitrate fee disputes under Part 137 of the Rules of the Chief Administrator.

(c) Instead of providing the client with a written letter of engagement, an attorney may comply with the provisions of subdivision (a) by entering into a signed written retainer agreement with the client, before or within a reasonable time after commencing the representation, provided that the agreement addresses the matters set forth in subdivision (b).

§1215.2 Exceptions

This section shall not apply to

(1) representation of a client where the fee to be charged is expected to be less than $3000,

(2) representation where the attorney's services are of the same general kind as previously rendered to and paid for by the client, or

(3) representation in domestic relations matters subject to Part 1400 of the Joint Rules of the Appellate Division (22 NYCRR), or

(4) representation where the attorney is admitted to practice in another jurisdiction and maintains no office in the State of New York, or where no material portion of the services are to be rendered in New York.

North Carolina: Rule 1.5(a) and Rule 1.5(b) are taken verbatim from DR 2-106(A) and (B) of the old ABA Model Code of Professional Responsibility. Rule 1.5(d)(1) adds that a lawyer "may charge and collect a contingent fee for representation in a criminal or civil asset forfeiture proceeding if not otherwise prohibited by law." Rule 1.5(f) provides as follows:

(f) Any lawyer having a dispute with a client regarding a fee for legal services must:

(1) make reasonable efforts to advise his or her client of the existence of the North Carolina State Bar's program of nonbinding fee arbitration at least 30 days prior to initiating legal proceedings to collect the disputed fee; and

(2) participate in good faith in nonbinding arbitration of the fee dispute if such is subject to the jurisdiction of any duly constituted fee arbitration committee of the North Carolina State Bar or any of its constituent district bars if the client submits a proper request for fee arbitration.

Ohio: DR 2-107(A) requires client consent after written disclosure to the client of "the terms of the division and the identity of all lawyers sharing in the fee." In addition, Ohio's DR 2-107(B) mandates that when lawyers who are sharing fees under DR 2-107 get into a fee dispute, "fees shall be divided in accordance with mediation or arbitration provided by a local bar association. Disputes that cannot be resolved by a local bar association shall be referred to the Ohio State Bar Association for mediation or arbitration." Ohio's DR 2-101(E)(1)(d)(ii) provides that if a lawyer's advertisement listing flat-rate services does not include a client's matter or an hourly fee, the client will be entitled, without obligation, to a specific written estimate of the "fee likely to be charged." Effective January 1, 2000, Ohio's DR 2-101(H)(1) requires any communication sent directly to a prospective client within thirty days after an accident or disaster to enclose a document entitled "Understanding Your Rights" which includes the following final paragraph:

> **9. How much will it cost?** In deciding whether to hire a particular lawyer, you should discuss, and the lawyer's written fee agreement should reflect:
>
> a. How is the lawyer to be paid? If you already have a settlement offer, how will that affect a contingent fee arrangement?
>
> b. How are the expenses involved in your case, such as telephone calls, deposition costs, and fees for expert witnesses, to be paid? Will these costs be advanced by the lawyer or charged to you as they are incurred? Since you are obligated to pay all expenses even if you lose your case, how will payment be arranged?
>
> c. Who will handle your case? If the case goes to trial, who will be the trial attorney?

Pennsylvania: Rule 1.5(b) requires a written fee agreement if a lawyer has not regularly represented a client. Pennsylvania Rule 1.5(e) requires only that "(1) the client is advised of and does not object to the participation of all the lawyers involved, and (2) the total fee of the lawyers is not illegal or clearly excessive. . . ."

Rhode Island: Rule 1.5(b) provides that if a lawyer has not regularly represented a client, the basis or rate of the fee "shall" be communicated to the client in writing. The rule also requires lawyers to send quarterly bills unless the client agrees to a different billing schedule or unless the fee is fixed or contingent. Rule 1.4 ("Communication") requires lawyers to take "reasonable steps to inform the client" about various aspects of the attorney-client relationship, including attorney fees.

Texas: Rule 1.04(a) forbids "illegal" or "unconscionable" fees and lists the same considerations as in Rule 1.5. The Texas Rules do not forbid contingent fees in family law matters but the Comment says they are "rarely justified." Texas Rule 1.04(f) provides that a division "or agreement for division" of a fee between lawyers who are not in the same firm shall not be made unless the division is "(i) in proportion to the professional services performed by each lawyer; (ii) made with a forwarding lawyer; or (iii) made, by written agreement with the client, with a lawyer who assumes joint responsibility for the representation. . . ."

Utah: Rule 1.5(b) provides as follows:

> (b) When the lawyer has not regularly represented the client, and it is reasonably foreseeable that the total attorneys fees to the client will exceed $750.00, the basis or rate of the fee shall be communicated to the client, in writing, before or within a reasonable time after commencing the representation.

Virginia: Rule 1.5(b) provides in part: "The lawyer's fee shall be adequately explained to the client." Rule 1.5(d)(1) forbids contingent fees in "a domestic relations matter, except in rare instances." Comment [3a] says that those rare instances include situations where "the parties are divorced and reconciliation is not a realistic prospect." Rule 1.5(e) requires full disclosure to the client when lawyers are dividing a fee. The "terms of the division of the fee" must be "disclosed to the client," the client must consent, the total fee must be reasonable, and the fee division and client consent must be "obtained in advance of the rendering of legal services." However, while a writing is said to be preferable, none is required.

Washington: Rule 1.5(a)(8) has the following criterion for evaluating the reasonableness of a fee: "Whether the fee agreement or confirming writing demonstrates that the client had received a reasonable and fair disclosure of material elements of the fee agreement and of the lawyer's billing practices." Rule 1.5(d)(1) adds that a fee may not be contingent on securing an "annulment of marriage," but an exception permits contingent fees in "postdissolution proceedings." Rule 1.5(e)(1) permits a division of fees if the division "is between the lawyer and a duly authorized lawyer referral service of either the Washington State Bar Association or of one of the county bar associations of this state."

Wyoming: Rule 1.5(e)(1) requires that a division of fees between lawyers must be in proportion to the services performed by each lawyer "*and*" by written agreement with the client, each lawyer assumes joint responsibility. Wyoming prohibits a lawyer from receiving a fee solely for making a referral.

Related Materials

ABA Commission on Billable Hours: In 2001, ABA President Robert Hirshon appointed the Commission on the Billable Hour. In August of 2002, the commission issued its report, which is available (together with other useful materials on the billable hour) at www.abanet.org/careercounsel/billable.html. The commission's purpose is eloquently explained in the preface to the report, which provides, in pertinent part, as follows:

> It has become increasingly clear that many of the legal profession's contemporary woes intersect at the billable hour. The 1960s marked the coming of age of the billable hour. . . .
>
> Today, unintended consequences of the billable hours model have permeated the profession. A recent study by the ABA shows that many young attorneys are leaving the profession due to a lack of balance in their lives. The unending drive for billable hours has had a negative effect not only on family and personal relationships, but on the public service role that lawyers traditionally have played in society. The elimination of discretionary time has taken a toll on pro bono work and our profession's ability to be involved in our communities. At the same time, professional development, workplace stimulation, mentoring and lawyer/client relationships have all suffered as a result of billable hour pressures.
>
> The profession is paying the price. Disaffection with the practice of law is illustrated by a feeling of frustration and isolation on the part of newer lawyers who, due to time-billing pressures, are not being as well mentored as in the past. Time pressures also result in less willingness on the part of lawyers to be collegial, which only exacerbates work load since it necessitates that everything be put in writing. Not coincidentally, public respect for lawyers has been waning since the 1970s. All this at a time when lawyers are less interested in climbing the corporate ladder and more interested in life balance. Many lawyers indicate that they would gladly take a substantial pay cut in exchange for a decrease in billable hours. . . .

. . . The billable hour is fundamentally about quantity over quality, repetition over creativity. With no gauge for intangibles such as productivity, creativity, knowledge or technological advancements, the billable hours model is a counter-intuitive measure of value. Alternatives that encourage efficiency and improve processes not only increase profits and provide early resolution of legal matters, but are less likely to garner ethical concerns.

That said, the outright elimination of time billing is not a likely proposition. In fact, time billing as one aspect of price-setting for legal services is an appropriate and necessary tool in certain situations. Our profession's goal, however, should be to adopt innovative billing methods that provide an accurate measure of value to the client and, at the same time, make the practice of law more fulfilling and enjoyable.

ABA Formal Ethics Opinions: See ABA Formal Ethics Ops. 87-354 (1987), 93-373 (1993), 93-379 (1993), 94-389 (1994), 00-418 (2000), 00-420 (2000), and 01-415 (2001).

ABA Model Rules for Fee Arbitration: In 1992, the ABA Commission on Evaluation of Disciplinary Enforcement ("the McKay Commission") recommended that each state establish mandatory arbitration for fee disputes. At its February 1995 Mid-Year Meeting, to assist the states in carrying out this recommendation, the ABA House of Delegates adopted Model Rules for Fee Arbitration. The ABA Model Rules for Fee Arbitration make fee arbitration mandatory if the client requests it. Some states go further than the ABA Model Rules by making fee arbitration binding as well as mandatory. (A few states do not mandate fee arbitration, but make it binding if the lawyer and client agree to arbitrate the dispute.) No states mandate fee arbitration at the option of the lawyer. For further information, contact Charlotte (Becky) Stretch at the ABA Center for Professional Responsibility, 541 North Fairbanks Court, Chicago, IL 60611, phone 312-988-5297.

American Academy of Matrimonial Lawyers: The "Bounds of Advocacy" drafted by the American Academy of Matrimonial Lawyers states:

Fees

Many divorce clients have never before hired an attorney and are vulnerable because of fear and insecurity. Matrimonial lawyers and their clients may not have the long-standing relationship out of which business lawyers and their clients often evolve an understanding about fees.

It is not unusual for one party to a divorce to lack sufficient funds to pay an attorney. This lack of resources, various strictures against contingent fee contracts, the unwillingness of some courts to redress the economic imbalance between the parties with fee awards, and the tendency of overwrought clients to misunderstand the fee agreement or to blame their attorneys for undesirable results can make collection of fees extremely difficult.

These factors help to explain why the records of fee dispute committees indicate that the number of disputes arising from family law cases is several times greater than those from any other category. Thus, financial arrangements with clients should be clearly explained, agreed upon, and documented.

2.3 All transactions in which an attorney obtains security for fees should be properly documented.

Comment to Rule 2.3

All security agreements should be arm's-length transactions. When taking mortgages on real property from a client, the client should be independently represented. If an attorney takes personal property as security, it must be appraised, photographed and identified by a qualified appraiser in order to establish concretely its precise identity and value. The attorney must then secure it in a safe place (usually a safe deposit box) where there is no danger that it can be removed, substituted, or lost.

American Lawyer's Code of Conduct: Rule 5.4, regarding division of fees among lawyers, provides:

> Lawyers who are not openly associated in the same firm shall not share a fee unless: (a) the division reflects the proportion of work performed by each attorney and the normal billing rate of each; or (b) the client has been informed pursuant to Rule 5.2 of the fact of fee-sharing and the effect on the total fee, and the client consents.

> *Comment to Rule 5.4*
>
> Rule 5.4, governing the division of fees by lawyers not openly associated in the same firm, is less restrictive than any other provision or proposal known to the Commission. . . .
>
> It must be emphasized that the purpose of allowing fee splitting is to encourage lawyers to refer clients to competent specialists. . . .

ALCC Rule 5.6(d) permits contingent fee agreements even in criminal cases. The ALCC Comment to Rule 5.6(d) provides:

> Rule 5.6(d) permits fees to be contingent in whole or in part on the outcome of any case. . . . The principal reason is that, as a practical matter, most people would not be in a position to seek vindication of their legal rights, however meritorious, if litigating those rights could result in substantial financial loss as well as loss in time and the other burdens of litigation. . . .
>
> There is even more reason for allowing contingent fees for the accused in criminal cases, because the accused who goes to prison, thereby losing any opportunity to earn a living, is far less able to pay a fee than is the accused who is acquitted. Also, lawyers would accept such arrangements only when the defense appeared sufficiently strong to warrant it, and the unscrupulous lawyer would be no more likely to fabricate a defense to earn a contingent fee than to earn a retainer. . . .

Costs and Expenses: Rule 1.5 governs costs and expenses as well as legal fees. In ABA Formal Ethics Opinion 93-379 (1993), the ABA discussed the application of Rule 1.5 to various billing problems, including several situations involving costs and expenses.

IRS Regulations: In the regulations governing practice before the Internal Revenue Service, 31 C.F.R. §10.28 prohibits an "unconscionable" fee for representing a client in a matter before the Internal Revenue Service and prohibits a contingent fee for preparing an original return, but permits a contingent fee for preparing an amended return or a claim for refund "if the practitioner reasonably anticipates at the time the fee arrangement is entered into that the amended return or claim will receive substantive review by the Service."

Private Securities Litigation Reform Act: In 1995, over President Clinton's veto, Congress passed the Private Securities Litigation Reform Act, 15 U.S.C. §77z-1. Title I of the new statute, entitled "Reduction of Abusive Litigation," combats unreasonable fees in such litigation by providing that total attorney fees and expenses awarded by a court "shall not exceed a reasonable percentage of the amount of any damages and prejudgment interest actually paid to the class." §77z-1(b). According to the committee report, this provision is intended to replace the "lodestar" method of computing fees and to give courts flexibility to determine reasonable fees and expenses on a case-by-case basis.

Restatement of the Law Governing Lawyers: See Restatement §§17, 19, 34, 35, 37–43, and 47 in our chapter on the Restatement later in this volume.

Rule 1.6 Confidentiality of Information

Editors' Note. At its August 2001 Annual Meeting, the ABA House of Delegates rejected certain parts of the Ethics 2000 Commission's proposal to amend Rule 1.6. The rejected provisions are reprinted after the heading "2002 Amendments" in the Legislative History below.

(a) A lawyer shall not reveal information relating to the representation of a client unless the client ~~consents after consultation, except for disclosures that are~~ gives informed consent, the disclosure is impliedly authorized in order to carry out the representation~~, and except as stated in~~ or the disclosure is permitted by paragraph (b).

(b) A lawyer may reveal ~~such~~ information relating to the representation of a client to the extent the lawyer reasonably believes necessary:

(1) to prevent ~~the client from committing a criminal act that the lawyer believes is likely to result in imminent~~ reasonably certain death or substantial bodily harm; ~~or~~

(2) to secure legal advice about the lawyer's compliance with these Rules;

~~(2)~~ (3) to establish a claim or defense on behalf of the lawyer in a controversy between the lawyer and the client, to establish a defense to a criminal charge or civil claim against the lawyer based upon conduct in which the client was involved, or to respond to allegations in any proceeding concerning the lawyer's representation of the client; or

(4) to comply with other law or a court order.

COMMENT

~~[1] The lawyer is part of a judicial system charged with upholding the law. One of the lawyer's functions is to advise clients so that they avoid any violation of the law in the proper exercise of their rights.~~

~~[2] The observance of the ethical obligation of a lawyer to hold inviolate confidential information of the client not only facilitates the full development of facts essential to proper representation of the client but also encourages people to seek early legal assistance.~~

~~[3] Almost without exception, clients come to lawyers in order to determine what their rights are and what is, in the maze of laws and regu-~~

lations, deemed to be legal and cor~~rect. The common law recognizes that the client's confidences must be protected from disclosure. Based upon experience, lawyers know that almost all clients follow the advice given, and the law is upheld.~~

[1] This Rule governs the disclosure by a lawyer of information relating to the representation of a client during the lawyer's representation of the client. See Rule 1.18 for the lawyer's duties with respect to information provided to the lawyer by a prospective client, Rule 1.9(c)(2) for the lawyer's duty not to reveal information relating to the lawyer's prior representation of a former client and Rules 1.8(b) and 1.9(c)(1) for the lawyer's duties with respect to the use of such information to the disadvantage of clients and former clients.

~~[4]~~ [2] A fundamental principle in the client-lawyer relationship is that, in the absence of the client's informed consent, the lawyer ~~maintain confidentiality of~~ must not reveal information relating to the representation. See Rule 1.0(e) for the definition of informed consent. This contributes to the trust that is the hallmark of the client-lawyer relationship. The client is thereby encouraged to seek legal assistance and to communicate fully and frankly with the lawyer even as to embarrassing or legally damaging subject matter. The lawyer needs this information to represent the client effectively and, if necessary, to advise the client to refrain from wrongful conduct. Almost without exception, clients come to lawyers in order to determine their rights and what is, in the complex of laws and regulations, deemed to be legal and correct. Based upon experience, lawyers know that almost all clients follow the advice given, and the law is upheld.

~~[5]~~ [3] The principle of client-lawyer confidentiality is given effect ~~in two~~ by related bodies of law~~,~~: the attorney-client privilege, ~~(which includes~~ the work product doctrine~~) in the law of evidence~~ and the rule of confidentiality established in professional ethics. The attorney-client privilege ~~applies~~ and work-product doctrine apply in judicial and other proceedings in which a lawyer may be called as a witness or otherwise required to produce evidence concerning a client. The rule of client-lawyer confidentiality applies in situations other than those where evidence is sought from the lawyer through compulsion of law. The confidentiality rule, for example, applies not ~~merely~~ only to matters communicated in confidence by the client but also to all information relating to the representation, whatever its source. A lawyer may not disclose such information except as authorized or required by the Rules of Professional Conduct or other law. See also Scope.

~~[6] The requirement of maintaining confidentiality of information relating to representation applies to government lawyers who may disagree with the policy goals that their representation is designed to advance.~~

[4] Paragraph (a) prohibits a lawyer from revealing information relating to the representation of a client. This prohibition also applies to disclosures by a lawyer that do not in themselves reveal protected information

but could reasonably lead to the discovery of such information by a third person. A lawyer's use of a hypothetical to discuss issues relating to the representation is permissible so long as there is no reasonable likelihood that the listener will be able to ascertain the identity of the client or the situation involved.

Authorized Disclosure

~~[7]~~ [5] ~~A~~ Except to the extent that the client's instructions or special circumstances limit that authority, a lawyer is impliedly authorized to make disclosures about a client when appropriate in carrying out the representation~~, except to the extent that the client's instructions or special circumstances limit that authority~~. In ~~litigation~~ some situations, for example, a lawyer may ~~disclose information by admitting~~ be impliedly authorized to admit a fact that cannot properly be disputed or~~, in negotiation by making~~ to make a disclosure that facilitates a satisfactory conclusion to a matter. ~~[8]~~ Lawyers in a firm may, in the course of the firm's practice, disclose to each other information relating to a client of the firm, unless the client has instructed that particular information be confined to specified lawyers.

Disclosure Adverse to Client

~~[9]~~ [6] ~~The~~ Although the public interest is usually best served by a strict rule requiring lawyers to preserve the confidentiality of information relating to the representation of their clients, the confidentiality rule is subject to limited exceptions. ~~In becoming privy to information about a client, a lawyer may foresee that the client intends serious harm to another person. However, to the extent a lawyer is required or permitted to disclose a client's purposes, the client will be inhibited from revealing facts which would enable the lawyer to counsel against a wrongful course of action. The public is better protected if full and open communication by the client is encouraged than if it is inhibited.~~ Paragraph (b)(1) recognizes the overriding value of life and physical integrity and permits disclosure reasonably necessary to prevent reasonably certain death or substantial bodily harm. Such harm is reasonably certain to occur if it will be suffered imminently or if there is a present and substantial threat that a person will suffer such harm at a later date if the lawyer fails to take action necessary to eliminate the threat. Thus, a lawyer who knows that a client has accidentally discharged toxic waste into a town's water supply may reveal this information to the authorities if there is a present and substantial risk that a person who drinks the water will contract a life-threatening or debilitating disease and the lawyer's disclosure is necessary to eliminate the threat or reduce the number of victims.

~~[10] Several situations must be distinguished.~~

~~[11] First, the lawyer may not counsel or assist a client in conduct that is criminal or fraudulent. See Rule 1.2(d). Similarly, a lawyer has a duty under Rule 3.3(a)(4) not to use false evidence. This duty is essentially a special instance of the duty prescribed in Rule 1.2(d) to avoid assisting a client in criminal or fraudulent conduct.~~

~~[12] Second, the lawyer may have been innocently involved in past conduct by the client that was criminal or fraudulent. In such a situation the lawyer has not violated Rule 1.2(d), because to "counsel or assist" criminal or fraudulent conduct requires knowing that the conduct is of that character.~~

~~[13] Third, the lawyer may learn that a client intends prospective conduct that is criminal and likely to result in imminent death or substantial bodily harm. As stated in paragraph (b)(1), the lawyer has professional discretion to reveal information in order to prevent such consequences. The lawyer may make a disclosure in order to prevent homicide or serious bodily injury which the lawyer reasonably believes is intended by a client. It is very difficult for a lawyer to "know" when such a heinous purpose will actually be carried out, for the client may have a change of mind.~~

~~[14] The lawyer's exercise of discretion requires consideration of such factors as the nature of the lawyer's relationship with the client and with those who might be injured by the client, the lawyer's own involvement in the transaction and factors that may extenuate the conduct in question. Where practical, the lawyer should seek to persuade the client to take suitable action. In any case, a disclosure adverse to the client's interest should be no greater than the lawyer reasonably believes necessary to the purpose. A lawyer's decision not to take preventive action permitted by paragraph (b)(1) does not violate this Rule.~~

[7] A lawyer's confidentiality obligations do not preclude a lawyer from securing confidential legal advice about the lawyer's personal responsibility to comply with these Rules. In most situations, disclosing information to secure such advice will be impliedly authorized for the lawyer to carry out the representation. Even when the disclosure is not impliedly authorized, paragraph (b)(2) permits such disclosure because of the importance of a lawyer's compliance with the Rules of Professional Conduct.

~~Dispute Concerning a Lawyer's Conduct~~

~~[18]~~ [8] Where a legal claim or disciplinary charge alleges complicity of the lawyer in a client's conduct or other misconduct of the lawyer involving representation of the client, the lawyer may respond to the extent the lawyer reasonably believes necessary to establish a defense. The same is true with respect to a claim involving the conduct or representation of a former client. Such a charge can arise in a civil, criminal, disciplinary or other proceeding and can be based on a wrong allegedly committed by the lawyer against the client or on a wrong alleged by a third person, for example, a person claiming to have been defrauded by the lawyer and client acting together. The lawyer's right to respond arises when an assertion of such complicity has been made. Paragraph (b)~~(2)~~(3) does not require the lawyer to await the commencement of an action or proceeding that charges such complicity, so that the defense may be established by responding directly to a third party who has made such an assertion. The right to defend also applies, of course, ~~applies~~ where a proceeding has been commenced. ~~Where practicable and not prejudicial to the lawyer's ability to establish the defense, the lawyer should advise the client of the third party's assertion and request that the client respond appropriately. In any event, disclosure should be no greater than the lawyer reasonably believes is necessary to vindicate innocence, the disclosure should be made in a manner which limits access to the information to the tribunal or other persons having a need to know it, and appropriate protective orders or other arrangements should be sought by the lawyer to the fullest extent practicable.~~

~~[19]~~ [9] ~~If the lawyer is charged with wrongdoing in which the client's conduct is implicated, the rule of confidentiality should not prevent the lawyer from defending against the charge. Such a charge can arise in a civil, criminal or professional disciplinary proceeding, and can be based on a wrong allegedly committed by the lawyer against the client, or on a wrong alleged by a third person; for example, a person claiming to have been defrauded by the lawyer and client acting together.~~ A lawyer entitled to a fee is permitted by paragraph (b)~~(2)~~(3) to prove the services rendered in an action to collect it. This aspect of the rule expresses the principle that the beneficiary of a fiduciary relationship may not exploit it to the detriment of the fiduciary. ~~As stated above, the lawyer must make every effort practicable to avoid unnecessary disclosure of information relating to a representation, to limit disclosure to those having the need to know it, and to obtain protective orders or make other arrangements minimizing the risk of disclosure.~~

[10] Other law may require that a lawyer disclose information about a client. Whether such a law supersedes Rule 1.6 is a question of law beyond the scope of these Rules. When disclosure of information relating to the representation appears to be required by other law, the lawyer must discuss the matter with the client to the extent required by Rule 1.4. If, however, the other law supersedes this Rule and requires disclosure, paragraph (b)(4) permits the lawyer to make such disclosures as are necessary to comply with the law.

[11] A lawyer may be ordered to reveal information relating to the representation of a client by a court or by another tribunal or governmental entity claiming authority pursuant to other law to compel the disclosure. Absent informed consent of the client to do otherwise, the lawyer should assert on behalf of the client all nonfrivolous claims that the order

is not authorized by other law or that the information sought is protected against disclosure by the attorney-client privilege or other applicable law. In the event of an adverse ruling, the lawyer must consult with the client about the possibility of appeal to the extent required by Rule 1.4. Unless review is sought, however, paragraph (b)(4) permits the lawyer to comply with the court's order.

[12] Paragraph (b) permits disclosure only to the extent the lawyer reasonably believes the disclosure is necessary to accomplish one of the purposes specified. Where practicable, the lawyer should first seek to persuade the client to take suitable action to obviate the need for disclosure. In any case, a disclosure adverse to the client's interest should be no greater than the lawyer reasonably believes necessary to accomplish the purpose. If the disclosure will be made in connection with a judicial proceeding, the disclosure should be made in a manner that limits access to the information to the tribunal or other persons having a need to know it and appropriate protective orders or other arrangements should be sought by the lawyer to the fullest extent practicable.

[13] Paragraph (b) permits but does not require the disclosure of information relating to a client's representation to accomplish the purposes specified in paragraphs (b)(1) through (b)(4). In exercising the discretion conferred by this Rule, the lawyer may consider such factors as the nature of the lawyer's relationship with the client and with those who might be injured by the client, the lawyer's own involvement in the transaction and factors that may extenuate the conduct in question. A lawyer's decision not to disclose as permitted by paragraph (b) does not violate this Rule. Disclosure may be required, however, by other Rules. Some Rules require disclosure only if such disclosure would be permitted by paragraph (b). See Rules 1.2(d), 4.1(b), 8.1 and 8.3. Rule 3.3, on the other hand, requires disclosure in some circumstances regardless of whether such disclosure is permitted by this Rule. See Rule 3.3(c).

Withdrawal

~~[15]~~ [14] If the lawyer's services will be used by the client in materially furthering a course of criminal or fraudulent conduct, the lawyer must withdraw, as stated in Rule 1.16(a)(1). ~~[16]~~ After withdrawal the lawyer is required to refrain from making disclosure of the client's confidences, except as otherwise permitted in Rule 1.6. Neither this Rule nor Rule 1.8(b) nor Rule 1.16(d) prevents the lawyer from giving notice of the fact of withdrawal, and the lawyer may also withdraw or disaffirm any opinion, document, affirmation, or the like. ~~[17]~~ Where the client is an organization, the lawyer may be in doubt whether contemplated conduct will actually be carried out by the organization. Where necessary to guide conduct in connection with this Rule, the lawyer may make inquiry within the organization as indicated in Rule 1.13(b).

~~Disclosures Otherwise Required or Authorized~~

~~[20] The attorney-client privilege is differently defined in various jurisdictions. If a lawyer is called as a witness to give testimony concerning a client, absent waiver by the client, paragraph (a) requires the lawyer to invoke the privilege when it is applicable. The lawyer must comply with the final orders of a court or other tribunal of competent jurisdiction requiring the lawyer to give information about the client.~~

~~[21] The Rules of Professional Conduct in various circumstances permit or require a lawyer to disclose information relating to the representation. See Rules 2.2, 2.3, 3.3 and 4.1. In addition to these provisions, a lawyer may be obligated or permitted by other provisions of law to give information about a client. Whether another provision of law supersedes Rule 1.6 is a matter of interpretation beyond the scope of these Rules, but a presumption should exist against such a supersession.~~

Acting Competently to Preserve Confidentiality

[15] A lawyer must act competently to safeguard information relating to the representation of a client against inadvertent or unauthorized disclosure by the lawyer or other persons who are participating in the representation of the client or who are subject to the lawyer's supervision. See Rules 1.1, 5.1 and 5.3.

[16] When transmitting a communication that includes information relating to the representation of a client, the lawyer must take reasonable precautions to prevent the information from coming into the hands of unintended recipients. This duty, however, does not require that the lawyer use special security measures if the method of communication affords a reasonable expectation of privacy. Special circumstances, however, may warrant special precautions. Factors to be considered in determining the reasonableness of the lawyer's expectation of confidentiality include the sensitivity of the information and the extent to which the privacy of the communication is protected by law or by a confidentiality agreement. A client may require the lawyer to implement special security measures not required by this Rule or may give informed consent to the use of a means of communication that would otherwise be prohibited by this Rule.

Former Client

~~[22]~~ [17] The duty of confidentiality continues after the client-lawyer relationship has terminated. See Rule 1.9(c)(2). See Rule 1.9(c)(1) for the prohibition against using such information to the disadvantage of the former client.

Canon and Code Antecedents

ABA Canons of Professional Ethics: Canon 37 provided as follows:

37. Confidences of a Client

It is the duty of a lawyer to preserve his client's confidences. This duty outlasts the lawyer's employment, and extends as well to his employees; and neither of them should accept employment which involves or may involve the disclosure or use of these confidences, either for the private advantage of the lawyer or his employees or to the disadvantage of the client, without his knowledge and consent, and even though there are other available sources of such information. A lawyer should not continue employment when he discovers that this obligation prevents the performance of his full duty to his former or to his new client.

If a lawyer is accused by his client, he is not precluded from disclosing the truth in respect to the accusation. The announced intention of a client to commit a crime is not included within the confidences which he is bound to respect. He may properly make such disclosures as may be necessary to prevent the act or protect those against whom it is threatened.

ABA Model Code of Professional Responsibility: Compare DR 4-101(A)-(C) (reprinted later in this volume).

Cross-References in Other Rules

Scope ¶17: "Most of the duties flowing from the client-lawyer relationship attach only after the client has requested the lawyer to render legal services and the lawyer has agreed to do so. But there are some duties, such as that of confidentiality under **Rule 1.6**, that attach when the lawyer agrees to consider whether a client-lawyer relationship shall be established."

Rule 1.0, Comment 6: "Many of the Rules of Professional Conduct require the lawyer to obtain the informed consent of a client or other person before accepting or continuing representation or pursuing a course of conduct (see Rules 1.2(c), **1.6(a)** and 1.7(b))."

Rule 1.8(f)(3): "A lawyer shall not accept compensation for representing a client from one other than the client unless information relating to representation of a client is protected as required by **Rule 1.6**."

Rule 1.8, Comment 5: It is prohibited to partake in the "disadvantageous use of client information unless the client gives informed consent, except as permitted or required by these Rules. See Rules 1.2(d), **1.6**, 1.9(c), 3.3, 4.1(b), 8.1 and 8.3."

Rule 1.8, Comment 12: "If, however, the fee arrangement creates a conflict of interest for the lawyer. . . . The lawyer must conform to the requirements of **Rule 1.6** concerning confidentiality."

Rule 1.9(b): "A lawyer shall not knowingly represent a person in the same or a substantially related matter in which a firm with which the lawyer formerly was associated had previously represented a client whose interests are materially adverse to that person and about whom the lawyer had acquired information protected by **Rules 1.6** and 1.9(c) that is material to the matter. . . ."

Rule 1.9, Comment 5: "Paragraph (b) operates to disqualify the lawyer only when the lawyer involved has actual knowledge of information protected by **Rules 1.6** and 1.9(c)."

Rule 1.9, Comment 7: "Independent of the question of disqualification of a firm, a lawyer changing professional association has a continuing duty to preserve confidentiality of information about a client formerly represented. See **Rules 1.6** and 1.9(c)."

Rule 1.10(b)(2) restricts representation when "any lawyer remaining in the firm has information protected by **Rules 1.6** and 1.9(c) that is material to the matter."

Rule 1.10, Comment 5: When a lawyer who represents or formerly represented a client leaves a firm, the firm may not represent a person with interests adverse to that client where the matter is the same or substantially related and "any other lawyer currently in the firm has material information protected by **Rules 1.6** and 1.9(c)."

Rule 1.12, Comment 3: "Although lawyers who serve as third-party neutrals do not have information concerning the parties that is protected under **Rule 1.6**, they typically owe the parties an obligation of confidentiality under law or codes of ethics governing third-party neutrals."

Rule 1.13, Comment 2: "When one of the constituents of an organizational client communicates with the organization's lawyer in that person's organizational capacity, the communication is protected by **Rule 1.6**. Thus, by way of example, if an organizational client requests its lawyer to investigate allegations of wrongdoing, interviews made in the course of that investigation between the lawyer and the client's employees or other constituents are covered by **Rule 1.6**. This does not mean, however, that constituents of an organizational client are the clients of the lawyer. The lawyer may not disclose to such constituents information relating to the representation except for disclosures explicitly or impliedly authorized by the organizational client in order to carry out the representation or as otherwise permitted by **Rule 1.6**."

Rule 1.13, Comment 5: "[T]his Rule does not limit or expand the lawyer's responsibility under **Rule 1.6**, 1.8, 1.16, 3.3 or 4.1."

Rule 1.14(c): "Information relating to the representation of a client with diminished capacity is protected by **Rule 1.6**. When taking protective action pursuant to paragraph (b), the lawyer is impliedly authorized under **Rule 1.6(a)** to reveal information about the client, but only to the extent reasonably necessary to protect the client's interests."

Rule 1.14, Comment 8: "Disclosure of the client's diminished capacity could adversely affect the client's interests. . . . Information relating to the representation is protected by **Rule 1.6**. Therefore, unless authorized to do so, the lawyer may not disclose such information."

Rule 1.16, Comment 3: "Lawyers should be mindful of their obligations to both clients and the court under **Rules 1.6** and 3.3."

Rule 1.17, Comment 7: "Negotiations between seller and prospective purchaser prior to disclosure of information relating to a specific representation of an identifiable client no more violate the confidentiality provisions of Model **Rule 1.6** than do preliminary discussions concerning the possible association of another lawyer or mergers between firms, with respect to which client consent is not required. Providing the purchaser access to client-specific information relating to the representation and to the file, however, requires client consent."

Rule 1.17, Comment 11: A lawyer selling a law practice has "the obligation to protect information relating to the representation (see **Rules 1.6** and 1.9)."

Rule 2.3(c): "Except as disclosure is authorized in connection with a report of an evaluation, information relating to the evaluation is otherwise protected by **Rule 1.6**."

Rule 2.3, Comment 5: "Information relating to an evaluation is protected by **Rule 1.6**. In many situations, providing an evaluation to a third party poses no significant risk to the client; thus, the lawyer may be impliedly authorized to disclose information to carry out the representation. See **Rule 1.6(a)**. Where, however, it is reasonably likely that providing the evaluation will affect the client's interests materially and adversely, the lawyer must first obtain the client's consent after the client has been adequately informed concerning the important possible effects on the client's interests. See **Rules 1.6(a)** and 1.0(e)."

Rule 3.3(c): "The duties stated in paragraphs (a) and (b) continue to the conclusion of the proceeding, and apply even if compliance requires disclosure of information otherwise protected by **Rule 1.6**."

Rule 3.3, Comment 10: "If withdrawal from the representation is not permitted or will not undo the effect of the false evidence, the advocate must make such disclosure to the tribunal as is reasonably necessary to remedy the situation, even if doing so requires the lawyer to reveal information that otherwise would be protected by **Rule 1.6**."

Rule 3.3, Comment 15: "In connection with a request for permission to withdraw that is premised on a client's misconduct, a lawyer may reveal information relating to the representation only to the extent reasonably necessary to comply with this Rule or as otherwise permitted by **Rule 1.6**."

Rule 4.1 (b): "In the course of representing a client a lawyer shall not knowingly fail to disclose a material fact when disclosure is necessary to avoid assisting a criminal or fraudulent act by a client, unless disclosure is prohibited by **Rule 1.6**."

Rule 4.1, Comment 3: "If the lawyer can avoid assisting a client's crime or fraud only by disclosing this information, then under paragraph (b) the lawyer is required to do so, unless the disclosure is prohibited by **Rule 1.6**."

Rule 5.7, Comment 10: "When a lawyer is obliged to accord the recipients of such services the protections of those Rules that apply to the client-lawyer relationship, the lawyer must . . . scrupulously adhere to the requirements of **Rule 1.6** relating to disclosure of confidential information."

Rule 6.5, Comment 2: Regarding "a lawyer who provides short-term limited legal services pursuant to this Rule, "[e]xcept as provided in this Rule, the Rules of Professional Conduct, including **Rules 1.6** and 1.9(c), are applicable to the limited representation."

Rule 8.1(b): "[T]his rule does not require disclosure of information otherwise protected by **Rule 1.6**."

Rule 8.1, Comment 3: "A lawyer representing an applicant for admission to the bar, or representing a lawyer who is the subject of a disciplinary inquiry or proceeding, is governed by the rules applicable to the client-lawyer relationship, including **Rule 1.6** and, in some cases, Rule 3.3."

Rule 8.3(c): "This Rule does not require disclosure of information otherwise protected by **Rule 1.6** — or information gained by a lawyer or judge while participating in an approved lawyers assistance program."

Rule 8.3, Comment 2: "A report about misconduct is not required where it would involve violation of **Rule 1.6**."

Legislative History of Model Rule 1.6

1979 Unofficial Pre-Circulation Draft:

(a) In giving testimony or providing evidence concerning a client's affairs, a lawyer shall not disclose matter concerning the client except as permitted under the applicable law of evidentiary privilege. In other circumstances, a lawyer shall not disclose information about a client acquired in serving the client in a professional capacity except as stated in paragraphs (b), (c) and (d).

(b) A lawyer shall disclose information about a client when directed to do so by the client and may do so when disclosure is necessary in the representation.

(c) A lawyer shall disclose information about a client

(1) to the extent necessary to prevent the client from committing an act that would seriously endanger the life or safety of a person, result in wrongful detention or incarceration of a person or wrongful destruction of substantial property, or corrupt judicial or governmental procedure;

(2) when disclosure by the lawyer is required by law or the rules of professional conduct.

(d) A lawyer may disclose information about a client

(1) to the extent necessary to prevent or rectify the consequences of a deliberately wrongful act by the client in which the lawyer's services are or were involved, except when the lawyer has been employed after the commission of such an act to represent the client concerning the act or its consequences. . . .

1980 Discussion Draft:

(b) A lawyer shall disclose information about a client to the extent it appears necessary to prevent the client from committing an act that would result in death or serious bodily harm to another person, and to the extent required by law or the rules of professional conduct.

(c) A lawyer may disclose information about a client only:

(1) For the purposes of serving the client's interest, unless it is information the client has specifically requested not to be disclosed;

(2) To the extent it appears necessary to prevent or rectify the consequences of a deliberately wrongful act by the client, except when the lawyer has been employed after the commission of such an act to represent the client concerning the act or its consequences. . . .

1981 Draft:

(b) A lawyer may reveal such information to the extent the lawyer believes necessary:

(1) to serve the client's interests, unless it is information the client has specifically requested not to be disclosed;

(2) to prevent the client from committing a criminal or fraudulent act that the lawyer believes is likely to result in death or substantial bodily harm, or substantial injury to the financial interest or property of another;

(3) to rectify the consequences of a client's criminal or fraudulent act in the commission of which the lawyer's services had been used. . . .

1982 Draft:

(b) A lawyer may reveal such information to the extent the lawyer reasonably believes necessary:

(1) to prevent the client from committing a criminal or fraudulent act that the lawyer reasonably believes is likely to result in death or substantial bodily harm, or in substantial injury to the financial interests or property of another;

> (2) to rectify the consequences of a client's criminal or fraudulent act in the furtherance of which the lawyer's services had been used. . . .

1991 Proposal: At the ABA's August 1991 Annual Meeting, the Standing Committee on Ethics and Professional Responsibility proposed an amendment to Rule 1.6(b) that would have permitted a lawyer to reveal information that the lawyer reasonably believed necessary to "rectify the consequences of a client's criminal or fraudulent act in the commission of which the lawyer's services had been used." The House of Delegates defeated this proposal by a vote of 251 to 158. The rejected amendment was virtually identical to the Kutak Commission draft that was rejected by the ABA in 1982. By rejecting the 1991 proposal to amend the text of Rule 1.6, the House of Delegates also rejected the following amendments to various paragraphs of the Comment to Rule 1.6:

> To the extent a lawyer is prohibited from making disclosure, the interests of the potential victim are sacrificed in favor of preserving the client's confidences even though the client's purpose is wrongful.
>
> Generally speaking, information relating to the representation must be kept confidential. . . . However, where the client is or has been engaged in criminal or fraudulent conduct or the integrity of the lawyer's own conduct is involved, the principle of confidentiality may have to yield, depending on the lawyer's knowledge about and relationship to the conduct in question, and the seriousness of the conduct.
>
> Even if the [lawyer's] involvement was innocent . . . the fact remains that the lawyer's professional services were made the instrument of the client's crime or fraud. The lawyer, therefore, has a legitimate interest in being able to rectify the consequences of such conduct, and has the professional right, although not a professional duty, to rectify the situation. Exercising that right may require revealing information relating to the representation.

2002 Amendments: At its February 2002 Mid-Year Meeting, the ABA House of Delegates adopted without change most of the ABA Ethics 2000 Commission proposal to amend Rule 1.6 and its Comment. However, at its August 2001 Annual Meeting, the House of Delegates had voted against a proposed new subparagraph in Rule 1.6(b) that would have permitted a lawyer to reveal information relating to the representation of a client to the extent the lawyer reasonably believes necessary:

> (2) to prevent the client from committing a crime or fraud that is reasonably certain to result in substantial injury to the financial interests or property interests of another and in furtherance of which the client has used or is using the lawyer's services;

After the House of Delegates defeated proposed subparagraph (b)(2), the Ethics 2000 Commission withdrew the following proposed subparagraph (b)(3) — before a vote was taken — that would have allowed disclosure:

> (3) to prevent, mitigate or rectify substantial injury to the financial interests or property of another that is reasonably certain to result or has resulted from the client's commission of a crime or fraud in furtherance of which the client has used the lawyer's services;

The rejected subparagraphs (b)(2) and (b)(3) would have been accompanied by the following two new proposed paragraphs of the Comment to Rule 1.6:

> [7] Paragraph (b)(2) is a limited exception to the rule of confidentiality that permits the lawyer to reveal information to the extent necessary to enable affected

persons or appropriate authorities to prevent the client from committing a crime or a fraud, as defined in Rule 1.0(d), that is reasonably certain to result in substantial injury to the financial or property interests of another and in furtherance of which the client has used or is using the lawyer's services. Such a serious abuse of the client-lawyer relationship by the client forfeits the protection of this Rule. The client can, of course, prevent such disclosure by refraining from the wrongful conduct. Although paragraph (b)(2) does not require the lawyer to reveal the client's misconduct, the lawyer may not counsel or assist the client in conduct the lawyer knows is criminal or fraudulent. See Rule 1.2(d). See also Rule 1.16 with respect to the lawyer's obligation or right to withdraw from the representation of the client in such circumstances. Where the client is an organization, the lawyer may be in doubt whether contemplated conduct will actually be carried out by the organization. Where necessary to guide conduct in connection with this Rule, the lawyer may make inquiry within the organization as indicated in Rule 1.13(b).

[8] Paragraph (b)(3) addresses the situation in which the lawyer does not learn of the client's crime or fraud until after it has been consummated. Although the client no longer has the option of preventing disclosure by refraining from the wrongful conduct, there will be situations in which the loss suffered by the affected person can be prevented, rectified or mitigated. In such situations, the lawyer may disclose information relating to the representation to the extent necessary to enable the affected persons to prevent or mitigate reasonably certain losses or to attempt to recoup their losses. Paragraph (b)(3) does not apply when a person who has committed a crime or fraud thereafter employs a lawyer for representation concerning that offense.

The Reporter's Explanation Memo regarding proposed subparagraphs (b)(2) and (b)(3) provided, in relevant part, as follows:

*Model Rule 1.6 — Reporter's Explanation of Changes**

Paragraph (b)(2): Add paragraph permitting disclosure to prevent client crimes or frauds reasonably certain to cause substantial economic injury and in which client has used or is using lawyer's services.

The Commission recommends that a lawyer be permitted to reveal information relating to the representation to the extent necessary to prevent the client from committing a crime or fraud reasonably certain to result in substantial economic loss, but only when the lawyer's services have been or are being used in furtherance of the crime or fraud. Use of the lawyer's services for such improper ends constitutes a serious abuse of the client-lawyer relationship. The client's entitlement to the protection of the Rule must be balanced against the prevention of the injury that would otherwise be suffered and the interest of the lawyer in being able to prevent the misuse of the lawyer's services. Moreover, with respect to future conduct, the client can easily prevent the harm of disclosure by refraining from the wrongful conduct. See also Comment [7].

Support for the Commission's proposal can be found in the eight jurisdictions that permit disclosure when clients threaten crimes or frauds likely to result in substantial injury to the financial or property interests of another and the 25 jurisdictions that permit a lawyer to reveal the intention of a client to commit any crime. The Commission's proposal is also in accord with Section 67 of the American Law Institute's Restatement of the Law Governing Lawyers.

*Committee Reports, and the Reporter's Explanation of Changes contained therein, do not represent official policy of the ABA. They are for information only, and the opinions are those of the authors of the report.

Paragraph (b)(3): Add paragraph permitting disclosure to prevent, mitigate or rectify substantial economic loss resulting from client crime or fraud in which client has used lawyer's services.

The rationale for this exception is the same as that for paragraph (b)(2), the only difference being that the client no longer can prevent disclosure by refraining from the crime or fraud. See also Comment [8]. The Commission believes that the interests of the affected persons in mitigating or recouping their substantial losses and the interest of the lawyer in undoing a wrong in which the lawyer's services were unwittingly used outweigh the interests of a client who has so abused the client-lawyer relationship. Support for the Commission's proposal can be found in the 13 jurisdictions that permit disclosure to rectify the consequences of a crime or fraud in the commission of which the client used the lawyer's services. The proposal is also in accord with Section 67 of the American Law Institute's Restatement of the Law Governing Lawyers.

Selected State Variations

Editors' Note. American jurisdictions have adopted many variations on Rule 1.6 and its exceptions. Under DR 4-101(C)(3) of the old ABA Model Code of Professional Responsibility, a lawyer was authorized to reveal the intention of a client to commit a crime and the information necessary to prevent the crime. Until 2002, Rule 1.6(b)(1) limited that authority to crimes "likely to result in imminent death or substantial bodily harm." Among the questions addressed in state variations are the following:

- whether to continue the Code's authority to reveal any prospective crime, even if the crime will not cause death or substantial bodily harm;
- whether to extend the authority to conduct other than criminal conduct (such as conduct that is reckless, fraudulent, or illegal, but not criminal);
- whether to keep the authority permissive or, instead, to mandate revelation of prospective criminal or harmful conduct;
- if revelation is mandatory, the prospective conduct that will be subject to the mandatory duty to reveal;
- whether to distinguish the right or obligation to disclose depending upon whether the lawyer's information is protected by the attorney-client privilege or only protected by the ethical duty of confidentiality.

Alaska, Connecticut, Maryland, New Hampshire, New Mexico, North Dakota, Pennsylvania, Utah, and Wisconsin permit a lawyer to reveal information necessary to prevent the client from committing a criminal act "likely to result in substantial injury to the financial interest or property of another" (or words to that effect). Maryland permits the same when the act is only fraudulent.

Alaska and Pennsylvania eliminate the word "imminent" in Rule 1.6(b).

Arizona, Arkansas, Colorado, Idaho, Illinois, Indiana, Kansas, Michigan, Minnesota, Mississippi, North Carolina, Ohio, Washington, and ***Wyoming*** essentially retain the old Model Code formulation — they all permit a lawyer to reveal "the intention of a client to commit a crime" (or use words to that effect).

Arizona, Connecticut, Illinois, Nevada, North Dakota, and ***Texas*** mandate disclosure of information to prevent the client from committing serious violent crimes.

California: B & P Code §6068(e) provides that it is the duty of an attorney "[t]o maintain inviolate the confidence, and at every peril to himself or herself to preserve the secrets, of his or her client." (California's Rules of Professional Conduct do not expressly cover confidentiality.) Section 956.5 of the California Evidence Code, reprinted in our chapter on privilege and work product, suspends the privilege when the lawyer "reasonably believes" that disclosure is necessary to prevent a criminal act "likely to result in death or substantial bodily harm."

Connecticut: Rule 1.6 does not contain the word "imminent" before "death or substantial bodily harm."

Connecticut, Maryland, Michigan, Nevada, North Carolina, Pennsylvania, and ***Wisconsin*** permit lawyers to reveal confidential information "to rectify the consequences of a client's criminal or fraudulent act in the furtherance of which the lawyer's services were used" (or words to that effect).

District of Columbia: D.C. Rule 1.6 differs significantly from the ABA Model Rule — see District of Columbia Rules of Professional Conduct below.

Florida provides that a lawyer "shall reveal" information the lawyer believes "necessary (1) to prevent a client from committing a crime or (2) to prevent death or substantial bodily harm to another." In addition, Florida Rule 1.6(c) permits a lawyer to reveal information necessary "(1) To serve the client's interest unless it is information the client specifically requires not to be disclosed . . . or (5) To comply with the Rules of Professional Conduct." Florida also adds Rule 1.6(d): "When required by a tribunal to reveal such information, a lawyer may first exhaust all appellate remedies." Finally, Florida adds Rule 1.6(e), which provides that "when disclosure is mandated or permitted, the lawyer shall disclose no more information than is required to meet the requirements or accomplish the purposes of this rule." Florida Rule 4-7.4(b)(2)(L), governing targeted mail, states: "A written communication seeking employment by a specific prospective client in a specific matter shall not reveal on the envelope, or on the outside of a self-mailing brochure or pamphlet, the nature of the client's legal problem."

Georgia: In the rules effective January 1, 2001, Rule 1.6(a) combines language from ABA Model Rule 1.6 with language from DR 4-101(A) of the ABA Model Code of Professional Responsibility, as follows:

> (a) A lawyer shall maintain in confidence all information gained in the professional relationship with a client, including information which the client has requested to be held inviolate or the disclosure of which would be embarrassing or would likely be detrimental to the client, unless the client consents after consultation, except for disclosures that are impliedly authorized in order to carry out the representation, or are required by these rules or other law, or by order of the Court.

Georgia's Rule 1.6(b)(1) permits a lawyer to reveal protected information which the lawyer reasonably believes necessary "(i) to avoid or prevent harm or substantial financial loss to another as a result of client criminal conduct or third party criminal conduct clearly in violation of the law" or "(ii) to prevent serious injury or death not otherwise covered" by subparagraph (i). Georgia adds Rule 1.6(b)(2)-(3) and (c), (d), and (e), which provide as follows:

> (2) In a situation described in Subsection (1), if the client has acted at the time the lawyer learns of the threat of harm or loss to a victim, use or disclosure is permissible only if the harm or loss has not yet occurred.

(3) Before using or disclosing information pursuant to Subsection (1), if feasible, the lawyer must make a good faith effort to persuade the client either not to act or, if the client has already acted, to warn the victim.

(c) The lawyer may, where the law does not otherwise require, reveal information to which the duty of confidentiality does not apply under paragraph (b) without being subjected to disciplinary proceedings.

(d) The lawyer shall reveal information under paragraph (b) as the applicable law requires.

(e) The duty of confidentiality shall continue after the client-lawyer relationship has terminated.

Illinois: Rule 1.6 provides:

(a) Except when required under Rule 1.6(b) or permitted under Rule 1.6(c), a lawyer shall not, during or after termination of the professional relationship with the client, use or reveal a confidence or secret of the client unless the client consents after disclosure.

(b) A lawyer shall reveal information about a client to the extent it appears necessary to prevent the client from committing an act that would result in death or serious bodily harm.

(c) A lawyer may use or reveal:

(1) confidences or secrets when permitted under these Rules or required by law or court order;

(2) the intention of a client to commit a crime in circumstances other than those enumerated in Rule 1.6(b); or

(3) confidences or secrets necessary to establish or collect the lawyer's fee or to defend the lawyer or the lawyer's employees or associates against an accusation of wrongful conduct.

(d) The relationship of trained intervenor and a lawyer or a judge who seeks or receives assistance through the Lawyer's Assistance Program, Inc., shall be the same as that of lawyer and client for purposes of the application of Rule 8.1, Rule 8.3, and Rule 1.6.

(e) Any information received by a lawyer in a formal proceeding before a trained intervenor, or panel of intervenors, of the Lawyer's Assistance Program, Inc., shall be deemed to have been received from a client for purposes of the application of Rule 1.6, Rule 8.1, and Rule 8.3.

Indiana: Rule 1.6 adds:

In the event of an attorney's physical or mental disability, or appointment of a Lawyers Assistance Committee as guardian or conservator of an attorney's client files, disclosure of the client names and files to the Program are deemed impliedly authorized in order to carry out the representation. . . .

Massachusetts: Rule 1.6 permits a lawyer to reveal — "and to the extent required by Rule 3.3 and Rule 4. 1(b), or Rule 8.3" requires a lawyer to reveal — confidential information "to prevent the commission of a criminal or fraudulent act that the lawyer reasonably believes is likely to result in death or substantial bodily harm or in substantial injury to the financial interests or property of another, or to prevent the wrongful execution or incarceration of another." Revelation is also permitted "to the extent the lawyer reasonably believes necessary to rectify client fraud in which the lawyer's services have been used, subject to Rule 3.3(e)."

Michigan essentially retains the language of DR 4-101 of the ABA Model Code of Professional Responsibility but deletes the self-defense exception in DR 4-101(C)(4) and adds an exception numbered Rule 1.6(c)(3), which allows a lawyer to reveal "confidences and secrets to the extent reasonably necessary to rectify the consequences of a client's illegal or fraudulent act in the furtherance of which the lawyer's services have been used."

New Jersey requires a lawyer to reveal confidential information "to prevent a client from committing a criminal, illegal or fraudulent act . . . likely to result in death or substantial bodily harm or substantial injury to the financial interest or property of another." New Jersey also requires a lawyer to reveal confidences to prevent a client from committing "a criminal, illegal or fraudulent act that the lawyer reasonably believes is likely to perpetrate a fraud upon a tribunal." New Jersey also permits (but does not require) a lawyer to reveal information necessary "to rectify the consequences of a client's criminal, illegal or fraudulent act in furtherance of which the lawyer's services had been used."

New York: Compare ABA Model Rule 1.6 to New York's DR 4-101 and DR 7-102(B).

North Carolina: Rule 1.6(b) (which is similar in purpose to ABA Model Rule 8.3(c)) adds that "confidential information" includes "information received by a lawyer then acting as an agent of a lawyers' or judges' assistance program approved by the North Carolina State Bar or the North Carolina Supreme Court regarding another lawyer or judge seeking assistance or to whom assistance is being offered." Rule 1.6(b) also adds that a "client" includes "lawyers seeking assistance" from approved lawyers' or judges' assistance programs. Rule 1.6(c) tracks DR 4-101(B) of the old ABA Model Code of Professional Responsibility.

Oregon: In 1995, Oregon added a new subparagraph DR 4-101(C)(5), which provides that a lawyer may reveal:

> (5) [t]he following information in discussions preliminary to the sale of a law practice under DR 2-111 with respect to each client potentially subject to the transfer: the client's identity; the identities of any adverse parties; the nature and extent of the legal services involved; and the fee and payment information. A potential purchasing lawyer shall have the same responsibilities as the selling lawyer to preserve confidences and secrets of such clients whether or not the sale of the practice closes or the client ultimately consents to representation by the purchasing lawyer.

Pennsylvania adds Rule 1.6(d), which provides: "The duty not to reveal information relating to representation of a client continues after the client-lawyer relationship has terminated." In addition, on June 28, 2001, Pennsylvania amended Rule 1.6 to allow a lawyer to reveal information relating to the representation of a client that the lawyer reasonably believes necessary to "effectuate the sale of a law practice consistent with Rule 1.17."

Texas: Rules 1.02(d) and (e) provide:

> (d) When a lawyer has confidential information clearly establishing that a client is likely to commit a criminal or fraudulent act that is likely to result in substantial injury to the financial interests or property of another, the lawyer shall promptly make reasonable efforts under the circumstances to dissuade the client from committing the crime or fraud.
>
> (e) When a lawyer has confidential information clearly establishing that the lawyer's client has committed a criminal or fraudulent act in the commission of which the lawyer's services have been used, the lawyer shall make reasonable efforts under the circumstances to persuade the client to take corrective action.

Texas Rule 1.05 distinguishes between "privileged information" and "unprivileged client information." The former is information protected by the attorney-client privilege. The latter "means all information relating to a client or furnished by the client, other than privileged information, acquired by the lawyer in the course of or by reason of the representation of the client." Both categories of information comprise a third category called "confidential information." A lawyer "may reveal confidential information" in eight instances, including when "the lawyer has reason to believe it is necessary to do so in order to prevent the client from committing a criminal or fraudulent act," and to "the extent revelation reasonably appears necessary to rectify the consequences of a client's criminal or fraudulent act in the commission of which the lawyer's services had been used." Rule 1.05(c)(7) and (8).

Utah: Rule 1.6(c) states:

> (c) Representation of a client includes counseling a lawyer(s) about the need for or availability of treatment for substance abuse or psychological or emotional problems by members of the Utah State Bar serving on the Lawyers Helping Lawyers Committee.

Virginia: Rule 1.6(a) contains the Code's definitions of "confidence" and "secret" without using these terms. A lawyer may reveal a client confidence "which clearly establishes that the client has, in the course of the representation, perpetrated upon a third party a fraud related to the subject matter of the representation." Rule 1.6(b)(3). The lawyer must "promptly" reveal "the intention of a client, as stated by the client, to commit a crime and the information necessary to prevent the crime," but if feasible must first give the client the opportunity to desist and must advise the client of the lawyer's obligation. If "the crime involves perjury by the client," the lawyer must advise the client that he or she "shall seek to withdraw as counsel." Rule 1.6(c)(1). Rule 1.6 (c)(2) also requires the lawyer to promptly reveal "information which clearly establishes that the client has, in the course of the representation, perpetrated a fraud related to the subject matter of the representation upon a tribunal." "[I]nformation is clearly established when the client acknowledges to the attorney that the client has perpetrated a fraud."

Washington adds Rule 1.6(c): "A lawyer may reveal to the tribunal confidences or secrets which disclose any breach of fiduciary responsibility by a client who is a guardian, personal representative, receiver or other court appointed fiduciary."

Related Materials

ABA Formal Ethics Opinions: See ABA Formal Ethics Ops. 90-358 (1990), 92-365 (1992), 92-368 (1992), 93-370 (1993), 93-372 (1993), 94-380 (1994), 94-382 (1994), 94-385 (1994), 95-393 (1995), 97-405 (1997), 98-411 (1998), and 99-413 (1999).

ABA Standards for Imposing Lawyer Sanctions:

> 4.21. Disbarment is generally appropriate when a lawyer, with the intent to benefit the lawyer or another, knowingly reveals information relating to representation of a client not otherwise lawfully permitted to be disclosed, and this disclosure causes injury or potential injury to a client.
>
> 4.22. Suspension is generally appropriate when a lawyer knowingly reveals information relating to the representation of a client not otherwise lawfully permitted to be disclosed, and this disclosure causes injury or potential injury to a client.
>
> 4.23. Reprimand is generally appropriate when a lawyer negligently reveals information relating to representation of a client not otherwise lawfully permitted to be disclosed and this disclosure causes injury or potential injury to a client.

4.24. Admonition is generally appropriate when a lawyer negligently reveals information relating to representation of a client not otherwise lawfully permitted to be disclosed and this disclosure causes little or no actual or potential injury to a client.

American Academy of Matrimonial Lawyers: The "Bounds of Advocacy" drafted by the American Academy of Matrimonial Lawyers contains the following provisions and commentary:

Comment to Rule 2.10

. . . To the extent specifically authorized by the client, the lawyer may discuss choices with third parties, provided all concerned are aware that such discussions may waive any attorney-client privilege. . . .

Both the client and the person paying for the representation must be informed at the outset that nothing related by the client in confidence will be disclosed without the client's consent. The duty to protect confidential information also requires that the attorney raise the issue of the effect on confidentiality of the parents, friends, lovers, children or employers' being present. Usually, the presence of a third person not necessary to the rendition of legal services waives the attorney-client privilege. For this and other reasons, an attorney should discourage family members and other third persons from participating in client conferences. In addition to the potential loss of confidentiality, a more accurate account of the client's desires and best interests can usually be obtained when third persons are not present.

2.26. An attorney should disclose evidence of a substantial risk of physical or sexual abuse of a child by the attorney's client.

Comment to Rule 2.26

While engaged in efforts on the client's behalf, the matrimonial lawyer may become convinced that the client has abused one of the children. Or the client, who seems a good parent, has a live-in lover who has abused one of the children. Under traditional analysis in most jurisdictions, the attorney should refuse to assist the client. The attorney may withdraw if the client will not be adversely affected and the court grants any required permission. . . .

In the most extreme cases, the attorney may reveal information reasonably believed necessary "to prevent the client from committing a criminal act that the lawyer believes is likely to result in imminent death or substantial bodily harm." Many states permit the attorney to reveal the intention of the client to commit any crime and the information necessary to prevent it. The rules do not appear to address, however, revelation of conduct that may be severely detrimental to the well-being of the child, but not criminal.

Notwithstanding the importance of the attorney-client privilege, the obligation of the matrimonial lawyer to consider the welfare of children, coupled with the client's lack of any legitimate interest in preventing his attorney from revealing information to protect the children from likely physical abuse, requires disclosure of a substantial risk of abuse and the information necessary to prevent it. If the client insists on seeking custody or unsupervised visitation, even without the attorney's assistance, the attorney should report specific knowledge of child abuse to the authorities for the protection of the child.

American Lawyer's Code of Conduct: The terminology section states:

A client's confidence, protected by this Code, includes any information obtained by the client's lawyer in the course of and by reason of the lawyer-client relationship.

Rules 1.1 through 1.6 provide:

1.1. Beginning with the initial interview with a prospective client, a lawyer shall strive to establish and maintain a relationship of trust and confidence with the client. The lawyer shall impress upon the client that the lawyer cannot adequately serve the client without knowing everything that might be relevant to the client's problem, and that the client should not withhold information that the client might think is embarrassing or harmful to the client's interests. The lawyer shall explain to the client the lawyer's obligation of confidentiality.

1.2. Without the client's knowing and voluntary consent, a lawyer shall not directly or indirectly reveal a confidence of a client or former client, or use it in any way detrimental to the interests of the client, except as provided in Rules 1.3 to 1.6, and Rule 6.5. . . .

1.3. A lawyer may reveal a client's confidence to the extent required to do so by law, rule of court, or court order, but only after good faith efforts to test the validity of the law, rule, or order have been exhausted.

1.4. A lawyer may reveal a client's confidence when the lawyer knows that a judge or juror in a pending proceeding in which the lawyer is involved has been bribed or subjected to extortion. In such a case, the lawyer shall use all reasonable means to protect the client, consistent with preventing the case from going forward with a corrupted judge or juror.

1.5. A lawyer may reveal a client's confidence to the extent necessary to defend the lawyer or the lawyer's associate or employee against charges of criminal, civil, or professional misconduct asserted by the client, or against formally instituted charges of such conduct in which the client is implicated.

[1.6. A lawyer may reveal a client's confidence when and to the extent that the lawyer reasonably believes that divulgence is necessary to prevent imminent danger to human life. The lawyer shall use all reasonable means to protect the client's interests that are consistent with preventing loss of life.]

Commission's Note: Rule 1.6 was not approved by the Commission [on Professional Responsibility of the Roscoe Pound Foundation], but was supported by so many members that it is included in this Revised Draft as a Supplemental Rule.

Comment to Rules 1.1-1.6

These Rules reject the previously recognized exception permitting lawyers to violate confidentiality to collect an unpaid fee. The reason for the exception — the lawyer's financial interest — is not sufficiently weighty to justify impairing confidentiality. On the other hand, a limited exception is permitted, when a lawyer or the lawyer's associate is formally charged with criminal or unprofessional conduct. . . .

This Code rejects permitting violation of confidentiality in all cases of "future (or continuing) crimes." First, the category of "crimes" is too broad; it lumps offenses that are openly done and relatively harmless, with those that are clandestine and involve life and death. At the same time, the requirement of a crime may be too narrow; if saving a life, for example, is sufficiently important to justify an exception to confidentiality, then the exception should not turn on technicalities. . . .

Attorney-Client Privilege: Wigmore's treatise on the law of evidence defines the attorney-client privilege as follows:

(1) Where legal advice of any kind is sought (2) from a professional legal advisor in his capacity as such, (3) the communications relating to that purpose, (4) made in confidence (5) by the client, (6) are at his [the client's] instance permanently protected (7) from disclosure by himself or the legal advisor, (8) except the protection be waived.

For more detailed descriptions of the attorney-client privilege, see "Attorney-Client Privilege and Work Product Provisions" later in this volume.

Cellular Telephone Calls: At the ABA's 1999 Annual Meeting, the ABA House of Delegates passed a resolution encouraging courts and bar disciplinary authorities to recognize explicitly that cellular telephone communications are protected by the attorney-client privilege.

Child Abuse Reporting Statutes: Many states have statutes that require citizens to report child abuse. A good example is Georgia's statute, which provides as follows:

> When any person . . . has reason to believe that a child has been subjected to incest, molestation, sexual exploitation, sexual abuse, physical abuse or neglect, or who observes a child being subjected to conditions or circumstances which would reasonably result in sexual abuse, physical abuse or neglect, he shall immediately notify the nearest peace office, law enforcement agency or office of the division.

However, it is a subject of debate whether a lawyer is obligated to comply with such reporting statutes if a report would violate Rule 1.6.

Department of Justice "Principles": A June 16, 1999 memorandum to all U.S. Attorneys entitled "Bringing Criminal Charges Against Corporations" contains twelve "Principles" to be weighed in deciding whether to prosecute corporations. A May 12, 2000 letter to Deputy Attorney General Eric Holder from Maud Mater, President of the American Corporate Counsel Association, complains about two of the Principles. Principle II urges U.S. Attorneys to consider a corporation's "timely and voluntary disclosure of wrongdoing and its willingness to cooperate in the investigation of its agents, including, if necessary, the waiver of the corporate attorney-client and work product privileges." Principle VI provides that in determining whether to charge a corporation, its "willingness to cooperate with the government's investigation may be [a] relevant factor," and in gauging the level of cooperation, "the prosecutor may consider the corporation's willingness to . . . disclose the complete results of its internal investigation, and to waive the attorney-client privilege and work product privileges."

E-mail Communications: Many ethics committees and commentators have considered whether communications by e-mail are protected by the attorney-client privilege. Some states have passed statutes protecting e-mail communications. For example, in 1998 New York enacted a new statute, CPLR §4548, which provides as follows:

> No communication privileged under this article shall lose its privileged character for the sole reason that it is communicated by electronic means or because persons necessary for the delivery or facilitation of such electronic communication may have access to the content of the communication.

Law firms are also concerned about privilege and confidentiality for e-mail. King & Spalding, for example, puts the following disclaimer on its web site:

> We would be pleased to communicate with you by e-mail. However, if you communicate with us through this World Wide Web site or otherwise in connection with a matter for which we do not already represent you, your communication may not be treated as privileged or confidential. If you communicate with us by e-mail in connection with a matter for which we already represent you, please remember that internet e-mail is not secure and you should avoid sending sensitive or confidential internet e-mail messages unless they are adequately encrypted.

Federal Prison Monitoring of Attorney-Client Communications: On October 31, 2001, effective immediately, the United States Bureau of Prisons issued an interim rule, 28 C.F.R. §503(d), that permits the federal government to monitor conversations between prisoners and their attorneys under certain circumstances. The regulation provides as follows:

> (d) In any case where the Attorney General specifically so orders, based on information from the head of a federal law enforcement or intelligence agency that reasonable suspicion exists to believe that a particular inmate may use communications with attorneys or their agents to further or facilitate acts of terrorism, the Director, Bureau of Prisons, shall, in addition to the special administrative measures imposed under paragraph (a) of this section, provide appropriate procedures for the monitoring or review of communications between that inmate and attorneys or attorneys' agents who are traditionally covered by the attorney-client privilege, for the purpose of deterring future acts that could result in death or serious bodily injury to persons, or substantial damage to property that would entail the risk of death or serious bodily injury to persons. . . .
>
> (2) Except in the case of prior court authorization, the Director, Bureau of Prisons, shall provide written notice to the inmate and to the attorneys involved, prior to the initiation of any monitoring or review under this paragraph (d). The notice shall explain:
>
> (i) That, notwithstanding the provisions of part 540 of this chapter or other rules, all communications between the inmate and attorneys may be monitored, to the extent determined to be reasonably necessary for the purpose of deterring future acts of violence or terrorism;
>
> (ii) That communications between the inmate and attorneys or their agents are not protected by the attorney-client privilege if they would facilitate criminal acts or a conspiracy to commit criminal acts, or if those communications are not related to the seeking or providing of legal advice.
>
> (3) The Director, Bureau of Prisons, with the approval of the Assistant Attorney General for the Criminal Division, shall employ appropriate procedures to ensure that all attorney-client communications are reviewed for privilege claims and that any properly privileged materials (including, but not limited to, recordings of privileged communications) are not retained during the course of the monitoring. To protect the attorney-client privilege and to ensure that the investigation is not compromised by exposure to privileged material relating to the investigation or to defense strategy, a privilege team shall be designated, consisting of individuals not involved in the underlying investigation. The monitoring shall be conducted pursuant to procedures designed to minimize the intrusion into privileged material or conversations. Except in cases where the person in charge of the privilege team determines that acts of violence or terrorism are imminent, the privilege team shall not disclose any information unless and until such disclosure has been approved by a federal judge."

Federal Rules of Civil Procedure: Except in specified categories of proceedings or to the extent otherwise stipulated between the parties or ordered by the court, Rule 26(a) of the Federal Rules of Civil Procedure, as amended effective December 1, 2000, provides that each party to a civil suit "must, without awaiting a discovery request, provide to other parties" various categories of information, including: (A) the name, address, and telephone of each individual likely to have discoverable information (including the identity of any person who may be used at trial as an expert); (B) a copy or description of all documents, data compilations, and tangible things in the party's possession, custody or control and that the disclosing party may use to support its claims or defenses; (C) a computation of any category of damages claimed by the disclosing party; and (D) any insurance agreement that may cover the judgment or a corresponding indemnification obligation. These provisions relate to ABA Model Rule 1.6 because clients who take part in litigation in federal court may be deemed to have "impliedly authorized" the disclosures mandated by Rule 26(a). For more information about the Federal Rules of Civil Procedure (and other federal court rules), check the official web site of the United States Courts at www.uscourts.gov or call John Rabiej, Chief of the Rules Committee Support Office, at (202) 273-1820.

Model Rules of Professional Conduct for Federal Lawyers: Rule 1.6(b) provides: "A federal lawyer shall reveal such information to the extent the Federal lawyer reasonably believes necessary to prevent the client from committing a criminal act that the Federal lawyer believes is likely to result in imminent death or substantial bodily harm, or imminent and significant impairment of national security or defense." The Comment also cautions that government lawyers have confidentiality obligations under many federal statutes and regulations, so "in addition to determining the extent to which Rule 1.6 applies to a given situation, it is always advisable for Government lawyers to review the applicable Federal law . . . and to consult with their supervisors."

Restatement of the Law Governing Lawyers: See Restatement §§14, 15, 41, and 59–93 in our chapter on the Restatement later in this volume.

Rule 1.7 Conflict of Interest: ~~General Rule~~ Current Clients

~~(a) A lawyer shall not represent a client if the representation of that client will be directly adverse to another client, unless:~~

~~(1) the lawyer reasonably believes the representation will not adversely affect the relationship with the other client; and~~

~~(2) each client consents after consultation.~~

~~(b) A lawyer shall not represent a client if the representation of that client may be materially limited by the lawyer's responsibilities to another client or to a third person, or by the lawyer's own interests, unless:~~

~~(1) the lawyer reasonably believes the representation will not be adversely affected; and~~

~~(2) the client consents after consultation. When representation of multiple clients in a single matter is undertaken, the consulta-~~

~~**tion shall include explanation of the implications of the common representation and the advantages and risks involved.**~~

(a) Except as provided in paragraph (b), a lawyer shall not represent a client if the representation involves a concurrent conflict of interest. A concurrent conflict of interest exists if:

(1) the representation of one client will be directly adverse to another client; or

(2) there is a significant risk that the representation of one or more clients will be materially limited by the lawyer's responsibilities to another client, a former client or a third person or by a personal interest of the lawyer.

(b) Notwithstanding the existence of a concurrent conflict of interest under paragraph (a), a lawyer may represent a client if:

(1) the lawyer reasonably believes that the lawyer will be able to provide competent and diligent representation to each affected client;

(2) the representation is not prohibited by law;

(3) the representation does not involve the assertion of a claim by one client against another client represented by the lawyer in the same litigation or other proceeding before a tribunal; and

(4) each affected client gives informed consent, confirmed in writing.

COMMENT

~~Loyalty to a Client~~ General Principles

[1] Loyalty ~~is an~~ and independent judgment are essential ~~element~~ elements in the lawyer's relationship to a client. Concurrent conflicts of interest can arise from the lawyer's responsibilities to another client, a former client or a third person or from the lawyer's own interests. For specific Rules regarding certain concurrent conflicts of interest, see Rule 1.8. For former client conflicts of interest, see Rule 1.9. For conflicts of interest involving prospective clients, see Rule 1.18. For definitions of "informed consent" and "confirmed in writing," see Rule 1.0(e) and (b).

[2] Resolution of a conflict of interest problem under this Rule requires the lawyer to: 1) clearly identify the client or clients; 2) determine whether a conflict of interest exists; 3) decide whether the representation may be undertaken despite the existence of a conflict, i.e., whether the conflict is consentable; and 4) if so, consult with the clients affected under paragraph (a) and obtain their informed consent, confirmed in writing. The clients affected under paragraph (a) include both of the clients referred to in paragraph (a)(1) and the one or more clients whose representation might be materially limited under paragraph (a)(2).

[3] ~~An impermissible~~ A conflict of interest may exist before representation is undertaken, in which event the representation ~~should~~ must be declined, unless the lawyer obtains the informed consent of each client under the conditions of paragraph (b). ~~The~~ To determine whether a conflict of interest exists, a lawyer should adopt reasonable procedures, appropriate for the size and type of firm and practice, to determine in both litigation and non-litigation matters the ~~parties~~ persons and issues involved ~~and to determine whether there are actual or potential conflicts of interest.~~ See also Comment to Rule 5.1. Ignorance caused by a failure to institute such procedures will not excuse a lawyer's violation of this Rule. As to whether a client-lawyer relationship exists or, having once been established, is continuing, see Comment to Rule 1.3 and Scope.

~~[2]~~ [4] If ~~such~~ a conflict arises after representation has been undertaken, the lawyer ~~should~~ ordinarily must withdraw from the representation, unless the lawyer has obtained the informed consent of the client under the conditions of paragraph (b). See Rule 1.16. Where more than one client is involved ~~and the lawyer withdraws because a conflict arises after representation~~, whether the lawyer may continue to represent any of the clients is determined both by the lawyer's ability to comply with duties owed to the former client and by the lawyer's ability to represent adequately the remaining client or clients, given the lawyer's duties to the former client. See Rule 1.9. See also ~~Rule 2.2(c)~~ Comments [5] and [29]. ~~As to whether a client-lawyer relationship exists or, having once been established, is continuing, see Comment to Rule 1.3 and Scope.~~

[5] Unforeseeable developments, such as changes in corporate and other organizational affiliations or the addition or realignment of parties in litigation, might create conflicts in the midst of a representation, as when a company sued by the lawyer on behalf of one client is bought by another client represented by the lawyer in an unrelated matter. Depending on the circumstances, the lawyer may have the option to withdraw from one of the representations in order to avoid the conflict. The lawyer must seek court approval where necessary and take steps to minimize harm to the clients. See Rule 1.16. The lawyer must continue to protect the confidences of the client from whose representation the lawyer has withdrawn. See Rule 1.9(c).

Identifying Conflicts of Interest: Directly Adverse

~~[3]~~ [6] ~~As a general proposition, loyalty~~ Loyalty to a current client prohibits undertaking representation directly adverse to that client without that client's informed consent. ~~Paragraph (a) expresses that general rule.~~ Thus, absent consent, a lawyer ~~ordinarily~~ may not act as an advocate in one matter against a person the lawyer represents in some other matter, even ~~if it is~~ when the matters are wholly unrelated. The client as to whom the representation is directly adverse is likely to feel betrayed, and the resulting damage to the client-lawyer relationship is likely to impair the lawyer's ability to represent the client effectively. In addition, the client on whose behalf the adverse representation is undertaken reasonably may fear that the lawyer will pursue that client's case less effectively out of deference to the other client, i.e., that the representation may be materially limited by the lawyer's interest in retaining the current client. Similarly, a directly adverse conflict may arise when a lawyer is required to cross-examine a client who appears as a witness in a lawsuit involving another client, as when the testimony will be damaging to the client who is represented in the lawsuit. On the other hand, simultaneous representation in unrelated matters of clients whose interests are only ~~generally~~ economically adverse, such as representation of competing economic enterprises in unrelated litigation, does not ordinarily constitute a conflict of interest and thus may not require consent of the respective clients. ~~Paragraph (a) applies only when the representation of one client would be directly adverse to the other.~~

[7] Directly adverse conflicts can also arise in transactional matters. For example, if a lawyer is asked to represent the seller of a business in negotiations with a buyer represented by the lawyer, not in the same transaction but in another, unrelated matter, the lawyer could not undertake the representation without the informed consent of each client.

Identifying Conflicts of Interest: Material Limitation

~~[4]~~ [8] ~~Loyalty to a client is also impaired when~~ Even where there is no direct adverseness, a conflict of interest exists if there is a significant risk that a ~~lawyer cannot~~ lawyer's ability to consider, recommend or carry out an appropriate course of action for the client ~~because~~ will be materially limited as a result of the lawyer's other responsibilities or interests. For example, a lawyer asked to represent several individuals seeking to form a joint venture is likely to be materially limited in the lawyer's ability to recommend or advocate all possible positions that each might take because of the lawyer's duty of loyalty to the others. The conflict in effect forecloses alternatives that would otherwise be available to the client. ~~Paragraph (b) addresses such situations. A possible conflict~~ The mere possibility of subsequent harm does not itself ~~preclude the representation~~ require disclosure and consent. The critical questions are the likelihood that a ~~conflict~~ difference in interests will eventuate and, if it does, whether it will materially interfere with the lawyer's independent professional judgment in considering alternatives or foreclose courses of action that reasonably should be pursued on behalf of the client. ~~Consideration should be given to whether the client wishes to accommodate the other interest involved.~~

Lawyer's ~~Interests~~ Responsibilities to Former Clients and Other Third Persons

[9] In addition to conflicts with other current clients, a lawyer's duties of loyalty and independence may be materially limited by responsibilities to former clients under Rule 1.9 or by the lawyer's responsibilities to other persons, such as fiduciary duties arising from a lawyer's service as a trustee, executor or corporate director.

Personal Interest Conflicts

~~[6]~~ [10] The lawyer's own interests should not be permitted to have an adverse effect on representation of a client. For example, ~~a lawyer's need for income should not lead the lawyer to undertake matters that cannot be handled competently and at a reasonable fee. See Rules 1.1 and 1.5. If~~ if the probity of a lawyer's own conduct in a transaction is in serious question, it may be difficult or impossible for the lawyer to give a client detached advice. ~~A~~ Similarly, when a lawyer has discussions concerning possible employment with an opponent of the lawyer's client, or with a law firm representing the opponent, such discussions could materially limit the lawyer's representation of the client. In addition, a lawyer may not allow related business interests to affect representation, for example, by referring clients to an enterprise in which the lawyer has an undisclosed financial interest. See Rule 1.8 for specific Rules pertaining to a number of personal interest conflicts, including business transactions with clients. See also Rule 1.10 (personal interest conflicts under Rule 1.7 ordinarily are not imputed to other lawyers in a law firm).

[11] When lawyers representing different clients in the same matter or in substantially related matters are closely related by blood or marriage, there may be a significant risk that client confidences will be revealed and that the lawyer's family relationship will interfere with both loyalty and independent professional judgment. As a result, each client is entitled to know of the existence and implications of the relationship between the lawyers before the lawyer agrees to undertake the representation. Thus, a lawyer related to another lawyer, e.g., as parent, child, sibling or spouse, ordinarily may not represent a client in a matter where that lawyer is representing another party, unless each client gives informed consent. The disqualification arising from a close family relationship is personal and ordinarily is not imputed to members of firms with whom the lawyers are associated. See Rule 1.10.

[12] A lawyer is prohibited from engaging in sexual relationships with a client unless the sexual relationship predates the formation of the client-lawyer relationship. See Rule 1.8(j).

Interest of Person Paying for a Lawyer's Service

~~[10]~~ [13] A lawyer may be paid from a source other than the client, including a co-client, if the client is informed of that fact and consents and the arrangement does not compromise the lawyer's duty of loyalty or independent judgment to the client. See Rule 1.8(f). ~~For example, when an insurer and its insured have conflicting interests in a matter arising from a liability insurance agreement, and the insurer is required to provide special counsel for the insured, the arrangement should assure the special counsel's professional independence. So also, when a corporation and its directors or employees are involved in a controversy in which they have conflicting interests, the corporation may provide funds for separate legal representation of the directors or employees, if the clients consent after consultation and the arrangement ensures the lawyer's professional independence.~~ If acceptance of the payment from any other source presents a significant risk that the lawyer's representation of the client will be materially limited by the lawyer's own interest in accommodating the person paying the lawyer's fee or by the lawyer's responsibilities to a payer who is also a co-client, then the lawyer must comply with the requirements of paragraph (b) before accepting the representation, including determining whether the conflict is consentable and, if so, that the client has adequate information about the material risks of the representation.

~~Consultation and Consent~~ Prohibited Representations

~~[5]~~ [14] ~~A client~~ Ordinarily, clients may consent to representation notwithstanding a conflict. However, as indicated in paragraph ~~(a)(1) with respect to representation directly adverse to a client, and paragraph~~ (b)~~(1) with respect to material limitations on representation of a client, when a disinterested lawyer would conclude that the client should not agree to the representation under the circumstances~~, some conflicts are nonconsentable, meaning that the lawyer involved cannot properly ask for such agreement or provide representation on the basis of the client's consent. When the lawyer is representing more than one client ~~is involved~~, the question of ~~conflict consentability~~ must be resolved as to each client. ~~Moreover, there may be circumstances where it is impossible to make the disclosure necessary to obtain consent. For example, when the lawyer represents different clients in related matters and one of the clients refuses to consent to the disclosure necessary to permit the other client to make an informed decision, the lawyer cannot properly ask the latter to consent.~~

[15] Consentability is typically determined by considering whether the interests of the clients will be adequately protected if the clients are permitted to give their informed consent to representation burdened by

a conflict of interest. Thus, under paragraph (b)(1), representation is prohibited if in the circumstances the lawyer cannot reasonably conclude that the lawyer will be able to provide competent and diligent representation. See Rule 1.1 (competence) and Rule 1.3 (diligence).

[16] Paragraph (b)(2) describes conflicts that are nonconsentable because the representation is prohibited by applicable law. For example, in some states substantive law provides that the same lawyer may not represent more than one defendant in a capital case, even with the consent of the clients, and under federal criminal statutes certain representations by a former government lawyer are prohibited, despite the informed consent of the former client. In addition, decisional law in some states limits the ability of a governmental client, such as a municipality, to consent to a conflict of interest.

[17] Paragraph (b)(3) describes conflicts that are nonconsentable because of the institutional interest in vigorous development of each client's position when the clients are aligned directly against each other in the same litigation or other proceeding before a tribunal. Whether clients are aligned directly against each other within the meaning of this paragraph requires examination of the context of the proceeding. Although this paragraph does not preclude a lawyer's multiple representation of adverse parties to a mediation (because mediation is not a proceeding before a "tribunal" under Rule 1.0(m)), such representation may be precluded by paragraph (b)(1).

Informed Consent

[18] Informed consent requires that each affected client be aware of the relevant circumstances and of the material and reasonably foreseeable ways that the conflict could have adverse effects on the interests of that client. See Rule 1.0(e) (informed consent). The information required depends on the nature of the conflict and the nature of the risks involved. When representation of multiple clients in a single matter is undertaken, the information must include the implications of the common representation, including possible effects on loyalty, confidentiality and the attorney-client privilege and the advantages and risks involved. See Comments [30] and [31] (effect of common representation on confidentiality).

[19] Under some circumstances it may be impossible to make the disclosure necessary to obtain consent. For example, when the lawyer represents different clients in related matters and one of the clients refuses to consent to the disclosure necessary to permit the other client to make an informed decision, the lawyer cannot properly ask the latter to consent. In some cases the alternative to common representation can be that each party may have to obtain separate representation with the possibility of incurring additional costs. These costs, along with the benefits of securing separate representation, are factors that may be considered by the af-

fected client in determining whether common representation is in the client's interests.

Consent Confirmed in Writing

[20] Paragraph (b) requires the lawyer to obtain the informed consent of the client, confirmed in writing. Such a writing may consist of a document executed by the client or one that the lawyer promptly records and transmits to the client following an oral consent. See Rule 1.0(b). See also Rule 1.0(n) (writing includes electronic transmission). If it is not feasible to obtain or transmit the writing at the time the client gives informed consent, then the lawyer must obtain or transmit it within a reasonable time thereafter. See Rule 1.0(b). The requirement of a writing does not supplant the need in most cases for the lawyer to talk with the client, to explain the risks and advantages, if any, of representation burdened with a conflict of interest, as well as reasonably available alternatives, and to afford the client a reasonable opportunity to consider the risks and alternatives and to raise questions and concerns. Rather, the writing is required in order to impress upon clients the seriousness of the decision the client is being asked to make and to avoid disputes or ambiguities that might later occur in the absence of a writing.

Revoking Consent

[21] A client who has given consent to a conflict may revoke the consent and, like any other client, may terminate the lawyer's representation at any time. Whether revoking consent to the client's own representation precludes the lawyer from continuing to represent other clients depends on the circumstances, including the nature of the conflict, whether the client revoked consent because of a material change in circumstances, the reasonable expectations of the other client and whether material detriment to the other clients or the lawyer would result.

Consent to Future Conflict

[22] Whether a lawyer may properly request a client to waive conflicts that might arise in the future is subject to the test of paragraph (b). The effectiveness of such waivers is generally determined by the extent to which the client reasonably understands the material risks that the waiver entails. The more comprehensive the explanation of the types of future representations that might arise and the actual and reasonably foreseeable adverse consequences of those representations, the greater the likelihood that the client will have the requisite understanding. Thus, if the

client agrees to consent to a particular type of conflict with which the client is already familiar, then the consent ordinarily will be effective with regard to that type of conflict. If the consent is general and open-ended, then the consent ordinarily will be ineffective, because it is not reasonably likely that the client will have understood the material risks involved. On the other hand, if the client is an experienced user of the legal services involved and is reasonably informed regarding the risk that a conflict may arise, such consent is more likely to be effective, particularly if, e.g., the client is independently represented by other counsel in giving consent and the consent is limited to future conflicts unrelated to the subject of the representation. In any case, advance consent cannot be effective if the circumstances that materialize in the future are such as would make the conflict nonconsentable under paragraph (b).

Conflicts in Litigation

~~[7]~~ [23] Paragraph ~~(a)~~ (b)(3) prohibits representation of opposing parties in the same litigation, regardless of the clients' consent. ~~Simultaneous~~ On the other hand, simultaneous representation of parties whose interests in litigation may conflict, such as coplaintiffs or codefendants, is governed by paragraph ~~(b)~~ (a)(2). ~~An impermissible~~ A conflict may exist by reason of substantial discrepancy in the parties' testimony, incompatibility in positions in relation to an opposing party or the fact that there are substantially different possibilities of settlement of the claims or liabilities in question. Such conflicts can arise in criminal cases as well as civil. The potential for conflict of interest in representing multiple defendants in a criminal case is so grave that ordinarily a lawyer should decline to represent more than one codefendant. On the other hand, common representation of persons having similar interests in civil litigation is proper if ~~the risk of adverse effect is minimal and~~ the requirements of paragraph (b) are met. ~~Compare Rule 2.2 involving intermediation between clients.~~

~~[8] Ordinarily, a lawyer may not act as advocate against a client the lawyer represents in some other matter, even if the other matter is wholly unrelated. However, there are circumstances in which a lawyer may act as advocate against a client. For example, a lawyer representing an enterprise with diverse operations may accept employment as an advocate against the enterprise in an unrelated matter if doing so will not adversely affect the lawyer's relationship with the enterprise or conduct of the suit and if both clients consent upon consultation. By the same token, government lawyers in some circumstances may represent government employees in proceedings in which a government agency is the opposing party. The propriety of concurrent representation can depend on the nature of the litigation. For example, a suit charging fraud entails conflict to a degree not involved in a suit for a declaratory judgment concerning statutory interpretation.~~

~~[9] A lawyer may represent parties having antagonistic positions on a legal question that has arisen in different cases, unless representation of either client would be adversely affected. Thus, it is ordinarily not improper to assert such positions in cases pending in different trial courts, but it may be improper to do so in cases pending at the same time in an appellate court.~~

[24] Ordinarily a lawyer may take inconsistent legal positions in different tribunals at different times on behalf of different clients. The mere fact that advocating a legal position on behalf of one client might create precedent adverse to the interests of a client represented by the lawyer in an unrelated matter does not create a conflict of interest. A conflict of interest exists, however, if there is a significant risk that a lawyer's action on behalf of one client will materially limit the lawyer's effectiveness in representing another client in a different case; for example, when a decision favoring one client will create a precedent likely to seriously weaken the position taken on behalf of the other client. Factors relevant in determining whether the clients need to be advised of the risk include: where the cases are pending, whether the issue is substantive or procedural, the temporal relationship between the matters, the significance of the issue to the immediate and long-term interests of the clients involved and the clients' reasonable expectations in retaining the lawyer. If there is significant risk of material limitation, then absent informed consent of the affected clients, the lawyer must refuse one of the representations or withdraw from one or both matters.

[25] When a lawyer represents or seeks to represent a class of plaintiffs or defendants in a class-action lawsuit, unnamed members of the class are ordinarily not considered to be clients of the lawyer for purposes of applying paragraph (a)(1) of this Rule. Thus, the lawyer does not typically need to get the consent of such a person before representing a client suing the person in an unrelated matter. Similarly, a lawyer seeking to represent an opponent in a class action does not typically need the consent of an unnamed member of the class whom the lawyer represents in an unrelated matter.

~~Other Conflict Situations~~ Nonlitigation Conflicts

~~[11]~~ [26] Conflicts of interest under paragraphs (a)(1) and (a)(2) arise in contexts other than litigation ~~sometimes may be difficult to assess~~. For a discussion of directly adverse conflicts in transactional matters, see Comment [7]. Relevant factors in determining whether there is significant potential for ~~adverse effect~~ material limitation include the duration and intimacy of the lawyer's relationship with the client or clients involved, the functions being performed by the lawyer, the likelihood that ~~actual conflict~~ disagreements will arise and the likely prejudice to the client from the conflict ~~if it does arise~~. The question is often one of proximity and degree. See Comment [8].

~~[13]~~ [27] ~~Conflict~~ For example, conflict questions may ~~also~~ arise in estate planning and estate administration. A lawyer may be called upon to prepare wills for several family members, such as husband and wife, and, depending upon the circumstances, a conflict of interest may ~~arise~~ be present. In estate administration the identity of the client may be unclear under the law of a particular jurisdiction. Under one view, the client is the fiduciary; under another view the client is the estate or trust, including its beneficiaries. ~~The~~ In order to comply with conflict of interest rules, the lawyer should make clear the lawyer's relationship to the parties involved.

~~[12]~~ [28] Whether a conflict is consentable depends on the circumstances. For example, a lawyer may not represent multiple parties to a negotiation whose interests are fundamentally antagonistic to each other, but common representation is permissible where the clients are generally aligned in interest even though there is some difference in interest among them. Thus, a lawyer may seek to establish or adjust a relationship between clients on an amicable and mutually advantageous basis; for example, in helping to organize a business in which two or more clients are entrepreneurs, working out the financial reorganization of an enterprise in which two or more clients have an interest or arranging a property distribution in settlement of an estate. The lawyer seeks to resolve potentially adverse interests by developing the parties' mutual interests. Otherwise, each party might have to obtain separate representation, with the possibility of incurring additional cost, complication or even litigation. Given these and other relevant factors, the clients may prefer that the lawyer act for all of them.

Special Considerations in Common Representation

[29] In considering whether to represent multiple clients in the same matter, a lawyer should be mindful that if the common representation fails because the potentially adverse interests cannot be reconciled, the result can be additional cost, embarrassment and recrimination. Ordinarily, the lawyer will be forced to withdraw from representing all of the clients if the common representation fails. In some situations, the risk of failure is so great that multiple representation is plainly impossible. For example, a lawyer cannot undertake common representation of clients where contentious litigation or negotiations between them are imminent or contemplated. Moreover, because the lawyer is required to be impartial between commonly represented clients, representation of multiple clients is improper when it is unlikely that impartiality can be maintained. Generally, if the relationship between the parties has already assumed antagonism, the possibility that the clients' interests can be adequately served by common representation is not very good. Other relevant factors are whether the lawyer subsequently will represent both parties on a con-

tinuing basis and whether the situation involves creating or terminating a relationship between the parties.

[30] A particularly important factor in determining the appropriateness of common representation is the effect on client-lawyer confidentiality and the attorney-client privilege. With regard to the attorney-client privilege, the prevailing rule is that, as between commonly represented clients, the privilege does not attach. Hence, it must be assumed that if litigation eventuates between the clients, the privilege will not protect any such communications, and the clients should be so advised.

[31] As to the duty of confidentiality, continued common representation will almost certainly be inadequate if one client asks the lawyer not to disclose to the other client information relevant to the common representation. This is so because the lawyer has an equal duty of loyalty to each client, and each client has the right to be informed of anything bearing on the representation that might affect that client's interests and the right to expect that the lawyer will use that information to that client's benefit. See Rule 1.4. The lawyer should, at the outset of the common representation and as part of the process of obtaining each client's informed consent, advise each client that information will be shared and that the lawyer will have to withdraw if one client decides that some matter material to the representation should be kept from the other. In limited circumstances, it may be appropriate for the lawyer to proceed with the representation when the clients have agreed, after being properly informed, that the lawyer will keep certain information confidential. For example, the lawyer may reasonably conclude that failure to disclose one client's trade secrets to another client will not adversely affect representation involving a joint venture between the clients and agree to keep that information confidential with the informed consent of both clients.

[32] When seeking to establish or adjust a relationship between clients, the lawyer should make clear that the lawyer's role is not that of partisanship normally expected in other circumstances and, thus, that the clients may be required to assume greater responsibility for decisions than when each client is separately represented. Any limitations on the scope of the representation made necessary as a result of the common representation should be fully explained to the clients at the outset of the representation. See Rule 1.2(c).

[33] Subject to the above limitations, each client in the common representation has the right to loyal and diligent representation and the protection of Rule 1.9 concerning the obligations to a former client. The client also has the right to discharge the lawyer as stated in Rule 1.16.

Organizational Clients

[34] A lawyer who represents a corporation or other organization does not, by virtue of that representation, necessarily represent any constituent or affiliated organization, such as a parent or subsidiary. See Rule 1.13(a). Thus, the lawyer for an organization is not barred from accepting representation

adverse to an affiliate in an unrelated matter, unless the circumstances are such that the affiliate should also be considered a client of the lawyer, there is an understanding between the lawyer and the organizational client that the lawyer will avoid representation adverse to the client's affiliates, or the lawyer's obligations to either the organizational client or the new client are likely to limit materially the lawyer's representation of the other client.

~~[14]~~ [35] A lawyer for a corporation or other organization who is also a member of its board of directors should determine whether the responsibilities of the two roles may conflict. The lawyer may be called on to advise the corporation in matters involving actions of the directors. Consideration should be given to the frequency with which such situations may arise, the potential intensity of the conflict, the effect of the lawyer's resignation from the board and the possibility of the corporation's obtaining legal advice from another lawyer in such situations. If there is material risk that the dual role will compromise the lawyer's independence of professional judgment, the lawyer should not serve as a director or should cease to act as the corporation's lawyer when conflicts of interest arise. The lawyer should advise the other members of the board that in some circumstances matters discussed at board meetings while the lawyer is present in the capacity of director might not be protected by the attorney-client privilege and that conflict of interest considerations might require the lawyer's recusal as a director or might require the lawyer and the lawyer's firm to decline representation of the corporation in a matter.

~~Conflict Charged by an Opposing Party~~

~~[15] Resolving questions of conflict of interest is primarily the responsibility of the lawyer undertaking the representation. In litigation, a court may raise the question when there is reason to infer that the lawyer has neglected the responsibility. In a criminal case, inquiry by the court is generally required when a lawyer represents multiple defendants. Where the conflict is such as clearly to call in question the fair or efficient administration of justice, opposing counsel may properly raise the question. Such an objection should be viewed with caution, however, for it can be misused as a technique of harassment. See Scope.~~

Canon and Code Antecedents

ABA Canons of Professional Ethics: Canon 6 provided as follows:

6. Adverse Influences and Conflicting Interests

It is the duty of a lawyer at the time of retainer to disclose to the client all the circumstances of his relations to the parties, and any interest in or connection with the controversy, which might influence the client in the selection of counsel.

It is unprofessional to represent conflicting interests, except by express consent of all concerned given after a full disclosure of the facts. Within the meaning of this canon, a lawyer represents conflicting interests when, in behalf of one client, it is his duty to contend for that which duty to another client requires him to oppose.

The obligation to represent the client with undivided fidelity and not to divulge his secrets or confidences forbids also the subsequent acceptance of retainers or employment from others in matters adversely affecting any interest of the client with respect to which confidence has been reposed.

ABA Model Code of Professional Responsibility: Compare DR 5-101(A), DR 5-105(A), DR 5-105(C), and DR 5-107(B) (reprinted later in this volume).

Cross-References in Other Rules

Rule 1.0, Comment 6: "Many of the Rules of Professional Conduct require the lawyer to obtain the informed consent of a client or other person before accepting or continuing representation or pursuing a course of conduct (see Rules 1.2(c), 1.6(a) and **1.7(b)**)."

Rule 1.0, Comment 7: "A number of Rules require that a person's consent be confirmed in writing. See **Rules 1.7(b)** and 1.9(a)."

Rule 1.8, Comment 3: "The risk to a client is greatest when the client expects the lawyer to represent the client in the transaction itself or when the lawyer's financial interest otherwise poses a significant risk that the lawyer's representation of the client will be materially limited by the lawyer's financial interest in the transaction. Here the lawyer's role requires that the lawyer must comply, not only with the requirements of paragraph (a), but also with the requirements of **Rule 1.7**. Under that Rule, the lawyer must disclose the risks associated with the lawyer's dual role as both legal adviser and participant in the transaction, such as the risk that the lawyer will structure the transaction or give legal advice in a way that favors the lawyer's interests at the expense of the client. Moreover, the lawyer must obtain the client's informed consent. In some cases, the lawyer's interest may be such that **Rule 1.7** will preclude the lawyer from seeking the client's consent to the transaction."

Rule 1.8, Comment 8: "This Rule does not prohibit a lawyer from seeking to have the lawyer or a partner or associate of the lawyer named as executor of the client's estate or to another potentially lucrative fiduciary position. Nevertheless, such appointments will be subject to the general conflict of interest provision in **Rule 1.7** when there is a significant risk that the lawyer's interest in obtaining the appointment will materially limit the lawyer's independent professional judgment in advising the client concerning the choice of an executor or other fiduciary."

Rule 1.8, Comment 12: "Sometimes, it will be sufficient for the lawyer to obtain the client's informed consent regarding the fact of the payment and the identity of the third-party payer. If, however, the fee arrangement creates a conflict of interest for the lawyer, then the lawyer must comply with **Rule 1.7**. . . . Under **Rule 1.7(a)**, a conflict of interest exists if there is significant risk that the lawyer's representation of the client will be materially limited by the lawyer's own interest in the fee arrangement or by the lawyer's responsibilities to the third-party payer. . . . Under **Rule 1.7(b)**, the lawyer may accept or continue the representation with the informed consent of each affected client, unless the conflict is nonconsentable under that paragraph. Under **Rule 1.7(b)**, the informed consent must be confirmed in writing."

Rule 1.8, Comment 13: "Differences in willingness to make or accept an offer of settlement are among the risks of common representation of multiple clients by a single lawyer. Under **Rule 1.7**, this is one of the risks that should be discussed before undertaking the representation. . . ."

Rule 1.8, Comment 18: In the situation of client-lawyer sexual relationships, "before proceeding with the representation . . . , the lawyer should consider whether the lawyer's ability to represent the client will be materially limited by the relationship. See **Rule 1.7(a)(2)**."

Rule 1.9, Comment 9: "With regard to the effectiveness of an advance waiver, see Comment [22] to **Rule 1.7**."

Rule 1.10(a): "While lawyers are associated in a firm, none of them shall knowingly represent a client when any one of them practicing alone would be prohibited from doing so by **Rules 1.7** or 1.9, unless the prohibition is based on a personal interest of the prohibited lawyer and does not present a significant risk of materially limiting the representation of the client by the remaining lawyers in the firm."

Rule 1.10(c): "A disqualification prescribed by this rule may be waived by the affected client under the conditions stated in **Rule 1.7**."

Rule 1.10, Comment 5: Despite Rule 1.10(b), a law firm "may not represent a person with interests adverse to those of a present client of the firm, which would violate **Rule 1.7**."

Rule 1.10, Comment 6: "Rule 1.10(c) removes imputation with the informed consent of the affected client or former client under the conditions stated in **Rule 1.7**. The conditions stated in **Rule 1.7** require the lawyer to determine that the representation is not prohibited by **Rule 1.7(b)**. . . . For a discussion of the effectiveness of client waivers of conflicts that might arise in the future, see **Rule 1.7**, Comment [22]."

Rule 1.11(d): "Except as law may otherwise expressly permit, a lawyer currently serving as a public officer or employee is subject to **Rules 1.7** and 1.9."

Rule 1.11, Comment 1: "A lawyer who has served or is currently serving as a public officer or employee is personally subject to the Rules of Professional Conduct, including the prohibition against concurrent conflicts of interest stated in **Rule 1.7**."

Rule 1.11, Comment 9: "Paragraphs (a) and (d) do not prohibit a lawyer from jointly representing a private party and a government agency when doing so is permitted by **Rule 1.7** and is not otherwise prohibited by law."

Rule 1.13(e): "A lawyer representing an organization may also represent any of its directors, officers, employees, members, shareholders or other constituents, subject to the provisions of **Rule 1.7**. If the organization's consent to the dual representation is required by **Rule 1.7**, the consent shall be given by an appropriate official of the organization other than the individual who is to be represented, or by the shareholders."

Rule 1.13, Comment 11: "[I]f the claim involves serious charges of wrongdoing by those in control of the organization, a conflict may arise between the lawyer's duty to the organization and the lawyer's relationship with the board. In those circumstances, **Rule 1.7** governs who should represent the directors and the organization."

Rule 1.17, Comment 11: A lawyer selling a law practice has an "obligation to avoid disqualifying conflicts, and to secure the client's informed consent for those conflicts that can be agreed to (see **Rule 1.7** regarding conflicts and Rule 1.0(e) for the definition of informed consent)."

Rule 1.18, Comment 4: "If the prospective client wishes to retain the lawyer, and if consent is possible under **Rule 1.7**, then consent from all affected present or former clients must be obtained before accepting the representation."

Rule 3.7(b): "A lawyer may act as advocate in a trial in which another lawyer in the lawyer's firm is likely to be called as a witness unless precluded from doing so by **Rule 1.7** or Rule 1.9."

Rule 3.7, Comment 4: In determining whether the lawyer should be disqualified, "[i]t is relevant that one or both parties could reasonably foresee that the lawyer would probably be a witness. The conflict of interest principles stated in **Rules 1.7**, 1.9 and 1.10 have no application to this aspect of the problem."

Rule 3.7, Comment 6: "In determining if it is permissible to act as advocate in a trial in which the lawyer will be a necessary witness, the lawyer must also consider that the dual role may give rise to a conflict of interest that will require compliance with **Rules 1.7** or 1.9. For example, if there is likely to be substantial conflict between the testimony of the client and that of the lawyer, the representation involves a conflict of interest that requires compliance with **Rule 1.7**. . . . If there is a conflict of interest, the lawyer must secure the client's informed consent, confirmed in writing. In some cases, the lawyer will be precluded from seeking the client's consent. See **Rule 1.7**."

Rule 3.7, Comment 7: "If, however, the testifying lawyer would also be disqualified by **Rule 1.7** or Rule 1.9 from representing the client in the matter, other lawyers in the firm will be precluded from representing the client by Rule 1.10 unless the client gives informed consent under the conditions stated in **Rule 1.7**."

Rule 5.2, Comment 2: "[I]f a question arises whether the interests of two clients conflict under **Rule 1.7**, the supervisor's reasonable resolution of the question should protect the subordinate professionally if the resolution is subsequently challenged."

Rule 5.7, Comment 10: "When a lawyer is obliged to accord the recipients of such services the protections of those Rules that apply to the client-lawyer relationship, the lawyer must take special care to heed the proscriptions of the Rules addressing conflict of interest (**Rules 1.7** through 1.11, especially **Rules 1.7** and 1.8(a), (b) and (f)). . . ."

Rule 6.3(a): "The lawyer shall not knowingly participate in a decision or action of the organization if participating in the decision or action would be incompatible with the lawyer's obligations to a client under **Rule 1.7**. . . ."

Rule 6.4, Comment 1: "In determining the nature and scope of participation in such activities, a lawyer should be mindful of obligations to clients under other Rules, particularly **Rule 1.7**."

Rule 6.5(a): "A lawyer who, under the auspices of a program sponsored by a nonprofit organization or court, provides short-term limited legal services to a client without expectation by either the lawyer or the client that the lawyer will provide continuing representation in the matter is subject to **Rules 1.7** and 1.9(a) only if the lawyer knows that the representation of the client involves a conflict of interest; and is subject to Rule 1.10 only if the lawyer knows that another lawyer associated with the lawyer in a law firm is disqualified by **Rule 1.7** or 1.9(a) with respect to the matter."

Rule 6.5, Comment 1: "Legal services organizations, courts and various nonprofit organizations have established programs through which lawyers provide short-term limited legal services. . . . Such programs are normally operated under circumstances in which it is not feasible for a lawyer to systematically screen for conflicts of interest as is generally required before undertaking a representation. See, e.g., **Rules 1.7**, 1.9 and 1.10."

Rule 6.5, Comment 3: "[P]aragraph (a) requires compliance with **Rules 1.7** or 1.9(a) only if the lawyer knows that the representation presents a conflict of interest for the lawyer, and with Rule 1.10 only if the lawyer knows that another lawyer in the lawyer's firm is disqualified by **Rules 1.7** or 1.9(a) in the matter."

Rule 6.5, Comment 4: "Paragraph (a)(2) requires the participating lawyer to comply with Rule 1.10 when the lawyer knows that the lawyer's firm is disqualified by **Rules 1.7** or 1.9(a)."

Rule 6.5, Comment 5: "If, after commencing a short-term limited representation in accordance with this Rule, a lawyer undertakes to represent the client in the matter on an ongoing basis, **Rules 1.7**, 1.9(a) and 1.10 become applicable."

Rule 7.2, Comment 8: "Conflicts of interest created by such [reciprocal referral] arrangements are governed by **Rule 1.7**."

Legislative History of Model Rule 1.7

1980 Discussion Draft (then Rule 1.8) provided as follows:

> In circumstances in which a lawyer has interests, commitments, or responsibilities that may adversely affect the representation of a client, a lawyer shall not represent the client unless:
>
> (a) the Services contemplated in the representation can otherwise be performed in accordance with the rules of professional conduct; and
>
> (b) the client consents after adequate disclosure of the circumstances.

1981 Draft:

> (a) A lawyer shall not represent a client if the lawyer's ability to consider, recommend or carry out a course of action on behalf of the client will be adversely affected by the lawyer's responsibilities to another client or to a third person, or by the lawyer's own interests.
>
> (b) When a lawyer's own interests or other responsibilities might adversely affect the representation of a client, the lawyer shall not represent the client unless:
>
> (1) the lawyer reasonably believes the other responsibilities or interests involved will not adversely affect the best interest of the client; and . . .

1982 Draft was adopted.

1987 Amendment: The ABA House of Delegates added the last sentence of Comment 1 to Rule 1.7, and placed other parts of Comment 1 into a separate paragraph, which is now Comment 2.

2002 Amendments: At its February 2002 Mid-Year Meeting, the ABA House of Delegates adopted without change the ABA Ethics 2000 Commission proposal to amend Rule 1.7 and its Comment.

Selected State Variations

Alaska adds Rule 1.7(c), which provides that a lawyer "shall act with reasonable diligence in determining whether a conflict of interest, as described in paragraphs (a) and (b) of this rule, or Rules 1.8, 1.9 and 1.10 exists." Alaska's Comment explains: "Substantial delay in litigation may occur as a result of a conflict of interest unless prompt efforts are made to discover any such conflicts. A lawyer should take all reasonable measures to determine whether or not a conflict of interest exists . . . ."

California: See Rule 3-310 (Avoiding the Representation of Adverse Interests). Section 2860 of the California Civil Code, adopted after the important decision in San Diego Credit Union v. Cumis, 162 Cal. App. 3d 358, 208 Cal. Rptr. 494 (1984), seeks to reconcile the multiple interests at stake when an insurance company has a duty to defend an insured whose interests might not be congruent with those of the insurer. The first paragraph of §2860 provides:

> (a) If the provisions of a policy of insurance impose a duty to defend upon an insurer and a conflict of interest arises which creates a duty on the part of the insurer to provide independent counsel to the insured, the insurer shall provide independent counsel to represent the insured unless, at the time the insured is informed that a possible conflict may arise or does exist, the insured expressly waives, in writing, the right to independent counsel. An insurance contract may contain a provision which sets forth the method of selecting that counsel consistent with this section.

The full text of §2860 is set out below in our chapter on Selected California Statutes.

In addition, §1424(a)(1) of the California Penal Code, entitled "Disqualification of the District Attorney," establishes special procedures for any motion to disqualify a D.A. from performing any authorized duty. Such a motion must be served at least ten court days before the motion is heard and "shall contain a statement of the facts setting forth the grounds for the claimed disqualification and the legal authorities relied upon by the moving party and shall be supported by affidavits of witnesses who are competent to testify to the facts set forth in the affidavit." The motion may not be granted unless the evidence shows that "a conflict of interest exists that would render it unlikely that the defendant would receive a fair trial." If the motion is brought at or before the preliminary hearing, "it may not be renewed in the trial court on the basis of facts that were raised or could have been raised at the time of the original motion."

Colorado: Rule 1.7 adds section (c):

> For the purposes of this Rule, a client's consent cannot be validly obtained in those instances in which a disinterested lawyer would conclude that the client should not agree to the representation under the circumstances of the particular situation.

District of Columbia: D.C. Rule 1.7 differs significantly from the ABA Model Rule — see District of Columbia Rules of Professional Conduct below.

Florida: Rule 1.7(a)(1) applies when "the representation will not adversely affect the lawyer's responsibilities to and relationship with the other client."

Georgia: In the rules effective January 1, 2001, Georgia draws heavily on the Restatement of the Law Governing Lawyers. Georgia Rule 1.7 provides, in full, as follows:

> (a) A lawyer shall not represent or continue to represent a client if there is a significant risk that the lawyer's own interests or the lawyer's duties to another client, a former client, or a third person will materially and adversely affect the representation of the client, except as permitted in (b).

(b) If client consent is permissible a lawyer may represent a client notwithstanding a significant risk of material and adverse effect if each affected or former client consents, preferably in writing, to the representation after:

(1) consultation with the lawyer,

(2) having received in writing reasonable and adequate information about the material risks of the representation, and

(3) having been given the opportunity to consult with independent counsel.

(c) Client consent is not permissible if the representation:

(1) is prohibited by law or these rules;

(2) includes the assertion of a claim by one client against another client represented by the lawyer in the same or substantially related proceeding; or

(3) involves circumstances rendering it reasonably unlikely that the lawyer will be able to provide adequate representation to one or more of the affected clients.

Louisiana imports into the text of Rule 1.7 the first sentence of the Comment to the pre-2002 version of ABA Model Rule 1.7: "Loyalty is an essential element in the lawyer's relationship to a client."

Maine: As amended effective July 1, 2001, Rule 3.4(a) provides as follows:

(a) *Disclosure of Interest.* Before commencing any professional representation, a lawyer shall disclose to the prospective client any relationship or interest of the lawyer or of any partner, associate or affiliated lawyer, that might reasonably give rise to a conflict of interest under these rules. A lawyer has a continuing duty to disclose to the client any information that, in light of circumstances arising after the commencement of representation, might reasonably give rise to such a conflict of interest.

Massachusetts: Rule 1.7 is identical to the ABA rule, but the Comment is substantially different. Among other things, it addresses: the situation of the lawyer who represents one member of a corporate family while opposing another member of the family; the issue of confidentiality and privilege in multiple representation; and the responsibilities of lawyers who represent classes. Comment [6] states that "a lawyer should not accept referrals from a referral source . . . if the lawyer's desire to continue to receive referrals from that source or the lawyer's relationship to that source would discourage or would reasonably be viewed as discouraging the lawyer from representing the client zealously."

New Jersey Rules 1.7(a)(2) and 1.7(b)(2) each add that "a public entity cannot consent to any such representation." New Jersey also adds Rule 1.7(c):

(c) This rule shall not alter the effect of case law or ethics opinions to the effect that:

(1) in certain cases or categories of cases involving conflicts or apparent conflicts, consent to continued representation is immaterial, and

(2) in certain cases or situations creating an appearance of impropriety rather than an actual conflict, multiple representation is not permissible, that is, in those situations in which an ordinary knowledgeable citizen acquainted with the facts would conclude that the multiple representation poses substantial risk of disservice to either the public interest or the interest of one of the clients.

With respect to mortgage transactions, New Jersey has an unusual conflict of interest statute, §46:10A-6(b), that provides as follows:

If a lender makes a written offer to a borrower to make a loan secured by real property located in this State, the lender shall disclose, in writing, prominently and in bold type, to the borrower before the acceptance of the offer by the borrower, that the interests of the borrower and lender are or may be different and may conflict, and that the lender's attorney represents only the lender and not the borrower and the borrower is, therefore, advised to employ an attorney of the borrower's choice licensed to practice law in this State to represent the interests of the borrower.

New York: Compare ABA Model Rule 1.7 to New York's DR 5-101, DR 5-105, and DR 9-101(D).

North Carolina: Rule 1.7(c) provides as follows:

(c) A lawyer shall have a continuing obligation to evaluate all situations involving potentially conflicting interests, and shall withdraw from the representation of any party the lawyer cannot adequately represent without using the confidential information of another client or a former client except as Rule 1.6 allows.

Ohio adds new subdivisions DR 5-101(A)(2) and (3) that provide as follows:

(2) Notwithstanding the consent of the client, a lawyer shall not knowingly prepare, draft, or supervise the preparation or execution of a will, codicil, or inter vivos trust for a client in which any of the following are named as beneficiary:

(a) the lawyer;

(b) the lawyer's law partner or a shareholder of the lawyer's firm;

(c) an associate, paralegal, law clerk, or other employee in the lawyer's firm or office;

(d) a lawyer acting "of counsel" in the lawyer's firm;

(e) the spouses, siblings, natural or adoptive children, or natural or adoptive parents of any of those described in . . . this rule.

(3) Division (A)(2) of this rule shall not apply if the client is related by blood or marriage to the beneficiary within the third degree of relationship as defined by the law of Ohio.

Texas: Rule 1.06 provides:

(a) A lawyer shall not represent opposing parties to the same litigation.

(b) In other situations and except to the extent permitted by paragraph (c), a lawyer shall not represent a person if the representation of that person:

(1) involves a substantially related matter in which that person's interests are materially and directly adverse to the interests of another client of the lawyer or the lawyer's firm; or

(2) reasonably appears to be or become adversely limited by the lawyer's or law firm's responsibilities to another client or to a third person or by the lawyer's or law firm's own interests.

(c) A lawyer may represent a client in the circumstances described in (b) if:

(1) the lawyer reasonably believes the representation of each client will not be materially affected; and

(2) each affected or potentially affected client consents to such representation after full disclosure of the existence, nature, implications, and possible adverse consequences of the common representation and the advantages involved, if any.

(d) A lawyer who has represented multiple parties in a matter shall not thereafter represent any of such parties in a dispute among the parties arising out of the matter, unless prior consent is obtained from all such parties to the dispute.

(e) If a lawyer has accepted representation in violation of this Rule, or if multiple representation properly accepted becomes improper under this Rule, the lawyer shall promptly withdraw from one or more representations to the extent necessary for any remaining representation not to be in violation of these Rules.

> (f) If a lawyer would be prohibited by this Rule from engaging in particular conduct, no other lawyer while a member or associated with that lawyer's firm may engage in that conduct.

The Texas rule thus allows a lawyer to oppose a current client if the matter is not "substantially related" to matters currently handled on behalf of the client. However, in In re Dresser Industries, Inc., 972 F.2d 540 (5th Cir. 1992), the Fifth Circuit refused to apply Texas Rule 1.06 and disqualified a law firm suing a current client in a class action securities case. The *Dresser* court said that conflicts of interest in federal litigation are governed by "national standards," including ABA Model Rule 1.7 and the Restatement of the Law Governing Lawyers.

Washington: Under Rules 1.7(a)(2) and 1.7(b)(2), client consent is effective only if each client "consents *in writing* after consultation and a full disclosure of the material facts (following authorization from the other client to make such a disclosure)." In addition, in 1995, Washington added Rule 1.7(c), which provides as follows:

> (c) For purposes of this rule, when a lawyer who is not a public officer or employee represents a discrete governmental agency or unit that is part of a broader governmental entity, the lawyer's client is the particular governmental agency or unit represented, and not the broader governmental entity of which the agency or unit is a part, unless:
>
> (1) Otherwise provided in a written agreement between the lawyer and the governmental agency or unit; or
>
> (2) The broader governmental entity gives the lawyer timely written notice to the contrary, in which case the client shall be designated by such entity. Notice under this subsection shall be given by the person designated by law as the chief legal officer of the broader governmental entity, or in the absence of such designation, by the chief executive officer of the entity.

Wisconsin requires that consent under Rule 1.7(a) and (b) be in writing after consultation.

Related Materials

ABA Formal Ethics Opinions: See ABA Formal Ethics Ops. 92-365 (1992), 92-368 (1992), 93-372 (1993), 95-390 (1995), 97-406 (1997), and 97-407 (1997).

ABA Report on Lawyers as Directors: In April 1998, the ABA Section of Litigation's Task Force on the Independent Lawyer issued a lengthy report entitled "The Lawyer-Director: Implications for Independence." The report examines problems that may arise when a lawyer for a public or privately held corporation also serves as a director of the corporation. The report discourages lawyers from serving as both lawyer and director at the same time, but also suggests precautionary measures for lawyers who do serve in both capacities simultaneously.

ABA Standards for Imposing Lawyer Sanctions:

4.3. Failure to Avoid Conflicts of Interest

> 4.31. Disbarment is generally appropriate when a lawyer, without the informed consent of client(s):
>
> (a) engages in representation of a client knowing that the lawyer's interests are adverse to the client's with the intent to benefit the lawyer or another, and causes serious or potentially serious injury to the client; or

(b) simultaneously represents clients that the lawyer knows have adverse interests with the intent to benefit the lawyer or another, and causes serious or potentially serious injury to a client; or

(c) represents a client in a matter substantially related to a matter in which the interests of a present or former client are materially adverse, and knowingly uses information relating to the representation of a client with the intent to benefit the lawyer or another, and causes serious or potentially serious injury to a client.

4.32. Suspension is generally appropriate when a lawyer knows of a conflict of interest and does not fully disclose to a client the possible effect of that conflict, and causes injury or potential injury to a client.

4.33. Reprimand is generally appropriate when a lawyer is negligent in determining whether the representation of a client may be materially affected by the lawyer's own interests, or whether the representation will adversely affect another client, and causes injury or potential injury to a client.

4.34. Admonition is generally appropriate when a lawyer engages in an isolated instance of negligence in determining whether the representation of a client may be materially affected by the lawyer's own interests, or whether the representation will adversely affect another client, and causes little or no actual or potential injury to a client.

American Academy of Matrimonial Lawyers: The "Bounds of Advocacy" contains the following provisions and commentary:

2.10. An Attorney should not permit a client's relatives, friends, lovers, employers, or other third persons to interfere with the representation, affect the attorney's independent professional judgment, or make decisions affecting the representation, except with the client's express consent.

Comment to Rule 2.10

Third persons often try to play a part in matrimonial cases. Frequently, the client has requested that one or more of these persons be present at conferences and consulted about major decisions. . . . While it is important for persons going through a divorce to receive advice and support from those they trust, the client, with the advice of the attorney, should make the decisions with which the client must ultimately live.

2.16. An attorney should never have a sexual relationship with a client or opposing counsel during the time of the representation.

Comment to Rule 2.16

Persons in need of a matrimonial lawyer are often in a highly vulnerable emotional state. Some degree of social contact (particularly if a social relationship existed prior to the events that occasioned the representation) may be desirable, but a more intimate relationship may endanger both the client's welfare and the lawyer's objectivity.

Attorneys are expected to maintain personal relationships with other attorneys, but must be sensitive to the threat to independent judgment and the appearance of impropriety when an intimate relationship exists with opposing counsel or others involved in the proceedings.

2.22. An attorney should not simultaneously represent both a client and a person with whom the client is sexually involved.

Comment to Rule 2.22

A matrimonial lawyer is often asked to represent a client and the client's lover. Joint representation may make it difficult to advise the client of the need to recover from the emotional trauma of divorce, the desirability of a prenuptial agreement, or the dangers of early remarriage. The testimony of either might be adverse to the other at deposition or trial. In addition, the client may desire to waive support payments because she believes she is going to marry her lover. The inherent conflicts in attempting to represent both the client and her lover render such representation improper. Even when the client's new partner is not represented by the attorney, but wishes to participate in consultations and other aspects of the representation, the attorney must be alert to the danger of the client's undermining her own best interests in an effort to accommodate her new partner.

2.23. In representing a parent, an attorney should consider the welfare of children.

Bankruptcy Law: Lawyers handling federal bankruptcy matters are subject to stringent statutes prohibiting conflicts of interest. One of the most prominent bankruptcy statutes is 11 U.S.C. §327, which provides, in part:

> (a) Except as otherwise provided in this section, the trustee, with the court's approval, may employ one or more attorneys, accountants, appraisers, auctioneers, or other professional persons, that do not hold or represent an interest adverse to the estate, and that are disinterested persons, to represent or assist the trustee in carrying out the trustee's duties under this title. . . .
>
> (c) In a case under chapter 7, 12, or 11 of this title, a person is not disqualified for employment under this section solely because of such person's employment by or representation of a creditor, unless there is objection by another creditor or the United States trustee, in which case the court shall disapprove such employment if there is an actual conflict of interest. . . .
>
> (e) The trustee, with the court's approval, may employ . . . an attorney that has represented the debtor, if in the best interest of the estate, and if such attorney does not represent or hold any interest adverse to the debtor or to the estate with respect to the matter on which such attorney is to be employed.

IRS Regulations: In the regulations governing practice before the Internal Revenue Service, 31 C.F.R. §10.29, entitled "Conflicting Interests," provides as follows: "No attorney . . . shall represent conflicting interests in his practice before the Internal Revenue Service, except by express consent of all directly interested parties after full disclosure has been made."

Paralegal Conflicts: Courts and bar association ethics committees are devoting increasing attention to conflicts caused by paralegals and other members of a lawyer's staff. Guideline 7 of the ABA Model Guidelines for the Utilization of Legal Assistant Services (adopted in 1991) provides:

> A lawyer should take reasonable measures to prevent conflicts of interest resulting from a legal assistant's other employment or interests insofar as such other employment or interests would present a conflict of interest if it were that of the lawyer.

Private Securities Litigation Reform Act: The Federal Private Securities Litigation Reform Act requires courts hearing securities lawsuits to determine whether a plaintiff's lawyer's ownership of securities creates a conflict of interest that disqualifies the lawyer from representing the class.

Restatement of the Law Governing Lawyers: See Restatement §§14, 15, 108, 121, 122, 125, 128–130, and 135 in our chapter on the Restatement later in this volume.

Rule 1.8 Conflict of Interest: ~~Prohibited Transactions~~ Current Clients: Specific Rules

(a) A lawyer shall not enter into a business transaction with a client or knowingly acquire an ownership, possessory, security or other pecuniary interest adverse to a client unless~~:~~:

(1) the transaction and terms on which the lawyer acquires the interest are fair and reasonable to the client and are fully disclosed and transmitted in writing ~~to the client~~ in a manner ~~which~~ that can be reasonably understood by the client;

(2) the client is advised in writing of the desirability of seeking and is given a reasonable opportunity to seek the advice of independent legal counsel ~~in~~ on the transaction; and

(3) the client ~~consents~~ gives informed consent, in a writing ~~thereto~~ signed by the client, to the essential terms of the transaction and the lawyer's role in the transaction, including whether the lawyer is representing the client in the transaction.

(b) A lawyer shall not use information relating to representation of a client to the disadvantage of the client unless the client ~~consents after consultation~~ gives informed consent, except as permitted or required by ~~Rule 1.6 or Rule 3.3~~ these Rules.

(c) A lawyer shall not solicit any substantial gift from a client, including a testamentary gift, or prepare on behalf of a client an instrument giving the lawyer or a person related to the lawyer ~~as parent, child, sibling, or spouse~~ any substantial gift ~~from a client, including a testamentary~~ unless the lawyer or other recipient of the gift~~, except where the client~~ is related to the ~~donee~~ client. For purposes of this paragraph, related persons include a spouse, child, grandchild, parent, grandparent or other relative or individual with whom the lawyer or the client maintains a close, familial relationship.

(d) Prior to the conclusion of representation of a client, a lawyer shall not make or negotiate an agreement giving the lawyer literary or media rights to a portrayal or account based in substantial part on information relating to the representation.

(e) A lawyer shall not provide financial assistance to a client in connection with pending or contemplated litigation, except that:

(1) a lawyer may advance court costs and expenses of litigation, the repayment of which may be contingent on the outcome of the matter; and

(2) a lawyer representing an indigent client may pay court costs and expenses of litigation on behalf of the client.

(f) A lawyer shall not accept compensation for representing a client from one other than the client unless:

(1) the client ~~consents after consultation~~ gives informed consent;

(2) there is no interference with the lawyer's independence of professional judgment or with the client-lawyer relationship; and

(3) information relating to representation of a client is protected as required by Rule 1.6.

(g) A lawyer who represents two or more clients shall not participate in making an aggregate settlement of the claims of or against the clients, or in a criminal case an aggregated agreement as to guilty or nolo contendere pleas, unless each client ~~consents after consultation, including~~ gives informed consent, in a writing signed by the client. The lawyer's disclosure ~~of~~ shall include the existence and nature of all the claims or pleas involved and of the participation of each person in the settlement.

(h) A lawyer shall not:

(1) make an agreement prospectively limiting the lawyer's liability to a client for malpractice unless ~~permitted by law and~~ the client is independently represented in making the agreement~~,~~; or

(2) settle a claim or potential claim for such liability with an unrepresented client or former client ~~without first advising~~ unless that person is advised in writing ~~that~~ of the desirability of seeking and is given a reasonable opportunity to seek the advice of independent ~~representation is appropriate~~ legal counsel in connection therewith.

~~(i) A lawyer related to another lawyer as parent, child, sibling or spouse shall not represent a client in a representation directly adverse to a person whom the lawyer knows is represented by the other lawyer except upon consent by the client after consultation regarding the relationship.~~

~~(j)~~ (i) A lawyer shall not acquire a proprietary interest in the cause of action or subject matter of litigation the lawyer is conducting for a client, except that the lawyer may:

(1) acquire a lien ~~granted~~ authorized by law to secure the lawyer's fee or expenses; and

(2) contract with a client for a reasonable contingent fee in a civil case.

(j) A lawyer shall not have sexual relations with a client unless a consensual sexual relationship existed between them when the client-lawyer relationship commenced.

(k) While lawyers are associated in a firm, a prohibition in the foregoing paragraphs (a) through (i) that applies to any one of them shall apply to all of them.

COMMENT

Business Transactions Between Client and Lawyer

[1] ~~As a general principle, all transactions between client and lawyer should be fair and reasonable to the client. In such transactions a review~~

~~by independent counsel on behalf of the client is often advisable. Furthermore, a lawyer may not exploit information relating to the representation to the client's disadvantage. For example, a lawyer who has learned that the client is investing in specific real estate may not, without the client's consent, seek to acquire nearby property where doing so would adversely affect the client's plan for investment. Paragraph (a)~~ A lawyer's legal skill and training, together with the relationship of trust and confidence between lawyer and client, create the possibility of overreaching when the lawyer participates in a business, property or financial transaction with a client, for example, a loan or sales transaction or a lawyer investment on behalf of a client. The requirements of paragraph (a) must be met even when the transaction is not closely related to the subject matter of the representation, as when a lawyer drafting a will for a client learns that the client needs money for unrelated expenses and offers to make a loan to the client. The Rule applies to lawyers engaged in the sale of goods or services related to the practice of law, for example, the sale of title insurance or investment services to existing clients of the lawyer's legal practice. See Rule 5.7. It also applies to lawyers purchasing property from estates they represent. It does not apply to ordinary fee arrangements between client and lawyer, which are governed by Rule 1.5, although its requirements must be met when the lawyer accepts an interest in the client's business or other nonmonetary property as payment of all or part of a fee. In addition, the Rule does not~~, however,~~ apply to standard commercial transactions between the lawyer and the client for products or services that the client generally markets to others, for example, banking or brokerage services, medical services, products manufactured or distributed by the client, and utilities' services. In such transactions, the lawyer has no advantage in dealing with the client, and the restrictions in paragraph (a) are unnecessary and impracticable.

[2] Paragraph (a)(1) requires that the transaction itself be fair to the client and that its essential terms be communicated to the client, in writing, in a manner that can be reasonably understood. Paragraph (a)(2) requires that the client also be advised, in writing, of the desirability of seeking the advice of independent legal counsel. It also requires that the client be given a reasonable opportunity to obtain such advice. Paragraph (a)(3) requires that the lawyer obtain the client's informed consent, in a writing signed by the client, both to the essential terms of the transaction and to the lawyer's role. When necessary, the lawyer should discuss both the material risks of the proposed transaction, including any risk presented by the lawyer's involvement, and the existence of reasonably available alternatives and should explain why the advice of independent legal counsel is desirable. See Rule 1.0(e) (definition of informed consent).

[3] The risk to a client is greatest when the client expects the lawyer to represent the client in the transaction itself or when the lawyer's financial interest otherwise poses a significant risk that the lawyer's representation of the client will be materially limited by the lawyer's financial

interest in the transaction. Here the lawyer's role requires that the lawyer must comply, not only with the requirements of paragraph (a), but also with the requirements of Rule 1.7. Under that Rule, the lawyer must disclose the risks associated with the lawyer's dual role as both legal adviser and participant in the transaction, such as the risk that the lawyer will structure the transaction or give legal advice in a way that favors the lawyer's interests at the expense of the client. Moreover, the lawyer must obtain the client's informed consent. In some cases, the lawyer's interest may be such that Rule 1.7 will preclude the lawyer from seeking the client's consent to the transaction.

[4] If the client is independently represented in the transaction, paragraph (a)(2) of this Rule is inapplicable, and the paragraph (a)(1) requirement for full disclosure is satisfied either by a written disclosure by the lawyer involved in the transaction or by the client's independent counsel. The fact that the client was independently represented in the transaction is relevant in determining whether the agreement was fair and reasonable to the client as paragraph (a)(1) further requires.

Use of Information Related to Representation

[5] Use of information relating to the representation to the disadvantage of the client violates the lawyer's duty of loyalty. Paragraph (b) applies when the information is used to benefit either the lawyer or a third person, such as another client or business associate of the lawyer. For example, if a lawyer learns that a client intends to purchase and develop several parcels of land, the lawyer may not use that information to purchase one of the parcels in competition with the client or to recommend that another client make such a purchase. The Rule does not prohibit uses that do not disadvantage the client. For example, a lawyer who learns a government agency's interpretation of trade legislation during the representation of one client may properly use that information to benefit other clients. Paragraph (b) prohibits disadvantageous use of client information unless the client gives informed consent, except as permitted or required by these Rules. See Rules 1.2(d), 1.6, 1.9(c), 3.3, 4.1(b), 8.1 and 8.3.

Gifts to Lawyers

~~[2]~~ [6] A lawyer may accept a gift from a client, if the transaction meets general standards of fairness. For example, a simple gift such as a present given at a holiday or as a token of appreciation is permitted. If a client offers the lawyer a more substantial gift, paragraph (c) does not prohibit the lawyer from accepting it, although such a gift may be voidable by the client under the doctrine of undue influence, which treats client gifts as presumptively fraudulent. In any event, due to concerns about overreaching and imposition on clients, a lawyer may not suggest that a substantial gift be made to the lawyer or for the lawyer's benefit, except where the lawyer is related to the client as set forth in paragraph (c).

[7] If effectuation of a substantial gift requires preparing a legal instrument such as a will or conveyance~~, however,~~ the client should have the detached advice that another lawyer can provide. ~~Paragraph (c) recognizes an~~ The sole exception to this Rule is where the client is a relative of the donee ~~or the gift is not substantial~~.

[8] This Rule does not prohibit a lawyer from seeking to have the lawyer or a partner or associate of the lawyer named as executor of the client's estate or to another potentially lucrative fiduciary position. Nevertheless, such appointments will be subject to the general conflict of interest provision in Rule 1.7 when there is a significant risk that the lawyer's interest in obtaining the appointment will materially limit the lawyer's independent professional judgment in advising the client concerning the choice of an executor or other fiduciary. In obtaining the client's informed consent to the conflict, the lawyer should advise the client concerning the nature and extent of the lawyer's financial interest in the appointment, as well as the availability of alternative candidates for the position.

Literary Rights

~~[3]~~ [9] An agreement by which a lawyer acquires literary or media rights concerning the conduct of the representation creates a conflict between the interests of the client and the personal interests of the lawyer. Measures suitable in the representation of the client may detract from the publication value of an account of the representation. Paragraph (d) does not prohibit a lawyer representing a client in a transaction concerning literary property from agreeing that the lawyer's fee shall consist of a share in ownership in the property, if the arrangement conforms to Rule 1.5 and ~~paragraph (j)~~ paragraphs (a) and (i).

Financial Assistance

[10] Lawyers may not subsidize lawsuits or administrative proceedings brought on behalf of their clients, including making or guaranteeing loans to their clients for living expenses, because to do so would encourage clients to pursue lawsuits that might not otherwise be brought and because such assistance gives lawyers too great a financial stake in the litigation. These dangers do not warrant a prohibition on a lawyer lending a client court costs and litigation expenses, including the expenses of medical examination and the costs of obtaining and presenting evidence, because these advances are virtually indistinguishable from contingent fees and help ensure access to the courts. Similarly, an exception allowing

lawyers representing indigent clients to pay court costs and litigation expenses regardless of whether these funds will be repaid is warranted.

Person Paying for a Lawyer's Services

[4] Paragraph (f) requires disclosure of the fact that the lawyer's services are being paid for by a third party. Such an arrangement must also conform to the requirements of Rule 1.6 concerning confidentiality and Rule 1.7 concerning conflict of interest. Where the client is a class, consent may be obtained on behalf of the class by court-supervised procedure.

[11] Lawyers are frequently asked to represent a client under circumstances in which a third person will compensate the lawyer, in whole or in part. The third person might be a relative or friend, an indemnitor (such as a liability insurance company) or a co-client (such as a corporation sued along with one or more of its employees). Because third-party payers frequently have interests that differ from those of the client, including interests in minimizing the amount spent on the representation and in learning how the representation is progressing, lawyers are prohibited from accepting or continuing such representations unless the lawyer determines that there will be no interference with the lawyer's independent professional judgment and there is informed consent from the client. See also Rule 5.4(c) (prohibiting interference with a lawyer's professional judgment by one who recommends, employs or pays the lawyer to render legal services for another).

[12] Sometimes, it will be sufficient for the lawyer to obtain the client's informed consent regarding the fact of the payment and the identity of the third-party payer. If, however, the fee arrangement creates a conflict of interest for the lawyer, then the lawyer must comply with Rule 1.7. The lawyer must also conform to the requirements of Rule 1.6 concerning confidentiality. Under Rule 1.7(a), a conflict of interest exists if there is significant risk that the lawyer's representation of the client will be materially limited by the lawyer's own interest in the fee arrangement or by the lawyer's responsibilities to the third-party payer (for example, when the third-party payer is a co-client). Under Rule 1.7(b), the lawyer may accept or continue the representation with the informed consent of each affected client, unless the conflict is nonconsentable under that paragraph. Under Rule 1.7(b), the informed consent must be confirmed in writing.

Aggregate Settlements

[13] Differences in willingness to make or accept an offer of settlement are among the risks of common representation of multiple clients by a single lawyer. Under Rule 1.7, this is one of the risks that should be discussed before undertaking the representation, as part of the process of obtaining

the clients' informed consent. In addition, Rule 1.2(a) protects each client's right to have the final say in deciding whether to accept or reject an offer of settlement and in deciding whether to enter a guilty or nolo contendere plea in a criminal case. The rule stated in this paragraph is a corollary of both these Rules and provides that, before any settlement offer or plea bargain is made or accepted on behalf of multiple clients, the lawyer must inform each of them about all the material terms of the settlement, including what the other clients will receive or pay if the settlement or plea offer is accepted. See also Rule 1.0(e) (definition of informed consent). Lawyers representing a class of plaintiffs or defendants, or those proceeding derivatively, may not have a full client-lawyer relationship with each member of the class; nevertheless, such lawyers must comply with applicable rules regulating notification of class members and other procedural requirements designed to ensure adequate protection of the entire class.

Limiting Liability and Settling Malpractice Claims

~~[5] Paragraph (h) is not intended to apply to customary qualifications and limitations in legal opinions and memoranda.~~

[14] Agreements prospectively limiting a lawyer's liability for malpractice are prohibited unless the client is independently represented in making the agreement because they are likely to undermine competent and diligent representation. Also, many clients are unable to evaluate the desirability of making such an agreement before a dispute has arisen, particularly if they are then represented by the lawyer seeking the agreement. This paragraph does not, however, prohibit a lawyer from entering into an agreement with the client to arbitrate legal malpractice claims, provided such agreements are enforceable and the client is fully informed of the scope and effect of the agreement. Nor does this paragraph limit the ability of lawyers to practice in the form of a limited-liability entity, where permitted by law, provided that each lawyer remains personally liable to the client for his or her own conduct and the firm complies with any conditions required by law, such as provisions requiring client notification or maintenance of adequate liability insurance. Nor does it prohibit an agreement in accordance with Rule 1.2 that defines the scope of the representation, although a definition of scope that makes the obligations of representation illusory will amount to an attempt to limit liability.

[15] Agreements settling a claim or a potential claim for malpractice are not prohibited by this Rule. Nevertheless, in view of the danger that a lawyer will take unfair advantage of an unrepresented client or former client, the lawyer must first advise such a person in writing of the appropriateness of independent representation in connection with such a settlement. In addition, the lawyer must give the client or former client a reasonable opportunity to find and consult independent counsel.

~~Family Relationships Between Lawyers~~

~~[6] Paragraph (i) applies to related lawyers who are in different firms. Related lawyers in the same firm are governed by Rules 1.7, 1.9, and 1.10. The disqualification stated in paragraph (i) is personal and is not imputed to members of firms with whom the lawyers are associated.~~

~~Acquisition of~~ Acquiring Proprietary Interest in Litigation

~~[7]~~ [16] Paragraph ~~(j)~~ (i) states the traditional general rule that lawyers are prohibited from acquiring a proprietary interest in litigation. ~~This~~ Like paragraph (e), the general rule~~, which~~ has its basis in common law champerty and maintenance~~,~~ and is designed to avoid giving the lawyer too great an interest in the representation. In addition, when the lawyer acquires an ownership interest in the subject of the representation, it will be more difficult for a client to discharge the lawyer if the client so desires. The Rule is subject to specific exceptions developed in decisional law and continued in these Rules~~, such as the exception for reasonable contingent fees set forth in Rule 1.5 and the exception for certain advances of the costs of litigation set forth in paragraph (e)~~. The exception for certain advances of the costs of litigation is set forth in paragraph (e). In addition, paragraph (i) sets forth exceptions for liens authorized by law to secure the lawyer's fees or expenses and contracts for reasonable contingent fees. The law of each jurisdiction determines which liens are authorized by law. These may include liens granted by statute, liens originating in common law and liens acquired by contract with the client. When a lawyer acquires by contract a security interest in property other than that recovered through the lawyer's efforts in the litigation, such an acquisition is a business or financial transaction with a client and is governed by the requirements of paragraph (a). Contracts for contingent fees in civil cases are governed by Rule 1.5.

Client-Lawyer Sexual Relationships

[17] The relationship between lawyer and client is a fiduciary one in which the lawyer occupies the highest position of trust and confidence. The relationship is almost always unequal; thus, a sexual relationship between lawyer and client can involve unfair exploitation of the lawyer's fiduciary role, in violation of the lawyer's basic ethical obligation not to use the trust of the client to the client's disadvantage. In addition, such a relationship presents a significant danger that, because of the lawyer's emotional involvement, the lawyer will be unable to represent the client with-

out impairment of the exercise of independent professional judgment. Moreover, a blurred line between the professional and personal relationships may make it difficult to predict to what extent client confidences will be protected by the attorney-client evidentiary privilege, since client confidences are protected by privilege only when they are imparted in the context of the client-lawyer relationship. Because of the significant danger of harm to client interests and because the client's own emotional involvement renders it unlikely that the client could give adequate informed consent, this Rule prohibits the lawyer from having sexual relations with a client regardless of whether the relationship is consensual and regardless of the absence of prejudice to the client.

[18] Sexual relationships that predate the client-lawyer relationship are not prohibited. Issues relating to the exploitation of the fiduciary relationship and client dependency are diminished when the sexual relationship existed prior to the commencement of the client-lawyer relationship. However, before proceeding with the representation in these circumstances, the lawyer should consider whether the lawyer's ability to represent the client will be materially limited by the relationship. See Rule 1.7(a)(2).

[19] When the client is an organization, paragraph (j) of this Rule prohibits a lawyer for the organization (whether inside counsel or outside counsel) from having a sexual relationship with a constituent of the organization who supervises, directs or regularly consults with that lawyer concerning the organization's legal matters.

Imputation of Prohibitions

[20] Under paragraph (k), a prohibition on conduct by an individual lawyer in paragraphs (a) through (i) also applies to all lawyers associated in a firm with the personally prohibited lawyer. For example, one lawyer in a firm may not enter into a business transaction with a client of another member of the firm without complying with paragraph (a), even if the first lawyer is not personally involved in the representation of the client. The prohibition set forth in paragraph (j) is personal and is not applied to associated lawyers.

Canon and Code Antecedents

ABA Canons of Professional Ethics: Canons 10, 11, and 38 provided as follows:

10. Acquiring Interest in Litigation

The lawyer should not purchase any interest in the subject matter of the litigation which he is conducting.

11. Dealing with Trust Property

The lawyer should refrain from any action whereby for his personal benefit or gain he abuses or takes advantage of the confidence reposed in him by his client.

Money of the client or collected for the client or other trust property coming into the possession of the lawyer should be reported and accounted for promptly, and should not under any circumstances be commingled with his own or be used by him.

38. Compensation, Commissions and Rebates

A lawyer should accept no compensation, commissions, rebates or other advantages from others without the knowledge and consent of his client after full disclosure.

ABA Model Code of Professional Responsibility: Compare DR 4-101(B)(3), DR 5-103(A), DR 5-103(B), DR 5-104(A), DR 5-104(B), DR 5-106, DR 5-107(A)(1), and DR 6-102(A) (reprinted later in this volume).

Cross-References in Other Rules

Rule 1.0, Comment 7: Certain "Rules require that a client's consent be obtained in a writing signed by the client. See, e.g., **Rules 1.8(a) and (g)**."

Rule 1.2, Comment 8: "All agreements concerning a lawyer's representation of a client must accord with the Rules of Professional Conduct and other law. See, e.g., Rules 1.1, **1.8** and 5.6."

Rule 1.5, Comment 4: "A lawyer may accept property in payment for services, such as an ownership interest in an enterprise, providing this does not involve acquisition of a proprietary interest in the cause of action or subject matter of the litigation contrary to **Rule 1.8(i)**. However, a fee paid in property instead of money may be subject to the requirements of **Rule 1.8(a)**. . . ."

Rule 1.6, Comment 1: See "**Rules 1.8(b)** and 1.9(c)(1) for the lawyer's duties with respect to the use of such information to the disadvantage of clients and former clients."

Rule 1.6, Comment 14: "Neither this Rule nor **Rule 1.8(b)** nor Rule 1.16(d) prevents the lawyer from giving notice of the fact of withdrawal."

Rule 1.7, Comment 1: "For specific Rules regarding certain concurrent conflicts of interest, see **Rule 1.8**."

Rule 1.7, Comment 10: "See **Rule 1.8** for specific Rules pertaining to a number of personal interest conflicts, including business transactions with clients."

Rule 1.7, Comment 12: "A lawyer is prohibited from engaging in sexual relationships with a client unless the sexual relationship predates the formation of the client-lawyer relationship. See **Rule 1.8(j)**."

Rule 1.7, Comment 13: "A lawyer may be paid from a source other than the client, including a co-client, if the client is informed of that fact and consents and the arrangement does not compromise the lawyer's duty of loyalty or independent judgment to the client. See **Rule 1.8(f)**."

Rule 1.10, Comment 8: "Where a lawyer is prohibited from engaging in certain transactions under **Rule 1.8**, paragraph (k) of that Rule, and not this Rule, determines whether that prohibition also applies to other lawyers associated in a firm with the personally prohibited lawyer."

Rule 1.13, Comment 5: "[T]his Rule does not limit or expand the lawyer's responsibility under Rule 1.6, **1.8**, 1.16, 3.3 or 4.1."

Rule 5.4, Comment 2: Rule 5.4 "expresses traditional limitations on permitting a third party to direct or regulate the lawyer's professional judgment in rendering legal services to another. See also **Rule 1.8(f)**. . . ."

Rule 5.7, Comment 5: "When a client-lawyer relationship exists with a person who is referred by a lawyer to a separate law-related service entity controlled by the lawyer, individually or with others, the lawyer must comply with **Rule 1.8(a)**."

Rule 5.7, Comment 10: "When a lawyer is obliged to accord the recipients of such services the protections of those Rules that apply to the client-lawyer relationship, the lawyer must take special care to heed the proscriptions of the Rules addressing conflict of interest (**Rules 1.7 through 1.11**, especially Rules 1.7 and **1.8(a), (b) and (f)**). . . ."

Legislative History of Model Rule 1.8

1979 Unofficial Pre-Circulation Draft:

> (e) A lawyer shall not provide financial assistance to a client in connection with pending or contemplated litigation, except that a lawyer may advance expenses, including:
>
> *Alternative (1):* Court costs, expenses of investigation, medical and other experts, and obtaining and presenting evidence.
>
> *Alternative (2):* Court costs, expenses of litigation, and living expenses.

1980 Discussion Draft (then called Rule 1.9):

> (f) A lawyer may serve as general counsel to a corporation or other organization of which the lawyer is a director only if:
>
> (1) There is adequate disclosure to and consent by all persons having an investment interest in the organization; or
>
> (2) When doing so would not involve serious risk of conflict between the lawyer's responsibilities as general counsel and those as director.

1981 and 1982 Drafts were substantially the same as adopted, except that Rule 1.8(f) contained no restrictions other than the client's consent "after consultation."

2002 Amendments: At its February 2002 Mid-Year Meeting, the ABA House of Delegates adopted without change the ABA Ethics 2000 Commission proposal to amend Rule 1.8 and its Comment.

Selected State Variations

Alabama adds Rule 1.8(e)(3), which provides as follows:

> (3) a lawyer may advance or guarantee emergency financial assistance to the client, the repayment of which may not be contingent on the outcome of the matter, provided that no promise or assurance of financial assistance was made to the client by the lawyer, or on the lawyer's behalf, prior to the employment of the lawyer.

Alabama Rule 1.8(f) allows a lawyer to accept compensation from one other than the client without client consent if the lawyer "is appointed pursuant to an insurance contract." Alabama also adds Rule 1.8(k), which provides as follows:

> (k) In no event shall a lawyer represent both parties in a divorce or domestic relations proceeding, or in matters involving custody of children, alimony or child support, whether or not contested. In an uncontested proceeding of this nature a lawyer may have contact with the non-represented party and shall be deemed to have complied with this prohibition if the non-represented party knowingly executes a document that is filed in such proceeding acknowledging:
>
> (1) that the lawyer does not and cannot appear or serve as the lawyer for the non-represented party;
>
> (2) that the lawyer represents only the client and will use the lawyer's best efforts to protect the client's best interests;
>
> (3) that the non-represented party has the right to employ counsel of the party's own choosing and has been advised that it may be in the party's best interest to do so; and
>
> (4) that having been advised of the foregoing, the non-represented party has requested the lawyer to prepare an answer and waiver under which the cause may be submitted without notice and such other pleadings and agreements as may be appropriate.

Arizona: In 1994, the State Bar filed a petition with the Arizona Supreme Court in support of a new Rule 1.17 that would have prohibited a lawyer from initiating abusive or exploitative sexual conduct with a client. The Arizona Supreme Court denied the petition. The Court's one-sentence opinion said that the current rules already covered the issues and that the proposed rule raised more questions than it answered.

California: See Rule 3-300 (Avoiding Adverse Interests — compare to Model Rule 1.8(a)); Rule 3-310(F) (compare to Model Rule 1.8(f)); Rule 3-310(D) (compare to Model Rule 1.8(g)); Rule 3-320 (Relationship with Other Party's Lawyer — compare to Model Rule 1.8(i)); Rule 3-400 (Limiting Liability to Client — compare to Model Rule 1.8(h)); and Rule 4-210 (Payment of Personal or Business Expenses Incurred by or for a Client — compare to Model Rule 1.8(e)).

In 1999, California added a new Article 10.5 to its Business and Professions Code to prohibit lawyers from selling "financial products" such as long-term care insurance, life insurance, and annuities to their clients (and recent former clients) unless the attorneys make the extensive disclosures specified in the statute. Section 6175.5 of the new law provides that a lawyer's violation of the law "shall be cause for discipline by the State Bar."

Colorado: Rule 1.8(i) adds "cohabiting relationship" to the list of relationships that require disclosure and consent prior to representation. In addition, Rule 23.3 of the Colorado Rules of Civil Procedure requires that every contingent fee agreement contain "a stipulation that the client, except as permitted by the Rules of Professional Conduct, including Rule 1.8(e), is to be liable for expenses, such stipulation including an estimate of such expenses, authority of the attorney to incur the expenses and make disbursements, a maximum limitation not to be exceeded without the client's further written authority."

Connecticut: Rule 1.8(a) applies to a client "or former client," and Rule 1.8(a)(2) requires that the client "or former client is advised in writing that the client or former client should consider seeking the advice of independent counsel in the transaction and" is given a reasonable opportunity to do so. Connecticut also adds Rule 1.8(a)(4), which provides as follows:

> (4) With regard to a business transaction, the lawyer advises the client or former client in writing either (i) that the lawyer will provide legal services to the client or former client concerning the transaction, or (ii) that the lawyer is involved as a business person only and not as a lawyer representing the client or former client and that the lawyer is not one to whom the client or former client can turn for legal advice concerning the transaction.

In addition, Connecticut's version of Rule 1.8(b) deletes the phrase "except as permitted or required by Rule 1.6 or Rule 3.3."

District of Columbia: D.C. Rule 1.8(d) and (i) differ significantly from the ABA Model Rule — see District of Columbia Rules of Professional Conduct below.

Florida: In 1994, the Florida Supreme Court rejected a petition by 50 Florida lawyers (opposed by The Florida Bar) to amend Florida's version of Rule 1.8(e). The court stated:

> [The] proposed amendment would permit a personal injury lawyer to assist a client in obtaining a third-party loan for ordinary living expense (food, clothing, shelter, and transportation). The lawyer would agree to act as trustee for the lender to ensure repayment from the proceeds of any recovery obtained. The Bar argues that the proposed amendment will result in inevitable conflicts of interest among lawyer, client, and lending institution, as well as discouraging settlements. We agree.

Georgia: In the rules effective January 1, 2001, Rule 1.8(a) applies "if the client expects the lawyer to exercise the lawyer's professional judgment therein for the protection of the client." Rule 1.8(i) adds that the disqualification of a lawyer due to a parent, child, sibling, or spousal relationship "is personal and is not imputed to members of firms with whom the lawyers are associated." Georgia adds that the maximum penalty for a violating Rule 1.8(b) (which relates to confidentiality) is disbarment, but the maximum penalty for violating any other provision of Rule 1.8 is only a public reprimand. Georgia also adds a new sentence to the first paragraph of the Comment stating that "[t]he client should be fully informed of the true nature of the lawyer's interest or lack of interest in all aspects of the transaction."

Illinois: The Illinois versions of Rule 1.8(a) and 1.8(c) largely track DR 5-104 of the old ABA Model Code of Professional Responsibility — see Model Code below. Illinois omits Rule 1.8(b), and modifies Rule 1.8(e) as follows:

> (d) While representing a client in connection with contemplated or pending litigation, a lawyer shall not advance or guarantee financial assistance to the client, except that a lawyer may advance or guarantee the expenses of litigation, including, but not limited to, court costs, expenses of investigation, expenses of medical examination, and costs of obtaining and presenting evidence if:
>
> (1) the client remains ultimately liable for such expenses; or
>
> (2) the repayment is contingent on the outcome of the matter; or
>
> (3) the client is indigent.

Illinois modifies Rule 1.8(h) as follows:

> (g) A lawyer shall not settle a claim against the lawyer made by an unrepresented client or former client without first advising that person in writing that independent representation is appropriate in connection therewith.

Illinois adds the following new subparagraph to Rule 1.8:

> (h) A lawyer shall not enter into an agreement with a client or former client limiting or purporting to limit the right of the client or former client to file or pursue any complaint before the Attorney Registration and Disciplinary Commission.

Related to Rule 1.8(h), in June of 2000, in reaction to a January 2000 appellate court decision holding that public defenders did not have sovereign immunity from legal malpractice suits, see Johnson v. Halloran, 728 N.E.2d 490 (Ill. App. 1st Dist.), aff'd, 742 N.E.2d 741 (Ill. 2000), the Illinois legislature enacted the Public and Appellate Defender Immunity Act, 745 Ill. Comp. Stat. §19/1, which provides that public defenders are not liable "for any damages in tort, contract or otherwise, in which the plaintiff seeks damages by reason of legal or professional malpractice, except for willful and wanton misconduct." Another statute, 55 Ill. Comp. Stat. §5/5-1003, requires counties to indemnify public defenders for liability resulting from acts undertaken in the performance of their duties.

Regarding sex with clients, the Illinois Supreme Court never acted on a 1996 proposal to prohibit lawyers from initiating sexual relationships with their clients, but in In re Rinella, 175 Ill. 2d 504, 677 N.E.2d 909, 222 Ill. Dec. 375 (1997), the court suspended a lawyer for three years for having sexual relations with three different clients (and then lying about it during the Bar's investigation). The court said that no lawyer could reasonably have considered such conduct acceptable under the existing ethics rules even though the rules do not expressly address sex with clients.

Indiana: Rule 1.8(k) prohibits a part-time prosecutor from "representing a private client in any matter wherein exists an issue upon which said prosecutor has statutory prosecutorial authority or responsibilities." The rule does not prohibit representation in "tort cases in which investigation and any prosecution of infractions has terminated," or in "family law matters involving no issue subject to prosecutorial authority or responsibilities."

Louisiana adds the following prior to Rule 1.8(a): "As a general principle, all transactions between client and lawyer should be fair and reasonable to the client. Furthermore, a lawyer may not exploit his representation of a client or information relating to the representation to the client's disadvantage."

Maryland also allows a gift if "the client is represented by independent counsel in connection with the gift."

Massachusetts: Rule 1.8(b) forbids a lawyer to use confidential information "for the lawyer's advantage or the advantage of a third person" without consent.

Michigan: Rule 1.8(e)(1) requires nonindigent clients to remain ultimately responsible for advanced costs and expenses.

Minnesota: Rule 1.8(e)(3) allows a lawyer to guarantee a loan necessary for a client to withstand litigation delay. In addition, Minnesota Rule 1.8(k) provides as follows:

> A lawyer shall not have sexual relations with a current client unless a consensual relationship existed between them when the lawyer-client relationship commenced. For purposes of this paragraph:
>
> (1) "Sexual relations" means sexual intercourse or any other intentional touching of the intimate parts of a person or causing the person to touch the intimate parts of the lawyer.
>
> (2) If the client is an organization, any individual who oversees the representation and gives instructions to the lawyer on behalf of the organization shall be deemed to be the client. In-house attorneys while representing governmental

or corporate entities are governed by Rule 1.7(b) rather than by this rule with respect to sexual relations with other employees of the entity they represent.

(3) This paragraph does not prohibit a lawyer from engaging in sexual relations with a client of the lawyer's firm provided that the lawyer has no involvement in the performance of the legal work for the client.

(4) If a party other than the client alleges violation of this paragraph, and the complaint is not summarily dismissed, the Director [of the Office of Professional Responsibility], in determining whether to investigate the allegation and whether to charge any violation based on the allegations, shall consider the client's statement regarding whether the client would be unduly burdened by the investigation or charge.

Mississippi: Effective October 21, 1999, Mississippi adopted the following unique Rule 1.8(e)(2) that permits a lawyer to advance medical and living expenses to a client under certain circumstances:

(2) A lawyer representing a client may, in addition to the above, advance the following costs and expenses on behalf of the client, which shall be repaid upon successful conclusion of the matter.

(a) Reasonable and necessary medical expenses associated with treatment for the injury giving rise to the litigation or administrative proceeding for which the client seeks legal representation; and

(b) Reasonable and necessary living expenses incurred.

The expenses enumerated in paragraph 2 above can only be advanced to a client under dire and necessitous circumstances, and shall be limited to minimal living expenses of minor sums such as those necessary to prevent foreclosure or repossession or for necessary medical treatment. There can be no payment of expenses under paragraph 2 until the expiration of 60 days after the client has signed a contract of employment with counsel. Such payments under paragraph 2 cannot include a promise of future payments, and counsel cannot promise any such payments in any type of communication to the public, and such funds may only be advanced after due diligence and inquiry into the circumstances of the client.

Payments under paragraph 2 shall be limited to $1,500 to any one party by any lawyer or group or succession of lawyers during the continuation of any litigation unless, upon ex parte application, such further payment has been approved by the Standing Committee on Ethics of the Mississippi Bar. An attorney contemplating such payment must exercise due diligence to determine whether such party has received any such payments from another attorney during the continuation of the same litigation. Without approval of the Standing Committee on Ethics, such payments shall not in the aggregate exceed $1,500. Upon denial of such application, the decision thereon shall be subject to review by the Mississippi Supreme Court on petition of the attorney seeking leave to make further payments. Payments under paragraph 2 aggregating $1,500 or less shall be reported by the lawyer making the payment to the Standing Committee on Ethics within seven (7) days following the making of each such payment. Applications for approval by the Standing Committee on Ethics as required hereunder and notices to the Standing Committee on Ethics of payments aggregating $1,500 or less, shall be confidential.

Montana provides as follows:

(3) a lawyer may, for the sole purpose of providing basic living expenses, guarantee a loan from a regulated financial institution whose usual business in-

volves making loans if such loan is reasonably needed to enable the client to withstand delay in litigation that would otherwise put substantial pressure on the client to settle a case because of financial hardship rather than on the merits, provided the client remains ultimately liable for the repayment of the loan without regard to the outcome of the litigation and, further provided that neither the lawyer nor anyone on his/her behalf offers, promises or advertises such financial assistance before being retained by the client.

New Jersey: Rule 1.8(a)(2) adds that the client must be "advised of the desirability of seeking and is given a reasonable opportunity to seek the advice of independent counsel of the client's choice." New Jersey permits agreements prospectively limiting malpractice only when the client rejects the lawyer's advice and the lawyer continues to represent the client. The balance of Rule 1.8(h) is the same as the ABA Model Rule. New Jersey also adds a Rule 1.8(k) making the provisions of Rule 1.7(c) applicable to Rule 1.8. See Selected State Variations under Rule 1.7.

New Mexico: N.M. Stat. Ann. 36-2-13.1(A) provides that "an attorney who engages a court reporter to perform court reporting services shall be jointly and severally liable with the client for whom the services were performed" for all of the court reporter's charges.

New York: Compare ABA Model Rule 1.8(a) to New York's DR 5-104. Compare Rule 1.8(b) to New York's DR 4-101(B). Compare Rule 1.8(c) to New York EC's 5-5 and 5-6. Compare Rule 1.8(d) to New York's DR 5-104(B). Compare Rule 1.8(e) to New York's DR 5-103(B). Compare Rule 1.8(f) to New York's DR 5-107(A) and (B). Compare Rule 1.8(g) to New York's DR 5-106. Compare Rule 1.8(h) to New York's DR 6-102. Compare Rule 1.8(i) to New York's DR 5-103(A). Compare Rule 1.8(j) to New York's DR 5-111. Compare Rule 1.8(k) to New York's DR 5-105(D).

North Dakota adds Rule 1.8(e)(3), which permits a lawyer to "guarantee a loan reasonably needed to enable the client to withstand delay in litigation that would otherwise put substantial pressure on the client to settle a case because of financial hardship rather than on the merits, provided the client remains ultimately liable for repayment of the loan" and the lawyer did not promise financial assistance before the client retained the lawyer. North Dakota also adds Rule 1.8(i), which allows a lawyer to make an agreement prospectively limiting the lawyer's liability for malpractice in an "emergency" where (1) it is "impractical" to refer to, consult with, or associate with another lawyer, or (2) the client has "unequivocally rejected" the lawyer's advice to consult with or associate with another lawyer and the client "unequivocally" requests the lawyer's "immediate services" after the lawyer has advised the client that the lawyer "does not have the ordinary skill required to give competent representation in the matter." North Dakota Rule 1.8(g) provides that the rule restricting aggregate settlements applies "other than in class actions." In addition, North Dakota adds Rule 1.8(j), which restricts the practice of law by a part-time prosecutor or judge in certain circumstances.

Ohio: DR 5-101(A)(2) provides that "[n]otwithstanding the consent of the client, a lawyer shall not knowingly prepare, draft, or supervise the preparation or execution of a will, codicil, or *inter vivos* trust for a client" that names as beneficiary "(a) the lawyer; (b) the lawyer's law partner or a shareholder of the lawyer's firm; (c) an associate, paralegal, law clerk, or other employee in the lawyer's firm or office; (d) a lawyer acting 'of counsel' in the lawyer's firm; (e) the spouses, siblings, natural or adoptive children, or natural or adoptive parents of any of those described in divisions (A)(2)(a) through (d) of this rule." However, the rule does not apply "if the client is related by blood or marriage to the beneficiary within the third degree of relationship as defined by the law of Ohio." In 1999, Ohio amended DR 5-103(B) to conform to ABA Model Rule 1.5(e)(1), which permits a lawyer to advance or guarantee the expenses of litigation and make repayment "contingent on the outcome of the matter."

Relating to Rule 1.8(h), effective July 1, 2001, Ohio adopted a new DR 1-104 that requires all attorneys (except government and in-house attorneys) to notify their clients in writing if their legal malpractice insurance is less than $100,000 per occurrence or $300,000 in the aggregate, or if their malpractice insurance is terminated. The new rule specifies the precise form of the required written notice and the client's acknowledgment.

Pennsylvania: Rule 1.8(a) requires the lawyer to advise the client to seek independent advice. In addition, Rule 1.8(c) applies only where the relative is "within the third degree of relationship." Pennsylvania has not adopted a rule governing sexual relations with clients, but in 1997, the Pennsylvania State Bar's Ethics Committee published Formal Op. 97-100 (1997), which opined that sex with clients is unethical. The opinion included a proposed rule to prohibit sex with clients, but the committee did not forward the proposal to the Bar's board because the board was unlikely to approve it. Instead, the Ethics Committee took the unusual step of issuing the opinion and proposal in a pamphlet circulated widely among the bar.

Texas: Rule 1.08(c) and (d) provides:

> (c) Prior to the conclusion of all aspects of the matter giving rise to the lawyer's employment, a lawyer shall not make or negotiate an agreement with a client, prospective client, or former client giving the lawyer literary or media rights to a portrayal or account based in substantial part on information relating to the representation.
>
> (d) A lawyer shall not provide financial assistance to a client in connection with pending or contemplated litigation or administrative proceedings, except that:
>
> > (1) a lawyer may advance or guarantee court costs, expenses of litigation or administrative proceedings, and reasonably necessary medical and living expenses, the repayment of which may be contingent on the outcome of the matter; and
> >
> > (2) a lawyer representing an indigent client may pay court costs and expenses of litigation on behalf of the client.

Utah: Utah adds a new subparagraph (g) to Rule 8.4, which provides that a lawyer shall not engage in "sexual relations with a client that exploit the lawyer client relationship." Rule 8.4(b)(2) provides:

> Except for a spousal relationship or a sexual relationship that existed at the commencement of the lawyer client relationship, sexual relations between a lawyer and a client shall be presumed to be exploitative. This presumption is rebuttable.

The Comment to Utah's new rule states that when the client is an organization, the "client" includes "any individual who oversees the client's interests in the representation and gives instructions to the lawyer on behalf of the organization." The Comment also states that Rule 8.4(g) "applies only to a lawyer who is directly involved in the representation of the client."

Virginia: Rule 1.8(b) forbids the use of information "for the advantage of the lawyer or of a third person or to the disadvantage of the client." Rule 1.8(e)(1) requires a client ultimately to be liable for court costs and expenses. Rule 1.8(h) contains an exception where the lawyer is "an employee" of the client "as long as the client is independently represented in making the agreement" prospectively limiting the lawyer's liability for malpractice.

Washington omits ABA Model Rule 1.8(e)(2). The United States District Court for the Western District of Washington has adopted Local General Rule 9, which provides:

Prohibition of Bias

Litigation, inside and outside the courtroom in the United States District Court for the Western District of Washington, must be free from prejudice and bias in any form. Fair and equal treatment must be accorded all courtroom participants, whether judges, attorneys, witnesses, litigants, jurors, or court personnel. The duty to be respectful of others includes the responsibility to avoid comment or behavior that can be reasonably interpreted as manifesting prejudice or bias toward another on the basis of categories such as gender, race, ethnicity, religion, disability, age, or sexual orientation.

In June 2000, the Washington Supreme Court adopted a new Rule 1.8(k) providing that a lawyer shall not:

(1) have sexual relationship with a current client of the lawyer unless a consensual sexual relationship existed between them at the time the lawyer/client relationship commenced; or

(2) have sexual relations with a representative of a current client if the sexual relations would, or would likely, damage or prejudice the client in the representation.

(3) For purposes of Rule 1.8(k), "lawyer" means any lawyer who assists in the representation of the client, but does not include any other firm members who provide no such assistance.

The new rule is almost identical to a proposed rule that the Washington Supreme Court rejected without explanation in 1995. Its adoption was apparently prompted by a sex-with-clients scandal involving a former president of the Washington State Bar.

Wisconsin: In 1995, Wisconsin adopted the following Rule 1.8(k):

(1)(i): "Sexual relations" means sexual intercourse or any other intentional touching of the intimate parts of a person or causing the person to touch the intimate parts of the lawyer.

(ii) If the client is an organization, "client" means any individual who oversees the representation and gives instructions to the lawyer on behalf of the organization.

(2) A lawyer shall not have sexual relations with a current client unless a consensual sexual relationship existed between them when the lawyer-client relationship commenced.

(3) In-house attorneys representing governmental or corporate entities are governed by Rule 1.7(b) rather than by this paragraph with respect to sexual relations with other employees of the entity they represent.

Related Materials

ABA Formal Ethics Opinions: See ABA Formal Ethics Ops. 00-416 (2000) and 00-418 (2000).

ABA Tort and Insurance Practice Section (TIPS): In April 1991, TIPS approved Guidelines for the Selection and Performance of Retained Counsel. The Guidelines are reprinted in the Fall 1991 issue of The Brief. The following provisions relate to Rule 1.8(f):

> c. *Relationships Involving Three Parties — Attorney, Insured, and Insurer — Must Be Balanced with Legal and Contractual Obligations*
>
> Counsel is charged with a high degree of care and fidelity to the client. When counsel is retained by an insurer to represent an insured, counsel's duty is owed to both clients to the extent that the interests of each party are aligned. When the interests of the insurer and the insured conflict, counsel's primary duty is to the insured.
>
> When counsel is retained by an insurer to represent an insured and a conflict exists between insured and insurer, counsel for the insured may not provide counsel to the insurer. All potential conflicts between insurer and insured must be identified and disclosed in detail to the insured by the insurer.
>
> If the insurer agrees to retain counsel to defend an insured (a) under a reservation of rights to deny coverage or (b) while contending that some of the allegations asserted against the insured are not covered by the insurance policy, counsel's primary duty is to the insured. In such a case, counsel should defend the action so as to avoid prejudice to, or impairment of, the rights of the insured.
>
> Where there are matters within the policy coverage and matters potentially outside the policy coverage, the insurer should advise the insured of the excess exposure and inform the insured of the right to retain personal counsel.

American Lawyer's Code of Conduct: Rules 5.6, 8.7, and 8.8 provide:

> 5.6. A lawyer shall not give money or anything of substantial value to any person in order to induce that person to become or to remain a client, or to induce that person to retain or to continue the lawyer as counsel on behalf of someone else. However, a lawyer may (a) advance money to a client on any terms that are fair; (b) give money to a client as an act of charity; (c) give money to a client to enable the client to withstand delays in litigation that would otherwise induce the client to settle a case because of financial hardship, rather than on the merits of the client's claim; or (d) charge a fee that is contingent in whole or in part on the outcome of the case.
>
> 8.7. A lawyer shall not enter into a commercial transaction or other business relationship with a person who is or was recently a client, unless that person is represented by independent counsel. This Rule does not affect the specific transactions covered by Chapter V of this Code, relating to retainer agreements and financial arrangements with clients.
>
> 8.8. A lawyer shall not commence having sexual relations with a client during the lawyer-client relationship.

Malpractice Insurance: Although Model Rule 1.8(h) prohibits lawyers from prospectively limiting their liability to clients for legal malpractice, no jurisdiction except Oregon requires its lawyers to maintain legal malpractice insurance. (South Dakota requires uninsured lawyers to state this fact on their letterhead but does not require insurance.) Consequently, a surprising number of lawyers do not carry malpractice insurance. A Massachusetts survey published in 1997 revealed that about 25 percent of the lawyers who responded said they did not carry professional liability insurance. The lawyers most likely to be insured were partners (97.4 percent) and associates (94.7 percent) in private law firms. Sole practitioners fell in the middle (75 percent). The lawyers least likely to be insured were lawyers employed by corporations (28.6 percent) and public service lawyers (17.4 percent). However, some Lawyer Referral Services operated by bar associations will not refer potential clients to lawyers who lack malpractice insurance. For example, the Massachusetts State Bar requires lawyers listed in its Lawyer Referral Service to carry at least a $250,000/$500,000 policy.

Restatement of the Law Governing Lawyers: See Restatement §§16, 18, 36, 43, 46, 54, 126, and 127 in our chapter on the Restatement later in this volume.

Rule 1.9 ~~Conflict of Interest:~~ Duties to Former ~~Client~~ Clients

(a) A lawyer who has formerly represented a client in a matter shall not thereafter represent another person in the same or a substantially related matter in which that person's interests are materially adverse to the interests of the former client unless the former client ~~consents after consultation~~ gives informed consent, confirmed in writing.

(b) A lawyer shall not knowingly represent a person in the same or a substantially related matter in which a firm with which the lawyer formerly was associated had previously represented a client

(1) whose interests are materially adverse to that person; and

(2) about whom the lawyer had acquired information protected by Rules 1.6 and 1.9(c) that is material to the matter;

unless the former client ~~consents after consultation~~ gives informed consent, confirmed in writing.

(c) A lawyer who has formerly represented a client in a matter or whose present or former firm has formerly represented a client in a matter shall not thereafter:

(1) use information relating to the representation to the disadvantage of the former client except as ~~Rule 1.6 or Rule 3.3~~ these Rules would permit or require with respect to a client, or when the information has become generally known; or

(2) reveal information relating to the representation except as ~~Rule 1.6 or Rule 3.3~~ these Rules would permit or require with respect to a client.

COMMENT

[1] After termination of a client-lawyer relationship, a lawyer has certain continuing duties with respect to confidentiality and conflicts of interest and thus may not represent another client except in conformity with this Rule. ~~The principles in Rule 1.7 determine whether the interests of the present and former client are adverse. Thus~~ Under this Rule, for example, a lawyer could not properly seek to rescind on behalf of a new client a contract drafted on behalf of the former client. So also a lawyer

who has prosecuted an accused person could not properly represent the accused in a subsequent civil action against the government concerning the same transaction. Nor could a lawyer who has represented multiple clients in a matter represent one of the clients against the others in the same or a substantially related matter after a dispute arose among the clients in that matter, unless all affected clients give informed consent. See Comment [9]. Current and former government lawyers must comply with this Rule to the extent required by Rule 1.11.

[2] The scope of a "matter" for purposes of this Rule ~~may depend~~ depends on the facts of a particular situation or transaction. The lawyer's involvement in a matter can also be a question of degree. When a lawyer has been directly involved in a specific transaction, subsequent representation of other clients with materially adverse interests in that transaction clearly is prohibited. On the other hand, a lawyer who recurrently handled a type of problem for a former client is not precluded from later representing another client in a ~~wholly~~ factually distinct problem of that type even though the subsequent representation involves a position adverse to the prior client. Similar considerations can apply to the reassignment of military lawyers between defense and prosecution functions within the same military jurisdictions. The underlying question is whether the lawyer was so involved in the matter that the subsequent representation can be justly regarded as a changing of sides in the matter in question.

[3] Matters are "substantially related" for purposes of this Rule if they involve the same transaction or legal dispute or if there otherwise is a substantial risk that confidential factual information as would normally have been obtained in the prior representation would materially advance the client's position in the subsequent matter. For example, a lawyer who has represented a businessperson and learned extensive private financial information about that person may not then represent that person's spouse in seeking a divorce. Similarly, a lawyer who has previously represented a client in securing environmental permits to build a shopping center would be precluded from representing neighbors seeking to oppose rezoning of the property on the basis of environmental considerations; however, the lawyer would not be precluded, on the grounds of substantial relationship, from defending a tenant of the completed shopping center in resisting eviction for nonpayment of rent. Information that has been disclosed to the public or to other parties adverse to the former client ordinarily will not be disqualifying. Information acquired in a prior representation may have been rendered obsolete by the passage of time, a circumstance that may be relevant in determining whether two representations are substantially related. In the case of an organizational client, general knowledge of the client's policies and practices ordinarily will not preclude a subsequent representation; on the other hand, knowledge of specific facts gained in a prior representation that are relevant to the matter in question ordinarily will preclude such a representation. A former client is not required to reveal the confidential information learned by the

lawyer in order to establish a substantial risk that the lawyer has confidential information to use in the subsequent matter. A conclusion about the possession of such information may be based on the nature of the services the lawyer provided the former client and information that would in ordinary practice be learned by a lawyer providing such services.

Lawyers Moving Between Firms

~~[3]~~ [4] When lawyers have been associated within a firm but then end their association, the question of whether a lawyer should undertake representation is more complicated. There are several competing considerations. First, the client previously represented by the former firm must be reasonably assured that the principle of loyalty to the client is not compromised. Second, the rule should not be so broadly cast as to preclude other persons from having reasonable choice of legal counsel. Third, the rule should not unreasonably hamper lawyers from forming new associations and taking on new clients after having left a previous association. In this connection, it should be recognized that today many lawyers practice in firms, that many lawyers to some degree limit their practice to one field or another, and that many move from one association to another several times in their careers. If the concept of imputation were applied with unqualified rigor, the result would be radical curtailment of the opportunity of lawyers to move from one practice setting to another and of the opportunity of clients to change counsel.

~~[4] Reconciliation of these competing principles in the past has been attempted under two rubrics. One approach has been to seek per se rules of disqualification. For example, it has been held that a partner in a law firm is conclusively presumed to have access to all confidences concerning all clients of the firm. Under this analysis, if a lawyer has been a partner in one law firm and then becomes a partner in another law firm, there may be a presumption that all confidences known by the partner in the first firm are known to all partners in the second firm. This presumption might properly be applied in some circumstances, especially where the client has been extensively represented, but may be unrealistic where the client was represented only for limited purposes. Furthermore, such a rigid rule exaggerates the difference between a partner and an associate in modern law firms.~~

~~[5] The other rubric formerly used for dealing with disqualification is the appearance of impropriety proscribed in Canon 9 of the ABA Model Code of Professional Responsibility. This rubric has a two-fold problem. First, the appearance of impropriety can be taken to include any new client-lawyer relationship that might make a former client feel anxious. If that meaning were adopted, disqualification would become little more than a question of subjective judgment by the former client. Second, since "impropriety" is undefined, the term "appearance of impropriety" is~~

~~question-begging. It therefore has to be recognized that the problem of disqualification cannot be properly resolved either by simple analogy to a lawyer practicing alone or by the very general concept of appearance of impropriety.~~

~~Confidentiality~~

~~[8]~~ [5] Paragraph (b) operates to disqualify the lawyer only when the lawyer involved has actual knowledge of information protected by Rules 1.6 and 1.9~~(b)~~(c). Thus, if a lawyer while with one firm acquired no knowledge or information relating to a particular client of the firm, and that lawyer later joined another firm, neither the lawyer individually nor the second firm is disqualified from representing another client in the same or a related matter even though the interests of the two clients conflict. See Rule 1.10(b) for the restrictions on a firm once a lawyer has terminated association with the firm.

[6] ~~Preserving confidentiality is a question of access to information. Access to information, in turn, is essentially a question of fact in~~ Application of paragraph (b) depends on a situation's particular ~~circumstances~~ facts, aided by inferences, deductions or working presumptions that reasonably may be made about the way in which lawyers work together. A lawyer may have general access to files of all clients of a law firm and may regularly participate in discussions of their affairs; it should be inferred that such a lawyer in fact is privy to all information about all the firm's clients. In contrast, another lawyer may have access to the files of only a limited number of clients and participate in discussions of the affairs of no other clients; in the absence of information to the contrary, it should be inferred that such a lawyer in fact is privy to information about the clients actually served but not those of other clients. In such an inquiry, the burden of proof should rest upon the firm whose disqualification is sought.

~~[7] Application of paragraph (b) depends on a situation's particular facts. In such an inquiry, the burden of proof should rest upon the firm whose disqualification is sought.~~

~~[9]~~ [7] Independent of the question of disqualification of a firm, a lawyer changing professional association has a continuing duty to preserve confidentiality of information about a client formerly represented. See Rules 1.6 and 1.9(c).

~~Adverse Positions~~

~~[10] The second aspect of loyalty to a client is the lawyer's obligation to decline subsequent representations involving positions adverse to a former client arising in substantially related matters. This obligation requires~~

abstention from adverse representation by the individual lawyer involved, ~~but does not properly entail abstention of other lawyers through imputed disqualification. Hence, this aspect of the problem is governed by Rule 1.9(a). Thus, if a lawyer left one firm for another, the new affiliation would not preclude the firms involved from continuing to represent clients with adverse interests in the same or related matters, so long as the conditions of paragraphs (b) and (c) concerning confidentiality have been met.~~

~~[11]~~ [8] ~~Information~~ Paragraph (c) provides that information acquired by the lawyer in the course of representing a client may not subsequently be used or revealed by the lawyer to the disadvantage of the client. However, the fact that a lawyer has once served a client does not preclude the lawyer from using generally known information about that client when later representing another client.

~~[12]~~ [9] ~~Disqualification from subsequent representation is~~ The provisions of this Rule are for the protection of former clients and can be waived ~~by them. A waiver is effective only if there is disclosure of the circumstances, including the lawyer's intended role in behalf of the new client~~ if the client gives informed consent, which consent must be confirmed in writing under paragraphs (a) and (b). See Rule 1.0(e). ~~[13]~~ With regard to ~~an opposing party's raising a question of conflict of interest~~ the effectiveness of an advance waiver, see Comment [22] to Rule 1.7. With regard to disqualification of a firm with which a lawyer is or was formerly associated, see Rule 1.10.

Canon and Code Antecedents

ABA Canons of Professional Ethics: Canon 37 provided as follows:

37. Confidences of a Client

It is the duty of a lawyer to preserve his client's confidences. This duty outlasts the lawyer's employment, and extends as well to his employees; and neither of them should accept employment which involves or may involve the disclosure or use of these confidences, either for the private advantage of the lawyer or his employees or to the disadvantage of the client, without his knowledge and consent, and even though there are other available sources of such information. A lawyer should not continue employment when he discovers that this obligation prevents the performance of his full duty to his former or to his new client.

If a lawyer is accused by his client, he is not precluded from disclosing the truth in respect to the accusation. The announced intention of a client to commit a crime is not included within the confidences which he is bound to respect. He may properly make such disclosures as may be necessary to prevent the act or protect those against whom it is threatened.

ABA Model Code of Professional Responsibility: Compare DR 5-105(C) (reprinted later in this volume).

Cross-References in Other Rules

Rule 1.0, Comment 7: "A number of Rules require that a person's consent be confirmed in writing. See Rules 1.7(b) and **1.9(a)**."

Rule 1.6, Comment 1: See "Rules 1.8(b) and **1.9(c)(1)** for the lawyer's duties with respect to the use of such information to the disadvantage of clients and former clients."

Rule 1.6, Comment 17: "The duty of confidentiality continues after the client-lawyer relationship has terminated. See **Rule 1.9(c)(2).** See **Rule 1.9(c)(1)** for the prohibition against using such information to the disadvantage of the former client."

Rule 1.7, Comment 1: "For former client conflicts of interest, see **Rule 1.9**."

Rule 1.7, Comment 4: "Where more than one client is involved, whether the lawyer may continue to represent any of the clients is determined both by the lawyer's ability to comply with duties owed to the former client and by the lawyer's ability to represent adequately the remaining client or clients, given the lawyer's duties to the former client. See **Rule 1.9**."

Rule 1.7, Comment 5: "The lawyer must continue to protect the confidences of the client from whose representation the lawyer has withdrawn. See **Rule 1.9(c)**."

Rule 1.7, Comment 9: "In addition to conflicts with other current clients, a lawyer's duties of loyalty and independence may be materially limited by responsibilities to former clients under **Rule 1.9**. . . ."

Rule 1.7, Comment 33: "Subject to the above limitations, each client in the common representation has the right to loyal and diligent representation and the protection of **Rule 1.9** concerning the obligations to a former client."

Rule 1.8, Comment 5: It is prohibited to partake in the "disadvantageous use of client information unless the client gives informed consent, except as permitted or required by these Rules. See Rules 1.2(d), 1.6, **1.9(c)**, 3.3, 4.1(b), 8.1 and 8.3."

Rule 1.10(a): "While lawyers are associated in a firm, none of them shall knowingly represent a client when any one of them practicing alone would be prohibited from doing so by Rules 1.7 or **1.9**, unless the prohibition is based on a personal interest of the prohibited lawyer and does not present a significant risk of materially limiting the representation of the client by the remaining lawyers in the firm."

Rule 1.10(b)(2) restricts representation when "any lawyer remaining in the firm has information protected by Rules 1.6 and **1.9(c)** that is material to the matter."

Rule 1.10, Comment 2: "When a lawyer moves from one firm to another, the situation is governed by **Rules 1.9(b)** and 1.10(b)."

Rule 1.10, Comment 5: When a lawyer who represents or formerly represented a client leaves a firm, the firm may not represent a person with interests adverse to that client where the matter is the same or substantially related and "any other lawyer currently in the firm has material information protected by Rules 1.6 and **1.9(c)**."

Rule 1.11(a): "Except as law may otherwise expressly permit, a lawyer who has formerly served as a public officer or employee of the government is subject to Rule 1.9(c). . . ."

Rule 1.11(d): "Except as law may otherwise expressly permit, a lawyer currently serving as a public officer or employee is subject to Rules 1.7 and **1.9**."

Rule 1.17, Comment 11: A lawyer selling a law practice has an "obligation to protect information relating to the representation (see Rules 1.6 and **1.9**)."

Rule 1.18(b): "Even when no client-lawyer relationship ensues, a lawyer who has had discussions with a prospective client shall not use or reveal information learned in the consultation, except as **Rule 1.9** would permit with respect to information of a former client."

Rule 1.18, Comment 3: When a prospective client reveals information, "Paragraph (b) prohibits the lawyer from using or revealing that information, except as permitted by **Rule 1.9**, even if the client or lawyer decides not to proceed with the representation."

Rule 3.7(b): "A lawyer may act as advocate in a trial in which another lawyer in the lawyer's firm is likely to be called as a witness unless precluded from doing so by Rule 1.7 or **Rule 1.9**."

Rule 3.7, Comment 4: "It is relevant that one or both parties could reasonably foresee that the lawyer would probably be a witness. The conflict of interest principles stated in Rules 1.7, **1.9** and 1.10 have no application to this aspect of the problem."

Rule 3.7, Comment 6: "In determining if it is permissible to act as advocate in a trial in which the lawyer will be a necessary witness, the lawyer must also consider that the dual role may give rise to a conflict of interest that will require compliance with Rules 1.7 or **1.9**. . . . [A] lawyer who might be permitted to simultaneously serve as an advocate and a witness by paragraph (a)(3) might be precluded from doing so by **Rule 1.9**."

Rule 3.7, Comment 7: "If, however, the testifying lawyer would also be disqualified by Rule 1.7 or **Rule 1.9** from representing the client in the matter, other lawyers in the firm will be precluded from representing the client by Rule 1.10 unless the client gives informed consent under the conditions stated in Rule 1.7."

Rule 5.7, Comment 10: "When a lawyer is obliged to accord the recipients of such services the protections of those Rules that apply to the client-lawyer relationship, the lawyer must take special care to heed the proscriptions of the Rules addressing conflict of interest (**Rules 1.7 through 1.11**, especially Rules 1.7 and 1.8(a), (b) and (f)). . . ."

Rule 6.5(a): "A lawyer who, under the auspices of a program sponsored by a nonprofit organization or court, provides short-term limited legal services to a client without expectation by either the lawyer or the client that the lawyer will provide continuing representation in the matter is subject to Rules 1.7 and **1.9(a)** only if the lawyer knows that the representation of the client involves a conflict of interest; and is subject to Rule 1.10 only if the lawyer knows that another lawyer associated with the lawyer in a law firm is disqualified by Rule 1.7 or **1.9(a)** with respect to the matter."

Rule 6.5, Comment 1: "Legal services organizations, courts and various nonprofit organizations have established programs through which lawyers provide short-term limited legal services. . . . Such programs are normally operated under circumstances in which it is not feasible for a lawyer to systematically screen for conflicts of interest as is generally required before undertaking a representation. See, e.g., Rules 1.7, **1.9** and 1.10."

Rule 6.5, Comment 2: Regarding "a lawyer who provides short-term limited legal services pursuant to this Rule . . . [e]xcept as provided in this Rule, the Rules of Professional Conduct, including Rules 1.6 and **1.9(c)**, are applicable to the limited representation."

Rule 6.5, Comment 3: "[P]aragraph (a) requires compliance with Rules 1.7 or **1.9(a)** only if the lawyer knows that the representation presents a conflict of interest for the lawyer, and with Rule 1.10 only if the lawyer knows that another lawyer in the lawyer's firm is disqualified by Rules 1.7 or **1.9(a)** in the matter."

Rule 6.5, Comment 4: "Paragraph (a)(2) requires the participating lawyer to comply with Rule 1.10 when the lawyer knows that the lawyer's firm is disqualified by Rules 1.7 or **1.9(a)**."

Rule 6.5, Comment 5: "If, after commencing a short-term limited representation in accordance with this Rule, a lawyer undertakes to represent the client in the matter on an ongoing basis, Rules 1.7, **1.9(a)** and 1.10 become applicable."

Legislative History of Model Rule 1.9

1980 Discussion Draft: Rule 1.9(c) (then Rule 1.10(a)(2)) provided that a lawyer who has represented a client in a matter shall not thereafter "make use of information acquired in service to the client in a manner disadvantageous to the client . . . unless the information has become generally known *or accessible.*"

1981 Draft was substantially the same as adopted.

1982 Draft was adopted.

1989 Amendments: At its February 1989 Mid-Year Meeting, the ABA House of Delegates moved former Rule 1.10(b) to its current position as Rule 1.9(b), amended and renumbered former Rule 1.9(b) as current Rule 1.9(c), and made some minor amendments to the balance of Rule 1.9. The Comments to Rules 1.9 and 1.10 were changed to correspond to these amendments. The Committee Report to the House of Delegates gave the following explanation for amending Rule 1.9(c):*

> The addition of explanatory language to . . . paragraph (c), is intended to eliminate another oversight in the drafting of Rule 1.9. The added language makes clear that a lawyer's duty of confidentiality with respect to former clients applies to clients who were personally represented by the lawyer and to clients who, although not personally represented by the lawyer, were represented by the lawyer's firm. In addition, a prohibition on the "revelation" of confidential information is added to Rule 1.9. As originally drafted, Rule 1.9 prohibited only the "use" of such information to the disadvantage of the former client. . . . The Comments to Rules 1.9 and 1.10 are amended in conformity with the amendments to the black letter Rules.

2002 Amendments: At its February 2002 Mid-Year Meeting, the ABA House of Delegates adopted without change the ABA Ethics 2000 Commission proposal to amend Rule 1.9 and its Comment.

Selected State Variations

California: See Rule 3-310(E) (regarding employment adverse to former clients), and B & P Code §6068(e) (regarding client confidences).

District of Columbia: D.C. Rule 1.9 differs significantly from the ABA Model Rule — see District of Columbia Rules of Professional Conduct below.

*Committee Reports do not represent official policy of the ABA. They are for information only, and the opinions are those of the authors of the report.

Georgia: In the rules effective January 1, 2001, Georgia adopts ABA Model Rule 1.9 nearly verbatim, but Georgia's Comment deletes paragraph 3 of the ABA Comment.

Illinois Rule 1.10(b) and (e) provide:

> (b) When a lawyer becomes associated with a firm, the firm may not represent a person in a matter that the firm knows or reasonably should know is the same or substantially related to a matter in which the newly associated lawyer, or a firm with which that lawyer was associated, had previously represented a client whose interests are materially adverse to that person unless:
>
> (1) the newly associated lawyer has no information protected by Rule 1.6 or Rule 1.9 that is material to the matter; or
>
> (2) the newly associated lawyer is screened from any participation in the matter. . . .
>
> (e) For purposes of Rule 1.10, Rule 1.11, and Rule 1.12, a lawyer in a firm will be deemed to have been screened from any participation in a matter if:
>
> (1) the lawyer has been isolated from confidences, secrets, and material knowledge concerning the matter;
>
> (2) the lawyer has been isolated from all contact with the client or any agent, officer, or employee of the client and any witness for or against the client;
>
> (3) the lawyer and the firm have been precluded from discussing the matter with each other; and
>
> (4) the firm has taken affirmative steps to accomplish the foregoing.

Massachusetts: Rule 1.9(c) also forbids a lawyer to use confidential information "to the lawyer's advantage, or to the advantage of a third person" without consent.

Michigan: Rule 1.10(b) permits firms to avoid disqualification based on a personally disqualified lawyer who was formerly with another firm if: "(1) the disqualified lawyer is screened from any participation in the matter and is apportioned no part of the fee therefrom; and (2) written notice is promptly given to the appropriate client to enable it to ascertain compliance with the provisions of this rule."

Nebraska: DR 5-109 protects former clients from conflicts with any "support person," including "law clerks, paralegals, legal assistants, secretaries, messengers, and other support personnel employed by the law firm." DR 5-109(B) prohibits a lawyer from knowingly allowing a support person, without a former client's consent, "to participate or assist in the representation of a current client in the same or a substantially related matter in which another lawyer or firm with which the support person formerly was associated had previously represented a client" if the former client's interests are materially adverse to the current client and "the support person has acquired confidential information that is material to the matter" — which will be assumed "unless the support person demonstrates otherwise." Moreover, if a support person is personally disqualified, then the disqualification is imputed to the entire law firm unless the former client consents or there "is no genuine threat that confidential information of the former client will be used with material adverse effect on the former client because the confidential client information communicated to the support person while associated with the former firm is not likely to be significant in the current client's case."

New Jersey adds the following language in Rule 1.10(d): "When lawyers terminate an association in a firm, none of them, nor any other lawyer with whom any of them subsequently becomes associated shall knowingly represent a client when doing so involves a material risk of violating Rule 1.6 or 1.9." Rule 1.9(a) requires "a full disclosure of the circumstances" to the former client as a condition of consent. Rule 1.9(c) applies New Jersey's Rule 1.7(c) to Rule 1.9. See Rule 1.7, Selected State Variations.

New York: Compare ABA Model Rule 1.9 to New York's DR 5-108(A) and (B).

Oregon: DR 5-105(H) and (I) permit screening but require "the personally disqualified lawyer" and his or her firm to serve affidavits at the outset and, on request, the conclusion of the matter attesting to the screen and its observance.

Texas Rule 1.09 provides:

> (a) Without prior consent, a lawyer who personally has formerly represented a client in a matter shall not thereafter represent another person in a matter adverse to the former client:
>
> (1) in which such other person questions the validity of the lawyer's services or work product for the former client;
>
> (2) if the representation in reasonable probability will involve a violation of Rule 1.05; or
>
> (3) if it is the same or a substantially related matter.

Virginia: Rule 1.9(a) requires the consent of both the present and former client. Rule 1.9(c)(1) prohibits a lawyer to "use information relating to or gained in the course of the representation to the disadvantage of the former client."

Related Materials

ABA Formal Ethics Opinions: See ABA Formal Ethics Ops. 94-381 (1994), 95-395 (1995), 96-400 (1996), 97-407 (1997), 97-409 (1997), and 99-415 (1999).

ABA Standards for Imposing Lawyer Sanctions: See Standard 4.3 in the Related Materials following Model Rule 1.7.

American Academy of Matrimonial Lawyers: The "Bounds of Advocacy" contains the following rule and comment:

> 3.5. An attorney should discourage the client from interfering in the spouse's effort to obtain effective representation.
>
> Comment to Rule 3.5
>
> Clients who file or anticipate the filing of a divorce proceeding occasionally telephone or interview numerous attorneys as a means of denying their spouse access to effective representation. The attorney should discourage such practices and should not assist the client, for example, by responding to the client's request for a list of matrimonial lawyers if improper motives are suspected. When the client has already contacted other lawyers for the purpose of disqualifying them, the client's attorney should attempt to persuade the client to waive any conflicts so created.

Restatement of the Law Governing Lawyers: See Restatement §§15, 33, 121, 122, and 132 in our chapter on the Restatement later in this volume.

Sixth Amendment: In Holloway v. Arkansas, 435 U.S. 475 (1978), the Court held that the "Sixth Amendment requires automatic reversal when a trial court fails to conduct an inquiry after either a timely conflict objection, or if a court knows or reasonably should know that a particular conflict exists." In Cuyler v. Sullivan, 446 U.S. 335 (1980), the Court ruled that this "automatic reversal" rule did not apply when the trial court is not informed or is not on notice of a conflict. If a conflict is later alleged, the Sixth Amendment requires a defendant to "establish that an actual conflict of interest adversely affected his lawyer's performance." *Holloway* and *Sullivan* both involved concurrent conflicts. In Mickens v. Taylor, 122 S. Ct. 1237 (2002), the conflict at issue was successive. The murder defendant was represented by a lawyer who, until a week before his appointment as defendant's counsel, had been representing the alleged victim of the defendant's homicide on an unrelated criminal matter. The judge who dismissed the criminal charges against the now-deceased murder victim appointed the victim's lawyer to represent his alleged murderer a week later. The Court held that these facts did not require "automatic reversal" as in *Holloway*. "Since this was not a case in which [as in *Holloway*] counsel protested his inability simultaneously to represent multiple defendants . . . it was at least necessary, to void the conviction, for petitioner to establish that the conflict of interest adversely affected his counsel's performance." The Court left open the possibility that a future defendant who alleged only a successive conflict might not even enjoy *Sullivan*'s test for establishing ineffectiveness, but would instead be required to satisfy the stricter Sixth Amendment effectiveness test set out in Strickland v. Washington, 466 U.S. 668 (1984).

Rule 1.10 ~~Imputed Disqualification~~ Imputation of Conflicts of Interest: General Rule

Editors' Note. At its August 2001 Annual Meeting, the ABA House of Delegates rejected certain parts of the Ethics 2000 Commission's proposal to amend Rule 1.10. The rejected provisions are reprinted after the heading "2002 Amendments" in the Legislative History below.

(a) While lawyers are associated in a firm, none of them shall knowingly represent a client when any one of them practicing alone would be prohibited from doing so by Rules 1.7~~, 1.8(c),~~ or 1.9 ~~or 2.2~~, unless the prohibition is based on a personal interest of the prohibited lawyer and does not present a significant risk of materially limiting the representation of the client by the remaining lawyers in the firm.

(b) When a lawyer has terminated an association with a firm, the firm is not prohibited from thereafter representing a person with interests materially adverse to those of a client represented by the formerly associated lawyer and not currently represented by the firm, unless:

(1) the matter is the same or substantially related to that in which the formerly associated lawyer represented the client; and

(2) any lawyer remaining in the firm has information protected by Rules 1.6 and 1.9(c) that is material to the matter.

(c) A disqualification prescribed by this rule may be waived by the affected client under the conditions stated in Rule 1.7.

(d) The disqualification of lawyers associated in a firm with former or current government lawyers is governed by Rule 1.11.

COMMENT

Definition of "Firm"

[1] For purposes of the Rules of Professional Conduct, the term "firm" ~~includes~~ denotes lawyers in a ~~private firm, and~~ law partnership, professional corporation, sole proprietorship or other association authorized to practice law; or lawyers employed in a legal services organization or the legal department of a corporation or other organization~~, or in a legal services organization~~. See Rule 1.0(c). Whether two or more lawyers constitute a firm within this definition can depend on the specific facts. ~~For example, two practitioners who share office space and occasionally consult or assist each other ordinarily would not be regarded as constituting a firm. However, if they present themselves to the public in a way suggesting that they are a firm or conduct themselves as a firm, they should be regarded as a firm for purposes of the Rules. The terms of any formal agreement between associated lawyers are relevant in determining whether they are a firm, as is the fact that they have mutual access to information concerning the clients they serve. Furthermore, it is relevant in doubtful cases to consider the underlying purpose of the Rule that is involved. A group of lawyers could be regarded as a firm for purposes of the rule that the same lawyer should not represent opposing parties in litigation, while it might not be so regarded for purposes of the rule that information acquired by one lawyer is attributed to another.~~ See Rule 1.0, Comments [2]-[4].

~~[2] With respect to the law department of an organization, there is ordinarily no question that the members of the department constitute a firm within the meaning of the Rules of Professional Conduct. However, there can be uncertainty as to the identity of the client. For example, it may not be clear whether the law department of a corporation represents a subsidiary or an affiliated corporation, as well as the corporation by which the members of the department are directly employed. A similar question can arise concerning an unincorporated association and its local affiliates.~~

~~[3] Similar questions can also arise with respect to lawyers in legal aid. Lawyers employed in the same unit of a legal service organization constitute a firm, but not necessarily those employed in separate units. As in the case of independent practitioners, whether the lawyers should be treated as associated with each other can depend on the particular rule that is involved, and on the specific facts of the situation.~~

~~[5] Different provisions are thus made for movement of a lawyer from one private firm to another and for movement of a lawyer between a private firm and the government. The government is entitled to protection of its client confidences and, therefore, to the protections provided in Rules 1.6, 1.9 and 1.11. However, if the more extensive disqualification in~~

~~Rule 1.10 were applied to former government lawyers, the potential effect on the government would be unduly burdensome. The government deals with all private citizens and organizations and, thus, has a much wider circle of adverse legal interests than does any private law firm. In these circumstances, the government's recruitment of lawyers would be seriously impaired if Rule 1.10 were applied to the government. On balance, therefore, the government is better served in the long run by the protections stated in Rule 1.11.~~

Principles of Imputed Disqualification

~~[6]~~ [2] The rule of imputed disqualification stated in paragraph (a) gives effect to the principle of loyalty to the client as it applies to lawyers who practice in a law firm. Such situations can be considered from the premise that a firm of lawyers is essentially one lawyer for purposes of the rules governing loyalty to the client, or from the premise that each lawyer is vicariously bound by the obligation of loyalty owed by each lawyer with whom the lawyer is associated. Paragraph (a) operates only among the lawyers currently associated in a firm. When a lawyer moves from one firm to another, the situation is governed by Rules 1.9(b) and 1.10(b).

[3] The rule in paragraph (a) does not prohibit representation where neither questions of client loyalty nor protection of confidential information are presented. Where one lawyer in a firm could not effectively represent a given client because of strong political beliefs, for example, but that lawyer will do no work on the case and the personal beliefs of the lawyer will not materially limit the representation by others in the firm, the firm should not be disqualified. On the other hand, if an opposing party in a case were owned by a lawyer in the law firm, and others in the firm would be materially limited in pursuing the matter because of loyalty to that lawyer, the personal disqualification of the lawyer would be imputed to all others in the firm.

[4] The rule in paragraph (a) also does not prohibit representation by others in the law firm where the person prohibited from involvement in a matter is a nonlawyer, such as a paralegal or legal secretary. Nor does paragraph (a) prohibit representation if the lawyer is prohibited from acting because of events before the person became a lawyer, for example, work that the person did while a law student. Such persons, however, ordinarily must be screened from any personal participation in the matter to avoid communication to others in the firm of confidential information that both the nonlawyers and the firm have a legal duty to protect. See Rules 1.0(k) and 5.3.

~~[7]~~ [5] Rule 1.10(b) operates to permit a law firm, under certain circumstances, to represent a person with interests directly adverse to those of a client represented by a lawyer who formerly was associated with the firm. The Rule applies regardless of when the formerly associated lawyer represented the client. However, the law firm may not represent a person with interests adverse to those of a present client of the firm, which would violate Rule 1.7. Moreover, the firm may not represent the person where the matter is the same or substantially related to that in which the formerly associated lawyer represented the client and any other lawyer currently in the firm has material information protected by Rules 1.6 and 1.9(c).

[6] Rule 1.10(c) removes imputation with the informed consent of the affected client or former client under the conditions stated in Rule 1.7. The conditions stated in Rule 1.7 require the lawyer to determine that the representation is not prohibited by Rule 1.7(b) and that each affected client or former client has given informed consent to the representation, confirmed in writing. In some cases, the risk may be so severe that the conflict may not be cured by client consent. For a discussion of the effectiveness of client waivers of conflicts that might arise in the future, see Rule 1.7, Comment [22]. For a definition of informed consent, see Rule 1.0(e).

~~[4]~~ [7] Where a lawyer has joined a private firm after having represented the government, ~~the situation~~ imputation is governed by Rule 1.11~~(a) and~~ (b) and (c)~~;~~, not this Rule. Under Rule 1.11(d), where a lawyer represents the government after having served ~~private~~ clients, ~~the situation is governed by Rule 1.11(c)(1). The individual lawyer involved is bound by the Rules generally, including Rules 1.6, 1.7 and 1.9~~ in private practice, nongovernmental employment or in another government agency, former-client conflicts are not imputed to government lawyers associated with the individually disqualified lawyer.

[8] Where a lawyer is prohibited from engaging in certain transactions under Rule 1.8, paragraph (k) of that Rule, and not this Rule, determines whether that prohibition also applies to other lawyers associated in a firm with the personally prohibited lawyer.

Canon and Code Antecedents

ABA Canons of Professional Ethics: No comparable Canon.

ABA Model Code of Professional Responsibility: Compare DR 5-105(D) (reprinted later in this volume).

Cross-References in Other Rules

Rule 1.7, Comment 10: "See Rule 1.8 for specific Rules pertaining to a number of personal interest conflicts, including business transactions with clients. See also **Rule 1.10** (personal interest conflicts under Rule 1.7 ordinarily are not imputed to other lawyers in a law firm)."

Rule 1.7, Comment 11: "The disqualification arising from a close family relationship is personal and ordinarily is not imputed to members of firms with whom the lawyers are associated. See **Rule 1.10**."

Rule 1.9, Comment 5: "See **Rule 1.10(b)** for the restrictions on a firm once a lawyer has terminated association with the firm."

Rule 1.9, Comment 9: "With regard to disqualification of a firm with which a lawyer is or was formerly associated, see **Rule 1.10**."

Rule 1.11, Comment 2: "**Rule 1.10** is not applicable to the conflicts of interest addressed by this Rule."

Rule 1.11, Comment 3: "As with paragraphs (a)(1) and (d)(1), **Rule 1.10** is not applicable to the conflicts of interest addressed by these paragraphs."

Rule 1.18, Comment 7: "Under paragraph (c), the prohibition in this Rule is imputed to other lawyers as provided in **Rule 1.10**. . . ."

Rule 3.7, Comment 4: "It is relevant that one or both parties could reasonably foresee that the lawyer would probably be a witness. The conflict of interest principles stated in Rules 1.7, 1.9 and **1.10** have no application to this aspect of the problem."

Rule 3.7, Comment 7: "If, however, the testifying lawyer would also be disqualified by Rule 1.7 or Rule 1.9 from representing the client in the matter, other lawyers in the firm will be precluded from representing the client by **Rule 1.10** unless the client gives informed consent under the conditions stated in Rule 1.7."

Rule 5.7, Comment 10: "When a lawyer is obliged to accord the recipients of such services the protections of those Rules that apply to the client-lawyer relationship, the lawyer must take special care to heed the proscriptions of the Rules addressing conflict of interest (**Rules 1.7 through 1.11**, especially Rules 1.7 and 1.8(a), (b) and (f)). . . ."

Rule 6.5(a): "A lawyer who, under the auspices of a program sponsored by a nonprofit organization or court, provides short-term limited legal services to a client without expectation by either the lawyer or the client that the lawyer will provide continuing representation in the matter is subject to Rules 1.7 and 1.9(a) only if the lawyer knows that the representation of the client involves a conflict of interest; and is subject to **Rule 1.10** only if the lawyer knows that another lawyer associated with the lawyer in a law firm is disqualified by Rule 1.7 or 1.9(a) with respect to the matter."

Rule 6.5(b): "Except as provided in paragraph (a)(2), **Rule 1.10** is inapplicable to a representation governed by this Rule."

Rule 6.5, Comment 1: "Legal services organizations, courts and various nonprofit organizations have established programs through which lawyers provide short-term limited legal services. . . . Such programs are normally operated under circumstances in which it is not feasible for a lawyer to systematically screen for conflicts of interest as is generally required before undertaking a representation. See, e.g., Rules 1.7, 1.9 and **1.10**."

Rule 6.5, Comment 3: "[P]aragraph (a) requires compliance with Rules 1.7 or 1.9(a) only if the lawyer knows that the representation presents a conflict of interest for the lawyer . . . and with **Rule 1.10** only if the lawyer knows that another lawyer in the lawyer's firm is disqualified by Rules 1.7 or 1.9(a) in the matter."

Rule 6.5, Comment 4: "[P]aragraph (b) provides that **Rule 1.10** is inapplicable to a representation governed by this Rule except as provided by paragraph (a)(2). Paragraph (a)(2) requires the participating lawyer to comply with **Rule 1.10** when the lawyer knows that the lawyer's firm is disqualified by Rules 1.7 or 1.9(a)."

Rule 6.5, Comment 5: "If, after commencing a short-term limited representation in accordance with this Rule, a lawyer undertakes to represent the client in the matter on an ongoing basis, Rules 1.7, 1.9(a) and **1.10** become applicable."

Legislative History of Model Rule 1.10

1980 Discussion Draft had no comparable provision on imputed disqualification.

1981 Draft:

> (b) When lawyers terminate an association in a firm, none of them, nor any other lawyer with whom any of them subsequently become associated, shall undertake or continue representation that involves a material risk of revealing information relating to representation of a client in violation of Rule 1.6, or of making use of information to the disadvantage of a former client in violation of Rule 1.9.

1982 Draft:

> (b) When lawyers terminate an association in a firm, none of them, nor any other lawyer with whom any of them subsequently becomes associated, shall knowingly represent a client when doing so involves a material risk of violating Rule 1.6 or Rule 1.9.

1989 Amendments: At its 1989 Mid-Year Meeting, the House of Delegates amended Rule 1.10 by moving former Rule 1.10(b) to its current position as Rule 1.9(b), by moving the corresponding Comment paragraphs to Rule 1.9's Comment, by moving former Rule 1.10(c) to current Rule 1.10(b), by adding a phrase to new Rule 1.10(b), and by moving former Rule 1.10(d) to its current position as Rule 1.10(c). An excerpt from the Committee Report explaining the changes is reprinted in the Legislative History following Rule 1.9. The Committee's explanation regarding the amendment to former Rule 1.10(c) states:

> Paragraph (c) (now paragraph (b)) of Rule 1.10 was never intended to permit the representation of a client whose interests are directly adverse to the interests of a present client of a firm. Such representation would violate Rule 1.7. In order to make it clear that when a lawyer leaves a law firm, this paragraph does not override the proscription in Rule 1.7, the limiting words "and not currently represented by the firm" are proposed to be added to Rule 1.10(b).

2002 Amendments: At its August 2001 Annual Meeting, the ABA House of Delegates adopted the ABA Ethics 2000 Commission proposal to amend Rules 1.10(a) and (d) without change, but rejected the Ethics 2000 Commission's proposal to amend Rule 1.10(c). (The Ethics 2000 Commission did not propose any changes to Rule 1.10(b).) The August 2001 votes were confirmed at the ABA's February 2002 Mid-Year Meeting. The rejected proposals would have permitted a law firm to use timely "screens" and related measures to overcome a former client's objections to an adverse representation. The rejected provisions of Rule 1.10(c) provided as follows:

> (c) When a lawyer becomes associated with a firm, no lawyer associated in the firm shall knowingly represent a person in a matter in which that lawyer is disqualified under Rule 1.9 unless:
>
> (1) the personally disqualified lawyer is timely screened from any

participation in the matter and is apportioned no part of the fee therefrom; and

(2) written notice is promptly given to any affected former client to enable it to ascertain compliance with the provisions of this Rule.

By rejecting the proposed text of Rule 1.10(c), the ABA also rejected three proposed comments that would have explained the proposed language. The three rejected Comments provided as follows:

> [6] Where the conditions of paragraph (c) are met, imputation is removed, and consent to the new representation is not required. Lawyers should be aware, however, that courts may impose more stringent obligations in ruling upon motions to disqualify a lawyer from pending litigation.
>
> [7] Requirements for screening procedures are stated in Rule 1.0(k). Paragraph (c)(2) does not prohibit the screened lawyer from receiving a salary or partnership share established by prior independent agreement, but that lawyer may not receive compensation directly related to the matter in which the lawyer is disqualified.
>
> [8] Notice, including a description of the screened lawyer's prior representation and of the screening procedures employed, generally should be given as soon as practicable after the need for screening becomes apparent.

The Reporter's Explanation Memo regarding the rejected Comments provided, in relevant part, as follows:

> *Model Rule 1.10 — Reporter's Explanation of Changes**
>
> A number of jurisdictions now provide that former-client conflicts of lawyers who have moved laterally are not imputed to the new law firm if the personally disqualified lawyer has been timely screened from participation in the matter and the former client is notified of the screen. The Commission is recommending that current Rule 1.10 be amended to permit nonconsensual screening of lawyers who have joined a law firm.
>
> The Commission is persuaded that nonconsensual screening in these cases adequately balances the interests of the former client in confidentiality of information, the interests of current clients in hiring the counsel of their choice (including a law firm that may have represented the client in similar matters for many years) and the interests of lawyers in mobility, particularly when they are moving involuntarily because their former law firms have downsized, dissolved or drifted into bankruptcy. There are presently seven jurisdictions that permit screening of laterals by Rule. The testimony the Commission has heard indicates that there have not been any significant numbers of complaints regarding lawyers' conduct under these Rules.

In addition, at its February 2002 Mid-Year Meeting, the ABA House of Delegates adopted with little change the Ethics 2000 Commission proposals to add two new rules to the Model Rules (Rules 1.18 and 6.5) to govern imputed conflicts of interest regarding two special categories of clients — prospective clients who ultimately did not retain a lawyer, and clients consulting a lawyer who (under the auspices of a program sponsored by a nonprofit organization or court) is providing "short-term limited legal services to a client without expectation by either the lawyer or the client that the lawyer will provide continuing representation in the matter." For more information about these rules, see the Legislative History following Rules 1.18 and 6.5 below.

*Committee Reports, and the Reporter's Explanation of Changes contained therein, do not represent official policy of the ABA. They are for information only, and the opinions are those of the authors of the report.

Selected State Variations

Alaska: Rule 1.10(b)(2) applies not only if any *lawyer* in the firm has information protected by Rule 1.6 or 1.9(c), but also if "the *firm* retains records containing such information."

California: No equivalent.

District of Columbia: D.C. Rule 1.10 differs significantly from the ABA Model Rule—see District of Columbia Rules of Professional Conduct below.

Georgia: In the rules effective January 1, 2001, Georgia adopted the pre-2002 version of ABA Model Rule 1.10 and its Comment essentially verbatim.

Illinois extends the prohibition of Rule 1.10(a) to any lawyer who "knows or reasonably should know" that another lawyer in the firm is disqualified. Illinois also adds a new provision, Rule 1.10(e), to define "screened." This new provision is quoted in the Selected State Variations following Rule 1.9.

Massachusetts: Rule 1.10(d) provides for screening a "personally disqualified lawyer" if he or she "had neither substantial involvement nor substantial material information relating to the matter . . . and is apportioned no part of the fee therefrom." Rule 1.10(e) describes an appropriate screen, which includes a requirement of an affidavit from the lawyer and the firm describing the screening procedures. Provision is made for court review of the adequacy of screens.

New Jersey adds the following Rule 1.10(e):

> A disqualification prescribed by this rule may be waived by the affected client under the conditions stated in Rule 1.7 except where prohibited by law or regulation, such as the prohibition against a public entity waiving an attorney conflict of interest.

New York: Compare Model Rule 1.10 to New York's DR 5-105(D) and (E) and DR 5-108(C).

Pennsylvania: Rule 1.10(b) permits firms to avoid disqualification based on a personally disqualified lawyer who was formerly with another firm if: "(1) the disqualified lawyer is screened from any participation in the matter and is apportioned no part of the fee therefrom; and (2) written notice is promptly given to the appropriate client to enable it to ascertain compliance with the provisions of this rule."

Texas: Rule 1.09 provides:

> (b) Except to the extent authorized by Rule 1.10 [concerning government lawyers], when lawyers are or have become members of or associated with a firm, none of them shall knowingly represent a client if any one of them practicing alone would be prohibited from doing so by paragraph (a).
>
> (c) When the association of a lawyer with a firm has terminated, the lawyers who were then associated with that lawyer shall not knowingly represent a client if the lawyer whose association with that firm has terminated would be prohibited from doing so by paragraph (a)(1) or if the representation in reasonable probability will involve a violation of Rule 1.05.

Related Materials

ABA Formal Ethics Opinions: See ABA Formal Ethics Op. 97-407 (1997).

Model Rules of Professional Conduct for Federal Lawyers: Rule 1.10(a) provides that "Government lawyers working in the same Federal Agency are not automatically disqualified from representing a client because any of them practicing alone would be prohibited from doing so by Rules 1.7, 1.8(c), 1.9 or 2.2." The Comment states:

> The circumstances of Government service may require representation of opposing sides by Government lawyers working in the same Federal Agency. Such representation is permissible so long as conflicts of interest are avoided and independent judgment, zealous representation, and protection of client confidences are not compromised. Thus, the principle of imputed disqualification is not automatically controlling for Government lawyers. The knowledge, action, and conflicts of interest of one Government lawyer are not to be imputed to another simply because they operate from the same office. . . .

Restatement of the Law Governing Lawyers: See Restatement §§15, 33, 121, 122, and 132 in our chapter on the Restatement later in this volume.

Rule 1.11 ~~Successive~~ Special Conflicts of Interest for Former and Current Government Officers and ~~Private Employment~~ Employees

(a) Except as law may otherwise expressly permit, a lawyer who has formerly served as a public officer or employee of the government:

(1) is subject to Rule 1.9(c); and

(2) shall not otherwise represent a ~~private~~ client in connection with a matter in which the lawyer participated personally and substantially as a public officer or employee, unless the appropriate government agency ~~consents after consultation~~ gives its informed consent, confirmed in writing, to the representation.

(b) ~~No~~ When a lawyer is disqualified from representation under paragraph (a), no lawyer in a firm with which that lawyer is associated may knowingly undertake or continue representation in such a matter unless:

(1) the disqualified lawyer is timely screened from any participation in the matter and is apportioned no part of the fee therefrom; and

(2) written notice is promptly given to the appropriate government agency to enable it to ascertain compliance with the provisions of this rule.

~~(b)~~ (c) Except as law may otherwise expressly permit, a lawyer having information that the lawyer knows is confidential government information about a person acquired when the lawyer was a public officer or employee, may not represent a private client whose interests are adverse to that person in a matter in which the information could be used to the material disadvantage of that person. As used in this Rule, the term "confidential government information" means information that has been obtained under governmental authority and which, at the time this Rule is applied, the government is prohibited

by law from disclosing to the public or has a legal privilege not to disclose and which is not otherwise available to the public. A firm with which that lawyer is associated may undertake or continue representation in the matter only if the disqualified lawyer is timely screened from any participation in the matter and is apportioned no part of the fee therefrom.

~~(c)~~ (d) Except as law may otherwise expressly permit, a lawyer currently serving as a public officer or employee:

(1) is subject to Rules 1.7 and 1.9; and

(2) shall not:

~~(1)~~ (i) participate in a matter in which the lawyer participated personally and substantially while in private practice or nongovernmental employment, unless ~~under applicable law no one is, or by lawful delegation may be, authorized to act in the lawyer's stead in the matter~~ the appropriate government agency gives its informed consent, confirmed in writing; or

~~(2)~~ (ii) negotiate for private employment with any person who is involved as a party or as lawyer for a party in a matter in which the lawyer is participating personally and substantially, except that a lawyer serving as a law clerk to a judge, other adjudicative officer or arbitrator may negotiate for private employment as permitted by Rule 1.12(b) and subject to the conditions stated in Rule 1.12(b).

~~(d)~~ (e) As used in this Rule, the term "matter" includes:

(1) any judicial or other proceeding, application, request for a ruling or other determination, contract, claim, controversy, investigation, charge, accusation, arrest or other particular matter involving a specific party or parties, and

(2) any other matter covered by the conflict of interest rules of the appropriate government agency.

~~(e) As used in this Rule, the term "confidential government information" means information which has been obtained under governmental authority and which, at the time this rule is applied, the government is prohibited by law from disclosing to the public or has a legal privilege not to disclose, and which is not otherwise available to the public.~~

COMMENT

~~[1] This Rule prevents a lawyer from exploiting public office for the advantage of a private client. It is a counterpart of Rule 1.10(b), which applies to lawyers moving from one firm to another.~~

~~[2]~~ [1] A lawyer ~~representing a government agency, whether employed or specially retained by the government,~~ who has served or is currently serving as a public officer or employee is personally subject to the

Rules of Professional Conduct, including the prohibition against ~~representing adverse interests~~ concurrent conflicts of interest stated in Rule 1.7 ~~and the protections afforded former clients in Rule 1.9~~. In addition, such a lawyer ~~is~~ may be subject to ~~Rule 1.11 and to~~ statutes and government regulations regarding conflict of interest. Such statutes and regulations may circumscribe the extent to which the government agency may give consent under this Rule. See Rule 1.0(e) for the definition of informed consent.

[2] Paragraphs (a)(1), (a)(2) and (d)(1) restate the obligations of an individual lawyer who has served or is currently serving as an officer or employee of the government toward a former government or private client. Rule 1.10 is not applicable to the conflicts of interest addressed by this Rule. Rather, paragraph (b) sets forth a special imputation rule for former government lawyers that provides for screening and notice. Because of the special problems raised by imputation within a government agency, paragraph (d) does not impute the conflicts of a lawyer currently serving as an officer or employee of the government to other associated government officers or employees, although ordinarily it will be prudent to screen such lawyers.

[3] Paragraphs (a)(2) and (d)(2) apply regardless of whether a lawyer is adverse to a former client and are thus designed not only to protect the former client, but also to prevent a lawyer from exploiting public office for the advantage of another client. For example, a lawyer who has pursued a claim on behalf of the government may not pursue the same claim on behalf of a later private client after the lawyer has left government service, except when authorized to do so by the government agency under paragraph (a). Similarly, a lawyer who has pursued a claim on behalf of a private client may not pursue the claim on behalf of the government, except when authorized to do so by paragraph (d). As with paragraphs (a)(1) and (d)(1), Rule 1.10 is not applicable to the conflicts of interest addressed by these paragraphs.

~~[3]~~ [4] ~~Where~~ This Rule represents a balancing of interests. On the one hand, where the successive clients are a ~~public~~ government agency and ~~a private~~ another client, public or private, the risk exists that power or discretion vested in that agency ~~public authority~~ might be used for the special benefit of ~~a private~~ the other client. A lawyer should not be in a position where benefit to ~~a private~~ the other client might affect performance of the lawyer's professional functions on behalf of the government ~~public authority~~. Also, unfair advantage could accrue to the ~~private~~ other client by reason of access to confidential government information about the client's adversary obtainable only through the lawyer's government service. ~~However~~ On the other hand, the rules governing lawyers presently or formerly employed by a government agency should not be so restrictive as to inhibit transfer of employment to and from the government. The government has a legitimate need to attract qualified lawyers as well as to maintain high ethical standards. Thus a former government lawyer is disqualified only from particular matters in which the lawyer participated personally and substantially. The provisions for screening and waiver in paragraph (b) are necessary to prevent the disqualification rule from imposing too severe a deterrent against entering public service. The limitation of disqualification in paragraphs (a)(2) and (d)(2) to matters involving a specific party or parties, rather than extending disqualification to all substantive issues on which the lawyer worked, serves a similar function.

~~[4]~~ [5] When ~~the client is an agency of~~ a lawyer has been employed by one government agency and then moves to a second government agency, it may be appropriate to treat that second agency ~~should be treated~~ as ~~a private~~ another client for purposes of this Rule ~~if the lawyer thereafter represents an agency of another government~~, as when a lawyer ~~represents~~ is employed by a city and subsequently is employed by a federal agency. However, because the conflict of interest is governed by paragraph (d), the latter agency is not required to screen the lawyer as paragraph (b) requires a law firm to do. The question of whether two government agencies should be regarded as the same or different clients for conflict of interest purposes is beyond the scope of these Rules. See Rule 1.13 Comment [6].

~~[5]~~ [6] Paragraphs ~~(a)(1) and~~ (b) and (c) contemplate a screening arrangement. See Rule 1.0(k) (requirements for screening procedures). These paragraphs do not prohibit a lawyer from receiving a salary or partnership share established by prior independent agreement~~. They prohibit~~, but that lawyer may not receive compensation directly relating the lawyer's compensation to the fee in the matter in which the lawyer is disqualified.

[7] Notice, including a description of the screened lawyer's prior representation and of the screening procedures employed, generally should be given as soon as practicable after the need for screening becomes apparent.

~~[6] Paragraph (a)(2) does not require that a lawyer give notice to the government agency at a time when premature disclosure would injure the client; a requirement for premature disclosure might preclude engagement of the lawyer. Such notice is, however, required to be given as soon as practicable in order that the government agency will have a reasonable opportunity to ascertain that the lawyer is complying with Rule 1.11 and to take appropriate action if it believes the lawyer is not complying.~~

~~[7]~~ [8] Paragraph ~~(b)~~ (c) operates only when the lawyer in question has knowledge of the information, which means actual knowledge; it does not operate with respect to information that merely could be imputed to the lawyer.

~~[8]~~ [9] Paragraphs (a) and ~~(c)~~ (d) do not prohibit a lawyer from jointly representing a private party and a government agency when doing so is permitted by Rule 1.7 and is not otherwise prohibited by law.

~~[9] Paragraph (c) does not disqualify other lawyers in the agency with which the lawyer in question has become associated.~~

[10] For purposes of paragraph (e) of this Rule, a "matter" may continue in another form. In determining whether two particular matters are

the same, the lawyer should consider the extent to which the matters involve the same basic facts, the same or related parties, and the time elapsed.

Canon and Code Antecedents

ABA Canons of Professional Ethics: No comparable Canon.

ABA Model Code of Professional Responsibility: Compare DR 9-101(B) (reprinted later in this volume).

Cross-References in Other Rules

Rule 1.0, Comment 8: "Screened" "applies to situations where screening of a personally disqualified lawyer is permitted to remove imputation of a conflict of interest under **Rules 1.11**, 1.12 or 1.18."

Rule 1.9, Comment 1: "Current and former government lawyers must comply with this Rule to the extent required by **Rule 1.11**."

Rule 1.10(d): "The disqualification of lawyers associated in a firm with former or current government lawyers is governed by **Rule 1.11**."

Rule 1.10, Comment 7: "Where a lawyer has joined a private firm after having represented the government, imputation is governed by **Rule 1.11(b) and (c)**. . . . Under **Rule 1.11(d)**, where a lawyer represents the government after having served clients in private practice, nongovernmental employment or in another government agency, former-client conflicts are not imputed to government lawyers associated with the individually disqualified lawyer."

Rule 1.12, Comment 1: "This Rule generally parallels **Rule 1.11**. . . . Compare the Comment to **Rule 1.11**."

Rule 5.7, Comment 10: "When a lawyer is obliged to accord the recipients of such services the protections of those Rules that apply to the client-lawyer relationship, the lawyer must take special care to heed the proscriptions of the Rules addressing conflict of interest (Rules 1.7 through **1.11**, especially Rules 1.7 and 1.8(a), (b) and (f)). . . ."

Legislative History of Model Rule 1.11

1980 Discussion Draft:

> . . . (e) If a lawyer is required by this rule to decline representation on account of personal and substantial participation in a matter, except where the participation was as a judicial law clerk, no lawyer in a firm with the disqualified lawyer may accept such employment. . . .

1981 and 1982 Drafts were substantially the same as adopted.

2002 Amendments: In its May 2001 report to the ABA House of Delegates, the Ethics 2000 Commission proposed several changes to Rule 1.11, including a proposed new section (a)(1) to make clear that a lawyer who has formerly served as a public officer or governmental employee "is subject to Rules 1.9(a) and (b), except that 'matter' is defined as in paragraph (e) of this Rule." Before the House of Delegates debated the proposal at its February 2002 Mid-Year Meeting, however, the Commission revised its proposal by deleting the quoted paragraph (and renumbering the remaining sections of Rule 1.11(a) accordingly). At its February 2002 Mid-Year Meeting, the ABA House of Delegates adopted without change the revised ABA Ethics 2000 Commission proposal to amend Rule 1.11 and its Comment.

Selected State Variations

Arizona, Connecticut, Florida, Illinois, New Jersey, and ***Pennsylvania*** omit the law clerk exception to ABA Model Rule 1.11(c)(2).

California has no direct counterpart.

District of Columbia: D.C. Rule 1.11 differs significantly from the ABA Model Rule — see District of Columbia Rules of Professional Conduct below.

Georgia: In the rules effective January 1, 2001, Georgia adopted the pre-2002 version of ABA Model Rule 1.11 and its Comment essentially verbatim. In addition, Georgia adopted a new Rule 9.5 that provides as follows:

Rule 9.5 Lawyer as a Public Official

> (a) A lawyer who is a public official and represents the State, a municipal corporation in the State, the United States government, their agencies or officials, is bound by the provisions of these Rules.
>
> (b) No provision of these Rules shall be construed to prohibit such a lawyer from taking a legal position adverse to the State, a municipal corporation in the State, the United States government, their agencies or officials, when such action is authorized or required by the U.S. Constitution, the Georgia Constitution or statutes of the United States or Georgia.

Illinois: Rule 1.11(a) covers any lawyer who knows "or reasonably should know" of the former government lawyer's prior participation. Rules 1.11(a)(1) and 1.11(b) condition the exceptions on apportioning the disqualified lawyer "no specific share" of the fee.

Iowa adds DR 8-101(b): "County attorneys and assistant county attorneys shall not engage in the defense of an accused in any criminal matter during the time they are holding this public office."

Massachusetts: The law clerk exception in Rule 1.11(c)(2) is extended to law clerks working for mediators.

Missouri: Missouri Rule 1.11(c) omits the "law clerk" exception in ABA Model Rule 1.11(d)(2)(ii) as amended in 2002. In addition, effective October 19, 2001, Missouri amended its version of Rule 1.11 by dropping the word "Successive" from the title of the rule and inserting the following new paragraph (d):

> (d)(1) A lawyer who also holds public office, whether full or part-time, shall not engage in activities in which his or her personal or professional interests are or foreseeably could be in conflict with his or her official duties or responsibilities. A lawyer holding public office shall not attempt to influence any agency of any political subdivision of which such lawyer is a public officer, other than as a part of his or her official duties, or except as authorized in sections 105.450 to 105.496, RSMo.

(2) No lawyer in a firm in which a lawyer holding a public office is associated may undertake or continue representation in a matter in which the lawyer who holds public office would be disqualified, unless the lawyer holding public office is screened in the manner set forth in Rule 4.1.11(a).

New Hampshire adds a Rule 1.11A dealing with the responsibilities of "a lawyer actively engaged in the practice of law, who is a member of [a] governmental body."

New Jersey: Rules 1.11(a) and 1.11(b) provide:

> (a) Except as law may otherwise expressly permit, a lawyer shall not represent a private client in connection with a matter (1) in which the lawyer participated personally and substantially as a public officer or employee, (2) about which the lawyer acquired knowledge of confidential information as a public officer or employee, or (3) for which the lawyer had substantial responsibility as a public officer or employee.
>
> (b) An appearance of impropriety may arise from a lawyer representing a private client in connection with a matter that relates to the lawyer's former employment as public officer or employee even if the lawyer did not personally and substantially participate in it, have actual knowledge of it, or substantial responsibility for it. In such an event, the lawyer may not represent a private client, but a firm with which that lawyer is associated may undertake or continue representation if: (1) the disqualified lawyer is screened from any participation in the matter and is apportioned no part of the fee therefrom, and (2) written notice is promptly given to the appropriate government agency to enable it to ascertain compliance with the provisions of this rule.

New York: Compare ABA Model Rule 1.11 to New York's DR 9-101(B).

Pennsylvania provides in its comment that paragraphs (a)(1) and (b) "do not prohibit a lawyer from receiving a salary or distribution of firm profits established by prior independent agreement. They prohibit directly relating the attorney's compensation to the fee in the matter in which the lawyer is disqualified."

Rhode Island: Rule 1.11(a) excludes the words "personally and substantially" and provides that a lawyer "shall not represent a private client in connection with a matter in which the lawyer participated as a public officer or employee." Rhode Island also adds the following subparagraph (b) to Rule 1.11:

> Notwithstanding any other provisions of this Rule, a lawyer who has been employed by any government office or agency shall not represent a private client before that government office or agency for a period of one year following the termination of such employment.

Texas: Rules 1.10(c) and (d) apply to information that a lawyer "knows or should know" is confidential government information. Rule 1.10(f) specifically excludes "regulation-making" and "rule-making" from the definition of "matter."

Virginia replaces ABA Model Rule 1.11(a) with the language from DR 8-101(A) of the old ABA Model Code of Professional Responsibility, and modifies Rule 1.11(b) by allowing representation when "the private client and the appropriate government agency consent after consultation."

Related Materials

ABA Formal Ethics Opinions: See ABA Formal Ethics Op. 97-409 (1997).

American Lawyer's Code of Conduct: Rules 9.14 and 9.15 provide:

> 9.14. A lawyer shall not accept private employment relating to any matter in which the lawyer participated personally and substantially while in public service.

9.15. When a lawyer is disqualified from representing a client under Rule 9.14, no partner or associate of the lawyer, and no one with an of counsel relationship to the lawyer, shall represent the client.

Comment to Rules 9.14-9.15

. . . The principal argument in favor of permitting a screening-waiver device is that the government would find it impossible to hire competent lawyers if the screening-waiver exception is rejected, because lawyers would fear becoming unemployable. But if concern over the denial of waivers would indeed result in the unemployability of former government lawyers, that problem would prevail as long as there were any significant risk that waivers would be denied in particular cases. That is, unless the waiver device were a sham, and waivers were to be granted as a matter of course whenever requested, the asserted risks of hiring former government employees would still discourage law firms from employing them, and would thus discourage lawyers from entering government service.

In fact, however, no instance has ever been given of a government employee who would be rendered unemployable by the rejection of a waiver-screening exception. Unquestionably, a particular lawyer might have to forgo employment with a particular law firm, or even with three or four firms, but that is hardly the sweeping effect that has been projected by opponents of the ethical rule.

"Confidential Government Information": Model Rule 1.11(c) defines "confidential government information" to include information the government is "prohibited by law from disclosing" or "has a legal privilege not to disclose, " and (having satisfied one of those two criteria) that also is "not otherwise available to the public." As to prohibitions, various federal statutes prohibit disclosure—see, e.g., the Privacy Act, 5 U.S.C. §552a, and the Trade Secrets Act, 18 U.S.C. §1905. As to privileges, the government has successfully claimed various privileges under Federal Rule of Evidence 501, including the executive privilege, the deliberate privilege, the national security privilege, and the attorney-client privilege. As to availability to the public, the Freedom of Information Act (FOIA), 5 U.S.C. §552, makes a broad range of government information available to the public on demand.

IRS Regulations: In the regulations governing practice before the Internal Revenue Service, 31 C.F.R. §10.26, entitled "Practice by Former Government Employees, Their Partners and Their Associates," sets forth elaborate restrictions on former government attorneys and their law firms.

Restatement of the Law Governing Lawyers: See Restatement §§74, 97, 124, 133 in our chapter on the Restatement later in this volume.

"Revolving Door" Provisions: Rule 1.11(e)(2) refers to "the conflict of interest rules of the appropriate government agency." All former lawyers for the federal government are covered by the "revolving door" provision in 18 U.S.C. §207, which prohibits former government lawyers from opposing the government, either directly or in matters in which the government has "a direct and substantial interest," for two years after leaving government, if the lawyer was involved in the matter while in federal government service. See 5 C.F.R. §2637 for the general implementation of 18 U.S.C. §207. In addition, several agencies of the federal government have their own "revolving door" provisions. See e.g., 45 C.F.R. §680 (National Science Foundation), 32 C.F.R. §1690 (Selective Service System), 22 C.F.R. §18 (Foreign Service). Many states have enacted parallel provisions.

Rule 1.12 Former Judge ~~or~~, Arbitrator, Mediator or Other Third-Party Neutral

(a) Except as stated in paragraph (d), a lawyer shall not represent anyone in connection with a matter in which the lawyer participated personally and substantially as a judge or other adjudicative officer~~,~~ ~~arbitrator~~ or law clerk to such a person or as an arbitrator, mediator or other third-party neutral, unless all parties to the proceeding give informed consent ~~after consultation~~, confirmed in writing.

(b) A lawyer shall not negotiate for employment with any person who is involved as a party or as lawyer for a party in a matter in which the lawyer is participating personally and substantially as a judge or other adjudicative officer or as an arbitrator, mediator or other third-party neutral. A lawyer serving as a law clerk to a judge~~,~~ or other adjudicative officer ~~or arbitrator~~ may negotiate for employment with a party or lawyer involved in a matter in which the clerk is participating personally and substantially, but only after the lawyer has notified the judge~~,~~ or other adjudicative officer ~~or arbitrator~~.

(c) If a lawyer is disqualified by paragraph (a), no lawyer in a firm with which that lawyer is associated may knowingly undertake or continue representation in the matter unless:

(1) the disqualified lawyer is timely screened from any participation in the matter and is apportioned no part of the fee therefrom; and

(2) written notice is promptly given to the parties and any appropriate tribunal to enable ~~it~~ them to ascertain compliance with the provisions of this rule.

(d) An arbitrator selected as a partisan of a party in a multimember arbitration panel is not prohibited from subsequently representing that party.

COMMENT

[1] This Rule generally parallels Rule 1.11. The term "personally and substantially" signifies that a judge who was a member of a multimember court, and thereafter left judicial office to practice law, is not prohibited from representing a client in a matter pending in the court, but in which the former judge did not participate. So also the fact that a former judge exercised administrative responsibility in a court does not prevent the former judge from acting as a lawyer in a matter where the judge had previously exercised remote or incidental administrative responsibility that did not affect the merits. Compare the Comment to Rule 1.11. The term "adjudicative officer" includes such officials as judges pro tempore, referees, special masters, hearing officers and other parajudicial officers, and also lawyers who serve as part-time judges. Compliance Canons A(2),

B(2) and C of the Model Code of Judicial Conduct provide that a part-time judge, judge pro tempore or retired judge recalled to active service, may not "act as a lawyer in any proceeding in which he served as a judge or in any other proceeding related thereto." Although phrased differently from this Rule, those Rules correspond in meaning.

[2] Like former judges, lawyers who have served as arbitrators, mediators or other third-party neutrals may be asked to represent a client in a matter in which the lawyer participated personally and substantially. This Rule forbids such representation unless all of the parties to the proceedings give their informed consent, confirmed in writing. See Rule 1.0(e) and (b). Other law or codes of ethics governing third-party neutrals may impose more stringent standards of personal or imputed disqualification. See Rule 2.4.

[3] Although lawyers who serve as third-party neutrals do not have information concerning the parties that is protected under Rule 1.6, they typically owe the parties an obligation of confidentiality under law or codes of ethics governing third-party neutrals. Thus, paragraph (c) provides that conflicts of the personally disqualified lawyer will be imputed to other lawyers in a law firm unless the conditions of this paragraph are met.

[4] Requirements for screening procedures are stated in Rule 1.0(k). Paragraph (c)(1) does not prohibit the screened lawyer from receiving a salary or partnership share established by prior independent agreement, but that lawyer may not receive compensation directly related to the matter in which the lawyer is disqualified.

[5] Notice, including a description of the screened lawyer's prior representation and of the screening procedures employed, generally should be given as soon as practicable after the need for screening becomes apparent.

Canon and Code Antecedents

ABA Canons of Professional Ethics: Canon 36 provided as follows:

36. Retirement from Judicial Position or Public Employment

A lawyer should not accept employment as an advocate in any matter upon the merits of which he has previously acted in a judicial capacity.

A lawyer, having once held public office or having been in the public employ, should not after his retirement accept employment in connection with any matter which he has investigated or passed upon while in such office or employ.

ABA Model Code of Professional Responsibility: Compare DR 5-105(C) and DR 9-101(A) (reprinted later in this volume).

Cross-References in Other Rules

Preamble, ¶13: "Some of these Rules apply directly to lawyers who are or have served as third-party neutrals. See, e.g., **Rules 1.12** and 2.4."

Rule 1.0, Comment 8: "Screened" "applies to situations where screening of a personally disqualified lawyer is permitted to remove imputation of a conflict of interest under Rules 1.11, **1.12** or 1.18."

Rule 1.11(d): "[A] lawyer serving as a law clerk to a judge, other adjudicative officer or arbitrator may negotiate for private employment as permitted by **Rule 1.12(b)** and subject to the conditions stated in **Rule 1.12(b)**."

Rule 2.4, Comment 4: "A lawyer who serves as a third-party neutral subsequently may be asked to serve as a lawyer representing a client in the same matter. The conflicts of interest that arise for both the individual lawyer and the lawyer's law firm are addressed in **Rule 1.12**."

Legislative History of Model Rule 1.12

1980 Discussion Draft (then Rules 1.11(d), 1.11(e), and 1.11(f)):

> (d) A lawyer who has served as a judge in an adjudicatory proceeding shall not thereafter represent anyone in connection with the subject matter of the proceeding.
>
> (e) If a lawyer is required by this rule to decline representation on account of personal and substantial participation in a matter, except where the participation was as a judicial law clerk, no lawyer in a firm with the disqualified lawyer may accept such employment.
>
> (f) . . . The disqualification stated in paragraph (d) may be waived by the consent of all parties to the adjudication.

1981 and 1982 Drafts: Substantially the same as adopted.

2002 Amendments: At its February 2002 Mid-Year Meeting, the ABA House of Delegates adopted with only minor changes the ABA Ethics 2000 Commission proposal to amend Rule 1.12 and its Comment.

Selected State Variations

California has no direct counterpart to Rule 1.12.

District of Columbia: D.C. Rule 1.12 differs significantly from the ABA Model Rule — see District of Columbia Rules of Professional Conduct below.

Georgia: In the rules effective January 1, 2001, Georgia adopts ABA Model Rule 1.12 and its Comment almost verbatim. However, Georgia Rule 1.12(b) adds that a law clerk who accepts employment with a party or lawyer involved in a matter in which the clerk is participating personally and substantively "shall promptly provide written notice of acceptance of employment to all counsel of record in all such matters in which the prospective employee is involved."

Illinois: Rule 1.12(c) covers any lawyer who "knows or reasonably should know" of the former judge's or arbitrator's disqualification. Rule 1.12(c)(1) requires that the disqualified lawyer receive "no specific share" of the fee.

Massachusetts: The law clerk exception in Rule 1.12(b) is extended to law clerks working for mediators.

New Jersey deletes Rule 1.12(c).

New York: Compare ABA Model Rule 1.12 to New York's EC 5-20 and DR 9-101(A).

Texas has no equivalent to Rule 1.12(d).

Related Materials

Restatement of the Law Governing Lawyers: See Restatement §124 in our chapter on the Restatement later in this volume.

Code of Conduct for Law Clerks: In a student piece entitled Ethics for Judicial Clerks, 4 Geo. L.J. 771, 786-790 (1991), the author proposes a Code of Conduct for Law Clerks. Proposed Canon 3(D) of this Code, which relates to Model Rule 1.12(b), provides:

> A law clerk should inform the appointing judge of any circumstance or activity of the law clerk that might serve as a basis for disqualification of the judge, e.g., a prospective employment relation with a law firm, association of the law clerk's spouse with a law firm or litigant, etc.

Rule 1.13 Organization as Client

(a) A lawyer employed or retained by an organization represents the organization acting through its duly authorized constituents.

(b) If a lawyer for an organization knows that an officer, employee or other person associated with the organization is engaged in action, intends to act or refuses to act in a matter related to the representation that is a violation of a legal obligation to the organization, or a violation of law which reasonably might be imputed to the organization, and is likely to result in substantial injury to the organization, the lawyer shall proceed as is reasonably necessary in the best interest of the organization. In determining how to proceed, the lawyer shall give due consideration to the seriousness of the violation and its consequences, the scope and nature of the lawyer's representation, the responsibility in the organization and the apparent motivation of the person involved, the policies of the organization concerning such matters and any other relevant considerations. Any measures taken shall be designed to minimize disruption of the organization and the risk of revealing information relating to the representation to persons outside the organization. Such measures may include among others:

(1) asking for reconsideration of the matter;

(2) advising that a separate legal opinion on the matter be sought for presentation to appropriate authority in the organization; and

(3) referring the matter to higher authority in the organization, including, if warranted by the seriousness of the matter, referral to the highest authority that can act ~~in~~ on behalf of the organization as determined by applicable law.

(c) If, despite the lawyer's efforts in accordance with paragraph (b), the highest authority that can act on behalf of the organization insists upon action, or a refusal to act, that is clearly a violation of law and is likely to result in substantial injury to the organization, the lawyer may resign in accordance with Rule 1.16.

(d) In dealing with an organization's directors, officers, employees, members, shareholders or other constituents, a lawyer shall explain the identity of the client when ~~it is apparent~~ the lawyer knows or reasonably should know that the organization's interests are adverse to those of the constituents with whom the lawyer is dealing.

(e) A lawyer representing an organization may also represent any of its directors, officers, employees, members, shareholders or other constituents, subject to the provisions of Rule 1.7. If the organization's consent to the dual representation is required by Rule 1.7, the consent shall be given by an appropriate official of the organization other than the individual who is to be represented, or by the shareholders.

COMMENT

The Entity as the Client

[1] An organizational client is a legal entity, but it cannot act except through its officers, directors, employees, shareholders and other constituents. Officers, directors, employees and shareholders are the constituents of the corporate organizational client. The duties defined in this Comment apply equally to unincorporated associations. "Other constituents" as used in this Comment means the positions equivalent to officers, directors, employees and shareholders held by persons acting for organizational clients that are not corporations.

[2] When one of the constituents of an organizational client communicates with the organization's lawyer in that person's organizational capacity, the communication is protected by Rule 1.6. Thus, by way of example, if an organizational client requests its lawyer to investigate allegations of wrongdoing, interviews made in the course of that investigation between the lawyer and the client's employees or other constituents are covered by Rule 1.6. This does not mean, however, that constituents of an organizational client are the clients of the lawyer. The lawyer may not disclose to such constituents information relating to the representation except for disclosures explicitly or impliedly authorized by the organizational client in order to carry out the representation or as otherwise permitted by Rule 1.6.

[3] When constituents of the organization make decisions for it, the decisions ordinarily must be accepted by the lawyer even if their utility or prudence is doubtful. Decisions concerning policy and operations, including ones entailing serious risk, are not as such in the lawyer's province. However, different considerations arise when the lawyer knows that the organization may be substantially injured by action of a constituent that is in violation of law. In such a circumstance, it may be reasonably necessary for the lawyer to ask the constituent to reconsider the matter. If that fails, or if the matter is of sufficient seriousness and impor-

tance to the organization, it may be reasonably necessary for the lawyer to take steps to have the matter reviewed by a higher authority in the organization. Clear justification should exist for seeking review over the head of the constituent normally responsible for it. The stated policy of the organization may define circumstances and prescribe channels for such review, and a lawyer should encourage the formulation of such a policy. Even in the absence of organization policy, however, the lawyer may have an obligation to refer a matter to higher authority, depending on the seriousness of the matter and whether the constituent in question has apparent motives to act at variance with the organization's interest. Review by the chief executive officer or by the board of directors may be required when the matter is of importance commensurate with their authority. At some point it may be useful or essential to obtain an independent legal opinion.

[4] ~~In an extreme case, it may be reasonably necessary for the lawyer to refer the matter to the~~ The organization's highest authority~~. Ordinarily, that is~~ to whom a matter may be referred ordinarily will be the board of directors or similar governing body. However, applicable law may prescribe that under certain conditions the highest authority reposes elsewhere, for example, in the independent directors of a corporation.

Relation to Other Rules

[5] The authority and responsibility provided in ~~paragraph (b)~~ this Rule are concurrent with the authority and responsibility provided in other Rules. In particular, this Rule does not limit or expand the lawyer's responsibility under Rule 1.6, 1.8, 1.16, 3.3 or 4.1. If the lawyer's services are being used by an organization to further a crime or fraud by the organization, Rule 1.2(d) can be applicable.

Government Agency

[6] The duty defined in this Rule applies to governmental organizations. ~~However, when the client is a governmental organization, a different balance may be appropriate between maintaining confidentiality and assuring that the wrongful official act is prevented or rectified, for public business is involved. In addition, duties of lawyers employed by the government or lawyers in military service may be defined by statutes and regulation. Therefore, defining~~ Defining precisely the identity of the client and prescribing the resulting obligations of such lawyers may be more difficult in the government context and is a matter beyond the scope of these Rules. See Scope [18]. Although in some circumstances the client may be a specific agency, it ~~is generally~~ may also be a branch of government, such as the executive branch, or the government as a whole. For example, if

the action or failure to act involves the head of a bureau, either the department of which the bureau is a part or the relevant branch of government ~~as a whole~~ may be the client for ~~purpose~~ purposes of this Rule. Moreover, in a matter involving the conduct of government officials, a government lawyer may have authority under applicable law to question such conduct more extensively than that of a lawyer for a private organization in similar circumstances. Thus, when the client is a governmental organization, a different balance may be appropriate between maintaining confidentiality and assuring that the wrongful act is prevented or rectified, for public business is involved. In addition, duties of lawyers employed by the government or lawyers in military service may be defined by statutes and regulation. This Rule does not limit that authority. See ~~note on~~ Scope.

Clarifying the Lawyer's Role

[7] There are times when the organization's interest may be or become adverse to those of one or more of its constituents. In such circumstances the lawyer should advise any constituent, whose interest the lawyer finds adverse to that of the organization of the conflict or potential conflict of interest, that the lawyer cannot represent such constituent, and that such person may wish to obtain independent representation. Care must be taken to assure that the individual understands that, when there is such adversity of interest, the lawyer for the organization cannot provide legal representation for that constituent individual, and that discussions between the lawyer for the organization and the individual may not be privileged.

[8] Whether such a warning should be given by the lawyer for the organization to any constituent individual may turn on the facts of each case.

Dual Representation

[9] Paragraph (e) recognizes that a lawyer for an organization may also represent a principal officer or major shareholder.

Derivative Actions

[10] Under generally prevailing law, the shareholders or members of a corporation may bring suit to compel the directors to perform their legal obligations in the supervision of the organization. Members of unincorporated associations have essentially the same right. Such an action may be brought nominally by the organization, but usually is, in fact, a legal controversy over management of the organization.

[11] The question can arise whether counsel for the organization may defend such an action. The proposition that the organization is the lawyer's client does not alone resolve the issue. Most derivative actions are a normal incident of an organization's affairs, to be defended by the organization's lawyer like any other suit. However, if the claim involves serious charges of wrongdoing by those in control of the organization, a conflict may arise between the lawyer's duty to the organization and the lawyer's relationship with the board. In those circumstances, Rule 1.7 governs who should represent the directors and the organization.

Canon and Code Antecedents

ABA Canons of Professional Ethics: No comparable Canon.
ABA Model Code of Professional Responsibility: Compare DR 5-107(B) (reprinted later in this volume).

Cross-References in Other Rules

Rule 1.4, Comment 6: "When the client is an organization or group, it is often impossible or inappropriate to inform every one of its members about its legal affairs; ordinarily, the lawyer should address communications to the appropriate officials of the organization. See **Rule 1.13**."
Rule 1.6, Comment 14: If "the lawyer may be in doubt whether contemplated conduct will actually be carried out by the organization . . . the lawyer may make inquiry within the organization as indicated in **Rule 1.13(b)**."
Rule 1.7, Comment 34: "A lawyer who represents a corporation or other organization does not, by virtue of that representation, necessarily represent any constituent or affiliated organization, such as a parent or subsidiary. See **Rule 1.13(a)**."
Rule 1.11, Comment 5: "The question of whether two government agencies should be regarded as the same or different clients for conflict of interest purposes is beyond the scope of these Rules. See **Rule 1.13** Comment [6]."
Rule 4.3, Comment 1: "For misunderstandings that sometimes arise when a lawyer for an organization deals with an unrepresented constituent, see **Rule 1.13(d)**."

Legislative History of Model Rule 1.13

1980 Discussion Draft:

An Organization as the Client

(a) A lawyer employed or retained by an organization represents the organization as distinct from its directors, officers, employees, members, shareholders, or other constituents.

(b) If a lawyer for an organization knows that an officer, employee, or other person associated with the organization is engaged in or intends action, or a refusal to act, that is a violation of law and is likely to result in significant harm to the organization, the lawyer shall use reasonable efforts to prevent the harm. [The rest of subparagraph (b) was substantially the same as adopted.]

(c) If, despite the lawyer's efforts in accordance with paragraph (b), the highest authority that can act on behalf of the organization insists upon action, or a refusal to act, that is clearly a violation of law and is likely to result in substantial injury to the organization, the lawyer may take further remedial action, including disclosure of client confidences to the extent necessary, if the lawyer reasonably believes such action to be in the best interest of the organization.

(d) A lawyer representing an organization may also represent any of its directors, officers, members, or shareholders subject to the provisions of Rule 1.8. A lawyer undertaking such dual representation shall disclose that fact to an appropriate official of the organization other than the person so represented.

(e) When a shareholder or member of an organization brings a derivative action, the lawyer for the organization may act as its advocate only as permitted by Rule 1.8.

(f) In dealing with an organization's officials and employees, a lawyer shall explain the identity of the client when necessary to avoid embarrassment or unfairness to them.

1981 Draft: Rule 1.13(a) was the same as 1980 Draft. In Rule 1.13(b), a lawyer discovering conduct likely to result in "material" injury (rather than "significant" injury) to the corporation was to "proceed as is reasonably necessary in the best interest of the organization." Rule 1.13(c), describing remedial action, provided:

> Such action may include revealing information relating to the representation of the organization only if the lawyer reasonably believes that:
>
> (1) the highest authority in the organization has acted to further the personal or financial interests of members of that authority which are in conflict with the interests of the organization; and
>
> (2) revealing the information is necessary in the best interest of the organization.

1982 Draft: Substantially the same as 1981 Draft.

2002 Amendments: At its February 2002 Mid-Year Meeting, the ABA House of Delegates adopted without change the ABA Ethics 2000 Commission proposal to amend Rule 1.13 and its Comment.

Selected State Variations

Alaska: Rule 1.13(c), after stating that a lawyer may resign, adds "and shall act in accordance with the provisions of Rule 1.6." Rule 1.13(d) requires a lawyer to explain the identity of the client and "that the lawyer's first duty is to the client."

California: See Rule 3-600 (Organization as Client).

Colorado: Rule 1.13(a) adds that "the lawyer owes allegiance to the organization itself, and not its individual stockholders, directors, officers, employees, representatives or other persons connected with the entity." In addition, Rule 1.13(e) permits a lawyer to represent both the entity and its constituents "only in those instances in which the representation will not affect the lawyer's allegiance to the entity itself."

District of Columbia: D.C. Rule 1.13 differs significantly from the ABA Model Rule — see District of Columbia Rules of Professional Conduct below.

Georgia: In the rules effective January 1, 2001, Georgia adopted the pre-2002 version of ABA Model Rule 1.13 and its Comment almost verbatim, but added the following new paragraph (f): " 'Organization' as used herein includes governmental entities."

Maryland and ***Michigan:*** In both states, Rule 1.13(c) tracks the Kutak Commission's 1981 draft verbatim by providing that "remedial action" may, if necessary, include "revealing information otherwise protected by Rule 1.6" — but "only if the lawyer reasonably believes that: (1) the highest authority in the organization has acted to further the personal or financial interests of members of the authority which are in conflict with the interests of the organization; and (2) revealing the information is necessary in the best interest of the organization."

Michigan: Rule 1.13(a) tracks the Kutak Commission's 1980 draft by providing that a lawyer for an organization represents the organization "as distinct from" its directors, officers, employees, members, shareholders, or other constituents.

Minnesota deletes "and is likely to result in substantial injury to the organization" from Rule 1.13(b). In Rule 1.13(c), Minnesota provides: "If despite the lawyer's efforts in accordance with paragraph (b), a violation of law appears likely, the lawyer may resign in accordance with Rule 1.16 and if the violation is criminal or fraudulent, may reveal it."

New Jersey retains the language of Rule 1.13(a) as it appeared in the Kutak Commission's 1980 Draft: "(a) A lawyer employed or retained by an organization represents the organization as distinct from its directors, officers, employees, members, shareholders or other constituents." However, in 1996 New Jersey also added that for purposes of Rules 4.2 and 4.3 "the organization's lawyer shall be deemed to represent not only the organizational entity but also the members of its litigation control group," which is defined as follows:

> Members of the litigation control group shall be deemed to include current agents and employees responsible for, or significantly involved in, the determination of the organization's legal position in the matter whether or not in litigation, provided, however, that "significant involvement" requires involvement greater, and other than, the supplying of factual information or data respecting the matter. Former agents and employees who were members of the litigation control group shall presumptively be deemed to be represented in the matter by the organization's lawyer but may at any time disavow said representation.

New Jersey adds to Rule 1.13(c) that "remedial action" may include "revealing information otherwise protected by RPC 1.6" — but only if the lawyer reasonably believes that:

> (1) the highest authority in the organization has acted to further the personal or financial interests of members of that authority which are in conflict with the interests of the organization; and
> (2) revealing information is necessary in the best interest of the organization.

New Jersey Rule 1.13(d) requires a lawyer to explain the identity of the client "when the lawyer believes that such explanation is necessary to avoid misunderstanding. . . ."

New Jersey also adds a new subparagraph (f) that defines the term "organization" in Rule 1.13 to include "any corporation, partnership, association, joint stock company, union, trust, pension fund, unincorporated association, proprietorship or other business entity, state or local government or political subdivision thereof, or non-profit organization."

New York: Compare ABA Model Rule 1.13 to New York's DR 5-109.

Pennsylvania omits the phrases "the apparent motivation of the person involved" and "the policies of the organization concerning such matters" from Rule 1.13(b).

Texas: Rule 1.12(a) says that a lawyer retained or employed by an organization "represents the entity." Texas Rule 1.12(d) relieves the lawyer of responsibilities to the entity when the lawyer properly withdraws from the representation.

Texas Rule 1.12(e) (equivalent to ABA Model Rule 1.13(d)) requires a lawyer to explain the identity of the client "when explanation appears reasonably necessary to avoid misunderstanding. . . ."

Washington omits Rule 1.13.

Related Materials

ABA Formal Ethics Opinions: See ABA Formal Ethics Ops. 91-361 (1991), 92-365 (1992), and 99-415 (1999).

American Lawyer's Code of Conduct: Rule 2.5 provides:

> A lawyer representing a corporation shall, as early as possible in the lawyer-client relationship, inform the board of directors of potential conflicts that might develop among the interests of the board, corporate officers, and shareholders. The lawyer shall receive from the board instructions in advance as to how to resolve such conflicts, and shall take reasonable steps to ensure that officers with whom the lawyer deals, and the shareholders, are made aware of how the lawyer has been instructed to resolve conflicts of interest.

Model Rules of Professional Conduct for Federal Lawyers: Rule 1.13 provides (with emphasis added):

> (a) Except when representing another client pursuant to paragraphs (e), (f) and (g), a *Government lawyer represents the Federal Agency that employs the Government lawyer.* Government lawyers are often formally employed by a Federal Agency but assigned to an organizational element within the Federal Agency. Unless otherwise specifically provided, the Federal Agency, not the organizational element, is ordinarily considered the client. The Federal Agency acts through its authorized officials. These officials include the heads of organizational elements within the Federal Agency. When a Government lawyer is assigned to an organizational element and designated to provide legal services and advice to the head of that organization, the client-lawyer relationship exists between the Government lawyer and the Federal Agency, as represented by the head of the organization. *The head of the organization may only invoke the attorney-client privilege or the rule of confidentiality for the benefit of the Federal Agency.* In so invoking either the attorney-client privilege or attorney-client confidentiality on behalf of the Federal Agency, the head of the organization is subject to being overruled by higher agency authority.
>
> (b) . . . [The measures a Government lawyer may take] may include, among others: . . .
>
> (3) Advising the person that the lawyer is ethically obligated to preserve the interests of the Federal agency and, as a result, must consider discussing the mat-

ter with supervisory lawyers within the Government lawyer's office or at a higher level within the Federal Agency.

(c) If, despite the Government lawyer's efforts in accordance with paragraph (b), the highest authority that can act concerning the matter insists upon action, or refusal to act, that is clearly a violation of law, the Government lawyer shall terminate representation with respect to the matter in question. In no event may the Government lawyer participate or assist in the illegal activity. . . .

(e) A Government lawyer shall not form a client-lawyer relationship or represent a client other than the Federal Agency unless specifically authorized or authorized by competent authority. . . .

(g) A Government lawyer who has been duly assigned or authorized to represent an individual who is subject to disciplinary action or administrative proceedings, or to provide civil legal assistance to an individual, has, for those purposes, a lawyer-client relationship with that individual.

The Comment to these Rules states, in part, as follows:

Except when a Government lawyer is assigned to represent the interest of another client, the Federal Agency that employs the Government lawyer is the client. This principle is critical to the application of these Rules, since the identity of the client affects significant confidentiality and conflict issues.

. . . Although arguments have been made that the Government lawyer's ultimate obligation is to serve the public interest or the "government as a whole," for practical purposes, these may be unworkable ethical guidelines, particularly with regard to client control and confidentiality.

A Federal Agency may, of course, establish different client-lawyer obligations by Executive or court order, regulation, or statute. See e.g., 5 U.S.C. 2302.

Restatement of the Law Governing Lawyers: See Restatement §§73, 85, 96, 97, 131 in our chapter on the Restatement later in this volume.

SEC Rules: In July of 2002, in the midst of public outrage over corporate scandals at Enron, Tyco, WorldCom, Global Crossing, and other companies, Congress enacted the Sarbanes-Oxley Act of 2002 (which passed the Senate as the Public Company Accounting Reform and Investor Protection Act). Among the provisions of this lengthy and complex act is the following §307, which is closely related to ABA Model Rules 1.13(b) and (c):

(d) *Rule of Professional Responsibility for Attorneys.* Not later than 180 days after the date of enactment of this section, the [Securities and Exchange] Commission shall establish rules, in the public interest and for the protection of investors, setting forth minimum standards of professional conduct for attorneys appearing and practicing before the Commission in any way in the representation of issuers, including a rule —

(1) requiring an attorney to report evidence of a material violation of securities law or breach of fiduciary duty or similar violation by the company or any agent thereof, to the chief legal counsel or the chief executive officer of the company (or the equivalent thereof) and

(2) if the counsel or officer does not appropriately respond to the evidence (adopting, as necessary, appropriate remedial measures or sanctions with respect to the violation), requiring the attorney to report the evidence to the audit committee of the board of directors of the issuer or to another committee of the board of directors comprised solely of directors not employed directly or indirectly by the issuer, or to the board of directors.

Rule 1.14 Client ~~Under a Disability~~ with Diminished Capacity

(a) When a client's ~~ability~~ capacity to make adequately considered decisions in connection with ~~the~~ a representation is ~~impaired~~ diminished, whether because of minority, mental ~~disability~~ impairment or for some other reason, the lawyer shall, as far as reasonably possible, maintain a normal client-lawyer relationship with the client.

(b) ~~A lawyer may seek the appointment of a guardian or take other protective action with respect to a client only when~~ When the lawyer reasonably believes that the client has diminished capacity, is at risk of substantial physical, financial or other harm unless action is taken and cannot adequately act in the client's own interest, the lawyer may take reasonably necessary protective action, including consulting with individuals or entities that have the ability to take action to protect the client and, in appropriate cases, seeking the appointment of a guardian ad litem, conservator or guardian.

(c) Information relating to the representation of a client with diminished capacity is protected by Rule 1.6. When taking protective action pursuant to paragraph (b), the lawyer is impliedly authorized under Rule 1.6(a) to reveal information about the client, but only to the extent reasonably necessary to protect the client's interests.

COMMENT

[1] The normal client-lawyer relationship is based on the assumption that the client, when properly advised and assisted, is capable of making decisions about important matters. When the client is a minor or suffers from a diminished mental capacity ~~disorder or disability~~, however, maintaining the ordinary client-lawyer relationship may not be possible in all respects. In particular, ~~an~~ a severely incapacitated person may have no power to make legally binding decisions. Nevertheless, a client ~~lacking legal competence~~ with diminished capacity often has the ability to understand, deliberate upon, and reach conclusions about matters affecting the client's own well-being. ~~Furthermore, to an increasing extent the law recognizes intermediate degrees of competence.~~ For example, children as young as five or six years of age, and certainly those of ten or twelve, are regarded as having opinions that are entitled to weight in legal proceedings concerning their custody. So also, it is recognized that some persons of advanced age can be quite capable of handling routine financial matters while needing special legal protection concerning major transactions.

[2] The fact that a client suffers a disability does not diminish the lawyer's obligation to treat the client with attention and respect. ~~If the person has no guardian or legal representative, the lawyer often must act as de facto guardian.~~ Even if the person ~~does have~~ has a legal representa-

tive, the lawyer should as far as possible accord the represented person the status of client, particularly in maintaining communication.

[3] The client may wish to have family members or other persons participate in discussions with the lawyer. When necessary to assist in the representation, the presence of such persons generally does not affect the applicability of the attorney-client evidentiary privilege. Nevertheless, the lawyer must keep the client's interests foremost and, except for protective action authorized under paragraph (b), must look to the client, and not family members, to make decisions on the client's behalf.

~~[3]~~ [4] If a legal representative has already been appointed for the client, the lawyer should ordinarily look to the representative for decisions on behalf of the client. ~~If a legal representative has not been appointed, the lawyer should see to such an appointment where it would serve the client's best interests. Thus, if a disabled client has substantial property that should be sold for the client's benefit, effective completion of the transaction ordinarily requires appointment of a legal representative. In many circumstances, however, appointment of a legal representative may be expensive or traumatic for the client. Evaluation of these considerations is a matter of professional judgment on the lawyer's part.~~ In matters involving a minor, whether the lawyer should look to the parents as natural guardians may depend on the type of proceeding or matter in which the lawyer is representing the minor. ~~[4]~~ If the lawyer represents the guardian as distinct from the ward, and is aware that the guardian is acting adversely to the ward's interest, the lawyer may have an obligation to prevent or rectify the guardian's misconduct. See Rule 1.2(d).

Taking Protective Action

[5] If a lawyer reasonably believes that a client is at risk of substantial physical, financial or other harm unless action is taken, and that a normal client-lawyer relationship cannot be maintained as provided in paragraph (a) because the client lacks sufficient capacity to communicate or to make adequately considered decisions in connection with the representation, then paragraph (b) permits the lawyer to take protective measures deemed necessary. Such measures could include: consulting with family members, using a reconsideration period to permit clarification or improvement of circumstances, using voluntary surrogate decisionmaking tools such as durable powers of attorney or consulting with support groups, professional services, adult-protective agencies or other individuals or entities that have the ability to protect the client. In taking any protective action, the lawyer should be guided by such factors as the wishes and values of the client to the extent known, the client's best interests and the goals of intruding into the client's decisionmaking autonomy to the least extent feasible, maximizing client capacities and respecting the client's family and social connections.

[6] In determining the extent of the client's diminished capacity, the lawyer should consider and balance such factors as: the client's ability to articulate reasoning leading to a decision; variability of state of mind and ability to appreciate consequences of a decision; the substantive fairness of a decision; and the consistency of a decision with the known long-term commitments and values of the client. In appropriate circumstances, the lawyer may seek guidance from an appropriate diagnostician.

[7] If a legal representative has not been appointed, the lawyer should consider whether appointment of a guardian ad litem, conservator or guardian is necessary to protect the client's interests. Thus, if a client with diminished capacity has substantial property that should be sold for the client's benefit, effective completion of the transaction may require appointment of a legal representative. In addition, rules of procedure in litigation sometimes provide that minors or persons with diminished capacity must be represented by a guardian or next friend if they do not have a general guardian. In many circumstances, however, appointment of a legal representative may be more expensive or traumatic for the client than circumstances in fact require. Evaluation of such circumstances is a matter entrusted to the professional judgment of the lawyer. In considering alternatives, however, the lawyer should be aware of any law that requires the lawyer to advocate the least restrictive action on behalf of the client.

Disclosure of the Client's Condition

~~[5]~~ [8] ~~Rules of procedure in litigation generally provide that minors or persons suffering mental disability shall be represented by a guardian or next friend if they do not have a general guardian. However, disclosure~~ Disclosure of the client's ~~disability can~~ diminished capacity could adversely affect the client's interests. For example, raising the question of ~~disability~~ diminished capacity could, in some circumstances, lead to proceedings for involuntary commitment. Information relating to the representation is protected by Rule 1.6. Therefore, unless authorized to do so, the lawyer may not disclose such information. When taking protective action pursuant to paragraph (b), the lawyer is impliedly authorized to make the necessary disclosures, even when the client directs the lawyer to the contrary. Nevertheless, given the risks of disclosure, paragraph (c) limits what the lawyer may disclose in consulting with other individuals or entities or seeking the appointment of a legal representative. At the very least, the lawyer should determine whether it is likely that the person or entity consulted with will act adversely to the client's interests before discussing matters related to the client. The lawyer's position in such cases is an unavoidably difficult one. ~~The lawyer may seek guidance from an appropriate diagnostician.~~

Emergency Legal Assistance

~~[6]~~ <u>[9]</u> In an emergency where the health, safety or a financial interest of a person ~~under a disability~~ <u>with seriously diminished capacity</u> is threatened with imminent and irreparable harm, a lawyer may take legal action on behalf of such a person even though the person is unable to establish a client-lawyer relationship or to make or express considered judgments about the matter, when the ~~disabled~~ person or another acting in good faith on that person's behalf has consulted <u>with</u> the lawyer. Even in such an emergency, however, the lawyer should not act unless the lawyer reasonably believes that the person has no other lawyer, agent or other representative available. The lawyer should take legal action on behalf of the ~~disabled~~ person only to the extent reasonably necessary to maintain the status quo or otherwise avoid imminent and irreparable harm. A lawyer who undertakes to represent a person in such an exigent situation has the same duties under these Rules as the lawyer would with respect to a client.

~~[7]~~ <u>[10]</u> A lawyer who acts on behalf of a ~~disabled~~ person <u>with seriously diminished capacity</u> in an emergency should keep the confidences of the ~~disabled~~ person as if dealing with a client, disclosing them only to the extent necessary to accomplish the intended protective action. The lawyer should disclose to any tribunal involved and to any other counsel involved the nature of his or her relationship with the ~~disabled~~ person. The lawyer should take steps to regularize the relationship or implement other protective solutions as soon as possible. Normally, a lawyer would not seek compensation for such emergency actions taken ~~on behalf of a disabled person~~.

Canon and Code Antecedents

ABA Canons of Professional Ethics: No comparable Canon.

ABA Model Code of Professional Responsibility: No comparable Disciplinary Rule.

Cross-References in Other Rules

Rule 1.2, Comment 4: "In a case in which the client appears to be suffering diminished capacity, the lawyer's duty to abide by the client's decisions is to be guided by reference to **Rule 1.14**."

Rule 1.4, Comment 6: A client is to be provided with information appropriate for a "comprehending and responsible adult. However, . . . this standard may be impracticable, for example, where the client is a child or suffers from diminished capacity. See **Rule 1.14**."

Rule 1.16, Comment 6: "If the client has severely diminished capacity, the client may lack the legal capacity to discharge the lawyer, and in any event the discharge may be seriously adverse to the client's interests. The lawyer should make special effort to help the client consider the consequences and may take reasonably necessary protective action as provided in **Rule 1.14**."

Legislative History of Model Rule 1.14

1980 Discussion Draft:

> . . . (b) A lawyer shall secure the appointment of a guardian or other legal representative, or seek a protective order with respect to a client, when doing so is necessary in the client's best interests.

1981 Draft: Rule 1.14(a) was the same as the version finally adopted. Rule 1.14(b) required a lawyer to seek appointment of a guardian or a protective order "only when the lawyer reasonably believes that the client cannot adequately communicate or exercise judgment in the client-lawyer relationship."

1982 Draft was adopted.

1995 Proposal: In May 1995, the ABA Commission on Legal Problems of the Elderly filed a proposal to amend Rule 1.14. However, the proposal was withdrawn during the ABA's August 1995 Annual Meeting. The proposal would not have touched Rule 1.14(a), but would have revised Rule 1.14(b) and added new sections 1.14(c), (d), and (e) so that those sections would have provided as follows:

> (b) A lawyer may take protective action or seek the appointment of a guardian only when the lawyer reasonably believes the client cannot adequately act in the client's own interest.
>
> (c) While it might be necessary to disclose information, the disclosure should be strictly limited to that which is necessary to accomplish the protective purpose.
>
> (d) (1) A lawyer is an agent who acts upon the authority of a principal. In many cases, the lawyer will have a pre-existing relationship with a person or that person's family. In the absence of such a pre-existing relationship or a contractual agreement, express or implied, a lawyer generally may not act on behalf of a client.
>
> (2) In certain circumstances, a lawyer may act as lawyer for a purported client even without express or limited agreement from the purported client, and may take those actions necessary to maintain the status quo or to avoid irreversible harm, if
>
> (i) An emergency situation exists in which the purported client's substantial health, safety, financial, or liability interests would be irreparably damaged;
>
> (ii) The purported client, in the lawyer's good faith judgment, lacks the ability to make or express considered judgments about action required to be taken because of an impairment of decision-making capacity;
>
> (iii) Time is of the essence; and
>
> (iv) The lawyer reasonably believes in good faith that no other lawyer who has an established relationship with the purported client is available or willing to act on behalf of the purported client.
>
> (3) A "purported client" is a person who has contact with a lawyer and who would be a client but for the inability to enter into an express agreement.
>
> (e) The lawyer should not be subject to professional discipline for invoking or failing to invoke the permissive conduct authorized by 1.14(b) if the lawyer has a reasonable basis for his or her action or inaction.

The proposal was accompanied by an eleven-page report, which explained that the genesis of the proposal was a conference on Ethical Issues in Representing Older Clients held at Fordham University Law School in December 1993. Much of the report quoted or cited papers from that conference, which are published in 62 Fordham L. Rev. (March 1994).

1997 Amendment: At its 1997 Mid-Year Meeting the ABA House of Delegates voted to add two new paragraphs to the Comment to Rule 1.14. (The amendment did not alter the text of Rule 1.14 or the existing Comment.) The new paragraphs, which were co-sponsored by the ABA Standing Committee on Ethics and Professional Responsibility and the ABA Commission on Legal Problems of the Elderly, are an outgrowth of amendments to the text of Rule 1.14 that the Commission proposed in 1995. They explain what a lawyer should do in an "emergency" that threatens the health, safety or financial interest of a disabled person who is not yet a client. The new paragraphs should be read in conjunction with ABA Ethics Op. 96-404 (1996), which addressed ethical issues that arise when existing clients are no longer mentally capable of handling their own affairs. The House of Delegates approved the new paragraphs exactly as proposed, by an overwhelming voice vote. We reprint here excerpts from the ABA Committee Report submitted in support of the 1997 amendment.

*ABA Report Explaining 1997 Amendment to Comment**

> [A] lawyer may reasonably conclude that an elderly person who has not been judged incompetent is in need of emergency legal assistance, but is, or appears to be, unable to make decisions on his or her own behalf — including a decision to retain a lawyer. Such situations fall most naturally within the spirit of Model Rule 1.14 ("Client Under a Disability"). The question is whether it is ethically permissible for a lawyer to take legal action on behalf of a disabled person who cannot, in the first instance, form a client-lawyer relationship.
>
> The question whether and under what circumstances a lawyer may take emergency legal action on behalf of a disabled person who is not a client is not, of course, unique to the representation of the elderly. It may arise in a variety of practice settings where individuals appear to be in need of immediate legal assistance but are unable to make adequately considered decisions in connection with initiating legal representation.
>
> Most of the duties arising under the Model Rules (the most notable exception being that of confidentiality) attach only after the formation of a client-lawyer relationship, and the Rules are silent with respect to any forms of representation that do not arise from such relationship. . . .
>
> However, the Committee believes that such emergency action is permissible under the Model Rules, if properly limited. . . .

2002 Amendments: At its February 2002 Mid-Year Meeting, the ABA House of Delegates adopted without change the ABA Ethics 2000 Commission proposal to amend Rule 1.14 and its Comment.

Selected State Variations

California has no counterpart to Rule 1.14.

Colorado: Rule 1.14(b) contains the following additional language:

> Not only can the mental, physical or other condition of the client impose additional responsibilities on the lawyer, the fact that a client is impaired does not relieve the lawyer of the obligation to obtain information from the client to the extent possible.

*Committee Reports do not represent official policy of the ABA. They are for information only, and the opinions are those of the authors of the report.

Georgia: In the rules effective January 1, 2001, Georgia adopted the pre-2002 version of ABA Model Rule 1.14 verbatim, but omitted the word "only" from Rule 1.14(b) and deleted the paragraphs of the Comment relating to emergency legal assistance.

Massachusetts: Rule 1.14(b) permits a lawyer who reasonably believes that a client lacks capacity as described in Rule 1.14(a) to consult "family members, adult protective agencies, or other individuals or entities that have authority to protect the client, and, if it reasonably appears necessary, the lawyer may seek the appointment of a guardian ad litem, conservator, or guardian, as the case may be."

New York: Compare ABA Model Rule 1.14 to New York's EC 7-11 and EC 7-12.

Pennsylvania substitutes "should" for "shall" in Rule 1.14(a).

South Carolina has adopted a set of "guidelines" for lawyers (and non-lawyer professionals) who are appointed as guardians ad litem for children in most family court cases. The guidelines can be found at www.scbar.org/guidelines_for_guardian_ad_litem.htm.

Texas: Rule 1.02(g) provides:

> A lawyer shall take reasonable action to secure the appointment of a guardian or other legal representative for, or seek other protective orders with respect to, a client whenever the lawyer reasonably believes that the client lacks legal competence and that such action should be taken to protect the client.

Related Materials

American Academy of Matrimonial Lawyers: The "Bounds of Advocacy" contains the following provision:

> 1.2 An attorney should be sensitive to common emotional and psychological problems. When an attorney believes that such problems are interfering with effective representation or with the client's ability to function, he should suggest that the client seek the help of a mental health professional.

ABA Formal Ethics Opinions: See ABA Formal Ethics Ops. 92-364 (1992) and 96-404 (1996).

Americans with Disabilities Act: All lawyers, especially those whose clients include people with disabilities, must adhere to Title III of the Americans with Disabilities Act, which took effect in January 1992. Section 302(a) of Title III, 42 U.S.C. §12182(a), states the general rule:

> No individual shall be discriminated against on the basis of disability in the full and equal enjoyment of the goods, services, facilities, privileges, advantages, or accommodations of any place of public accommodation by any person who owns, leases (or leases to), or operates a place of public accommodation.

(A "public accommodation" includes any law firm open to the public.)

Restatement of the Law Governing Lawyers: See Restatement §24 in our chapter on the Restatement later in this volume.

Rule 1.15 Safekeeping Property

(a) A lawyer shall hold property of clients or third persons that is in a lawyer's possession in connection with a representation separate from the lawyer's own property. Funds shall be kept in a separate account maintained in the state where the lawyer's office is situated, or elsewhere with the consent of the client or third person. Other property shall be identified as such and appropriately safeguarded. Complete records of such account funds and other property shall be kept by the lawyer and shall be preserved for a period of [five years] after termination of the representation.

(b) A lawyer may deposit the lawyer's own funds in a client trust account for the sole purpose of paying bank service charges on that account, but only in an amount necessary for that purpose.

(c) A lawyer shall deposit into a client trust account legal fees and expenses that have been paid in advance, to be withdrawn by the lawyer only as fees are earned or expenses incurred.

~~(b)~~ (d) Upon receiving funds or other property in which a client or third person has an interest, a lawyer shall promptly notify the client or third person. Except as stated in this rule or otherwise permitted by law or by agreement with the client, a lawyer shall promptly deliver to the client or third person any funds or other property that the client or third person is entitled to receive and, upon request by the client or third person, shall promptly render a full accounting regarding such property.

~~(c)~~ (e) When in the course of representation a lawyer is in possession of property in which ~~both~~ two or more persons (one of whom may be the lawyer ~~and another person~~) claim interests, the property shall be kept separate by the lawyer until ~~there is an accounting and severance of their interests. If a dispute arises concerning their respective interests, the portion in dispute shall be kept separate by the lawyer until~~ the dispute is resolved. The lawyer shall promptly distribute all portions of the property as to which the interests are not in dispute.

COMMENT

[1] A lawyer should hold property of others with the care required of a professional fiduciary. Securities should be kept in a safe deposit box, except when some other form of safekeeping is warranted by special circumstances. All property that is the property of clients or third persons ~~should~~, including prospective clients, must be kept separate from the lawyer's business and personal property and, if monies, in one or more trust accounts. Separate trust accounts may be warranted when administering estate monies or acting in similar fiduciary capacities. A lawyer should maintain on a current basis books and records in accordance with generally accepted accounting practice and comply with any recordkeeping rules

established by law or court order. See, e.g., ABA Model Financial Recordkeeping Rule.

[2] While normally it is impermissible to commingle the lawyer's own funds with client funds, paragraph (b) provides that it is permissible when necessary to pay bank service charges on that account. Accurate records must be kept regarding which part of the funds are the lawyer's.

~~[2]~~ [3] Lawyers often receive funds from ~~third parties from~~ which the lawyer's fee will be paid. ~~If there is risk that the client may divert the funds without paying the fee, the~~ The lawyer is not required to remit ~~the portion from which the fee is to be paid~~ to the client funds that the lawyer reasonably believes represent fees owed. However, a lawyer may not hold funds to coerce a client into accepting the lawyer's contention. The disputed portion of the funds ~~should~~ must be kept in a trust account and the lawyer should suggest means for prompt resolution of the dispute, such as arbitration. The undisputed portion of the funds shall be promptly distributed.

~~[3]~~ [4] ~~Third~~ Paragraph (e) also recognizes that third parties~~, such as a client's creditors,~~ may have ~~just~~ lawful claims against specific funds or other property in a lawyer's custody, such as a client's creditor who has a lien on funds recovered in a personal injury action. A lawyer may have a duty under applicable law to protect such third-party claims against wrongful interference by the client~~, and accordingly may~~. In such cases, when the third-party claim is not frivolous under applicable law, the lawyer must refuse to surrender the property to the client until the claims are resolved. ~~However, a~~ A lawyer should not unilaterally assume to arbitrate a dispute between the client and the third party, but, when there are substantial grounds for dispute as to the person entitled to the funds, the lawyer may file an action to have a court resolve the dispute.

~~[4]~~ [5] The obligations of a lawyer under this Rule are independent of those arising from activity other than rendering legal services. For example, a lawyer who serves only as an escrow agent is governed by the applicable law relating to fiduciaries even though the lawyer does not render legal services in the transaction and is not governed by this Rule.

~~[5]~~ [6] A ~~"clients' security~~ lawyers' fund" for client protection provides a means through the collective efforts of the bar to reimburse persons who have lost money or property as a result of dishonest conduct of a lawyer. Where such a fund has been established, a lawyer must participate where it is mandatory, and, even when it is voluntary, the lawyer should participate.

Canon and Code Antecedents

ABA Canons of Professional Ethics: Canon 11 provided as follows:

11. Dealing with Trust Property

The lawyer should refrain from any action whereby for his personal benefit or gain he abuses or takes advantage of the confidence reposed in him by his client.

> Money of the client or collected for the client or other trust property coming into the possession of the lawyer should be reported and accounted for promptly, and should not under any circumstances be commingled with his own or be used by him.

ABA Model Code of Professional Responsibility: Compare DR 9-102(A) and DR 9-102(B) (reprinted later in this volume).

Cross-References in Other Rules

Rule 1.16, Comment 9: "Even if the lawyer has been unfairly discharged by the client, a lawyer must take all reasonable steps to mitigate the consequences to the client. The lawyer may retain papers as security for a fee only to the extent permitted by law. See **Rule 1.15**."

Rule 1.18, Comment 9: "For a lawyer's duties when a prospective client entrusts valuables or papers to the lawyer's care, see **Rule 1.15**."

Legislative History of Model Rule 1.15

1980 Discussion Draft (then Rule 1.12) provided in (a) that funds "shall be kept in a trust account." Subparagraph (d) provided:

> (d) When a lawyer and another person both have interests in property, the property shall be treated by the lawyer as trust property until an accounting and severance of their interests. If a dispute arises concerning their respective interests, the portion in dispute shall be treated as trust property until the dispute is resolved.

1981 and 1982 Drafts were substantially the same as adopted.

2002 Amendments: At its February 2002 Mid-Year Meeting, the ABA House of Delegates adopted without change the ABA Ethics 2000 Commission proposal to amend Rule 1.15 and its Comment.

Selected State Variations

Alabama: Rule 1.15(a) provides that "[n]o personal funds of a lawyer shall ever be deposited in such a trust account, except (1) unearned attorney fees that are being held until earned, and (2) funds sufficient to cover maintenance fees, such as service charges, on the account." Rule 1.15(g) requires lawyers to maintain short-term or nominal client funds in an interest-bearing account that remits the interest at least quarterly to the Alabama Law Foundation or the Alabama Civil Justice Foundation. Rules 1.15(i) and (j) state the many purposes of the Alabama Law Foundation and the Alabama Civil Justice Foundation.

Alaska adds Rule 1.15(d), which provides that unless a lawyer submits an election not to participate, "a lawyer or law firm shall establish and maintain an interest bearing insured depository account into which must be deposited funds of clients which are nominal in amount or are expected to be held for a short period of time." The rule then sets forth detailed rules governing such accounts.

California: See Rule 4-100 (Preserving Identity of Funds and Property of a Client) and accompanying standards.

In addition, §710 of the California Probate Code, entitled "Preservation of Documents Transferred to Attorney," provides that "[i]f a document is deposited with an attorney, the attorney . . . shall use ordinary care for preservation of the document . . . whether or not consideration is given, and shall hold the document in a safe, vault, safe deposit box, or other secure place where it will be reasonably protected against loss or destruction." Probate Code §711 provides that if a document deposited with an attorney is lost or destroyed, "the attorney shall give notice of the loss or destruction to the depositor. . . ." However, §712 provides that an attorney "is not liable for loss or destruction of the document if the depositor has actual notice of the loss or destruction and a reasonable opportunity to replace the document, and the attorney offers without charge either to assist the depositor in replacing the document, or to prepare a substantially similar document and assist in its execution."

Colorado: Colorado Rule 1.15(f)(6) requires that attorneys maintain trust funds in financial institutions "approved by the Regulation Counsel" (Colorado's disciplinary authority). A financial institution will be "approved" only if it files an agreement to "report to the Regulation Counsel in the event any properly payable trust account instrument is presented against insufficient funds, irrespective of whether the instrument is honored."

In May of 2000, construing Colorado Rule 1.15(f)(1) (which requires "any advance payment of fees that has not been earned" to be deposited into a trust account), the Colorado Supreme Court held that an attorney "must keep advance fees in a separate trust account until the attorney performs legal services or otherwise confers a benefit on the client. . . ." See In re Sather, 2000 WL 655914 (Colo. May 22, 2000), *modified on denial of rehearing* (June 12, 2000). However, because "many attorneys collect flat fees in advance of performing work and place the fees in their operating accounts upon receipt" and its holding in *Sather* would therefore have "widespread practical implications," the Supreme Court asked the Colorado Bar Association to "solicit widespread comment from practicing attorneys and then draft proposed Rules that would implement the ethical principles that we today announce." In May of 2001, the Colorado Bar Association forwarded a proposed rule to the Colorado Supreme Court. After considerable discussion in bar association committees, the Colorado Supreme Court adopted the following new Rule 1.15(f) effective July 1, 2002:

> Fees are not earned until the lawyer confers a benefit on the client or performs a legal service for the client. Advances of unearned fees are the property of the client and shall be deposited in the lawyer's trust account pursuant to Rule 1.15(f)(1) until earned. If advances of unearned fees are in the form of property other than funds, then the lawyer shall hold such property separate from the lawyer's own property pursuant to Rule 1.15(a).

Connecticut adds Rule 1.15(d), which generally requires lawyers to deposit client funds in an interest-bearing account if the funds are less than $10,000 or are expected to be held for no more than 60 business days. The interest provides funding for "(i) the delivery of legal services to the poor by nonprofit corporations whose principal purpose is providing legal services to the poor and (ii) law school scholarships based on financial need." The rule contains detailed provisions, amended in 1997, regarding interest rates, recordkeeping, reporting, audits, and other matters. The final subparagraph provides:

> Nothing in this section shall prevent a lawyer or law firm from depositing a client's funds, regardless of the amount of such funds or the period for which such

funds are expected to be held, in a separate interest-bearing account established on behalf of and for the benefit of the client.

Delaware adds a long list of requirements to Rule 1.15.

District of Columbia: D.C. Rule 1.15 differs significantly from the ABA Model Rule, and D.C.'s version of Rule 1.17 deals with notification of trust account overdrafts — see District of Columbia Rules of Professional Conduct below.

Florida: Chapter 5 of the Supreme Court Rules extensively regulates lawyer trust accounts.

Georgia: In the rules effective January 1, 2001, Georgia Rule 1.15(I) generally tracks ABA Model Rule 1.15, with some modification. Georgia adds Rule 1.15(II) to govern trust accounts and IOLTA accounts, and Rule 1.15(III) to govern trust account recordkeeping, overdraft notification, and auditing by disciplinary authorities. Rule 1.15(III) requires that lawyers deposit trust funds in a financial institution that agrees "to report to the State Disciplinary Board whenever any properly payable instrument is presented against a lawyer trust account containing insufficient funds, and the instrument is not honored." The Comment to Rule 1.15(III) explains the overdraft agreement as follows:

> [2] The overdraft agreement requires that all overdrafts be reported to the Office of General Counsel of the State Bar of Georgia whether or not the instrument is honored. It is improper for a lawyer to accept "overdraft privileges" or any other arrangement for a personal loan on a client trust account, particularly in exchange for the institution's promise to delay or not to report an overdraft. . . .
>
> [3] The overdraft notification provision is not intended to result in the discipline of every lawyer who overdraws a trust account. The lawyer or institution may explain occasional errors. The provision merely intends that the Office of General Counsel receive an early warning of improprieties so that corrective action, including audits for cause, may be taken.

Illinois: Rule 1.15(g), a highly unusual provision adopted in 1998 at the urging of the real estate bar, provides: "In the closing of a real estate transaction, a lawyer's disbursement of funds deposited but not collected shall not violate his or her duty pursuant to this Rule 1.15 if, prior to the closing, the lawyer has established a segregated Real Estate Funds Account (REFA) maintained solely for the receipt and disbursement of such funds," and (among other requirements) the lawyer deposits only "good funds," which include only seven specified forms of deposits, including "(a) a certified check, (b) a check issued by the State of Illinois, the United States, or a political subdivision . . . , (c) a cashier's check, teller's check, bank money order, or official bank check . . . , (d) a check drawn on the trust account of any lawyer or real estate broker licensed under the law of any state, . . . [or] (f) a check drawn on the account of or issued by a lender approved by the United States Department of Housing and Urban Development. . . ." Rule 1.15(g) ends by stating: "Without limiting the rights of the lawyer against any person, it shall be the responsibility of the disbursing lawyer to reimburse the trust account for such funds that are not collected."

Massachusetts: Rule 1.15 has extensive provisions for deposit of client funds in IOLTA accounts. Rule 1.15(f) contains provisions to ensure that disciplinary authorities are notified in the event a lawyer's check is dishonored.

Michigan provides for IOLTA accounts in Rule 1.15(d).

Missouri: Rules 1.15(d) through (g) and Appendix 1 to Supreme Court Rule 4 govern the Missouri Lawyer Trust Account Foundation.

New Jersey: Under Rule 1.15(a) funds must be deposited in New Jersey institutions, without exception. Lawyers may deposit personal funds sufficient to pay bank charges. No accounting of property is required under Rule 1.15(b). New Jersey adds 1.15(d), referring lawyers to section 1:21-6 of the Court Rules on recordkeeping.

New York: Compare ABA Model Rule 1.15 to New York's DR 9-102.

Ohio: Effective April 1, 2002, Ohio adopted extensive new rules to govern IOLTA accounts. Among other things, the new rules (a) require each attorney, law firm, legal professional association, or ancillary business related to the practice of law in which the attorney is the principal to establish and maintain an IOLTA or IOTA account for the deposit of client funds held in a common escrow or trust account; (b) specify when and how an attorney must establish the account; (c) require the depositing attorney to assist the Ohio Legal Assistance Foundation (OLAF) to ensure that the deposits are maintained by an eligible participating bank at the greatest available return; and (d) summarize the consequences of noncompliance. The full text of the rules, with related information, appears on the OLAF web site at www.olaf.org/ioltaiota/Rules/rulesfinal.shtml. Ohio Stat. §§4705.09 and 4705.10 also govern IOLTA accounts.

Pennsylvania: Rules 1.15(d)-(1) institute and describe Pennsylvania's mandatory IOLTA program.

Virginia: Rule 1.15 substantially incorporates provisions from the former Code as adopted in the state and is significantly different from the Model Rule. Virginia Rule 1.15(d) prescribes the responsibility of lawyers who receive funds or other property in a fiduciary capacity.

Related Materials

ABA Financial Recordkeeping Rule: At its February 1993 Mid-Year Meeting, the ABA House of Delegates overwhelmingly approved a Model Financial Recordkeeping Rule. The rule was sponsored by the ABA Standing Committee on Lawyers' Responsibility for Client Protection and was uncontroversial. The purpose of the rule is to provide detailed guidance for compliance with Model Rule 1.15. The rule details ten separate categories of records that a lawyer must keep current and must retain for five years after termination of a representation. It also contains rules regarding deposits, withdrawals, and bookkeeping for lawyer trust accounts, and provides guidelines for dealing with trust accounts upon the dissolution of a law firm or the sale of a law practice.

ABA Random Audit Rule: At its August 1993 Annual Meeting, by the narrow vote of 110 to 105, the ABA House of Delegates approved a Model Rule for the Random Audit of Lawyer Trust Accounts. Like the Model Financial Recordkeeping Rule, the Random Audit Rule was sponsored by the ABA Standing Committee on Lawyers' Responsibility for Client Protection. The rule was controversial and was opposed by the ABA Section on General Practice, which is composed mainly of sole practitioners and small firms. The Random Audit Rule provides as follows:

Random Audits of Lawyer Trust Accounts

(a) The [Supreme Court] shall approve procedures to randomly select lawyer or law firm trust accounts for audit.

(b) An audit of a lawyer or law firm trust account conducted pursuant to this rule shall be commenced by the issuance of an investigative subpoena to compel the production of records relating to a lawyer's or law firm's trust accounts. The subpoena shall contain a certification that it was issued in compliance with this rule; that the lawyer or law firm was selected at random; and that there exist no grounds to believe that professional misconduct has occurred with respect to the accounts being audited. The subpoena shall be served at least [10] business days before commencement of the audit.

(c) With respect to each audit conducted pursuant to this rule, the examiner shall:

(1) determine whether the lawyer's or law firm's records and accounts are being maintained in accordance with applicable rules of court; and

(2) employ sampling techniques to examine "selected accounts," unless discrepancies are found which indicate a need for a more detailed audit. "Selected accounts" may include money, securities and other trust assets held by the lawyer or law firm; safe deposit boxes and similar devices; deposit records; cancelled checks or their equivalent; and any other records which pertain to trust transactions affecting the lawyer's or law firm's practice of law.

(d) The examiner shall prepare a written report containing the examiner's findings, a copy of which shall be provided to the audited lawyer or law firm.

(e) In the event that the audit report asserts deficiencies in the audited lawyer's or law firm's records or procedures, the lawyer or law firm shall, within [10] business days after receipt of the report, provide evidence that the alleged deficiencies are incorrect, or that they have been corrected. If corrective action requires additional time, the lawyer or law firm shall apply for an extension of time to a date certain in which to correct the deficiencies cited in the audit report.

(f) All records produced for an audit conducted pursuant to this rule shall remain confidential, and their contents shall not be disclosed in violation of the attorney-client privilege.

(g) Records produced for an audit conducted pursuant to this rule may be disclosed to:

(1) the lawyer disciplinary agency or to a court to the extent disclosure is necessary for the purposes of the particular audit;

(2) the lawyer disciplinary agency for the purposes of a disciplinary proceeding; and

(3) any other person, including a law enforcement agency, with the permission of the Supreme Court.

(h) A lawyer or law firm shall cooperate in an audit conducted pursuant to this rule, and shall answer all questions pertaining thereto, unless the lawyer or law firm claims a privilege or right which is available to the lawyer or law firm under applicable state or federal law. A lawyer's or law firm's failure to cooperate in an audit conducted pursuant to this rule shall constitute professional misconduct.

(i) No lawyer or law firm shall be subject to an audit conducted pursuant to this rule more frequently than once every [three] years.

*Report of the Standing Committee on Lawyers' Responsibility for Client Protection**

[R]andom audits are a proven deterrent to the misuse of money and property in the practice of law. The examination of trust accounts by court-paid auditors also

*Committee Reports do not represent official policy of the ABA. They are for information only, and the opinions are those of the authors of the report.

provides practitioners with expert and practical assistance in maintaining necessary records and supporting books of account. . . .

The Model Rule proposes a basic structure and system for a random audit program, including such procedural safeguards as adequate prior notice before the commencement of an audit; written audit reports; the opportunity for an audited lawyer or law firm to respond to an examiner's report; the preservation of confidentiality for law client records; and the frequency of audits conducted by random selection. . . .

ABA Standards for Imposing Lawyer Sanctions:

4.11. Disbarment is generally appropriate when a lawyer knowingly converts client property and causes injury or potential injury to a client.

4.12. Suspension is generally appropriate when a lawyer knows or should know that he is dealing improperly with client property and causes injury or potential injury to a client.

4.13. Reprimand is generally appropriate when a lawyer is negligent in dealing with client property and causes injury or potential injury to a client.

4.14. Admonition is generally appropriate when a lawyer is negligent in dealing with client property and causes little or no actual or potential injury to a client.

Client Protection Funds: In keeping with Comment 6 of Rule 1.15, many states have established client protection funds (sometimes called client security funds) for the purpose of reimbursing clients who have lost money or property as a result of dishonest conduct by lawyers. For example, chapter 7 of Florida's Supreme Court Rules authorizes establishment of a Clients' Security Fund "to provide monetary relief to persons who suffer reimbursable losses as a result of misappropriation, embezzlement, or other wrongful taking or conversion" by a Florida lawyer. In several states, these client protection funds have paid out so many claims that they have run out of money. The ABA adopted Model Rules for Lawyers' Funds for Client Protection at its 1989 Annual Meeting. These Model Rules replaced similar rules first adopted in 1981, then called Model Rules for Clients' Security Funds. For further information about client protection funds, see the web site of the National Client Protection Organization at www.ncpo.org.

IOLTA Programs: ABA Model Rule 1.15(a) requires lawyers to hold funds belonging to clients or others in a special separate account usually referred to as a "lawyer trust account." (Common examples of such funds include the down payment on a house, or a settlement check from an insurance company in a personal injury case.) Every state has a similar rule. Since some of these client and third-party funds are too small or are held for too short a time to justify opening a separate bank account, lawyers usually pool these small or short-term funds in a single account. For many years, lawyers deposited these pooled funds into non-interest-bearing accounts because it was too difficult to allocate small amounts of interest to individual clients or third parties. In the late 1970s, however, states began requiring lawyers to deposit these small or short-term funds into interest-bearing accounts at banks that agreed to remit the interest directly to a special state-administered fund created for this purpose. (The first such program was created by Florida in 1978.) The programs establishing and administering these special state funds are typically referred to as "IOLTA" programs, which stands for "interest on lawyer trust accounts" (or in some states simply as "IOLA" programs). By 1995, every state had adopted some form of IOLTA program, and these programs often generate literally millions of dollars per year. (In Illinois, for example, the IOLTA program raised $3,971,932 in fiscal 2001 after all bank charges and fees. The national total from all state IOLTA programs was about $140 million annually at last count.) The funds from IOLTA programs are generally distributed to legal services offices, law school clinics, and other programs that provide legal services to the poor or work to improve the administration of justice.

In the mid-1990s, the Washington Legal Foundation challenged the Texas IOLTA program, arguing that the mandatory remittal of interest on lawyer trust accounts constituted an unconstitutional "taking" of client property without compensation, thus violating the Fifth Amendment. (The Washington Legal Foundation's web site describes it as "a public interest law and policy center" that "devotes a substantial portion of its resources to promoting economic liberty and a limited and accountable government.") The United States Supreme Court eventually heard the case, but the decision was inconclusive. The Court held 5-4 that the interest on lawyer trust accounts was indeed "property" for purposes of the Takings Clause, but the Court remanded the case for a determination of the key question: had there been a "taking" (and, if so, what constituted just compensation)? See Phillips v. Washington Legal Foundation, 524 U.S. 156 (1998). (Proceedings on remand are still in litigation.)

In June of 2002, however, the Supreme Court granted certiorari in Washington Legal Foundation v. Legal Foundation of Washington, 122 S. Ct. 2355 (2002). The case will review a Ninth Circuit en banc opinion holding that Washington State's mandatory rules governing Interest on Lawyers' Trust Accounts (IOLTA) do not amount to an unconstitutional taking of clients' property. Oral arguments are scheduled for January of 2003. Every state in the country has some form of IOLTA program similar to Washington State's program, so the case is likely to have a nationwide impact on state regulation of lawyer trust accounts.

Model Rules of Professional Conduct for Federal Lawyers add a new subparagraph (d) that provides: "When property of a client or third party is admitted into evidence or otherwise included in the record of a proceeding, the Federal lawyer should take reasonable action to ensure its prompt return."

Restatement of the Law Governing Lawyers: See Restatement §§43–46 in our chapter on the Restatement later in this volume.

Rule 1.16 Declining or Terminating Representation

(a) Except as stated in paragraph (c), a lawyer shall not represent a client or, where representation has commenced, shall withdraw from the representation of a client if:

(1) the representation will result in violation of the rules of professional conduct or other law;

(2) the lawyer's physical or mental condition materially impairs the lawyer's ability to represent the client; or

(3) the lawyer is discharged.

(b) Except as stated in paragraph (c), a lawyer may withdraw from representing a client if:

(1) withdrawal can be accomplished without material adverse effect on the interests of the client~~, or if:~~;

~~(1)~~ (2) the client persists in a course of action involving the lawyer's services that the lawyer reasonably believes is criminal or fraudulent;

~~(2)~~ (3) the client has used the lawyer's services to perpetrate a crime or fraud;

~~(3)~~ (4) ~~a~~ the client insists upon ~~pursuing an objective~~ taking action that the lawyer considers repugnant or ~~imprudent~~ with which the lawyer has a fundamental disagreement;

~~(4)~~ (5) the client fails substantially to fulfill an obligation to the lawyer regarding the lawyer's services and has been given reasonable warning that the lawyer will withdraw unless the obligation is fulfilled;

~~(5)~~ (6) the representation will result in an unreasonable financial burden on the lawyer or has been rendered unreasonably difficult by the client; or

~~(6)~~ (7) other good cause for withdrawal exists.

(c) A lawyer must comply with applicable law requiring notice to or permission of a tribunal when terminating a representation. When ordered to do so by a tribunal, a lawyer shall continue representation notwithstanding good cause for terminating the representation.

(d) Upon termination of representation, a lawyer shall take steps to the extent reasonably practicable to protect a client's interests, such as giving reasonable notice to the client, allowing time for employment of other counsel, surrendering papers and property to which the client is entitled and refunding any advance payment of fee or expense that has not been earned or incurred. The lawyer may retain papers relating to the client to the extent permitted by other law.

COMMENT

[1] A lawyer should not accept representation in a matter unless it can be performed competently, promptly, without improper conflict of interest and to completion. Ordinarily, a representation in a matter is completed when the agreed-upon assistance has been concluded. See Rules 1.2(c) and 6.5. See also Rule 1.3, Comment [4].

Mandatory Withdrawal

[2] A lawyer ordinarily must decline or withdraw from representation if the client demands that the lawyer engage in conduct that is illegal or violates the Rules of Professional Conduct or other law. The lawyer is not obliged to decline or withdraw simply because the client suggests such a course of conduct; a client may make such a suggestion in the hope that a lawyer will not be constrained by a professional obligation.

[3] When a lawyer has been appointed to represent a client, withdrawal ordinarily requires approval of the appointing authority. See also Rule 6.2. Similarly, court approval or notice to the court is often required by applicable law before a lawyer withdraws from pending litigation. Difficulty may be encountered if withdrawal is based on the client's demand that the lawyer engage in unprofessional conduct. The court may ~~wish~~ request an explanation for the withdrawal, while the lawyer may be bound to keep confidential the facts that would constitute such an explanation. The lawyer's statement that professional considerations require termination of the representation ordinarily should be accepted as sufficient. Lawyers should be mindful of their obligations to both clients and the court under Rules 1.6 and 3.3.

Discharge

[4] A client has a right to discharge a lawyer at any time, with or without cause, subject to liability for payment for the lawyer's services. Where future dispute about the withdrawal may be anticipated, it may be advisable to prepare a written statement reciting the circumstances.

[5] Whether a client can discharge appointed counsel may depend on applicable law. A client seeking to do so should be given a full explanation of the consequences. These consequences may include a decision by the appointing authority that appointment of successor counsel is unjustified, thus requiring self-representation by the client.

[6] If the client ~~is mentally incompetent~~ has severely diminished capacity, the client may lack the legal capacity to discharge the lawyer, and in any event the discharge may be seriously adverse to the client's interests. The lawyer should make special effort to help the client consider the consequences and~~, in an extreme case,~~ may ~~initiate proceedings for a conservatorship or similar protection of the client. See~~ take reasonably necessary protective action as provided in Rule 1.14.

Optional Withdrawal

[7] A lawyer may withdraw from representation in some circumstances. The lawyer has the option to withdraw if it can be accomplished without material adverse effect on the client's interests. Withdrawal is also justified if the client persists in a course of action that the lawyer reasonably believes is criminal or fraudulent, for a lawyer is not required to be associated with such conduct even if the lawyer does not further it. Withdrawal is also permitted if the lawyer's services were misused in the past even if that would materially prejudice the client. The lawyer may also withdraw where the client insists on ~~a~~ taking action that the lawyer considers repugnant or ~~imprudent objective~~ with which the lawyer has a fundamental disagreement.

[8] A lawyer may withdraw if the client refuses to abide by the terms of an agreement relating to the representation, such as an agreement concerning fees or court costs or an agreement limiting the objectives of the representation.

Assisting the Client upon Withdrawal

[9] Even if the lawyer has been unfairly discharged by the client, a lawyer must take all reasonable steps to mitigate the consequences to the client. The lawyer may retain papers as security for a fee only to the extent permitted by law. ~~Whether or not a lawyer for an organization may under certain unusual circumstances have a legal obligation to the organization after withdrawing or being discharged by the organization's highest authority is beyond the scope of these Rules.~~ See Rule 1.15.

Canon and Code Antecedents

ABA Canons of Professional Ethics: Canons 7 and 44 provided as follows:

7. Professional Colleagues and Conflicts of Opinion

A client's proffer of assistance of additional counsel should not be regarded as evidence of want of confidence, but the matter should be left to the determination of the client. A lawyer should decline association as colleague if it is objectionable to the original counsel, but if the lawyer first retained is relieved, another may come into the case.

When lawyers jointly associated in a cause cannot agree as to any matter vital to the interest of the client, the conflict of opinion should be frankly stated to him for his final determination. His decision should be accepted unless the nature of the difference makes it impracticable for the lawyer whose judgment has been overruled to co-operate effectively. In this event it is his duty to ask the client to relieve him.

Efforts, direct or indirect, in any way to encroach upon the professional employment of another lawyer, are unworthy of those who should be brethren at the Bar; but, nevertheless, it is the right of any lawyer, without fear or favor, to give proper advice to those seeking relief against unfaithful or neglectful counsel, generally after communication with the lawyer of whom the complaint is made.

44. Withdrawal from Employment as Attorney or Counsel

The right of an attorney or counsel to withdraw from employment, once assumed, arises only from good cause. Even the desire or consent of the client is not always sufficient. The lawyer should not throw up the unfinished task to the detriment of his client except for reasons of honor or self-respect. If the client insists upon an unjust or immoral course in the conduct of his case, or if he persists over the attorney's remonstrance in presenting frivolous defenses, or if he deliberately disregards an agreement or obligation as to fees or expenses, the lawyer may be warranted in withdrawing on due notice to the client, allowing him time to employ another lawyer. So also when a lawyer discovers that his client has no case and the client is determined to continue it; or even if the lawyer finds himself incapable of conducting the case effectively. Sundry other instances may arise in which withdrawal is to be justified. Upon withdrawing from a case after a retainer has been paid, the attorney should refund such part of the retainer as has not been clearly earned.

ABA Model Code of Professional Responsibility: Compare DR 2-109(A), DR 2-110(A), DR 2-110(B), and DR 2-110(C) (reprinted later in this volume).

Cross-References in Other Rules

Rule 1.2, Comment 2: When a lawyer and client disagree, the "lawyer should also consult with the client and seek a mutually acceptable resolution of the disagreement. If such efforts are unavailing and the lawyer has a fundamental disagreement with the client, the lawyer may withdraw from the representation. See **Rule 1.16(b)(4)**. Conversely, the client may resolve the disagreement by discharging the lawyer. See **Rule 1.16(a)(3)**."

Rule 1.2, Comment 10: "A lawyer may not continue assisting a client in conduct that the lawyer originally supposed was legally proper but then discovers is criminal or fraudulent. The lawyer must, therefore, withdraw from the representation of the client in the matter. See **Rule 1.16(a)**."

Rule 1.3, Comment 4: "Unless the relationship is terminated as provided in **Rule 1.16,** a lawyer should carry through to conclusion all matters undertaken for a client."

Rule 1.5, Comment 4: "A lawyer may require advance payment of a fee, but is obliged to return any unearned portion. See **Rule 1.16(d)**."

Rule 1.6, Comment 14: "If the lawyer's services will be used by the client in materially furthering a course of criminal or fraudulent conduct, the lawyer must withdraw, as stated in **Rule 1.16(a)(1)**. Neither this Rule nor Rule 1.8(b) nor **Rule 1.16(d)** prevents the lawyer from giving notice of the fact of withdrawal."

Rule 1.7, Comment 4: "If a conflict arises after representation has been undertaken, the lawyer ordinarily must withdraw from the representation, unless the lawyer has obtained the informed consent of the client under the conditions of paragraph (b). See **Rule 1.16**."

Rule 1.7, Comment 5: When unforeseeable circumstances create conflicts the "lawyer must seek court approval where necessary and take steps to minimize harm to the clients. See **Rule 1.16**."

Rule 1.7, Comment 33: Each client in the common representation "has the right to discharge the lawyer as stated in **Rule 1.16**."

Rule 1.13(c): "If, despite the lawyer's efforts in accordance with paragraph (b), the highest authority that can act on behalf of the organization insists upon action, or a refusal to act, that is clearly a violation of law and is likely to result in substantial injury to the organization, the lawyer may resign in accordance with **Rule 1.16**."

Rule 1.13, Comment 5: "[T]his Rule does not limit or expand the lawyer's responsibility under Rule 1.6, 1.8, **1.16**, 3.3 or 4.1."

Rule 1.17, Comment 12: "If approval of the substitution of the purchasing lawyer for the selling lawyer is required by the rules of any tribunal in which a matter is pending, such approval must be obtained before the matter can be included in the sale (see **Rule 1.16**)."

Rule 3.3, Comment 15: "The lawyer may . . . be required by **Rule 1.16(a)** to seek permission of the tribunal to withdraw if the lawyer's compliance with this Rule's duty of candor results in such an extreme deterioration of the client-lawyer relationship that the lawyer can no longer competently represent the client. Also see **Rule 1.16(b)** for the circumstances in which a lawyer will be permitted to seek a tribunal's permission to withdraw."

Legislative History of Model Rule 1.16

1980 Discussion Draft: Rule 1.16(b) provided:

> (b) Except as stated in paragraph (c), a lawyer may withdraw from representing a client if:
>
> (1) Withdrawal can be effected without material prejudice to the client;
>
> (2) The client persists in a course of conduct that is illegal or unjust; or
>
> (3) The client fails to fulfill an obligation to the lawyer regarding the lawyer's services.

1981 and 1982 Drafts were substantially the same as adopted.

2002 Amendments: At its February 2002 Mid-Year Meeting, the ABA House of Delegates adopted without change the ABA Ethics 2000 Commission proposal to amend Rule 1.16 and its Comment.

Selected State Variations

California: See Rule 3-700 (Termination of Employment).

Florida: Rule 4-1.16(d) provides that, upon termination: "The lawyer may retain papers and other property relating to or belonging to the client to the extent permitted by law."

Georgia: In the rules effective January 1, 2001, Rule 1.16 generally tracks ABA Model Rule 1.16, but Georgia Rule 1.16(c) provides that "[w]hen a lawyer withdraws it shall be done in compliance with applicable laws and rules."

Illinois: Rule 1.16 is substantially the same as DR 2-110.

Massachusetts: Rule 1.16(e) provides:

> A lawyer must make available to a former client, within a reasonable time following the client's request for his or her file, the following:
>
> 1. all papers, documents, and other materials the client supplied to the lawyer. The lawyer may at his or her own expense retain copies of any such materials.
>
> 2. all pleadings and other papers filed with or by the court or served by or upon any party. The client may be required to pay any copying charge consistent with the lawyer's actual cost for these materials, unless the client has already paid for such materials.
>
> 3. all investigatory or discovery documents for which the client has paid the lawyer's out-of-pocket costs, including but not limited to medical records, photographs, tapes, disks, investigative reports, expert reports, depositions, and demonstrative evidence. The lawyer may at his or her own expense retain copies of any such materials.
>
> 4. if the lawyer and the client have not entered into a contingent fee agreement, the client is entitled only to that portion of the lawyer's work

product (as defined in subparagraph (6) below) for which the client has paid.

5. if the lawyer and the client have entered into a contingent fee agreement, the lawyer must provide copies of the lawyer's work product (as defined in subparagraph (6) below). The client may be required to pay any copying charge consistent with the lawyer's actual cost for the copying of these materials.

6. for purposes of this paragraph (e), work product shall consist of documents and tangible things prepared in the course of the representation of the client by the lawyer or at the lawyer's direction by his or her employee, agent, or consultant, and not described in paragraphs (2) or (3) above. Examples of work product include without limitation legal research, records of witness interviews, reports of negotiations, and correspondence.

7. notwithstanding anything in this paragraph (e) to the contrary, a lawyer may not refuse, on grounds of nonpayment, to make available materials in the client's file when retention would prejudice the client unfairly.

New York: Compare ABA Model Rule 1.16 to New York's DR 2-110.

North Carolina: Rule 1.16(a) adds language from DR 2-110(B)(1) and (C)(1) of the old ABA Model Code — see Model Code Comparison above. Rule 1.7(c) mandates that a lawyer "withdraw from the representation of any party the lawyer cannot adequately represent without using the confidential information of another client or a former client except as Rule 1.6 allows."

Oregon: DR 2-110(C)(7) provides that a lawyer may withdraw if:

> (7) [t]he lawyer has sold all or part of the lawyer's practice in compliance with the requirements of DR 2-111. The selling lawyer shall comply with the requirements of DR 2-110(A) if the selling lawyer intends to withdraw from representation of the client even if the client objects to the transfer of its legal work to the purchasing lawyer.

Texas: Rule 1.15(d) adds: "The lawyer may retain papers relating to the client to the extent permitted by other law only if such retention will not prejudice the client in the subject matter of the representation."

Virginia: Rule 1.16(b)(1) substitutes "illegal or unjust" for "criminal or fraudulent," and Rule 1.16(e) specifies in some detail the papers to which a client is entitled after a lawyer withdraws and whether the client or the lawyer must bear the cost of duplication. The client's entitlement does not depend upon "whether or not the client has paid the fees and costs owed a lawyer."

Related Materials

ABA Formal Ethics Opinions: See ABA Formal Ethics Ops. 92-366 (1992) and 94-384 (1994).

American Lawyer's Code of Conduct: Rules 5.5 and 6.5 provide:

> 5.5. A lawyer shall not impose a lien upon any part of a client's files, except upon the lawyer's own work product, and then only to the extent that the work product has not been paid for. This work-product exception shall be inapplicable when the client is in fact unable to pay, or when withholding the lawyer's work product would present a significant risk to the client of imprisonment, deportation, destruction of essential evidence, loss of custody of a child, or similar irreparable harm.
>
> 6.5. In any matter other than criminal litigation, a lawyer may withdraw from representing a client if the lawyer comes to know that the client has knowingly

induced the lawyer to take the case or to take action on behalf of the client on the basis of material misrepresentations about the facts of the case, and if withdrawal can be accomplished without a direct violation of confidentiality.

Model Rules of Professional Conduct for Federal Lawyers: Rule 1.16(c) provides: "When properly ordered to do so by a tribunal or other competent authority, a Federal lawyer shall continue representation notwithstanding good cause for terminating the representation."

Restatement of the Law Governing Lawyers: See Restatement §§31–33, 40, and 46 in our chapter on the Restatement later in this volume.

Rule 1.17 Sale of Law Practice

A lawyer or a law firm may sell or purchase a law practice, or an area of practice, including good will, if the following conditions are satisfied:

(a) The seller ceases to engage in the private practice of law, or in the area of practice that has been sold, [in the geographic area] [in the jurisdiction] (a jurisdiction may elect either version) in which the practice has been conducted;

(b) The entire practice, or the entire area of practice, is sold ~~as an entirety~~ to ~~another lawyer~~ one or more lawyers or law ~~firm~~ firms;

(c) ~~Actual~~ The seller gives written notice ~~is given~~ to each of the seller's clients regarding:

(1) the proposed sale;

~~(2) the terms of any proposed change in the fee arrangement authorized by paragraph (d);~~

~~(3)~~ (2) the client's right to retain other counsel or to take possession of the file; and

~~(4)~~ (3) the fact that the client's consent to the ~~sale~~ transfer of the client's files will be presumed if the client does not take any action or does not otherwise object within ninety (90) days of receipt of the notice.

If a client cannot be given notice, the representation of that client may be transferred to the purchaser only upon entry of an order so authorizing by a court having jurisdiction. The seller may disclose to the court in camera information relating to the representation only to the extent necessary to obtain an order authorizing the transfer of a file.

(d) The fees charged clients shall not be increased by reason of the sale. ~~The purchaser may, however, refuse to undertake the representation unless the client consents to pay the purchaser fees at a rate not exceeding the fees charged by the purchaser for rendering substantially similar services prior to the initiation of the purchase negotiations.~~

COMMENT

[1] The practice of law is a profession, not merely a business. Clients are not commodities that can be purchased and sold at will. Pursuant to

this Rule, when a lawyer or an entire firm ceases to practice, or ceases to practice in an area of law, and ~~another lawyer~~ other lawyers or ~~firm takes~~ firms take over the representation, the selling lawyer or firm may obtain compensation for the reasonable value of the practice as may withdrawing partners of law firms. See Rules 5.4 and 5.6.

Termination of Practice by the Seller

[2] The requirement that all of the private practice, or all of an area of practice, be sold is satisfied if the seller in good faith makes the entire practice, or the area of practice, available for sale to the ~~purchaser~~ purchasers. The fact that a number of the seller's clients decide not to be represented by the ~~purchaser~~ purchasers but take their matters elsewhere, therefore, does not result in a violation. ~~Neither does a return~~ Return to private practice as a result of an unanticipated change in circumstances does not necessarily result in a violation. For example, a lawyer who has sold the practice to accept an appointment to judicial office does not violate the requirement that the sale be attendant to cessation of practice if the lawyer later resumes private practice upon being defeated in a contested or a retention election for the office or resigns from a judiciary position.

[3] The requirement that the seller cease to engage in the private practice of law does not prohibit employment as a lawyer on the staff of a public agency or a legal services entity that provides legal services to the poor, or as in-house counsel to a business.

[4] The Rule permits a sale of an entire practice attendant upon retirement from the private practice of law within the jurisdiction. Its provisions, therefore, accommodate the lawyer who sells the practice upon the occasion of moving to another state. Some states are so large that a move from one locale therein to another is tantamount to leaving the jurisdiction in which the lawyer has engaged in the practice of law. To also accommodate lawyers so situated, states may permit the sale of the practice when the lawyer leaves the geographic area rather than the jurisdiction. The alternative desired should be indicated by selecting one of the two provided for in Rule 1.17(a).

[5] This Rule also permits a lawyer or law firm to sell an area of practice. If an area of practice is sold and the lawyer remains in the active practice of law, the lawyer must cease accepting any matters in the area of practice that has been sold, either as counsel or co-counsel or by assuming joint responsibility for a matter in connection with the division of a fee with another lawyer as would otherwise be permitted by Rule 1.5(e). For example, a lawyer with a substantial number of estate planning matters and a substantial number of probate administration cases may sell the estate planning portion of the practice but remain in the practice of law by concentrating on probate administration; however, that practitioner may not thereafter accept any estate planning matters. Although a lawyer who

<u>leaves a jurisdiction or geographical area typically would sell the entire practice, this Rule permits the lawyer to limit the sale to one or more areas of the practice, thereby preserving the lawyer's right to continue practice in the areas of the practice that were not sold.</u>

~~Single Purchaser~~ <u>Sale of Entire Practice or Entire Area of Practice</u>

~~[5]~~ <u>[6]</u> The Rule requires ~~a single purchaser~~ <u>that the seller's entire practice, or an entire area of practice, be sold</u>. The prohibition against ~~piecemeal~~ sale of ~~a~~ <u>less than an entire</u> practice <u>area</u> protects those clients whose matters are less lucrative and who might find it difficult to secure other counsel if a sale could be limited to substantial fee-generating matters. The ~~purchaser is~~ <u>purchasers are</u> required to undertake all client matters in the practice <u>or practice area</u>, subject to client consent. ~~If~~ <u>This requirement is satisfied</u>, however, ~~the~~ <u>even if a</u> purchaser is unable to undertake ~~all~~ <u>a particular</u> client ~~matters~~ <u>matter</u> because of a conflict of interest ~~in a specific matter respecting which the purchaser is not permitted by Rule 1.7 or another rule to represent the client, the requirement that there be a single purchaser is nevertheless satisfied~~.

Client Confidences, Consent and Notice

~~[6]~~ <u>[7]</u> Negotiations between seller and prospective purchaser prior to disclosure of information relating to a specific representation of an identifiable client no more violate the confidentiality provisions of Model Rule 1.6 than do preliminary discussions concerning the possible association of another lawyer or mergers between firms, with respect to which client consent is not required. Providing the purchaser access to client-specific information relating to the representation and to the file, however, requires client consent. The Rule provides that before such information can be disclosed by the seller to the purchaser the client must be given actual written notice of the contemplated sale, including the identity of the purchaser ~~and any proposed change in the terms of future representation~~, and must be told that the decision to consent or make other arrangements must be made within 90 days. If nothing is heard from the client within that time, consent to the sale is presumed.

~~[7]~~ <u>[8]</u> A lawyer or law firm ceasing to practice cannot be required to remain in practice because some clients cannot be given actual notice of the proposed purchase. Since these clients cannot themselves consent to the purchase or direct any other disposition of their files, the Rule requires an order from a court having jurisdiction authorizing their transfer or other disposition. The Court can be expected to determine whether reasonable efforts to locate the client have been exhausted, and whether the absent client's legitimate interests will be served by authorizing the transfer of the file so that the purchaser may continue the representation. Preservation of client confidences requires that the petition for a court order be considered in camera. (A procedure by which such an order can be obtained needs to be established in jurisdictions in which it presently does not exist.)

~~[8]~~ [9] All the elements of client autonomy, including the client's absolute right to discharge a lawyer and transfer the representation to another, survive the sale of the practice or area of practice.

Fee Arrangements Between Client and Purchaser

~~[9]~~ [10] The sale may not be financed by increases in fees charged the clients of the practice. Existing agreements between the seller and the client as to fees and the scope of the work must be honored by the purchaser~~, unless the client consents after consultation. The purchaser may, however, advise the client that the purchaser will not undertake the representation unless the client consents to pay the higher fees the purchaser usually charges. To prevent client financing of the sale, the higher fee the purchaser may charge must not exceed the fees charged by the purchaser for substantially similar service rendered prior to the initiation of the purchase negotiations~~.

~~[10] The purchaser may not intentionally fragment the practice which is the subject of the sale by charging significantly different fees in substantially similar matters. Doing so would make it possible for the purchaser to avoid the obligation to take over the entire practice by charging arbitrarily higher fees for less lucrative matters, thereby increasing the likelihood that those clients would not consent to the new representation.~~

Other Applicable Ethical Standards

[11] Lawyers participating in the sale of a law practice or a practice area are subject to the ethical standards applicable to involving another lawyer in the representation of a client. These include, for example, the seller's obligation to exercise competence in identifying a purchaser qualified to assume the practice and the purchaser's obligation to undertake the representation competently (see Rule 1.1); the obligation to avoid disqualifying conflicts, and to secure ~~client~~ the client's informed consent ~~after consultation~~ for those conflicts that can be agreed to (see Rule 1.7 regarding conflicts and Rule 1.0(e) for the definition of informed consent); and the obligation to protect information relating to the representation (see Rules 1.6 and 1.9).

[12] If approval of the substitution of the purchasing lawyer for the selling lawyer is required by the rules of any tribunal in which a matter is

pending, such approval must be obtained before the matter can be included in the sale (see Rule 1.16).

Applicability of the Rule

[13] This Rule applies to the sale of a law practice by representatives of a deceased, disabled or disappeared lawyer. Thus, the seller may be represented by a non-lawyer representative not subject to these Rules. Since, however, no lawyer may participate in a sale of a law practice which does not conform to the requirements of this Rule, the representatives of the seller as well as the purchasing lawyer can be expected to see to it that they are met.

[14] Admission to or retirement from a law partnership or professional association, retirement plans and similar arrangements, and a sale of tangible assets of a law practice do not constitute a sale or purchase governed by this Rule.

[15] This Rule does not apply to the transfers of legal representation between lawyers when such transfers are unrelated to the sale of a practice <u>or an area of practice</u>.

Canon and Code Antecedents

ABA Canons of Professional Ethics: No comparable Canon.

ABA Model Code of Professional Responsibility: No comparable Disciplinary Rule.

Cross-References in Other Rules

Rule 5.4(a)(2) provides that "a lawyer who purchases the practice of a deceased, disabled, or disappeared lawyer may, pursuant to the provisions of **Rule 1.17**, pay to the estate or other representative of that lawyer the agreed-upon purchase price."

Rule 5.6, Comment 3: "This Rule does not apply to prohibit restrictions that may be included in the terms of the sale of a law practice pursuant to **Rule 1.17**."

Rule 7.2(b)(3) permits a lawyer to "pay for a law practice in accordance with **Rule 1.17**."

Legislative History of Model Rule 1.17

1993 Adoption: Rule 1.17 was adopted by the ABA House of Delegates at the ABA's February 1990 Mid-Year Meeting. It was not proposed in any form in Kutak Commission drafts. The proposal to add Rule 1.17 to the Model Rules was initiated by the State Bar of California, based on California Rule 2-300, and was joined by the ABA Section of General Practice and the ABA Section of Law

Practice Management. The Committee Report submitted to the House of Delegates in support of adding Rule 1.17 explained the Rule as follows:*

Impetus for Formulation of the Rule

Protection of Clients

[California] Rule of Professional Conduct 2-300 and proposed Model Rule 1.17 are consumer protection measures designed to address the disparity between the treatment of the clients of sole practitioners and the clients of law firms when the attorney handling the client matter leaves the practice, by ensuring that the client matters handled by sole practitioners are attended to when the sole practitioner leaves the practice.

If the attorney leaving the practice is or was part of a law firm, in most cases, the firm continues to handle the matter. In the majority of situations, the transition for the client is very smooth. However, if the attorney was in sole practice, the transition is not so smooth because there is no law firm standing ready to continue to handle the client matter. The clients of sole practitioners who leave the practice of law are relatively unprotected because there are no regulations in place to protect them during the transition.

Sole Practitioners in Unfair Financial Position

In addition to the issues of the client protection, sole practitioners are in an unfair financial position concerning the "good will" of their law practice. The "good will" of a business is "the expectation of continued public patronage.". . . Attorneys, like other business persons, may sell the physical assets of their law practice, such as equipment, the library or the furniture. However, case authority and ethics opinions held that the sale of "good will" of a law practice is unethical and against public policy. . . .

Treatment of "good will" in other contexts presents a mixed picture. For example, attorneys who are members of firms with two or more members may ethically enter into retirement agreements which may require lump sum payments that implicitly include sums for the attorney's share of the firm's "good will."

The estate of a deceased attorney may receive payments from the attorney who completes the unfinished client matters of the deceased attorney. However, in the absence of a rule like that which is being proposed, the payments are limited to the "proportion of the total compensation which fairly represents the services rendered by the deceased member" and thus do not permit an allowance for "good will."

Pursuant to agreements entered into between an attorney not in sole practice and the attorney's firm, partner or associate, the estate of the attorney may receive payments over a reasonable period of time after the attorney's death. Note that there is no requirement that the payments be related to any services the attorney performed. Thus, it appears that the payments to the estate can include the value of "good will."

In marital dissolution proceedings, the "good will" of the attorney-spouse's share in his or her law practice may be valued for the purpose of determining the community or other divisible assets.

This inconsistent treatment of "good will" resulted in a series of awkward results: the estate of a sole practitioner could not receive payment for the "good will" of the law practice, while the estate of an attorney who was a member of a law firm could; upon retirement, an attorney who was a member of a law firm could receive compensation including "good will," while the compensation received by a sole practitioner could not include "good will"; the "good will" of a sole practice may be considered an asset of the marital community for purposes of a dissolution, but could not be sold.

*Committee Reports do not represent official policy of the ABA. They are for information only, and the opinions are those of the authors of the report.

2002 Amendments: At its February 2002 Mid-Year Meeting, the ABA House of Delegates adopted with some changes the ABA Ethics 2000 Commission proposal to amend Rule 1.17 and its Comment. The proposal would have allowed the sale only of an "entire practice," but the House of Delegates voted to allow the sale of "an area of practice."

Selected State Variations

California: See Rule 2-300 (Sale or Purchase of a Law Practice of a Member Living or Deceased).

District of Columbia: D.C. has not adopted any rule permitting the sale of a law practice. (D.C. Rule 1.17 deals with trust account overdrafts, not the sale of a law practice — see District of Columbia Rules of Professional Conduct below.)

Florida omits the requirement in ABA Model Rule 1.17(a) that the seller cease practicing law, and adds or modifies several provisions, including the following:

> (c) *Court Approval Required.* If a representation involves pending litigation, there shall be no substitution of counsel or termination of representation unless authorized by the court. . . .
>
> (d) *Client Objections.* If a client objects to the proposed substitution of counsel, the seller shall comply with the requirements of rule 4-1.16(d) [which governs withdrawal]; . . .
>
> (f) *Existing Fee Contracts Controlling.* The purchaser shall honor the fee agreements that were entered into between the seller and the seller's clients. The fees charged clients shall not be increased by reason of the sale.

Florida's Comment to subparagraph (f) provides:

> The sale may not be financed by increases in fees charged the clients of the practice. Existing agreements between the seller and the client as to fees and the scope of the work must be honored by the purchaser. This obligation of the purchaser is a factor that can be taken into account by seller and purchaser when negotiating the sale price of the practice.

Georgia: In the rules effective January 1, 2001, Georgia adopted the pre-2002 version of ABA Model Rule 1.17 verbatim except that Georgia deleted paragraph (a) (requiring that the seller stop practicing law).

Hawaii: Rule 1.17(c)(1) requires notice to the client not only of the proposed sale but also "the identity of the purchaser." Rule 1.17(d) provides: "Existing agreements between the seller and the client as to fees and the scope of the work must be honored by the purchaser, unless the client consents in writing after consultation."

Idaho: Rule 1.17(a) allows the sale of a law practice by a lawyer who ceases to engage in the private practice of law "or in the substantive practice area subject of the sale" in the geographic area in which the practice has been conducted. Rule 1.17(b) permits the practice "or part thereof" to be sold to another lawyer or law firm. Idaho omits Rule 1.17(d).

Illinois: In 1991, the Illinois State Bar Association recommended that the Supreme Court adopt Rule 1.17, but the Supreme Court did not adopt it. In 1993, the Supreme Court's Committee on Rules held public hearings on a new recommendation to adopt 1.17, but in 1997, the Court issued an order stating, "Petition *denied*," without explanation.

Michigan adds Rule 1.17(e), which permits the "sale of the good will of a law practice . . . conditioned upon the seller ceasing to engage in the private practice of law for a reasonable period of time within the geographical area in which the practice has been conducted."

Minnesota forbids the buyer from raising fees "by reason of the sale for a period of at least one year from the date of the sale." All existing fee agreements must be honored for one year from the date of the sale. All pro bono and reduced fee matters must be continued to completion. The notice to clients must include a "summary of the buying lawyer's or law firm's professional background, including education and experience and the length of time that the buyer lawyer or members of the buying law firm has been in practice." The transaction may but need not include a promise by the selling lawyer that he or she will not engage in law practice "for a reasonable period of time within a reasonable geographic area and will not advertise for or solicit clients within that area for that time."

Mississippi: In 1999, Mississippi adopted a version of Rule 1.17 that largely tracks ABA Model Rule 1.17 but adds Rule 1.18(e), which defines "good will" as "reputation, including use of the lawyer or law firm's name that will probably generate future business," and provides that "any use of the lawyer or law firm's name, after the sale or purchase of the subject law practice has been completed, must be accompanied with a notice that the selling lawyer or law firm is no longer engaged in the active practice of law." Moreover, under Rule 1.17(f), "if the selling lawyer or law firm returns to the practice of law, then use of the selling lawyer or law firm's name must be discontinued by the purchasing lawyer or law firm."

New Jersey: Rule 1.17 permits a lawyer or firm to sell or purchase a law practice, including goodwill, if the seller is ceasing to engage in private law practice in New Jersey, the practice is sold as an entirety except for cases in which a conflict is present, and certain notices are given to the clients of the seller and by publication in the New Jersey Law Journal and the New Jersey Lawyer at least 30 days in advance of the sale.

New York: Compare ABA Model Rule 1.17 to New York's DR 2-111.

North Carolina: Rule 1.17(b) permits the sale of legal fields of a practice to a distinct purchaser "provided that such purchasers concentrate in those legal fields." Rule 1.17(c)(4) requires only 30 days' notice. North Carolina also adds Rule 1.17(d), which provides that if a conflict of interest disqualifies the purchaser from representing a client, then "the seller's notice to the client shall advise the client to retain substitute counsel to assume the client's representation . . . ," and Rule 1.17(g), which provides that the purchaser "does not have to pay the entire sales price for the seller's law practice in one lump sum" and expressly allows the seller to finance the purchaser's acquisition, but adds that the seller "shall have no say regarding the purchaser's conduct of the law practice."

Oklahoma requires the seller to have a reasonable basis for believing that the buyer has the knowledge and skill to handle the matters being transferred, or obtains reasonable assurance that the buyer will either acquire such knowledge and skill or associate with another lawyer who possesses the requisite knowledge and skill. Oklahoma also requires the seller to advise each client about any funds or property being held for the client, including advance fees.

Oregon: DR 2-111 permits the sale of a law practice, but Oregon's rule contains somewhat more stringent notice provisions than ABA Model Rule 1.17, and

Oregon provides that the client's consent to the transfer of legal work to the purchasing lawyer will be presumed if the client does not object "within forty-five (45) days after the date the notice was mailed." Oregon also provides:

> (F) If substitution of counsel is required by the rules of a tribunal in which a matter is pending, the selling lawyer shall assure that substitution of counsel is made.
>
> (G) The fees charged clients shall not be increased by reason of the sale except upon agreement of the client.
>
> (H) The sale of a law practice may be conditioned on the selling lawyer's ceasing to engage in the private practice of law or some particular area of practice for a reasonable period within the geographic area in which the practice has been conducted.

Pennsylvania: Effective June 28, 2001, Pennsylvania adopted a version of Rule 1.17 that differs significantly from the 2002 version of ABA Model Rule 1.17. For example, Pennsylvania permits the sale of a law practice only by the "personal representative or estate of a deceased lawyer or a lawyer disabled from the practice of law. . . ." Moreover, Pennsylvania Rule 1.17(b) requires that the seller must sell the practice "as an entirety to a single lawyer." Rule 1.17(c) adds: "Existing agreements between the seller and the client concerning fees and the scope of work must be honored by the purchaser, unless the client consents in writing after consultation." In addition, Rule 1.17(d) and (f) provide:

> (d) The agreement of sale shall include a clear statement of the respective responsibilities of the parties to maintain and preserve the records and files of the seller's practice, including client files.
>
> (f) The sale shall not be effective as to any client for whom the proposed sale would create a conflict of interest for the purchaser or who cannot be represented by the purchaser because of other requirements of the Pennsylvania Rules of Professional Conduct or rules of the Pennsylvania Supreme Court governing the practice of law in Pennsylvania, unless such conflict, requirement or rule can be waived by the client and is in fact waived by the client in writing.

Pennsylvania simultaneously amended Rule 1.6 to allow the disclosure of confidential information "to effectuate the sale of a law practice consistent with Rule 1.17."

South Dakota: In 1998, South Dakota adopted a version of Rule 1.17 that largely tracks the ABA rule but expressly provides that the "estate of a deceased lawyer may be a seller."

Virginia: Virginia's rule permits the sale of a partial law practice, but the client's "refusal to consent to the transfer of the client's matter will be presumed" if the client does nothing after receiving notice.

Wisconsin: Rule 1.17(d) states that the sale "may not be financed by increases in fees charged the clients of the practice. Existing agreements between the seller and the client as to fees and the scope of the work must be honored by the purchaser, unless the client consents in writing after consultation."

Related Materials

Restatement of the Law Governing Lawyers: The Restatement has no provision comparable to ABA Model Rule 1.17.

Rule 1.18 Duties to Prospective Client

Editors' Note. Rule 1.18 is entirely new. The ABA House of Delegates added it to the Model Rules at its February 2002 Mid-Year Meeting, based on the proposal submitted by the ABA Ethics 2000 Commission. For more information, see the entry entitled "2002 Amendments" in the Legislative History below.

(a) A person who discusses with a lawyer the possibility of forming a client-lawyer relationship with respect to a matter is a prospective client.

(b) Even when no client-lawyer relationship ensues, a lawyer who has had discussions with a prospective client shall not use or reveal information learned in the consultation, except as Rule 1.9 would permit with respect to information of a former client.

(c) A lawyer subject to paragraph (b) shall not represent a client with interests materially adverse to those of a prospective client in the same or a substantially related matter if the lawyer received information from the prospective client that could be significantly harmful to that person in the matter, except as provided in paragraph (d). If a lawyer is disqualified from representation under this paragraph, no lawyer in a firm with which that lawyer is associated may knowingly undertake or continue representation in such a matter, except as provided in paragraph (d).

screening – **(d) When the lawyer has received disqualifying information as defined in paragraph (c), representation is permissible if:**

(1) both the affected client and the prospective client have given informed consent, confirmed in writing, or:

(2) the lawyer who received the information took reasonable measures to avoid exposure to more disqualifying information than was reasonably necessary to determine whether to represent the prospective client; and

(i) the disqualified lawyer is timely screened from any participation in the matter and is apportioned no part of the fee therefrom; and

(ii) written notice is promptly given to the prospective client.

COMMENT

[1] Prospective clients, like clients, may disclose information to a lawyer, place documents or other property in the lawyer's custody, or rely on the lawyer's advice. A lawyer's discussions with a prospective client

usually are limited in time and depth and leave both the prospective client and the lawyer free (and sometimes required) to proceed no further. Hence, prospective clients should receive some but not all of the protection afforded clients.

[2] Not all persons who communicate information to a lawyer are entitled to protection under this Rule. A person who communicates information unilaterally to a lawyer, without any reasonable expectation that the lawyer is willing to discuss the possibility of forming a client-lawyer relationship, is not a "prospective client" within the meaning of paragraph (a).

[3] It is often necessary for a prospective client to reveal information to the lawyer during an initial consultation prior to the decision about formation of a client-lawyer relationship. The lawyer often must learn such information to determine whether there is a conflict of interest with an existing client and whether the matter is one that the lawyer is willing to undertake. Paragraph (b) prohibits the lawyer from using or revealing that information, except as permitted by Rule 1.9, even if the client or lawyer decides not to proceed with the representation. The duty exists regardless of how brief the initial conference may be.

[4] In order to avoid acquiring disqualifying information from a prospective client, a lawyer considering whether or not to undertake a new matter should limit the initial interview to only such information as reasonably appears necessary for that purpose. Where the information indicates that a conflict of interest or other reason for non-representation exists, the lawyer should so inform the prospective client or decline the representation. If the prospective client wishes to retain the lawyer, and if consent is possible under Rule 1.7, then consent from all affected present or former clients must be obtained before accepting the representation.

[5] A lawyer may condition conversations with a prospective client on the person's informed consent that no information disclosed during the consultation will prohibit the lawyer from representing a different client in the matter. See Rule 1.0(e) for the definition of informed consent. If the agreement expressly so provides, the prospective client may also consent to the lawyer's subsequent use of information received from the prospective client.

[6] Even in the absence of an agreement, under paragraph (c), the lawyer is not prohibited from representing a client with interests adverse to those of the prospective client in the same or a substantially related matter unless the lawyer has received from the prospective client information that could be significantly harmful if used in the matter.

[7] Under paragraph (c), the prohibition in this Rule is imputed to other lawyers as provided in Rule 1.10, but, under paragraph (d)(1), imputation may be avoided if the lawyer obtains the informed consent, confirmed in writing, of both the prospective and affected clients. In the alternative, imputation may be avoided if the conditions of paragraph (d)(2) are met and all disqualified lawyers are timely screened and written notice

is promptly given to the prospective client. See Rule 1.0(k) (requirements for screening procedures). Paragraph (d)(2)(i) does not prohibit the screened lawyer from receiving a salary or partnership share established by prior independent agreement, but that lawyer may not receive compensation directly related to the matter in which the lawyer is disqualified.

[8] Notice, including a general description of the subject matter about which the lawyer was consulted, and of the screening procedures employed, generally should be given as soon as practicable after the need for screening becomes apparent.

[9] For the duty of competence of a lawyer who gives assistance on the merits of a matter to a prospective client, see Rule 1.1. For a lawyer's duties when a prospective client entrusts valuables or papers to the lawyer's care, see Rule 1.15.

Cross-References in Other Rules

Scope, ¶17: "Most of the duties flowing from the client-lawyer relationship attach only after the client has requested the lawyer to render legal services and the lawyer has agreed to do so. But there are some duties, such as that of confidentiality under Rule 1.6, that attach when the lawyer agrees to consider whether a client-lawyer relationship shall be established. See **Rule 1.18**."

Rule 1.0, Comment 8: The definition of "screened" "applies to situations where screening of a personally disqualified lawyer is permitted to remove imputation of a conflict of interest under Rules 1.11, 1.12 or **1.18**."

Rule 1.6, Comment 1: Regarding disclosure: "See **Rule 1.18** for the lawyer's duties with respect to information provided to the lawyer by a prospective client."

Rule 1.7, Comment 1: "For conflicts of interest involving prospective clients, see **Rule 1.18**."

Legislative History of Model Rule 1.18

2002 Amendments: Rule 1.18 was added to the Model Rules in February of 2002. The new rule and its Comment were based on a proposal by the ABA Ethics 2000 Commission, which the ABA House of Delegates adopted without change. The Reporter's Explanation Memo that accompanied the Ethics 2000 Commission proposal provided, in relevant part, as follows:

*Model Rule 1.18 — Reporter's Explanation of Changes**

Rule 1.18 is a proposed new Rule in response to the Commission's concern that important events occur in the period during which a lawyer and prospective client are considering whether to form a client-lawyer relationship. For the most part, the current Model Rules do not address that pre-retention period.

*Committee Reports, and the Reporter's Explanation of Changes contained therein, do not represent official policy of the ABA. They are for information only, and the opinions expressed are those of the authors.

Paragraph (a) defines the limited circumstances to which this Rule applies by defining who qualifies as a "prospective client."

Paragraph (b) identifies the duty to treat all communications with a prospective client as confidential. This obligation is a well-settled matter under the law of attorney-client privilege, and the fact that Model Rule 1.9 does not now technically cover these communications is an omission that this proposal corrects.

Paragraph (c) extends the application of Rule 1.9 to prohibit representation adverse to the prospective client in the same or a substantially related matter. Unlike Rule 1.9, however, this Rule does so only if the lawyer received information from the prospective client that could be "significantly harmful" to that person in the later representation.

The prospective client situation justifies that different treatment because, prior to the representation decision, there is an inevitable period in which it is in the interest of the prospective client to share enough information with the lawyer to determine whether there is a conflict of interest or simple incompatibility. The lawyer may learn very early in the consultation, for example, that the party adverse to the prospective client is a client of the lawyer's firm. If the discussion stops before "significantly harmful" information is shared, it seems that the law firm's regular client should not be denied counsel of its choice if a substantially related matter arises.

Paragraph (c) also extends the prohibition of this Rule to associated lawyers, except as provided in paragraph (d).

Paragraph (d) makes clear that the prohibition imposed by this Rule can be waived with the informed consent, confirmed in writing, of both the former prospective client and the client on whose behalf the lawyer later plans to take action adverse to the former prospective client. The expression of this requirement is parallel to that in Rules 1.7 and 1.9.

In the event that "significantly harmful" information is revealed, paragraph (d) provides that the lawyer who received the information may be screened from any involvement in the subsequent matter but others in the law firm may represent the adverse party.

The next portion of the Reporter's Explanation of Changes discussed the Comment to Rule 1.18, as follows:

[1] This Comment highlights three ways in which lawyers may assume obligations to prospective clients: disclosure of information, taking possession of documents or property and giving legal advice. It also explains the inevitably tentative quality of the initial consultation and suggests the reason for giving prospective clients somewhat less than the protection offered former clients by Rule 1.9.

[2] This Comment explains that lawyers are not disqualified when a person unilaterally communicates information to the lawyer without any reasonable expectation that the lawyer will agree to discuss the possibility of forming a client-lawyer relationship.

[3] This Comment explains the lawyer's obligation to preserve confidences of the prospective client, no matter what right the lawyer or law firm may have to undertake later adverse representation.

[4] This Comment first explains that a lawyer should obtain only the information required to determine whether to undertake the representation. If a conflict of interest is found to exist, the lawyer should decline the representation or obtain the required consent from all affected clients.

[5] This Comment identifies consent in advance of the consultation as one way to avoid later concerns about adverse use of the information obtained. Such an option was expressly approved in ABA Standing Committee on Ethics and Professional Responsibility Formal Opinion 90-358.

[6] This Comment reiterates the right of a lawyer to undertake representation adverse to a prospective client from whom no "significantly harmful" information was obtained.

[7] This Comment describes how the imputation otherwise required by paragraph (c) may be avoided by either obtaining the informed consent of the prospective and affected clients or by screening under the conditions stated in paragraph (d)(1).

[8] This Comment addresses the requirements of paragraph (d)(2).

[9] This Comment is a cross-reference to existing Rules that deal with two of the three issues identified in Comment [1]. Any advice a lawyer gives must be competent under Rule 1.1, and Rule 1.15 requires a lawyer to care for property of "third persons," which would include prospective clients.

Selected State Variations

New York has no direct counterpart to ABA Model Rule 1.18, but compare New York's DR 5-108(A).

Related Materials

Restatement of the Law Governing Lawyers: See Restatement §15 in our chapter on the Restatement later in this volume.

ARTICLE 2. COUNSELOR

Rule 2.1 Advisor

In representing a client, a lawyer shall exercise independent professional judgment and render candid advice. In rendering advice, a lawyer may refer not only to law but to other considerations such as moral, economic, social and political factors, that may be relevant to the client's situation.

COMMENT

Scope of Advice

[1] A client is entitled to straightforward advice expressing the lawyer's honest assessment. Legal advice often involves unpleasant facts and alternatives that a client may be disinclined to confront. In presenting advice, a lawyer endeavors to sustain the client's morale and may put advice in as acceptable a form as honesty permits. However, a lawyer should not be deterred from giving candid advice by the prospect that the advice will be unpalatable to the client.

[2] Advice couched in narrow legal terms may be of little value to a client, especially where practical considerations, such as cost or effects on other people, are predominant. Purely technical legal advice, therefore, can sometimes be inadequate. It is proper for a lawyer to refer to relevant moral and ethical considerations in giving advice. Although a lawyer is not a moral advisor as such, moral and ethical considerations impinge upon most legal questions and may decisively influence how the law will be applied.

[3] A client may expressly or impliedly ask the lawyer for purely technical advice. When such a request is made by a client experienced in legal matters, the lawyer may accept it at face value. When such a request is made by a client inexperienced in legal matters, however, the lawyer's responsibility as advisor may include indicating that more may be involved than strictly legal considerations.

[4] Matters that go beyond strictly legal questions may also be in the domain of another profession. Family matters can involve problems within the professional competence of psychiatry, clinical psychology or social work; business matters can involve problems within the competence of the accounting profession or of financial specialists. Where consultation with a professional in another field is itself something a competent lawyer would recommend, the lawyer should make such a recommendation. At the same time, a lawyer's advice at its best often consists of recommending a course of action in the face of conflicting recommendations of experts.

Offering Advice

[5] In general, a lawyer is not expected to give advice until asked by the client. However, when a lawyer knows that a client proposes a course of action that is likely to result in substantial adverse legal consequences to the client, <u>the lawyer's</u> duty to the client under Rule 1.4 may require that the lawyer ~~act~~ <u>offer advice</u> if the client's course of action is related to the representation. <u>Similarly, when a matter is likely to involve litigation, it may be necessary under Rule 1.4 to inform the client of forms of dispute resolution that might constitute reasonable alternatives to litigation.</u> A lawyer ordinarily has no duty to initiate investigation of a client's affairs or to give advice that the client has indicated is unwanted, but a lawyer may initiate advice to a client when doing so appears to be in the client's interest.

Canon and Code Antecedents

ABA Canons of Professional Ethics: No comparable Canon.

ABA Model Code of Professional Responsibility: Compare DR 5-107(B) (reprinted later in this volume).

Cross-References in Other Rules

Rule 7.2, Comment 8: "[R]eciprocal referral arrangements must not interfere with the lawyer's professional judgment as to making referrals or as to providing substantive legal services. See **Rules 2.1** and 5.4(c)."

Legislative History of Model Rule 2.1

1980 Discussion Draft: The Introduction to the section entitled "Attorney as Advisor" contained the following paragraph:

> The lawyer's professional function historically originated as attorney and advocate, that is, appearing on behalf of a party to litigation. Giving legal advice evolved from giving advice about how to proceed in litigation. Today, serving as advisor is the lawyer's predominant role.

Rule 2.1 provided:

Independence and Candor

> In advising a client a lawyer shall exercise independent and candid professional judgment, uncontrolled by the interests or wishes of a third person, or by the lawyer's own interests or wishes.

In addition, Rule 2.2 (now incorporated into Rule 2.1) provided:

Scope of Advice

> In rendering advice a lawyer may refer to all relevant considerations unless in the circumstances it is evident that the client desires advice confined to strictly legal considerations.

1981 and 1982 Drafts were the same as adopted.

2002 Amendments: At its February 2002 Mid-Year Meeting, the ABA House of Delegates adopted with only minor changes the ABA Ethics 2000 Commission proposal to amend the Comment to Rule 2.1. (The Ethics 2000 Commission did not propose any changes to the text of Rule 2.1.)

Selected State Variations

California has no direct counterpart to Rule 2.1.

Colorado: Rule 2.1 provides that "[i]n a matter involving or expected to involve litigation, a lawyer should advise the client of alternative forms of dispute resolution which might reasonably be pursued to attempt to resolve the legal dispute or to reach the legal objective sought." The Colorado Comment to this sentence states that depending on the circumstances, "it may be appropriate for the lawyer to discuss with the client factors such as cost, speed, effects on existing relationships, confidentiality and privacy, scope of relief, statutes of limitation, and relevant procedural rules and statutes."

Georgia: In the rules effective January 1, 2001, Georgia adopted the first sentence of ABA Model Rule 2.1 verbatim. However, Georgia moved the second sentence of the ABA rule to Comment 2 and added the following new sentence to the text of the rule: "A lawyer should not be deterred from giving candid advice by the prospect that the advice will be unpalatable to the client."

Hawaii: Rule 2.1 suggests that lawyers advise clients about ADR if a matter may involve litigation.

New York: Compare ABA Model Rule 2.1 to New York's EC 7-8.

Pennsylvania: Rule 2.1 provides that a lawyer "should" (rather than "shall") exercise independent professional judgment and render candid advice.

Texas: Rule 2.01 begins, "In advising or otherwise representing a client . . . ," and Texas deletes the second sentence of ABA Model Rule 2.1.

Related Materials

American Academy of Matrimonial Lawyers: The "Bounds of Advocacy" contains the following rules and comments:

> 2.12. An attorney should advise the client of the emotional and economic impact of divorce and the possibility or advisability of reconciliation.
>
> Comment to Rule 2.12
>
> . . . An attorney should ask if reconciliation might be possible, or at least whether the client is receptive to counseling. If the client exhibits uncertainty or ambivalence, the lawyer should assist in obtaining a counselor. In no event should an attorney urge a client to file suit, unless necessary to protect the client's interests.
>
> . . . Although few attorneys are qualified to do personal counseling, a thorough discussion of the probable emotional and monetary repercussions of divorce is permissible.
>
> If the client has begun counseling in hopes of reconciliation, the matrimonial lawyer should attempt to mitigate litigation-related activities that might prejudice marital harmony. It is important, however, for the attorney to be mindful that clients may make damaging admissions during joint marriage counseling. One spouse may use a "breathing spell" afforded by counseling to deplete the marital estate. The lawyer should advise the client of these risks and take precautions to protect the client in the interim.
>
> 2.14. An attorney should advise the client of the potential effect of the client's conduct on a custody dispute.
>
> Comment to Rule 2.14
>
> Predivorce conduct of the parents may significantly affect custody decisions. . . . Suggesting that the client spend more time with the child and consult from time-to-time with the child's doctor, teacher, and babysitter is appropriate. It is also proper to describe the potentially harmful legal consequences of an adulterous relationship, substance abuse, or other inappropriate behavior.
>
> The lawyer must consider whether the custody claim will be made in good faith. If not, the lawyer must advise the client of the harmful consequences of a meritless custody claim to the client, the child, and the client's spouse. If the client still demands advice to build a spurious custody case or to use a custody claim as a bargaining chip or as a means of inflicting revenge . . . the lawyer should withdraw.

Restatement of the Law Governing Lawyers: See Restatement §94 in our chapter on the Restatement later in this volume.

Rule 2.2 Intermediary

Editors' Note. At its February 2002 Mid-Year Meeting, based on a recommendation by the ABA Ethics 2000 Commission, the ABA House of Delegates completely deleted Rule 2.2 and its Comment from the Model Rules. At the same time, also based on a proposal by the Ethics 2000 Commission, the House of Delegates added a new Rule 2.4 ("Lawyer Serving as Third-Party Neutral"). For more information, see the entry entitled "2002 Amendments" in the Legislative History following this rule and Rule 2.4.

(a) A lawyer may act as intermediary between clients if:

(1) the lawyer consults with each client concerning the implications of the common representation, including the advantages and risks involved, and the effect on the attorney-client privileges, and obtains each client's consent to the common representation;

(2) the lawyer reasonably believes that the matter can be resolved on terms compatible with the clients' best interests, that each client will be able to make adequately informed decisions in the matter and that there is little risk of material prejudice to the interests of any of the clients if the contemplated resolution is unsuccessful; and

(3) the lawyer reasonably believes that the common representation can be undertaken impartially and without improper effect on other responsibilities the lawyer has to any of the clients.

(b) While acting as intermediary, the lawyer shall consult with each client concerning the decisions to be made and the considerations relevant in making them, so that each client can make adequately informed decisions.

(c) A lawyer shall withdraw as intermediary if any of the clients so requests, or if any of the conditions stated in paragraph (a) is no longer satisfied. Upon withdrawal, the lawyer shall not continue to represent any of the clients in the matter that was the subject of the intermediation.

COMMENT

[1] A lawyer acts as intermediary under this Rule when the lawyer represents two or more parties with potentially conflicting interests. A key factor in defining the relationship is whether the parties share responsibility for the lawyer's fee, but the common representation may be inferred from other circumstances. Because confusion can arise as to the lawyer's role where each party is not separately represented, it is important that the lawyer make clear the relationship.

~~[2] The Rule does not apply to a lawyer acting as arbitrator or mediator between or among parties who are not clients of the lawyer, even where the lawyer has been appointed with the concurrence of the parties. In performing such a role the lawyer may be subject to applicable codes of ethics, such as the Code of Ethics for Arbitration in Commercial Disputes prepared by a joint Committee of the American Bar Association and the American Arbitration Association.~~

~~[3] A lawyer acts as intermediary in seeking to establish or adjust a relationship between clients on an amicable and mutually advantageous basis; for example, in helping to organize a business in which two or more clients are entrepreneurs, working out the financial reorganization of an enterprise in which two or more clients have an interest, arranging a property distribution in settlement of an estate or mediating a dispute between clients. The lawyer seeks to resolve potentially conflicting interests by developing the parties' mutual interests. The alternative can be that each party may have to obtain separate representation, with the possibility in some situations of incurring additional cost, complication or even litigation. Given these and other relevant factors, all the clients may prefer that the lawyer act as intermediary.~~

~~[4] In considering whether to act as intermediary between clients, a lawyer should be mindful that if the intermediation fails the result can be additional cost, embarrassment and recrimination. In some situations the risk of failure is so great that intermediation is plainly impossible. For example, a lawyer cannot undertake common representation of clients between whom contentious litigation is imminent or who contemplate contentious negotiations. More generally, if the relationship between the parties has already assumed definite antagonism, the possibility that the clients' interests can be adjusted by intermediation ordinarily is not very good.~~

~~[5] The appropriateness of intermediation can depend on its form. Forms of intermediation range from informal arbitration, where each client's case is presented by the respective client and the lawyer decides the outcome, to mediation, to common representation where the clients' interests are substantially though not entirely compatible. One form may be appropriate in circumstances where another would not. Other relevant factors are whether the lawyer subsequently will represent both parties on a continuing basis and whether the situation involves creating a relationship between the parties or terminating one.~~

~~Confidentiality and Privilege~~

~~[6] A particularly important factor in determining the appropriateness of intermediation is the effect on client-lawyer confidentiality and the attorney-client privilege. In a common representation, the lawyer is still required both to keep each client adequately informed and to maintain~~

confidentiality of information relating to the representation. See R~~ules 1.4 and 1.6. Complying with both requirements while acting as intermediary requires a delicate balance. If the balance cannot be maintained, the common representation is improper. With regard to the attorney-client privilege, the prevailing rule is that as between commonly represented clients the privilege does not attach. Hence, it must be assumed that if litigation eventuates between the clients, the privilege will not protect any such communications, and the clients should be so advised.~~

~~[7] Since the lawyer is required to be impartial between commonly represented clients, intermediation is improper when that impartiality cannot be maintained. For example, a lawyer who has represented one of the clients for a long period and in a variety of matters might have difficulty being impartial between that client and one to whom the lawyer has only recently been introduced.~~

~~Consultation~~

~~[8] In acting as intermediary between clients, the lawyer is required to consult with the clients on the implications of doing so, and proceed only upon consent based on such a consultation. The consultation should make clear that the lawyer's role is not that of partisanship normally expected in other circumstances.~~

~~[9] Paragraph (b) is an application of the principle expressed in Rule 1.4. Where the lawyer is intermediary, the clients ordinarily must assume greater responsibility for decisions than when each client is independently represented.~~

~~Withdrawal~~

~~[10] Common representation does not diminish the rights of each client in the client-lawyer relationship. Each has the right to loyal and diligent representation, the right to discharge the lawyer as stated in Rule 1.16, and the protection of Rule 1.9 concerning obligations to a former client.~~

Canon and Code Antecedents

ABA Canons of Professional Ethics: No comparable Canon.

ABA Model Code of Professional Responsibility: Compare DR 5-105(B) and DR 5-105(C) (reprinted later in this volume).

Cross-References in Other Rules

None.

Legislative History of Model Rule 2.2

1980 Discussion Draft (then Rules 5.1 and 5.2) began with the following Introduction:

Intermediary Between Clients

A lawyer acts as intermediary in seeking to establish or adjust a relationship between clients on an amicable and mutually advantageous basis. A lawyer acts as intermediary, for example, in drafting the documents organizing a business in which two or more clients are entrepreneurs but have differing financial or personal interests in the enterprise. A lawyer acts as intermediary in working out a plan of financial reorganization for an enterprise on behalf of two or more clients who have differing financial interests in the enterprise, or in arranging the distribution of specific property in settlement of an estate among distributees. Under some circumstances, a lawyer may act as intermediary between spouses in arranging the terms of an uncontested separation or divorce settlement. A lawyer may act as intermediary in mediating a dispute between clients.

In all such situations, the lawyer seeks to resolve potentially conflicting interests by developing the parties' mutual interests. . . . In some nonlitigation situations, the stakes involved may be so modest that separate representation of the parties is financially impractical. Given these factors, all the clients may prefer that the lawyer act as intermediary. If they do, and if the lawyer's independent professional judgment indicates that acting as intermediary will further the clients' mutual interest, a lawyer may undertake that function.

This Rule does not deal with a lawyer acting as mediator or arbitrator between parties with whom the lawyer does not have a client-lawyer relationship, nor does it govern a situation where a lawyer represents a party in negotiation with a party who is unrepresented. A lawyer acts as intermediary under this Rule when the lawyer represents both parties. A key factor in defining the relationship is whether the parties share responsibility for paying the lawyer's fee, but the existence of a joint or common representation can be inferred from other circumstances. Because confusion can arise as to the lawyer's role and responsibility where each party is not separately represented, it is important that the lawyer make clear whom he represents in such situations.

Rules 5.1 and 5.2 of the 1980 Discussion Draft provided:

Conditions for Acting as an Intermediary

(a) A lawyer may act as an intermediary between clients if:

(1) the possibility of adjusting the clients' interests is strong; and

(2) each client will be able to make adequately informed decisions in the matter, and there is little likelihood that any of the clients will be significantly prejudiced if the contemplated adjustment of interests is unsuccessful; and

(3) the lawyer can act impartially and without improper effect on other services the lawyer is performing for any of the clients; and

(4) the lawyer fully explains to each client the implications of the common representation, including the advantages and risks involved, and obtains each client's consent to the common representation.

(b) Before serving as intermediary a lawyer shall explain fully to each client the decisions to be made and the considerations relevant to making them, so that each client can make adequately informed decisions.

Withdrawal as an Intermediary

> A lawyer shall withdraw as intermediary if any of the clients so requests, if the conditions stated in Rule 5.1 cannot be met, or if it becomes apparent that a mutually advantageous adjustment of interests cannot be made. Upon withdrawal, the lawyer may continue to represent any of the clients only to the extent compatible with the lawyer's responsibilities to the other client or clients.

1981 Draft: Rule 2.2(c) required a lawyer to withdraw if the conditions in (a) could not be met "or if in the light of subsequent events the lawyer reasonably should know that a mutually advantageous resolution cannot be achieved."

1982 Draft: Rule 2.2(a)(1) was substantially the same as adopted except that it did not require the lawyer to explain "the effect on the attorney-client privileges." Rule 2.2(c)'s second sentence provided: "Upon withdrawal, the lawyer shall not continue to represent any of the clients unless doing so is clearly compatible with the lawyer's responsibilities to the other client or clients." The remainder of Rule 2.2 was substantially the same as adopted.

2002 Amendments: At its February 2002 Mid-Year Meeting, the ABA House of Delegates adopted without change the ABA Ethics 2000 Commission proposal to delete Rule 2.2 and its Comment and to move discussion of common representation to Rule 1.7's Comment. The Reporter's explanation for this deletion stated:

> [T]he Commission believes that the ideas expressed therein are better dealt with in the Comment to Rule 1.7. There is much in Rule 2.2 and its Comment that applies to all examples of common representation and ought to appear in Rule 1.7. Moreover, there is less resistance to common representation today than there was in 1983; thus, there is no longer any particular need to establish the propriety of common representation through a separate Rule.

Selected State Variations

Alaska: Rule 2.2 adds paragraph (d), which prohibits a lawyer who represents a client in divorce, dissolution, custody, alimony, child support, or marital property settlement cases from acting as an intermediary in the same case.

California: See Rule 3-310(B) (generally governing concurrent conflicts — California has no direct counterpart to Rule 2.2).

Colorado: Rule 2.2(a) provides that when acting as an intermediary, the lawyer must provide "full disclosure in writing" of the implications of common representation, and that the client's consent must also be "in writing."

District of Columbia: D.C. Rule 2.2(b) differs significantly from the ABA Model Rule — see District of Columbia Rules of Professional Conduct below.

Georgia: In the rules effective January 1, 2001, Georgia's version of Rule 2.2 differs significantly from former ABA Model Rule 2.2. Essentially, Georgia has adopted only Rule 2.2(c), moving Rule 2.2(a)(2) and (3) to paragraph 6 of the Comment and deleting ABA Model Rule 2.2(a)(1) and 2.2(b). The Comment, however, adopts the Comment to ABA Model Rule 2.2 nearly verbatim.

Illinois omits Rule 2.2.

Iowa: DR 5-105(A) provides: "In no event shall a lawyer represent both parties in dissolution of marriage proceedings whether or not contested or involving custody of children, alimony, child support, or property settlement."

Massachusetts has no equivalent to Rule 2.2, but Comments 12 through 12F to Rule 1.7 provide guidance concerning joint representation.

New Jersey makes Rule 2.2 "subject to the provisions of Rule 1.7."

New York: Compare former ABA Model Rule 2.2 to New York's EC 5-20 and DR 5-105.

Texas: In the Texas equivalent of former ABA Model Rule 2.2, Rule 1.07(a)(3) prohibits a lawyer from serving as an intermediary unless the lawyer "obtains each client's written consent to the common representation." Texas omits paragraphs (d) and (e) of former ABA Model Rule 2.2.

Virginia adds Rule 2.2(d), which states: "A lawyer shall not act as intermediary between clients in certain matters relating to divorce, annulment or separation — specifically child custody, child support, visitation, spousal support, and maintenance or division of property."

Virginia also has two rules that do not appear in the Model Rules. Rule 2.10 is entitled "Third Party Neutral." Rule 2.11 is entitled "Mediator." The text of those rules, in relevant part, is as follows:

Virginia Rule 2.10 Third Party Neutral

(a) A third party neutral assists parties in reaching a voluntary settlement of a dispute through a structured process known as a dispute resolution proceeding. The third party neutral does not represent any party.

(b) A lawyer who serves as a third party neutral

(1) shall inform the parties of the difference between the lawyer's role as third party neutral and the lawyer's role as one who represents a client;

(2) shall encourage unrepresented parties to seek legal counsel before an agreement is executed; and

(3) may encourage and assist the parties in reaching a resolution of their dispute; but

(4) may not compel or coerce the parties to make an agreement.

(c) A lawyer may serve as a third party neutral only if the lawyer has not previously represented and is not currently representing one of the parties in connection with the subject matter of the dispute resolution proceeding. . . .

(g) A lawyer who serves as a third party neutral shall not charge a fee contingent on the outcome of the resolution proceeding.

(h) This Rule does not apply to intermediation, which is covered by Rule 2.2.

Virginia Rule 2.11 Mediator

(a) A lawyer-mediator is a third party neutral (see Rule 2.10) who facilitates communication between the parties and, without deciding the issues or imposing a solution on the parties, enables them to understand and resolve their dispute.

(b) Prior to agreeing to mediate and throughout the mediation process a lawyer-mediator should reasonably determine that:

(1) mediation is an appropriate process for the parties;

(2) each party is able to participate effectively within the context of the mediation process; and

(3) each party is willing to enter and participate in the process in good faith.

(c) A lawyer-mediator may offer legal information if all parties are present or separately to the parties if they consent. The lawyer-mediator shall inform unrepresented parties or those parties who are not accompanied by legal counsel about the importance of reviewing the lawyer-mediator's legal information with legal counsel.

(d) A lawyer-mediator may offer evaluation of, for example, strengths and weaknesses of positions, assess the value and cost of alternatives to settlement or assess the barriers to settlement (collectively referred to as evaluation) only if such evaluation is incidental to the facilitative role and does not interfere with the lawyer-mediator's impartiality or the self-determination of the parties. . . .

Rule 2.3 Evaluation for Use by Third Persons

(a) A lawyer may ~~undertake~~ <u>provide</u> an evaluation of a matter affecting a client for the use of someone other than the client if~~: (1)~~ the lawyer reasonably believes that making the evaluation is compatible with other aspects of the lawyer's relationship with the client~~; and~~<u>.</u>

~~(2)~~ <u>(b) When the lawyer knows or reasonably should know that the evaluation is likely to affect the client's interests materially and adversely, the lawyer shall not provide the evaluation unless</u> the client ~~consents after consultation~~ <u>gives informed consent</u>.

~~(b)~~ <u>(c)</u> Except as disclosure is ~~required~~ <u>authorized</u> in connection with a report of an evaluation, information relating to the evaluation is otherwise protected by Rule 1.6.

COMMENT

Definition

[1] An evaluation may be performed at the client's direction ~~but~~ <u>or when impliedly authorized in order to carry out the representation. See Rule 1.2. Such an evaluation may be</u> for the primary purpose of establishing information for the benefit of third parties; for example, an opinion concerning the title of property rendered at the behest of a vendor for the information of a prospective purchaser, or at the behest of a borrower for the information of a prospective lender. In some situations, the evaluation may be required by a government agency; for example, an opinion concerning the legality of the securities registered for sale under the securities laws. In other instances, the evaluation may be required by a third person, such as a purchaser of a business.

~~[2] Lawyers for the government may be called upon to give a formal opinion on the legality of contemplated government agency action. In making such an evaluation, the government lawyer acts at the behest of the government as the client but for the purpose of establishing the limits of the agency's authorized activity. Such an opinion is to be distinguished from confidential legal advice given agency officials. The critical question is whether the opinion is to be made public.~~

~~[3]~~ [2] A legal evaluation should be distinguished from an investigation of a person with whom the lawyer does not have a client-lawyer relationship. For example, a lawyer retained by a purchaser to analyze a vendor's title to property does not have a client-lawyer relationship with the vendor. So also, an investigation into a person's affairs by a government lawyer, or by special counsel by a government lawyer, or by special counsel employed by the government, is not an evaluation as that term is used in this Rule. The question is whether the lawyer is retained by the person whose affairs are being examined. When the lawyer is retained by that person, the general rules concerning loyalty to client and preservation of confidences apply, which is not the case if the lawyer is retained by someone else. For this reason, it is essential to identify the person by whom the lawyer is retained. This should be made clear not only to the person under examination, but also to others to whom the results are to be made available.

~~Duty~~ Duties Owed to Third Person and Client

~~[4]~~ [3] When the evaluation is intended for the information or use of a third person, a legal duty to that person may or may not arise. That legal question is beyond the scope of this Rule. However, since such an evaluation involves a departure from the normal client-lawyer relationship, careful analysis of the situation is required. The lawyer must be satisfied as a matter of professional judgment that making the evaluation is compatible with other functions undertaken in behalf of the client. For example, if the lawyer is acting as advocate in defending the client against charges of fraud, it would normally be incompatible with that responsibility for the lawyer to perform an evaluation for others concerning the same or a related transaction. Assuming no such impediment is apparent, however, the lawyer should advise the client of the implications of the evaluation, particularly the lawyer's responsibilities to third persons and the duty to disseminate the findings.

Access to and Disclosure of Information

~~[5]~~ [4] The quality of an evaluation depends on the freedom and extent of the investigation upon which it is based. Ordinarily a lawyer should have whatever latitude of investigation seems necessary as a matter of professional judgment. Under some circumstances, however, the terms of the evaluation may be limited. For example, certain issues or sources may be categorically excluded, or the scope of search may be limited by time constraints or the noncooperation of persons having relevant information. Any such limitations that are material to the evaluation should be described in the report. If after a lawyer has commenced an evaluation, the client refuses to comply with the terms upon which it was understood the evaluation was to have been made, the lawyer's obligations are determined by law, having reference to the terms of the client's agreement and the surrounding circumstances. In no circumstances is the lawyer permitted to knowingly make a false statement of material fact or law in providing an evaluation under this Rule. See Rule 4.1.

Obtaining Client's Informed Consent

[5] Information relating to an evaluation is protected by Rule 1.6. In many situations, providing an evaluation to a third party poses no significant risk to the client; thus, the lawyer may be impliedly authorized to disclose information to carry out the representation. See Rule 1.6(a). Where, however, it is reasonably likely that providing the evaluation will affect the client's interests materially and adversely, the lawyer must first obtain the client's consent after the client has been adequately informed concerning the important possible effects on the client's interests. See Rules 1.6(a) and 1.0(e).

Financial Auditors' Requests for Information

[6] When a question concerning the legal situation of a client arises at the instance of the client's financial auditor and the question is referred to the lawyer, the lawyer's response may be made in accordance with procedures recognized in the legal profession. Such a procedure is set forth in the American Bar Association Statement of Policy Regarding Lawyers' Responses to Auditors' Requests for Information, adopted in 1975.

Canon and Code Antecedents

ABA Canons of Professional Ethics: No comparable Canon.

ABA Model Code of Professional Responsibility: No comparable Disciplinary Rule.

Cross-References in Other Rules

None.

Legislative History of Model Rule 2.3

1980 Discussion Draft (then Rules 6.1 through 6.3):

Confidential Evaluation (Rule 6.1)

A lawyer undertakes a confidential evaluation of a matter affecting a client when a report of the evaluation is to be given to the client alone and to be disclosed to others only at the direction of the client.

Independent Evaluation (Rule 6.2)

(a) A lawyer undertakes an independent evaluation of a matter affecting a client when a report of the evaluation is to be given to someone other than the client. A lawyer may make an independent evaluation if:

(1) Making the evaluation is compatible with other aspects of the lawyer's relationship with the client; and

(2) The terms upon which the evaluation is made are clearly described, particularly the lawyer's access to information and the persons to whom the report of the evaluation is to be made; and

(3) The client agrees that the lawyer may, within the terms upon which the evaluation is made, disclose information about the client, including matter otherwise confidential or privileged, that the lawyer determines ought to be disclosed in making a fair and accurate evaluation; and

(4) After adequate disclosure of the terms upon which the evaluation is to be made and their implications for the client, the client requests the lawyer to make the evaluation.

(b) In reporting the evaluation, the lawyer shall indicate any limitations on the scope of the inquiry that are reasonably necessary to a proper interpretation of the report.

(c) If, after a lawyer has commenced an independent evaluation, the client refuses to comply with the terms upon which it is to be made, the lawyer shall give to the person for whom the evaluation is intended the fullest report that can be made in the circumstances.

(d) Except as disclosure is required in connection with a report of the evaluation, information relating to an independent evaluation is confidential under Rule 1.7.

Financial Auditors' Requests for Information (Rule 6.3)

When a question concerning the legal situation of a client arises at the instance of the client's financial auditor and the question is referred to the lawyer, the lawyer's response shall be made in accordance with procedures recognized in the legal profession unless some other procedure is established after consent by the client upon adequate disclosure.

1981 Draft: Rule 2.3(a)(2) provided:

the terms upon which the evaluation is to be made are stated in writing, particularly the terms relating to the lawyer's access to information, the contemplated disclosure of otherwise confidential information and the persons to whom report of the evaluation is to be made . . . .

Rule 2.3(b) provided: "In reporting the evaluation, the lawyer shall indicate any material limitations that were imposed on the scope of the inquiry or on the disclosure of information."

1982 Draft: Rule 2.3(a)(2) required that "the conditions of the evaluation [be] described to the client in writing, including contemplated disclosure of information otherwise protected by Rule 1.6. . . ."

2002 Amendments: At its February 2002 Mid-Year Meeting, the ABA House of Delegates adopted without change the ABA Ethics 2000 Commission proposal to amend Rule 2.3 and its Comment.

Selected State Variations

California has no direct counterpart to Rule 2.3.

Florida adds the following new subparagraph:

> *Limitation on Scope of Evaluation.* In reporting the evaluation, the lawyer shall indicate any material limitations that were imposed on the scope of the inquiry or on the disclosure of information.

Georgia: In the rules effective January 1, 2001, Georgia adopted the pre-2002 version of ABA Model Rule 2.3 and its Comment verbatim.

New Jersey adds a requirement that "the conditions of the evaluation are described to the client in writing, including contemplated disclosure of information otherwise protected by Rule 1.6."

New York has no counterpart to ABA Model Rule 2.3.

Texas: Rule 2.02 deletes paragraph (b) of ABA Model Rule 2.3.

Virginia adopts Rule 2.3 but adds a paragraph (c) which states: "Except as disclosure is required in connection with a report of an evaluation, information relating to the evaluation is otherwise protected by Rule 1.6."

Related Materials

IRS Regulations: In the regulations governing practice before the Internal Revenue Service, 31 C.F.R. §10.33, entitled "Tax Shelter Opinions," provides that any practitioner who "provides a tax shelter opinion analyzing the Federal tax effects of a tax shelter investment" must comply with a stringent set of requirements. For example, regarding factual matters, §10.33(a)(1)(i) provides that a practitioner "must make inquiry as to all relevant facts, be satisfied that the material facts are accurately and completely described in the offering materials, and assure that any representations as to future activities are clearly identified, reasonable and complete"; and §10.33(a)(1)(ii) provides that a practitioner "may not accept as true asserted facts pertaining to the tax shelter which he/she should not, based on his/her background and knowledge, reasonably believe to be true." However, a practitioner "need not conduct an audit or independent verification of the asserted facts, or assume that a client's statement of the facts cannot be relied upon, unless he/she has reason to believe that any relevant facts asserted to him/her are untrue."

Legal Opinion Letters: A major area governed by Rule 2.3 is the "legal opinion letter" — a letter issued by a lawyer to a third party (typically a buyer or lender) assuring that the lawyer believes the transaction is legal, the seller is authorized to sell, etc. Banks, opposing parties, and others often rely upon such legal opinion letters, and a satisfactory legal opinion letter from the seller's or borrower's lawyer is often a condition of sale or a condition of making a loan. The ABA Section of Business Law has developed a Legal Opinion Accord that addresses numerous issues raised by legal opinion letters issued to third parties. The Legal Opinion Accord, which had its genesis in a 1989 conference in

Silverado, California, is reprinted with extensive commentary in Third-Party Legal Opinion Report, Including the Legal Opinion Accord, of the Section of Business Law, American Bar Association, 47 Bus. Law. 167 (1991).

In 1994, a Rhode Island statute took effect prohibiting any financial institution from requiring a private borrower's lawyer to issue a legal opinion letter as a condition of making a loan. As amended, the statute provides, in pertinent part, as follows:

> *§19-9-7. Attorneys' Opinions*
>
> (a) Except as provided in subsections (b)-(d), no lending institution making a loan in this state or any attorney, agent or representative for such lending institution shall directly or indirectly, as a condition of the making of a loan or advance, require any attorney representing a borrower in such loan transaction to give an opinion in relation to the validity, binding effect, or enforceability of any of the loan documents or the availability of remedies thereunder.
>
> (b) Subsection (a) shall not apply to any transaction in which the state, or any municipality in the state . . . is the borrower.
>
> (c) Subsection (a) shall not apply to transactions involving the public sale or underwriting of bonds, debentures, or other securities.
>
> (d) Subsection (a) shall not prohibit, as part of a loan transaction, any requirement or condition with respect to opinions dealing with the authority and status of a borrower and matters relating to collateral.
>
> (e) No opinion obtained in violation of this section may be relied on for any purpose, and no such opinion shall give rise to or form the basis for any action against any attorney or firm rendering such opinion. Any lending institution, and any attorney, agent or representative of any lending institution knowingly violating this section shall be subject to such action as may be lawfully imposed by the regulatory authority or court which has licensing or disciplinary authority over the lending institution, attorney or other individual in question.

Restatement of the Law Governing Lawyers: See Restatement §§51 and 95 in our chapter on the Restatement later in this volume.

Rule 2.4 Lawyer Serving as Third-Party Neutral

Editors' Note. Rule 2.4 is entirely new. The ABA House of Delegates added it to the Model Rules at its February 2002 Mid-Year Meeting, essentially based on the proposal submitted by the ABA Ethics 2000 Commission. For more information, see the entry entitled "2002 Amendments" in the Legislative History following this rule.

(a) A lawyer serves as a third-party neutral when the lawyer assists two or more persons who are not clients of the lawyer to reach a resolution of a dispute or other matter that has arisen between them. Service as a third-party neutral may include service as an arbitrator, a mediator or in such other capacity as will enable the lawyer to assist the parties to resolve the matter.

(b) A lawyer serving as a third-party neutral shall inform unrepresented parties that the lawyer is not representing them. When the lawyer knows or reasonably should know that a party does not understand the lawyer's role in the matter, the lawyer shall explain the difference between the lawyer's role as a third-party neutral and a lawyer's role as one who represents a client.

COMMENT

[1] Alternative dispute resolution has become a substantial part of the civil justice system. Aside from representing clients in dispute-resolution processes, lawyers often serve as third-party neutrals. A third-party neutral is a person, such as a mediator, arbitrator, conciliator or evaluator, who assists the parties, represented or unrepresented, in the resolution of a dispute or in the arrangement of a transaction. Whether a third-party neutral serves primarily as a facilitator, evaluator or decisionmaker depends on the particular process that is either selected by the parties or mandated by a court.

[2] The role of a third-party neutral is not unique to lawyers, although, in some court-connected contexts, only lawyers are allowed to serve in this role or to handle certain types of cases. In performing this role, the lawyer may be subject to court rules or other law that apply either to third-party neutrals generally or to lawyers serving as third-party neutrals. Lawyer-neutrals may also be subject to various codes of ethics, such as the Code of Ethics for Arbitration in Commercial Disputes prepared by a joint committee of the American Bar Association and the American Arbitration Association or the Model Standards of Conduct for Mediators jointly prepared by the American Bar Association, the American Arbitration Association and the Society of Professionals in Dispute Resolution.

[3] Unlike nonlawyers who serve as third-party neutrals, lawyers serving in this role may experience unique problems as a result of differences between the role of a third-party neutral and a lawyer's service as a client representative. The potential for confusion is significant when the parties are unrepresented in the process. Thus, paragraph (b) requires a lawyer-neutral to inform unrepresented parties that the lawyer is not representing them. For some parties, particularly parties who frequently use dispute-resolution processes, this information will be sufficient. For others, particularly those who are using the process for the first time, more information will be required. Where appropriate, the lawyer should inform unrepresented parties of the important differences between the lawyer's role as third-party neutral and a lawyer's role as a client representative, including the inapplicability of the attorney-client evidentiary privilege. The extent of disclosure required under this paragraph will depend on the particular parties involved and the subject matter of the

proceeding, as well as the particular features of the dispute-resolution process selected.

[4] A lawyer who serves as a third-party neutral subsequently may be asked to serve as a lawyer representing a client in the same matter. The conflicts of interest that arise for both the individual lawyer and the lawyer's law firm are addressed in Rule 1.12.

[5] Lawyers who represent clients in alternative dispute-resolution processes are governed by the Rules of Professional Conduct. When the dispute-resolution process takes place before a tribunal, as in binding arbitration (see Rule 1.0(m)), the lawyer's duty of candor is governed by Rule 3.3. Otherwise, the lawyer's duty of candor toward both the third-party neutral and other parties is governed by Rule 4.1.

Canon and Code Antecedents

ABA Canons of Professional Ethics: No comparable Canon.

ABA Model Code of Professional Responsibility: No comparable Disciplinary Rule.

Cross-References in Other Rules

Preamble, ¶3: "Some of these Rules apply directly to lawyers who are or have served as third-party neutrals. See, e.g., Rules 1.12 and **2.4**."

Rule 1.12, Comment 2: "Other law or codes of ethics governing third-party neutrals may impose more stringent standards of personal or imputed disqualification. See **Rule 2.4**."

Legislative History of Model Rule 2.4

2002 Amendments: Rule 2.4 was added to the Model Rules in February of 2002. The new rule and its Comment were based on a proposal by the ABA Ethics 2000 Commission, which the ABA House of Delegates adopted without change. The Reporter's Explanation Memo that accompanied the Ethics 2000 Commission proposal provided, in relevant part, as follows:

*Model Rule 2.4 — Reporter's Explanation of Changes**

The role of third-party neutral is not unique to lawyers, but the Commission recognizes that lawyers are increasingly serving in these roles. Unlike nonlawyers who serve as neutrals, lawyers may experience unique ethical problems, for example, those arising from possible confusion about the nature of the lawyer's role. The Commission notes that there have been a number of attempts by various organiza-

*Committee Reports, and the Reporter's Explanation of Changes contained therein, do not represent official policy of the ABA. They are for information only, and the opinions expressed are those of the authors.

tions to promulgate codes of ethics for neutrals (e.g., aspirational codes for arbitrators or mediators or court enacted rules governing court-sponsored mediators), but such codes do not typically address the special problems of lawyers. The Commission's proposed approach is designed to promote dispute resolution parties' understanding of the lawyer-neutral's role.

Paragraph (a) defines the term "third-party neutral" and emphasizes assistance at the request of the parties who participate in the resolution of disputes and other matters.

Paragraph (b) requires the lawyer serving as a third-party neutral to inform unrepresented parties in all cases that the lawyer does not represent them. The potential for confusion is sufficiently great to mandate this requirement in all cases involving unrepresented parties. Consistent with the standard of Rule 4.3, paragraph (b) requires the lawyer to explain the differences in a lawyer's role as a third-party neutral and the role of a lawyer representing a party in situations where the lawyer knows or reasonably should know that the unrepresented party does not understand the lawyer's role as a third-party neutral.

(The next part of the Reporter's Explanation of Changes discussed the Comment to Rule 2.4.)

[1] This introductory Comment describes dispute-resolution processes and notes that the specific role of the third-party neutral may depend on whether the process is court-annexed or private.

[2] This Comment cross-references other law and ethics codes applicable to lawyers serving as third-party neutrals. The Commission believes the referenced material will be helpful to lawyers unfamiliar with existing standards in this area.

[3] This Comment explains the rationale for the requirement of paragraph (b) that lawyers inform unrepresented parties that the lawyer is not representing them and, in some cases, explain the differences between the lawyer's role as neutral and the role of a lawyer representing a party.

[4] This Comment cross-references Rule 1.12, which addresses the conflicts of interest that arise when a lawyer-neutral or that lawyer's firm is asked to represent a client in a matter that is the same as a matter in which the lawyer served as a third-party neutral.

[5] This Comment distinguishes between the lawyer's duty of candor in an arbitration and in other dispute resolution proceedings. Because a binding arbitration is a "tribunal" as defined in Rule 1.0(m), the lawyer's duty of candor in such a proceeding is governed by Rule 3.3. In other dispute-resolution proceedings, the lawyer's duty of candor toward the third-party neutral and the other parties is governed by Rule 4.1.

Editors' Note. Comment 2 to Rule 2.4 notes that lawyer-neutrals "may also be subject to various codes of ethics. . . ." The Related Materials below include a few examples:

ABA Standards of Practice for Lawyer Mediators in Family Disputes: In 1984, the ABA House of Delegates formally adopted Standards for Lawyer Mediators in Family Disputes.

American Academy of Matrimonial Lawyers: The "Bounds of Advocacy" contains the following rules and commentary:

1.4 An attorney should be knowledgeable about alternative ways to resolve matrimonial disputes.

Comment to Rule 1.4

. . . Alternative dispute resolution mechanisms may establish a positive tone for continuing post-divorce relations by avoiding the animosity and pain of court battles. Parents who litigate their custody disputes are more likely to believe the process had a detrimental effect on relations with the divorcing spouse than parents whose custody disputes are mediated. When resolution requires complex trade-offs, the parties may be better able than the court to forge a resolution that addresses their individual values and needs. Alternatives to litigation are often less expensive; however, the client should be informed that such mechanisms may not necessarily reduce the cost because the matrimonial lawyer may need to prepare the case as thoroughly as for trial. Thus, it is essential that matrimonial lawyers have sufficient knowledge about alternative dispute resolution to enable them to understand its advantages and disadvantages. The attorney may then be able to determine when it is appropriate to recommend alternative methods to the client.

1.5 An attorney should act as a mediator or arbitrator only if competent to do so.

2.15 An attorney should encourage the settlement of marital disputes through negotiation, mediation, or arbitration.

Comment to Rule 2.15

. . . In many cases, the parties will have continuing contact with each other and need to cooperate for years to come. There is evidence that parties to a matrimonial dispute are more willing to abide by an agreement voluntarily entered into than by a court-ordered resolution following litigation. And, there is increasing evidence of the destructive effect on the children of protracted, adversarial proceedings between the spouses. It is therefore in the family's interest to seek to settle disputes cooperatively.

2.20 An attorney should not represent both husband and wife even if they do not wish to obtain independent representation.

Comment to Rule 2.20

The temptation to represent potentially conflicting interests is particularly difficult to resist in family disputes. Often the attorney is the "family lawyer" and previously represented husband, wife, family corporations, and even the children. Serving as an intermediary between husband and wife is not prohibited by the RPC. However, it is impossible for the attorney to provide impartial advice to both parties, and even a seemingly amicable separation or divorce may result in bitter litigation over financial matters or custody. A matrimonial lawyer should not attempt to represent both husband and wife even with the consent of both.

The attorney may be asked to represent family members in a nonlitigation setting. If separation or divorce is foreseeable or if one of the parents desires defense in a battered child action, the lawyer may see her role as counselor or negotiator for all concerned. This temptation should be resisted. However, this Standard does not apply in adoption proceedings or other matters where the spouses' positions are not adverse.

Association of Family Conciliation Courts Model Standards of Practice for Family and Divorce Mediation: In 1984, the Association of Family and Conciliation Courts promulgated standards "intended to assist public and private, voluntary and mandatory mediation" (Preamble). They can be found in the December 1984 Dispute Resolution Forum published by the National Institute for Dispute Resolution.

Code of Ethics for Arbitrators in Commercial Disputes: A Joint Committee of the ABA and the American Arbitration Association (AAA) has prepared a code of ethics for commercial arbitrators. It is expressly mentioned in Comment 2 to Rule 2.4.

"Lawyer for the Situation." During the Senate hearings on the nomination of Louis Brandeis to the Supreme Court, Brandeis was criticized for alleged conflicts of interest in a complex bankruptcy where he said he was "counsel for the situation." The phrase "lawyer for the situation" has since mystified and intrigued legal scholars. A thorough recounting of the origin of the phrase is found in A. Todd, Justice on Trial: The Case of Louis D. Brandeis (1964); John Dzienkowski, Lawyers as Intermediaries: The Representation of Multiple Clients in the Modern Legal Profession, 1992 U. Ill. L. Rev. 741 (1992); and John Frank, The Legal Ethics of Louis D. Brandeis, 17 Stan. L. Rev. 683, 699-702 (1965).

Model Rules of Professional Conduct for Federal Lawyers: Federal lawyers are permitted to act as intermediaries only between two individuals. After withdrawal as an intermediary, a federal lawyer may continue to represent some of the clients in the same matter if each client consents.

Restatement of the Law Governing Lawyers: See Restatement §130 in our chapter on the Restatement later in this volume.

Selected State Variations

New York has no direct counterpart to ABA Model Rule 2.4, but compare New York's EC 5-20.

Related Materials

Restatement of the Law Governing Lawyers: See Restatement §§103 and 130 in our chapter on the Restatement later in this volume.

ARTICLE 3. ADVOCATE

Rule 3.1 Mertitorious Claims and Contentions

A lawyer shall not bring or defend a proceeding, or assert or controvert an issue therein, unless there is a basis <u>in law and fact</u> for doing so that is not frivolous, which includes a good faith argument for an extension, modification or reversal of existing law. A lawyer for the defendant in a criminal proceeding, or the respondent in a proceeding

that could result in incarceration, may nevertheless so defend the proceeding as to require that every element of the case be established.

COMMENT

[1] The advocate has a duty to use legal procedure for the fullest benefit of the client's cause, but also a duty not to abuse legal procedure. The law, both procedural and substantive, establishes the limits within which an advocate may proceed. However, the law is not always clear and never is static. Accordingly, in determining the proper scope of advocacy, account must be taken of the law's ambiguities and potential for change.

[2] The filing of an action or defense or similar action taken for a client is not frivolous merely because the facts have not first been fully substantiated or because the lawyer expects to develop vital evidence only by discovery. What is required of lawyers, however, is that they inform themselves about the facts of their clients' cases and the applicable law and determine that they can make good faith arguments in support of their clients' positions. Such action is not frivolous even though the lawyer believes that the client's position ultimately will not prevail. The action is frivolous, however, if the ~~client desires to have the action taken primarily for the purpose of harassing or maliciously injuring a person, or, if the~~ lawyer is unable either to make a good faith argument on the merits of the action taken or to support the action taken by a good faith argument for an extension, modification or reversal of existing law.

[3] The lawyer's obligations under this Rule are subordinate to federal or state constitutional law that entitles a defendant in a criminal matter to the assistance of counsel in presenting a claim or contention that otherwise would be prohibited by this Rule.

Canon and Code Antecedents

ABA Canons of Professional Ethics: Canons 5, 15, 30, and 31 provided as follows:

5. The Defense or Prosecution of Those Accused of Crime

It is the right of the lawyer to undertake the defense of a person accused of crime, regardless of his personal opinion as to the guilt of the accused; otherwise innocent persons, victims only of suspicious circumstances, might be denied proper defense. Having undertaken such defense, the lawyer is bound, by all fair and honorable means, to present every defense that the law of the land permits, to the end that no person may be deprived of life or liberty, but by due process of law.

The primary duty of a lawyer engaged in public prosecution is not to convict, but to see that justice is done. The suppression of facts or the secreting of witnesses capable of establishing the innocence of the accused is highly reprehensible.

15. How Far a Lawyer May Go in Supporting a Client's Cause

Nothing operates more certainly to create or to foster popular prejudice against lawyers as a class, and to deprive the profession of that full measure of public esteem and confidence which belongs to the proper discharge of its duties than does the false claim, often set up by the unscrupulous in defense of questionable transactions, that it is the duty of the lawyer to do whatever may enable him to succeed in winning his client's cause.

It is improper for a lawyer to assert in argument his personal belief in his client's innocence or in the justice of his cause.

The lawyer owes "entire devotion to the interest of the client, warm zeal in the maintenance and defense of his rights and the exertion of his utmost learning and ability," to the end that nothing be taken or be withheld from him, save by the rules of law, legally applied. No fear of judicial disfavor or public unpopularity should restrain him from the full discharge of his duty. In the judicial forum the client is entitled to the benefit of any and every remedy and defense that is authorized by the law of the land, and he may expect his lawyer to assert every such remedy or defense. But it is steadfastly to be borne in mind that the great trust of the lawyer is to be performed within and not without the bounds of the law. The office of attorney does not permit, much less does it demand of him for any client, violation of law or any manner of fraud or chicane. He must obey his own conscience and not that of his client.

30. Justifiable and Unjustifiable Litigations

The lawyer must decline to conduct a civil cause or to make a defense when convinced that it is intended merely to harass or to injure the opposite party or to work oppression or wrong. But otherwise it is his right, and, having accepted retainer, it becomes his duty to insist upon the judgment of the Court as to the legal merits of his client's claim. His appearance in Court should be deemed equivalent to an assertion on his honor that in his opinion his client's case is one proper for judicial determination.

31. Responsibility for Litigation

No lawyer is obliged to act either as adviser or advocate for every person who may wish to become his client. He has the right to decline employment. Every lawyer upon his own responsibility must decide what employment he will accept as counsel, what causes he will bring into Court for plaintiffs, what cases he will contest in Court for defendants. The responsibility for advising as to questionable transactions, for bringing questionable suits, for urging questionable defenses, is the lawyer's responsibility. He cannot escape it by urging as an excuse that he is only following his client's instructions.

ABA Model Code of Professional Responsibility: Compare DR 7-102(A)(1) and DR 7-102(A)(2) (reprinted later in this volume).

Cross-References in Other Rules

Rule 3.3, Comment 3: "An advocate is responsible for pleadings and other documents prepared for litigation, but is usually not required to have personal knowledge of matters asserted therein, for litigation documents ordinarily present assertions by the client, or by someone on the client's behalf, and not assertions by the lawyer. Compare **Rule 3.1**."

Legislative History of Model Rule 3.1

1980 Discussion Draft contained the following Introduction to Article 3:

> As advocate, a lawyer presents evidence and argument before a tribunal in behalf of a client. The advocate's duty in the adversary system is to present the client's case as persuasively as possible, leaving presentation of the opposing case to the other party. An advocate may not present a claim or defense lacking serious merit for the purpose of delay, although an advocate for the defendant in a criminal case may insist on proof of the offense charged. An advocate does not vouch for the justness of a client's cause but only its legal merit.

In addition, Rule 3.1 provided:

> (a) A lawyer shall not:
>
> (1) file a complaint, motion, or pleading other than one that puts the prosecution to its proof in a criminal case, unless according to the lawyer's belief there is good ground to support it; . . .

1982 and 1982 Drafts were substantially the same as adopted.

2002 Amendments: At its February 2002 Mid-Year Meeting, the ABA House of Delegates adopted without change the ABA Ethics 2000 Commission proposal to amend Rule 3.1 and its Comment.

Selected State Variations

Alabama: Rule 3.1(a) tracks the language of DR 7-102(A)(1) — see Model Code Comparison above.

California: See Rule 3-200 (Prohibited Objectives of Employment) and B & P Code §6068(c). In addition, California Civil Code §§128.5, 128.6, and 128.7 provide sanctions for bad faith lawsuits and for frivolous litigation tactics.

Colorado: In 1999, when Colorado amended Rule 1.2(c) to permit a lawyer to "provide limited representation to pro se parties . . . ," the state simultaneously added the following new Rule 11(b) to the state's sanctions rule, C.R.C.P. 11:

> *Limited Representation*
>
> (b) . . . Pleadings or papers filed by the pro se party that were prepared with the drafting assistance of the attorney shall include the attorney's name, address, telephone number and registration number. . . . The attorney in providing such drafting assistance may rely on the pro se party's representation of facts, unless the attorney has reason to believe that such representations are false or materially insufficient, in which instance the attorney shall make an independent reasonable inquiry into the facts. . . .

Merely "helping to draft the pleading or paper filed by the pro se party" constitutes a certification by the attorney that the document is "(1) well-grounded in fact based upon a reasonable inquiry of the pro se party by the attorney, . . . and (3) is not interposed for any improper purpose, such as to harass or to cause unnecessary delay or needless increase in the cost of litigation."

District of Columbia: D.C. Rule 3.1 differs significantly from ABA Model Rule 3.1 — see District of Columbia Rules of Professional Conduct below.

Georgia: In the rules effective January 1, 2001, Georgia rejects ABA Model Rule 3.1 and instead retains the language of DR 7-102(A)(1) (2) from the ABA Model Code of Professional Responsibility. Georgia adopts the first two paragraphs of the ABA Comment to ABA Model Rule 3.1 verbatim, but adds the following two new paragraphs:

> [3] It is not ethically improper for a lawyer to file a lawsuit before complete factual support for the claim has been established provided that the lawyer determines that a reasonable lawyer would conclude that there is a reasonable possibility that facts supporting the cause of action can be established after the filing of the claim; and provided further that the lawyer is not required by rules of procedure, or otherwise to represent that the cause of action has an adequate factual basis. If after filing it is discovered that the lawsuit has no merit, the lawyer will dismiss the lawsuit or in the alternative withdraw.
>
> [4] The decision of a court that a claim is not meritorious is not necessarily conclusive of a violation of this Rule.

New Jersey adds "the lawyer knows or reasonably believes" after "unless" in the first sentence.

New York: Compare ABA Model Rule 3.1 to New York's DR 7-102(A)(1) and (A)(2).

Texas: Rule 3.01 ends after "frivolous."

Virginia adopts Rule 3.1.

Related Materials

ABA Civil Discovery Standards: At its 1999 Annual Meeting, the ABA House of Delegates formally approved lengthy Civil Discovery Standards (53 pages) that the ABA Section of Litigation developed to help courts and lawyers deal with discovery issues that frequently occur in civil litigation but that often fall outside the scope of the statutes and court rules governing civil discovery.

American Academy of Matrimonial Lawyers: The "Bounds of Advocacy" drafted by the American Academy of Matrimonial Lawyers contains the following provision and commentary:

> 2.25 An attorney should not contest child custody or visitation for either financial leverage or vindictiveness.
>
> Comment to Rule 2.25
>
> Clients in contested dissolutions sometimes ask attorneys to contest custody even though they concede that the other spouse is the better parent. It is improper for the matrimonial lawyer to assist the client in such conduct. Proper consideration of the welfare of the children requires that they not be used as pawns in the adversary process. If despite the attorney's advice the client persists, the attorney should seek to withdraw.

Federal Rules of Civil Procedure: Rule 11(b), which closely parallels Model Rule 3.1, provides that a lawyer's signature on a pleading, written motion, or other paper certifies, among other things, that "to the best of [his or her] knowledge, information, and belief, formed after an inquiry reasonable under the circumstances," the document

> (1) it is not being presented for any improper purpose, such as to harass or to cause unnecessary delay or needless increase in the cost of litigation;
>
> (2) the claims, defenses, and other legal contentions therein are warranted by existing law or by a nonfrivolous argument for the extension, modification, or reversal of existing law or the establishment of new law;
>
> (3) the allegations and other factual contentions have evidentiary support or, if specifically so identified, are likely to have evidentiary support after a reasonable opportunity for further investigation or discovery; and
>
> (4) the denials of factual contentions are warranted on the evidence or, if specifically so identified, are reasonably based on a lack of information or belief.

Sanctions must be "limited to what is sufficient to deter repetition of such conduct or comparable conduct." When a party makes a motion for sanctions, a safe-harbor provision gives the targeted party three weeks to withdraw the offending document before the motion can be decided. A court cannot award a monetary sanction against a party who has voluntarily dismissed or settled claims before the court issues its order to show cause. Sanctions may include an order to pay a penalty into court, "directives of a nonmonetary nature," and, if imposed after motion, an order to pay attorney's fees and "other expenses incurred as a direct result of the violation." A party (as opposed to a lawyer) who signs a document is not subject to a monetary sanction for violation of paragraph (2) above. Absent "exceptional circumstances, a law firm shall be held jointly responsible for violations committed by its partners, associates, and employees."

Federal Rules of Appellate Procedure: Rule 38 provides that "If a court of appeals shall determine that an appeal is frivolous, it may award just damages and single or double costs to the appellee."

Fee Award Statutes: Dozens of state and federal statutes permit courts to award attorney fees to a prevailing party in litigation if the opposing party's position is frivolous or unjustified. In federal criminal prosecutions, for example, 18 U.S.C. §3006A provides that a court "may" award reasonable attorney fees and other litigation expenses to a federal criminal defendant (other than one represented by assigned counsel paid for by the public) "where the court finds that the position of the United States was vexatious, frivolous, or in bad faith, unless the court finds that special circumstances make such an award unjust." Similarly, in federal civil cases to which the United States is a party, the Equal Access to Justice Act, 28 U.S.C. §2412, provides that a court "shall" award attorney fees to the prevailing party if the government's position in the litigation was not "substantially justified" unless "special circumstances make an award unjust."

IRS Regulations: In the regulations governing practice before the Internal Revenue Service, 31 C.F.R. §10.34(a)(1) provides that a practitioner "may not sign a return as a preparer if the practitioner determines that the return contains a position that does not have a realistic possibility of being sustained on its merits (the realistic possibility standard) unless the position is not frivolous and is adequately disclosed to the Service." Section 10.34(a)(4)(i) provides that a position is considered to have a "realistic possibility" of being sustained on its merits "if a reasonable and well-informed analysis by a person knowledgeable in the tax law would lead such a person to conclude that the position has approximately a one in three, or greater, likelihood of being sustained on its merits."

Private Securities Litigation Reform Act: In December of 1995, Congress passed the Private Securities Litigation Reform Act, 15 U.S.C. §77z-1. Title I, entitled "Reduction of Abusive Litigation," requires courts to make specific findings as to whether all attorneys in private securities fraud suits have complied with Rule 11 of the Federal Rules of Civil Procedure. The law also establishes a rebuttable presumption that a losing party should pay all of a prevailing party's costs and attorney fees as an appropriate sanction for violating Rule 11 — but a party may rebut this presumption by showing that (1) the violation was de minimis, or (2) imposing fees and costs would be an undue burden and would be unjust. Finally, the law gives courts express authority to require counsel for either side or both sides to post a bond to cover fees and expenses that the court may ultimately award.

Restatement of the Law Governing Lawyers: See Restatement §§57 and 110 in our chapter on the Restatement later in this volume.

Rule 3.2 Expediting Litigation

A lawyer shall make reasonable efforts to expedite litigation consistent with the interests of the client.

COMMENT

[1] Dilatory practices bring the administration of justice into disrepute. ~~Delay should not be indulged merely for the convenience of the advocates, or~~ Although there will be occasions when a lawyer may properly seek a postponement for personal reasons, it is not proper for a lawyer to routinely fail to expedite litigation solely for the convenience of the advocates. Nor will a failure to expedite be reasonable if done for the purpose of frustrating an opposing party's attempt to obtain rightful redress or repose. It is not a justification that similar conduct is often tolerated by the bench and bar. The question is whether a competent lawyer acting in good faith would regard the course of action as having some substantial purpose other than delay. Realizing financial or other benefit from otherwise improper delay in litigation is not a legitimate interest of the client.

Canon and Code Antecedents

ABA Canons of Professional Ethics: No comparable Canon.

ABA Model Code of Professional Responsibility: Compare DR 7-101(A)(1) and DR 7-102(A)(1) (reprinted later in this volume).

Cross-References in Other Rules

None.

Legislative History of Model Rule 3.2

1980 Discussion Draft (then Rule 3.3(a)) provided:

> A lawyer shall make every effort consistent with the legitimate interests of the client to expedite litigation. Realizing financial or other benefit from otherwise improper delay in litigation is not a legitimate interest of the client. A lawyer shall not engage in any procedure or tactic having no substantial purpose other than delay or increasing the cost of litigation to another party.

1981 Draft: "A lawyer shall make reasonable effort consistent with the *legitimate* interests of the client to expedite litigation."

1982 Draft was adopted.

2002 Amendments: At its February 2002 Mid-Year Meeting, the ABA House of Delegates adopted without change the ABA Ethics 2000 Commission proposal to amend the Comment to Rule 3.2. (The Ethics 2000 Commission did not propose any changes to the text of Rule 3.2.)

Selected State Variations

California: See B & P Code §6128(b). (California's Rules of Professional Conduct have no comparable provision.)

District of Columbia: D.C. Rule 3.2(a) differs significantly from the ABA Model Rule — see District of Columbia Rules of Professional Conduct below.

Georgia: In the rules effective January 1, 2001, Georgia adopted ABA Model Rule 3.2 and the first sentence of the ABA Comment verbatim. However, Georgia replaced the remainder of the ABA Comment with a new paragraph that states: "The reasonableness of a lawyer's effort to expedite litigation must be judged by all of the controlling factors. 'Reasonable efforts' do not equate to 'instant efforts' and are sufficient if reasonable under the relevant circumstances."

New Jersey adds "and shall treat with courtesy and consideration all persons involved in the legal process" at the end of Rule 3.2.

New York has no counterpart to ABA Model Rule 3.2.

Texas: Rule 3.02 provides:

> In the course of litigation, a lawyer shall not take a position that unreasonably increases the costs or other burdens of the case or that unreasonably delays resolution of the matter.

Virginia omits Rule 3.2.

Related Materials

Alternative Dispute Resolution ("ADR"): Some lawyers believe that the obligation in Rule 3.2 to "expedite litigation" includes the obligation to inform a client about ADR methods as alternatives to litigation. For example, a Texas Bar Association Creed states: "I will advise my client regarding the availability of mediation [and] arbitration. . . ." Similarly, the Houston Bar Association has adopted guidelines stating: "When appropriate, I will counsel my client with respect to mediation, arbitration, and other alternative methods of dispute resolution." The Chicago Bar Association has circulated a draft proposal to amend Rule 3.2 to provide: "A lawyer shall make reasonable efforts to expedite or *minimize the cost of* litigation, *including the possible use of alternative dispute resolution processes,* consistent with the interests of the client." (Emphasis added.) In the context of Rule 2.1, Colorado, Georgia, and Hawaii already require lawyers to advise clients about ADR, and numerous state and federal courts have adopted mandatory ADR to move litigation along more quickly and inexpensively.

Federal Rules of Appellate Procedure: Rule 38, entitled "Damages for Delay," provides as follows: "If a court of appeals shall determine that an appeal is frivolous, it may award just damages and single or double costs to the appellee."

Federal Rules of Civil Procedure: Fed. R. Civ. P. 1 provides that the Federal Rules of Civil Procedure "shall be construed to secure the just, *speedy*, and inexpensive determination of every action [emphasis added]." Fed. R. Civ. P. 11, the broadest and most frequently invoked sanctions rule, requires attorneys to sign every pleading, motion, or other paper to certify that (among other things) the paper is "not being presented for any improper purpose, such as to harass or to *cause unnecessary delay* or needless increase in the cost of litigation . . . [emphasis added]." Fed. R. Civ. P. 26(g), part of the general rule governing discovery, requires a similar certification pertaining to discovery requests, responses, and objections. Fed. R. Civ. P. 56(g), part of the rule on summary judgment, provides sanctions whenever the court finds "that any of the affidavits presented pursuant to this rule are presented in bad faith *or solely for the purpose of delay* [emphasis added]."

Federal Rules of Evidence: Rule 102 of the Federal Rules of Evidence provides that the Rules shall be construed to secure "elimination of unjustifiable expense and delay. . . ."

Model Rules of Professional Conduct for Federal Lawyers: Rule 3.2 provides: "A Federal lawyer shall make reasonable efforts to expedite litigation and other proceedings consistent with the interests of the client *and the lawyer's responsibilities to the tribunal to avoid unwarranted delay* [emphasis added]."

Restatement of the Law Governing Lawyers: The Restatement has no comparable provision.

28 U.S.C. §1927: A major federal statutory provision available to penalize litigants who engage in abusive delay and other improper litigation tactics is 28 U.S.C. §1927, which provides as follows:

> *Counsel's Liability for Excessive Costs*
>
> Any attorney . . . who so multiplies the proceedings in any case unreasonably and vexatiously may be required by the court to satisfy personally the excess costs, expenses, and attorneys' fees reasonably incurred because of such conduct.

Rule 3.3 Candor Toward the Tribunal

(a) A lawyer shall not knowingly:

(1) make a false statement of ~~material~~ fact or law to a tribunal <u>or fail to correct a false statement of material fact or law previously made to the tribunal by the lawyer</u>;

~~(2) fail to disclose a material fact to a tribunal when disclosure is necessary to avoid assisting a criminal or fraudulent act by the client;~~

~~(3)~~ (2) fail to disclose to the tribunal legal authority in the controlling jurisdiction known to the lawyer to be directly adverse to the position of the client and not disclosed by opposing counsel; or

~~(4)~~ (3) offer evidence that the lawyer knows to be false. If a lawyer, the lawyer's client, or a witness called by the lawyer, has offered material evidence and the lawyer comes to know of its falsity, the lawyer shall take reasonable remedial measures, including, if necessary, disclosure to the tribunal. A lawyer may refuse to offer evidence, other than the testimony of a defendant in a criminal matter, that the lawyer reasonably believes is false.

(b) A lawyer who represents a client in an adjudicative proceeding and who knows that a person intends to engage, is engaging or has engaged in criminal or fraudulent conduct related to the proceeding shall take reasonable remedial measures, including, if necessary, disclosure to the tribunal.

~~(b)~~ (c) The duties stated in ~~paragraph~~ paragraphs (a) and (b) continue to the conclusion of the proceeding, and apply even if compliance requires disclosure of information otherwise protected by Rule 1.6.

~~(c) A lawyer may refuse to offer evidence that the lawyer reasonably believes is false.~~

(d) In an ex parte proceeding, a lawyer shall inform the tribunal of all material facts known to the lawyer that will enable the tribunal to make an informed decision, whether or not the facts are adverse.

COMMENT

[1] This Rule governs the conduct of a lawyer who is representing a client in the proceedings of a tribunal. See Rule 1.0(m) for the definition of "tribunal." It also applies when the lawyer is representing a client in an ancillary proceeding conducted pursuant to the tribunal's adjudicative authority, such as a deposition. Thus, for example, paragraph (a)(3) requires a lawyer to take reasonable remedial measures if the lawyer comes to know that a client who is testifying in a deposition has offered evidence that is false.

~~[1]~~ [2] ~~The advocate's task is~~ This Rule sets forth the special duties of lawyers as officers of the court to avoid conduct that undermines the integrity of the adjudicative process. A lawyer acting as an advocate in an adjudicative proceeding has an obligation to present the client's case with persuasive force. Performance of that duty while maintaining confidences of the client, however, is qualified by the advocate's duty of candor to the tribunal. ~~However~~ Consequently, ~~an advocate does~~ although a lawyer in an adversary proceeding is not required to present an impartial exposition of the law or to vouch for the evidence submitted in a cause;, the lawyer must not allow the tribunal is responsible for assessing its probative value to be misled by false statements of law or fact or evidence that the lawyer knows to be false.

Representations by a Lawyer

[2] [3] An advocate is responsible for pleadings and other documents prepared for litigation, but is usually not required to have personal knowledge of matters asserted therein, for litigation documents ordinarily present assertions by the client, or by someone on the client's behalf, and not assertions by the lawyer. Compare Rule 3.1. However, an assertion purporting to be on the lawyer's own knowledge, as in an affidavit by the lawyer or in a statement in open court, may properly be made only when the lawyer knows the assertion is true or believes it to be true on the basis of a reasonably diligent inquiry. There are circumstances where failure to make a disclosure is the equivalent of an affirmative misrepresentation. The obligation prescribed in Rule 1.2(d) not to counsel a client to commit or assist the client in committing a fraud applies in litigation. Regarding compliance with Rule 1.2(d), see the Comment to that Rule. See also the Comment to Rule 8.4(b).

Misleading Legal Argument

[3] [4] Legal argument based on a knowingly false representation of law constitutes dishonesty toward the tribunal. A lawyer is not required to make a disinterested exposition of the law, but must recognize the existence of pertinent legal authorities. Furthermore, as stated in paragraph (a)(3)(2), an advocate has a duty to disclose directly adverse authority in the controlling jurisdiction that has not been disclosed by the opposing party. The underlying concept is that legal argument is a discussion seeking to determine the legal premises properly applicable to the case.

False Offering Evidence

[4] When evidence that a lawyer knows to be false is provided by a person who is not the client, the lawyer must refuse to offer it regardless of the client's wishes.

[5] When false evidence is offered by the client, however, a conflict may arise between the lawyer's duty to keep the client's revelations confidential and the duty of candor to the court. Upon ascertaining that material evidence is false, the lawyer should seek to persuade the client that

the evidence should not be offered or~~, if it has been offered, that its false character should immediately be disclosed. If the persuasion is ineffective, the lawyer must take reasonable remedial measures.~~

[5] Paragraph (a)(3) requires that the lawyer refuse to offer evidence that the lawyer knows to be false, regardless of the client's wishes. This duty is premised on the lawyer's obligation as an officer of the court to prevent the trier of fact from being misled by false evidence. A lawyer does not violate this Rule if the lawyer offers the evidence for the purpose of establishing its falsity.

[6] If a lawyer knows that the client intends to testify falsely or wants the lawyer to introduce false evidence, the lawyer should seek to persuade the client that the evidence should not be offered. If the persuasion is ineffective and the lawyer continues to represent the client, the lawyer must refuse to offer the false evidence. If only a portion of a witness's testimony will be false, the lawyer may call the witness to testify but may not elicit or otherwise permit the witness to present the testimony that the lawyer knows is false.

[7] The duties stated in paragraphs (a) and (b) apply to all lawyers, including defense counsel in criminal cases. In some jurisdictions, however, courts have required counsel to present the accused as a witness or to give a narrative statement if the accused so desires, even if counsel knows that the testimony or statement will be false. The obligation of the advocate under the Rules of Professional Conduct is subordinate to such requirements. See also Comment [9].

[8] The prohibition against offering false evidence only applies if the lawyer knows that the evidence is false. A lawyer's reasonable belief that evidence is false does not preclude its presentation to the trier of fact. A lawyer's knowledge that evidence is false, however, can be inferred from the circumstances. See Rule 1.0(f). Thus, although a lawyer should resolve doubts about the veracity of testimony or other evidence in favor of the client, the lawyer cannot ignore an obvious falsehood.

~~Refusing to Offer Proof Believed to Be False~~

~~[14]~~ [9] ~~Generally speaking,~~ Although paragraph (a)(3) only prohibits a lawyer ~~has authority~~ from offering evidence the lawyer knows to be false, it permits the lawyer to refuse to offer testimony or other proof that the lawyer reasonably believes is ~~untrustworthy~~ false. Offering such proof may reflect adversely on the lawyer's ability to discriminate in the quality of evidence and thus impair the lawyer's effectiveness as an advocate. ~~In criminal cases, however, a lawyer may, in some jurisdictions, be denied this authority by constitutional requirements governing the right to counsel.~~ Because of the special protections historically provided criminal defendants, however, this Rule does not permit a lawyer to refuse to offer the testimony of such a client where the lawyer reasonably believes but does not know that the testimony will be false. Unless the lawyer knows the testimony will be false, the lawyer ~~must honor~~ the client's decision to testify. See also Comment [7].

~~Perjury by a Criminal Defendant~~

~~[7] Whether an advocate for a criminally accused has the same duty of disclosure has been intensely debated. While it is agreed that the lawyer should seek to persuade the client to refrain from perjurious testimony, there has been dispute concerning the lawyer's duty when that persuasion fails. If the confrontation with the client occurs before trial, the lawyer ordinarily can withdraw. Withdrawal before trial may not be possible, however, either because trial is imminent, or because the confrontation with the client does not take place until the trial itself, or because no other counsel is available.~~

~~[8] The most difficult situation, therefore, arises in a criminal case where the accused insists on testifying when the lawyer knows that the testimony is perjurious. The lawyer's effort to rectify the situation can increase the likelihood of the client's being convicted as well as opening the possibility of a prosecution for perjury. On the other hand, if the lawyer does not exercise control over the proof, the lawyer participates, although in a merely passive way, in deception of the court.~~

~~[9] Three resolutions of this dilemma have been proposed. One is to permit the accused to testify by a narrative without guidance through the lawyer's questioning. This compromises both contending principles; it exempts the lawyer from the duty to disclose false evidence but subjects the client to an implicit disclosure of information imparted to counsel. Another suggested resolution, of relatively recent origin, is that the advocate be entirely excused from the duty to reveal perjury if the perjury is that of the client. This is a coherent solution but makes the advocate a knowing instrument of perjury.~~

~~[10] The other resolution of the dilemma is that the lawyer must reveal the client's perjury if necessary to rectify the situation. A criminal accused has a right to the assistance of an advocate, a right to testify and a right of confidential communication with counsel. However, an accused should not have a right to assistance of counsel in committing perjury. Furthermore, an advocate has an obligation, not only in professional ethics but under the law as well, to avoid implication in the commission of perjury or other falsification of evidence. See Rule 1.2(d).~~

Remedial Measures

~~[11]~~ [10] ~~If perjured testimony or false~~ Having offered material evidence ~~has been offered~~ in the belief that it was true, a lawyer may subsequently come to know that the evidence is false. Or, a lawyer may be surprised when the lawyer's client, or another witness called by the lawyer, offers testimony the lawyer knows to be false, either during the lawyer's direct examination or in response to cross-examination by the opposing lawyer. In such situations or if the lawyer knows of the falsity of testimony elicited from the client during a deposition, the lawyer must take reasonable remedial measures. In such situations, the advocate's proper course ~~ordinarily~~ is to remonstrate with the client confidentially, advise the client of the lawyer's duty of candor to the tribunal and seek the client's cooperation with respect to the withdrawal or correction of the false statements or evidence. If that fails, the advocate ~~should seek to withdraw if that will remedy the situation~~ must take further remedial action. If withdrawal from the representation is not permitted or will not ~~remedy the situation or is impossible~~ undo the effect of the false evidence, the advocate ~~should~~ must make such disclosure to the ~~court~~ tribunal as is reasonably necessary to remedy the situation, even if doing so requires the lawyer to reveal information that otherwise would be protected by Rule 1.6. It is for the ~~court~~ tribunal then to determine what should be done — making a statement about the matter to the trier of fact, ordering a mistrial or perhaps nothing. ~~If the false testimony was that of the client, the client may controvert the lawyer's version of their communication when the lawyer discloses the situation to the court. If there is an issue whether the client has committed perjury, the lawyer cannot represent the client in resolution of the issue, and a mistrial may be unavoidable. An unscrupulous client might in this way attempt to produce a series of mistrials and thus escape prosecution. However, a second such encounter could be construed as a deliberate abuse of the right to counsel and as such a waiver of the right to further representation.~~

~~[6]~~ [11] ~~Except in the defense of a criminal accused, the rule generally recognized is that, if necessary to rectify the situation, an advocate must disclose the existence of the client's deception to the court or to the other party. Such a~~ The disclosure of a client's false testimony can result in grave consequences to the client, including not only a sense of betrayal but also loss of the case and perhaps a prosecution for perjury. But the alternative is that the lawyer cooperate in deceiving the court, thereby subverting the truth-finding process which the adversary system is designed to implement. See Rule 1.2(d). Furthermore, unless it is clearly understood that the lawyer will act upon the duty to disclose the existence of false evidence, the client can simply reject the lawyer's advice to reveal the false evidence and insist that the lawyer keep silent. Thus the client could in effect coerce the lawyer into being a party to fraud on the court.

Preserving Integrity of Adjudicative Process

[12] Lawyers have a special obligation to protect a tribunal against criminal or fraudulent conduct that undermines the integrity of the adjudicative process, such as bribing, intimidating or otherwise unlawfully com-

municating with a witness, juror, court official or other participant in the proceeding, unlawfully destroying or concealing documents or other evidence or failing to disclose information to the tribunal when required by law to do so. Thus, paragraph (b) requires a lawyer to take reasonable remedial measures, including disclosure if necessary, whenever the lawyer knows that a person, including the lawyer's client, intends to engage, is engaging or has engaged in criminal or fraudulent conduct related to the proceeding.

~~Constitutional Requirements~~

~~[12] The general rule that an advocate must reveal the existence of perjury with respect to a material fact, even that of a client — applies to defense counsel in criminal cases, as well as in other instances. However, the definition of the lawyer's ethical duty in such a situation may be qualified by constitutional provisions for due process and the right to counsel in criminal cases. In some jurisdictions these provisions have been construed to require that counsel present an accused as a witness if the accused wishes to testify, even if counsel knows the testimony will be false. The obligation of the advocate under these Rules is subordinate to such a constitutional requirement.~~

Duration of Obligation

[13] A practical time limit on the obligation to rectify ~~the presentation of~~ false evidence or false statements of law and fact has to be established. The conclusion of the proceeding is a reasonably definite point for the termination of the obligation. A proceeding has concluded within the meaning of this Rule when a final judgment in the proceeding has been affirmed on appeal or the time for review has passed.

Ex Parte Proceedings

~~[15]~~ [14] Ordinarily, an advocate has the limited responsibility of presenting one side of the matters that a tribunal should consider in reaching a decision; the conflicting position is expected to be presented by the opposing party. However, in any ex parte proceeding, such as an application for a temporary restraining order, there is no balance of presentation by opposing advocates. The object of an ex parte proceeding is nevertheless to yield a substantially just result. The judge has an affirmative responsibility to accord the absent party just consideration. The lawyer for the represented party has the correlative duty to make disclosures of material facts known to the lawyer and that the lawyer reasonably believes are necessary to an informed decision.

Withdrawal

[15] Normally, a lawyer's compliance with the duty of candor imposed by this Rule does not require that the lawyer withdraw from the representation of a client whose interests will be or have been adversely affected by the lawyer's disclosure. The lawyer may, however, be required by Rule 1.16(a) to seek permission of the tribunal to withdraw if the lawyer's compliance with this Rule's duty of candor results in such an extreme deterioration of the client-lawyer relationship that the lawyer can no longer competently represent the client. Also see Rule 1.16(b) for the circumstances in which a lawyer will be permitted to seek a tribunal's permission to withdraw. In connection with a request for permission to withdraw that is premised on a client's misconduct, a lawyer may reveal information relating to the representation only to the extent reasonably necessary to comply with this Rule or as otherwise permitted by Rule 1.6.

Canon and Code Antecedents

ABA Canons of Professional Ethics: Canons 22 and 41 provided as follows:

22. Candor and Fairness

The conduct of the lawyer before the Court and with other lawyers should be characterized by candor and fairness.

It is not candid or fair for the lawyer knowingly to misquote the contents of a paper, the testimony of a witness, the language or the argument of opposing counsel, or the language of a decision or a textbook; or with knowledge of its invalidity, to cite as authority a decision that has been overruled, or a statute that has been repealed; or in argument to assert as a fact that which has not been proved, or in those jurisdictions where a side has the opening and closing arguments to mislead his opponent by concealing or withholding positions in his opening argument upon which his side then intends to rely.

It is unprofessional and dishonorable to deal other than candidly with the facts in taking the statements of witnesses, in drawing affidavits and other documents, and in the presentation of causes.

A lawyer should not offer evidence which he knows the Court should reject, in order to get the same before the jury by argument for its admissibility, nor should he address to the Judge arguments upon any point not properly calling for determination by him. Neither should he introduce into an argument, addressed to the court, remarks or statements intended to influence the jury or bystanders.

These and all kindred practices are unprofessional and unworthy of an officer of the law charged, as is the lawyer, with the duty of aiding in the administration of justice.

41. Discovery of Imposition and Deception

When a lawyer discovers that some fraud or deception has been practiced, which has unjustly imposed upon the court or a party, he should endeavor to rectify it; at first by advising his client, and if his client refuses to forego the advantage thus unjustly gained, he should promptly inform the injured person or his counsel, so that they may take appropriate steps.

ABA Model Code of Professional Responsibility: Compare DR 7-102(A)(3), DR 7-102(A)(4), DR 7-102(A)(5), DR 7-102(B)(1), and DR 7-106(B)(1) (reprinted later in this volume).

Cross-References in Other Rules

Rule 1.6, Comment 13: "**Rule 3.3** . . . requires disclosure in some circumstances regardless of whether such disclosure is permitted by this Rule. See **Rule 3.3(c)**."

Rule 1.8, Comment 5: It is prohibited to partake in the "disadvantageous use of client information unless the client gives informed consent, except as permitted or required by these Rules. See Rules 1.2(d), 1.6, 1.9(c), **3.3**, 4.1(b), 8.1 and 8.3."

Rule 1.13, Comment 5: "[T]his Rule does not limit or expand the lawyer's responsibility under Rule 1.6, 1.8, 1.16, **3.3** or 4.1."

Rule 1.16, Comment 3: "Lawyers should be mindful of their obligations to both clients and the court under Rules 1.6 and **3.3**."

Rule 2.4, Comment 5: "When the dispute-resolution process takes place before a tribunal, as in binding arbitration (see Rule 1.0(m)), the lawyer's duty of candor is governed by **Rule 3.3**."

Rule 3.9: "A lawyer representing a client before a legislative body or administrative agency in a nonadjudicative proceeding shall disclose that the appearance is in a representative capacity and shall conform to the provisions of **Rules 3.3(a)** through **(c)**, 3.4(a) through (c), and 3.5."

Rule 3.9, Comment 1: "In representation before bodies such as legislatures, municipal councils, and executive and administrative agencies acting in a rule-making or policy-making capacity" lawyers must deal "honestly and in conformity with applicable rules of procedure. See **Rules 3.3(a)** through **(c)**, 3.4(a) through (c) and 3.5."

Rule 8.1, Comment 3: "A lawyer representing an applicant for admission to the bar, or representing a lawyer who is the subject of a disciplinary inquiry or proceeding, is governed by the rules applicable to the client-lawyer relationship, including Rule 1.6 and, in some cases, **Rule 3.3**."

Legislative History of Model Rule 3.3

1980 Discussion Draft (then Rule 3.1) provided:

> (a) A lawyer shall not: . . .
>
> (3) except as provided in paragraph (f), offer evidence that the lawyer is convinced beyond a reasonable doubt is false, or offer without suitable explanation evidence that the lawyer knows is substantially misleading; or
>
> (4) make a representation about existing legal authority that the lawyer knows to be inaccurate or so incomplete as to be substantially misleading.
>
> (b) Except as provided in paragraph (f), if a lawyer discovers that evidence or testimony presented by the lawyer is false, the lawyer shall disclose that fact and take suitable measures to rectify the consequences, even if doing so requires disclosure of a confidence of the client or disclosure that the client is implicated in the falsification.
>
> (c) If a lawyer discovers that the tribunal has not been apprised of legal authority known to the lawyer that would probably have a substantial effect on the determination of a material issue, the lawyer shall advise the tribunal of that authority.

(d) Except as provided in paragraph (f), a lawyer shall disclose a fact known to the lawyer, even if the fact is adverse, when disclosure:

(1) is required by law or the Rules of Professional Conduct; or

(2) is necessary to correct a manifest misapprehension resulting from a previous representation the lawyer has made to the tribunal.

(e) Except as provided in paragraph (f), a lawyer may apprise another party of evidence favorable to that party and may refuse to offer evidence that the lawyer believes with substantial reason to be false.

(f) A lawyer for a defendant in a criminal case:

(1) is not required to apprise the prosecutor or the tribunal of evidence adverse to the accused, except as law may otherwise provide;

(2) may not disclose facts as required by paragraph (d) if doing so is prohibited by applicable law;

(3) shall offer evidence regardless of belief as to whether it is false if the client so demands and applicable law requires that the lawyer comply with such a demand.

(g) A prosecutor has the further duty of disclosure stated in Rule 3.10.

1981 Draft was substantially the same as adopted except for the following parts of subparagraph (a):

> (a) A lawyer shall not knowingly:
>
> (1) make a false statement of fact or law to a tribunal, or fail to disclose a fact in circumstances where the failure to make the disclosure is the equivalent of the lawyer's making a material misrepresentation;
>
> (2) fail to make a disclosure of fact necessary to prevent a fraud on the tribunal. . . .

1982 Draft was adopted.

2002 Amendments: At its February 2002 Mid-Year Meeting, the ABA House of Delegates adopted without change the ABA Ethics 2000 Commission proposal to amend Rule 3.3 and its Comment.

Selected State Variations

Arizona: At the end of Rule 3.3(a)(2) and (4), Arizona adds: "except as required by applicable law."

California: See Rule 5-200 (Trial Conduct), and B & P Code §6068(d) (regarding false statements to a judge) and §6128(a) (regarding intention to deceive a court).

District of Columbia: D.C. Rule 3.3 differs significantly from the ABA Model Rule — see District of Columbia Rules of Professional Conduct below.

Florida: Rule 3.3 provides that a lawyer shall not

> (a)(4) Permit any witness, including a criminal defendant, to offer testimony or other evidence that the lawyer knows to be false. A lawyer may not offer testimony which he knows to be false in the form of a narrative unless so ordered by the tribunal. . . .

Florida also provides in Rule 3.3(b) that the "duties stated in paragraph (a) continue beyond the conclusion of the proceeding. . . ." Florida has also added the following new paragraph to the Comment to Rule 3.3:

> Although the offering of perjured testimony or false evidence is considered a fraud on the tribunal, these situations are distinguishable from that of a client who, upon

being arrested, provides false identification to a law enforcement officer. The client's past act of lying to a law enforcement officer does not constitute a fraud on the tribunal, and thus does not trigger the disclosure obligation under this rule, because a false statement to an arresting officer is unsworn and occurs prior to the institution of a court proceeding. If the client testifies, the lawyer must attempt to have the client respond to any questions truthfully or by asserting an applicable privilege. Any false statements by the client in the course of the court proceeding will trigger the duties under this rule.

Georgia: In the rules effective January 1, 2001, Georgia adopted the pre-2002 version of ABA Model Rule 3.3 and its Comment essentially verbatim, except that Georgia has deleted the last sentence of ABA Comment 6.

Hawaii: At the end of Rule 3.3(a)(4), Hawaii commands lawyers to "take remedial measures to the extent necessary to rectify the consequences." Rule 3.3(d) applies to ex parte proceedings "except grand jury proceedings and applications for search warrants," and at the end Rule 3.3(d) Hawaii adds "disclosure of which is not otherwise prohibited by law."

Illinois Rule 3.3(a) provides:

> (a) In appearing in a professional capacity before a tribunal, a lawyer shall not:
>
> (1) make a statement of material fact or law to a tribunal which the lawyer knows or reasonably should know is false; . . .
>
> (5) participate in the creation or preservation of evidence when the lawyer knows or reasonably should know the evidence is false; . . .
>
> (8) fail to disclose the identities of the clients represented and of the persons who employed the lawyer unless such information is privileged or irrelevant; . . .
>
> (12) fail to use reasonable efforts to restrain and to prevent clients from doing those things that the lawyer ought not to do;
>
> (13) suppress any evidence that the lawyer or client has a legal obligation to reveal or produce; . . .
>
> (b) The duties stated in paragraph (a) are continuing duties and apply even if compliance requires disclosure of information otherwise protected by Rule 1.6.

Illinois also adds to its Rule 1.2 the following subparagraphs, which substantially retain the language of DR 7-102(B) of the Code of Professional Responsibility as amended in 1974 (see Model Code Comparison to Rule 3.3 above):

> (g) A lawyer who knows a client has, in the course of the representation, perpetrated a fraud upon a person or tribunal shall promptly call upon the client to rectify the same, and if the client refuses or is unable to do so, the lawyer shall reveal the fraud to the affected person or tribunal, except when the information is protected as a privileged communication.
>
> (h) A lawyer who knows that a person other than the client has perpetrated a fraud upon a tribunal shall promptly reveal the fraud to the tribunal.

Iowa: DR 7-102(b)(2) requires a lawyer to disclose a client's fraud "except when barred from doing so by Iowa code section 622.10. If barred from doing so by section 622.10, the lawyer shall immediately withdraw from representation of the client unless the client fully discloses the fraud to the person or tribunal."

Maryland adds the following subparagraph (e): "notwithstanding paragraphs (a) through (d), a lawyer for an accused in a criminal case need not disclose that the accused intends to testify falsely or has testified falsely if the lawyer reasonably believes that the disclosure would jeopardize any constitutional right of the accused."

Massachusetts: Rule 3.3(b) states that the conclusion of the proceedings includes "all appeals." Rule 3.3(e) permits a lawyer representing a criminal defendant to elicit false testimony in narrative fashion if withdrawal is not otherwise possible without prejudicing the defendant. However, "the lawyer shall not argue the probative value of the false testimony in closing argument or in any other proceedings, including appeals." A lawyer who is unable to withdraw when he or she knows that a criminal defendant will testify falsely "may not prevent the client from testifying" but must not "examine the client in such a manner as to elicit any testimony from the client the lawyer knows to be false." Comment [2A] to Rule 3.3 provides that the word "assisting" in Rule 3.3(a)(2) "is not limited to conduct that makes the lawyer liable as an aider, abettor or joint tortfeasor," but "is intended to guide the conduct of the lawyer as an officer of the court as a prophylactic measure to protect against the contamination of the judicial process. Thus, for example, a lawyer who knows that a client has committed fraud on a tribunal and has refused to rectify it must disclose the fraud to avoid assisting the client's fraudulent act." However, this obligation would not apply to a lawyer for a criminal defendant.

New Jersey adds the following subparagraph (a)(5): "fail to disclose to the tribunal a material fact with knowledge that the tribunal may tend to be misled by such failure." New Jersey adds the client's "illegal" acts to Rule 3.3(a)(2). In Rule 1.6(b)(2), New Jersey requires a lawyer to reveal confidences to prevent a client from committing "a criminal, illegal or fraudulent act that the lawyer reasonably believes is likely to perpetrate a fraud upon a tribunal."

New York: Compare ABA Model Rule 3.3(a) to New York's DR 7-102(A)(3) and (5) and DR 7-106(B)(1). Compare Rule 3.3(b) and (c) to New York's DR 4-101(C)(5) and DR 7-102(A)(4) and (B). New York has no counterpart to Rule 3.3(d).

Texas: Rule 3.03(b) and (c) provides:

> (b) If a lawyer has offered material evidence and comes to know of its falsity, the lawyer shall make a good faith effort to persuade the client to authorize the lawyer to correct or withdraw the false evidence. If such efforts are unsuccessful, the lawyer shall take reasonable remedial measures, including disclosure of the true facts.
>
> (c) The duties stated in paragraphs (a) and (b) continue until remedial legal measures are no longer reasonably possible.

Paragraph 15 of the Comment to Texas Rule 3.03 states:

> A lawyer may refuse to offer evidence that the lawyer reasonably believes is untrustworthy, even if the lawyer does not know that the evidence is false. That discretion should be exercised cautiously, however, in order not to impair the legitimate interests of the client. Where a client wishes to have such suspect evidence introduced, generally the lawyer should do so and allow the finder of fact to assess its probative value. A lawyer's obligations under paragraphs (a)(2), (a)(5) and (b) of this Rule are not triggered by the introduction of testimony or other evidence that is believed by the lawyer to be false, but not known to be so.

Virginia: Rule 3.3(a)(1) omits the word "material" before "fact or law." Rule 3.3(a)(2) omits the word "material" before "fact." Rule 3.3(a)(3) omits the word "directly" before "adverse." The Comment explains that "directly" was deleted "in the belief that the limiting effect of that term could seriously dilute the paragraph's meaning." Virginia omits Rule 3.3(b). It adds a paragraph (d) which provides: "A lawyer who receives information clearly establishing that a person other than a client has perpetrated a fraud upon a tribunal shall promptly reveal the fraud to the tribunal."

Washington's version of Rule 3.3(b) does *not* allow disclosure of information protected by Rule 1.6.

Related Materials

ABA Formal Ethics Opinions: See ABA Formal Ethics Ops. 87-352 (1987), 93-376 (1993) and 98-412 (1998).

ABA Standards for Criminal Justice: See Defense Function Standard 4-7.5. The original draft of The Defense Function contained the following version of Standard 4-7.7:

> (a) If the defendant has admitted to defense counsel facts which establish guilt and counsel's independent investigation established that the admissions are true but the defendant insists on the right to trial, counsel must strongly discourage the defendant against taking the witness stand to testify perjuriously.
>
> (b) If, in advance of trial, the defendant insists that he or she will take the stand to testify perjuriously, the lawyer may withdraw from the case, if that is feasible, seeking leave of the court if necessary, but the court should not be advised of the lawyer's reason for seeking to do so.
>
> (c) If withdrawal from the case is not feasible or is not permitted by the court, or if the situation arises immediately preceding trial or during the trial and the defendant insists upon testifying perjuriously in his or her own behalf, it is unprofessional conduct for the lawyer to lend aid to the perjury or use the perjured testimony. Before the defendant takes the stand in these circumstances, the lawyer should make a record of the fact that the defendant is taking the stand against the advice of counsel in some appropriate manner without revealing the fact to the court. The lawyer may identify the witness as the defendant and may ask appropriate questions of the defendant when it is believed that the defendant's answers will not be perjurious. As to matters for which it is believed the defendant will offer perjurious testimony, the lawyer should seek to avoid direct examination of the defendant in the conventional manner; instead, the lawyer should ask the defendant if he or she wishes to make any additional statement concerning the case to the trier or triers of the facts. A lawyer may not later argue the defendant's known false version of facts to the jury as worthy of belief, and may not recite or rely upon the false testimony in his or her closing argument.

When Standard 4-7.7 was published, it was accompanied by the following official Editorial Note written by the ABA:

> This proposed standard was approved by the ABA Standing Committee on Association Standards for Criminal Justice but was withdrawn prior to submission of this chapter to the ABA House of Delegates. Instead, the question of what should be done in situations dealt with by the standard has been deferred until the ABA Special Commission on Evaluation of Professional Standards [the Kutak Commission] reports its final recommendations.

The final recommendation of the Kutak Commission is found in the original version of ABA Model Rule 3.3 and its Comment. In particular, the original Comment 9 to Rule 3.3 (deleted in 2002) expressly referred to the "narrative" suggested in Standard 4-7.7, but both Rule 3.3 and its Comment appeared to reject the narrative proposal. ABA Formal Ethics Opinion 87-353 (1987) did so explicitly. See also Nix v. Whiteside, 475 U.S. 157 (1986). Nevertheless, some courts continue to approve the narrative method, and at least three jurisdictions (D.C., Florida, and Massachusetts) expressly permit a narrative in certain circumstances.

ABA Standards for Imposing Lawyer Sanctions:

6.11. Disbarment is generally appropriate when a lawyer, with the intent to deceive the court, makes a false statement, submits a false document, or improperly withholds material information, and causes serious or potentially serious injury to a party, or causes a significant or potentially significant adverse effect on the legal proceeding.

6.12. Suspension is generally appropriate when a lawyer knows that false statements or documents are being submitted to the court or that material information is improperly being withheld, and takes no remedial action, and causes injury or potential injury to a party to the legal proceeding, or causes an adverse or potentially adverse effect on the legal proceeding.

6.13. Reprimand is generally appropriate when a lawyer is negligent either in determining whether statements or documents are false or in taking remedial action when material information is being withheld, and causes injury or potential injury to a party to the legal proceeding, or causes an adverse or potentially adverse effect on the legal proceeding.

6.14. Admonition is generally appropriate when a lawyer engages in an isolated instance of neglect in determining whether submitted statements or documents are false or in failing to disclose material information upon learning of its falsity, and causes little or no actual or potential injury to a party, or causes little or no adverse or potentially adverse effect on the legal proceeding.

6.31. Disbarment is generally appropriate when a lawyer:

. . . (b) makes an ex parte communication with a judge or juror with intent to affect the outcome of the proceeding, and causes serious or potentially serious injury to a party, or causes significant or potentially significant interference with the outcome of the legal proceeding. . . .

American Academy of Matrimonial Lawyers: The "Bounds of Advocacy" contains the following rule and comment:

3.11 An attorney should not seek an ex parte order without prior notice to opposing counsel except in exigent circumstances.

Comment to Rule 3.11

There are few things more damaging to a client's confidence in his lawyer, or to relationships between lawyers, than for a party to be served with an ex parte order about which his lawyer knows nothing. Even where there are exigent circumstances (substantial physical or financial risk to the client), or local rules permit ex parte proceedings, notice to, or the appearance of, opposing counsel usually will not prevent appropriate relief from issuing.

IRS Regulations: In the regulations governing practice before the Internal Revenue Service, 31 C.F.R. §10.21 provides in pertinent part as follows:

§10.21. Knowledge of Client's Omission

Each attorney . . . who, having been retained by a client with respect to a matter administered by the Internal Revenue Service, knows that the client has not complied with the revenue laws of the United States or has made an error in or omission from any return, document, affidavit, or other paper which the client is required by the revenue laws of the United States to execute, shall advise the client promptly of the fact of such noncompliance, error, or omission.

Federal Rules of Civil Procedure: Under Fed. R. Civ. P. 26(e), parties have a duty to supplement all discovery information given to the other side, either under the "automatic disclosure" provisions of Rule 26(a)(1) or in response to a party's specific request.

Model Rules of Professional Conduct for Federal Lawyers add a new Rule 3.3(a)(5), which states that a federal lawyer shall not "[d]isobey an obligation or order imposed by a tribunal, unless done openly before the tribunal in a good faith assertion that no valid obligation or order should exist." (This rule is similar to Rule 3.4(c), but the Federal Lawyers version of that rule covers only obligations to opposing parties and counsel.)

Restatement of the Law Governing Lawyers: See Restatement §§111, 112, 118 and 120 in our chapter on the Restatement later in this volume.

Rule 3.4 Fairness to Opposing Party and Counsel

A lawyer shall not:

(a) unlawfully obstruct another party's access to evidence or unlawfully alter, destroy or conceal a document or other material having potential evidentiary value. A lawyer shall not counsel or assist another person to do any such act;

(b) falsify evidence, counsel or assist a witness to testify falsely, or offer an inducement to a witness that is prohibited by law;

(c) knowingly disobey an obligation under the rules of a tribunal, except for an open refusal based on an assertion that no valid obligation exists;

(d) in pretrial procedure, make a frivolous discovery request or fail to make reasonably diligent effort to comply with a legally proper discovery request by an opposing party;

(e) in trial, allude to any matter that the lawyer does not reasonably believe is relevant or that will not be supported by admissible evidence, assert personal knowledge of facts in issue except when testifying as a witness, or state a personal opinion as to the justness of a cause, the credibility of a witness, the culpability of a civil litigant or the guilt or innocence of an accused; or

(f) request a person other than a client to refrain from voluntarily giving relevant information to another party unless:

(1) the person is a relative or an employee or other agent of a client; and

(2) the lawyer reasonably believes that the person's interests will not be adversely affected by refraining from giving such information.

COMMENT

[1] The procedure of the adversary system contemplates that the evidence in a case is to be marshalled competitively by the contending parties. Fair competition in the adversary system is secured by prohibitions against destruction or concealment of evidence, improperly influencing witnesses, obstructive tactics in discovery procedure, and the like.

[2] Documents and other items of evidence are often essential to establish a claim or defense. Subject to evidentiary privileges, the right of an opposing party, including the government, to obtain evidence through discovery or subpoena is an important procedural right. The exercise of that right can be frustrated if relevant material is altered, concealed or destroyed. Applicable law in many jurisdictions makes it an offense to destroy material for purpose of impairing its availability in a pending proceeding or one whose commencement can be foreseen. Falsifying evidence is also generally a criminal offense. Paragraph (a) applies to evidentiary material generally, including computerized information. Applicable law may permit a lawyer to take temporary possession of physical evidence of client crimes for the purpose of conducting a limited examination that will not alter or destroy material characteristics of the evidence. In such a case, applicable law may require the lawyer to turn the evidence over to the police or other prosecuting authority, depending on the circumstances.

[3] With regard to paragraph (b), it is not improper to pay a witness's expenses or to compensate an expert witness on terms permitted by law. The common law rule in most jurisdictions is that it is improper to pay an occurrence witness any fee for testifying and that it is improper to pay an expert witness a contingent fee.

[4] Paragraph (f) permits a lawyer to advise employees of a client to refrain from giving information to another party, for the employees may identify their interests with those of the client. See also Rule 4.2.

Canon and Code Antecedents

ABA Canons of Professional Ethics: Canons 3, 15, 25, and 39 provided as follows:

3. Attempts to Exert Personal Influence on the Court

Marked attention and unusual hospitality on the part of a lawyer to a Judge, uncalled for by the personal relations of the parties, subject both the Judge and the lawyer to misconstructions of motive and should be avoided. A lawyer should not communicate or argue privately with the Judge as to the merits of a pending cause, and he deserves rebuke and denunciation for any device or attempt to gain from a Judge special personal consideration or favor. A self-respecting independence in the discharge of professional duty, without denial or diminution of the courtesy and respect due the Judge's station, is the only proper foundation for cordial personal and official relations between Bench and Bar.

15. How Far a Lawyer May Go in Supporting a Client's Cause

Nothing operates more certainly to create or to foster popular prejudice against lawyers as a class, and to deprive the profession of that full measure of public esteem and confidence which belongs to the proper discharge of its duties than does the false claim, often set up by the unscrupulous in defense of questionable transactions, that it is the duty of the lawyer to do whatever may enable him to succeed in winning his client's cause.

It is improper for a lawyer to assert in argument his personal belief in his client's innocence or in the justice of his cause.

The lawyer owes "entire devotion to the interest of the client, warm zeal in the maintenance and defense of his rights and the exertion of his utmost learning and ability," to the end that nothing be taken or be withheld from him, save by the rules of law, legally applied. No fear of judicial disfavor or public unpopularity should restrain him from the full discharge of his duty. In the judicial forum the client is entitled to the benefit of any and every remedy and defense that is authorized by the law of the land, and he may expect his lawyer to assert every such remedy or defense. But it is steadfastly to be borne in mind that the great trust of the lawyer is to be performed within and not without the bounds of the law. The office of attorney does not permit, much less does it demand of him for any client, violation of law or any manner of fraud or chicane. He must obey his own conscience and not that of his client.

25. Taking Technical Advantage of Opposite Counsel; Agreements With Him

A lawyer should not ignore known customs or practice of the Bar or of a particular Court, even when the law permits, without giving timely notice to the opposing counsel. As far as possible, important agreements, affecting the rights of clients, should be reduced to writing; but it is dishonorable to avoid performance of an agreement fairly made because it is not reduced to writing, as required by rules of Court.

39. Witnesses

A lawyer may properly interview any witness or prospective witness for the opposing side in any civil or criminal action without the consent of opposing counsel or party. In doing so, however, he should scrupulously avoid any suggestion calculated to induce the witness to suppress or deviate from the truth, or in any degree to affect his free and untrammeled conduct when appearing at the trial or on the witness stand.

ABA Model Code of Professional Responsibility: Compare DR 7-102(A)(6), DR 7-104(A)(2), DR 7-106(A), DR 7-106(C)(1), DR 7-106(C)(2), DR 7-106(C)(3), DR 7-106(C)(4), DR 7-106(C)(5), DR 7-106(C)(7), DR 7-109(A), and DR 7-109(C) (reprinted later in this volume).

Cross-References in Other Rules

Rule 1.4, Comment 7: "Rules or court orders governing litigation may provide that information supplied to a lawyer may not be disclosed to the client. **Rule 3.4(c)** directs compliance with such rules or orders."

Rule 3.6, Comment 2: "Special rules of confidentiality may validly govern proceedings in juvenile, domestic relations and mental disability proceedings, and perhaps other types of litigation. **Rule 3.4(c)** requires compliance with such rules."

Rule 3.9: "A lawyer representing a client before a legislative body or administrative agency in a nonadjudicative proceeding shall disclose that the appearance is in a representative capacity and shall conform to the provisions of Rules 3.3(a) through (c), **3.4(a)** through **(c)**, and 3.5."

Rule 3.9, Comment 1: "In representation before bodies such as legislatures, municipal councils, and executive and administrative agencies acting in a rule-making or policy-making capacity" lawyers must deal "honestly and in conformity with applicable rules of procedure. See Rules 3.3(a) through (c), **3.4(a)** through **(c)** and 3.5."

Rule 4.2, Comment 7: "If a constituent of the organization is represented in the matter by his or her own counsel, the consent by that counsel to a communication will be sufficient for purposes of this Rule. Compare **Rule 3.4(f)**."

Legislative History of Model Rule 3.4

1980 Discussion Draft (then Rule 3.2):

> (a) A lawyer shall be fair to other parties and their counsel, accord them their procedural rights, and fulfill obligations under the procedural law and established practices of the tribunal.
>
> (b) A lawyer shall not:
>
> (1) improperly obstruct another party's access to evidence, destroy, falsify or conceal evidence, or use illegal methods of obtaining evidence;
>
> (2) disobey an obligation under procedural law, except for an open refusal based on a good faith belief that no valid obligation exists;
>
> (3) refer in a proceeding to a matter that the lawyer has no reasonable basis to believe is relevant thereto, or does not reasonably expect will be supported by admissible evidence;
>
> (4) make a knowing misrepresentation of fact or law to an opposing party or counsel;
>
> (5) interview or otherwise communicate with a party who the lawyer knows is represented by other counsel concerning the subject matter of the representation, except with the consent of that party's counsel or as authorized by law.

In addition, the 1980 Discussion Draft contained the following Rule 2.5:

> *Alteration or Destruction of Evidence*
>
> A lawyer shall not advise a client to alter or destroy a document or other material when the lawyer reasonably should know that the material is relevant to a pending proceeding or one that is clearly foreseeable.

1981 Draft: Substantially the same as finally adopted, except subparagraph (a), which provided:

> A lawyer shall not:
>
> (a) unlawfully obstruct another party's access to evidence or alter, destroy or conceal a document or other material that the lawyer knows or reasonably

should know is relevant to a pending proceeding or one that is reasonably foreseeable. A lawyer shall not counsel or assist another person to do any such act;

1982 Draft was adopted.

2002 Amendments: At its February 2002 Mid-Year Meeting, the ABA House of Delegates adopted with only minor changes the ABA Ethics 2000 Commission proposal to amend the Comment to Rule 3.4. (The Ethics 2000 Commission did not propose any changes to the text of Rule 3.4.)

Selected State Variations

Alabama adds two exceptions that allow a lawyer to ask a non-client not to give information to another party: "(2) the person may be required by law to refrain from disclosing the information; or (3) the information pertains to covert law enforcement investigations in process, such as the use of undercover law enforcement agents."

California: See Rule 5-200 (Trial Conduct), Rule 5-310 (Prohibited Contact with Witnesses), and B & P Code §§6068(d), 6103, and 6128(a). In addition, California Penal Code §135, which was enacted in 1872, provides as follows:

> *Destroying or Concealing Documentary Evidence*
>
> *Destroying evidence.* Every person who, knowing that any book, paper, record, instrument in writing, or other matter or thing, is about to be produced in evidence upon any trial, inquiry, or investigation whatever, authorized by law, willfully destroys or conceals the same, with intent thereby to prevent it from being produced, is guilty of a misdemeanor.

Connecticut, retaining language from DR 7-105, forbids a lawyer to "present, participate in presenting, or threaten to present criminal charges solely to obtain an advantage in a civil matter." Rule 3.4(7).

Delaware: Rule 3.4(b) provides that a lawyer shall not:

> falsify evidence, counsel or assist a witness to testify falsely, or pay, offer to pay or acquiesce in the payment of compensation, or participate in offering any inducement to a witness contingent upon the content of his testimony or the outcome of the case. But a lawyer may advance, guarantee or acquiesce in the payment of:
>
> (i) expenses reasonably incurred by a witness in attending or testifying;
>
> (ii) reasonable compensation to a witness for his loss of time in attending or testifying;
>
> (iii) a reasonable fee for the professional services of an expert witness.

District of Columbia: D.C. Rule 3.4(a) differs significantly from the ABA Model Rule — see District of Columbia Rules of Professional Conduct below.

Florida: Rule 3.4(a) applies to evidence that a lawyer "knows or reasonably should know is relevant to a pending or a reasonably foreseeable proceeding . . . ." Rule 3.4(b) provides that a lawyer shall not "fabricate" (instead of "falsify") evidence. In addition, amplifying Comment 3 to ABA Model Rule 3.4, Florida Rule 3.4(b) provides:

> [A] lawyer may pay a witness reasonable expenses incurred by the witness in attending or testifying at proceedings; a reasonable, noncontingent fee for the professional services of an expert witness; and reasonable compensation to reimburse a witness for the loss of compensation incurred by reason of preparing for, attending, or testifying at proceedings.

Florida Rule 3.4(d) eliminates the phrase "to make a reasonably diligent effort" and instead provides that a lawyer shall not "*intentionally* fail to comply with a legally proper discovery request by an opposing party." Florida Rules 3.4(g) and (h), which became effective on October 1, 1998, track and expand upon the old DR 7-105 by providing that a lawyer must not present, participate in presenting, or threaten to present either criminal charges or "disciplinary charges under these rules" solely to obtain an advantage in a civil manner.

Georgia: In the rules effective January 1, 2001, Georgia adopted Rule 3.4(a) verbatim, but in Rule 3.4(b) Georgia borrowed language based on DR 7-109(c) of the ABA Model Code of Professional Responsibility (see Model Code Comparison above). Georgia omitted subparagraphs (c), (d), and (e) of ABA Model Rule 3.4 entirely. Georgia adopted Rule 3.4(f), but added that a lawyer may request a person not to volunteer information to another party "if the information is subject to the assertion of a privilege by the client."

Georgia also added a new Rule 3.4(g), based on ABA Model Rule 4.4, which provides that a lawyer shall not "use methods of obtaining evidence that violate the legal rights of the opposing party or counsel," and a new Rule 3.4(h), taken verbatim from DR 7-105 of the ABA Model Code, which provides that a lawyer shall not "present, participate in presenting or threaten to present criminal charges solely to obtain an advantage in a civil matter."

Illinois provides, in Rule 3.3(a)(15), that a lawyer shall not "pay, offer to pay, or acquiesce in the payment of compensation to a witness contingent upon the content of the witness' testimony or the outcome of the case, but a lawyer may advance, guarantee, or acquiesce in the payment of expenses reasonably incurred in attending or testifying, and a reasonable fee for the professional services of an expert witness." In addition, Illinois omits Rules 3.4(c)-(d) and moves an amplified version of Rule 3.4(e) to Illinois Rule 3.3(a)(10).

Massachusetts: Rule 3.4(g) tracks DR 7-109(C) of the old ABA Model Code of Professional Responsibility. Rule 3.4(h) forbids a lawyer to "present, participate in presenting, or threaten to present criminal or disciplinary charges solely to obtain an advantage in a private civil matter." Rule 3.4(i) says that a lawyer shall not "in appearing in a professional capacity before a tribunal, engage in conduct manifesting bias or prejudice based on race, sex, religion, national origin, disability, age, or sexual orientation against a party, witness, counsel, or other person. This paragraph does not preclude legitimate advocacy when [the same factors or a similar one] is an issue in the proceeding."

New Jersey: Rule 3.4(d) refers to "requests" and "efforts" in the plural so that a violation will depend on showing a "pattern of behavior."

New York: Compare ABA Model Rule 3.4(a) to New York's DR 7-109(A). Compare Rule 3.4(b) to New York's DR 7-102(A)(6) and DR 7-109(C). Compare Rule 3.4(c) to New York's DR 7-106(A). New York has no counterpart to Rule 3.4(d). Compare Rule 3.4(e) to New York's DR 7-106(C). Compare Rule 3.4(f) to New York's DR 7-104(A)(2) and DR 7-109(B).

North Carolina: Rule 3.4(b) adds language from DR 7-109(B) of the old ABA Model Code of Professional Responsibility by providing that a lawyer shall not "counsel or assist a witness to hide or leave the jurisdiction for the purpose of being unavailable as a witness." In Rule 3.4(f)(1), North Carolina limits the "employee" exception to a "managerial employee."

Ohio has adopted a lengthy DR 7-111, entitled "Confidential Information," which provides, in part, as follows:

> (A)(1) A lawyer shall not disclose or cause to be disclosed, without appropriate authorization, information regarding the probable or actual decision in a case or legal proceeding pending before a court, including the vote of a justice, judge, or court in a case pending before the Supreme Court, a court of appeals, or a panel of judges of a trial court, prior to the announcement of the decision by the court or journalization of an opinion, entry, or other document reflecting that decision under either of the following circumstances:
>
> (a) The probable or actual decision is confidential because of statutory or rule provisions;
>
> (b) The probable or actual decision clearly has been designated to the justice or judge as confidential when confidentiality is warranted because of the status of the proceedings or the circumstances under which the information was received and preserving confidentiality is necessary to the proper conduct of court business.

Subparagraph (B)(1) adds that no lawyer shall "obtain or attempt to obtain" information whose disclosure would violate DR 7-111(A)(1).

Pennsylvania: Rule 3.4(b) and (c) retain the substance of DR 7-109(C). Pennsylvania adds at the end of Rule 3.4(d)(2) "and such conduct is not prohibited by Rule 4.2."

Texas: Rule 3.04(b) retains the substance of DR 7-109(C) (see Model Code Comparison above). Rule 3.04(a), (c), and (d) provide, in pertinent part:

> A lawyer shall not:
>
> (a) unlawfully obstruct another party's access to evidence; in anticipation of a dispute unlawfully alter, destroy or conceal a document or other material that a competent lawyer would believe has potential or actual evidentiary value; . . .
>
> (c) except as stated in paragraph (d), in representing a client before a tribunal:
>
> (1) habitually violate an established rule of procedure or of evidence; . . .
>
> (4) ask any question intended to degrade a witness or other person except where the lawyer reasonably believes that the question will lead to relevant and admissible evidence; or
>
> (5) engage in conduct intended to disrupt the proceedings.
>
> (d) knowingly disobey, or advise the client to disobey, an obligation under the standing rules of or a ruling by a tribunal except for an open refusal based either on an assertion that no valid obligation exists or on the client's willingness to accept any sanctions arising from such disobedience.

Regarding the word "unlawfully" in Rule 3.04(a), Texas Penal Law §37.09 makes it a felony if a person "knowing that an investigation or official proceeding is pending or in progress . . . alters, destroys, or conceals any record, document, or thing with intent to impair its verity, legibility, or availability as evidence. . . ." The section does not apply to items that are "privileged or . . . work product."

Virginia adopts Rule 3.4 with several changes. Drawing on the prior Virginia Code, paragraphs (a) and (b) provide as follows:

> Lawyers shall not:
>
> (a) Obstruct another party's access to evidence or alter, destroy or conceal a document or other material having potential evidentiary value for the purpose of obstructing a party's access to evidence. A lawyer shall not counsel or assist another person to do any such act.
>
> (b) Advise or cause a person to secret himself or herself or to leave the jurisdiction of the tribunal for the purpose of making that person unavailable as a witness therein.

Rule 3.4(c) incorporates language from DR 7-109(C) regarding permissible payments to witnesses. Rule 3.4's other provisions are changed in various respects, also drawing on the prior Virginia Code.

Washington deletes subparagraph (f).

Related Materials

ABA Formal Ethics Opinions: See ABA Formal Ethics Ops. 93-378 (1993) and 96-402 (1996).

ABA Standards for Criminal Justice: See Prosecution Function Standards 3-5.2, 3-5.6; Defense Function Standards 4-1.2, 4-4.3, 4-4.5, 4-4.6, 4-7.1. Standard 4-4.6 is especially important because it concerns a criminal defense lawyer's obligations upon the receipt of physical evidence. In addition, Standard 11-6.3 provides:

> Neither the counsel for the parties nor other prosecution or defense personnel should advise persons (other than the defendant) who have relevant material or information to refrain from discussing the case with opposing counsel or showing opposing counsel any relevant material, nor should they otherwise impede opposing counsel's investigation of the case.

ABA Standards for Imposing Lawyer Sanctions:

6.2. Abuse of the Legal Process

> 6.21. Disbarment is generally appropriate when a lawyer knowingly violates a court order or rule with the intent to obtain a benefit for the lawyer or another, and causes serious injury or potentially serious injury to a party, or causes serious or potentially serious interference with a legal proceeding.
>
> 6.22. Suspension is appropriate when a lawyer knows that he is violating a court order or rule, and there is injury or potential injury to a client or a party, or interference or potential interference with a legal proceeding.

See also Standard 6.3 printed in the Related Materials following Model Rule 4.2.

Contempt of Court: Various statutes and rules make it a civil or criminal offense to disobey the rules of a tribunal, and give judges power to punish such contempt of court with fines or imprisonment. For example, Rule 42(a) of the Federal Rules of Criminal Procedure provides that a criminal contempt "may be punished summarily if the judge certifies that the judge saw or heard the conduct constituting the contempt and that it was committed in the actual presence of the court." For a statute defining conduct constituting contempt of court, see §1209 of the California Code of Civil Procedure.

Federal Rules of Appellate Procedure: Fed. R. App. P. 46(c) provides that a federal court of appeals, after notice and hearing, may discipline an attorney who practices before it for conduct unbecoming a member of the bar or for failure to comply with any court rule.

Federal Rules of Civil Procedure: Various provisions of the rules of procedure penalize the kinds of behavior condemned in Rule 3.4. With respect to Rule 3.4(c), Fed. R. Civ. P. 41(b) provides: "For failure of the plaintiff to prosecute or to comply with these rules or any order of court, a defendant may move for dismissal of an action or of any claim against the defendant," and such a dismissal ordinarily "operates as an adjudication upon the merits." Fed. R. Civ. P. 45(e) provides: "Failure by any person without adequate excuse to obey a subpoena served upon that person may be deemed a contempt of the court from which the subpoena issued." With respect to Rule 3.4(d), Fed. R. Civ. P. 26(g) provides sanctions for improper or bad faith conduct in discovery, and Fed. R. Civ. P. 37, gives courts power to compel a party to respond to discovery requests and to sanction an unjustified failure to respond to discovery.

Model Rules of Professional Conduct for Federal Lawyers clarify that Rule 3.4 applies to an obligation "to an opposing party and counsel." (The Rules for Federal Lawyers address obligations to a tribunal in a new Rule 3.3(a)(5), quoted after Rule 3.3.) The Comment to Rule 3.4 states:

> A federal lawyer who receives . . . an item of physical evidence implicating the client in criminal conduct shall disclose the location of or shall deliver that item to proper authorities when required by law or court order. Thus, if a Federal lawyer receives contraband, the Federal lawyer has no legal right to possess it and must always surrender it to lawful authorities. If a Federal lawyer receives stolen property, the Federal lawyer must surrender it to the owner or lawful authority to avoid violating the law. . . . When a client informs the Federal lawyer about the existence of material having potential evidentiary value adverse to the client or when the client presents, but does not relinquish possession of, such material to the Federal lawyer, the Federal lawyer should inform the client of the Federal lawyer's legal and ethical obligations regarding evidence. Frequently, the best course for the Federal lawyer is to refrain from either taking possession of such material or advising the client as to what course of action should be taken regarding it. . . . If a Federal lawyer discloses the location of or delivers an item of physical evidence to proper authorities, it should be done in the way best designed to protect the client's interest. The Federal lawyer should consider methods of return or disclosure that best protect (a) the client's identity; (b) the client's words concerning the item; (c) other confidential information; and (d) the client's privilege against self-incrimination. . . .
>
> With regard to paragraph (c), a "rule of a tribunal" includes Rule 6(e) of the Federal Rules of Criminal Procedure governing discussion of grand jury testimony.

Restatement of the Law Governing Lawyers: See Restatement §§94, 105, 107, 110 and 116-119 in our chapter on the Restatement later in this volume.

Witness Tampering: Federal law makes it a crime to kill, intimidate, or harass a witness, victim, or informant in an official proceeding, and many states have parallel laws. The main federal statute is found at 18 U.S.C. §1512.

18 U.S.C. §201(c) and (d), reprinted below in our chapter on Federal Conflict and Confidentiality Provisions, make it a crime to give "anything of value to any person, for or because of the testimony . . . to be given by such person as a witness upon a trial. . . ." The prohibition does not apply to, among other things, payment of "the reasonable cost of travel and subsistence incurred and the reasonable value of time lost in attendance at any such trial . . . or in the case of expert witnesses, a reasonable fee for time spent in the preparation. . . ."

Rule 3.5 Impartiality and Decorum of the Tribunal

A lawyer shall not:

(a) seek to influence a judge, juror, prospective juror or other official by means prohibited by law;

(b) communicate ex parte with such a person ~~except as permitted~~ during the proceeding unless authorized to do so by law or court order;

(c) communicate with a juror or prospective juror after discharge of the jury if:

(1) the communication is prohibited by law or court order;

(2) the juror has made known to the lawyer a desire not to communicate; or

(3) the communication involves misrepresentation, coercion, duress or harassment; or

~~(c)~~ (d) engage in conduct intended to disrupt a tribunal.

COMMENT

[1] Many forms of improper influence upon a tribunal are proscribed by criminal law. Others are specified in the ABA Model Code of Judicial Conduct, with which an advocate should be familiar. A lawyer is required to avoid contributing to a violation of such provisions.

[2] During a proceeding a lawyer may not communicate ex parte with persons serving in an official capacity in the proceeding, such as judges, masters or jurors, unless authorized to do so by law or court order.

[3] A lawyer may on occasion want to communicate with a juror or prospective juror after the jury has been discharged. The lawyer may do so unless the communication is prohibited by law or a court order but must respect the desire of the juror not to talk with the lawyer. The lawyer may not engage in improper conduct during the communication.

~~[2]~~ [4] The advocate's function is to present evidence and argument so that the cause may be decided according to law. Refraining from abusive or obstreperous conduct is a corollary of the advocate's right to speak on behalf of litigants. A lawyer may stand firm against abuse by a judge but should avoid reciprocation; the judge's default is no justification for similar dereliction by an advocate. An advocate can present the cause, protect the record for subsequent review and preserve professional integrity by patient firmness no less effectively than by belligerence or theatrics.

[5] The duty to refrain from disruptive conduct applies to any proceeding of a tribunal, including a deposition. See Rule 1.0(m).

Canon and Code Antecedents

ABA Canons of Professional Ethics: Canons 17 and 23 provided as follows:

17. Ill-Feeling and Personalities Between Advocates

Clients, not lawyers, are the litigants. Whatever may be the ill-feeling existing between clients, it should not be allowed to influence counsel in their conduct and demeanor toward each other or toward suitors in the case. All personalities between counsel should be scrupulously avoided. In the trial of a cause it is indecent to allude to the personal history or the personal peculiarities and idiosyncrasies of counsel on the other side. Personal colloquies between counsel which cause delay and promote unseemly wrangling should also be carefully avoided.

23. Attitude Toward Jury

All attempts to curry favor with juries by fawning, flattery or pretended solicitude for their personal comfort are unprofessional. Suggestions of counsel, looking to the comfort or convenience of jurors, and propositions to dispense with argument, should be made to the Court out of the jury's hearing. A lawyer must never converse privately with jurors about the case; and both before and during the trial he should avoid communicating with them, even as to matters foreign to the cause.

ABA Model Code of Professional Responsibility: Compare DR 7-106(C)(6), DR 7-108(A), DR 7-108(B), and DR 7-110(B) (reprinted later in this volume).

Cross-References in Other Rules

Rule 3.9: "A lawyer representing a client before a legislative body or administrative agency in a nonadjudicative proceeding shall disclose that the appearance is in a representative capacity and shall conform to the provisions of Rules 3.3(a) through (c), 3.4(a) through (c), and **3.5**."

Rule 3.9, Comment 1: "In representation before bodies such as legislatures, municipal councils, and executive and administrative agencies acting in a rule-making or policy-making capacity" lawyers must deal "honestly and in conformity with applicable rules of procedure. See Rules 3.3(a) through (c), 3.4(a) through (c) and **3.5**."

Legislative History of Model Rule 3.5

1980 Discussion Draft (then called Rule 3.7) provided as follows:

(a) A lawyer shall assist a tribunal in maintaining impartiality and conducting the proceedings with decorum.

(b) A lawyer shall not:

(1) seek improperly to influence a judge, juror, or other decision-maker, or, except as permitted by law, communicate ex parte with such a person;

(2) seek improperly to influence a witness;

(3) be abusive or obstreperous;

(4) refuse to comply with an obligation of procedural law or an order of the tribunal, except for an open refusal based on a good faith belief that compliance is not legally required.

1981 Draft was substantially the same as adopted, except that subparagraph (a) used the phrase "other decision-maker" instead of "other official."

1982 Draft was adopted.

2002 Amendments: At its February 2002 Mid-Year Meeting, the ABA House of Delegates adopted without change the ABA Ethics 2000 Commission proposal to amend Rule 3.5 and its Comment.

Selected State Variations

Arkansas: Subparagraph (b) provides that a lawyer shall not "communicate ex parte with such a person *on the merits of the cause* except as permitted by law."

California: See Rule 5-300 (Contact with Officials).

Delaware adds the following language to subparagraph (c): "or engage in undignified or discourteous conduct which is degrading to a tribunal."

Florida, Maryland, and ***Minnesota*** add language to Rule 3.5 drawing on DR 7-108 — see ABA Model Code of Professional Responsibility below.

Georgia: In the rules effective January 1, 2001, Georgia adopted the three subparagraphs of the pre-2002 version of Rule 3.5 verbatim but altered the introductory phrase to make clear that the prohibitions apply "without regard to whether the lawyer represents a client in the matter." Georgia also expands the Comment to Rule 3.5 to eight paragraphs.

Illinois: Rule 3.5 tracks DR 7-108 almost verbatim, but adds the following paragraph (h) prompted by the bribery and "loan" scandals uncovered in Chicago courts during Operation Greylord in the 1980's:

> (h) A lawyer shall not give or lend anything of value to a judge, official, or employee of a tribunal, except those gifts or loans which a judge or a member of the judge's family may receive under Rule 65(C)(4) of the Code of Judicial Conduct, and except that a lawyer may: make a gift, bequest, loan or campaign contribution to a judge that the judge is permitted to accept under the Code of Judicial Conduct, provided that no campaign contribution to a judge or candidate for judical office may be made other than by means of a check, draft, or other instrument payable to or to the order of an entity which the lawyer reasonably believes to be a political committee supporting such judge or candidate, provided further, however, that the provision of volunteer services by a lawyer to a political committee shall not be deemed to violate this Rule.

Illinois Rule 3.5 also adds a new subparagraph (i) that tracks language from DR 7-110.

Massachusetts: Rule 3.5(d) restricts the ability of lawyers connected to a case to initiate a communication with a member of the jury after discharge without leave of the court.

Michigan: Rule 3.5(c) forbids a lawyer to "engage in undignified or discourteous conduct toward the tribunal."

New York: Compare ABA Model Rule 3.5(a) to New York's DR 9-101(C). Compare Rule 3.5(b) to New York's DR 7-108(B) and (C) and DR 7-110(B). Compare Rule 3.5(c) to New York's DR 7-108. Compare Rule 3.5(d) to New York's DR 7-106(C)(6).

North Carolina: Rule 3.5 adds language from various provisions of the old ABA Model Code of Professional Responsibility, including DR 7-106(C)(5)-(7), DR 7-108(D), (F), and (G), and DR 7-110(B).

Pennsylvania: Rule 3.5(c) provides that a lawyer shall not engage in conduct "disruptive" to a tribunal.

Texas: Rule 3.05 is substantially the same as DR 7-110(B) of the old ABA Model Code of Professional Responsibility. Rule 3.06 borrows heavily from DR 7-108, but rearranges the order somewhat, adds references to an "alternate juror," and provides in Rule 3.06(A)(2) that a lawyer shall not "seek to influence a venireman or juror concerning the merits of a pending matter by means prohibited by law or applicable rules of practice or procedure."

Virginia Rule 3.5(a)(2) adds that a lawyer shall not "before discharge of the jury from further consideration of a case, ask questions of or make comments to a member of that jury that are calculated merely to harass or embarrass the juror or to influence the juror's actions in future jury service." Rule 3.5(e) contains exceptions to the rule against ex parte communications with a judge.

Related Materials

ABA Model Code of Judicial Conduct, cited in Rule 3.5, Comment 1, is reprinted in full later in this volume.

ABA Standards for Criminal Justice: See Prosecution Function Standard 3-2.8 (Relations with the Courts and Bar), Standard 3-5.2 (Courtroom Professionalism), Standard 3-5.4 (Relations with Jury), and Defense Function Standard 4-7.1 (Courtroom Professionalism) and Standard 4-7.3 (Relations with Jury). See also ABA Standards for Special Functions of the Trial Judge.

ABA Standards for Imposing Lawyer Sanctions: See Standard 6.3, which is reprinted in the Related Materials following Model Rule 4.2.

Federal Rules of Civil Procedure: Rule 65(b), governing ex parte communications in proceedings to obtain temporary restraining orders, provides, in pertinent part, as follows:

> *Temporary Restraining Order; Notice; Hearing; Duration.* A temporary restraining order may be granted without written or oral notice to the adverse party or that party's attorney only if (1) it clearly appears from specific facts shown by affidavit or by the verified complaint that immediate and irreparable injury, loss, or damage will result to the applicant before the adverse party or that party's attorney can be heard in opposition, and (2) the applicant's attorney certifies to the court in writing the efforts, if any, which have been made to give the notice and the reasons supporting the claim that notice should not be required. . . .

Model Rules of Professional Conduct for Federal Lawyers: Rule 3.5(a) prohibits a federal lawyer from seeking to influence "a tribunal, a member of a tribunal, a prospective member of a tribunal, or other official by means prohibited by law."

Obstruction of Justice: Various federal and state statutes make it a crime to obstruct justice. For example, 18 U.S.C. §1503, entitled "Influencing or Injuring Officer or Juror Generally," makes it illegal to use "threats or force . . . to influence, intimidate, or impede any grand or petit juror, or officer in or of any court of the United States . . . in the discharge of his duty"; and 18 U.S.C. §1512, entitled "Tampering with a Witness, Victim or an Informant," makes it a crime to kill, intimidate, harass, or threaten a witness, victim or informant in connection with an official proceeding.

Restatement of the Law Governing Lawyers: See Restatement §§112, 113, and 115 in our chapter on the Restatement later in this volume.

Rule 3.6 Trial Publicity

(a) A lawyer who is participating or has participated in the investigation or litigation of a matter shall not make an extrajudicial statement that ~~a reasonable person would expect to~~ <u>the lawyer knows</u>

or reasonably should know will be disseminated by means of public communication and will have a substantial likelihood of materially prejudicing an adjudicative proceeding in the matter.

(b) Notwithstanding paragraph (a), a lawyer may state:

(1) the claim, offense or defense involved and, except when prohibited by law, the identity of the persons involved;

(2) information contained in a public record;

(3) that an investigation of a matter is in progress;

(4) the scheduling or result of any step in litigation;

(5) a request for assistance in obtaining evidence and information necessary thereto;

(6) a warning of danger concerning the behavior of a person involved, when there is reason to believe that there exists the likelihood of substantial harm to an individual or to the public interest; and

(7) in a criminal case, in addition to subparagraphs (1) through (6):

(i) the identity, residence, occupation and family status of the accused;

(ii) if the accused has not been apprehended, information necessary to aid in apprehension of that person;

(iii) the fact, time and place of arrest; and

(iv) the identity of investigating and arresting officers or agencies and the length of the investigation.

(c) Notwithstanding paragraph (a), a lawyer may make a statement that a reasonable lawyer would believe is required to protect a client from the substantial undue prejudicial effect of recent publicity not initiated by the lawyer or the lawyer's client. A statement made pursuant to this paragraph shall be limited to such information as is necessary to mitigate the recent adverse publicity.

(d) No lawyer associated in a firm or government agency with a lawyer subject to paragraph (a) shall make a statement prohibited by paragraph (a).

COMMENT

[1] It is difficult to strike a balance between protecting the right to a fair trial and safeguarding the right of free expression. Preserving the right to a fair trial necessarily entails some curtailment of the information that may be disseminated about a party prior to trial, particularly where trial by jury is involved. If there were no such limits, the result would be the practical nullification of the protective effect of the rules of forensic decorum and the exclusionary rules of evidence. On the other hand, there are vital social interests served by the free dissemination of information about events having legal consequences and about legal proceedings themselves. The

public has a right to know about threats to its safety and measures aimed at assuring its security. It also has a legitimate interest in the conduct of judicial proceedings, particularly in matters of general public concern. Furthermore, the subject matter of legal proceedings is often of direct significance in debate and deliberation over questions of public policy.

[2] Special rules of confidentiality may validly govern proceedings in juvenile, domestic relations and mental disability proceedings, and perhaps other types of litigation. Rule 3.4(c) requires compliance with such rules.

[3] The Rule sets forth a basic general prohibition against a lawyer's making statements that the lawyer knows or should know will have a substantial likelihood of materially prejudicing an adjudicative proceeding. Recognizing that the public value of informed commentary is great and the likelihood of prejudice to a proceeding by the commentary of a lawyer who is not involved in the proceeding is small, the rule applies only to lawyers who are, or who have been involved in the investigation or litigation of a case, and their associates.

[4] Paragraph (b) identifies specific matters about which a lawyer's statements would not ordinarily be considered to present a substantial likelihood of material prejudice, and should not in any event be considered prohibited by the general prohibition of paragraph (a). Paragraph (b) is not intended to be an exhaustive listing of the subjects upon which a lawyer may make a statement, but statements on other matters may be subject to paragraph (a).

[5] There are, on the other hand, certain subjects that are more likely than not to have a material prejudicial effect on a proceeding, particularly when they refer to a civil matter triable to a jury, a criminal matter, or any other proceeding that could result in incarceration. These subjects relate to:

(1) the character, credibility, reputation or criminal record of a party, suspect in a criminal investigation or witness, or the identity of a witness, or the expected testimony of a party or witness;
(2) in a criminal case or proceeding that could result in incarceration, the possibility of a plea of guilty to the offense or the existence or contents of any confession, admission, or statement given by a defendant or suspect or that person's refusal or failure to make a statement;
(3) the performance or results of any examination or test or the refusal or failure of a person to submit to an examination or test, or the identity or nature of physical evidence expected to be presented;
(4) any opinion as to the guilt or innocence of a defendant or suspect in a criminal case or proceeding that could result in incarceration;
(5) information that the lawyer knows or reasonably should know is likely to be inadmissible as evidence in a trial and that would, if disclosed, create a substantial risk of prejudicing an impartial trial; or

(6) the fact that a defendant has been charged with a crime, unless there is included therein a statement explaining that the charge is merely an accusation and that the defendant is presumed innocent until and unless proven guilty.

[6] Another relevant factor in determining prejudice is the nature of the proceeding involved. Criminal jury trials will be most sensitive to extrajudicial speech. Civil trials may be less sensitive. Non-jury hearings and arbitration proceedings may be even less affected. The Rule will still place limitations on prejudicial comments in these cases, but the likelihood of prejudice may be different depending on the type of proceeding.

[7] Finally, extrajudicial statements that might otherwise raise a question under this Rule may be permissible when they are made in response to statements made publicly by another party, another party's lawyer, or third persons, where a reasonable lawyer would believe a public response is required in order to avoid prejudice to the lawyer's client. When prejudicial statements have been publicly made by others, responsive statements may have the salutary effect of lessening any resulting adverse impact on the adjudicative proceeding. Such responsive statements should be limited to contain only such information as is necessary to mitigate undue prejudice created by the statements made by others.

<u>[8] See Rule 3.8(f) for additional duties of prosecutors in connection with extrajudicial statements about criminal proceedings.</u>

Canon and Code Antecedents

ABA Canons of Professional Ethics: Canon 20 provided as follows:

20. Newspaper Discussion of Pending Litigation

Newspaper publications by a lawyer as to pending or anticipated litigation may interfere with a fair trial in the Courts and otherwise prejudice the due administration of justice. Generally they are to be condemned. If the extreme circumstances of a particular case justify a statement to the public, it is unprofessional to make it anonymously. An *ex parte* reference to the facts should not go beyond quotation from the records and papers on file in the court; but even in extreme cases it is better to avoid any *ex parte* statement.

ABA Model Code of Professional Responsibility: Compare DR 7-107 (reprinted later in this volume).

Cross-References in Other Rules

Rule 3.8(f) provides that the prosecutor of a criminal case shall "exercise reasonable care to prevent investigators . . . or other persons . . . from making an extrajudicial statement that the prosecutor would be prohibited from making under **Rule 3.6** or this Rule."

Rule 3.8, Comment 5: "Paragraph (f) supplements **Rule 3.6**, which prohibits extrajudicial statements that have a substantial likelihood of prejudicing an adjudicatory proceeding. . . . Nothing in this Comment is intended to restrict the statements which a prosecutor may make which comply with **Rule 3.6(b)** or **3.6(c)**."

Legislative History of Model Rule 3.6

1980 Discussion Draft (then Rule 3.8) was essentially an amalgam and reorganization of DR 7-107, except that paragraphs (F), (I), (J) of DR 7-107 were deleted, and the following new provisions were added.

> (a) To ensure a fair trial, a lawyer involved in the investigation of a criminal matter or in criminal or civil litigation shall not, except as provided in paragraph (b), make an extrajudicial statement:
>
> (2) when the matter under investigation or in litigation is a criminal case or a civil case triable to a jury and the statement relates to:
>
> (v) information the lawyer knows or reasonably should know would be inadmissible as evidence in a trial;
>
> (vi) any other matter that similarly creates a serious and imminent risk of prejudicing an impartial trial.
>
> (b) A lawyer involved in the investigation or litigation of a matter may state without elaboration;
>
> (6) in a criminal case:
>
> (vi) that the accused denies the charges.
>
> (c) When evidence or information received in or relating to a proceeding is by law or order of a tribunal to be kept confidential, the lawyer shall not unlawfully disclose the evidence or information.

1981 Draft was the same as adopted, except (b)(7)(iii), which provided: "the fact, time, and place of arrest, *resistance, pursuit and use of weapons.*"

1982 Draft was adopted.

1994 Amendment: At its August 1994 Annual Meeting, by a voice vote, the ABA House of Delegates significantly amended Rule 3.6 for the first time since its original adoption in 1983. The amendment reflected three years of drafting spurred by the Supreme Court's decision in Gentile v. Nevada State Bar, 501 U.S. 1030 (1991), which cast doubt on the constitutionality of some parts of Rule 3.6. (Companion amendments to Rule 3.8 were approved at the same time, also to conform to *Gentile.*)

The amendment to Rule 3.6 has three purposes: (1) it lists various types of information that a lawyer may disclose in out-of-court statements despite the general ban on extrajudicial statements substantially likely to prejudice a court proceeding; (2) it creates a "safe harbor" that allows a lawyer to protect clients against undue prejudice resulting from recent publicity not initiated by the lawyer or client; and (3) it makes clear that all lawyers in a firm or government agency are governed by Rule 3.6. For a legislative-style version of the Rule showing exactly what was added and deleted by the 1994 amendment, see our 1995 edition.

The 1994 amendment also substantially rewrote the Comment and Code Comparison, deleting former paragraph [2] of the Comment and adding paragraphs 3 through 7. The deleted paragraph of the Comment had stated as follows:

> [2] No body of rules can simultaneously satisfy all interests of fair trial and all those of free expression. The formula in this Rule is based upon the ABA Model

Code of Professional Responsibility and the ABA Standards Relating to Fair Trial and Free Press, as amended in 1978.

The amendment was co-sponsored by the ABA Standing Committee on Ethics and Professional Responsibility and the ABA Criminal Justice Section. Below are substantial excerpts from the joint ABA report explaining the amendments.

*Excerpts from ABA Report Explaining 1994 Amendments**

In *Gentile,* a criminal defense lawyer challenged disciplinary action taken against him by the State Bar of Nevada under its version of Rule 3.6, because of certain remarks made by him at a press conference relating to his client's anticipated defense. The lawyer challenged the state's action on grounds that his extrajudicial statements were protected by the First Amendment, and that in any event his remarks were within the Rule's "safe harbor" provision.

The Supreme Court unanimously upheld the Rule's "substantial likelihood of material prejudice" test. However, a majority of five Justices held the Rule void for vagueness as interpreted and applied by the Nevada State Bar in the circumstances of the case. . . . The five members of the Court who reversed the state's disciplinary action noted that the safe harbor provision of Rule 3.6 allows a criminal lawyer to explain the "general" nature of his client's defense "without elaboration," and pointed out that the terms "general" and "elaboration" have "no settled usage or tradition of interpretation in law." As worded, they said, the provision gives a lawyer "no principle for determining when his remarks pass from the safe harbor of the general to the forbidden sea of the elaborated," and creates "a trap for the wary as well as the unwary."

The Standing Committee on Ethics and Professional Responsibility . . . proposes to revise the Rule's safe harbor provision by deleting the qualifying terms which the Supreme Court held unconstitutionally vague. . . .

The Committee adopted a proposal from the Criminal Justice Section to place in the text of the Rule a provision entitling a lawyer to respond where adverse publicity has been initiated by an opposing party or third persons, in order to avoid substantial undue prejudice to the lawyer's client. The Committee felt that in this situation, the danger of the second statement prejudicing the proceeding is minimized, and the rights of the client can be protected.

The Committee . . . felt that for completeness, the Rule must also extend to lawyers associated with those participating in a matter, and those who formerly participated in a matter. The need for lawyers outside a proceeding to interpret those proceedings to the public is so great, and the right of comment on government process so fundamental that the Committee felt that the lawyers affected by speech restrictions of Rule 3.6 should be clearly and narrowly defined.

The Committee also considered whether Rule 3.6 should be limited to criminal cases, or to cases involving jury trials. While a convincing argument can be made that there is less chance of prejudice from statements made in the course of a civil proceeding than in the context of a criminal matter, and in a bench trial than in a jury trial, it is the Committee's view that the nature of the proceeding and the identity of the trier of fact are relevant to but not dispositive of the issue of likelihood of prejudice. . . .

*Committee Reports do not represent official policy of the ABA. They are for information only, and the opinions are those of the authors of the report.

2002 Amendments: At its February 2002 Mid-Year Meeting, the ABA House of Delegates adopted without change the ABA Ethics 2000 Commission proposal to amend Rule 3.6 and its Comment.

Selected State Variations

Arizona, Connecticut, Florida, Minnesota, Montana, New Jersey, and ***Pennsylvania*** omit from Rule 3.6(a) the phrase "who is participating or has participated in the investigation or litigation of a matter. . . ." Arizona also omits paragraphs (c) and (d) of ABA Model Rule 3.6, and elevates paragraph 5 of the ABA Comment to the text of Rule 3.6.

California: See Rule 5-120 (Trial Publicity) and B&P §6103.7 (commanding the State Bar to propose a rule governing trial publicity).

District of Columbia: D.C. Rule 3.6 differs significantly from the ABA Model Rule — see District of Columbia Rules of Professional Conduct below.

Florida: Rule 3.6(a) applies to a statement that will have a substantial likelihood of materially prejudicing an adjudicative proceeding due to the statement's "creation of an imminent and substantial detrimental effect on that proceeding." Florida deletes ABA Model Rules 3.6(b), (c), and (d), and substitutes the following Rule 3.6(b):

> *Statements of Third Parties.* A lawyer shall not counsel or assist another person to make such a statement. Counsel shall exercise reasonable care to prevent investigators, employees, or other persons assisting in or associated with a case from making extrajudicial statements that are prohibited under this rule.

Georgia: In the rules effective January 1, 2001, Georgia adopted subparagraphs (a), (c), and (d) of the pre-2002 version of Rule 3.6 verbatim, but relegated subparagraph (b) to a new paragraph 5A of the Comment, which notes that there are "certain subjects which are more likely than not to have no material prejudicial effect on a proceeding." The Comment then lists all of the items in ABA Model Rule 3.6(b) as examples of things that a lawyer may "usually" state.

Illinois: The Illinois Supreme Court amended Rule 3.6 effective October 22, 1999, but on November 23, 1999, in response to a petition for reconsideration filed by several federal, state, and county prosecutors, the court stayed implementation of the amended rule. On March 16, 2000, the court lifted the stay and ordered that the amended rule (and a companion amendment to Rule 3.8) be "effective immediately." The amended rule prohibits an extrajudicial statement if the lawyer "knows or reasonably should know that it would pose a serious and imminent threat to the fairness of an adjudicative proceeding." The amended rule then borrows heavily from DR 7-107 of the ABA Model Code of Professional Responsibility and language taken verbatim from ABA Model Rule 3.6(b), (c), and (d), but adds some language not found in either DR 7-107 or ABA Model Rule 3.6.

Michigan places Rules 3.6(b) and (c) in its Comment to Rule 3.6.

Minnesota shortens Rule 3.6(a) and deletes subparagraphs (b), (c) and (d) of Rule 3.6 in their entirety.

Montana adds the following language to (b)(4): "or a substantial likelihood of materially prejudicing the outcome of a hearing or trial."

New Jersey substitutes "reasonable lawyer" for "reasonable person" in Rule 3.6(a). Rule 3.6(b)(1) ordinarily prohibits a lawyer from making a statement about the identity of a witness "other than the victim of a crime."

New York: Compare ABA Model Rule 3.6 to New York's DR 7-107.

North Carolina: Rule 3.6 moves most of paragraph 5 of the Comment to ABA Model Rule 3.6 into the text of the rule. North Carolina omits paragraphs (c) and (d) of ABA Model Rule 3.6 and substitutes its own version of Rule 3.6(d), which provides that Rule 3.6 does not "preclude a lawyer from replying to charges of misconduct publicly made against the lawyer or from participating in the proceedings of legislative, administrative, or other investigative bodies." Finally, North Carolina adds a new Rule 3.6(e), similar to ABA Model Rule 3.8(f) as amended in 2002, which requires a lawyer to exercise "reasonable care to prevent the lawyer's employees from making statements the lawyer would be prohibited from making" under Rule 3.6.

Ohio: In 1996, Ohio repealed its old DR 7-107 and adopted a new DR 7-107 substantively identical to the 1994 version of ABA Model Rule 3.6.

Oregon: DR 7-107(A) prohibits a lawyer from making an extrajudicial statement that a reasonable person would expect to be disseminated by means of public communication if the lawyer intends to affect the fact-finding process or the lawyer knows or reasonably should know that the statement poses "a serious and imminent threat to the fact-finding process" in an adjudicative proceeding and acts with indifference to that effect. Oregon DR 7-107(B) provides that DR 7-107(A) "does not preclude a lawyer from replying to charges of misconduct publicly made against the lawyer or from participating in the proceedings of legislative, administrative or other investigative bodies." Oregon DR 7-107(C) requires a lawyer to "exercise reasonable care to prevent the lawyer's employees from making an extrajudicial statement that the lawyer would be prohibited from making under DR 7-107 (A)."

Texas: Rule 3.07 is substantially similar to North Carolina Rule 3.06(a)-(c) — see North Carolina entry above. Texas Rule 3.07(a) adds that a lawyer "shall not counsel or assist another person to make" a statement that the rule would prohibit the lawyer from making.

Utah: In 1997, Utah amended Rule 3.6 to conform substantially to ABA Model Rule 3.6 as amended in 1994.

Virginia: Rule 3.6 provides:

> (a) A lawyer participating in or associated with the investigation or the prosecution or the defense of a criminal matter that may be tried by a jury shall not make or participate in making an extrajudicial statement that a reasonable person would expect to be disseminated by means of public communication that the lawyer knows, or should know, will have a substantial likelihood of interfering with the fairness of the trial by a jury.
>
> (b) A lawyer shall exercise reasonable care to prevent employees and associates from making an extrajudicial statement that the lawyer would be prohibited from making under this Rule.

Related Materials

ABA Standards of Criminal Justice: See Prosecution Function Standard 3-1.4 (Public Statements). See also Standards Relating to Fair Trial and Free Press (excerpted at pp. 544-548 of our 1997 edition).

Code of Federal Regulations: See 28 C.F.R. §50.2, reprinted later in this volume in the material on Federal Conflicts and Confidentiality Provisions.

Model Rules of Professional Conduct for Federal Lawyers: Rule 3.6(a) prohibits extrajudicial statements likely to prejudice an adjudicative proceeding "or an official review process thereof." Rule 3.6(b)(4) makes clear that Rule 3.6 applies to any proceeding that could result in incarceration "or other adverse action." The Rules for Federal Lawyers also add Rule 3.6(d), which provides: "The protection and release of information in matters pertaining to the Government shall be consistent with law."

Restatement of the Law Governing Lawyers: See Restatement §109 in our chapter on the Restatement later in this volume.

Rule 3.7 Lawyer as Witness

(a) A lawyer shall not act as advocate at a trial in which the lawyer is likely to be a necessary witness ~~except where~~ unless:

(1) the testimony relates to an uncontested issue;

(2) the testimony relates to the nature and value of legal services rendered in the case; or

(3) disqualification of the lawyer would work substantial hardship on the client.

(b) A lawyer may act as advocate in a trial in which another lawyer in the lawyer's firm is likely to be called as a witness unless precluded from doing so by Rule 1.7 or Rule 1.9.

COMMENT

[1] Combining the roles of advocate and witness can prejudice the tribunal and the opposing party and can also involve a conflict of interest between the lawyer and client.

Advocate-Witness Rule

[2] The tribunal has proper objection when the trier of fact may be confused or misled by a lawyer serving as both advocate and witness. The opposing party has proper objection where the combination of roles may prejudice that party's rights in the litigation. A witness is required to testify on the basis of personal knowledge, while an advocate is expected to explain and comment on evidence given by others. It may not be clear whether a statement by an advocate-witness should be taken as proof or as an analysis of the proof.

[3] To protect the tribunal, paragraph (a) prohibits a lawyer from simultaneously serving as advocate and necessary witness except in those

circumstances specified in paragraphs (a)(1) through (a)(3). Paragraph (a)(1) recognizes that if the testimony will be uncontested, the ambiguities in the dual role are purely theoretical. Paragraph (a)(2) recognizes that where the testimony concerns the extent and value of legal services rendered in the action in which the testimony is offered, permitting the lawyers to testify avoids the need for a second trial with new counsel to resolve that issue. Moreover, in such a situation the judge has firsthand knowledge of the matter in issue; hence, there is less dependence on the adversary process to test the credibility of the testimony.

[4] Apart from these two exceptions, paragraph (a)(3) recognizes that a balancing is required between the interests of the client and those of the tribunal and the opposing party. Whether the tribunal is likely to be misled or the opposing party is likely to suffer prejudice depends on the nature of the case, the importance and probable tenor of the lawyer's testimony, and the probability that the lawyer's testimony will conflict with that of other witnesses. Even if there is risk of such prejudice, in determining whether the lawyer should be disqualified, due regard must be given to the effect of disqualification on the lawyer's client. It is relevant that one or both parties could reasonably foresee that the lawyer would probably be a witness. The ~~principle of imputed disqualification~~ conflict of interest principles stated in ~~Rule~~ Rules 1.7, 1.9 and 1.10 ~~has~~ have no application to this aspect of the problem.

[5] Because the tribunal is not likely to be misled when a lawyer acts as advocate in a trial in which another lawyer in the lawyer's firm will testify as a necessary witness, paragraph (b) permits the lawyer to do so except in situations involving a conflict of interest.

Conflict of Interest

~~[5]~~ [6] ~~Whether the combination of roles involves an improper~~ In determining if it is permissible to act as advocate in a trial in which the lawyer will be a necessary witness, the lawyer must also consider that the dual role may give rise to a conflict of interest ~~with respect to the client is determined by Rule~~ that will require compliance with Rules 1.7 or 1.9. For example, if there is likely to be substantial conflict between the testimony of the client and that of the lawyer ~~or a member of the lawyer's firm~~, the representation ~~is improper~~ involves a conflict of interest that requires compliance with Rule 1.7. This would be true even though the lawyer might not be prohibited by paragraph (a) from simultaneously serving as advocate and witness because the lawyer's disqualification would work a substantial hardship on the client. Similarly, a lawyer who might be permitted to simultaneously serve as an advocate and a witness by paragraph (a)(3) might be precluded from doing so by Rule 1.9. The problem can arise whether the lawyer is called as a witness on behalf of the client or is called by the opposing party.

Determining whether or not such a conflict exists is primarily the responsibility of the lawyer involved. If there is a conflict of interest, the lawyer must secure the client's informed consent, confirmed in writing. In some cases, the lawyer will be precluded from seeking the client's consent. See ~~Comment to~~ Rule 1.7. ~~If a lawyer who is a member of a firm may not act as both advocate and witness by reason of conflict of interest, Rule 1.10 disqualifies the firm also.~~ See Rule 1.0(b) for the definition of "confirmed in writing" and Rule 1.0(e) for the definition of "informed consent."

[7] Paragraph (b) provides that a lawyer is not disqualified from serving as an advocate because a lawyer with whom the lawyer is associated in a firm is precluded from doing so by paragraph (a). If, however, the testifying lawyer would also be disqualified by Rule 1.7 or Rule 1.9 from representing the client in the matter, other lawyers in the firm will be precluded from representing the client by Rule 1.10 unless the client gives informed consent under the conditions stated in Rule 1.7.

Canon and Code Antecedents

ABA Canons of Professional Ethics: Canon 19 provided as follows:

19. Appearance of Lawyer as Witness for His Client

When a lawyer is a witness for his client, except as to merely formal matters, such as the attestation or custody of an instrument and the like, he should leave the trial of the case to other counsel. Except when essential to the ends of justice, a lawyer should avoid testifying in court in behalf of his client.

ABA Model Code of Professional Responsibility: Compare DR 5-101(B), DR 5-101(B)(1), DR 5-101(B)(2), DR 5-102(A), and DR 5-102(B) (reprinted later in this volume).

Cross-References in Other Rules

None.

Legislative History of Model Rule 3.7

1980 Discussion Draft (then Rule 3.9) prohibited a lawyer from acting as an advocate, "except on the lawyer's own behalf, in litigation in which the lawyer's own conduct is a material issue or in which the lawyer is likely to be a witness," unless the lawyer satisfied exceptions that were substantially the same as finally adopted.

1981 Draft was substantially the same as adopted.

1982 Draft was adopted.

2002 Amendments: At its February 2002 Mid-Year Meeting, the ABA House of Delegates adopted without change the ABA Ethics 2000 Commission proposal to amend Rule 3.7 and its Comment.

Selected State Variations

Arkansas totally deletes subparagraph (b).

California: See Rule 5-210 (Member as Witness).

District of Columbia: D.C. Rule 3.7(b) differs significantly from the ABA Model Rule — see District of Columbia Rules of Professional Conduct below.

Florida: Rule 3.7 prohibits a lawyer from acting as advocate at a trial where the lawyer is likely to be a necessary witness "on behalf of the client" unless various exceptions apply. The exceptions are drawn from DR 5-101(B) of the ABA Model Code — see the ABA Model Code of Professional Responsibility (reprinted later in this volume).

Georgia: In the rules effective January 1, 2001, Georgia adopted the pre-2002 version of ABA Model Rule 3.7 substantially verbatim.

Illinois: Rule 3.7 distinguishes between a witness on behalf of a client and a witness not on behalf of a client. Illinois Rule 3.7(a) essentially tracks DR 5-101(B), and Illinois Rule 3.7(b) essentially tracks DR 5-102(B).

New Mexico deletes subparagraph (a)(3).

New York: Compare ABA Model Rule 3.7 to New York's DR 5-102.

Texas: Rule 3.08(a) disqualifies a lawyer "if the lawyer knows or believes that the lawyer is or may be a witness necessary to establish an essential fact on behalf of the lawyer's client," unless specified exceptions apply. The exceptions are substantially identical to DR 5-101(B)(1)-(3) of the ABA Model Code of Professional Responsibility, but Texas adds an exception if "(4) the lawyer is a party to the action and is appearing pro se," and Texas applies the "substantial hardship" exception only if "the lawyer has promptly notified opposing counsel that the lawyer expects to testify in the matter. . . ." Texas Rules 3.08(b) and (c) provide as follows:

> (b) A lawyer shall not continue as an advocate in a pending adjudicatory proceeding if the lawyer believes that the lawyer will be compelled to furnish testimony that will be substantially adverse to the lawyer's client, unless the client consents after full disclosure.
>
> (c) Without the client's informed consent, a lawyer may not act as advocate in an adjudicatory proceeding in which another lawyer in the lawyer's firm is prohibited by paragraphs (a) or (b) from serving as advocate. If the lawyer to be called as a witness could not also serve as an advocate under this Rule, that lawyer shall not take an active role before the tribunal in the presentation of the matter.

Virginia: In Rule 3.7(a), Virginia substitutes "adversarial proceeding" for "trial." In addition, Virginia inserts as Rule 3.7(b) language from DR 5-102(B) to deal with situations in which a lawyer learns that he or she may be called as a witness "other than on behalf of the client" after having accepted the representation.

Washington's version of subparagraph (a)(3) is as follows: "the trial judge finds that disqualification of the lawyer would work a substantial hardship on the client and that the likelihood of the lawyer being a necessary witness was not reasonably foreseeable before trial." Washington also adds the following new subparagraph (c): "the lawyer has been called by the opposing party and the court rules that the lawyer may continue to act as an advocate."

Related Materials

Model Rules of Professional Conduct for Federal Lawyers: Rule 3.7(a)(2) permits a lawyer to testify to "the nature, value, *and quality* of legal services rendered in the case."

Restatement of the Law Governing Lawyers: See Restatement §109 in our chapter on the Restatement later in this volume.

Rule 3.8 Special Responsibilities of a Prosecutor

The prosecutor in a criminal case shall:

(a) refrain from prosecuting a charge that the prosecutor knows is not supported by probable cause;

(b) make reasonable efforts to assure that the accused has been advised of the right to, and the procedure for obtaining, counsel and has been given reasonable opportunity to obtain counsel;

(c) not seek to obtain from an unrepresented accused a waiver of important pretrial rights, such as the right to a preliminary hearing;

(d) make timely disclosure to the defense of all evidence or information known to the prosecutor that tends to negate the guilt of the accused or mitigates the offense, and, in connection with sentencing, disclose to the defense and to the tribunal all unprivileged mitigating information known to the prosecutor, except when the prosecutor is relieved of this responsibility by a protective order of the tribunal;

~~(e)~~ [See paragraph (f).]

~~(f)~~ (e) not subpoena a lawyer in a grand jury or other criminal proceeding to present evidence about a past or present client unless the prosecutor reasonably believes:

(1) the information sought is not protected from disclosure by any applicable privilege;

(2) the evidence sought is essential to the successful completion of an ongoing investigation or prosecution; and

~~(3)~~ there is no other feasible alternative to obtain the information~~.~~;

~~(g)~~ (f) except for statements that are necessary to inform the public of the nature and extent of the prosecutor's action and that serve a legitimate law enforcement purpose, refrain from making extrajudicial comments that have a substantial likelihood of heightening public condemnation of the accused and ~~(e)~~ exercise reasonable care to prevent investigators, law enforcement personnel, employees or other persons assisting or associated with the prosecutor in a criminal case from making an extrajudicial statement that the prosecutor would be prohibited from making under Rule 3.6 or this Rule.

COMMENT

[1] A prosecutor has the responsibility of a minister of justice and not simply that of an advocate. This responsibility carries with it specific obligations to see that the defendant is accorded procedural justice and that guilt is decided upon the basis of sufficient evidence. Precisely how far the prosecutor is required to go in this direction is a matter of debate and varies in different jurisdictions. Many jurisdictions have adopted the ABA Standards of Criminal Justice Relating to the Prosecution Function, which in turn are the product of prolonged and careful deliberation by lawyers experienced in both criminal prosecution and defense. ~~See also Rule 3.3(d), governing *ex parte* proceedings, among which grand jury proceedings are included.~~ Applicable law may require other measures by the prosecutor and knowing disregard of those obligations or a systematic abuse of prosecutorial discretion could constitute a violation of Rule 8.4.

[2] In some jurisdictions, a defendant may waive a preliminary hearing and thereby lose a valuable opportunity to challenge probable cause. Accordingly, prosecutors should not seek to obtain waivers of preliminary hearings or other important pretrial rights from unrepresented accused persons. Paragraph (c) does not apply, however, to an accused appearing *pro se* with the approval of the tribunal. Nor does it forbid the lawful questioning of ~~a~~ an uncharged suspect who has knowingly waived the rights to counsel and silence.

[3] The exception in paragraph (d) recognizes that a prosecutor may seek an appropriate protective order from the tribunal if disclosure of information to the defense could result in substantial harm to an individual or to the public interest.

[4] Paragraph ~~(f)~~ (e) is intended to limit the issuance of lawyer subpoenas in grand jury and other criminal proceedings to those situations in which there is a genuine need to intrude into the client-lawyer relationship.

[5] Paragraph ~~(g)~~ (f) supplements Rule 3.6, which prohibits extrajudicial statements that have a substantial likelihood of prejudicing an adjudicatory proceeding. In the context of a criminal prosecution, a prosecutor's extrajudicial statement can create the additional problem of increasing public condemnation of the accused. Although the announcement of an indictment, for example, will necessarily have severe consequences for the accused, a prosecutor can, and should, avoid comments which have no legitimate law enforcement purpose and have a substantial likelihood of increasing public opprobrium of the accused. Nothing in this Comment is intended to restrict the statements which a prosecutor may make which comply with Rule 3.6(b) or 3.6(c).

[6] Like other lawyers, prosecutors are subject to Rules 5.1 and 5.3, which relate to responsibilities regarding lawyers and nonlawyers who work for or are associated with the lawyer's office. Paragraph (f) reminds the prosecutor of the importance of these obligations in connection with

the unique dangers of improper extrajudicial statements in a criminal case. In addition, paragraph (f) requires a prosecutor to exercise reasonable care to prevent persons assisting or associated with the prosecutor from making improper extrajudicial statements, even when such persons are not under the direct supervision of the prosecutor. Ordinarily, the reasonable care standard will be satisfied if the prosecutor issues the appropriate cautions to law-enforcement personnel and other relevant individuals.

Canon and Code Antecedents

ABA Canons of Professional Ethics: Canon 5 provided as follows:

5. The Defense or Prosecution of Those Accused of Crime

It is the right of the lawyer to undertake the defense of a person accused of crime, regardless of his personal opinion as to the guilt of the accused; otherwise innocent persons, victims only of suspicious circumstances, might be denied proper defense. Having undertaken such defense, the lawyer is bound, by all fair and honorable means, to present every defense that the law of the land permits, to the end that no person may be deprived of life or liberty, but by due process of law.

The primary duty of a lawyer engaged in public prosecution is not to convict, but to see that justice is done. The suppression of facts or the secreting of witnesses capable of establishing the innocence of the accused is highly reprehensible.

ABA Model Code of Professional Responsibility: Compare DR 7-103(A) and DR 7-103(B) (reprinted later in this volume).

Cross-References in Other Rules

Rule 3.6, Comment 8: "See **Rule 3.8(f)** for additional duties of prosecutors in connection with extrajudicial statements about criminal proceedings."

Legislative History of Model Rule 3.8

1980 Discussion Draft (then Rule 3.10) provided as follows:

The prosecutor in a criminal case shall:

(a) refrain from prosecuting a charge that the prosecutor knows is not supported by probable cause;

(b) advise the defendant of the right to counsel and provide assistance in obtaining counsel;

(c) not induce an unrepresented defendant to surrender important procedural rights, such as the right to a preliminary hearing;

(d) seek all evidence, whether or not favorable to the accused, and make timely disclosure to the defense of all evidence supporting innocence of mitigating the offense;

(e) not discourage a person from giving relevant information to the defense;

(f) in connection with sentencing, disclose to the defendant and to the court all unprivileged information known to the prosecution that is relevant thereto.

1980 Discussion Draft also contained a separate rule, with no counterpart in the Rules as adopted, that read as follows:

Special Responsibilities of Defense Counsel in a Criminal Case

A lawyer for the accused in a criminal case, shall not:

(a) agree to represent a person proposing to commit a crime, except as part of a good faith effort to determine the validity, scope, meaning, or application of the law;

(b) act in a case in which the lawyer's partner or other professional associate is or has been the prosecutor;

(c) accept payment of fees by one person for the defense of another except with the consent of the accused after adequate disclosure; or

(d) charge a contingent fee.

1981 Draft: Substantially the same as adopted, except subparagraph (d), which included an obligation to "make reasonable efforts to seek all evidence, whether or not favorable to the defendant," but did not refer to protective orders. Also, the 1981 Draft did not include subparagraph (e) of the rule as adopted.

1982 Draft: Same as adopted, except that the 1982 Draft did not include subparagraph (e) of the rule as adopted.

1990 Amendment: At its 1990 Mid-Year Meeting, the ABA House of Delegates added subparagraph (f) (now (e)) to Rule 3.8 and added paragraph 4 to the Comment. The reasons for adding Rule 3.8(f) were explained by the ABA's Standing Committee on Ethics and Professional Responsibility as follows:

*Excerpt from ABA Report Explaining 1990 Amendment**

Any rule regulating subpoenas to lawyers must, at a minimum, provide for full protection of the privilege.

A subpoena rule which does no more than recognize the attorney-client privilege, however, will ignore other important aspects of the relationship between a client and his attorney. . . . Because information protected by the attorney-client privilege is not coterminous with information which an ethical attorney is supposed to hold confidential, there is much information in the hands of an attorney which remains exposed to the subpoena power, even if that power is limited by the privilege. For example, the prevailing judicial position is that, absent special circumstances, an attorney may be compelled by subpoena to reveal information about the identity of the client and the size and source of the fee — information frequently sought by government attorneys. Similarly, an attorney in possession of documents received from a client in the course of a case may be compelled by subpoena to produce those documents, assuming that the client personally could be compelled to produce the documents were they in the client's hands.

*Committee Reports do not represent official policy of the ABA. They are for information only, and the opinions are those of the authors of the report.

> Since a subpoena may compel production of information which, though unprivileged, is certainly confidential under Rule 1.6 and DR 4-101, the mere issuance of the subpoena undermines the client's confidence and trust. . . .
>
> . . . Confronted by a powerful adversary and by a seemingly bewildering array of procedures, with their liberty at stake, clients rightfully expect that their lawyer will, within the constraints of the law and the profession's code of ethics, zealously argue their case at every turn. There could be few things more destructive of this expectation than the spectacle of their own attorney forced by their adversary to supply information detrimental to their interest.

1994 Amendment: At its August 1994 Annual Meeting, by a voice vote, the ABA House of Delegates amended Rule 3.8 for the second time since its original adoption in 1983. The amendment added a new subparagraph (g) (now (f)) that permits prosecutors to make statements "necessary to inform the public of the nature and extent of the prosecutor's action and that serve a legitimate law enforcement purpose," even if these statements may heighten "public condemnation of the accused." The amendment added a corresponding paragraph to the Comment. The amendment supplements the 1994 amendment to Rule 3.6, which generally governs extrajudicial statements by lawyers.

The amendment was co-sponsored by the ABA Standing Committee on Ethics and Professional Responsibility and the ABA Criminal Justice Section, which submitted a joint report in support of the 1994 amendment to Rule 3.6 and Rule 3.8. We reprint below the small portion of the joint ABA report explaining the amendment to Rule 3.8. (Excerpts from the remainder of the report, which provides further background and context for the amendment, are found in the Legislative History section following Rule 3.6.)

*Excerpts from ABA Report Explaining 1994 Amendment**

> In connection with its proposed revision of Rule 3.6, the Committee also proposes to add a new section (g) to Rule 3.8, prohibiting gratuitous comments by a prosecutor which have a substantial likelihood of increasing public opprobrium toward the accused. Not only can pretrial publicity taint the fairness of a trial, but it can also subject the accused to unfair and unnecessary condemnation before the trial takes place. Because of a prosecutor's special power and visibility, a prosecutor should use special care to avoid such publicity.

1995 Amendment: At its August 1995 Annual Meeting, the ABA House of Delegates voted 187-113 to amend Rule 3.8 by deleting subparagraph (f)(2), which had required prosecutors to obtain "prior judicial approval after an opportunity for an adversarial hearing" before serving a subpoena on a lawyer in a grand jury or other criminal proceeding to seek evidence about the lawyer's past or present clients. The ABA also removed the last sentence of Comment 4 to Rule 3.8, which had explained the need for judicial approval. The amendment was jointly sponsored by the ABA's Standing Committee on Ethics and Professional

*Committee Reports do not represent official policy of the ABA. They are for information only, and the opinions are those of the authors of the report.

Responsibility and the ABA Criminal Justice Section. Below are excerpts from the joint Committee Report explaining the amendment.

*Excerpt from ABA Report Explaining 1995 Amendment**

Subparagraph (2) of Rule 3.8(f) is an anomaly in the Model Rules. Rather than stating a substantive ethical precept, it sets out a type of implementing requirement that is properly established by rules of criminal procedure rather than established as an ethical norm. Moreover, while nominally addressed to the conduct of prosecutors, subparagraph (2) affects the operation of courts and grand juries by "requir[ing] the erection of novel court procedures and interject[ing] an additional layer of judicial supervision over the grand jury subpoena process." Baylson v. Disciplinary Board, 764 F. Supp. 328, 337 (E D. Pa. 1991). The procedural obligations it seeks to impose as a matter of professional ethics have no parallel in any other enforceable provision of the Model Rules.

We therefore recommend deletion of subparagraph (2) of Rule 3.8(f), with its requirement of prior judicial approval of a lawyer subpoena and an opportunity for an adversarial proceeding. The limiting description of the circumstances in which a prosecutor could ethically issue such a subpoena, set forth in subparagraph (1), would remain unchanged. The proposed amendment would remove the feature of the rule that courts have found objectionable, and we expect this will lead to the more widespread adoption of it substantive provisions by state bars.

2002 Amendments: At its February 2002 Mid-Year Meeting, the ABA House of Delegates adopted without change the ABA Ethics 2000 Commission proposal to amend Rule 3.8 and its Comment. The amendment to the text of Rule 3.8 was stylistic only.

Selected State Variations

Alaska deletes section (c) from its version of Rule 3.8.

Arizona, Connecticut, Florida, and ***Michigan*** omit paragraphs (e) and (f) of ABA Model Rule 3.8 as amended in 2002.

California: See Rule 5-110 (Performing the Duty of Member in Government Service) and Rule 5-220 (Suppression of Evidence).

Colorado: Paragraphs (a), (b), (d), and (e) of Colorado Rule 3.8 are substantially identical to ABA Model Rule 3.8 as amended in 2002, but Colorado Rule 3.8(c) provides that a prosecutor shall not seek to obtain from an unrepresented accused a waiver of important pretrial rights "such as the right to a preliminary hearing, except that this does not apply to an accused appearing pro se with the approval of the tribunal. Nor does it forbid the lawful questioning of a suspect who has waived the rights to counsel and silence." Colorado omits paragraph (f) of ABA Model Rule 3.8 as amended in 2002, except that the obligation to "exercise reasonable care" regarding investigators and others is contained in Colorado Rule 3.8(e).

*Committee Reports do not represent official policy of the ABA. They are for information only, and the opinions are those of the authors of the report.

District of Columbia: D.C. Rule 3.8 differs significantly from the ABA Model Rule — see District of Columbia Rules of Professional Conduct below.

Florida omits paragraphs (b), (e), and (f) of ABA Model Rule 3.8 as amended in 2002.

Georgia: In the rules effective January 1, 2001, Georgia adopted much of ABA Model Rule 3.8 verbatim. However, in place of subparagraphs (b) and (c), Georgia substitutes the simple caution that a prosecutor shall "refrain from making any effort to prevent the accused from exercising a reasonable effort to obtain counsel." Georgia also shortens Rule 3.8(d) by eliminating the part that begins "in connection with sentencing." Georgia also limits the application of Rule 3.8(e) to statements the prosecutor would be prohibited from making under Rule 3.6(g) (as opposed to the entire rule).

Hawaii: Rule 3.8 applies to a "public prosecutor or other government lawyer." Rule 3.8(a) applies to a charge that the lawyer knows "or it is obvious" is not supported by probable cause.

Illinois: The Illinois Supreme Court amended Rule 3.8 effective October 22, 1999, but on November 23, 1999, in response to a petition for reconsideration filed by several federal, state, and county prosecutors, the court stayed implementation of the amended rule. On March 16, 2000, the court lifted the stay and ordered that the amended rule (and a companion amendment to Rule 3.6) be "effective immediately."

On March 1, 2001, effective immediately, the Illinois Supreme Court added a new paragraph (a) at the beginning of Rule 3.8. The new paragraph says: "The duty of a public prosecutor or other government lawyer is to seek justice, not merely to convict." The Court's order, IL Order 00-15 (March 1, 2000), quoted the following Committee Comments written by the Special Supreme Court Committee on Capital Cases to explain the new paragraph:

> Paragraph (a) of Rule 3.8 is substantially similar to Standard 3-1.2(c) of the American Bar Association (ABA) Standards for Criminal Justice (3d ed. 1993); however, paragraph (a) of Rule 3.8 restates a principle that is far older than the ABA standard. In 1924, the Illinois Supreme Court reversed a conviction for murder, noting that:
>
>> "The State's attorney in his official capacity is the representative of all the people, including the defendant, and it was as much his duty to safeguard the constitutional rights of the defendant as those of any other citizen." People v. Cochran, 313 Ill. 508, 526 (1924).
>
> In 1935, the United States Supreme Court described the duty of a federal prosecutor in the following passage:
>
>> "The United States Attorney is the representative not of an ordinary party to a controversy, but of a sovereignty whose obligation to govern impartially is as compelling as its obligation to govern at all; and whose interest, therefore, in a criminal prosecution is not that it shall win a case, but that justice shall be done. As such, he is in a peculiar and very definite sense the servant of the law, the twofold aim of which is that guilt shall not escape or innocence suffer. He may prosecute with earnestness and vigor — indeed, he should do so. But, while he may strike hard blows, he is not at liberty to strike foul ones. It is as much his duty to refrain from improper methods calculated to produce a wrongful conviction as it is to use every legitimate means to bring about a just one." Berger v. United States, 295 U.S. 78, 88 . . . (1935).
>
> Paragraph (a) of Rule 3.8 does not set an exact standard, but one good prosecutors will readily recognize and have always adhered to in the discharge of their

> duties. Specific standards, such as those in Rules 3.3, 3.4, 3.5, 3.6, the remaining paragraphs of Rule 3.8, and other applicable rules provide guidance for specific situations. Paragraph (a) of Rule 3.8 is intended to remind prosecutors that the touchstone of ethical conduct is the duty to act fairly, honestly, and honorably.

The remainder of Illinois Rule 3.8 begins with language taken almost verbatim from DR 7-103(A) and (B) of the ABA Model Code of Professional Responsibility. It continues with language drawn from ABA Model Rule 3.8(e) and (g), but the Illinois rule applies only when extrajudicial statements "would pose a serious and imminent threat" of heightening public condemnation of the accused.

Illinois omits subparagraphs (b), (c), and (e) of ABA Model Rule 3.8, but the omission of Rule 3.8(f) reflects a bitter struggle too complex to recount here.

Louisiana: In 1993, the Louisiana Supreme Court suspended Rule 3.8(f) (the subpoena provision) as applied to federal prosecutors.

Maryland's version of subparagraph (e) extends only to an "employee or other person under the control of a prosecutor."

Massachusetts: Rule 3.8(c) allows prosecutors to seek waivers of important pretrial rights from unrepresented defendants only if "a court has first obtained from the accused a knowing and intelligent written waiver of counsel." Rule 3.8(f) forbids a prosecutor to subpoena a lawyer to a grand jury or other criminal proceeding to present evidence about a past or present client unless:

> (1) the prosecutor reasonably believes:
> (i) the information sought is not protected from disclosure by any applicable privilege;
> (ii) the evidence sought is essential to the successful completion of an ongoing investigation or prosecution; and
> (iii) there is no other feasible alternative to obtain the information; and
> (2) the prosecutor obtains prior judicial approval after an opportunity for an adversarial proceeding.

In addition, Massachusetts adds paragraphs (h), (i), and (j) to Rule 3.8, which provide that a prosecutor in a criminal case shall:

> (h) not assert personal knowledge of the facts in issue, except when testifying as a witness;
> (i) not assert a personal opinion as to the justness of a cause, as to the credibility of a witness, as to the culpability of a civil litigant, or as to the guilt or innocence of an accused; but the prosecutor may argue, on analysis of the evidence, for any position or conclusion with respect to the matters stated herein; and
> (j) not intentionally avoid pursuit of evidence because the prosecutor believes it will damage the prosecution's case or aid the accused.

The federal court version of Massachusetts Rule 3.8(f), Local Rule 3.8(f), was declared invalid in Stern v. U.S. District Court for the District of Massachusetts, 16 F. Supp. 2d 88 (1st Cir. 2000), *rehearing and rehearing en banc denied,* 2000 U.S. App. LEXIS 14486 (1st Cir., June 22, 2000) (concluding that "the adoption of Local Rule 3.8(f) exceeded the district court's lawful authority to regulate both grand jury and trial subpoenas" in federal courts).

New Jersey: Rule 3.8(c) provides that a prosecutor shall "not seek to obtain from an unrepresented accused a waiver of important post-indictment pretrial rights." New Jersey omits paragraphs (e) and (f) of ABA Model Rule 3.8 as amended in 2002.

New York: Compare ABA Model Rule 3.8(a) to New York's DR 7-103(A). Rule 3.8(b) and (c) have no New York counterparts. Compare Rule 3.8(d) to New York's DR 7-103(B). Rule 3.8(e) has no New York counterpart. Compare Rule 3.8(f) to New York's DR 1-104(B) and (C) and DR 7-107(A).

North Carolina: Rule 3.8(f) adds that the prosecutor shall not "participate in the application for the issuance of a search warrant to a lawyer for the seizure of information of a past or present client in connection with an investigation of someone other than the lawyer," unless the conditions stated in ABA Model Rule 3.8(e) as amended in 2002 are satisfied.

Pennsylvania: Rule 3.10 forbids a prosecutor, without judicial approval, to subpoena a lawyer before a grand jury or other tribunal investigating criminal conduct if the prosecutor seeks to compel evidence concerning a current or former client of the lawyer.

Pennsylvania omits ABA Model Rule 3.8(f) as amended in 2002.

Texas: Rule 3.09(a) provides that a prosecutor shall refrain from prosecuting "or threatening to prosecute" a charge that the prosecutor knows is not supported by probable cause. Texas Rules 3.09(b) and (c) provide that a prosecutor shall:

> (b) refrain from conducting or assisting in a custodial interrogation of an accused unless the prosecutor has made reasonable efforts to be assured that the accused has been advised of any right to, and the procedure for obtaining, counsel and has been given reasonable opportunity to obtain counsel;
>
> (c) not initiate or encourage efforts to obtain from an unrepresented accused a waiver of important pre-trial, trial or post-trial rights.

Texas omits paragraph (e) and the first half of paragraph (f) of ABA Model Rule 3.8 as amended in 2002 but retains the obligation to exercise reasonable care to prevent "persons employed or controlled by the prosecutor" in a criminal case from making an extrajudicial statement that the prosecutor would be prohibited from making under Rule 3.07.

Virginia's Rule 3.8 states that a prosecutor shall:

> (b) not knowingly take advantage of an unrepresented defendant.
>
> (c) not instruct or encourage a person to withhold information from the defense after a party has been charged with an offense.
>
> (d) make timely disclosure to counsel for the defendant, or to the defendant if he has no counsel, of the existence of evidence which the prosecutor knows tends to negate the guilt of the accused, mitigate the degree of the offense, or reduce the punishment, except when disclosure is precluded or modified by order of a court; . . .

Virginia omits paragraph (e) and the first half of paragraph (f) of ABA Model Rule 3.8 as amended in 2002 and replaces the duty to "exercise reasonable care to prevent" in the second half of amended ABA Model Rule 3.8(f) with a mandate that a prosecutor not "direct or encourage" others to make statements that Rule 3.6 would prohibit the prosecutor from making.

Related Materials

ABA Standards for Criminal Justice: See Prosecution Function Standard 3-3.9(a) (Discretion in the Charging Decision), Standard 3-3.11 (Disclosure of Evidence by the Prosecutor), and Standard 3-4.1 (Availability for Plea Discussions).

ABA Standards for Imposing Lawyer Sanctions: See Standard 5.2 printed in the Related Materials following Model Rule 8.4.

American Lawyer's Code of Conduct: Chapter 9 of the ALCC, entitled "Responsibilities of Government Lawyers," contains the following provisions:

> 9.3. A lawyer serving as public prosecutor shall not seek or sign formal charges, or proceed to trial, unless a fair-minded juror could conclude beyond a reasonable doubt that the accused is guilty, on the basis of all of the facts that are known to the prosecutor and likely to be admissible into evidence. . . .
>
> 9.5. A lawyer serving as public prosecutor shall not use unconscionable pressures in plea bargaining, such as charging an accused in several counts for what is essentially a single offense, or charging an accused with a more serious offense than is warranted under Rule 9.3. . . .
>
> 9.7. A lawyer serving as public prosecutor shall promptly make available to defense counsel, without request for it, any information that the prosecutor knows is likely to be useful to the defense. . . .
>
> 9.9. A lawyer serving as public prosecutor, who knows that a defendant is not receiving or has not received effective assistance of counsel, shall promptly advise the court, on the record when possible.

Attorney Fee Forfeiture: A topic often intertwined with subpoenas to defense attorneys is attorney fee forfeiture — seizing an attorney's fees when the government can prove that they are the fruit of federal drug crimes or RICO violations. In 1989, the Supreme Court decided two cases on fee forfeiture, Caplin & Drysdale v. United States, 491 U.S. 617 (1989), and United States v. Monsanto, 491 U.S. 600 (1989).

Department of Justice Guidelines: The United States Department of Justice maintains internal guidelines limiting the circumstances under which Justice Department lawyers may issue subpoenas to criminal defense lawyers. See D.O.J. Subpoena Guidelines §9-2.161(B) and (F).

Due Process Clause: The constitutional basis for the disclosure obligations in Rule 3.8(d) is found in Brady v. Maryland, 373 U.S. 83, 87 (1963), which held that "the suppression by the prosecution of evidence favorable to an accused upon request violates due process where the evidence is material. . . ."

Federal Rules of Criminal Procedure: Rules 16 and 26.2 of the Federal Rules of Criminal Procedure impose disclosure obligations on both sides in criminal cases. Before trial, Rule 16(a)(1) provides that federal prosecutors must allow a criminal defendant to inspect four categories of information, including: (A) any relevant written or recorded statements made by the defendant; (B) a copy of the defendant's prior criminal record; (C) books, papers, documents, photographs, tangible objects, buildings or places that are material to the preparation of the defense, or are intended for use by the government as evidence in chief at trial, or were obtained from or belong to the defendant; and (D) results or reports of physical or mental examinations, and scientific tests or experiments, which are material to the preparation of the defense or which the government intends to use as evidence in chief at trial. However, Rules 16(a)(2) and (3) provide that the government's duty to disclose does not apply to the prosecutor's work product ("reports, memoranda, or other internal government documents made by the attorney for the government or other government agents in connection with the investigation or prosecution of the case") or to statements made by the government's witnesses or prospective witnesses "except as provided by 18 U.S.C. §3500."

Conversely, Rule 16(b)(1) provides that if the government complies with a defendant's request for documents and tangible objects, or scientific tests and reports, then the defendant must permit the government to inspect and copy the same categories of materials in the control of the defendant. However, Rule 16(b)(2) protects the defense attorney's work product. Rule 16(c) imposes a continuing duty to disclose on both sides, and Rule 16(d) provides for protective orders or sanctions, including an order to "prohibit the party from introducing evidence not disclosed."

At trial, Rule 26.2(a) provides that after any witness other than the defendant has testified on direct examination, the court, on motion of a party who did not call the witness, shall order whichever side called the witness to produce "any statement of the witness that is in their possession and that relates to the subject matter concerning which the witness has testified."

Guidelines for the Issuance of Search Warrants: In 1990, the ABA's Criminal Justice Section issued Guidelines for the Issuance of Search Warrants, many of which directly or indirectly apply to prosecutors.

Model Rules of Professional Conduct for Federal Lawyers: Rule 3.8(a) mandates that a prosecutor shall "[r]efrain from prosecuting a charge that the prosecutor knows is not supported by probable cause, or if not authorized to decline the prosecution of a charge to recommend to the appropriate authority that any charge not warranted by the evidence be withdrawn." Rule 3.8(d) requires timely disclosure only to the defense, not to the tribunal. Rule 3.8(f) obligates a prosecutor to "[r]espect the attorney-client privilege of defendants and not diminish the privilege through investigative or judicial processes."

Restatement of the Law Governing Lawyers: See Restatement §§57, 97, and 109 in our chapter on the Restatement later in this volume.

Witness Statements: In federal criminal trials, a prosecutor's "timely disclosure" of witness statements is governed by 18 U.S.C. §3500 (often called the Jencks Act), which provides, in pertinent part:

§3500. Demands for Production of Statements and Reports of Witnesses

(b) After a witness called by the United States has testified on direct examination, the court shall, on motion of the defendant, order the United States to produce any statement (as hereinafter defined) of the witness in the possession of the United States which relates to the subject matter as to which the witness has testified. If the entire contents of any such statement relate to the subject matter of the testimony of the witness, the court shall order it to be delivered directly to the defendant for his examination and use.

Rule 3.9 Advocate in Nonadjudicative Proceedings

A lawyer representing a client before a legislative body or administrative ~~tribunal~~ agency in a nonadjudicative proceeding shall disclose that the appearance is in a representative capacity and shall conform to the provisions of Rules 3.3(a) through (c), 3.4(a) through (c), and 3.5.

COMMENT

[1] In representation before bodies such as legislatures, municipal councils, and executive and administrative agencies acting in a rule-making

or policy-making capacity, lawyers present facts, formulate issues and advance argument in the matters under consideration. The decision-making body, like a court, should be able to rely on the integrity of the submissions made to it. A lawyer appearing before such a body ~~should~~ must deal with ~~the tribunal~~ it honestly and in conformity with applicable rules of procedure. See Rules 3.3(a) through (c), 3.4(a) through (c) and 3.5.

[2] Lawyers have no exclusive right to appear before nonadjudicative bodies, as they do before a court. The requirements of this Rule therefore may subject lawyers to regulations inapplicable to advocates who are not lawyers. However, legislatures and administrative agencies have a right to expect lawyers to deal with them as they deal with courts.

[3] This Rule only applies when a lawyer represents a client in connection with an official hearing or meeting of a governmental agency or a legislative body to which the lawyer or the lawyer's client is presenting evidence or argument. It does not apply to representation of a client in a negotiation or other bilateral transaction with a governmental agency~~; representation~~ or in connection with an application for a license or other privilege or the client's compliance with generally applicable reporting requirements, such as the filing of income-tax returns. Nor does it apply to the representation of a client in connection with an investigation or examination of the client's affairs conducted by government investigators or examiners. Representation in such ~~a transaction~~ matters is governed by Rules 4.1 through 4.4.

Canon and Code Antecedents

ABA Canons of Professional Ethics: Canon 26 provided as follows:

26. Professional Advocacy Other Than Before Courts

A lawyer openly, and in his true character may render professional services before legislative or other bodies, regarding proposed legislation and in advocacy of claims before departments of government, upon the same principles of ethics which justify his appearance before the Courts; but it is unprofessional for a lawyer so engaged to conceal his attorneyship, or to employ secret personal solicitations, or to use means other than those addressed to the reason and understanding, to influence action.

ABA Model Code of Professional Responsibility: Compare DR 7-106(B)(1) (reprinted later in this volume).

Cross-References in Other Rules

None.

Legislative History of Model Rule 3.9

1980 Draft (then Rule 3.12) provided as follows:

(a) A lawyer representing a client before a legislative or administrative tribunal in a nonadjudicative proceeding shall deal fairly with the body conducting the proceeding and with other persons making presentations therein and their counsel.

(b) A lawyer in such a proceeding shall:

(1) identify the client on whose behalf the lawyer appears, unless the identity of the client is privileged;

(2) conform to the provisions of Rules 3.1 and 3.4.

1981 and 1982 Drafts were the same as adopted.

2002 Amendments: At its February 2002 Mid-Year Meeting, the ABA House of Delegates adopted without change the ABA Ethics 2000 Commission proposal to amend Rule 3.9 and its Comment.

Selected State Variations

Alaska replaces the phrase "legislative or administrative tribunal" with the phrase "legislative committee or administrative agency."

California has no direct counterpart.

Georgia: In the rules effective January 1, 2001, Georgia adopted the pre-2002 version of ABA Model Rule 3.9 and its Comment essentially verbatim.

Illinois omits Rule 3.9.

New Jersey deletes the cross-reference to Rule 3.5(b) in Rule 3.9.

New York: Compare ABA Model Rule 3.9 to New York EC's 7-15, 7-16, and 8-5.

North Carolina omits Rule 3.9.

Pennsylvania does not incorporate Rule 3.4(c) in Rule 3.9.

Virginia omits Rule 3.9.

Related Materials

ABA Canons: Canon 26 provided:

26. Professional Advocacy Other Than Before Courts

A lawyer openly, and in his true character may render professional services before legislative or other bodies, regarding proposed legislation and in advocacy of claims before departments of government, upon the same principles of ethics which justify his appearance before the Courts; but it is unprofessional for a lawyer so engaged to conceal his attorneyship, or to employ secret personal solicitations, or to use means other than those addressed to the reason and understanding, to influence action.

ABA Standards for Criminal Justice: See Prosecution Function Standards 3-3.1, 3-3.9, and 3-3.11.

Lobbying Laws: The federal government and all states have laws regulating lobbyists, including lawyers. On the federal level, the most prominent statute is the Lobbying Disclosure Act of 1995, 2 U.S.C. §§1601-1612, which requires registration of federal lobbyists and regulates their conduct. Lawyer-lobbyists are also regulated by a host of other federal statutes and regulations, including the Foreign Agents Registration Act, the Byrd Amendment, the HUD Reform Act of 1989, Federal Acquisition Regulations, and Office of Management and Budget Regulations. These statutes and regulations are thoroughly explained in a publication by the ABA

Section of Administrative Law and Regulatory Practice entitled The Lobbying Manual: A Compliance Guide for Lawyers and Lobbyists (2d ed. 1998).

On the state level, an example of a lobbying law is 25 Illinois Consolidated Statutes 170/1 through 170/12 (the "Lobbyist Registration Act"), which requires registration of any person who "undertakes to influence executive, legislative or administrative action." State and federal lobbying laws and regulations are discussed in detail in Abner Mikva & Eric Lane, The Legislative Process (Aspen 2d ed. 2002).

Restatement of the Law Governing Lawyers: See Restatement §104 in our chapter on the Restatement later in this volume.

ARTICLE 4. TRANSACTIONS WITH PERSONS OTHER THAN CLIENTS

Rule 4.1 Truthfulness in Statements to Others

In the course of representing a client a lawyer shall not knowingly:

(a) make a false statement of material fact or law to a third person; or

(b) fail to disclose a material fact when disclosure is necessary to avoid assisting a criminal or fraudulent act by a client, unless disclosure is prohibited by Rule 1.6.

COMMENT

Misrepresentation

[1] A lawyer is required to be truthful when dealing with others on a client's behalf, but generally has no affirmative duty to inform an opposing party of relevant facts. A misrepresentation can occur if the lawyer incorporates or affirms a statement of another person that the lawyer knows is false. Misrepresentations can also occur by ~~failure to act~~ partially true but misleading statements or omissions that are the equivalent of affirmative false statements. For dishonest conduct that does not amount to a false statement or for misrepresentations by a lawyer other than in the course of representing a client, see Rule 8.4.

Statements of Fact

[2] This Rule refers to statements of fact. Whether a particular statement should be regarded as one of fact can depend on the circumstances. Under generally accepted conventions in negotiation, certain types of statements ordinarily are not taken as statements of material fact. Estimates of price or value placed on the subject of a transaction and a

party's intentions as to an acceptable settlement of a claim are ordinarily in this category, and so is the existence of an undisclosed principal except where nondisclosure of the principal would constitute fraud. Lawyers should be mindful of their obligations under applicable law to avoid criminal and tortious misrepresentation.

Crime or Fraud by Client

[3] Under Rule 1.2(d), a lawyer is prohibited from counseling or assisting a client in conduct that the lawyer knows is criminal or fraudulent. Paragraph (b) ~~recognizes that~~ states a specific application of the principle set forth in Rule 1.2(d) and addresses the situation where a client's crime or fraud takes the form of a lie or misrepresentation. Ordinarily, a lawyer can avoid assisting a client's crime or fraud by withdrawing from the representation. Sometimes it may be necessary for the lawyer to give notice of the fact of withdrawal and to disaffirm an opinion, document, affirmation or the like. In extreme cases, substantive law may require a lawyer to disclose ~~certain~~ information relating to the representation to avoid being deemed to have assisted the client's crime or fraud. ~~The requirement of~~ If the lawyer can avoid assisting a client's crime or fraud only by disclosing this information, then under paragraph (b) the lawyer is required to do so, unless the disclosure ~~created by this paragraph is, however, subject to the obligations created~~ is prohibited by Rule 1.6.

Canon and Code Antecedents

ABA Canons of Professional Ethics: No comparable Canon.

ABA Model Code of Professional Responsibility: Compare DR 7-102(A)(3) and DR 7-102(A)(5) (reprinted later in this volume).

Cross-References in Other Rules

Rule 1.2, Comment 10: "A lawyer may not continue assisting a client in conduct that the lawyer originally supposed was legally proper but then discovers is criminal or fraudulent. The lawyer must, therefore, withdraw from the representation. . . . In some cases, withdrawal alone might be insufficient. It may be necessary for the lawyer to give notice of the fact of withdrawal and to disaffirm any opinion, document, affirmation or the like. See **Rule 4.1**."

Rule 1.6, Comment 13: Some Rules require "disclosure of information relating to a client's representation to accomplish the purposes specified in paragraphs (b)(1) through (b)(4)," only if such disclosure would be permitted by paragraph (b). See **Rules** 1.2(d), **4.1(b)**, 8.1 and 8.3.

Rule 1.8, Comment 5: It is prohibited to partake in the "disadvantageous use of client information unless the client gives informed consent, except as permitted or required by these Rules. See Rules 1.2(d), 1.6, 1.9(c), 3.3, **4.1(b)**, 8.1 and 8.3."

Rule 1.13, Comment 5: "[T]his Rule does not limit or expand the lawyer's responsibility under **Rule** 1.6, 1.8, 1.16, 3.3 or **4.1**."

Rule 2.3, Comment 4: "In no circumstances is the lawyer permitted to knowingly make a false statement of material fact or law in providing an evaluation under this Rule. See **Rule 4.1**."

Rule 2.4, Comment 5: "When the dispute-resolution process takes place before a tribunal, as in binding arbitration (see Rule 1.0(m)), the lawyer's duty of candor is governed by Rule 3.3. Otherwise, the lawyer's duty of candor toward both the third-party neutral and other parties is governed by **Rule 4.1**."

Rule 3.9, Comment 3: This Rule "does not apply to representation of a client in a negotiation or other bilateral transaction with a governmental agency. . . . Representation in such matters is governed by **Rules 4.1** through 4.4."

Legislative History of Model Rule 4.1

1980 Discussion Draft contained the following Introduction:

Negotiator

. . . A negotiator should seek the most advantageous result for the client that is consistent with the requirements of law and the lawyer's responsibilities under the Rules of Professional Conduct. As negotiator, a lawyer should consider not only the client's short-run advantage but also his or her long-run interests, such as the state of future relations between the parties. The lawyer should help the client appreciate the interests and position of the other party and should encourage concessions that will effectuate the client's larger objectives. A lawyer should not transform a bargaining situation into a demonstration of toughness or hypertechnicality or forget that the purely legal aspects of an agreement are often subordinate to its practical aspects. When the alternative to reaching agreement is likely to be litigation, the lawyer should be aware that, although litigation is wholly legitimate as a means of resolving controversy, a fairly negotiated settlement generally yields a better conclusion. A lawyer should also recognize that the lawyer's own interest in resorting to litigation may be different from a client's interest in doing so.

A lawyer's style in negotiations can have great influence on the character of the negotiations—whether they are restrained, open, and business-like, or acrimonious and permeated with distrust. Whatever their outcome, negotiations should be conducted in a civil and forthright manner. Nevertheless, it must be recognized that in negotiations a lawyer is the agent for the client and not an arbitrator or mediator. Negotiation is in part a competition for advantage between parties who have the legal competence to settle their own affairs. A lawyer as negotiator should not impose an agreement on the client, even if the lawyer believes the agreement is in the client's best interests. By the same token, a lawyer does not necessarily endorse the substance of an agreement arrived at through his or her efforts.

1980 Discussion Draft of Rule 4.1 (then called Rule 4.2) provided as follows:

Fairness to Other Participants

(a) In conducting negotiations a lawyer shall be fair in dealing with other participants.

> (b) A lawyer shall not make a knowing misrepresentation of fact or law, or fail to disclose a material fact known to the lawyer, even if adverse, when disclosure is:
>
> (1) required by law or the Rules of Professional Conduct; or
>
> (2) necessary to correct a manifest misapprehension of fact or law resulting from a previous representation made by the lawyer or known by the lawyer to have been made by the client. . . .

1980 Discussion Draft also contained the following provision (then called Rule 4.3) that has no equivalent in the Rules as adopted:

> *Illegal, Fraudulent, or Unconscionable Transactions*
>
> A lawyer shall not conclude an agreement, or assist a client in concluding an agreement, that the lawyer knows or reasonably should know is illegal, contains legally prohibited terms, would work a fraud, or would be held to be unconscionable as a matter of law.

1981 Draft: Subparagraph (a) was substantially the same as adopted. Subparagraph (b) provided that a lawyer must not:

> (b) knowingly fail to disclose a fact to a third person when:
>
> (1) in the circumstances failure to make the disclosure is equivalent to making a material misrepresentation;
>
> (2) disclosure is necessary to prevent assisting a criminal or fraudulent act, as required by Rule 1.2(d); or
>
> (3) disclosure is necessary to comply with other law.

1982 Draft: Substantially the same as adopted, except that Rule 4.1(b) provided: "The duties stated in this Rule apply even if compliance requires disclosure of information otherwise protected by Rule 1.6."

2002 Amendments: At its February 2002 Mid-Year Meeting, the ABA House of Delegates adopted without change the ABA Ethics 2000 Commission proposal to amend the Comment to Rule 4.1. (The Ethics 2000 Commission did not propose any changes to the text of Rule 4.1.)

Selected State Variations

California: See B & P Code §6128(a).

Colorado: Rule 4.1(a) applies to a false "or misleading" statement, and Colorado omits the word "material" before "fact."

Georgia: In the rules effective January 1, 2001, Georgia adopted the pre-2002 version of ABA Model Rule 4.1 and its Comment essentially verbatim.

Illinois: Rule 4.1(a) prohibits a lawyer from making "a statement of material fact or law to a third person which statement the lawyer knows or reasonably should know is false."

Indiana: Rule 4.1(b) provides simply that a lawyer shall not knowingly "fail to disclose that which is required by law to be revealed."

Kansas states the final clause of Rule 4.1(b) as follows: "unless disclosure is prohibited by or made discretionary under Rule 1.6."

Maryland adds a separate subparagraph providing: "The duties stated in this Rule apply even if compliance requires disclosure of information otherwise protected by Rule 1.6."

Massachusetts: Comment 3 to Rule 4.1 defines "assisting" to refer "to that level of assistance that would render a third party liable for another's crime or fraud." Compare the definition of "assisting" in the comment to Massachusetts Rule 3.3.

Michigan has not adopted Rule 4.1(b). See also Michigan's version of Rule 1.6(c)(3), which is noted in the Comment to Michigan's Rule 4.1.

Mississippi deletes the wording in Rule 4.1(b), "unless disclosure is prohibited by Rule 1.6."

New Jersey: Rule 4.1 applies the duties of that Rule even if it requires revelation of information protected by Rule 1.6.

New York: Compare ABA Model Rule 4.1 to New York's DR 4-101(C)(5), DR 7-102(A)(5), and DR 7-102(B).

North Carolina deletes Rule 4.1(b).

Texas: Rule 4.01(b) provides in full that a lawyer shall not "fail to disclose a material fact to a third person when disclosure is necessary to avoid making the lawyer a party to a criminal act or knowingly assisting a fraudulent act perpetrated by a client."

Virginia: Rule 4.1 omits the word "material" in both paragraphs (a) and (b). The words "to a third person" are deleted from Rule 4.1(a). The final clause in Rule 4.1(b) subordinating the obligation to Rule 1.6 is also deleted. Comment 1 is expanded by adding "or by knowingly failing to correct false statements made by the lawyer's client or someone acting on behalf of the client" at the end of the final sentence of the Comment.

Related Materials

ABA Formal Ethics Opinions: See ABA Formal Ethics Op. 93-378 (1993).

American Academy of Matrimonial Lawyers: The "Bounds of Advocacy" contains the following rules and comments:

> 3.3 An attorney should not induce or rely on a mistake by opposing counsel as to matters agreed upon to obtain an unfair benefit for the client.
>
> Comment to Rule 3.3
>
> The need for trust between attorneys, even those representing opposing sides in a dispute, requires more than simply avoiding fraudulent and intentionally deceitful conduct. Misunderstandings should be corrected and not relied upon in the hope they will benefit the client. Thus, for example, the attorney reducing an oral agreement to writing not only should avoid misstating the understanding, but should correct inadvertent errors by opposing counsel that do not reflect prior understandings or agreements. Whether or not conduct or statements by opposing counsel that are not necessarily in her client's best interests should be corrected may not always be clear and will depend on the particular facts of a case. The crucial consideration should be whether the attorney induced the misunderstanding or is aware that opposing counsel's statements do not accurately reflect any prior agreement. It is thus unlikely that tactical, evidentiary or legal errors made by opposing counsel at trial require correction.
>
> 3.4 An attorney should not overstate his authority to settle nor represent that he has authority which he does not have.

Comment to Rule 3.4

> . . . A matrimonial lawyer who is uncertain of his authority — or simply does not believe that opposing counsel is entitled to such information — should either truthfully disclose his uncertainty, or state that he is unwilling or unable to respond at all.

Ethical Guidelines for Settlement Negotiations: In August of 2002, the ABA Section of Litigation issued a comprehensive set of Ethical Guidelines for Settlement Negotiations. They cover settlement negotiations generally, issues relating to lawyers and their clients, and issues relating to a lawyer's negotiations with opposing parties. The Guidelines are available in full at www.abanet.org/litigation/ethics.

Restatement of the Law Governing Lawyers: See Restatement §§51, 56 and 98 in our chapter on the Restatement later in this volume.

Rule 4.2 Communication with Person Represented by Counsel

In representing a client, a lawyer shall not communicate about the subject of the representation with a person the lawyer knows to be represented by another lawyer in the matter, unless the lawyer has the consent of the other lawyer or is authorized to do so by law ~~to do so~~ or a court order.

COMMENT

[1] This Rule contributes to the proper functioning of the legal system by protecting a person who has chosen to be represented by a lawyer in a matter against possible overreaching by other lawyers who are participating in the matter, interference by those lawyers with the client-lawyer relationship and the uncounseled disclosure of information relating to the representation.

~~[3]~~ [2] This Rule ~~also~~ applies to communications with any person~~, whether or not a party to a formal adjudicative proceeding, contract or negotiation,~~ who is represented by counsel concerning the matter to which the communication relates.

[3] The Rule applies even though the represented person initiates or consents to the communication. A lawyer must immediately terminate communication with a person if, after commencing communication, the lawyer learns that the person is one with whom communication is not permitted by this Rule.

~~[1]~~ [4] This Rule does not prohibit communication with a represented person, or an employee or agent of such a person, concerning matters outside the representation. For example, the existence of a controversy between a government agency and a private party, or between two organizations, does not prohibit a lawyer for either from communicating with nonlawyer representatives of the other regarding a separate matter.

~~Also, parties~~ Nor does this Rule preclude communication with a represented person who is seeking advice from a lawyer who is not otherwise representing a client in the matter. A lawyer may not make a communication prohibited by this Rule through the acts of another. See Rule 8.4(a). Parties to a matter may communicate directly with each other, and a lawyer is not prohibited from advising a client concerning a communication that the client is legally entitled to make. Also, a lawyer having independent justification or legal authorization for communicating with a represented person is permitted to do so. ~~Communications authorized by law include, for example, the right of a party to a controversy with a government agency to speak with government officials about the matter.~~

[5] Communications authorized by law may include communications by a lawyer on behalf of a client who is exercising a constitutional or other legal right to communicate with the government. ~~[2]~~ Communications authorized by law may also include ~~constitutionally permissible~~ investigative activities of lawyers representing governmental entities, directly or through investigative agents, prior to the commencement of criminal or civil enforcement proceedings~~, when there is applicable judicial precedent that either has found the activity permissible under this Rule or has found this Rule inapplicable. However, the Rule imposes ethical restrictions that go beyond those imposed by constitutional provisions.~~ When communicating with the accused in a criminal matter, a government lawyer must comply with this Rule in addition to honoring the constitutional rights of the accused. The fact that a communication does not violate a state or federal constitutional right is insufficient to establish that the communication is permissible under this Rule.

[6] A lawyer who is uncertain whether a communication with a represented person is permissible may seek a court order. A lawyer may also seek a court order in exceptional circumstances to authorize a communication that would otherwise be prohibited by this Rule, for example, where communication with a person represented by counsel is necessary to avoid reasonably certain injury.

~~[4]~~ [7] In the case of ~~an~~ a represented organization, this Rule prohibits communications ~~by a lawyer for another person or entity concerning the matter in representation~~ with ~~persons having a managerial responsibility on behalf~~ a constituent of the organization~~, and with any other person~~ who supervises, directs or regularly consults with the organization's lawyer concerning the matter or has authority to obligate the organization with respect to the matter or whose act or omission in connection with ~~that~~ the matter may be imputed to the organization for purposes of civil or criminal liability ~~or whose statement may constitute an admission on the part of the organization~~. Consent of the organization's lawyer is not required for communication with a former constituent. If ~~an agent or employee~~ a constituent of the organization is represented in the matter by his or her own counsel, the consent by that counsel to a communication will be sufficient for purposes of this Rule. Compare Rule 3.4(f). In communicating with a current or former constituent of an organization, a lawyer must not use methods of obtaining evidence that violate the legal rights of the organization. See Rule 4.4.

~~[5]~~ [8] The prohibition on communications with a represented person only applies~~, however,~~ in circumstances where the lawyer knows that the person is in fact represented in the matter to be discussed. This means that the lawyer has actual knowledge of the fact of the representation; but such actual knowledge may be inferred from the circumstances. See ~~Terminology~~ Rule 1.0(f). ~~Such an inference may arise in circumstances where there is substantial reason to believe that the person with whom communication is sought is represented in the matter to be discussed.~~ Thus, the lawyer cannot evade the requirement of obtaining the consent of counsel by closing eyes to the obvious.

~~[6]~~ [9] In the event the person with whom the lawyer communicates is not known to be represented by counsel in the matter, the lawyer's communications are subject to Rule 4.3.

Canon and Code Antecedents

ABA Canons of Professional Ethics: Canon 9 provided as follows:

9. Negotiations with Opposite Party

A lawyer should not in any way communicate upon the subject of controversy with a party represented by counsel; much less should he undertake to negotiate or compromise the matter with him, but should deal only with his counsel. It is incumbent upon the lawyer most particularly to avoid everything that may tend to mislead a party not represented by counsel, and he should not undertake to advise him as to the law.

ABA Model Code of Professional Responsibility: Compare DR 7-104(A)(1) (reprinted later in this volume).

Cross-References in Other Rules

Rule 3.4, Comment 4: "Paragraph (f) permits a lawyer to advise employees of a client to refrain from giving information to another party, for the employees may identify their interests with those of the client. See also **Rule 4.2**."

Rule 3.9, Comment 3: This transaction "does not apply to representation of a client in a negotiation or other bilateral transaction with a governmental agency. . . . Representation in such matters is governed by **Rules 4.1** through **4.4**."

Legislative History of Model Rule 4.2

1980 Discussion Draft (then Rule 3.2(b)(5)) provided that a lawyer shall not "interview or otherwise communicate with a party who the lawyer knows is represented by other counsel concerning the subject matter of the representation, except with the consent of that party's counsel or as authorized by law."

1981 Draft was substantially the same as adopted.

1982 Draft was adopted.

1994 Proposal: In May of 1994, the ABA's Standing Committee on Ethics and Professional Responsibility submitted a proposed amendment to Rule 4.2 that was intended to be considered at the ABA's August 1994 Annual Meeting. In June of 1994, however, after receiving some criticism of the proposal, the Standing Committee withdrew the proposal to circulate it for public comment.

The withdrawn 1994 proposal would have substituted the word "person" for "party" and would have added the phrase "or reasonably should know" to the text of the rule. Thus, underscoring proposed additions and striking over deletions, Rule 4.2 would have provided:

> In representing a client, a lawyer shall not communicate about the subject of the representation with a ~~party~~ <u>person</u> the lawyer knows <u>or reasonably should know</u> to be represented by another lawyer in the matter, unless the lawyer has the consent of the other lawyer or is authorized by law to do so.

A proposed addition to the Comment stated:

> Because of the interest in ensuring that persons have the assistance of counsel who represent them in a matter, a lawyer has an affirmative obligation to act as would a lawyer of reasonable prudence and competence to ascertain whether a person is represented in a matter before undertaking further communication on that matter with that person; and if the person is so represented, to communicate only as the Rule allows.

The Standing Committee's report in support of the proposed amendment explained:*

> The situation presented by the current language of the Rule permits a lawyer who believes or suspects that a person is represented in the matter by another lawyer to subvert the purpose and spirit of the Rule by avoiding learning whether that belief or suspicion is correct. The protection of represented persons the Rule is designed to foster, and the ability of those persons to receive counsel from their lawyers in dealings with counsel for other persons in the matter, would be enhanced by an amendment to Model Rule 4.2 requiring a lawyer contemplating communicating with other persons to act as a lawyer of reasonable prudence and competence would act under the circumstances and to *ascertain* whether the person with whom communication is sought is represented in the matter by another lawyer.
>
> The Standing Committee has also taken the occasion presented by this amendment to clarify the fact that the Rule protects represented persons whether or not they are, in a formal sense, actual or prospective "parties" to a proceeding or transaction. . . .

1995 Amendment: At the ABA's 1995 Annual Meeting, the House of Delegates voted to amend Rule 4.2 by changing the word "party" to "person" in Rule 4.2. (Unlike the withdrawn 1994 proposal, the 1995 proposal did not add the phrase "or reasonably should know" to the Rule.) The House of Delegates also added three new paragraphs to the Comment (paragraphs 2, 5, and 6) and revised the three existing paragraphs. The amendment was overwhelmingly approved on a voice vote, so no exact vote count was taken. For a legislative-style version of the Rule and Comment underscoring new material and striking out deleted material, see our 1996 edition.

*Committee Reports do not represent official policy of the ABA. They are for information only and represent only the opinions of the authors.

The sole sponsor of the 1995 amendment was the ABA Standing Committee on Ethics and Professional Responsibility. The United States Department of Justice, which followed its own rules on communications with represented parties and persons (reprinted in the Special Section at the end of our 1996 edition), officially opposed the amendment and spoke against it during the House of Delegates debate. The ABA Section on Criminal Justice voted against the amendment. The Standing Committee's report in support of the amendment was lengthy (about ten single-spaced pages). We reprint the most important portions of the report below (with all citations omitted).

*Excerpt from ABA Report Explaining 1995 Amendment**

[II] C. SUBSTITUTION OF THE WORD "PERSON" FOR "PARTY"

In choosing whether "party" or "person" better describes the proper scope of the Rule, the Standing Committee has not sought to ascertain original intent or assess the relative precedential weight that should be assigned to the divided authority, but instead has addressed the question of what the meaning of the Rule *should* be, in light of the purposes the Rule is designed to serve.

In this light, it seems clear to the Committee that the appropriate operative term is "person," and not "party," for neither the need to protect uncounselled persons against being taken advantage of by opposing counsel nor the importance of preserving the client-attorney relationship is limited to those circumstances where the represented person is a party to an adjudicative or other formal proceeding. The interests sought to be protected by the Rule may equally well be involved when litigation is merely under consideration, even though it has not actually been instituted, and the persons who are potentially parties to the litigation have retained counsel with respect to the matter in dispute.

Concerns regarding the need to protect uncounselled persons against the wiles of opposing counsel and preserving the attorney-client relationship may also be involved where a person is a target of a criminal investigation, knows this, and has retained counsel to advise him with respect to the investigation. The same concerns may be involved where a "third-party" witness furnishes testimony in an investigation or proceeding and, even though not a formal party, has seen fit to retain counsel to advise him with respect thereto. Such concerns are equally applicable in a non-adjudicatory context, such as a commercial transaction involving a sale, a lease or some other form of contract.

E. OBJECTIONS TO THE PROPOSED CHANGE IN THE RULE

. . . The Rule now applies, and as amended would continue to apply, only where the person to be contacted is known to be represented with respect to the particular matter that is the subject of the prospective communication. The fact that a particular entity or person has retained a lawyer for one matter does not mean that the representation extends to any other matter; and even a general representation for all purposes, such as might be asserted by inside counsel for a corporation, does not, for purposes of the Rule, necessarily imply a representation with respect to a matter that has not in fact been brought to the attention of such counsel. . . .

*Committee Reports do not represent official policy of the ABA. They are for information only and represent only the opinions of the authors.

III. The Proposed Change to Clarify That an Attorney's Knowledge Regarding Representation May Be Inferred from the Circumstances

C. REASONS FOR THE PROPOSED CHANGE

It would not . . . be reasonable to require a lawyer in all circumstances where the lawyer wishes to speak to a third person in the course of his representation of a client first to inquire whether the person is represented by counsel: among other things, such a routine inquiry would unnecessarily complicate perfectly routine fact-finding, and might well unnecessarily obstruct such fact-finding by conveying a suggestion that there was a need for counsel in circumstances where there was none, and thus discouraging witnesses from talking. In consequence, the Rule's requirement of securing permission of counsel is reasonably limited to those circumstances where the inquiring lawyer *knows* that the person to whom he wants to speak is represented by counsel with respect to the subject of the communication.

However, a lawyer should not be able to ignore the obvious and then claim lack of certain knowledge, thus excusing a failure to secure consent of counsel whose likely involvement should have been obvious. . . . [A] lawyer may not avoid Rule 4.2 by closing eyes to what is plainly to be seen.

The proposed final paragraph of the Comment points out that if a lawyer does not know that a person with whom he or she wishes to communicate is represented by counsel, then the lawyer must assume that he or she is dealing with an unrepresented person, and so subject to the restrictions of Rule 4.3 . . . which requires reasonable assurance that the person with whom they are communicating does not misunderstand the role the lawyer is playing in the matter.

1999 Proposal (withdrawn): In 1999, in an effort to resolve years of stalemated negotiations between the United States Department of Justice (representing all federal government lawyers) and the Conference of Chief Justices (representing the high courts of the fifty states and the District of Columbia), the ABA's Standing Committee on Ethics and Professional Responsibility proposed to add the following new paragraphs (b) and (c) to Rule 4.2:

(b) A government lawyer supervising a criminal or civil law enforcement investigation may authorize an investigative agent to communicate with a person represented in the matter prior to the arrest of or the filing of a formal criminal charge or civil complaint against that person in the matter, if the lawyer makes reasonable efforts to ensure that the agent's conduct is compatible with paragraph (c).

(c) Unless permitted to do otherwise by the consent of the represented person's lawyer, a lawyer communicating with a represented person pursuant to this Rule shall not

(1) seek information protected by the attorney-client privilege or as attorney work product;

(2) attempt to induce the represented person to forego representation by or disregard the advice of his or her lawyer; or

(3) initiate or engage in negotiation of an agreement, settlement or plea with respect to the matter in which the person is represented by a lawyer, except as authorized by law or court order.

The Standing Committee also proposed extensively amending the comment to Rule 4.2. One of the proposed new paragraphs provided as follows:

Ordinarily a lawyer may not direct an investigative agent to communicate with a represented person in circumstances where the lawyer would be prohibited from

> doing so by this Rule. . . . This prohibition is qualified by paragraph (b) of this Rule to permit government lawyers to supervise criminal and civil law enforcement investigations. The lawyer representing the government in the matter must not directly and personally communicate with the represented person unless otherwise permitted to do so by paragraph (a) of this Rule. In addition, the lawyer must make reasonable efforts to ensure that investigative agents comply with paragraph (c). "Investigative agent" includes an informant acting under the direction of the government lawyer or investigative agent. . . .

The Committee Report explaining the proposed changes noted that Department of Justice lawyers have for years "expressed concerns that Rule 4.2 imposes undue restrictions on law enforcement investigations directly or by creating ambiguities as to the allowable parameters of investigative methods." The ABA entered into discussions with the Department of Justice in an effort to address the Department of Justice's concerns, and the ABA put forth the above proposal hoping that the Department of Justice would endorse it. However, the Department of Justice did not endorse it, so the ABA withdrew it from consideration shortly before the ABA's 1999 Annual Meeting. Discussions between the ABA and the Department of Justice are continuing, however, and the ABA Ethics 2000 Commission proposed (and the ABA adopted) revisions to Rule 4.2 and its Comment that reflect some of the Department of Justice's concerns. For information about other historical developments pertaining to Rule 4.2, see the Related Materials following Rule 4.2.

2002 Amendments: At its February 2002 Mid-Year Meeting, the ABA House of Delegates adopted with only minor changes the ABA Ethics 2000 Commission proposal to amend Rule 4.2 and its Comment.

Selected State Variations

Alaska, Connecticut, and ***Pennsylvania*** restrict communication with a "party or person."

Arizona: Rule 4.2 restricts communication with a "party."

California: See Rule 2-100 (Communication with a Represented Party).

Colorado: In 1999, Colorado amended Rule 1.2(c) to permit "limited representation of a pro se party." Colorado simultaneously amended the Comment to Rule 4.2 (but not the text of the rule) to provide that a pro se party to whom such limited representation has been provided is "unrepresented for purposes of this rule unless the lawyer has knowledge to the contrary." Colorado also amended Rule 5 of its Rules of Civil Procedure to provide that such limited representation of a pro se party "shall not constitute an entry of appearance by the attorney . . . and does not authorize or require the service of papers upon the attorney."

District of Columbia: D.C. Rule 4.2 differs significantly from the ABA Model Rule — see District of Columbia Rules of Professional Conduct below.

Florida generally tracks Model Rule 4.2 but adds:

> [A]n attorney may, without such prior consent, communicate with another's client in order to meet the requirements of any statute or contract requiring notice or service of process directly on an adverse party, in which event the communication shall be strictly restricted to that required by statute or contract, and a copy shall be provided to the adverse party's attorney.

Georgia: In the rules effective January 1, 2001, Georgia closely tracks ABA Model Rule 4.2 but replaces the phrase "authorized by law" with the phrase "authorized to do so by constitutional law or statute." Georgia also adds a new subparagraph (b) that provides: "Attorneys for the State and Federal Government shall be subject to this Rule in the same manner as other attorneys in this State."

Illinois provides that a lawyer shall not communicate "or cause another to communicate" with a represented "party."

Louisiana adds: "A lawyer shall not effect the prohibited communication through a third person, including the lawyer's client."

Minnesota adds a second sentence to Rule 4.2 that provides:

> A party who is a lawyer may communicate directly with another party unless expressly instructed to avoid communication by the lawyer for the other party, or unless the other party manifests a desire to communicate only through counsel.

New Jersey: Rule 4.2 provides as follows:

> In representing a client, a lawyer shall not communicate about the subject of the representation with a person the lawyer knows, or by the exercise of reasonable diligence should know, to be represented by another lawyer in the matter, including members of an organization's litigation control group as defined by RPC 1.13, unless the lawyer has the consent of the other lawyer, or is authorized by law to do so, or unless the sole purpose of the communication is to ascertain whether the person is in fact represented. Reasonable diligence shall include, but not be limited to, a specific inquiry of the person as to whether that person is represented by counsel. Nothing in this rule shall, however, preclude a lawyer from counseling or representing a member or former member of an organization's litigation control group who seeks independent legal advice.

Rule 4.2 must be read in conjunction with New Jersey's Rule 1.13, which defines the phrase "litigation control group"as follows:

> For the purposes of RPC 4.2 and 4.3 . . . the organization's lawyer shall be deemed to represent not only the organizational entity but also the members of its litigation control group. Members of the litigation control group shall be deemed to include current agents and employees responsible for, or significantly involved in, the determination of the organization's legal position in the matter whether or not in litigation, provided, however, that "significant involvement" requires involvement greater, and other than, the supplying of factual information or data respecting the matter. Former agents and employees who were members of the litigation control group shall presumptively be deemed to be represented in the matter by the organization's lawyer but may at any time disavow said representation.

New Mexico adds a sentence to Rule 4.2: "Except for persons having a managerial responsibility on behalf of the organization, an attorney is not prohibited from communicating directly with employees of a corporation, partnership or other entity about the subject matter of the representation even though the corporation, partnership or entity itself is represented by counsel."

New York: Compare ABA Model Rule 4.2 to New York's DR 7-104(A)(1) and DR 7-104(B).

North Carolina adds a Rule 4.2(b) that borrows from DR 7-110(B) by providing as follows:

> (b) Notwithstanding section (a) above, in representing a client who has a dispute with a government agency or body, a lawyer may communicate about the sub-

ject of the representation with the elected officials who have authority over such government agency or body, even if the lawyer knows that the government agency or body is represented by another lawyer in the matter, but such communications may only occur under the following circumstances:

(1) in writing, if a copy of the writing is promptly delivered to opposing counsel;

(2) orally, upon adequate notice to opposing counsel; or

(3) in the course of official proceedings.

Oregon: DR 7-104(A)(1) prohibits a lawyer from communicating with a represented party on the subject of the representation "or on directly related subjects," but DR 7-104(A)(1)(c) makes an exception if "a written agreement requires a written notice or demand to be sent to such other person, in which case a copy of such notice or demand shall also be sent to such other person's lawyer." Oregon further provides that the prohibition in DR 7-104(A)(1) "includes a lawyer representing the lawyer's own interests."

Texas: Rule 4.02 provides:

(a) In representing a client, a lawyer shall not communicate or cause or encourage another to communicate about the subject of the representation with a person, organization or entity of government the lawyer knows to be represented by another lawyer regarding that subject, unless the lawyer has the consent of the other lawyer or is authorized by law to do so.

(b) In representing a client a lawyer shall not communicate or cause another to communicate about the subject of representation with a person or organization a lawyer knows to be employed or retained for the purpose of conferring with or advising another lawyer about the subject of the representation, unless the lawyer has the consent of the other lawyer or is authorized by law to do so.

(c) For the purpose of this rule, "organization or entity of government" includes: (1) those persons presently having a managerial responsibility with an organization or entity of government that relates to the subject of the representation, or (2) those persons presently employed by such organization or entity and whose act or omission in connection with the subject of representation may make the organization or entity of government vicariously liable for such act or omission.

(d) When a person, organization, or entity of government that is represented by a lawyer in a matter seeks advice regarding that matter from another lawyer, the second lawyer is not prohibited by paragraph (a) from giving such advice without notifying or seeking consent of the first lawyer.

Related Materials

ABA Formal Ethics Opinions: See ABA Formal Ethics Ops. 92-362 (1992), 95-396 (1995), and 97-408 (1997).

ABA Standards for Criminal Justice: See Prosecution Function Standard 3-4.1(b).

ABA Standards for Imposing Lawyer Sanctions:

6.3. Improper Communications with Individuals in the Legal System

6.31. Disbarment is generally appropriate when a lawyer:

(a) intentionally tampers with a witness and causes serious or potentially serious injury to a party, or causes significant or potentially significant interference with the outcome of the legal proceeding; or . . .

(c) improperly communicates with someone in the legal system other than a witness, judge, or juror with the intent to influence or affect the outcome of the proceeding, and causes significant or potentially significant interference with the outcome of the legal proceeding.

6.32. Suspension is generally appropriate when a lawyer engages in communication with an individual in the legal system when the lawyer knows that such communication is improper, and causes injury or potential injury to a party or causes interference or potential interference with the outcome of the legal proceeding.

6.33. Reprimand is generally appropriate when a lawyer is negligent in determining whether it is proper to engage in communication with an individual in the legal system, and causes injury or potential injury to a party or interference or potential interference with the outcome of the legal proceeding.

American Lawyer's Code of Conduct: Rule 3.9 provides: "[A] lawyer may send a written offer of settlement directly to an adverse party, seven days or more after that party's attorney has received the same offer of settlement in writing."

Department of Justice Rules: In 1989, U.S. Attorney General Richard Thornburgh issued a memorandum stating that until an indictment Rule 4.2 did not apply to Department of Justice employees and their agents and investigators. Thornburgh argued that (1) the Supremacy Clause prohibited state ethics rules from controlling federal employees, and (2) federal undercover investigations, including undercover contacts with suspects or unindicted grand jury targets represented by counsel, were "authorized by law" within the meaning of Rule 4.2. In 1991, however, a federal court held that the "Thornburgh Memorandum" did not have the force of law and dismissed an indictment because a prosecutor had contacted a defendant represented by counsel without being "authorized by law." United States v. Lopez, 765 F. Supp. 1433 (N.D. Cal. 1991), *vacated on other grounds,* 989 F.2d 1032 (9th Cir. 1993). The first Bush administration sought to remedy the problem by publishing the Thornburgh Memorandum in the Federal Register on November 20, 1992, so that it would, after an appropriate period for public comment, attain the force of law. However, the proposal did not become law before the inauguration of President Clinton. The Clinton administration withdrew the proposal on January 22, 1993, two days after taking office.

On July 26, 1993, under Attorney General Janet Reno, the Department of Justice republished the Thornburgh memorandum with only minor changes for 30 days of public comment on both the text of the proposal and on comments previously received in response to the November 1992 publication. (See 58 Fed. Reg. 39976.) Criticism was again harsh. On March 3, 1994, the Department of Justice circulated a third revised rule for public comment. (See 59 Fed. Reg. 10086.) Finally, effective September 6, 1994, the Department of Justice issued a "final rule" on the subject, sometimes called the "Reno rules." (See 59 Fed. Reg. 39910, formerly codified at 28 C.F.R. Part 77.) The final rule was expressly intended "to preempt the entire field of rules concerning" contacts by government attorneys with represented parties. (We reprinted the full text of the "Reno rules" in our Special Section at the end of the 1996 edition.)

In O'Keefe v. McDonnell Douglas Corp., 132 F.3d 1252 (8th Cir. 1998), the Court held that the Department of Justice had no authority to promulgate the Reno Rules. Thereafter, Congress passed and the President signed 28 U.S.C. §530B, entitled "Ethical Standards for Attorneys for the Government," which provides that federal government attorneys are subject to the same ethical standards as other attorneys practicing in the same state. The statute also commanded the Attorney General to amend the Department of Justice's rules "to assure compliance with this section." (The full text of §530B is reprinted below in these Related Materials.) Pursuant to the statutory directive, the Attorney General has amended 28 C.F.R. Part 77.

Ethical Standards for Attorneys for the Government: In 1998, Congress enacted a new statute, 28 U.S.C. §530B (often called the "McDade Amendment," after its main sponsor in the House of Representatives), which provides as follows:

§530B. Ethical Standards for Attorneys for the Government

> (a) An attorney for the Government shall be subject to State laws and rules, and local Federal court rules, governing attorneys in each State where such attorney engages in that attorney's duties, to the same extent and in the same manner as other attorneys in that State.
>
> (b) The Attorney General shall make and amend rules of the Department of Justice to assure compliance with this section.
>
> (c) As used in this section, the term "attorney for the Government" includes any attorney described in section 77.2(a) of part 77 of title 28 of the Code of Federal Regulations and also includes any independent counsel, or employee of such a counsel, appointed under chapter 40.

Federal Rules of Civil Procedure: Rule 5(b) provides: "Whenever under these rules service is required or permitted to be made upon a party represented by an attorney the service shall be made upon the attorney unless service on the party is ordered by the court."

Federal Rules of Evidence: Rule 802(d)(2)(D), often cited in opinions regarding Rule 4.2, provides:

> (d) *Statements which are not hearsay.* A statement is not hearsay if—
>
> (2) *Admission by party-opponent.* The statement is offered against a party and is . . .
>
> (D) a statement by the party's agent or servant concerning a matter within the scope of the agency or employment made during the existence of the relationship . . . .

Joint Proposal by U.S. Department of Justice and Conference of Chief Justices: In December 1997, the Conference of Chief Justices (representing all state courts) and the United States Department of Justice (representing all federal lawyers) circulated a joint proposal to amend Rule 4.2. The proposal, the product of more than two years of negotiations, represented a compromise between the DOJ's position that the so-called "Reno rules" (28 C.F.R. Part 77) govern all federal lawyers and the CCJ's position that state rules govern all federal lawyers. The tentative plan was for the DOJ to withdraw the Reno rules in states that adopted the proposed amendment to Rule 4.2. The Conference of Chief Justices solicited public comments on the proposal, and determined that the public comments and other discussion evidenced "a decided lack of consensus in the national legal community as to both the principles underlying the draft and the specific language of the proposal." The Conference also noted that the ABA and various other groups were "actively considering" proposals to amend Rule 4.2. Therefore, on August 6, 1998 the Conference passed a resolution stating that it was "premature for the Conference to take action on the draft at this time." In our Special Section at the end of our 1999 edition we reprinted the full text of the joint proposal to amend Rule 4.2 (together with a proposed Comment) and the full text of the Conference's 1998 resolution regarding the joint proposal.

Model Rules of Professional Conduct for Federal Lawyers: Rule 4.2 provides as follows:

> (a) In representing a client, a Federal lawyer shall not communicate about the subject of the representation with a party the lawyer knows to be represented by another lawyer in the matter, unless the Federal lawyer has the consent of the other lawyer; [or] in a criminal matter, the individual initiates the communication with the Government lawyer and voluntarily and knowingly waives the right to counsel for the purposes of that communication; or the Federal lawyer otherwise is authorized by law to do so.
>
> (b) This Rule does not prohibit communications by a Non-Government lawyer with Federal Agency officials who have the authority to resolve a matter affecting the lawyer's client, whether or not the lawyer's communications relate to matters that are the subject of the representation, provided that the lawyer discloses the lawyer's identity; the fact that the lawyer represents a client in a matter involving the official's Federal Agency; and that the matter is being handled for the Federal Agency by a Government lawyer.

The Comment explains:

> In a criminal case there may be times when communications between a defendant and a Federal Agency without notice to defense counsel is in the interest of the defendant. Some communications will serve to protect the defendant and to identify sham representations. For example, in certain criminal enterprises, such as organized crime or drug rings, a defendant may wish to cooperate with a Federal Agency, but the counsel may also be the counsel of others involved in the enterprise. To insure that in such instances there is no abuse, this rule would permit communications by the defendant with the Government lawyer, as long as the defendant voluntarily and knowingly waives the right to counsel.

Restatement of the Law Governing Lawyers: See Restatement §§99–102 in our chapter on the Restatement later in this volume.

Rule 4.3 Dealing with Unrepresented Person

In dealing on behalf of a client with a person who is not represented by counsel, a lawyer shall not state or imply that the lawyer is disinterested. When the lawyer knows or reasonably should know that the unrepresented person misunderstands the lawyer's role in the matter, the lawyer shall make reasonable efforts to correct the misunderstanding. <u>The lawyer shall not give legal advice to an unrepresented person, other than the advice to secure counsel, if the lawyer knows or reasonably should know that the interests of such a person are or have a reasonable possibility of being in conflict with the interests of the client.</u>

COMMENT

[1] An unrepresented person, particularly one not experienced in dealing with legal matters, might assume that a lawyer is disinterested in loyalties or is a disinterested authority on the law even when the lawyer represents a client. ~~During the course of a lawyer's representation of a client, the lawyer should not give advice to an unrepresented person other than the advice to obtain counsel.~~ <u>In order to avoid a misunderstanding, a lawyer will typically need to identify the lawyer's client and, where necessary, explain that the client has interests opposed to those of the unrepresented person. For misunderstandings that sometimes arise when a lawyer for an organization deals with an unrepresented constituent, see Rule 1.13(d).</u>

<u>[2] The Rule distinguishes between situations involving unrepresented persons whose interests may be adverse to those of the lawyer's client and those in which the person's interests are not in conflict with the client's. In the former situation, the possibility that the lawyer will compromise the unrepresented person's interests is so great that the Rule prohibits the giving of any advice, apart from the advice to obtain counsel. Whether a lawyer is giving impermissible advice may depend on the experience and sophistication of the unrepresented person, as well as the setting in which the behavior and comments occur. This Rule does not prohibit a lawyer from negotiating the terms of a transaction or settling a dispute with an unrepresented person. So long as the lawyer has explained that the lawyer represents an adverse party and is not representing the person, the lawyer may inform the person of the terms on which the lawyer's client will enter into an agreement or settle a matter, prepare documents that require the person's signature and explain the lawyer's own view of the meaning of the document or the lawyer's view of the underlying legal obligations.</u>

Canon and Code Antecedents

ABA Canons of Professional Ethics: Canon 9 provided as follows:

9. Negotiations with Opposite Party

A lawyer should not in any way communicate upon the subject of controversy with a party represented by counsel; much less should he undertake to negotiate or compromise the matter with him, but should deal only with his counsel. It is incumbent upon the lawyer most particularly to avoid everything that may tend to mislead a party not represented by counsel, and he should not undertake to advise him as to the law.

ABA Model Code of Professional Responsibility: Compare DR 7-104(A)(2) (reprinted later in this volume).

Cross-References in Other Rules

Rule 3.9, Comment 3: This transaction "does not apply to representation of a client in a negotiation or other bilateral transaction with a governmental agency. . . . Representation in such matters is governed by **Rules 4.1** through **4.4.**"

Rule 4.2, Comment 9: "In the event the person with whom the lawyer communicates is not known to be represented by counsel in the matter, the lawyer's communications are subject to **Rule 4.3**."

Legislative History of Model Rule 4.3

1980 Discussion Draft (then Rule 3.6) provided as follows:

Appearing Against an Unrepresented Party

When an opposing party is unrepresented, a lawyer shall refrain from unfairly exploiting that party's ignorance of the law or the practices of the tribunal.

1981 Draft was substantially the same as adopted.

1982 Draft was adopted.

2002 Amendments: At its February 2002 Mid-Year Meeting, the ABA House of Delegates adopted without change the ABA Ethics 2000 Commission proposal to amend Rule 4.3 and its Comment.

Selected State Variations

California: No comparable provision.

Colorado adds to Rule 4.3 the following sentence taken from the old ABA Model Code: "The lawyer shall not give advice to the unrepresented person other than to secure counsel." In 1999, Colorado amended Rule 1.2 to permit "limited representation" of pro se parties. Colorado simultaneously amended the Comment to Rule 4.3 (but not the text of the rule) to provide that a lawyer "must comply with the requirements of this rule for pro se parties to whom limited representation has been provided . . . . Such parties are considered to be unrepresented for purposes of this rule."

District of Columbia: D.C. Rule 4.3 differs significantly from the ABA Model Rule — see District of Columbia Rules of Professional Conduct below.

Georgia: In the rules effective January 1, 2001, Georgia adopted the pre-2002 version of ABA Model Rule 4.3 and its Comment, but Georgia added two new subparagraphs to the text of the rule. These provide that a lawyer shall not:

(b) give advice other than the advice to secure counsel; and

(c) initiate any contact with a potentially adverse party in a matter concerning personal injury or wrongful death or otherwise related to an accident or disaster involving the person to whom the contact is addressed or a relative of that person, unless the accident or disaster occurred more than 30 days prior to the contact.

Louisiana: Rule 4.3 provides:

> A lawyer shall assume that an unrepresented person does not understand the lawyer's role in a matter and the lawyer shall carefully explain to the unrepresented person the lawyer's role in the matter.
>
> During the course of a lawyer's representation of a client, the lawyer should not give advice to a non-represented person other than the advice to obtain counsel.

Massachusetts, North Carolina, and ***Pennsylvania*** add the following language from DR 7-104(A)(2) of the ABA Model Code of Professional Responsibility to their versions of Rule 4.3:

> During the course of a lawyer's representation of a client, a lawyer shall not give advice to a person who is not represented by a lawyer, other than the advice to secure counsel, if the interests of such person are or have a reasonable possibility of being in conflict with the interests of the lawyer's client.

New Jersey adopts ABA Model Rule 4.3, but New Jersey's rule must be read in conjunction with New Jersey Rule 1.13(a), which provides that for the purposes of Rules 4.2 and 4.3, a lawyer employed or retained to represent an organization represents not only the organization but also the members of its "litigation control group," which includes "current agents and employees responsible for, or significantly involved in, the determination of the organization's legal position in the matter . . . ." Former employees who were members of the litigation control group "shall presumptively be deemed to be represented in the matter by the organization's lawyer but may at any time disavow said representation."

New York: Compare ABA Model Rule 4.3 to New York's DR 7-104(A)(2).

Virginia adopts Rule 4.3 but adds a paragraph (b) derived from DR 7-103(B).

Related Materials

ABA Standards for Criminal Justice: See Prosecution Function Standards 3-3.2(b) and 3-3.10(c).

American Academy of Matrimonial Lawyers: The "Bounds of Advocacy" contains the following provision and commentary:

> 2.21 An attorney should not advise an unrepresented party.
>
> Comment to Rule 2.21
>
> Once it becomes apparent that an opposing party intends to proceed without a lawyer, the attorney should, at the earliest opportunity, inform the opposing party in writing as follows:
>
> 1. I am your spouse's lawyer.
> 2. I do not and will not represent you.
> 3. I will at all times look out for your spouse's interests, not yours.
> 4. Any statements I make to you about this case should be taken by you as negotiation or argument on behalf of your spouse and not as advice to you as to your best interest.
> 5. I urge you to obtain your own lawyer.

Restatement of the Law Governing Lawyers: See Restatement §103 in our chapter on the Restatement later in this volume.

Rule 4.4 Respect for Rights of Third Persons

(a) In representing a client, a lawyer shall not use means that have no substantial purpose other than to embarrass, delay, or burden a third person, or use methods of obtaining evidence that violate the legal rights of such a person.

(b) A lawyer who receives a document relating to the representation of the lawyer's client and knows or reasonably should know that the document was inadvertently sent shall promptly notify the sender.

COMMENT

[1] Responsibility to a client requires a lawyer to subordinate the interests of others to those of the client, but that responsibility does not imply that a lawyer may disregard the rights of third persons. It is impractical to catalogue all such rights, but they include legal restrictions on methods of obtaining evidence from third persons and unwarranted intrusions into privileged relationships, such as the client-lawyer relationship.

[2] Paragraph (b) recognizes that lawyers sometimes receive documents that were mistakenly sent or produced by opposing parties or their lawyers. If a lawyer knows or reasonably should know that a such a document was sent inadvertently, then this Rule requires the lawyer to promptly notify the sender in order to permit that person to take protective measures. Whether the lawyer is required to take additional steps, such as returning the original document, is a matter of law beyond the scope of these Rules, as is the question of whether the privileged status of a document has been waived. Similarly, this Rule does not address the legal duties of a lawyer who receives a document that the lawyer knows or reasonably should know may have been wrongfully obtained by the sending person. For purposes of this Rule, "document" includes e-mail or other electronic modes of transmission subject to being read or put into readable form.

[3] Some lawyers may choose to return a document unread, for example, when the lawyer learns before receiving the document that it was inadvertently sent to the wrong address. Where a lawyer is not required by applicable law to do so, the decision to voluntarily return such a document is a matter of professional judgment ordinarily reserved to the lawyer. See Rules 1.2 and 1.4.

Canon and Code Antecedents

ABA Canons of Professional Ethics: Canon 18 provided as follows:

18. Treatment of Witnesses and Litigants

> A lawyer should always treat adverse witnesses and suitors with fairness and due consideration, and he should never minister to the malevolence or prejudices of a client in the trial or conduct of a cause. The client cannot be made the keeper of the lawyer's conscience in professional matters. He has no right to demand that his counsel shall abuse the opposite party or indulge in offensive personalities. Improper speech is not excusable on the ground that it is what the client would say if speaking in his own behalf.

ABA Model Code of Professional Responsibility: Compare DR 7-102(A)(1), DR 7-106(C)(2), DR 7-108(D), and DR 7-108(E) (reprinted later in this volume).

Cross-References in Other Rules

Rule 3.9, Comment 3: This transaction "does not apply to representation of a client in a negotiation or other bilateral transaction with a governmental agency. . . . Representation in such matters is governed by **Rules** 4.1 through **4.4**."

Rule 4.2, Comment 7: "In communicating with a current or former constituent of an organization, a lawyer must not use methods of obtaining evidence that violate the legal rights of the organization. See **Rule 4.4**."

Legislative History of Model Rule 4.4

1980 Discussion Draft (then Rule 3.4) provided as follows:

> (a) In preparing and presenting a cause, a lawyer shall respect the interests of third persons, including witnesses, jurors, and persons incidentally concerned with the proceeding. . . .

1981 and 1982 Drafts were the same as adopted.

2002 Amendments: Before the February 2002 Mid-Year Meeting of the ABA House of Delegates, the ABA Ethics 2000 Commission revised its May 2001 proposal to amend Rule 4.4 by adding the language "relating to the representation of the lawyer's client" and revising the Rule 4.4 Comment accordingly. At its February 2002 Mid-Year Meeting, the ABA House of Delegates adopted without change the ABA Ethics 2000 Commission's revised proposal to amend Rule 4.4 and its Comment.

Selected State Variations

California: See Rule 3-200(A) (Prohibited Objectives of Employment); Rule 5-100 (Threatening Criminal, Administrative, or Disciplinary Charges); Rule 5-310(B) (Prohibited Contact with Witnesses); B & P Code §§6068(c), 6068(f), 6068(g), and 6128(b).

Florida: Rule 5.1(a) applies to any lawyer who is "a partner, proprietor, shareholder, member of a limited liability company, officer, director, or manager in an authorized business entity . . . as defined elsewhere in these rules, or who has supervisory authority over another lawyer in the law department of an enterprise or government agency. . . ."

Georgia: In the rules effective January 1, 2001, Georgia adopts ABA Model Rule 4.4 and its Comment verbatim.

New York has no direct counterpart to ABA Model Rule 4.4(a) or (b), but New York prohibits various forms of misconduct toward witnesses, jurors, and others in DR 7-102(A)(1), DR 7-106(C)(2), and DR 7-108(D) and (E).

Pennsylvania: Rule 4.4 omits the prohibition on using "means that have no substantial purpose other than to embarrass, delay or burden a third person."

Texas: Rule 4.04(b) forbids lawyers to present or threaten disciplinary or criminal charges "solely to gain an advantage in a civil matter" or civil, criminal, or disciplinary charges "solely" to prevent participation by a complainant or witness in a disciplinary matter.

Virginia omits the word "substantial" from its version of Rule 4.4.

Related Materials

ABA Standards for Criminal Justice: See Prosecution Function Standards 3-2.9(b), 3-3.1(c), and 3-5.7(a); Defense Function Standards 4-1.2(b) and (d), 4-4.2, 4-7.1(e), and 4-7.6(a).

Restatement of the Law Governing Lawyers: See Restatement §§30, 51, 56, 102, and 106 in our chapter on the Restatement later in this volume.

ARTICLE 5. LAW FIRMS AND ASSOCIATIONS

Rule 5.1 Responsibilities of ~~a Partner or~~ Partners, Managers, and Supervisory ~~Lawyer~~ Lawyers

(a) A partner in a law firm, and a lawyer who individually or together with other lawyers possesses comparable managerial authority in a law firm, shall make reasonable efforts to ensure that the firm has in effect measures giving reasonable assurance that all lawyers in the firm conform to the Rules of Professional Conduct.

(b) A lawyer having direct supervisory authority over another lawyer shall make reasonable efforts to ensure that the other lawyer conforms to the Rules of Professional Conduct.

(c) A lawyer shall be responsible for another lawyer's violation of the Rules of Professional Conduct if:

(1) the lawyer orders or, with knowledge of the specific conduct, ratifies the conduct involved; or

(2) the lawyer is a partner or has comparable managerial authority in the law firm in which the other lawyer practices, or has

direct supervisory authority over the other lawyer, and knows of the conduct at a time when its consequences can be avoided or mitigated but fails to take reasonable remedial action.

COMMENT

[1] ~~Paragraphs~~ Paragraph (a) ~~and (b) refer~~ applies to lawyers who have ~~supervisory~~ managerial authority over the professional work of a firm ~~or legal department of a government agency~~. See Rule 1.0(c). This includes members of a partnership ~~and~~, the shareholders in a law firm organized as a professional corporation, and members of other associations authorized to practice law; lawyers having ~~supervisory~~ comparable managerial authority in ~~the~~ a legal services organization or a law department of an enterprise or government agency; and lawyers who have intermediate managerial responsibilities in a firm. Paragraph (b) applies to lawyers who have supervisory authority over the work of other lawyers in a firm.

[2] Paragraph (a) requires lawyers with managerial authority within a firm to make reasonable efforts to establish internal policies and procedures designed to provide reasonable assurance that all lawyers in the firm will conform to the Rules of Professional Conduct. Such policies and procedures include those designed to detect and resolve conflicts of interest, identify dates by which actions must be taken in pending matters, account for client funds and property and ensure that inexperienced lawyers are properly supervised.

~~[2]~~ [3] ~~The~~ Other measures that may be required to fulfill the responsibility prescribed in ~~paragraphs~~ paragraph (a) ~~and (b)~~ can depend on the firm's structure and the nature of its practice. In a small firm of experienced lawyers, informal supervision and ~~occasional admonition~~ periodic review of compliance with the required systems ordinarily ~~might be sufficient~~ will suffice. In a large firm, or in practice situations in which intensely difficult ethical problems frequently arise, more elaborate ~~procedures~~ measures may be necessary. Some firms, for example, have a procedure whereby junior lawyers can make confidential referral of ethical problems directly to a designated senior partner or special committee. See Rule 5.2. Firms, whether large or small, may also rely on continuing legal education in professional ethics. In any event, the ethical atmosphere of a firm can influence the conduct of all its members and ~~a lawyer having authority over the work of another~~ the partners may not assume that ~~the subordinate lawyer~~ all lawyers associated with the firm will inevitably conform to the Rules.

~~[3]~~ [4] Paragraph (c)~~(1)~~ expresses a general principle of personal responsibility for acts of another. See also Rule 8.4(a).

~~[4]~~ [5] Paragraph (c)(2) defines the duty of a partner or other lawyer having comparable managerial authority in a law firm, as well as a lawyer who has direct supervisory authority over performance of specific legal work by another lawyer. Whether a lawyer has supervisory authority in particular circumstances is a question of fact. Partners ~~of a private firm~~ and lawyers with comparable authority have at least indirect responsibility for all work being done by the firm, while a partner or manager in charge of a particular matter ordinarily also has ~~direct authority over~~ supervisory responsibility for the work of other firm lawyers engaged in the matter. Appropriate remedial action by a partner or managing lawyer would depend on the immediacy of ~~the partner's~~ that lawyer's involvement and the seriousness of the misconduct. ~~The~~ A supervisor is required to intervene to prevent avoidable consequences of misconduct if the supervisor knows that the misconduct occurred. Thus, if a supervising lawyer knows that a subordinate misrepresented a matter to an opposing party in negotiation, the supervisor as well as the subordinate has a duty to correct the resulting misapprehension.

~~[5]~~ [6] Professional misconduct by a lawyer under supervision could reveal a violation of paragraph (b) on the part of the supervisory lawyer even though it does not entail a violation of paragraph (c) because there was no direction, ratification or knowledge of the violation.

~~[6]~~ [7] Apart from this Rule and Rule 8.4(a), a lawyer does not have disciplinary liability for the conduct of a partner, associate or subordinate. Whether a lawyer may be liable civilly or criminally for another lawyer's conduct is a question of law beyond the scope of these Rules.

[8] The duties imposed by this Rule on managing and supervising lawyers do not alter the personal duty of each lawyer in a firm to abide by the Rules of Professional Conduct. See Rule 5.2(a).

Canon and Code Antecedents

ABA Canons of Professional Ethics: No comparable Canon.

ABA Model Code of Professional Responsibility: Compare DR 1-102 and DR 1-103(A) (reprinted later in this volume).

Cross-References in Other Rules

Rule 1.6, Comment 15: "A lawyer must act competently to safeguard information relating to the representation of a client against inadvertent or unauthorized disclosure by the lawyer or other persons who are participating in the representation of the client or who are subject to the lawyer's supervision (see **Rules** 1.1, **5.1** and 5.3)."

Rule 1.7, Comment 3: "To determine whether a conflict of interest exists, a lawyer should adopt reasonable procedures, appropriate for the size and type of firm and practice, to determine in both litigation and non-litigation matters the persons and issues involved. See also Comment to **Rule 5.1**."

Rule 3.8, Comment 6: "Like other lawyers, prosecutors are subject to **Rules 5.1** and 5.3, which relate to responsibilities regarding lawyers and nonlawyers who work for or are associated with the lawyer's office."

Rule 5.3, Comment 2: "Paragraph (a) requires lawyers with managerial authority within a law firm to make reasonable efforts to establish internal policies and procedures designed to provide reasonable assurance that nonlawyers in the firm will act in a way compatible with the Rules of Professional Conduct. See Comment [1] to **Rule 5.1**."

Legislative History of Model Rule 5.1

1980 Discussion Draft of Rule 5.1 (then Rule 7.2) provided as follows:

Responsibilities of a Supervisory Lawyer

(a) A lawyer having supervisory authority over another lawyer shall make a reasonable effort to see that the conduct of the lawyer under supervision conforms to the Rules of Professional Conduct.

(b) A lawyer is chargeable with another lawyer's violation of the Rules of Professional Conduct if:

(1) the lawyer orders or ratifies the conduct involved; or

(2) the lawyer has supervisory responsibility over the other lawyer and has knowledge of the conduct at a time when its consequences can be avoided or mitigated but fails to take appropriate remedial action.

1981 Draft was substantially the same as adopted, except that Rule 5.2(a) applied to "all lawyers in the firm, including other partners. . . ."

1982 Draft was adopted.

2002 Amendments: At its February 2002 Mid-Year Meeting, the ABA House of Delegates adopted without change the ABA Ethics 2000 Commission proposal to amend Rule 5.1 and its Comment.

Selected State Variations

California: See Rule 1-100(B) (defining "law firm" and "associate").

Georgia: In the rules effective January 1, 2001, Georgia adopted the pre-2002 version of ABA Model Rule 5.1 and its Comment essentially verbatim.

Illinois provides that "[e]ach" partner or lawyer shall make the reasonable efforts specified in Rule 5.1(a) and (b).

New Jersey begins Rule 5.1(a) with: "Every law firm and organization authorized by the Court Rules to practice law in this jurisdiction . . ." instead of "A partner in a law firm." Rule 5.1(c)(2) applies only to lawyers having "direct supervisory authority"; it deletes the phrase "is a partner or has comparable managerial authority in the law firm in which the other lawyer practices."

New York: Compare ABA Model Rule 5.1 to New York's DR 1-104(A)-(D).

North Carolina: Rule 5.1(c)(1) applies only when the lawyer in question "orders the conduct involved" — it omits the words "or, with knowledge of the specific conduct, ratifies." Rule 5.1(c)(2) applies only to a lawyer who has "direct supervisory authority over the other lawyer" — it omits the clause "partner or has comparable managerial authority in the law firm in which the other lawyer practices."

Texas: The text of Texas Rule 5.01 has no equivalent to ABA Model Rules 5.1(a) and (b) as amended in 2002, but Comment 6 to Texas Rule 5.01 provides:

> Wholly aside from the dictates of these rules for discipline, a lawyer in a position of authority in a firm or government agency or over another lawyer should feel a moral compunction to make reasonable efforts to ensure that the office, firm, or agency has in effect appropriate procedural measures giving reasonable assurance that all lawyers in the office conform to these rules. This moral obligation, although not required by these rules, should fall also upon lawyers who have intermediate managerial responsibilities in the law department of an organization or government agency.

Texas Rule 5.01(b), which is similar to ABA Model Rule 5.1(c)(2), also applies to "the general counsel of a government agency's legal department."

Virginia adopts Rule 5.1.

Related Materials

Model Rules of Professional Conduct for Federal Lawyers add the following new subparagraphs to Rule 5.1:

> (c) A Federal lawyer, who is a supervisory lawyer, is responsible for ensuring that the subordinate lawyer is properly trained and is competent to perform the duties to which the subordinate lawyer is assigned.
>
> (d) A Government lawyer, who is a supervisory lawyer, should encourage subordinate lawyers to participate in pro bono publico service activities and the activities of bar associations and law reform organizations.

Partnership Law: Model Rule 5.1 roughly parallels the financial liability of general partners for the acts of others in the partnership. Section 13 of the Uniform Partnership Act, which has been adopted in nearly every state, provides:

> *§13. Partnership Bound by Partner's Wrongful Act*
>
> Where, by any wrongful act or omission of any partner acting in the ordinary course of the business of the partnership or with the authority of his co-partners, loss or injury is caused to any person, not being a partner in the partnership, or any penalty is incurred, the partnership is liable therefor to the same extent as the partner so acting or omitting to act.

Restatement of the Law Governing Lawyers: See Restatement §§11 and 58 in our chapter on the Restatement later in this volume.

Rule 5.2 Responsibilities of a Subordinate Lawyer

(a) A lawyer is bound by the Rules of Professional Conduct notwithstanding that the lawyer acted at the direction of another person.

(b) A subordinate lawyer does not violate the Rules of Professional Conduct if that lawyer acts in accordance with a supervisory lawyer's reasonable resolution of an arguable question of professional duty.

COMMENT

[1] Although a lawyer is not relieved of responsibility for a violation by the fact that the lawyer acted at the direction of a supervisor, that fact may be relevant in determining whether a lawyer had the knowledge required to render conduct a violation of the Rules. For example, if a subordinate filed a frivolous pleading at the direction of a supervisor, the subordinate would not be guilty of a professional violation unless the subordinate knew of the document's frivolous character.

[2] When lawyers in a supervisor-subordinate relationship encounter a matter involving professional judgment as to ethical duty, the supervisor may assume responsibility for making the judgment. Otherwise a consistent course of action or position could not be taken. If the question can reasonably be answered only one way, the duty of both lawyers is clear and they are equally responsible for fulfilling it. However, if the question is reasonably arguable, someone has to decide upon the course of action. That authority ordinarily reposes in the supervisor, and a subordinate may be guided accordingly. For example, if a question arises whether the interests of two clients conflict under Rule 1.7, the supervisor's reasonable resolution of the question should protect the subordinate professionally if the resolution is subsequently challenged.

Canon and Code Antecedents

ABA Canons of Professional Ethics: No comparable Canon.

ABA Model Code of Professional Responsibility: No comparable Disciplinary Rule.

Cross-References in Other Rules

Rule 5.1, Comment 3: "Some firms . . . have a procedure whereby junior lawyers can make confidential referral of ethical problems directly to a designated senior partner or special committee. See **Rule 5.2**."

Rule 5.1, Comment 8: "The duties imposed by this Rule on managing and supervising lawyers do not alter the personal duty of each lawyer in a firm to abide by the Rules of Professional Conduct. See **Rule 5.2(a)**."

Legislative History of Model Rule 5.2

1980 Discussion Draft (then Rule 7.3) provided as follows:

> (a) A lawyer acting under the supervisory authority of another person is bound by the Rules of Professional Conduct notwithstanding the fact that the lawyer's conduct was ordered by the supervisor.

1981 Draft was substantially the same as adopted.

1982 Draft was adopted.

2002 Amendments: The ABA Ethics 2000 Commission did not propose any changes to the text or Comment of Rule 5.2.

Selected State Variations

California: No comparable provision.

Georgia: In the rules effective January 1, 2001, Georgia adopted ABA Model Rule 5.2 and its Comment essentially verbatim.

New York: Compare ABA Model Rule 5.2 to New York's DR 1-104(E) and (F).

Ohio has no provision comparable to ABA Model Rule 5.2.

Virginia omits Rule 5.2.

Related Materials

Restatement of the Law Governing Lawyers: See Restatement §12 in our chapter on the Restatement later in this volume.

Rule 5.3 Responsibilities Regarding Nonlawyer Assistants

With respect to a nonlawyer employed or retained by or associated with a lawyer:

(a) a partner, and a lawyer who individually or together with other lawyers possesses comparable managerial authority in a law firm shall make reasonable efforts to ensure that the firm has in effect measures giving reasonable assurance that the person's conduct is compatible with the professional obligations of the lawyer;

(b) a lawyer having direct supervisory authority over the nonlawyer shall make reasonable efforts to ensure that the person's conduct is compatible with the professional obligations of the lawyer; and

(c) a lawyer shall be responsible for conduct of such a person that would be a violation of the Rules of Professional Conduct if engaged in by a lawyer if:

(1) the lawyer orders or, with the knowledge of the specific conduct, ratifies the conduct involved; or

(2) the lawyer is a partner or has comparable managerial authority in the law firm in which the person is employed, or has direct supervisory authority over the person, and knows of the conduct at a time when its consequences can be avoided or mitigated but fails to take reasonable remedial action.

COMMENT

[1] Lawyers generally employ assistants in their practice, including secretaries, investigators, law student interns, and paraprofessionals. Such assistants, whether employees or independent contractors, act for the lawyer in rendition of the lawyer's professional services. A lawyer ~~should~~ must give such assistants appropriate instruction and supervision concerning the ethical aspects of their employment, particularly regarding the obligation not to disclose information relating to representation of the client, and should be responsible for their work product. The measures employed in supervising nonlawyers should take account of the fact that they do not have legal training and are not subject to professional discipline.

[2] Paragraph (a) requires lawyers with managerial authority within a law firm to make reasonable efforts to establish internal policies and procedures designed to provide reasonable assurance that nonlawyers in the firm will act in a way compatible with the Rules of Professional Conduct. See Comment [1] to Rule 5.1. Paragraph (b) applies to lawyers who have supervisory authority over the work of a nonlawyer. Paragraph (c) specifies the circumstances in which a lawyer is responsible for conduct of a nonlawyer that would be a violation of the Rules of Professional Conduct if engaged in by a lawyer.

Canon and Code Antecedents

ABA Canons of Professional Ethics: No comparable Canon.

ABA Model Code of Professional Responsibility: Compare DR 4-101(D) (reprinted later in this volume).

Cross-References in Other Rules

Rule 1.6, Comment 15: "A lawyer must act competently to safeguard information relating to the representation of a client against inadvertent or unauthorized disclosure by the lawyer or other persons who are participating in the representation of the client or who are subject to the lawyer's supervision (see **Rules** 1.1, 5.1 and **5.3**)."

Rule 1.10, Comment 4: Paragraph (a) does not "prohibit representation if the lawyer is prohibited from acting because of events before the person became a lawyer. . . . Such persons, however, ordinarily must be screened from any personal participation in the matter to avoid communication to others in the firm of confidential information that both the nonlawyers and the firm have a legal duty to protect. See **Rules** 1.0(k) and **5.3**."

Rule 3.8, Comment 6: "Like other lawyers, prosecutors are subject to **Rules** 5.1 and **5.3**, which relate to responsibilities regarding lawyers and nonlawyers who work for or are associated with the lawyer's office."

Rule 5.5, Comment 1: "Paragraph (b) does not prohibit a lawyer from employing the services of paraprofessionals and delegating functions to them, so long as the lawyer supervises the delegated work and retains responsibility for their work. See **Rule 5.3**."

Rule 5.7, Comment 8: When rendering both legal and law-related services in the same matter, "a lawyer will be responsible for assuring that both the lawyer's conduct and, to the extent required by **Rule 5.3**, that of nonlawyer employees in the distinct entity that the lawyer controls complies in all respects with the Rules of Professional Conduct."

Rule 7.2, Comment 5: "See **Rule 5.3** for the duties of lawyers and law firms with respect to the conduct of nonlawyers who prepare marketing materials for them."

Rule 7.2, Comment 7: "A lawyer who accepts assignments or referrals from a legal service plan or referrals from a lawyer referral service must act reasonably to assure that the activities of the plan or service are compatible with the lawyer's professional obligations. See **Rule 5.3**."

Legislative History of Model Rule 5.3

1980 Discussion Draft (then Rule 7.4) provided:

> *Supervision of Nonlawyer Assistants*
>
> A lawyer shall use reasonable effort to ensure that nonlawyers employed or retained by the lawyer conduct themselves in a manner compatible with the professional obligations of the lawyer.

1981 Draft was substantially the same as adopted.

1982 Draft was adopted.

2002 Amendments: At its February 2002 Mid-Year Meeting, the ABA House of Delegates adopted without change the ABA Ethics 2000 Commission proposal to amend Rule 5.3 and its Comment.

Selected State Variations

Alabama: Rule 7.6, entitled "Professional Cards of Nonlawyers," provides as follows:

> A lawyer shall not cause or permit a business card of a nonlawyer which contains the lawyer's or firm's name to contain a false or misleading statement or omission to the effect that the nonlawyer is a lawyer. A business card of a nonlawyer is not false and misleading which clearly identifies the nonlawyer as a "Legal Assistant," provided that the individual is employed in that capacity by a lawyer or law firm, that the lawyer or law firm supervises and is responsible for the law related tasks assigned to and performed by such individual, and that the lawyer or law firm has authorized the use of such cards.

California: No comparable provision.

Georgia: In the rules effective January 1, 2001, Georgia adopted the pre-2002 version of ABA Model Rule 5.3 and its Comment verbatim, but also added a new subparagraph (d) that provides as follows:

> (d) a lawyer shall not allow any person who has been suspended or disbarred and who maintains a presence in an office where the practice of law is conducted by the lawyer, to:
>
> (1) represent himself or herself as a lawyer or person with similar status;
>
> (2) have any contact with the clients of the lawyer either in person, by telephone or in writing; or
>
> (3) have any contact with persons who have legal dealings with the office either in person, by telephone or in writing.

Georgia's Comment to subparagraph (d) provides:

> [2] The prohibitions of paragraph (d) apply to professional conduct and not to social conversation unrelated to the representation of clients or legal dealings of the law office, or the gathering of general information in the course of working in a law office. The thrust of the restriction is to prevent the unauthorized practice of law in a law office by a person who has been suspended or disbarred.

Illinois: Rule 5.3(a) applies to "[t]he lawyer, and, in a law firm, each partner," and refers to the professional obligations of the lawyer "and the firm." Illinois Rule 5.3(b) applies to "each" lawyer having direct supervisory authority.

Indiana has adopted a series of "Guidelines" entitled "Use of Legal Assistants." Among other topics, the Guidelines cover "Permissible Delegation," "Prohibited Delegation," "Identification on Letterhead," and "Legal Assistant Ethics."

New Hampshire: Supreme Court Rule 35, titled "Guidelines for the Utilization by Lawyers of the Services of Legal Assistants under the New Hampshire Rules of Professional Conduct," contains nine rules for using the services of legal assistants in compliance with Rule 5.3. For example, Rule 1 provides:

> It is the responsibility of the lawyer to take all steps reasonably necessary to ensure that a legal assistant for whose work the lawyer is responsible does not provide legal advice or otherwise engage in the unauthorized practice of law; provided, however, that with adequate lawyer supervision the legal assistant may provide information concerning legal matters and otherwise act as permitted under these rules.

New Jersey: Rule 5.3(a) provides that "every lawyer or organization authorized by the Court Rules to practice law in this jurisdiction shall adopt and maintain reasonable efforts to ensure that the conduct of nonlawyers retained or employed by the lawyer, law firm or organization is compatible with the professional obligations of the lawyer." In addition, New Jersey has added Rule 5.3(c)(3), which provides that a lawyer is responsible for the conduct of a nonlawyer employee if "the lawyer has failed to make reasonable investigation of circumstances that would disclose past instances of conduct by the nonlawyer incompatible with the professional obligations of a lawyer, which evidence a propensity for such conduct."

New York: Compare ABA Model Rule 5.3 to New York's DR 1-104(C) and (D) and DR 4-101(D).

North Carolina: Rule 5.3(c)(1) applies only when the lawyer in question "orders the conduct involved" — it omits the words "or, with knowledge of the specific conduct, ratifies." Rule 5.3(c)(2) applies only to a lawyer who has "direct supervisory authority over the other lawyer"— it omits the clause "partner or has comparable managerial authority in the law firm in which the person is employed."

Pennsylvania replaces "shall" with "should" in its version of Rules 5.3(a) and (b).

Texas relegates ABA Model Rule 5.3(a) to Comment 2 after Texas Rule 5.03. The Comment provides, in essence, that "[e]ach lawyer in a position of authority in a law firm or in a government agency should make reasonable efforts to ensure that the organization" has measures reasonably assuring that the conduct of nonlawyers "employed or retained by or associated with the firm or legal department" is compatible with the professional obligations of the lawyer. This ethical obligation "includes lawyers having supervisory authority or intermediate managerial responsibilities in the law department of any enterprise or government agency." Texas Rule 5.03(b), which is equivalent to ABA Model Rule 5.3(c), subjects a lawyer to discipline for a nonlawyer's misconduct if:

(1) the lawyer orders, encourages, or permits the conduct involved; or

(2) the lawyer:

(i) is a partner in the law firm in which the person is employed, retained by, or associated with; or is the general counsel of a government agency's legal department in which the person is employed, retained by or associated with; or has direct supervisory authority over such person; and

(ii) with knowledge of such misconduct by the nonlawyer knowingly fails to take reasonable remedial action to avoid or mitigate the consequences of that person's misconduct.

Virginia: Rule 5.3 is substantially the same as the Model Rule except that Virginia adds the phrase "or should have known" after "knows" in Rule 5.3(c)(2).

Related Materials

ABA Formal Ethics Opinions: See ABA Formal Ethics Op. 95-398 (1995).

ABA Guidelines for Approval of Paralegal Education Programs: The ABA has adopted Guidelines for the Approval of Paralegal Education Programs. These guidelines are enforced by an ABA Approval Commission that examines and approves paralegal education programs. There are currently around 700 paralegal education programs in the United States, of which about 185 are approved by the ABA. Approved programs include programs in colleges (B.A. programs), in community colleges (A.A. programs), and in proprietary institutions (certificate or degree programs). Some universities even offer a master's degree in paraprofessionalism. The ABA works closely with the American Association for Paralegal Education (see entry below).

ABA Model Guidelines for the Utilization of Legal Assistant Services: The ABA has adopted Model Guidelines for the Utilization of Legal Assistant Services. Guidelines 1 and 6 provide as follows:

> 1. A lawyer is responsible for all of the professional actions of a legal assistant performing legal assistant services at the lawyer's direction and should take reasonable measures to ensure that the legal assistant's conduct is consistent with the lawyer's obligations under the ABA Model Rules of Professional Conduct. . . .
>
> 6. It is the responsibility of a lawyer to take reasonable measures to ensure that all client confidences are preserved by a legal assistant.

ABA Standards for Criminal Justice: See Prosecution Function Standards 3-3.1(a) and (c); Defense Function Standard 4-4.2.

American Association for Paralegal Education (www.aafpe.org): The American Association for Paralegal Education (AAfPE) is an organization for those who educate paralegals. The AAfPE represents approximately 250 paralegal training programs across America and works closely with the ABA Approval Commission to ensure that paralegal programs are providing quality education to paralegals.

Independent Paralegals: Some states allow "independent paralegals" (also called "freelance paralegals") who are retained by lawyers on an "as needed" basis but are not employees of the law firm. See, e.g., In re Opinion No. 24 of the Committee on the Unauthorized Practice of Law, 128 N.J. 114, 607 A.2d 962 (1992). Because Rule 5.3 covers non-lawyers who are "retained by or associated with" a lawyer, the rule reaches independent paralegals.

Legal Assistant Managers Association (www.lamanet.org): The Legal Assistant Managers Association (LAMA) represents approximately 400 "legal assistant managers" whose job is to supervise paralegals in traditional law firm settings. LAMA strongly supports efforts to expand the role of paralegals who are employed by law firms or government agencies. For example, LAMA believes that paralegals should be permitted to appear on behalf of clients at administrative hearings and record depositions, to conduct real estate closings, and to prepare routine corporate filings, guardianship papers, and adoption papers. LAMA also supports establishing formal qualifications for paralegals and establishing a system to address complaints about unethical paralegals.

National Association of Legal Assistants (www.nala.org): The National Association of Legal Assistants, Inc. (NALA), founded in 1975 and headquartered in Tulsa, Oklahoma, is an organization of about 17,000 legal assistants. NALA has published Model Standards and Guidelines for Utilization of Legal Assistants Annotated. The Guidelines "represent a statement of how the legal assistant may function in the law office," and may thus help lawyers understand their supervisory responsibilities under Model Rule 5.3. The Guidelines set minimum educational standards for legal assistants. Excerpts from the Guidelines are reprinted in the Related Materials following Rule 5.5 ("Unauthorized Practice of Law").

NALA has also adopted a very brief Code of Ethics and Professional Responsibility for legal assistants. Canon 8 of this code, which is the reciprocal of ABA Model Rule 5.3, provides: "It is the obligation of the legal assistant to avoid conduct which would cause the lawyer to be unethical or even to appear to be unethical, and loyalty to the employer is incumbent upon the legal assistant."

Restatement of the Law Governing Lawyers: See Restatement §§11 and 58 in our chapter on the Restatement later in this volume.

Student Practice Rules: Many states have student practice rules that permit law students to represent clients under certain conditions. These rules often require lawyers to provide a certain degree of supervision over law students. For example, Florida Rule 11-1.2(a) provides as follows:

> An eligible law student may appear in any court or before any administrative tribunal in this state on behalf of any indigent person if the person on whose behalf the student is appearing has indicated in writing consent to that appearance and the supervising lawyer has also indicated in writing approval of that appearance. In those cases in which an indigent has a right to appointed counsel, the supervising attorney shall be personally present at all critical stages of the proceeding. In all cases, the supervising attorney shall be personally present when required by the court or administrative tribunal who shall determine the extent of the eligible law student's participation in the proceeding.

Unauthorized Practice of Law: A lawyer who fails to supervise a paralegal adequately may be assisting the paralegal in the unauthorized practice of law, in violation of Rule 5.5. (For examples of statutes governing the unauthorized practice of law, see the Related Materials following ABA Model Rule 5.5 below.)

Rule 5.4 Professional Independence of a Lawyer

(a) A lawyer or law firm shall not share legal fees with a nonlawyer, except that:

(1) an agreement by a lawyer with the lawyer's firm, partner, or associate may provide for the payment of money, over a reasonable period of time after the lawyer's death, to the lawyer's estate or to one or more specified persons;

(2) a lawyer who purchases the practice of a deceased, disabled, or disappeared lawyer may, pursuant to the provisions of Rule 1.17, pay to the estate or other representative of that lawyer the agreed-upon purchase price; ~~and~~

(3) a lawyer or law firm may include nonlawyer employees in a compensation or retirement plan, even though the plan is based in whole or in part on a profit-sharing arrangement; and

(4) a lawyer may share court-awarded legal fees with a nonprofit organization that employed, retained or recommended employment of the lawyer in the matter.

(b) A lawyer shall not form a partnership with a nonlawyer if any of the activities of the partnership consist of the practice of law.

(c) A lawyer shall not permit a person who recommends, employs, or pays the lawyer to render legal services for another to direct or regulate the lawyer's professional judgment in rendering such legal services.

(d) A lawyer shall not practice with or in the form of a professional corporation or association authorized to practice law for a profit, if:

(1) a nonlawyer owns any interest therein, except that a fiduciary representative of the estate of a lawyer may hold the stock or interest of the lawyer for a reasonable time during administration;

(2) a nonlawyer is a corporate director or officer thereof or occupies the position of similar responsibility in any form of association other than a corporation; or

(3) a nonlawyer has the right to direct or control the professional judgment of a lawyer.

COMMENT

[1] The provisions of this Rule express traditional limitations on sharing fees. These limitations are to protect the lawyer's professional in-

dependence of judgment. Where someone other than the client pays the lawyer's fee or salary, or recommends employment of the lawyer, that arrangement does not modify the lawyer's obligation to the client. As stated in paragraph (c), such arrangements should not interfere with the lawyer's professional judgment.

[2] This Rule also expresses traditional limitations on permitting a third party to direct or regulate the lawyer's professional judgment in rendering legal services to another. See also Rule 1.8(f) (lawyer may accept compensation from a third party as long as there is no interference with the lawyer's independent professional judgment and the client gives informed consent).

Canon and Code Antecedents

ABA Canons of Professional Ethics: Canons 33, 34, and 35 provided as follows:

33. Partnerships — Names

Partnerships among lawyers for the practice of their profession are very common and are not to be condemned. In the formation of partnerships and the use of partnership names care should be taken not to violate any law, custom, or rule of court locally applicable. Where partnerships are formed between lawyers who are not all admitted to practice in the courts of the state, care should be taken to avoid any misleading name or representation which would create a false impression as to the professional position or privileges of the member not locally admitted. In the formation of partnerships for the practice of law, no person should be admitted or held out as a practitioner or member who is not a member of the legal profession duly authorized to practice, and amenable to professional discipline. In the selection and use of a firm name, no false, misleading, assumed or trade name should be used. The continued use of the name of a deceased or former partner, when permissible by local custom, is not unethical, but care should be taken that no imposition or deception is practiced through this use. When a member of the firm, on becoming a judge, is precluded from practicing law, his name should not be continued in the firm name.

Partnerships between lawyers and members of other professions or nonprofessional persons should not be formed or permitted where any part of the partnership's employment consists of the practice of law.

34. Division of Fees

No division of fees for legal services is proper, except with another lawyer, based upon a division of service or responsibility.

35. Intermediaries

The professional services of a lawyer should not be controlled or exploited by any lay agency, personal or corporate, which intervenes between client and lawyer. A lawyer's responsibilities and qualifications are individual. He should avoid all relations which direct the performance of his duties by or in the interest of such intermediary. A lawyer's relation to his client should be personal, and the responsibility should be direct to the client. Charitable societies rendering aid to the indigents are not deemed such intermediaries.

A lawyer may accept employment from any organization, such as an association, club or trade organization, to render legal services in any matter in which the organization, as an entity, is interested, but this employment should not include the rendering of legal services to the members of such an organization in respect to their individual affairs.

ABA Model Code of Professional Responsibility: Compare DR 3-102(A), DR 3-103(B), DR 5-107(B), and DR 5-107(C) (reprinted later in this volume).

Cross-References in Other Rules

Rule 1.8, Comment 11: "See also **Rule 5.4(c)** (prohibiting "interference with a lawyer's professional judgment by one who recommends, employs or pays the lawyer to render legal services for another)."

Rule 1.17, Comment 1: "[W]hen a lawyer or an entire firm ceases to practice, or ceases to practice in an area of law, and other lawyers or firms take over the representation, the selling lawyer or firm may obtain compensation for the reasonable value of the practice as may withdrawing partners of law firms. See **Rules 5.4** and 5.6."

Rule 7.2, Comment 8: "[R]eciprocal referral arrangements must not interfere with the lawyer's professional judgment as to making referrals or as to providing substantive legal services. See **Rules** 2.1 and **5.4(c)**."

Legislative History of Model Rule 5.4

1980 Discussion Draft (then Rule 7.5) provided as follows:

Professional Independence of a Firm

A lawyer shall not practice with a firm in which an interest is owned or managerial authority is exercised by a nonlawyer, unless services can be rendered in conformity with the Rules of Professional Conduct. The terms of the relationship shall expressly provide that:

(a) there is no interference with the lawyer's independence of professional judgment or with the client-lawyer relationship; and

(b) the confidences of clients are protected as required by Rule 1.7; and

(c) the arrangement does not involve advertising or solicitation prohibited by Rules 9.2 and 9.3; and

(d) the arrangement does not result in charging a client a fee which violates Rule 1.6.

1981 Draft:

Professional Independence of a Firm

A lawyer may be employed by an organization in which a financial interest is held or managerial authority is exercised by a non-lawyer, or by a lawyer acting in a capacity other than that of representing clients, such as a business corporation, insurance company, legal services organization or government agency, but only if the terms of the relationship provide in writing that:

(a) there is no interference with the lawyer's independence of professional judgment or with the client-lawyer relationship;

(b) information relating to representation of a client is protected as required by Rule 1.6;

(c) the arrangement does not involve advertising or personal contract with prospective clients prohibited by Rules 7.2 and 7.3; and

(d) the arrangement does not result in charging a fee that violates Rule 1.5.

The ***1982 Draft*** was substantially the same as 1981 Draft.

1983 Version: The version of Rule 5.4 finally adopted in 1983 was proposed as an amendment by the ABA's General Practice Section as a substitute for the Kutak Commission's draft. Rule 5.4 was the only proposed rule from the 1982 Draft that was completely rejected and rewritten by the House of Delegates in 1983.

1990 Amendment: At its February 1990 Mid-Year Meeting, the ABA House of Delegates amended Rule 5.4(a)(2) to conform to Rule 1.17 (permitting the sale of a law practice), which was added to the Rules at the same meeting. (There was no Committee Report to explain the change, but the reason for the change is obvious.) The former version of Rule 5.4(a)(2) provided that "a lawyer who undertakes to complete unfinished legal business of a deceased lawyer may pay to the estate of the deceased lawyer that proportion of the total compensation which fairly represents the services rendered by the deceased lawyer."

2002 Amendments: At its February 2002 Mid-Year Meeting, the ABA House of Delegates adopted without change the ABA Ethics 2000 Commission proposal to amend Rule 5.4 and its Comment.

Selected State Variations

Arizona, Connecticut, Florida, Pennsylvania, and ***Texas*** use the following language in place of ABA Model Rule 5.4(a)(2):

> (2) a lawyer who undertakes to complete unfinished legal business of a deceased lawyer may pay to the estate of the deceased lawyer that proportion of the total compensation which fairly represents the services rendered by the deceased lawyer.

California: See Rule 1-310 (Forming a Partnership with a Non-Lawyer) and Rule 1-320 (Financial Arrangements with Non-Lawyers).

District of Columbia: D.C. Rule 5.4 differs significantly from the ABA Model Rule — see District of Columbia Rules of Professional Conduct below.

Illinois does not permit the sale of a law practice, so Rule 5.4(a)(2) applies only to a lawyer "who undertakes to complete unfinished legal business of a deceased lawyer . . . ," and makes no reference to a "disabled or disappeared" lawyer. Illinois Rule 5.4(d)(2) permits a non-lawyer to serve as secretary for a professional corporation or for-profit association authorized to practice law "if such secretary performs only ministerial duties."

Florida: Florida Rule 4-8.6 describes the business entities through which lawyers may practice law and forbids practice other than through "officers, directors, partners, agents, or employees who are qualified to render legal services in this state." Further, only persons who are so qualified may serve as "a partner, manager, director, or executive officer" of such an entity.

Georgia: In the rules effective January 1, 2001, Georgia adopted the pre-2002 version of ABA Model Rule 5.4 and its Comment verbatim, but also added a new subparagraph (a)(4), which permits a lawyer who undertakes to complete the unfinished business of a deceased lawyer to "pay to the estate of the deceased lawyer that proportion of the total compensation which fairly represents the services rendered by the deceased lawyer."

Maryland: Rule 8.5(b) imposes responsibility on lawyers admitted elsewhere who supervise Maryland lawyers.

Massachusetts: Rule 5.4(a) allows a lawyer or law firm to share "a statutory or tribunal-approved" legal fee with "a qualified legal assistance organization that referred the matter to the lawyer or law firm" if the organization is not for profit and tax-exempt, the fee is made in connection with a proceeding to advance the organization's purposes, and the client consents. The Comment to this rule explains that the "financial needs of these organizations, which serve important public ends, justify a limited exception to the prohibition against fee-sharing with nonlawyers." The Comment also explains that the exception does not extend to fees generated in connection with proceedings unrelated to the organization's tax-exempt purpose, "such as generating business income for the organization." Massachusetts Rule 5.4(b) prohibits a lawyer from forming a partnership "or other business entity" with a nonlawyer if any of the activities of the "entity" consist of the practice of law. Massachusetts amended Rule 5.4 in relatively minor ways effective October 1, 1999.

Missouri: Rule 5.4(d) provides that a lawyer "shall not practice with or in the form of a professional corporation, *limited liability company,* or association authorized to practice law for a profit" if the conditions in the subparagraphs apply. Rule 5.4(d)(2) prohibits such practice if a nonlawyer is "a manager of the limited liability company."

New Jersey: Rule 5.4 permits a lawyer to share legal fees with the estate of a deceased lawyer or the representative of a disabled lawyer where the first lawyer has assumed responsibility for the deceased or disabled lawyer's cases.

New York: Compare ABA Model Rule 5.4(a) to New York's DR 1-107(A)(2), DR 2-103(B), and DR 3-102. Compare Rule 5.4(b) to New York's DR 1-107 and DR 3-103. Compare Rule 5.4(c) to New York's DR 1-107(A)(2) and DR 5-107(A) and (B). Compare Rule 5.4(d) to New York's DR 1-107(A)(2) and DR 5-107(C).

North Carolina: North Carolina adds the following language to Rule 5.4(a):

> (3) a lawyer who undertakes to complete unfinished legal business of a deceased lawyer or a disbarred lawyer may pay to the estate of the deceased lawyer or to the disbarred lawyer that proportion of the total compensation which fairly represents the services rendered by the deceased lawyer or the disbarred lawyer.

North Carolina also omits ABA Model Rule 5.4(d)(2) as amended in 2002.

Ohio: DR 3-102(A)(4) allows a lawyer participating in a qualified lawyer referral service to "pay to the service a fee calculated as a percentage of legal fees earned by the lawyer in his or her capacity as a lawyer to whom the service has referred a matter." This percentage fee may be "in addition to any reasonable membership or registration fee established by the service."

Pennsylvania provides in Rule 5.4(d) that a lawyer shall not practice with or in the form of a professional corporation or other form of association organized for profit if "a nonlawyer is the beneficial owner of any interest therein [with an exception for an estate representative]; a nonlawyer is a corporate director or officer thereof or occupies the position of similar responsibility in any form of association other than a corporation; [or] . . . in the case of any form of association other than a professional corporation, the organic law governing the internal affairs of the association provides the equity owners of the association with greater liability protection than is available to the shareholders of a professional corporation." These provisions do not apply "to a lawyer employed in the legal department of a corporation or other organization."

Rhode Island: On February 15, 2002, the Rhode Island Supreme Court rejected a proposal to add an exception to Rule 5.4(a) that would allow a lawyer or law firm "to share a statutory or tribunal-approved fee award, or a settlement in a matter eligible for such an award," with a tax exempt, non profit organization that referred the matter to the lawyer or law firm. In an opinion announcing the rejection, the court noted that under Rhode Island statute §11-27-3, such a fee-sharing arrangement, except with the Legal Aid Society, would amount to a criminal violation and would constitute the unauthorized practice of law. See In re Rule Amendments to Rules 5.4(a) and 7.2(c) of Rules of Professional Conduct, 2002 WL 649020 (R.I. 2002).

Texas: Under Texas Rule 5.04(a)(1), either a lawyer's agreement or a lawful court order may provide for the payment of money over time to the lawyer's estate "to or for the benefit of the lawyer's heirs or personal representatives, beneficiaries, or former spouse, after the lawyer's death or as otherwise provided by law or court order."

Related Materials

ABA Commission on Multidisciplinary Practice: In 1998, the ABA appointed a Commission on Multidisciplinary Practice ("MDP Commission") to study and report on the scope and manner of efforts by accounting firms and other nonlawyer professional service firms to provide legal services to the public. (Unauthorized practice of law statutes and ethics rules like Rule 5.4 currently make it improper for lawyers to offer legal services to the public through non-law entities, but lawyers in some professional service firms owned by nonlawyers are alleged to be doing so anyway. In many European countries nonlawyer professional service firms are permitted to offer both legal and nonlegal services to the public, and large accounting firms have been aggressively acquiring European law firms.) The MDP Commission's Reporter was Professor Mary Daly of Fordham University School of Law. During 1998 and 1999, the MDP Commission held public hearings, received public comments in writing, and issued a "Background Paper" and a series of "Hypotheticals and Models" to focus public discussion. The MDP Commission's first report, issued in June of 1999, recommended far-reaching proposals to revamp the ABA Model Rules of Professional Conduct to permit nonlawyers to become partners with lawyers in MDPs that offer clients legal and nonlegal services provided the nonlawyers in an MDP agree to be bound by the ethics rules that govern lawyers. At the ABA's August 1999 Annual Meeting, the House of Delegates voted overwhelmingly (304 to 98) to reject the MDP Commission's recommendations. Instead, the ABA adopted a resolution not to change the ABA Model Rules to permit multidisciplinary practice "unless and until additional study demonstrates that such changes will further the public interest without sacrificing or compromising lawyer independence and the legal profession's tradition of loyalty to clients."

Despite this setback, the MDP Commission continued to hold hearings and to solicit public comments. In December of 1999, the MDP Commission issued an "Updated Background and Informational Report and Request for Comments." At the ABA's February 2000 Mid-Year Meeting, the House of Delegates discussed and debated multidisciplinary practice and the MDP Commission held a public hearing. Shortly afterwards, the MDP Commission issued a thoughtful "Postscript" summarizing and responding to the major points raised at the Mid-Year Meeting. In July of 2000, the MDP Commission issued another report to the House of Delegates, this time with more modest proposals. However, at the ABA's July 2000 Annual Meeting, the House of Delegates voted 314-106 to reject the MDP Commission's report and instead to adopt a recommendation that the ABA continue to prohibit partnerships with non-lawyers and continue to prohibit non-lawyer equity interests in law firms. In our Special Section at the end of our 2001 edition, we reprinted the MDP Commission's July 2000 report and the ABA's July 2000 recommendation. For additional information, including copies of public comments and all of the MDP Commission's reports, visit www.abanet.org/cpr/ multicom.html.

ABA Formal Ethics Opinions: See ABA Formal Ethics Ops. 87-355 (1987), 91-360 (1991), 93-374 (1993), 95-392 (1995), and 01-423 (2001).

ABA Model Guidelines for the Utilization of Legal Assistant Services: In 1992, the ABA House of Delegates approved Model Guidelines for the Utilization of Legal Assistant Services. Guideline 9 provides:

> A lawyer may not split legal fees with a legal assistant nor pay a legal assistant for the referral of legal business. A lawyer may compensate a legal assistant based on the quantity and quality of the legal assistant's work and the value of that work to a law practice, but the legal assistant's compensation may not be contingent, by advance agreement, upon the profitability of the lawyer's practice.

American Lawyer's Code of Conduct: Rule 4.7 provides:

> If a lawyer forms a partnership with a nonlawyer for the purpose of more effectively serving clients' interests, the terms of the partnership shall be consistent with the lawyer's obligations under this Code, with particular reference to Rule 2.1, requiring undivided fidelity to the client.

IRS Regulations: In the regulations governing practice before the Internal Revenue Service, 31 C.F.R. §10.24 provides that no attorney practicing before the IRS shall "knowingly and directly or indirectly . . . [e]mploy or accept assistance from any person who is under disbarment or suspension from practice" before the IRS or "share fees with, any such person . . . ."

Limited Liability Companies: Rule 5.4(d) governs lawyers who practice with or in the form of "a professional association or association authorized to practice law for a profit" if certain enumerated circumstances apply. Some states have expressly extended coverage of Rule 5.4(d) to limited liability companies (sometimes called LLC's), which combine the benefits of partnership taxation rules with the benefits of limited liability for corporations. All states except Illinois have enacted statutes permitting LLC's or their close cousins, limited liability partnerships (LLP's).

Model Rules of Professional Conduct for Federal Lawyers insert a substantially different version of Rule 5.4, which provides:

> (a) A Federal lawyer is expected to exercise professional independence of judgment during the representation of a client, consistent with these Rules.

(b) Notwithstanding a Government lawyer's status as a Government employee, a Government lawyer detailed or assigned to represent an individual Government employee or another person as the client is expected to exercise loyalty and professional independence during the representation, consistent with these Rules and to the same extent as required by a Non-Government lawyer in private practice.

(c) A Supervisory Government lawyer may not base an adverse evaluation or other prejudicial action against a Subordinate Government lawyer on the Subordinate Government lawyer's exercise of professional independence under (b) above.

(d) A Government lawyer shall obey the lawful orders of superiors when representing the United States and individual clients, but a Government lawyer shall not permit a nonlawyer to direct or regulate the Government lawyer's professional judgment in rendering legal services.

(e) A Non-Government lawyer shall not permit a nonlawyer who recommends, employs, or pays the Non-Government lawyer to render legal services for another to direct or regulate the Non-Government lawyer's professional judgment in rendering legal services.

(f) A Non-Government lawyer shall comply with the Rules of Professional Conduct or other applicable laws of the jurisdiction in which the Non-Government lawyer is licensed or is practicing law concerning the limitations on sharing fees and the organizational form of their practice.

The Comment, which has no parallel in the ABA Model Rules, states (with headings omitted):

A Federal lawyer subjected to outside pressures that might impair or give the appearance of impairing the effectiveness of the representation should make full disclosure of the pressures to the client. If the Federal lawyer or the client believes the effectiveness of the representation has been or will be impaired thereby, the lawyer should take proper steps to withdraw from representation of the client.

This Rule recognizes that a Government lawyer is a Government employee required by law to obey the lawful orders of superiors. Nevertheless, the practice of law requires the exercise of judgment solely for the benefit of the client and free of compromising influences and loyalties. Thus, when a Government lawyer is assigned to represent an individual client, neither the lawyer's personal interests, the interests of other clients, nor the interests of third persons should affect the loyalty to the individual client.

Rather than adopting specific rules on the sharing of fees or the organizational makeup of law practices that would apply only to Non-Government lawyers practicing before the Federal Agency, the Federal Agency defers on this matter to the rules and applicable laws of the jurisdictions in which these Non-Government lawyers are licensed.

Restatement of the Law Governing Lawyers: See Restatement §§10 and 134 in our chapter on the Restatement later in this volume.

Rule 5.5 Unauthorized Practice of Law; Multijurisdictional Practice of Law

Editors' Note. At its August 2002 Annual Meeting, the ABA House of Delegates significantly amended Rule 5.5. The amendments were based on a proposal by the ABA Commission on Multijurisdictional Practice. For further information, see the entry titled "2002 Amendments" in the Legislative History following this rule.

(a) A lawyer shall not~~: (a)~~ practice law in a jurisdiction ~~where doing so violates~~ in violation of the regulation of the legal profession in that jurisdiction~~;~~, or ~~(b)~~ assist ~~a person who is not a member of the bar~~ another in ~~the performance of activity that constitutes the unauthorized practice of law~~ doing so.

(b) A lawyer who is not admitted to practice in this jurisdiction shall not:

(1) except as authorized by these Rules or other law, establish an office or other systematic and continuous presence in this jurisdiction for the practice of law; or

(2) hold out to the public or otherwise represent that the lawyer is admitted to practice law in this jurisdiction.

(c) A lawyer admitted in another United States jurisdiction, and not disbarred or suspended from practice in any jurisdiction, may provide legal services on a temporary basis in this jurisdiction that:

(1) are undertaken in association with a lawyer who is admitted to practice in this jurisdiction and who actively participates in the matter;

(2) are in or reasonably related to a pending or potential proceeding before a tribunal in this or another jurisdiction, if the lawyer, or a person the lawyer is assisting, is authorized by law or order to appear in such proceeding or reasonably expects to be so authorized;

(3) are in or reasonably related to a pending or potential arbitration, mediation, or other alternative dispute resolution proceeding in this or another jurisdiction, if the services arise out of or are reasonably related to the lawyer's practice in a jurisdiction in which the lawyer is admitted to practice and are not services for which the forum requires pro hac vice admission; or

(4) are not within paragraphs (c)(2) or (c)(3) and arise out of or are reasonably related to the lawyer's practice in a jurisdiction in which the lawyer is admitted to practice.

(d) A lawyer admitted in another United States jurisdiction, and not disbarred or suspended from practice in any jurisdiction, may provide legal services in this jurisdiction that:

(1) are provided to the lawyer's employer or its organizational affiliates and are not services for which the forum requires pro hac vice admission; or

(2) are services that the lawyer is authorized by federal or other law to provide in this jurisdiction.

COMMENT

[1] A lawyer may practice law only in a jurisdiction in which the lawyer is authorized to practice. A lawyer may be admitted to practice law

in a jurisdiction on a regular basis or may be authorized by court rule or order or by law to practice for a limited purpose or on a restricted basis. Paragraph (a) applies to unauthorized practice of law by a lawyer, whether through the lawyer's direct action or by the lawyer assisting another person.

~~[1]~~ [2] The definition of the practice of law is established by law and varies from one jurisdiction to another. Whatever the definition, limiting the practice of law to members of the bar protects the public against rendition of legal services by unqualified persons. ~~Paragraph (b)~~ This Rule does not prohibit a lawyer from employing the services of paraprofessionals and delegating functions to them, so long as the lawyer supervises the delegated work and retains responsibility for their work. See Rule 5.3.

[3] ~~Likewise, it does not prohibit lawyers from providing~~ A lawyer may provide professional advice and instruction to nonlawyers whose employment requires knowledge of the law; for example, claims adjusters, employees of financial or commercial institutions, social workers, accountants and persons employed in government agencies. Lawyers also may assist independent nonlawyers, such as paraprofessionals, who are authorized by the law of a jurisdiction to provide particular law-related services. In addition, a lawyer may counsel nonlawyers who wish to proceed pro se.

[4] Other than as authorized by law or this Rule, a lawyer who is not admitted to practice generally in this jurisdiction violates paragraph (b) if the lawyer establishes an office or other systematic and continuous presence in this jurisdiction for the practice of law. Presence may be systematic and continuous even if the lawyer is not physically present here. Such a lawyer must not hold out to the public or otherwise represent that the lawyer is admitted to practice law in this jurisdiction. See also Rules 7.1(a) and 7.5(b).

[5] There are occasions in which a lawyer admitted to practice in another United States jurisdiction, and not disbarred or suspended from practice in any jurisdiction, may provide legal services on a temporary basis in this jurisdiction under circumstances that do not create an unreasonable risk to the interests of their clients, the public or the courts. Paragraph (c) identifies four such circumstances. The fact that conduct is not so identified does not imply that the conduct is or is not authorized. With the exception of paragraphs (d)(1) and (d)(2), this Rule does not authorize a lawyer to establish an office or other systematic and continuous presence in this jurisdiction without being admitted to practice generally here.

[6] There is no single test to determine whether a lawyer's services are provided on a "temporary basis" in this jurisdiction, and may therefore be permissible under paragraph (c). Services may be "temporary" even though the lawyer provides services in this jurisdiction on a recurring basis, or for an extended period of time, as when the lawyer is representing a client in a single lengthy negotiation or litigation.

[7] Paragraphs (c) and (d) apply to lawyers who are admitted to practice law in any United States jurisdiction, which includes the District of Columbia and any state, territory or commonwealth of the United States. The word "admitted" in paragraph (c) contemplates that the lawyer is authorized to practice in the jurisdiction in which the lawyer is admitted and excludes a lawyer who while technically admitted is not authorized to practice, because, for example, the lawyer is on inactive status.

[8] Paragraph (c)(1) recognizes that the interests of clients and the public are protected if a lawyer admitted only in another jurisdiction associates with a lawyer licensed to practice in this jurisdiction. For this paragraph to apply, however, the lawyer admitted to practice in this jurisdiction must actively participate in and share responsibility for the representation of the client.

[9] Lawyers not admitted to practice generally in a jurisdiction may be authorized by law or order of a tribunal or an administrative agency to appear before the tribunal or agency. This authority may be granted pursuant to formal rules governing admission pro hac vice or pursuant to informal practice of the tribunal or agency. Under paragraph (c)(2), a lawyer does not violate this Rule when the lawyer appears before a tribunal or agency pursuant to such authority. To the extent that a court rule or other law of this jurisdiction requires a lawyer who is not admitted to practice in this jurisdiction to obtain admission pro hac vice before appearing before a tribunal or administrative agency, this Rule requires the lawyer to obtain that authority.

[10] Paragraph (c)(2) also provides that a lawyer rendering services in this jurisdiction on a temporary basis does not violate this Rule when the lawyer engages in conduct in anticipation of a proceeding or hearing in a jurisdiction in which the lawyer is authorized to practice law or in which the lawyer reasonably expects to be admitted pro hac vice. Examples of such conduct include meetings with the client, interviews of potential witnesses, and the review of documents. Similarly, a lawyer admitted only in another jurisdiction may engage in conduct temporarily in this jurisdiction in connection with pending litigation in another jurisdiction in which the lawyer is or reasonably expects to be authorized to appear, including taking depositions in this jurisdiction.

[11] When a lawyer has been or reasonably expects to be admitted to appear before a court or administrative agency, paragraph (c)(2) also permits conduct by lawyers who are associated with that lawyer in the matter, but who do not expect to appear before the court or administrative agency. For example, subordinate lawyers may conduct research, review documents, and attend meetings with witnesses in support of the lawyer responsible for the litigation.

[12] Paragraph (c)(3) permits a lawyer admitted to practice law in another jurisdiction to perform services on a temporary basis in this jurisdiction if those services are in or reasonably related to a pending or potential arbitration, mediation, or other alternative dispute resolution

proceeding in this or another jurisdiction, if the services arise out of or are reasonably related to the lawyer's practice in a jurisdiction in which the lawyer is admitted to practice. The lawyer, however, must obtain admission pro hac vice in the case of a court-annexed arbitration or mediation or otherwise if court rules or law so require.

[13] Paragraph (c)(4) permits a lawyer admitted in another jurisdiction to provide certain legal services on a temporary basis in this jurisdiction that arise out of or are reasonably related to the lawyer's practice in a jurisdiction in which the lawyer is admitted but are not within paragraphs (c)(2) or (c)(3). These services include both legal services and services that nonlawyers may perform but that are considered the practice of law when performed by lawyers.

[14] Paragraphs (c)(3) and (c)(4) require that the services arise out of or be reasonably related to the lawyer's practice in a jurisdiction in which the lawyer is admitted. A variety of factors evidence such a relationship. The lawyer's client may have been previously represented by the lawyer, or may be resident in or have substantial contacts with the jurisdiction in which the lawyer is admitted. The matter, although involving other jurisdictions, may have a significant connection with that jurisdiction. In other cases, significant aspects of the lawyer's work might be conducted in that jurisdiction or a significant aspect of the matter may involve the law of that jurisdiction. The necessary relationship might arise when the client's activities or the legal issues involve multiple jurisdictions, such as when the officers of a multinational corporation survey potential business sites and seek the services of their lawyer in assessing the relative merits of each. In addition, the services may draw on the lawyer's recognized expertise developed through the regular practice of law on behalf of clients in matters involving a particular body of federal, nationally uniform, foreign, or international law.

[15] Paragraph (d) identifies two circumstances in which a lawyer who is admitted to practice in another United States jurisdiction, and is not disbarred or suspended from practice in any jurisdiction, may establish an office or other systematic and continuous presence in this jurisdiction for the practice of law as well as provide legal services on a temporary basis. Except as provided in paragraphs (d)(1) and (d)(2), a lawyer who is admitted to practice law in another jurisdiction and who establishes an office or other systematic or continuous presence in this jurisdiction must become admitted to practice law generally in this jurisdiction.

[16] Paragraph (d)(1) applies to a lawyer who is employed by a client to provide legal services to the client or its organizational affiliates, i.e., entities that control, are controlled by, or are under common control with the employer. This paragraph does not authorize the provision of personal legal services to the employer's officers or employees. The paragraph applies to in-house corporate lawyers, government lawyers and others who are employed to render legal services to the employer. The lawyer's ability to represent the employer outside the jurisdiction in which

the lawyer is licensed generally serves the interests of the employer and does not create an unreasonable risk to the client and others because the employer is well situated to assess the lawyer's qualifications and the quality of the lawyer's work.

[17] If an employed lawyer establishes an office or other systematic presence in this jurisdiction for the purpose of rendering legal services to the employer, the lawyer may be subject to registration or other requirements, including assessments for client protection funds and mandatory continuing legal education.

[18] Paragraph (d)(2) recognizes that a lawyer may provide legal services in a jurisdiction in which the lawyer is not licensed when authorized to do so by federal or other law, which includes statute, court rule, executive regulation or judicial precedent.

[19] A lawyer who practices law in this jurisdiction pursuant to paragraphs (c) or (d) or otherwise is subject to the disciplinary authority of this jurisdiction. See Rule 8.5(a).

[20] In some circumstances, a lawyer who practices law in this jurisdiction pursuant to paragraphs (c) or (d) may have to inform the client that the lawyer is not licensed to practice law in this jurisdiction. For example, that may be required when the representation occurs primarily in this jurisdiction and requires knowledge of the law of this jurisdiction. See Rule 1.4(b).

[21] Paragraphs (c) and (d) do not authorize communications advertising legal services to prospective clients in this jurisdiction by lawyers who are admitted to practice in other jurisdictions. Whether and how lawyers may communicate the availability of their services to prospective clients in this jurisdiction is governed by Rules 7.1 to 7.5.

Canon and Code Antecedents

ABA Canons of Professional Ethics: Canon 47 provided as follows:

47. Aiding the Unauthorized Practice of Law

No lawyer shall permit his professional services, or his name, to be used in aid of, or to make possible, the unauthorized practice of law by any lay agency, personal or corporate.

ABA Model Code of Professional Responsibility: Compare DR 3-101(A) and DR 3-101(B) (reprinted later in this volume).

Cross-References in Other Rules

None.

Legislative History of Model Rule 5.5

1980 Discussion Draft (then Rule 10.4(d) and (e)) provided that it was "professional misconduct" for a lawyer to "(d) practice law in a jurisdiction in violation of the regulation of the legal profession in that jurisdiction; or (e) aid a person who is not a member of the bar in the performance of activity that constitutes the practice of law."

1981 and 1982 Drafts (then Rule 8.4(d) and (e)) were the same as adopted.

2002 Amendments: At its August 2002 Annual Meeting, by voice vote the ABA House of Delegates approved significant amendments to ABA Model Rule 5.5. These amendments were proposed by the ABA Commission on Multijurisdictional Practice, which was formed in July 2000 to consider a host of issues pertaining to the practice of law by lawyers in jurisdictions where they are not admitted to practice, either permanently or pro hac vice. (The ABA Ethics 2000 Commission also considered amendments to Rule 5.5 but eventually deferred to the Commission on Multijurisdictional Practice, which was studying the issues much more comprehensively.)

The full report of the ABA Commission on Multijurisdictional Practice regarding Rule 5.5 and related issues, which runs more than 60 pages, may be found at www.abanet.org/cpr (click on "Commission on Multijurisdictional Practice," then look for "REVISED FINAL REPORT, AS ADOPTED AUGUST 12, 2002" and pick the appropriate segments). We excerpt here (with footnotes omitted) the portions of that report that relate most directly to the 2002 amendments to Rule 5.5:

*Excerpts from Final Report by the ABA Commission on Multijurisdictional Practice in Support of Amendments to Rule 5.5**

Rule 5.5 of the ABA *Model Rules of Professional Conduct* (Unauthorized Practice of Law) currently prohibits a lawyer from practicing law in a jurisdiction where doing so violates the regulation of the legal profession in that jurisdiction and from assisting a person who is not a member of the bar in the unauthorized practice of law. The MJP Commission proposes to re-title the Rule "Unauthorized Practice of Law; Multijurisdictional Practice of Law." Additionally, the Commission proposes two sets of amendments to the Rule.

First, Rule 5.5 would be clarified and strengthened by adoption of amended sections 5.5(a) and (b). As amended, Rule 5.5(a) would make clear that a lawyer is prohibited not only from engaging in the unauthorized practice of law, but also from assisting another in the unauthorized practice of law. Proposed Rule 5.5(b) would make clear that, except when authorized by law or rule, a lawyer may not establish an office or other systematic and continuous presence for the practice of law in a jurisdiction in which the lawyer is not admitted to practice. Nor may the lawyer hold out to the public or otherwise represent that the lawyer is admitted to practice law in that jurisdiction.

*Committee Reports do not represent official policy of the ABA. They are for information only and represent only the opinions of the authors.

Second, the standards identified in proposed sections 5.5(c) and (d) would recognize specific exceptions to otherwise applicable restrictions on the practice of law by out-of-state lawyers, in order to facilitate multijurisdictional law practice in identifiable situations that serve the interests of clients and the public and do not create an unreasonable regulatory risk. These standards draw on the prior work of the Ethics 2000 Commission, the American Law Institute's Restatement of the Law Governing Lawyers, the ABA Standing Committee on Ethics and Professional Responsibility, the ABA Section of Business Law, other ABA entities and state and local bar associations.

The Ethics 2000 Commission anticipated the MJP Commission's work by proposing for inclusion in ABA Model Rule 5.5 exceptions to the general rule that a lawyer may practice law only in a jurisdiction in which the lawyer is licensed. The Ethics 2000 Commission's proposed multijurisdictional practice standards were specific applications of the general principle that, under certain circumstances, it is in the public interest for a lawyer admitted in one United States jurisdiction to be allowed to provide legal services in another United States jurisdiction because the interests of the lawyer's client will be served if the lawyer is permitted to render the particular services, and doing so does not create an unreasonable risk to the interests of the lawyer's client, the public or the courts. In such circumstances, it should not be the unauthorized practice of law for a lawyer admitted in another United States jurisdiction to provide legal services in a jurisdiction in which the lawyer is not admitted. To similar effect, RESTATEMENT (THIRD) OF THE LAW GOVERNING LAWYERS §3(3) identified specific situations where a lawyer not admitted to practice law in a jurisdiction may provide legal services to a client in that jurisdiction.

The MJP Commission worked to develop, refine and harmonize the Ethics 2000 Commission's initial list of multijurisdictional practice standards and the Restatement provision in light of the study conducted by the MJP Commission. Both before and after the Commission issued its Interim Report, the Commission received extremely helpful proposals for developing and refining the provisions of proposed Rule 5.5. The Commission drew liberally on the suggestions it received.

The multijurisdictional practice standards will not eliminate all uncertainty regarding interstate law practice but will provide a framework for the activities that the Commission believes should be authorized. In identifying these new standards, the Commission has taken a conservative approach, addressing only those classes of conduct that do not pose unacceptable risks to the public interest. Because the exercise of determining what constitutes authorized conduct requires judgment and balancing, the application of the new standards leaves room for individual opinion and judicial interpretation.

While the MJP Commission's proposed Model Rule 5.5 identifies situations in which United States lawyers may practice law outside the jurisdictions in which they are licensed, the adoption of this rule by state judiciaries may not, in itself, provide the necessary authorization to out-of-state lawyers. As discussed earlier, restrictions on unauthorized practice of law are also embodied in laws and rules that differ from state to state. Particularly in jurisdictions in which the UPL [Unauthorized Practice of Law] restrictions are contained in legislation, state legislative reform may also be necessary.

Proposed Model Rule 5.5(a) would make clear that a lawyer may not assist another, whether a lawyer or nonlawyer, in the unauthorized practice of law. Existing Rule 5.5 has two provisions: Rule 5.5(a) forbids a lawyer from engaging in the practice of law in a jurisdiction where doing so violates the regulation of the legal profession in that jurisdiction and Rule 5.5(b) forbids a lawyer from assisting a person who is not a member of the bar in the performance of activity that constitutes the unauthorized practice of law. The Commission proposes combining and refining these restrictions into a single provision, which would provide that "[a] lawyer shall not practice law in a jurisdiction, or assist *another* in doing so, in violation of the regulation of the legal profession in that jurisdiction." (Emphasis added.) However, this would not effect a substantive change to the Model Rules, since this is simply a specific application of Model Rule 8.4(a) (Misconduct), which prohibits a lawyer from "knowingly assist[ing]" another in violating the Rules of Professional Conduct.

Proposed Model Rule 5.5(b) would prohibit a lawyer from establishing an office or maintaining a systematic and continuous presence in a jurisdiction, except as authorized by the Model Rules or other law; and it would also prohibit a lawyer from representing that the lawyer is admitted in a jurisdiction if the lawyer is not admitted. Nothing in the proposed rule would authorize lawyers to open an office or otherwise establish a permanent law practice in states where they are not licensed or otherwise authorized to do so. Nor would any part of the proposed rule permit lawyers to hold themselves out as licensed to practice law in jurisdictions where they are not in fact licensed. The amendments recommended by the Commission make these limitations clear. . . . [T]he Commission has developed a separate recommendation on "admission on motion" directed at lawyers seeking to establish a law practice in jurisdictions where they are not currently licensed to practice law. . . .

Proposed Model Rule 5.5(c)(1) would allow work on a temporary basis in a state by an out-of-state lawyer who is associated in the matter with a lawyer who is admitted to practice in the jurisdiction and who actively participates in the representation. This provision would promote the client's interest in counsel of choice in many circumstances where the client has good reason to engage both a local and an out-of-state lawyer. One recurring example is where local counsel recommends engaging the assistance of a lawyer with special or particularized expertise. Another is where the client has a prior or ongoing relationship with the out-of-state lawyer in whom the client has particular confidence and whose advice is sought in evaluating the services of the local counsel. Lawyers who assist litigation counsel but who do not themselves appear in judicial proceedings would also be covered by this provision.

For this provision to apply, the lawyer admitted to practice in the jurisdiction could not serve merely as a conduit for the out-of-state lawyer, but would have to share actual responsibility for the representation. When that condition is met, the state's regulatory interest in protecting the interests of both clients and the public is adequately served. The lawyer who is licensed in the jurisdiction will have an opportunity to oversee the out-of-state lawyer's work and to assure that the work is performed competently and ethically. The local lawyer, having been found to have the requisite fitness and character to practice law in the state, is presumptively qualified to carry out this responsibility.

This provision would permit a lawyer to provide legal services on a temporary basis in an office of the lawyer's firm outside the lawyer's home state, as long as the lawyer is in a genuine co-counsel relationship with a lawyer of the firm who is licensed in the jurisdiction. However, this provision is not intended to cover associates who rotate among a law firm's offices for periods that would be longer than "temporary."

Proposed Model Rule 5.5(c)(2) would allow lawyers to provide services ancillary to pending or prospective litigation. Specifically, it would permit a lawyer's temporary presence in a state where the lawyer is not presently admitted to practice, if (a) the lawyer's services are in anticipation of litigation reasonably expected to be filed in a state where the lawyer is admitted or expects to be admitted *pro hac vice,* or (b) the lawyer's services are ancillary to pending litigation in which the lawyer lawfully appears (or reasonably expects to appear), either because the lawyer is licensed in the jurisdiction where the litigation takes place or because the lawyer has been or reasonably expects to be admitted *pro hac vice* to participate in the litigation. This provision would not supplant *pro hac vice* requirements, however. In order to appear before a tribunal in a state where the lawyer is not licensed, the out-of-state lawyer would be required to comply with existing *pro hac vice* provisions.

When a lawyer represents a party in a pending lawsuit in a jurisdiction in which the lawyer is licensed to practice law or in a pending litigation in which the lawyer appears *pro hac vice,* this provision would cover work related to the lawsuit that is performed in other states. Often, a lawyer representing a party in pending litigation must travel outside the jurisdiction where the litigation takes place in order to interview or depose witnesses, review documents, conduct negotiations, and perform other necessary work. It is generally recognized that work of this nature, insofar as it does not involve appearances in court by the out-of-state lawyer, is and should be permissible. It would be exceedingly costly and inefficient for a party to retain separate counsel in every state in which work must be performed ancillary to a pending litigation, and requiring parties to do so would not strongly serve any regulatory interest, since lawyers in litigation are generally supervised adequately by the courts before which they appear.

Additionally, this provision would cover work of a similar nature in connection with prospective litigation when there is a reasonable expectation that the lawsuit will be filed in a jurisdiction in which the lawyer is admitted to practice law or reasonably expects to be admitted *pro hac vice.* Prior to the filing of a lawsuit in a particular jurisdiction, lawyers may need to perform a variety of tasks, such as interviewing witnesses and reviewing documents, which may occur in multiple states. As in the case of pending litigation, in the context of prospective litigation it would be exceedingly costly and inefficient to require a party to retain separate counsel in every state in which such preliminary work must be done.

This provision would also cover supporting work by assisting lawyers who do not appear before the tribunal and are not themselves admitted *pro hac vice*. When a group of lawyers from an out-of-state law firm works collectively on a substantial litigation, it is understood that those lawyers who are making formal appearances in court or in depositions must seek *pro hac vice* admission, but it is customary for assisting lawyers not to do so if they serve exclusively in certain supporting roles, such as conducting legal research and drafting documents. The Commission's proposed amendment would establish that as long as the supervisory lawyers involved in the litigation are or reasonably expect to be authorized to appear in the proceeding, this type of supporting legal work by assisting lawyers is permissible, even if some of it is performed outside the states in which the assisting lawyers are licensed.

Proposed Model Rule 5.5(c)(2) would also make clear that jurisdictional restrictions do not apply when out-of-state lawyers are authorized by law or court order to appear before a tribunal or administrative agency in the jurisdiction. As the Ethics 2000 Commission provided in Comment [3] to its proposed provision on this subject,

> Lawyers not admitted to practice generally in the jurisdiction may be authorized by law or order of a tribunal or an administrative agency to appear before the tribunal or agency. Such authority may be granted pursuant to formal rules governing admission *pro hac vice* or pursuant to informal practice of the tribunal or agency.

To avoid confusion, the proposed Rule would incorporate the substance of this Comment.

Proposed Model Rule 5.5(c)(3) would allow a lawyer to provide services on a temporary basis in a jurisdiction in which the lawyer is not licensed to practice law in connection with the representation of clients in pending or anticipated arbitrations, mediations or other alternative dispute resolution ("ADR") proceedings, where the work arises out of or is reasonably related to the lawyer's practice in a jurisdiction in which the lawyer is admitted to practice. The provision would not apply, however, when participation in an ADR proceeding is governed by a *pro hac vice* provision.

It is generally recognized that, in the ADR context, there is often a strong justification for choosing a lawyer who is not admitted to practice law in the jurisdiction in which the proceeding takes place but who has an ongoing relationship with the client, who is admitted to practice in the jurisdiction in which the client is located, or has developed a particular knowledge or expertise that would be advantageous in providing the representation. Admission to practice law in the jurisdiction in which the proceeding takes place may be relatively unimportant, in part, because that jurisdiction may have no relation to the law governing the proceeding or to the dispute. Unlike litigation, in ADR parties may select the site of the proceeding simply on the basis of convenience. At times, as in the case of international arbitrations, a site is chosen precisely because it has no connection to either party or to the dispute. Thus, in ADR proceedings, the in-state lawyer is not ordinarily better qualified than other lawyers by virtue of greater familiarity with state law, state legal processes and state institutions. Further, as noted by the ABA Section of Litigation in its comments to the Commission, "Clients have important considerations in ADR, which include confidentiality, consistency, uniformity, costs, and convenience. After all, non-binding ADR procedures usually require client 'buy in' to succeed. Denying a client her preferred counsel could hamper early ADR efforts and impede prompt resolution of disputes." It is for these reasons that many found the *Birbrower* decision [Birbrower, Montalbano, Condon & Frank, P.C. v. Superior Court, 949 P.2d 1 (Cal. 1998)] troubling, and that the California legislature subsequently adopted a law temporarily authorizing out-of-state lawyers to represent clients in arbitration proceedings.

This proposed provision would not address the work of arbitrators, mediators and others serving in ADR proceedings in comparable non-representative roles. It is questionable whether work as an adjudicator or "neutral" in an ADR proceeding comprises the practice of law for purposes of UPL restrictions. Assuming it does, this work would typically be covered by the proposed provision, discussed below in Model Rule 5.5(c)(4), applicable to providing services that arise out of or are reasonably related to the lawyer's practice in a jurisdiction in which the lawyer is admitted to practice.

Proposed Model Rule 5.5(c)(4) would permit, on a temporary basis, transactional representation, counseling and other non-litigation work that arises out of or is reasonably related to the lawyer's practice in a jurisdiction in which the lawyer is admitted to practice. This provision would address legal services provided by the lawyer *outside* the lawyer's state of admission that are related to the lawyer's practice *in* the home state. The provision is drawn from §3(3) of the Restatement (Third) of the Law Governing Lawyers. The Commission's proposed Comment to Rule 5.5 offers guidance as to its scope and limitations, and it is anticipated that courts and other authorities would provide additional guidance.

This provision is intended, first, to cover services that are ancillary to a particular matter in the home state. For example, in order to conduct negotiations on behalf of a home state client or in connection with a home state matter, the lawyer may need to meet with the client and/or other parties to the transaction outside the lawyer's home state. A client should be able to have a single lawyer conduct all aspects of a transaction, even though doing so requires traveling to different states. It is reasonable that the lawyer be one who practices law in the client's state or in a state with a connection to the legal matter that is the subject of the representation. In such circumstances, it should be sufficient to rely on the lawyer's home state as the jurisdiction with the primary responsibility to ensure that the lawyer has the requisite character and fitness to practice law; the home state has a substantial interest in ensuring that all aspects of the lawyer's provision of legal services, wherever they occur, are conducted competently and professionally.

Second, this provision would respect preexisting and ongoing client-lawyer relationships by permitting a client to retain a lawyer to work on multiple related matters, including some having no connection to the jurisdiction in which the lawyer is licensed. Clients who have multiple or recurring legal matters in multiple jurisdictions have an interest in retaining a single lawyer or law firm to provide legal representation in all the related matters. In general, clients are better served by having a sustained relationship with a lawyer or law firm in whom the client has confidence. Through past experience, the client can gain some assurance that the lawyer performs work competently and can work more efficiently by drawing on past experience regarding the client, its business, and its objectives. In order to retain the client's business, lawyers representing clients in multiple matters have a strong incentive to work competently, and to engage other counsel to provide legal services work that they are not qualified to render.

Third, this provision would authorize legal services to be provided on a temporary basis outside the lawyer's home state by a lawyer who, through the course of regular practice in the lawyer's home state, has developed a recognized expertise in a body of law that is applicable to the client's particular matter. This could include expertise regarding nationally applicable bodies of law, such as federal, international or foreign law. A client has an interest in retaining a specialist in federal tax, securities or antitrust law, or the law of a foreign jurisdiction, regardless of where the lawyer has been admitted to practice law. This could also include expertise regarding the law of the lawyer's home state if that law governs the matter, since a client has an interest in retaining a lawyer who is admitted in the jurisdiction whose law governs the particular matter and who has experience regarding that law. The provision would, thus, bring the law into line with prevalent law practices. For example, many lawyers who specialize in federal law currently practice nationally, without regard to jurisdictional restrictions, which are unenforced. The same is true of lawyers specializing in other law that applies across state lines.

To be covered by this provision, the lawyer's contact with any particular host state would have to be temporary. As the California Supreme Court Advisory Task Force noted in its preliminary report on MJP,

> clients often request an out-of-state transactional or other nonlitigating lawyer to come temporarily to [a host state] to provide legal services on a discrete matter. In many circumstances, such conduct poses no significant threat to the public or the legal system, particularly where the attorney is representing a client located in another state [or] has a longstanding relationship with the client. . . .

When a lawyer seeks to practice law regularly in a state, to open an office for the solicitation of clients, or otherwise to establish a practice in the state, however, the state has a more substantial interest in regulating the lawyer's law practice by requiring the lawyer to gain admission to the bar. Although the line between the "temporary" practice of law and the "regular" or "established" practice of law is not a bright one, the line can become clearer over time as Rule 5.5 is interpreted by courts, disciplinary authorities, committees of the bar, and other relevant authorities.

Additionally, for this provision to apply, the lawyer's work in the host state must arise out of or be reasonably related to the lawyer's practice in the home state, so that as a matter of efficiency or for other reasons, the client's interest in retaining the lawyer should be respected. For example, if a corporate client is seeking legal advice about its environmental liability or about its employment relations in each of the twenty states in which it has plants, it is likely to be unnecessarily costly and inefficient for the client to retain twenty different lawyers. Likewise, if a corporate client is seeking to open a retail store in each of twenty states, the client may be best served by retaining a single lawyer to assist it in coordinating its efforts. On the other hand, work for an out-of-state client with whom the lawyer has no prior professional relationship and for whom the lawyer is performing no other work ordinarily will not have the requisite relationship to the lawyer's practice where the matter involves a body of law in which the lawyer does not have special expertise. In the context of determining whether work performed outside the lawyer's home state is reasonably related to the lawyer's practice in the home state, as is true in the many other legal contexts in which a "reasonableness" standard is employed, some judgment must be exercised.

Proposed Model Rule 5.5(d)(1) would permit a lawyer employed by an organizational entity (e.g., an in-house corporate lawyer or a government lawyer), admitted in another United States jurisdiction, to provide legal services in a jurisdiction in which the lawyer is not admitted, other than representations for which *pro hac vice* admission is required, on behalf of the employer, an affiliated entity (i.e., an entity controlling, controlled by, or under common control with, the lawyer's organizational employer). This proposed provision would authorize the employed lawyer to give advice to the employer-client or assist in transactions on the employer-client's behalf in jurisdictions where the lawyer does not maintain an office. This provision would not apply, however, to appearances in judicial and agency proceedings that are subject to *pro hac vice* provisions; to participate in such proceedings, out-of-state employed lawyers, like other out-of-state lawyers, would be required to seek and obtain admission *pro hac vice*.

This proposed provision reflects well-accepted contemporary law practice. Corporations and similar entities with ongoing and recurring legal issues have an interest in retaining in-house lawyers to provide legal assistance with respect to those matters, wherever they arise. In recent years, in-house corporate lawyers' work has grown increasingly national and global along with the business of corporate clients. The organization's interest in being provided legal assistance in an efficient, cost-effective and competent manner by a lawyer in whom it reposes confidence is furthered by permitting an organization to employ a lawyer to assist it with recurring matters. From a regulatory perspective, a lawyer who is employed to represent an organization on an ongoing basis poses less of a risk to the client and the public than a lawyer retained by an individual on a one-time basis, since, as the California report observed, an in-house lawyer is "under the constant scrutiny of his or her employer."

The proposed provision would allow an out-of-state lawyer to work permanently from the office of a corporate, government or other organizational employer. This is consistent with the explicit understanding in many jurisdictions. In New Jersey, for example, established practice by an employed lawyer is authorized by opinion. In other states, this practice is authorized by a court rule or statute that requires the employed lawyer to apply to the admissions authority and receive permission to practice to this limited extent. The Commission is unaware of significant regulatory concerns raised by the practice in these jurisdictions and, accordingly, recommends that ABA Model Rule 5.5 be amended to recognize this practice.

Comment [16] to Rule 5.5 clarifies that paragraph (d)(1) would not authorize representing the employer's officers or employees solely in their personal capacity. Nor would this provision authorize representation of customers of the corporate employer, or other third parties, if the lawyer is not licensed to practice law in the jurisdiction. Comment [17] to Rule 5.5 makes clear that the employed lawyer who has an office in the jurisdiction must comply with registration requirements and any other requirements that are applicable.

Proposed Model Rule 5.5(d)(2) would permit a lawyer to render legal services in a jurisdiction in which the lawyer is not licensed to practice law when authorized to do so by federal law or other law. Among other things, the proposed provision would make clear that in a jurisdiction that has adopted rules permitting established practice by foreign lawyers who serve as legal consultants, a lawyer may establish a law practice in the jurisdiction as permitted by such a rule.

Because it is axiomatic that a lawyer may perform work when authorized by federal law to do so, the Ethics 2000 Commission initially proposed relegating a provision to this effect to a Comment to Model Rule 5.5. However, the MJP Commission has been told that it is important to lawyers who perform such work that this provision be codified in black letter law, because at times they have been threatened with sanctions for violating state UPL laws. Although this qualification of jurisdictional restrictions would apparently apply to federal prosecutors and federal patent attorneys, among others, the Commission has not undertaken to identify every federal law that authorizes particular work and thereby may preempt state UPL laws. Nor has the Commission attempted to identify every state law that specifically authorizes out-of-state lawyers to render particular legal services in the state as an exception to the state's general UPL restriction.

Selected State Variations

California: See Rule 1-300 (Unauthorized Practice of Law) and State Bar Act §§6125-6127 (Unlawful Practice of Law). In addition, in 1998 California enacted a "Legal Document Assistant" statute, §§6400-6416 of the California Business & Professions Code, that permits qualified non-lawyers, upon registration with the state, to provide the following "self-help" services to unrepresented people:

> (1) Completing legal documents in a ministerial manner, selected by a person who is representing himself or herself in a legal matter, by typing or otherwise completing the documents at the person's specific direction.
>
> (2) Providing general published factual information that has been written or approved by an attorney, pertaining to legal procedures, rights or obligations to a person who is representing himself or herself in a legal matter, to assist the person in representing himself or herself. This service in and of itself, shall not require registration as a legal document assistant.
>
> (3) Making published legal documents available to a person who is representing himself or herself in a legal matter.
>
> (4) Filing and serving legal forms and documents at the specific direction of a person who is representing himself or herself in a legal matter.

Connecticut adds that a lawyer may not assist a person "who has resigned from the bar or who has been suspended, disbarred, or placed on inactive status" in activities constituting the unauthorized practice of law.

District of Columbia: D.C. Rule 5.5 is identical to ABA Model Rule 5.5. In addition, D.C. has developed one of the most detailed unauthorized practice rules in the country (D.C. Rule 49), which provides in pertinent part as follows:

> (a) *General Rule.* No person shall engage in the practice of law in the District of Columbia or in any manner hold out as authorized or competent to practice law in the District of Columbia unless enrolled as an active member of the District of Columbia Bar, except as otherwise permitted by these Rules.
>
> (b) *Definitions* . . . .
>
> (2) "Practice of Law" means the provision of professional legal advice or services where there is a client relationship of trust or reliance. One is presumed to be practicing law when engaging in any of the following conduct on behalf of another:
>
> (A) Preparing any legal document, including any deeds, mortgages, assignments, discharges, leases, trust instruments or any other instruments intended to affect interests in real or personal property, wills, codicils, instruments intended to affect the disposition of property of decedents' estates, other instruments intended to affect or secure legal rights, and contracts except routine agreements incidental to a regular course of business;
>
> (B) Preparing or expressing legal opinions;
>
> (C) Appearing or acting as an attorney in any tribunal;
>
> (D) Preparing any claims, demands or pleadings of any kind, or any written documents containing legal argument or interpretation of law, for filing in any court, administrative agency or other tribunal;
>
> (E) Providing advice or counsel as to how any of the activities described in subparagraph (A) through (D) might be done, or whether they were done, in accordance with applicable law;
>
> (F) Furnishing an attorney or attorneys, or persons, to render the services described in subparagraphs (A) through (E) above.
>
> (3) "In the District of Columbia" means conduct in, or conduct from an office or location within, the District of Columbia, where the person's presence in the District of Columbia is not of incidental or occasional duration. . . .

The rule contains exceptions for (among others): lawyers who advise the federal government; out-of-state lawyers in their first 360 days of employment by the District of Columbia; and lawyers who serve as in-house counsel for a regular employer who "does not reasonably expect that it is receiving advice from a person authorized to practice law in the District of Columbia."

Florida: Effective February 8, 2001, Florida adopted a new Rule 1-3.10 to replace its old pro hac vice rule, Rule 1-3.2(a). The new rule combines provisions formerly found in the old rule with some entirely new provisions. It provides, in part:

> *Rule 1-3.10. Appearances by Non-Florida Lawyers*
>
> (a) *Non-Florida Lawyers With Professional Business in Florida.* A practicing lawyer of another state, in good standing, may, upon association of a member of The Florida Bar, in good standing, and verified motion be permitted to practice upon such conditions as the court deems appropriate under the circumstances of the case. Such lawyer shall comply with the applicable portions of this rule and the Florida Rules of Judicial Administration.
>
> (1) *Application of Rules Regulating The Florida Bar.* Lawyers permitted to appear by this rule shall be subject to these Rules Regulating The Florida Bar while engaged in the permitted representation.
>
> (2) *General Practice Prohibited.* Non-Florida lawyers shall not be permitted to engage in a general practice before Florida courts. For purposes of this rule more than

> 3 appearances within a 365-day period in separate and unrelated representations shall be presumed to be a "general practice," provided, however, that the court shall have discretion to allow other appearances upon a showing that the appearances are not a "general practice" or that denial will work a substantial hardship on the client.
>
> (3) *Effect of Professional Discipline or Contempt.* Non-Florida lawyers who have been disciplined or held in contempt by reason of misconduct committed while engaged in representation that is permitted by this rule shall thereafter be denied admission under this rule and the applicable provisions of the Florida Rules of Judicial Administration. . . .

Supreme Court Rule 3-6.1 expressly permits lawyers and law firms to employ suspended, disbarred, or resigned attorneys on the same terms as other lay persons, provided the employing lawyer or firm gives notice and reports periodically to the Bar's staff counsel, and provided that "[n]o suspended, resigned, or disbarred attorney shall have direct contact with any client or receive, disburse, or otherwise handle trust funds or property."

Rule 4-7.11, which governs lawyer referral services, prohibits a Florida lawyer from accepting referrals unless a service "refers clients only to persons lawfully permitted to practice law in Florida when the services to be rendered constitute the practice of law in Florida."

Chapter 17 of the Rules Regulating the Florida Bar, entitled "Authorized House Counsel Rule," authorizes attorneys licensed to practice in jurisdictions other than Florida to be "permitted to undertake said activities in Florida while exclusively employed by a business organization without the requirement of taking the bar examination."

Georgia: In the rules effective January 1, 2001, Georgia adopted the pre-2002 version of ABA Model Rule 5.5 and its Comment essentially verbatim.

Maryland reinforces Rule 5.5 with the following variation on Rule 8.5 that reaches lawyers who are not admitted to practice in Maryland:

> (b) A lawyer not admitted by the Court of Appeals to practice in this State is subject to the disciplinary authority of this State for conduct that constitutes a violation of these Rules and that:
>
> (1) involves the practice of law in this State by that lawyer. . . .

Missouri: Rule 5.5(c) prohibits the practice of law by a lawyer reported for failure to comply with Missouri Continuing Legal Education requirements.

Missouri Supreme Court Rule 8.105 authorizes limited admission to the bar for in-house counsel. Rule 8.105(a) provides as follows:

> A lawyer admitted to the practice of law in another state or territory of the United States may receive a limited license to practice law in this state when the lawyer is employed in Missouri as a lawyer exclusively for: a corporation, its subsidiaries or affiliates; an association; a business; or a governmental entity whose lawful business consists of activities other than the practice of law or the provision of legal services.

Attorneys operating under the limited license may not perform legal work for anyone other than their employer unless they are granted *pro hac vice* status. A limited license is valid for five years but is automatically terminated if the lawyer's employment terminates before that.

Missouri Supreme Court Rule 9.05 permits foreign (i.e., non-American) lawyers to work in Missouri as "foreign legal consultants." This rule addressed concerns of the state's largest law firm, which has offices in Saudi Arabia, Germany, England, and other foreign countries.

Missouri Supreme Court Rule 13.06 allows a full-time law teacher at a Missouri law school to supervise clinical students without being admitted to the Missouri bar if the teacher: (1) provides legal services only in connection with the law school's clinical program; (2) receives compensation only from the law school; (3) is a member in good standing of the bar of another American jurisdiction; (4) has not been denied admission to a bar or been disciplined for professional misconduct within the last five years; and (5) certifies in writing that he or she has read and is familiar with the Missouri Rules of Professional Conduct.

New Jersey expressly permits nonprofit corporations to practice law, and permits attorneys to assist them, provided certain conditions are met. Supreme Court Rule 1:21-1(d) provides:

> (d) *Legal Services Organizations.* Nonprofit organizations incorporated in this or any other state for the purpose of providing legal services to the poor or functioning as a public interest law firm, and other federally tax exempt legal services organizations or trusts, such as those defined by 26 U.S.C.A. 120(b) and 501(c)(20), which provide legal services to a defined and limited class of clients, may practice law in their own names through staff attorneys who are members of the bar of the State of New Jersey, provided that: (1) the legal work serves the intended beneficiaries of the organizational purpose, (2) the staff attorney responsible for the matter signs all papers prepared by the organization, and (3) the relationship between staff attorney and client meets the attorney's professional responsibilities to the client and is not subject to interference, control, or direction by the organization's board or employees except for a supervising attorney who is a member of the New Jersey bar.

New Jersey Rule 1:21-1 requires that every attorney practicing law in New Jersey maintain "a bona fide office for the practice of law" in New Jersey no matter where the attorney is domiciled. The rule continues as follows:

> A bona fide office is more than a maildrop, a summer home that is unattended during a substantial portion of the year, an answering service unrelated to a place where business is conducted or a place where an on-site agent of the attorney receives and transmits messages only. For the purpose of this section, a bona fide office is a place where clients are met, files are kept, the telephone is answered, mail is received and the attorney or a responsible person acting on the attorney's behalf can be reached in person and by telephone during normal business hours to answer questions posed by the courts, clients or adversaries and to ensure that competent advice from the attorney can be obtained within a reasonable period of time. An attorney who practices law in this state and fails to maintain a bona fide office in this State shall be deemed to be in violation of RPC 5.5(a). . . .

New York: Compare ABA Model Rule 5.5 to New York's DR 3-101. New York defines the unauthorized practice of law by statute in §§478 and 484 of the New York Judiciary Law (reprinted below in our Selected Provisions of the New York Judiciary Law). In addition, New York Judiciary Law §495 generally prohibits corporations from practicing law, but exempts "non-profit organizations whether incorporated or unincorporated . . . which furnish legal services as an incidental activity in furtherance of their primary purpose" and "organizations which have as their primary purpose the furnishing of legal services to indigent persons."

North Carolina adds the following two new paragraphs to Rule 5.5:

> (c) A lawyer or law firm shall not employ a disbarred or suspended lawyer as a law clerk or legal assistant if that individual was associated with such lawyer or law firm at any time on or after the date of the acts which resulted in disbarment or suspension through and including the effective date of disbarment or suspension.

(d) A lawyer or law firm employing a disbarred or suspended lawyer as a law clerk or legal assistant shall not represent any client represented by the disbarred or suspended lawyer or by any lawyer with whom the disbarred or suspended lawyer practiced during the period on or after the date of the acts which resulted in disbarment or suspension through and including the effective date of the disbarment or suspension.

In addition, under 27 NCAC 1E, §.0200, no law firm with offices in both North Carolina and one or more other jurisdictions "may do business in North Carolina without first obtaining a certificate of registration from the North Carolina State Bar" unless "all attorneys associated with the law firm . . . or any law firm or professional organization that is in partnership with said law firm . . . are licensed to practice law in North Carolina."

Virginia: Rule 5.5 adds language dealing with the responsibilities of the law firm that employs a lawyer who has been suspended or disbarred for professional misconduct.

Washington: In 1983, Washington adopted Admission to Practice Rule 12, which establishes a "Limited Practice Board" and authorizes qualified nonlawyers to "select, prepare and complete legal documents" incident to real estate closings and personal property transactions. The central provision of Rule 12 provides as follows:

(d) Scope of Practice Authorized by Limited Practice Rule

[A] person certified as a closing officer under this rule may select, prepare and complete documents in a form previously approved by the Board for use in closing a loan, extension of credit, sale or other transfer of real or personal property. Such documents shall be limited to deeds, promissory notes, guaranties, deeds of trust, reconveyances, mortgages, satisfactions, security agreements, releases, Uniform Commercial Code documents, assignments, contracts, real estate excise tax affidavits, and bills of sale. Other documents may be from time to time approved by the Board.

Certified closing officers may render services authorized by Rule 12 only if they abide by stringent conditions. Rule 12 also establishes a licensing procedure, an examination, a continuing education requirement, a grievance procedure, and other administrative features for certified closing officers. A separate Rule 12.1 establishes a strict escrow account requirement for certified closing officers.

Effective September 1, 2001, after years of study, the Washington Supreme Court adopted new General Rule 24, which provides, in part, as follows:

General Rule 24. Definition of the Practice of Law

(a) *General Definition.* The practice of law is the application of legal principles and judgment with regard to the circumstances or objectives of another entity or person(s) which require the knowledge and skill of a person trained in the law. This includes but is not limited to:

(1) Giving advice or counsel to others as to their legal rights or the legal rights or responsibilities of others for fees or other consideration.

(2) Selection, drafting, or completion of legal documents or agreements which affect the legal rights of an entity or person(s).

(3) Representation of another entity or person(s) in a court, or in a formal administrative adjudicative proceeding or other formal dispute resolution

process or in an administrative adjudicative proceeding in which legal pleadings are filed or a record is established as the basis for judicial review.

(4) Negotiation of legal rights or responsibilities on behalf of another entity or person(s).

(b) *Exceptions and Exclusions.* Whether or not they constitute the practice of law, the following are permitted:

(1) Practicing law authorized by a limited license to practice pursuant to Admission to Practice Rules 8 (special admission for: a particular purpose or action; indigent representation; educational purposes; emeritus membership; house counsel), 9 (legal interns), 12 (limited practice for closing officers), or 14 (limited practice for foreign law consultants).

(2) Serving as a court house facilitator pursuant to court rule.

(3) Acting as a lay representative authorized by administrative agencies or tribunals.

(4) Serving in a neutral capacity as a mediator, arbitrator, conciliator, or facilitator.

(5) Participation in labor negotiations, arbitrations or conciliations arising under collective bargaining rights or agreements.

(6) Providing assistance to another to complete a form provided by a court for protection under RCW chapters 10.14 (harassment) or 26.50 (domestic violence prevention) when no fee is charged to do so.

(7) Acting as a legislative lobbyist.

(8) Sale of legal forms in any format.

(9) Activities which are preempted by Federal law.

(10) Such other activities that the Supreme Court has determined by published opinion do not constitute the unlicensed or unauthorized practice of law or that have been permitted under a regulatory system established by the Supreme Court.

(c) *Nonlawyer Assistants.* Nothing in this rule shall affect the ability of nonlawyer assistants to act under the supervision of a lawyer in compliance with Rule 5.3 of the Rules of Professional Conduct.

(d) *General Information.* Nothing in this rule shall affect the ability of a person or entity to provide information of a general nature about the law and legal procedures to members of the public. . . .

Rule 24 was accompanied by a new General Rule 25 creating a "Practice of Law Board," which has power to issue advisory opinions, investigate the unauthorized practice of law and recommend to the Supreme Court "that non-lawyers be authorized to engage in certain defined activities that otherwise constitute the practice of law."

Related Materials

ABA Commission on Multidisciplinary Practice. In 1998, the ABA appointed a Commission on Multidisciplinary Practice ("MDP Commission") to study and report on the scope and manner of efforts by accounting firms and other nonlawyer professional service firms to provide legal services to the public. Currently, lawyers who provide legal services to the public through nonlawyer professional service firms are violating Rule 5.5(b) by assisting nonlawyers in "the performance of activity that constitutes the unauthorized practice of law." In June of 1999, the MDP Commission issued a report recommending that non-law entities be permitted to offer legal services to the public through licensed lawyers under certain conditions, but the ABA rejected the MDP Commission's recommendations and instead adopted a resolution not to change the ABA Model Rules to permit multidisciplinary practice "unless and until additional study demonstrates that such changes will further the public interest without sacrificing or compromising lawyer independence and the legal profession's tradition of loyalty to clients." Nevertheless, the MDP Commission continued its work and in July of 2000 issued another report to the House of Delegates, this time with more modest proposals. However, at the ABA's July 2000 Annual Meeting, the House of Delegates voted 314-106 to reject the MDP Commission's report and instead adopted a recommendation that the ABA continue to prohibit partnerships with non-lawyers and non-lawyer equity interests in law firms. In the Special Section of our 2001 edition, we reprinted the MDP Commission's July 2000 report and the ABA's July 2000 recommendation ("Resolution 10F"). For further information, visit the web site of the ABA Center for Professional Responsibility at www.abanet.org/cpr/multicom.html.

ABA Commission on Multijurisdictional Practice (MJP Commission): In July of 2000, in response to professional concerns about the regulation of "multijurisdictional" law practice (meaning the practice of law by lawyers in jurisdictions where they are not admitted), the ABA appointed a Commission on Multijurisdictional Practice (commonly called the "MJP Commission"). The MJP Commission's chairperson is attorney Wayne Positan of New Jersey, and its Reporter is Professor Bruce Green of Fordham Law School. (Professor Stephen Gillers, a co-author of this book, is one of 12 members of the Commission.) The ABA instructed the MJP Commission to undertake four specific responsibilities:

(1) "Research, study and report on the application of current ethics and bar admission rules to the multijurisdictional practice of law";
(2) "analyze the impact of those rules on the practice of in-house counsel, transactional lawyers, litigators and arbitrators and on lawyers and law firms maintaining offices and practicing in multiple state and federal jurisdictions";
(3) "make policy recommendations to govern the multijurisdictional practice of law that serve the public interest and take any other actions as may be necessary to carry out its jurisdictional mandate"; and
(4) "review international issues related to multijurisdictional practice in the United States."

The MJP Commission actively solicited public comments, held public hearings around the country, and issued an Interim Report in November 2001. In May 2002, after reviewing public comments on the Interim Report, the MJP Commission issued its Final Report, which contained nine specific recommendations. At the ABA's August 2002 Annual Meeting, the House of Delegates amended Rule 5.5 (and Rule 8.5) exactly as proposed by the MJP Commission. The House of Delegates also approved all of the Commission's remaining recommendations, which are summarized below in excerpts from the MJP Commission's Final Report. In fact, so few speakers opposed the MJP Commission's proposals that the House of Delegates approved all but one of them by voice vote. The only proposal generating enough controversy to require counting was the proposed ABA Model Rule for Admission on Motion (meaning admission without taking the bar exam, based on years of practice elsewhere), which passed by a vote of 257-150.

The full MJP Commission Report, which runs more than 60 pages, is available at www.abanet.org/cpr (click on "Commission on Multijurisdictional Practice" and look for "REVISED FINAL REPORT, AS ADOPTED AUGUST 12, 2002"). We reprint here excerpts (with footnotes omitted) from the Final Report's "Introduction and Overview" and its "Summary of Recommendations." Additional excerpts elaborating on the recommendation to amend Rules 5.5 and 8.5 may be found in the Legislative History following those rules.

*Excerpts from MJP Commission's Final Report**

Introduction and Overview

. . . The predicate for this national study undertaken by the American Bar Association was the dynamic change and evolution in nature and scope of legal practice during the past century, facilitated by a transformation in communications, transportation and technology.

In the early twentieth century, states adopted "unauthorized practice of law" (UPL) provisions that apply equally to lawyers licensed in other states and to nonlawyers. These laws prohibit lawyers from engaging in the practice of law except in states in which they are licensed or otherwise authorized to practice law. UPL restrictions have long been qualified by *pro hac vice* provisions, which allow courts or administrative agencies to authorize an out-of-state lawyer to represent a client in a particular case before the tribunal. In recent years, some jurisdictions have adopted provisions authorizing out-of-state lawyers to perform other legal work in the jurisdiction.

Jurisdictional restrictions on law practice were not historically a matter of concern, because most clients' legal matters were confined to a single state and a lawyer's familiarity with that state's law was a qualification of particular importance. However, the wisdom of the application of UPL laws to licensed lawyers has been questioned repeatedly since the 1960s in light of the changing nature of clients' legal needs and the changing nature of law practice. Both the law and the transactions in which lawyers assist clients have increased in complexity, requiring a growing number of lawyers to concentrate in particular areas of practice rather than being generalists in state law. Often, the most significant qualification to render assistance in a legal matter is not knowledge of any given state's law, but knowledge of federal or international law or familiarity with a particular type of business or personal transaction or legal proceeding. Additionally, modern transportation and communications technology have enabled clients to travel easily and transact business throughout the country, and even internationally. Because of this globalization of business and finance, clients sometimes now need lawyers to assist them in transactions in multiple jurisdictions (state and national) or to advise them about multiple jurisdictions' laws.

Although client needs and legal practices have evolved, lawyer regulation has not yet responded effectively to that evolution. As the work of lawyers has become more varied, specialized and national in scope, it has become increasingly uncertain when a lawyer's work (other than as a trial

*Committee Reports do not represent official policy of the ABA. They are for information only, and the opinions are those of the authors of the Report.

lawyer in court) implicates the UPL law of a jurisdiction in which the lawyer is not licensed. Lawyers recognize that the geographic scope of a lawyer's practice must be adequate to enable the lawyer to serve the legal needs of clients in a national and global economy. They have expressed concern that if UPL restrictions are applied literally to United States lawyers who perform any legal work outside the jurisdictions in which they are admitted to practice, the laws will impede lawyers' ability to meet their clients' multistate and interstate legal needs efficiently and effectively.

This concern was sharpened by the California Supreme Court decision, *Birbrower, Montalbano, Condon & Frank, P.C. v. Superior Court of Santa Clara County*, 949 P.2d 1 (Cal. 1998), which held that lawyers not licensed to practice law in California violated California's misdemeanor UPL provision when they assisted a California corporate client in connection with an impending California arbitration under California law, and were therefore barred from recovering fees under a written fee agreement for services the lawyers rendered while they were physically or "virtually" in California. Although the state law was subsequently and temporarily amended to allow out-of-state lawyers to obtain permission to participate in certain California arbitrations, concerns have persisted.

In response to professional concerns about the regulation of multijurisdictional law practice, ABA President Martha Barnett appointed this Commission in July 2000. . . .

Summary of Recommendations

"Multijurisdictional practice" ("MJP") describes the legal work of a lawyer in a jurisdiction in which the lawyer is not admitted to practice law. As this report discusses, a wide variety of practices falling within this rubric have been called to the attention of the MJP Commission. The guiding principle that informs the Commission's recommendations is simple to state: we searched for the proper balance between the interests of a state in protecting its residents and justice system, on the one hand; and the interests of clients in a national and international economy in the ability to employ or retain counsel of choice efficiently and economically. A key word here is "balance." Our challenges did not lend themselves to mathematical solutions. Rather, accommodating our state-based system of bar admission, which we fully support, with the realities of modern life and our tradition of respect for client choice required the exercise of informed judgment. Our judgment was informed not only by the diverse experience and perspectives of the members of the Commission and its liaisons, but also by the wealth of testimony, written and spoken, of which we have been the most fortunate beneficiary.

The Commission's recommendations are, in summary, as follows:

1. The ABA affirm its support for the principle of state judicial regulation of the practice of law.

2. The ABA re-title Rule 5.5 of the Model Rules of Professional Conduct as "Unauthorized Practice of Law; Multijurisdictional Practice of Law."

The ABA amend Rule 5.5(a) of the ABA *Model Rules of Professional Conduct* to provide that a lawyer may not practice law in a jurisdiction, or assist another in doing so, in violation of the regulations of the legal profession in that jurisdiction.

The ABA adopt proposed Rule 5.5(b) to prohibit a lawyer from establishing an office or other systematic and continuous presence in a jurisdiction, unless permitted to do so by law, or another provision of Rule 5.5; or holding out to the public or otherwise representing that the lawyer is admitted to practice law in a jurisdiction in which the lawyer is not admitted.

The ABA adopt proposed Rule 5.5(c) to identify circumstances in which a lawyer who is admitted in a United States jurisdiction, and not disbarred or suspended from practice in any jurisdiction, may practice law on a temporary basis in another jurisdiction. These would include:

> Work on a temporary basis in association with a lawyer admitted to practice law in the jurisdiction, who actively participates in the representation;
>
> Services ancillary to pending or prospective litigation or administrative agency proceedings in a state where the lawyer is admitted or expects to be admitted *pro hac vice* or is otherwise authorized to appear;
>
> Representation of clients in, or ancillary to, an alternative dispute resolution ("ADR") setting, such as arbitration or mediation; and
>
> Non-litigation work that arises out of or is reasonably related to the lawyer's practice in a jurisdiction in which the lawyer is admitted to practice.

The ABA adopt proposed Rule 5.5(d) to identify multijurisdictional practice standards relating to (i) legal services by a lawyer who is an employee of a client and (ii) legal services that the lawyer is authorized by federal or other law to render in a jurisdiction in which the lawyer is not licensed to practice law.

3. The ABA amend Rule 8.5 of the ABA *Model Rules of Professional Conduct* in order to clarify the authority of a jurisdiction to discipline lawyers licensed in another jurisdiction who practice law within their jurisdiction pursuant to the provisions of Rule 5.5 or other law.

4. The ABA amend Rules 6 and 22 of the ABA *Model Rules for Lawyer Disciplinary Enforcement* to promote effective disciplinary enforcement with respect to lawyers who engage in the multijurisdictional practice of law and to renew efforts to encourage states to adopt Rule 22, which provides for reciprocal discipline.

5. The ABA should encourage the use of the National Lawyer Regulatory Data Bank to promote interstate disciplinary enforcement mechanisms and urge jurisdictions to adopt the International Standard Lawyer Numbering System®. The ABA should also urge jurisdictions to require lawyers to report to the lawyer regulatory agency in the jurisdiction in which they are licensed, all other jurisdictions in which they are licensed and any status changes in those other jurisdictions.

6. The ABA adopt the proposed *Model Rule on Pro Hac Vice Admission* to govern the admission of lawyers to practice law before courts and administrative agencies *pro hac vice* in jurisdictions in which the lawyer is not admitted to practice.

7. With regard to the establishment of a law practice on a permanent basis in a jurisdiction in which a lawyer is not admitted to practice, the ABA adopt the proposed *Model Rule on Admission by Motion* to facilitate the licensing of the lawyer, if the lawyer is admitted to practice in another United States jurisdiction, has been engaged in the active practice of law for a significant period of time and is in good standing in all jurisdictions where admitted.

8. With regard to lawyers admitted to practice only in non-United States jurisdictions, the ABA encourage United States jurisdictions to adopt the ABA *Model Rule for the Licensing of Legal Consultants* or to conform their already existing rule to the Model Rule.

9. With regard to lawyers who seek to provide legal services in the United States and are admitted to practice law only in non-United States jurisdictions, the ABA adopt the proposed *Model Rule on Temporary Practice by Foreign Lawyers* to identify circumstances where it is not the unauthorized practice of law for a lawyer admitted in a non-United States jurisdiction to provide legal services on a temporary basis for a client in a United States jurisdiction.

ABA Commission on Non-Lawyer Practice: In 1992, the American Bar Association appointed a 17-member Commission on Non-Lawyer Practice to examine all aspects of work done by non-lawyers and to make recommendations in a formal report. The Commission was composed of both lawyers and non-lawyers (including representatives from two national paralegal organizations) and held hearings in nine cities around the country, taking live testimony from 337 witnesses and reviewing over 12,000 pages of additional written statements, studies, statutes, reports, and scholarly articles. The Commission issued a final report in 1995, but the ABA Board of Governors did not reappoint the Commission on Non-lawyer Practice, which therefore automatically ceased to exist on August 31, 1995. The report was never transmitted to the ABA House of Delegates for approval.

ABA Model Guidelines for the Utilization of Legal Assistant Services: In August of 1991, the ABA House of Delegates adopted Model Guidelines for the Utilization of Legal Assistant Services. These Model Guidelines drew upon similar guidelines already existing or proposed in 17 states. The most interesting guidelines relating to the unauthorized practice of law provide as follows:

> *Guideline 2:* Provided the lawyer maintains responsibility for the work product, a lawyer may delegate to a legal assistant any task normally performed by a lawyer except those tasks proscribed to one not licensed as a lawyer by statute, court rule, [etc.].
>
> *Guideline 3:* A lawyer may not delegate to a legal assistant:
>
> (a) Responsibility for establishing an attorney-client relationship.
>
> (b) Responsibility for establishing the amount of a fee to be charged for a legal service.
>
> (c) Responsibility for a legal opinion rendered to a client.
>
> *Guideline 4:* It is the lawyer's responsibility to take reasonable measures to ensure that clients, courts, and other lawyers are aware that a legal assistant, whose services are utilized by the lawyer in performing legal services, is not licensed to practice law.

ABA Model Rule for the Licensing of Foreign Legal Consultants: At its August 1993 Annual Meeting, the ABA House of Delegates approved a Model Rule for the Licensing of Foreign Legal Consultants. The rule was proposed by the ABA's Section of International Law and Practice and was motivated by concern that foreign countries may not allow American lawyers to practice abroad if foreign lawyers cannot practice in America. The rule, which is modeled on similar rules already in effect in New York and Washington, D.C., allows a state to license a "legal consultant" without requiring an examination if the applicant has been a member in good standing of a foreign bar for five of the past seven years. Legal consultants are not full-fledged lawyers; the rule limits the scope of their practice. However, they are subject to all disciplinary rules.

ABA Model Rule on Admission by Motion: At its August 2002 Annual Meeting, by a vote of 257-150, the ABA adopted a Model Rule on Admission by Motion. The rule was part of the package proposed by the ABA Commission on Multijurisdictional Practice. About half the states already permit admission on motion, meaning that lawyers admitted in one jurisdiction may gain admission in another jurisdiction without taking the new jurisdiction's bar examination provided they meet certain criteria. The ABA Model Rule on Admission by Motion provides as follows:

> 1. An applicant who meets the requirements of (a) through (h) of this Rule may, upon motion, be admitted to the practice of law in this jurisdiction.
>
> The applicant shall:
>
> (a) have been admitted to practice law in another state, territory, or the District of Columbia;
>
> (b) hold a first professional degree in law (J.D. or LL.B.) from a law school approved by the Council of the Section of Legal Education and Admission to the Bar of the American Bar Association at the time the graduate matriculated;
>
> (c) have been primarily engaged in the active practice of law in one or more states, territories or the District of Columbia for five of the seven years immediately preceding the date upon which the application is filed;
>
> (d) submit evidence of a passing score on the Multistate Professional Responsibility Examination as it is established in this jurisdiction;
>
> (e) establish that the applicant is currently a member in good standing in all jurisdictions where admitted;
>
> (f) establish that the applicant is not currently subject to lawyer discipline or the subject of a pending disciplinary matter in any other jurisdiction;
>
> (g) establish that the applicant possesses the character and fitness to practice law in this jurisdiction; and
>
> (h) designate the Clerk of the jurisdiction's highest court for service of process.
>
> 2. For the purposes of this rule, the "active practice of law" shall include the following activities, if performed in a jurisdiction in which the applicant is admitted, or if performed in a jurisdiction that affirmatively permits such activity by a lawyer not admitted to practice; however, in no event shall activities listed under (2)(e) and (f) that were performed in advance of bar admission in the jurisdiction to which application is being made be accepted toward the durational requirement:
>
> (a) Representation of one or more clients in the private practice of law;
>
> (b) Service as a lawyer with a local, state, or federal agency, including military service;
>
> (c) Teaching law at a law school approved by the Council of the Section of Legal Education and Admissions to the Bar of the American Bar Association;
>
> (d) Service as a judge in a federal, state, territorial or local court of record;
>
> (e) Service as a judicial law clerk; or
>
> (f) Service as corporate counsel.
>
> 3. For the purposes of this Rule, the active practice of law shall not include work that, as undertaken, constituted the unauthorized practice of law in the jurisdiction in which it was performed or in the jurisdiction in which the clients receiving the unauthorized services were located.
>
> 4. An applicant who has failed a bar examination administered in this jurisdiction within five years of the date of filing an application under this rule shall not be eligible for admission on motion.

ABA Model Rule on Pro Hac Vice Admission: At its August 2002 Annual Meeting, the ABA adopted a lengthy and detailed Model Rule on Pro Hac Vice Admission. The rule was part of the package proposed by the ABA Commission on Multijurisdictional Practice because the ABA Section of Litigation reported to the MJP Commission that a more uniform pro hac vice procedure "would be strongly preferable to the disparate requirements now in place." The ABA Section of Tort and Insurance Practice and the International Association of Defense Counsel (IADC) expressed similar views and worked with the Section of Litigation to develop the proposed Model Rule on Pro Hac Vice Admission. The full rule can be found at www.abanet.org/cpr (click on "Commission on Multijurisdictional Practice," then look for "Report 201F"). For more information, see the entry below entitled "Pro Hac Vice Admission" in these Related Materials.

ABA Model Rules for Advisory Opinions on Unauthorized Practice of Law: In 1984, the ABA House of Delegates adopted Model Rules for Advisory Opinions on Unauthorized Practice of Law, which set forth model procedures for committees and courts to follow in issuing opinions on unauthorized practice. These rules, according to their Preamble, recognize the need "to prevent harm to the public from the unauthorized practice of law and to make public a clear and timely understanding of what is the unauthorized practice of law."

ABA Resolution on Unauthorized Practice: At its 1999 Annual Meeting, by a vote of 305-118, the ABA House of Delegates passed a resolution sponsored by the Ohio State Bar Association urging every jurisdiction to "establish and implement effective procedures for the discovery and investigation of any apparent violation of its laws prohibiting the unauthorized practice of law and to pursue active enforcement of those laws." The resolution also requires the ABA to "establish and support a mechanism for identifying and reporting to state, local, and territorial bar associations and designated authorities instances of persons or organizations engaging in the unauthorized practice of law in more than one jurisdiction." The report submitted in support of the resolution noted that statutes prohibiting the unauthorized practice of law, which are in force in virtually every state, have not been enforced aggressively or effectively. The report added: "It is becoming more apparent that unlicensed and unsupervised persons are peddling legal services to the public and that adequate protection to the public is not being provided."

European Community Law on Multijurisdictional Practice: The fifteen member states of the European Community ("EC") are much more permissive of cross border practice than are American jurisdictions. This difference is especially notable because the members of the EC are different nations, not different states within a single nation. In an online interview with www.CrossingtheBar.com, Professor Laurel Terry, of Penn State Dickinson School of Law, was asked to explain the system in the EC. Here is the question and her answer.*

Question: There appears to be a fair amount of misinformation circulating about what lawyers in Europe are able to do by way of multijurisdictional practice. Could you explain the general scheme of things there for the benefit of U.S. lawyers unfamiliar with the licensing of lawyers there?

 For the full text of Professor Terry's interview, visit www.CrossingtheBar.com.

Answer: I will respond to your question first and thereafter explain why I have put the terms "European Community" and "EC" in quotation marks in my answer. The "European Community" or "EC" has adopted three laws or "directives" that are relevant to your question asking "what lawyers in Europe are able to do by way of multi-jurisdictional practice." The first directive is over twenty years old and governs the temporary provision of legal services in an EC Member State by EC lawyers from a different Member State. The name of this directive is "COUNCIL DIRECTIVE of 22 March 1977 to facilitate the effective exercise by lawyers of freedom to provide services (77/249/EEC), O.J. L. 78/17(1977)" [hereafter Lawyers' Services Directive 77/249].

The Lawyers' Services Directive 77/249 authorizes lawyers from one EC country to offer temporary legal services in another EC country. In effect, a law license from one EC country is given "full faith and credit" in the second country. Or, to state it differently, the EC has adopted a system of "mutual recognition", in which each EC country agrees to recognize the qualifications of lawyers from another EC country. ("Mutual recognition" requirements often are viewed as the opposite of "harmonization" requirements, in which each country must adopt identical or "harmonized" provisions.)

One of the key points of the Lawyers' Services Directive 77/249 is that there is no automatic registration requirement, although the Host State may ask the "transient" lawyer to establish his or her qualifications as a lawyer. The directive requires the transient lawyer to use the professional title used in the Home State [original] jurisdiction when the lawyer temporarily practices in the Host State. The directive also specifies the rules of conduct that apply to the transient lawyer. The directive permits the Member State to place limitations on the transient lawyer's scope of practice. For example, an EC Member State may exclude the transient lawyer from preparing formal documents to administer estates of deceased persons or documents creating or transferring interests in land. The Member State may also require the transient lawyer to be introduced to the presiding judge or bar president and require a lawyer involved in litigation to work in conjunction with a lawyer who practices before the judicial authority in question. For a more detailed discussion of this directive, see Roger J. Goebel, Lawyers in the European Community: Progress Towards Community-Wide Rights of Practice, 15 Fordham Int'l L. J. 556, 576-585 (1991-1992).

The second major law that regulates multijurisdictional practice by European lawyers is entitled "COUNCIL DIRECTIVE of 21 December 1988 on a general system for the recognition of higher-education diplomas awarded on completion of professional education and training of at least three years' duration (89/48/EEC), O.J.L. 19/16 (1989)" [hereafter "Diplomas Directive"]. Unlike the Lawyers Services Directive 77/249, which applies to the temporary provision of legal services in another Member State, the Diplomas Directive was intended to cover permanent establishment. Furthermore, the Diplomas Directive is not limited to the legal profession. The Diplomas Directive requires mutual recognition by EC Member States of higher education diplomas and regulated professional licenses for those professions which are not subject to a separate directive.

Under the Diplomas Directive, the Host State can require that the transient professional either take an aptitude test or complete an adaptation period of not more than three years. For the legal profession, it is the Host State, not the individual, who has the right to determine whether to require an adaptation period or aptitude test. All EC jurisdictions except Denmark have opted to require an aptitude test rather than an adaptation period. Information about these requirements and the contents of the aptitude tests are available from an excellent website maintained by Professor Julian Lonbay of the University of Birmingham. See http://www.iel.bham.ac.uk/ (and select "Lawyers" from the left-hand menu).

The third important EC law governing lawyers addresses the topic of permanent establishment of lawyers. This law is relatively new and has not yet been implemented in all EC Member States. The law is entitled "Directive 98/5/EC of the European Parliament and of the Council of 16 February 1998 to facilitate practice of the profession of lawyer on a permanent basis in a Member State other than that in which the qualification was obtained, O.J.L. 77/36 (1998)" [hereafter "Lawyers' Establishment Directive 98/5"].

Because the Lawyers' Establishment Directive specifically addresses the topic of establishment of lawyers, one might expect that the Diplomas Directive would no longer be relevant to the issue of multijurisdictional practice by European lawyers. The Diplomas Directive remains relevant, however, because the Lawyers' Establishment Directive incorporates by reference some of the provisions of the Diplomas Directive and allows lawyers to become established using the methods specified in the Diplomas Directive.

It is beyond the scope of this interview to completely describe the Lawyers' Establishment Directive, which has been discussed in several law review articles. See, e.g., Roger J. Goebel, The Liberalization of Interstate Legal Practice in the European Union: Lessons for the United States?, 34 Int'l L. 307 (2000); see also Laurel S. Terry, A Case Study of the Hybrid Model For Facilitating Cross-Border Legal Practice: The Agreement Between the American Bar Association and the Brussels Bars, 21 Fordham Int'l L.J. 1382 (1998) (comparing the EC scheme of multijurisdictional practice with the other major global MJP schemes). In a nutshell, however, the Lawyers' Establishment Directive permits a lawyer from one EC Member State to practice law on a permanent basis in another EC Member State. In other words, each EC Member State will "recognize" the qualifications obtained in another EC Member State and give "full faith and credit" to those qualifications.

The Lawyers' Establishment Directive requires the transient lawyer to register with the Host State. The directive specifies the rules of conduct that apply in different situations and makes the transient lawyer subject to discipline in the Host State. Initially, the transient lawyer practices under the lawyer's Home State title.

Similar to the Lawyers' Services Directive, the Lawyers' Establishment Directive places some limits on the transient lawyer's scope of practice. For example, the Host State may elect to exclude the transient lawyer from preparing formal documents to administer estates of deceased persons or documents creating or transferring interests in land. The Member State may also require a lawyer involved in litigation to work in conjunction with a lawyer who practices before the judicial authority in question. These "scope of practice" limitations are relatively narrow, however. Except for the specified limitations, the transient lawyer may practice Home State law, EC law, international law, and Host State law.

Interestingly, the Lawyers' Establishment Directive provides two different methods by which the transient lawyer may become "integrated" into the Host State profession, with the ability to thereafter use the Host State's title of lawyer. First, the transient lawyer may become integrated under the methods specified in the Diplomas Directive. Alternatively, the transient lawyer may become integrated into the Host State's profession if the transient lawyer has "effectively and regularly pursued for a period of at least three years an activity in the host Member State in the law of that State including Community law. . . ." In my view, this directive permits a French lawyer to move to Germany, practice EC law for three years, and thereafter become a full-fledged German Rechtsanwalt, with the right to use the title of Rechtsanwalt. The French lawyer can do this without an examination or special requirements, other than registration with the proper German authorities. In sum, the multijurisdictional practice laws that apply to European lawyers are significantly more liberal than the multijurisdictional provisions found in many U.S. states. The EC temporary practice MJP rules have been in place for over twenty years, with very little history of problems. The permanent practice rules have been in place a much shorter time and do not yet have a significant track record.

The EC's multijurisdictional practice scheme is constitutionally required because of treaty provisions guaranteeing freedom of mobility. Despite this constitutional mandate, I would note that in my view, it should have been much more difficult to develop a European multijurisdictional practice system than a U.S. multijurisdictional practice system. Although it is true that there are only fifteen EC Member States, in many of these states, lawyers are licensed on a local basis, rather than a national basis. Therefore, the EC, like the US, had to cope with a large number of different regulators. In addition, there are significant language barriers involved in developing a European multijurisdictional practice system. An added difficulty is the fact that some EC Member States have a civil law system and other Member States have a common law system. Moreover, there are some significant differences even among Member States that have a civil law system.

In short, the EC overcame significant practical barriers when it developed its multijurisdictional practice rules for European lawyers.

At this point, I would like to explain why I initially put the terms "European Community" and "EC" in quotation marks. It is somewhat difficult to speak about the "European Community" because there are, in fact, three "European Communities," not one. Three separate initiating treaties established the European Coal and Steel Community (ECSC); the European Atomic Energy Community (Euratom); and the European Economic Community (EEC). The 1957 Treaty of Rome, which created the EEC, together with the subsequent law relating to the EEC, is currently what is meant when the shorthand term "European Community" or "EC" is used.

At its initiation in 1957, the EC had six Member States. Currently there are fifteen Member States, but additional countries have petitioned to join the EC. In 1985, a conference was held in Luxembourg to amend the Treaty of Rome that created the EEC. The resulting amendments are contained in a document called the Single European Act (SEA). Numerous changes occurred, including an agreement to complete a single internal market by 1992. A second set of major amendments was adopted on February 7, 1992 at Maastricht, the Netherlands, in the Treaty on European Union (TEU). The TEU contained significant new agreements on economic and political integration and also created a new entity called the "European Union." The core of the "European Union"consists of the European Community, rather than the European Economic Community. The

TEU was followed by the 1997 Amsterdam Treaty which adopted further provisions concerning economic and political integration. For ease of use, the official EU website includes a document entitled "Consolidated Version of the Treaty Establishing the European Community." This document has not been officially adopted, but consolidates in a useful fashion the original European Community treaty and subsequent amendments. It is found at http://europa.eu.int/eur-lex/en/treaties/dat/ec_cons_treaty_en.pdf.

In-House Lawyers: At least ten jurisdictions (D.C., Florida, Kansas, Kentucky, Maryland, Minnesota, Missouri, Ohio, Oklahoma, and South Carolina) have statutes or court rules that permit in-house lawyers to provide legal services to their employers, subject to certain limitations, without committing the unauthorized practice of law. Various other states have issued court decisions or ethics opinions stating that in-house lawyers who serve only their employer are not engaged in unauthorized practice. (California, however, rejected a special admission category for in-house lawyers in 1987.)

(When we went to press in September 2002, the Virginia State Bar was considering a proposed rule that would require, by January 1, 2004, any in-house lawyer working for a Virginia employer either to become a regularly admitted active member of the Virginia State Bar or to obtain a "Corporate Counsel Certificate" that would enable the lawyer to be an active member of the Virginia State Bar but would limit the lawyer's practice to representing the employer.) For a comprehensive chart assembled by the American Corporate Counsel Association (ACCA) briefly describing the law or policy of every state regarding admission for in-house attorneys, see www.abanet.org/cpr/ mjp-uplchart.html.

IRS Regulations: In the regulations governing practice before the Internal Revenue Service, 31 C.F.R. §10.3 is in essence the opposite of an unauthorized practice law in that it expressly authorizes certain categories of non-lawyers to appear before the IRS as "enrolled agents" on the same terms (or nearly the same terms) as attorneys. According to §10.4, a nonlawyer who is neither a CPA nor an enrolled actuary may be eligible for "enrolled agent" status (a) if he passes an examination given by the IRS or (b) if he is a former IRS employee who has "not engaged in any conduct which would justify the suspension or disbarment of any attorney, certified public accountant, or enrolled agent under the provisions of this part and who, by virtue of his past service and technical experience in the Internal Revenue Service has qualified for such enrollment . . . ." Enrolled agents may be granted either limited or unlimited rights to practice before the IRS, in the discretion of the Director of Practice at the IRS. However, §10.32 provides that "[n]othing in the regulations in this part shall be construed as authorizing persons not members of the bar to practice law."

Model Rules of Professional Conduct for Federal Lawyers: Rule 5.5(a) provides that "[e]xcept as authorized by law," a federal lawyer shall not practice in a jurisdiction where doing so violates the regulation of the legal profession in that jurisdiction.

National Association of Legal Assistants (www.nala.org): The National Association of Legal Assistants, an organization of 18,000 paralegals with its headquarters in Tulsa, Oklahoma and an excellent web site at www.nala.org, publishes the NALA Code of Ethics and Professional Responsibility and the NALA Model Standards and Guidelines for Utilization of Legal Assistants. Canon 3 of the NALA Code of Ethics provides:

> A legal assistant must not: (a) engage in, encourage, or contribute to any act which could constitute the unauthorized practice of law; and (b) establish attorney-client relationships, set fees, give legal opinions or advice or represent a client before a court or agency unless so authorized by that court or agency; and (c) engage in conduct or take any action which would assist or involve the attorney in a violation of professional ethics or give the appearance of professional impropriety.

The NALA Guidelines (which are more detailed than the NALA Code of Ethics) include Guideline 5, which generally permits a legal assistant to perform "any function delegated by an attorney, including but not limited to the following":

> 1. Conduct client interviews and maintain general contact with the client after the establishment of the attorney-client relationship, so long as the client is aware of the status and function of the legal assistant, and the client contact is under the supervision of the attorney.
> 2. Locate and interview witnesses, so long as the witnesses are aware of the status and function of the legal assistant.
> 3. Conduct investigations and statistical and documentary research for review by the attorney.
> 4. Conduct legal research for review by the attorney.
> 5. Draft legal documents for review by the attorney.
> 6. Draft correspondence and pleadings for review by and signature of the attorney.
> 7. Summarize depositions, interrogatories, and testimony for review by the attorney.
> 8. Attend executions of wills, real estate closings, depositions, court or administrative hearings and trials with the attorney.
> 9. Author and sign letters provided the legal assistant's status is clearly indicated and the correspondence does not contain independent legal opinions or legal advice.

National Federation of Paralegal Associations (www.paralegals.org): The National Federation of Paralegal Associations, Inc. (NFPA), founded in 1974 and headquartered in Kansas City, Missouri, is an organization of approximately 18,000 paralegals, almost all of whom are traditional paralegals working in corporations or private law firms. In May of 1993, the NFPA adopted a Model Code of Ethics and Professional Responsibility. The Preamble of the NFPA Code states that paralegals "should strive to expand the paralegal role in the delivery of legal services." However, the NFPA does not support the delivery of legal services directly to the public by paralegals who are not supervised by lawyers. The NFPA views paralegals as complements to lawyers, not competitors to lawyers.

Pro Hac Vice Admission: In all states, courts have authority to admit out-of-state lawyers to practice before the court "pro hac vice," meaning for a particular matter. A typical example of a pro hac vice admission provision is Michigan Rule 15, which provides:

> Any person who is duly licensed to practice law in another state . . . or in any foreign country, may be permitted to engage in the trial of a specific case in a court or before an administrative tribunal in this State when associated with and on motion of an active member of the State Bar of Michigan who appears of record in the case. Such temporary permission may be revoked by the court summarily at any time for misconduct.

District of Columbia Rule 49(b)(7) is far more complex. It prohibits a lawyer from applying for admission pro hac vice in more than five cases pending in D.C. courts per calendar year, absent "exceptional cause," and requires each applicant for admission pro hac vice to file a sworn statement declaring, among other things:

> (3) that there are no disciplinary complaints pending against me for violation of the rules of the courts of those states, (4) that I have not been suspended or disbarred for disciplinary reasons from practice in any court, (5) that I am associated with _________ (name member and give his/her Bar number) . . . , (6) that I do not practice or hold out to practice law in the District of Columbia. . . .

The applicant must also acknowledge "the power and jurisdiction of the courts of the District of Columbia" over his professional conduct, and agree to be bound by the D.C. Rules of Professional Conduct in the matter if admitted pro hac vice. The court where the litigation is pending may grant, deny, or withdraw the admission pro hac vice "in its discretion."

In California (and perhaps in other jurisdictions), a lawyer may also be admitted pro hac vice in arbitration proceedings—see California Code of Civil Procedure §1282.4 (reprinted in our California Materials later in this volume).

Approximately 20 states charge a fee to out-of-state attorneys who appear pro hac vice in state courts. (Federal courts do not charge any similar fee.) In April 2002, the Texas State Bar's Board of Directors approved a proposal to impose a $200 fee for each pro hac vice appearance. When this book went to press in September of 2002, the Texas Supreme Court had not yet acted on the proposal.

Restatement of the Law Governing Lawyers: See Restatement §§2-4 in our chapter on the Restatement later in this volume.

Tax Court Rules of Practice: The Tax Court Rules of Practice permit qualified non-lawyers to practice before the Tax Court. For example, Tax Court Rule 200(a)(3), as amended in 1998, allows non-lawyers to be admitted to practice before the Tax Court if they pay a fee and pass a written examination (and, in the court's discretion, an oral examination as well).

Unauthorized Practice Laws: Most states have enacted statutes making it a crime to engage in the unauthorized practice of law. California Business and Professions Code §6126 ("Unauthorized Practice or Advertising as Misdemeanor") is typical:

> Any person advertising or holding himself or herself out as practicing or entitled to practice law or otherwise practicing law who is not an active member of the State Bar, is guilty of a misdemeanor.

A more detailed statute is found in Florida, where §454.23 ("Penalties") provides as follows:

> Any person not licensed or otherwise authorized by the Supreme Court of Florida who shall practice law or assume or hold himself or herself out to the public as qualified to practice in this state, or who willfully pretends to be, or willfully takes or uses any name, title, addition, or description implying that he or she is qualified, or recognized by law as qualified, to act as a lawyer in this state, and any person entitled to practice who shall violate any provisions of this chapter, shall be guilty of a misdemeanor of the first degree . . . .

A different definition of the unauthorized practice of law is contained in Georgia Statutes Annotated §15-19-50 ("Practice of law defined"), which provides:

> The practice of law in this state is defined as: (1) Representing litigants in court and preparing pleadings and other papers incident to any action or special proceedings in any court or other judicial body; (2) Conveyancing; (3) The preparation of

legal instruments of all kinds whereby a legal right is secured; (4) The rendering of opinions as to the validity or invalidity of titles to real or personal property; (5) The giving of any legal advice; and (6) Any action taken for others in any matter connected with the law.

In 1999, Texas enacted a statute governing web sites, CD-ROM's, and other electronic media. Texas Government Code §81.101(c) provides:

> In this chapter, the "practice of law" does not include the design, creation, publication, distribution, display or sale, including publication, distribution, display, or sale by means of an Internet web site, of written materials, books, forms, computer software, or similar products if the products clearly and conspicuously state that the products are not a substitute for the advice of an attorney. This subsection does not authorize the use of the products or similar media in violation of Chapter 83 [dealing with unauthorized practice in connection with title to real estate and other unrelated matters] and does not affect the applicability or enforceability of that chapter.

For a highly detailed rule governing unauthorized practice, see District of Columbia Rule 49, described in our Selected State Variations following Rule 5.5. For a remarkable collection of the unauthorized practice laws and court rules in every American jurisdiction, compiled by the Attorneys' Liability Assurance Society (ALAS), see www.abanet.org/cpr/mjp-uplrules.html. For an alternative collection of unauthorized practice materials, see www.CrossingtheBar.com.

In many states, the state bar has authority to enforce the unauthorized practice laws. In Florida, for example, the board of governors of the state bar acts "as an arm of the Supreme Court of Florida for the purpose of seeking to prohibit the unauthorized practice of law by investigating, prosecuting, and reporting" incidents involving unlicensed practice. See Florida Supreme Court Rule 1-8.2 and Chapter 10 of those Rules (setting forth detailed procedures for investigating and prosecuting unauthorized practice cases).

Rule 5.6 Restrictions on Right to Practice

A lawyer shall not participate in offering or making:

(a) a partnership ~~or~~, shareholders, operating, employment, or other similar type of agreement that restricts the right of a lawyer to practice after termination of the relationship, except an agreement concerning benefits upon retirement; or

(b) an agreement in which a restriction on the lawyer's right to practice is part of the settlement of a client controversy ~~between private parties~~.

COMMENT

[1] An agreement restricting the right of ~~partners or associates~~ lawyers to practice after leaving a firm not only limits their professional autonomy but also limits the freedom of clients to choose a lawyer. Paragraph (a) prohibits such agreements except for restrictions incident to provisions concerning retirement benefits for service with the firm.

[2] Paragraph (b) prohibits a lawyer from agreeing not to represent other persons in connection with settling a claim on behalf of a client.

[3] This Rule does not apply to prohibit restrictions that may be included in the terms of the sale of a law practice pursuant to Rule 1.17.

Canon and Code Antecedents

ABA Canons of Professional Ethics: No comparable Canon.

ABA Model Code of Professional Responsibility: Compare DR 2-108 (reprinted later in this volume).

Cross-References in Other Rules

Rule 1.2, Comment 8: "All agreements concerning a lawyer's representation of a client must accord with the Rules of Professional Conduct and other law." See **Rules** 1.1, 1.8 and **5.6**.

Rule 1.17, Comment 1 provides that "when a lawyer or an entire firm ceases to practice, or ceases to practice in an area of law, and other lawyers or firms take over the representation, the selling lawyer or firm may obtain compensation for the reasonable value of the practice as may withdrawing partners of law firms. See **Rules** 5.4 and **5.6**."

Legislative History of Model Rule 5.6

1980 and 1981 Drafts had no equivalent to Rule 5.6.

1982 Draft was adopted.

2002 Amendments: Before the February 2002 Mid-Year Meeting of the ABA House of Delegates, the ABA Ethics 2000 Commission revised its May 2001 proposal to amend Rule 5.6 by replacing "controversy between private parties" with "client controversy" at the end of Rule 5.6(b), making clear that this Rule applies to settlements between private parties and the government, not just to settlements between private parties. At its February 2002 Mid-Year Meeting, the ABA House of Delegates adopted without change the ABA Ethics 2000 Commission revised proposal to amend Rule 5.6 and its Comment.

Selected State Variations

California: See Rule 1-500 (Agreements Restricting a Member's Practice).

Florida: In 1997, without amending the text of Rule 5.6, Florida added the following new paragraph to the Comment to its version of Rule 5.6:

> This rule is not a per se prohibition against severance agreements between lawyers and law firms. Severance agreements containing reasonable and fair compensation provisions designed to avoid disputes required by time-consuming quantum meruit analysis are not prohibited by this rule. Severance agreements, on the other hand, that contain punitive clauses, the effect of which are to restrict competition or encroach upon a client's inherent right to select counsel, are prohibited. . . .

Georgia: In the rules effective January 1, 2001, Georgia adopted the pre-2002 version of ABA Model Rule 5.6 and its Comment essentially verbatim. (Before Georgia's new rules took effect, Georgia's DR 2-108(B) permitted a lawyer to agree in a settlement not to "accept any other representation arising out of a transaction or event embraced in the subject matter of the controversy or suit thus settled.") In addition, relevant to ABA Model Rule 5.6(b), Georgia also added the following new Rule 9.2:

> In connection with the settlement of a controversy or suit involving misuse of funds held in a fiduciary capacity, a lawyer shall not enter into an agreement that the person bringing the claim will be prohibited or restricted from filing a disciplinary complaint, or will be required to request the dismissal of a pending disciplinary complaint concerning that conduct.

New York: Compare ABA Model Rule 5.6 to New York's DR 2-108.

Pennsylvania: As amended effective June 28, 2001, Pennsylvania Rule 5.6(a) generally tracks the 2002 version of ABA Model Rule 5.6(a), but Pennsylvania also permits an agreement that restricts the rights of a lawyer to practice as part of "an agreement for the sale of a law practice consistent with Rule 1.17."

Texas: Rule 5.06(b) adds that "as part of the settlement of a disciplinary proceeding against a lawyer an agreement may be made placing restrictions on the right of that lawyer to practice."

Virginia modifies Rule 5.6(b) to forbid "an agreement in which a broad restriction of the lawyer's right to practice is part of the settlement of a controversy, except where such a restriction is approved by a tribunal or a governmental entity."

Related Materials

ABA Formal Ethics Opinions: See ABA Formal Ethics Ops. 93-371 (1993), 94-381 (1994), 95-394 (1995), and 00-417 (2000).

Arbitration Provisions: Many law partnership agreements contain terms giving greater benefits to those who do not compete with the firm after they leave. Departing lawyers often argue that such terms violate Rule 5.6(a). To reduce the expense of litigating these disputes, many partnership agreements contain arbitration agreements. These arbitration provisions are encouraged by legal malpractice insurers. In Pennsylvania, for example, the well-known Bertholon-Rowland Agencies has sometimes given a 5 percent "quality of management credit" (i.e., discount) on professional liability policies that contain the following paragraph:

> Any controversy or claim arising out of or relating to the dissolution of the partnership, or relating to a partner's withdrawal from the partnership, shall be settled through mediation conducted in accordance with the then-existing rules of the Pennsylvania Bar Association Lawyer Dispute Resolution Program (the "PBA Program"). Any issues that are not resolved through such mediation shall be submitted for arbitration conducted in accordance with the then-existing rules of the PBA Program. . . .

Non-compete Provisions: Some law firm partnership agreements contain provisions that pay greater severance payments to departing lawyers who do not compete with the firm than to those who do compete. In a variation, severance payments to departing partners may be based on a sliding scale so that partners who earn more after they leave will receive less than partners who earn less (such as partners who leave to enter public service or to take a public interest job).

Many of these provisions have been held invalid under Rule 5.6(a), and others are currently being challenged in litigation.

Restatement of the Law Governing Lawyers: See Restatement §§9 and 13 in our chapter on the Restatement later in this volume.

Rule 5.7 Responsibilities Regarding Law-Related Services

(a) A lawyer shall be subject to the Rules of Professional Conduct with respect to the provision of law-related services, as defined in paragraph (b), if the law-related services are provided:

(1) by the lawyer in circumstances that are not distinct from the lawyer's provision of legal services to clients; or

(2) in other circumstances by ~~a separate~~ an entity controlled by the lawyer individually or with others if the lawyer fails to take reasonable measures to assure that a person obtaining the law-related services knows that the services ~~of the separate entity~~ are not legal services and that the protections of the client-lawyer relationship do not exist.

(b) The term "law-related services" denotes services that might reasonably be performed in conjunction with and in substance are related to the provision of legal services, and that are not prohibited as unauthorized practice of law when provided by a nonlawyer.

COMMENT

[1] When a lawyer performs law-related services or controls an organization that does so, there exists the potential for ethical problems. Principal among these is the possibility that the person for whom the law-related services are performed fails to understand that the services may not carry with them the protections normally afforded as part of the client-lawyer relationship. The recipient of the law-related services may expect, for example, that the protection of client confidences, prohibitions against representation of persons with conflicting interests, and obligations of a lawyer to maintain professional independence apply to the provision of law-related services when that may not be the case.

[2] Rule 5.7 applies to the provision of law-related services by a lawyer even when the lawyer does not provide any legal services to the person for whom the law-related services are performed and whether the law-related services are performed through a law firm or a separate entity. The Rule identifies the circumstances in which all of the Rules of Professional Conduct apply to the provision of law-related services. Even when those circumstances do not exist, however, the conduct of a lawyer involved in the provision of law-related services is subject to those Rules

that apply generally to lawyer conduct, regardless of whether the conduct involves the provision of legal services. See, e.g., Rule 8.4.

[3] When law-related services are provided by a lawyer under circumstances that are not distinct from the lawyer's provision of legal services to clients, the lawyer in providing the law-related services must adhere to the requirements of the Rules of Professional Conduct as provided in ~~Rule 5.7~~ paragraph (a)(1). Even when the law-related and legal services are provided in circumstances that are distinct from each other, for example through separate entities or different support staff within the law firm, the Rules of Professional Conduct apply to the lawyer as provided in paragraph (a)(2) unless the lawyer takes reasonable measures to assure that the recipient of the law-related services knows that the services are not legal services and that the protections of the client-lawyer relationship do not apply.

[4] Law-related services also may be provided through an entity that is distinct from that through which the lawyer provides legal services. If the lawyer individually or with others has control of such an entity's operations, the Rule requires the lawyer to take reasonable measures to assure that each person using the services of the entity knows that the services provided by the entity are not legal services and that the Rules of Professional Conduct that relate to the client-lawyer relationship do not apply. A lawyer's control of an entity extends to the ability to direct its operation. Whether a lawyer has such control will depend upon the circumstances of the particular case.

[5] When a client-lawyer relationship exists with a person who is referred by a lawyer to a separate law-related service entity controlled by the lawyer, individually or with others, the lawyer must comply with Rule 1.8(a).

[6] In taking the reasonable measures referred to in paragraph (a)(2) to assure that a person using law-related services understands the practical effect or significance of the inapplicability of the Rules of Professional Conduct, the lawyer should communicate to the person receiving the law-related services, in a manner sufficient to assure that the person understands the significance of the fact, that the relationship of the person to the business entity will not be a client-lawyer relationship. The communication should be made before entering into an agreement for provision of or providing law-related services, and preferably should be in writing.

[7] The burden is upon the lawyer to show that the lawyer has taken reasonable measures under the circumstances to communicate the desired understanding. For instance, a sophisticated user of law-related services, such as a publicly held corporation, may require a lesser explanation than someone unaccustomed to making distinctions between legal services and law-related services, such as an individual seeking tax advice from a lawyer-accountant or investigative services in connection with a lawsuit.

[8] Regardless of the sophistication of potential recipients of law-

related services, a lawyer should take special care to keep separate the provision of law-related and legal services in order to minimize the risk that the recipient will assume that the law-related services are legal services. The risk of such confusion is especially acute when the lawyer renders both types of services with respect to the same matter. Under some circumstances the legal and law-related services may be so closely entwined that they cannot be distinguished from each other, and the requirement of disclosure and consultation imposed by paragraph (a)(2) of the Rule cannot be met. In such a case a lawyer will be responsible for assuring that both the lawyer's conduct and, to the extent required by Rule 5.3, that of nonlawyer employees in the distinct entity that the lawyer controls complies in all respects with the Rules of Professional Conduct.

[9] A broad range of economic and other interests of clients may be served by lawyers' engaging in the delivery of law-related services. Examples of law-related services include providing title insurance, financial planning, accounting, trust services, real estate counseling, legislative lobbying, economic analysis, social work, psychological counseling, tax preparation, and patent, medical or environmental consulting.

[10] When a lawyer is obliged to accord the recipients of such services the protections of those Rules that apply to the client-lawyer relationship, the lawyer must take special care to heed the proscriptions of the Rules addressing conflict of interest (Rules 1.7 through 1.11, especially Rules 1.7~~(b)~~(a)(2) and 1.8(a), (b) and (f)), and to scrupulously adhere to the requirements of Rule 1.6 relating to disclosure of confidential information. The promotion of the law-related services must also in all respects comply with Rules 7.1 through 7.3, dealing with advertising and solicitation. In that regard, lawyers should take special care to identify the obligations that may be imposed as a result of a jurisdiction's decisional law.

[11] When the full protections of all of the Rules of Professional Conduct do not apply to the provision of law-related services, principles of law external to the Rules, for example, the law of principal and agent, govern the legal duties owed to those receiving the services. Those other legal principles may establish a different degree of protection for the recipient with respect to confidentiality of information, conflicts of interest and permissible business relationships with clients. See also Rule 8.4 (Misconduct).

Canon and Code Antecedents

ABA Canons of Professional Ethics: No comparable Canon.

ABA Model Code of Professional Responsibility: No comparable Disciplinary Rule.

Cross-References in Other Rules

Rule 1.8, Comment 1: "The Rule applies to lawyers engaged in the sale of goods or services related to the practice of law. See **Rule 5.7**."

Legislative History of Model Rule 5.7

1980, 1981, and 1982 Drafts: None of the Kutak Commission drafts had any provision equivalent to Rule 5.7.

1991 Adoption: Rule 5.7 was originally added to the Model Rules at the ABA's 1991 Annual Meeting. The rule as adopted in 1991 was proposed by the ABA's Litigation Section, which had been intensively studying ancillary businesses for several years. Before the House of Delegates voted on the Litigation Section's proposal, it rejected by voice vote an alternative version of Rule 5.7 that had been proposed by the ABA's Standing Committee on Ethics and Professional Responsibility. After rejecting the Standing Committee's proposal, the House of Delegates voted 197-186 to adopt the Litigation Section's version of Rule 5.7. The original version of Rule 5.7 provided as follows:

Provision of Ancillary Services

(a) A lawyer shall not practice law in a law firm which owns a controlling interest in, or operates, an entity which provides non-legal services which are ancillary to the practice of law, or otherwise provides such ancillary non-legal services, except as provided in paragraph (b).

(b) A lawyer may practice law in a law firm which provides non-legal services which are ancillary to the practice of law if:

(1) The ancillary services are provided solely to clients of the law firm and are incidental to, in connection with and concurrent to, the provision of legal services by the law firm to such clients;

(2) Such ancillary services are provided solely by employees of the law firm itself and not by a subsidiary or other affiliate of the law firm;

(3) The law firm makes appropriate disclosure in writing to its clients; and

(4) The law firm does not hold itself out as engaging in any non-legal activities except in conjunction with the provision of legal services, as provided in this rule.

(c) One or more lawyers who engage in the practice of law in a law firm shall neither own a controlling interest in, nor operate, an entity which provides non-legal services which are ancillary to the practice of law, nor otherwise provide such ancillary non-legal services, except that their firms may provide such services as provided in paragraph (b).

(d) Two or more lawyers who engage in the practice of law in separate law firms shall neither own a controlling interest in, nor operate, an entity which provides non-legal services which are ancillary to the practice of law, nor otherwise provide such ancillary non-legal services.

The Comment to the 1991 version of Rule 5.7 was nineteen paragraphs, making it one of the longest comments in the Model Rules. The following excerpt from the original Comment explains the origin and purpose of the 1991 version of Rule 5.7:

Excerpt from Comment to 1991 Version of Rule 5.7

[1] For many years, lawyers have provided to their clients non-legal services which are ancillary to the practice of law. Such services included title insurance, trust services and patent consulting. In most instances, these ancillary non-legal services were provided to law firm clients in connection with, and concurrent to, the provision of legal services by the lawyer or law firm. The provision of such services afforded benefits to clients, including making available a greater range of services

from one source and maintaining technical expertise in various fields within a law firm. However, the provision of both legal and ancillary non-legal services raises ethical concerns, including conflicts of interest, confusion on the part of clients and possible loss (or inapplicability) of the attorney-client privilege, which may not have been addressed adequately by the other Model Rules of Professional Conduct.

[2] Eventually, law firms began to form affiliates, largely staffed by non-lawyers, to provide ancillary non-legal services to both clients and customers who were not clients for legal services. In addition to exacerbating the ethical problems of conflicts of interest, confusion and threats to confidentiality, the large-scale movement of law firms into ancillary non-legal businesses raised serious professionalism concerns, including compromising lawyers' independent judgment, the loss of the bar's right to self-regulation and the provision of legal services by entities controlled by non-lawyers.

[3] Rule 5.7 addresses both the ethical and professionalism concerns implicated by the provision of ancillary non-legal services by lawyers and law firms. It preserves the ability of lawyers to provide additional services to their clients and maintain within the law firm a broad range of technical expertise. However, Rule 5.7 restricts the ability of law firms to provide ancillary non-legal services through affiliates to non-client customers and clients alike, the rendition of which raises serious ethical and professionalism concerns.

1992 Deletion: The original version of Rule 5.7 was deleted from the ABA Model Rules in its entirety at the ABA's 1992 Annual Meeting. The report urging deletion of the rule was jointly submitted by the Illinois State Bar Association, the ABA Standing Committee on Lawyers Title Guaranty Funds, and six ABA sections. The House of Delegates voted 190-183 to delete the rule. Rule 5.7 was the first rule ever to be deleted from the Model Rules.

1994 Version: The version of Rule 5.7 in effect from 1994 to 2002 was adopted by the ABA House of Delegates by a margin of 237-183 at the ABA's February 1994 Mid-Year Meeting. From August 1992 (when the original version of Rule 5.7 was deleted) until February 1994 (when the new version was adopted), the Model Rules did not contain any version of Rule 5.7. After the 1992 vote to delete the original rule, House of Delegates Chair Phil Anderson of Arkansas appointed a Special Committee on Ancillary Business Services to "review the work that had been done by various Association entities on the subject of ancillary business activities of lawyers, and to make a recommendation to the House of Delegates for an appropriate position on that subject." The Special Committee, chaired by William G. Paul, recommended that the ABA adopt the 1994 version of Rule 5.7. Here are excerpts from the Special Committee's Report in support of the 1994 version of Rule 5.7:

*Excerpt from Report of the Special House of Delegates Committee on Ancillary Business in Support of the 1994 Version of Rule 5.7**

[T]he Committee is satisfied that law-related services are being provided wherever lawyers practice, that law-related services are often provided by separate entities, and that there has been no reported disciplinary infraction or malpractice claim resulting from the provision of law-related services. . . . Several respondents expressed concern about potential confusion on the part of recipients of law-related services regarding the

*Committee Reports do not represent official policy of the ABA. They are for information only, and the opinions are those of the authors of the report.

nature of their relationship with the lawyer, although no instances of actual confusion were reported to the Committee. Responses also indicated a profusion of law-related services, some traditional in the jurisdiction, and others of more recent origin. These include not only the provision of trust services, title insurance, accounting and escrow services, but also the furnishing of insurance investigation, psychological counseling, lobbying, arbitration and mediation, registered corporate agent representation, and environmental consulting services. The Committee believes that the list of law-related services is not only long, but growing longer.

The Committee concluded that law-related services should not be prohibited. Instead, the Committee proposes adoption of a rule that specifically treats lawyers' dealings with recipients of law-related services. The proposed rule supplements existing Rules that apply to such relationships. . . .

Examples of law-related services are provided in the Comment to the proposed Rule, but these are by no means exhaustive. The Committee found that the types of law-related services are virtually unlimited, and that new types continue to be developed. Accordingly, the definition is intended to encompass a wide range of services whether or not the services are of a type currently being provided. . . .

Even when the recipient of law-related services is not a client of the lawyer, the law of principal and agent affords the recipient significant protections against disclosure or use of confidence, conflicts of interest, and self-dealing. The Committee notes, in this context, that it found no justification for affording recipients of law-related services through separate entities greater protection than that to which they would otherwise be entitled solely because lawyers control the separate entity.

2002 Amendments: In its May 2001 report to the ABA House of Delegates, the ABA Ethics 2000 Commission proposed to amend the Comment, but not the text, of Rule 5.7. Before the House of Delegates acted on the proposal, however, the Commission revised its proposal to broaden the text of Rule 5.7(a)(2) so that it would apply to law-related services provided directly by a lawyer or the lawyer's law firm. At its February 2002 Mid-Year Meeting, the ABA House of Delegates adopted without change the ABA Ethics 2000 Commission revised proposal to amend Rule 5.7 and its Comment.

Selected State Variations

District of Columbia has not adopted a rule equivalent to ABA Model Rule 5.7, but has adopted a version of Rule 5.4 that permits non-lawyers to become partners under certain circumstances — see District of Columbia Rules of Professional Conduct below.

Georgia: In the rules effective January 1, 2001, Georgia adopted the pre-2002 version of ABA Model Rule 5.7 and its Comment essentially verbatim.

Maine adopted a version Rule 5.7 based almost verbatim on the ABA Model Rule in 1997 — see Maine Rule 3.2(h). The Advisory Committee Note to Rule 3.2(h) states, in part:

> In Maine the scope of "law-related services" as opposed to legal services may be quite broad, in view of the indefinite meaning of "unauthorized practice." It may be that in this jurisdiction any service other than litigation is a "law-related service." Familiar examples would include, however, the preparation of a federal income tax return, lobbying and such activities as real estate brokerage and marital counseling. . . . [T]itle insurance is the most common example of law-related services provided through a separate entity by a Maine law firm.

New York: Compare ABA Model Rule 5.7 to New York's DR 1-106.

Ohio has no provision comparable to ABA Model Rule 5.7.

Pennsylvania, which adopted a version of Rule 5.7 in 1996, was the first state to do so. The Pennsylvania rule, which differs significantly from ABA Model Rule 5.7, provides as follows:

> *Rule 5.7 Responsibilities Regarding Nonlegal Services*
>
> (a) A lawyer who provides nonlegal services to a recipient that are not distinct from legal services provided to that recipient is subject to the Rules of Professional Conduct with respect to the provision of both legal and nonlegal services.
>
> (b) A lawyer who provides nonlegal services to a recipient that are distinct from any legal services provided to the recipient is subject to the Rules of Professional Conduct with respect to the nonlegal services if the lawyer knows or reasonably should know that the recipient might believe that the recipient is receiving the protection of a client-lawyer relationship.
>
> (c) A lawyer who is an owner, controlling party, employee, agent, or is otherwise affiliated with an entity providing nonlegal services to a recipient is subject to the Rules of Professional Conduct with respect to the nonlegal services if the lawyer knows or reasonably should know that the recipient might believe that the recipient is receiving the protection of a client-lawyer relationship.
>
> (d) Paragraph (b) or (c) does not apply if the lawyer makes reasonable efforts to avoid any misunderstanding by the recipient receiving nonlegal services. Those efforts must include advising the recipient that the services are not legal services and that the protection of a client-lawyer relationship does not exist with respect to the provision of nonlegal services to the recipient.

Virginia omits Rule 5.7.

Related Materials

Professionalism Report: The ABA's Stanley Commission Report on Professionalism, 112 F.R.D. 243 (1986), called the trend toward law firm involvement in nonlegal services "disturbing" and urged the ABA to "initiate a study to see what, if any, controls or prohibitions should be imposed."

Restatement of the Law Governing Lawyers: The Restatement has no provision comparable to ABA Model Rule 5.7.

ARTICLE 6. PUBLIC SERVICE

Rule 6.1 Voluntary Pro Bono Publico Service

Every lawyer has a professional responsibility to provide legal services to those unable to pay. A lawyer should aspire to render at least (50) hours of pro bono publico legal services per year. In fulfilling this responsibility, the lawyer should:

(a) provide a substantial majority of the (50) hours of legal services without fee or expectation of fee to:

(1) persons of limited means or

(2) charitable, religious, civic, community, governmental and educational organizations in matters that are designed primarily to address the needs of persons of limited means; and

(b) provide any additional services through:

(1) delivery of legal services at no fee or substantially reduced fee to individuals, groups or organizations seeking to secure or protect civil rights, civil liberties or public rights, or charitable, religious, civic, community, governmental and educational organizations in matters in furtherance of their organizational purposes, where the payment of standard legal fees would significantly deplete the organization's economic resources or would be otherwise inappropriate;

(2) delivery of legal services at a substantially reduced fee to persons of limited means; or

(3) participation in activities for improving the law, the legal system or the legal profession.

In addition, a lawyer should voluntarily contribute financial support to organizations that provide legal services to persons of limited means.

COMMENT

[1] Every lawyer, regardless of professional prominence or professional workload, has a responsibility to provide legal services to those unable to pay, and personal involvement in the problems of the disadvantaged can be one of the most rewarding experiences in the life of a lawyer. The American Bar Association urges all lawyers to provide a minimum of 50 hours of pro bono services annually. States, however, may decide to choose a higher or lower number of hours of annual service (which may be expressed as a percentage of a lawyer's professional time) depending upon local needs and local conditions. It is recognized that in some years a lawyer may render greater or fewer hours than the annual standard specified, but during the course of his or her legal career, each lawyer should render on average per year, the number of hours set forth in this Rule. Services can be performed in civil matters or in criminal or quasi-criminal matters for which there is no government obligation to provide funds for legal representation, such as post-conviction death penalty appeal cases.

[2] Paragraphs (a)(1) and (2) recognize the critical need for legal services that exists among persons of limited means by providing that a substantial majority of the legal services rendered annually to the disadvantaged be furnished without fee or expectation of fee. Legal services under

these paragraphs consist of a full range of activities, including individual and class representation, the provision of legal advice, legislative lobbying, administrative rule making and the provision of free training or mentoring to those who represent persons of limited means. The variety of these activities should facilitate participation by government lawyers, even when restrictions exist on their engaging in the outside practice of law.

[3] Persons eligible for legal services under paragraphs (a)(1) and (2) are those who qualify for participation in programs funded by the Legal Services Corporation and those whose incomes and financial resources are slightly above the guidelines utilized by such programs but, nevertheless, cannot afford counsel. Legal services can be rendered to individuals or to organizations such as homeless shelters, battered women's centers and food pantries that serve those of limited means. The term "governmental organizations" includes, but is not limited to, public protection programs and sections of governmental or public sector agencies.

[4] Because service must be provided without fee or expectation of fee, the intent of the lawyer to render free legal services is essential for the work performed to fall within the meaning of paragraphs (a)(1) and (2). Accordingly, services rendered cannot be considered pro bono if an anticipated fee is uncollected, but the award of statutory attorneys' fees in a case originally accepted as pro bono would not disqualify such services from inclusion under this section. Lawyers who do receive fees in such cases are encouraged to contribute an appropriate portion of such fees to organizations or projects that benefit persons of limited means.

[5] While it is possible for a lawyer to fulfill the annual responsibility to perform pro bono services exclusively through activities described in paragraphs (a)(1) and (2), to the extent that any hours of service remained unfulfilled, the remaining commitment can be met in a variety of ways as set forth in paragraph (b). Constitutional, statutory or regulatory restrictions may prohibit or impede government and public sector lawyers and judges from performing the pro bono services outlined in paragraphs (a)(1) and (2). Accordingly, where those restrictions apply, government and public sector lawyers and judges may fulfill their pro bono responsibility by performing services outlined in paragraph (b).

[6] Paragraph (b)(1) includes the provision of certain types of legal services to those whose incomes and financial resources place them above limited means. It also permits the pro bono lawyer to accept a substantially reduced fee for services. Examples of the types of issues that may be addressed under this paragraph include First Amendment claims, Title VII claims and environmental protection claims. Additionally, a wide range of organizations may be represented, including social service, medical research, cultural and religious groups.

[7] Paragraph (b)(2) covers instances in which lawyers agree to and receive a modest fee for furnishing legal services to persons of limited means. Participation in judicare programs and acceptance of court

appointments in which the fee is substantially below a lawyer's usual rate are encouraged under this section.

[8] Paragraph (b)(3) recognizes the value of lawyers engaging in activities that improve the law, the legal system or the legal profession. Serving on bar association committees, serving on boards of pro bono or legal services programs, taking part in Law Day activities, acting as a continuing legal education instructor, a mediator or an arbitrator and engaging in legislative lobbying to improve the law, the legal system or the profession are a few examples of the many activities that fall within this paragraph.

[9] Because the provision of pro bono services is a professional responsibility, it is the individual ethical commitment of each lawyer. Nevertheless, there may be times when it is not feasible for a lawyer to engage in pro bono services. At such times a lawyer may discharge the pro bono responsibility by providing financial support to organizations providing free legal services to persons of limited means. Such financial support should be reasonably equivalent to the value of the hours of service that would have otherwise been provided. In addition, at times it may be more feasible to satisfy the pro bono responsibility collectively, as by a firm's aggregate pro bono activities.

[10] Because the efforts of individual lawyers are not enough to meet the need for free legal services that exists among persons of limited means, the government and the profession have instituted additional programs to provide those services. Every lawyer should financially support such programs, in addition to either providing direct pro bono services or making financial contributions when pro bono service is not feasible.

[11] Law firms should act reasonably to enable and encourage all lawyers in the firm to provide the pro bono legal services called for by this Rule.

~~[11]~~ [12] The responsibility set forth in this Rule is not intended to be enforced through disciplinary process.

Canon and Code Antecedents

ABA Canons of Professional Ethics: No comparable Canon.

ABA Model Code of Professional Responsibility: No comparable Disciplinary Rule.

Cross-References in Other Rules

Rule 6.2, Comment 1: "All lawyers have a responsibility to assist in providing pro bono publico service. See **Rule 6.1**."

Legislative History of Model Rule 6.1

1980 Discussion Draft of Rule 6.1 (then Rule 8.1) provided as follows: "A lawyer shall render unpaid public interest legal services. . . . A lawyer shall make an annual report concerning such service to appropriate regulatory authority."

1981 and 1982 Drafts were the same as adopted in 1983, except that neither draft contained the final clause, "by financial support for organizations that provide legal services to persons of limited means."

1983-1993 Rule: The version of Rule 6.1 originally adopted by the ABA in 1983 (which remained in effect until its amendment in 1993) provided as follows:

> A lawyer should render public interest legal service. A lawyer may discharge this responsibility by providing professional services at no fee or a reduced fee to persons of limited means or to public service or charitable groups or organizations, by service in activities for improving the law, the legal system or the legal profession, and by financial support for organizations that provide legal services to persons of limited means.

1993 Amendment: At its 1993 Mid-Year Meeting, the ABA House of Delegates voted to amend Rule 6.1 substantially and to rewrite its Comment entirely. The amendment passed by the close vote of 228-215. The principal sponsor and author of the amended rule was the ABA's Standing Committee on Lawyers' Public Service Responsibility (SCLPSR).

Because amendments to the Model Rules are usually proposed by the ABA's Standing Committee on Ethics and Professional Responsibility, SCLPSR held a number of joint meetings with that committee. However, SCLPSR and the Standing Committee on Ethics and Professional Responsibility were unable to agree on a joint proposal. The Standing Committee on Ethics and Professional Responsibility had three major problems with the amendment: (1) the Standing Committee on Ethics and Professional Responsibility opposed setting a specific target number of hours of pro bono service per year (preferring a word like "substantial" instead of a number); (2) it opposed urging lawyers to allocate most of their pro bono hours to serving the poor (out of concern that pro bono work for civil rights, the environment, and other important areas would diminish); and (3) it would have favored a "buy-out" provision allowing lawyers to substitute financial support for personal service.

We reprint below excerpts from the Committee Report issued by SCLPSR and its five co-sponsors in support of the 1993 amendment to Rule 6.1:

*Excerpts from ABA Committee Report Supporting 1993 Amendment to Rule 6.1**

The Current Crisis in the Delivery of Legal Services to the Poor

[B]ecause the legal problems of the economically disadvantaged often involve areas of basic need such as minimum levels of income and entitlements, shelter, utilities and child support, their inability to obtain legal services can have dire consequences. For example, the failure of a poor person to have effective legal counsel in an eviction proceeding may well result in homelessness; the failure to have legal counsel present at a public aid hearing may result in the denial of essential food or medical benefits.

The inability of the poor to obtain needed legal services has been well documented: since 1983, when Rule 6.1 was adopted, at least one national and 13 statewide studies assessing the legal needs of the poor have been conducted. Of

*Committee Reports do not represent official policy of the ABA. They are for information only, and the opinions are those of the authors of the report.

those studies reporting unmet legal need, there has been a consistent finding that only about 15%-20% of the legal needs of the poor are being addressed. The legal need studies also confirmed that unmet need exists in critical areas such as public benefits, utilities, shelter, medical benefits and family matters. . . .

The Committee firmly believes that the private bar alone cannot be expected to fill the gap for service that exists among the poor. Rather, the federal government, through adequate funding of the Legal Services Corporation (LSC), should bear the major responsibility for addressing the problem. Although the federal government has never provided sufficient funding for the LSC, during the past decade funding has fallen even further, causing the crisis of unmet legal needs among the poor to be exacerbated. Specifically, in FY 1981, the annual budget for LSC was $321 million, while in FY 1991, the annual budget was only $328 million. Given the fact that the consumer price index increased by well over 50% from 1980 to 1990 and that during that same time period the poverty population is estimated to have increased by 15.4%, funding for LSC is clearly inadequate.

The Association . . . must again turn to members of the private bar and call upon them to help ease the crisis that exists in the provision of legal services to the poor. The Committee believes that one effective means of doing this is by revising Model Rule 6.1 to reflect a new emphasis on service to the disadvantaged. . . .

III. Discussion of the Proposed Revisions to Rule 6.1

In order to clarify that Rule 6.1 remains a voluntary aspirational standard, the words "aspire to" have been added to the first sentence of the Rule. The first sentence also contains one of the most notable changes proposed to Rule 6.1: the addition of language that specifies the minimum number of hours of activity on an annual basis that would be necessary to fulfill the pro bono responsibility. . . . The Committee believes that while 50 hours is a reasonable standard, each state should retain the flexibility to determine the standard that is best for it, based upon local needs and local conditions . . . as Oregon did in adopting a pro bono resolution calling upon all lawyers to render 80 hours of pro bono service annually.

To address the crisis in the delivery of legal services to the poor, the proposed revision provides that a substantial majority of the annual hours of pro bono legal services should be rendered at no cost to persons of limited means or to organizations in matters which are designed primarily to address the needs of persons of limited means. The Committee purposely chose the words "substantial majority" to make clear that a simple majority of the hours would not suffice. While the Committee recognizes the value and importance of other types of pro bono activity, it strongly believes that due to the enormity of the unmet need for legal services that exists among the disadvantaged, the provision of legal services to that group must be given priority over all other types of pro bono service. . . .

In addition to voluntarily rendering pro bono service, the revised Rule 6.1 calls upon every lawyer to voluntarily make financial contributions to organizations providing legal services to persons of limited means. In those cases in which a lawyer determines that it is not feasible to render legal services and makes a financial contribution instead, he or she is expected to make an additional contribution pursuant to the last sentence of the new Rule. . . .

It is the Committee's intent that the ethical responsibilities set forth in Rule 6.1 apply to all lawyers and not just those currently engaged in the practice of law. . . .

Although neither the Rule nor the Comment explicitly so states, it should be self evident that every lawyer is expected to provide the same quality of legal services to pro bono clients as he or she would provide to paying clients. . . . Therefore, to the extent that an attorney is unfamiliar with a given area of the law, he or she is expected to seek advice or training in that area before advising a client, either for a fee or on a pro bono basis. Many pro bono programs provide free training on a wide range of topics to assist their volunteer attorneys in attaining competency to handle the cases referred to them. The Committee strongly endorses the provision of these training events and urges pro bono attorneys to take advantage of them whenever possible.

[T]he Comment to the revised Rule explicitly states that the pro bono responsibility is not intended to be enforced through the disciplinary process. Thus as drafted, revised Rule 6.1 does not mandate pro bono. Although the Committee recognizes that since 1988, mandatory pro bono proposals have been considered in many states and remain under active consideration in several of them, it nevertheless believes that it is not practical nor feasible at this time to address the issue of mandatory pro bono on a national level. Rather, the Committee views the question of mandatory pro bono as an issue that needs to be examined by state and local bar associations.

2002 Amendments: At its February 2002 Mid-Year Meeting, the ABA House of Delegates adopted with only minor changes the ABA Ethics 2000 Commission proposal to amend Rule 6.1 and its Comment. Comment 11 was not in the Commission's proposal but rather was added by the House of Delegates.

Selected State Variations

Arizona: Rule 6.1 contains the following key provisions:

(a) A lawyer should voluntarily render public interest legal service. A lawyer may discharge this responsibility by rendering a minimum of fifty hours of service per calendar year. . . .

(c) A law firm or other group of lawyers may satisfy their responsibility under this Rule, if they desire, collectively. For example, the designation of one or more lawyers to work on pro bono publico matters may be attributed to other lawyers within the firm or group who support the representation. . . .

(d) The efforts of individual lawyers are not enough to meet the needs of the poor. The profession and government have instituted programs to provide direct delivery of legal services to the poor. The direct support of such programs is an alternative expression of support to provide law in the public interest, and a lawyer is encouraged to provide financial support for organizations that provide legal services to persons of limited means or to the Arizona Bar Foundation for the direct delivery of legal services to the poor.

California: No comparable provision.

Colorado: In 1999, the Colorado Supreme Court *rejected* a recommendation by the state's Judicial Advisory Council to institute mandatory pro bono reporting. The court said that mandatory reporting was a step toward mandatory pro bono, and "[s]ince we are unwilling to arrive at that destination, we are also unwilling to take the first step."

Connecticut, Michigan, New Jersey, and ***Pennsylvania,*** among others, retain the original version of ABA Model Rule 6.1 as adopted in 1983, which provided:

A lawyer should render public interest service. A lawyer may discharge this responsibility by providing professional services at no fee or a reduced fee to persons of limited means or to public service or charitable groups or organizations, by service in activities for improving the law, the legal system or the legal profession, and by financial support for organizations that provide legal services to persons of limited means.

District of Columbia: D.C. Rule 6.1 differs significantly from the ABA Model Rule — see District of Columbia Rules of Professional Conduct below.

Florida: In 1993, in a divided opinion, the Florida Supreme Court adopted an elaborate new pro bono rule, which took effect on October 1, 1993. See 630 So. 2d 501 (Fla. 1993). The bar subsequently sought to eliminate the mandatory reporting requirements of the rule but the Florida Supreme Court refused to do so at 696 So. 2d 734 (1997). In Schwarz v. Kogan, 132 F.3d 1387 (11th Cir. 1998), the Court upheld Florida's rule against a federal constitutional challenge. The rule provides as follows:

4-6.1 Pro Bono Public Service

(a) *Professional Responsibility.* Each member of The Florida Bar in good standing, as part of that member's professional responsibility, should (1) render pro bono legal services to the poor or (2) participate, to the extent possible, in other pro bono service activities that directly relate to the legal needs of the poor. This professional responsibility does not apply to members of the judiciary or their staffs or to government lawyers who are prohibited from performing legal services by constitutional, statutory, rule, or regulatory prohibitions. Neither does this professional responsibility apply to those members of The Bar who are retired, inactive, or suspended, or who have been placed on the inactive list for incapacity not related to discipline.

(b) *Discharge of the Professional Responsibility to Provide Pro Bono Legal Service to the Poor.* The professional responsibility to provide pro bono legal services as established under this rule is aspirational rather than mandatory in nature. The failure to fulfill one's professional responsibility under this rule will not subject a lawyer to discipline. The professional responsibility to provide pro bono legal service to the poor may be discharged by:

(1) annually providing at least 20 hours of pro bono legal service to the poor; or

(2) making an annual contribution of at least $350 to a legal aid organization.

(c) *Collective Discharge of the Professional Responsibility to Provide Pro Bono Legal Service to the Poor.* Each member of the bar should strive to individually satisfy the member's professional responsibility to provide pro bono legal service to the poor. Collective satisfaction of this professional responsibility is permitted by law firms only under a collective satisfaction plan that has been filed previously with the circuit pro bono committee and only when providing pro bono legal service to the poor:

(1) in a major case or matter involving a substantial expenditure of time and resources; or

(2) through a full-time community or public service staff; or

(3) in any other manner that has been approved by the circuit pro bono committee in the circuit in which the firm practices.

(d) *Reporting Requirement.* Each member of the bar shall annually report whether the member has satisfied the member's professional responsibility to provide pro bono legal services to the poor. Each member shall report this information through a simplified reporting form that is made a part of the member's annual dues statement. . . . The failure to report this information shall constitute a disciplinary offense under these rules. . . .

Florida also adds a lengthy new Rule 6.5 (Voluntary Pro Bono Plan) that organizes various bar and court committees whose purpose is to encourage and facilitate pro bono work by Florida lawyers. Among other things, Rule 6.5(c)(2) instructs every judicial circuit to "(a) prepare in written form a circuit pro bono plan after evaluating the needs of the circuit and making a determination of present available pro bono services; (b) implement the plan and monitor its results; [and] (c) submit an annual report to The Florida Bar standing committee. . . ." Rule 6.5(d) provides:

> The following are suggested pro bono service opportunities that should be included in each circuit plan:
>
> (1) representation of clients through case referral;
> (2) interviewing of prospective clients;
> (3) participation in pro se clinics and other clinics in which lawyers provide advice and counsel;
> (4) acting as co-counsel on cases or matters with legal assistance providers and other pro bono lawyers;
> (5) providing consultation services to legal assistance providers for case reviews and evaluations;
> (6) participation in policy advocacy;
> (7) providing training to the staff of legal assistance providers and other volunteer pro bono attorneys;
> (8) making presentations to groups of poor persons regarding their rights and obligations under the law;
> (9) providing legal research;
> (10) providing guardian ad litem services;
> (11) providing assistance in the formation and operation of legal entities for groups of poor persons; and
> (12) serving as a mediator or arbitrator at no fee to the client-eligible party.

Georgia: In the rules effective January 1, 2001, Georgia adopted the version of ABA Model Rule 6.1 that was in effect immediately before it was amended in February 2002, but Georgia Rule 6.1 adds: "No reporting rules or requirements may be imposed without specific permission of the Supreme Court granted through amendments to these Rules. There is no disciplinary penalty for a violation of this Rule."

Illinois omits Rule 6.1 and explains why in its Preamble:

> It is the responsibility of those licensed as officers of the court to use their training, experience and skills to provide services in the public interest for which compensation may not be available. It is the responsibility of those who manage law firms to create an environment that is hospitable to the rendering of a reasonable amount of uncompensated service by lawyers practicing in that firm.
>
> Service in the public interest may take many forms. These include but are not limited to *pro bono* representation of persons unable to pay for legal services and assistance in the organized bar's efforts at law reform. An individual lawyer's efforts in these areas is evidence of the lawyer's good character and fitness to practice law, and the efforts of the bar as a whole are essential to the bar's maintenance of professionalism.
>
> [T]his concept is not appropriate for a disciplinary code, because an appropriate disciplinary standard regarding *pro bono* and public service is difficult, if not impossible, to articulate. That ABA Model Rule 6.1 itself uses the word "should" instead of "shall" in describing this duty reflects the uncertainty of the ABA on this issue.

Kentucky: Rule 6.1, entitled "Donated Legal Services," provides as follows:

> A lawyer is encouraged to voluntarily render public interest legal service. A lawyer is encouraged to accept and fulfill this responsibility to the public by rendering

a minimum of fifty (50) hours of service per calendar year by providing professional services at no fee or a reduced fee to persons of limited means, and/or by financial support for organizations that provide legal services to persons of limited means. Donated legal services may be reported on the annual dues statement furnished by the Kentucky Bar Association. Lawyers rendering a minimum of fifty (50) hours of donated legal service shall receive a recognition award for such service from the Kentucky Bar Association.

Massachusetts: Rule 6.1 states that a lawyer "should provide annually at least 25 hours of pro bono publico legal services for the benefit of persons of limited means." Alternatively, the lawyer should "contribute from $250 to 1 percent of the lawyer's annual taxable, professional income to one or more organizations that provide or support legal services to persons of limited means." This provision does not state whether the lawyer should contribute the greater or the lesser of these sums.

Montana has adopted the pre-2002 version of ABA Model Rule 6.1 but adds the following two sentences at the end of the rule: "The responsibility above set forth in this rule is a goal to which each lawyer should aspire. The rule will not be enforced through any form of disciplinary process."

New Mexico: Rule 16-601 conforms closely to ABA Model Rule 6.1, except that New Mexico has modified the last sentence of Rule 6.1 by providing that a lawyer may "alternatively, fulfill this aspiration by contributing financial support to organizations that provide legal services to persons of limited means, in the amount of three hundred fifty dollars ($350.00) per year."

New York: Compare ABA Model Rule 6.1 to New York EC's 2-25, 8-3, and 8-9.

North Carolina omits Rule 6.1, but Paragraph 6 of North Carolina's Preamble contains language almost identical to the original version of ABA Model Rule 6.1 (see "1983-1993 Rule" in the Legislative History above). However, North Carolina states that every lawyer should render public interest legal service "and provide civic leadership."

Texas omits Rule 6.1, but Paragraph 6 of the Texas Preamble addresses pro bono services. Among other things, the Preamble states: "The provision of free legal services to those unable to pay reasonable fees is a moral obligation of each lawyer as well as the profession generally."

Virginia: Rule 6.1 says that a lawyer "should render at least 2 percent per year of the lawyer's professional time to pro bono publico legal services," which the Rule defines. A law firm or group of lawyers may satisfy their responsibility under the Rule collectively. Further, "direct financial support of programs that provide direct delivery of legal services to meet the need described" in the Rule "is an alternative method for fulfilling a lawyer's responsibility."

Wyoming: Rule 6.1 largely tracks ABA Model Rule 6.1, but Wyoming adds a new paragraph (b) providing: "In the alternative, a lawyer should voluntarily contribute $500.00 per year to any existing non-profit organization which provides direct legal assistance to persons of limited means . . . ."

Related Materials

ABA Model Guidelines for the Utilization of Legal Assistant Services: In 1991, the ABA House of Delegates approved Model Guidelines for the Utilization of

Legal Assistant Services. Guideline 10 provides: "A lawyer who employs a legal assistant should facilitate the legal assistant's participation in appropriate continuing education and pro bono publico activities."

ABA Standards for Programs Providing Civil Pro Bono Legal Services to Persons of Limited Means: At its February 1996 Mid-Year Meeting, the ABA House of Delegates approved Standards for Programs Providing Civil Pro Bono Legal Services to Persons of Limited Means, which were drafted by the ABA Standing Committee on Lawyers' Public Service Responsibility ("SCLPSR"). The standards provide guidance to newly established pro bono programs and furnish a basis for evaluating and improving existing programs. The introduction to the standards notes that organized pro bono programs have grown in number at a remarkable rate, from 80 in 1980 to more than 900 in 1995. The standards cover such things as fundraising, conflicts of interest, communication with clients, training of volunteers, and case acceptance policy. The standards replace the ABA's Standards for Providers of Civil Legal Services to the Poor, which were originally adopted in 1961 and last revised in 1986. For more information about the standards, contact Gwendolyn Rowan at the ABA Center for Professional Responsibility, 541 N. Fairbanks Court, Chicago, IL 60611, (312) 988-5756.

American Lawyer's Code of Conduct: The Comment to Chapter 8 of the ALCC states:

> This Code has no rule requiring each lawyer to do a particular amount of uncompensated public interest or *pro bono publico* work, on pain of professional discipline. That does not mean that the attorney members of the Commission are unwilling to perform such services or that the non-lawyer members do not want to share in the benefits of *pro bono* work. Rather, it is apparent to the Commission that such a rule would be inherently so vague as to be unenforceable and unenforced, and therefore hypocritical.
>
> All lawyers should do work in the public interest. But some lawyers should not be telling other lawyers how much *pro bono* work they should be doing, and for whom, and disciplining them if they do not. Nor should codes of conduct purport to impose disciplinary requirements that the codifiers know will not be enforced.

Federal Statutes: Certain federal statutes may preclude federal government lawyers from doing any pro bono work adverse to any agency or department of the United States government. For example, 18 U.S.C. §205 makes it a criminal offense, punishable by up to five years in prison or a $50,000 fine, for a federal government lawyer to act as an "attorney for prosecuting any claim against the United States. . . ."

Law School Pro Bono Requirements: A number of law schools now require law students to engage in a specified amount of pro bono work as a condition of graduation. Columbia Law School, for example, requires all students to perform 40 hours of public interest service between the start of the second year and graduation. Students at Columbia can register to work at any of more than 500 public interest placements, covering a wide variety of work settings. Students who do not complete the 40 hours cannot graduate. For more information on the Columbia program, contact the Columbia Law School Public Interest Program, 435 W. 116th Street, Box E-16, New York, NY 10027, (212) 854-6158.

Model Rules of Professional Conduct for Federal Lawyers add a new subparagraph (b) providing that government lawyers "should provide pro bono legal services consistent with applicable law." In addition, Rule 5.1(d) provides that a supervisory government lawyer "should encourage subordinate lawyers to participate in pro bono publico service activities and the activities of bar associations and law reform organizations." However, the Comment to Rule 6.1 explains that "18 U.S.C. §205 and §209 and other laws, including those governing off-duty employment by members of the Armed Forces, may regulate a Government lawyer's ability to provide legal services on a pro bono basis outside the scope of the Government lawyer's official duties."

Restatement of the Law Governing Lawyers: The Restatement has no provision comparable to ABA Model Rule 6.1.

Statement of Principles by Chicago Law Firms: In 1991, 31 major Chicago law firms formally endorsed and committed to a Statement of Principles relating to pro bono work including that law firms "should make it a goal to contribute an average of at least 30 hours of legal services per lawyer per year to representing the poor or other persons and organizations who are unable to retain legal counsel and which serve the public interest."

Rule 6.2 Accepting Appointments

A lawyer shall not seek to avoid appointment by a tribunal to represent a person except for good cause, such as:

(a) representing the client is likely to result in violation of the Rules of Professional Conduct or other law;

(b) representing the client is likely to result in an unreasonable financial burden on the lawyer; or

(c) the client or the cause is so repugnant to the lawyer as to be likely to impair the client-lawyer relationship or the lawyer's ability to represent the client.

COMMENT

[1] A lawyer ordinarily is not obliged to accept a client whose character or cause the lawyer regards as repugnant. The lawyer's freedom to select clients is, however, qualified. All lawyers have a responsibility to assist in providing pro bono publico service. See Rule 6.1. An individual lawyer fulfills this responsibility by accepting a fair share of unpopular matters or indigent or unpopular clients. A lawyer may also be subject to appointment by a court to serve unpopular clients or persons unable to afford legal services.

Appointed Counsel

[2] For good cause a lawyer may seek to decline an appointment to represent a person who cannot afford to retain counsel or whose cause is

unpopular. Good cause exists if the lawyer could not handle the matter competently, see Rule 1.1, or if undertaking the representation would result in an improper conflict of interest, for example, when the client or the cause is so repugnant to the lawyer as to be likely to impair the client-lawyer relationship or the lawyer's ability to represent the client. A lawyer may also seek to decline an appointment if acceptance would be unreasonably burdensome, for example, when it would impose a financial sacrifice so great as to be unjust.

[3] An appointed lawyer has the same obligations to the client as retained counsel, including the obligations of loyalty and confidentiality, and is subject to the same limitations on the client-lawyer relationship, such as the obligation to refrain from assisting the client in violation of the Rules.

Canon and Code Antecedents

ABA Canons of Professional Ethics: Canon 4 provided as follows:

4. *When Counsel for an Indigent Prisoner*

> A lawyer assigned as counsel for an indigent prisoner ought not to ask to be excused for any trivial reason, and should always exert his best efforts in his behalf.

ABA Model Code of Professional Responsibility: No comparable Disciplinary Rule.

Cross-References in Other Rules

Rule 1.1, Comment 4: "A lawyer may accept representation where the requisite level of competence can be achieved by reasonable preparation. This applies as well to a lawyer who is appointed as counsel for an unrepresented person. See also **Rule 6.2**."

Rule 1.16, Comment 3: "When a lawyer has been appointed to represent a client, withdrawal ordinarily requires approval of the appointing authority. See also **Rule 6.2**."

Legislative History of Model Rule 6.2

1980 Discussion Draft and 1981 Draft were substantially the same as adopted, with only minor changes in phrasing.

1982 Draft was the same as adopted *except* that it completely omitted subparagraph (c).

2002 Amendments: The ABA Ethics 2000 Commission did not propose any changes to the text or Comment of Rule 6.2.

Selected State Variations

California: See B & P Code 6068(h). (California's Rules of Professional Conduct have no comparable provision.)

Georgia: In the rules effective January 1, 2001, Georgia shortens ABA Model Rule 6.2 to a single sentence: "For good cause a lawyer may seek to avoid appointment by a tribunal to represent a person." Georgia adopts the ABA Comment to Rule 6.2 essentially verbatim, but adds that the rule "is not intended to be enforced through disciplinary process."

New York: Compare ABA Model Rule 6.2 to New York EC's 2-29 and 2-30.

North Carolina omits Rule 6.2.

Related Materials

Federal Statutes: 28 U.S.C. §1915(d), which governs in forma pauperis status in civil cases, provides: "The court may request an attorney to represent any [person claiming in forma pauperis status] unable to employ counsel and may dismiss the case if the allegation of poverty is untrue. . . ." In Mallard v. United States District Court, 490 U.S. 296 (1989), the Supreme Court held that the word "request" does not give federal courts the power to compel lawyers to represent indigents in civil cases. The *Mallard* Court declined to rule on whether statutes (such as 18 U.S.C. §3005) that provide for the "assignment" or "appointment" of counsel in federal cases give courts power to compel unwilling attorneys to represent indigents.

Restatement of the Law Governing Lawyers: See Restatement §§9 and 13 in our chapter on the Restatement later in this volume.

Rule 6.3 Membership in Legal Services Organization

A lawyer may serve as a director, officer or member of a legal services organization, apart from the law firm in which the lawyer practices, notwithstanding that the organization serves persons having interests adverse to a client of the lawyer. The lawyer shall not knowingly participate in a decision or action of the organization:

(a) if participating in the decision or action would be incompatible with the lawyer's obligations to a client under Rule 1.7; or

(b) where the decision or action could have a material adverse effect on the representation of a client of the organization whose interests are adverse to a client of the lawyer.

COMMENT

[1] Lawyers should be encouraged to support and participate in legal service organizations. A lawyer who is an officer or a member of such an organization does not thereby have a client-lawyer relationship with persons served by the organization. However, there is potential conflict between the interests of such persons and the interests of the lawyer's clients. If the possibility of such conflict disqualified a lawyer from serving

on the board of a legal services organization, the profession's involvement in such organizations would be severely curtailed.

[2] It may be necessary in appropriate cases to reassure a client of the organization that the representation will not be affected by conflicting loyalties of a member of the board. Established, written policies in this respect can enhance the credibility of such assurances.

Canon and Code Antecedents

ABA Canons of Professional Ethics: No comparable Canon.

ABA Model Code of Professional Responsibility: No comparable Disciplinary Rule.

Cross-References in Other Rules

None.

Legislative History of Model Rule 6.3

1980 Discussion Draft (then Rule 8.2(c)) provided as follows:

> (c) A lawyer may serve as a director, member or officer of an organization involved in reform of the law or its administration notwithstanding the fact that the reform may affect interests of a client of the lawyer if:
>
> (1) when the interests of the client could be affected, the fact is disclosed in the course of deliberations on the matter, but the identity of the client need not be disclosed;
>
> (2) when the client could be adversely affected, the lawyer complies with Rule 1.8 with respect to the client; and
>
> (3) the lawyer takes no part in any decision that could result in a direct material benefit or detriment to the client.

1981 Draft was similar to the adopted version of Rule 6.3, except that it contained an additional requirement that "the organization complies with Rule 5.4 concerning the professional independence of its legal staff."

1982 Draft was adopted.

2002 Amendments: The ABA Ethics 2000 Commission did not propose any changes to the text or Comment of Rule 6.3.

Selected State Variations

California: See Rule 1-600 (Legal Service Programs).

Georgia: In the rules effective January 1, 2001, Georgia adopts ABA Model Rule 6.3 and its Comment essentially verbatim, but Georgia adds that there is "no disciplinary penalty for a violation of this Rule."

Illinois: Rule 6.3 applies only to a "not-for-profit" legal services organization.

Michigan: Rule 6.3 adds extensive rules governing lawyer participation in "not-for-profit referral service[s] that recommend legal services to the public."

New Jersey: Rule 6.3 requires that the organization comply with Rule 5.4 and states the limitation in (b) to include adverse effect on the interest of "a client or class of clients of the organization or upon the independence of professional judgment of a lawyer representing such a client."

New York: Compare ABA Model Rule 6.3 to New York's DR 5-110.

Ohio has no provision comparable to ABA Model Rule 6.3.

Related Materials

Restatement of the Law Governing Lawyers: See Restatement §§9 and 13 in our chapter on the Restatement later in this volume.

Rule 6.4 Law Reform Activities Affecting Client Interests

A lawyer may serve as a director, officer or member of an organization involved in reform of the law or its administration notwithstanding that the reform may affect the interests of a client of the lawyer. When the lawyer knows that the interests of a client may be materially benefited by a decision in which the lawyer participates, the lawyer shall disclose that fact but need not identify the client.

COMMENT

[1] Lawyers involved in organizations seeking law reform generally do not have a client-lawyer relationship with the organization. Otherwise, it might follow that a lawyer could not be involved in a bar association law reform program that might indirectly affect a client. See also Rule 1.2(b). For example, a lawyer specializing in antitrust litigation might be regarded as disqualified from participating in drafting revisions of rules governing that subject. In determining the nature and scope of participation in such activities, a lawyer should be mindful of obligations to clients under other Rules, particularly Rule 1.7. A lawyer is professionally obligated to protect the integrity of the program by making an appropriate disclosure within the organization when the lawyer knows a private client might be materially benefited.

Canon and Code Antecedents

ABA Canons of Professional Ethics: No comparable Canon.

ABA Model Code of Professional Responsibility: No comparable Disciplinary Rule.

Cross-References in Other Rules

None.

Legislative History of Model Rule 6.4

1980 Discussion Draft (then Rule 8.2(a) and (b)) provided as follows:

Conflict of Interest in Pro Bono Publico Service

(a) A lawyer engaged in service pro bono publico shall avoid improper conflicts of interest therein.

(b) A lawyer may serve as a director, officer, or member of an organization providing legal services to persons of limited means notwithstanding that such services are provided to persons having interests adverse to a client of the lawyer if:

(1) the organization complies with Rule 7.5 [now Rule 5.4(c)] concerning the professional independence of its legal staff;

(2) when the interests of a client of the lawyer could be affected, the lawyer takes no part in any decision by the organization that could have a material adverse effect on the interest of a client of the organization or upon the independence of professional judgment of a lawyer representing such a client; and

(3) the lawyer otherwise complies with Rule 1.8 with respect to the lawyer's client.

1981 Draft:

A lawyer may serve as a director, officer or member of an organization involved in reform of the law or its administration notwithstanding the fact that the reform may affect the interests of a client of the lawyer if the lawyer takes no part in any decision that could have a direct material effect on the client.

1982 Draft was adopted.

2002 Amendments: The ABA Ethics 2000 Commission did not propose any changes to the text or Comment of Rule 6.4.

Selected State Variations

California: No comparable provision.

District of Columbia adds a paragraph (a) to its version of Rule 6.4 — see District of Columbia Rules of Professional Conduct below.

Florida replaces "materially benefitted" with "materially affected" in the second sentence of Rule 6.4.

Georgia: In the rules effective January 1, 2001, Georgia adopts ABA Model Rule 6.4 and its Comment essentially verbatim, but Georgia adds that "[t]here is no disciplinary penalty for a violation of this Rule."

Illinois: Rule 6.4 applies when the "actions" of the organization may affect a client's interests, rather than when the "reform" may affect the client's interests.

New York: Compare ABA Model Rule 6.4 to New York EC 8-4 and DR 5-110.

Ohio has no provision comparable to ABA Model Rule 6.4.

Texas: Rule 1.13 (Conflicts: Public Interest Activities) is similar to ABA Model Rule 6.3 as amended in 2002, but the Texas rule also governs a lawyer's activities in a "civic, charitable or law reform organization." Texas Rule 1.13 omits the clause "notwithstanding that the organization serves persons having interests adverse to a client of the lawyer."

Virginia omits Rule 6.4.

Related Materials

Model Rules of Professional Conduct for Federal Lawyers: Rule 6.4 adds a sentence providing that a federal lawyer "shall not knowingly participate in a decision or action of the organization if participating in the decision would be incompatible with the Federal lawyer's obligations to the client under Rule 1.7."

Rule 6.5 Nonprofit and Court-Annexed Limited Legal Services Programs

Editors' Note. Rule 6.5 is entirely new. The ABA House of Delegates added it to the Model Rules at its February 2002 Mid-Year Meeting, adopting the proposal submitted by the ABA Ethics 2000 Commission. For more information, see the entry titled "2002 Amendments" in the Legislative History following this rule.

(a) A lawyer who, under the auspices of a program sponsored by a nonprofit organization or court, provides short-term limited legal services to a client without expectation by either the lawyer or the client that the lawyer will provide continuing representation in the matter:

(1) is subject to Rules 1.7 and 1.9(a) only if the lawyer knows that the representation of the client involves a conflict of interest; and

(2) is subject to Rule 1.10 only if the lawyer knows that another lawyer associated with the lawyer in a law firm is disqualified by Rule 1.7 or 1.9(a) with respect to the matter.

(b) Except as provided in paragraph (a)(2), Rule 1.10 is inapplicable to a representation governed by this Rule.

COMMENT

[1] Legal services organizations, courts and various nonprofit organizations have established programs through which lawyers provide

short-term limited legal services — such as advice or the completion of legal forms — that will assist persons to address their legal problems without further representation by a lawyer. In these programs, such as legal-advice hotlines, advice-only clinics or pro se counseling programs, a client-lawyer relationship is established, but there is no expectation that the lawyer's representation of the client will continue beyond the limited consultation. Such programs are normally operated under circumstances in which it is not feasible for a lawyer to systematically screen for conflicts of interest as is generally required before undertaking a representation. See, e.g., Rules 1.7, 1.9 and 1.10.

[2] A lawyer who provides short-term limited legal services pursuant to this Rule must secure the client's informed consent to the limited scope of the representation. See Rule 1.2(c). If a short-term limited representation would not be reasonable under the circumstances, the lawyer may offer advice to the client but must also advise the client of the need for further assistance of counsel. Except as provided in this Rule, the Rules of Professional Conduct, including Rules 1.6 and 1.9(c), are applicable to the limited representation.

[3] Because a lawyer who is representing a client in the circumstances addressed by this Rule ordinarily is not able to check systematically for conflicts of interest, paragraph (a) requires compliance with Rules 1.7 or 1.9(a) only if the lawyer knows that the representation presents a conflict of interest for the lawyer, and with Rule 1.10 only if the lawyer knows that another lawyer in the lawyer's firm is disqualified by Rules 1.7 or 1.9(a) in the matter.

[4] Because the limited nature of the services significantly reduces the risk of conflicts of interest with other matters being handled by the lawyer's firm, paragraph (b) provides that Rule 1.10 is inapplicable to a representation governed by this Rule except as provided by paragraph (a)(2). Paragraph (a)(2) requires the participating lawyer to comply with Rule 1.10 when the lawyer knows that the lawyer's firm is disqualified by Rules 1.7 or 1.9(a). By virtue of paragraph (b), however, a lawyer's participation in a short-term limited legal services program will not preclude the lawyer's firm from undertaking or continuing the representation of a client with interests adverse to a client being represented under the program's auspices. Nor will the personal disqualification of a lawyer participating in the program be imputed to other lawyers participating in the program.

[5] If, after commencing a short-term limited representation in accordance with this Rule, a lawyer undertakes to represent the client in the matter on an ongoing basis, Rules 1.7, 1.9(a) and 1.10 become applicable.

Cross-References in Other Rules

Rule 1.16, Comment 1: "Ordinarily, a representation in a matter is completed when the agreed-upon assistance has been concluded. See **Rules** 1.2(c) and **6.5**. See also Rule 1.3, Comment [4]."

Canon and Code Antecedents

ABA Canons of Professional Ethics: No comparable Canon.

ABA Model Code of Professional Responsibility: No comparable Disciplinary Rule.

Legislative History

2002 Amendments: Rule 6.5 was added to the Model Rules in February 2002. The new rule and its Comment were based on a proposal by the ABA Ethics 2000 Commission, which the ABA House of Delegates adopted without change. The Reporter's Explanation that accompanied the Ethics 2000 Commission proposal provided, in relevant part, as follows:

*Model Rule 6.5 — Reporter's Explanation of Changes**

Rule 6.5 is a new Rule in response to the Commission's concern that a strict application of the conflict-of-interest rules may be deterring lawyers from serving as volunteers in programs in which clients are provided short-term limited legal services under the auspices of a nonprofit organization or a court-annexed program. The paradigm is the legal-advice hotline or pro se clinic, the purpose of which is to provide short-term limited legal assistance to persons of limited means who otherwise would go unrepresented.

Paragraph (a) limits Rule 6.5 to situations in which lawyers provide clients short-term limited legal services under the auspices of a program sponsored by a nonprofit organization or court. The Commission believes that the proposed relaxation of the conflict rules does not pose a significant risk to clients when the lawyer is working in a program sponsored by a nonprofit organization or a court and will eliminate an impediment to lawyer participation in such programs. See Comment [1].

Paragraph (a)(1) provides that the lawyer is subject to the requirements of Rules 1.7 and 1.9(a) only if the lawyer knows that the representation involves a conflict of interest. The purpose is to make it unnecessary for the lawyer to do a comprehensive conflicts check in a practice setting in which it normally is not feasible to do so. See Comment [3]. In cases in which the lawyer knows of a conflict of interest, however, compliance with Rules 1.7 and 1.9(a) is required.

Paragraph (a)(2) provides that a lawyer participating in a short-term legal services program must comply with Rule 1.10 if the lawyer knows that a lawyer with whom the lawyer is associated in a firm would be disqualified from handling the matter by Rules 1.7 or 1.9(a). By otherwise exempting a representation governed by this Rule from Rule 1.10, however, paragraph (b) protects lawyers associated with the participating lawyer from a vicarious disqualification that might otherwise be required. Thus, as explained in Comment [4], a lawyer's participation in a short-term limited legal services program will not preclude the lawyer's firm from undertaking or continuing the representation of a client with interests adverse to a client being represented under the program's auspices. Nor will a personal disqualification of a lawyer participating in the program be imputed to other lawyers participating in the program. Given the limited nature of the representation provided in nonprofit short-term limited legal ser-

*Committee Reports, and the Reporter's Explanation of Changes contained therein, do not represent official policy of the ABA. They are for information only, and the opinions are those of the authors.

vices programs, the Commission thinks that the protections afforded clients by Rule 1.10 are not necessary except in the circumstances specified in paragraph (a)(2).

The remainder of the Reporter's Explanation of Changes tracks each paragraph of the Comment to Rule 6.5. To view this part of the report, visit the web site of the ABA Center for Professional Responsibility at www.abanet.org/cpr (click on "Ethics 2000 Commission").

Selected State Variations

New York has no counterpart to ABA Model Rule 6.5.

Related Materials

Restatement of the Law Governing Lawyers: See Restatement §§121 and 123 in our chapter on the Restatement later in this volume.

ARTICLE 7. INFORMATION ABOUT LEGAL SERVICES

Rule 7.1 Communications Concerning a Lawyer's Services

A lawyer shall not make a false or misleading communication about the lawyer or the lawyer's services. A communication is false or misleading if it~~: (a)~~ contains a material misrepresentation of fact or law, or omits a fact necessary to make the statement considered as a whole not materially misleading~~;~~.

~~**(b) is likely to create an unjustified expectation about results the lawyer can achieve, or states or implies that the lawyer can achieve results by means that violate the Rules of Professional Conduct or other law; or**~~

~~**(c) compares the lawyer's services with other lawyers' services, unless the comparison can be factually substantiated.**~~

COMMENT

[1] This Rule governs all communications about a lawyer's services, including advertising permitted by Rule 7.2. Whatever means are used to make known a lawyer's services, statements about them ~~should~~ must be truthful. ~~The prohibition in paragraph (b) of statements that may create~~

“unjustified ~~expectations” would ordinarily preclude advertisements about results obtained on behalf of a client, such as the amount of a damage award or the lawyer’s record in obtaining favorable verdicts, and advertisements containing client endorsements. Such information may create the unjustified expectation that similar results can be obtained for others without reference to the specific factual and legal circumstances.~~

[2] Truthful statements that are misleading are also prohibited by this Rule. A truthful statement is misleading if it omits a fact necessary to make the lawyer’s communication considered as a whole not materially misleading. A truthful statement is also misleading if there is a substantial likelihood that it will lead a reasonable person to formulate a specific conclusion about the lawyer or the lawyer’s services for which there is no reasonable factual foundation.

[3] An advertisement that truthfully reports a lawyer’s achievements on behalf of clients or former clients may be misleading if presented so as to lead a reasonable person to form an unjustified expectation that the same results could be obtained for other clients in similar matters without reference to the specific factual and legal circumstances of each client’s case. Similarly, an unsubstantiated comparison of the lawyer’s services or fees with the services or fees of other lawyers may be misleading if presented with such specificity as would lead a reasonable person to conclude that the comparison can be substantiated. The inclusion of an appropriate disclaimer or qualifying language may preclude a finding that a statement is likely to create unjustified expectations or otherwise mislead a prospective client.

[4] See also Rule 8.4(e) for the prohibition against stating or implying an ability to influence improperly a government agency or official or to achieve results by means that violate the Rules of Professional Conduct or other law.

Canon and Code Antecedents

ABA Canons of Professional Ethics: Canons 27 and 43 provided as follows:

27. Advertising, Direct or Indirect

It is unprofessional to solicit professional employment by circulars, advertisements, through touters or by personal communications or interviews not warranted by personal relations. Indirect advertisements for professional employment such as furnishing or inspiring newspaper comments, or procuring his photograph to be published in connection with causes in which the lawyer has been or is engaged or concerning the manner of their conduct, the magnitude of the interest involved, the importance of the lawyer’s position, and all other like self-laudation, offend the traditions and lower the tone of our profession and are reprehensible; but the customary use of simple professional cards is not improper.

Publication in reputable law lists in a manner consistent with the standards of conduct imposed by these canons of brief biographical and informative data is permissible. Such data must not be misleading and may include only a statement of the lawyer's name and the names of his professional associates; addresses, telephone numbers, cable addresses; branches of the profession practiced; date and place of birth and admission to the bar; schools attended; with dates of graduation, degrees and other educational distinctions; public or quasi-public offices; posts of honor; legal authorships; legal teaching positions; memberships and offices in bar associations and committees thereof, in legal and scientific societies and legal fraternities; foreign language ability; the fact of listings in other reputable law lists; the names and addresses of references; and, with their written consent, the names of clients regularly represented. A certificate of compliance with the Rules and Standards issued by the Standing Committee on Law Lists may be treated as evidence that such list is reputable.

It is not improper for a lawyer who is admitted to practice as a proctor in admiralty to use that designation on his letterhead or shingle or for a lawyer who has complied with the statutory requirements of admission to practice before the patent office, to so use the designation "patent attorney" or "patent lawyer" or "trademark attorney" or "trademark lawyer" or any combination of those terms.

43. Approved Law Lists

It shall be improper for a lawyer to permit his name to be published in a law list the conduct, management or contents of which are calculated or likely to deceive or injure the public or the profession, or to lower the dignity or standing of the profession.

ABA Model Code of Professional Responsibility: Compare DR 2-101 (reprinted later in this volume).

Cross-References in Other Rules

Rule 5.5, Comment 21: "Whether and how lawyers may communicate the availability of their services to prospective clients in this jurisdiction is governed by **Rules 7.1** to 7.5."

Rule 5.7, Comment 10: "The promotion of the law-related services must also in all respects comply with **Rules 7.1** through 7.3, dealing with advertising and solicitation."

Rule 7.2(a): "Subject to the requirements of **Rules 7.1** and 7.3, a lawyer may advertise services through written, recorded or electronic communication, including public media."

Rule 7.3, Comment 3: The "potential for informal review is itself likely to help guard against statements and claims that might constitute false and misleading communications, in violation of **Rule 7.1**."

Rule 7.3, Comment 5: "[A]ny solicitation which contains information which is false or misleading within the meaning of **Rule 7.1** . . . is prohibited."

Rule 7.3, Comment 8: "Lawyers who participate in a legal service plan must reasonably assure that the plan sponsors are in compliance with **Rules 7.1**, 7.2 and 7.3(b). See 8.4(a)."

Rule 7.4, Comment 1: Communications claiming specialization "are subject to the 'false and misleading' standard applied in **Rule 7.1** to communications concerning a lawyer's services."

Rule 7.5(a): "A lawyer shall not use a firm name, letterhead or other professional designation that violates **Rule 7.1**. A trade name may be used by a lawyer in private practice if it does not imply a connection with a government agency or with a public or charitable legal services organization and is not otherwise in violation of **Rule 7.1**."

Legislative History of Model Rule 7.1

1980 Discussion Draft of Rule 7.1 (then Rule 9.1) was substantially the same as adopted, except that the first sentence prohibited a lawyer from making any "false, *fraudulent,* or misleading statement. . . ."

1981 and 1982 Drafts were the same as adopted.

2002 Amendments: At its February 2002 Mid-Year Meeting, the ABA House of Delegates adopted with only minor changes the ABA Ethics 2000 Commission proposal to amend Rule 7.1 and its Comment.

Selected State Variations

Editors' Note. For a comprehensive collection of the full text of the ethics rules governing lawyer advertising in most states, see the web site maintained by the American Bar Association's Commission on Responsibility in Client Development at www.abanet.org/adrules.

Alaska: Rule 7.1 adds language prohibiting a lawyer from making a false or misleading communication regarding "any prospective client's need for legal services."

Arizona: Communications and advertisements concerning a lawyer's services must be "predominantly informational," which is defined to mean that "in both quantity and quality, the communication of factual information rationally related to the need for and selection of an attorney predominates." Rule 7.1(b).

California: See Rule 1-400 (Advertising and Solicitation) and the accompanying Standards showing presumptive violations of Rule 1-400. See also B&P Code §§6157-6159.2; California Labor Code §139.45 ("the Industrial Medical Council and the administrative director shall take particular care to preclude any advertisements with respect to industrial injuries or illnesses that are false or mislead the public with respect to workers' compensation. In promulgating rules with respect to advertising, the State Bar . . . shall also take particular care to achieve the same goal"); and California Labor Code §5432 (requiring every advertisement soliciting workers' compensation clients to state conspicuously: "Making a false or fraudulent workers' compensation claim is a felony subject to up to 5 years in prison or a fine of up to $50,000 or double the value of the fraud, whichever is greater, or by both imprisonment and fine").

Colorado: Rule 7.2(c) provides that "unsolicited communications concerning a lawyer's services mailed to prospective clients shall be sent only by regular U.S. mail, not by registered mail or other forms of restricted delivery."

District of Columbia: D.C. Rule 7.1 differs significantly from the ABA Model Rule, and covers some material from ABA Model Rule 7.4, which D.C. omits — see District of Columbia Rules of Professional Conduct below.

Florida: Florida's lawyer advertising rules, which were extensively amended in 1999, are far more comprehensive and detailed than the ABA Model Rules of Professional Conduct. For example, Rule 4-7.2 provides:

> (a)(2) *Location of Practice.* All advertisements and written communications provided for under these rules shall disclose, by city or town, 1 or more bona fide office locations of the lawyer or lawyers who will actually perform the services advertised. . . . For the purposes of this rule, a bona fide office is defined as a physical location maintained by the lawyer or law firm where the lawyer or law firm reasonably expects to furnish legal services in a substantial way on a regular and continuing basis. If an advertisement or written communication lists a telephone number in connection with a specified geographic area other than an area containing a bona fide office, appropriate qualifying language must appear in the advertisement.

Rule 4-7.2(a) requires that all portrayals of persons, things, or events "must be objectively relevant to the selection of an attorney and shall not be deceptive, misleading, or manipulative." A lawyer shall not advertise "an area of practice in which the advertising lawyer or law firm does not currently practice law."

Rule 4-7.2(c) requires illustrations to "present information that is directly related and objectively relevant to a viewer's possible need for legal services in a specific type of matter." The Comment notes that "a drawing of a fist, to suggest the lawyer's ability to achieve results, would be barred," but a lawyer could illustrate advertisements with "the scales of justice . . . , a picture of the lawyer, or a map of the office location."

Rule 4-7.3(b) requires that all lawyer advertisements must contain the following disclosure: "The hiring of a lawyer is an important decision that should not be based solely upon advertisements. Before you decide, ask us to send you free written information about our qualifications and experience." A separate rule, Rule 4-7.9, prescribes the written information that lawyers must provide to potential clients on request.

Rule 4-7.5(b), subtitled "Appearance on Television or Radio," strictly regulates advertisements on the "electronic media."

Florida Rule 4-7.7 requires lawyers to file all advertisements with the "standing committee on advertising . . . either prior to or concurrently with the lawyer's first dissemination of the advertisement or written communication . . . ." If the committee does not approve or disapprove the ad within 15 days, "the advertisement will be deemed approved." If the committee disapproves of an advertisement, it "shall advise the lawyer that dissemination or continued dissemination of the advertisement or written communication may result in professional discipline," and the committee's finding may be offered as evidence in a grievance proceeding. However, Florida Rule 4-7.8 exempts various categories of advertisements from the standing committee's review.

Information requested by potential clients is governed by Florida Rule 4-7.9, which provides that whenever a potential client requests information regarding a lawyer or law firm, the lawyer or law firm "shall promptly furnish (by mail if requested) the extensive written (including computer-accessed) information" described later in the rule. Information provided pursuant to a potential client's request may contain "factually verifiable statements concerning past results obtained by the lawyer or law firm" if the statements are not misleading.

In 1997, the Standing Committee on Advertising issued "Internet Guidelines," which generally require lawyers to submit both a hard copy of the homepage and the URL (i.e., the Internet address) to the Standing Committee on Advertising. However, information beyond the homepage "will be treated as information provided to prospective clients at their request" and need not be filed, and homepages that contain "no audio or photographs or illustrations" and only specified information are "exempt" from filing.

Georgia: In the rules effective January 1, 2001, Georgia generally tracks the pre-2002 version of ABA Model Rule 7.1, but Georgia adds special subparagraphs requiring specified disclaimers in all advertisements mentioning contingent fees or stating "no fee unless you win or collect" or any similar phrase. Such advertisements must conspicuously present a disclaimer stating: "Court costs and other additional expenses of legal action usually must be paid by the client. Contingent fees are not permitted in all types of cases."

Iowa has among the most restrictive rules in the country on advertising and solicitation. Iowa prohibits not only false or misleading communications but also any "self-laudatory" statement or "any statement or claim . . . which appeals to the emotions, prejudices, or likes or dislikes of a person. . . ." Iowa also continues to specify the precise categories of information a lawyer may advertise, basically along the lines of DR 2-101(B) of the ABA Model Code, and requires all information to be "presented in a dignified manner." With respect to legal fees, Iowa prohibits "all subjective characterizations," including terms such as "cut-rate," "lowest," "reasonable," "moderate," "very reasonable," "give-away," "below-cost," or "special."

Massachusetts: Rule 7.1 tracks ABA Model Rule 7.1(a) but relegates subparagraphs (b) and (c) of the pre-2002 version of ABA Rule 7.1 to the Comment.

Mississippi: Rule 7.5(e) provides: "Upon reasonable request by The Mississippi Bar, a lawyer shall promptly provide proof that any statement or claim made in any advertisement or written communication, as well as the information furnished to a prospective client," is not "directly or inherently" or "potentially" false or misleading. In addition, Mississippi Rule 7.5(f) provides that advertising offering to "represent a client in a particular type of matter, without appropriate qualification, shall be presumed to be misleading if the lawyer reasonably believes that a lawyer or law firm not associated with the originally retained lawyer or law firm will be associated or act as primary counsel in representing the client."

Missouri: Rule 7.1 adds that a communication is false or misleading if it:

> (e) contains a representation of, or implication of, fact regarding the quality of legal services which is not susceptible to reasonable verification by the public;
>
> (f) contains any statistical data or other information based on past performance which is not susceptible to reasonable verification by the public;
>
> (g) contains any paid testimonial about, or paid endorsement of, the lawyer, without identifying the fact that payment has been made or, if the testimonial or endorsement is not made by an actual client, without identifying that fact;
>
> (h) contains a simulated description of the lawyer, his partners or associates, his offices or facilities, or his services without identifying the fact that the description is a simulation . . . .

Nevada: Supreme Court Rule 195 provides that a communication is false or misleading if it "[c]ontains a testimonial or endorsement."

New Jersey adds a Rule 7.1(a)(4) specifying what a legal advertisement can say about fees.

New Mexico adds Rule 16-701(A)(5), which provides that a communication is false or misleading if it "states or implies that the lawyer is a specialist in any field of law other than as specifically permitted by Rule 16-704."

New York: Compare ABA Model Rule 7.1 to New York's DR 2-101.

North Carolina provides that a "dramatization depicting a fictional situation is misleading unless it . . . contains a conspicuous written or oral statement at the beginning and end of the communication, explaining that the communication contains a dramatization and does not depict actual events or real persons."

Ohio: DR 2-101 prohibits any communication that is "unfair"; or that "[s]eeks employment in connection with matters in which the lawyer or law firm does not intend to actively participate in the representation, but that the lawyer or law firm intends to refer to other counsel" (except a pro bono organization); or that is "subjectively self-laudatory" or is not presented in a "dignified manner"; or "[c]ontains characterizations of rates or fees chargeable by the lawyer or law firm, such as 'cut-rate,' 'lowest,' 'giveaway,' 'below cost,' 'discount,' and 'special.' "

Pennsylvania provides in Rule 7.7, entitled Lawyer Referral Service, as follows:

> (a) A lawyer shall not accept referrals from a lawyer referral service if the service engaged in communication with the public or direct contact with prospective clients in a manner that would violate the Rules of Professional Conduct if the communication or contact were made by the lawyer.
>
> (b) A "lawyer referral service" is any person, group of persons, association, organization or entity that receives a fee or charge for referring or causing the direct or indirect referral of a potential client to a lawyer drawn from a specific group or panel of lawyers.

Pennsylvania Rule 7.1(b) provides that a communication is false or misleading if it:

> is likely to create an unjustified expectation about results the lawyer can achieve, such as the amount of previous damage awards, the lawyer's record in obtaining favorable verdicts, or client endorsements, or states or implies that the lawyer can achieve results by means that violate the rules of professional conduct or other law.

Rule 7.1(d) provides that a communication would be considered false or misleading if it "contains subjective claims as to the quality of legal services or a lawyer's credentials that are not capable of measurement or verification."

South Carolina: Rule 7.2 includes the following paragraphs:

> (f) A lawyer shall not make statements in advertisements which are merely self-laudatory or which describe or characterize the quality of the lawyer's services; provided that this provision shall not apply to information furnished to a prospective client at that person's request or to information supplied to existing clients.
>
> (g) Every advertisement that contains information about the lawyer's fee shall disclose whether the client will be liable for any expenses in addition to the fee and, if the fee will be a percentage of the recovery, whether the percentage will be computed before deducting the expenses.

These restrictions have special significance for lawyers who are not licensed in South Carolina because Rule 418 of the South Carolina court rules makes it "misconduct" for an out-of-state lawyer to violate South Carolina's advertising rules and provides for severe sanctions, including fee forfeiture, for any lawyer who solicits a matter in violation of those rules. For more on Rule 418, see the South Carolina entry in the Selected State Variations following ABA Model Rule 8.5.

Virginia's version of Rule 7.1 gives additional examples of what would make a communication false or misleading. Virginia also requires "ADVERTISING MATERIAL" to appear as a legend on direct mail solicitations. Prominence is specified. Registered mail and other forms of restricted delivery are forbidden.

Related Materials

ABA Aspirational Goals for Lawyer Advertising: In August of 1988, the ABA's House of Delegates endorsed a series of "aspirational" goals written by the ABA's Commission on Advertising. These goals are nonbinding and are not grounds for discipline. They are intended to permit lawyers to advertise "effectively yet with dignity." We reprint the following excerpts:*

Preamble

[E]mpirical evidence suggests that undignified advertising can detract from the public's confidence in the legal profession and respect for the justice system.

Under present case law, the matter of dignity is widely believed to be so subjective as to be beyond the scope of constitutionally permitted regulation. Nevertheless, it seems entirely proper for the organized bar to suggest non-binding aspirational goals urging lawyers who wish to advertise to do so in a dignified manner. . . .

Aspirational Goals

6. Lawyers should consider that the use of inappropriately dramatic music, unseemly slogans, hawkish spokespersons, premium offers, slapstick routines or outlandish settings in advertising does not instill confidence in the lawyer or the legal profession and undermines the serious purpose of legal services and the judicial system. . . .

9. Lawyers should design their advertising to attract legal matters which they are competent to handle.

10. Lawyers should be concerned with making legal services more affordable to the public. Lawyer advertising may be designed to build up client bases so that efficiencies of scale may be achieved that will translate into more affordable legal services.

ABA Commission on Responsibility in Client Development (formerly the ABA Commission on Advertising): In 1978, the ABA appointed a Commission on Advertising. Commission members over the years have included private lawyers, disciplinary counsel, a lawyer for an advertising agency, nonlawyers, and others. In 1994, the ABA Commission on Advertising held public hearings around the country to explore whether advertising by lawyers was contributing to perceived decline in the public's opinion of lawyers, and whether lawyer advertising was helping a significant number of people, especially the poor, to locate lawyers. In 1995, the Commission issued a final report and recommendations. In 1998, the Commission published a "white paper" entitled "A Re-Examination of the ABA Model Rules of Professional Conduct Pertaining to Client Development in Light of Emerging Technologies." Later in 1998, proposals were circulated to abolish the Commission, but protests from many parts of the profession persuaded the ABA to continue funding the Commission and its work.

In 1999, the Commission on Advertising changed its name to the Commission on Responsibility in Client Development to better reflect its mission. For more information about the Commission and its work, contact the Commission's Staff Counsel, William Hornsby, 541 North Fairbanks Court, Chicago, Illinois 60611, phone 312-988-5761, or visit the Commission's web site at www.abanet.org/legalservices/advertising.html.

ABA Formal Ethics Opinions: See ABA Formal Ethics Ops. 94-388 (1994) and 95-391 (1995).

IRS Regulations: In the regulations governing practice before the Internal Revenue Service, 31 C.F.R. §10.30 provides that no attorney eligible to practice before the IRS shall, with respect to any IRS matter, use any form of public communication containing "(i) A false, fraudulent, unduly influencing, coercive, or unfair statement or claim; or (ii) a misleading or deceptive statement or claim."

Lanham Act: 15 U.S.C. §1125(a), provides in pertinent part:

> (a) *Civil action*
>
> (1) Any person who . . . uses in commerce any word, term, name, symbol, or device, or any combination thereof, or any false designation of origin, false or misleading description of fact, or false or misleading representation of fact, which —
>
> (A) is likely to cause confusion, or to cause mistake, or to deceive as to the affiliation, connection, or association of such person with another person, or as to the origin, sponsorship, or approval of his or her goods, services, or commercial activities by another person, or
>
> (B) in commercial advertising or promotion, misrepresents the nature, characteristics, qualities, or geographic origin of his or her or another person's goods, services, or commercial activities,
>
> shall be liable in a civil action by any person who believes that he or she is or is likely to be damaged by such act. . . .

In Haymond v. Lundy, 2001 WL 15956 (E.D. Pa. 2001), the court found false advertising by a lawyer to be actionable under §1125(a) of the Lanham Act.

National Federation of Paralegal Associations: In 1993, the National Federation of Paralegal Associations, Inc. adopted a Model Code of Ethics and Professional Responsibility. EC-6.1 and EC-6.2 of the Code provide:

> EC-6.1 A paralegal's title shall clearly indicate the individual's status and shall be disclosed in all business and professional communications to avoid misunderstandings and misconceptions about the paralegal's role and responsibilities.
>
> EC-6.2 A paralegal's title shall be included if the paralegal's name appears on business cards, letterhead, brochures, directories, and advertisements.

Restatement of the Law Governing Lawyers: The Restatement has no provision comparable to ABA Model Rule 7.1.

Rule 7.2 Advertising

Editors' Note. The ABA amended Rule 7.2 in February 2002 and again in August 2002. The February 2002 amendments were based on a proposal by the ABA Ethics 2000 Commission. The August 2002 amendments, which added a new subparagraph (b)(4) and a new Comment 8, were based on a proposal by the ABA Standing Committee on Ethics and Professional Responsibility. For details about these amendments, see the entry entitled "2002 Amendments" in the Legislative History following this rule.

(a) Subject to the requirements of Rules 7.1 and 7.3, a lawyer may advertise services through ~~public media, such as a telephone directory, legal directory, newspaper or other periodical, outdoor advertising, radio or television, or through~~ written ~~or~~, recorded or electronic communication, including public media.

~~(b) A copy or recording of an advertisement or communication shall be kept for two years after its last dissemination along with a record of when and where it was used.~~

~~(c)~~ (b) A lawyer shall not give anything of value to a person for recommending the lawyer's services except that a lawyer may

(1) pay the reasonable costs of advertisements or communications permitted by this Rule;

(2) pay the usual charges of a ~~not-for-profit lawyer referral service or~~ legal service ~~organization~~ plan or a not-for-profit or qualified lawyer referral service. A qualified lawyer referral service is a lawyer referral service that has been approved by an appropriate regulatory authority; and

(3) pay for a law practice in accordance with Rule 1.17; and

(4) refer clients to another lawyer or a nonlawyer professional pursuant to an agreement not otherwise prohibited under these Rules that provides for the other person to refer clients or customers to the lawyer, if

(i) the reciprocal referral agreement is not exclusive, and

(ii) the client is informed of the existence and nature of the agreement.

~~(d)~~ (c) Any communication made pursuant to this rule shall include the name and office address of at least one lawyer or law firm responsible for its content.

COMMENT

[1] To assist the public in obtaining legal services, lawyers should be allowed to make known their services not only through reputation but also through organized information campaigns in the form of advertising. Advertising involves an active quest for clients, contrary to the tradition that a lawyer should not seek clientele. However, the public's need to know about legal services can be fulfilled in part through advertising. This need is particularly acute in the case of persons of moderate means who have not made extensive use of legal services. The interest in expanding public information about legal services ought to prevail over considerations of tradition. Nevertheless, advertising by lawyers entails the risk of practices that are misleading or overreaching.

[2] This Rule permits public dissemination of information concerning a lawyer's name or firm name, address and telephone number; the kinds of services the lawyer will undertake; the basis on which the lawyer's fees are determined, including prices for specific services and payment and credit arrangements; a lawyer's foreign language ability; names of references and, with their consent, names of clients regularly represented; and other information that might invite the attention of those seeking legal assistance.

[3] Questions of effectiveness and taste in advertising are matters of speculation and subjective judgment. Some jurisdictions have had extensive prohibitions against television advertising, against advertising going beyond specified facts about a lawyer, or against "undignified" advertising. Television is now one of the most powerful media for getting information to the public, particularly persons of low and moderate income; prohibiting television advertising, therefore, would impede the flow of information about legal services to many sectors of the public. Limiting the

information that may be advertised has a similar effect and assumes that the bar can accurately forecast the kind of information that the public would regard as relevant. Similarly, electronic media, such as the Internet, can be an important source of information about legal services, and lawful communication by electronic mail is permitted by this Rule. But see Rule 7.3(a) for the prohibition against the solicitation of a prospective client through a real-time electronic exchange that is not initiated by the prospective client.

[4] Neither this Rule nor Rule 7.3 prohibits communications authorized by law, such as notice to members of a class in class action litigation.

~~Record of Advertising~~

~~[5] Paragraph (b) requires that a record of the content and use of advertising be kept in order to facilitate enforcement of this Rule. It does not require that advertising be subject to review prior to dissemination. Such a requirement would be burdensome and expensive relative to its possible benefits, and may be of doubtful constitutionality.~~

Paying Others to Recommend a Lawyer

~~[6]~~ [5] ~~A lawyer is allowed to pay for advertising permitted by this Rule and for the purchase of a law practice in accordance with the provisions of Rule 1.17, but otherwise is~~ Lawyers are not permitted to pay ~~another person~~ others for channeling professional work. ~~This restriction does not prevent an organization or person other than the lawyer from advertising or recommending the lawyer's services. Thus, a legal aid agency or prepaid legal services plan may pay to advertise legal services provided under its auspices. Likewise, a lawyer may participate in not-for-profit lawyer referral programs and pay the usual fees charged by such programs. Paragraph (c) does not prohibit paying regular compensation to an assistant, such as a secretary, to prepare communications permitted by this Rule.~~ Paragraph (b)(1), however, allows a lawyer to pay for advertising and communications permitted by this Rule, including the costs of print directory listings, on-line directory listings, newspaper ads, television and radio airtime, domain-name registrations, sponsorship fees, banner ads, and group advertising. A lawyer may compensate employees, agents and vendors who are engaged to provide marketing or client-development services, such as publicists, public-relations personnel, business-development staff and web site designers. See Rule 5.3 for the duties of lawyers and law firms with respect to the conduct of nonlawyers who prepare marketing materials for them.

[6] A lawyer may pay the usual charges of a legal service plan or a not-for-profit or qualified lawyer referral service. A legal service plan is a pre-

paid or group legal service plan or a similar delivery system that assists prospective clients to secure legal representation. A lawyer referral service, on the other hand, is any organization that holds itself out to the public as a lawyer referral service. Such referral services are understood by laypersons to be consumer-oriented organizations that provide unbiased referrals to lawyers with appropriate experience in the subject matter of the representation and afford other client protections, such as complaint procedures or malpractice insurance requirements. Consequently, this Rule only permits a lawyer to pay the usual charges of a not-for-profit or qualified lawyer referral service. A qualified lawyer referral service is one that is approved by an appropriate regulatory authority as affording adequate protections for prospective clients. See, e.g., the American Bar Association's Model Supreme Court Rules Governing Lawyer Referral Services and Model Lawyer Referral and Information Service Quality Assurance Act (requiring that organizations that are identified as lawyer referral services (i) permit the participation of all lawyers who are licensed and eligible to practice in the jurisdiction and who meet reasonable objective eligibility requirements as may be established by the referral service for the protection of prospective clients; (ii) require each participating lawyer to carry reasonably adequate malpractice insurance; (iii) act reasonably to assess client satisfaction and address client complaints; and (iv) do not refer prospective clients to lawyers who own, operate or are employed by the referral service).

[7] A lawyer who accepts assignments or referrals from a legal service plan or referrals from a lawyer referral service must act reasonably to assure that the activities of the plan or service are compatible with the lawyer's professional obligations. See Rule 5.3. Legal service plans and lawyer referral services may communicate with prospective clients, but such communication must be in conformity with these Rules. Thus, advertising must not be false or misleading, as would be the case if the communications of a group advertising program or a group legal services plan would mislead prospective clients to think that it was a lawyer referral service sponsored by a state agency or bar association. Nor could the lawyer allow in-person, telephonic, or real-time contacts that would violate Rule 7.3.

Editors' Note. The changes to paragraphs 1 through 7 of the Comment to Rule 7.2 were proposed by the ABA Ethics 2000 Commission and were approved by the ABA House of Delegates in February 2002. Paragraph 8 of the Comment was proposed by the ABA Standing Committee on Ethics and Professional Responsibility and was approved by the ABA in August 2002 at the same time that the House approved new Rule 7.2(b)(4), which paragraph 8 of the Comment explains.

[8] A lawyer also may agree to refer clients to another lawyer or a nonlawyer professional, in return for the undertaking of that person to

refer clients or customers to the lawyer. Such reciprocal referral arrangements must not interfere with the lawyer's professional judgment as to making referrals or as to providing substantive legal services. See Rules 2.1 and 5.4(c). Except as provided in Rule 1.5(e), a lawyer who receives referrals from a lawyer or nonlawyer professional must not pay anything solely for the referral, but the lawyer does not violate paragraph (b) of this Rule by agreeing to refer clients to the other lawyer or nonlawyer professional, so long as the reciprocal referral agreement is not exclusive and the client is informed of the referral agreement. Conflicts of interest created by such agreements are governed by Rule 1.7. Reciprocal referral agreements should not be of indefinite duration and should be reviewed periodically to determine whether they comply with these Rules. This Rule does not restrict referrals or divisions of revenues or net income among lawyers within firms comprised of multiple entities.

Canon and Code Antecedents

ABA Canons of Professional Ethics: Canons 28, 40, and 46 provided as follows:

28. Stirring Up Litigation, Directly or Through Agents

It is unprofessional for a lawyer to volunteer advice to bring a lawsuit, except in rare cases where ties of blood, relationship or trust make it his duty to do so. Stirring up strife and litigation is not only unprofessional, but it is indictable at common law. It is disreputable to hunt up defects in titles or other causes of action and inform thereof in order to be employed to bring suit or collect judgment, or to breed litigation by seeking out those with claims for personal injuries or those having any other grounds of action in order to secure them as clients, or to employ agents or runners for like purposes, or to pay or reward, directly or indirectly, those who bring or influence the bringing of such cases to his office, or to remunerate policemen, court or prison officials, physicians, hospital *attaches* or others who may succeed, under the guise of giving disinterested friendly advice, in influencing the criminal, the sick and the injured, the ignorant or others, to seek his professional services. A duty to the public and to the profession devolves upon every member of the Bar having knowledge of such practices upon the part of any practitioner immediately to inform thereof, to the end that the offender may be disbarred.

40. Newspapers

A lawyer may with propriety write articles for publications in which he gives information upon the law; but he should not accept employment from such publications to advise inquirers in respect to their individual rights.

46. Notice to Local Lawyers

A lawyer available to act as an associate of other lawyers in a particular branch of the law or legal service may send to local lawyers only and publish in his local legal journal, a brief and dignified announcement of his availability to serve other lawyers in connection therewith. The announcement should be in a form which does not constitute a statement or representation of special experience or expertness.

ABA Model Code of Professional Responsibility: Compare DR 2-101(B), DR 2-101(D), DR 2-101(I), DR 2-103(B), and DR 2-103(D) (reprinted later in this volume).

Cross-References in Other Rules

Rule 5.5, Comment 21: "Whether and how lawyers may communicate the availability of their services to prospective clients in this jurisdiction is governed by **Rules 7.1 to 7.5**."

Rule 5.7, Comment 10: "The promotion of the law-related services must also in all respects comply with **Rules 7.1 through 7.3**, dealing with advertising and solicitation."

Rule 7.1, Comment 1: "This Rule governs all communications about a lawyer's services, including advertising permitted by **Rule 7.2**."

Rule 7.3, Comment 2: "This potential for abuse inherent in direct in-person, live telephone or real-time electronic solicitation of prospective clients justifies its prohibition, particularly since lawyer advertising and written and recorded communication permitted under **Rule 7.2** offer alternative means of conveying necessary information to those who may be in need of legal services."

Rule 7.3, Comment 3: "The contents of advertisements and communications permitted under **Rule 7.2** can be permanently recorded so that they cannot be disputed and may be shared with others who know the lawyer."

Rule 7.3, Comment 5: "[I]f after sending a letter or other communication to a client as permitted by **Rule 7.2** the lawyer receives no response, any further effort to communicate with the prospective client may violate the provisions of Rule 7.3(b)."

Rule 7.3, Comment 6: Rule 7.3 does not prohibit lawyers from communicating with representatives of organizations or groups regarding group or prepaid legal service plans because such communications "are functionally similar to and serve the same purpose as advertising permitted under **Rule 7.2**."

Rule 7.3, Comment 8: "Lawyers who participate in a legal service plan must reasonably assure that the plan sponsors are in compliance with **Rules** 7.1, **7.2** and 7.3(b). See 8.4(a)."

Legislative History of Model Rule 7.2

1980 Discussion Draft (then Rule 9.2) provided as follows:

> (b) A copy or record of an advertisement in its entirety shall be kept for one year after its dissemination.
>
> (c) A lawyer shall not give anything of value to a person for recommending the lawyer's services, except that a lawyer may pay the reasonable cost of advertising permitted by this rule.

1981 and 1982 Drafts were substantially the same as adopted, except that subparagraph (a) permitted any "written communication not involving personal contract."

1989 Amendments: In 1989, the ABA House of Delegates made minor amendments to Rule 7.2(a) and (c). The ABA did not amend the Comment to Rule 7.2.

1990 Amendment: At its 1990 Mid-Year Meeting, the ABA House of Delegates added subparagraph 7.2(c)(3) to reflect the addition of Rule 1.17.

2002 Amendments: At its February 2002 Mid-Year Meeting, the ABA House of Delegates adopted with only minor changes the ABA Ethics 2000 Commission proposal to amend Rule 7.2 and its Comment.

In addition, at its August 2002 Annual Meeting, the ABA House of Delegates added a new subparagraph (b)(4) to Rule 7.2 based on a proposal by the ABA Standing Committee on Ethics and Professional Responsibility. (The Standing Committee's 2002 proposal was very similar to a proposal that the Standing Committee withdrew before the House of Delegates met in August of 2001, but the 2002 proposal added one new sentence to the Comment to Rule 7.5 — see the Legislative History following that rule.) We reprint in full the following Report that the Standing Committee submitted in support of its proposal to add Rule 7.2(b)(4):

*ABA Committee Report Submitted in Support of 2002 Amendment**

In July 2000 the House of Delegates adopted Resolution 10F relating to the issue of multi-disciplinary practice. By that resolution, the Standing Committee on Ethics and Professional Responsibility was directed to review the Model Rules of Professional Conduct, in consultation with state, local, and territorial bar associations and interested ABA Sections, Divisions and Committees, and to recommend any changes the Committee believed necessary

> "to assure that there are safeguards in the [Model Rules of Professional Conduct] relating to strategic alliances and other contractual relationships with non-legal professional services providers consistent with the statement of principles in [Resolution 10F]."

The Committee reviewed the Model Rules and Resolution 10F as directed by the House of Delegates. It considered the "strategic alliance" or "contractual relationship" arrangements identified in Resolution 10F to be arrangements by professional services providers and lawyers to steer business to each other on a systematic and regular basis. Such arrangements may range from a simple understanding generally to refer business to each other to an agreement that includes sharing space, computer systems, and the like to reduce costs by obtaining economies of scale or other efficiencies.

The Committee took into account the "core values" of the profession as described in paragraph 1 of Resolution 10F: the duty of loyalty, the duty to exercise independent professional judgment for the benefit of the client, the duty to protect client confidences, and the traditional prohibitions against sharing legal fees with nonlawyers and against ownership and control of the practice of law by nonlawyers.

In October 2000 the Committee circulated a memorandum identifying possible changes to the Model Rules that it felt would alert lawyers to the circumstances in which strategic alliances could present ethical problems, and requested comments and suggestions regarding the proposed changes by January 2001. Contact was made with presidents and executive directors of state, local, and territorial bar associations; chairs and staff liaisons of ABA Sections and Divisions; the high courts of the fifty states and the District of Columbia; chief disciplinary counsel in all jurisdictions; and a number of other entities. In all, over five hundred letters were sent so-

*Committee Reports do not represent official policy of the ABA. They are for information only and the opinions are those of the authors of the report.

liciting comment. Six responses were received, each of which was taken into account by the Committee in preparing this Recommendation.

In August 2001 the Committee in Report 113 recommended changes to Comment language under Rule 1.7 and changes to the text and Comment under Rule 7.2. The New York State Bar Association ("NYSBA") asked the Committee to withdraw the Recommendation in Report 113 from consideration by the House at that time to enable it to file their own proposal to deal with cross-referral arrangements between lawyers and other professionals. It was to be based upon Disciplinary Rules and Ethical Considerations in the New York Code of Professional Conduct that had just gained approval by the New York courts. The Committee accordingly withdrew its Report from consideration.

The Committee resubmitted its proposal for consideration at the Midyear 2002 Meeting, at which time the NYSBA submitted a Report and Recommendation proposing considerably more extensive amendments to the Model Rules, addressing both reciprocal referral agreements between lawyers and non-legal professional services firms and certain forms of "multidisciplinary practice" in which lawyers and law firms might be permitted to offer their services. Once again at the Midyear Meeting, in consideration of the possibility of developing a proposal acceptable to both sponsoring entities, the Standing Committee withdrew its Report and Recommendation; the NYSBA did so as well.

Subsequent to the Midyear 2002 Meeting, the NYSBA communicated with the Standing Committee to report that the NYSBA had determined, after all, that the changes to New York's Code of Professional Responsibility in this area, although needed in New York because of the absence of commentary in its Code, were not necessary in the revised format of the ABA Model Rules. The NYSBA therefore decided not to submit a proposal to the House of Delegates for consideration at this Meeting. It did, however, recommend one amendment to the Comment to Model Rule 7.5 ("Firm Names and Letterheads"), in light of its concern that law firms engaged in offering certain services jointly with other nonlawyer professionals not create confusion by adding names of nonlawyer professionals to their law firm names. The Standing Committee agrees with this recommendation of the NYSBA, and therefore recommends that such an amendment be made, appearing in the final sentence of Comment [1] to Model Rule 7.5.

The Committee presents to the House once again its conclusion that when lawyers enter into cross-referral agreements with other lawyers and nonlawyer professionals, clients need to be informed of those agreements in order to decide whether to accept the lawyer's suggestions to use the other professionals' services. A per se prohibition against exclusive referral arrangements also is required, to ensure that a lawyer is free to exercise independent professional judgment when counseling clients to consult with other professionals. Each of these concepts is therefore embodied in the Committee's proposed changes to the black-letter of Rule 7.2(b).

The Committee also believes that the Comment to Rule 7.2(b) should be amplified to address lawyers' participation in referral arrangements in the context of related Model Rules. For example, the independent professional judgment required of a lawyer who is making referrals to other professionals is set out in Rules 2.1 and 5.4(c), which are therefore included in the Comment. Similarly, the Comment notes that actual payment by a lawyer to a referring nonlawyer professional for the referral itself is prohibited, except in the narrow lawyer-to-lawyer referral situation that is permitted under Rule 1.5(e)'s exception to the prohibition against fee-sharing. Finally, reference is made in the Comment to Rule 1.7 ("Conflict of Interest"), to remind lawyers that they must not allow their contractual relationships for reciprocal referrals, which might be considered "related business interests," to adversely affect the representation of their clients.

The Committee believes that these proposed amendments to Model Rule 7.2 and its Comment, addressing reciprocal referral agreements between lawyers and other lawyers or nonlawyer professionals, and its amendment to Model Rule 7.5's Comment, will provide necessary and helpful safeguards to the ethical practice of law, as contemplated by the House in its Report 10F in August 2000, and therefore urges their adoption.

Selected State Variations

Editors' Note. For a comprehensive collection of the full text of the ethics rules governing lawyer advertising in most states, see the web site maintained by the American Bar Association's Commission on Responsibility in Client Development at www.abanet.org/adrules.

Arizona: Rule 7.2(f)(1) forbids a lawyer to send a written communication to a prospective client about a specific matter if the lawyer knows or reasonably should know that the recipient has a lawyer in the matter. Arizona also requires advertising lawyers or firms to provide clients on request with "a factual statement detailing the background, training, and experience" of the lawyer or firm. Rule 7.2(a).

California: See Rule 1-400 (Advertising and Solicitation) and the Standards adopted by the State Bar pursuant to Rule 1-400; Business & Professions Code §6129 (prohibiting lawyers from purchasing claims), §§6155 and 6156 (governing lawyer referral services), and §§6157-6159.2 (governing advertising).

Connecticut: Rule 7.2(e) requires lawyers who advertise a fee or fee arrangement to specify "whether and to what extent the client will be responsible for any court costs and expenses of litigation."

District of Columbia omits Rule 7.2, but see Rule 7.1(c) in District of Columbia Rules of Professional Conduct below.

Florida: Rule 4-7.1 expressly permits attorneys to advertise through "computer-accessed communications" and through "recorded messages the public may access by dialing a telephone number." Regarding referral services, Florida Rule 4 7.4(b)(2) provides that "[e]very written communication disseminated by a lawyer referral service shall be accompanied by a written statement detailing the background, training, and experience of each lawyer to whom the recipient may be referred." Rule 4-7.11 titled "Lawyer Referral Services," sets forth elaborate requirements for lawyer referral services.

Chapter 8 of the Florida Supreme Court Rules sets forth extensive requirements for the operation of lawyer referral services by local bar associations, and no local bar association may operate a referral service without the express approval of the state bar. Chapter 9 of the Florida Supreme Court Rules provides detailed regulations governing group and prepaid legal service plans, and defines such plans as follows in Rule 9-1.2:

> (a) *"Group Legal Services."* Group legal services are plans by which legal services are rendered to individual members of a group identifiable in terms of some common interest.
>
> (b) *"Prepaid Legal Services Plans."* Prepaid legal services plans are programs in which the cost of the services are prepaid by the group member or by some other person or organization in the member's behalf.

Georgia: In the rules effective January 1, 2001, Georgia adopted the pre-2002 version of ABA Model Rules 7.2(a) and (b) essentially verbatim, and adopted most of the ABA Comment. However, Georgia moved Rule 7.2(c) and the corresponding ABA Comment to Georgia Rule 7.3(c) and modified and expanded the exceptions in ABA Rule 7.2(c) regarding lawyer referral services. The Comment adds that a lawyer "may not indirectly engage in promotional activities through a lay public relations or marketing firm if such activities would be prohibited by these Rules if engaged in directly by the lawyer."

Illinois prohibits giving anything of value for recommending "or having recommended" the lawyer's services.

Iowa: DR 2-101 restricts both written and broadcast advertising to "the geographic area in which the lawyer maintains offices or in which a significant part of the lawyer's clientele resides. . . ." With respect to radio and television, Iowa permits information to be "articulated only by a single non-dramatic voice, not that of the lawyer, and with no other background sound," and on television, "no visual display shall be allowed except that allowed in print as articulated by the announcer."

Maryland adds Rule 7.2(e), which provides that "[a]n advertisement or communication indicating that no fee will be charged in the absence of a recovery shall also disclose whether the client will be liable for any expenses."

Massachusetts: Rule 7.2(a) adds that lawyers may advertise in "an electronic or computer accessed directory." A new Comment 3A provides, in part, as follows:

> The advertising and solicitation rules can generally be applied to computer-accessed or other similar types of communications by analogizing the communication to its hard-copy form. Thus, because it is not a communication directed to a specific recipient, a web site or home page would generally be considered advertising subject to this rule, rather than solicitation subject to Rule 7.3. . . .

Michigan: Rule 6.3(b), drawing on language from DR 2-103(D) of the ABA Model Code of Professional Responsibility and other ABA guidelines, permits a lawyer to "participate in and pay the usual charges of a not-for-profit lawyer referral service that recommends legal services to the public if that service":

(1) maintains registration as a qualified service with the State Bar . . . ;

(2) is operated in the public interest for the purpose of referring prospective clients to lawyers; pro bono and public service legal programs; and government, consumer or other agencies that can best provide the assistance needed by clients, in light of their financial circumstances, spoken language, any disability, geographical convenience, and the nature and complexity of their problems;

(3) is open to all lawyers licensed and eligible to practice in this state who maintain an office within the geographical area served, and who:

(i) meet reasonable and objective requirements of experience . . . ;

(ii) pay reasonable registration and membership fees not to exceed an amount established by the State Bar to encourage widespread lawyer participation; and

(iii) maintain a policy of errors and omissions insurance, or provide proof of financial responsibility, in an amount at least equal to the minimum established by the State Bar;

(4) ensures that the combined fees and expenses charged a prospective client by a qualified service and a lawyer to whom the client is referred

not exceed the total charges the client would have incurred had no referral service been involved; and

(5) makes no fee-generating referral to any lawyer who has an ownership interest in, or who operates or is employed by, the qualified service, or who is associated with a law firm that has an ownership interest in, or operates or is employed by, a qualified service.

(c) . . .

(d) The State Bar or any aggrieved person may seek an injunction in the circuit court to enjoin violations of subrule (b). In the event the injunction is granted, the petitioner shall be entitled to reasonable costs and attorney fees.

(e) . . .

Missouri adds the following sentence to Rule 7.2(a): "All advertisements that state that legal services are available on a contingent or no-recovery-no-fee basis shall also state conspicuously that the client may be responsible for costs or expenses." Rule 10.1 governs lawyer referral services. The rule is based largely on the ABA Model Supreme Court Rules Governing Lawyer Referral Services (see Related Materials following Rule 7.2), but Missouri adds that any person violating the new rule shall be deemed to be engaged in the unauthorized practice of law.

New Jersey: In Felmeister & Isaacs, 518 A.2d 188, 208 (1986), the New Jersey Supreme Court set down the following guidelines:

> . . . All advertisements shall be predominantly informational. No drawings, animations, dramatizations, music, or lyrics shall be used in connection with televised advertising. No advertisement shall rely in any way on techniques to obtain attention that depend upon absurdity and that demonstrate a clear and intentional lack of relevance to the selection of counsel; included in this category are all advertisements that contain any extreme portrayal of counsel exhibiting characteristics clearly unrelated to legal competence.

New York: Compare ABA Model Rule 7.2(a) to New York's DR 2-101(F). Compare Rule 7.2(b) to New York's 1-107(C), DR 2-103(B), and DR 2-111. Compare Rule 7.2(c) to New York's DR 2-101(K).

Ohio: DR 2-101(A)(2) prohibits a lawyer from seeking employment if the lawyer "does not intend to actively participate in the representation" but instead intends to refer the matter to other counsel.

In 1999, Ohio extensively amended DR 2-103, authorizing lawyers to request referrals from any lawyer referral service that (a) "Operates in the public interest" for the purpose of referring prospective clients to lawyers, pro bono and public service programs, and government, consumer, or other agencies; (b) "Calls itself a lawyer referral service or a lawyer referral and information service;" (c) is open to all Ohio lawyers with offices in the service's geographical area who meet "reasonable, objectively determined experience requirements established by the service" and maintain malpractice insurance in an amount established by the service; (d) prohibits lawyers from charging clients "fees and or costs that exceed charges the client would have incurred had no lawyer referral service been involved;" (e) "Establishes procedures to survey periodically clients referred to determine client satisfaction" and to investigate and act on client complaints; and (f) "Establishes procedures for admitting, suspending, or removing lawyers from its roll of panelists". . . .

Pennsylvania omits Rule 7.2(d), but has adopted the following additional provisions in its version of Rule 7.2:

> (d) No advertisement or public communication shall contain an endorsement by a celebrity or public figure.

> (e) An advertisement or public communication that contains a paid endorsement shall disclose that the endorser is being paid or otherwise compensated for his or her appearance or endorsement.
>
> (f) A non-lawyer shall not portray a lawyer or imply that he or she is a lawyer in any advertisement or public communication . . . .
>
> (g) An advertisement or public communication shall not contain a portrayal of a client by a non-client; the re-enactment of any events or scenes; or, pictures or persons, which are not actual or authentic, without a disclosure that such depiction is a dramatization. . . .
>
> (i) All advertisements and written communications shall disclose the geographic location, by city or town, of the office in which the lawyer or lawyers who will actually perform the services advertised principally practice law. If the office location is outside the city or town, the county in which the office is located must be disclosed. . . .

Pennsylvania has also adopted Rule 7.7 which forbids lawyers to accept referrals from a lawyer referral service "if the service engaged in communication with the public or direct contact with prospective clients in a manner that would violate the Rules of Professional Conduct if the communication or contact were made by the lawyer."

Texas: Rule 7.02 forbids "false or misleading communication about the qualifications or the services of any lawyer or firm." A communication will violate the rule if, among other things, it creates "an unjustified expectation about results the lawyer can achieve" or "compares the lawyer's services with other lawyers' services, unless the comparison can be substantiated by reference to verifiable, objective data." In 1997, Texas adopted guidelines for advertising on the Internet, including a requirement that "homepages" be submitted for review.

Virginia: See discussion under Rule 7.1.

Related Materials

ABA Formal Ethics Opinions: See ABA Formal Ethics Op. 93-374 (1993).

ABA Model Supreme Court Rules Governing Lawyer Referral Services: In 1993, the ABA House of Delegates voted to adopt Model Supreme Court Rules Governing Lawyer Referral Services, as well as model legislation to implement the rules. (Because many referral services are run by non-lawyers, the regulation of referral services cannot be accomplished solely through the disciplinary machinery for lawyers.) The rules and legislation are modeled on legislation governing lawyer referral services in California, Florida, and Texas. The rules provide that a referral service may be "qualified" only if (1) membership on referral panels is open to all lawyers in a given geographic area who meet reasonable experience standards and pay a reasonable membership fee to be fixed by the state bar, and (2) the referral service establishes procedures for admitting and removing lawyers from referral lists, and (3) the service establishes panels in various specific fields of law so that callers can be matched with a lawyer experienced in a particular type of law. The rules reflect concern over sham referral services, often operated by lawyers who refer cases only to themselves.

ABA "Pay-to-Play" Resolution: At its 1997 Annual Meeting, the ABA adopted a resolution condemning so-called "pay-to-play" practices under which law firms in some jurisdictions allegedly are not considered eligible to perform government legal work unless they have made or solicited campaign contributions for the government officials who retain outside counsel or influence the selection of outside counsel. The 1997 resolution also directed the ABA President to appoint a Task Force to study the pay-to-play issue and report to the House of Delegates within a year. At its 1998 Annual Meeting, the ABA received a lengthy report from the Task Force and passed a resolution directing the ABA's Standing Committee on Ethics and Professional Responsibility to draft a new Model Rule 7.6 to govern pay-to play. The proposed rule was approved at the ABA's 2000 Mid-Year Meeting.

Criminal Statutes: Some states make it a crime for a non-lawyer to accept anything of value for referring a matter to a lawyer. For example, California Penal Code §3215 makes it a crime for anyone to receive money or any nonmonetary thing "as compensation or inducement for referring clients . . . ." Similarly, New York Judiciary Law §479 makes it a crime for any person to make it a business to solicit business for an attorney.

Restatement of the Law Governing Lawyers: The Restatement has no comparable provision.

Rule 7.3 Direct Contact with Prospective Clients

(a) A lawyer shall not by in-person ~~or~~, live telephone or real-time electronic contact solicit professional employment from a prospective client ~~with whom the lawyer has no family or prior professional relationship~~ when a significant motive for the lawyer's doing so is the lawyer's pecuniary gain, unless the person contacted:

(1) is a lawyer; or

(2) has a family, close personal, or prior professional relationship with the lawyer.

(b) A lawyer shall not solicit professional employment from a prospective client by written ~~or~~, recorded or electronic communication or by in-person ~~or~~, telephone or real-time electronic contact even when not otherwise prohibited by paragraph (a), if:

(1) the prospective client has made known to the lawyer a desire not to be solicited by the lawyer; or

(2) the solicitation involves coercion, duress or harassment.

(c) Every written ~~or~~, recorded or electronic communication from a lawyer soliciting professional employment from a prospective client known to be in need of legal services in a particular matter~~, and with whom the lawyer has no family or prior professional relationship,~~ shall include the words "Advertising Material" on the outside envelope, if any, and at the beginning and ending of any recorded or electronic communication, unless the recipient of the communication is a person specified in paragraphs (a)(1) or (a)(2).

(d) Notwithstanding the prohibitions in paragraph (a), a lawyer may participate with a prepaid or group legal service plan operated by an organization not owned or directed by the lawyer that uses in-person or telephone contact to solicit memberships or subscriptions

for the plan from persons who are not known to need legal services in a particular matter covered by the plan.

COMMENT

[1] There is a potential for abuse inherent in direct in-person ~~or~~, live telephone or real-time electronic contact by a lawyer with a prospective client known to need legal services. These forms of contact between a lawyer and a prospective client subject the layperson to the private importuning of the trained advocate in a direct interpersonal encounter. The prospective client, who may already feel overwhelmed by the circumstances giving rise to the need for legal services, may find it difficult fully to evaluate all available alternatives with reasoned judgment and appropriate self-interest in the face of the lawyer's presence and insistence upon being retained immediately. The situation is fraught with the possibility of undue influence, intimidation, and over-reaching.

[2] This potential for abuse inherent in direct in-person ~~or~~, live telephone or real-time electronic solicitation of prospective clients justifies its prohibition, particularly since lawyer advertising and written and recorded communication permitted under Rule 7.2 offer alternative means of conveying necessary information to those who may be in need of legal services. Advertising and written and recorded communications which may be mailed or autodialed make it possible for a prospective client to be informed about the need for legal services, and about the qualifications of available lawyers and law firms, without subjecting the prospective client to direct in-person ~~or~~, telephone or real-time electronic persuasion that may overwhelm the client's judgment.

[3] The use of general advertising and written ~~and~~, recorded or electronic communications to transmit information from lawyer to prospective client, rather than direct in-person ~~or~~, live telephone or real-time electronic contact, will help to assure that the information flows cleanly as well as freely. The contents of advertisements and communications permitted under Rule 7.2 ~~are~~ can be permanently recorded so that they cannot be disputed and may be shared with others who know the lawyer. This potential for informal review is itself likely to help guard against statements and claims that might constitute false and misleading communications, in violation of Rule 7.1. The contents of direct in-person ~~or~~, live telephone or real-time electronic conversations between a lawyer ~~to~~ and a prospective client can be disputed and ~~are~~ may not be subject to third-party scrutiny. Consequently, they are much more likely to approach (and occasionally cross) the dividing line between accurate representations and those that are false and misleading.

[4] There is far less likelihood that a lawyer would engage in abusive practices against an individual who is a former client, or with whom the lawyer has a ~~prior~~ close personal or ~~professional~~ family relationship, or

~~where~~ in situations in which the lawyer is motivated by considerations other than the lawyer's pecuniary gain. Nor is there a serious potential for abuse when the person contacted is a lawyer. Consequently, the general prohibition in Rule 7.3(a) and the requirements of Rule 7.3(c) are not applicable in those situations. Also, paragraph (a) is not intended to prohibit a lawyer from participating in constitutionally protected activities of public or charitable legal-service organizations or bona fide political, social, civic, fraternal, employee or trade organizations whose purposes include providing or recommending legal services to its members or beneficiaries.

[5] But even permitted forms of solicitation can be abused. Thus, any solicitation which contains information which is false or misleading within the meaning of Rule 7.1, which involves coercion, duress or harassment within the meaning of Rule 7.3(b)(2), or which involves contact with a prospective client who has made known to the lawyer a desire not to be solicited by the lawyer within the meaning of Rule 7.3(b)(1) is prohibited. Moreover, if after sending a letter or other communication to a client as permitted by Rule 7.2 the lawyer receives no response, any further effort to communicate with the prospective client may violate the provisions of Rule 7.3(b).

[6] This Rule is not intended to prohibit a lawyer from contacting representatives of organizations or groups that may be interested in establishing a group or prepaid legal plan for their members, insureds, beneficiaries or other third parties for the purpose of informing such entities of the availability of and details concerning the plan or arrangement which the lawyer or lawyer's firm is willing to offer. This form of communication is not directed to a prospective client. Rather, it is usually addressed to an individual acting in a fiduciary capacity seeking a supplier of legal services for others who may, if they choose, become prospective clients of the lawyer. Under these circumstances, the activity which the lawyer undertakes in communicating with such representatives and the type of information transmitted to the individual are functionally similar to and serve the same purpose as advertising permitted under Rule 7.2.

[7] The requirement in Rule 7.3(c) that certain communications be marked "Advertising Material" does not apply to communications sent in response to requests of potential clients or their spokespersons or sponsors. General announcements by lawyers, including changes in personnel or office location, do not constitute communications soliciting professional employment from a client known to be in need of legal services within the meaning of this Rule.

[8] Paragraph (d) of this Rule ~~would permit~~ permits a lawyer to participate with an organization which uses personal contact to solicit members for its group or prepaid legal service plan, provided that the personal contact is not undertaken by any lawyer who would be a provider of legal services through the plan. The organization ~~referred to in paragraph (d)~~ must not be owned by or directed (whether as manager or otherwise) by any lawyer or law firm that participates in the plan. For example, paragraph (d) would not permit a lawyer to create an organization controlled

directly or indirectly by the lawyer and use the organization for the in-person or telephone solicitation of legal employment of the lawyer through memberships in the plan or otherwise. The communication permitted by these organizations also must not be directed to a person known to need legal services in a particular matter, but is to be designed to inform potential plan members generally of another means of affordable legal services. Lawyers who participate in a legal service plan must reasonably assure that the plan sponsors are in compliance with Rules 7.1, 7.2 and 7.3(b). See Rule 8.4(a).

Canon and Code Antecedents

ABA Canons of Professional Ethics: Canon 28 provided as follows:

28. Stirring Up Litigation, Directly or Through Agents

> It is unprofessional for a lawyer to volunteer advice to bring a lawsuit, except in rare cases where ties of blood, relationship or trust make it his duty to do so. Stirring up strife and litigation is not only unprofessional, but it is indictable at common law. It is disreputable to hunt up defects in titles or other causes of action and inform thereof in order to be employed to bring suit or collect judgment, or to breed litigation by seeking out those with claims for personal injuries or those having any other grounds of action in order to secure them as clients, or to employ agents or runners for like purposes, or to pay or reward, directly or indirectly, those who bring or influence the bringing of such cases to his office, or to remunerate policemen, court or prison officials, physicians, hospital *attaches* or others who may succeed, under the guise of giving disinterested friendly advice, in influencing the criminal, the sick and the injured, the ignorant or others, to seek his professional services. A duty to the public and to the profession devolves upon every member of the Bar having knowledge of such practices upon the part of any practitioner immediately to inform thereof, to the end that the offender may be disbarred.

ABA Model Code of Professional Responsibility: Compare DR 2-104(A) (reprinted later in this volume).

Cross-References in Other Rules

Rule 5.5, Comment 21: "Whether and how lawyers may communicate the availability of their services to prospective clients in this jurisdiction is governed by **Rules 7.1 to 7.5**."

Rule 5.7, Comment 10: "The promotion of the law-related services must also in all respects comply with **Rules** 7.1 through **7.3**, dealing with advertising and solicitation."

Rule 7.2(a): "Subject to the requirements of **Rules** 7.1 and **7.3**, a lawyer may advertise services through written, recorded or electronic communication, including public media."

Rule 7.2, Comment 3: "[S]ee **Rule 7.3(a)** for the prohibition against the solicitation of a prospective client through a real-time electronic exchange that is not initiated by the prospective client."

Rule 7.2, Comment 4: "Neither this Rule nor **Rule 7.3** prohibits communications authorized by law, such as notice to members of a class in class action litigation."

Rule 7.2, Comment 7: A lawyer accepting assignments or referrals from a legal service plan or referrals from a lawyer referral service is not permitted to "allow in-person, telephonic, or real-time contacts that would violate **Rule 7.3**."

Legislative History of Model Rule 7.3

1980 Discussion Draft (then Rule 9.3) provided as follows:

Solicitation

(a) A lawyer shall not initiate contact with a prospective client if:

(1) the lawyer reasonably should know that the physical, emotional, or mental state of the person solicited is such that the person could not exercise reasonable judgment in employing a lawyer;

(2) the person solicited has made known a desire not to receive communications from the lawyer; or

(3) the solicitation involves coercion, duress, or harassment.

(b) subject to the requirements of paragraph (a), a lawyer may initiate contact with a prospective client in the following circumstances:

(1) if the prospective client is a close friend or relative of the lawyer;

(2) by a letter concerning a specific event or transaction if the letter is followed up only upon positive response from the addressee;

(3) under the auspices of a public or charitable legal services organization or a bona fide political, social, civic, fraternal, employee, or trade organization whose purposes include but are not limited to providing or recommending legal services.

(c) A lawyer shall not give another person anything of value to initiate contact with a prospective client on behalf of the lawyer.

1981 and 1982 Drafts both provided as follows:

Personal Contact with Prospective Clients

(a) A lawyer may initiate personal contact with a prospective client for the purpose of obtaining professional employment only in the following circumstances and subject to the requirements of paragraph (b):

(1) if the prospective client is a close friend, relative, former client or one whom the lawyer reasonably believes to be a client;

(2) under the auspices of a public or charitable legal services organization; or

(3) under the auspices of a bona fide political, social, civic, fraternal, employee or trade organization whose purposes include but are not limited to providing or recommending legal services, if the legal services are related to the principal purposes of the organization.

(b) A lawyer shall not contact, or send a written communication to, a prospective client for the purpose of obtaining professional employment if:

(1) the lawyer knows or reasonably should know that the physical, emotional or mental state of the person is such that the person could not exercise reasonable judgment in employing a lawyer;

(2) the person has made known to the lawyer a desire not to receive communications from the lawyer; or

(3) the communication involves coercion, duress or harassment.

1989 Amendments: At its February 1989 Mid-Year Meeting, the ABA House of Delegates substantially amended Rule 7.3 and its Comment. As originally promulgated, Rule 7.3 provided:

> A lawyer may not solicit professional employment from a prospective client with whom the lawyer has no family or prior professional relationship, by mail, in person or otherwise, when a significant motive for the lawyer's doing so is the lawyer's pecuniary gain. The term "solicit" includes contact in person, by telephone or telegraph, by letter or other writing, or by other communications directed to a specific recipient, but does not include letters addressed or advertising circulars distributed generally to persons not known to need legal services of the kind provided by the lawyer in a particular matter, but who are so situated that they might in general find such services useful.

When the ABA amended Rule 7.3 in 1989, it *completely deleted* the following two paragraphs from the original Comment to Rule 7.3:

> These dangers [of false and misleading representations] attend direct solicitation whether in-person or by mail. Direct mail solicitation cannot be effectively regulated by means less drastic than outright prohibition. One proposed safeguard is to require that the designation "Advertising" be stamped on any envelope containing a solicitation letter. This would do nothing to assure the accuracy and reliability of the contents. Another suggestion is that solicitation letters be filed with a state regulatory agency. This would be ineffective as a practical matter. State lawyer discipline agencies struggle for resources to investigate specific complaints, much less for those necessary to screen lawyers' mail solicitation material. Even if they could examine such materials, agency staff members are unlikely to know anything about the lawyer or about the prospective client's underlying problem. Without such knowledge they cannot determine whether the lawyer's representations are misleading. In any event, such review would be after the fact, potentially too late to avert the undesirable consequences of disseminating false and misleading material.
>
> General mailings not speaking to a specific matter do not pose the same danger of abuse as targeted mailings, and therefore are not prohibited by this Rule. The representations made in such mailings are necessarily general rather than tailored, less importuning than informative. They are addressed to recipients unlikely to be specially vulnerable at the time, hence who are likely to be more skeptical about unsubstantiated claims. General mailings not addressed to recipients involved in a specific legal matter or incident, therefore, more closely resemble permissible advertising rather than prohibited solicitation.

The amendments to Rules 7.2 and 7.3 were explained by the ABA's Standing Committee on Ethics and Professional Responsibility in a report that began as follows:

*ABA Committee Report Explaining 1989 Amendments to Rule 7.3**

> The Supreme Court of the United States, in Shapero v. Kentucky Bar Association, 486 U.S. 466 (1988), ruled that the First Amendment does not allow states to impose blanket bans on targeted mail solicitation by lawyers of prospective

*Committee Reports do not represent official policy of the ABA. They are for information only, and the opinions are those of the authors of the report.

clients. Held unconstitutional was a Kentucky Supreme Court rule identical to Model Rule 7.3. The principal purpose of the amendments proposed here is to bring the Model Rules into compliance with the *Shapero* decision. . . .

2002 Amendments: At its February 2002 Mid-Year Meeting, the ABA House of Delegates adopted with only minor changes the ABA Ethics 2000 Commission proposal to amend Rule 7.3 and its Comment.

Selected State Variations

Editors' Note. For a comprehensive collection of the full text of the ethics rules governing lawyer advertising in most states, see the web site maintained by the American Bar Association's Commission on Responsibility in Client Development at www.abanet.org/adrules.

Alabama: Targeted direct mail to prospective personal injury clients or their relatives is forbidden for 30 days following the injury. Rule 7.3(b)(1)(i). Direct mail solicitations of all kinds can only be sent "by regular mail," cannot resemble "a legal pleading, official government form or document (federal or state), or other legal document," and must contain the word " 'Advertisement' . . . prominently in red ink on each page of the written communication" and on the envelope. Further, if "the written communication is prompted by a specific occurrence [it] shall disclose how the lawyer obtained the information prompting the communication." Rule 7.3(b)(2).

Arizona: Targeted direct mail solicitation must be "clearly marked on the envelope and on the first page" as follows: "ADVERTISING MATERIAL: THIS IS A COMMERCIAL SOLICITATION." The rule continues: "Said notification shall be printed in red ink, in all capital letters, in type size at least double the largest type size used in the body of the communication." Rule 7.3(b).

California: See Rule 1-400 (Advertising and Solicitation) and B & P Code §§6152 and 6157-6158.2.

Colorado: Rule 7.3(c) imposes a waiting period of 30 days after an event causing personal injury or death before a lawyer may solicit professional employment in connection with the event. The communication "shall not reveal on the envelope or on the outside of a self-mailing brochure or pamphlet the nature of the prospective client's legal problem."

District of Columbia omits Rule 7.3. See District of Columbia Rules of Professional Conduct below.

Florida Rule 4-7.4(a) defines the term "solicit" to include (among other things) contact by "facsimile, or by other communication directed to a specific recipient." Rule 7-7.4(b)(1), which is essentially the rule upheld in Florida Bar v. Went for It, Inc., 515 U.S. 618 (1995), prohibits a lawyer from soliciting prospective clients in writing if:

> (A) the written communication concerns an action for personal injury or wrongful death or otherwise relates to an accident or disaster involving the person to whom the communication is addressed or a relative of that person, unless the ac-

> cident or disaster occurred more than 30 days prior to the mailing of the communication;
>
> (B) the written communication concerns a specific matter and the lawyer knows or reasonably should know that the person to whom the communication is directed is represented by a lawyer in the matter. . . .

Rule 4-7.4(b)(2) imposes stringent, detailed requirements on all written communications to prospective clients, including that each written communication must be filed with the standing committee on advertising, and the first sentence of every written communication prompted by a specific occurrence must be: "If you have already retained a lawyer for this matter, please disregard this letter," and the body of the letter must disclose how the lawyer obtained the information prompting the communication.

Florida Rule 4-7.6, which may be unique among state ethics rules, provides:

> *Rule 4-7.6 Computer-Accessed Communications*
>
> (a) *Definition.* For purposes of this subchapter, "computer-accessed communications" are defined as information regarding a lawyer's or law firm's services that is read, viewed, or heard directly through the use of a computer. . . .
>
> (b) *Internet Presence.* All World Wide Web sites and home pages accessed via the Internet that are controlled or sponsored by a lawyer or law firm and that contain information concerning the lawyer's or law firm's services:
>
> (1) shall disclose all jurisdictions in which the lawyer or members of the law firm are licensed to practice law;
>
> (2) shall disclose 1 or more bona fide office locations . . .
>
> (3) are considered to be information provided upon request and, therefore, are otherwise governed by the requirements of Rule 4-7.9.

A lawyer shall not send an "unsolicited electronic mail communication directly or indirectly to a prospective client for the purpose of obtaining professional employment" unless it complies with a host of requirements, including that the subject line of the communication must state "legal advertisement."

Georgia: In the rules effective January 1, 2001, Georgia's version of Rule 7.3 borrows from DR 2-103(A) of the ABA Model Code of Professional Responsibility by prohibiting a lawyer from soliciting professional employment as a private practitioner through direct personal contact or live telephone contact "with a non-lawyer who has not sought advice regarding employment of a lawyer." Georgia's Rule 7.3(a)(3) provides that a lawyer "shall not send, or knowingly permit to be sent, . . . a written communication to a prospective client" if: the written communication concerns an action for personal injury or wrongful death or otherwise relates to an accident or disaster involving the person to whom the communication is addressed or a relative of that person, unless the accident or disaster occurred more than 30 days prior to the mailing of the communication. Georgia has also moved its version of ABA Model Rule 7.2(b) to Georgia Rule 7.3(c) — see the Georgia entry following ABA Model Rule 7.2. Georgia omits ABA Model Rule 7.3(c), but adds a new Rule 7.3(e), based on DR 2-103(E) of the ABA Model Code, which provides that a lawyer "shall not accept employment when the lawyer knows or it is obvious that the person who seeks to employ the lawyer does so as a result of conduct by any person or organization prohibited under" these rules.

Illinois defines "solicit" as contact with a person "other than a lawyer. . . ." Illinois permits solicitation "under the auspices of a public or charitable legal services organization or a *bona fide* political, social, civic, charitable, religious, fraternal, employee or trade organization whose purposes include, but are not limited to, providing or recommending legal services."

Kentucky has adopted an elaborate Rule 7.60 entitled "Kentucky Disaster Response Plan." Article I of Rule 7.60 explains that one purpose of the Kentucky Disaster Response Plan is to address problems that occur when lawyers and non-lawyers who are not subject to disciplinary jurisdiction in Kentucky "engage in the provision of legal services, legal advice, and outright solicitation of persons and their families affected by a disastrous event." It is the policy of Rule 7.60 to "[m]onitor the conduct of all attorneys, both members and non-members of the Kentucky Bar Association, and thereby deter violations of the rules of ethical conduct . . . ."

Kentucky has also enacted a criminal statute, Ky. Rev. Stat. §21A.300, providing that for 30 days after "the filing of a criminal or civil action, or claim for damages, or a traffic citation, injury, accident, or disaster," an attorney or an attorney referral service "shall not directly solicit . . . a victim of the accident or disaster, or a relative of the victim, for the purpose of obtaining professional employment," and "shall not knowingly accept a referral from an attorney referral service" if the referral service has violated that prohibition. Under Ky. Rev. Stat. §21A.310, violation of the 30-day blackout law is a Class A misdemeanor, and may subject an attorney to professional discipline in addition to any criminal penalty.

Massachusetts: Rule 7.3(b)(1) prohibits solicitation if "the lawyer knows or reasonably should know that the physical, mental, or emotional state of the prospective client is such that there is a substantial potential that the person cannot exercise reasonable judgment in employing a lawyer"—but this prohibition does not apply to solicitation "not for a fee." Rule 7.3(d) prohibits solicitation in person "or by personal communication by telephone, electronic device, or otherwise," but under a new Rule 7.3(e) this prohibition does not apply to:

> (1) communications to members of the bar of any state or jurisdiction;
>
> (2) communications to individuals who are (A) the grandparents of the lawyer or the lawyer's spouse, (B) descendants of the grandparents of the lawyer or the lawyer's spouse, or (C) the spouse of any of the foregoing persons; . . . and
>
> (4) communications with organizations engaged in trade or commerce . . . , non-profit entities, or governmental entities . . . .

Missouri's version of Rule 7.3 generally follows the Kutak Commission's 1981 and 1982 drafts of Rule 7.3. However, in 1995, the Missouri Supreme Court added the following sentence to Rule 7.3(c):

> A written communication sent and received or a personal contact made within a reasonable period after an incident giving rise to personal injury or death is presumed to be written at a time or made at a time when the writer knows or reasonably should know that the physical, emotional, or mental state of the person makes it unlikely that the person would exercise reasonable judgment in employing a lawyer.

Missouri also adds the following new subparagraph (d) to Rule 7.3: "All communications or personal contacts made pursuant to this Rule 7.3 that state that legal services are available on a contingent or no-recovery-no-fee basis shall also state conspicuously that the client may be responsible for costs or expenses."

Montana Rule 7.3(d) prohibits a lawyer from contacting a prospective client if "the lawyer reasonably should know that the person is already represented by another lawyer."

Nevada: Supreme Court Rule 197 provides: "Written communication directed to a specific prospective client who may need legal services due to a particular transaction or occurrence is prohibited in Nevada within 45 days of the transaction or occurrence giving rise to the communication."

New Jersey: In 1997, to control solicitation after mass disasters, New Jersey adopted a new Rule 7.3(b)(4), which provides that a lawyer shall not contact, or send a written communication to, a prospective client for the purpose of obtaining professional employment if "(4) the communication involves unsolicited direct contact with a prospective client within thirty days after a specific mass-disaster event, when such contact concerns potential compensation arising from the event." In response to the State Bar Association's concerns that out-of-state attorneys would continue to solicit New Jersey victims and their families after mass disasters, the Court's Clerk issued a statement saying that it "has jurisdiction over out-of-state attorneys who make such solicitations to prospective claimants in New Jersey."

With respect to events other than mass disasters, New Jersey Rule 7.3(b)(5) generally permits targeted mail if it (among other things):

> (iii) contains an additional notice . . . that the recipient may, if the letter is inaccurate or misleading, report same to the Committee on Attorney Advertising, Hughes Justice Complex, CN 037, Trenton, New Jersey 08625.

New York: Compare ABA Model Rule 7.3 to New York's DR 2-101(F) and DR 2-103(A) and (C). In addition, New York Judiciary Law §479 (reprinted below in our Selected Provisions of the New York Judiciary Law) prohibits certain forms of solicitation.

North Carolina amended its Rule 7.3 in 2002 to define the criteria for a "prepaid or group legal services plan" that will satisfy Rule 7.3(d).

Ohio: Targeted direct mail solicitation must disclose "accurately and fully the manner in which the lawyer . . . became aware of and verified the identity and specific legal need of the addressee." It must also disclaim "any prior acquaintance or contact with the addressee and avoid any personalization in approach unless the facts are otherwise." The lawyer may not express "any predetermined evaluation of the merits of the addressee's case." In addition, effective January 1, 2000, Ohio added a new DR 2-101(H)(1) requiring that if a lawyer sends a communication to a prospective client or a relative of a prospective client within thirty days of an accident or disaster that gives rise to a potential claim for personal injury or wrongful death, a document entitled "Understanding Your Rights" must be enclosed with the communication. The required document consists of nine paragraphs providing such advice as: "Make and keep records"; "You do not have to sign anything"; "There is a time limit to file an insurance claim"; "Legal assistance may be appropriate"; "How to find an attorney"; "Check a lawyer's qualifications"; and a final paragraph that provides as follows:

> **9. How much will it cost?** In deciding whether to hire a particular lawyer, you should discuss, and the lawyer's written fee agreement should reflect:
>
> a. How is the lawyer to be paid? If you already have a settlement offer, how will that affect a contingent fee arrangement?

b. How are the expenses involved in your case, such as telephone calls, deposition costs, and fees for expert witnesses, to be paid? Will these costs be advanced by the lawyer or charged to you as they are incurred? Since you are obligated to pay all expenses even if you lose your case, how will payment be arranged?

c. Who will handle your case? If the case goes to trial, who will be the trial attorney?

Also, effective April 1, 2001, Ohio adopted a new rule requiring that before mailing a written solicitation of legal business to a party who has been named as a defendant in a civil action, a lawyer "shall verify that the party has been served with notice of the action filed against that party. Service shall be verified by consulting the docket of the court in which the action was filed . . . ."

Oregon: DR 2-101(H) requires that "communications sent via electronic mail" must include "the word 'advertisement' in type that is larger and darker than the type used for the text of the communication, if possible, or if that is not possible, then set off from the text at the beginning and end of the communication." DR 10-101(J) defines "electronic communication" to include "on-line legal lists and directories, web pages, messages sent to news groups, listservers, and bulletin boards; messages sent via electronic mail; and real time interactive communications such as conversations in internet chat groups and conference areas and video conferencing."

Pennsylvania has not adopted Rules 7.3(c) or (d).

Rhode Island: Rule 7.3(b)(2)(A) provides that a lawyer shall not send a written solicitation to a prospective client concerning "a specific matter" if "the lawyer knows or reasonably should know that the person to whom the communication is directed is represented by a lawyer in the matter."

South Carolina: Rules 7.3(c)(2) and (3) require that every written or recorded solicitation "must include the following statements":

> (A) "You may wish to consult your lawyer or another lawyer instead of me (us). You may obtain information about other lawyers by consulting the Yellow Pages or by calling the South Carolina Bar Lawyer Referral Service at 799-7100 in Columbia or toll-free at 1-800-868-2284. If you have already engaged a lawyer in connection with the legal matter referred to in this communication, you should direct any questions you have to that lawyer;" and
>
> (B) "The exact nature of your legal situation will depend on many facts not known to me (us) at this time. You should understand that the advice and information in this communication is general and that your own situation may vary." . . .
>
> (3) Each written or recorded solicitation must include the following statement: "ANY COMPLAINTS ABOUT THIS LETTER (OR RECORDING) OR THE REPRESENTATIONS OF ANY LAWYER MAY BE DIRECTED TO THE COMMISSION ON LAWYER CONDUCT, POST OFFICE BOX 11330, COLUMBIA, SOUTH CAROLINA, 29211—TELEPHONE NUMBER 803-734-2038." Where the solicitation is written, this statement must be printed in capital letters and in a size no smaller than that used in the body of the communication.

Rule 418 of the South Carolina court rules makes it "misconduct" for an out-of-state lawyer to violate South Carolina's advertising rules and provides for severe sanctions, including fee forfeiture, for any lawyer who solicits a matter in violation of those rules. For more on Rule 418, see the South Carolina entry in the Selected State Variations following ABA Model Rule 8.5.

Texas: Rule 7.06 provides that a lawyer "shall not accept or continue employment when the lawyer knows or reasonably should know that the person who seeks the lawyer's services does so as a result of conduct prohibited by these Rules." Texas Rule 7.03(a) provides that a lawyer "shall not by in-person or telephone contact seek professional employment concerning a matter arising out of a particular occurrence or event . . . when a significant motive for the lawyer's doing so is the lawyer's pecuniary gain." This rule does not apply to family members of current or former clients. In addition, under §38.12 of the Texas Penal Code it is a crime if a lawyer, "with intent to obtain an economic benefit . . . (2) solicits employment, either in person or by telephone, for himself or for another. . . ." Section 38.01(11) of the Texas Penal Code defines the phrase "solicits employment" as follows:

> "Solicits employment" means to communicate in person or by telephone or written communication with a prospective client or a member of the prospective client's family concerning legal representation arising out of a particular occurrence or event, or series of occurrences or events, or concerning an existing legal problem of the prospective client, for the purpose of providing legal representation to the prospective client, when neither the person receiving the communication nor anyone acting on that person's behalf has requested the communication.

The rule does not appear to prohibit in-person or telephone contact with prospective clients where the contact is not prompted by a specific event.

Virginia: Rule 7.3 permits in-person solicitation that is noncoercive and not misleading. However, such solicitation "for compensation in a personal injury or wrongful death claim of a prospective client with whom the lawyer has no family or prior professional relationship" is forbidden.

Related Materials

American Prepaid Legal Services Institute: Under ABA Model Rule 7.3(d), lawyers may participate with "a prepaid or group legal service plan operated by an organization not owned or directed by the lawyer" in certain circumstances. For more information about prepaid legal services, visit the web site maintained by the American Prepaid Legal Services Institute ("API") at www.aplsi.org. The API is a professional trade organization representing the legal services plan industry. It is affiliated with the American Bar Association and is headquartered in Chicago, Illinois.

ATLA Code of Conduct: In July 1988, following unfavorable press coverage of lawyer solicitation at various mass disaster sites, the membership of the Association of Trial Lawyers of America (ATLA), which consists largely of plaintiffs' personal injury lawyers, adopted a Code of Conduct that includes the following provisions relating to solicitation:

> 1. No ATLA member shall personally, or through a representative, contact any party, or an aggrieved survivor in an attempt to solicit a potential client when there has been no request for such contact from the injured party, an aggrieved survivor, or a relative of either, or the injured parties' union representative.
>
> 2. No ATLA member shall go to the scene of an event which caused injury unless requested to do so by an interested party, an aggrieved survivor, a relative of either, or by an attorney representing an injured party or survivor.

> 3. No ATLA member shall initiate a television appearance or initiate any comment to any news media concerning an event causing injury within 10 days of the event unless the member forgoes any financial return from the compensation of those injured or killed, provided, however, that an individual designated by a bar association to state the official position of such bar association may initiate such media contact to communicate such position. . . .
>
> 6. No ATLA member shall personally, or through a representative, initiate personal contact with a potential client (who is not a client, former client, relative or close personal friend of the attorney) for the purpose of advising that individual of the possibility of an unrecognized legal claim for damages unless the member forgoes any financial interest in the compensation of the injured party.

Aviation Disaster Family Assistance Act: In 1996, amidst allegations that lawyers had improperly solicited relatives of the victims of the crashes of ValueJet Flight 109 in the Florida Everglades and TWA Flight 800 off Long Island, Congress passed the Aviation Disaster Family Assistance Act, 49 U.S.C. §1136(g)(2). As amended in 2000, that statute restricts solicitation of air crash victims and their relatives as follows:

> *Unsolicited communications.* In the event of an accident involving an air carrier . . . no unsolicited communication concerning a potential action for personal injury or wrongful death may be made by an attorney (including any associate, agent, employee, or other representative of an attorney) or any potential party to the litigation to an individual injured in the accident, or to a relative of an individual involved in the accident, before the 45th day following the date of the accident.

"Jail Mail": In 1996, to make it more difficult for private criminal defense attorneys to send targeted mail to potential clients who were recently arrested (so-called "jail mail"), California amended Government Code §6254(f) to require any person requesting an arrestee's address to declare under penalty of perjury that the information "shall not be used directly or indirectly to sell a product or service . . . ." In Los Angeles Police Dep't v. United Reporting Publishing Corp., 120 S. Ct. 483 (1999), the United States Supreme Court held that this statute is not *facially* invalid, but left open the possibility that it may be invalid as applied.

Restatement of the Law Governing Lawyers: See Restatement §9 in our chapter on the Restatement later in this volume.

Rule 7.4 Communication of Fields of Practice and Specialization

(a) A lawyer may communicate the fact that the lawyer does or does not practice in particular fields of law. ~~A lawyer shall not state or imply that the lawyer has been recognized or certified as a specialist in a particular field of law except as follows:~~

~~(a)~~ (b) ~~a~~ A lawyer admitted to engage in patent practice before the United States Patent and Trademark Office may use the designation "Patent Attorney" or a substantially similar designation~~;~~.

~~(b)~~ (c) ~~a~~ A lawyer engaged in Admiralty practice may use the designation "Admiralty," "Proctor in Admiralty" or a substantially similar designation~~; and~~.

~~**(c) [for jurisdictions where there is a regulatory authority granting certification or approving organizations that grant certification] a lawyer may communicate the fact that the lawyer has been certified as a specialist in a field of law by a named organization or authority but only if:**~~

~~**(1) such certification is granted by the appropriate regulatory authority or by an organization which has been approved by the appropriate regulatory authority to grant such certification; or**~~

~~**(2) such certification is granted by an organization that has not yet been approved by, or has been denied the approval available from, the appropriate regulatory authority, and the absence or denial of approval is clearly stated in the communication, and in any advertising subject to Rule 7.2, such statement appears in the same sentence that communicates the certification.**~~

~~**(c) [for jurisdictions where there is no procedure either for certification of specialties or for approval of organizations granting certification] a lawyer may communicate the fact that the lawyer has been certified as a specialist in a field of law by a named organization, provided that the communication clearly states that there is no procedure in this jurisdiction for approving certifying organizations. If, however, the named organization has been accredited by the American Bar Association to certify lawyers as specialists in a particular field of law, the communication need not contain such a statement.**~~

(d) A lawyer shall not state or imply that a lawyer is certified as a specialist in a particular field of law, unless:

(1) the lawyer has been certified as a specialist by an organization that has been approved by an appropriate state authority or that has been accredited by the American Bar Association; and

(2) the name of the certifying organization is clearly identified in the communication.

COMMENT

[1] ~~This~~ Paragraph (a) of this Rule permits a lawyer to indicate areas of practice in communications about the lawyer's services. If a lawyer practices only in certain fields, or will not accept matters except in a specified field or fields, the lawyer is permitted to so indicate. A lawyer is generally permitted to state that the lawyer is a "specialist," practices a "specialty," or "specializes in" particular fields, but such communications are subject to the "false and misleading" standard applied in Rule 7.1 to communications concerning a lawyer's services.

[2] ~~However, a lawyer may not communicate that the lawyer has been recognized or certified as a specialist in a particular field of law, ex-~~

cept as provided by this R~~ule. Recognition of specialization in patent matters is a matter of~~ Paragraph (b) recognizes the long-established policy of the Patent and Trademark Office~~, as reflected in paragraph (a)~~ for the designation of lawyers practicing before the Office. Paragraph ~~(b)~~ (c) recognizes that designation of ~~admiralty~~ Admiralty practice has a long historical tradition associated with maritime commerce and the federal courts.

[3] Paragraph ~~(c) provides for certification~~ (d) permits a lawyer to state that the lawyer is certified as a specialist in a field of law ~~when a state authorizes an appropriate regulatory authority to grant such certification or when the state grants other organizations the right to grant certification~~ if such certification is granted by an organization approved by an appropriate state authority or accredited by the American Bar Association or another organization, such as a state bar association, that has been approved by the state authority to accredit organizations that certify lawyers as specialists. Certification ~~procedures imply~~ signifies that an objective entity has recognized ~~a lawyer's higher~~ an advanced degree of ~~specialized ability~~ knowledge and experience in the specialty area greater than is suggested by general licensure to practice law. ~~Those objective entities~~ Certifying organizations may be expected to apply standards of ~~competence,~~ experience ~~and~~, knowledge and proficiency to insure that a lawyer's recognition as a specialist is meaningful and reliable. In order to insure that consumers can obtain access to useful information about an organization granting certification, the name of the certifying organization ~~or agency~~ must be included in any communication regarding the certification.

~~[4] Lawyers may also be certified as specialists by organizations that either have not yet been approved to grant such certification or have been disapproved. In such instances, the consumer may be misled as to the significance of the lawyer's status as a certified specialist. The Rule therefore requires that a lawyer who chooses to communicate recognition by such an organization also clearly state the absence or denial of the organization's authority to grant such certification. Since lawyer advertising through public media and written or recorded communications invites the greatest danger of misleading consumers, the absence or denial of the organization's authority to grant certification must be clearly stated in such advertising in the same sentence that communicates the certification.~~

~~[5] In jurisdictions where no appropriate regulatory authority has a procedure for approving organizations granting certification, the Rule requires that a lawyer clearly state such lack of procedure. If, however, the named organization has been accredited by the American Bar Association to certify lawyers as specialists in a particular field of law, the communication need not contain such a statement.~~

Canon and Code Antecedents

ABA Canons of Professional Ethics: Canons 45 and 46 provided as follows:

45. Specialists

The canons of the American Bar Association apply to all branches of the legal profession; specialists in particular branches are not to be considered as exempt from the application of these principles.

46. Notice to Local Lawyers

A lawyer available to act as an associate of other lawyers in a particular branch of the law or legal service may send to local lawyers only and publish in his local legal journal, a brief and dignified announcement of his availability to serve other lawyers in connection therewith. The announcement should be in a form which does not constitute a statement or representation of special experience or expertness.

ABA Model Code of Professional Responsibility: Compare DR 2-105(A) (reprinted later in this volume).

Cross-References in Other Rules

Rule 5.5, Comment 21: "Whether and how lawyers may communicate the availability of their services to prospective clients in this jurisdiction is governed by **Rules 7.1** to **7.5**."

Legislative History of Model Rule 7.4

1979 Unofficial Pre-Circulation Draft (then Rule 9.3) provided, in pertinent part, as follows:

(a) A lawyer whose practice is limited to specified types of legal matters may communicate that fact except as otherwise provided by regulations governing specialization. A lawyer may indicate that he or she is a specialist only as permitted by paragraphs (b) and (c) and as follows: [Insert applicable provisions on designation of specialization.]

The remainder of the 1979 Draft was substantially the same as adopted.

1980 Discussion Draft was substantially the same as adopted.

1981 and 1982 Drafts were the same as adopted.

1989 Amendments: At its February 1989 Mid-Year Meeting, the ABA House of Delegates substantially amended the Comment (but not the text) to Rule 7.4. The changes were explained in the following report:

*ABA Committee Report Explaining 1989 Amendment to Rule 7.4**

Rule 7.4 prohibits a lawyer from stating or implying that he or she is a "specialist," with certain limited exceptions. The Rule further provides for designation of specialty in accordance with the rules of the particular jurisdiction. Rule 7.4(c).

*Committee Reports do not represent official policy of the ABA. They are for information only, and the opinions are those of the authors of the report.

This rule operates only to prohibit factually inaccurate or misleading information. . . .

As presently written, however, the Comment to Rule 7.4 *also* prohibits statements that the lawyer's practice is "limited to" or "concentrated in" certain fields, under the theory that these terms also connote formal recognition of the lawyer as a "specialist." . . . The use of the words "limited to" or "concentrated in" in denoting areas of practice do not clearly imply *formal* recognition as a "specialist" and simply do not pose sufficient danger of misleading to warrant a proscription of their use. . . .

Therefore, the Comment to Rule 7.4 should not prohibit statements that a lawyer's practice is "limited to" or "concentrated in" a particular field.

1992 Amendments: At its 1992 Annual Meeting, the ABA House of Delegates substantially amended Rule 7.4 and its Comment to conform the rule to the holding of Peel v. Attorney Registration and Disciplinary Commission, 496 U.S. 91 (1990). The amendments are explained in the following committee report:

*ABA Committee Report Explaining 1992 Amendment to Rule 7.4**

Background

The findings in a recent survey conducted by the ABA Young Lawyers Division . . . revealed that 64 percent of all lawyers in private practice spend at least 50 percent of their time in one substantive field of law. Further, this phenomenon is not limited to large firms. Fifty-five percent of sole practitioners responding to the survey were found to spend half or more of their time in just one field.

Lawyer specialization has proliferated largely without formal recognition by the organized bar or state and federal regulators. An ABA committee concluded in 1967 that in spite of the apparent unwillingness of the bar either to control lawyer specialization or to accept its regulation, "the fact of specialization persists and expands and the need to recognize the fact and regulate its existence and growth becomes steadily more apparent." . . .

The *Peel* Decision

In 1990 the legal specialization issue was addressed again by the Supreme Court in *Peel v. Attorney Registration and Disciplinary Commission*. . . .

The *Peel* decision invalidated the broad prohibition of ABA Model Rule 7.4 on lawyers' communications about their specialties, holding that states may not categorically ban a truthful communication by a lawyer that he or she is certified as a specialist by a bona fide private certifying organization.

The National Board of Trial Advocacy, whose certification was at issue in the *Peel* case, had certified lawyers as civil and criminal trial specialists for many years. The *Peel* decision has now spurred other private organizations to establish lawyer certification programs. The American Bankruptcy Board of Certification, a nonprofit organization sponsored by the American Bankruptcy Institute, is beginning to certify qualified lawyers as specialists, offering separate certification in business and consumer bankruptcy. The Commercial Law League of America recently announced its lawyer certification program in bankruptcy and creditors' rights law.

Other private groups such as the National Organization of Social Security Claimants Representatives and the National Academy of Elder Law Attorneys are contemplating certification plans. It is conceivable that even law schools, CLE providers and ABA Sections will become certifiers.

*Committee Reports do not represent official policy of the ABA. They are for information only, and the opinions are those of the authors of the report.

> The proposed amendment of Model Rule 7.4 would bring the ABA Model Rules of Professional Conduct into compliance with the *Peel* decision. . . . Amending Model Rule 7.4 as we have proposed will help to insure protection of the users of legal services while authorizing legitimate, truthful advertising claims of lawyer specialists.

1994 Amendments: At its August 1994 Annual Meeting, the ABA House of Delegates amended Rule 7.4 by adding a single new sentence at the end of the existing rule and an identical sentence to the end of the Comment. (The amendment made no deletions.) The new sentence brought Rule 7.4 into line with the ABA's system for accrediting organizations that certify lawyers as specialists. (The ABA Standing Committee on Specialization began approving such organizations in 1993.) In essence, the amendment makes it unnecessary for lawyers in states without certifying procedures to use a disclaimer when claiming certification by an ABA-accredited organization. This is the first time that the American Bar Association has been mentioned by name anywhere in the ABA Model Rules of Professional Conduct.

Below are excerpts from the joint report and recommendation submitted by the two co-sponsors in support of the amendment.

*ABA Committee Report Explaining 1994 Amendment to Rule 7.4**

> The purpose of this recommendation is to harmonize Model Rule 7.4 with the Association's newly enacted procedure for accrediting organizations that certify specialists in particular areas of the law. . . .
>
> In August, 1993 the Standing Committee on Specialization reported to the House that six specialty certification programs . . . had met the Standards. The Standing Committee on Specialization therefore recommended that those programs be accredited, which recommendation was approved by the House.
>
> However, under the 1992 amendments, a lawyer who is certified by one of those accredited programs, and who practices in a State that has not yet adopted a procedure for approving certifying organizations, would have to add, to any communication setting forth his or her certification, a statement to the effect that there is no procedure in that particular jurisdiction for approving certifying organizations. Many lawyers believe that such a disclaimer would dilute the positive fact of certification; therefore, those lawyers would end up refraining from publicizing their certification rather than adding the required statement, even though the certifying organization had been fully accredited by the ABA. As a consequence, the value of the ABA accreditation would be considerably diminished.
>
> The Standing Committee on Specialization and the Standing Committee on Ethics and Professional Responsibility believe that Rule 7.4 should now be further amended to permit any accreditations authorized by the House to have their intended effect and be given recognition in those states which have not yet created a mechanism for approving organizations that grant certification.

2002 Amendments: At its February 2002 Mid-Year Meeting, the ABA House of Delegates adopted without change the ABA Ethics 2000 Commission proposal to amend Rule 7.4 and its Comment.

*Committee Reports do not represent official policy of the ABA. They are for information only, and the opinions are those of the authors of the report.

Selected State Variations

Arizona: Rule 7.4(c) permits a lawyer to state that he or she is "certified by a national entity which has standards for certification substantially the same as those established by" the Arizona Board of Legal Specialization. The Board must have recognized the entity as having equivalent standards.

Arkansas provides: "A lawyer who has been recognized as a specialist under the Arkansas Plan of Specialization approved by the Arkansas Supreme Court may communicate the fact during the period he or she is a 'Board Recognized Specialist in [insert field of law].' "

California: See Standard 11 following Rule 1-400.

Colorado: Rule 7.4 permits lawyers to advertise areas of practice in which they will accept referrals, and to advertise availability as a consultant in specific areas.

District of Columbia: D.C. omits Rule 7.4, but covers communication of fields of practice and certification in a general and limited fashion in Rule 7.1(a) — see District of Columbia Rules of Professional Conduct below.

Florida: Rule 4-7.9(c)(2), governing information that must be provided to a prospective client upon request, provides that if a lawyer or law firm "claims special expertise in the representation of clients in special matters or publicly limits the lawyer's or law firm's practice to special types of cases or clients, written information setting forth the factual details of the lawyer's experience, expertise, background, and training in such matters" shall be available to potential clients.

Pursuant to Supreme Court Rule 6-1.2, the Florida Bar has promulgated the following notice to the public:

> Attorneys indicating they are "board certified" have been identified by The Florida Bar as having special knowledge, skills, and proficiency in their areas of practice. "Florida Bar Designated" attorneys have met minimum experience and educational requirements under the Florida Designation Plan. "Florida Bar Members" may list their areas of practice in the Yellow Pages without meeting any specific criteria.

The rules governing Florida's designation and certification plans set forth special criteria for more than 25 separate fields of law practice.

Georgia: In the rules effective January 1, 2001, Georgia's version of Rule 7.4 is much shorter than ABA Model Rule 7.4. After tracking the first sentence of ABA Model Rule 7.4 verbatim, Georgia eliminates the rest of the ABA rule and states simply: "A lawyer who is a specialist in a particular field of law by experience, specialized training or education, or is certified by a recognized and bona fide professional entity, may communicate such specialty or certification so long as the statement is not false or misleading."

Illinois, whose old rule on specialization (DR 2-105) was struck down in Peel v. Attorney Registration and Disciplinary Commission of Illinois, 496 U.S. 91 (1990), promulgated a new rule six weeks after the *Peel* decision. The new rule requires that any lawyer advertisement using the terms "certified," "specialist," "expert," or similar terms must meet two conditions:

> (1) the reference must be truthful and verifiable and may not be misleading in violation of Rule 7.1;
>
> (2) the reference must state that the Supreme Court of Illinois does not recognize certifications of specialties in the practice of law and that the certificate, award or recognition is not a requirement to practice law in Illinois.

Iowa prohibits lawyers from advertising "[f]ixed fees or range of fees for specific legal services" except in the following twelve specified areas of law: (1) abstract examinations and title opinions, (2) uncontested divorces "involving no disagreement concerning custody of children, alimony, child support, or property settlement," (3) wills "leaving all property outright to one beneficiary and contingently to one beneficiary or class or beneficiaries," (4) income tax returns for wage earners, (5) uncontested personal bankruptcies, (6) changes of name, (7) simple residential deeds, (8) residential purchase and sale agreements, (9) residential leases, (10) residential mortgages and notes, (11) powers of attorney, and (12) bills of sale. In addition, Iowa prohibits a lawyer from advertising fixed fees for these services "as an indirect means of attracting clients for whom he performs other legal services not related to the specific legal services publicized."

Massachusetts: Rule 7.4(a) permits lawyers to hold themselves out as "specialists in particular services, fields, and areas of law if the holding out does not include a false or misleading communication." The rule defines "holding out" to include "(1) a statement that the lawyer concentrates in, specializes in, is certified in, has expertise in, or limits practice to a particular service, field, or area of law, (2) directory listings, including electronic, computer-accessed or other similar types of directory listings, by particular service, field, or area of law, and (3) any other association of the lawyer's name with a particular service, field, or area of law." A new Comment 3A to Massachusetts Rule 7.2 provides, in part:

> Depending upon the topic or purpose of the newsgroup, bulletin board, or chat group, the posting might also constitute an association of the lawyer or law firm's name with a particular service, field, or area of law amounting to a claim of specialization under Rule 7.4 and would therefore be subject to the restrictions of that rule.

Michigan: Rule 7.4 stops after the first sentence of ABA Model Rule 7.4.

Minnesota adds that a lawyer "shall not state that the lawyer is a certified specialist if the lawyer's certification has terminated, or if the statement is otherwise contrary to the terms of such certification."

Mississippi: In 1999, the Mississippi Supreme Court amended Rule 7.6(a) to permit lawyers to advertise a specialty certification without disclaimer "if that certification or designation is granted by an organization or authority whose specialty certification or designation program is accredited by the American Bar Association." But if the certifying organization or authority is not accredited by the ABA, then the lawyer "must disclose such fact and further disclose that there is no procedure in Mississippi for approving certifying or designating organizations and authorities." The amendment was necessary because portions of Mississippi's former rule on advertising a specialty certification were declared unconstitutional in Schwartz v. Welch, 890 F. Supp. 565 (S.D. Miss. 1996).

Missouri provides that a lawyer other than an admiralty or patent attorney shall not state or imply that the lawyer is a specialist "unless the communication contains a disclaimer that neither the Supreme Court of Missouri nor The Missouri Bar reviews or approves certifying organizations or specialist designations."

Montana provides:

> (c) A lawyer who is a specialist in a certain field of law by experience in the field, by specialized training or education in the field, or by certification by an authoritative professional entity in the field may communicate the fact of his or her specialty where such communication is not false or misleading under Rule 7.1.

New Hampshire provides:

> A lawyer who publicly discloses fields of law in which the lawyer or the law firm practices or states that his or her practice is limited to one or more fields of law shall do so by using descriptive language that is accurate, straightforward, truthful and dignified.

New Jersey provides in Rule 7.4(b):

> A lawyer may communicate that the lawyer has been certified as a specialist or certified in a field of practice only when the communication is not false or misleading, states the name of the certifying organization, and states that the certification has been granted by the Supreme Court of New Jersey or by an organization that has been approved by the American Bar Association. If the certification has been granted by an organization that has not been approved, or has been denied approval, by the Supreme Court of New Jersey or the American Bar Association, the absence or denial of such approval shall be clearly identified in each such communication by the lawyer.

New York: Compare ABA Model Rule 7.4 to New York's DR 2-105.

Pennsylvania: Lawyers may advertise that they are certified by organizations approved by the Supreme Court. The Supreme Court may approve an organization upon recommendation of the State Bar Association if the court finds that advertising by the lawyer of such certification "will provide meaningful information, which is not false, misleading or deceptive, for use of the public in selecting or retaining a lawyer." Certification must be available to all lawyers "who meet objective and consistently applied standards relevant to practice in the area of law to which the certification relates."

Texas: Rule 7.04(b)(2) permits lawyers to advertise that they have been certified as specialists by the Texas Board of Legal Specialization or by an organization that has been:

> accredited by the Texas Board of Legal Specialization as a bona fide organization that admits to membership or grants certification only on the basis of objective, exacting, publicly available standards (including high standards of individual character, conduct, and reputation) that are reasonably relevant to the special training or special competence that is implied and that are in excess of the level of training and competence generally required for admission to the Bar. . . .

Rule 7.04(b)(3) requires lawyers to state, "with respect to each area advertised in which the lawyer has not been awarded a Certificate of Special Competence by the Texas Board of Legal Specialization," that the lawyer is "Not Certified by the Texas Board of Legal Specialization." In a November 1998 referendum, Texas lawyers voted to delete the "not certified" requirement, but on June 21, 1999 the Texas Supreme Court invalidated the referendum because fewer than 51 percent of all Texas lawyers voted in it. Therefore, the "old" Rule 7.04 and its "not certified" requirement remains in effect.

Related Materials

ABA Model Plan of Specialization: In 1979, the ABA House of Delegates adopted the Model Plan of Specialization proposed by the ABA Standing Committee on Specialization. The plan is reprinted in the ABA/BNA Lawyers' Manual on Professional Conduct.

ABA Standards for Accreditation of Specialty Certification Programs for Lawyers: In 1992, when the ABA amended Rule 7.4 to allow lawyers to advertise that they were "certified" by private organizations as specialists, the ABA also asked a special committee to develop standards for accrediting private organizations that issue specialty certifications to lawyers. In 1993, the ABA House of Delegates adopted Standards for Accreditation of Specialty Certification Programs for Lawyers. The ABA Standards are strict, and the ethics rules of some states expressly allow lawyers to claim specialty certification only by an entity that has been accredited by the ABA. Under the ABA Standards, organizations must be made up primarily of lawyers and must not certify lawyers unless the lawyers meet five distinct criteria: (1) they have been involved in the specialty area for at least the past three years; (2) they devote at least 25 percent of their practice to the specialty area; (3) they have passed a written examination of "suitable length and complexity"; (4) they have been favorably recommended by five or more lawyers or judges knowledgeable in the specialty area; and (5) they have taken at least 36 hours of CLE in the specialty area during the three years before applying for certification as a specialist. The task of accrediting certifying organizations under the Standards was given to the ABA's Standing Committee on Specialization.

Since 1993, the ABA has voted to accredit more than ten specialty certification programs. A complete list of these programs is available at the ABA's specialization web page, www.abanet.org/specialization.

At its 1999 Annual Meeting, the ABA amended the Standards for Accreditation of Specialty Certification Programs for Lawyers by extending the accreditation period from three years to five years. The Standing Committee on Specialization is currently working with various private groups to help them develop additional certification programs that meet the ABA Standards. The Standing Committee on Specialization also hosts an annual National Roundtable on Lawyer Specialty Certification. For further information about specialization, call the Staff Counsel of the ABA's Standing Committee on Specialization at (312) 988-5753, or visit the Committee's web site at www.abanet.org/specialization.

Paralegal Certification: Since 1976, the National Association of Legal Assistants ("NALA") has administered a certifying examination for paralegals. The exam tests Communications, Ethics, Legal Research, Human Relations and Interviewing Techniques, Judgment & Analytical Ability, Legal Terminology, and Substantive Law. The substantive law section consists of five "mini-examinations" covering the American Legal System and four substantive areas selected by examinees from the following list: Administrative Law, Bankruptcy, Business Organizations/Corporations, Contracts, Family Law, Criminal Law and Procedure, Litigation, Probate and Estate Planning, and Real Estate. Passing the exam entitles a paralegal to the designation "Certified Legal Assistant" (or "CLA"). In 1999, approximately 1,500 candidates took the CLA exam. In addition, paralegals who hold the CLA credential may take four-hour specialty certification examinations in the areas of Bankruptcy, Civil Litigation, Corporations/Business Law, Criminal Law and Procedure, Intellectual Property, Estate Planning and Probate, and Real Estate. The CLA credential is awarded for a period of five years. To maintain CLA status after the initial five-year period expires, legal assistants must participate in at least 50 hours of continuing legal education programs or individual study programs during the five-year period. The

NALA may revoke the CLA designation for a variety of reasons, including "[v]iolation of the NALA Code of Ethics and Professional Responsibility." For more information, check the NALA's web site at www.nala.org.

Restatement of the Law Governing Lawyers: The Restatement has no provision comparable to ABA Model Rule 7.4.

Rule 7.5 Firm Names and Letterheads

(a) A lawyer shall not use a firm name, letterhead or other professional designation that violates Rule 7.1. A trade name may be used by a lawyer in private practice if it does not imply a connection with a government agency or with a public or charitable legal services organization and is not otherwise in violation of Rule 7.1.

(b) A law firm with offices in more than one jurisdiction may use the same name or other professional designation in each jurisdiction, but identification of the lawyers in an office of the firm shall indicate the jurisdictional limitations on those not licensed to practice in the jurisdiction where the office is located.

(c) The name of a lawyer holding a public office shall not be used in the name of a law firm, or in communications on its behalf, during any substantial period in which the lawyer is not actively and regularly practicing with the firm.

(d) Lawyers may state or imply that they practice in a partnership or other organization only when that is the fact.

COMMENT

[1] A firm may be designated by the names of all or some of its members, by the names of deceased members where there has been a continuing succession in the firm's identity or by a trade name such as the "ABC Legal Clinic." A lawyer or law firm may also be designated by a distinctive web site address or comparable professional designation. Although the United States Supreme Court has held that legislation may prohibit the use of trade names in professional practice, use of such names in law practice is acceptable so long as it is not misleading. If a private firm uses a trade name that includes a geographical name such as "Springfield Legal Clinic," an express disclaimer that it is a public legal aid agency may be required to avoid a misleading implication. It may be observed that any firm name including the name of a deceased partner is, strictly speaking, a trade name. The use of such names to designate law firms has proven a useful means of identification. However, it is misleading to use the name of a lawyer not associated with the firm or a predecessor of the firm, or the name of a nonlawyer.

> **Editors' Note.** The last clause of Comment 1 ("or the name of a nonlawyer") was added at the ABA's August 2002 Annual Meeting — see the entry entitled "2002 Amendments" in the Legislative History below for more information.

[2] With regard to paragraph (d), lawyers sharing office facilities, but who are not in fact ~~partners~~ associated with each other in a law firm, may not denominate themselves as, for example, "Smith and Jones," for that title suggests ~~partnership in the practice of~~ that they are practicing law together in a firm.

Canon and Code Antecedents

ABA Canons of Professional Ethics: Canon 33 provided as follows:

33. Partnerships — Names

Partnerships among lawyers for the practice of their profession are very common and are not to be condemned. In the formation of partnerships and the use of partnership names care should be taken not to violate any law, custom, or rule of court locally applicable. Where partnerships are formed between lawyers who are not all admitted to practice in the courts of the state, care should be taken to avoid any misleading name or representation which would create a false impression as to the professional position or privileges of the member not locally admitted. In the formation of partnerships for the practice of law, no person should be admitted or held out as a practitioner or member who is not a member of the legal profession duly authorized to practice, and amenable to professional discipline. In the selection and use of a firm name, no false, misleading, assumed or trade name should be used. The continued use of the name of a deceased or former partner, when permissible by local custom, is not unethical, but care should be taken that no imposition or deception is practiced through this use. When a member of the firm, on becoming a judge, is precluded from practicing law, his name should not be continued in the firm name.

Partnerships between lawyers and members of other professions or nonprofessional persons should not be formed or permitted where any part of the partnership's employment consists of the practice of law.

ABA Model Code of Professional Responsibility: Compare DR 2-102(A), DR 2-102(B), DR 2-102(C), and DR 2-102(D) (reprinted later in this volume).

Cross-References in Other Rules

Rule 5.5, Comment 21: "Whether and how lawyers may communicate the availability of their services to prospective clients in this jurisdiction is governed by **Rules** 7.1 to **7.5**."

Legislative History of Model Rule 7.5

1980 Discussion Draft (then Rule 9.5) did not include the clause in subparagraph (b) requiring lawyers to indicate their jurisdictional limitations, and did not contain subparagraph (d).

1981 Draft was generally the same as adopted, except that Rule 7.5(d) provided: "Lawyers shall not hold themselves out as practicing in a law firm unless the association is in fact a firm."

1982 Draft was adopted.

2002 Amendments: At its February 2002 Mid-Year Meeting, the ABA House of Delegates adopted without change the ABA Ethics 2000 Commission proposal to amend Rule 7.5 and its Comment.

In addition, at the ABA's August 2002 Annual Meeting, the House of Delegates approved a proposal by the ABA Standing Committee on Ethics and Professional Responsibility to add the final clause ("or the name of a nonlawyer") to Comment 1 of Rule 7.5. The Report submitted by the Standing Committee in support of this proposal (and a companion proposal to amend Rule 7.2) noted that the Standing Committee had consulted with the New York State Bar Association, which recommended amending Rule 7.5 to address "its concern that law firms engaged in offering certain services jointly with other nonlawyer professionals not create confusion by adding names of nonlawyer professionals to their law firm names." The Standing Committee agreed with this recommendation, and therefore recommended adding the final clause of Comment 1 to Model Rule 7.5. The House of Delegates approved the recommendation.

Selected State Variations

Alaska adds subparagraph (e): "The term 'of counsel' shall be used only to refer to a lawyer who has a close continuing relationship with the firm."

Arizona deletes the clause in subparagraph (a) beginning, "if it does not imply a connection. . . ."

California: See Standards 6 through 9 following Rule 1-400. In addition, §16952 of the California Corporations Law, entitled "Requirements for Name," provides that the name of a registered limited liability partnership must contain the words "Registered Limited Liability Partnership" or "Limited Liability Partnership" or one of the abbreviations "L.L.P.," "LLP," "R.L.L.P.," or "RLLP" as the last words or letters of its name.

Colorado's Rule 7.5(d) permits the use of the name of "deceased or retired members of the firm or of a predecessor firm in a continuing line of succession," as in DR 2-102(B) of the ABA Model Code.

Florida: Rule 4-7.10(b) permits a lawyer to practice under a trade name if the name is "not deceptive" and "does not imply that the firm is something other than a private law firm." The same rule permits a lawyer to use the term "legal clinic" or "legal services" in conjunction with the lawyer's own name "if the lawyer's practice is devoted to providing routine legal services for fees that are lower than the prevailing rate in the community for those services."

Rule 4-7.10(c) provides that a lawyer who advertises under a trade or fictitious name "shall be in violation of this rule unless the same name is the law firm name that appears on the lawyer's letterhead, business cards, office sign, and fee contracts, and appears with the lawyer's signature on pleadings and other legal documents."

The Comment to Rule 4-7.10 gives two examples of terms that imply that a firm is something other than a private law firm: "academy" and "institute." It also notes that a lawyer may not advertise under "a nonsense name designed to obtain an advantageous position for the lawyer in alphabetical directory listings unless the lawyer actually practices under that nonsense name."

Georgia: In the rules effective January 1, 2001, Georgia adopted the pre-2002 version of ABA Model Rule 7.5(b), (c), and (d) verbatim, but substituted the following two paragraphs for ABA Model Rule 7.5(a):

> (a) A lawyer shall not use a firm name, letterhead or other professional designation that violates Rule 7.1. . . .
>
> (e) A trade name may be used by a lawyer in private practice if:
>
> (1) the trade name includes the name of at least one of the lawyers practicing under said name. A law firm name consisting solely of the name or names of deceased or retired members of the firm does not have to include the name of an active member of the firm; and
>
> (2) the trade name does not imply a connection with a government entity, with a public or charitable legal services organization or any other organization, association or institution or entity, unless there is, in fact, a connection.

Georgia's Comment to Rule 7.5 differs significantly from the ABA Comment.

Illinois amplifies Rule 7.5(c) as follows:

> (a) A lawyer who assumes a judicial, legislative, or public executive or administrative post or office shall not permit the lawyer's name to remain in the name of a law firm or to be used in professional notices of the firm during any substantial period in which the lawyer is not actively and regularly practicing law as a member of the firm. . . .

Iowa: DR 2-101(G) prohibits a lawyer from using the word "clinic" in any public communication "unless the practice of the lawyer or his firm is limited to routine matters for which the costs of rendering the service can be substantially reduced because of the repetitive nature of the services performed and the use of standardized forms and office procedures."

Massachusetts: Rule 7.5(a) adds that "[u]se of such names in law practice is acceptable so long as it is not misleading." Massachusetts adds to ABA Comment 2 that the term "associates" implies practice in either a partnership or sole proprietorship form and "may not be used by a group in which the individual members disclaim the joint or vicarious responsibility inherent in such forms of business in the absence of an effective disclaimer of such responsibility."

Missouri deletes the second sentence of Rule 7.5(a), and adds two new subparagraphs providing as follows:

> (b) A lawyer's firm name shall include the name of the lawyer, the name of another lawyer in the firm or the name of a deceased or retired member of the firm in a continuing line of succession.
>
> (c) A lawyer's firm name shall not include the name of any person other than a present member of the firm or a deceased or retired member of the firm in a continuing line of succession.

Nevada: Rule 199, which is the only one of its kind in the nation, provides, in part, as follows: "*Firm names.* It shall be unprofessional conduct to use a firm name for a law firm unless each and every person whose name is used is a member of the state bar in good standing and a bona fide member of the firm." When we went to press in September of 2002, Rule 199 was the subject of a preliminary injunction as a result of lawsuits filed by two out-of-state law firms challenging the rule's constitutionality.

New Jersey: Rule 7.5 provides, in part:

> (b) A law firm with offices in more than one jurisdiction may use the same name in each jurisdiction. In New Jersey, identification of all lawyers of the firm, in advertisements, on letterheads or anywhere else that the firm name is used, shall indicate the jurisdictional limitations on those not licensed to practice in New Jersey. Where the name of an attorney not licensed to practice in this State is used in a firm name, any advertisement, letterhead or other communication containing the firm name must include the name of at least one licensed New Jersey attorney who is responsible for the firm's New Jersey practice or the local office thereof. . . .
>
> (d) Lawyers may state or imply that they practice in a partnership only if the persons designated in the firm name and the principal members of the firm share in the responsibility and liability for the firm's performance of legal services.
>
> (e) A law firm name may include additional identifying language such as "& Associates" only when such language is accurate and descriptive of the firm. Any firm name including additional identifying language such as "Legal Services" or other similar phrases shall inform all prospective clients in the retainer agreement or other writing that the law firm is not affiliated or associated with a public, quasi-public or charitable organization. However, no firm shall use the phrase "legal aid" in its name or in any additional identifying language.
>
> (f) In any case in which an organization practices under a trade name as permitted by paragraph (a) above, the name or names of one or more of its principally responsible attorneys, licensed to practice in this State, shall be displayed on all letterheads, signs, advertisements and cards or other places where the trade name is used.

New York: Compare ABA Model Rule 7.5(a) to New York's DR 2-102(A)-(B). Compare Rule 7.5(b) to New York's DR 2-102(D). Compare Rule 7.5(c) to New York's DR 2-102(B) (last sentence). Compare Rule 7.5(d) to New York's DR 2-102(C).

North Carolina: Rule 7.5(c) provides that a law firm with offices only in North Carolina may not list a lawyer who is not licensed to practice law in North Carolina as a lawyer "affiliated" with the firm "unless the listing properly identifies the jurisdiction in which the lawyer is licensed and states that the lawyer is not licensed in North Carolina." Comment 3 explains that the revised rule "does not prohibit the employment by a law firm of a lawyer who is licensed to practice in another jurisdiction, but not in North Carolina, provided the lawyer's practice is limited to areas that do not require a North Carolina law license such as immigration law, federal tort claims, military law, and the like." However, the firm may not include the out-of-state lawyer's name on the firm letterhead, and all communications by the out-of-state lawyer on behalf of the firm "must indicate the jurisdiction in which the lawyer is licensed as well as the fact that the lawyer is not licensed in North Carolina."

Ohio DR 2-102(G) specifically provides rules for use of the term "legal clinic" in a firm name. The Rule envisions that a legal clinic will provide "standardized and multiple legal services."

Virginia combines the language of DR 2-102 and Model Rule 7.5.

Related Materials

ABA Formal Ethics Opinions: See ABA Formal Ethics Op. 84-351 (1984), 90-357 (1990), and 95-391 (1995).

Partnership Law: Rule 7.4(d) prohibits lawyers from stating or implying that they are partners if they are not. Section 7 of the Uniform Partnership Act, entitled "Rules for Determining the Existence of a Partnership," provides: "(4) The receipt by a person of a share of the profits of a business is prima facie evidence that he is a partner in the business. . . ." The subparagraph then lists five exceptions to this general rule.

Restatement of the Law Governing Lawyers: The Restatement has no provision comparable to ABA Model Rule 7.5.

Rule 7.6 Political Contributions to Obtain Government Legal Engagements or Appointments by Judges

A lawyer or law firm shall not accept a government legal engagement or an appointment by a judge if the lawyer or law firm makes a political contribution or solicits political contributions for the purpose of obtaining or being considered for that type of legal engagement or appointment.

COMMENT

[1] Lawyers have a right to participate fully in the political process, which includes making and soliciting political contributions to candidates for judicial and other public office. Nevertheless, when lawyers make or solicit political contributions in order to obtain an engagement for legal work awarded by a government agency, or to obtain appointment by a judge, the public may legitimately question whether the lawyers engaged to perform the work are selected on the basis of competence and merit. In such a circumstance, the integrity of the profession is undermined.

[2] The term "political contribution" denotes any gift, subscription, loan, advance or deposit of anything of value made directly or indirectly to a candidate, incumbent, political party or campaign committee to influence or provide financial support for election to or retention in judicial or other government office. Political contributions in initiative and referendum elections are not included. For purposes of this Rule, the term "political contribution" does not include uncompensated services.

[3] Subject to the exceptions below, (i) the term "government legal engagement" denotes any engagement to provide legal services that a public official has the direct or indirect power to award; and (ii) the term "appointment by a judge" denotes an appointment to a position such as referee, commissioner, special master, receiver, guardian or other similar position that is made by a judge. Those terms do not, however, include (a) substantially uncompensated services; (b) engagements or appointments made on the basis of experience, expertise, professional qualifications and cost following a request for proposal or other process that is free from

influence based upon political contributions; and (c) engagements or appointments made on a rotational basis from a list compiled without regard to political contributions.

[4] The term "lawyer or law firm" includes a political action committee or other entity owned or controlled by a lawyer or law firm.

[5] Political contributions are for the purpose of obtaining or being considered for a government legal engagement or appointment by a judge if, but for the desire to be considered for the legal engagement or appointment, the lawyer or law firm would not have made or solicited the contributions. The purpose may be determined by an examination of the circumstances in which the contributions occur. For example, one or more contributions that in the aggregate are substantial in relation to other contributions by lawyers or law firms, made for the benefit of an official in a position to influence an award of a government legal engagement, and followed by an award of the legal engagement to the contributing or soliciting lawyer or the lawyer's firm would support an inference that the purpose of the contributions was to obtain the engagement, absent other factors that weigh against existence of the proscribed purpose. Those factors may include among others that the contribution or solicitation was made to further a political, social, or economic interest or because of an existing personal, family, or professional relationship with a candidate.

[6] If a lawyer makes or solicits a political contribution under circumstances that constitute bribery or another crime, Rule 8.4(b) is implicated.

Canon and Code Antecedents

ABA Canons of Professional Ethics: No comparable Canon.

ABA Model Code of Professional Responsibility: No comparable Disciplinary Rule.

Cross-References in Other Rules

None.

Legislative History of Model Rule 7.6

1997 Proposal and Resolution: At the ABA's August 1997 Annual Meeting, the Association of the Bar of the City of New York proposed that the ABA adopt a detailed and highly restrictive "pay-to-play" rule. The heart of the proposal provided as follows:

> *3. Prohibitions On Certain Government Finance Engagements*
>
> (a) No lawyer shall undertake a Government Finance Engagement awarded by an Official of an Issuer within two years after making either a Political

Contribution or a Political Solicitation; provided, however, that this Rule shall not prohibit a lawyer from undertaking a Government Finance Engagement with a particular Official of an Issuer if:

(i)(A) the only Political Contribution made by the lawyer to that Official of an Issuer within the previous two years was (I) for a position for which the lawyer was entitled to vote and (II) not in excess of $250 for each stage of the electoral campaign (i.e., primary and general election) and (B) the lawyer did not make any political contribution in excess of $1,000 to any political party or committee of the State or of any political subdivision, agency or instrumentality thereof; or

(ii) the only Political Solicitation made by the lawyer on behalf of that Official of an Issuer or any political party or committee of the State or of any political subdivision, agency or instrumentality thereof, was for Political Contributions made within the previous two years for an Official of an Issuer for whom the lawyer was entitled to vote, no Political Contribution solicited was in excess of $100 to the Official of an Issuer for each complete electoral campaign (primary and general election combined), and the aggregate of all Political Contributions solicited in any such campaign within the previous two years did not exceed $2,500. . . .

(b) Notwithstanding subsection (a), any lawyer who is personally involved in the undertaking of Government Finance Engagements who solicits Political Contributions in any amount at the request of an Official of an Issuer or one of the Official's subordinates, is prohibited from undertaking a Government Finance Engagement awarded by that Official of an Issuer for a period of two years. . . .

(c) To the extent that a lawyer is prohibited from undertaking a Government Finance Engagement by operation of this Rule, the law firm employing such lawyer (whether or not that lawyer is admitted to practice in New York) shall also be prohibited from undertaking a Government Finance Engagement . . . .

(d) If a law firm or a political action committee controlled by a law firm itself makes a Political Contribution or a Political Solicitation that would operate to prohibit a lawyer from undertaking certain Government Finance Engagements, the law firm is likewise prohibited from undertaking such Government Finance Engagements for the same two year period that would be applicable to lawyer prohibited through operation of the Rule.

The ABA House of Delegates did not approve the New York City Bar's proposal. Instead, the House of Delegates approved a resolution (a) condemning pay-to-play practices wherever they existed, and (b) calling for the creation of a Task Force that would study the problems created by a pay-to-play system, develop appropriate professional standards or rules on the subject, and report to the House of Delegates within a year.

The following month, in keeping with this resolution, newly elected ABA President Jerome Shestack appointed a Task Force on Lawyer's Political Contributions. The twelve-member Task Force was chaired by John W. Martin Jr., Chairman and General Counsel of Ford Motor Company, and included such distinguished members as former CIA and FBI Director William H. Webster, former United States Senator Howard H. Baker Jr., then-current Securities and Exchange Commission General Counsel Harvey J. Goldschmid, and former SEC Commissioner Stephen J. Friedman. The Task Force collected and reviewed empirical data and media reporting on pay-to-play practices and considered possible approaches the ABA might take to discourage or prevent them.

1998 Resolution: Shortly before the ABA's 1998 Annual Meeting, the ABA Task Force on Lawyer's Political Contributions issued a sharply divided report. The Task Force unanimously condemned pay-to-play practices and urged the

ABA to adopt a new Model Rule making pay-to-play practices unethical. The Task Force also recommended broader disclosure of campaign contributions. However, the Task Force was almost equally split as to whether a new Model Rule alone would be sufficient, and what the new Model Rule should say. Six of the Task Force members favored a strict rule that would disqualify both lawyers who made political contributions and their law firms, require lawyers to publicly disclose their political contributions, and require lawyers facing disciplinary charges to show that their political contributions were not made to obtain government legal work. Five other Task Force members believed that requiring lawyers to disclose their contributions and to prove that the contributions were not made to obtain government work would be ineffective and would have an undue chilling effect on the First Amendment rights of lawyers to take part in the political process.

In the end, the House of Delegates refused to adopt a new Model Rule but instead adopted the following resolution:

> RESOLVED, That the American Bar Association urges the following actions be taken to address any conduct by lawyers making or soliciting campaign contributions to public officials for the purpose of being considered or retained for government legal engagements.
>
> (1) All state, territorial and local bar associations should unequivocally condemn any arrangement under which the selection or consideration of lawyers to be retained for government legal engagements depends, in whole or in part, on whether the lawyer has made or solicited campaign contributions.
>
> (2) State, territorial and local government entities should create, establish and maintain full and effective systems for the reporting and disclosure of campaign contributions to candidates for elective public office so that the public may have reasonable notice of contributions made by lawyers or law firms, and where they have not, bar and disciplinary authorities should adopt rules that require disclosure of campaign contributions by lawyers and law firms to government officials in a position to influence the award of legal engagements to the contributor.
>
> (3) Merit procurement processes should be adopted for the selection of lawyers performing legal services for government agencies as a means of ensuring that no political contribution or solicitation has influenced the selection.
>
> (4) The Standing Committee on Ethics and Professional Responsibility is directed to report to the House of Delegates by its 1999 Annual Meeting a proposed Model Rule that declares that a lawyer or law firm shall not make a political contribution or solicitation for the purpose of obtaining or being considered for a legal engagement. . . .

Regarding paragraph (4) of the resolution, which directed the ABA Standing Committee on Ethics and Professional Responsibility to draft a proposed new model rule by 1999, a motion was made to give the Standing Committee "discretion" to address the problem of pay-to-play either by amending the comment to an existing rule, or by issuing a formal ethics opinion, or by proposing a new model rule. That motion failed by a vote of 158-151.

1999 Proposal: At the ABA's August 1999 Annual Meeting, the ABA House of Delegates voted 164 to 146 not to add proposed Rule 7.6 to the Model Rules of Professional Conduct. We reprint below substantial excerpts from the report submitted by the ABA Standing Committee on Ethics and Professional Responsibility in support of the rejected rule.

*ABA Committee Report Submitted in Support of Rejected Rule 7.6**

. . . The practice commonly known as "pay-to-play" addressed by the Rule is a system whereby lawyers and law firms are considered for or awarded either government legal engagements or appointments by a judge only upon their making or soliciting contributions for the political campaigns of officials who are in a position to "steer" such business their way. . . .

The Committee notes at the outset, however, that although lawyers and their political contributions are an important component of the pay-to-play system, lawyers are not the most important players in such a system. The primary actor in any pay-to-play situation is the public official who, depending upon the style of his or her participation in the system, may be acting in dereliction of official duties. For this reason, the rules of professional conduct governing lawyer behavior should not be relied upon as the primary method of preventing the practice of pay-to-play. Rather, consistent and diligent enforcement of statutory provisions governing fair campaign finance practices and the conduct of public officials is the most fundamental method of addressing the problem of pay-to-play. The fundamental harm done by a pay-to-play system is the harm that befalls the public when a government official, motivated by campaign contributions, chooses lawyers or law firms that may not be the best qualified to perform legal services on the public's behalf. Thus it is the integrity of a basic governmental process, and not just the integrity of the legal profession, that is undermined when such action by a public official is tolerated.

The Committee also notes that a second method of protecting against the evils of a pay-to-play system exists, and it also lies outside the scope of rules governing lawyer conduct: the use of uniform procurement or acquisition procedures for the placement of legal services engagements by government entities and the granting of appointments by judges. The Association has strongly supported . . . fundamental principles of competition in public acquisitions. . . .

The Standing Committee therefore notes emphatically that where there is aggressive enforcement of prohibitions against pay-to-play conduct by public officials, and where there is reliance on uniform procurement codes and procedures in the placement of legal engagements and in appointments by judges, the need to focus on lawyer conduct will be diminished . . . .

Background for Developing a Model Rule

. . . In carrying out its charge, the Task Force expanded the scope of its investigation in two important ways. Initial concerns had focused on the existence of the phenomenon in the area of municipal finance engagements. The Task Force's review revealed at least some evidence that the practice occurs in a wider range of practice areas. Early proposals for a Model Rule limited in application to lawyers engaged in municipal finance work were therefore put aside and the Task Force focused on developing a Rule of wider application.

The Task Force also discovered that a similar system was sometimes in evidence as well in the context of appointments of lawyers made by judges following the making or soliciting of substantial contributions to the judges' election campaigns.

Development of the Prosposed Rule

The Committee used the Task Force Report . . . to develop two possible "trial" rules addressing lawyers' roles in the pay-to-play system. One was almost verbatim

*Committee Reports do not represent official policy of the ABA. They are for information only, and the opinions are those of the authors of the report.

the recommendation that had been made by the Task Force, prohibiting political contributions when the purpose of such contributions was the obtaining of legal business.* Because the Committee questioned the wisdom of basing the restriction solely on a lawyer's purpose for making political contributions, and recognized the difficulty of proving "purpose," it developed a second rule that approached the pay-to-play problem from a different perspective, prohibiting lawyers from accepting legal engagements where the awarding of the engagements was based upon lawyer's political contributions. Each draft rule was accompanied by extensive commentary that was intended, among other things, to establish criteria whereby a contributing lawyer's "purpose" could be proven.

The Committee circulated these trial drafts widely for comment and answered questions about them at a public hearing in February 1999. . . . The following summary of the Committee's findings in each of these areas explains the Committee's ultimate decision to advance the proposed Model Rule presented here, which represents a combination of its two initial alternative proposals with refinements.

CONSTITUTIONAL ISSUES

. . . The Committee undertook a review of recent First Amendment jurisprudence treating legislatively-enacted campaign contribution limits. It found, not surprisingly, that limitations on the making and solicitation of political contributions must be predicated on the need to protect a valid state interest; that they must be narrowly drawn; and that their language must be sufficiently clear as to provide fair notice of when and how they operate, thereby satisfying the requirements of due process. . . .

ENACTED OR PROPOSED REGULATIONS

The Committee examined numerous regulations that have been either adopted or proposed in different forums to regulate lawyers' contributions to political campaigns in connection with "pay-to-play" type problems. They ranged from federal criminal statutes (18 U.S.C. Sec. 201) relating to the most egregious violations (bribery or the giving of illegal gratuities) to a considerably more narrowly-drawn Association of the Bar of the City of New York proposal which, like Municipal Securities Rulemaking Board Rule GS-37, applicable to municipal finance professionals, would prohibit a lawyer or law firm from undertaking a municipal finance engagement within a certain period of time after having made a contribution in excess of a de minimis amount to a public official of influencing the public finance engagement.

The Committee recognizes that in some circumstances, the Model Rules of Professional Conduct already apply to lawyers' participation in pay-to-play. For example, the prophylactic effect of criminal statutes potentially applicable to pay-to-play participation by lawyers already has a parallel in the Model Rules of Professional Conduct: a lawyer whose style of participation in pay-to-play is so egregious as to result in conviction of bribery or a similar serious crime would also violate Model Rule 8.4 ("Misconduct"). Model Rule 7.2(c), which prohibits a lawyer from giving anything of value to another for recommending the lawyer for employment, may in some pay-to-play circumstances also be applicable . . . .

*The proposal just mentioned was included in the Committee Report as part of "Appendix A." It provided as follows: "A lawyer or law firm shall not make a political contribution or solicit political contributions for the purpose of obtaining or being considered for a government legal engagement or an appointment by a judge." — EDS.

The House has, however, adopted the Task Force's position that the Association should adopt more stringent restrictions on pay-to-play than these Model Rules would afford. The Rule submitted herewith accords with that position.

Enforcement Issues

. . . A common and understandable concern of the bar counsel was the number of elements that would need to be proven in order to find that a lawyer's conduct in making political contributions constituted a violation of either draft rule. In this regard, bar counsel comment echoed that of other commentators, both proponents and opponents of either draft rule.

The successful enforcement of each of the draft proposals was considered to depend on the ability of disciplinary counsel to prove an element of purpose, whether it were the purpose of the lawyer making the contribution, or the purpose of the official or judge in giving the engagement or appointment to reward the lawyer's contribution.

It was also noted that any rule that prohibited a lawyer from accepting a legal engagement—no matter what other provision it contained—would not, as a practical matter, be enforced against those participants in pay-to-play who might have an improper purpose in making contributions, but who do not obtain a legal engagement. The proposed Rule therefore combines the elements of proof of purpose and proof that a lawyer has accepted a legal engagement that the political contributions were intended to influence.

The lawyer's purpose in making or soliciting political contributions was deemed by many commentators to be the most significant test in determining if a Rule violation exists. Hence, it has been retained in the submitted Rule along with carefully crafted standards in the Comments designed to explain how "purpose" will be identified.

Disciplinary counsel who provided comment on the draft proposals also appeared generally unpersuaded that pay-to-play exists as a significant problem. Hence self-enforcement of this Rule to stem pay-to-play practices by lawyers and law firms is an even more important consideration than it is in enforcement of certain other Model Rules.

The Proposed Model Rule

The new Model Rule would provide:

> A lawyer or law firm shall not accept a government legal engagement or an appointment by a judge if the lawyer or law firm makes a political contribution or solicits political contributions for the purpose of obtaining or being considered for that type of legal engagement or appointment.

. . . Two safe harbors are established within the definitions in Comment [3]. The first excludes from government legal engagements and appointments by judges those awarded based on merit in a request-for-proposal ("RFP") process "that is free from influence based upon political contributions." The second excludes awards made on a rotational basis from lists compiled "without regard to political contributions." Also excluded under both definitions are "substantially uncompensated services."

In addition, Comment [5] seeks to explain when the proscribed purpose is or is not present. In formulating this Comment, the Committee became convinced that language was essential that would permit lawyers to make political contributions to personal friends or clients or to candidates whose causes they support while remaining eligible to accept government legal engagements or appointments by judges. Accordingly, for the proscribed purpose to be found, it must be shown that, "but for the desire to be considered for the legal engagement or appointment, the lawyer or law firm would not have made or solicited the contributions."

Comment [5] also provides an example of facts from which, absent other factors to the contrary, it may be fairly inferred that the proscribed purpose is present: substantial contributions for a candidate who can influence the selection of the lawyer to perform the work, followed by selection of the contributor. Factors weighing against the inference set forth in Comment [5] include the existence of a prior family or professional relationship or the desire to further a political or social cause. Unlike awards made in the circumstances described in Comment [3] that are excluded from the Rule's prohibition, the circumstances in Comment [5] are merely examples of factors that should be taken into account, among all others that are relevant, in order to determine if the proscribed purpose is present.

2000 Amendment: At the ABA's February 2000 Mid-Year Meeting, the House of Delegates voted 266-157 to adopt the very same version of Rule 7.6 and its Comment that the delegates had rejected in 1999. In 2000, however, the proposed rule was sponsored not only by the ABA Standing Committee on Ethics and Professional Responsibility (which had been the sole sponsor in 1999), but also by the ABA Section of Business Law, the ABA Section of State and Local Government Law, and the Association of the Bar of the City of New York. (The New York City Bar had sponsored the original proposal to add a pay-to-play rule back in 1997.) The report submitted in support of the new rule was nearly identical to the report submitted in 1999, but it began with the following passages explaining the 1999 proposal and why it failed:

*ABA Committee Report Submitted in Support of Rule 7.6 as Adopted**

. . . At the 1999 Annual Meeting, the House of Delegates, by a vote of 164 to 146, rejected the Standing Committee's proposal.

The Sponsors believe that the very important issue of pay-to-play should be reconsidered by the House. The [1999] vote was taken very late in the session after a substantial number of delegates had departed (only 310 of the 530 members of the House were present and voting) and without adequate opportunity for balanced debate (only one "pro" speaker, other than the moving sponsor, was recognized before a tired House called the question). Accordingly, the Sponsors resubmit the proposed Model Rule 7.6 governing lawyers' political contributions to the House of Delegates at the 2000 Midwinter Meeting.

2002 Amendments: The ABA Ethics 2000 Commission did not propose any changes to Rule 7.6 or its Comment.

Selected State Variations

Georgia: In the rules effective January 1, 2001, Georgia omits Rule 7.6.

New York: Compare ABA Model Rule 7.6 to New York EC's 2-37 and 2-38.

*Committee Reports do not represent official policy of the ABA. They are for information only, and the opinions are those of the authors of the report.

Related Materials

Municipal Securities Rulemaking Board Rule GS 37: This rule, which was cited in the ABA Committee Report submitted in support of Rule 7.6, prohibits municipal finance professionals from undertaking a municipal finance engagement within a certain period of time after having made a contribution in excess of a de minimis amount to a public official capable of influencing the public finance engagement.

Restatement of the Law Governing Lawyers: The Restatement has no provision comparable to ABA Model Rule 7.6.

ARTICLE 8. MAINTAINING THE INTEGRITY OF THE PROFESSION

Rule 8.1 Bar Admission and Disciplinary Matters

An applicant for admission to the bar, or a lawyer in connection with a bar admission application or in connection with a disciplinary matter, shall not:

(a) knowingly make a false statement of material fact; or

(b) fail to disclose a fact necessary to correct a misapprehension known by the person to have arisen in the matter, or knowingly fail to respond to a lawful demand for information from an admissions or disciplinary authority, except that this rule does not require disclosure of information otherwise protected by Rule 1.6.

COMMENT

[1] The duty imposed by this Rule extends to persons seeking admission to the bar as well as to lawyers. Hence, if a person makes a material false statement in connection with an application for admission, it may be the basis for subsequent disciplinary action if the person is admitted, and in any event may be relevant in a subsequent admission application. The duty imposed by this Rule applies to a lawyer's own admission or discipline as well as that of others. Thus, it is a separate professional offense for a lawyer to knowingly make a misrepresentation or omission in connection with a disciplinary investigation of the lawyer's own conduct. ~~This~~ Paragraph (b) of this Rule also requires correction of any prior misstatement in the matter that the applicant or lawyer may have made and affirmative clarification of any misunderstanding on the part of the admissions or disciplinary authority of which the person involved becomes aware.

[2] This Rule is subject to the provisions of the fifth amendment of the United States Constitution and corresponding provisions of state constitutions. A person relying on such a provision in response to a question, however, should do so openly and not use the right of nondisclosure as a justification for failure to comply with this Rule.

[3] A lawyer representing an applicant for admission to the bar, or representing a lawyer who is the subject of a disciplinary inquiry or proceeding, is governed by the rules applicable to the client-lawyer relationship, including Rule 1.6 and, in some cases, Rule 3.3.

Canon and Code Antecedents

ABA Canons of Professional Ethics: No comparable Canon.

ABA Model Code of Professional Responsibility: Compare DR 1-101(A), DR 1-101(B), and DR 1-102(A)(5) (reprinted later in this volume).

Cross-References in Other Rules

Rule 1.6, Comment 13: Some Rules require "disclosure of information relating to a client's representation to accomplish the purposes specified in paragraphs (b)(1) through (b)(4)," only if such disclosure would be permitted by paragraph (b). See Rules 1.2(d), 4.1(b), **8.1** and 8.3.

Rule 1.8, Comment 5: It is prohibited to partake in the "disadvantageous use of client information unless the client gives informed consent, except as permitted or required by these Rules. See Rules 1.2(d), 1.6, 1.9(c), 3.3, 4.1(b), **8.1** and 8.3."

Legislative History of Model Rule 8.1

1980 Discussion Draft of Rule 8.1 was substantially the same as adopted, except that subparagraph (a) prohibited a lawyer from making "a knowing misrepresentation of fact," and subparagraph (b) did not include the clause beginning "or knowingly fail to respond. . . ."

1981 and 1982 Drafts were substantially the same as adopted.

2002 Amendments: At its February 2002 Mid-Year Meeting, the ABA House of Delegates adopted without change the ABA Ethics 2000 Commission proposal to amend the Comment to Rule 8.1. (The Ethics 2000 Commission did not propose any changes to the text of Rule 8.1.)

Selected State Variations

California: See Rule 1-200 (False Statement Regarding Admission to the State Bar).

Colorado: Rule 8.1 adds "reinstatement" to the list of proceedings to which the rule applies. Colorado also adds that 8.1(b) does not "prohibit a good faith challenge to the demand for such information."

Georgia: In the rules effective January 1, 2001, Georgia adopted ABA Model Rule 8.1 and the pre-2002 version of its Comment substantially verbatim. In addition, Georgia has adopted a new Rule 9.3, entitled "Cooperation with Disciplinary Authority," which provides: "During the investigation of a grievance filed under these Rules, the lawyer complained against shall respond to disciplinary authorities in accordance with State Bar Rules." Georgia's Comment to this provision states:

> [1] Much of the work in the disciplinary process is performed by volunteer lawyers and lay persons. In order to make good use of their valuable time, it is imperative that the lawyer complained against cooperate with the investigation. In particular, the lawyer must file a sworn response with the member of the Investigative Panel charged with the responsibility of investigating the complaint.
>
> [2] Nothing in this Rule prohibits a lawyer from responding by making a Fifth Amendment objection, if appropriate. However, disciplinary proceedings are civil in nature and the use of a Fifth Amendment objection will give rise to a presumption against the lawyer.

Illinois: Rule 8.1(b) provides that a lawyer "shall not further the application for admission to the bar of another person known by the lawyer to be unqualified in respect to character, education, or any other relevant attribute."

Michigan: Effective July 30, 2001, Michigan added the following new language to its version of ABA Model Rule 8.1:

> (b) An applicant for admission to the bar
>
> (1) shall not engage in the unauthorized practice of law (this does not apply to activities permitted under MCR 8.120), and
>
> (2) has a continuing obligation, until the date of admission, to inform the standing committee on character and fitness, in writing, if any answers in the applicant's affidavit of personal history change or cease to be true.

New York: Compare ABA Model Rule 8.1 to New York's DR 1-101.

Pennsylvania: Rule 8.1 retains the language of DR 1-101 of the ABA Model Code of Professional Responsibility verbatim, except that Pennsylvania Rule 8.1(a) applies not only to an application for bar admission but also to "any disciplinary proceeding."

Virginia adopted the "broader coverage" of the ABA Rule over DR 1-101 and made the ABA rule "even broader" by adding language to cover certifications and licensing renewal. The Virginia rule also imposes "an affirmative duty of cooperation with lawful demands for information" and makes it a "separate violation to obstruct any investigation by a disciplinary or admissions authority."

Related Materials

ABA Model Rules for Lawyer Disciplinary Enforcement: At its 1989 Annual Meeting, the ABA adopted a revised set of Model Rules for Lawyer Disciplinary Enforcement. These replaced the 1985 version of the Model Rules for Lawyer Disciplinary Enforcement, which had themselves replaced the 1979 Standards for Lawyer Discipline Proceedings.

Character and Fitness Standards: Nearly every state requires bar applicants to meet certain standards for "character and fitness." In New York, for example, 22 N.Y.C.R.R. §602.1(b) provides: "Every completed application shall be referred for investigation of the applicant's character and fitness to a committee on character and fitness. . . ." In Illinois, §2 of the Illinois Attorney Act provides that no person shall be entitled to receive a law license "until he shall have obtained a certificate of his good moral character from a circuit court." Neither state has adopted written standards defining good character.

Model Rules of Professional Conduct for Federal Lawyers: Rule 8.1 also applies to an "applicant for admission to a bar or employment as a lawyer with a Federal Agency, [and] a Federal lawyer seeking the right to practice before a Federal Agency. . . ."

Restatement of the Law Governing Lawyers: See Restatement §2 in our chapter on the Restatement later in this volume.

Rule 8.2 Judicial and Legal Officials

(a) A lawyer shall not make a statement that the lawyer knows to be false or with reckless disregard as to its truth or falsity concerning the qualifications or integrity of a judge, adjudicatory officer or public legal officer, or of a candidate for election or appointment to judicial or legal office.

(b) A lawyer who is a candidate for judicial office shall comply with the applicable provisions of the Code of Judicial Conduct.

COMMENT

[1] Assessments by lawyers are relied on in evaluating the professional or personal fitness of persons being considered for election or appointment to judicial office and to public legal offices, such as attorney general, prosecuting attorney and public defender. Expressing honest and candid opinions on such matters contributes to improving the administration of justice. Conversely, false statements by a lawyer can unfairly undermine public confidence in the administration of justice.

[2] When a lawyer seeks judicial office, the lawyer should be bound by applicable limitations on political activity.

[3] To maintain the fair and independent administration of justice, lawyers are encouraged to continue traditional efforts to defend judges and courts unjustly criticized.

Canon and Code Antecedents

ABA Canons of Professional Ethics: Canons 1 and 2 provided as follows:

1. The Duty of the Lawyer to the Courts

It is the duty of the lawyer to maintain towards the Courts a respectful attitude, not for the sake of the temporary incumbent of the judicial office, but for the maintenance of its supreme importance. Judges, not being wholly free to defend themselves, are peculiarly entitled to receive the support of the Bar against unjust criticism and clamor. Whenever there is proper ground for serious complaint of a judicial officer, it is the right and duty of the lawyer to submit his grievances to the proper authorities. In such cases, but not otherwise, such charges should be encouraged and the person making them should be protected.

2. The Selection of Judges

It is the duty of the Bar to endeavor to prevent political considerations from outweighing judicial fitness in the selections of Judges. It should protest earnestly and actively against the appointment or election of those who are unsuitable for the Bench; and it should strive to have elevated thereto only those willing to forego other employments, whether of a business, political or other character, which may embarrass their free and fair consideration of questions before them for decision. The aspiration of lawyers for judicial position should be governed by an impartial estimate of their ability to add honor to the office and not by a desire for the distinction the position may bring to themselves.

ABA Model Code of Professional Responsibility: Compare DR 8-102(A), DR 8-102(B), and DR 8-103 (reprinted later in this volume).

Cross-References in Other Rules

None.

Legislative History of Model Rule 8.2

1980 Discussion Draft (then Rule 10.2): Subparagraph (a) provided: "A lawyer who is a candidate for judicial office shall comply with the applicable provisions of the code of judicial conduct." Subparagraph (b) was the same as adopted.

1981 and 1982 Drafts were substantially the same as adopted.

2002 Amendments: The ABA Ethics 2000 Commission did not propose any changes to the text or Comment of Rule 8.2.

Selected State Variations

California: See B & P Code §6068(b).

District of Columbia omits Rule 8.2.

Florida: Rule 8.2(b) also applies to statements about a "mediator, arbitrator, . . . juror or member of the venire. . . ."

Georgia: In the rules effective January 1, 2001, Georgia omits ABA Model Rule 8.2(a) but adopts Rule 8.2(b) and the ABA Comment to Rule 8.2 verbatim.

Maine: In 1998, Maine abrogated its prior version of Rule 8.2 and adopted a new rule, numbered Rule 3.2(c), that closely tracks ABA Model Rule 8.2.

Maryland provides:

(b) A candidate for judicial position shall not make or suffer others to make for him, promises of conduct in office which appeal to the cupidity or prejudices of the appointing or electing powers; he shall not announce in advance his conclusions of law on disputed issues to secure class support, and he shall do nothing while a candidate to create the impression that if chosen, he will administer his office with bias, partiality or improper discrimination.

New Jersey: Rule 8.2(b) provides that a lawyer who "has been confirmed for judicial office" shall comply with the applicable provisions of the Code of Judicial Conduct. The rule does not apply to lawyers who are only candidates for judicial office.

New York: Compare ABA Model Rule 8.2(a) to New York's DR 8-102. Compare Rule 8.2(b) to New York's DR 8-103.

Pennsylvania: Rule 8.2 replaces all of ABA Model Rule 8.2(a) with language taken verbatim from DR 8-102(A) and (B) and 8-103(A) of the ABA Model Code of Professional Responsibility.

Virginia: Rule 8.2 provides, in its entirety: "A lawyer shall not make a statement that the lawyer knows to be false or with reckless disregard as to its truth or falsity concerning the qualifications or integrity of a judge or other judicial officer."

Related Materials

ABA Code of Judicial Conduct: Rule 8.2(b) requires candidates for judicial office to "comply with the applicable provisions of the code of judicial conduct." The applicable provisions for judicial candidates are found in Canon 5 of the ABA's 1990 Code of Judicial Conduct, reprinted below in this volume.

Restatement of the Law Governing Lawyers: See Restatement §114 in our chapter on the Restatement later in this volume.

Rule 8.3 Reporting Professional Misconduct

(a) A lawyer ~~having knowledge~~ who knows that another lawyer has committed a violation of the Rules of Professional Conduct that raises a substantial question as to that lawyer's honesty, trustworthiness or fitness as a lawyer in other respects, shall inform the appropriate professional authority.

(b) A lawyer ~~having knowledge~~ who knows that a judge has committed a violation of applicable rules of judicial conduct that raises a substantial question as to the judge's fitness for office shall inform the appropriate authority.

(c) This Rule does not require disclosure of information otherwise protected by Rule 1.6 or information gained by a lawyer or judge while ~~serving as a member of~~ participating in an approved lawyers assistance program ~~to the extent that such information would be confidential if it were communicated subject to the attorney-client privilege~~.

COMMENT

[1] Self-regulation of the legal profession requires that members of the profession initiate a disciplinary investigation when they know of a vi-

olation of the Rules of Professional Conduct. Lawyers have a similar obligation with respect to judicial misconduct. An apparently isolated violation may indicate a pattern of misconduct that only a disciplinary investigation can uncover. Reporting a violation is especially important where the victim is unlikely to discover the offense.

[2] A report about misconduct is not required where it would involve violation of Rule 1.6. However, a lawyer should encourage a client to consent to disclosure where prosecution would not substantially prejudice the client's interests.

[3] If a lawyer were obliged to report every violation of the Rules, the failure to report any violation would itself be a professional offense. Such a requirement existed in many jurisdictions but proved to be unenforceable. This Rule limits the reporting obligation to those offenses that a self-regulating profession must vigorously endeavor to prevent. A measure of judgment is, therefore, required in complying with the provisions of this Rule. The term "substantial" refers to the seriousness of the possible offense and not the quantum of evidence of which the lawyer is aware. A report should be made to the bar disciplinary agency unless some other agency, such as a peer review agency, is more appropriate in the circumstances. Similar considerations apply to the reporting of judicial misconduct.

[4] The duty to report professional misconduct does not apply to a lawyer retained to represent a lawyer whose professional conduct is in question. Such a situation is governed by the Rules applicable to the client-lawyer relationship.

[5] Information about a lawyer's or judge's misconduct or fitness may be received by a lawyer in the course of that lawyer's participation in an approved lawyers or judges assistance program. In that circumstance, providing for ~~the confidentiality of such information~~ an exception to the reporting requirements of paragraphs (a) and (b) of this Rule encourages lawyers and judges to seek treatment through such a program. Conversely, without such ~~confidentiality~~ an exception, lawyers and judges may hesitate to seek assistance from these programs, which may then result in additional harm to their professional careers and additional injury to the welfare of clients and the public. ~~The Rule therefore exempts the lawyer from the reporting requirements of paragraphs (a) and (b) with respect to information that would be privileged if the relationship between the impaired lawyer or judge and the recipient of the information were that of a client and a lawyer. On the other hand, a lawyer who receives such information would nevertheless be required to comply with the Rule 8.3 reporting provisions to report misconduct if the impaired lawyer or judge indicates an intent to engage in illegal activity, for example, the conversion of client funds to his or her use.~~ These Rules do not otherwise address the confidentiality of information received by a lawyer or judge participating in an approved lawyers assistance program; such an obligation, however, may be imposed by the rules of the program or other law.

Canon and Code Antecedents

ABA Canons of Professional Ethics: Canon 29 provided as follows:

29. Upholding the Honor of the Profession

> Lawyers should expose without fear or favor before the proper tribunals corrupt or dishonest conduct in the profession, and should accept without hesitation employment against a member of the Bar who has wronged his client. The counsel upon the trial of a cause in which perjury has been committed owe it to the profession and to the public to bring the matter to the knowledge of the prosecuting authorities. The lawyer should aid in guarding the Bar against the admission to the profession of candidates unfit or unqualified because deficient in either moral character or education. He should strive at all times to uphold the honor and to maintain the dignity of the profession and to improve not only the law but the administration of justice.

ABA Model Code of Professional Responsibility: Compare DR 1-103(A) (reprinted later in this volume).

Cross-References in Other Rules

Rule 1.6, Comment 13: Some Rules require "disclosure of information relating to a client's representation to accomplish the purposes specified in paragraphs (b)(1) through (b)(4)," only if such disclosure would be permitted by paragraph (b). See Rules 1.2(d), 4.1(b), 8.1 and **8.3**.

Rule 1.8, Comment 5: It is prohibited to partake in the "disadvantageous use of client information unless the client gives informed consent, except as permitted or required by these Rules. See Rules 1.2(d), 1.6, 1.9(c), 3.3, 4.1(b), 8.1 and **8.3**."

Legislative History of Model Rule 8.3

1980 Discussion Draft (then Rule 10.3) provided:

> A lawyer having information indicating that another lawyer has committed a substantial violation of the Rules of Professional Conduct shall report the information to the appropriate disciplinary authority.

1981 Draft was substantially the same as adopted, except that it did not include any equivalent to Rule 8.3(b).

1982 Draft was adopted.

1991 Amendments: At its August 1991 Annual Meeting, the ABA House of Delegates added the clause beginning "or information gained . . ." to Rule 8.3(c). The following excerpts from the Report of the ABA Standing Committee on Ethics and Professional Responsibility explain the rationale and scope of the amendments:

*ABA Committee Report Explaining 1991 Amendments to Rule 8.3**

> The serious concerns that have arisen recently as a result of "lawyer impairment" have led to the creation of special programs throughout the nation to assist

*Committee Reports do not represent official policy of the ABA. They are for information only, and the opinions are those of the authors of the report.

lawyers and judges who face alcohol or drug addiction or other serious problems which threaten to affect or have already affected the performance of their professional responsibilities. More than forty-four such programs, commonly known as "Lawyer and Judge Assistance Programs" have been established by state courts or state and local bar associations.

... The Committee believes that it is in the interest of the legal profession and the public that the ABA Model Rules be amended to provide for the confidentiality of information that is furnished by the impaired lawyer or judge.

Under the amendment to Model Rule 8.3, the protection of information obtained in the circumstances of a lawyer's or judge's participation in an assistance program is similar to the protection ordinarily provided by the attorney-client privilege. Where the attorney-client privilege would not apply because the information relates to the intention to commit a crime, for example where a lawyer indicates the intention to continue to convert client funds to his or her own use, such information may be disclosed to the appropriate authority, permitting the recipient of the information to comply with the obligation imposed upon him or her by paragraphs (a) or (b). In such situations concerns other than the recovery of the impaired lawyer or judge necessarily outweigh the impaired lawyer's or judge's right to confidentiality. ... Although the Committee recognizes that disclosure of such information by one member of the profession to the detriment of a professional colleague is painful and difficult, it considers such a situation indistinguishable from other situations in which important public policy considerations require disclosure of confidential information. To extend the confidentiality protection to a lawyer's or judge's intention to commit a crime likely to result in significant harm to others, moreover, would lend support to claims that the profession is unable or unwilling to live up to its obligation to regulate itself in the public interest.

2002 Amendments: At its February 2002 Mid-Year Meeting, the ABA House of Delegates adopted without change the ABA Ethics 2000 Commission proposal to amend Rule 8.3 and its Comment.

Selected State Variations

Arizona: Rule 8.3(c) does not require disclosure of information otherwise protected by Rule 1.6 or information gained by a lawyer "while participating in an approved lawyers' assistance program that would otherwise be subject to reporting under paragraphs (a) and (b) of this rule."

Arkansas: Rule 8.3(c) generally exempts lawyers working with the Arkansas Lawyer Assistance Program from mandatory reporting obligations "unless it appears . . . that the attorney in question, after entry into the ALAP, is failing to desist from said violation, or is failing to cooperate with a program of assistance to which said attorney has agreed, or is engaged in the sale of a controlled substance or theft of property constituting a felony under Arkansas law, or the equivalent thereof if the offense is not within the State's jurisdiction."

California: No comparable provision.

Connecticut: Rule 8.3(a) contains the following additional sentence: "A lawyer may not condition settlement of a civil dispute involving allegations of improprieties on the part of a lawyer on an agreement that the subject misconduct not be reported to the appropriate disciplinary authority."

Connecticut Rule 8.3(c) tracks the pre-2002 version of ABA Model Rule 8.3(c), but also applies to a lawyer "while serving as a member of a bar association professional ethics committee."

Florida: Effective February 8, 2001, Florida added a new Rule 8.3(d) that provides:

> *Limited Exception for LOMAS Counsel.* A lawyer employed by or acting on behalf of the Law Office Management Assistance Service (LOMAS) shall not have an obligation to disclose knowledge of the conduct of another member . . . if the lawyer employed by or acting on behalf of LOMAS acquired the knowledge while engaged in a LOMAS review of the other lawyer's practice. *Provided further,* however, that if the LOMAS review is conducted as a part of a disciplinary sanction this limitation shall not be applicable and a report shall be made to the appropriate disciplinary agency.

Georgia: In the rules effective January 1, 2001, Georgia adopted the pre-2002 version of ABA Model Rule 8.3(a) and (b) essentially verbatim, but changed "shall" to "should" in both paragraphs. Georgia also deleted all of ABA Model Rule 8.3(c) and added that "[t]here is no disciplinary penalty for a violation of this Rule." Georgia has also adopted a special self-reporting provision, Rule 9.1, which requires members of the Georgia Bar to notify the State Bar of Georgia of (a) all other jurisdictions in which they are admitted to practice law and the dates of admission; and (b) "the conviction of any felony or of a misdemeanor involving moral turpitude where the underlying conduct relates to the lawyer's fitness to practice law, within sixty days of conviction."

Georgia has also adopted a special Rule 9.2 regarding agreements not to report. It provides as follows:

> In connection with the settlement of a controversy or suit involving misuse of funds held in a fiduciary capacity, a lawyer shall not enter into an agreement that the person bringing the claim will be prohibited or restricted from filing a disciplinary complaint, or will be required to request the dismissal of a pending disciplinary complaint concerning that conduct.

Georgia's Comment to Rule 9.2 provides:

> [1] The disciplinary system provides protection to the general public from those lawyers who are not morally fit to practice law. One problem in the past has been the lawyer who settles the civil claim/disciplinary complaint with the injured party on the basis that the injured party not bring a disciplinary complaint or request the dismissal of a pending disciplinary complaint. The lawyer is then is free to injure other members of the general public.
>
> [2] To prevent such abuses in settlements, this rule prohibits a lawyer from settling any controversy or suit involving misuse of funds on any basis which prevents the person bringing the claim from pursuing a disciplinary complaint.

Illinois: Rule 8.3(a) requires a lawyer to report knowledge "not otherwise protected as a confidence by these Rules or by law" that a lawyer has committed specified violations. Rule 8.3(c) provides that upon proper request of a tribunal or disciplinary authority, "a lawyer possessing information not otherwise protected as a confidence by these Rules or by law concerning another lawyer or a judge shall fully reveal such information." Rule 8.3(d) provides:

> A lawyer who has been disciplined as a result of a lawyer disciplinary action brought before any body other than the Illinois Attorney Registration and Disciplinary Commission shall report that fact to the Commission.

Kansas adds the following to Rule 8.3(c):

> In addition, a lawyer is not required to disclose information concerning any such violation which is discovered through participation in a Substance Abuse Committee,

> Service to the Bar Committee, or similar committees sponsored by a state or local bar association, or by participation in a self-help organization such as Alcoholics Anonymous, through which aid is rendered to another lawyer who may be impaired in the practice of law.

In addition, Rule 223 of the Kansas Rules Relating to Discipline of Attorneys, entitled "Immunity," provides: "Complaints, reports, or testimony in the course of disciplinary proceedings under these Rules shall be deemed to be made in the course of judicial proceedings. All participants shall be entitled to judicial immunity and all rights, privileges and immunities afforded public officials and other participants in actions filed in the courts of this state."

Massachusetts: Rule 8.3 tracked the pre-2002 version of ABA Model Rule 8.3, but the rule was the subject of vigorous debate. The old Massachusetts Code of Professional Responsibility had no mandatory reporting rule. In 1997 the Supreme Judicial Court proposed a mandatory reporting rule, but many members of the bar objected, so in 1998 the Court adopted an interim rule providing that a lawyer "should" report another lawyer's serious misconduct, then amended Rule 8.3 by replacing "should" with "shall" effective March 1, 1998. In 1999, the Court amended the Comment to Rule 8.3 to read as follows:

> [3] A lawyer must report misconduct that, if proven and without regard to mitigation, would likely result in an order of suspension or disbarment, including misconduct that would constitute a "serious crime" . . . . Section 12(3) of Rule 4:01 provides that a serious crime is "any felony, and . . . any lesser crime a necessary element of which . . . includes interference with the administration of justice, false swearing, misrepresentation, fraud, willful failure to file income tax returns, deceit, bribery, extortion, misappropriation, theft, or an attempt or a conspiracy, or solicitation of another, to commit [such a crime]." In addition to conviction of a felony, misappropriation of client funds or perjury before a tribunal are common examples of reportable conduct. . . .
>
> [3A] In most situations, a lawyer may defer making a report under this Rule until the matter has been concluded, but the report should be made as soon as practicable thereafter. An immediate report is ethically compelled, however, when a client or third person will likely be injured by a delay in reporting, such as where the lawyer has knowledge that another lawyer has embezzled client or fiduciary funds and delay may impair the ability to recover the funds.

Michigan adds the word "significant" before "violation" in Rule 8.3(a) and Rule 8.3(b). The duty under this rule is suspended if the lawyer gained the information "while serving as an employee or volunteer of the substance abuse counseling program of the State Bar of Michigan, to the extent that the information would be protected under Rule 1.6 from disclosure if it were a communication between lawyer and client." Rule 8.3(c)(2).

New Jersey adds Rule 8.3(d), which provides as follows:

> Paragraph (a) of this Rule shall not apply to knowledge obtained as a result of participation in a Lawyers Assistance Program established by the Supreme Court and administered by the New Jersey State Bar Association, except as follows:
>
> > (i) if the effect of discovered ethics infractions on the practice of an impaired attorney is irremediable or poses a substantial and imminent threat to the interests of clients, then attorney volunteers, peer counselors, or program staff have a duty to disclose the infractions to the disciplinary authorities, and attorney volunteers have the obligation to apply immediately for the

appointment of a conservator, who also has the obligation to report ethics infractions to disciplinary authorities; and

(ii) attorney volunteers or peer counselors assisting the impaired attorney in conjunction with his or her practice have the same responsibility as any other lawyer to deal candidly with clients, but that responsibility does not include the duty to disclose voluntarily, without inquiry by the client, information of past violations or present violations that did not or do not pose a serious danger to clients.

New York: Compare ABA Model Rule 8.3 to New York's DR 1-103. In addition, §499 of the New York Judiciary Law (reprinted below in our Selected Provisions of the New York Judiciary Law) protects communications between a lawyer and a lawyer assistance program to the same extent as communications between attorneys and their clients.

North Carolina: Rule 1.6(b) provides that "confidential information" includes (among other things) "information received by a lawyer then acting as an agent of a lawyers' or judges' assistance program approved by the North Carolina State Bar or the North Carolina Supreme Court regarding another lawyer or judge seeking assistance or to whom assistance is being offered." North Carolina Rule 1.15-2(o) provides as follows: "(o) *Duty to Report Misappropriation.* A lawyer who discovers or reasonably believes that entrusted property has been misappropriated or misapplied shall promptly inform the North Carolina State Bar." Finally, North Carolina Rule 8.3(d) provides: "A lawyer who has been disciplined in any state or federal court for a violation of the Rules of Professional Conduct in effect in such state or federal court will inform the secretary of such action in writing no later than 30 days after entry of the order of discipline."

Ohio: DR 1-103(C) extends a privilege if a lawyer obtains knowledge of another lawyer's wrongdoing while working for a Bar Association substance abuse committee.

Oregon: DR 1-103(F) provides: "A lawyer who is the subject of a complaint or referral to the State Lawyers Assistance Committee shall . . . cooperate with the committee and its designees, including: . . . (4) participating in and complying with a remedial program established by the committee or its designees."

Pennsylvania: Rule 8.3(c) adds that the rule does not require disclosure of "information learned by a lawyer while serving as a sobriety, financial or practice monitor for another lawyer (except for information required to be reported by the order appointing the monitor) or while participating in an alcohol or substance abuse rehabilitation program, to the extent that the information would be protected by Rule 1.6 if it had been communicated in the context of an attorney-client relationship."

Texas: Rules 8.03(a) and (b) generally track ABA Model Rules 8.3(a) and (b), but the balance of the Texas rule is as follows:

> (c) A lawyer having knowledge or suspecting that another lawyer or judge whose conduct the lawyer is required to report pursuant to paragraphs (a) or (b) of this Rule is impaired by chemical dependency on alcohol or drugs or by mental illness may report that person to an approved peer assistance program rather than to an appropriate disciplinary authority. If a lawyer elects that option, the lawyer's report to the approved peer assistance program shall disclose any disciplinary violations that the reporting lawyer would otherwise have to disclose to the authorities referred to in paragraphs (a) and (b).

(d) This rule does not require disclosure of knowledge or information otherwise protected as confidential information:

(1) by Rule 1.05 or

(2) by any statutory or regulatory provisions applicable to the counseling activities of the approved peer assistance program.

Virginia adds an additional paragraph to Rule 8.3 which requires that if a lawyer is serving as a third party neutral and in that capacity receives confidential information about another lawyer's misconduct, the lawyer/neutral "shall attempt to obtain the parties' written agreement to waive confidentiality and permit disclosure of such information to the appropriate professional authority." Rule 8.3(c).

Related Materials

ABA Commission on Lawyer Assistance Programs: In 1988, the ABA formed a Commission on Impaired Attorneys to encourage and assist state and local bar associations in establishing programs to assist addicted lawyers and judges. In 1995, the House of Delegates adopted the Commission's Model Lawyer Assistance Program, which is designed to assist state and local bar associations in developing and maintaining effective programs to identify and assist lawyers, judges, and law students impaired by alcoholism, drugs, or mental health problems. In 1996, the ABA changed the name of the Commission on Impaired Attorneys to the Commission on Lawyer Assistance Programs (COLAP). (Rule 8.3(c) expressly refers to lawyer assistance programs.) The Commission reviews lawyer assistance programs, makes recommendations for expanding and improving the programs, holds an annual National Workshop for Lawyer Assistance Programs, and circulates guidelines and policies. For further information, contact the Commission's Staff Director, Donna Spilis, at the ABA Center for Professional Responsibility, 541 North Fairbanks Court, Chicago, IL 60011, telephone 312-988-5359, or visit the Commission's web site at www.abanet.org/cpr/colap.

ABA Formal Ethics Opinions: See ABA Formal Ethics Op. 94-383 (1994).

Oath of Office: All states require new attorneys to take an oath upon being admitted to the bar. In Illinois, for example, §4 of the Attorney Act requires every new attorney to take the following oath:

> I do solemnly swear (or affirm, as the case may be), that I will support the constitution of the United States and the constitution of the state of Illinois, and that I will faithfully discharge the duties of the office of attorney and counselor at law to the best of my ability.

Reporting Obligations by Courts and Non-lawyers: Certain judges and non-lawyers may also be obligated to report lawyer misconduct. For example, California Business and Professions Code §6086.7 requires courts to notify the State Bar whenever an attorney is held in contempt or commits other specified wrongs, and California Insurance Code §1872.83 requires certain government officials to report incidents of lawyer fraud to lawyer disciplinary authorities.

Restatement of the Law Governing Lawyers: See Restatement §§2 and 5 in our chapter on the Restatement later in this volume.

Rule 8.4 Misconduct

It is professional misconduct for a lawyer to:

(a) violate or attempt to violate the Rules of Professional Conduct, knowingly assist or induce another to do so, or do so through the acts of another;

(b) commit a criminal act that reflects adversely on the lawyer's honesty, trustworthiness or fitness as a lawyer in other respects;

(c) engage in conduct involving dishonesty, fraud, deceit or misrepresentation;

(d) engage in conduct that is prejudicial to the administration of justice;

(e) state or imply an ability to influence improperly a government agency or official or to achieve results by means that violate the Rules of Professional Conduct or other law; or

(f) knowingly assist a judge or judicial officer in conduct that is a violation of applicable rules of judicial conduct or other law.

COMMENT

[1] Lawyers are subject to discipline when they violate or attempt to violate the Rules of Professional Conduct, knowingly assist or induce another to do so or do so through the acts of another, as when they request or instruct an agent to do so on the lawyer's behalf. Paragraph (a), however, does not prohibit a lawyer from advising a client concerning action the client is legally entitled to take.

~~[1]~~ [2] Many kinds of illegal conduct reflect adversely on fitness to practice law, such as offenses involving fraud and the offense of willful failure to file an income tax return. However, some kinds of offenses carry no such implication. Traditionally, the distinction was drawn in terms of offenses involving "moral turpitude." That concept can be construed to include offenses concerning some matters of personal morality, such as adultery and comparable offenses, that have no specific connection to fitness for the practice of law. Although a lawyer is personally answerable to the entire criminal law, a lawyer should be professionally answerable only for offenses that indicate lack of those characteristics relevant to law practice. Offenses involving violence, dishonesty, breach of trust, or serious interference with the administration of justice are in that category. A pattern of repeated offenses, even ones of minor significance when considered separately, can indicate indifference to legal obligation.

~~[2]~~ [3] A lawyer who, in the course of representing a client, knowingly manifests by words or conduct, bias or prejudice based upon race, sex, religion, national origin, disability, age, sexual orientation or socioeconomic status, violates paragraph (d) when such actions are prejudicial to the administration of justice. Legitimate advocacy respecting the foregoing factors does not violate paragraph (d). A trial judge's finding that peremptory challenges were exercised on a discriminatory basis does not alone establish a violation of this rule.

~~[3]~~ [4] A lawyer may refuse to comply with an obligation imposed by law upon a good faith belief that no valid obligation exists. The provisions of Rule 1.2(d) concerning a good faith challenge to the validity, scope, meaning or application of the law apply to challenges of legal regulation of the practice of law.

~~[4]~~ [5] Lawyers holding public office assume legal responsibilities going beyond those of other citizens. A lawyer's abuse of public office can suggest an inability to fulfill the professional role of lawyers. The same is true of abuse of positions of private trust such as trustee, executor, administrator, guardian, agent and officer, director or manager of a corporation or other organization.

Canon and Code Antecedents

ABA Canons of Professional Ethics: Canon 29 provided as follows:

29. Upholding the Honor of the Profession

Lawyers should expose without fear or favor before the proper tribunals corrupt or dishonest conduct in the profession, and should accept without hesitation employment against a member of the Bar who has wronged his client. The counsel upon the trial of a cause in which perjury has been committed owe it to the profession and to the public to bring the matter to the knowledge of the prosecuting authorities. The lawyer should aid in guarding the Bar against the admission to the profession of candidates unfit or unqualified because deficient in either moral character or education. He should strive at all times to uphold the honor and to maintain the dignity of the profession and to improve not only the law but the administration of justice.

ABA Model Code of Professional Responsibility: Compare DR 1-102(A) and DR 9-101(C) (reprinted later in this volume).

Cross-References in Other Rules

Preamble, ¶13: "[T]here are Rules that apply to lawyers who are not active in the practice of law or to practicing lawyers even when they are acting in a nonprofessional capacity. . . . See **Rule 8.4**."

Rule 3.3, Comment 3: "Regarding compliance with Rule 1.2(d), see the Comment to that Rule. See also the Comment to **Rule 8.4(b)**."

Rule 3.8, Comment 1: "Applicable law may require other measures by the prosecutor and knowing disregard of those obligations or a systematic abuse of prosecutorial discretion could constitute a violation of **Rule 8.4**."

Rule 4.1, Comment 1: "For dishonest conduct that does not amount to a false statement or for misrepresentations by a lawyer other than in the course of representing a client, see **Rule 8.4**."

Rule 4.2, Comment 4: "A lawyer may not make a communication prohibited by this Rule through the acts of another. See **Rule 8.4(a)**."

Rule 5.1, Comment 4: "Paragraph (c) expresses a general principle of personal responsibility for acts of another. See also **Rule 8.4(a)**."

Rule 5.1, Comment 7: "Apart from this Rule and **Rule 8.4(a)**, a lawyer does not have disciplinary liability for the conduct of a partner, associate or subordinate."

Rule 5.7, Comment 2: "[T]he conduct of a lawyer involved in the provision of law-related services is subject to those Rules that apply generally to lawyer conduct, regardless of whether the conduct involves the provision of legal services. See, e.g., **Rule 8.4**."

Rule 5.7, Comment 11: "When the full protections of all of the Rules of Professional Conduct do not apply to the provision of law-related services, principles of law external to the Rules, for example, the law of principal and agent, govern the legal duties owed to those receiving the services. . . . See also **Rule 8.4** (Misconduct)."

Rule 7.1, Comment 4: "See also **Rule 8.4(e)** for the prohibition against stating or implying an ability to influence improperly a government agency or official or to achieve results by means that violate the Rules of Professional Conduct or other law."

Rule 7.3, Comment 8: "Lawyers who participate in a legal service plan must reasonably assure that the plan sponsors are in compliance with Rules 7.1, 7.2 and 7.3(b). **See 8.4(a)**."

Rule 7.6, Comment 6: "If a lawyer makes or solicits a political contribution under circumstances that constitute bribery or another crime, **Rule 8.4(b)** is implicated."

Legislative History of Model Rule 8.4

1980 Discussion Draft (then Rule 10.4) provided:

> It is professional misconduct for a lawyer to:
>
> (a) violate the Rules of Professional Conduct or knowingly aid another to do so;
>
> (b) commit a crime or other deliberately wrongful act that reflects adversely on the lawyer's honesty, trustworthiness, or fitness in other respects to practice law;
>
> (c) state or imply an ability to influence improperly a government agency or official;
>
> (d) practice law in a jurisdiction in violation of the regulation of the legal profession in that jurisdiction; or
>
> (e) aid a person who is not a member of the bar in the performance of activity that constitutes the practice of law.

1981 and 1982 Drafts: Subparagraph (b) of both drafts provided that it was misconduct for a lawyer to "commit a criminal *or fraudulent* act that reflects adversely . . . ," and neither draft included subparagraphs (c) and (d) of the rule as adopted. Subparagraphs (e) and (f) of both drafts were moved to Rule 5.5 of the Rules as adopted.

1994 Proposals: Two competing "anti-discrimination" proposals, each in the form of a new subparagraph (g) to Rule 8.4, were on the agenda at the ABA's February 1994 Mid-Year Meeting. However, at the last minute both proposals were withdrawn, and the competing sponsors announced their intention to work together to develop a single proposal. The two proposals withdrawn in 1994 differed mainly in their scope. The narrower proposal was submitted by the ABA Standing Committee on Ethics and Professional Responsibility. It provided that it would be professional misconduct for a lawyer to:

> (g) knowingly manifest by words or conduct, in the course of representing a client, bias or prejudice based upon race, sex, religion, national origin, disability, age, sexual orientation or socio-economic status. This paragraph does not apply to a lawyer's confidential communications to a client or preclude legitimate advocacy with respect to the foregoing factors.

The Report submitted in support of the Standing Committee's 1994 proposal explained the proposed language as follows:*

> The Committee's proposed amendment has three essential aspects.
>
> The first is its limitation to situations in which the lawyer is representing a client in a legal matter. . . .
>
> The second aspect is the Rule's identification of particular types of bias or prejudice that are to be prohibited. . . . The proposed amendment establishes a standard of conduct broader than that mandated by statutory enactments; this standard enables the profession to set an example of fairness and impartiality that is at the core of its commitment to the public interest. . . .
>
> The third aspect of the rule comprises its exceptions. In order to avoid inquiry into a lawyer's confidential communications to a client, the rule excepts those communications from its ambit. The rule, as well, does not preclude legitimate advocacy by the lawyer with respect to the specified factors. An example of this would be when the national origin of a party is a factor in selecting a jury for a particular case. The Committee did not, however, intend by use of the word advocacy to limit the applicability of the exception to lawyer conduct in formal proceedings; the exception is intended to apply with equal force to the lawyer's counseling function.

A broader proposal was submitted by the ABA Young Lawyers Division. It provided that it would be professional misconduct for a lawyer to:

> (g) commit a discriminatory act prohibited by law or to harass a person on the basis of sex, race, age, creed, religion, color, national origin, disability, sexual orientation or marital status, where the act of discrimination or harassment is committed in connection with a lawyer's professional activities.

The Report submitted in support of the Young Lawyers Division's 1994 proposal explained the proposed language as follows:

> The amendment is designed to regulate conduct in all manifestations of a lawyer's professional activities, and thereby avoid the inexplicable nuances of a rule which would allow reprehensible behavior to go unchecked merely because it is calculatedly inflicted outside the courtroom or after a case is concluded. Encompassing the all too common courtroom antics, the proposed rule will reach also to each situation where a lawyer is engaged in endeavors associated with professional activities.
>
> The proposed amendment will apply to professional activities regardless of whether the lawyer is representing a client. Implicit therein is the notion that the administration of justice must be protected from offensive conduct committed by officers of the court in all instances where a lawyer is called upon by virtue of the distinction of being a member of our profession. To do otherwise makes a mockery of

*Committee Reports do not represent official policy of the ABA. They are for information only, and the opinions are those of the authors of the report.

> the concept of fair and impartial administration of justice for all, and enhances the perception that lawyers are somehow outside or above the law. . . .
>
> The proposal must regulate a lawyer's conduct both inside and outside the courtroom because all lawyers represent the judicial system each time they act within their professional capacity. A public perception of fairness and equality within the judicial system is essential to maintaining the integrity of the system. The proposed resolution is not unlike existing model rules that prohibit lawyers from "engaging in conduct that is prejudicial to the administration of justice," and these rules might serve as a guide to its application.

1995 Resolution: After the Young Lawyers Division and the Standing Committee on Ethics and Professional Responsibility withdrew their competing 1994 proposals to add a new subparagraph 8.4(g), the Young Lawyers Division worked with the Standing Committee and other ABA entities in an attempt to produce a unified proposal to present to the House of Delegates. That attempt failed, partly because of concerns that a rule prohibiting bias and prejudice could infringe First Amendment rights. The Young Lawyers Division therefore decided to recommend a resolution to the House of Delegates condemning bias and prejudice by lawyers and encouraging affirmative steps to discourage bias and prejudice. The resolution passed. The full text of the resolution is reprinted in the Related Materials following this rule under the heading "ABA Resolution Against Bias and Prejudice."

1998 Mid Year Proposals: As in 1994 and 1995, proposals condemning bias and prejudice were withdrawn on the eve of the ABA meeting. A proposed amendment to the text of Rule 8.4, sponsored by the ABA's Criminal Justice Section, would have made it professional misconduct to:

> (1) commit, in the course of representing a client, any verbal or physical discriminatory act, on account of race, ethnicity, or gender, if intended to abuse litigants, jurors, witnesses, court personnel, opposing counsel or other lawyers, or to gain a tactical advantage; or
>
> (2) engage, in the course of representing a client, in any continuing course of verbal or physical discriminatory conduct, on account of race, ethnicity or gender, in dealings with litigants, jurors, witnesses, court personnel, opposing counsel or other lawyers, if such conduct constitutes harassment.

A competing proposal, sponsored by the ABA's Standing Committee on Ethics and Professional Responsibility, would not have amended the text of Rule 8.4 but would have added the following new paragraph to the comment:

> A lawyer who, in the course of representing a client, knowingly manifests by words or conduct, bias or prejudice based on race, sex, religion, national origin, disability, age, sexual orientation or socioeconomic status, violates paragraph (d) [of Rule 8.4] when such actions are prejudicial to the administration of justice. Legitimate advocacy respecting the foregoing factors does not violate paragraph (d).

1998 Amendment: After the 1998 Mid-Year Meeting proposals to amend the text of Rule 8.4 were withdrawn, the sponsors realized that the House of Delegates would not support an amendment to the text of Rule 8.4 but might support an amendment to the Comment. Eventually, the ABA's Standing Committee on Ethics and Professional Responsibility (later joined by the Section on Criminal Justice and the ABA Commission on Minorities in the Profession) proposed adding a new paragraph 2 to the Comment to make clear that words and conduct manifesting bias or prejudice in the course of representing a client violate Rule 8.4(d) when such actions are prejudicial to the administration of justice. The proposal to amend the Comment passed by a voice vote. We reprint the following excerpts (with most citations omitted) from the report of the ABA Standing Committee on Ethics and Professional Responsibility in support of the amendment:

*Excerpts from ABA Report Explaining 1998 Amendment to Comment to Rule 8.4**

. . . For a lawyer to display bias or discrimination in the course of representing a client, whether in the courtroom or a conference room discredits the fundamental principles that all people are equal before the law, and that controversies should be resolved according to their merits under the law.

. . . In 1993 and 1994, attempts to develop a clear and constitutionally enforceable black-letter rule of professional conduct on this subject proved difficult, controversial, and divisive. The need for a statement by the Association nevertheless was recognized and, at the 1995 Annual Meeting, a policy statement was adopted by the House condemning certain manifestations of bias or prejudice by lawyers and calling for development of an educational campaign that would enable lawyers to recognize, avoid, and themselves condemn such conduct. The problem, however, remains a serious one.

Formulation of a black-letter rule barring unacceptable conduct while preserving legitimate advocacy and First Amendment freedoms is a difficult task because manifestations of bias and prejudice may include protected speech and because race, gender and other factors are sometimes legitimate subjects of consideration and comment in the legal process. At the heart of the First Amendment is the right to free speech regarding matters relating to the functioning of government, including the judicial process. . . .

When a personal attack is made upon a judge, witness, or court official for the sole purpose of ridicule or harassment, however, such speech does not enjoy First Amendment protection. See e.g., Matter of Vincenti, 152 N.J. 253, 262-63, 704 A.2d 927, 932 (N.J. 1998) (lawyer made insinuations about a witness's sexual orientation by making sashaying motions and questioning her use of purple paper for taking notes in her office); In re Williams, 414 N.W.2d 394, 397 (Minn. 1987), *appeal dismissed* by 485 U.S. 950 (1988) (lawyer stated to opposing counsel at a deposition, "[d]on't use your little sheeny Hebrew tricks on me, Rosen."); Matter of Vincenti, 114 N.J. 275, 279, 554 A.2d 470, 472 (N.J. 1998) (lawyer commented to opposing counsel, "I see you are turning black again."). . . .

The Standing Committee believes that the recently-created Commission on Evaluation of the Model Rules of Professional Conduct ("ETHICS 2000") ought to consider whether an amendment to the Model Rules should be proposed and if so, how that rule should be crafted. In the meantime, however, the Standing Committee believes that the Comment to the existing model rule prohibiting conduct prejudicial to the administration of justice should be amended to make explicit that expressions of bias and prejudice are among the actions of a lawyer that can prejudice the administration of justice and subject a lawyer to disciplinary action.

. . . Three important issues are addressed in the proposed new Comment: (1) the context in which expressions of bias or prejudice will be subject to possible discipline; (2) the specific characteristics that must not be the basis for bias or prejudice;

*Committee Reports do not represent official policy of the ABA. They are for information only, and the opinions are those of the authors of the report.

and (3) a guarantee that the rule is not intended and will be ineffective to diminish a lawyer's advocacy where a listed characteristic is at issue in a matter. This report addresses these three issues.

The amended Comment identifies as conduct subject to scrutiny that which occurs "in the course of representing a client." . . . Conduct and communications by a lawyer other than in the course of representing a client are not intended to be made subject to review under the revised Comment.

The characteristics that must not be the basis of biased or prejudicial conduct or speech in the representation of clients are identical to those included in the directive of the Model Judicial Code [Canon 3(B)(6)] to judges regarding lawyer conduct occurring before them. . . . Although only some of these characteristics presently enjoy special constitutional protection, their inclusion in the Model Code of Judicial Conduct reflects this Association's view that all of them are, for the purpose of the fair administration of justice, unacceptable bases for bias or prejudice. . . .

The Comment specifically states that the application of Rule 8.4 (d) does not extend to a lawyer's legitimate advocacy. . . .

We have included language in the Comment to address a concern of the criminal bar, namely whether a finding by a trial judge that a lawyer exercised a peremptory challenge in a discriminatory manner could be considered a per se violation of this Rule. We think that it should not. A trial court may find that a lawyer has exercised a peremptory challenge with impermissible, discriminatory intent if it disbelieves the lawyer's neutral explanation for striking the juror. See, Batson v. Kentucky, 476 U.S. 79, 98 (1986). Although we note that some reasons for striking a juror such as location of residence, age, level of education, or prior involvement by the juror or a family member with the law are easily verifiable, neutral grounds for striking the juror, more subjective reasons such as body language, eye contact, or tone of voice are less subject to verification, placing the trial court in the difficult position of deciding whether a seemingly neutral reason is sufficient or indicative of the lawyer's conscious or unconscious discrimination. . . .

The Comment, reasonably interpreted, is meant only to reach conduct of such a nature or frequency that it is prejudicial to the administration of justice. Single incidents that suggest or imply bias or prejudice, or expressions of so slight a nature that they do not give serious offense are not necessarily prejudicial to the administration of justice and therefore violative of Rule 8.4(d). The determination of when this threshold is met is left to the disciplinary process, which will properly be informed by a variety of considerations that may differ from one situation or jurisdiction to another.

2002 Amendments: At its February 2002 Mid-Year Meeting, the ABA House of Delegates adopted with only minor changes the ABA Ethics 2000 Commission proposal to amend Rule 8.4 and its Comment.

Selected State Variations

Alabama: Rule 3.10 provides that a lawyer "shall not present, participate in presenting, or threaten to present criminal charges solely to obtain an advantage in a civil matter," as provided in DR 7-105 of the ABA Model Code.

Alaska's version of Rule 8.4 omits paragraph (d). (See Alaska Rule 3.8.) The comment states that the phrase "prejudicial to the administration of justice" was too vague. Alaska also adds a paragraph, based on DR 7-108(D) from the Model Code, that prohibits a lawyer from harassing or embarrassing jurors or from seeking to influence the juror's actions in future jury service. (See Alaska Rule 3.10.)

California: See Rule 2-400 (Prohibited Discriminatory Conduct in a Law Practice). In addition, California Business and Professions Code §125.6 (Discrimination in the Performance of Licensed Activity) permits the State to discipline any licensed attorney who "refuses to perform the licensed activity" or "makes any discrimination, or restriction in the performance of the licensed activity, because of the applicant's race, color, sex, religion, ancestry, disability, marital status, or national origin."

In addition, Business & Professions Code §490.5 permits the State to suspend a lawyers's license if the lawyer "is not in compliance with a child support order or judgment." California also provides, in Rule 290(a) of the Rules of Procedure of the State Bar, that (unless otherwise ordered by the Supreme Court), a member of the bar "shall be required to satisfactorily complete the State Bar Ethics School in all dispositions or decisions involving the imposition of discipline, unless the member previously completed the course within the prior two years." In cases of lesser sanctions, Rule 956(a) of the California Rules of Court provides that the State Bar "may attach conditions, effective for a reasonable time, to a public or private reproval administered upon a member of the State Bar. Conditions so attached shall be based upon a finding by the State Bar that protection of the public and interests of the attorney will be served."

Colorado: Rule 1.2(f) makes it misconduct to "engage in conduct which violates accepted standards of legal ethics" or to engage in conduct that:

> exhibits or is intended to appeal to or engender bias against a person on account of that person's race, gender, religion, national origin, disability, age, sexual orientation, or socioeconomic status, whether that conduct is directed to other counsel, court personnel, witnesses, parties, judges, judicial officers, or any persons involved in the legal process.

Colorado also includes a Rule 4.5 that retains the old Model Code prohibition, found in DR 7-105(A), against threatening criminal prosecution to gain an advantage in a civil proceeding.

Connecticut: Gen. Stat. §1-25 prescribes the following oath for attorneys:

> You solemnly swear that you will do no falsehood, nor consent to any to be done in court, and, if you know of any to be done, you will give information thereof to the judges, or one of them, that it may be reformed; you will not wittingly or willingly promote, sue or cause to be sued, any false or unlawful suit, or give aid, or consent, to the same; you will delay no person for lucre or malice; but will exercise the office of attorney, within the court wherein you may practice, according to the best of your learning and discretion, and with fidelity, as well to the court as to your client; so help you God.

District of Columbia: D.C. Rule 8.4(d) differs significantly from the ABA Model Rule, and D.C. adds Rule 9.1, which prohibits discrimination in employment — see District of Columbia Rules of Professional Conduct below.

Florida adds a new subparagraph (h) making it professional misconduct for a lawyer to "willfully refuse, as determined by a court of competent jurisdiction, to timely pay a child support obligation." The Comment explaining the new subparagraph says that the provision was added so that lawyers will be treated like other professionals in Florida.

Florida also provides that a lawyer shall not:

> (d) engage in conduct in connection with the practice of law that is prejudicial to the administration of justice, including to knowingly, or through callous indifference,

> disparage, humiliate, or discriminate against litigants, jurors, witnesses, court personnel, or other lawyers on any basis, including, but not limited to, on account of race, ethnicity, gender, religion, national origin, disability, marital status, sexual orientation, age, socioeconomic status, employment, or physical characteristic.

However, in 1994, the Florida Supreme Court *rejected* two proposals to address discriminatory employment practices, saying:

> We do not adopt either of these proposals because this Court's constitutional authority over the courts of Florida and attorney admission and discipline does not extend to the employment practices of lawyers.

In 1995, the Florida Supreme Court adopted a new Rule 4-8.4(i), which provides that a lawyer shall not "engage in sexual conduct with a client that exploits the lawyer-client relationship."

In addition the Florida Supreme Court has promulgated Rule 3-4.7, which provides:

> Violation of the oath taken by an attorney to support the constitutions of the United States and the State of Florida is ground for disciplinary action. Membership in, alliance with, or support of any organization, group, or party advocating or dedicated to the overthrow of the government by violence or by any means in violation of the Constitution of the United States or constitution of this state shall be a violation of the oath.

Effective February 8, 2001, Florida amended Rule 4-8.4(g) by specifying various time limits for responding to inquiries or subpoenas issued by bar counsel, a grievance committee, or the Florida Bar Board of Governors.

Georgia: In the rules effective January 1, 2001, Georgia's version of Rule 8.4 differs significantly from the ABA Model Rule. Georgia adopts ABA Model Rule 8.4(a) verbatim, but deletes ABA Model Rule 8.4(b) in favor of two subparagraphs making it a rules violation to be "convicted of a felony" or to be "convicted of a misdemeanor involving moral turpitude where the underlying conduct relates to the lawyer's fitness to practice law." Rule 8.4(a)(4) — Georgia's equivalent to ABA Model Rule 8.4(c) — makes it improper to engage in "professional" conduct involving dishonesty, fraud, deceit or misrepresentation. Georgia adds a new Rule 8.4(a)(5) that makes it improper for a lawyer to "fail to pay any final judgment or rule absolute rendered against such lawyer for money collected by him or her as a lawyer within ten (10) days after the time appointed in the order or judgment" — and the record of the judgment is "conclusive evidence unless obtained without valid service of process." A new Rule 8.4(d) provides that Rule 8.4(a)(1) "does not apply to Part Six of the Georgia Rules of Professional Conduct" (which covers pro bono work, court appointments, legal service organizations, and law reform organizations). Georgia deletes ABA Model Rules 8.4(d), (e), and (f).

For Georgia attorneys seeking guidance on their ethical conduct, Georgia Supreme Court Rule 4-401 authorizes the Georgia State Bar's Office of General Counsel to "render Informal Advisory Opinions concerning the Office of the General Counsel's interpretation of the Canons of Ethics or any of the grounds for disciplinary action as applied to a given state of facts." However, the rule cautions that an Informal Advisory Opinion is merely "the personal opinion of the issuing attorney of the Office of the General Counsel and is neither a defense to any complaint nor binding on the State Disciplinary Board, the Supreme Court of Georgia, or the State Bar of Georgia." Rules 4-402 and 4-403 describe the procedures by which the Supreme Court of Georgia issues Formal Advisory Opinions, and subparagraph (e) provides: "It shall be a complete defense to any grievance or formal complaint under these rules that the member complained against has acted in accordance with and in reasonable reliance upon any such Formal Advisory Opinion issued by the Supreme Court of Georgia."

Illinois: Effective March 26, 2001, the Illinois Supreme Court amended Rule 8.4(a)(9)(A) to provide that a lawyer shall not "violate a Federal, State or local statute or ordinance that prohibits discrimination based on race, sex, religion, national origin, *disability, age, sexual orientation or socioeconomic status* by conduct that reflects adversely on the lawyer's fitness as a lawyer." (The italicized terms were not previously mentioned in the rule.) Effective July 6, 2001, Illinois similarly amended Rule 8.4(a)(5) to prohibit "adverse discriminatory treatment of litigants, jurors, witnesses, lawyers, and others, based on race, sex, religion, national origin, disability, age, sexual orientation, or socioeconomic status."

Illinois Rule 8.4(a)(8) provides that a lawyer shall not "avoid in bad faith the repayment of an education loan guaranteed by the Illinois Student Assistance Commission or other governmental entity." Subparagraph (a)(8) does not prohibit a lawyer from discharging a student loan in a bankruptcy proceeding, but does provide that "the discharge shall not preclude a review of the attorney's conduct to determine if it constitutes bad faith." (A parallel Illinois statute provides that the state shall not issue or renew a law license for a person who has defaulted on a student loan, unless the person has established a satisfactory repayment plan and payment record.) Illinois Rule 8.4(b) borrows from DR 8-101(A)(1) and (2) of the ABA Model Code but adds new language providing that a lawyer holding public office shall not

> represent any client, including a municipal corporation or other public body, in the promotion or defeat of legislative or other proposals pending before the public body of which such lawyer is a member or by which such lawyer is employed.

Louisiana adds Rule 8.4(g), which forbids a lawyer "except upon the expressed assertion of a constitutional privilege, to fail to cooperate with the Office of Disciplinary Counsel in its investigation of alleged misconduct."

Massachusetts: Rule 8.4(h) continues language from the Code of Professional Responsibility that forbids a lawyer to "engage in any other conduct that adversely reflects on his or her fitness to practice law." This language is not in the Model Rules. Comment [5] states that such conduct is subject to discipline even if it "does not constitute a criminal, dishonest, or fraudulent or other act specifically described in the other paragraphs of this rule."

Michigan has adopted a rule numbered 6.5 and entitled "Professional Conduct," which provides:

> (a) A lawyer shall treat with courtesy and respect all persons involved in the legal process. A lawyer shall take particular care to avoid treating such a person discourteously or disrespectfully because of the person's race, gender, or other protected personal characteristic. To the extent possible, a lawyer shall require subordinate lawyers and nonlawyer assistants to provide such courteous and respectful treatment.
>
> (b) A lawyer serving as an adjudicative officer shall, without regard to a person's race, gender, or other protected personal characteristic, treat every person fairly, with courtesy and respect. To the extent possible, the lawyer shall require staff and others who are subject to the adjudicative officer's direction and control to

provide such fair, courteous, and respectful treatment to persons who have contact with the adjudicative tribunal.

In addition, the Michigan Court Rules include the following Rule 9.104:

Rule 9.104 Grounds for Discipline in General; Adjudication Elsewhere

The following acts or omissions by an attorney, individually or in concert with another person, are misconduct and grounds for discipline, whether or not occurring in the course of an attorney-client relationship:

(1) conduct prejudicial to the proper administration of justice;

(2) conduct that exposes the legal profession or the courts to obloquy, contempt, censure, or reproach;

(3) conduct that is contrary to justice, ethics, honesty, or good morals;

(4) conduct that violates the standards or rules of professional responsibility adopted by the Supreme Court;

(5) conduct that violates a criminal law of a state or of the United States;

(6) knowing misrepresentation of any facts or circumstances surrounding a request for investigation or complaint;

(7) failure to answer a request for investigation or complaint in conformity with MCR 9.113 and 9.115(D);

(8) contempt of the board or a hearing panel; or

(9) violation of an order of discipline.

Proof of an adjudication of misconduct in a disciplinary proceeding by another state or a United States court is conclusive proof of misconduct in a disciplinary proceeding in Michigan. The only issues to be addressed in the Michigan proceeding are whether the respondent was afforded due process of law in the course of the original proceedings and whether imposition of identical discipline in Michigan would be clearly inappropriate.

Minnesota: Rule 8.4 makes it professional misconduct for a lawyer to:

(g) harass a person on the basis of sex, race, age, creed, religion, color, national origin, disability, sexual preference or marital status in connection with a lawyer's professional activities; or

(h) commit a discriminatory act, prohibited by federal, state, or local statute or ordinance, that reflects adversely on the lawyer's fitness as a lawyer. Whether a discriminatory act reflects adversely on a lawyer's fitness as a lawyer shall be determined after consideration of all the circumstances, including (1) the seriousness of the act, (2) whether the lawyer knew that it was prohibited by statute or ordinance, (3) whether it was part of a pattern of prohibited conduct, and (4) whether it was committed in connection with the lawyer's professional activities.

New Jersey: Rule 8.4(g) makes it professional misconduct for a lawyer to "engage, in a professional capacity, in conduct involving discrimination (except employment discrimination unless resulting in a final agency or judicial determination) because of race, color, religion, age, sex, sexual orientation, national origin, language, marital status, socio-economic status, or handicap, where the conduct is intended or likely to cause harm." The Supreme Court's comment states that the rule

would, for example, cover activities in the court house, such as a lawyer's treatment of court support staff, as well as conduct more directly related to litigation; activities related to practice outside of the court house, whether or not related to litigation, such as treatment of other attorneys and their staff; bar association and similar activities; and activities in the lawyer's office and firm. Except to the extent that they are closely related to the foregoing, purely private activities are not intended to be covered by this rule amendment, although they may possibly constitute a violation of some other ethical rule. Nor is employment discrimination in hiring, firing, promotion, or partnership status intended to be covered unless it has resulted in either an agency or judicial determination of discriminatory conduct.

New York: Compare ABA Model Rule 8.4(a)-(d) and (f) to New York's DR 1-102. Compare Rule 8.4(e) to New York's DR 9-101(C).

North Carolina adds a new Rule 6.5 that tracks DR 8-101 of the old ABA Model Code of Professional Responsibility by prohibiting lawyers who hold "public office" from abusing their public positions. Also, North Carolina adds Rule 8.4(g), which borrows from DR 7-101(A)(3) of the old Code by providing that a lawyer shall not "intentionally prejudice or damage his or her client during the course of the professional relationship, except as may be required by Rule 3.3."

Ohio: In 1994, Ohio adopted DR 1-102(B), which provides:

> (B) A lawyer shall not engage, in a professional capacity, in conduct involving discrimination prohibited by law because of race, color, religion, age, gender, sexual orientation, national origin, marital status, or disability. This prohibition does not apply to a lawyer's confidential communication to a client or preclude legitimate advocacy where race, color, religion, age, gender, sexual orientation, national origin, marital status, or disability is relevant to the proceeding where the advocacy is made.

Oregon: DR 7-105(A) continues the old ABA Model Code prohibition on threatening to present criminal charges solely to obtain an advantage in a civil matter, but continues:

> A lawyer may threaten to present such charges if, but only if, the lawyer reasonably believes the charge to be true and if the purpose of the lawyer is to compel or induce the person threatened to take reasonable action to make good the wrong which is the subject of the charge.

Relating to Rule 8.4(c), in November 2000, in response to the widely publicized Oregon Supreme Court decision in In re Gatti, 330 Or. 517, 8 P.3d 966 (2000) (disciplining a lawyer in private practice who misrepresented his identity in order to obtain information about suspected medical insurance fraud), the Oregon State Bar proposed adding a new subparagraph to DR 1-102 saying that "it is not misconduct for a lawyer to supervise or advise about lawful covert activity in the investigation of violations of civil or criminal law or constitutional rights . . . ." The Oregon Supreme Court declined to adopt that proposal, but the State Bar submitted a revised proposal to the court in the fall of 2001, and on January 29, 2002, the Oregon Supreme Court added a new DR 1-102(D) that provides as follows:

> (D) Notwithstanding DR 1-102(A)(1), (A)(3) and (A)(4) and DR 7-102(A)(5), it shall not be professional misconduct for a lawyer to advise clients or others about or to supervise lawful covert activity in the investigation of violations of civil or criminal law or constitutional rights, provided the lawyer's conduct is otherwise in compliance with these disciplinary rules. "Covert activity," as used in this rule, means an effort to obtain information on unlawful activity through the use of misrepresentations or other subterfuge. "Covert activity" may be commenced by a lawyer or involve a lawyer as an advisor or supervisor only when the lawyer in good faith believes there is a reasonable possibility that unlawful activity has taken place, is taking place or will take place in the foreseeable future.

Rhode Island adds a Rule 9.1 that establishes an ethics advisory panel to be appointed by the Supreme Court, and states: "Any lawyer who acts in accordance with an opinion given by the panel shall be conclusively presumed to have abided by the Rules of Professional Conduct."

Texas: In 1994, Texas adopted Rule 5.08, entitled "Prohibited Discriminatory Activities," which provides as follows:

> (a) A lawyer shall not willfully, in connection with an adjudicatory proceeding, except as provided in paragraph (b), manifest, by words or conduct, bias or prejudice based on race, color, national origin, religion, disability, age, sex, or sexual orientation towards any person involved in that proceeding in any capacity.
>
> (b) Paragraph (a) does not apply to a lawyer's decision whether to represent a particular person in connection with an adjudicatory proceeding, nor to the process of jury selection, nor to communications protected as "confidential information" under these Rules. See Rule 1.05(a), (b). It also does not preclude advocacy in connection with an adjudicatory proceeding involving any of the factors set out in paragraph (a) if that advocacy:
>
> (i) is necessary in order to address any substantive or procedural issues raised by the proceeding; and
>
> (ii) is conducted in conformity with applicable rulings and orders of a tribunal and applicable rules of practice and procedure.

Texas Rule 8.04 forbids a lawyer to "engage in conduct that constitutes barratry as defined by the laws of this state." Rule 8.04(a)(2) forbids a lawyer to "commit a serious crime or commit any other criminal act that reflects adversely on the lawyer's honesty, trustworthiness or fitness as a lawyer in other respects." Rule 8.04(b) defines "serious crime" to include "barratry; any felony involving moral turpitude; any misdemeanor involving theft, embezzlement, or fraudulent or reckless misappropriation of money or other property; or any attempt, conspiracy, or solicitation of another to commit any of the foregoing crimes."

Virginia omits Rule 8.4(d), which forbids "conduct that is prejudicial to the administration of justice."

Related Materials

ABA Formal Ethics Opinions: See ABA Formal Ethics Op. 94-383 (1994).

ABA Model Rules for Disciplinary Enforcement: In 1989, the ABA adopted Model Rules for Disciplinary Enforcement, which set forth model procedures for state disciplinary agencies to follow. They are reprinted in full in the ABA/BNA Lawyer's Manual on Professional Conduct. In 1993, 1999, and 2002, the ABA amended these rules. Amended Rule 19 provides for immediate interim suspension of a lawyer found guilty of a serious crime. Amended Rule 25 provides that a lawyer who is disbarred may not apply for reinstatement for five years and requires a disbarred lawyer to pass the bar examination as a condition of reinstatement. (The ABA also rejected a proposal to prohibit applications for reinstatement for at least eight years after disbarment.)

ABA Resolution Against Bias and Prejudice: In 1995, after various ABA committees could not agree on a new Model Rule prohibiting bias and prejudice, the House of Delegates passed a resolution recommended by the ABA Young Lawyers Division to condemn bias and prejudice by lawyers in their professional activities and to encourage affirmative steps to discourage bias and prejudice among lawyers. The full resolution provides as follows:

RESOLVED, That the American Bar Association:

(a) condemns the manifestation by lawyers in the course of their professional activities, by words or conduct, of bias or prejudice against clients, opposing parties and their counsel, other litigants, witnesses, judges and court personnel, jurors and others, based upon race, sex, religion, national origin, disability, age, sexual orientation or socio-economic status, unless such words or conduct are otherwise permissible as legitimate advocacy on behalf of a client or a cause;

(b) opposes unlawful discrimination by lawyers in the management or operation of a law practice in hiring, promoting, discharging or otherwise determining the conditions of employment, or accepting or terminating representation of a client;

(c) condemns any conduct by lawyers that would threaten, harass, intimidate or denigrate any other person on the basis of the aforementioned categories and characteristics;

(d) discourages members from belonging to any organization that practices invidious discrimination on the basis of the aforementioned categories and characteristics;

(e) encourages affirmative steps such as continuing education, studies, and conferences to discourage the speech and conduct described above.

ABA Standards for Imposing Lawyer Sanctions:

5.1. Failure to Maintain Personal Integrity

5.11. Disbarment is generally appropriate when:

(a) a lawyer engages in serious criminal conduct a necessary element of which includes intentional interference with the administration of justice, false swearing, misrepresentation, fraud, extortion, misappropriation, or theft; or the sale, distribution or importation of controlled substances; or the intentional killing of another; or an attempt or conspiracy or solicitation of another to commit any of these offenses; or

(b) a lawyer engages in any other intentional conduct involving dishonesty, fraud, deceit, or misrepresentation that seriously adversely reflects on the lawyer's fitness to practice.

5.12. Suspension is generally appropriate when a lawyer knowingly engages in criminal conduct which does not contain the elements listed in Standard 5.11 and that seriously adversely reflects on the lawyer's fitness to practice.

5.13. Reprimand is generally appropriate when a lawyer knowingly engages in any other conduct that involves dishonesty, fraud, deceit, or misrepresentation and that adversely reflects on the lawyer's fitness to practice law.

5.14. Admonition is generally appropriate when a lawyer engages in any other conduct that reflects adversely on the lawyer's fitness to practice law.

5.2. Failure to Maintain the Public Trust

5.21. Disbarment is generally appropriate when a lawyer in an official or governmental position knowingly misuses the position with the intent to obtain a significant benefit or advantage for himself or another, or with the intent to cause serious or potentially serious injury to a party or to the integrity of the legal process.

5.22. Suspension is generally appropriate when a lawyer in an official or governmental position knowingly fails to follow proper procedures or rules and causes injury or potential injury to a party or to the integrity of the legal process.

8.0. Prior Discipline Orders

8.1. Disbarment is generally appropriate when a lawyer:

(a) intentionally or knowingly violates the terms of a prior disciplinary order and such violation causes injury or potential injury to a client, the public, the legal system, or the profession; or

(b) has been suspended for the same or similar misconduct, and intentionally or knowingly engages in further acts of misconduct that cause injury or potential injury to a client, the public, the legal system, or the profession.

8.2. Suspension is generally appropriate when a lawyer has been reprimanded for the same or similar misconduct and engages in further acts of misconduct that cause injury or potential injury to a client, the public, the legal system, or the profession.

Discrimination Statutes: Some state ethics rules, such as New York's DR 1-102(A)(6) and California's Rule 2-400(B), prohibit bias and discrimination only to the extent that the conduct would violate federal or state substantive laws prohibiting discrimination. Under federal law, the main statutes prohibiting discrimination in employment are: Title VII of the Civil Rights Act of 1964 (prohibiting discrimination in employment based on race, sex, religion, or national origin); the Americans with Disabilities Act (prohibiting discrimination in employment and public accommodations based on disability or the perception of a disability); and the Age Discrimination in Employment Act (prohibiting discrimination in employment based on age). Most states have parallel laws, and some state laws reach further than the federal statutes, prohibiting employment discrimination based on such things as sexual orientation, color, and marital status in addition to the federal criteria. In addition, many state laws prohibit acts of bias and discrimination going beyond employment discrimination, and some state ethics rules make it professional misconduct to violate these laws as well.

Federal Rules of Appellate Procedure: Fed. R. App. P. 46(b) and (c) give federal courts of appeals power to suspend or disbar or "take any appropriate disciplinary action against any attorney who practices before it for conduct unbecoming a member of the bar or for failure to comply with these rules or any rule of court."

IRS Regulations: In the regulations governing practice before the Internal Revenue Service, 31 C.F.R. §10.50 authorizes the Secretary of the Treasury to suspend or disbar any practitioner from practice before the IRS "who is shown to be incompetent or disreputable, who refuses to comply with any regulation in this part, or who, with intent to defraud, willfully and knowingly misleads or threatens a client or prospective client." "Disreputable conduct" is defined in §10.51 to encompass a long list of misdeeds, including conviction of any crime under federal revenue laws; conviction of any offense involving "dishonesty, or breach of trust"; knowingly giving false or misleading information to "any tribunal authorized to pass upon Federal tax matters, in connection with any matter pending or likely to be pending before them . . ."; misappropriating client funds; "[c]ontemptuous conduct in connection with practice before the Internal Revenue Service, including the use of abusive language, making false accusations and statements knowing them to be false, or circulating or publishing malicious or libelous matter"; or "[g]iving a false opinion, knowingly, recklessly, or through gross incompetence, including an opinion which is intentionally or recklessly misleading, or a pattern of providing incompetent opinions on questions arising under the Federal tax laws."

Misconduct: Many states define "misconduct" by statute or court rule. In Washington, D.C., for example, §2(b) of the rules governing disciplinary proceedings provides: "Acts or omissions by an attorney . . . which violate the attorney's oath of office or the rules or code of professional conduct currently in effect in the District of Columbia shall constitute misconduct and shall be grounds for discipline, whether or not the act or omission occurred in the course of an attorney-client relationship. . . ."

Restatement of the Law Governing Lawyers: See Restatement §§1, 5, 37, and 113 in our chapter on the Restatement later in this volume.

Securities and Exchange Commission Rules: SEC Rule 2(e) provides that the SEC may impose a censure or temporarily or permanently deny a lawyer (or other professional) the right to practice before the SEC if the lawyer has engaged in "unethical or improper professional conduct."

Statutes of Limitations: Some states have adopted statutes of limitations for disciplinary matters. For example, in 1995, the Florida Supreme Court adopted the following statute of limitations provision:

> *Rule 3-7.16 Limitation on Time to Bring Complaint*
>
> (a) *Time for Inquiries and Complaints.* Inquiries raised or complaints presented by or to The Florida Bar under these rules shall be commenced within 6 years from the time the matter giving rise to the inquiry or complaint is discovered or, with due diligence, should have been discovered.
>
> (b) *Exception for Theft or Conviction of a Felony Criminal Offense.* There shall be no limit on the time in which to present or bring a matter alleging theft or conviction of a felony criminal offense by a member of The Florida Bar.
>
> (c) *Tolling Based on Fraud, Concealment or Misrepresentation.* In matters covered by this rule where it can be shown that fraud, concealment, or intentional misrepresentation of fact prevented the discovery of the matter giving rise to the inquiry or complaint, the limitation of time in which to bring an inquiry or complaint within this rule shall be tolled.

Rule 8.5 Disciplinary Authority; Choice of Law

Editors' Note. At its August 2002 Annual Meeting, the ABA House of Delegates significantly amended Rule 8.5 and its Comment. Most of the amendments were proposed by the ABA Commission on Multijurisdictional Practice. For further information, see the entry titled "2002 Amendments" in the Legislative History following this rule.

(a) *Disciplinary Authority.* A lawyer admitted to practice in this jurisdiction is subject to the disciplinary authority of this jurisdiction, regardless of where the lawyer's conduct occurs. A lawyer not admitted in this jurisdiction is also subject to the disciplinary authority of this jurisdiction if the lawyer provides or offers to provide any legal services in this jurisdiction. A lawyer may be subject to the disciplinary authority of both this jurisdiction and another jurisdiction ~~where the lawyer is admitted~~ for the same conduct.

(b) *Choice of Law.* In any exercise of the disciplinary authority of this jurisdiction, the rules of professional conduct to be applied shall be as follows:

(1) for conduct in connection with a ~~proceeding in~~ matter pending before a ~~court before which a lawyer has been admitted to practice (either generally or for purposes of that proceeding)~~ tribunal, the rules ~~to be applied shall be the rules~~ of the jurisdiction in which the ~~court~~ tribunal sits, unless the rules of the ~~court~~ tribunal provide otherwise; and

(2) for any other conduct, the rules of the jurisdiction in which the lawyer's conduct occurred, or, if the predominant effect of the conduct is in a different jurisdiction, the rules of that jurisdiction shall be applied to the conduct. A lawyer shall not be subject to discipline if the lawyer's conduct conforms to the rules of a jurisdiction in which the lawyer reasonably believes the predominant effect of the lawyer's conduct will occur.

~~(i) if the lawyer is licensed to practice only in this jurisdiction, the rules to be applied shall be the rules of this jurisdiction, and~~

~~(ii) if the lawyer is licensed to practice in this and another jurisdiction, the rules to be applied shall be the rules of the admitting jurisdiction in which the lawyer principally practices; provided, however, that if particular conduct clearly has its predominant effect in another jurisdiction in which the lawyer is licensed to practice, the rules of that jurisdiction shall be applied to that conduct.~~

COMMENT

Disciplinary Authority

[1] ~~Paragraph (a) restates~~ It is longstanding law that the conduct of a lawyer admitted to practice in this jurisdiction is subject to the disciplinary authority of this jurisdiction. Extension of the disciplinary authority of this jurisdiction to other lawyers who provide or offer to provide legal services in this jurisdiction is for the protection of the citizens of this jurisdiction. Reciprocal enforcement of a jurisdiction's disciplinary findings and sanctions will further advance the purposes of this Rule. See Rules 6 and 22, ABA Model Rules for Lawyer Disciplinary Enforcement. A lawyer who is subject to the disciplinary authority of the jurisdiction under Rule 8.5(a) appoints [an official to be designated by this Court] to receive service of process in this jurisdiction. The fact that the lawyer is subject to the disciplinary authority of this jurisdiction may be a factor in determining whether personal jurisdiction may be asserted over the lawyer for civil matters.

Choice of Law

[2] A lawyer may be potentially subject to more than one set of rules of professional conduct which impose different obligations. The lawyer may be licensed to practice in more than one jurisdiction with differing rules, or may be admitted to practice before a particular court with rules that differ from those of the jurisdiction or jurisdictions in which the lawyer is licensed to practice. ~~In the past, decisions have not developed clear or consistent guidance as to which rules apply in such circumstances.~~ Additionally, the lawyer's conduct may involve significant contacts with more than one jurisdiction.

[3] Paragraph (b) seeks to resolve such potential conflicts. Its premise is that minimizing conflicts between rules, as well as uncertainty about which rules are applicable, is in the best interest of both clients and the profession (as well as the bodies having authority to regulate the profession). Accordingly, it takes the approach of (i) providing that any particular conduct of a lawyer shall be subject to only one set of rules of professional conduct, ~~and~~ (ii) making the determination of which set of rules applies to particular conduct as straightforward as possible, consistent with recognition of appropriate regulatory interests of relevant jurisdictions, and (iii) providing protection from discipline for lawyers who act reasonably in the face of uncertainty.

[4] Paragraph (b)(1) provides that as to a lawyer's conduct relating to a proceeding ~~in~~ pending before a ~~court before which the lawyer is admitted to practice (either generally or pro hac vice)~~ tribunal, the lawyer shall be subject only to the rules of professional conduct of that ~~court~~ tribunal. As to all other conduct, including conduct in anticipation of a proceeding not yet pending before a tribunal, paragraph (b)(2) provides that a lawyer ~~licensed to practice only in this jurisdiction shall be subject to the rules of professional conduct of this jurisdiction, and that a lawyer licensed in multiple jurisdictions shall be subject only to the rules of the jurisdiction where he or she (as an individual, not his or her firm) principally practices, but with one exception: if particular conduct clearly has its predominant effect in another admitting jurisdiction, then only the rules of that jurisdiction shall apply. The intention is for the latter exception to be a narrow one. It would be appropriately applied, for example, to a situation in which a lawyer admitted in, and principally practicing in, State A, but also admitted in State B, handled an acquisition by a company whose headquarters and operations were in State B of another, similar such company. The exception would not appropriately be applied, on the other hand, if the lawyer handled an acquisition by a company whose headquarters and operations were in State A of a company whose headquarters and main operations were in State A, but which also had some operations in State B~~ shall be subject to the rules of the jurisdiction in which the lawyer's conduct occurred, or, if the predominant effect of the conduct is in another jurisdiction, the rules of that jurisdiction shall be

<u>applied to the conduct. In the case of conduct in anticipation of a proceeding that is likely to be before a tribunal, the predominant effect of such conduct could be where the conduct occurred, where the tribunal sits or in another jurisdiction</u>.

<u>[5] When a lawyer's conduct involves significant contacts with more than one jurisdiction, it may not be clear whether the predominant effect of the lawyer's conduct will occur in a jurisdiction other than the one in which the conduct occurred. So long as the lawyer's conduct conforms to the rules of a jurisdiction in which the lawyer reasonably believes the predominant effect will occur, the lawyer shall not be subject to discipline under this Rule.</u>

~~[5]~~ <u>[6]</u> If two admitting jurisdictions were to proceed against a lawyer for the same conduct, they should, applying this rule, identify the same governing ethics rules. They should take all appropriate steps to see that they do apply the same rule to the same conduct, and in all events should avoid proceeding against a lawyer on the basis of two inconsistent rules.

~~[6]~~ <u>[7]</u> The choice of law provision ~~is not intended to apply to~~ <u>applies to lawyers engaged in</u> transnational practice<u>, unless international law, treaties or other agreements between competent regulatory authorities in the affected jurisdictions provide otherwise</u>. ~~Choice of law in this context should be the subject of agreements between jurisdictions or of appropriate international law.~~

Canon and Code Antecedents

ABA Canons of Professional Ethics: No comparable Canon.

ABA Model Code of Professional Responsibility: No comparable Disciplinary Rule.

Cross-References in Other Rules

Rule 5.5, Comment 19: "A lawyer who practices law in this jurisdiction pursuant to paragraph (c) or (d) or otherwise is subject to the disciplinary authority of this jurisdiction. See **Rule 8.5(a)**."

Legislative History of Model Rule 8.5

1980 Discussion Draft had no comparable provision.

1981 Draft was substantially the same as the 1982 draft (see next entry).

1982 Draft was adopted in 1983, and consisted of a single sentence: "A lawyer admitted to practice in this jurisdiction is subject to the disciplinary authority of this jurisdiction although engaged in practice elsewhere."

1993 Amendment: At its August 1993 Annual Meeting, the ABA House of Delegates voted to amend Rule 8.5 by rephrasing the first sentence of paragraph (a) (which had been the only sentence in the entire rule), by adding a second sentence to paragraph (a), and by adding an entirely new paragraph (b). The purpose of the new paragraph (b) is to provide guidelines for deciding which jurisdiction's disciplinary rules apply to lawyers who are licensed (either generally or pro hac vice) to practice in more than one jurisdiction. The amendment also included a wholesale revision of the Comment, replacing the three existing paragraphs with six completely new paragraphs, five of which explain the new choice-of-law rules contained in paragraph (b).

The amendment was proposed by the ABA's Standing Committee on Ethics and Professional Responsibility. We reprint here excerpts from the committee report submitted in support of the amendment (with most citations omitted):

*ABA Committee Report Explaining 1993 Amendment to Rule 8.5**

The objective of this proposed change in Rule 8.5 is to bring some measure of certainty and clarity to the frequently encountered, and often difficult, decisions a lawyer must make when encountering a situation in which the lawyer is potentially subject to differing ethical requirements of more than one jurisdiction. It is generally the case that such decisions cannot await an authoritative ruling or advisory opinion from an independent source.

The most compelling circumstance of a lawyer caught between conflicting ethical obligations in all likelihood is that where a lawyer has become aware of a client's fraud committed in the course of the lawyer's representation, and the rule of one jurisdiction with authority over the lawyer would require disclosure of the fraud and that of another jurisdiction with authority would forbid it. But this is by no means the only circumstance in which the problem arises. . . .

The problem of lack of clear guidance that this proposal seeks to address is exacerbated by the fact that existing authority as to choice of law in the area of ethics rules is unclear and inconsistent. Some authorities suggest that particular conduct should be subject to only one set of rules, while others suggest that more than one set of rules can apply simultaneously to the same conduct. Widely differing approaches to how to identify the applicable rules have been taken. . . .

The proposed amendment to Rule 8.5 seeks to provide clear answers to these problems in nearly all cases. In litigation, the ethical rules of the tribunal, and only those rules, would apply. In other matters, the multiply admitted lawyer would be subject only to the rules of the jurisdiction where he or she principally practices, except when the particular conduct clearly has its predominant effect in another admitting jurisdiction. . . .

[I]t might be argued that, because of the exception for particular conduct that clearly has its predominant effect in another jurisdiction, the proposal falls short of achieving perfect clarity and certainty. This is indeed true, and there may be instances in which it is difficult to define the "particular conduct" and to decide whether it has its "predominant effect" in one jurisdiction or another. However, to provide for no exception would allow substantial conduct to occur in a second admitting jurisdiction without being subject to that jurisdiction's rules; and the exception has been crafted in a manner that is intended to minimize to the extent possible the difficulty of applying it in particular cases. . . .

2002 Amendments: At its August 2002 Annual Meeting, by voice vote, the ABA House of Delegates approved significant amendments to ABA Model Rule 8.5. Most of these amendments were proposed by the ABA Commission on

*Committee Reports do not represent official policy of the ABA. They are for information only, and the opinions are those of the authors of the report.

Multijurisdictional Practice, which was formed in July 2000 to consider a host of issues pertaining to the practice of law by lawyers in jurisdictions where they are not admitted to practice, either permanently or pro hac vice. (The ABA Ethics 2000 Commission had also discussed amendments to Rule 8.5, but eventually decided to defer to the Commission on Multijurisdictional Practice, which was studying the issues more comprehensively.) However, the last two sentences of Comment 1 (regarding service of process and personal jurisdiction) were added based on negotiations between the MJP Commission and lawyers from the Ohio State Bar Association. The Ohio lawyers wanted to ensure that lawyers who harmed clients in states where they were not admitted would be amenable to disciplinary and civil jurisdiction in those states.

The full 60-page Final Report of the ABA Commission on Multijurisdictional Practice regarding Rule 8.5 and related issues — which is well worth reading — may be found at www.abanet.org/cpr (click on "Commission on Multijurisdictional Practice" and look for "REVISED FINAL REPORT, AS ADOPTED AUGUST 12, 2002"). We excerpt here (with footnotes omitted) the portions of that report that relate most directly to the 2002 Amendments to Rule 8.5:

*Excerpts from Final Report of the ABA Commission on Multijurisdictional Practice in Support of Amendments to Rule 8.5**

It is important that state regulatory authorities acknowledge the increasing prevalence of cross-border law practice and respond appropriately. Allowances must be made for effectively regulating lawyers who practice law outside the states in which they are licensed. Sanctions must be available both against lawyers who do unauthorized work outside their home states and against those who violate rules of professional conduct when they engage in otherwise permissible multijurisdictional law practice.

The Ethics 2000 Commission proposed amending Rule 8.5(a) (Disciplinary Authority) to make clear that a jurisdiction in which a lawyer engages in disciplinary misconduct may sanction the lawyer regardless of whether the lawyer is licensed to practice law in that jurisdiction. Most significantly, a sentence would be added to provide that: "A lawyer not admitted in this jurisdiction is also subject to the disciplinary authority of this jurisdiction if the lawyer provides or offers to provide any legal services in this jurisdiction." The proposal is consistent with existing ABA policy, as embodied in Rule 6 of the *ABA Model Rules for Lawyer Disciplinary Enforcement.* As the Ethics 2000 Commission noted, "this is an appropriate Rule to adopt in the *Model Rules of Professional Conduct,* given that a jurisdiction in which a lawyer is not admitted may be the one most interested in disciplining the lawyer for improper conduct." As a further enhancement to this Rule, the MJP Commission recommends that the following statement be added to the end of Comment [1]: "Reciprocal enforcement of a jurisdiction's disciplinary findings and sanctions will further advance the purposes of this Rule. See Rules 6 and 22, ABA *Model Rules for Lawyer Disciplinary Enforcement.*"

Additionally, the Ethics 2000 Commission proposed amending Rule 8.5(b) (Choice of Law) in two principal respects. First, a number of changes would clarify the choice of law rule applicable to lawyers participating in adjudications. It would provide that a lawyer who participates in a formal adjudication before any "tribunal" — and not only a "court" — is bound by the rules of professional conduct of the jurisdiction in which the tribunal sits or by the rules of the tribunal itself if they provide otherwise.

*Committee Reports do not represent official policy of the ABA. They are for information only and represent only the opinions of the authors.

Second, the Ethics 2000 Commission proposed changing the choice of law rule applicable to legal work outside the context of adjudications. The current rule provides that a lawyer is governed by the rules of professional conduct of the jurisdiction in which the lawyer is licensed. When a lawyer is licensed in multiple jurisdictions, it identifies a principle to determine which of the jurisdictions' rules apply. The proposed amendment recognizes that when lawyers engage in multijurisdictional practice, the jurisdiction in which they practice has an interest in enforcing compliance with its rules of professional conduct. Under the proposed amendment, the applicable rules would be those of the jurisdiction in which lawyer's conduct had its predominant effect or, where the conduct did not have its predominant effect in a single jurisdiction, the rules of the jurisdiction in which the conduct occurred. However, a lawyer who acts reasonably in the face of uncertainty about which jurisdiction's rules apply would not be subject to discipline. Rule 1.0 (Terminology) of the ABA *Model Rules of Professional Conduct* provides that reasonable, when used in reference to a lawyer's actions, denotes the conduct of a reasonably prudent and competent lawyer.

Selected State Variations

Alaska: Rule 8.5 extends the state's disciplinary authority to a lawyer not admitted to practice in Alaska but who "engages in the practice of law pursuant to court rule or order."

Arizona, Connecticut, Florida and ***New Jersey*** (among others) maintain the original one-sentence version of ABA Model Rule 8.5 that was in effect from 1983 to 1993, which provides: "A lawyer admitted to practice in this jurisdiction is subject to the disciplinary authority of this jurisdiction although engaged in practice elsewhere."

California: See B & P Code §6002.1(a)(4). California Rule 1-100(D), entitled "Geographic Scope of Rules," specifies application of California's Rules to members of the state bar and to lawyers from other jurisdictions.

Florida has not adopted Rule 8.5(b), but a special provision on lawyer advertising, Rule 4-7.1(b), as amended in December of 1999, provides as follows:

> (b) *Advertisements Not Disseminated in Florida.* These rules shall not apply to any advertisement broadcast or disseminated in another jurisdiction in which the advertising lawyer is admitted if such advertisement complies with the rules governing lawyer advertising in that jurisdiction and is not intended for broadcast or dissemination within the state of Florida.

In December of 1999, the Florida Supreme Court *rejected* a proposed rule which would have provided that "lawyers, whether or not admitted to practice law in Florida, who solicit or advertise for legal employment in Florida or who target solicitations or advertisements for legal employment at Florida residents . . . must do so only in accordance with the applicable provisions of these Rules Regulating The Florida Bar." (The court simultaneously rejected a companion proposal to subject lawyers to Florida's advertising rules and procedures if they "disseminate advertisements within Florida or target advertisements at Florida residents.") The Bar said that the proposals stemmed directly from the "offensive and improper practices of some non-Florida attorneys who converged on the survivors of those killed in the ValuJet airplane crash in the Everglades in May of 1996." In rejecting the proposals, the Supreme Court said: "We find the proposed rules unnecessary. Out-of-state lawyers are not lawyers who are subject to the Rules Regulating the Florida Bar; rather, they are 'nonlawyers' subject to chapter 10 unlicensed practice of law charges if they . . . engage in improper solicitation or advertising in Florida."

Georgia: In the rules effective January 1, 2001, Georgia adopted the pre-2002 version of ABA Model Rule 8.5 and its Comment nearly verbatim. In addition, Georgia has adopted a new Rule 9.4, entitled "Reciprocal Discipline," which provides:

> (a) Disbarment or suspension by another jurisdiction is a ground for discipline in the State of Georgia.
>
> (b) The record of disbarment or suspension in another jurisdiction shall be conclusive evidence of such disbarment or suspension and shall be admissible in disciplinary proceedings.

Georgia's Comment to Rule 9.4 states:

> [1] If a lawyer has been the subject of disciplinary proceedings in another jurisdiction which resulted in the lawyer being suspended or disbarred, that outcome will be the basis for discipline in Georgia without a retrial of the underlying charges. Often if a Georgia lawyer is the subject of a disciplinary proceeding in another jurisdiction, it is because the offense occurred in that jurisdiction. To retry the underlying charges would be a needless waste of time and resources.
>
> [2] This rule does not necessarily adopt the disciplinary sanction imposed by the other jurisdiction as the sanction in Georgia. The lawyer will be able to present mitigating evidence in the Georgia proceedings, including evidence as to the rule and the procedure used in the other jurisdiction.

Maryland: Rule 8.5 includes the following provision that reaches lawyers who are admitted in other states but not Maryland:

> (b) A lawyer not admitted by the Court of Appeals to practice in this State is subject to the disciplinary authority of this State for conduct that constitutes a violation of these Rules and that:
>
> (1) involves the practice of law in this State by that lawyer, or
>
> (2) involves that lawyer holding himself or herself out as practicing law in this State, or
>
> (3) involves the practice of law in this State by another lawyer over whom that lawyer has the obligation of supervision or control.

Massachusetts has not adopted Rule 8.5(b). When the Supreme Judicial Court adopted new rules in June of 1997, the Court deemed further study necessary because Rule 8.5(b) "has revealed many instances in which its application seems problematic."

Michigan: The second sentence of Rule 8.5 provides: "A lawyer who is licensed to practice in another jurisdiction and who is admitted to practice in this jurisdiction is subject to the disciplinary authority of this jurisdiction." Michigan has not adopted Rule 8.5(b).

Montana: In 1996, the Montana Supreme Court adopted the following new Rule 8.5, entitled "Jurisdiction and Certification," to insure that out-of-state lawyers who practice law in Montana will "be aware of and be subject to" Montana's Rules of Professional Conduct:

> A lawyer who is not an active member in good standing of the State Bar of Montana and who seeks to practice in any court of this State pro hac vice, by motion, or before being otherwise admitted to the practice of law in this State, shall,

> prior to engaging in the practice of law in this State, certify in writing and under oath to this Court that, except as to Rules 6.1 through 6.4, he or she will be bound by these Rules of Professional Conduct in his or her practice of law in this State and will be subject to the disciplinary authority of this State. . . .

New York: Compare ABA Model Rule 8.5 to New York's EC 2-10 (last sentence) and DR 1-105.

North Dakota: A North Dakota lawyer is subject to discipline in that state "even though the conduct of the lawyer giving rise to the discipline may have occurred outside of this jurisdiction and even when that conduct may subject or has subjected the lawyer to discipline by another jurisdiction." In addition, persons not licensed in North Dakota but eligible to practice elsewhere are subject to the disciplinary authority of North Dakota if they "actually engage in this jurisdiction in the practice of law."

Ohio has no provision comparable to ABA Model Rule 8.5.

Rhode Island: Rule 8.5 uses the original version of ABA Model Rule 8.5, plus the following new additional sentence: "A lawyer engaged in practice in another jurisdiction who is specially admitted to appear before the courts of this jurisdiction on an ad hoc basis shall be subject to these rules."

South Carolina: South Carolina Appellate Court Rule 418, which took effect on July 1, 1999, requires any "unlicensed lawyer" (defined as "any person who is admitted to practice law in another jurisdiction but who is not admitted to practice law in South Carolina") to comply with South Carolina's advertising rules (Rules 7.1 through 7.5) if the unlicensed lawyer engages in any of six specified forms of advertising or solicitation. The six forms include: (1) "in-person contact with a potential client which occurs in South Carolina"; (2) a "telephone communication" (including a fax to a potential client at a South Carolina phone number); (3) a "letter or other document sent" to a South Carolina address; (4) an "advertisement on a radio or television station located in South Carolina"; (5) an advertisement in "a South Carolina newspaper or any other publication which is primarily distributed in South Carolina"; or (6) "[a]ny other form of advertising or solicitation which is specifically targeted at potential clients in South Carolina." (The rule does not expressly address web sites or e-mail.)

Rule 418(c) provides that it is "misconduct" for an unlicensed lawyer to violate or attempt to violate South Carolina's advertising rules, and gives South Carolina's Commission on Lawyer Conduct "jurisdiction over allegations that an unlicensed lawyer has committed misconduct." Regarding sanctions, Rule 418(d) provides:

> *Sanctions for Misconduct.* An unlicensed lawyer who commits misconduct under this rule may receive a letter of caution or any form of discipline contained in Rule 7(b)(4)–(10) of the Rules for Lawyer Disciplinary Enforcement. In addition, an unlicensed lawyer who has committed misconduct under this rule may be ordered to refund all fees paid to the unlicensed lawyer pursuant to any contract of employment arising out of the advertising or solicitation. Misconduct under this rule may also be punished as a contempt of the Supreme Court, and the Supreme Court may issue injunctions against future violations.

Texas: Rule 8.05(b) provides as follows:

(b) A lawyer admitted to practice in this state is also subject to the disciplinary authority of this state for:

(1) an advertisement in the public media that does not comply with these rules and that is broadcast or disseminated in another jurisdiction,

even if the advertisement complies with the rules governing lawyer advertisements in that jurisdiction, if the broadcast or dissemination of the advertisement is intended to be received by prospective clients in this state and is intended to secure employment to be performed in this state; and

(2) a written solicitation communication that does not comply with these rules and that is mailed in another jurisdiction, even if the communication complies with the rules governing written solicitation communications by lawyers in that jurisdiction, if the communication is mailed to an addressee in this state or is intended to secure employment to be performed in this state.

Related Materials

ABA Model Rules of Lawyer Disciplinary Enforcement: Comment 1 to ABA Model Rule 8.5 expressly mentions Rules 6 and 22 of the ABA Model Rules for Lawyer Disciplinary Enforcement. As amended at ABA's August 2002 Annual Meeting pursuant to proposals by the ABA Commission on Multijurisdictional Practice, Rules 6 and 22 provide, in relevant part, as follows:

Rule 6. Jurisdiction

A. *Lawyers Admitted to Practice.* Any lawyer admitted to practice law in this jurisdiction, including any formerly admitted lawyer with respect to acts committed prior to resignation, suspension, disbarment, or transfer to inactive status . . . and any lawyer specially admitted by a court of this jurisdiction for a particular proceeding and any lawyer not admitted in this jurisdiction who practices law or renders or offers to render any legal services in this jurisdiction, is subject to the disciplinary jurisdiction of this court and the board.

Rule 22. Reciprocal Discipline and Reciprocal Disability Inactive Status

A. *Disciplinary Counsel Duty to Obtain Order of Discipline or Disability Inactive Status from Other Jurisdiction.* Upon being disciplined or transferred to disability inactive status in another jurisdiction, a lawyer admitted to practice in [this jurisdiction] shall promptly inform disciplinary counsel of the discipline or transfer. . . .

D. *Discipline to be Imposed.* . . . [T]his court shall impose the identical discipline or disability inactive status unless disciplinary counsel or the lawyer demonstrates, or this court finds that it clearly appears upon the face of the record from which the discipline is predicated, that:

(1) The procedure was so lacking in notice or opportunity to be heard as to constitute a deprivation of due process; or
(2) There was such infirmity of proof establishing the misconduct as to give rise to the clear conviction that the court could not, consistent with its duty, accept as final the conclusion on that subject; or
(3) The discipline imposed would result in grave injustice; or be offensive to the public policy of the jurisdiction; or
(4) The reason for the original transfer to disability inactive status no longer exists.

If this court determines that any of those elements exists, this court shall enter such other order as it deems appropriate. The burden is on the party seeking different discipline in this jurisdiction to demonstrate that the imposition of the same discipline is not appropriate.

E. *Conclusiveness of Adjudication in Other Jurisdictions.* In all other aspects, a final adjudication in another jurisdiction that a lawyer, whether or not admitted in that jurisdiction, has been guilty of misconduct or should be transferred to disability inactive status shall establish conclusively the misconduct or the disability for purposes of a disciplinary or disability proceeding in this state.

Federal Government Attorneys: In 1998, Congress passed 28 U.S.C. §530B, entitled "Ethical Standards for Attorneys for the Government," which provides, in part:

(a) An attorney for the Government shall be subject to State laws and rules, and local Federal court rules, governing attorneys in each State where such attorney engages in that attorney's duties, to the same extent and in the same manner as other attorneys in that State.

Federal Rules of Appellate Procedure: Fed. R. App. P. 46(b) provides:

When it is shown to the court that any member of its bar has been suspended or disbarred from practice in any other court of record, or has been guilty of conduct unbecoming a member of the bar of the court, the member will be subject to suspension or disbarment by the court.

Limitations on Jurisdiction: A state's willingness to exercise jurisdiction over a lawyer licensed only in other states may depend on whether the alleged misconduct was directly related to the practice of law. Florida, for example, provides in Supreme Court Rule 3-4.1 that "[j]urisdiction over an attorney of another state who is not a member of The Florida Bar shall be limited to conduct as an attorney in relation to the business for which the attorney was permitted to practice in this state. . . ."

Model Rules of Professional Conduct for Federal Lawyers: Rule 8.5 provides:

(a) A Federal lawyer shall comply with the rules of professional conduct applicable to the Federal Agency that employs the Government lawyer or the Federal Agency before which the Federal lawyer practices.

(b) If the Federal Agency has not adopted or promulgated rules of professional conduct, the Federal lawyer shall comply with the rules of professional conduct of the state bars in which the Federal lawyer is admitted to practice.

The Comment to this rule states:

While the Federal lawyer may remain subject to the governing authority of their licensing jurisdiction, the Federal lawyer is also subject to these Rules. However, when a Government lawyer is engaged in the conduct of Federal Agency legal functions, whether servicing the Federal Agency as a client or serving an individual client in the course of official duties, these Rules are regarded as superseding any conflicting rules applicable in the jurisdictions in which the Government lawyer may be licensed.

Restatement of the Law Governing Lawyers: See Restatement §§1 and 5 in our chapter on the Restatement later in this volume.

INDEX TO THE MODEL RULES

Editors' Note. This index was originally prepared by the American Bar Association following the February 2002 Amendments to the ABA Model Rules of Professional Conduct. It has been enhanced by the authors of this volume and has been updated to reflect amendments to the Model Rules through the ABA's August 2002 Annual Meeting.

A

Abuse of process, Rule 3.1 (Comment)
Accepting appointments, Rule 6.2
Accounting for funds, Rule 1.15
Acquiring interest in litigation, Rule 1.8(i)
  contingent fee, Rule 1.8(i)(2)
Adjudicative officers
  disqualification of former, Rule 1.12(a)
  negotiating for private employment, Rule 1.12(b)
Administration of justice
  conduct prejudicial to, Rule 8.4(d)
  interference with, Rule 8.4 (Comment)
  lawyer's duty to seek improvment in, Preamble
Administration of law, participation in, Rule 6.4
Administrative agencies and tribunals, appearance before, Rule 3.9
Administrator, fee for representation of, Rule 1.5 (Comment)
Admiralty practice, communication of, Rule 7.4(c)
Admission to practice, Rule 8.1
Advance fee payments
  deposit of, Rule 1.15(c)
  propriety of, Rule 1.5 (Comment)
Adversary system, duty of lawyer to, Preamble
Adverse legal authority, lawyer's duty to disclose, Rule 3.3(a)(2)
Advertising. (*See also* Solicitation, Letterheads, Firm name.)
  class action members, to notify, Rule 7.2 (Comment)
  communications concerning a lawyer's services generally, Rule 7.1
  comparison with services of other lawyers, Rule 7.1 (Comment)
  fields of practice, Rule 7.4
  mail, Rule 7.3
  permitted forms, Rule 7.2
  prior results, Rule 7.1 (Comment)
  specialization, Rule 7.4
Advice to client
  candor, duty of, Rule 2.1
  legal services program, Rule 6.5 (Comment)
  used to engage in criminal or fraudulent conduct, Rule 1.2 (Comment)
  when lawyer not competent in area, Rule 1.1 (Comment)
Advice to unrepresented person, Rule 4.3
Advisor, lawyer as, Preamble, Rule 2.1
Advocate
  in nonadjudicative proceedings, Rule 3.9
  lawyer as, Preamble
Alteration of documents, Rule 3.4(a)
Alternative dispute resolution, Rule 2.4 (Comment)
  duty to inform of, Rule 2.1 (Comment)
Ancillary businesses (or services), Rule 5.7
Appeal
  advising client of possibility, Rule 1.3 (Comment)
  contingent fee, Rule 1.5 (Comment)
  government lawyer's authority, Scope
Appointed counsel
  accepting appointments, Rule 6.2
  discharge by client, Rule 1.16 (Comment)
  endorsement of client's views, Rule 1.2(b)
  obtaining appointments by judges, Rule 7.6
  requirement of competence, Rule 1.1 (Comment)
  withdrawal by, Rule 1.16 (Comment)

Arbitration, fee disputes, Rule 1.5 (Comment)
Arbitrator
- codes of ethics, Rule 1.12 (Comment), Rule 2.4 (Comment)
- conflict of interest, Rule 1.12
- former, negotiating for private employment, Rule 1.12(b)
- lawyer as, Rule 2.4
- partisan in multimember panel, Rule 1.12(d)

Area of practice, sale of, Rule 1.17
Association with competent lawyer, Rule 1.1 (Comment)
Associations, unincorporated, Rule 1.13 (Comment)
Attorney-client privilege
- common representation, Rule 1.7 (Comment)
- dispute resolution, Rule 2.4 (Comment)
- distinguished from confidentiality rule, Rule 1.6 (Comment)

Attorney general, authority of, Scope
Auditors' requests for information, Rule 2.3 (Comment)
Authority of lawyer
- decision-making authority, Rule 1.2(a)
- government lawyer, Scope

Autonomy of legal profession, Preamble

B

Bank charges, Rule 1.15(b)
"Belief," "believes," defined, Rule 1.0(a)
Beneficiary, fiduciary client, lawyer's obligation toward, Rule 1.2 (Comment)
Bias, words or conduct manifesting, Rule 8.4 (Comment)
Board of directors
- lawyer member, Rule 1.7 (Comment)
- organization as client, Rule 1.13

Bodily harm, client's intent to commit serious, Rule 1.6(b)(1)
Breach of trust, offense involving, Rule 8.4 (Comment)
Bribery
- of officials, Rule 3.5(a)
- of witness, Rule 3.4(b)
- remediation, Rule 3.3 (Comment)

Business affairs of lawyer
- adverse to client, Rule 1.8(a)
- conflict of interest, Rule 1.7 (Comment)
- duty to conduct in compliance with law, Preamble
- law-related services, Rule 5.7

C

Campaign contributions, Rule 7.6
Candid advice, Rule 2.1
Candidate for judicial office, Rule 8.2(b)
Candidate for public office, contributions to, Rule 7.6
Candor toward tribunal, Rule 3.3
Cause of action, violation of Rules as basis for, Scope
Certification as specialist, Rule 7.4(d)
Champerty, law of, Rule 1.8 (Comment)
Child client, Rule 1.14
- communication with, Rule 1.4 (Comment)

Child of lawyer
- client of, Rule 1.7 (Comment)
- gift to, Rule 1.8(c)

Choice of law, Rule 8.5(b)
Citizen, lawyer as, Preamble
Civil disobedience, to test validity of statute or regulation, Rule 1.2 (Comment)
Civil liability, violation of Rules as basis for, Scope
Class actions
- conflict of interest, Rule 1.7 (Comment)
- fee determination, Rule 1.5 (Comment)
- notice to members, Rule 7.2 (Comment)

Client-lawyer relationship
- existence of defined by substantive law, Scope
- informed understanding, lawyer's role, Preamble
- law-related services, Rule 5.7(a)(2)

Client protection, fund for
- participation in, Rule 1.15 (Comment)

Client's identity
- duty to disclose, Rule 1.13(d)
- government agency, Rule 1.11 (Comment), Rule 1.13 (Comment)

organizational client, Rule 1.0, (Comment), Rule 1.13 (Comment)
Client's security fund. (*See* Client protection, fund for.)
Clinic, legal, Rule 6.5 (Comment)
Code of Judicial Conduct, Rule 1.12 (Comment), Rule 3.5 (Comment), Rule 8.2(b)
Comments, do not expand lawyer's responsibilities, Scope
Common representation, Rule 1.7 (Comment), Rule 1.9 (Comment)
Communication
  concerning lawyer's services, Rule 7.1
  duty to maintain with client, Preamble, Rule 1.4
  safeguarding confidentiality, Rule 1.6 (Comment)
  with represented party, Rule 4.2
  with third persons, Rule 4.1
  with unrepresented persons, Rule 4.3
  withholding information from client, Rule 1.4 (Comment)
Competence
  duty of, Preamble, Rule 1.16 (Comment)
Competent representation
  requirements of, Rule 1.1
Compliance with Rules, Preamble, Scope
Concealment
  duty to avoid, Rule 1.2 (Comment)
  of documents, Rule 3.3 (Comment), Rule 3.4(a)
Confidences of client
  attachment of duty, Scope
  common representation, Rule 1.7 (Comment)
  consent required to reveal, Rule 1.6(a)
  corporate client, Rule 1.13 (Comment)
  disclosure of, Preamble, Rule 1.6(b)
  disclosure to disciplinary authorities, Rule 8.1(b), Rule 8.3 (Comment)
  disclosure when charged with wrongdoing, Rule 1.6(b)(3)
  duty to preserve, Preamble, Rule 1.6(a)
  evaluation, information used in preparing, Rule 2.3(c)
  former client, Rule 1.9(c)
  government client, Rule 1.11(c)
  imputed to members of firm, Rule 1.0 (Comment)
  lawyer assistance program, Rule 8.3(c)
  maintenance of, serves public interest, Preamble, Rule 1.6 (Comment), Rule 8.3 (Comment)
  perjury by client, Rule 3.3(c)
  prospective client, Rule 1.18(b)
  public interest in preserving, Preamble, Rule 1.6 (Comment)
  with diminished capacity, Rule 1.14(c)
  withdrawal, facts constituting explanation for, Rule 1.16 (Comment)
Confirmed in writing, defined, Rule 1.0(b)
Conflict of laws, Rule 8.5 (Comment)
Conflict of interest
  acquiring interest in litigation, Rule 1.8(i)
  advocate, when acting as, Rule 1.7 (Comment)
  aggregate agreements, Rule 1.8(g)
  ancillary business activity, Rule 5.7
  business interests of lawyer, Rule 1.7 (Comment)
  business transaction with client, Rule 1.8(a)
  consent of client to, Rule 1.7(b)(4), Rule 1.8(a)(3), Rule 1.8(b), Rule 1.8(f)(1), Rule 1.8(g), Rule 1.9(a), Rule 1.9(b), Rule 1.11(a)(2), Rule 1.12(a), Rule 1.18(d)(1)
  co-parties, representation of, Rule 1.7 (Comment)
  current client, concurrent conflict, Rule 1.7
  declining employment because of, Rule 1.7 (Comment)
  estate planning or administration, Rule 1.7 (Comment)
  existing client, interest adverse to client, Rule 1.7(a)(1)
  fee paid by one other than client, Rule 1.7 (Comment), Rule 1.8(f), Rule 5.4(c)
  former client, Rule 1.9
  former judge or other neutral, Rule 1.12
  general rule, Rule 1.7
  government client, Rule 1.11
  imputation, Rule 1.10
  interest of lawyer adverse to client, Rule 1.7(a)(2)
  lawyer as third party neutral, Rule 2.4 (Comment)

legal services corporation, lawyer serves as director of, Rule 6.3
legal services program, Rule 6.5
"matter" defined, Rule 1.11(e)
multiple representation in mediation, Rule 1.7 (Comment)
negotiation, Rule 1.7 (Comment)
prospective client, Rule 1.18(c)
responsibility for firm, Rule 5.1 (Comment)
sexual relations with client, Rule 1.8(j)
third person, interest adverse to client, Rule 1.7(a)(2)
unrelated matters, Rule 1.7 (Comment)
waiver of future, Rule 1.7 (Comment)
withdrawal because of, Rule 1.7 (Comment)
Conflicting responsibilities, Preamble
Conscience, Preamble
Consent by client
communication regarding decisions requiring, Rule 1.4(a)(1)
to common representation, Rule 1.7 (Comment)
to conflict of interest, Rule 1.7(b)(4), Rule 1.8(a)(3), Rule 1.8(b), Rule 1.8(f)(1), Rule 1.8(g), Rule 1.9(a), Rule 1.9(b), Rule 1.11(a)(2), Rule 1.12(a), Rule 1.18(d)(1)
to disclosure of professional misconduct, Rule 8.3 (Comment)
to evaluation for use by third persons, Rule 2.3(b)
to limited representation, Rule 1.2(c), Rule 6.5 (Comment)
to reveal confidences, Rule 1.6(a)
Constitutional law
governing authority of government lawyer, Scope
Consultation
duty, Rule 1.2(a), Rule 1.4(a)(2)
Contingent fee
civil cases, Rule 1.8(i)(2)
costs and expenses advanced by lawyer, Rule 1.8(e)(1)
criminal cases, Rule 1.5(d)(2)
domestic relations cases, Rule 1.5(d)(1)
expert witness, Rule 3.4 (Comment)
prohibited representations, Rule 1.5(d)
requirements of, Rule 1.5(c)
Continuing legal education, Rule 1.1 (Comment)
Corporate legal department, Rule 1.0(c), Rule 1.10 (Comment)
Corporate representation. (*See* Organization, representation of.)
Corporation, communicating with employees and officers of, Rule 4.2 (Comment)
Costs advanced to client, Rule 1.8(e)(1)
Court. (*See also* Tribunal.)
authority over legal profession, Preamble
candor, duty of, Rule 3.3
legal services program, Rule 6.5
offering false evidence to, Rule 3.3(a)(3)
Court order
allowing communication with represented person, Rule 4.2
disclosure of client confidences pursuant to, Rule 1.6(b)(4)
Court rules, relation to Rules, Scope
Creditors of client
claim funds of client, Rule 1.15 (Comment)
Criminal conduct
by lawyer, Rule 8.4(b)
counseling or assisting client to engage in, Rule 1.2(d), Rule 3.3(b), Rule 4.1(b)
withdrawal when client persists in, Rule 1.2 (Comment), Rule 1.6 (Comment), Rule 1.13(c), Rule 1.16(b)(2), Rule 3.3 (Comment), Rule 4.1 (Comment)
Criminal representation
aggregate plea bargain on behalf of multiple defendants, Rule 1.8(g)
codefendants, representation of, Rule 1.7 (Comment)
contingent fee for, Rule 1.5(d)(2)
decision-making authority, Rule 1.2(a)
frivolous defense, Rule 3.1
perjury by client, Rule 3.3(a)(3)
trial publicity, Rule 3.6

D

Deceased lawyer
avoiding neglect of matters of, Rule 1.3 (Comment)

payments to estate of, Rule 5.4(a)(2)
Deceit by lawyer, Rule 8.4(c)
Declining representation
causes, Rule 1.16(a)
conflict of interest, Rule 1.7 (Comment)
refusing to accept appointment, Rule 6.2
when political contributions have been made, Rule 7.6
Decorum of tribunal, Rule 3.5
Delay, Rule 4.4(a)
Delivery of funds or property, Rule 1.15(d)
Deposition
disruption, Rule 3.5 (Comment)
false statement, Rule 3.3 (Comment)
Derivative actions, Rule 1.13 (Comment)
Destruction of potential evidence, Rule 3.3 (Comment), Rule 3.4(a)
Dilatory practices, Rule 3.2 (Comment)
Diligence, Preamble, Rule 1.3
Diminished capacity of client, Rule 1.2 (Comment), Rule 1.4 (Comment), Rule 1.14
discharge of lawyer, Rule 1.16 (Comment)
Diminished capacity of lawyer, Rule 1.16(a)(2)
avoiding neglect of client matters, Rule 1.3 (Comment)
Direct contact with prospective clients, Rule 7.3
Directors of organization, Rule 1.13
Disaffirmation, Rule 1.2 (Comment), Rule 1.6 (Comment), Rule 4.1 (Comment)
Discharge of lawyer, Rule 1.16(a)(3), Rule 1.16 (Comment)
Disciplinary authority, Rule 8.5(a)
Disciplinary proceedings
disclosure of client confidences in connection with, Rule 1.6(b)(3)
failure to comply with requests for information, Rule 8.1(b)
jurisdiction, Rule 8.5
reporting professional misconduct, Rule 8.3
Discipline, violation of Rules as basis for, Scope
Disclosure of
client confidences, Rule 1.6(b)
client's criminal conduct, Rule 3.3(b)
client's diminished capacity, Rule 1.14 (Comment)
client's interests when lawyer participates in law reform activities, Rule 6.4
fee division, Rule 1.5(e)(2)
material fact to avoid assisting client crime or fraud, Rule 4.1(b)
Discovery
obstructive tactics, Rule 3.4(d)
refusing to comply, Rule 3.4(d)
Discretion of lawyer, where Rule cast in "may," Scope
Dishonesty, conduct involving, Rule 8.4(c)
Disruptive conduct, Rule 3.5(d)
Disputes with client
confidentiality exception, Rule 1.6(b)(3)
fees, Rule 1.5 (Comment)
Disqualification. (*See also* Imputed disqualification.)
former judge, Rule 1.12(a)
violation of Rules not necessarily warranting, Scope
waiver by client, Rule 1.9 (Comment), Rule 1.10(d)
Division of fees
requirements of, Rule 1.5(e)
with nonlawyer, Rule 5.4(a)
Documents
alteration of, Rule 3.3 (Comment), Rule 3.4(a)
inadvertent receipt of, Rule 4.4(b)
Domestic relations, contingent fee in, Rule 1.5(d)(1)
Dual representation of organization and constituent, Rule 1.13(e)

E

Economic factors relevant to client's situation, Rule 2.1
Education, legal, Preamble
Embarrassing third persons, Rule 4.4(a)
Emergency, advice in matter, Rule 1.1 (Comment)
Employees of client, Rule 1.13, Rule 3.4(f)(1)
Employees of lawyer
imputation of conflicts, Rule 1.10 (Comment)
responsibilitiy for, Rule 5.3

Employment agreement restricting right to practice, Rule 5.6(a)
Escrow agent, Rule 1.15 (Comment)
Estate planning, conflicts of interest in, Rule 1.7 (Comment)
Evaluation
- confidential information used in preparing, Rule 2.3(c)
- third person, prepared at client's request for, Rule 2.3

Evaluator, lawyer as, Preamble, Rule 2.4 (Comment)
Evidence
- destruction of, Rule 3.4(a)
- methods of obtaining, Rule 4.4(a)
- obstructing access to, Rule 3.4(a)
- offering false, Rule 3.3(a)(3)

Ex parte communications with member of tribunal, Rule 3.5(b)
Ex parte proceedings, Rule 3.3(d)
Executor, lawyer's fee for representation of, Rule 1.5 (Comment)
Expediting litigation, Rule 3.2
Expenses of litigation
- client's right to determine, Rule 1.2 (Comment)
- contingent fee, Rule 1.5(c)
- indigent client, paying on behalf of, Rule 1.8(e)(2)
- lawyer advancing to client, Rule 1.8(e)(1)
- reasonableness, Rule 1.5(a)
- termination of representation, Rule 1.16(d)

Expert witness. (*See* Witness.)
Expertise, competent representation, Rule 1.1 (Comment)

F

Failure to disclose adverse legal authority, Rule 3.3(a)(2)
Fairness to opposing party and counsel, Rule 3.4
False communications concerning lawyer's services, Rule 7.1
False statement to tribunal, Rule 3.3(a)(1)
Falsification of evidence, Rule 3.3 (Comment), Rule 3.4(b)
Family of client with diminished capacity, Rule 1.14 (Comment)
Family of lawyer
- client of lawyer-relative, Rule 1.7 (Comment)
- gift to, Rule 1.8(c)

Fees
- acquiring ownership interest in enterprise as, Rule 1.5 (Comment)
- advance fee payments, Rule 1.5 (Comment)
- advertising of, Rule 7.2 (Comment)
- arbitration of, Rule 1.5 (Comment)
- communication to client, Rule 1.5(b)
- contingent, prohibited representations, Rule 1.5(d)
- contingent, requirements of, Rule 1.5(c)
- determination of, Rule 1.5(a)
- disclosure of confidential information to collect, Rule 1.6(b)(3)
- division with lawyer, Rule 1.5(e)
- division with nonlawyer, Rule 5.4(a)
- division with nonprofit organization, Rule 5.4(a)(4)
- former government lawyer, Rule 1.11(b)(1), Rule 1.11(c)
- paid by someone other than client, Rule 1.7 (Comment), Rule 1.8(f), Rule 5.4(c)
- reasonableness of, Rule 1.5(a)
- termination of representation, Rule 1.16(d)

Fiduciary
- lawyer's obligation toward beneficiary, Rule 1.2 (Comment)
- standard for holding property of others, Rule 1.15 (Comment)

Field of practice, communication of, Rule 7.4
Fifth Amendment in bar admission and disciplinary matters, Rule 8.1 (Comment)
Financial assistance to client, Rule 1.8(c)
Firm. (*See* Law firm.)
Former client. (*See* Conflict of interest.)
Former government lawyer
- "confidential government information" defined, Rule 1.11(c)
- conflict of interest, Rule 1.7 (Comment), Rule 1.11
- "matter" defined, Rule 1.11(e)

Former judge. (*See* Judges.)
"Fraud," defined, Rule 1.0(d)
"Fraudulent," defined, Rule 1.0(d)
Fraudulent conduct

counseling or assisting client to engage in, Rule 1.2(d), Rule 4.1(b)
engaging in, Rule 8.4(c)
remediation, Rule 3.3 (Comment)
withdrawal when client persists in, Rule 1.2 (Comment), Rule 1.6 (Comment), Rule 1.13(c), Rule 1.16(b)(2)
Frivolous claims and defenses, Rule 3.1
Frivolous discovery request, Rule 3.4(d)
Funds of client
handling of, Rule 1.15
lawyer claims interest in, Rule 1.15(e)
responsibility of firm, Rule 5.1 (Comment)

G

Gift to lawyer by client, Rule 1.8(c)
Government agency
appearance before, Rule 3.9
communication with, Rule 4.2 (Comment)
conflict of interest, Rule 1.11
constitutes firm, Rule 1.10 (Comment), Rule 5.1 (Comment)
improper influence on, Rule 8.4(e)
representation of, Rule 1.13 (Comment)
Government lawyer
authority of, Scope
communication with accused by, Rule 4.2 (Comment)
conflict of interest, Rule 1.11(d)
duties of, Rule 1.13 (Comment)
representing multiple clients, Scope
subject to Rules, Rule 1.11 (Comment)
supervisory responsibilities, Rule 5.1 (Comment)
Government legal engagements, Rule 7.6
Guardian of client with diminished capacity
acting adversely to ward, Rule 1.14 (Comment)
appointment of, Rule 1.14(b)

H

Harass, law's procedures used to, Preamble
Harm, client's intent to commit serious bodily, Rule 1.6(b)(1)
Hearing officers. (*See* Adjudicative officers.)
Homicide, client's intent to commit, Rule 1.6(b)(1)
Hotlines, Rule 6.5 (Comment)
Hypotheticals, Rule 1.6 (Comment)

I

Identity of client, conflicts of interest, Rule 1.0 (Comment)
explaining, Rule 1.13(d)
government agency, Rule 1.11 (Comment)
organization, Rule 1.13 (Comment)
Impartiality and decorum of tribunal, Rule 3.5
Imperatives in rules, Scope
Imputed disqualification
firm of former judge or other neutral, Rule 1.12(c)
firm of political contributor, Rule 7.6
former client, Rule 1.9 (Comment)
general rule, Rule 1.10
government lawyers, Rule 1.11(b)
legal services program, Rule 6.5(a)(2), Rule 6.5(b)
prospective client, Rule 1.18(c)
types of conflicts, Rule 1.8(k)
witness, when member of firm serves as, Rule 3.7(b)
Incompetent client
appointment of guardian for, Rule 1.14(b)
representation of, Rule 1.14(a)
Independence of legal profession, Preamble, Rule 5.4
Independent professional judgment, duty to exercise, Rule 2.1, Rule 5.4(c), Rule 5.4(d)(3)
Indigent client
legal representation, Preamble, Rule 1.2 (Comment), Rule 6.1
paying court costs on behalf of, Rule 1.8(e)(2)
Information
used to disadvantage of client, Rule 1.8(b)
withholding from client, Rule 1.4 (Comment)
"Informed consent," defined, Rule 1.0(e)

Injury, client's intent to commit serious bodily, Rule 1.6(b)(1)
Interest, acquisition by lawyer
adverse to client, Rule 1.8(a)
in litigation, Rule 1.8(i)
Intimidation by lawyer, prohibitions on, Preamble, Rule 3.3 (Comment)
Investigation of client's affairs, Rule 2.1 (Comment)

J

Judgment, exercise of, Preamble
Judges
contributions to, Rule 7.6
duty to show respect for, Preamble
ex parte communication with, Rule 3.5(b)
former judge, disqualification, Rule 1.12
improper influence on, Rule 3.3 (Comment), Rule 3.5(a)
lawyers assistance program, confidentiality, Rule 8.3(c)
misconduct by, Rule 8.3(b), Rule 8.4(f)
statements about, Rule 8.2(a)
Jurisdiction, Rule 8.5(a)
Juror
communication with, Rule 3.5(b), Rule 3.5(c)
improper influence on, Rule 3.3 (Comment), Rule 3.5(a)
Jury trial, client's right to waive, Rule 1.2(a)

K

Knowledge
defined, Rule 1.0(f)
factors, Rule 1.1 (Comment)
lawyer's role, Preamble
of client's intent to commit homicide or serious bodily harm, Rule 1.6 (Comment)

L

Law clerk, negotiating for private employment, Rule 1.12(b)
Law firm
defined, Rule 1.0(c), Rule 1.10 (Comment)
disclosure of client information in, Rule 1.6 (Comment)
disqualification, Rule 1.10(a), Rule 1.10(b)
former government lawyer, disqualification, Rule 1.11(b), Rule 1.11(c)
former judge or arbitrator, disqualification, Rule 1.12(c)
legal services program, disqualification, Rule 6.5(b)
name, Rule 7.5(a)
nonlawyer assistants, Rule 1.10 (Comment), Rule 5.3
partner, manager or supervisory lawyer, Rule 5.1
political action committee, Rule 7.6 (Comment)
political contributions by, Rule 7.6
prospective client, disqualification, Rule 1.18(c)
subordinate lawyer, Rule 5.2
Law practice, sale of, Rule 1.17
Law reform activities, affecting clients' interests, Rule 6.4
Law-related services, Rule 5.7
Lawyer as witness, Rule 3.7
Lawyer referral services, costs of, Rule 7.2(b)(2)
Lawyers assistance program, confidentiality, Rule 8.3(c)
Lawyer's fund for client protection, Rule 1.15 (Comment)
Learned profession, lawyer as member of, Preamble
Legal advice, disclosure of client confidences when seeking, Rule 1.6(b)(2)
Legal aid, constitutes law firm, Rule 1.0 (Comment), Rule 1.10 (Comment)
Legal assistants
conflict of interest, Rule 1.10 (Comment)
responsibilities of lawyer, Rule 5.3
Legal education, duty to work to strengthen, Preamble
Legal representative of client with diminished capacity, Rule 1.14 (Comment)
Legal services organization
constitutes law firm, Rule 1.0 (Comment), Rule 1.10 (Comment), Rule 5.1 (Comment)

limited legal services, Rule 6.5 (Comment)
membership in, Rule 6.3
Legal service plan
cost of, Rule 7.2(b)(2)
participation in, Rule 7.3(d)
Legislature, appearance before on behalf of client, Rule 3.9
Letterheads
false or misleading, Rule 7.5(a)
jurisdictional limitations of firm's members, Rule 7.5(b)
public officials, Rule 7.5(c)
Liability to client, agreements limiting, Rule 1.8(h)
Licensure statutes, relation to Rules, Scope
Lien to secure fees and expenses, Rule 1.8(i)(1)
Limited legal services, Rule 6.5
Literary rights concerning representation, Rule 1.8(d)
Litigation
acquiring interest in, Rule 1.8(i)
conflict of interest, Rule 1.7(b)(3)
expedite, duty to, Rule 3.2
information, Rule 1.4 (Comment)
Loyalty to client, Rule 1.7 (Comment)

M

Mail contact with prospective clients, Rule 7.3
Maintenance, law of, Rule 1.8 (Comment)
Malpractice, limiting liability to client for, Rule 1.8(h)
Mandatory withdrawal, Rule 1.16(a)
Matter, substantially related, Rule 1.9 (Comment), Rule 1.11(e)
Media rights concerning representation, Rule 1.8(d)
Mediation of fee disputes, Rule 1.5 (Comment)
Mediator
codes of ethics, Rule 1.12 (Comment), Rule 2.4 (Comment)
disqualification of former, Rule 1.12
lawyer as, Rule 2.4
Mental impairment of client, Rule 1.14(a)
client decisions, Rule 1.2 (Comment)
communication with client, Rule 1.4 (Comment)
Mental impairment of lawyer, Rule 1.16(a)(2)
avoiding neglect of client matters, Rule 1.3 (Comment)
Meritorious claims and contentions, Rule 3.1
Military lawyers
duties of, Rule 1.13 (Comment)
representation of adverse interests, Rule 1.9 (Comment)
Minor client, Rule 1.14 (Comment)
Misconduct
forms of, Rule 8.4
reporting, Rule 8.3
Misrepresentation
advertisements, Rule 7.1
bar admission and disciplinary matters, Rule 8.1
firm names and letterhead, Rule 7.5
misconduct, Rule 8.4(c)
negligent, Rule 1.0(d)
to court, Rule 3.3
to third person, Rule 4.1(a)
Moral factors relevant to client's situation, Rule 2.1
Moral turpitude offenses, Rule 8.4 (Comment)
Multiple representation. (*See* Common representation.)
Multistate law practice, Rule 8.5

N

Negotiation
conflicting interests, representation of, Rule 1.7 (Comment)
statements made during, Rule 4.1 (Comment)
Negotiator, lawyer as, Preamble
Nonadjudicative proceedings, Rule 3.9
Nonlawyer assistants
conflict of interest, Rule 1.10 (Comment)
responsibilities of lawyer, Rule 5.3
Nonlawyers
division of fees with, Rule 5.4(a)
partnership, Rule 5.4(b)
professional corporation, Rule 5.4(d)
Nonlegal services, provision of, Rule 5.7
Nonprofit legal services program, Rule 6.5

Nonprofit organization, division of fees with, Rule 5.4(a)(4)
Notice of receipt of funds or other property, Rule 1.15(d)

O

Objectives of the representation, client's right to determine, Rule 1.2(a)
Obstruction of party's access to evidence, Rule 3.3 (Comment), Rule 3.4(a)
Officer of legal system, Preamble
Opinions
  evaluation for use by third persons, Rule 2.3
  limit on malpractice liability, Rule 1.8 (Comment)
Opposing party
  communication with represented party, Rule 4.2
  communication with unrepresented party, Rule 4.3
  duty of fairness to, Rule 3.4
Optional withdrawal, Rule 1.16(b)
Organization, representation of
  board of directors, lawyer on, Rule 1.7 (Comment)
  communication with, Rule 1.4 (Comment)
  communication with constituents of, Rule 4.2 (Comment)
  conflict of interest, Rule 1.7 (Comment)
  constituents, representing, Rule 1.13(e)
  identity of client, Rule 1.13(a), Rule 1.13(d)
  intended conduct, Rule 1.6 (Comment)
  law department of, Rule 1.0 (Comment), Rule 1.10 (Comment), Rule 5.1 (Comment)
  misconduct, client engaged in, Rule 1.13(b)
  officers of, Rule 1.13

P

Papers, retention of, Rule 1.16(d)
Parent of lawyer
  client of, Rule 1.7 (Comment)
  gift to, Rule 1.8(c)
Partner
  defined, Rule 1.0(g)
  nonlawyer, Rule 5.4(b)
  supervision of lawyers, Rule 5.1
  supervision of nonlawyers, Rule 5.3
Partnership
  agreement restricting right to practice, Rule 5.6(a)
  name, Rule 7.5(d)
Patent practice, advertising, Rule 7.4(b)
Pay-to-play, Rule 7.6
Peer approval, Preamble
Peer review agency, reporting misconduct to, Rule 8.3 (Comment)
Perjury
  criminal defendant, Rule 3.3 (Comment)
  disclosure of, Rule 3.3(a)(3)
Permissive rules, Scope
Personal affairs of lawyer, duty to conduct in compliance with law, Preamble
Physical condition of lawyer, Rule 1.16(a)(2)
Plea bargain, client's right to accept or reject, Rule 1.2(a)
Pleadings, verification of, Rule 3.3 (Comment)
Political contributions by lawyers to public officials' campaigns, Rule 7.6
Political factors relevant to client's situation, Rule 2.1
Practice area, sale of, Rule 1.17
Preamble, role of, Scope
Precedent, failure to disclose to court, Rule 3.3(a)(2)
Prejudice, words or conduct manifesting, Rule 8.4 (Comment)
Prepaid legal services, advertising for, Rule 7.2 (Comment), Rule 7.3(d)
Pro bono publico service, Rule 6.1
Procedural law, lawyer's professional responsibilities prescribed by, Preamble, Scope
Procedural use of Rules, Scope
Procrastination, Rule 1.3 (Comment)
Professional corporation
  defined as firm, Rule 1.0(c)
  formation of, Rule 5.4(d)
  shareholders' responsibilities, Rule 5.1 (Comment)

Professional role, Scope
Promptness, Preamble
Property of client
payment for services, Rule 1.5 (Comment)
prospective client, Rule 1.18 (Comment)
return upon termination of representation, Rule 1.16(d)
safekeeping, Rule 1.15
Prosecutor
communication with accused, Rule 4.2 (Comment)
representing former defendant, Rule 1.9 (Comment)
special responsibilities of, Rule 3.8
subpoena to lawyer, Rule 3.8(e)
trial publicity, Rule 3.6, Rule 3.8(f)
Prospective client, Rule 1.18
Protective order, Rule 1.6 (Comment)
Psychiatrist, withholding diagnosis, Rule 1.4 (Comment)
Public interest in preserving client confidences, Preamble, Rule 1.6 (Comment)
Public citizen, lawyer's duty as, Preamble
Public interest legal services. (*See* Pro bono publico service.)
Public office
abuse of, Rule 8.4 (Comment)
negotiating private employment while holding, Rule 1.11(d)(2)(ii)
Public officials
firm's use of name, Rule 7.5(d)
improper influence, Rule 8.4(e)
lawyers' contributions to election campaigns of, Rule 7.6
respect for, Preamble
Public service, Preamble
Publicity, trial, Rule 3.6(g)
special responsibilities of prosecutor, Rule 3.8(f)
Purchase of a law practice, Rule 1.17

Q

Quality of service, improvement, Preamble

R

"Reasonable," defined, Rule 1.0(h)
Recordkeeping, property of client, Rule 1.15(a)
Referral
to other professionals, Rule 2.1 (Comment)
when lawyer not competent to handle matter, Rule 1.1 (Comment)
Referral services, costs of, Rule 7.2(b)(2)
Referees. (*See* Adjudicative officers.)
Reform of the law, Preamble, Rule 6.4
Regulation, validity or interpretation, Rule 1.2 (Comment)
Regulation of legal profession, self-governance, Preamble
Remedial measures when false evidence offered, Rule 3.3(a)(3)
Reporting misconduct, Rule 8.3
Representation of client
decision-making authority of lawyer and client, Rule 1.2(a)
declining or terminating, Rule 1.2 (Comment), Rule 1.16
scope, lawyer's right to limit, Rule 1.2(c)
Representative of client, lawyer as, Preamble, Rule 2.4 (Comment)
Representative, legal, of client with diminished capacity, Rule 1.14 (Comment)
Represented party, communication with, Rule 4.2
Responsibility for observing Rules, Preamble
Restrictions on right to practice
partnership or employment agreement, Rule 5.6(a)
settlement agreement, Rule 5.6(b)
Rule of reason, Scope

S

Safekeeping of property, Rule 1.15
Sale of law practice, Rule 1.17
Sanction, severity of, Scope
Scope of representation, Rule 1.1 (Comment), Rule 1.2
"Screened," defined, Rule 1.0(k)
Screening
disqualified former government lawyer, Rule 1.11(b)(1)
disqualified former judge or other neutral, Rule 1.12(c)
nonlawyer assistants, Rule 1.10 (Comment)
prospective client, Rule 1.18(d)(2)

Securities, safekeeping, Rule 1.15 (Comment)
Self-regulation, Preamble
Settlement
- aggregate, Rule 1.8(g)
- client's right to refuse, Rule 1.2(a)
- contingent fee, Rule 1.5(c)
- government lawyer's authority, Scope
- informing client of settlement offers, Rule 1.4 (Comment)
- restricting right to practice, Rule 5.6(b)

Sexual relations with client, Rule 1.8(i)
Shareholders of organization, Rule 1.13
Sibling of lawyer
- client of, Rule 1.7 (Comment)
- gift to, Rule 1.8(c)

"Signed," defined, Rule 1.0(n)
Solicitation, prohibition on, Rule 7.3
Special masters. (*See* Adjudicative officers.)
Specialization, communication of, Rule 7.4(d)
Spouse of lawyer
- client of, Rule 1.7 (Comment)
- gift to, Rule 1.8(c)

State's attorney, authority of, Scope
Statute of limitations, Rule 1.3 (Comment)
Statutes
- conflict of interest, agency consent to, Rule 1.11 (Comment)
- shape lawyer's role, Scope
- validity or interpretation, Rule 1.2 (Comment)

Subordinate lawyer, responsibilities of, Rule 5.2
Subpoena to lawyer, by prosecutor, Rule 3.8(e)
Substantive law
- defines existence of client-lawyer relationship, Scope
- lawyer's professional responsibilities prescribed by, Preamble
- relation to Rules, Scope

Supervision
- of lawyer, Rule 5.1
- of nonlawyer, Rule 5.3

T

Taxation, escaping liability, Rule 1.2 (Comment)
Termination of representation, Rule 1.2 (Comment), Rule 1.16
- records of funds and other property, Rule 1.15(a)

Testamentary gifts, Rule 1.8(c)
Testimony of client in criminal trial
- false, Rule 3.3(a)(3)
- right to decide to give, Rule 1.2(a)

Testimony of lawyer. (*See* Lawyer as witness.)
Third-party neutral, Preamble, Rule 1.12, Rule 2.4
Third persons
- evaluation for use by, Rule 2.3
- respect for rights of, Rule 4.4
- statements to, Rule 4.1

Trade names, Rule 7.5(a)
Transactions with persons other than client. (*See* Third persons.)
Trial conduct
- allusion to irrelevant or inadmissible evidence, Rule 3.4(e)
- disruptive conduct, Rule 3.5(d)

Trial publicity, Rule 3.6
- special responsibilities of prosecutor, Rule 3.8(f)

Tribunal
- continued representation ordered by, Rule 1.16(c)
- defined, Rule 1.0(m)
- disobeying obligation of, Rule 3.4(c)
- impartiality and decorum of, Rule 3.5

Trust accounts, Rule 1.15
- responsibility for firm, Rule 5.1 (Comment)

Truthfulness in statements to third persons, Rule 4.1

U

Unauthorized practice of law
- assisting in, Rule 5.5(b)
- engaging in, Rule 5.5(a)

Unrepresented person
- dealing with, Rule 4.3
- in alternative dispute resolution, Rule 2.4(b)

Unincorporated associations, Rule 1.13 (Comment)

V

Violation of Rules of Professional Conduct. (*See also* Misconduct.)
- declining or terminating representation, Rule 1.16(a)(1)

Violence, Rule 8.4 (Comment)

W

Waiver
future conflict of interest, Rule 1.7 (Comment)
prosecutor obtaining from criminal defendant, Rule 3.8(c)
Withdrawal, Rule 1.16
conflict of interest, Rule 1.7 (Comment)
discharge, Rule 1.16(a)(3)
incapacity, Rule 1.16(a)(2)
mandatory, Rule 1.16(a)
method of, Rule 1.3 (Comment)
notice of, Rule 1.6 (Comment)
optional, Rule 1.16(b)
property of client, Rule 1.16(d)
when client persists in criminal or fraudulent conduct, Rule 1.2 (Comment), Rule 1.6 (Comment), Rule 1.13(c), Rule 1.16(b)(2), Rule 3.3 (Comment), Rule 4.1 (Comment)
Withholding information from client, Rule 1.4 (Comment)
Witness
bribing, Rule 3.3 (Comment), Rule 3.4(b)
client's right to decide whether to testify, Rule 1.2(a)
expenses, payment of, Rule 3.4 (Comment)
expert, payment of, Rule 3.4 (Comment)
lawyer as, Rule 1.6 (Comment), Rule 3.7
Workload management, Rule 1.3 (Comment)
Work product privilege, confidentiality rule, Rule 1.6 (Comment)
"Writing," defined, Rule 1.0(n)

Z

Zealous representation
opposing party well represented, Preamble
requirement of, Rule 1.3 (Comment)

Restatement of the Law Governing Lawyers*

Editors' Introduction. The Restatement of the Law Governing Lawyers is published by the American Law Institute ("the ALI"), an organization established in 1923 "to promote the clarification and simplification of the law and its better adaptation to social needs." The ALI drafts restatements of the law in many fields (e.g., contracts, agency, and torts).

In 1986, realizing that the regulation of lawyers had become a specialized and highly developed field of law, the ALI began organizing the massive project of drafting a restatement of the law governing lawyers. The ALI appointed Professor Charles Wolfram as the Reporter, and named Professors John Leubsdorf, Thomas Morgan, and Linda Mullenix as Assistant Reporters. From 1988 through 1997, the ALI annually published paperback drafts of various sections of the Restatement, together with an extensive Comment, Illustrations, and a Reporter's Note regarding each section. (We began publishing draft Restatement sections in our 1992 edition.)

In 1998, the full membership of the ALI approved the entire draft and sent it on to the Reporters to make final changes (in consultation with the various groups within the ALI) to reflect amendments and discussions over the years. In the fall of 2000, the final version of the Restatement of the Law Governing Lawyers was published. With all of the Comments, Illustrations, and Reporter's Notes, it runs over 1,000 pages. The book can be ordered in softcover or hardcover from the ALI's web site at www.ali.org (click on "Publications Catalog").

In our Related Materials following each ABA Model Rule of Professional Conduct, we cross-reference the Restatement sections most relevant to the rule at hand. However, some ABA Model Rules have no counterpart in the Restatement, and some Restatement sections have no counterpart in the ABA Model Rules.

We reprint below all of the black letter sections from the full Restatement of the Law Governing Lawyers, without any of the Comments, Illustrations, or Reporter's Notes. Our version of the Restatement is based on the final version of the Restatement as published in late summer of 2000. At the end of the Restatement, we include two tables we have compiled to show the Restatement sections that correspond to each ABA Model Rule of Professional Conduct and the converse.

Contents

CHAPTER 1 REGULATION OF THE LEGAL PROFESSION

TOPIC 1. REGULATION OF LAWYERS — IN GENERAL

§1. Regulation of Lawyers — In General

TOPIC 2. PROCESS OF PROFESSIONAL REGULATION

Title A. Admission to Practice Law

§2. Admission to Practice Law

Title B. Authorized and Unauthorized Practice

§3. Jurisdictional Scope of the Practice of Law by a Lawyer

§4. Unauthorized Practice by a Nonlawyer

Title C. Professional Discipline

§5. Professional Discipline

TOPIC 3. CIVIL JUDICIAL REMEDIES IN GENERAL

§6. Judicial Remedies Available to a Client or Nonclient for Lawyer Wrongs

§7. Judicial Remedies Available to a Lawyer for Client Wrongs

TOPIC 4. LAWYER CRIMINAL OFFENSES

§8. Lawyer Criminal Offenses

TOPIC 5. LAW-FIRM STRUCTURE AND OPERATION

Title A. Association of Lawyers in Law Organizations

§9. Law-Practice Organizations — In General

Title B. Limitation on Nonlawyer Involvement in a Law Firm

§10. Limitations on Nonlawyer Involvement in a Law Firm

Title C. Supervision of Lawyers and Nonlawyers Within an Organization

§11. A Lawyer's Duty of Supervision

§12. Duty of a Lawyer Subject to Supervision

Title D. Restrictions on the Right to Practice Law

§13. Restrictions on the Right to Practice Law

CHAPTER 2 THE CLIENT-LAWYER RELATIONSHIP

TOPIC 1. CREATING A CLIENT-LAWYER RELATIONSHIP

§14. Formation of a Client-Lawyer Relationship

§15. A Lawyer's Duties to a Prospective Client

TOPIC 2. SUMMARY OF THE DUTIES UNDER A CLIENT-LAWYER RELATIONSHIP

§16. A Lawyer's Duties to a Client — In General
§17. A Client's Duties to a Lawyer
§18. Client-Lawyer Contracts
§19. Agreements Limiting Client or Lawyer Duties

TOPIC 3. AUTHORITY TO MAKE DECISIONS

§20. A Lawyer's Duty to Inform and Consult with a Client
§21. Allocating the Authority to Decide Between a Client and a Lawyer
§22. Authority Reserved to a Client
§23. Authority Reserved to a Lawyer
§24. A Client with Diminished Capacity

TOPIC 4. A LAWYER'S AUTHORITY TO ACT FOR A CLIENT

§25. Appearance Before a Tribunal
§26. A Lawyer's Actual Authority
§27. A Lawyer's Apparent Authority
§28. A Lawyer's Knowledge; Notification to a Lawyer; and Statements of a Lawyer
§29. A Lawyer's Act or Advice as Mitigating or Avoiding a Client's Responsibility
§30. A Lawyer's Liability to a Third Person for Conduct on Behalf of a Client

TOPIC 5. ENDING A CLIENT-LAWYER RELATIONSHIP

§31. Termination of a Lawyer's Authority
§32. Discharge by a Client and Withdrawal by a Lawyer
§33. A Lawyer's Duties When a Representation Terminates

CHAPTER 3 CLIENT AND LAWYER: THE FINANCIAL AND PROPERTY RELATIONSHIP

TOPIC 1. LEGAL CONTROLS ON ATTORNEY FEES

§34. Reasonable and Lawful Fees
§35. Contingent-Fee Arrangements
§36. Forbidden Client-Lawyer Financial Arrangements
§37. Partial or Complete Forfeiture of a Lawyer's Compensation

TOPIC 2. A LAWYER'S CLAIM TO COMPENSATION

§38. Client-Lawyer Fee Contracts
§39. A Lawyer's Fee in the Absence of a Contract
§40. Fees on Termination

TOPIC 3. FEE-COLLECTION PROCEDURES

§41. Fee-Collection Methods
§42. Remedies and the Burden of Persuasion
§43. Lawyer Liens

TOPIC 4. PROPERTY AND DOCUMENTS OF CLIENTS AND OTHERS

§44. Safeguarding and Segregating Property
§45. Surrendering Possession of Property
§46. Documents Relating to a Representation

TOPIC 5. FEE-SPLITTING WITH A LAWYER NOT IN THE SAME FIRM

§47. Fee-Splitting Between Lawyers Not in the Same Firm

CHAPTER 4 LAWYER CIVIL LIABILITY

TOPIC 1. LIABILITY FOR PROFESSIONAL NEGLIGENCE AND BREACH OF FIDUCIARY DUTY

§48. Professional Negligence — Elements and Defenses Generally
§49. Breach of Fiduciary Duty — Generally
§50. Duty of Care to a Client
§51. Duty of Care to Certain Nonclients
§52. The Standard of Care
§53. Causation and Damages
§54. Defenses; Prospective Liability Waiver; Settlement with a Client

TOPIC 2. OTHER CIVIL LIABILITY

§55. Civil Remedies of a Client Other Than for Malpractice
§56. Liability to a Client or Nonclient Under General Law
§57. Nonclient Claims — Certain Defenses and Exceptions to Liability

TOPIC 3. VICARIOUS LIABILITY

§58. Vicarious Liability

CHAPTER 5 CONFIDENTIAL CLIENT INFORMATION

TOPIC 1. CONFIDENTIALITY RESPONSIBILITIES OF LAWYERS

Title A. A Lawyer's Confidentiality Duties
§59. Definition of "Confidential Client Information"
§60. A Lawyer's Duty to Safeguard Confidential Client Information

Title B. Using or Disclosing Confidential Client Information
§61. Using or Disclosing Information to Advance Client Interests
§62. Using or Disclosing Information with Client Consent
§63. Using or Disclosing Information When Required by Law
§64. Using or Disclosing Information in a Lawyer's Self-Defense
§65. Using or Disclosing Information in a Compensation Dispute
§66. Using or Disclosing Information to Prevent Death or Serious Bodily Harm
§67. Using or Disclosing Information to Prevent, Rectify, or Mitigate Substantial Financial Loss

TOPIC 2. THE ATTORNEY-CLIENT PRIVILEGE

Title A. The Scope of the Privilege
§68. Attorney-Client Privilege
§69. Attorney-Client Privilege — "Communication"
§70. Attorney-Client Privilege — "Privileged Persons"
§71. Attorney-Client Privilege — "In Confidence"
§72. Attorney-Client Privilege — Legal Assistance as the Object of a Privileged Communication

Title B. The Attorney-Client Privilege for Organizational and Multiple Clients
§73. The Privilege for an Organizational Client
§74. The Privilege for a Governmental Client
§75. The Privilege of Co-Clients
§76. The Privilege in Common-Interest Arrangements

Title C. Duration of the Attorney-Client Privilege; Waivers and Exceptions
§77. Duration of a Privilege
§78. Agreement, Disclaimer, or Failure to Object
§79. Subsequent Disclosure
§80. Putting Assistance or a Communication in Issue
§81. A Dispute Concerning a Decedent's Disposition of Property
§82. Client Crime or Fraud
§83. Lawyer Self-Protection
§84. Fiduciary-Lawyer Communications
§85. Communications Involving a Fiduciary Within an Organization

Title D. Invoking the Privilege and Its Exceptions
§86. Invoking the Privilege and Its Exceptions

TOPIC 3. THE LAWYER WORK-PRODUCT IMMUNITY

Title A. The Scope of the Lawyer Work-Product Immunity
§87. Lawyer Work-Product Immunity
§88. Ordinary Work Product
§89. Opinion Work Product

Title B. Procedural Administration of the Lawyer Work-Product Immunity
§90. Invoking the Lawyer Work-Product Immunity and Its Exceptions

Title C. Waivers and Exceptions to the Work-Product Immunity
§91. Voluntary Acts
§92. Use of Lawyer Work Product in Litigation
§93. Client Crime or Fraud

CHAPTER 6 REPRESENTING CLIENTS — IN GENERAL

TOPIC 1. LAWYER FUNCTIONS IN REPRESENTING CLIENTS — IN GENERAL
§94. Advising and Assisting a Client — In General
§95. An Evaluation Undertaken for a Third Person

TOPIC 2. REPRESENTING ORGANIZATIONAL CLIENTS
§96. Representing an Organization as Client
§97. Representing a Governmental Client

TOPIC 3. LAWYER DEALINGS WITH A NONCLIENT

Title A. Dealings with a Nonclient — Generally
§98. Statements to a Nonclient

Title B. Contact with a Represented Nonclient
§ 99. A Represented Nonclient — The General Anti-Contact Rule
§100. Definition of a Represented Nonclient
§101. A Represented Governmental Agency or Officer
§102. Information of a Nonclient Known to be Legally Protected

Title C. Dealings with an Unrepresented Nonclient
§103. Dealings with an Unrepresented Nonclient

TOPIC 4. LEGISLATIVE AND ADMINISTRATIVE MATTERS
§104. Representing a Client in Legislative and Administrative Matters

CHAPTER 7 REPRESENTING CLIENTS IN LITIGATION

TOPIC 1. ADVOCACY IN GENERAL
§105. Complying with Law and Tribunal Rulings
§106. Dealing with Other Participants in Proceedings
§107. Prohibited Forensic Tactics
§108. An Advocate as a Witness
§109. An Advocate's Public Comment on Pending Litigation

TOPIC 2. LIMITS ON ADVOCACY
§110. Frivolous Advocacy
§111. Disclosure of Legal Authority
§112. Advocacy in Ex Parte and Other Proceedings

TOPIC 3. ADVOCATES AND TRIBUNALS
§113. Improperly Influencing a Judicial Officer
§114. A Lawyer's Statements Concerning a Judicial Officer
§115. Lawyer Contact with a Juror

TOPIC 4. ADVOCATES AND EVIDENCE
§116. Interviewing and Preparing a Prospective Witness
§117. Compensating a Witness
§118. Falsifying or Destroying Evidence
§119. Physical Evidence of a Client Crime
§120. False Testimony or Evidence

CHAPTER 8 CONFLICTS OF INTEREST

TOPIC 1. CONFLICTS OF INTEREST — IN GENERAL
§121. The Basic Prohibition of Conflicts of Interest
§122. Client Consent to a Conflict of Interest
§123. Imputation of a Conflict of Interest to an Affiliated Lawyer
§124. Removing Imputation

TOPIC 2. CONFLICTS OF INTEREST BETWEEN A LAWYER AND A CLIENT
§125. A Lawyer's Personal Interest Affecting the Representation of a Client
§126. Business Transactions Between a Lawyer and a Client
§127. A Client Gift to a Lawyer

TOPIC 3. CONFLICTS OF INTEREST AMONG CURRENT CLIENTS
§128. Representing Clients with Conflicting Interests in Civil Litigation
§129. Conflicts of Interest in Criminal Litigation
§130. Multiple Representation in a Nonlitigated Matter
§131. Conflicts of Interest in Representing an Organization

TOPIC 4. CONFLICTS OF INTEREST WITH A FORMER CLIENT
§132. A Representation Adverse to the Interests of a Former Client
§133. A Former Government Lawyer or Officer

TOPIC 5. CONFLICTS OF INTEREST DUE TO A LAWYER'S OBLIGATION TO A THIRD PERSON
§134. Compensation or Direction of a Lawyer by a Third Person
§135. A Lawyer with a Fiduciary or Other Legal Obligation to a Nonclient

CHAPTER 1 REGULATION OF THE LEGAL PROFESSION

TOPIC 1. REGULATION OF LAWYERS — IN GENERAL

§1. Regulation of Lawyers — In General

Upon admission to the bar of any jurisdiction, a person becomes a lawyer and is subject to applicable law governing such matters as professional discipline, procedure and evidence, civil remedies, and criminal sanctions.

TOPIC 2. PROCESS OF PROFESSIONAL REGULATION

Title A. Admission to Practice Law

§2. Admission to Practice Law

In order to become a lawyer and qualify to practice law in a jurisdiction of admission, a prospective lawyer must comply with requirements of the jurisdiction relating to such matters as education, other demonstration of competence such as success in a bar examination, and character.

Title B. Authorized and Unauthorized Practice

§3. Jurisdictional Scope of the Practice of Law by a Lawyer

A lawyer currently admitted to practice in a jurisdiction may provide legal services to a client:

(1) at any place within the admitting jurisdiction;

(2) before a tribunal or administrative agency of another jurisdiction or the federal government in compliance with requirements for temporary or regular admission to practice before that tribunal or agency; and

(3) at a place within a jurisdiction in which the lawyer is not admitted to the extent that the lawyer's activities arise out of or are otherwise reasonably related to the lawyer's practice under Subsection (1) or (2).

§4. Unauthorized Practice by a Nonlawyer

A person not admitted to practice as a lawyer (see §2) may not engage in the unauthorized practice of law, and a lawyer may not assist a person to do so.

Title C. Professional Discipline

§5. Professional Discipline

(1) A lawyer is subject to professional discipline for violating any provision of an applicable lawyer code.

(2) A lawyer is also subject to professional discipline under Subsection (1) for attempting to commit a violation, knowingly assisting or inducing another to do so, or knowingly doing so through the acts of another.

(3) A lawyer who knows of another lawyer's violation of applicable rules of professional conduct raising a substantial question of the lawyer's honesty or trustworthiness or the lawyer's fitness as a lawyer in some other respect must report that information to appropriate disciplinary authorities.

TOPIC 3. CIVIL JUDICIAL REMEDIES IN GENERAL

§6. Judicial Remedies Available to a Client or Nonclient for Lawyer Wrongs

For a lawyer's breach of a duty owed to the lawyer's client or to a nonclient, judicial remedies may be available through judgment or or-

der entered in accordance with the standards applicable to the remedy awarded, including standards concerning limitation of remedies. Judicial remedies include the following:

(1) awarding a sum of money as damages;

(2) providing injunctive relief, including requiring specific performance of a contract or enjoining its nonperformance;

(3) requiring restoration of a specific thing or awarding a sum of money to prevent unjust enrichment;

(4) ordering cancellation or reformation of a contract, deed, or similar instrument;

(5) declaring the rights of the parties, such as determining that an obligation claimed by the lawyer to be owed to the lawyer is not enforceable;

(6) punishing the lawyer for contempt;

(7) enforcing an arbitration award;

(8) disqualifying a lawyer from a representation;

(9) forfeiting a lawyer's fee (see §37);

(10) denying the admission of evidence wrongfully obtained;

(11) dismissing the claim or defense of a litigant represented by the lawyer;

(12) granting a new trial; and

(13) entering a procedural or other sanction.

§7. Judicial Remedies Available to a Lawyer for Client Wrongs

A lawyer may obtain a remedy based on a present or former client's breach of a duty to the lawyer if the remedy:

(1) is appropriate under applicable law governing the remedy; and

(2) does not put the lawyer in a position prohibited by an applicable lawyer code.

TOPIC 4. LAWYER CRIMINAL OFFENSES

§8. Lawyer Criminal Offenses

The traditional and appropriate activities of a lawyer in representing a client in accordance with the requirements of the applicable lawyer code are relevant factors for the tribunal in assessing the propriety of the lawyer's conduct under the criminal law. In other respects, a lawyer is guilty of an offense for an act committed in the course of representing a client to the same extent and on the same basis as would a nonlawyer acting similarly.

TOPIC 5. LAW-FIRM STRUCTURE AND OPERATION

Title A. Association of Lawyers in Law Organizations

§9. Law-Practice Organizations — In General

(1) A lawyer may practice as a solo practitioner, as an employee of another lawyer or law firm, or as a member of a law firm constituted as a partnership, professional corporation, or similar entity.

(2) A lawyer employed by an entity described in Subsection (1) is subject to applicable law governing the creation, operation, management, and dissolution of the entity.

(3) Absent an agreement with the firm providing a more permissive rule, a lawyer leaving a law firm may solicit firm clients:

(a) prior to leaving the firm:

(i) only with respect to firm clients on whose matters the lawyer is actively and substantially working; and

(ii) only after the lawyer has adequately and timely informed the firm of the lawyer's intent to contact firm clients for that purpose; and

(b) after ceasing employment in the firm, to the same extent as any other nonfirm lawyer.

Title B. Limitation on Nonlawyer Involvement in a Law Firm

§10. Limitations on Nonlawyer Involvement in a Law Firm

(1) A nonlawyer may not own any interest in a law firm, and a nonlawyer may not be empowered to or actually direct or control the professional activities of a lawyer in the firm.

(2) A lawyer may not form a partnership or other business enterprise with a nonlawyer if any of the activities of the enterprise consist of the practice of law.

(3) A lawyer or law firm may not share legal fees with a person not admitted to practice as a lawyer, except that:

(a) an agreement by a lawyer with the lawyer's firm or another lawyer in the firm may provide for payment, over a reasonable period of time after the lawyer's death, to the lawyer's estate or to one or more specified persons;

(b) a lawyer who undertakes to complete unfinished legal business of a deceased lawyer may pay to the estate of the deceased lawyer

a portion of the total compensation that fairly represents services rendered by the deceased lawyer; and

(c) a lawyer or law firm may include nonlawyer employees in a compensation or retirement plan, even though the plan is based in whole or in part on a profit-sharing arrangement.

Title C. Supervision of Lawyers and Nonlawyers Within an Organization

§11. A Lawyer's Duty of Supervision

(1) A lawyer who is a partner in a law-firm partnership or a principal in a law firm organized as a corporation or similar entity is subject to professional discipline for failing to make reasonable efforts to ensure that the firm has in effect measures giving reasonable assurance that all lawyers in the firm conform to applicable lawyer-code requirements.

(2) A lawyer who has direct supervisory authority over another lawyer is subject to professional discipline for failing to make reasonable efforts to ensure that the other lawyer conforms to applicable lawyer-code requirements.

(3) A lawyer is subject to professional discipline for another lawyer's violation of the rules of professional conduct if:

(a) the lawyer orders or, with knowledge of the specific conduct, ratifies the conduct involved; or

(b) the lawyer is a partner or principal in the law firm, or has direct supervisory authority over the other lawyer, and knows of the conduct at a time when its consequences can be avoided or mitigated but fails to take reasonable remedial measures.

(4) With respect to a nonlawyer employee of a law firm, the lawyer is subject to professional discipline if either:

(a) the lawyer fails to make reasonable efforts to ensure:

(i) that the firm in which the lawyer practices has in effect measures giving reasonable assurance that the nonlawyer's conduct is compatible with the professional obligations of the lawyer; and

(ii) that conduct of a nonlawyer over whom the lawyer has direct supervisory authority is compatible with the professional obligations of the lawyer; or

(b) the nonlawyer's conduct would be a violation of the applicable lawyer code if engaged in by a lawyer, and

(i) the lawyer orders or, with knowledge of the specific conduct, ratifies the conduct; or

(ii) the lawyer is a partner or principal in the law firm, or has direct supervisory authority over the nonlawyer, and knows of the conduct at a time when its consequences can be avoided or mitigated but fails to take reasonable remedial measures.

§12. Duty of a Lawyer Subject to Supervision

(1) For purposes of professional discipline, a lawyer must conform to the requirements of an applicable lawyer code even if the lawyer acted at the direction of another lawyer or other person.

(2) For purposes of professional discipline, a lawyer under the direct supervisory authority of another lawyer does not violate an applicable lawyer code by acting in accordance with the supervisory lawyer's direction based on a reasonable resolution of an arguable question of professional duty.

Title D. Restrictions on the Right to Practice Law

§13. Restrictions on the Right to Practice Law

(1) A lawyer may not offer or enter into a law-firm agreement that restricts the right of the lawyer to practice law after terminating the relationship, except for a restriction incident to the lawyer's retirement from the practice of law.

(2) In settling a client claim, a lawyer may not offer or enter into an agreement that restricts the right of the lawyer to practice law, including the right to represent or take particular action on behalf of other clients.

CHAPTER 2 THE CLIENT-LAWYER RELATIONSHIP

TOPIC 1. CREATING A CLIENT-LAWYER RELATIONSHIP

§14. Formation of a Client-Lawyer Relationship

A relationship of client and lawyer arises when:

(1) a person manifests to a lawyer the person's intent that the lawyer provide legal services for the person; and either

(a) the lawyer manifests to the person consent to do so; or

(b) the lawyer fails to manifest lack of consent to do so, and the lawyer knows or reasonably should know that the person reasonably relies on the lawyer to provide the services; or

(2) a tribunal with power to do so appoints the lawyer to provide the services.

§15. A Lawyer's Duties to a Prospective Client

(1) When a person discusses with a lawyer the possibility of their forming a client-lawyer relationship for a matter and no such relationship ensues, the lawyer must:

(a) not subsequently use or disclose confidential information learned in the consultation, except to the extent permitted with respect to confidential information of a client or former client as stated in §§61–67;

(b) protect the person's property in the lawyer's custody as stated in §§44–46; and

(c) use reasonable care to the extent the lawyer provides the person legal services.

(2) A lawyer subject to Subsection (1) may not represent a client whose interests are materially adverse to those of a former prospective client in the same or a substantially related matter when the lawyer or another lawyer whose disqualification is imputed to the lawyer under §§123 and 124 has received from the prospective client confidential information that could be significantly harmful to the prospective client in the matter, except that such a representation is permissible if:

(a)(i) any personally prohibited lawyer takes reasonable steps to avoid exposure to confidential information other than information appropriate to determine whether to represent the prospective client, and (ii) such lawyer is screened as stated in §124(2)(b) and (c); or

(b) both the affected client and the prospective client give informed consent to the representation under the limitations and conditions provided in §122.

TOPIC 2. SUMMARY OF THE DUTIES UNDER A CLIENT-LAWYER RELATIONSHIP

§16. A Lawyer's Duties to a Client — In General

To the extent consistent with the lawyer's other legal duties and subject to the other provisions of this Restatement, a lawyer must, in matters within the scope of the representation:

(1) proceed in a manner reasonably calculated to advance a client's lawful objectives, as defined by the client after consultation;

(2) act with reasonable competence and diligence;

(3) comply with obligations concerning the client's confidences and property, avoid impermissible conflicting interests, deal honestly with the client, and not employ advantages arising from the client-lawyer relationship in a manner adverse to the client; and

(4) fulfill valid contractual obligations to the client.

§17. A Client's Duties to a Lawyer

Subject to the other provisions of this Restatement, in matters covered by the representation a client must:

(1) compensate a lawyer for services and expenses as stated in Chapter 3;

(2) indemnify the lawyer for liability to which the client has exposed the lawyer without the lawyer's fault; and

(3) fulfill any valid contractual obligations to the lawyer.

§18. Client-Lawyer Contracts

(1) A contract between a lawyer and client concerning the client-lawyer relationship, including a contract modifying an existing contract, may be enforced by either party if the contract meets other applicable requirements, except that:

(a) if the contract or modification is made beyond a reasonable time after the lawyer has begun to represent the client in the matter (see §38(1)), the client may avoid it unless the lawyer shows that the contract and the circumstances of its formation were fair and reasonable to the client; and

(b) if the contract is made after the lawyer has finished providing services, the client may avoid it if the client was not informed of facts needed to evaluate the appropriateness of the lawyer's compensation or other benefits conferred on the lawyer by the contract.

(2) A tribunal should construe a contract between client and lawyer as a reasonable person in the circumstances of the client would have construed it.

§19. Agreements Limiting Client or Lawyer Duties

(1) Subject to other requirements stated in this Restatement, a client and lawyer may agree to limit a duty that a lawyer would otherwise owe to the client if:

(a) the client is adequately informed and consents; and

(b) the terms of the limitation are reasonable in the circumstances.

(2) A lawyer may agree to waive a client's duty to pay or other duty owed to the lawyer.

TOPIC 3. AUTHORITY TO MAKE DECISIONS

§20. A Lawyer's Duty to Inform and Consult with a Client

(1) A lawyer must keep a client reasonably informed about the mat-

ter and must consult with a client to a reasonable extent concerning decisions to be made by the lawyer under §§21–23.

(2) A lawyer must promptly comply with a client's reasonable requests for information.

(3) A lawyer must notify a client of decisions to be made by the client under §§21–23 and must explain a matter to the extent reasonably necessary to permit the client to make informed decisions regarding the representation.

§21. Allocating the Authority to Decide Between a Client and a Lawyer

As between client and lawyer:

(1) A client and lawyer may agree which of them will make specified decisions, subject to the requirements stated in §§18, 19, 22, 23, and other provisions of this Restatement. The agreement may be superseded by another valid agreement.

(2) A client may instruct a lawyer during the representation, subject to the requirements stated in §§22, 23, and other provisions of this Restatement.

(3) Subject to Subsections (1) and (2) a lawyer may take any lawful measure within the scope of representation that is reasonably calculated to advance a client's objectives as defined by the client, consulting with the client as required by §20.

(4) A client may ratify an act of a lawyer that was not previously authorized.

§22. Authority Reserved to a Client

(1) As between client and lawyer, subject to Subsection (2) and §23, the following and comparable decisions are reserved to the client except when the client has validly authorized the lawyer to make the particular decision: whether and on what terms to settle a claim; how a criminal defendant should plead; whether a criminal defendant should waive jury trial; whether a criminal defendant should testify; and whether to appeal in a civil proceeding or criminal prosecution.

(2) A client may not validly authorize a lawyer to make the decisions described in Subsection (1) when other law (such as criminal-procedure rules governing pleas, jury-trial waiver, and defendant testimony) requires the client's personal participation or approval.

(3) Regardless of any contrary contract with a lawyer, a client may revoke a lawyer's authority to make the decisions described in Subsection (1).

§23. Authority Reserved to a Lawyer

As between client and lawyer, a lawyer retains authority that may not be overridden by a contract with or an instruction from the client:

(1) to refuse to perform, counsel, or assist future or ongoing acts in the representation that the lawyer reasonably believes to be unlawful;

(2) to make decisions or take actions in the representation that the lawyer reasonably believes to be required by law or an order of a tribunal.

§24. A Client with Diminished Capacity

(1) When a client's capacity to make adequately considered decisions in connection with the representation is diminished, whether because of minority, physical illness, mental disability, or other cause, the lawyer must, as far as reasonably possible, maintain a normal client-lawyer relationship with the client and act in the best interests of the client as stated in Subsection (2).

(2) A lawyer representing a client with diminished capacity as described in Subsection (1) and for whom no guardian or other representative is available to act, must, with respect to a matter within the scope of the representation, pursue the lawyer's reasonable view of the client's objectives or interests as the client would define them if able to make adequately considered decisions on the matter, even if the client expresses no wishes or gives contrary instructions.

(3) If a client with diminished capacity as described in Subsection (1) has a guardian or other person legally entitled to act for the client, the client's lawyer must treat that person as entitled to act with respect to the client's interests in the matter, unless:

(a) the lawyer represents the client in a matter against the interests of that person; or

(b) that person instructs the lawyer to act in a manner that the lawyer knows will violate the person's legal duties toward the client.

(4) A lawyer representing a client with diminished capacity as described in Subsection (1) may seek the appointment of a guardian or take other protective action within the scope of the representation when doing so is practical and will advance the client's objectives or interests, determined as stated in Subsection (2).

TOPIC 4. A LAWYER'S AUTHORITY TO ACT FOR A CLIENT

§25. Appearance Before a Tribunal

A lawyer who enters an appearance before a tribunal on behalf of a

person is presumed to represent that person as a client. The presumption may be rebutted.

§26. A Lawyer's Actual Authority

A lawyer's act is considered to be that of a client in proceedings before a tribunal or in dealings with third persons when:

(1) the client has expressly or impliedly authorized the act;

(2) authority concerning the act is reserved to the lawyer as stated in §23; or

(3) the client ratifies the act.

§27. A Lawyer's Apparent Authority

A lawyer's act is considered to be that of the client in proceedings before a tribunal or in dealings with a third person if the tribunal or third person reasonably assumes that the lawyer is authorized to do the act on the basis of the client's (and not the lawyer's) manifestations of such authorization.

§28. A Lawyer's Knowledge; Notification to a Lawyer; and Statements of a Lawyer

(1) Information imparted to a lawyer during and relating to the representation of a client is attributed to the client for the purpose of determining the client's rights and liabilities in matters in which the lawyer represents the client, unless those rights or liabilities require proof of the client's personal knowledge or intentions or the lawyer's legal duties preclude disclosure of the information to the client.

(2) Unless applicable law otherwise provides, a third person may give notification to a client, in a matter in which the client is represented by a lawyer, by giving notification to the client's lawyer, unless the third person knows of circumstances reasonably indicating that the lawyer's authority to receive notification has been abrogated.

(3) A lawyer's unprivileged statement is admissible in evidence against a client as if it were the client's statement if either:

(a) the client authorized the lawyer to make a statement concerning the subject; or

(b) the statement concerns a matter within the scope of the representation and was made by the lawyer during it.

§29. A Lawyer's Act or Advice as Mitigating or Avoiding a Client's Responsibility

(1) When a client's intent or mental state is in issue, a tribunal may consider otherwise admissible evidence of a lawyer's advice to the client.

(2) In deciding whether to impose a sanction on a person or to relieve a person from a criminal or civil ruling, default, or judgment, a tribunal may consider otherwise admissible evidence to prove or disprove that the lawyer who represented the person did so inadequately or contrary to the client's instructions.

§30. A Lawyer's Liability to a Third Person for Conduct on Behalf of a Client

(1) For improper conduct while representing a client, a lawyer is subject to professional discipline as stated in §5, to civil liability as stated in Chapter 4, and to prosecution as provided in the criminal law (see §7).

(2) Unless at the time of contracting the lawyer or third person disclaimed such liability, a lawyer is subject to liability to third persons on contracts the lawyer entered into on behalf of a client if:

(a) the client's existence or identity was not disclosed to the third person; or

(b) the contract is between the lawyer and a third person who provides goods or services used by lawyers and who, as the lawyer knows or reasonably should know, relies on the lawyer's credit.

(3) A lawyer is subject to liability to a third person for damages for loss proximately caused by the lawyer's acting without authority from a client under §26 if:

(a) the lawyer tortiously misrepresents to the third person that the lawyer has authority to make a contract, conveyance, or affirmation on behalf of the client and the third person reasonably relies on the misrepresentation; or

(b) the lawyer purports to make a contract, conveyance, or affirmation on behalf of the client, unless the lawyer manifests that the lawyer does not warrant that the lawyer is authorized to act or the other party knows that the lawyer is not authorized to act.

TOPIC 5. ENDING A CLIENT-LAWYER RELATIONSHIP

§31. Termination of a Lawyer's Authority

(1) A lawyer must comply with applicable law requiring notice to or permission of a tribunal when terminating a representation and with an order of a tribunal requiring the representation to continue.

(2) Subject to Subsection (1) and §33, a lawyer's actual authority to represent a client ends when:

(a) the client discharges the lawyer;

(b) the client dies or, in the case of a corporation or similar organization, loses its capacity to function as such;

(c) the lawyer withdraws;

(d) the lawyer dies or becomes physically or mentally incapable of providing representation, is disbarred or suspended from practicing law, or is ordered by a tribunal to cease representing a client; or

(e) the representation ends as provided by contract or because the lawyer has completed the contemplated services.

(3) A lawyer's apparent authority to act for a client with respect to another person ends when the other person knows or should know of facts from which it can be reasonably inferred that the lawyer lacks actual authority, including knowledge of any event described in Subsection (2).

§32. Discharge by a Client and Withdrawal by a Lawyer

(1) Subject to Subsection (5), a client may discharge a lawyer at any time.

(2) Subject to Subsection (5), a lawyer may not represent a client or, where representation has commenced, must withdraw from the representation of a client if:

(a) the representation will result in the lawyer's violating rules of professional conduct or other law;

(b) the lawyer's physical or mental condition materially impairs the lawyer's ability to represent the client; or

(c) the client discharges the lawyer.

(3) Subject to Subsections (4) and (5), a lawyer may withdraw from representing a client if:

(a) withdrawal can be accomplished without material adverse effect on the interests of the client;

(b) the lawyer reasonably believes withdrawal is required in circumstances stated in Subsection (2);

(c) the client gives informed consent;

(d) the client persists in a course of action involving the lawyer's services that the lawyer reasonably believes is criminal, fraudulent, or in breach of the client's fiduciary duty;

(e) the lawyer reasonably believes the client has used or threatens to use the lawyer's services to perpetrate a crime or fraud;

(f) the client insists on taking action that the lawyer considers repugnant or imprudent;

(g) the client fails to fulfill a substantial financial or other obligation to the lawyer regarding the lawyer's services and the lawyer has given the client reasonable warning that the lawyer will withdraw unless the client fulfills the obligation;

(h) the representation has been rendered unreasonably difficult by the client or by the irreparable breakdown of the client-lawyer relationship; or

(i) other good cause for withdrawal exists.

(4) In the case of permissive withdrawal under Subsections (3)(f)–(i), a lawyer may not withdraw if the harm that withdrawal would cause significantly exceeds the harm to the lawyer or others in not withdrawing.

(5) Notwithstanding Subsections (1)–(4), a lawyer must comply with applicable law requiring notice to or permission of a tribunal when terminating a representation and with a valid order of a tribunal requiring the representation to continue.

§33. A Lawyer's Duties When a Representation Terminates

(1) In terminating a representation, a lawyer must take steps to the extent reasonably practicable to protect the client's interests, such as giving notice to the client of the termination, allowing time for employment of other counsel, surrendering papers and property to which the client is entitled, and refunding any advance payment of fee the lawyer has not earned.

(2) Following termination of a representation, a lawyer must:

(a) observe obligations to a former client such as those dealing with client confidences (see Chapter 5), conflicts of interest (see Chapter 8), client property and documents (see §§44–46), and fee collection (see §41);

(b) take no action on behalf of a former client without new authorization and give reasonable notice, to those who might otherwise be misled, that the lawyer lacks authority to act for the client;

(c) take reasonable steps to convey to the former client any material communication the lawyer receives relating to the matter involved in the representation; and

(d) take no unfair advantage of a former client by abusing knowledge or trust acquired by means of the representation.

CHAPTER 3 CLIENT AND LAWYER: THE FINANCIAL AND PROPERTY RELATIONSHIP

TOPIC 1. LEGAL CONTROLS ON ATTORNEY FEES

§34. Reasonable and Lawful Fees

A lawyer may not charge a fee larger than is reasonable in the circumstances or that is prohibited by law.

§35. Contingent-Fee Arrangements

(1) A lawyer may contract with a client for a fee the size or payment of which is contingent on the outcome of a matter, unless the contract violates §34 or another provision of this Restatement or the size or payment of the fee is:

(a) contingent on success in prosecuting or defending a criminal proceeding; or

(b) contingent on a specified result in a divorce proceeding or a proceeding concerning custody of a child.

(2) Unless the contract construed in the circumstances indicates otherwise, when a lawyer has contracted for a contingent fee, the lawyer is entitled to receive the specified fee only when and to the extent the client receives payment.

§36. Forbidden Client-Lawyer Financial Arrangements

(1) A lawyer may not acquire a proprietary interest in the cause of action or subject matter of litigation that the lawyer is conducting for a client, except that the lawyer may:

(a) acquire a lien as provided by §43 to secure the lawyer's fee or expenses; and

(b) contract with a client for a contingent fee in a civil case except when prohibited as stated in §35.

(2) A lawyer may not make or guarantee a loan to a client in connection with pending or contemplated litigation that the lawyer is conducting for the client, except that the lawyer may make or guarantee a loan covering court costs and expenses of litigation, the repayment of which to the lawyer may be contingent on the outcome of the matter.

(3) A lawyer may not, before the lawyer ceases to represent a client, make an agreement giving the lawyer literary or media rights to a portrayal or account based in substantial part on information relating to the representation.

§37. Partial or Complete Forfeiture of a Lawyer's Compensation

A lawyer engaging in clear and serious violation of duty to a client may be required to forfeit some or all of the lawyer's compensation for the matter. Considerations relevant to the question of forfeiture include the gravity and timing of the violation, its willfulness, its effect on the value of the lawyer's work for the client, any other threatened or actual harm to the client, and the adequacy of other remedies.

TOPIC 2. A LAWYER'S CLAIM TO COMPENSATION

§38. Client-Lawyer Fee Contracts

(1) Before or within a reasonable time after beginning to represent a client in a matter, a lawyer must communicate to the client, in writing when applicable rules so provide, the basis or rate of the fee, unless the communication is unnecessary for the client because the lawyer has previously represented that client on the same basis or at the same rate.

(2) The validity and construction of a contract between a client and a lawyer concerning the lawyer's fees are governed by §18.

(3) Unless a contract construed in the circumstances indicates otherwise:

(a) a lawyer may not charge separately for the lawyer's general office and overhead expenses;

(b) payments that the law requires an opposing party or that party's lawyer to pay as attorney-fee awards or sanctions are credited to the client, not the client's lawyer, absent a contrary statute or court order; and

(c) when a lawyer requests and receives a fee payment that is not for services already rendered, that payment is to be credited against whatever fee the lawyer is entitled to collect.

§39. A Lawyer's Fee in the Absence of a Contract

If a client and lawyer have not made a valid contract providing for another measure of compensation, a client owes a lawyer who has performed legal services for the client the fair value of the lawyer's services.

§40. Fees on Termination

If a client-lawyer relationship ends before the lawyer has completed the services due for a matter and the lawyer's fee has not been forfeited under §37:

(1) a lawyer who has been discharged or withdraws may recover the lesser of the fair value of the lawyer's services as determined under §39 and the ratable proportion of the compensation provided by any otherwise enforceable contract between lawyer and client for the services performed; except that

(2) the tribunal may allow such a lawyer to recover the ratable proportion of the compensation provided by such a contract if:

(a) the discharge or withdrawal is not attributable to misconduct of the lawyer;

(b) the lawyer has performed severable services; and

(c) allowing contractual compensation would not burden the client's choice of counsel or the client's ability to replace counsel.

TOPIC 3. FEE-COLLECTION PROCEDURES

§41. Fee-Collection Methods

In seeking compensation claimed from a client or former client, a lawyer may not employ collection methods forbidden by law, use confidential information (as defined in Chapter 5) when not permitted under §65, or harass the client.

§42. Remedies and the Burden of Persuasion

(1) A fee dispute between a lawyer and a client may be adjudicated in any appropriate proceeding, including a suit by the lawyer to recover an unpaid fee, a suit for a refund by a client, an arbitration to which both parties consent unless applicable law renders the lawyer's consent unnecessary, or in the court's discretion a proceeding ancillary to a pending suit in which the lawyer performed the services in question.

(2) In any such proceeding the lawyer has the burden of persuading the trier of fact, when relevant, of the existence and terms of any fee contract, the making of any disclosures to the client required to render a contract enforceable, and the extent and value of the lawyer's services.

§43. Lawyer Liens

(1) Except as provided in Subsection (2) or by statute or rule, a lawyer does not acquire a lien entitling the lawyer to retain the client's property in the lawyer's possession in order to secure payment of the lawyer's fees and disbursements. A lawyer may decline to deliver to a client or former client an original or copy of any document prepared by the lawyer or at the lawyer's expense if the client or former client has not paid all fees and disbursements due for the lawyer's work in preparing the document and nondelivery would not unreasonably harm the client or former client.

(2) Unless otherwise provided by statute or rule, client and lawyer may agree that the lawyer shall have a security interest in property

of the client recovered for the client through the lawyer's efforts, as follows:

(a) the lawyer may contract in writing with the client for a lien on the proceeds of the representation to secure payment for the lawyer's services and disbursements in that matter;

(b) the lien becomes binding on a third party when the party has notice of the lien;

(c) the lien applies only to the amount of fees and disbursements claimed reasonably and in good faith for the lawyer's services performed in the representation; and

(d) the lawyer may not unreasonably impede the speedy and inexpensive resolution of any dispute concerning those fees and disbursements or the lien.

(3) A tribunal where an action is pending may in its discretion adjudicate any fee or other dispute concerning a lien asserted by a lawyer on property of a party to the action, provide for custody of the property, release all or part of the property to the client or lawyer, and grant such other relief as justice may require.

(4) With respect to property neither in the lawyer's possession nor recovered by the client through the lawyer's efforts, the lawyer may obtain a security interest on property of a client only as provided by other law and consistent with §§18 and 126. Acquisition of such a security interest is a business or financial transaction with a client within the meaning of §126.

TOPIC 4. PROPERTY AND DOCUMENTS OF CLIENTS AND OTHERS

§44. Safeguarding and Segregating Property

(1) A lawyer holding funds or other property of a client in connection with a representation, or such funds or other property in which a client claims an interest, must take reasonable steps to safeguard the funds or property. A similar obligation may be imposed by law on funds or other property so held and owned or claimed by a third person. In particular, the lawyer must hold such property separate from the lawyer's property, keep records of it, deposit funds in an account separate from the lawyer's own funds, identify tangible objects, and comply with related requirements imposed by regulatory authorities.

(2) Upon receiving funds or other property in a professional capacity and in which a client or third person owns or claims an interest, a lawyer must promptly notify the client or third person. The lawyer must promptly render a full accounting regarding such property upon request by the client or third person.

§45. Surrendering Possession of Property

(1) Except as provided in Subsection (2), a lawyer must promptly deliver, to the client or nonclient so entitled, funds or other property in the lawyer's possession belonging to a client or nonclient.

(2) A lawyer may retain possession of funds or other property of a client or non-client if:

(a) the client or non-client consents;

(b) the lawyer's client is entitled to the property, the lawyer appropriately possesses the property for purposes of the representation, and the client has not asked for delivery of the property;

(c) the lawyer has a valid lien on the property (see §43);

(d) there are substantial grounds for dispute as to the person entitled to the property; or

(e) delivering the property to the client or non-client would violate a court order or other legal obligation of the lawyer.

§46. Documents Relating to a Representation

(1) A lawyer must take reasonable steps to safeguard documents in the lawyer's possession relating to the representation of a client or former client.

(2) On request, a lawyer must allow a client or former client to inspect and copy any document possessed by the lawyer relating to the representation, unless substantial grounds exist to refuse.

(3) Unless a client or former client consents to non-delivery or substantial grounds exist for refusing to make delivery, a lawyer must deliver to the client or former client, at an appropriate time and in any event promptly after the representation ends, such originals and copies of other documents possessed by the lawyer relating to the representation as the client or former client reasonably needs.

(4) Notwithstanding Subsections (2) and (3), a lawyer may decline to deliver to a client or former client an original or copy of any document under circumstances permitted by §43(1).

TOPIC 5. FEE-SPLITTING WITH A LAWYER NOT IN THE SAME FIRM

§47. Fee-Splitting Between Lawyers Not in the Same Firm

A division of fees between lawyers who are not in the same firm may be made only if:

(1) (a) the division is in proportion to the services performed by each lawyer or (b) by agreement with the client, the lawyers assume joint responsibility for the representation;

(2) the client is informed of and does not object to the fact of division, the terms of the division, and the participation of the lawyers involved; and

(3) the total fee is reasonable (see §34).

CHAPTER 4 LAWYER CIVIL LIABILITY

TOPIC 1. LIABILITY FOR PROFESSIONAL NEGLIGENCE AND BREACH OF FIDUCIARY DUTY

§48. Professional Negligence — Elements and Defenses Generally

In addition to the other possible bases of civil liability described in §§49, 55, and 56, a lawyer is civilly liable for professional negligence to a person to whom the lawyer owes a duty of care within the meaning of §50 or §51, if the lawyer fails to exercise care within the meaning of §52 and if that failure is a legal cause of injury within the meaning of §53, unless the lawyer has a defense within the meaning of §54.

§49. Breach of Fiduciary Duty — Generally

In addition to the other possible bases of civil liability described in §§48, 55, and 56, a lawyer is civilly liable to a client if the lawyer breaches a fiduciary duty to the client set forth in §16(3) and if that failure is a legal cause of injury within the meaning of §53, unless the lawyer has a defense within the meaning of §54.

§50. Duty of Care to a Client

For purposes of liability under §48, a lawyer owes a client the duty to exercise care within the meaning of §52 in pursuing the client's lawful objectives in matters covered by the representation.

§51. Duty of Care to Certain Nonclients

For purposes of liability under §48, a lawyer owes a duty to use care within the meaning of §52 in each of the following circumstances:

(1) to a prospective client, as stated in §15;

(2) to a nonclient when and to the extent that:

(a) the lawyer or (with the lawyer's acquiescence) the lawyer's client invites the nonclient to rely on the lawyer's opinion or provision of other legal services, and the nonclient so relies; and

(b) the nonclient is not, under applicable tort law, too remote from the lawyer to be entitled to protection;

(3) to a nonclient when and to the extent that:

(a) the lawyer knows that a client intends as one of the primary objectives of the representation that the lawyer's services benefit the nonclient;

(b) such a duty would not significantly impair the lawyer's performance of obligations to the client; and

(c) the absence of such a duty would make enforcement of those obligations to the client unlikely; and

(4) to a nonclient when and to the extent that:

(a) the lawyer's client is a trustee, guardian, executor, or fiduciary acting primarily to perform similar functions for the nonclient;

(b) the lawyer knows that appropriate action by the lawyer is necessary with respect to a matter within the scope of the representation to prevent or rectify the breach of a fiduciary duty owed by the client to the nonclient, where (i) the breach is a crime or fraud or (ii) the lawyer has assisted or is assisting the breach;

(c) the nonclient is not reasonably able to protect its rights; and

(d) such a duty would not significantly impair the performance of the lawyer's obligations to the client.

§52. The Standard of Care

(1) For purposes of liability under §§48 and 49, a lawyer who owes a duty of care must exercise the competence and diligence normally exercised by lawyers in similar circumstances.

(2) Proof of a violation of a rule or statute regulating the conduct of lawyers:

(a) does not give rise to an implied cause of action for professional negligence or breach of fiduciary duty;

(b) does not preclude other proof concerning the duty of care in Subsection (1) or the fiduciary duty; and

(c) may be considered by a trier of fact as an aid in understanding and applying the standard of Subsection (1) or §49 to the extent that (i) the rule or statute was designed for the protection of persons in the position of the claimant and (ii) proof of the content and construction of such a rule or statute is relevant to the claimant's claim.

§53. Causation and Damages

A lawyer is liable under §48 or §49 only if the lawyer's breach of a duty of care or breach of fiduciary duty was a legal cause of injury, as determined under generally applicable principles of causation and damages.

§54. Defenses; Prospective Liability Waiver; Settlement with a Client

(1) Except as otherwise provided in this Section, liability under §§48 and 49 is subject to the defenses available under generally applicable principles of law governing respectively actions for professional negligence and breach of fiduciary duty. A lawyer is not liable under §48 or §49 for any action or inaction the lawyer reasonably believed to be required by law, including a professional rule.

(2) An agreement prospectively limiting a lawyer's liability to a client for malpractice is unenforceable.

(3) The client or former client may rescind an agreement settling a claim by the client or former client against the person's lawyer if:

(a) the client or former client was subjected to improper pressure by the lawyer in reaching the settlement; or

(b) (i) the client or former client was not independently represented in negotiating the settlement, and (ii) the settlement was not fair and reasonable to the client or former client.

(4) For purposes of professional discipline, a lawyer may not:

(a) make an agreement prospectively limiting the lawyer's liability to a client for malpractice; or

(b) settle a claim for such liability with an unrepresented client or former client without first advising that person in writing that independent representation is appropriate in connection therewith.

TOPIC 2. OTHER CIVIL LIABILITY

§55. Civil Remedies of a Client Other Than for Malpractice

(1) A lawyer is subject to liability to a client for injury caused by breach of contract in the circumstances and to the extent provided by contract law.

(2) A client is entitled to restitutionary, injunctive, or declaratory remedies against a lawyer in the circumstances and to the extent provided by generally applicable law governing such remedies.

§56. Liability to a Client or Nonclient Under General Law

Except as provided in §57 and in addition to liability under

§§48–55, a lawyer is subject to liability to a client or nonclient when a nonlawyer would be in similar circumstances.

§57. Nonclient Claims — Certain Defenses and Exceptions to Liability

(1) In addition to other absolute or conditional privileges, a lawyer is absolutely privileged to publish matter concerning a nonclient if:

(a) the publication occurs in communications preliminary to a reasonably anticipated proceeding before a tribunal or in the institution or during the course and as a part of such a proceeding;

(b) the lawyer participates as counsel in that proceeding; and

(c) the matter is published to a person who may be involved in the proceeding, and the publication has some relation to the proceeding.

(2) A lawyer representing a client in a civil proceeding or procuring the institution of criminal proceedings by a client is not liable to a nonclient for wrongful use of civil proceedings or for malicious prosecution if the lawyer has probable cause for acting, or if the lawyer acts primarily to help the client obtain a proper adjudication of the client's claim in that proceeding.

(3) A lawyer who advises or assists a client to make or break a contract, to enter or dissolve a legal relationship, or to enter or not enter a contractual relation, is not liable to a nonclient for interference with contract or with prospective contractual relations or with a legal relationship, if the lawyer acts to advance the client's objectives without using wrongful means.

TOPIC 3. VICARIOUS LIABILITY

§58. Vicarious Liability

(1) A law firm is subject to civil liability for injury legally caused to a person by any wrongful act or omission of any principal or employee of the firm who was acting in the ordinary course of the firm's business or with actual or apparent authority.

(2) Each of the principals of a law firm organized as a general partnership without limited liability is liable jointly and severally with the firm.

(3) A principal of a law firm organized other than as a general partnership without limited liability as authorized by law is vicariously liable for the acts of another principal or employee of the firm to the extent provided by law.

CHAPTER 5 CONFIDENTIAL CLIENT INFORMATION

TOPIC 1. CONFIDENTIALITY RESPONSIBILITIES OF LAWYERS

Title A. A Lawyer's Confidentiality Duties

§59. Definition of "Confidential Client Information"

Confidential client information consists of information relating to representation of a client, other than information that is generally known.

§60. A Lawyer's Duty to Safeguard Confidential Client Information

(1) Except as provided in §§61–67, during and after representation of a client:

(a) the lawyer may not use or disclose confidential client information as defined in §59 if there is a reasonable prospect that doing so will adversely affect a material interest of the client or if the client has instructed the lawyer not to use or disclose such information;

(b) the lawyer must take steps reasonable in the circumstances to protect confidential client information against impermissible use or disclosure by the lawyer's associates or agents that may adversely affect a material interest of the client or otherwise than as instructed by the client.

(2) Except as stated in §62, a lawyer who uses confidential information of a client for the lawyer's pecuniary gain other than in the practice of law must account to the client for any profits made.

Title B. Using or Disclosing Confidential Client Information

§61. Using or Disclosing Information to Advance Client Interests

A lawyer may use or disclose confidential client information when the lawyer reasonably believes that doing so will advance the interests of the client in the representation.

§62. Using or Disclosing Information with Client Consent

A lawyer may use or disclose confidential client information when the client consents after being adequately informed concerning the use or disclosure.

§63. Using or Disclosing Information When Required by Law

A lawyer may use or disclose confidential client information when required by law, after the lawyer takes reasonably appropriate steps to assert that the information is privileged or otherwise protected against disclosure.

§64. Using or Disclosing Information in a Lawyer's Self-Defense

A lawyer may use or disclose confidential client information when and to the extent that the lawyer reasonably believes necessary to defend the lawyer or the lawyer's associate or agent against a charge or threatened charge by any person that the lawyer or such associate or agent acted wrongfully in the course of representing a client.

§65. Using or Disclosing Information in a Compensation Dispute

A lawyer may use or disclose confidential client information when and to the extent that the lawyer reasonably believes necessary to permit the lawyer to resolve a dispute with the client concerning compensation or reimbursement that the lawyer reasonably claims the client owes the lawyer.

§66. Using or Disclosing Information to Prevent Death or Serious Bodily Harm

(1) A lawyer may use or disclose confidential client information when the lawyer reasonably believes that its use or disclosure is necessary to prevent reasonably certain death or serious bodily harm to a person.

(2) Before using or disclosing information under this Section, the lawyer must, if feasible, make a good-faith effort to persuade the client not to act. If the client or another person has already acted, the lawyer must, if feasible, advise the client to warn the victim or to take other action to prevent the harm and advise the client of the lawyer's ability to use or disclose information as provided in this Section and the consequences thereof.

(3) A lawyer who takes action or decides not to take action permitted under this Section is not, solely by reason of such action or inaction, subject to professional discipline, liable for damages to the lawyer's client or any third person, or barred from recovery against a client or third person.

§67. Using or Disclosing Information to Prevent, Rectify, or Mitigate Substantial Financial Loss

(1) A lawyer may use or disclose confidential client information when the lawyer reasonably believes that its use or disclosure is necessary to prevent a crime or fraud, and:

(a) the crime or fraud threatens substantial financial loss;

(b) the loss has not yet occurred;

(c) the lawyer's client intends to commit the crime or fraud either personally or through a third person; and

(d) the client has employed or is employing the lawyer's services in the matter in which the crime or fraud is committed.

(2) If a crime or fraud described in Subsection (1) has already occurred, a lawyer may use or disclose confidential client information when the lawyer reasonably believes its use or disclosure is necessary to prevent, rectify, or mitigate the loss.

(3) Before using or disclosing information under this Section, the lawyer must, if feasible, make a good-faith effort to persuade the client not to act. If the client or another person has already acted, the lawyer must, if feasible, advise the client to warn the victim or to take other action to prevent, rectify, or mitigate the loss. The lawyer must, if feasible, also advise the client of the lawyer's ability to use or disclose information as provided in this Section and the consequences thereof.

(4) A lawyer who takes action or decides not to take action permitted under this Section is not, solely by reason of such action or inaction, subject to professional discipline, liable for damages to the lawyer's client or any third person, or barred from recovery against a client or third person.

TOPIC 2. THE ATTORNEY-CLIENT PRIVILEGE

Title A. The Scope of the Privilege

§68. Attorney-Client Privilege

Except as otherwise provided in this Restatement, the attorney-client privilege may be invoked as provided in §86 with respect to:

(1) a communication
(2) made between privileged persons
(3) in confidence
(4) for the purpose of obtaining or providing legal assistance for the client.

§69. Attorney-Client Privilege — "Communication"

A communication within the meaning of §68 is any expression through which a privileged person, as defined in §70, undertakes to convey information to another privileged person and any document or other record revealing such an expression.

§70. Attorney-Client Privilege — "Privileged Persons"

Privileged persons within the meaning of §68 are the client (including a prospective client), the client's lawyer, agents of either who facilitate communications between them, and agents of the lawyer who facilitate the representation.

§71. Attorney-Client Privilege — "In Confidence"

A communication is in confidence within the meaning of §68 if, at the time and in the circumstances of the communication, the communicating person reasonably believes that no one will learn the contents of the communication except a privileged person as defined in §70 or another person with whom communications are protected under a similar privilege.

§72. Attorney-Client Privilege — Legal Assistance as the Object of a Privileged Communication

A communication is made for the purpose of obtaining or providing legal assistance within the meaning of §68 if it is made to or to assist a person:

(1) who is a lawyer or who the client or prospective client reasonably believes to be a lawyer; and

(2) whom the client or prospective client consults for the purpose of obtaining legal assistance.

Title B. The Attorney-Client Privilege for Organizational and Multiple Clients

§73. The Privilege for an Organizational Client

When a client is a corporation, unincorporated association, partnership, trust, estate, sole proprietorship, or other for-profit or not-for-profit organization, the attorney-client privilege extends to a communication that:

(1) otherwise qualifies as privileged under §§68–72;

(2) is between an agent of the organization and a privileged person as defined in §70;

(3) concerns a legal matter of interest to the organization; and

(4) is disclosed only to:

(a) privileged persons as defined in §70; and

(b) other agents of the organization who reasonably need to know of the communication in order to act for the organization.

§74. The Privilege for a Governmental Client

Unless applicable law otherwise provides, the attorney-client privilege extends to a communication of a governmental organization as stated in §73 and of an individual employee or other agent of a governmental organization as a client with respect to his or her personal interest as stated in §§68–72.

§75. The Privilege of Co-Clients

(1) If two or more persons are jointly represented by the same lawyer in a matter, a communication of either co-client that otherwise qualifies as privileged under §§68–72 and relates to matters of common interest is privileged as against third persons, and any co-client may invoke the privilege, unless it has been waived by the client who made the communication.

(2) Unless the co-clients have agreed otherwise, a communication described in Subsection (1) is not privileged as between the co-clients in a subsequent adverse proceeding between them.

§76. The Privilege in Common-Interest Arrangements

(1) If two or more clients with a common interest in a litigated or nonlitigated matter are represented by separate lawyers and they agree

to exchange information concerning the matter, a communication of any such client that otherwise qualifies as privileged under §§68–72 that relates to the matter is privileged as against third persons. Any such client may invoke the privilege, unless it has been waived by the client who made the communication.

(2) Unless the clients have agreed otherwise, a communication described in Subsection (1) is not privileged as between clients described in Subsection (1) in a subsequent adverse proceeding between them.

Title C. Duration of the Attorney-Client Privilege; Waivers and Exceptions

§77. Duration of the Privilege

Unless waived (see §§78–80) or subject to exception (see §§81–85), the attorney-client privilege may be invoked as provided in §86 at any time during or after termination of the relationship between client or prospective client and lawyer.

§78. Agreement, Disclaimer, or Failure to Object

The attorney-client privilege is waived if the client, the client's lawyer, or another authorized agent of the client:

(1) agrees to waive the privilege;

(2) disclaims protection of the privilege and

(a) another person reasonably relies on the disclaimer to that person's detriment; or

(b) reasons of judicial administration require that the client not be permitted to revoke the disclaimer; or

(3) in a proceeding before a tribunal, fails to object properly to an attempt by another person to give or exact testimony or other evidence of a privileged communication.

§79. Subsequent Disclosure

The attorney-client privilege is waived if the client, the client's lawyer, or another authorized agent of the client voluntarily discloses the communication in a non-privileged communication.

§80. Putting Assistance or a Communication in Issue

(1) The attorney-client privilege is waived for any relevant communication if the client asserts as to a material issue in a proceeding that:

(a) the client acted upon the advice of a lawyer or that the advice was otherwise relevant to the legal significance of the client's conduct; or

(b) a lawyer's assistance was ineffective, negligent, or otherwise wrongful.

(2) The attorney-client privilege is waived for a recorded communication if a witness:

(a) employs the communication to aid the witness while testifying; or

(b) employed the communication in preparing to testify, and the tribunal finds that disclosure is required in the interests of justice.

§81. A Dispute Concerning a Decedent's Disposition of Property

The attorney-client privilege does not apply to a communication from or to a decedent relevant to an issue between parties who claim an interest through the same deceased client, either by testate or intestate succession or by an inter vivos transaction.

§82. Client Crime or Fraud

The attorney-client privilege does not apply to a communication occurring when a client:

(a) consults a lawyer for the purpose, later accomplished, of obtaining assistance to engage in a crime or fraud or aiding a third person to do so, or

(b) regardless of the client's purpose at the time of consultation, uses the lawyer's advice or other services to engage in or assist a crime or fraud.

§83. Lawyer Self-Protection

The attorney-client privilege does not apply to a communication that is relevant and reasonably necessary for a lawyer to employ in a proceeding:

(1) to resolve a dispute with a client concerning compensation or reimbursement that the lawyer reasonably claims the client owes the lawyer; or

(2) to defend the lawyer or the lawyer's associate or agent against a charge by any person that the lawyer, associate, or agent acted wrongfully during the course of representing a client.

§84. Fiduciary-Lawyer Communications

In a proceeding in which a trustee of an express trust or similar fiduciary is charged with breach of fiduciary duties by a beneficiary, a communication otherwise within §68 is nonetheless not privileged if the communication:

(a) is relevant to the claimed breach; and

(b) was between the trustee and a lawyer (or other privileged person within the meaning of §70) who was retained to advise the trustee concerning the administration of the trust.

§85. Communications Involving a Fiduciary Within an Organization

In a proceeding involving a dispute between an organizational client and shareholders, members, or other constituents of the organization toward whom the directors, officers, or similar persons managing the organization bear fiduciary responsibilities, the attorney-client privilege of the organization may be withheld from a communication otherwise within §68 if the tribunal finds that:

(a) those managing the organization are charged with breach of their obligations toward the shareholders, members, or other constituents or toward the organization itself;

(b) the communication occurred prior to the assertion of the charges and relates directly to those charges; and

(c) the need of the requesting party to discover or introduce the communication is sufficiently compelling and the threat to confidentiality sufficiently confined to justify setting the privilege aside.

Title D. Invoking the Privilege and Its Exceptions

§86. Invoking the Privilege and Its Exceptions

(1) When an attempt is made to introduce in evidence or obtain discovery of a communication privileged under §68:

(a) A client, a personal representative of an incompetent or deceased client, or a person succeeding to the interest of a client may invoke or waive the privilege, either personally or through counsel or another authorized agent.

(b) A lawyer, an agent of the lawyer, or an agent of a client from whom a privileged communication is sought must invoke the privilege when doing so appears reasonably appropriate, unless the client:

(i) has waived the privilege; or

(ii) has authorized the lawyer or agent to waive it.

(c) Notwithstanding failure to invoke the privilege as specified in Subsections (1)(a) and (1)(b), the tribunal has discretion to invoke the privilege.

(2) A person invoking the privilege must ordinarily object contemporaneously to an attempt to disclose the communication and, if the objection is contested, demonstrate each element of the privilege under §68.

(3) A person invoking a waiver of or exception to the privilege (§§78–85) must assert it and, if the assertion is contested, demonstrate each element of the waiver or exception.

TOPIC 3. THE LAWYER WORK-PRODUCT IMMUNITY

Title A. The Scope of the Lawyer Work-Product Immunity

§87. Lawyer Work-Product Immunity

(1) Work product consists of tangible material or its intangible equivalent in unwritten or oral form, other than underlying facts, prepared by a lawyer for litigation then in progress or in reasonable anticipation of future litigation.

(2) Opinion work product consists of the opinions or mental impressions of a lawyer; all other work product is ordinary work product.

(3) Except for material which by applicable law is not so protected, work product is immune from discovery or other compelled disclosure to the extent stated in §§88 (ordinary work product) and 89 (opinion work product) when the immunity is invoked as described in §90.

§88. Ordinary Work Product

When work product protection is invoked as described in §90, ordinary work product (§87(2)) is immune from discovery or other compelled disclosure unless either an exception recognized in §§91–93 applies or the inquiring party:

(1) has a substantial need for the material in order to prepare for trial; and

(2) is unable without undue hardship to obtain the substantial equivalent of the material by other means.

§89. Opinion Work Product

When work product protection is invoked as described in §90, opinion work product (§87(2)) is immune from discovery or other com-

pelled disclosure unless either the immunity is waived or an exception applies (§§91–93) or extraordinary circumstances justify disclosure.

Title B. Procedural Adminstration of the Lawyer Work-Product Immunity

§90. Invoking the Lawyer Work-Product Immunity and Its Exceptions

(1) Work-product immunity may be invoked by or for a person on whose behalf the work product was prepared.

(2) The person invoking work-product immunity must object and, if the objection is contested, demonstrate each element of the immunity.

(3) Once a claim of work product has been adequately supported, a person entitled to invoke a waiver or exception must assert it and, if the assertion is contested, demonstrate each element of the waiver or exception.

Title C. Waivers and Exceptions to the Work-Product Immunity

§91. Voluntary Acts

Work-product immunity is waived if the client, the client's lawyer, or another authorized agent of the client:

(1) agrees to waive the immunity;

(2) disclaims protection of the immunity and:

(a) another person reasonably relies on the disclaimer to that person's detriment; or

(b) reasons of judicial administration require that the client not be permitted to revoke the disclaimer; or

(3) in a proceeding before a tribunal, fails to object properly to an attempt by another person to give or exact testimony or other evidence of work product; or

(4) discloses the material to third persons in circumstances in which there is a significant likelihood that an adversary or potential adversary in anticipated litigation will obtain it.

§92. Use of Lawyer Work Product in Litigation

(1) Work-product immunity is waived for any relevant material if the client asserts as to a material issue in a proceeding that:

(a) the client acted upon the advice of a lawyer or that the advice was otherwise relevant to the legal significance of the client's conduct; or

(b) a lawyer's assistance was ineffective, negligent, or otherwise wrongful.

(2) The work-product immunity is waived for recorded material if a witness

(a) employs the material to aid the witness while testifying, or

(b) employed the material in preparing to testify, and the tribunal finds that disclosure is required in the interests of justice.

§93. Client Crime or Fraud

Work-product immunity does not apply to materials prepared when a client consults a lawyer for the purpose, later accomplished, of obtaining assistance to engage in a crime or fraud or to aid a third person to do so or uses the materials for such a purpose.

CHAPTER 6 REPRESENTING CLIENTS — IN GENERAL

TOPIC 1. LAWYER FUNCTIONS IN REPRESENTING CLIENTS — IN GENERAL

§94. Advising and Assisting a Client — In General

(1) A lawyer who counsels or assists a client to engage in conduct that violates the rights of a third person is subject to liability:

(a) to the third person to the extent stated in §§51 and 56–57; and

(b) to the client to the extent stated in §§50, 55, and 56.

(2) For purposes of professional discipline, a lawyer may not counsel or assist a client in conduct that the lawyer knows to be criminal or fraudulent or in violation of a court order with the intent of facilitating or encouraging the conduct, but the lawyer may counsel or assist a client in conduct when the lawyer reasonably believes:

(a) that the client's conduct constitutes a good-faith effort to determine the validity, scope, meaning, or application of a law or court order; or

(b) that the client can assert a nonfrivolous argument that the client's conduct will not constitute a crime or fraud or violate a court order.

(3) In counseling a client, a lawyer may address non-legal aspects of a proposed course of conduct, including moral, reputational, economic, social, political, and business aspects.

§95. An Evaluation Undertaken for a Third Person

(1) In furtherance of the objectives of a client in a representation, a lawyer may provide to a nonclient the results of the lawyer's investigation and analysis of facts or the lawyer's professional evaluation or opinion on the matter.

(2) When providing the information, evaluation, or opinion under Subsection (1) is reasonably likely to affect the client's interests materially and adversely, the lawyer must first obtain the client's consent after the client is adequately informed concerning important possible effects on the client's interests.

(3) In providing the information, evaluation, or opinion under Subsection (1), the lawyer must exercise care with respect to the nonclient to the extent stated in §51(2) and not make false statements prohibited under §98.

TOPIC 2. REPRESENTING ORGANIZATIONAL CLIENTS

§96. Representing an Organization as Client

(1) When a lawyer is employed or retained to represent an organization:

(a) the lawyer represents the interests of the organization as defined by its responsible agents acting pursuant to the organization's decision-making procedures; and

(b) subject to Subsection (2), the lawyer must follow instructions in the representation, as stated in §21(2), given by persons authorized so to act on behalf of the organization.

(2) If a lawyer representing an organization knows of circumstances indicating that a constituent of the organization has engaged in action or intends to act in a way that violates a legal obligation to the organization that will likely cause substantial injury to it, or that reasonably can be foreseen to be imputable to the organization and likely to result in substantial injury to it, the lawyer must proceed in what the lawyer reasonably believes to be the best interests of the organization.

(3) In the circumstances described in Subsection (2), the lawyer may, in circumstances warranting such steps, ask the constituent to reconsider the matter, recommend that a second legal opinion be sought, and seek review by appropriate supervisory authority within the organization, including referring the matter to the highest authority that can act in behalf of the organization.

§97. Representing a Governmental Client

A lawyer representing a governmental client must proceed in the representation as stated in §96, except that the lawyer:

(1) possesses such rights and responsibilities as may be defined by law to make decisions on behalf of the governmental client that are within the authority of a client under §§22 and 21(2);

(2) except as otherwise provided by law, must proceed as stated in §§96(2) and 96(3) with respect to an act of a constituent of the governmental client that violates a legal obligation that will likely cause substantial public or private injury or that reasonably can be foreseen to be imputable to and thus likely result in substantial injury to the client;

(3) if a prosecutor or similar lawyer determining whether to file criminal proceedings or take other steps in such proceedings, must do so only when based on probable cause and the lawyer's belief, formed after due investigation, that there are good factual and legal grounds to support the step taken; and

(4) must observe other applicable restrictions imposed by law on those similarly functioning for the governmental client.

TOPIC 3. LAWYER DEALINGS WITH A NONCLIENT

Title A. Dealings with a Nonclient — Generally

§98. Statements to a Nonclient

A lawyer communicating on behalf of a client with a nonclient may not:

(1) knowingly make a false statement of material fact or law to the nonclient,

(2) make other statements prohibited by law; or

(3) fail to make a disclosure of information required by law.

Title B. Contact with a Represented Nonclient

§99. A Represented Nonclient — The General Anti-Contact Rule

(1) A lawyer representing a client in a matter may not communicate about the subject of the representation with a nonclient whom the lawyer knows to be represented in the matter by another lawyer or with a representative of an organizational nonclient so represented as defined in §100, unless:

(a) the communication is with a public officer or agency to the extent stated in §101;

(b) the lawyer is a party and represents no other client in the matter;

(c) the communication is authorized by law;

(d) the communication reasonably responds to an emergency; or

(e) the other lawyer consents.

(2) Subsection (1) does not prohibit the lawyer from assisting the client in otherwise proper communication by the lawyer's client with a represented nonclient.

§100. Definition of a Represented Nonclient

Within the meaning of §99, a represented nonclient includes:

(1) a natural person represented by a lawyer; and:

(2) a current employee or other agent of an organization represented by a lawyer:

(a) if the employee or other agent supervises, directs, or regularly consults with the lawyer concerning the matter or if the agent has power to compromise or settle the matter;

(b) if the acts or omissions of the employee or other agent may be imputed to the organization for purposes of civil or criminal liability in the matter; or

(c) if a statement of the employee or other agent, under applicable rules of evidence, would have the effect of binding the organization with respect to proof of the matter.

§101. A Represented Governmental Agency or Officer

(1) Unless otherwise provided by law (see §99(1)(c)) and except as provided in Subsection (2), the prohibition stated in §99 against contact with a represented nonclient does not apply to communications with employees of a represented governmental agency or with a governmental officer being represented in the officer's official capacity.

(2) In negotiation or litigation by a lawyer of a specific claim of a client against a governmental agency or against a governmental officer in the officer's official capacity, the prohibition stated in §99 applies, except that the lawyer may contact any officer of the government if permitted by the agency or with respect to an issue of general policy.

§102. Information of a Nonclient Known to Be Legally Protected

A lawyer communicating with a nonclient in a situation permitted under §99 may not seek to obtain information that the lawyer reasonably

should know the nonclient may not reveal without violating a duty of confidentiality to another imposed by law.

Title C. Dealings with an Unrepresented Nonclient

§103. Dealings with an Unrepresented Nonclient

In the course of representing a client and dealing with a nonclient who is not represented by a lawyer:

(1) the lawyer may not mislead the nonclient, to the prejudice of the nonclient, concerning the identity and interests of the person the lawyer represents; and

(2) when the lawyer knows or reasonably should know that the unrepresented nonclient misunderstands the lawyer's role in the matter, the lawyer must make reasonable efforts to correct the misunderstanding when failure to do so would materially prejudice the nonclient.

TOPIC 4. LEGISLATIVE AND ADMINISTRATIVE MATTERS

§104. Representing a Client in Legislative and Administrative Matters

A lawyer representing a client before a legislature or administrative agency:

(1) must disclose that the appearance is in a representative capacity and not misrepresent the capacity in which the lawyer appears;

(2) must comply with applicable law and regulations governing such representations; and

(3) except as applicable law otherwise provides:

(a) in an adjudicative proceeding before a government agency or involving such an agency as a participant, has the legal rights and responsibilities of an advocate in a proceeding before a judicial tribunal; and

(b) in other types of proceedings and matters, has the legal rights and responsibilities applicable in the lawyer's dealings with a private person.

CHAPTER 7 REPRESENTING CLIENTS IN LITIGATION

TOPIC 1. ADVOCACY IN GENERAL

§105. Complying with Law and Tribunal Rulings

In representing a client in a matter before a tribunal, a lawyer must comply with applicable law, including rules of procedure and evidence and specific tribunal rulings.

§106. Dealing with Other Participants in Proceedings

In representing a client in a matter before a tribunal, a lawyer may not use means that have no substantial purpose other than to embarrass, delay, or burden a third person or use methods of obtaining evidence that are prohibited by law.

§107. Prohibited Forensic Tactics

In representing a client in a matter before a tribunal, a lawyer may not, in the presence of the trier of fact:

(1) state a personal opinion about the justness of a cause, the credibility of a witness, the culpability of a civil litigant, or the guilt or innocence of an accused, but the lawyer may argue any position or conclusion adequately supported by the lawyer's analysis of the evidence; or

(2) allude to any matter that the lawyer does not reasonably believe is relevant or that will not be supported by admissible evidence.

§108. An Advocate as a Witness

(1) Except as provided in Subsection (2), a lawyer may not represent a client in a contested hearing or trial of a matter in which:

(a) the lawyer is expected to testify for the lawyer's client; or

(b) the lawyer does not intend to testify but (i) the lawyer's testimony would be material to establishing a claim or defense of the client, and (ii) the client has not consented as stated in §122 to the lawyer's intention not to testify.

(2) A lawyer may represent a client when the lawyer will testify as stated in Subsection (1)(a) if:

(a) the lawyer's testimony relates to an issue that the lawyer reasonably believes will not be contested or to the nature and value of legal services rendered in the proceeding;

(b) deprivation of the lawyer's services as advocate would work a substantial hardship on the client; or

(c) consent has been given by

(i) opposing parties who would be adversely affected by the lawyer's testimony and,

(ii) if relevant, the lawyer's client, as stated in §122 with respect to any conflict of interest between lawyer and client (see §125) that the lawyer's testimony would create.

(3) A lawyer may not represent a client in a litigated matter pending before a tribunal when the lawyer or a lawyer in the lawyer's firm will give testimony materially adverse to the position of the lawyer's client or materially adverse to a former client of any such lawyer with respect to a matter substantially related to the earlier representation, unless the affected client has consented as stated in §122 with respect to any conflict of interest between lawyer and client (see §125) that the testimony would create.

(4) A tribunal should not permit a lawyer to call opposing trial counsel as a witness unless there is a compelling need for the lawyer's testimony.

§109. An Advocate's Public Comment on Pending Litigation

(1) In representing a client in a matter before a tribunal, a lawyer may not make a statement outside the proceeding that a reasonable person would expect to be disseminated by means of public communication when the lawyer knows or reasonably should know that the statement will have a substantial likelihood of materially prejudicing a juror or influencing or intimidating a prospective witness in the proceeding. However, a lawyer may in any event make a statement that is reasonably necessary to mitigate the impact on the lawyer's client of substantial, undue, and prejudicial publicity recently initiated by one other than the lawyer or the lawyer's client.

(2) A prosecutor must, except for statements necessary to inform the public of the nature and extent of the prosecutor's action and that serve a legitimate law-enforcement purpose, refrain from making extrajudicial comments that have a substantial likelihood of heightening public condemnation of the accused.

TOPIC 2. LIMITS ON ADVOCACY

§110. Frivolous Advocacy

(1) A lawyer may not bring or defend a proceeding or assert or controvert an issue therein, unless there is a basis for doing so that is not

frivolous, which includes a good-faith argument for an extension, modification, or reversal of existing law.

(2) Notwithstanding Subsection (1), a lawyer for the defendant in a criminal proceeding or the respondent in a proceeding that could result in incarceration may so defend the proceeding as to require that the prosecutor establish every necessary element.

(3) A lawyer may not make a frivolous discovery request, fail to make a reasonably diligent effort to comply with a proper discovery request of another party, or intentionally fail otherwise to comply with applicable procedural requirements concerning discovery.

§111. Disclosure of Legal Authority

In representing a client in a matter before a tribunal, a lawyer may not knowingly:

(1) make a false statement of a material proposition of law to the tribunal; or

(2) fail to disclose to the tribunal legal authority in the controlling jurisdiction known to the lawyer to be directly adverse to the position asserted by the client and not disclosed by opposing counsel.

§112. Advocacy in Ex Parte and Other Proceedings

In representing a client in a matter before a tribunal, a lawyer applying for ex parte relief or appearing in another proceeding in which similar special requirements of candor apply must comply with the requirements of §110 and §§118–120 and further:

(1) must not present evidence the lawyer reasonably believes is false;

(2) must disclose all material and relevant facts known to the lawyer that will enable the tribunal to reach an informed decision; and

(3) must comply with any other applicable special requirements of candor imposed by law.

TOPIC 3. ADVOCATES AND TRIBUNALS

§113. Improperly Influencing a Judicial Officer

(1) A lawyer may not knowingly communicate ex parte with a judicial officer before whom a proceeding is pending concerning the matter, except as authorized by law.

(2) A lawyer may not make a gift or loan prohibited by law to a judicial officer, attempt to influence the officer otherwise than by legally

proper procedures, or state or imply an ability so to influence a judicial officer.

§114. A Lawyer's Statements Concerning a Judicial Officer

A lawyer may not knowingly or recklessly make publicly a false statement of fact concerning the qualifications or integrity of an incumbent of a judicial office or a candidate for election to such an office.

§115. Lawyer Contact with a Juror

A lawyer may not:

(1) except as allowed by law, communicate with or seek to influence a person known by the lawyer to be a member of a jury pool from which the jury will be drawn;

(2) except as allowed by law, communicate with or seek to influence a member of a jury; or

(3) communicate with a juror who has been excused from further service:

(a) when that would harass the juror or constitute an attempt to influence the juror's actions as a juror in future cases; or

(b) when otherwise prohibited by law.

TOPIC 4. ADVOCATES AND EVIDENCE

§116. Interviewing and Preparing a Prospective Witness

(1) A lawyer may interview a witness for the purpose of preparing the witness to testify.

(2) A lawyer may not unlawfully obstruct another party's access to a witness.

(3) A lawyer may not unlawfully induce or assist a prospective witness to evade or ignore process obliging the witness to appear to testify.

(4) A lawyer may not request a person to refrain from voluntarily giving relevant testimony or information to another party, unless:

(a) the person is the lawyer's client in the matter; or

(b)(i) the person is not the lawyer's client but is a relative or employee or other agent of the lawyer or the lawyer's client, and (ii) the lawyer reasonably believes compliance will not materially and adversely affect the person's interests.

§117. Compensating a Witness

A lawyer may not offer or pay to a witness any consideration:

(1) in excess of the reasonable expenses of the witness incurred and the reasonable value of the witness's time spent in providing evidence, except that an expert witness may be offered and paid a noncontingent fee;

(2) contingent on the content of the witness's testimony or the outcome of the litigation; or

(3) otherwise prohibited by law.

§118. Falsifying or Destroying Evidence

(1) A lawyer may not falsify documentary or other evidence.

(2) A lawyer may not destroy or obstruct another party's access to documentary or other evidence when doing so would violate a court order or other legal requirements, or counsel or assist a client to do so.

§119. Physical Evidence of a Client Crime

With respect to physical evidence of a client crime, a lawyer:

(1) may, when reasonably necessary for purposes of the representation, take possession of the evidence and retain it for the time reasonably necessary to examine it and subject it to tests that do not alter or destroy material characteristics of the evidence; but

(2) following possession under subsection (1), the lawyer must notify prosecuting authorities of the lawyer's possession of the evidence or turn the evidence over to them.

§120. False Testimony or Evidence

(1) A lawyer may not:

(a) knowingly counsel or assist a witness to testify falsely or otherwise to offer false evidence;

(b) knowingly make a false statement of fact to the tribunal;

(c) offer testimony or other evidence as to an issue of fact known by the lawyer to be false.

(2) If a lawyer has offered testimony or other evidence as to a material issue of fact and comes to know of its falsity, the lawyer must take reasonable remedial measures and may disclose confidential client information when necessary to take such a measure.

(3) A lawyer may refuse to offer testimony or other evidence that the lawyer reasonably believes is false, even if the lawyer does not know it to be false.

CHAPTER 8 CONFLICTS OF INTEREST

TOPIC 1. CONFLICTS OF INTEREST — IN GENERAL

§121. The Basic Prohibition of Conflicts of Interest

Unless all affected clients and other necessary persons consent to the representation under the limitations and conditions provided in §122, a lawyer may not represent a client if the representation would involve a conflict of interest. A conflict of interest is involved if there is a substantial risk that the lawyer's representation of the client would be materially and adversely affected by the lawyer's own interests or by the lawyer's duties to another current client, a former client, or a third person.

§122. Client Consent to a Conflict of Interest

(1) A lawyer may represent a client notwithstanding a conflict of interest prohibited by §121 if each affected client or former client gives informed consent to the lawyer's representation. Informed consent requires that the client or former client have reasonably adequate information about the material risks of such representation to that client or former client.

(2) Notwithstanding the informed consent of each affected client or former client, a lawyer may not represent a client if:

(a) the representation is prohibited by law;

(b) one client will assert a claim against the other in the same litigation; or

(c) in the circumstances, it is not reasonably likely that the lawyer will be able to provide adequate representation to one or more of the clients.

§123. Imputation of a Conflict of Interest to an Affiliated Lawyer

Unless all affected clients consent to the representation under the limitations and conditions provided in §122 or unless imputation hereunder is removed as provided in §124, the restrictions upon a lawyer imposed by §§125–135 also restrict other affiliated lawyers who:

(1) are associated with that lawyer in rendering legal services to others through a law partnership, professional corporation, sole proprietorship, or similar association;

(2) are employed with that lawyer by an organization to render legal services either to that organization or to others to advance the interests or objectives of the organization; or

(3) share office facilities without reasonably adequate measures to protect confidential client information so that it will not be available to other lawyers in the shared office.

§124. Removing Imputation

(1) Imputation specified in §123 does not restrict an affiliated lawyer when the affiliation between the affiliated lawyer and the personally prohibited lawyer that required the imputation has been terminated, and no material confidential information of the client, relevant to the matter, has been communicated by the personally prohibited lawyer to the affiliated lawyer or that lawyer's firm.

(2) Imputation specified in §123 does not restrict an affiliated lawyer with respect to a former-client conflict under §132, when there is no substantial risk that confidential information of the former client will be used with material adverse effect on the former client because:

(a) any confidential client information communicated to the personally prohibited lawyer is unlikely to be significant in the subsequent matter;

(b) the personally prohibited lawyer is subject to screening measures adequate to eliminate participation by that lawyer in the representation; and

(c) timely and adequate notice of the screening has been provided to all affected clients.

(3) Imputation specified in §123 does not restrict a lawyer affiliated with a former government lawyer with respect to a conflict under §133 if:

(a) the personally prohibited lawyer is subject to screening measures adequate to eliminate involvement by that lawyer in the representation; and

(b) timely and adequate notice of the screening has been provided to the appropriate government agency and to affected clients.

TOPIC 2. CONFLICTS OF INTEREST BETWEEN A LAWYER AND A CLIENT

§125. A Lawyer's Personal Interest Affecting the Representation of a Client

Unless the affected client consents to the representation under the limitations and conditions provided in §122, a lawyer may not represent

a client if there is a substantial risk that the lawyer's representation of the client would be materially and adversely affected by the lawyer's financial or other personal interests.

§126. Business Transactions Between a Lawyer and a Client

A lawyer may not participate in a business or financial transaction with a client, except a standard commercial transaction in which the lawyer does not render legal services, unless:

(1) the client has adequate information about the terms of the transaction and the risks presented by the lawyer's involvement in it;

(2) the terms and circumstances of the transaction are fair and reasonable to the client; and

(3) the client consents to the lawyer's role in the transaction under the limitations and conditions provided in §122 after being encouraged, and given a reasonable opportunity, to seek independent legal advice concerning the transaction.

§127. A Client Gift to a Lawyer

(1) A lawyer may not prepare any instrument effecting any gift from a client to the lawyer, including a testamentary gift, unless the lawyer is a relative or other natural object of the client's generosity and the gift is not significantly disproportionate to those given other donees similarly related to the donor.

(2) A lawyer may not accept a gift from a client, including a testamentary gift, unless:

(a) the lawyer is a relative or other natural object of the client's generosity;

(b) the value conferred by the client and the benefit to the lawyer are insubstantial in amount; or

(c) the client, before making the gift, has received independent advice or has been encouraged, and given a reasonable opportunity, to seek such advice.

TOPIC 3. CONFLICTS OF INTEREST AMONG CURRENT CLIENTS

§128. Representing Clients with Conflicting Interests in Civil Litigation

Unless all affected clients consent to the representation under the limitations and conditions provided in §122, a lawyer in civil litigation may not:

(1) represent two or more clients in a matter if there is a substantial risk that the lawyer's representation of one client would be materially and adversely affected by the lawyer's duties to another client in the matter; or

(2) represent one client to assert or defend a claim against or brought by another client currently represented by the lawyer, even if the matters are not related.

§129. Conflicts of Interest in Criminal Litigation

Unless all affected clients consent to the representation under the limitations and conditions provided in §122, a lawyer in a criminal matter may not represent:

(1) two or more defendants or potential defendants in the same matter; or

(2) a single defendant, if the representation would involve a conflict of interest as defined in §121.

§130. Multiple Representation in a Nonlitigated Matter

Unless all affected clients consent to the representation under the limitations and conditions provided in §122, a lawyer may not represent two or more clients in a matter not involving litigation if there is a substantial risk that the lawyer's representation of one or more of the clients would be materially and adversely affected by the lawyer's duties to one or more of the other clients.

§131. Conflicts of Interest in Representing an Organization

Unless all affected clients consent to the representation under the limitations and conditions provided in §122, a lawyer may not represent both an organization and a director, officer, employee, shareholder, owner, partner, member, or other individual or organization associated with the organization if there is a substantial risk that the lawyer's representation of either would be materially and adversely affected by the lawyer's duties to the other.

TOPIC 4. CONFLICTS OF INTEREST WITH A FORMER CLIENT

§132. A Representation Adverse to the Interests of a Former Client

Unless both the affected present and former clients consent to the representation under the limitations and conditions provided in §122, a

lawyer who has represented a client in a matter may not thereafter represent another client in the same or a substantially related matter in which the interests of the former client are materially adverse. The current matter is substantially related to the earlier matter if:

(1) the current matter involves the work the lawyer performed for the former client; or

(2) there is a substantial risk that representation of the present client will involve the use of information acquired in the course of representing the former client, unless that information has become generally known.

§133. A Former Government Lawyer or Officer

(1) A lawyer may not act on behalf of a client with respect to a matter in which the lawyer participated personally and substantially while acting as a government lawyer or officer unless both the government and the client consent to the representation under the limitations and conditions provided in §122.

(2) A lawyer who acquires confidential information while acting as a government lawyer or officer may not:

(a) if the information concerns a person, represent a client whose interests are materially adverse to that person in a matter in which the information could be used to the material disadvantage of that person; or

(b) if the information concerns the governmental client or employer, represent another public or private client in circumstances described in §132(2).

TOPIC 5. CONFLICTS OF INTEREST DUE TO A LAWYER'S OBLIGATION TO A THIRD PERSON

§134. Compensation or Direction of a Lawyer by a Third Person

(1) A lawyer may not represent a client if someone other than the client will wholly or partly compensate the lawyer for the representation, unless the client consents under the limitations and conditions provided in §122 and knows of the circumstances and conditions of the payment.

(2) A lawyer's professional conduct on behalf of a client may be directed by someone other than the client if:

(a) the direction does not interfere with the lawyer's independence of professional judgment;

(b) the direction is reasonable in scope and character, such as by reflecting obligations borne by the person directing the lawyer; and

(c) the client consents to the direction under the limitations and conditions provided in §122.

§135. A Lawyer with a Fiduciary or Other Legal Obligation to a Nonclient

Unless the affected client consents to the representation under the limitations and conditions provided in §122, a lawyer may not represent a client in any matter with respect to which the lawyer has a fiduciary or other legal obligation to another if there is a substantial risk that the lawyer's representation of the client would be materially and adversely affected by the lawyer's obligation.

TABLE COMPARING ABA MODEL RULES OF PROFESSIONAL CONDUCT TO RESTATEMENT OF THE LAW GOVERNING LAWYERS

ABA Model Rule	Comparable Restatement Sections
1.1	16, 17, 29, 48–50, 52, 53-55
1.2	16, 21-23, 26, 51, 67, 82, 93, 94, 120
1.3	16
1.4	20
1.5	17, 19, 34, 35, 37–43, 47
1.6	14, 15, 41, 59–93
1.7	14, 15, 108, 121, 122, 125, 128–130, 135
1.8	16, 18, 36, 43, 46, 54, 126, 127
1.9	15, 33, 121, 122, 132
1.10	15, 123, 124
1.11	74, 97, 124, 133
1.12	124
1.13	73, 85, 96, 97, 131
1.14	24
1.15	43–46
1.16	31–33, 40, 46
1.17	No comparable Restatement provision
1.18	15
2.1	94
2.2	130
2.3	51, 95
2.4	No comparable Restatement provision
3.1	57, 110
3.2	No comparable Restatement provision
3.3	111, 112, 118, 120

ABA Model Rule	Comparable Restatement Sections
3.4	94, 105, 107, 110, 116–119
3.5	112, 113, 115
3.6	109
3.7	108
3.8	57, 97, 109
3.9	104
4.1	51, 56, 98
4.2	99–102
4.3	103
4.4	30, 51, 56, 102, 106
5.1	11, 58
5.2	12
5.3	11, 58
5.4	10, 134
5.5	2–4
5.6	9, 13
5.7	No comparable Restatement provision
6.1	No comparable Restatement provision
6.2	14
6.3	No comparable Restatement provision
6.4	No comparable Restatement provision
6.5	No comparable Restatement provision
7.1	No comparable Restatement provision
7.2	No comparable Restatement provision
7.3	9
7.4	No comparable Restatement provision
7.5	No comparable Restatement provision
7.6	No comparable Restatement provision
8.1	2
8.2	14
8.3	2, 5
8.4	1, 5, 37, 113
8.5	1, 5

TABLE COMPARING RESTATEMENT OF THE LAW GOVERNING LAWYERS TO ABA MODEL RULES OF PROFESSIONAL CONDUCT

Restatement Section	Comparable ABA Model Rule
1	8.4, 8.5
2	5.5, 8.1, 8.3
3	5.5
4	5.5
5	8.3, 8.4, 8.5

Restatement of the Law Governing Lawyers

Restatement Section	Comparable ABA Model Rule
6	No comparable provision
7	No comparable provision
8	No comparable provision
9	5.6, 7.3
10	5.4
11	5.1, 5.3
12	5.2
13	5.6
14	1.6, 1.7, 6.2
15	1.6, 1.7, 1.9, 1.10
16	1.1, 1.2, 1.3, 1.8
17	1.1, 1.5
18	1.8
19	1.5
20	1.4
21	1.2
22	1.2
23	1.2
24	1.14
25	No comparable provision
26	1.2
27	No comparable provision
28	No comparable provision
29	1.1
30	4.4
31	1.16
32	1.16
33	1.9, 1.16
34	1.5
35	1.5
36	1.8
37	1.5, 8.4
38	1.5
39	1.5
40	1.5, 1.16
41	1.5, 1.6
42	1.5
43	1.5, 1.8, 1.15
44	1.15
45	1.15
46	1.8, 1.15, 1.16
47	1.5
48	1.1
49	1.1
50	1.1

Restatement Section	Comparable ABA Model Rule
51	1.2, 2.3, 4.1, 4.4
52	1.1
53	1.1
54	1.1, 1.8
55	1.1
56	4.1, 4.4
57	3.1, 3.8
58	5.1, 5.3
59	1.6
60	1.6
61	1.6
62	1.6
63	1.6
64	1.6
65	1.6
66	1.6
67	1.2, 1.6
68	1.6
69	1.6
70	1.6
71	1.6
72	1.6
73	1.6, 1.13
74	1.6, 1.11
75	1.6
76	1.6
77	1.6
78	1.6
79	1.6
80	1.6
81	1.6
82	1.2, 1.6
83	1.6
84	1.6
85	1.6, 1.13
86	1.6
87	1.6
88	1.6
89	1.6
90	1.6
91	1.6
92	1.6
93	1.2, 1.6
94	1.2, 2.1, 3.4
95	2.3

Restatement of the Law Governing Lawyers

Restatement Section	Comparable ABA Model Rule
96	1.13
97	1.11, 1.13, 3.8
98	4.1
99	4.2
100	4.2
101	4.2
102	4.2, 4.4
103	4.3
104	3.9
105	3.4
106	4.4
107	3.4
108	1.7, 3.7
109	3.6, 3.8
110	3.1, 3.4
111	3.3
112	3.3, 3.5
113	3.5, 8.4
114	8.2
115	3.5
116	3.4
117	3.4
118	3.3, 3.4
119	3.4
120	1.2, 3.3
121	1.7, 1.9
122	1.7, 1.9
123	1.1
124	1.10, 1.11, 1.12
125	1.7
126	1.8
127	1.8
128	1.7
129	1.7
130	1.7, 2.2
131	1.13
132	1.9
133	1.11
134	5.4
135	1.7

ABA Model Code of Professional Responsibility*

In effect as of August 1983

Editors' Introduction. From 1908 to 1969, the ABA's formal position on matters of legal ethics was embodied in the ABA's Canons of Professional Ethics. In 1964, however, amidst growing dissatisfaction with the Canons, the ABA appointed a Special Committee on the Evaluation of Ethical Standards (the "Wright Committee") to study the Canons. The Wright Committee drafted a proposed Code of Professional Responsibility, which was ultimately approved by the ABA House of Delegates in August of 1969. By 1980, nearly every state had adopted a Code of Professional Responsibility modeled on the ABA Code. Since 1983, however, about 45 jurisdictions have revised their ethical rules to conform, in some degree, to the Model Rules of Professional Conduct. Many of the Model Rules, however, closely parallel their counterparts in the Model Code. (After each set of Disciplinary Rules, we have included a table relating Model Code provisions to the comparable provisions in the Model Rules.)

The Code was amended a number of times during the 1970's, principally in response to Supreme Court opinions concerning advertising and group legal services. The version of the Model Code reprinted here is the version that was in effect at the time the ABA adopted the Model Rules in August 1983. However, because the ABA has not amended the Model Code in more than two decades and does not intend to amend it in the future, and because only a handful of states continue to use the Code's Ethical Considerations (EC's) and the Code's awkward numbering system, we reprint only the Canons and the Disciplinary Rules. We have omitted all footnotes, whose main purpose was to relate the Code to the old ABA Canons of Professional Ethics, and we have omitted all of the Ethical Considerations. (Those who want to study the EC's should consult the New York Code of Professional Responsibility, which is reprinted later in this volume. The New York Code includes many EC's based on the ABA Model Code and uses the same numbering system as the Code.)

Contents

Preamble
Preliminary Statement

Canon 1. A Lawyer Should Assist in Maintaining the Integrity and Competence of the Legal Profession

DR 1-101. Maintaining Integrity and Competence of the Legal Profession
DR 1-102. Misconduct
DR 1-103. Disclosure of Information to Authorities

Canon 2. A Lawyer Should Assist the Legal Profession in Fulfilling Its Duty to Make Legal Counsel Available

DR 2-101. Publicity
DR 2-102. Professional Notices, Letterheads and Offices
DR 2-103. Recommendation of Professional Employment
DR 2-104. Suggestion of Need of Legal Services
DR 2-105. Limitation of Practice
DR 2-106. Fees for Legal Services
DR 2-107. Division of Fees Among Lawyers
DR 2-108. Agreements Restricting the Practice of a Lawyer
DR 2-109. Acceptance of Employment
DR 2-110. Withdrawal from Employment

Canon 3. A Lawyer Should Assist in Preventing the Unauthorized Practice of Law

DR 3-101. Aiding Unauthorized Practice of Law
DR 3-102. Dividing Legal Fees with a Non-Lawyer
DR 3-103. Forming a Partnership with a Non-Lawyer

Canon 4. A Lawyer Should Preserve the Confidences and Secrets of a Client

DR 4-101. Preservation of Confidences and Secrets of a Client

Canon 5. A Lawyer Should Exercise Independent Professional Judgment on Behalf of a Client

DR 5-101. Refusing Employment When the Interests of the Lawyer May Impair His Independent Professional Judgment
DR 5-102. Withdrawal as Counsel When the Lawyer Becomes a Witness
DR 5-103. Avoiding Acquisition of Interest in Litigation

DR 5-104. Limiting Business Relations with a Client
DR 5-105. Refusing to Accept or Continue Employment If the Interests of Another Client May Impair the Independent Professional Judgment of the Lawyer
DR 5-106. Settling Similar Claims of Clients
DR 5-107. Avoiding Influence by Others Than the Client

Canon 6. A Lawyer Should Represent a Client Competently

DR 6-101. Failing to Act Competently
DR 6-102. Limiting Liability to Client

Canon 7. A Lawyer Should Represent a Client Zealously Within the Bounds of the Law

DR 7-101. Representing a Client Zealously
DR 7-102. Representing a Client Within the Bounds of the Law
DR 7-103. Performing the Duty of Public Prosecutor or Other Government Lawyer
DR 7-104. Communicating with One of Adverse Interest
DR 7-105. Threatening Criminal Prosecution
DR 7-106. Trial Conduct
DR 7-107. Trial Publicity
DR 7-108. Communication with or Investigation of Jurors
DR 7-109. Contact with Witnesses
DR 7-110. Contact with Officials

Canon 8. A Lawyer Should Assist in Improving the Legal System

DR 8-101. Action as a Public Official
DR 8-102. Statements Concerning Judges and Other Adjudicatory Officers
DR 8-103. Lawyer Candidate for Judicial Office

Canon 9. A Lawyer Should Avoid Even the Appearance of Professional Impropriety

DR 9-101. Avoiding Even the Appearance of Impropriety
DR 9-102. Preserving Identity of Funds and Property of a Client

Definitions

PREAMBLE

The continued existence of a free and democratic society depends upon recognition of the concept that justice is based upon the rule of law grounded in respect for the dignity of the individual and his capacity through reason for enlightened self-government. Law so grounded makes justice possible, for only through such law does the dignity of the individual attain respect and protection. Without it, individual rights become subject to unrestrained power, respect for law is destroyed, and rational self-government is impossible.

Lawyers, as guardians of the law, play a vital role in the preservation of society. The fulfillment of this role requires an understanding by lawyers of their relationship with and function in our legal system. A consequent obligation of lawyers is to maintain the highest standards of ethical conduct.

In fulfilling his professional responsibilities, a lawyer necessarily assumes various roles that require the performance of many difficult tasks. Not every situation which he may encounter can be foreseen, but fundamental ethical principles are always present to guide him. Within the framework of these principles, a lawyer must with courage and foresight be able and ready to shape the body of the law to the ever-changing relationships of society.

The Model Code of Professional Responsibility points the way to the aspiring and provides standards by which to judge the transgressor. Each lawyer must find within his own conscience the touchstone against which to test the extent to which his actions should rise above minimum standards. But in the last analysis it is the desire for the respect and confidence of the members of his profession and of the society which he serves that should provide to a lawyer the incentive for the highest possible degree of ethical conduct. The possible loss of that respect and confidence is the ultimate sanction. So long as its practitioners are guided by these principles, the law will continue to be a noble profession. This is its greatness and its strength, which permit of no compromise.

PRELIMINARY STATEMENT

In furtherance of the principles stated in the Preamble, the American Bar Association has promulgated this Model Code of Professional Responsibility, consisting of three separate but interrelated parts: Canons, Ethical Considerations, and Disciplinary Rules. The Model Code is designed to be adopted by appropriate agencies both as an inspirational guide to the members of the profession and as a basis for disciplinary action when the conduct of a lawyer falls below the required minimum standards stated in the Disciplinary Rules.

Obviously the Canons, Ethical Considerations, and Disciplinary

Rules cannot apply to non-lawyers; however, they do define the type of ethical conduct that the public has a right to expect not only of lawyers but also of their non-professional employees and associates in all matters pertaining to professional employment. A lawyer should ultimately be responsible for the conduct of his employees and associates in the course of the professional representation of the client.

The Canons are statements of axiomatic norms, expressing in general terms the standards of professional conduct expected of lawyers in their relationships with the public, with the legal system, and with the legal profession. They embody the general concepts from which the Ethical Considerations and the Disciplinary Rules are derived.

The Ethical Considerations are aspirational in character and represent the objectives toward which every member of the profession should strive. They constitute a body of principles upon which the lawyer can rely for guidance in many specific situations.

The Disciplinary Rules, unlike the Ethical Considerations, are mandatory in character. The Disciplinary Rules state the minimum level of conduct below which no lawyer can fall without being subject to disciplinary action. Within the framework of fair trial, the Disciplinary Rules should be uniformly applied to all lawyers, regardless of the nature of their professional activities. The Model Code makes no attempt to prescribe either disciplinary procedures or penalties for violation of a Disciplinary Rule, nor does it undertake to define standards for civil liability of lawyers for professional conduct. The severity of judgment against one found guilty of violating a Disciplinary Rule should be determined by the character of the offense and the attendant circumstances. An enforcing agency, in applying the Disciplinary Rules, may find interpretive guidance in the basic principles embodied in the Canons and in the objectives reflected in the Ethical Considerations.

CANON 1. A LAWYER SHOULD ASSIST IN MAINTAINING THE INTEGRITY AND COMPETENCE OF THE LEGAL PROFESSION

DR 1-101 Maintaining Integrity and Competence of the Legal Profession

(A) A lawyer is subject to discipline if he has made a materially false statement in, or if he has deliberately failed to disclose a material fact requested in connection with, his application for admission to the bar.

(B) A lawyer shall not further the application for admission to the bar of another person known by him to be unqualified in respect to character, education, or other relevant attribute.

DR 1-102 Misconduct

(A) A lawyer shall not:

(1) Violate a Disciplinary Rule.

(2) Circumvent a Disciplinary Rule through actions of another.

(3) Engage in illegal conduct involving moral turpitude.

(4) Engage in conduct involving dishonesty, fraud, deceit, or misrepresentation.

(5) Engage in conduct that is prejudicial to the administration of justice.

(6) Engage in any other conduct that adversely reflects on his fitness to practice law.

DR 1-103 Disclosure of Information to Authorities

(A) A lawyer possessing unprivileged knowledge of a violation of DR 1-102 shall report such knowledge to a tribunal or other authority empowered to investigate or act upon such violation.

(B) A lawyer possessing unprivileged knowledge or evidence concerning another lawyer or a judge shall reveal fully such knowledge or evidence upon proper request of a tribunal or other authority empowered to investigate or act upon the conduct of lawyers or judges.

Model Rules Comparison

Model Code	*ABA Model Rules*
DR 1-101	Rule 8.1(a)
DR 1-102(A)(1)	Rule 8.4(a)
DR 1-102(A)(2)	Rules 5.1(c), 5.3(b), 8.4(a)
DR 1-102(A)(3)	Rule 8.4(b), (f)
DR 1-102(A)(4)	Rules 3.3(a)(1), (2), & (4), 3.4(a), (b), 4.1, 8.4(c), (f)
DR 1-102(A)(5)	Rules 3.1 through 3.9, Rules 8.1, 8.4(d) & (f)
DR 1-102(A)(6)	Rules 3.4(b), 8.4(b), (f)
DR 1-103(A)	Rules 5.1, 8.3
DR 1-103(B)	Rule 8.1(b)

CANON 2. A LAWYER SHOULD ASSIST THE LEGAL PROFESSION IN FULFILLING ITS DUTY TO MAKE LEGAL COUNSEL AVAILABLE

DR 2-101 Publicity

(A) A lawyer shall not, on behalf of himself, his partner, associate or any other lawyer affiliated with him or his firm, use or participate in the use of any form of public communication containing a false, fraudulent, misleading, deceptive, self-laudatory or unfair statement or claim.

(B) In order to facilitate the process of informed selection of a lawyer by potential consumers of legal services, a lawyer may publish or broadcast, subject to DR 2-103, the following information in print media distributed or over television or radio broadcast in the geographic area or areas in which the lawyer resides or maintains offices or in which a significant part of the lawyer's clientele resides, provided that the information disclosed by the lawyer in such publication or broadcast complies with DR 2-101(A), and is presented in a dignified manner:

(1) Name, including name of law firm and names of professional associates; addresses and telephone numbers;

(2) One or more fields of law in which the lawyer or law firm practices, a statement that practice is limited to one or more fields of law, or a statement that the lawyer or law firm specializes in a particular field of law practice, to the extent authorized under DR 2-105;

(3) Date and place of birth;

(4) Date and place of admission to the bar of state and federal courts;

(5) Schools attended, with dates of graduation, degrees and other scholastic distinctions;

(6) Public or quasi-public offices;

(7) Military service;

(8) Legal authorships;

(9) Legal teaching positions;

(10) Memberships, offices, and committee assignments, in bar associations;

(11) Membership and offices in legal fraternities and legal societies;

(12) Technical and professional licenses;

(13) Memberships in scientific, technical and professional associations and societies;

(14) Foreign language ability;

(15) Names and addresses of bank references;

(16) With their written consent, names of clients regularly represented;

(17) Prepaid or group legal services programs in which the lawyer participates;

(18) Whether credit cards or other credit arrangements are accepted;

(19) Office and telephone answering service hours;

(20) Fee for an initial consultation;

(21) Availability upon request of a written schedule of fees and/or an estimate of the fee to be charged for specific services;

(22) Contingent fee rates subject to DR 2-106(C), provided that the statement discloses whether percentages are computed before or after deduction of costs;

(23) Range of fees for services, provided that the statement discloses that the specific fee within the range which will be charged will vary depending upon the particular matter to be handled for each client and the client is entitled without obligation to an estimate of the fee within the range likely to be charged, in print size equivalent to the largest print used in setting forth the fee information;

(24) Hourly rate, provided that the statement discloses that the total fee charged will depend upon the number of hours which must be devoted to the particular matter to be handled for each client and the client is entitled to without obligation an estimate of the fee likely to be charged, in print size at least equivalent to the largest print used in setting forth the fee information;

(25) Fixed fees for specific legal services, the description of which would not be misunderstood or be deceptive, provided that the statement discloses that the quoted fee will be available only to clients whose matters fall into the services described and that the client is entitled without obligation to a specific estimate of the fee likely to be charged in print size at least equivalent to the largest print used in setting forth the fee information.

(C) Any person desiring to expand the information authorized for disclosure in DR 2-101(B), or to provide for its dissemination through other forums may apply to [the agency having jurisdiction under state law]. Any such application shall be served upon [the agencies having jurisdiction under state law over the regulation of the legal profession and consumer matters] who shall be heard, together with the applicant, on the issue of whether the proposal is necessary in light of the existing provisions of the Code, accords with standards of accuracy, reliability and truthfulness, and would facilitate the process of informed selection of lawyers by potential consumers of legal services. The relief granted in response to any such application shall be promulgated as an amendment to DR 2-101(B), universally applicable to all lawyers.

(D) If the advertisement is communicated to the public over television or radio, it shall be prerecorded, approved for broadcast by the lawyer, and a recording of the actual transmission shall be retained by the lawyer.

(E) If a lawyer advertises a fee for a service, the lawyer must render that service for no more than the fee advertised.

(F) Unless otherwise specified in the advertisement if a lawyer publishes any fee information authorized under DR 2-101(B) in a publication that is published more frequently than one time per month, the lawyer shall be bound by any representation made therein for a period of not less than 30 days after such publication. If a lawyer publishes any fee information authorized under DR 2-101(B) in a publication that is published once a month or less frequently, he shall be bound by any representation made therein until the publication of the succeeding issue. If a lawyer publishes any fee information authorized under DR 2-101(B) in a publication which has no fixed date for publication of a succeeding issue, the lawyer shall be bound by any representation made therein for a reasonable period of time after publication but in no event less than one year.

(G) Unless otherwise specified, if a lawyer broadcasts any fee information authorized under DR 2-101(B), the lawyer shall be bound by any representation made therein for a period of not less than 30 days after such broadcast.

(H) This rule does not prohibit limited and dignified identification of a lawyer as a lawyer as well as by name:

(1) In political advertisements when his professional status is germane to the political campaign or to a political issue.

(2) In public notices when the name and profession of a lawyer are required or authorized by law or are reasonably pertinent for a purpose other than the attraction of potential clients.

(3) In routine reports and announcements of a bona fide business, civic, professional, or political organization in which he serves as a director or officer.

(4) In and on legal documents prepared by him.

(5) In and on legal textbooks, treatises, and other legal publications, and in dignified advertisements thereof.

(I) A lawyer shall not compensate or give any thing of value to representatives of the press, radio, television, or other communication medium in anticipation of or in return for professional publicity in a news item.

DR 2-102 Professional Notices, Letterheads and Offices

(A) A lawyer or law firm shall not use or participate in the use of professional cards, professional announcement cards, office signs, letterheads, or similar professional notices or devices, except that the following may be used if they are in dignified form:

(1) A professional card of a lawyer identifying him by name and as a lawyer, and giving his addresses, telephone numbers, the name of his law firm, and any information permitted under DR 2-105. A professional card of a law firm may also give the names of members and associates. Such cards may be used for identification.

(2) A brief professional announcement card stating new or changed associations or addresses, change of firm name, or similar matters pertaining to the professional offices of a lawyer or law firm, which may be mailed to lawyers, clients, former clients, personal friends, and relatives. It shall not state biographical data except to the extent reasonably necessary to identify the lawyer or to explain the change in his association, but it may state the immediate past position of the lawyer. It may give the names and dates of predecessor firms in a continuing line of succession. It shall not state the nature of the practice except as permitted under DR 2-105.

(3) A sign on or near the door of the office and in the building directory identifying the law office. The sign shall not state the nature of the practice, except as permitted under DR 2-105.

(4) A letterhead of a lawyer identifying him by name and as a lawyer, and giving his addresses, telephone numbers, the name of his law firm, associates and any information permitted under DR 2-105. A letterhead of a law firm may also give the names of members and associates, and names and dates relating to deceased and retired members. A lawyer may be designated "Of Counsel" on a letterhead if he has a continuing relationship with a lawyer or law firm, other than as a partner or associate. A lawyer or law firm may be designated as "General Counsel" or by similar professional reference on stationery of a client if he or the firm devotes a substantial amount of professional time in the representation of that client. The letterhead of a law firm may give the names and dates of predecessor firms in a continuing line of succession.

(B) A lawyer in private practice shall not practice under a trade name, a name that is misleading as to the identity of the lawyer or lawyers practicing under such name, or a firm name containing names other than those of one or more of the lawyers in the firm, except that the name of a professional corporation or professional association may contain "P.C." or "P.A." or similar symbols indicating the nature of the organization, and if otherwise lawful a firm may use as, or continue to include in, its name the name or names of one or more deceased or retired members of the firm or of a predecessor firm in a continuing line of succession. A lawyer who assumes a judicial, legislative, or public executive or administrative post or office shall not permit his name to remain in the name of a law firm or to be used in professional notices of the firm during any significant period in which he is not actively and regularly practicing law as a member of the firm, and during such period other members of the firm shall not use his name in the firm name or in professional notices of the firm.

(C) A lawyer shall not hold himself out as having a partnership with one or more other lawyers or professional corporations unless they are in fact partners.

(D) A partnership shall not be formed or continued between or among lawyers licensed in different jurisdictions unless all enumera-

tions of the members and associates of the firm on its letterhead and in other permissible listings make clear the jurisdictional limitations on those members and associates of the firm not licensed to practice in all listed jurisdictions; however, the same firm name may be used in each jurisdiction.

(E) Nothing contained herein shall prohibit a lawyer from using or permitting the use of, in connection with his name, an earned degree or title derived therefrom indicating his training in the law.

DR 2-103 Recommendation of Professional Employment

(A) A lawyer shall not, except as authorized in DR 2-101(B), recommend employment as a private practitioner, of himself, his partner, or associate to a layperson who has not sought his advice regarding employment of a lawyer.

(B) A lawyer shall not compensate or give anything of value to a person or organization to recommend or secure his employment by a client, or as a reward for having made a recommendation resulting in his employment by a client, except that he may pay the usual and reasonable fees or dues charged by any of the organizations listed in DR 2-103(D).

(C) A lawyer shall not request a person or organization to recommend or promote the use of his services or those of his partner or associate, or any other lawyer affiliated with him or his firm, as a private practitioner, except as authorized in DR 2-101, and except that

(1) He may request referrals from a lawyer referral service operated, sponsored, or approved by a bar association and may pay its fees incident thereto.

(2) He may cooperate with the legal service activities of any of the offices or organizations enumerated in DR 2-103(D) (1) through (4) and may perform legal services for those to whom he was recommended by it to do such work if:

(a) The person to whom the recommendation is made is a member or beneficiary of such office or organization; and

(b) The lawyer remains free to exercise his independent professional judgment on behalf of his client.

(D) A lawyer or his partner or associate or any other lawyer affiliated with him or his firm may be recommended, employed or paid by, or may cooperate with, one of the following offices or organizations that promote the use of his services or those of his partner or associate or any other lawyer affiliated with him or his firm if there is no interference with the exercise of independent professional judgment in behalf of his client:

(1) A legal aid office or public defender office:

(a) Operated or sponsored by a duly accredited law school.

(b) Operated or sponsored by a bona fide nonprofit community organization.

(c) Operated or sponsored by a governmental agency.

(d) Operated, sponsored, or approved by a bar association.

(2) A military legal assistance office.

(3) A lawyer referral service operated, sponsored, or approved by a bar association.

(4) Any bona fide organization that recommends, furnishes or pays for legal services to its members or beneficiaries provided the following conditions are satisfied:

(a) Such organization, including any affiliate, is so organized and operated that no profit is derived by it from the rendition of legal services by lawyers, and that, if the organization is organized for profit, the legal services are not rendered by lawyers employed, directed, supervised or selected by it except in connection with matters where such organization bears ultimate liability of its member or beneficiary.

(b) Neither the lawyer, nor his partner, nor associate, nor any other lawyer affiliated with him or his firm, nor any non-lawyer, shall have initiated or promoted such organization for the primary purpose of providing financial or other benefit to such lawyer, partner, associate or affiliated lawyer.

(c) Such organization is not operated for the purpose of procuring legal work or financial benefit for any lawyer as a private practitioner outside of the legal services program of the organization.

(d) The member or beneficiary to whom the legal services are furnished, and not such organization, is recognized as the client of the lawyer in the matter.

(e) Any member or beneficiary who is entitled to have legal services furnished or paid for by the organization may, if such member or beneficiary so desires, select counsel other than that furnished, selected or approved by the organization for the particular matter involved; and the legal service plan of such organization provides appropriate relief for any member or beneficiary who asserts a claim that representation by counsel furnished, selected or approved would be unethical, improper or inadequate under the circumstances of the matter involved and the plan provides an appropriate procedure for seeking such relief.

(f) The lawyer does not know or have cause to know that such organization is in violation of applicable laws, rules of court and other legal requirements that govern its legal service operations.

(g) Such organization has filed with the appropriate disciplinary authority at least annually a report with respect to its legal service plan, if any, showing its terms, its schedule of benefits, its subscription charges, agreements with counsel, and financial results of its legal service activities or, if it has failed to do so, the lawyer does not know or have cause to know of such failure.

(E) A lawyer shall not accept employment when he knows or it is obvious that the person who seeks his services does so as a result of conduct prohibited under this Disciplinary Rule.

DR 2-104 Suggestion of Need of Legal Services

(A) A lawyer who has given in-person unsolicited advice to a layperson that he should obtain counsel or take legal action shall not accept employment resulting from that advice, except that:

(1) A lawyer may accept employment by a close friend, relative, former client (if the advice is germane to the former employment), or one whom the lawyer reasonably believes to be a client.

(2) A lawyer may accept employment that results from his participation in activities designed to educate laypersons to recognize legal problems, to make intelligent selection of counsel, or to utilize available legal services if such activities are conducted or sponsored by a qualified legal assistance organization.

(3) A lawyer who is recommended, furnished or paid by a qualified legal assistance organization enumerated in DR 2-103(D) (1) through (4) may represent a member or beneficiary thereof, to the extent and under the conditions prescribed therein.

(4) Without affecting his right to accept employment, a lawyer may speak publicly or write for publication on legal topics so long as he does not emphasize his own professional experience or reputation and does not undertake to give individual advice.

(5) If success in asserting rights or defenses of his client in litigation in the nature of a class action is dependent upon the joinder of others, a lawyer may accept, but shall not seek, employment from those contacted for the purpose of obtaining their joinder.

DR 2-105 Limitation of Practice

(A) A lawyer shall not hold himself out publicly as a specialist, as practicing in certain areas of law or as limiting his practice permitted under DR 2-101(B), except as follows:

(1) A lawyer admitted to practice before the United States Patent and Trademark Office may use the designation "Patents," "Patent Attorney," "Patent Lawyer," or "Registered Patent Attorney" or any combination of those terms, on his letterhead and office sign.

(2) A lawyer who publicly discloses fields of law in which the lawyer or the law firm practices or states that his practice is limited to one or more fields of law shall do so by using designations and

definitions authorized and approved by [the agency having jurisdiction of the subject under state law].

(3) A lawyer who is certified as a specialist in a particular field of law or law practice by [the authority having jurisdiction under state law over the subject of specialization by lawyers] may hold himself out as such, but only in accordance with the rules prescribed by that authority.

DR 2-106 Fees for Legal Services

(A) A lawyer shall not enter into an agreement for, charge, or collect an illegal or clearly excessive fee.

(B) A fee is clearly excessive when, after a review of the facts, a lawyer of ordinary prudence would be left with a definite and firm conviction that the fee is in excess of a reasonable fee. Factors to be considered as guides in determining the reasonableness of a fee include the following:

(1) The time and labor required, the novelty and difficulty of the questions involved, and the skill requisite to perform the legal service properly.

(2) The likelihood, if apparent to the client, that the acceptance of the particular employment will preclude other employment by the lawyer.

(3) The fee customarily charged in the locality for similar legal services.

(4) The amount involved and the results obtained.

(5) The time limitations imposed by the client or by the circumstances.

(6) The nature and length of the professional relationship with the client.

(7) The experience, reputation, and ability of the lawyer or lawyers performing the services.

(8) Whether the fee is fixed or contingent.

(C) A lawyer shall not enter into an arrangement for, charge, or collect a contingent fee for representing a defendant in a criminal case.

DR 2-107 Division of Fees Among Lawyers

(A) A lawyer shall not divide a fee for legal services with another lawyer who is not a partner in or associate of his law firm or law office, unless:

(1) The client consents to employment of the other lawyer after a full disclosure that a division of fees will be made.

(2) The division is made in proportion to the services performed and responsibility assumed by each.

(3) The total fee of the lawyers does not clearly exceed reasonable compensation for all legal services they rendered the client.

(B) This Disciplinary Rule does not prohibit payment to a former partner or associate pursuant to a separation or retirement agreement.

DR 2-108 Agreements Restricting the Practice of a Lawyer

(A) A lawyer shall not be a party to or participate in a partnership or employment agreement with another lawyer that restricts the right of a lawyer to practice law after the termination of a relationship created by the agreement, except as a condition to payment of retirement benefits.

(B) In connection with the settlement of a controversy or suit, a lawyer shall not enter into an agreement that restricts his right to practice law.

DR 2-109 Acceptance of Employment

(A) A lawyer shall not accept employment on behalf of a person if he knows or it is obvious that such person wishes to:

(1) Bring a legal action, conduct a defense, or assert a position in litigation, or otherwise have steps taken for him, merely for the purpose of harassing or maliciously injuring any person.

(2) Present a claim or defense in litigation that is not warranted under existing law, unless it can be supported by good faith argument for an extension, modification, or reversal of existing law.

DR 2-110 Withdrawal from Employment

(A) In general.

(1) If permission for withdrawal from employment is required by the rules of a tribunal, a lawyer shall not withdraw from employment in a proceeding before that tribunal without its permission.

(2) In any event, a lawyer shall not withdraw from employment until he has taken reasonable steps to avoid foreseeable prejudice to the rights of his client, including giving due notice to his client, allowing time for employment of other counsel, delivering to the client all papers and property to which the client is entitled, and complying with applicable laws and rules.

(3) A lawyer who withdraws from employment shall refund promptly any part of a fee paid in advance that has not been earned.

(B) *Mandatory withdrawal.* A lawyer representing a client before a tribunal, with its permission if required by its rules, shall withdraw from employment, and a lawyer representing a client in other matters shall withdraw from employment, if:

(1) He knows or it is obvious that his client is bringing the legal action, conducting the defense, or asserting a position in the litigation, or is otherwise having steps taken for him, merely for the purpose of harassing or maliciously injuring any person.

(2) He knows or it is obvious that his continued employment will result in violation of a Disciplinary Rule.

(3) His mental or physical condition renders it unreasonably difficult for him to carry out the employment effectively.

(4) He is discharged by his client.

(C) *Permissive withdrawal.* If DR 2-110 (B) is not applicable, a lawyer may not request permission to withdraw in matters pending before a tribunal, and may not withdraw in other matters, unless such request or such withdrawal is because:

(1) His client:

(a) Insists upon presenting a claim or defense that is not warranted under existing law and cannot be supported by good faith argument for an extension, modification, or reversal of existing law.

(b) Personally seeks to pursue an illegal course of conduct.

(c) Insists that the lawyer pursue a course of conduct that is illegal or that is prohibited under the Disciplinary Rules.

(d) By other conduct renders it unreasonably difficult for the lawyer to carry out his employment effectively.

(e) Insists, in a matter not pending before a tribunal, that the lawyer engage in conduct that is contrary to the judgment and advice of the lawyer but not prohibited under the Disciplinary Rules.

(f) Deliberately disregards an agreement or obligation to the lawyer as to expenses or fees.

(2) His continued employment is likely to result in a violation of a Disciplinary Rule.

(3) His inability to work with co-counsel indicates that the best interests of the client likely will be served by withdrawal.

(4) His mental or physical condition renders it difficult for him to carry out the employment effectively.

(5) His client knowingly and freely assents to termination of his employment.

(6) He believes in good faith, in a proceeding pending before a tribunal, that the tribunal will find the existence of other good cause for withdrawal.

Model Rules Comparison

Model Code	*ABA Model Rules*
DR 2-101(A)	Rule 7.1
DR 2-101(B)	Rules 7.1, 7.2(a)
DR 2-101(C)	Rules 7.1, 7.2
DR 2-101(D)	Rule 7.2(b)
DR 2-101(E)	Rule 7.1(a)
DR 2-101(F)	Rule 7.1
DR 2-101(G)	Rule 7.1
DR 2-101(H)	Rules 7.1, 7.2
DR 2-101(I)	Rule 7.2(c)
DR 2-102(A)	Rules 7.2(a), 7.4, 7.5
DR 2-102(B)	Rules 7.2(a), 7.5(a), (c)
DR 2-102(C)	Rule 7.5(d)
DR 2-102(D)	Rule 7.5(a), (b)
DR 2-102(E)	Rules 7.1(a), 7.4, 7.5(a)
DR 2-103(A)	Rules 7.2(a), 7.3
DR 2-103(B)	Rules 5.4(c), 7.2(a), (c)
DR 2-103(C)	Rules 5.4(a), 7.2(c), 7.3
DR 2-103(D)	Rules 5.4, 7.2(c), 7.3
DR 2-103(E)	Rules 1.16(a), 8.4(a)
DR 2-104	Rules 1.16(a), 7.3
DR 2-105	Rule 7.4
DR 2-106(A)	Rule 1.5(a)
DR 2-106(B)	Rule 1.5(a)
DR 2-106(C)	Rule 1.5(d)(2)
DR 2-107(A)	Rule 1.5(e)
DR 2-107(B)	Rule 5.4(a)(1)
DR 2-108(A)	Rule 5.6(a)
DR 2-108(B)	Rule 5.6(b)
DR 2-109(A)	Rules 1.16(a), 3.1, 3.2
DR 2-110(A)	Rule 1.16(c), (d)
DR 2-110(B)	Rules 1.16(a), 3.1, 4.4
DR 2-110(C)	Rules 1.2(e), 1.16(a), (b)

CANON 3. A LAWYER SHOULD ASSIST IN PREVENTING THE UNAUTHORIZED PRACTICE OF LAW

DR 3-101 Aiding Unauthorized Practice of Law

(A) A lawyer shall not aid a non-lawyer in the unauthorized practice of law.

(B) A lawyer shall not practice law in a jurisdiction where to do so would be in violation of regulations of the profession in that jurisdiction.

DR 3-102 Dividing Legal Fees with a Non-Lawyer

(A) A lawyer or law firm shall not share legal fees with a non-lawyer, except that:

(1) An agreement by a lawyer with his firm, partner, or associate may provide for the payment of money, over a reasonable period of time after his death, to his estate or to one or more specified persons.

(2) A lawyer who undertakes to complete unfinished legal business of a deceased lawyer may pay to the estate of the deceased lawyer that proportion of the total compensation which fairly represents the services rendered by the deceased lawyer.

(3) A lawyer or law firm may include non-lawyer employees in a compensation or retirement plan, even though the plan is based in whole or in part on a profit-sharing arrangement, providing such plan does not circumvent another Disciplinary Rule.

DR 3-103 Forming a Partnership with a Non-Lawyer

(A) A lawyer shall not form a partnership with a non-lawyer if any of the activities of the partnership consist of the practice of law.

	Model Code	*ABA Model Rules*
Model Rules Comparison	DR 3-101(A)	Rule 5.5(b)
	DR 3-101(B)	Rule 5.5(a)
	DR 3-102	Rule 5.4(a)
	DR 3-103	Rule 5.4(b)

CANON 4. A LAWYER SHOULD PRESERVE THE CONFIDENCES AND SECRETS OF A CLIENT

DR 4-101 Preservation of Confidences and Secrets of a Client

(A) "Confidence" refers to information protected by the attorney-client privilege under applicable law, and "secret" refers to other information gained in the professional relationship that the client has re-

quested be held inviolate or the disclosure of which would be embarrassing or would be likely to be detrimental to the client.

(B) Except when permitted under DR 4-101 (C), a lawyer shall not knowingly:

(1) Reveal a confidence or secret of his client.

(2) Use a confidence or secret of his client to the disadvantage of the client.

(3) Use a confidence or secret of his client for the advantage of himself or of a third person, unless the client consents after full disclosure.

(C) A lawyer may reveal:

(1) Confidences or secrets with the consent of the client or clients affected, but only after a full disclosure to them.

(2) Confidences or secrets when permitted under Disciplinary Rules or required by law or court order.

(3) The intention of his client to commit a crime and the information necessary to prevent the crime.

(4) Confidences or secrets necessary to establish or collect his fee or to defend himself or his employees or associates against an accusation of wrongful conduct.

(D) A lawyer shall exercise reasonable care to prevent his employees, associates, and others whose services are utilized by him from disclosing or using confidences or secrets of a client, except that a lawyer may reveal the information allowed by DR 4-101 (C) through an employee.

	Model Code	*ABA Model Rules*
Model Rules Comparison	DR 4-101(A)	Rule 1.6(a)
	DR 4-101(B)	Rules 1.6(a), (b), 1.8(b), 1.9(c)
	DR 4-101(C)	Rules 1.6, 1.9(c)
	DR 4-101(D)	Rules 5.1(a), (b), 5.3(a), (b)

CANON 5. A LAWYER SHOULD EXERCISE INDEPENDENT PROFESSIONAL JUDGMENT ON BEHALF OF A CLIENT

DR 5-101 Refusing Employment When the Interests of the Lawyer May Impair His Independent Professional Judgment

(A) Except with the consent of his client after full disclosure, a lawyer shall not accept employment if the exercise of his professional judgment on behalf of his client will be or reasonably may be affected by his own financial, business, property, or personal interests.

(B) A lawyer shall not accept employment in contemplated or pending litigation if he knows or it is obvious that he or a lawyer in his firm ought to be called as a witness, except that he may undertake the employment and he or a lawyer in his firm may testify:

(1) If the testimony will relate solely to an uncontested matter.

(2) If the testimony will relate solely to a matter of formality and there is no reason to believe that substantial evidence will be offered in opposition to the testimony.

(3) If the testimony will relate solely to the nature and value of legal services rendered in the case by the lawyer or his firm to the client.

(4) As to any matter, if refusal would work a substantial hardship on the client because of the distinctive value of the lawyer or his firm as counsel in the particular case.

DR 5-102 Withdrawal as Counsel When the Lawyer Becomes a Witness

(A) If, after undertaking employment in contemplated or pending litigation, a lawyer learns or it is obvious that he or a lawyer in his firm ought to be called as a witness on behalf of his client, he shall withdraw from the conduct of the trial and his firm, if any, shall not continue representation in the trial, except that he may continue the representation and he or a lawyer in his firm may testify in the circumstances enumerated in DR 5-101(B) (1) through (4).

(B) If, after undertaking employment in contemplated or pending litigation, a lawyer learns or it is obvious that he or a lawyer in his firm may be called as a witness other than on behalf of his client, he may continue the representation until it is apparent that his testimony is or may be prejudicial to his client.

DR 5-103 Avoiding Acquisition of Interest in Litigation

(A) A lawyer shall not acquire a proprietary interest in the cause of action or subject matter of litigation he is conducting for a client, except that he may:

(1) Acquire a lien granted by law to secure his fee or expenses.

(2) Contract with a client for a reasonable contingent fee in a civil case.

(B) While representing a client in connection with contemplated or pending litigation, a lawyer shall not advance or guarantee financial assistance to his client, except that a lawyer may advance or guarantee the expenses of litigation, including court costs, expenses of investigation, expenses of medical examination, and costs of obtaining and presenting evidence, provided the client remains ultimately liable for such expenses.

DR 5-104 Limiting Business Relations with a Client

(A) A lawyer shall not enter into a business transaction with a client if they have differing interests therein and if the client expects the lawyer to exercise his professional judgment therein for the protection of the client, unless the client has consented after full disclosure.

(B) Prior to conclusion of all aspects of the matter giving rise to his employment, a lawyer shall not enter into any arrangement or understanding with a client or a prospective client by which he acquires an interest in publication rights with respect to the subject matter of his employment or proposed employment.

DR 5-105 Refusing to Accept or Continue Employment If the Interests of Another Client May Impair the Independent Professional Judgment of the Lawyer

(A) A lawyer shall decline proffered employment if the exercise of his independent professional judgment in behalf of a client will be or is likely to be adversely affected by the acceptence of the proffered employment, or if it would be likely to involve him in representing differing interests, except to the extent permitted under DR 5-105(C).

(B) A lawyer shall not continue multiple employment if the exercise of his independent professional judgment in behalf of a client will be or is likely to be adversely affected by his representation of another client, or if it would be likely to involve him in representing differing interests, except to the extent permitted under DR 5-105(C).

(C) In the situations covered by DR 5-105 (A) and (B), a lawyer may represent multiple clients if it is obvious that he can adequately represent the interest of each and if each consents to the representation after full disclosure of the possible effect of such representation on the exercise of his independent professional judgment on behalf of each.

(D) If a lawyer is required to decline employment or to withdraw from employment under a Disciplinary Rule, no partner, or associate, or any other lawyer affiliated with him or his firm, may accept or continue such employment.

DR 5-106 Settling Similar Claims of Clients

(A) A lawyer who represents two or more clients shall not make or participate in the making of an aggregate settlement of the claims of or against his clients, unless each client has consented to the settlement after being advised of the existence and nature of all the claims involved in the proposed settlement, of the total amount of the settlement, and of the participation of each person in the settlement.

DR 5-107 Avoiding Influence by Others Than the Client

(A) Except with the consent of his client after full disclosure, a lawyer shall not:

(1) Accept compensation for his legal services from one other than his client.

(2) Accept from one other than his client any thing of value related to his representation of or his employment by his client.

(B) A lawyer shall not permit a person who recommends, employs, or pays him to render legal services for another to direct or regulate his professional judgment in rendering such legal services.

(C) A lawyer shall not practice with or in the form of a professional corporation or association authorized to practice law for a profit, if:

(1) A non-lawyer owns any interest therein, except that a fiduciary representative of the estate of a lawyer may hold the stock or interest of the lawyer for a reasonable time during administration;

(2) A non-lawyer is a corporate director or officer thereof; or

(3) A non-lawyer has the right to direct or control the professional judgment of a lawyer.

	Model Code	*ABA Model Rules*
Model Rules Comparison	DR 5-101(A)	Rules 1.7, 1.8(j), 6.3, 6.4
	DR 5-101(B)	Rules 1.7, 3.7
	DR 5-102(A)	Rules 1.7, 3.7
	DR 5-102(B)	Rules 1.7, 3.7
	DR 5-103(A)	Rules 1.5(c), 1.8(e), (j), 1.15
	DR 5-103(B)	Rule 1.8(e)
	DR 5-104(A)	Rules 1.7(b), 1.8(a)
	DR 5-104(B)	Rule 1.8(d)
	DR 5-105(A)	Rules 1.7, 2.2
	DR 5-105(B)	Rules 1.7, 1.13(e), 2.2
	DR 5-105(C)	Rules 1.7, 1.9, 1.13(e), 2.2

Model Rules Comparison	*Model Code*	*ABA Model Rules*
	DR 5-105(D)	Rules 1.10(a), 1.12(c)
	DR 5-106	Rule 1.8(g)
	DR 5-107(A)	Rules 1.7, 1.8(f)
	DR 5-107(B)	Rules 1.7, 1.8(f), 1.13(b), (c), 2.1, 5.4(c)
	DR 5-107(C)	Rule 5.4(d)

CANON 6. A LAWYER SHOULD REPRESENT A CLIENT COMPETENTLY

DR 6-101 Failing to Act Competently

(A) A lawyer shall not:

(1) Handle a legal matter which he knows or should know that he is not competent to handle, without associating with him a lawyer who is competent to handle it.

(2) Handle a legal matter without preparation adequate in the circumstances.

(3) Neglect a legal matter entrusted to him.

DR 6-102 Limiting Liability to Client

(A) A lawyer shall not attempt to exonerate himself from or limit his liability to his client for his personal malpractice.

Model Rules Comparison	*Model Code*	*ABA Model Rules*
	DR 6-101	Rules 1.1, 1.3, 1.4
	DR 6-102	Rule 1.8(h)

CANON 7. A LAWYER SHOULD REPRESENT A CLIENT ZEALOUSLY WITHIN THE BOUNDS OF THE LAW

DR 7-101 Representing a Client Zealously

(A) A lawyer shall not intentionally:

(1) Fail to seek the lawful objectives of his client through reasonably available means permitted by law and the Disciplinary Rules,

except as provided by DR 7-101 (B). A lawyer does not violate this Disciplinary Rule, however, by acceding to reasonable requests of opposing counsel which do not prejudice the rights of his client, by being punctual in fulfilling all professional commitments, by avoiding offensive tactics, or by treating with courtesy and consideration all persons involved in the legal process.

(2) Fail to carry out a contract of employment entered into with a client for professional services, but he may withdraw as permitted under DR 2-110, DR 5-102, and DR 5-105.

(3) Prejudice or damage his client during the course of the professional relationship, except as required under DR 7-102 (B).

(B) In his representation of a client, a lawyer may:

(1) Where permissible, exercise his professional judgment to waive or fail to assert a right or position of his client.

(2) Refuse to aid or participate in conduct that he believes to be unlawful, even though there is some support for an argument that the conduct is legal.

DR 7-102 Representing a Client Within the Bounds of the Law

(A) In his representation of a client, a lawyer shall not:

(1) File a suit, assert a position, conduct a defense, delay a trial, or take other action on behalf of his client when he knows or when it is obvious that such action would serve merely to harass or maliciously injure another.

(2) Knowingly advance a claim or defense that is unwarranted under existing law, except that he may advance such claim or defense if it can be supported by good faith argument for an extension, modification, or reversal of existing law.

(3) Conceal or knowingly fail to disclose that which he is required by law to reveal.

(4) Knowingly use perjured testimony or false evidence.

(5) Knowingly make a false statement of law or fact.

(6) Participate in the creation or preservation of evidence when he knows or it is obvious that the evidence is false.

(7) Counsel or assist his client in conduct that the lawyer knows to be illegal or fraudulent.

(8) Knowingly engage in other illegal conduct or conduct contrary to a Disciplinary Rule.

(B) A lawyer who receives information clearly establishing that:

(1) His client has, in the course of the representation, perpetrated a fraud upon a person or tribunal shall promptly call upon his client to rectify the same, and if his client refuses or is unable to do so, he shall reveal the fraud to the affected person or tribunal, except when the information is protected as a privileged communication.

(2) A person other than his client has perpetrated a fraud upon a tribunal shall promptly reveal the fraud to the tribunal.

DR 7-103 Performing the Duty of Public Prosecutor or Other Government Lawyer

(A) A public prosecutor or other government lawyer shall not institute or cause to be instituted criminal charges when he knows or it is obvious that the charges are not supported by probable cause.

(B) A public prosecutor or other government lawyer in criminal litigation shall make timely disclosure to counsel for the defendant, or to the defendant if he has no counsel, of the existence of evidence, known to the prosecutor or other government lawyer, that tends to negate the guilt of the accused, mitigate the degree of the offense, or reduce the punishment.

DR 7-104 Communicating with One of Adverse Interest

(A) During the course of his representation of a client a lawyer shall not:

(1) Communicate or cause another to communicate on the subject of the representation with a party he knows to be represented by a lawyer in that matter unless he has the prior consent of the lawyer representing such other party or is authorized by law to do so.

(2) Give advice to a person who is not represented by a lawyer, other than the advice to secure counsel, if the interests of such person are or have a reasonable possibility of being in conflict with the interests of his client.

DR 7-105 Threatening Criminal Prosecution

(A) A lawyer shall not present, participate in presenting, or threaten to present criminal charges solely to obtain an advantage in a civil matter.

DR 7-106 Trial Conduct

(A) A lawyer shall not disregard or advise his client to disregard a standing rule of a tribunal or a ruling of a tribunal made in the course of a proceeding, but he may take appropriate steps in good faith to test the validity of such rule or ruling.

(B) In presenting a matter to a tribunal, a lawyer shall disclose:

(1) Legal authority in the controlling jurisdiction known to him to be directly adverse to the position of his client and which is not disclosed by opposing counsel.

(2) Unless privileged or irrelevant, the identities of the clients he represents and of the persons who employed him.

(C) In appearing in his professional capacity before a tribunal, a lawyer shall not:

(1) State or allude to any matter that he has no reasonable basis to believe is relevant to the case or that will not be supported by admissible evidence.

(2) Ask any question that he has no reasonable basis to believe is relevant to the case and that is intended to degrade a witness or other person.

(3) Assert his personal knowledge of the facts in issue, except when testifying as a witness.

(4) Assert his personal opinion as to the justness of a cause, as to the credibility of a witness, as to the culpability of a civil litigant, or as to the guilt or innocence of an accused; but he may argue, on his analysis of the evidence, for any position or conclusion with respect to the matters stated herein.

(5) Fail to comply with known local customs of courtesy or practice of the bar or a particular tribunal without giving to opposing counsel timely notice of his intent not to comply.

(6) Engage in undignified or discourteous conduct which is degrading to a tribunal.

(7) Intentionally or habitually violate any established rule of procedure or of evidence.

DR 7-107 Trial Publicity

(A) A lawyer participating in or associated with the investigation of a criminal matter shall not make or participate in making an extrajudicial statement that a reasonable person would expect to be disseminated by means of public communication and that does more than state without elaboration:

(1) Information contained in a public record.

(2) That the investigation is in progress.

(3) The general scope of the investigation including a description of the offense and, if permitted by law, the identity of the victim.

(4) A request for assistance in apprehending a suspect or assistance in other matters and the information necessary thereto.

(5) A warning to the public of any dangers.

(B) A lawyer or law firm associated with the prosecution or defense of a criminal matter shall not, from the time of the filing of a complaint, information, or indictment, the issuance of an arrest warrant, or arrest until the commencement of the trial or disposition without trial, make or participate in making an extrajudicial statement that a reasonable person would expect to be disseminated by means of public communication and that relates to:

(1) The character, reputation, or prior criminal record (including arrests, indictments, or other charges of crime) of the accused.

(2) The possibility of a plea of guilty to the offense charged or to a lesser offense.

(3) The existence or contents of any confession, admission, or statement given by the accused or his refusal or failure to make a statement.

(4) The performance or results of any examinations or tests or the refusal or failure of the accused to submit to examinations or tests.

(5) The identity, testimony, or credibility of a prospective witness.

(6) Any opinion as to the guilt or innocence of the accused, the evidence, or the merits of the case.

(C) DR 7-107 (B) does not preclude a lawyer during such period from announcing:

(1) The name, age, residence, occupation, and family status of the accused.

(2) If the accused has not been apprehended, any information necessary to aid in his apprehension or to warn the public of any dangers he may present.

(3) A request for assistance in obtaining evidence.

(4) The identity of the victim of the crime.

(5) The fact, time, and place of arrest, resistance, pursuit, and use of weapons.

(6) The identity of investigating and arresting officers or agencies and the length of the investigation.

(7) At the time of seizure, a description of the physical evidence seized, other than a confession, admission, or statement.

(8) The nature, substance, or text of the charge.

(9) Quotations from or references to public records of the court in the case.

(10) The scheduling or result of any step in the judicial proceedings.

(11) That the accused denies the charges made against him.

(D) During the selection of a jury or the trial of a criminal matter, a lawyer or law firm associated with the prosecution or defense of a criminal matter shall not make or participate in making an extrajudicial statement that a reasonable person would expect to be disseminated by means of public communication and that relates to the trial, parties, or issues in the trial or other matters that are reasonably likely to interfere with a fair trial, except that he may quote from or refer without comment to public records of the court in the case.

(E) After the completion of a trial or disposition without trial of a criminal matter and prior to the imposition of sentence, a lawyer or law firm associated with the prosecution or defense shall not make or participate in making an extrajudicial statement that a reasonable person would expect to be disseminated by public communication and that is reasonably likely to affect the imposition of sentence.

(F) The foregoing provisions of DR 7-107 also apply to professional disciplinary proceedings and juvenile disciplinary proceedings when pertinent and consistent with other law applicable to such proceedings.

(G) A lawyer or law firm associated with a civil action shall not during its investigation or litigation make or participate in making an extrajudicial statement, other than a quotation from or reference to public records, that a reasonable person would expect to be disseminated by means of public communication and that relates to:

(1) Evidence regarding the occurrence or transaction involved.

(2) The character, credibility, or criminal record of a party, witness, or prospective witness.

(3) The performance or results of any examinations or tests or the refusal or failure of a party to submit to such.

(4) His opinion as to the merits of the claims or defenses of a party, except as required by law or administrative rule.

(5) Any other matter reasonably likely to interfere with a fair trial of the action.

(H) During the pendency of an administrative proceeding, a lawyer or law firm associated therewith shall not make or participate in making a statement, other than a quotation from or reference to public records, that a reasonable person would expect to be disseminated by means of public communication if it is made outside the official course of the proceeding and relates to:

(1) Evidence regarding the occurrences or transaction involved.

(2) The character, credibility, or criminal record of a party, witness, or prospective witness.

(3) Physical evidence or the performance or results of any examinations or tests or the refusal or failure of a party to submit to such.

(4) His opinion as to the merits of the claims, defenses, or positions of an interested person.

(5) Any other matter reasonably likely to interfere with a fair hearing.

(I) The foregoing provisions of DR 7-107 do not preclude a lawyer from replying to charges of misconduct publicly made against him or from participating in the proceedings of legislative, administrative, or other investigative bodies.

(J) A lawyer shall exercise reasonable care to prevent his employees and associates from making an extrajudicial statement that he would be prohibited from making under DR 7-107.

DR 7-108 Communication with or Investigation of Jurors

(A) Before the trial of a case a lawyer connected therewith shall not communicate with or cause another to communicate with anyone he knows to be a member of the venire from which the jury will be selected for the trial of the case.

(B) During the trial of a case:

(1) A lawyer connected therewith shall not communicate with or cause another to communicate with any member of the jury.

(2) A lawyer who is not connected therewith shall not communicate with or cause another to communicate with a juror concerning the case.

(C) DR 7-108 (A) and (B) do not prohibit a lawyer from communicating with veniremen or jurors in the course of official proceedings.

(D) After discharge of the jury from further consideration of a case with which the lawyer was connected, the lawyer shall not ask questions of or make comments to a member of that jury that are calculated merely to harass or embarrass the juror or to influence his actions in the future jury service.

(E) A lawyer shall not conduct or cause, by financial support or otherwise, another to conduct a vexatious or harassing investigation of either a venireman or a juror.

(F) All restrictions imposed by DR 7-108 upon a lawyer also apply to communications with or investigations of members of a family of a venireman or a juror.

(G) A lawyer shall reveal promptly to the court improper conduct by a venireman or a juror, or by another toward a venireman or a juror or a member of his family, of which the lawyer has knowledge.

DR 7-109 Contact with Witnesses

(A) A lawyer shall not suppress any evidence that he or his client has a legal obligation to reveal or produce.

(B) A lawyer shall not advise or cause a person to secrete himself or to leave the jurisdiction of a tribunal for the purpose of making him unavailable as a witness therein.

(C) A lawyer shall not pay, offer to pay, or acquiesce in the payment of compensation to a witness contingent upon the content of his testimony or the outcome of the case. But a lawyer may advance, guarantee, or acquiesce in the payment of:

(1) Expenses reasonably incurred by a witness in attending or testifying.

(2) Reasonable compensation to a witness for his loss of time in attending or testifying.

(3) A reasonable fee for the professional services of an expert witness.

DR 7-110 Contact with Officials

(A) A lawyer shall not give or lend any thing of value to a judge, official, or employee of a tribunal except as permitted by Section C(4) of Canon 5 of the Code of Judicial Conduct, but a lawyer may make a contribution to the campaign fund of a candidate for judicial office in conformity with Section B(2) under Canon 7 of the Code of Judicial Conduct.

(B) In an adversary proceeding, a lawyer shall not communicate, or cause another to communicate, as to the merits of the cause with a judge or an official before whom the proceeding is pending, except:

(1) In the course of official proceedings in the cause.

(2) In writing if he promptly delivers a copy of the writing to opposing counsel or to the adverse party if he is not represented by a lawyer.

(3) Orally upon adequate notice to opposing counsel or to the adverse party if he is not represented by a lawyer.

(4) As otherwise authorized by law, or by Section A(4) under Canon 3 of the Code of Judicial Conduct.

Model Rules Comparison

Model Code	*ABA Model Rules*
DR 7-101(A)	Rules 1.2(a), (d), 1.3, 3.2, 3.5(c), 4.4
DR 7-101(B)	Rules 1.2(a), (c), (d), 1.16(b)
DR 7-102(A)(1)	Rules 3.1, 3.2, 4.4
DR 7-102(A)(2)	Rule 3.1
DR 7-102(A)(3)	Rules 3.3(a)(2), (3), 4.1
DR 7-102(A)(4)	Rule 3.3(a)(4), (c)
DR 7-102(A)(5)	Rules 3.3(a)(1), 4.1
DR 7-102(A)(6)	Rules 1.2(b), 3.4(b)
DR 7-102(A)(7)	Rules 1.2(d), 3.3(a), 4.1
DR 7-102(A)(8)	Rules 1.2(d), 8.4(a), (b)
DR 7-102(B)	Rules 1.6(b), 3.3(a)(4), (b), 4.1(b)
DR 7-103(A)	Rule 3.8(a)
DR 7-103(B)	Rule 3.8(d)
DR 7-104	Rules 3.4(f), 4.2, 4.3
DR 7-105	None
DR 7-106(A)	Rules 1.2(d), 3.4(c), (d)

Model Rules Comparison

Model Code	ABA Model Rules
DR 7-106(B)	Rules 3.3(a)(3), 3.9
DR 7-106(C)	Rules 3.4(a), (c), (d), (e), 3.5, 4.4
DR 7-107(A)-(I)	Rule 3.6
DR 7-107(J)	Rules 5.1(a), (b), 5.3(a), (b)
DR 7-108(A)	Rule 3.5(a), (b)
DR 7-108(B)	Rules 3.5(a), (b), 5.1(c), 5.3(a), (b), 8.4(a)
DR 7-108(C)	Rule 3.5(a), (b)
DR 7-108(D)	Rules 3.5(b), 4.4
DR 7-108(E)	Rules 3.5(b), 4.4, 5.1(c), 5.3(a), (b), 8.4(a)
DR 7-108(F)	Rule 4.4
DR 7-108(G)	None
DR 7-109(A)	Rules 3.3(a)(2), 3.4(a)
DR 7-109(B)	Rule 3.4(a), (f)
DR 7-109(C)	Rule 3.4(b)
DR 7-110(A)	Rules 3.5(a), 8.4(f)
DR 7-110(B)	Rule 3.5(a), (b)

CANON 8. A LAWYER SHOULD ASSIST IN IMPROVING THE LEGAL SYSTEM

DR 8-101 Action as a Public Official

(A) A lawyer who holds public office shall not:

(1) Use his public position to obtain, or attempt to obtain, a special advantage in legislative matters for himself or for a client under circumstances where he knows or it is obvious that such action is not in the public interest.

(2) Use his public position to influence, or attempt to influence, a tribunal to act in favor of himself or of a client.

(3) Accept any thing of value from any person when the lawyer knows or it is obvious that the offer is for the purpose of influencing his action as a public official.

DR 8-102 Statements Concerning Judges and Other Adjudicatory Officers

(A) A lawyer shall not knowingly make false statements of fact concerning the qualifications of a candidate for election or appointment to a judicial office.

(B) A lawyer shall not knowingly make false accusations against a judge or other adjudicatory officer.

DR 8-103 Lawyer Candidate for Judicial Office

(A) A lawyer who is a candidate for judicial office shall comply with the applicable provisions of Canon 7 of the Code of Judicial Conduct.

	Model Code	*ABA Model Rules*
Model Rules Comparison	DR 8-101	Rules 1.11(c), 3.5(a), 8.4(e), (f)
	DR 8-102	Rule 8.2(a)
	DR 8-103	Rule 8.2(b)

CANON 9. A LAWYER SHOULD AVOID EVEN THE APPEARANCE OF PROFESSIONAL IMPROPRIETY

DR 9-101 Avoiding Even the Appearance of Impropriety

(A) A lawyer shall not accept private employment in a matter upon the merits of which he has acted in a judicial capacity.

(B) A lawyer shall not accept private employment in a matter in which he had substantial responsibility while he was a public employee.

(C) A lawyer shall not state or imply that he is able to influence improperly or upon irrelevant grounds any tribunal, legislative body, or public official.

DR 9-102 Preserving Identity of Funds and Property of a Client

(A) All funds of clients paid to a lawyer or law firm, other than advances for costs and expenses, shall be deposited in one or more identifiable bank accounts maintained in the state in which the law office is situated and no funds belonging to the lawyer or law firm shall be deposited therein except as follows:

(1) Funds reasonably sufficient to pay bank charges may be deposited therein.

(2) Funds belonging in part to a client and in part presently or potentially to the lawyer or law firm must be deposited therein, but the portion belonging to the lawyer or law firm may be withdrawn when due unless the right of the lawyer or law firm to receive it is disputed by the client, in which event the disputed portion shall not be withdrawn until the dispute is finally resolved.

(B) A lawyer shall:

(1) Promptly notify a client of the receipt of his funds, securities, or other properties.

(2) Identify and label securities and properties of a client promptly upon receipt and place them in a safe deposit box or other place of safekeeping as soon as practicable.

(3) Maintain complete records of all funds, securities, and other properties of a client coming into the possession of the lawyer and render appropriate accounts to his client regarding them.

(4) Promptly pay or deliver to the client as requested by a client the funds, securities, or other properties in the possession of the lawyer which the client is entitled to receive.

	Model Code	*ABA Model Rules*
Model Rules Comparison	DR 9-101(A)	Rule 1.12
	DR 9-101(B)	Rules 1.11(a), 1.12(a), (b)
	DR 9-101(C)	Rules 1.2(e), 7.1(b), 8.4(e)
	DR 9-102	Rules 1.4, 1.15

DEFINITIONS*

As used in the Disciplinary Rules of the Model Code of Professional Responsibility:

(1) "Differing interests" include every interest that will adversely affect either the judgment or the loyalty of a lawyer to a client, whether it be a conflicting, inconsistent, diverse, or other interest.

(2) "Law firm" includes a professional legal corporation.

(3) "Person" includes a corporation, an association, a trust, a partnership, and any other organization or legal entity.

(4) "Professional legal corporation" means a corporation, or an association treated as a corporation, authorized by law to practice law for profit.

*"Confidence" and "secret" are defined in DR 4-101(A).

(5) "State" includes the District of Columbia, Puerto Rico, and other federal territories and possessions.

(6) "Tribunal" includes all courts and all other adjudicatory bodies.

(7) "A Bar association" includes a bar association of specialists as referred to in DR 2-105(A)(1) or (3).

(8) "Qualified legal assistance organization" means an office or organization of one of the four types listed in DR 2-103(D)(1)-(4), inclusive that meets all the requirements thereof.

ABA Standards for Criminal Justice*

The Prosecution Function
The Defense Function

Editors' Introduction. In 1964, ABA President Louis F. Powell, Jr. (who later served on the United States Supreme Court) appointed a Special Committee on Standards for the Administration of Criminal Justice. The Special Committee included many distinguished figures, and was at one time chaired by Judge (later Chief Justice) Warren E. Burger. By 1973, the ABA House of Delegates had approved 17 sets of Standards, governing every phase of the criminal justice system.

In the early 1990's, the ABA amended many of the Standards. In 1991, the ABA House of Delegates approved a complete revision of Chapter 4, "The Defense Function," and in 1992 the House of Delegates approved substantial revisions to Chapter 3, "The Prosecution Function."

The Standards for Criminal Justice have been enormously influential. More than 40 states revised their criminal codes on the basis of the ABA Standards, and the Standards are cited dozens of times in each volume of federal court opinions. Two of the most important sets of Standards are "The Prosecution Function" and "The Defense Function." These Standards are intended to present in an organized way "guidelines that have long been adhered to by the best prosecutors and best defense advocates." We reprint here, without commentary, all of the black letter Standards for "The Prosecution Function" as amended in 1992, and "The Defense Function" as amended in 1991.

Contents

Chapter 3. The Prosecution Function

Part I. General Standards

3-1.3 Conflicts of Interest
3-1.4 Public Statements
3-1.5 Duty to Respond to Misconduct

Part II. Organization of the Prosecution Function

3-2.8 Relations with the Courts and Bar
3-2.9 Prompt Disposition of Criminal Charges
3-2.10 Supercession and Substitution of Prosecutor
3-2.11 Literary or Media Agreements

Part III. Investigation for Prosecution Decision

3-3.1 Investigative Function of Prosecutor
3-3.2 Relations with Victims and Prospective Witnesses
3-3.3 Relations with Expert Witnesses
3-3.4 Decision to Charge
3-3.5 Relations with Grand Jury
3-3.6 Quality and Scope of Evidence Before Grand Jury
3-3.7 Quality and Scope of Evidence for Information
3-3.8 Discretion as to Noncriminal Disposition
3-3.9 Discretion in the Charging Decision
3-3.10 Role in First Appearance and Preliminary Hearing
3-3.11 Disclosure of Evidence by the Prosecutor

Part IV. Plea Discussions

3-4.1 Availability for Plea Discussions
3-4.2 Fulfillment of Plea Discussions
3-4.3 Record of Reasons for Nolle Prosequi Disposition

Part V. The Trial

3-5.1 Calendar Control
3-5.2 Courtroom Professionalism
3-5.3 Selection of Jurors
3-5.4 Relations with Jury
3-5.5 Opening Statement
3-5.6 Presentation of Evidence
3-5.7 Examination of Witnesses
3-5.8 Argument to the Jury
3-5.9 Facts Outside the Record
3-5.10 Comments by Prosecutor After Verdict

Chapter 4. The Defense Function

Part I. General Standards

4-1.2 The Function of Defense Counsel
4-1.3 Delays; Punctuality; Workload
4-1.4 Public Statements

Part III. Lawyer-Client Relationship

4-3.1 Establishment of Relationship
4-3.2 Interviewing the Client
4-3.3 Fees
4-3.4 Obtaining Literary or Media Rights from the Accused
4-3.5 Conflicts of Interest
4-3.6 Prompt Action to Protect the Accused
4-3.7 Advice and Service on Anticipated Unlawful Conduct
4-3.8 Duty to Keep Client Informed

Part IV. Investigation and Preparation

4-4.1 Duty to Investigate
4-4.2 Illegal Investigation
4-4.3 Relations with Prospective Witnesses
4-4.4 Relations with Expert Witnesses
4-4.5 Compliance with Discovery Procedure
4-4.6 Physical Evidence

Part V. Control and Direction of Litigation

4-5.1 Advising the Accused
4-5.2 Control and Direction of the Case

Part VI. Disposition Without Trial

4-6.1 Duty to Explore Disposition Without Trial
4-6.2 Plea Discussions

Part VII. Trial

4-7.1 Courtroom Professionalism
4-7.2 Selection of Jurors
4-7.3 Relations with Jury
4-7.4 Opening Statement
4-7.5 Presentation of Evidence
4-7.6 Examination of Witnesses
4-7.7 Argument to the Jury
4-7.8 Facts Outside the Record

CHAPTER 3. THE PROSECUTION FUNCTION

Editors' Note. Chapter 3 was originally approved by the ABA in 1971. At its 1992 Mid-Year Meeting, the ABA approved substantial revisions to "The Prosecution Function." The version that follows reflects these 1992 revisions.

Part I. General Standards

Standard 3-1.3. Conflicts of Interest

(a) A prosecutor should avoid a conflict of interest with respect to his or her official duties.

(b) A prosecutor should not represent a defendant in criminal proceedings in a jurisdiction where he or she is also employed as a prosecutor.

(c) A prosecutor should not, except as law may otherwise expressly permit, participate in a matter in which he or she participated personally and substantially while in private practice or non-governmental employment unless under applicable law no one is, or by lawful delegation may be, authorized to act in the prosecutor's stead in the matter.

(d) A prosecutor who has formerly represented a client in a matter in private practice should not thereafter use information obtained from that representation to the disadvantage of the former client unless the rules of attorney-client confidentiality do not apply or the information has become generally known.

(e) A prosecutor should not, except as law may otherwise expressly permit, negotiate for private employment with any person who is involved as an accused or as an attorney or agent for an accused in a matter in which the prosecutor is participating personally and substantially.

(f) A prosecutor should not permit his or her professional judgment or obligations to be affected by his or her own political, financial, business, property, or personal interests.

(g) A prosecutor who is related to another lawyer as parent, child, sibling or spouse should not participate in the prosecution of a person who the prosecutor knows is represented by the other lawyer. Nor should a prosecutor who has a significant personal or financial relationship with another lawyer participate in the prosecution of a person who the prosecutor knows is represented by the other lawyer, unless the prosecutor's supervisor, if any, is informed and approves or unless there is no other prosecutor authorized to act in the prosecutor's stead.

(h) A prosecutor should not recommend the services of particular defense counsel to accused persons or witnesses unless requested by the accused person or witness to make such a recommendation, and should not make a referral that is likely to create a conflict of interest. Nor

should a prosecutor comment upon the reputation or abilities of defense counsel to an accused person or witness who is seeking or may seek such counsel's services unless requested by such person.

Standard 3-1.4. Public Statements

(a) A prosecutor should not make or authorize the making of an extrajudicial statement that a reasonable person would expect to be disseminated by means of public communication if the prosecutor knows or reasonably should know that it will have a substantial likelihood of prejudicing a criminal proceeding.

(b) A prosecutor should exercise reasonable care to prevent investigators, law enforcement personnel, employees or other persons assisting or associated with the prosecutor from making an extrajudicial statement that the prosecutor would be prohibited from making under this standard.

Standard 3-1.5. Duty to Respond to Misconduct

(a) Where a prosecutor knows that another person associated with the prosecutor's office is engaged in action, intends to act or refuses to act in a manner that is a violation of a legal obligation to the prosecutor's office or a violation of law, the prosecutor should follow the policies of the prosecutor's office concerning such matters. If such policies are unavailing or do not exist, the prosecutor should ask the person to reconsider the action or inaction which is at issue if such a request is aptly timed to prevent such misconduct and is otherwise feasible. If such a request for reconsideration is unavailing, inapt or otherwise not feasible or if the seriousness of the matter so requires, the prosecutor should refer the matter to higher authority in the prosecutor's office, including, if warranted by the seriousness of the matter, referral to the chief prosecutor.

(b) If, despite the prosecutor's efforts in accordance with section (a), the chief prosecutor insists upon action, or a refusal to act, that is clearly a violation of law, the prosecutor may take further remedial action, including revealing the information necessary to remedy this violation to other appropriate governmental officials not in the prosecutor's office.

Part II. Organization of the Prosecution Function

Standard 3-2.8. Relations with the Courts and Bar

(a) A prosecutor should not intentionally misrepresent matters of fact or law to the court.

(b) A prosecutor's duties necessarily involve frequent and regular official contacts with the judge or judges of the prosecutor's jurisdiction. In such contacts the prosecutor should carefully strive to preserve the appearance as well as the reality of the correct relationship which professional traditions, ethical codes, and applicable law require between advocates and judges.

(c) A prosecutor should not engage in unauthorized ex parte discussions with or submission of material to a judge relating to a particular case which is or may come before the judge.

(d) A prosecutor should not fail to disclose to the tribunal legal authority in the controlling jurisdiction known to the prosecutor to be directly adverse to the prosecutor's position and not disclosed by defense counsel.

(e) A prosecutor should strive to develop good working relationships with defense counsel in order to facilitate the resolution of ethical problems. In particular, a prosecutor should assure defense counsel that if counsel finds it necessary to deliver physical items which may be relevant to a pending case or investigation to the prosecutor, the prosecutor will not offer the fact of such delivery by defense counsel as evidence before a jury for purposes of establishing defense counsel's client's culpability. However, nothing in this Standard shall prevent a prosecutor from offering evidence of the fact of such delivery in a subsequent proceeding for the purpose of proving a crime or fraud in the delivery of the evidence.

Standard 3-2.9. Prompt Disposition of Criminal Charges

(a) A prosecutor should avoid unnecessary delay in the disposition of cases. A prosecutor should not fail to act with reasonable diligence and promptness in prosecuting an accused.

(b) A prosecutor should not intentionally use procedural devices for delay for which there is no legitimate basis.

(c) The prosecution function should be so organized and supported with staff and facilities as to enable it to dispose of all criminal charges promptly. The prosecutor should be punctual in attendance in court and in the submission of all motions, briefs, and other papers. The prosecutor should emphasize to all witnesses the importance of punctuality in attendance in court.

(d) A prosecutor should not intentionally misrepresent facts or otherwise mislead the court in order to obtain a continuance.

(e) A prosecutor, without attempting to get more funding for additional staff, should not carry a workload that, by reason of its excessive size, interferes with the rendering of quality representation, endangers the interests of justice in the speedy disposition of charges, or may lead to the breach of professional obligations.

Standard 3-2.10. Supercession and Substitution of Prosecutor

(a) Procedures should be established by appropriate legislation to the end that the governor or other elected state official is empowered by law to suspend and supersede a local prosecutor upon making a public finding, after reasonable notice and hearing, that the prosecutor is incapable of fulfilling the duties of office.

(b) The governor or other elected official should be empowered by law to substitute special counsel in the place of the local prosecutor in a particular case, or category of cases, upon making a public finding that this is required for the protection of the public interest.

Standard 3-2.11. Literary or Media Agreements

A prosecutor, prior to conclusion of all aspects of a matter, should not enter into any agreement or understanding by which the prosecutor acquires an interest in literary or media rights to a portrayal or account based in substantial part on information relating to that matter.

Part III. Investigation for Prosecution Decision

Standard 3-3.1. Investigative Function of Prosecutor

(a) A prosecutor ordinarily relies on police and other investigative agencies for investigation of alleged criminal acts, but the prosecutor has an affirmative responsibility to investigate suspected illegal activity when it is not adequately dealt with by other agencies.

(b) A prosecutor should not invidiously discriminate against or in favor of any person on the basis of race, religion, sex, sexual preference, or ethnicity in exercising discretion to investigate or to prosecute. A prosecutor should not use other improper considerations in exercising such discretion.

(c) A prosecutor should not knowingly use illegal means to obtain evidence or to employ or instruct or encourage others to use such means.

(d) A prosecutor should not discourage or obstruct communication between prospective witnesses and defense counsel. A prosecutor should not advise any person or cause any person to be advised to decline to give to the defense information which such person has the right to give.

(e) A prosecutor should not secure the attendance of persons for interviews by use of any communication which has the appearance or

color of a subpoena or similar judicial process unless the prosecutor is authorized by law to do so.

(f) A prosecutor should not promise not to prosecute for prospective criminal activity, except where such activity is part of an officially supervised investigative and enforcement program.

(g) Unless a prosecutor is prepared to forgo impeachment of a witness by the prosecutor's own testimony as to what the witness stated in an interview or to seek leave to withdraw from the case in order to present the impeaching testimony, a prosecutor should avoid interviewing a prospective witness except in the presence of a third person.

Standard 3-3.2. Relations with Victims and Prospective Witnesses

(a) A prosecutor should not compensate a witness, other than an expert, for giving testimony, but it is not improper to reimburse an ordinary witness for the reasonable expenses of attendance upon court, attendance for depositions pursuant to statute or court rule, or attendance for pretrial interviews. Payments to a witness may be for transportation and loss of income, provided there is no attempt to conceal the fact of reimbursement.

(b) A prosecutor should advise a witness who is to be interviewed of his or her rights against self-incrimination and the right to counsel whenever the law so requires. It is also proper for a prosecutor to so advise a witness whenever the prosecutor knows or has reason to believe that the witness may be the subject of a criminal prosecution. However, a prosecutor should not so advise a witness for the purpose of influencing the witness in favor of or against testifying.

(c) The prosecutor should readily provide victims and witnesses who request it information about the status of cases in which they are interested.

(d) The prosecutor should seek to insure that victims and witnesses who may need protections against intimidation are advised of and afforded such protections where feasible.

(e) The prosecutor should insure that victims and witnesses are given notice as soon as practicable of scheduling changes which will affect the victims' or witnesses' required attendance at judicial proceedings.

(f) The prosecutor should not require victims and witnesses to attend judicial proceedings unless their testimony is essential to the prosecution or is required by law. When their attendance is required, the prosecutor should seek to reduce to a minimum the time they must spend at the proceedings.

(g) The prosecutor should seek to insure that victims of serious crimes or their representatives are given timely notice of: (i) judicial proceedings relating to the victims' case; (ii) disposition of the case, including plea bargains, trial and sentencing; and (iii) any decision or action in the case which results in the accused's provisional or final release from custody.

(h) Where practical, the prosecutor should seek to insure that victims of serious crimes or their representatives are given an opportunity to consult with and to provide information to the prosecutor prior to the decision whether or not to prosecute, to pursue a disposition by plea, or to dismiss the charges.

Standard 3-3.3. Relations with Expert Witnesses

(a) A prosecutor who engages an expert for an opinion should respect the independence of the expert and should not seek to dictate the formation of the expert's opinion on the subject. To the extent necessary, the prosecutor should explain to the expert his or her role in the trial as an impartial expert called to aid the fact finders and the manner in which the examination of witnesses is conducted.

(b) A prosecutor should not pay an excessive fee for the purpose of influencing the expert's testimony or to fix the amount of the fee contingent upon the testimony the expert will give or the result in the case.

Standard 3-3.4. Decision to Charge

(a) The decision to institute criminal proceedings should be initially and primarily the responsibility of the prosecutor.

(b) Prosecutors should take reasonable care to ensure that investigators working at their direction or under their authority are adequately trained in the standards governing the issuance of arrest and search warrants and should inform investigators that they should seek the approval of a prosecutor in close or difficult cases.

(c) The prosecutor should establish standards and procedures for evaluating complaints to determine whether criminal proceedings should be instituted.

(d) Where the law permits a citizen to complain directly to a judicial officer or the grand jury, the citizen complainant should be required to present the complaint for prior approval to the prosecutor, and the prosecutor's action or recommendation thereon should be communicated to the judicial officer or grand jury.

Standard 3-3.5. Relations with Grand Jury

(a) Where the prosecutor is authorized to act as legal adviser to the grand jury, the prosecutor may appropriately explain the law and

express an opinion on the legal significance of the evidence but should give due deference to its status as an independent legal body.

(b) The prosecutor should not make statements or arguments in an effort to influence grand jury action in a manner which would be impermissible at trial before a petit jury.

(c) The prosecutor's communications and presentations to the grand jury should be on the record.

Standard 3-3.6. Quality and Scope of Evidence Before Grand Jury

(a) A prosecutor should only make statements or arguments to the grand jury and only present evidence to the grand jury which the prosecutor believes is appropriate or authorized under law for presentation to the grand jury. In appropriate cases, the prosecutor may present witnesses to summarize admissible evidence available to the prosecutor which the prosecutor believes he or she will be able to present at trial. The prosecutor should also inform the grand jurors that they have the right to hear any available witnesses, including eyewitnesses.

(b) No prosecutor should knowingly fail to disclose to the grand jury evidence which tends to negate guilt or mitigate the offense.

(c) A prosecutor should recommend that the grand jury not indict if he or she believes the evidence presented does not warrant an indictment under governing law.

(d) If the prosecutor believes that a witness is a potential defendant, the prosecutor should not seek to compel the witness's testimony before the grand jury without informing the witness that he or she may be charged and that the witness should seek independent legal advice concerning his or her rights.

(e) The prosecutor should not compel the appearance of a witness before the grand jury whose activities are the subject of the inquiry if the witness states in advance that if called he or she will exercise the constitutional privilege not to testify, unless the prosecutor intends to judicially challenge the exercise of the privilege or to seek a grant of immunity according to the law.

(f) A prosecutor in presenting a case to a grand jury should not intentionally interfere with the independence of the grand jury, preempt a function of the grand jury, or abuse the processes of the grand jury.

(g) Unless the law of the jurisdiction so permits, a prosecutor should not use the grand jury in order to obtain tangible, documentary or testimonial evidence to assist the prosecutor in preparation for trial of a defendant who has already been charged by indictment or information.

(h) Unless the law of the jurisdiction so permits, a prosecutor should not use the grand jury for the purpose of aiding or assisting in any administrative inquiry.

Standard 3-3.7. Quality and Scope of Evidence for Information

Where the prosecutor is empowered to charge by information, the prosecutor's decisions should be governed by the principles embodied in standards 3-3.6 and 3-3.9, where applicable.

Standard 3-3.8. Discretion as to Noncriminal Disposition

(a) The prosecutor should consider in appropriate cases the availability of noncriminal disposition, formal or informal, in deciding whether to press criminal charges which would otherwise be supported by probable cause; especially in the case of a first offender, the nature of the offense may warrant noncriminal disposition.

(b) Prosecutors should be familiar with the resources of social agencies which can assist in the evaluation of cases for diversion from the criminal process.

Standard 3-3.9. Discretion in the Charging Decision

(a) A prosecutor should not institute, or cause to be instituted, or permit the continued pendency of criminal charges when the prosecutor knows that the charges are not supported by probable cause. A prosecutor should not institute, cause to be instituted, or permit the continued pendency of criminal charges in the absence of sufficient admissible evidence to support a conviction.

(b) The prosecutor is not obliged to present all charges which the evidence might support. The prosecutor may in some circumstances and for good cause consistent with the public interest decline to prosecute, notwithstanding that sufficient evidence may exist which would support a conviction. Illustrative of the factors which the prosecutor may properly consider in exercising his or her discretion are:

(i) the prosecutor's reasonable doubt that the accused is in fact guilty;

(ii) the extent of the harm caused by the offense;

(iii) the disproportion of the authorized punishment in relation to the particular offense or the offender;

(iv) possible improper motives of a complainant;

(v) reluctance of the victim to testify;

(vi) cooperation of the accused in the apprehension or conviction of others; and

(vii) availability and likelihood of prosecution by another jurisdiction.

(c) A prosecutor should not be compelled by his or her supervisor to prosecute a case in which he or she has a reasonable doubt about the guilt of the accused.

(d) In making the decision to prosecute, the prosecutor should give no weight to the personal or political advantages or disadvantages which might be involved or to a desire to enhance his or her record of convictions.

(e) In cases which involve a serious threat to the community, the prosecutor should not be deterred from prosecution by the fact that in the jurisdiction juries have tended to acquit persons accused of the particular kind of criminal act in question.

(f) The prosecutor should not bring or seek charges greater in number or degree than can reasonably be supported with evidence at trial or than are necessary to fairly reflect the gravity of the offense.

(g) The prosecutor should not condition a dismissal of charges, nolle prosequi, or similar action on the accused's relinquishment of the right to seek civil redress unless the accused has agreed to the action knowingly and intelligently, freely and voluntarily, and where such waiver is approved by the court.

Standard 3-3.10. Role in First Appearance and Preliminary Hearing

(a) A prosecutor who is present at the first appearance (however denominated) of the accused before a judicial officer should not communicate with the accused unless a waiver of counsel has been entered, except for the purpose of aiding in obtaining counsel or in arranging for the pretrial release of the accused. A prosecutor should not fail to make reasonable efforts to assure that the accused has been advised of the right to, and the procedure for obtaining, counsel and has been given reasonable opportunity to obtain counsel.

(b) The prosecutor should cooperate in good faith in arrangements for release under the prevailing system for pretrial release.

(c) The prosecutor should not seek to obtain from an unrepresented accused a waiver of important pretrial rights, such as the right to a preliminary hearing.

(d) The prosecutor should not seek a continuance solely for the purpose of mooting the preliminary hearing by securing an indictment.

(e) Except for good cause, the prosecutor should not seek delay in the preliminary hearing after an arrest has been made if the accused is in custody.

(f) The prosecutor should ordinarily be present at a preliminary hearing where such hearing is required by law.

Standard 3-3.11. Disclosure of Evidence by the Prosecutor

(a) A prosecutor should not intentionally fail to make timely disclosure to the defense, at the earliest feasible opportunity, of the existence of all evidence or information which tends to negate the guilt of the accused or mitigate the offense charged or which would tend to reduce the punishment of the accused.

(b) A prosecutor should not fail to make a reasonably diligent effort to comply with a legally proper discovery request.

(c) A prosecutor should not intentionally avoid pursuit of evidence because he or she believes it will damage the prosecution's case or aid the accused.

Part IV. Plea Discussions

Standard 3-4.1. Availability for Plea Discussions

(a) The prosecutor should have and make known a general policy or willingness to consult with defense counsel concerning disposition of charges by plea.

(b) A prosecutor should not engage in plea discussions directly with an accused who is represented by defense counsel, except with defense counsel's approval. Where the defendant has properly waived counsel, the prosecuting attorney may engage in plea discussions with the defendant, although, where feasible, a record of such discussions should be made and preserved.

(c) A prosecutor should not knowingly make false statements or representations as to fact or law in the course of plea discussions with defense counsel or the accused.

Standard 3-4.2. Fulfillment of Plea Discussions

(a) A prosecutor should not make any promise or commitment assuring a defendant or defense counsel that a court will impose a specific sentence or a suspension of sentence; a prosecutor may properly advise the defense what position will be taken concerning disposition.

(b) A prosecutor should not imply a greater power to influence the disposition of a case than is actually possessed.

(c) A prosecutor should not fail to comply with a plea agreement, unless a defendant fails to comply with a plea agreement or other extenuating circumstances are present.

Standard 3-4.3. Record of Reasons for Nolle Prosequi Disposition

Whenever felony criminal charges are dismissed by way of nolle prosequi (or its equivalent), the prosecutor should make a record of the reasons for the action.

Part V. The Trial

Standard 3-5.1. Calendar Control

Control over the trial calendar should be vested in the court. The prosecuting attorney should advise the court of facts relevant in determining the order of cases on the court's calendar.

Standard 3-5.2. Courtroom Professionalism

(a) As an officer of the court, the prosecutor should support the authority of the court and the dignity of the trial courtroom by strict adherence to codes of professionalism and by manifesting a professional attitude toward the judge, opposing counsel, witnesses, defendants, jurors, and others in the courtroom.

(b) When court is in session, the prosecutor should address the court, not opposing counsel, on all matters relating to the case.

(c) Prosecutor should comply promptly with all orders and directives of the court, but the prosecutor has a duty to have the record reflect adverse rulings or judicial conduct which the prosecutor considers prejudicial. The prosecutor has a right to make respectful requests for reconsideration of adverse rulings.

(d) Prosecutors should cooperate with courts and the organized bar in developing codes of professionalism for each jurisdiction.

Standard 3-5.3. Selection of Jurors

(a) The prosecutor should prepare himself or herself prior to trial to discharge effectively the prosecution function in the selection of the jury and the exercise of challenges for cause and peremptory challenges.

(b) In those cases where it appears necessary to conduct a pretrial investigation of the background of jurors, investigatory methods of the prosecutor should neither harass nor unduly embarrass potential jurors or invade their privacy and, whenever possible, should be restricted to an investigation of records and sources of information already in existence.

(c) The opportunity to question jurors personally should be used solely to obtain information for the intelligent exercise of challenges. A prosecutor should not intentionally use the voir dire to present factual matter which the prosecutor knows will not be admissible at trial or to argue the prosecution's case to the jury.

Standard 3-5.4. Relations with Jury

(a) A prosecutor should not intentionally communicate privately with persons summoned for jury duty or impaneled as jurors prior to or during trial. The prosecutor should avoid the reality or appearance of any such communications.

(b) The prosecutor should treat jurors with deference and respect, avoiding the reality or appearance of currying favor by a show of undue solicitude for their comfort or convenience.

(c) After discharge of the jury from further consideration of a case, a prosecutor should not intentionally make comments to or ask questions of a juror for the purpose of harassing or embarrassing the juror in any way which will tend to influence judgment in future jury service. If the prosecutor believes that the verdict may be subject to legal challenge, he or she may properly, if no statute or rule prohibits such course, communicate with jurors to determine whether such challenge may be available.

Standard 3-5.5. Opening Statement

The prosecutor's opening statement should be confined to a statement of the issues in the case and the evidence the prosecutor intends to offer which the prosecutor believes in good faith will be available and admissible. A prosecutor should not allude to any evidence unless there is a good faith and reasonable basis for believing that such evidence will be tendered and admitted in evidence.

Standard 3-5.6. Presentation of Evidence

(a) A prosecutor should not knowingly offer false evidence, whether by documents, tangible evidence, or the testimony of witnesses, or fail to seek withdrawal thereof upon discovery of its falsity.

(b) A prosecutor should not knowingly and for the purpose of bringing inadmissible matter to the attention of the judge or jury offer inadmissible evidence, ask legally objectionable questions, or make other impermissible comments or arguments in the presence of the judge or jury.

(c) A prosecutor should not permit any tangible evidence to be displayed in the view of the judge or jury which would tend to prejudice fair consideration by the judge or jury until such time as a good faith tender of such evidence is made.

(d) A prosecutor should not tender tangible evidence in the view of the judge or jury if it would tend to prejudice fair consideration by the judge or jury unless there is a reasonable basis for its admission in evidence. When there is any substantial doubt about the admissibility of such evidence, it should be tendered by an offer of proof and a ruling obtained.

Standard 3-5.7. Examination of Witnesses

(a) The interrogation of all witnesses should be conducted fairly, objectively, and with due regard for the dignity and legitimate privacy of the witness, and without seeking to intimidate or humiliate the witness unnecessarily.

(b) The prosecutor's belief that the witness is telling the truth does not preclude cross-examination, but may affect the method and scope of cross-examination. A prosecutor should not use the power of cross-examination to discredit or undermine a witness if the prosecutor knows the witness is testifying truthfully.

(c) A prosecutor should not call a witness in the presence of the jury who the prosecutor knows will claim a valid privilege not to testify.

(d) A prosecutor should not ask a question which implies the existence of a factual predicate for which a good faith belief is lacking.

Standard 3-5.8. Argument to the Jury

(a) In closing argument to the jury, the prosecutor may argue all reasonable inferences from evidence in the record. The prosecutor should not intentionally misstate the evidence or mislead the jury as to the inferences it may draw.

(b) The prosecutor should not express his or her personal belief or opinion as to the truth or falsity of any testimony or evidence or the guilt of the defendant.

(c) The prosecutor should not use arguments calculated to appeal to the prejudices of the jury.

(d) The prosecutor should refrain from argument which would divert the jury from its duty to decide the case on the evidence.

Standard 3-5.9. Facts Outside the Record

The prosecutor should not intentionally refer to or argue on the basis of facts outside the record whether at trial or on appeal, unless such facts are matters of common public knowledge based on ordinary human experience or matters of which the court may take judicial notice.

Standard 3-5.10. Comments by Prosecutor After Verdict

The prosecutor should not make public comments critical of a verdict, whether rendered by judge or jury.

CHAPTER 4. THE DEFENSE FUNCTION

Editors' Note. Chapter 4 was originally approved by the ABA in 1971. As noted in the Editors' Introduction to this chapter, the ABA approved substantial revisions to "The Defense Function" at its 1991 Mid-Year Meeting.

Part I. General Standards

Standard 4-1.2. The Function of Defense Counsel

(a) Counsel for the accused is an essential component of the administration of criminal justice. A court properly constituted to hear a criminal case must be viewed as a tripartite entity consisting of the judge (and jury, where appropriate), counsel for the prosecution, and counsel for the accused.

(b) The basic duty defense counsel owes to the administration of justice and as an officer of the court is to serve as the accused's counselor and advocate with courage and devotion and to render effective, quality representation.

(c) Since the death penalty differs from other criminal penalties in its finality, defense counsel in a capital case should respond to this difference by making extraordinary efforts on behalf of the accused. Defense counsel should comply with the ABA Guidelines for the Appointment and Performance of Counsel in Death Penalty Cases.

(d) Defense counsel should seek to reform and improve the administration of criminal justice. When inadequacies or injustices in the substantive or procedural law come to defense counsel's attention, he or she should stimulate efforts for remedial action.

(e) Defense counsel, in common with all members of the bar, is subject to standards of conduct stated in statutes, rules, decisions of courts, and codes, canons, or other standards of professional conduct. Defense counsel has no duty to execute any directive of the accused which does not comport with law or such standards. Defense counsel is the professional representative of the accused, not the accused's alter ego.

(f) Defense counsel should not intentionally misrepresent matters of fact or law to the court.

(g) Defense counsel should disclose to the tribunal legal authority in the controlling jurisdiction known to defense counsel to be directly adverse to the position of the accused and not disclosed by the prosecutor.

(h) It is the duty of defense counsel to know and be guided by the standards of professional conduct as defined in codes and canons of the legal profession applicable in defense counsel's jurisdiction. Once representation has been undertaken, the functions and duties of defense counsel are the same whether defense counsel is assigned, privately retained, or serving in a legal aid or defender program.

Standard 4-1.3. Delays; Punctuality; Workload

(a) Defense counsel should act with reasonable diligence and promptness in representing a client.

(b) Defense counsel should avoid unnecessary delay in the disposition of cases. Defense counsel should be punctual in attendance upon court and in the submission of all motions, briefs, and other papers. Defense counsel should emphasize to the client and all witnesses the importance of punctuality in attendance in court.

(c) Defense counsel should not intentionally misrepresent facts or otherwise mislead the court in order to obtain a continuance.

(d) Defense counsel should not intentionally use procedural devices for delay for which there is no legitimate basis.

(e) Defense counsel should not carry a workload that, by reason of its excessive size, interferes with the rendering of quality representation, endangers the client's interest in the speedy disposition of charges, or may lead to the breach of professional obligations. Defense counsel should not accept employment for the purpose of delaying trial.

Standard 4-1.4. Public Statements

Defense counsel should not make or authorize the making of an extrajudicial statement that a reasonable person would expect to be disseminated by means of public communication if defense counsel knows or reasonably should know that it will have a substantial likelihood of prejudicing a criminal proceeding.

Part III. Lawyer-Client Relationship

Standard 4-3.1. Establishment of Relationship

(a) Defense counsel should seek to establish a relationship of trust and confidence with the accused and should discuss the objectives of the representation and whether defense counsel will continue to represent the accused if there is an appeal. Defense counsel should explain the necessity of full disclosure of all facts known to the client for an effective defense, and defense counsel should explain the extent to which counsel's obligation of confidentiality makes privileged the accused's disclosures.

(b) To ensure the privacy essential for confidential communication between defense counsel and client, adequate facilities should be available for private discussions between counsel and accused in jails, prisons, courthouses, and other places where accused persons must confer with counsel.

(c) Personnel of jails, prisons, and custodial institutions should be prohibited by law or administrative regulations from examining or otherwise interfering with any communication or correspondence between client and defense counsel relating to legal action arising out of charges or incarceration.

Standard 4-3.2. Interviewing the Client

(a) As soon as practicable, defense counsel should seek to determine all relevant facts known to the accused. In so doing, defense counsel should probe for all legally relevant information without seeking to influence the direction of the client's responses.

(b) Defense counsel should not instruct the client or intimate to the client in any way that the client should not be candid in revealing facts so as to afford defense counsel free rein to take action which would be precluded by counsel's knowing of such facts.

Standard 4-3.3. Fees

(a) Defense counsel should not enter into an agreement for, charge, or collect an illegal or unreasonable fee.

(b) In determining the amount of the fee in a criminal case, it is proper to consider the time and effort required, the responsibility assumed by counsel, the novelty and difficulty of the questions involved, the skill requisite to proper representation, the likelihood that other employment will be precluded, the fee customarily charged in the locality for similar services, the gravity of the charge, the experience,

reputation, and ability of defense counsel, and the capacity of the client to pay the fee.

(c) Defense counsel should not imply that his or her compensation is for anything other than professional services rendered by defense counsel or by others for defense counsel.

(d) Defense counsel should not divide a fee with a nonlawyer, except as permitted by applicable ethical codes of conduct.

(e) Defense counsel not in the same firm should not divide fees unless the division is in proportion to the services performed by each counsel or, by written agreement with the client, each counsel assumes joint responsibility for the representation, the client is advised of and does not object to the participation of all counsel involved, and the total fee is reasonable.

(f) Defense counsel should not enter into an arrangement for, charge, or collect a contingent fee for representing a defendant in a criminal case.

(g) When defense counsel has not regularly represented the client, defense counsel should communicate the basis or rate of the fee to the client, preferably in writing, before or within a reasonable time after commencing the representation.

Standard 4-3.4. Obtaining Literary or Media Rights from the Accused

Defense counsel, prior to conclusion of all aspects of the matter giving rise to his or her employment, should not enter into any agreement or understanding with a client or a prospective client by which defense counsel acquires an interest in literary or media rights to a portrayal or account based in substantial part on information relating to the employment or proposed employment.

Standard 4-3.5. Conflicts of Interest

(a) Defense counsel should not permit his or her professional judgment or obligations to be affected by his or her own political, financial, business, property, or personal interests.

(b) Defense counsel should disclose to the defendant at the earliest feasible opportunity any interest in or connection with the case or any other matter that might be relevant to the defendant's selection of counsel to represent him or her or counsel's continuing representation. Such disclosure should include communication of information reasonably sufficient to permit the client to appreciate the significance of any conflict or potential conflict of interest.

(c) Except for preliminary matters such as initial hearings or ap-

plications for bail, defense counsel who are associated in practice should not undertake to defend more than one defendant in the same criminal case if the duty to one of the defendants may conflict with the duty to another. The potential for conflict of interest in representing multiple defendants is so grave that ordinarily defense counsel should decline to act for more than one of several codefendants except in unusual situations when, after careful investigation, it is clear either that no conflict is likely to develop at trial, sentencing, or at any other time in the proceeding or that common representation will be advantageous to each of the codefendants represented and, in either case, that:

(i) the several defendants give an informed consent to such multiple representation; and

(ii) the consent of the defendants is made a matter of judicial record. In determining the presence of consent by the defendants, the trial judge should make appropriate inquiries respecting actual or potential conflicts of interest of counsel and whether the defendants fully comprehend the difficulties that defense counsel sometimes encounters in defending multiple clients.

(d) Defense counsel who has formerly represented a defendant should not thereafter use information related to the former representation to the disadvantage of the former client unless the information has become generally known or the ethical obligation of confidentiality otherwise does not apply.

(e) In accepting payment of fees by one person for the defense of another, defense counsel should be careful to determine that he or she will not be confronted with a conflict of loyalty since defense counsel's entire loyalty is due the accused. Defense counsel should not accept such compensation unless:

(i) the accused consents after disclosure;

(ii) there is no interference with defense counsel's independence of professional judgment or with the client-lawyer relationship; and

(iii) information relating to the representation of the accused is protected from disclosure as required by defense counsel's ethical obligation of confidentiality.

Defense counsel should not permit a person who recommends, employs, or pays defense counsel to render legal services for another to direct or regulate counsel's professional judgment in rendering such legal services.

(f) Defense counsel should not defend a criminal case in which counsel's partner or other professional associate is or has been the prosecutor in the same case.

(g) Defense counsel should not represent a criminal defendant in a jurisdiction in which he or she is also a prosecutor.

(h) Defense counsel who formerly participated personally and substantially in the prosecution of a defendant should not thereafter represent any person in the same or a substantially related matter. Defense counsel

who was formerly a prosecutor should not use confidential information about a person acquired when defense counsel was a prosecutor in the representation of a client whose interests are adverse to that person in a matter.

(i) Defense counsel who is related to a prosecutor as parent, child, sibling or spouse should not represent a client in a criminal matter where defense counsel knows that government is represented in the matter by such prosecutor. Nor should defense counsel who has a significant personal or financial relationship with a prosecutor represent a client in a criminal matter where defense counsel knows the government is represented in the matter by such prosecutor, except upon consent by the client after consultation regarding the relationship.

(j) Defense counsel should not act as surety on a bond either for the accused represented by counsel or for any other accused in the same or a related case.

(k) Except as law may otherwise expressly permit, defense counsel should not negotiate to employ any person who is significantly involved as an attorney or employee of the government in a matter in which defense counsel is participating personally and substantially.

Standard 4-3.6. Prompt Action to Protect the Accused

Many important rights of the accused can be protected and preserved only by prompt legal action. Defense counsel should inform the accused of his or her rights at the earliest opportunity and take all necessary action to vindicate such rights. Defense counsel should consider all procedural steps which in good faith may be taken, including, for example, motions seeking pretrial release of the accused, obtaining psychiatric examination of the accused when a need appears, moving for change of venue or continuance, moving for severance from jointly charged defendants, and seeking dismissal of the charges.

Standard 4-3.7. Advice and Service on Anticipated Unlawful Conduct

(a) It is defense counsel's duty to advise a client to comply with the law, but counsel may advise concerning the meaning, scope, and validity of a law.

(b) Defense counsel should not counsel a client in or knowingly assist a client to engage in conduct which defense counsel knows to be illegal or fraudulent but defense counsel may discuss the legal consequences of any proposed course of conduct with a client.

(c) Defense counsel should not agree in advance of the commission

of a crime that he or she will serve as counsel for the defendant, except as part of a bona fide effort to determine the validity, scope, meaning, or application of the law, or where the defense is incident to a general retainer for legal services to a person or enterprise engaged in legitimate activity.

(d) Defense counsel should not reveal information relating to representation of a client unless the client consents after consultation, except for disclosures that are impliedly authorized in order to carry out the representation and except that defense counsel may reveal such information to the extent he or she reasonably believes necessary to prevent the client from committing a criminal act that defense counsel believes is likely to result in imminent death or substantial bodily harm.

Standard 4-3.8. Duty to Keep Client Informed

(a) Defense counsel should keep the client informed of the developments in the case and the progress of preparing the defense and should promptly comply with reasonable requests for information.

(b) Defense counsel should explain developments in the case to the extent reasonably necessary to permit the client to make informed decisions regarding the representation.

Part IV. Investigation and Preparation

Standard 4-4.1. Duty to Investigate

(a) Defense counsel should conduct a prompt investigation of the circumstances of the case and explore all avenues leading to facts relevant to the merits of the case and the penalty in the event of conviction. The investigation should include efforts to secure information in the possession of the prosecution and law enforcement authorities. The duty to investigate exists regardless of the accused's admissions or statements to defense counsel of facts constituting guilt or the accused's stated desire to plead guilty.

(b) Defense counsel should not seek to acquire possession of physical evidence personally or through use of an investigator where defense counsel's sole purpose is to obstruct access to such evidence.

Standard 4-4.2. Illegal Investigation

Defense counsel should not knowingly use illegal means to obtain evidence or information or to employ, instruct, or encourage others to do so.

Standard 4-4.3. Relations with Prospective Witnesses

(a) Defense counsel, in representing an accused, should not use means that have no substantial purpose other than to embarrass, delay, or burden a third person, or use methods of obtaining evidence that violate the legal rights of such a person.

(b) Defense counsel should not compensate a witness, other than an expert, for giving testimony, but it is not improper to reimburse a witness for the reasonable expenses of attendance upon court, including transportation and loss of income, attendance for depositions pursuant to statute or court rule, or attendance for pretrial interviews, provided there is no attempt to conceal the fact of reimbursement.

(c) It is not necessary for defense counsel or defense counsel's investigator, in interviewing a prospective witness, to caution the witness concerning possible self-incrimination and the need for counsel.

(d) Defense counsel should not discourage or obstruct communication between prospective witnesses and the prosecutor. It is unprofessional conduct to advise any person other than a client, or cause such person to be advised, to decline to give to the prosecutor or defense counsel for codefendants information which such person has a right to give.

(e) Unless defense counsel is prepared to forgo impeachment of a witness by counsel's own testimony as to what the witness stated in an interview or to seek leave to withdraw from the case in order to present such impeaching testimony, defense counsel should avoid interviewing a prospective witness except in the presence of a third person.

Standard 4-4.4. Relations with Expert Witnesses

(a) Defense counsel who engages an expert for an opinion should respect the independence of the expert and should not seek to dictate the formation of the expert's opinion on the subject. To the extent necessary, defense counsel should explain to the expert his or her role in the trial as an impartial witness called to aid the fact finders and the manner in which the examination of witnesses is conducted.

(b) Defense counsel should not pay an excessive fee for the purpose of influencing an expert's testimony or fix the amount of the fee contingent upon the testimony an expert will give or the result in the case.

Standard 4-4.5. Compliance with Discovery Procedure

Defense counsel should make a reasonably diligent effort to comply with a legally proper discovery request.

Standard 4-4.6. Physical Evidence

(a) Defense counsel who receives a physical item under circumstances implicating a client in criminal conduct should disclose the location of or should deliver that item to law enforcement authorities only: (1) if required by law or court order, or (2) as provided in paragraph (d).

(b) Unless required to disclose, defense counsel should return the item to the source from whom defense counsel received it, except as provided in paragraphs (c) and (d). In returning the item to the source, defense counsel should advise the source of the legal consequences pertaining to possession or destruction of the item. Defense counsel should also prepare a written record of these events for his or her file, but should not give the source a copy of such record.

(c) Defense counsel may receive the item for a reasonable period of time during which defense counsel: (1) intends to return it to the owner; (2) reasonably fears that return of the item to the source will result in destruction of the item; (3) reasonably fears that return of the item to the source will result in physical harm to anyone; (4) intends to test, examine, inspect, or use the item in any way as part of defense counsel's representation of the client; or (5) cannot return it to the source. If defense counsel tests or examines the item, he or she should thereafter return it to the source unless there is reason to believe that the evidence might be altered or destroyed or used to harm another or return is otherwise impossible. If defense counsel retains the item, he or she should retain it in his or her law office in a manner that does not impede the lawful ability of law enforcement authorities to obtain the item.

(d) If the item received is contraband, i.e. an item, possession of which is in and of itself a crime, such as narcotics, defense counsel may suggest that the client destroy it where there is no pending case or investigation relating to this evidence and where such destruction is clearly not in violation of any criminal statute. If such destruction is not permitted by law or if in defense counsel's judgment he or she cannot retain the item, whether or not it is contraband, in a way that does not pose an unreasonable risk of physical harm to anyone, defense counsel should disclose the location of or should deliver the item to law enforcement authorities.

(e) If defense counsel discloses the location of or delivers the item to law enforcement authorities under paragraphs (a) or (d), or to a third party under paragraph (c)(1), he or she should do so in the way best designed to protect the client's interests.

[Standard 11-3.2(a) provides: "If either party intends to destroy or transfer out of its possession any objects or information otherwise discoverable under the standards, the party should give notice to the other

party sufficiently in advance to afford that party an opportunity to object or take other appropriate action."]

Part V. Control and Direction of Litigation

Standard 4-5.1. Advising the Accused

(a) After informing himself or herself fully on the facts and the law, defense counsel should advise the accused with complete candor concerning all aspects of the case, including a candid estimate of the probable outcome.

(b) Defense counsel should not intentionally understate or overstate the risks, hazards, or prospects of the case to exert undue influence on the accused's decision as to his or her plea.

(c) Defense counsel should caution the client to avoid communication about the case with witnesses, except with the approval of counsel, to avoid any contact with jurors or prospective jurors, and to avoid either the reality or the appearance of any other improper activity.

Standard 4-5.2. Control and Direction of the Case

(a) Certain decisions relating to the conduct of the case are ultimately for the accused and others are ultimately for defense counsel. The decisions which are to be made by the accused after full consultation with counsel include:

(i) what pleas to enter;
(ii) whether to accept a plea agreement;
(iii) whether to waive jury trial;
(iv) whether to testify in his or her own behalf; and
(v) whether to appeal.

(b) Strategic and tactical decisions should be made by defense counsel after consultation with the client where feasible and appropriate. Such decisions include what witnesses to call, whether and how to conduct cross-examination, what jurors to accept or strike, what trial motions should be made, and what evidence should be introduced.

(c) If a disagreement on significant matters of tactics or strategy arises between defense counsel and the client, defense counsel should make a record of the circumstances, counsel's advice and reasons, and the conclusion reached. The record should be made in a manner which protects the confidentiality of the lawyer-client relationship.

Part VI. Disposition Without Trial

Standard 4-6.1. Duty to Explore Disposition Without Trial

(a) Whenever the law, nature, and circumstances of the case permit, defense counsel should explore the possibility of an early diversion of the case from the criminal process through the use of other community agencies.

(b) Defense counsel may engage in plea discussions with the prosecutor. Under no circumstances should defense counsel recommend to a defendant acceptance of a plea unless appropriate investigation and study of the case has been completed, including an analysis of controlling law and the evidence likely to be introduced at trial.

Standard 4-6.2. Plea Discussions

(a) Defense counsel should keep the accused advised of developments arising out of plea discussions conducted with the prosecutor.

(b) Defense counsel should promptly communicate and explain to the accused all significant plea proposals made by the prosecutor.

(c) Defense counsel should not knowingly make false statements concerning the evidence in the course of plea discussions with the prosecutor.

(d) Defense counsel should not seek concessions favorable to one client by any agreement which is detrimental to the legitimate interests of a client in another case.

(e) Defense counsel representing two or more clients in the same or related cases should not participate in making an aggregated agreement as to guilty or nolo contendre pleas, unless each client consents after consultation, including disclosure of the existence and nature of all the claims or pleas involved.

Part VII. Trial

Standard 4-7.1. Courtroom Professionalism

(a) As an officer of the court, defense counsel should support the authority of the court and the dignity of the trial courtroom by strict adherence to codes of professionalism and by manifesting a professional attitude toward the judge, opposing counsel, witnesses, jurors, and others in the courtroom.

(b) Defense counsel should not engage in unauthorized ex parte discussions with or submission of material to a judge relating to a particular case which is or may come before the judge.

(c) When court is in session, defense counsel should address the court and should not address the prosecutor directly on all matters relating to the case.

(d) Defense counsel should comply promptly with all orders and directives of the court, but defense counsel has a duty to have the record reflect adverse rulings or judicial conduct which counsel considers prejudicial to his or her client's legitimate interests. Defense counsel has a right to make respectful requests for reconsiderations of adverse rulings.

(e) Defense counsel should cooperate with courts and the organized bar in developing codes of professionalism for each jurisdiction.

Standard 4-7.2. Selection of Jurors

(a) Defense counsel should prepare himself or herself prior to trial to discharge effectively his or her function in the selection of the jury, including the raising of any appropriate issues concerning the method by which the jury panel was selected and the exercise of both challenges for cause and peremptory challenges.

(b) In those cases where it appears necessary to conduct a pretrial investigation of the background of jurors, investigatory methods of defense counsel should neither harass nor unduly embarrass potential jurors or invade their privacy and, whenever possible, should be restricted to an investigation of records and sources of information already in existence.

(c) The opportunity to question jurors personally should be used solely to obtain information for the intelligent exercise of challenges. Defense counsel should not intentionally use the voir dire to present factual matter which defense counsel knows will not be admissible at trial or to argue counsel's case to the jury.

Standard 4-7.3. Relations with Jury

(a) Defense counsel should not intentionally communicate privately with persons summoned for jury duty or impaneled as jurors prior to or during the trial. Defense counsel should avoid the reality or appearance of any such communications.

(b) Defense counsel should treat jurors with deference and respect, avoiding the reality or appearance of currying favor by a show of undue solicitude for their comfort or convenience.

(c) After discharge of the jury from further consideration of a case, defense counsel should not intentionally make comments to or ask questions of a juror for the purpose of harassing or embarrassing the juror in any way which will tend to influence judgment in future jury service. If defense counsel believes that the verdict may be subject to legal

challenge, he or she may properly, if no statute or rule prohibits such course, communicate with jurors to determine whether such challenge may be available.

Standard 4-7.4. Opening Statement

Defense counsel's opening statement should be confined to a statement of the issues in the case and the evidence defense counsel believes in good faith will be available and admissible. Defense counsel should not allude to any evidence unless there is a good faith and reasonable basis for believing such evidence will be tendered and admitted in evidence.

Standard 4-7.5. Presentation of Evidence

(a) Defense counsel should not knowingly offer false evidence, whether by documents, tangible evidence, or the testimony of witnesses, or fail to take reasonable remedial measures upon discovery of its falsity.

(b) Defense counsel should not knowingly and for the purpose of bringing inadmissible matter to the attention of the judge or jury offer inadmissible evidence, ask legally objectionable questions, or make other impermissible comments or arguments in the presence of the judge or jury.

(c) Defense counsel should not permit any tangible evidence to be displayed in the view of the judge or jury which would tend to prejudice fair consideration of the case by the judge or jury until such time as a good faith tender of such evidence is made.

(d) Defense counsel should not tender tangible evidence in the presence of the judge or jury if it would tend to prejudice fair consideration of the case unless there is a reasonable basis for its admission in evidence. When there is any substantial doubt about the admissibility of such evidence, it should be tendered by an offer of proof and a ruling obtained.

Standard 4-7.6. Examination of Witnesses

(a) The interrogation of all witnesses should be conducted fairly, objectively, and with due regard for the dignity and legitimate privacy of the witness, and without seeking to intimidate or humiliate the witness unnecessarily.

(b) Defense counsel's belief or knowledge that the witness is telling the truth does not preclude cross-examination.

(c) Defense counsel should not call a witness in the presence of the jury who the lawyer knows will claim a valid privilege not to testify.

(d) Defense counsel should not ask a question which implies the existence of a factual predicate for which a good faith belief is lacking.

Standard 4-7.7. Argument to the Jury

(a) In closing argument to the jury, defense counsel may argue all reasonable inferences from the evidence in the record. Defense counsel should not intentionally misstate the evidence or mislead the jury as to the inferences it may draw.

(b) Defense counsel should not express a personal belief or opinion in his or her client's innocence or personal belief or opinion in the truth or falsity of any testimony or evidence.

(c) Defense counsel should not make arguments calculated to appeal to the prejudices of the jury.

(d) Defense counsel should refrain from argument which would divert the jury from its duty to decide the case on the evidence.

Standard 4-7.8. Facts Outside the Record

Defense counsel should not intentionally refer to or argue on the basis of facts outside the record whether at trial or on appeal, unless such facts are matters of common public knowledge based on ordinary human experience or matters of which the court can take judicial notice.

ABA Code of Judicial Conduct*

Editors' Introduction. The ABA first adopted Canons of Judicial Ethics in 1924. (The original spur for judicial canons was that Kennesaw Mountain Landis, the first Commissioner of Baseball, refused to resign as a federal judge after accepting the job of Commissioner.) With occasional amendments, the Canons of Judicial Ethics served the profession well for nearly 50 years and were adopted by most states. In 1969, however, the ABA created a Special Committee on Standards of Judicial Conduct, chaired by California Supreme Court Justice Roger Traynor, "to draw up modern standards and to replace the Canons of Judicial Ethics." In August 1972, the ABA House of Delegates formally adopted the Code of Judicial Conduct to replace the Canons. The ABA made minor changes in 1982 and 1984.

The ABA Code of Judicial Conduct proved widely influential. Nearly all states (plus the District of Columbia) eventually adopted codes of judicial conduct closely modeled on the 1972 ABA Code.

In August 1990, the ABA revised the Code of Judicial Conduct. Although it is like the 1972 Code in many regards, it also contains many differences, affecting such issues as judicial membership in exclusionary clubs and judicial responsibility to prohibit race and sex discrimination and other kinds of bias in the courtroom. For a legislative history of the 1990 Code, see L. Milord, The Development of the ABA Judicial Code (1992).

At the ABA's 1997 Annual Meeting, the House of Delegates voted to amend the 1990 Judicial Code for the first time since its adoption. The amendment substantially changed the Commentary to (but not the text of) Canon 5C(2), a provision that governs the solicitation and acceptance of campaign contributions by judges and judicial candidates who are "subject to public election" (as distinct from appointed judges). The amendment to the Commentary addresses widespread concern about "the appearance of impropriety that may arise when parties whose interests may come before a judge or the lawyers who represent such parties have made contributions to the election campaigns of judicial candidates." Shortly before the ABA's 1998 Annual Meeting, the ABA's elite Task Force on Lawyers' Political Contributions (which was appointed in

1997 to study so-called "pay-to-play" issues) issued a report recommending various amendments to the Code of Judicial Conduct "to protect the integrity and independence of judges and candidates for judicial office." The Task Force noted that judges in 42 states must stand for election in some fashion and that their need to raise campaign funds creates an appearance of impropriety. The Task Force therefore recommended amendments to Canon 5 of the Code of Judicial Conduct that would (a) require judicial candidates and/or their campaign committees to publicly disclose all campaign contributions from lawyers, (b) limit the amount of money a judicial candidate may accept from any one lawyer, law firm, political action committee, or political party, (c) require judges, upon motion, to recuse themselves from hearing any case in which a litigant or lawyer has contributed more than a specified amount to the judge's campaign, (d) prohibit judges from appointing a lawyer as a guardian, executor, special master, or other paid position if the lawyer, the lawyer's firm, or any employee of the firm has contributed more than a specified limit to the judge's campaign, and (e) require unopposed judicial candidates and judicial candidates who have campaign funds remaining after an election to return the surplus funds to contributors pro rata and/or give the funds to an entity to be determined by the jurisdiction. On the eve of the 1998 House of Delegates meeting, however, the Task Force withdrew all of its recommendations to amend the Code of Judicial Conduct so that the ABA's Judicial Division and other interested groups could have more time to study them. The Task Force ceased to exist after the ABA's 1998 Annual Meeting because of a "sunset" provision, but various members of the Task Force and its supporters announced that they hoped to offer revised proposals to amend the Code of Judicial Conduct in 1999.

That hope became a reality. In 1999, the ABA adopted a definition of the word "aggregate" and new provisions in Canons 3 and 5 as part of the Association's continuing efforts to address "concern about the relationship between lawyers making political contributions and the award of engagements to perform legal services in a variety of contexts."

According to the American Judicature Society, about 20 jurisdictions have adopted new codes of judicial conduct based on the 1990 ABA Model Code of Judicial Conduct. These are Arizona, Arkansas, California, Florida, Hawaii, Indiana, Kansas, Maine, Minnesota, Nebraska, Nevada, New Mexico, New York, North Dakota, Rhode Island, South Dakota, Utah, West Virginia, Wyoming, and the District of Columbia. In addition, the following jurisdictions have adopted various provisions of the 1990 Code: Colorado, Connecticut, Delaware, Georgia, Idaho, Illinois, Iowa, Kentucky, Louisiana, Maryland, Massachusetts, Missouri, New Jersey, Ohio, Texas, Washington, and Wisconsin. In these states, the number of provisions adopted from the 1990 Code varies widely. For example, Connecticut adopted only the ex parte communications provision of the 1990 Code, whereas Georgia has adopted the preamble, the terminology, and Canons 1 through 3 of the ABA Code. The United States Judicial Conference has adopted a Code of Judicial Conduct that includes some provisions from the 1990 ABA Code.

In June 2002, in a 5-4 opinion by Justice Scalia, the Supreme Court held that a Minnesota rule limiting judicial campaign speech violated the First Amendment. Republican Party of Minnesota v. White, 122 S. Ct. 2528 (2002). The state rule was derived from the 1972 ABA Code of Judicial

Conduct. See also Canon 5A(3)(d)(ii) of the 1990 ABA Code of Judicial Conduct, which will now have to be rewritten. Specifically, the Minnesota rule prohibited a judicial candidate to "announce his or her views on disputed legal or political issues." Lower federal courts and the Minnesota Supreme Court had interpreted this language to encompass only those disputed issues likely to come before the candidate if elected and not to forbid general discussion of case law and judicial philosophy. Another Minnesota provision, not before the Court, prohibited judicial candidates from making "pledges or promises of conduct in office." This prohibition also appears in Canon 5A(3)(d)(i) of the ABA Code. Justices O'Connor and Kennedy concurred in the Court's opinion and also wrote separate opinions. Justices Stevens, Souter, Ginsburg, and Breyer dissented in opinions by Justices Stevens and Ginsburg.

At the end of Canon 3, we reprint a remarkable press release from seven United States Supreme Court Justices specifying when the participation of a lawyer-relative or the law firm of a lawyer-relative in cases before them will cause them to recuse themselves.

Contents

MODEL CODE OF JUDICIAL CONDUCT (1990)

Preamble
Terminology

Canon

1. A Judge Shall Uphold the Integrity and Independence of the Judiciary
2. A Judge Shall Avoid Impropriety and the Appearance of Impropriety in All of the Judge's Activities
3. A Judge Shall Perform the Duties of Judicial Office Impartially and Diligently
   A. Judicial Duties in General
   B. Adjudicative Responsibilities
   C. Administrative Responsibilities
   D. Disciplinary Responsibilities
   E. Disqualification
   F. Remittal of Disqualification
4. A Judge Shall So Conduct the Judge's Extra-Judicial Activities as to Minimize the Risk of Conflict with Judicial Obligations
   A. Extra-Judicial Activities in General
   B. Avocational Activities
   C. Governmental, Civic or Charitable Activities
   D. Financial Activities
   E. Fiduciary Activities
   F. Service as Arbitrator or Mediator
   G. Practice of Law
   H. Compensation, Reimbursement and Reporting
   I. [Disclosure of Judge's Assets]

5. A Judge or Judicial Candidate Shall Refrain from Inappropriate Political Activity
   A. All Judges and Candidates
   B. Candidates Seeking Appointment to Judicial or Other Governmental Office
   C. Judges and Candidates Subject to Public Election
   D. Incumbent Judges
   E. Applicability
Application of the Code of Judicial Conduct
   A. [Definition of a Judge]
   B. Retired Judge Subject to Recall
   C. Continuing Part-Time Judge
   D. Periodic Part-Time Judge
   E. Pro Tempore Part-Time Judge
   F. Time for Compliance
Appendix. Judicial Ethics Committee

MODEL CODE OF JUDICIAL CONDUCT (1990)

PREAMBLE

Our legal system is based on the principle that an independent, fair and competent judiciary will interpret and apply the laws that govern us. The role of the judiciary is central to American concepts of justice and the rule of law. Intrinsic to all sections of this Code are the precepts that judges, individually and collectively, must respect and honor the judicial office as a public trust and strive to enhance and maintain confidence in our legal system. The judge is an arbiter of facts and law for the resolution of disputes and a highly visible symbol of government under the rule of law.

The Code of Judicial Conduct is intended to establish standards for ethical conduct of judges. It consists of broad statements called Canons, specific rules set forth in Sections under each Canon, a Terminology Section, an Application Section and Commentary. The text of the Canons and the Sections, including the Terminology and Application Sections, is authoritative. The Commentary, by explanation and example, provides guidance with respect to the purpose and meaning of the Canons and Sections. The Commentary is not intended as a statement of additional rules. When the text uses "shall" or "shall not," it is intended to impose binding obligations the violation of which can result in disciplinary action. When "should" or "should not" is used, the text is intended as hortatory and as a statement of what is or is not appropriate conduct but not as a binding rule under which a judge may be disciplined. When "may" is used, it denotes permissible discretion or, depending on the context, it refers to action that is not covered by specific proscriptions.

The Canons and Sections are rules of reason. They should be applied consistent with constitutional requirements, statutes, other court rules and decisional law and in the context of all relevant circumstances. The Code is to be construed so as not to impinge on the essential independence of judges in making judicial decisions.

The Code is designed to provide guidance to judges and candidates for judicial office and to provide a structure for regulating conduct through disciplinary agencies. It is not designed or intended as a basis for civil liability or criminal prosecution. Furthermore, the purpose of the Code would be subverted if the Code were invoked by lawyers for mere tactical advantage in a proceeding.

The text of the Canons and Sections is intended to govern conduct of judges and to be binding upon them. It is not intended, however, that every transgression will result in disciplinary action. Whether disciplinary action is appropriate, and the degree of discipline to be imposed, should be determined through a reasonable and reasoned application of the text and should depend on such factors as the seriousness of the transgression, whether there is a pattern of improper activity and the effect of the improper activity on others or on the judicial system. See ABA Standards Relating to Judicial Discipline and Disability Retirement.[1] The Code of Judicial Conduct is not intended as an exhaustive guide for the conduct of judges. They should also be governed in their judicial and personal conduct by general ethical standards. The Code is intended, however, to state basic standards which should govern the conduct of all judges and to provide guidance to assist judges in establishing and maintaining high standards of judicial and personal conduct.

1. Judicial disciplinary procedures adopted in the jurisdictions should comport with the requirements of due process. The ABA Standards Relating to Judicial Discipline and Disability Retirement are cited as an example of how these due process requirements may be satisfied.

TERMINOLOGY

Terms explained below are noted with an asterisk (*) in the Sections where they appear. In addition, the Sections where terms appear are referred to after the explanation of each term below.

"Appropriate authority" denotes the authority with responsibility for initiation of disciplinary process with respect to the violation to be reported. See Sections 3D(1) and 3D(2).

> **Editor's Note:** At its 1999 Annual Meeting, the ABA adopted the following definition of the word "aggregate" as an amendment to the Code of Judicial Conduct.

"Aggregate" in relation to contributions for a candidate under Sections 3E(1)(e) and 5C(3) and (4) denotes not only contributions in cash or in kind made directly to a candidate's committee or treasurer, but also, except in retention elections, all contributions made indirectly with the understanding that they will be used to support the election of the candidate or to oppose the election of the candidate's opponent.

"Candidate." A candidate is a person seeking selection for or retention in judicial office by election or appointment. A person becomes a candidate for judicial office as soon as he or she makes a public announcement of candidacy, declares or files as a candidate with the election or appointment authority, or authorizes solicitation or acceptance of contributions or support. The term "candidate" has the same meaning when applied to a judge seeking election or appointment to non-judicial office. See Preamble and Sections 5A, 5B, 5C and 5E.

"Continuing part-time judge." A continuing part-time judge is a judge who serves repeatedly on a part-time basis by election or under a continuing appointment, including a retired judge subject to recall who is permitted to practice law. See Application Section C.

"Court personnel" does not include the lawyers in a proceeding before a judge. See Sections 3B(7)(c) and 3B(9).

"De minimis" denotes an insignificant interest that could not raise reasonable question as to a judge's impartiality. See Sections 3E(1)(c) and 3E(1)(d).

"Economic interest" denotes ownership of a more than de minimis legal or equitable interest, or a relationship as officer, director, advisor or other active participant in the affairs of a party, except that:

(i) ownership of an interest in a mutual or common investment fund that holds securities is not an economic interest in such securities unless the judge participates in the management of the fund or a proceeding pending or impending before the judge could substantially affect the value of the interest;

(ii) service by a judge as an officer, director, advisor or other active participant in an educational, religious, charitable, fraternal or civic organization, or service by a judge's spouse, parent or child as an officer, director, advisor or other active participant in any organization does not create an economic interest in securities held by that organization;

(iii) a deposit in a financial institution, the proprietary interest of a policy holder in a mutual insurance company, of a depositor in a mutual savings association or of a member in a credit union, or a similar proprietary interest, is not an economic interest in the organization unless a proceeding pending or impending before the judge could substantially affect the value of the interest;

(iv) ownership of government securities is not an economic interest in the issuer unless a proceeding pending or impending before the judge could substantially affect the value of the securities.

See Sections 3E(1)(c) and 3E(2).

"Fiduciary" includes such relationships as executor, administrator, trustee, and guardian. See Sections 3E(2) and 4E.

"Knowingly," "knowledge," "known" or "knows" denotes actual knowledge of the fact in question. A person's knowledge may be inferred from circumstances. See Sections 3D, 3E(1), and 5A(3).

"Law" denotes court rules as well as statutes, constitutional provisions and decisional law. See Sections 2A, 3A, 3B(2), 3B(6), 4B, 4C, 4D(5), 4F, 4I, 5A(2), 5A(3), 5B(2), 5C(1), 5C(3) and 5D.

"Member of the candidate's family" denotes a spouse, child, grandchild, parent, grandparent or other relative or person with whom the candidate maintains a close familial relationship. See Section 5A(3)(a).

"Member of the judge's family" denotes a spouse, child, grandchild, parent, grandparent, or other relative or person with whom the judge maintains a close familial relationship. See Sections 4D(3), 4E and 4G.

"Member of the judge's family residing in the judge's household" denotes any relative of a judge by blood or marriage, or a person treated by a judge as a member of the judge's family, who resides in the judge's household. See Sections 3E(1) and 4D(5).

"Nonpublic information" denotes information that, by law, is not available to the public. Nonpublic information may include but is not limited to: information that is sealed by statute or court order, impounded or communicated in camera; and information offered in grand jury proceedings, presentencing reports, dependency cases or psychiatric reports. See Section 3B(11).

"Periodic part-time judge." A periodic part-time judge is a judge who serves or expects to serve repeatedly on a part-time basis but under a separate appointment for each limited period of service or for each matter. See Application Section D.

"Political organization" denotes a political party or other group, the principal purpose of which is to further the election or appointment of candidates to political office. See Sections 5A(1), 5B(2) and 5C(1).

"Pro tempore part-time judge." A pro tempore part-time judge is a judge who serves or expects to serve once or only sporadically on a part-time basis under a separate appointment for each period of service or for each case heard. See Application Section E.

"Public election." This term includes primary and general elections; it includes partisan elections, nonpartisan elections and retention elections. See Section 5C.

"Require." The rules prescribing that a judge "require" certain conduct of others are, like all of the rules in this Code, rules of reason. The use of the term "require" in that context means a judge is to exercise reasonable direction and control over the conduct of those persons subject to the judge's direction and control. See Sections 3B(3), 3B(4), 3B(5), 3B(6), 3B(9) and 3C(2).

"Third degree of relationship." The following persons are relatives within the third degree of relationship: great-grandparent, grandparent, parent, uncle, aunt, brother, sister, child, grandchild, great-grandchild, nephew or niece. See Section 3E(1)(d).

CANON 1. A JUDGE SHALL UPHOLD THE INTEGRITY AND INDEPENDENCE OF THE JUDICIARY

A. An independent and honorable judiciary is indispensable to justice in our society. A judge should participate in establishing, maintaining and enforcing high standards of conduct, and shall personally observe those standards so that the integrity and independence of the

judiciary will be preserved. The provisions of this Code are to be construed and applied to further that objective.

Commentary

Deference to the judgments and rulings of courts depends upon public confidence in the integrity and independence of judges. The integrity and independence of judges depends in turn upon their acting without fear or favor. Although judges should be independent, they must comply with the law, including the provisions of this Code. Public confidence in the impartiality of the judiciary is maintained by the adherence of each judge to this responsibility. Conversely, violation of this Code diminishes public confidence in the judiciary and thereby does injury to the system of government under law.

CANON 2. A JUDGE SHALL AVOID IMPROPRIETY AND THE APPEARANCE OF IMPROPRIETY IN ALL OF THE JUDGE'S ACTIVITIES

A. A judge shall respect and comply with the law* and shall act at all times in a manner that promotes public confidence in the integrity and impartiality of the judiciary.

Commentary

Public confidence in the judiciary is eroded by irresponsible or improper conduct by judges. A judge must avoid all impropriety and appearance of impropriety. A judge must expect to be the subject of constant public scrutiny. A judge must therefore accept restrictions on the judge's conduct that might be viewed as burdensome by the ordinary citizen and should do so freely and willingly.

The prohibition against behaving with impropriety or the appearance of impropriety applies to both the professional and personal conduct of a judge. Because it is not practicable to list all prohibited acts, the proscription is necessarily cast in general terms that extend to conduct by judges that is harmful although not specifically mentioned in the Code. Actual improprieties under this standard include violations of law, court rules or other specific provisions of this Code. The test for appearance of impropriety is whether the conduct would create in reasonable minds a perception that the judge's ability to carry out judicial responsibilities with integrity, impartiality and competence is impaired.

See also Commentary under Section 2C.

*Asterisked terms are defined in the Terminology Section. — Eds.

B. A judge shall not allow family, social, political or other relationships to influence the judge's judicial conduct or judgment. A judge shall not lend the prestige of judicial office to advance the private interests of the judge or others; nor shall a judge convey or permit others to convey the impression that they are in a special position to influence the judge. A judge shall not testify voluntarily as a character witness.

Commentary

Maintaining the prestige of judicial office is essential to a system of government in which the judiciary functions independently of the executive and legislative branches. Respect for the judicial office facilitates the orderly conduct of legitimate judicial functions. Judges should distinguish between proper and improper use of the prestige of office in all of their activities. For example, it would be improper for a judge to allude to his or her judgeship to gain a personal advantage such as deferential treatment when stopped by a police officer for a traffic offense. Similarly, judicial letterhead must not be used for conducting a judge's personal business.

A judge must avoid lending the prestige of judicial office for the advancement of the private interests of others. For example, a judge must not use the judge's judicial position to gain advantage in a civil suit involving a member of the judge's family. In contracts for publication of a judge's writings, a judge should retain control over the advertising to avoid exploitation of the judge's office. As to the acceptance of awards, see Section 4D(5)(a) and Commentary.

Although a judge should be sensitive to possible abuse of the prestige of office, a judge may, based on the judge's personal knowledge, serve as a reference or provide a letter of recommendation. However, a judge must not initiate the communication of information to a sentencing judge or a probation or corrections officer but may provide to such persons information for the record in response to a formal request.

Judges may participate in the process of judicial selection by cooperating with appointing authorities and screening committees seeking names for consideration, and by responding to official inquiries concerning a person being considered for a judgeship. See also Canon 5 regarding use of a judge's name in political activities.

A judge must not testify voluntarily as a character witness because to do so may lend the prestige of the judicial office in support of the party for whom the judge testifies. Moreover, when a judge testifies as a witness, a lawyer who regularly appears before the judge may be placed in the awkward position of cross-examining the judge. A judge may, however, testify when properly summoned. Except in unusual circumstances where the demands of justice require, a judge should discourage a party from requiring the judge to testify as a character witness.

C. A judge shall not hold membership in any organization that practices invidious discrimination on the basis of race, sex, religion or national origin.

Commentary

Membership of a judge in an organization that practices invidious discrimination gives rise to perceptions that the judge's impartiality is impaired. Section 2C refers to the current practices of the organization. Whether an organization practices invidious discrimination is often a complex question to which judges should be sensitive. The answer cannot be determined from a mere examination of an organization's current membership rolls but rather depends on how the organization selects members and other relevant factors, such as that the organization is dedicated to the preservation of religious, ethnic or cultural values of legitimate common interest to its members, or that it is in fact and effect an intimate, purely private organization whose membership limitations could not be constitutionally prohibited. Absent such factors, an organization is generally said to discriminate invidiously if it arbitrarily excludes from membership on the basis of race, religion, sex or national origin persons who would otherwise be admitted to membership. See New York State Club Assn., Inc. v. City of New York, 108 S. Ct. 2225, 101 L. Ed. 2d 1 (1988); Board of Directors of Rotary International v. Rotary Club of Duarte, 481 U.S. 537, 107 S. Ct. 1940 (1987), 95 L. Ed. 2d 474; Roberts v. United States Jaycees, 468 U.S. 609, 104 S. Ct. 3244, 82 L. Ed. 2d 462 (1984).

Although Section 2C relates only to membership in organizations that invidiously discriminate on the basis of race, sex, religion or national origin, a judge's membership in an organization that engages in any discriminatory membership practices prohibited by the law of the jurisdiction also violates Canon 2 and Section 2A and gives the appearance of impropriety. In addition, it would be a violation of Canon 2 and Section 2A for a judge to arrange a meeting at a club that the judge knows practices invidious discrimination on the basis of race, sex, religion or national origin in its membership or other policies, or for the judge to regularly use such a club. Moreover, public manifestation by a judge of the judge's knowing approval of invidious discrimination on any basis gives the appearance of impropriety under Canon 2 and diminishes public confidence in the integrity and impartiality of the judiciary, in violation of Section 2A.

When a person who is a judge in the date this Code becomes effective [in the jurisdiction in which the person is a judge][1] learns that an organization to which the judge belongs engages in invidious discrimination that would preclude membership under Section 2C or under Canon 2 and Section 2A, the judge is permitted, in lieu of resigning, to make immediate efforts to have the organization discontinue its invidiously discriminatory practices, but is required to suspend participation in any other activities of the organization. If the organization fails to discontinue its invidiously discriminatory practices as promptly as possible (and in all events within a year of the judge's first learning of the practices), the judge is required to resign immediately from the organization.

1. The language within the brackets should be deleted when the jurisdiction adopts this provision.

CANON 3. A JUDGE SHALL PERFORM THE DUTIES OF JUDICIAL OFFICE IMPARTIALLY AND DILIGENTLY

A. Judicial Duties in General

The judicial duties of a judge take precedence over all the judge's other activities. The judge's judicial duties include all the duties of the judge's office prescribed by law.* In the performance of these duties, the following standards apply.

B. Adjudicative Responsibilities

(1) A judge shall hear and decide matters assigned to the judge except those in which disqualification is required.

(2) A judge shall be faithful to the law* and maintain professional competence in it. A judge shall not be swayed by partisan interests, public clamor or fear of criticism.

(3) A judge shall require* order and decorum in proceedings before the judge.

(4) A judge shall be patient, dignified and courteous to litigants, jurors, witnesses, lawyers and others with whom the judge deals in an official capacity, and shall require* similar conduct of lawyers, and of staff, court officials and others subject to the judge's direction and control.

Commentary

The duty to hear all proceedings fairly and with patience is not inconsistent with the duty to dispose promptly of the business of the court. Judges can be efficient and businesslike while being patient and deliberate.

(5) A judge shall perform judicial duties without bias or prejudice. A judge shall not, in the performance of judicial duties, by words or conduct manifest bias or prejudice, including but not limited to bias or prejudice based upon race, sex, religion, national origin, disability, age, sexual orientation or socioeconomic status, and shall not permit staff, court officials and others subject to the judge's direction and control to do so.

Commentary

A judge must refrain from speech, gestures or other conduct that could reasonably be perceived as sexual harassment and must require the same standard of conduct of others subject to the judge's direction and control.

*Asterisked terms are defined in the Terminology Section. — Eds.

A judge must perform judicial duties impartially and fairly. A judge who manifests bias on any basis in a proceeding impairs the fairness of the proceeding and brings the judiciary into disrepute. Facial expression and body language, in addition to oral communication, can give to parties or lawyers in the proceeding, jurors, the media and others an appearance of judicial bias. A judge must be alert to avoid behavior that may be perceived as prejudicial.

(6) A judge shall require* lawyers in proceedings before the judge to refrain from manifesting, by words or conduct, bias or prejudice based upon race, sex, religion, national origin, disability, age, sexual orientation or socioeconomic status, against parties, witnesses, counsel or others. This Section 3B(6) does not preclude legitimate advocacy when race, sex, religion, national origin, disability, age, sexual orientation or socioeconomic status, or other similar factors, are issues in the proceeding.

(7) A judge shall accord to every person who has a legal interest in a proceeding, or that person's lawyer, the right to be heard according to law.* A judge shall not initiate, permit, or consider ex parte communications, or consider other communications made to the judge outside the presence of the parties concerning a pending or impending proceeding except that:

(a) Where circumstances require, ex parte communications for scheduling, administrative purposes or emergencies that do not deal with substantive matters or issues on the merits are authorized; provided:

(i) the judge reasonably believes that no party will gain a procedural or tactical advantage as a result of the ex parte communication, and

(ii) the judge makes provision promptly to notify all other parties of the substance of the ex parte communication and allows an opportunity to respond.

(b) A judge may obtain the advice of a disinterested expert on the law* applicable to a proceeding before the judge if the judge gives notice to the parties of the person consulted and the substance of the advice, and affords the parties reasonable opportunity to respond.

(c) A judge may consult with court personnel* whose function is to aid the judge in carrying out the judge's adjudicative responsibilities or with other judges.

(d) A judge may, with the consent of the parties, confer separately with the parties and their lawyers in an effort to mediate or settle matters pending before the judge.

(e) A judge may initiate or consider any ex parte communications when expressly authorized by law* to do so.

*Asterisked terms are defined in the Terminology Section. — Eds.

Commentary

The proscription against communications concerning a proceeding includes communications from lawyers, law teachers, and other persons who are not participants in the proceeding, except to the limited extent permitted.

To the extent reasonably possible, all parties or their lawyers shall be included in communications with a judge.

Whenever presence of a party or notice to a party is required by Section 3B(7), it is the party's lawyer, or if the party is unrepresented the party, who is to be present or to whom notice is to be given.

An appropriate and often desirable procedure for a court to obtain the advice of a disinterested expert on legal issues is to invite the expert to file a brief *amicus curiae*.

Certain ex parte communication is approved by Section 3B(7) to facilitate scheduling and other administrative purposes and to accommodate emergencies. In general, however, a judge must discourage ex parte communication and allow it only if all the criteria stated in Section 3B(7) are clearly met. A judge must disclose to all parties all ex parte communications described in Sections 3B(7)(a) and 3B(7)(b) regarding a proceeding pending or impending before the judge.

A judge must not independently investigate facts in a case and must consider only the evidence presented.

A judge may request a party to submit proposed findings of fact and conclusions of law, so long as the other parties are apprised of the request and are given an opportunity to respond to the proposed findings and conclusions.

A judge must make reasonable efforts, including the provision of appropriate supervision, to ensure that Section 3B(7) is not violated through law clerks or other personnel on the judge's staff.

If communication between the trial judge and the appellate court with respect to a proceeding is permitted, a copy of any written communication or the substance of any oral communication should be provided to all parties.

(8) A judge shall dispose of all judicial matters promptly, efficiently and fairly.

Commentary

In disposing of matters promptly, efficiently and fairly, a judge must demonstrate due regard for the rights of the parties to be heard and to have issues resolved without unnecessary cost or delay. Containing costs while preserving fundamental rights of parties also protects the interests of witnesses and the general public. A judge should monitor and supervise cases so as to reduce or eliminate dilatory practices, avoidable delays and unnecessary costs. A judge should encourage and seek to facilitate settlement, but parties should not feel coerced into surrendering the right to have their controversy resolved by the courts.

Prompt disposition of the court's business requires a judge to devote adequate time to judicial duties, to be punctual in attending court and expeditious in determining matters under submission, and to insist that court officials, litigants and their lawyers cooperate with the judge to that end.

(9) A judge shall not, while a proceeding is pending or impending in any court, make any public comment that might reasonably be expected to affect its outcome or impair its fairness or make any nonpublic comment that might substantially interfere with a fair trial or hearing. The judge shall require* similar abstention on the part of court personnel* subject to the judge's direction and control. This Section does not prohibit judges from making public statements in the course of their official duties or from explaining for public information the procedures of the court. This Section does not apply to proceedings in which the judge is a litigant in a personal capacity.

Commentary

The requirement that judges abstain from public comment regarding a pending or impending proceeding continues during any appellate process and until final disposition. This Section does not prohibit a judge from commenting on proceedings in which the judge is a litigant in a personal capacity, but in cases such as a writ of mandamus where the judge is a litigant in an official capacity, the judge must not comment publicly. The conduct of lawyers relating to trial publicity is governed by [Rule 3.6 of the ABA Model Rules of Professional Conduct]. (Each jurisdiction should substitute an appropriate reference to its rule.)

(10) A judge shall not commend or criticize jurors for their verdict other than in a court order or opinion in a proceeding, but may express appreciation to jurors for their service to the judicial system and the community.

Commentary

Commending or criticizing jurors for their verdict may imply a judicial expectation in future cases and may impair a juror's ability to be fair and impartial in a subsequent case.

(11) A judge shall not disclose or use, for any purpose unrelated to judicial duties, nonpublic information* acquired in a judicial capacity.

C. *Administrative Responsibilities*

(1) A judge shall diligently discharge the judge's administrative responsibilities without bias or prejudice and maintain professional competence in judicial administration, and should cooperate with other judges and court officials in the administration of court business.

*Asterisked terms are defined in the Terminology Section. — Eds.

(2) A judge shall require* staff, court officials and others subject to the judge's direction and control to observe the standards of fidelity and diligence that apply to the judge and to refrain from manifesting bias or prejudice in the performance of their official duties.

(3) A judge with supervisory authority for the judicial performance of other judges shall take reasonable measures to assure the prompt disposition of matters before them and the proper performance of their other judicial responsibilities.

(4) A judge shall not make unnecessary appointments. A judge shall exercise the power of appointment impartially and on the basis of merit. A judge shall avoid nepotism and favoritism. A judge shall not approve compensation of appointees beyond the fair value of services rendered.

Editors' Note: By voice vote at its 1999 Annual Meeting, the ABA adopted the following amendment to Canon 3C(5) of the Code of Judicial Conduct.

(5) A judge shall not appoint a lawyer to a position if the judge either knows that the lawyer has contributed more than [$] within the prior [ ] years to the judge's election campaign, or learns of such a contribution by means of a timely motion by a party or other person properly interested in the matter, unless**

(a) the position is substantially uncompensated;

(b) the lawyer has been selected in rotation from a list of qualified and available lawyers compiled without regard to their having made political contributions; or

(c) the judge or another presiding or administrative judge affirmatively finds that no other lawyer is willing, competent and able to accept the position.

Commentary

Appointees of a judge include assigned counsel, officials such as referees, commissioners, special masters, receivers and guardians and personnel such as clerks, secretaries and bailiffs. Consent by the parties to an appointment or an award of compensation does not relieve the judge of the obligation prescribed by Section 3C(4).

*Asterisked terms are defined in the Terminology Section. — Eds.

**This provision is meant to be applicable wherever judges are subject to public election; specific amount and time limitations, to be determined based on circumstances within the jurisdiction, should be inserted in the brackets.

D. Disciplinary Responsibilities

(1) A judge who receives information indicating a substantial likelihood that another judge has committed a violation of this Code should take appropriate action. A judge having knowledge* that another judge has committed a violation of this Code that raises a substantial question as to the other judge's fitness for office shall inform the appropriate authority.*

(2) A judge who receives information indicating a substantial likelihood that a lawyer has committed a violation of the Rules of Professional Conduct [substitute correct title if the applicable rules of lawyer conduct have a different title] should take appropriate action. A judge having knowledge* that a lawyer has committed a violation of the Rules of Professional Conduct [substitute correct title if the applicable rules of lawyer conduct have a different title] that raises a substantial question as to the lawyer's honesty, trustworthiness or fitness as a lawyer in other respects shall inform the appropriate authority.*

(3) Acts of a judge, in the discharge of disciplinary responsibilities, required or permitted by Sections 3D(1) and 3D(2) are part of a judge's judicial duties and shall be absolutely privileged, and no civil action predicated thereon may be instituted against the judge.

Commentary

Appropriate action may include direct communication with the judge or lawyer who has committed the violation, other direct action if available, and reporting the violation to the appropriate authority or other agency or body.

E. Disqualification

(1) A judge shall disqualify himself or herself in a proceeding in which the judge's impartiality might reasonably be questioned, including but not limited to instances where:

Commentary

Under this rule, a judge is disqualified whenever the judge's impartiality might reasonably be questioned, regardless whether any of the specific rules in Section 3E(1) apply. For example, if a judge were in the process of negotiating for employment with a law firm, the judge would be disqualified from any matters in which that law firm appeared, unless the disqualification was waived by the parties after disclosure by the judge.

*Asterisked terms are defined in the Terminology Section. — Eds.

A judge should disclose on the record information that the judge believes the parties or their lawyers might consider relevant to the question of disqualification, even if the judge believes there is no real basis for disqualification.

By decisional law, the rule of necessity may override the rule of disqualification. For example, a judge might be required to participate in judicial review of a judicial salary statute, or might be the only judge available in a matter requiring immediate judicial action, such as a hearing on probable cause or a temporary restraining order. In the latter case, the judge must disclose on the record the basis for possible disqualification and use reasonable efforts to transfer the matter to another judge as soon as practicable.

(a) the judge has a personal bias or prejudice concerning a party or a party's lawyer, or personal knowledge* of disputed evidentiary facts concerning the proceeding;

(b) the judge served as a lawyer in the matter in controversy, or a lawyer with whom the judge previously practiced law served during such association as a lawyer concerning the matter, or the judge has been a material witness concerning it;

Commentary

A lawyer in a government agency does not ordinarily have an association with other lawyers employed by that agency within the meaning of Section 3E(1)(b); a judge formerly employed by a government agency, however, should disqualify himself or herself in a proceeding if the judge's impartiality might reasonably be questioned because of such association.

(c) the judge knows* that he or she, individually or as a fiduciary, or the judge's spouse, parent or child wherever residing, or any other member of the judge's family residing in the judge's household,* has an economic interest* in the subject matter in controversy or in a party to the proceeding or has any other more than de minimis* interest that could be substantially affected by the proceeding;

(d) the judge or the judge's spouse, or a person within the third degree of relationship* to either of them, or the spouse of such a person:

(i) is a party to the proceeding, or an officer, director or trustee of a party;

(ii) is acting as a lawyer in the proceeding;

(iii) is known* by the judge to have a more than de minimis* interest that could be substantially affected by the proceeding;

(iv) is to the judge's knowledge* likely to be a material witness in the proceeding.

*Asterisked terms are defined in the Terminology Section. — Eds.

Editors' Note: By voice vote at its 1999 Annual Meeting, the ABA adopted the following amendment to the Code of Judicial Conduct.

(e) the judge knows or learns by means of a timely motion that a party or a party's lawyer has within the previous [ ] year[s] made aggregate* contributions to the judge's campaign in an amount that is greater than [[$] for an individual or [$] for an entity] [[is reasonable and appropriate for an individual or an entity]].**

Commentary

The fact that a lawyer in a proceeding is affiliated with a law firm with which a relative of the judge is affiliated does not of itself disqualify the judge. Under appropriate circumstances, the fact that "the judge's impartiality might reasonably be questioned" under Section 3E(1), or that the relative is known by the judge to have an interest in the law firm that could be "substantially affected by the outcome of the proceeding" under Section 3E(1)(d)(iii) may require the judge's disqualification.

(2) A judge shall keep informed about the judge's personal and fiduciary* economic interests,* and make a reasonable effort to keep informed about the personal economic interests of the judge's spouse and minor children residing in the judge's household.

F. Remittal of Disqualification

A judge disqualified by the terms of Section 3E may disclose on the record the basis of the judge's disqualification and may ask the parties and their lawyers to consider, out of the presence of the judge, whether to waive disqualification. If following disclosure of any basis for disqualification other than personal bias or prejudice concerning a party, the parties and lawyers, without participation by the judge, all agree that the judge should not be disqualified, and the judge is then willing to participate, the judge may participate in the proceeding. The agreement shall be incorporated in the record of the proceeding.

Commentary

A remittal procedure provides the parties an opportunity to proceed without delay if they wish to waive the disqualification. To assure that consideration

*Asterisked terms are defined in the Terminology Section. — Eds.

**This provision is meant to be applicable wherever judges are subject to public election. Where specific dollar amounts determined by local circumstances are not used, the "reasonable and appropriate" language should be used.

of the question of remittal is made independently of the judge, a judge must not solicit, seek or hear comment on possible remittal or waiver of the disqualification unless the lawyers jointly propose remittal after consultation as provided in the rule. A party may act through counsel if counsel represents on the record that the party has been consulted and consents. As a practical matter, a judge may wish to have all parties and their lawyers sign the remittal agreement.

Editors' Note. On November 1, 1993, in an unusual press release, seven Justices of the Supreme Court issued the following announcement, entitled "Statement of Recusal Policy." The Statement was signed by Chief Justice Rehnquist and Justices Stevens, Scalia, Thomas, O'Connor, Kennedy, and Ginsburg. Justices Blackmun and Souter did not sign.

STATEMENT OF RECUSAL POLICY

We have spouses, children or other relatives within the degree of relationship covered by 28 U.S.C. §455 who are or may become practicing attorneys. In connection with a case four Terms ago, the Chief Justice announced his policy (with which we are all in accord) regarding recusal when a covered relative is "an associate in the law firm representing one of the parties before this Court" but has "not participated in the case before the Court or at previous stages of the litigation." [The letter concluded that recusal was not required.] We think it desirable to set forth what our recusal policy will be in additional situations — specifically, when the covered lawyer has participated in the case at an earlier stage of the litigation, or when the covered lawyer is a *partner* in a firm appearing before us. Determining and announcing our policy in advance will make it evident that future decisions to recuse or not to recuse are unaffected by irrelevant circumstances of the particular case, and will provide needed guidance to our relatives and the firms to which they belong.

The provision of the recusal statute that deals specifically with a relative's involvement as a lawyer in the case requires recusal only when the covered relative "[i]s acting as a lawyer in the proceeding." §455(b)(5)(ii). It is well established that this provision requires personal participation in the representation, and not just membership in the representing firm, see, e.g., Potashnick v. Port City Constr. Co., 609 F.2d 1101, 1113 (CA5), *cert. denied,* 449 U.S. 820 (1980). It is also apparent, from use of the present tense, that current participation as a lawyer, and not merely past involvement in earlier stages of the litigation, is required.

A relative's partnership status, or participation in earlier stages of the litigation, is relevant, therefore, only under one of two less specific provisions of §455, which require recusal when the judge knows that the relative has "an interest that could be substantially affected by the outcome of the proceeding," §455(b)(5)(iii), or when for any reason the judge's "impartiality might reasonably be questioned," §455(a). We think that a relative's partnership in the firm appearing before us, or his or her previous work as a lawyer on a case that later comes before us, does not *automatically* trigger these provisions. If that were the intent of the law, the per se "lawyer-related recusal" requirement of §455(b)(5)(ii) would have expressed it. Per se recusal for a relative's membership in the partnership appearing here, or for a relative's work on the case below, would render the limitation of §455(b)(5)(ii) to *personal* work, and to *present* representation, meaningless.

We do not think it would serve the public interest to go beyond the requirements of the statute, and to recuse ourselves, out of an excess of caution, whenever a relative is a partner in the firm before us or acted as a lawyer at an earlier stage. Even one unnecessary recusal impairs the functioning of the Court. Given the size and number of today's national law firms, and the frequent appearance before us of many of them in a single case, recusal might become a common occurrence, and opportunities would be multiplied for "strategizing" recusals, that is, selecting law firms with an eye to producing the recusal of particular Justices. In this Court, where the absence of one Justice cannot be made up by another, needless recusal deprives litigants of the nine Justices to which they are entitled, produces the possibility of an even division on the merits of the case, and has a distorting effect upon the certiorari process, requiring the petitioner to obtain (under our current practice) four votes out of eight instead of four out of nine.

Absent some special factor, therefore, we will not recuse ourselves by reason of a relative's participation as a lawyer in earlier stages of the case. One such special factor, perhaps the most common, would be the relative's functioning as lead counsel below, so that the litigation is in effect "his" or "her" case and its outcome even at a later stage might reasonably be thought capable of substantially enhancing or damaging his or her professional reputation. We shall recuse ourselves whenever, to our knowledge, a relative has been lead counsel below.

Another special factor, of course, would be the fact that the amount of the relative's compensation could be substantially affected by the outcome here. That would require our recusal even if the relative had not worked on the case, but was merely a partner in the firm that shared the profits. It seems to us that in virtually every case before us with retained counsel there exists a genuine possibility that success or failure will affect the amount of the fee, and hence a genuine possibility that the outcome will have a substantial effect upon each partner's compensation. Since it is impractical to assure ourselves of the absence of such consequences in each individual case, we shall recuse ourselves from all cases in which appearances on behalf of parties are made by firms in which our relatives are partners, unless we have received from the firm written assurance that income from Supreme Court litigation is, on a permanent basis, excluded from our relatives' partnership shares.

CANON 4. A JUDGE SHALL SO CONDUCT THE JUDGE'S EXTRA-JUDICIAL ACTIVITIES AS TO MINIMIZE THE RISK OF CONFLICT WITH JUDICIAL OBLIGATIONS

A. Extra-Judicial Activities in General

A judge shall conduct all of the judge's extra-judicial activities so that they do not:

(1) cast reasonable doubt on the judge's capacity to act impartially as a judge;

(2) demean the judicial office; or

(3) interfere with the proper performance of judicial duties.

Commentary

Complete separation of a judge from extra-judicial activities is neither possible nor wise; a judge should not become isolated from the community in which the judge lives.

Expressions of bias or prejudice by a judge, even outside the judge's judicial activities, may cast reasonable doubt on the judge's capacity to act impartially as a judge. Expressions which may do so include jokes or other remarks demeaning individuals on the basis of their race, sex, religion, national origin, disability, age, sexual orientation or socioeconomic status. See Section 2C and accompanying Commentary.

B. Avocational Activities

A judge may speak, write, lecture, teach and participate in other extrajudicial activities concerning the law,* the legal system, the administration of justice and non-legal subjects, subject to the requirements of this Code.

Commentary

As a judicial officer and person specially learned in the law, a judge is in a unique position to contribute to the improvement of the law, the legal system, and the administration of justice, including revision of substantive and procedural law and improvement of criminal and juvenile justice. To the extent that time permits, a judge is encouraged to do so, either independently or through a bar association, judicial conference or other organization dedicated to the improvement of the law. Judges may participate in efforts to promote the fair administration of justice, the independence of the judiciary and the integrity of the legal profession and may express opposition to the persecution of lawyers and judges in other countries because of their professional activities.

In this and other Sections of Canon 4, the phrase "subject to the requirements of this Code" is used, notably in connection with a judge's governmental, civic or charitable activities. This phrase is included to remind judges that the use of permissive language in various Sections of the Code does not relieve a judge from the other requirements of the Code that apply to the specific conduct.

C. Governmental, Civic or Charitable Activities

(1) A judge shall not appear at a public hearing before, or otherwise consult with, an executive or legislative body or official except on matters concerning the law,* the legal system or the administration of justice or except when acting pro se in a matter involving the judge or the judge's interests.

*Asterisked terms are defined in the Terminology Section. — Eds.

Commentary

See Section 2B regarding the obligation to avoid improper influence.

(2) A judge shall not accept appointment to a governmental committee or commission or other governmental position that is concerned with issues of fact or policy on matters other than the improvement of the law,* the legal system or the administration of justice. A judge may, however, represent a country, state or locality on ceremonial occasions or in connection with historical, educational or cultural activities.

Commentary

Section 4C(2) prohibits a judge from accepting any governmental position except one relating to the law, legal system or administration of justice as authorized by Section 4C(3). The appropriateness of accepting extra-judicial assignments must be assessed in light of the demands on judicial resources created by crowded dockets and the need to protect the courts from involvement in extra-judicial matters that may prove to be controversial. Judges should not accept governmental appointments that are likely to interfere with the effectiveness and independence of the judiciary.

Section 4C(2) does not govern a judge's service in a nongovernmental position. See Section 4C(3) permitting service by a judge with organizations devoted to the improvement of the law, the legal system or the administration of justice and with educational, religious, charitable, fraternal or civic organizations not conducted for profit. For example, service on the board of a public educational institution, unless it were a law school, would be prohibited under Section 4C(2), but service on the board of a public law school or any private educational institution would generally be permitted under Section 4C(3).

(3) A judge may serve as an officer, director, trustee or non-legal advisor of an organization or governmental agency devoted to the improvement of the law,* the legal system or the administration of justice or of an educational, religious, charitable, fraternal or civic organization not conducted for profit, subject to the following limitations and the other requirements of this Code.

Commentary

Section 4C(3) does not apply to a judge's service in a governmental position unconnected with the improvement of the law, the legal system or the administration of justice; see Section 4C(2).

*Asterisked terms are defined in the Terminology Section. — Eds.

See Commentary to Section 4B regarding use of the phrase "subject to the following limitations and the other requirements of this Code."

As an example of the meaning of the phrase, a judge permitted by Section 4C(3) to serve on the board of a fraternal institution may be prohibited from such service by Sections 2C or 4A if the institution practices invidious discrimination or if service on the board otherwise casts reasonable doubt on the judge's capacity to act impartially as a judge.

Service by a judge on behalf of a civic or charitable organization may be governed by other provisions of Canon 4 in addition to Section 4C. For example, a judge is prohibited by Section 4G from serving as a legal advisor to a civic or charitable organization.

(a) A judge shall not serve as an officer, director, trustee or non-legal advisor if it is likely that the organization

(i) will be engaged in proceedings that would ordinarily come before the judge, or

(ii) will be engaged frequently in adversary proceedings in the court of which the judge is a member or in any court subject to the appellate jurisdiction of the court of which the judge is a member.

Commentary

The changing nature of some organizations and of their relationship to the law makes it necessary for a judge regularly to reexamine the activities of each organization with which the judge is affiliated to determine if it is proper for the judge to continue the affiliation. For example, in many jurisdictions charitable hospitals are now more frequently in court than in the past. Similarly, the boards of some legal aid organizations now make policy decisions that may have political significance or imply commitment to causes that may come before the courts for adjudication.

(b) A judge as an officer, director, trustee or non-legal advisor, or as a member or otherwise:

(i) may assist such an organization in planning fund-raising and may participate in the management and investment of the organization's funds, but shall not personally participate in the solicitation of funds or other fund-raising activities, except that a judge may solicit funds from other judges over whom the judge does not exercise supervisory or appellate authority;

(ii) may make recommendations to public and private fund-granting organizations on projects and programs concerning the law,* the legal system or the administration of justice;

*Asterisked terms are defined in the Terminology Section. — Eds.

(iii) shall not personally participate in membership solicitation if the solicitation might reasonably be perceived as coercive or, except as permitted in Section 4C(3)(b)(i), if the membership solicitation is essentially a fund-raising mechanism;

(iv) shall not use or permit the use of the prestige of judicial office for fund-raising or membership solicitation.

Commentary

A judge may solicit membership or endorse or encourage membership efforts for an organization devoted to the improvement of the law, the legal system or the administration of justice or a nonprofit educational, religious, charitable, fraternal or civic organization as long as the solicitation cannot reasonably be perceived as coercive and is not essentially a fund-raising mechanism. Solicitation of funds for an organization and solicitation of memberships similarly involve the danger that the person solicited will feel obligated to respond favorably to the solicitor if the solicitor is in a position of influence or control. A judge must not engage in direct, individual solicitation of funds or memberships in person, in writing or by telephone except in the following cases: 1) a judge may solicit for funds or memberships other judges over whom the judge does not exercise supervisory or appellate authority, 2) a judge may solicit other persons for membership in the organizations described above if neither those persons nor persons with whom they are affiliated are likely ever to appear before the court on which the judge serves and 3) a judge who is an officer of such an organization may send a general membership solicitation mailing over the judge's signature.

Use of an organization letterhead for fund-raising or membership solicitation does not violate Section 4C(3)(b) provided the letterhead lists only the judge's name and office or other position in the organization, and, if comparable designations are listed for other persons, the judge's judicial designation. In addition, a judge must also make reasonable efforts to ensure that the judge's staff, court officials and others subject to the judge's direction and control do not solicit funds on the judge's behalf for any purpose, charitable or otherwise.

A judge must not be a speaker or guest of honor at an organization's fund-raising event, but mere attendance at such an event is permissible if otherwise consistent with this Code.

D. Financial Activities

(1) A judge shall not engage in financial and business dealings that:

(a) may reasonably be perceived to exploit the judge's judicial position, or

(b) involve the judge in frequent transactions or continuing business relationships with those lawyers or other persons likely to come before the court on which the judge serves.

Commentary

The Time for Compliance provision of this Code (Application, Section F) postpones the time for compliance with certain provisions of this Section in some cases.

When a judge acquires in a judicial capacity information, such as material contained in filings with the court, that is not yet generally known, the judge must not use the information for private gain. See Section 2B; see also Section 3B(11).

A judge must avoid financial and business dealings that involve the judge in frequent transactions or continuing business relationships with persons likely to come either before the judge personally or before other judges in the judge's court. In addition, a judge should discourage members of the judge's family from engaging in dealings that would reasonably appear to exploit the judge's judicial position. This rule is necessary to avoid creating an appearance of exploitation of office or favoritism and to minimize the potential for disqualification. With respect to affiliation of relatives of judges with law firms appearing before the judge, see Commentary to Section 3E(1) relating to disqualification.

Participation by a judge in financial and business dealings is subject to the general prohibitions in Section 4A against activities that tend to reflect adversely on impartiality, demean the judicial office, or interfere with the proper performance of judicial duties. Such participation is also subject to the general prohibition in Canon 2 against activities involving impropriety or the appearance of impropriety and the prohibition in Section 2B against the misuse of the prestige of judicial office. In addition, a judge must maintain high standards of conduct in all of the judge's activities, as set forth in Canon 1. See Commentary for Section 4B regarding use of the phrase "subject to the requirements of this Code."

(2) A judge may, subject to the requirements of this Code, hold and manage investments of the judge and members of the judge's family,* including real estate, and engage in other remunerative activity.

Commentary

This Section provides that, subject to the requirements of this Code, a judge may hold and manage investments owned solely by the judge, investments owned solely by a member or members of the judge's family, and investments owned jointly by the judge and members of the judge's family.

(3) A judge shall not serve as an officer, director, manager, general partner, advisor or employee of any business entity except that a judge may, subject to the requirements of this Code, manage and participate in:

(a) a business closely held by the judge or members of the judge's family,* or

*Asterisked terms are defined in the Terminology Section. — Eds.

(b) a business entity primarily engaged in investment of the financial resources of the judge or members of the judge's family.

Commentary

Subject to the requirements of this Code, a judge may participate in a business that is closely held either by the judge alone, by members of the judge's family, or by the judge and members of the judge's family.

Although participation by a judge in a closely-held family business might otherwise be permitted by Section 4D(3), a judge may be prohibited from participation by other provisions of this Code when, for example, the business entity frequently appears before the judge's court or the participation requires significant time away from judicial duties. Similarly, a judge must avoid participating in a closely-held family business if the judge's participation would involve misuse of the prestige of judicial office.

(4) A judge shall manage the judge's investments and other financial interests to minimize the number of cases in which the judge is disqualified. As soon as the judge can do so without serious financial detriment, the judge shall divest himself or herself of investments and other financial interests that might require frequent disqualification.

(5) A judge shall not accept, and shall urge members of the judge's family residing in the judge's household* not to accept, a gift, bequest, favor or loan from anyone except for:

Commentary

Section 4D(5) does not apply to contributions to a judge's campaign for judicial office, a matter governed by Canon 5.

Because a gift, bequest, favor or loan to a member of the judge's family residing in the judge's household might be viewed as intended to influence the judge, a judge must inform those family members of the relevant ethical constraints upon the judge in this regard and discourage those family members from violating them. A judge cannot, however, reasonably be expected to know or control all of the financial or business activities of all family members residing in the judge's household.

(a) a gift incident to a public testimonial, books, tapes and other resource materials supplied by publishers on a complimentary basis for official use, or an invitation to the judge and the judge's spouse or guest to attend a bar-related function or an activity devoted to the improvement of the law,* the legal system or the administration of justice;

*Asterisked terms are defined in the Terminology Section. — Eds.

Commentary

Acceptance of an invitation to a law-related function is governed by Section 4D(5)(a); acceptance of an invitation paid for by an individual lawyer or group of lawyers is governed by Section 4D(5)(h).

A judge may accept a public testimonial or a gift incident thereto only if the donor organization is not an organization whose members comprise or frequently represent the same side in litigation, and the testimonial and gift are otherwise in compliance with other provisions of this Code. See Sections 4A(1) and 2B.

(b) a gift, award or benefit incident to the business, profession or other separate activity of a spouse or other family member of a judge residing in the judge's household, including gifts, awards and benefits for the use of both the spouse or other family member and the judge (as spouse or family member), provided the gift, award or benefit could not reasonably be perceived as intended to influence the judge in the performance of judicial duties;

(c) ordinary social hospitality;

(d) a gift from a relative or friend, for a special occasion, such as a wedding, anniversary or birthday, if the gift is fairly commensurate with the occasion and the relationship;

Commentary

A gift to a judge, or to a member of the judge's family living in the judge's household, that is excessive in value raises questions about the judge's impartiality and the integrity of the judicial office and might require disqualification of the judge where disqualification would not otherwise be required. See, however, Section 4D(5)(e).

(e) a gift, bequest, favor or loan from a relative or close personal friend whose appearance or interest in a case would in any event require disqualification under Section 3E;

(f) a loan from a lending institution in its regular course of business on the same terms generally available to persons who are not judges;

(g) a scholarship or fellowship awarded on the same terms and based on the same criteria applied to other applicants; or

(h) any other gift, bequest, favor or loan, only if: the donor is not a party or other person who has come or is likely to come or whose interests have come or are likely to come before the judge; and, if its value exceeds $150.00, the judge reports it in the same manner as the judge reports compensation in Section 4H.

Commentary

Section 4D(5)(h) prohibits judges from accepting gifts, favors, bequests or loans from lawyers or their firms if they have come or are likely to come before the judge; it also prohibits gifts, favors, bequests or loans from clients of lawyers or their firms when the clients' interests have come or are likely to come before the judge.

E. Fiduciary Activities

(1) A judge shall not serve as executor, administrator or other personal representative, trustee, guardian, attorney in fact or other fiduciary,* except for the estate, trust or person of a member of the judge's family,* and then only if such service will not interfere with the proper performance of judicial duties.

(2) A judge shall not serve as a fiduciary* if it is likely that the judge as a fiduciary will be engaged in proceedings that would ordinarily come before the judge, or if the estate, trust or ward becomes involved in adversary proceedings in the court on which the judge serves or one under its appellate jurisdiction.

(3) The same restrictions on financial activities that apply to a judge personally also apply to the judge while acting in a fiduciary* capacity.

Commentary

The Time for Compliance provision of this Code (Application, Section F) postpones the time for compliance with certain provisions of this Section in some cases.

The restrictions imposed by this Canon may conflict with the judge's obligation as a fiduciary. For example, a judge should resign as trustee if detriment to the trust would result from divestiture of holdings the retention of which would place the judge in violation of Section 4D(4).

F. Service as Arbitrator or Mediator

A judge shall not act as an arbitrator or mediator or otherwise perform judicial functions in a private capacity unless expressly authorized by law.*

Commentary

Section 4F does not prohibit a judge from participating in arbitration, mediation or settlement conferences performed as part of judicial duties.

*Asterisked terms are defined in the Terminology Section. — Eds.

G. Practice of Law

A judge shall not practice law. Notwithstanding this prohibition, a judge may act pro se and may, without compensation, give legal advice to and draft or review documents for a member of the judge's family.*

Commentary

This prohibition refers to the practice of law in a representative capacity and not in a pro se capacity. A judge may act for himself or herself in all legal matters, including matters involving litigation and matters involving appearances before or other dealings with legislative and other governmental bodies. However, in so doing, a judge must not abuse the prestige of office to advance the interests of the judge or the judge's family. See Section 2(B).

The Code allows a judge to give legal advice to and draft legal documents for members of the judge's family, so long as the judge receives no compensation. A judge must not, however, act as an advocate or negotiator for a member of the judge's family in a legal matter.

Canon 6, new in the 1972 Code, reflected concerns about conflicts of interest and appearances of impropriety arising from compensation for off-the-bench activities. Since 1972, however, reporting requirements that are much more comprehensive with respect to what must be reported and with whom reports must be filed have been adopted by many jurisdictions. The Committee believes that although reports of compensation for extra-judicial activities should be required, reporting requirements preferably should be developed to suit the respective jurisdictions, not simply adopted as set forth in a national model code of judicial conduct. Because of the Committee's concern that deletion of this Canon might lead to the misconception that reporting compensation for extra-judicial activities is no longer important, the substance of Canon 6 is carried forward as Section 4H in this Code for adoption in those jurisdictions that do not have other reporting requirements. In jurisdictions that have separately established reporting requirements, Section 4H(2) (Public Reporting) may be deleted and the caption for Section 4H modified appropriately.

H. Compensation, Reimbursement and Reporting

(1) Compensation and Reimbursement. A judge may receive compensation and reimbursement of expenses for the extra-judicial activities permitted by this Code, if the source of such payments does not give the appearance of influencing the judge's performance of judicial duties or otherwise give the appearance of impropriety.

(a) Compensation shall not exceed a reasonable amount nor shall

*Asterisked terms are defined in the Terminology Section. — Eds.

it exceed what a person who is not a judge would receive for the same activity.

(b) Expense reimbursement shall be limited to the actual cost of travel, food and lodging reasonably incurred by the judge and, where appropriate to the occasion, by the judge's spouse or guest. Any payment in excess of such an amount is compensation.

(2) Public Reports. A judge shall report the date, place and nature of any activity for which the judge received compensation, and the name of the payor and the amount of compensation so received. Compensation or income of a spouse attributed to the judge by operation of a community property law is not extra-judicial compensation to the judge. The judge's report shall be made at least annually and shall be filed as a public document in the office of the clerk of the court on which the judge serves or other office designated by law.*

Commentary

See Section 4D(5) regarding reporting of gifts, bequests and loans.

The Code does not prohibit a judge from accepting honoraria or speaking fees provided that the compensation is reasonable and commensurate with the task performed. A judge should ensure, however, that no conflicts are created by the arrangement. A judge must not appear to trade on the judicial position for personal advantage. Nor should a judge spend significant time away from court duties to meet speaking or writing commitments for compensation. In addition, the source of the payment must not raise any question of undue influence or the judge's ability or willingness to be impartial.

I. [Disclosure of Judge's Assets]

Disclosure of a judge's income, debts, investments or other assets is required only to the extent provided in this Canon and in Sections 3E and 3F, or as otherwise required by law.*

Commentary

Section 3E requires a judge to disqualify himself or herself in any proceeding in which the judge has an economic interest. See "economic interest" as explained in the Terminology Section. Section 4D requires a judge to refrain from engaging in business and from financial activities that might interfere with the impartial performance of judicial duties; Section 4H requires a judge to report all compensation the judge received for activities outside judicial office. A judge

*Asterisked terms are defined in the Terminology Section. — Eds.

has the rights of any other citizen, including the right to privacy of the judge's financial affairs, except to the extent that limitations established by law are required to safeguard the proper performance of the judge's duties.

CANON 5. A JUDGE OR JUDICIAL CANDIDATE SHALL REFRAIN FROM INAPPROPRIATE POLITICAL ACTIVITY[2]

A. All Judges and Candidates

(1) Except as authorized in Sections 5B(2), 5C(1) and 5C(3), a judge or a candidate* for election or appointment to judicial office shall not:

(a) act as a leader or hold an office in a political organization;*

(b) publicly endorse or publicly oppose another candidate for public office;

(c) make speeches on behalf of a political organization;

(d) attend political gatherings; or

(e) solicit funds for, pay an assessment to or make a contribution to a political organization or candidate, or purchase tickets for political party dinners or other functions.

Commentary

A judge or candidate for judicial office retains the right to participate in the political process as a voter.

2. Introductory Note to Canon 5: There is wide variation in the methods of judicial selection used, both among jurisdictions and within the jurisdictions themselves. In a given state, judges may be selected by one method initially, retained by a different method, and selected by still another method to fill interim vacancies.

According to figures compiled in 1987 by the National Center for State Courts, 32 states and the District of Columbia use a merit selection method (in which an executive such as a governor appoints a judge from a group of nominees selected by a judicial nominating commission) to select judges in the state either initially or to fill an interim vacancy. Of those 33 jurisdictions, a merit selection method is used in 18 jurisdictions to choose judges of courts of last resort, in 13 jurisdictions to choose judges of intermediate appellate courts, in 12 jurisdictions to choose judges of general jurisdiction courts and in 5 jurisdictions to choose judges of limited jurisdiction courts.

Methods of judicial selection other than merit selection include nonpartisan election (10 states use it for initial selection at all court levels, another 10 states use it for initial selection for at least one court level) and partisan election (8 states use it for initial selection at all court levels, another 7 states use it for initial selection for at least one level). In a small minority of the states, judicial selection methods include executive or legislative appointment (without nomination of a group of potential appointees by a judicial nominating commission) and court selection. In addition, the federal judicial system utilizes an executive appointment method. See State Court Organization 1987 (National Center for State Courts, 1988).

*Asterisked terms are defined in the Terminology Section. — Eds.

Where false information concerning a judicial candidate is made public, a judge or another judicial candidate having knowledge of the facts is not prohibited by Section 5A(1) from making the facts public.

Section 5A(1)(a) does not prohibit a candidate for elective judicial office from retaining during candidacy a public office such as county prosecutor, which is not "an office in a political organization."

Section 5A(1)(b) does not prohibit a judge or judicial candidate from privately expressing his or her views on judicial candidates or other candidates for public office.

A candidate does not publicly endorse another candidate for public office by having that candidate's name on the same ticket.

(2) A judge shall resign from judicial office upon becoming a candidate* for a non-judicial office either in a primary or in a general election, except that the judge may continue to hold judicial office while being a candidate for election to or serving as a delegate in a state constitutional convention if the judge is otherwise permitted by law* to do so.

(3) A candidate* for a judicial office:

(a) shall maintain the dignity appropriate to judicial office and act in a manner consistent with the integrity and independence of the judiciary, and shall encourage members of the candidate's family* to adhere to the same standards of political conduct in support of the candidate as apply to the candidate;

Commentary

Although a judicial candidate must encourage members of his or her family to adhere to the same standards of political conduct in support of the candidate that apply to the candidate, family members are free to participate in other political activity.

(b) shall prohibit employees and officials who serve at the pleasure of the candidate,* and shall discourage other employees and officials subject to the candidate's direction and control from doing on the candidate's behalf what the candidate is prohibited from doing under the Sections of this Canon;

(c) except to the extent permitted by Section 5C(2), shall not authorize or knowingly* permit any other person to do for the candidate* what the candidate is prohibited from doing under the Sections of this Canon;

(d) shall not:

(i) make pledges or promises of conduct in office other than the faithful and impartial performance of the duties of the office;

*Asterisked terms are defined in the Terminology Section. — Eds.

(ii) make statements that commit or appear to commit the candidate with respect to cases, controversies or issues that are likely to come before the court; or

(iii) knowingly* misrepresent the identity, qualifications, present position or other fact concerning the candidate or an opponent;

Commentary

Section 5A(3)(d) prohibits a candidate for judicial office from making statements that appear to commit the candidate regarding cases, controversies or issues likely to come before the court. As a corollary, a candidate should emphasize in any public statement the candidate's duty to uphold the law regardless of his or her personal views. See also Section 3B(9), the general rule on public comment by judges. Section 5A(3)(d) does not prohibit a candidate from making pledges or promises respecting improvements in court administration. Nor does this Section prohibit an incumbent judge from making private statements to other judges or court personnel in the performance of judicial duties. This Section applies to any statement made in the process of securing judicial office, such as statements to commissions charged with judicial selection and tenure and legislative bodies confirming appointment. See also Rule 8.2 of the ABA Model Rules of Professional Conduct.

(e) may respond to personal attacks or attacks on the candidate's record as long as the response does not violate Section 5A(3)(d).

B. Candidates Seeking Appointment to Judicial or Other Governmental Office

(1) A candidate* for appointment to judicial office or a judge seeking other governmental office shall not solicit or accept funds, personally or through a committee or otherwise, to support his or her candidacy.

(2) A candidate* for appointment to judicial office or a judge seeking other governmental office shall not engage in any political activity to secure the appointment except that:

(a) such persons may:

(i) communicate with the appointing authority, including any selection or nominating commission or other agency designated to screen candidates;

(ii) seek support or endorsement for the appointment from organizations that regularly make recommendations for reappointment or appointment to the office, and from individuals to the extent requested or required by those specified in Section 5B(2)(a); and

*Asterisked terms are defined in the Terminology Section. — Eds.

(iii) provide to those specified in Sections 5B(2)(a)(i) and 5B(2)(a)(ii) information as to his or her qualifications for the office;

(b) a non-judge candidate* for appointment to judicial office may, in addition, unless otherwise prohibited by law:*

(i) retain an office in a political organization,*

(ii) attend political gatherings, and

(iii) continue to pay ordinary assessments and ordinary contributions to a political organization or candidate and purchase tickets for political party dinners or other functions.

Commentary

Section 5B(2) provides a limited exception to the restrictions imposed by Sections 5A(1) and 5D. Under Section 5B(2), candidates seeking reappointment to the same judicial office or appointment to another judicial office or other governmental office may apply for the appointment and seek appropriate support.

Although under Section 5B(2) non-judge candidates seeking appointment to judicial office are permitted during candidacy to retain office in a political organization, attend political gatherings and pay ordinary dues and assessments, they remain subject to other provisions of this Code during candidacy. See Sections 5B(1), 5B(2)(a), 5E and Application Section.

C. Judges and Candidates Subject to Public Election

(1) A judge or a candidate* subject to public election* may, except as prohibited by law:*

(a) at any time

(i) purchase tickets for and attend political gatherings;

(ii) identify himself or herself as a member of a political party; and

(iii) contribute to a political organization;*

(b) when a candidate for election

(i) speak to gatherings on his or her own behalf;

(ii) appear in newspaper, television and other media advertisements supporting his or her candidacy;

(iii) distribute pamphlets and other promotional campaign literature supporting his or her candidacy; and

(iv) publicly endorse or publicly oppose other candidates for the same judicial office in a public election in which the judge or judicial candidate is running.

*Asterisked terms are defined in the Terminology Section. — Eds.

Commentary

Section 5C(1) permits judges subject to election at any time to be involved in limited political activity. Section 5D, applicable solely to incumbent judges, would otherwise bar this activity.

(2) A candidate* shall not personally solicit or accept campaign contributions or personally solicit publicly stated support. A candidate may, however, establish committees of responsible persons to conduct campaigns for the candidate through media advertisements, brochures, mailings, candidate forums and other means not prohibited by law. Such committees may solicit and accept reasonable campaign contributions, manage the expenditure of funds for the candidate's campaign and obtain public statements of support for his or her candidacy. Such committees are not prohibited from soliciting and accepting reasonable campaign contributions and public support from lawyers. A candidate's committee may solicit contributions and public support for the candidate's campaign no earlier than [one year] before an election and no later than [90] days after the last election in which the candidate participates during the election year. A candidate shall not use or permit the use of campaign contributions for the private benefit of the candidate or others.

Editors' Note. At the ABA's 1997 Annual Meeting, the House of Delegates voted to amend the Commentary to Canon 5C(2). (The ABA did not amend the text of Canon 5C(2).) The amendment was sponsored by the ABA's Standing Committee on Ethics and Professional Responsibility, which submitted a brief Report in support of the amendment. (Committee Reports do not represent official policy of the ABA. They are for information only, and the opinions are those of the authors of the report.)

The Committee Report noted that the ABA "strongly endorses merit selection of judges, as opposed to public election, in no small part because of the potential for conflicts of interest created by the solicitation and acceptance of significant amounts of money by committees established to manage judicial candidates' election campaigns." But the Report acknowledged that "the majority of judges are selected through the electoral process." The Report continued:

> [A]lthough permissible from a legal standpoint, the fund-raising that accompanies judicial campaigns frequently gives rise to conflicts of interest that may reflect adversely upon the impartiality of the judiciary. . . .
>
> The proposed amendment . . . suggests that election campaign contributions made by lawyers or others who appear before the judge may, by virtue of their size or source, raise questions about the judge's impartiality and be cause for disqualification.

Commentary

There is legitimate concern about a judge's impartiality when parties whose interests may come before a judge, or the lawyers who represent such parties, are

*Asterisked terms are defined in the Terminology Section. — Eds.

known to have made contributions to the election campaigns of judicial candidates. This is among the reasons that merit selection of judges is a preferable manner in which to select the judiciary. Notwithstanding that preference, Section 5C(2) recognizes that in many jurisdictions judicial candidates must raise funds to support their candidacies for election to judicial office. It therefore permits a candidate, other than a candidate for appointment, to establish campaign committees to solicit and accept public support and reasonable financial contributions. In order to guard against the possibility that conflicts of interest will arise, the candidate must instruct his or her campaign committees at the start of the campaign to solicit or accept only contributions that are reasonable and appropriate under the circumstances. Though not prohibited, campaign contributions of which a judge has knowledge, made by lawyers or others who appear before the judge may, by virtue of their size or source, raise questions about a judge's impartiality and be cause for disqualification as provided under Section 3(E).

Campaign committees established under Section 5C(2) should manage campaign finances responsibly, avoiding deficits that might necessitate post-election fund-raising, to the extent possible. Such committees must at all times comply with applicable statutory provisions governing their conduct.

Section 5C(2) does not prohibit a candidate from initiating an evaluation by a judicial selection commission or bar association, or, subject to the requirements of this Code, from responding to a request for information from any organization.

Editors' Note: By voice vote at its 1999 Annual Meeting, the ABA added the following two paragraphs, 3 and 4, to Canon 5C of the Code of Judicial Conduct and renumbered old paragraph 3 as paragraph 5.

(3) A candidate shall instruct his or her campaign committee(s) at the start of the campaign not to accept campaign contributions for any election that exceed, in the aggregate*, $[ ] from an individual or $[ ] from en entity. This limitation is in addition to the limitations provided in Section 5C(2).***

(4) In addition to complying with all applicable statutory requirements for disclosure of campaign contributions, campaign committees established by a candidate shall file with [ ] a report stating the name, address, occupation and employer of each person who has made campaign contributions to the committee whose value in the aggregate* exceed [$].*** The report must be filed within [ ]**** days following the election.**

*Asterisked terms are defined in the Terminology Section. — Eds.

**Each jurisdiction should identify an appropriate depository for the information required under this provision, giving consideration to the public's need for convenient and timely access to the information. Electronic filing is to be preferred.

***Jurisdictions wishing to adopt campaign contribution limits that are lower than generally applicable campaign finance regulations provide should adopt this provision, inserting appropriate dollar amounts where brackets appear.

****A time period chosen by the adopting jurisdiction should appear in the bracketed space.

(5) Except as prohibited by law,* a candidate* for judicial office in a public election* may permit the candidate's name: (a) to be listed on election materials along with the names of other candidates for elective public office, and (b) to appear in promotions of the ticket.

Commentary

Section 5C(3) provides a limited exception to the restrictions imposed by Section 5A(1).

D. Incumbent Judges

A judge shall not engage in any political activity except (i) as authorized under any other Section of this Code, (ii) on behalf of measures to improve the law,* the legal system or the administration of justice, or (iii) as expressly authorized by law.

Commentary

Neither Section 5D nor any other section of the Code prohibits a judge in the exercise of administrative functions from engaging in planning and other official activities with members of the executive and legislative branches of government. With respect to a judge's activity on behalf of measures to improve the law, the legal system and the administration of justice, see Commentary to Section 4B and Section 4C(1) and its Commentary.

E. Applicability

Canon 5 generally applies to all incumbent judges and judicial candidates.* A successful candidate, whether or not an incumbent, is subject to judicial discipline for his or her campaign conduct; an unsuccessful candidate who is a lawyer is subject to lawyer discipline for his or her campaign conduct. A lawyer who is a candidate for judicial office is subject to [Rule 8.2(b) of the ABA Model Rules of Professional Conduct]. (An adopting jurisdiction should substitute a reference to its applicable rule.)

*Asterisked terms are defined in the Terminology Section. — Eds.

APPLICATION OF THE CODE OF JUDICIAL CONDUCT

A. [Definition of a Judge]

Anyone, whether or not a lawyer, who is an officer of a judicial system[3] and who performs judicial functions, including an officer such as a magistrate, court commissioner, special master or referee, is a judge within the meaning of this Code. All judges shall comply with this Code except as provided below.

Commentary

The four categories of judicial service in other than a full-time capacity are necessarily defined in general terms because of the widely varying forms of judicial service. For the purposes of this Section, as long as a retired judge is subject to recall the judge is considered to "perform judicial functions." The determination of which category and, accordingly, which specific Code provisions apply to an individual judicial officer, depend upon the facts of the particular judicial service.

B. Retired Judge Subject to Recall

A retired judge subject to recall who by law is not permitted to practice law is not required to comply:

(1) except while serving as a judge, with Section 4F; and

(2) at any time with Section 4E.

C. Continuing Part-Time Judge

A continuing part-time judge:*

(1) is not required to comply

(a) except while serving as a judge, with Section 3B(9); and

(b) at any time with Sections 4C(2), 4D(3), 4E(1), 4F, 4G, 4H, 5A(1), 5B(2) and 5D.

(2) shall not practice law in the court on which the judge serves or in any court subject to the appellate jurisdiction of the court on which the

3. Applicability of this Code to administrative law judges should be determined by each adopting jurisdiction. Administrative law judges generally are affiliated with the executive branch of government rather than the judicial branch and each adopting jurisdiction should consider the unique characteristics of particular administrative law judge positions in adopting and adapting the Code for administrative law judges. See, e.g., Model Code of Judicial Conduct for Federal Administrative Law Judges, endorsed by the National Conference of Administrative Law Judges in February 1989.

*Asterisked terms are defined in the Terminology Section. — Eds.

judge serves, and shall not act as a lawyer in a proceeding in which the judge has served as a judge or in any other proceeding related thereto.

Commentary

When a person who has been a continuing part-time judge is no longer a continuing part-time judge, including a retired judge no longer subject to recall, that person may act as a lawyer in a proceeding in which he or she has served as a judge or in any other proceeding related thereto only with the express consent of all parties pursuant to [Rule 1.12(a) of the ABA Model Rules of Professional Conduct]. (An adopting jurisdiction should substitute a reference to its applicable rule.)

D. Periodic Part-Time Judge

A periodic part-time judge:*

(1) is not required to comply

(a) except while serving as a judge, with Section 3B(9);

(b) at any time, with Sections 4C(2), 4C(3)(a), 4D(1)(b), 4D(3), 4D(4), 4D(5), 4E, 4F, 4G, 4H, 5A(1), 5B(2) and 5D.

(2) shall not practice law in the court on which the judge serves or in any court subject to the appellate jurisdiction of the court on which the judge serves, and shall not act as a lawyer in a proceeding in which the judge has served as a judge or in any other proceeding related thereto.

Commentary

When a person who has been a periodic part-time judge is no longer a periodic part-time judge (no longer accepts appointments), that person may act as a lawyer in a proceeding in which he or she has served as a judge or in any other proceeding related thereto only with the express consent of all parties pursuant to [Rule 1.12(a) of the ABA Model Rules of Professional Conduct]. (An adopting jurisdiction should substitute a reference to its applicable rule.)

E. Pro Tempore Part-Time Judge

A pro tempore part-time judge:*

(1) is not required to comply

(a) except while serving as a judge, with Sections 2A, 2B, 3B(9) and 4C(1);

*Asterisked terms are defined in the Terminology Section. — Eds.

(b) at any time with Sections 2C, 4C(2), 4C(3)(a), 4C(3)(b), 4D(1)(b), 4D(3), 4D(4), 4D(5), 4E, 4F, 4G, 4H, 5A(1), 5A(2), 5B(2) and 5D.

(2) A person who has been a pro tempore part-time judge* shall not act as a lawyer in a proceeding in which the judge has served as a judge or in any other proceeding related thereto except as otherwise permitted by [Rule 1.12(a) of the ABA Model Rules of Professional Conduct]. (An adopting jurisdiction should substitute a reference to its applicable rule.)

F. Time for Compliance

A person to whom this Code becomes applicable shall comply immediately with all provisions of this Code except Sections 4D(2), 4D(3) and 4E and shall comply with these Sections as soon as reasonably possible and shall do so in any event within the period of one year.

Commentary

If serving as a fiduciary when selected as judge, a new judge may, notwithstanding the prohibitions in Section 4E, continue to serve as fiduciary but only for that period of time necessary to avoid serious adverse consequences to the beneficiary of the fiduciary relationship and in no event longer than one year. Similarly, if engaged at the time of judicial selection in a business activity, a new judge may, notwithstanding the prohibitions in Section 4D(3), continue in that activity for a reasonable period but in no event longer than one year.

APPENDIX. JUDICIAL ETHICS COMMITTEE

A. The [chief judge of the highest court of the jurisdiction] shall appoint a Judicial Ethics Committee consisting of [nine] members. [Five] members shall be judges; [two] members shall be non-judge lawyers; and [two] members shall be public members. Of the judicial members, one member shall be appointed from each of [the highest court, the intermediate levels of courts, and the trial courts]. The remaining judicial members shall be judges appointed from any of the above courts, but not from the [highest court of the jurisdiction]. The [chief judge] shall designate one of the members as chairperson. Members shall serve three-year terms; terms shall be staggered; and no individual shall serve for more than two consecutive terms.

B. The Judicial Ethics Committee so established shall have authority to:

(1) by the concurrence of a majority of its members, express its opinion on proper judicial conduct with respect to the provisions of

*Asterisked terms are defined in the Terminology Section. — Eds.

[the code of judicial conduct adopted by the jurisdiction and any other specified sections of law of the jurisdiction regarding the judiciary, such as financial reporting requirements], either on its own initiative, at the request of a judge or candidate for judicial office, or at the request of a court or an agency charged with the administration of judicial discipline in the jurisdiction, provided that an opinion may not be issued on a matter that is pending before a court or before such an agency except on request of the court or agency;

(2) make recommendations to [the highest court of the jurisdiction] for amendment of the Code of Judicial Conduct [of the jurisdiction]; and

(3) adopt rules relating to the procedures to be used in expressing opinions, including rules to assure a timely response to inquiries.

C. A judge or candidate for judicial office as defined in the Terminology Section of this Code who has requested and relied upon an opinion may not be disciplined for conduct conforming to that opinion.

D. An opinion issued pursuant to this rule shall be filed with [appropriate official of the judicial conference of the jurisdiction]. Such an opinion is confidential and not public information unless [the highest court of the jurisdiction] otherwise directs. However, the [appropriate official of the judicial conference of the jurisdiction] shall cause an edited version of each opinion to be prepared, in which the identity and geographic location of the person who has requested the opinion, the specific court involved, and the identity of other individuals, organizations or groups mentioned in the opinion are not disclosed. Opinions so edited shall be published periodically in the manner [the appropriate official of the judicial conference of the jurisdiction] deems proper.

Attorney-Client Privilege and Work Product Provisions

Attorney-Client Privilege and Work Product Provisions

Editors' Introduction. The ethical obligation of confidentiality is closely related to the evidentiary rules governing the attorney-client privilege and the procedural rules protecting attorney work product. The materials in this chapter show how the attorney-client privilege and the work product doctrine are treated in the Federal Rules of Evidence, the Federal Rules of Civil Procedure, New York's Civil Practice Law and Rules, the California Evidence Code, the California Code of Civil Procedure, and the Arizona Revised Statutes.

In our earlier editions, this chapter also included provisions from the American Law Institute's Restatement of the Law Governing Lawyers. However, the final version of the Restatement was published in August 2000, so we have moved the Restatement provisions on attorney-client privilege and work product to the chapter that includes the entire Restatement. The attorney-client privilege and work product provisions are found there at §§59–93 of the Restatement.

Contents

FEDERAL RULES OF EVIDENCE

Rule 501. General Rule
Proposed Rule 503. Lawyer-Client Privilege (not enacted)

FEDERAL RULES OF CIVIL PROCEDURE

Rule 26(b)(3). Trial Preparation: Materials
Rule 26(b)(4). Trial Preparation: Experts

NEW YORK CIVIL PRACTICE LAW AND RULES

§3101. Scope of Disclosure

§4503. Attorney
§4548. Privileged Communications; Electronic Communication Thereof

ARIZONA REVISED STATUTES

§12-2234. Attorney and Client

CALIFORNIA EVIDENCE CODE

§911. General Rule as to Privileges
§912. Waiver of Privilege
§915. Disclosure of Privileged Information in Ruling on Claim of Privilege
§917. Presumption That Certain Communications Are Confidential
§950. "Lawyer"
§951. "Client"
§952. "Confidential Communication Between Client and Lawyer"
§953. "Holder of the Privilege"
§954. Lawyer-Client Privilege
§955. When Lawyer Required to Claim Privilege
§956. Exception: Crime or Fraud
§956.5 Reasonable Belief That Disclosure of Confidential Communication Is Necessary to Prevent Criminal Act Resulting in Death or Bodily Harm; Exception to Privilege
§957. Exception: Parties Claiming Through Deceased Client
§958. Exception: Breach of Duty Arising out of Lawyer-Client Relationship
§959. Exception: Lawyer as Attesting Witness
§960. Exception: Intention of Deceased Client Concerning Writing Affecting Property Interest
§961. Exception: Validity of Writing Affecting Property Interest
§962. Exception: Joint Clients

CALIFORNIA CODE OF CIVIL PROCEDURE

§2018. Attorney's Work Product Protection

FEDERAL RULES OF EVIDENCE

Rule 501. General Rule

Except as otherwise required by the Constitution of the United States or provided by Act of Congress or in rules prescribed by the

Supreme Court pursuant to statutory authority, the privilege of a witness, person, government, State, or political subdivision thereof shall be governed by the principles of the common law as they may be interpreted by the courts of the United States in the light of reason and experience. However, in civil actions and proceedings, with respect to an element of a claim or defense as to which State law supplies the rule of decision, the privilege of a witness, person, government, State, or political subdivision thereof shall be determined in accordance with State law.

Editors' Note. When the Supreme Court transmitted the proposed Federal Rules of Evidence to Congress in 1973, they contained thirteen separate proposed rules on privileges, including Rule 503 (defining the lawyer-client privilege) and Rules 511, 512, and 513 (governing waiver, compelled disclosure of privileged material, and comment in court about a claim of privilege). The privilege rules were extremely controversial, however, and Congress rejected all of the proposed privilege rules. (Rule 501 — the only privilege rule in the rules today — was substantially altered by Congress before its enactment.) We reprint Rule 503 here because, despite its rejection, it is an accurate general statement of the law in many jurisdictions and has been adopted nearly verbatim in the evidence codes of some states (see, e.g., Rule 503 of the Texas Rules of Criminal Evidence).

Proposed Rule 503. Lawyer-Client Privilege (not enacted)

(a) *Definitions.* As used in this rule:

(1) A "client" is a person, public officer, or corporation, association, or other organization or entity, either public or private, who is rendered professional legal services by a lawyer, or who consults a lawyer with a view to obtaining professional legal services from him.

(2) A "lawyer" is a person authorized, or reasonably believed by the client to be authorized, to practice law in any state or nation.

(3) A "representative of the lawyer" is one employed to assist the lawyer in the rendition of professional legal services.

(4) A communication is "confidential" if not intended to be disclosed to third persons other than those to whom disclosure is in furtherance of the rendition of professional legal services to the client or those reasonably necessary for the transmission of the communication.

(b) *General rule of privilege.* A client has a privilege to refuse to disclose and to prevent any other person from disclosing confidential communications made for the purpose of facilitating the rendition of professional legal services to the client, (1) between himself or his representative and his lawyer or his lawyer's representative, or (2) between his lawyer and the lawyer's representative, or (3) by him or his lawyer to a lawyer representing another in a matter of common interest, or (4) between representatives of the client or between the client and a representative of the client, or (5) between lawyers representing the client.

(c) *Who may claim the privilege?* The privilege may be claimed by the client, his guardian or conservator, the personal representative of a deceased client, or the successor, trustee, or similar representative of a corporation, association, or other organization, whether or not in existence. The person who was the lawyer at the time of the communication may claim the privilege but only on behalf of the client. His authority to do so is presumed in the absence of evidence to the contrary.

(d) *Exceptions.* There is no privilege under this rule:

(1) *Furtherance of crime or fraud.* If the services of the lawyer were sought or obtained to enable or aid anyone to commit or plan to commit what the client knew or reasonably should have known to be a crime or fraud; or

(2) *Claimants through same deceased client.* As to a communication relevant to an issue between parties who claim through the same deceased client, regardless of whether the claims are by testate or intestate succession or by inter vivos transaction; or

(3) *Breach of duty by lawyer or client.* As to a communication relevant to an issue of breach of duty by the lawyer to his client or by the client to his lawyer; or

(4) *Document attested by lawyer.* As to a communication relevant to an issue concerning an attested document to which the lawyer is an attesting witness; or

(5) *Joint clients.* As to a communication relevant to a matter of common interest between two or more clients if the communication was made by any of them to a lawyer retained or consulted in common, when offered in an action between any of the clients.

FEDERAL RULES OF CIVIL PROCEDURE

Editors' Note. In federal courts, the work product doctrine is codified in Rules 26(b)(3)-(4) of the Federal Rules of Civil Procedure. These provisions were added to the rules by amendment in 1970 to resolve confusion and disagreement over the scope of the judicially created work product doctrine stemming from Hickman v. Taylor, 329 U.S. 495 (1947). Rule 26(b)(3) governs work product generally, including the mental opinions and impressions of lawyers, and Rule 26(b)(4) governs work product relating to experts. In 1993, Rule 26(b)(4) was extensively amended to the form reprinted here, but Rule 26(b)(3) was not amended at all. In addition, Rule 26(b)(5), governing claims of privilege or work product, was entirely new in 1993; there was no comparable provision in the Federal Rules of Civil Procedure until then. Neither provision was changed by the amendments to other parts of Rule 26 that took effect on December 1, 2000.

Readers should note that the Federal Rules of Criminal Procedure, in Rules 16(a)(2) and (b)(2), contain a kind of work product protection, but the criminal work product protection is subject to many exceptions, including Rule 26.2, which requires lawyers in criminal cases to turn over, upon request, any relevant statement made by a witness who has completed a direct examination at trial.

Rule 26. General Provisions Governing Discovery; Duty of Disclosure

. . . (b)(3) *Trial Preparation: Materials.* Subject to the provisions of subdivision (b)(4) of this rule, a party may obtain discovery of documents and tangible things otherwise discoverable under subdivision (b)(1) of this rule and prepared in anticipation of litigation or for trial by or for another party or by or for that other party's representative (including the other party's attorney, consultant, surety, indemnitor, insurer, or agent) only upon a showing that the party seeking discovery has substantial need of the materials in the preparation of the party's case and that the party is unable without undue hardship to obtain the substantial equivalent of the materials by other means. In ordering discovery of such materials when the required showing has been made, the court shall protect against disclosure of the mental impressions, conclusions, opinions, or legal theories of an attorney or other representative of a party concerning the litigation.

A party may obtain without the required showing a statement concerning the action or its subject matter previously made by that party. Upon request, a person not a party may obtain without the required showing a statement concerning the action or its subject matter previously made by that person.

(4) *Trial Preparation: Experts.*

(A) A party may depose any person who has been identified as an expert whose opinions may be presented at trial. If a report from the expert is required under subdivision (a)(2)(B), the deposition shall not be conducted until after the report is provided.

(B) A party may, through interrogatories or by deposition, discover facts known or opinions held by an expert who has been retained or specially employed by another party in anticipation of litigation or preparation for trial and who is not expected to be called as a witness at trial, only as provided in Rule 35(b) or upon a showing of exceptional circumstances under which it is impracticable for the party seeking discovery to obtain facts or opinions on the same subject by other means.

(C) Unless manifest injustice would result, (i) the court shall require that the party seeking discovery pay the expert a reasonable fee for time spent in responding to discovery under this subdivision; and (ii) with respect to discovery obtained under subdivision (b)(4)(B) of

this rule the court shall require, the party seeking discovery to pay the other party a fair portion of the fees and expenses reasonably incurred by the latter party in obtaining facts and opinions from the expert.

(5) *Claims of Privilege or Protection of Trial Preparation Materials.* When a party withholds information otherwise discoverable under these rules by claiming that it is privileged or subject to protection as trial preparation material, the party shall make the claim expressly and shall describe the nature of the documents, communications, or things not produced or disclosed in a manner that, without revealing information itself privileged or protected, will enable other parties to assess the applicability of the privilege or protection.

NEW YORK CIVIL PRACTICE LAW AND RULES

§3101. Scope of Disclosure

(a) *Generally.* There shall be full disclosure of all matter material and necessary in the prosecution or defense of an action, regardless of the burden of proof . . . .

(b) *Privileged matter.* Upon objection by a person entitled to assert the privilege, privileged matter shall not be obtainable.

(c) *Attorney's work product.* The work product of an attorney shall not be obtainable.

(d) *Trial preparation.*

1. Experts.

(i) Upon request, each party shall identify each person whom the party expects to call as an expert witness at trial and shall disclose in reasonable detail the subject matter on which each expert is expected to testify, the substance of the facts and opinions on which each expert is expected to testify, the qualifications of each expert witness and a summary of the grounds for each expert's opinion. However, where a party for good cause shown retains an expert an insufficient period of time before the commencement of trial to give appropriate notice thereof, the party shall not thereupon be precluded from introducing the expert's testimony at the trial solely on grounds of noncompliance with this paragraph. In that instance, upon motion of any party, made before or at trial, or on its own initiative, the court may make whatever order may be just. . . .

(iii) Further disclosure concerning the expected testimony of any expert may be obtained only by court order upon a showing of special circumstances and subject to restrictions as to scope and provisions concerning fees and expenses as the court may deem appropriate. . . .

2. *Materials.* Subject to the provisions of paragraph one of this

subdivision, materials otherwise discoverable under subdivision (a) of this section and prepared in anticipation of litigation or for trial by or for another party, or by or for that other party's representative (including an attorney, consultant, surety, indemnitor, insurer or agent), may be obtained only upon a showing that the party seeking discovery has substantial need of the materials in the preparation of the case and is unable without undue hardship to obtain the substantial equivalent of the materials by other means. In ordering discovery of the materials when the required showing has been made, the court shall protect against disclosure of the mental impressions, conclusions, opinions or legal theories of an attorney or other representative of a party concerning the litigation.

(e) *Party's statement.* A party may obtain a copy of his own statement. . . .

§4503. Attorney

(a) *Confidential communication privileged; non-judicial proceedings.* Unless the client waives the privilege, an attorney or his employee, or any person who obtains without the knowledge of the client evidence of a confidential communication made between the attorney or his employee and the client in the course of professional employment, shall not disclose, or be allowed to disclose such communication, nor shall the client be compelled to disclose such communication, in any action, disciplinary trial or hearing, or administrative action, proceeding or hearing conducted by or on behalf of any state, municipal or local governmental agency or by the legislature or any committee or body thereof. Evidence of any such communication obtained by any such person, and evidence resulting therefrom, shall not be disclosed by any state, municipal or local governmental agency or by the legislature or any committee or body thereof. The relationship of an attorney and client shall exist between a professional service corporation organized under article fifteen of the business corporation law to practice as an attorney and counselor-at-law and the clients to whom it renders legal services.

(b) *Wills.* (1) In any action involving the probate, validity or construction of a will, an attorney or his employee shall be required to disclose information as to the preparation, execution or revocation of any will or other relevant instrument, but he shall not be allowed to disclose any communications privileged under subdivision (a) wihch would tend to disgrace the memory of the decedent.

(2) *Personal representatives.* (A) For purposes of the attorney-client privilege, if the client is a personal representative and the attorney represents the personal representative in that capacity, in the absence of an agreement between the attorney and the personal representative to the contrary:

(i) No beneficiary of the estate is, or shall be treated as, the client of the attorney solely by reason of his or her status as beneficiary; and

(ii) The existence of a fiduciary relationship between the personal representative and a beneficiary of the estate does not by itself constitute or give rise to any waiver of the privilege for confidential communications made in the course of professional employment between the attorney or his or her employee and the personal representative who is the client.

(B) For purposes of this paragraph, "personal representative" shall mean (i) the administrator, administrator c.t.a., ancillary administrator, executor, preliminary executor, temporary administrator or trustee to whom letters have been issued within the meaning of subdivision thirty-four of section one hundred three of the surrogate's court procedure act, and (ii) the guardian of an incapacitated communicant if and to the extent that the order appointing such guardian under subdivision (c) of section 81.16 of the mental hygiene law or any subsequent order of any court expressly provides that the guardian is to be the personal representative of the incapacitated communicant for purposes of this section; "beneficiary" shall have the meaning set forth in subdivision eight of section one hundred three of the surrogate's court procedure act and "estate" shall have the meaning set forth in subdivision nineteen of section one hundred three of the surrogate's court procedure act.

Editors' Note. Paragraph (b)(2) of §4503 was signed into law by Governor Pataki on August 20, 2002.

§4548. Privileged Communications; Electronic Communication Thereof

No communication privileged under this article shall lose its privileged character for the sole reason that it is communicated by electronic means or because persons necessary for the delivery or facilitation of such electronic communication may have access to the content of the communication.

ARIZONA REVISED STATUTES

Editors' Note. In Samaritan Foundation v. Goodfarb, 862 P.2d 870 (Ariz. 1993), the Arizona Supreme Court rejected the broad view of the attorney-client privilege for corporations espoused in Upjohn Co. v. United States, 449 U.S. 383 (1981), and required a corporate defendant (a hospital) to disclose certain information gathered by the defendant's paralegals that the defendant contended was privileged. The following year, after intense lobbying from corporations, the Arizona Legislature enacted §12-2234 of the Arizona Revised Statute, which effectively overruled the *Samaritan* opinion. We reprint the entire statute.

§12-2234. Attorney and Client

A. In a civil action an attorney shall not, without the consent of his client, be examined as to any communication made by the client to him, or his advice given thereon in the course of professional employment. An attorney's paralegal, assistant, secretary, stenographer or clerk shall not, without the consent of his employer, be examined concerning any fact the knowledge of which was acquired in such capacity.

B. For purposes of subsection A, any communication is privileged between an attorney for a corporation, governmental entity, partnership, business, association or other similar entity or an employer and any employee, agent or member of the entity or employer regarding acts or omissions of or information obtained from the employee, agent or member if the communication is either:

1. For the purpose of providing legal advice to the entity or employer or to the employee, agent or member.

2. For the purpose of obtaining information in order to provide legal advice to the entity or employer or to the employee, agent or member.

C. The privilege defined in this section shall not be construed to allow the employee to be relieved of a duty to disclose the facts solely because they have been communicated to an attorney.

CALIFORNIA EVIDENCE CODE

§911. General Rule as to Privileges

Except as otherwise provided by statute:

(a) No person has a privilege to refuse to be a witness.

(b) No person has a privilege to refuse to disclose any matter or to refuse to produce any writing, object, or other thing.

(c) No person has a privilege that another shall not be a witness or shall not disclose any matter or shall not produce any writing, object, or other thing.

§912. Waiver of Privilege

(a) Except as otherwise provided in this section, the right of any person to claim a privilege provided by Section 954 (lawyer-client

privilege), 980 (privilege for confidential marital communications), 994 (physician-patient privilege), 1014 (psychotherapist-patient privilege), 1033 (privilege of penitent), 1034 (privilege of clergyman), or 1035.8 (sexual assault victim-counselor privilege) is waived with respect to a communication protected by such privilege if any holder of the privilege, without coercion, has disclosed a significant part of the communication or has consented to such disclosure made by anyone. Consent to disclosure is manifested by any statement or other conduct of the holder of the privilege indicating consent to the disclosure, including failure to claim the privilege in any proceeding in which the holder has the legal standing and opportunity to claim the privilege.

(b) Where two or more persons are joint holders of a privilege provided by Section 954 (lawyer-client privilege), 994 (physician-patient privilege), 1014 (psychotherapist-patient privilege), or 1035.8 (sexual assault victim-counselor privilege), a waiver of the right of a particular joint holder of the privilege to claim the privilege does not affect the right of another joint holder to claim the privilege. In the case of the privilege provided by Section 980 (privilege for confidential marital communications), a waiver of the right of one spouse to claim the privilege does not affect the right of the other spouse to claim the privilege.

(c) A disclosure that is itself privileged is not a waiver of any privilege.

(d) A disclosure in confidence of a communication that is protected by a privilege provided by Section 954 (lawyer-client privilege), 994 (physician-patient privilege), 1014 (psychotherapist-patient privilege), or 1035.8 (sexual assault victim-counselor privilege), when such disclosure is reasonably necessary for the accomplishment of the purpose for which the lawyer, physician, psychotherapist, or sexual assault counselor was consulted, is not a waiver of the privilege.

§915. Disclosure of Privileged Information or Attorney Work Product in Ruling on Claim of Privilege

(a) Subject to subdivision (b), the presiding officer may not require disclosure of information claimed to be privileged under this division or attorney work product under subdivision (c) of Section 2018 of the Code of Civil Procedure in order to rule on the claim of privilege; provided, however, that in any hearing conducted pursuant to subdivision (c) of Section 1524 of the Penal Code in which a claim of privilege is made and the court determines that there is no other feasible means to rule on the validity of the claim other than to require disclosure, the court shall proceed in accordance with subdivision (b).

(b) When a court is ruling on a claim of privilege under Article 9 (commencing with Section 1040) of Chapter 4 (official information and identity of informer) or under Section 1060 (trade secret) or under subdivision (b) of Section 2018 of the Code of Civil Procedure (attorney work product) and is unable to do so without requiring disclosure of the information claimed to be privileged, the court may require the person from whom disclosure is sought or the person authorized to claim the privilege, or both, to disclose the information in chambers out of the presence and hearing of all persons except the person authorized to claim the privilege and any other persons as the person authorized to claim the privilege is willing to have present. If the judge determines that the information is privileged, neither the judge nor any other person may ever disclose, without the consent of a person authorized to permit disclosure, what was disclosed in the course of the proceedings in chambers.

§917. Presumption That Certain Communications Are Confidential

Whenever a privilege is claimed on the ground that the matter sought to be disclosed is a communication made in confidence in the course of the lawyer-client, physician-patient, psychotherapist-patient, clergyman-penitent, or husband-wife relationship, the communication is presumed to have been made in confidence and the opponent of the claim of privilege has the burden of proof to establish that the communication was not confidential.

§950. "Lawyer"

As used in this article, "lawyer" means a person authorized, or reasonably believed by the client to be authorized, to practice law in any state or nation.

§951. "Client"

As used in this article, "client" means a person who, directly or through an authorized representative, consults a lawyer for the purpose of retaining the lawyer or securing legal service or advice from him in his professional capacity, and includes an incompetent (a) who himself so consults the lawyer or (b) whose guardian or conservator so consults the lawyer in behalf of the incompetent.

§952. "Confidential Communication Between Client and Lawyer"

As used in this article, "confidential communication between client and lawyer" means information transmitted between a client and his or her lawyer in the course of that relationship and in confidence by a means which, so far as the client is aware, discloses the information to no third persons other than those who are present to further the interest of the client in the consultation or those to whom disclosure is reasonably necessary for the transmission of the information or the accomplishment of the purpose for which the lawyer is consulted, and includes a legal opinion formed and the advice given by the lawyer in the course of that relationship. A communication between a client and his or her lawyer is not deemed lacking in confidentiality solely because the communication is transmitted by facsimile, cellular telephone, or other electronic means between the client and his or her lawyer.

§953. "Holder of the Privilege"

As used in this article, "holder of the privilege" means:

(a) The client when he has no guardian or conservator.

(b) A guardian or conservator of the client when the client has a guardian or conservator.

(c) The personal representative of the client if the client is dead.

(d) A successor, assign, trustee in dissolution, or any similar representative of a firm, association, organization, partnership, business trust, corporation, or public entity that is no longer in existence.

§954. Lawyer-Client Privilege

Subject to Section 912 and except as otherwise provided in this article, the client, whether or not a party, has a privilege to refuse to disclose, and to prevent another from disclosing, a confidential communication between client and lawyer if the privilege is claimed by:

(a) The holder of the privilege;

(b) A person who is authorized to claim the privilege by the holder of the privilege; or

(c) The person who was the lawyer at the time of the confidential communication, but such person may not claim the privilege if there is no holder of the privilege in existence or if he is otherwise instructed by a person authorized to permit disclosure.

The relationship of attorney and client shall exist between a law corporation as defined in Article 10 (commencing with Section 6160) of Chapter 4 of Division 3 of the Business and Professions Code and the persons to whom it renders professional services, as well as between such persons and members of the State Bar employed by such corporation to render services to such persons. The word "persons" as used in this subdivision includes partnerships, corporations, limited liability companies, associations and other groups and entities.

§955. When Lawyer Required to Claim Privilege

The lawyer who received or made a communication subject to the privilege under this article shall claim the privilege whenever he is present when the communication is sought to be disclosed and is authorized to claim the privilege under subdivision (c) of Section 954.

§956. Exception: Crime or Fraud

There is no privilege under this article if the services of the lawyer were sought or obtained to enable or aid anyone to commit or plan to commit a crime or a fraud.

§956.5. Reasonable Belief That Disclosure of Confidential Communication Is Necessary to Prevent Criminal Act Resulting in Death or Bodily Harm; Exception to Privilege

Editors' Note. Section 956.5 of the California Evidence Code was signed into law by the Governor of California in 1993 as an entirely new provision. The language closely parallels the wording of the pre-2002 version of Rule 1.6 of the ABA Model Rules of Professional Conduct, but omits the requirement in Rule 1.6 that the harm be "imminent."

There is no privilege under this article if the lawyer reasonably believes that disclosure of any confidential communication relating to representation of a client is necessary to prevent the client from committing a criminal act that the lawyer believes is likely to result in death or substantial bodily harm.

§957. Exception: Parties Claiming Through Deceased Client

There is no privilege under this article as to a communication relevant to an issue between parties all of whom claim through a deceased client, regardless of whether the claims are by testate or intestate succession or by inter vivos transaction.

§958. Exception: Breach of Duty Arising out of Lawyer-Client Relationship

There is no privilege under this article as to a communication relevant to an issue of breach, by the lawyer or by the client, of a duty arising out of the lawyer-client relationship.

§959. Exception: Lawyer as Attesting Witness

There is no privilege under this article as to a communication relevant to an issue concerning the intention or competence of a client executing an attested document of which the lawyer is an attesting witness, or concerning the execution or attestation of such a document.

§960. Exception: Intention of Deceased Client Concerning Writing Affecting Property Interest

There is no privilege under this article as to a communication relevant to an issue concerning the intention of a client, now deceased, with respect to a deed of conveyance, will, or other writing, executed by the client, purporting to affect an interest in property.

§961. Exception: Validity of Writing Affecting Property Interest

There is no privilege under this article as to a communication relevant to an issue concerning the validity of a deed of conveyance, will, or other writing, executed by a client, now deceased, purporting to affect an interest in property.

§962. Exception: Joint Clients

Where two or more clients have retained or consulted a lawyer upon a matter of common interest, none of them, nor the successor in interest of any of them, may claim a privilege under this article as to a communication made in the course of that relationship when such communication is offered in a civil proceeding between one of such clients (or his successor in interest) and another of such clients (or his successor in interest).

CALIFORNIA CODE OF CIVIL PROCEDURE

§2018. Attorney's Work Product Protection

(a) It is the policy of the state to: (1) preserve the rights of attorneys to prepare cases for trial with that degree of privacy necessary to encourage them to prepare their cases thoroughly and to investigate not only the favorable but the unfavorable aspects of those cases; and (2) to prevent attorneys from taking undue advantage of their adversary's industry and efforts.

(b) Subject to subdivision (c), the work product of an attorney is not discoverable unless the court determines that denial of discovery will unfairly prejudice the party seeking discovery in preparing that party's claim or defense or will result in an injustice.

(c) Any writing that reflects an attorney's impressions, conclusions, opinions, or legal research or theories shall not be discoverable under any circumstances.

(d) This section is intended to be a restatement of existing law relating to protection of work product. It is not intended to expand or reduce the extent to which work product is discoverable under existing law in any action.

(e) The State Bar may discover the work product of an attorney against whom disciplinary charges are pending when it is relevant to issues of breach of duty by the lawyer, subject to applicable client approval and to a protective order, where requested and for good cause, to ensure the confidentiality of work product except for its use by the State Bar in disciplinary investigations and its consideration under seal in State Bar Court proceedings. For purposes of this section, whenever a client has initiated a complaint against an attorney, the requisite client approval shall be deemed to have been granted.

(f) If an action between an attorney and his or her client or former client, no work product privilege under this section exists if the work product is relevant to an issue of breach by the attorney of a duty to the attorney's client arising out of the attorney-client relationship.

For purposes of this section, "client" means a client as defined in Section 951 of the Evidence Code.

Federal Statutes and Regulations

Federal Provisions on Conflicts, Confidentiality, and Crimes

Editors' Introduction. According to a federal statute that took effect in 1999, 28 U.S.C. §530B, lawyers for the federal government practicing in a given state must abide by the same state laws and ethics rules (including local federal court rules) that govern other attorneys practicing in that state. In addition, federal statutes and regulations amplify and reinforce many of the obligations imposed by rules of professional conduct. For example, lawyers who work for (or have worked for) the federal government are governed not only by state ethics rules on conflicts and confidentiality, but also by stringent federal statutes and regulations on those topics. The statutes and regulations that follow govern obstruction of justice, perjury, conflicts arising out of a government lawyer's financial interests, the use or revelation of confidential government information, and the propriety of a former government lawyer's representation of private clients in matters relating to work the lawyer did while in government service. Violation of the statutory provisions in Title 18 is a crime.

Since our last edition went to press, Congress has amended 18 U.S.C. §1512 and has added a new §1519. Both changes were mandated by the Sarbanes-Oxley Act of 2002, Pub. L. No. 107-204, a broad accounting and securities reform statute that was signed by President Bush on July 30, 2002. We reprint amended §1512 and new §1519 below.

Contents

SELECTED PROVISIONS FROM 18 U.S.C.

§201. Bribery of Public Officials and Witnesses

§202. Definitions

§207. Restrictions on Former Officers, Employees, and Elected Officials of the Executive and Legislative Branches

§208. Acts Affecting a Personal Financial Interest

§1503. Influencing or Injuring Officer or Juror Generally
§1505. Obstruction of Proceedings Before Departments, Agencies, and Committees
§1510. Obstruction of Criminal Investigations
§1512. Tampering with a Witness, Victim or an Informant
§1515. Definitions for Certain Provisions; General Provisions
§1519. Destruction, Alteration, or Falsification of Records in Federal Investigations and Bankruptcy
§1621. Perjury Generally
§1622. Subornation of Perjury
§1623. False Declarations before Grand Jury or Court
§1905. Disclosure of Confidential Information Generally
§3500. Demands for Production of Statements and Reports of Witnesses

SELECTED PROVISIONS FROM 28 U.S.C.

§530B. Ethical Standards for Attorneys for the Government
§535. Investigation of Crimes Involving Government Officers and Employees; Limitations

SELECTED PROVISIONS FROM 28 C.F.R. PART 50

§50.2. Release of Information by Personnel of the Department of Justice Relating to Criminal and Civil Proceedings
§50.19. Procedures to Be Followed by Government Attorneys Prior to Filing Recusal or Disqualification Motions

SELECTED PROVISIONS FROM 18 U.S.C.

§201. Bribery of Public Official and Witnesses . . .

(c) Whoever —

(1) . . .

(2) directly or indirectly, gives, offers or promises anything of value to any person, for or because of the testimony under oath or affirmation given or to be given by such person as a witness upon a trial, hearing, or other proceeding, before any court, any committee of either

House or both Houses of Congress, or any agency, commission, or officer authorized by the laws of the United States to hear evidence or take testimony, or for or because of such person's absence therefrom;

(3) directly or indirectly, demands, seeks, receives, accepts, or agrees to receive or accept anything of value personally for or because of the testimony under oath or affirmation given or to be given by such person as a witness upon any such trial, hearing, or other proceeding, or for or because of such person's absence therefrom;

shall be fined under this title or imprisoned for not more than two years, or both.

(d) Paragraphs (3) and (4) of subsection (b) and paragraphs (2) and (3) of subsection (c) shall not be construed to prohibit the payment or receipt of witness fees provided by law, or the payment, by the party upon whose behalf a witness is called and receipt by a witness, of the reasonable cost of travel and subsistence incurred and the reasonable value of time lost in attendance at any such trial, hearing, or proceeding, or in the case of expert witnesses, a reasonable fee for time spent in the preparation of such opinion, and in appearing and testifying.

§202. Definitions

. . . (b) For the purposes of sections 205 and 207 of this title, the term "official responsibility" means the direct administrative or operating authority, whether intermediate or final, and either exercisable alone or with others, and either personally or through subordinates, to approve, disapprove, or otherwise direct Government action.

(c) Except as otherwise provided in such sections, the terms "officer" and "employee" in sections 203, 205, 207 through 209, and 218 of this title shall not include the President, the Vice President, a Member of Congress, or a Federal judge.

§207. Restrictions on Former Officers, Employees, and Elected Officials of the Executive and Legislative Branches

(a) *Restrictions on all officers and employees of the executive branch and certain other agencies.* —

(1) *Permanent restrictions on representation on particular matters.* — Any person who is an officer or employee (including any special Government employee) of the executive branch of the United States (including any independent agency of the United States), or of the District of Columbia, and who, after the termination of his or her service or employment with the United States or the District of Columbia, knowingly makes, with the intent to influence, any communication to

or appearance before any officer or employee of any department, agency, court, or court-martial of the United States or the District of Columbia, on behalf of any other person (except the United States or the District of Columbia) in connection with a particular matter —

(A) in which the United States or the District of Columbia is a party or has a direct and substantial interest,

(B) in which the person participated personally and substantially as such officer or employee, and

(C) which involved a specific party or specific parties at the time of such participation,

shall be punished as provided in section 216 of this title.

(2) *Two-year restrictions concerning particular matters under official responsibility.* — Any person subject to the restrictions contained in paragraph (1) who, within 2 years after the termination of his or her service or employment with the United States or the District of Columbia, knowingly makes, with the intent to influence, any communication to or appearance before any officer or employee of any department, agency, court, or court-martial of the United States or the District of Columbia, on behalf of any other person (except the United States or the District of Columbia), in connection with a particular matter —

(A) in which the United States or the District of Columbia is a party or has a direct and substantial interest,

(B) which such person knows or reasonably should know was actually pending under his or her official responsibility as such officer or employee within a period of 1 year before the termination of his or her service or employment with the United States or the District of Columbia, and

(C) which involved a specific party or specific parties at the time it was so pending,

shall be punished as provided in section 216 of this title.

(3) *Clarification of restrictions.* — The restrictions contained in paragraphs (1) and (2) shall apply —

(A) in the case of an officer or employee of the executive branch of the United States (including any independent agency), only with respect to communications to or appearances before any officer or employee of any department, agency, court, or court-martial of the United States on behalf of any other person (except the United States), and only with respect to a matter in which the United States is a party or has a direct and substantial interest; and

(B) in the case of an officer or employee of the District of Columbia, only with respect to communications to or appearances before any officer or employee of any department, agency, or court of the District of Columbia on behalf of any other person (except the District of Columbia), and only with respect to a matter in which the District of Columbia is a party or has a direct and substantial interest.

(b) *One-year restrictions on aiding or advising.* —

(1) *In general.* — Any person who is a former officer or employee of the executive branch of the United States (including any independent agency) and is subject to the restrictions contained in subsection (a)(1), or any person who is a former officer or employee of the legislative branch or a former Member of Congress, who personally and substantially participated in any ongoing trade or treaty negotiation on behalf of the United States within the 1-year period preceding the date on which his or her service or employment with the United States terminated, and who had access to information concerning such trade or treaty negotiation which is exempt from disclosure under section 552 of title 5, which is so designated by the appropriate department or agency, and which the person knew or should have known was so designated, shall not, on the basis of that information, knowingly represent, aid, or advise any other person (except the United States) concerning such ongoing trade or treaty negotiation for a period of 1 year after his or her service or employment with the United States terminates. Any person who violates this subsection shall be punished as provided in section 216 of this title.

(2) *Definition.* — For purposes of this paragraph —

(A) the term "trade negotiation" means negotiations which the President determines to undertake to enter into a trade agreement pursuant to section 1102 of the Omnibus Trade and Competitiveness Act of 1988, and does not include any action taken before that determination is made; and

(B) the term "treaty" means an international agreement made by the President that requires the advice and consent of the Senate.

(c) *One-year restrictions on certain senior personnel of the executive branch and independent agencies.* —

(1) *Restrictions.* — In addition to the restrictions set forth in subsections (a) and (b), any person who is an officer or employee (including any special Government employee) of the executive branch of the United States (including an independent agency), who is referred to in paragraph (2), and who, within 1 year after the termination of his or her service or employment as such officer or employee, knowingly makes, with the intent to influence, any communication to or appearance before any officer or employee of the department or agency in which such person served within 1 year before such termination, on behalf of any other person (except the United States), in connection with any matter on which such person seeks official action by any officer or employee of such department or agency, shall be punished as provided in section 216 of this title.

(2) *Persons to whom restrictions apply.* — (A) Paragraph (1) shall

apply to a person (other than a person subject to the restrictions of subsection (d)) —

(i) employed at a rate of pay specified in or fixed according to subchapter II of chapter 53 of title 5,

(ii) employed in a position which is not referred to in clause (i) and for which the basic rate of pay, exclusive of any locality-based pay adjustment under section 5302 of title 5 (or any comparable adjustment pursuant to interim authority of the President), is equal to or greater than the rate of basic pay payable for level 5 of the Senior Executive Service,

(iii) appointed by the President to a position under section 105(a)(2)(B) of title 3 or by the Vice President to a position under section 106(a)(1)(B) of title 3, or

(iv) employed in a position which is held by an active duty commissioned officer of the uniformed services who is serving in a grade or rank for which the pay grade (as specified in section 201 of title 37) is pay grade O-7 or above.

(B)Paragraph (1) shall not apply to a special Government employee who serves less than 60 days in the 1-year period before his or her service or employment as such employee terminates.

(C) At the request of a department or agency, the Director of the Office of Government Ethics may waive the restrictions contained in paragraph (1) with respect to any position, or category of positions, referred to in clause (ii) or (iv) of subparagraph (A), in such department or agency if the Director determines that —

(i) the imposition of the restrictions with respect to such position or positions would create an undue hardship on the department or agency in obtaining qualified personnel to fill such position or positions, and

(ii) granting the waiver would not create the potential for use of undue influence or unfair advantage.

(d) *Restrictions on very senior personnel of the executive branch and independent agencies.* —

(1) *Restrictions.* — In addition to the restrictions set forth in subsections (a) and (b), any person who —

(A) serves in the position of Vice President of the United States,

(B) is employed in a position in the executive branch of the United States (including any independent agency) at a rate of pay payable for level I of the Executive Schedule or employed in a position in the Executive Office of the President at a rate of pay payable for level II of the Executive Schedule, or

(C) is appointed by the President to a position under section 105(a)(2)(A) of title 3 or by the Vice President to a position under section 106(a)(1)(A) of title 3, and who, within 1 year after the termination of that person's service in that position, knowingly makes, with the intent to influence, any communication to or appearance before any person described in paragraph (2), on behalf of any other person (except the United States), in connection with any matter on which such person seeks official action by any officer or employee of the executive branch of the United States, shall be punished as provided in section 216 of this title.

(2) *Persons who may not be contacted.* — The persons referred to in paragraph (1) with respect to appearances or communications by a person in a position described in subparagraph (A), (B), or (C) of paragraph (1) are —

(A) any officer or employee of any department or agency in which such person served in such position within a period of 1 year before such person's service or employment with the United States Government terminated, and

(B) any person appointed to a position in the executive branch which is listed in sections 5312, 5313, 5314, 5315, or 5316 of title 5.

(e) *Restrictions on members of Congress and officers and employees of the legislative branch.* —

(1) *Members of congress and elected officers.* — (A) Any person who is a Member of Congress or an elected officer of either House of Congress and who, within 1 year after that person leaves office, knowingly makes, with the intent to influence, any communication to or appearance before any of the persons described in subparagraph (B) or (C), on behalf of any other person (except the United States) in connection with any matter on which such former Member of Congress or elected officer seeks action by a Member, officer, or employee of either House of Congress, in his or her official capacity, shall be punished as provided in section 216 of this title.

(B) The persons referred to in subparagraph (A) with respect to appearances or communications by a former Member of Congress are any Member, officer, or employee of either House of Congress, and any employee of any other legislative office of the Congress.

(C) The persons referred to in subparagraph (A) with respect to appearances or communications by a former elected officer are any Member, officer, or employee of the House of Congress in which the elected officer served.

(2) *Personal staff.* — (A) Any person who is an employee of a Senator or an employee of a Member of the House of Representatives and who, within 1 year after the termination of that employment, knowingly makes, with the intent to influence, any communication to or appearance before any of the persons described in subparagraph (B), on behalf of any other person (except the United States) in connection with any matter on which such former employee seeks action by a Member, officer, or employee of either House of Congress, in his

or her official capacity, shall be punished as provided in section 216 of this title.

(B) The persons referred to in subparagraph (A) with respect to appearances or communications by a person who is a former employee are the following:

(i) the Senator or Member of the House of Representatives for whom that person was an employee; and

(ii) any employee of that Senator or Member of the House of Representatives.

(3) *Committee staff.* — Any person who is an employee of a committee of Congress and who, within 1 year after the termination of that person's employment on such committee, knowingly makes, with the intent to influence, any communication to or appearance before any person who is a Member or an employee of that committee or who was a Member of the committee in the year immediately prior to the termination of such person's employment by the committee, on behalf of any other person (except the United States) in connection with any matter on which such former employee seeks action by a Member, officer, or employee of either House of Congress, in his or her official capacity, shall be punished as provided in section 216 of this title.

(4) *Leadership staff.* — (A) Any person who is an employee on the leadership staff of the House of Representatives or an employee on the leadership staff of the Senate and who, within 1 year after the termination of that person's employment on such staff, knowingly makes, with the intent to influence, any communication to or appearance before any of the persons described in subparagraph (B), on behalf of any other person (except the United States) in connection with any matter on which such former employee seeks action by a Member, officer, or employee of either House of Congress, in his or her official capacity, shall be punished as provided in section 216 of this title.

(B) The persons referred to in subparagraph (A) with respect to appearances or communications by a former employee are the following:

(i) in the case of a former employee on the leadership staff of the House of Representatives, those persons are any Member of the leadership of the House of Representatives and any employee on the leadership staff of the House of Representatives; and

(ii) in the case of a former employee on the leadership staff of the Senate, those persons are any Member of the leadership of the Senate and any employee on the leadership staff of the Senate.

(5) *Other legislative offices.* — (A) Any person who is an employee of any other legislative office of the Congress and who, within 1 year after the termination of that person's employment in such office, knowingly makes, with the intent to influence, any communication to

or appearance before any of the persons described in subparagraph (B), on behalf of any other person (except the United States) in connection with any matter on which such former employee seeks action by any officer or employee of such office, in his or her official capacity, shall be punished as provided in section 216 of this title.

(B) The persons referred to in subparagraph (A) with respect to appearances or communications by a former employee are the employees and officers of the former legislative office of the Congress of the former employee.

(6) *Limitation on restrictions.* — (A) The restrictions contained in paragraphs (2), (3), and (4) apply only to acts by a former employee who, for at least 60 days, in the aggregate, during the 1-year period before that former employee's service as such employee terminated, was paid a rate of basic pay equal to or greater than an amount which is 75 percent of the basic rate of pay payable for a Member of the House of Congress in which such employee was employed.

(B) The restrictions contained in paragraph (5) apply only to acts by a former employee who, for at least 60 days, in the aggregate, during the 1-year period before that former employee's service as such employee terminated, was employed in a position for which the rate of basic pay, exclusive of any locality-based pay adjustment under section 5302 of title 5 (or any comparable adjustment pursuant to interim authority of the President), is equal to or greater than the basic rate of pay payable for level 5 of the Senior Executive Service.

(7) *Definitions.* — As used in this subsection —

(A) the term "committee of Congress" includes standing committees, joint committees, and select committees;

(B) a person is an employee of a House of Congress if that person is an employee of the Senate or an employee of the House of Representatives;

(C) the term "employee of the House of Representatives" means an employee of a Member of the House of Representatives, an employee of a committee of the House of Representatives, an employee of a joint committee of the Congress whose pay is disbursed by the Clerk of the House of Representatives, and an employee on the leadership staff of the House of Representatives;

(D) the term "employee of the Senate" means an employee of a Senator, an employee of a committee of the Senate, an employee of a joint committee of the Congress whose pay is disbursed by the Secretary of the Senate, and an employee on the leadership staff of the Senate;

(E) a person is an employee of a Member of the House of Representatives if that person is an employee of a Member of the House of Representatives under the clerk hire allowance;

(F) a person is an employee of a Senator if that person is an employee in a position in the office of a Senator;

(G) the term "employee of any other legislative office of the Congress" means an officer or employee of the Architect of the Capitol, the United States Botanic Garden, the General Accounting Office, the Government Printing Office, the Library of Congress, the Office of Technology Assessment, the Congressional Budget Office, the Copyright Royalty Tribunal, the United States Capitol Police, and any other agency, entity, or office in the legislative branch not covered by paragraph (1), (2), (3), or (4) of this subsection;

(H) the term "employee on the leadership staff of the House of Representatives" means an employee of the office of a Member of the leadership of the House of Representatives described in subparagraph (L), and any elected minority employee of the House of Representatives;

(I) the term "employee on the leadership staff of the Senate" means an employee of the office of a Member of the leadership of the Senate described in subparagraph (M);

(J) the term "Member of Congress" means a Senator or a Member of the House of Representatives;

(K) the term "Member of the House of Representatives" means a Representative in, or a Delegate or Resident Commissioner to, the Congress;

(L) the term "Member of the leadership of the House of Representatives" means the Speaker, majority leader, minority leader, majority whip, minority whip, chief deputy majority whip, chief deputy minority whip, chairman of the Democratic Steering Committee, chairman and vice chairman of the Democratic Caucus, chairman, vice chairman, and secretary of the Republican Conference, chairman of the Republican Research Committee, and chairman of the Republican Policy Committee, of the House of Representatives (or any similar position created on or after the effective date set forth in section 102(a) of the Ethics Reform Act of 1989);

(M) the term "Member of the leadership of the Senate" means the Vice President, and the President pro tempore, Deputy President pro tempore, majority leader, minority leader, majority whip, minority whip, chairman and secretary of the Conference of the Majority, chairman and secretary of the Conference of the Minority, chairman and co-chairman of the Majority Policy Committee, and chairman of the Minority Policy Committee, of the Senate (or any similar position created on or after the effective date set forth in section 102(a) of the Ethics Reform Act of 1989).

(f) *Restrictions relating to foreign entities.* —

(1) *Restrictions.* — Any person who is subject to the restrictions contained in subsection (c), (d), or (e) and who knowingly, within 1

year after leaving the position, office, or employment referred to in such subsection —

(A) represents a foreign entity before any officer or employee of any department or agency of the United States with the intent to influence a decision of such officer or employee in carrying out his or her official duties, or

(B) aids or advises a foreign entity with the intent to influence a decision of any officer or employee of any department or agency of the United States, in carrying out his or her official duties,

shall be punished as provided in section 216 of this title.

(2) *Special rule for trade representative.* — With respect to a person who is the United States Trade Representative or Deputy United States Trade Representative, the restrictions described in paragraph (1) shall apply to representing, aiding, or advising foreign entities at any time after the termination of that person's service as the United States Trade Representative.

(3) *Definition.* — For purposes of this subsection, the term "foreign entity" means the government of a foreign country as defined in section 1(e) of the Foreign Agents Registration Act of 1938, as amended, or a foreign political party as defined in section 1(f) of that Act.

(g) *Special rules for detailees.* — For purposes of this section, a person who is detailed from one department, agency, or other entity to another department, agency, or other entity shall, during the period such person is detailed, be deemed to be an officer or employee of both departments, agencies, or such entities.

(h) *Designations of separate statutory agencies and bureaus.* —

(1) *Designations.* — For purposes of subsection (c) and except as provided in paragraph (2), whenever the Director of the Office of Government Ethics determines that an agency or bureau within a department or agency in the executive branch exercises functions which are distinct and separate from the remaining functions of the department or agency and that there exists no potential for use of undue influence or unfair advantage based on past Government service, the Director shall by rule designate such agency or bureau as a separate department or agency. On an annual basis the Director of the Office of Government Ethics shall review the designations and determinations made under this subparagraph and, in consultation with the department or agency concerned, make such additions and deletions as are necessary. Departments and agencies shall cooperate to the fullest extent with the Director of the Office of Government Ethics in the exercise of his or her responsibilities under this paragraph.

(2) *Inapplicability of designations.* — No agency or bureau within the Executive Office of the President may be designated under paragraph (1) as a separate department or agency. No designation under paragraph (1) shall apply to persons referred to in subsection (c)(2)(A)(i) or (iii).

(i) *Definitions.* — For purposes of this section —

(1) the term "officer or employee", when used to describe the person to whom a communication is made or before whom an appearance is made, with the intent to influence, shall include —

(A) in subsections (a), (c), and (d), the President and the Vice President; and

(B) in subsection (f), the President, the Vice President, and Members of Congress;

(2) the term "participated" means an action taken as an officer or employee through decision, approval, disapproval, recommendation, the rendering of advice, investigation, or other such action; and

(3) the term "particular matter" includes any investigation, application, request for a ruling or determination, rulemaking, contract, controversy, claim, charge, accusation, arrest, or judicial or other proceeding. . . .

§208. Acts Affecting a Personal Financial Interest

(a) Except as permitted by subsection (b) hereof, whoever, being an officer or employee of the executive branch of the United States Government, or of any independent agency of the United States, a Federal Reserve bank director, officer, or employee, or an officer or employee of the District of Columbia, including a special Government employee, participates personally and substantially as a Government officer or employee, through decision, approval, disapproval, recommendation, the rendering of advice, investigation, or otherwise, in a judicial or other proceeding, application, request for a ruling or other determination, contract, claim, controversy, charge, accusation, arrest, or other particular matter in which, to his knowledge, he, his spouse, minor child, general partner, organization in which he is serving as officer, director, trustee, general partner or employee, or any person or organization with whom he is negotiating or has any arrangement concerning prospective employment, has a financial interest —

Shall be subject to the penalties set forth in section 216 of this title.

(b) Subsection (a) shall not apply —

(1) if the officer or employee first advises the Government official responsible for appointment to his or her position of the nature and circumstances of the judicial or other proceeding, application, request for a ruling or other determination, contract, claim, controversy, charge, accusation, arrest, or other particular matter and makes full disclosure of the financial interest and receives in advance a written determination made by such official that the interest is not so substantial as to be deemed likely to affect the integrity of the services which the Government may expect from such officer or employee;

(2) if, by regulation issued by the Director of the Office of Government Ethics, applicable to all or a portion of all officers and employees covered by this section, and published in the Federal Register, the financial interest has been exempted from the requirements of paragraph (a) as being too remote or too inconsequential to affect the integrity of the services of the Government officers or employees to which such regulation applies;

(3) in the case of a special Government employee serving on an advisory committee within the meaning of the Federal Advisory Committee Act (including an individual being considered for an appointment to such a position), the official responsible for the employee's appointment, after review of the financial disclosure report filed by the individual pursuant to section 107 of the Ethics in Government Act of 1978, certifies in writing that the need for the individual's services outweighs the potential for a conflict of interest created by the financial interest involved. . . .

(d)(1) Upon request, a copy of any determination granting an exemption under subsection (b)(1) or (b)(3) shall be made available to the public by the agency granting the exemption pursuant to the procedures set forth in section 105 of the Ethics in Government Act of 1978. In making such determination available, the agency may withhold from disclosure any information contained in the determination that would be exempt from disclosure under section 552 of title 5. For purposes of determinations under subsection (b)(3), the information describing each financial interest shall be no more extensive than that required of the individual in his or her financial disclosure report under the Ethics in Government Act of 1978.

(2) The Office of Government Ethics, after consultation with the Attorney General, shall issue uniform regulations for the issuance of waivers and exemptions under subsection (b) which shall —

(A) list and describe exemptions; and

(B) provide guidance with respect to the types of interests that are not so substantial as to be deemed likely to affect the integrity of the services the Government may expect from the employee.

§1503. Influencing or Injuring Officer or Juror Generally

(a) Whoever corruptly, or by threats or force, or by any threatening letter or communication, endeavors to influence, intimidate, or impede any grand or petit juror, or officer in or of any court of the United States, or officer who may be serving at any examination or other proceeding before any United States magistrate judge or other committing magistrate, in the discharge of his duty, or injures any such grand or petit juror in his person or property on account of any verdict or indictment assented to by him, or on account of his being or having been such juror, or injures any such officer, magistrate judge, or other committing magistrate in his person or property on account of the performance of his official duties, or corruptly or by threats or force, or by any threatening letter or communication, influences, obstructs, or impedes, or endeavors to influence, obstruct, or impede, the due administration of justice, shall be punished as provided in subsection (b). If the offense under this section occurs in connection with a trial of a criminal case, and the act in violation of this section involves the threat of physical force or physical force, the maximum term of imprisonment which may be imposed for the offense shall be the higher of that otherwise provided by law or the maximum term that could have been imposed for any offense charged in such case.

(b) The punishment for an offense under this section is -

(1) in the case of a killing, the punishment provided in sections 1111 and 1112;

(2) in the case of an attempted killing, or a case in which the offense was committed against a petit juror and in which a class A or B felony was charged, imprisonment for not more than 20 years, a fine under this title, or both; and

(3) in any other case, imprisonment for not more than 10 years, a fine under this title, or both.

§1505. Obstruction of Proceedings Before Departments, Agencies, and Committees

Whoever, with intent to avoid, evade, prevent, or obstruct compliance, in whole or in part, with any civil investigative demand duly and properly made under the Antitrust Civil Process Act, willfully withholds, misrepresents, removes from any place, conceals, covers up, destroys, mutilates, alters, or by other means falsifies any documentary material, answers to written interrogatories, or oral testimony, which is the subject of such demand; or attempts to do so or solicits another to do so; or

Whoever corruptly, or by threats or force, or by any threatening letter or communication influences, obstructs, or impedes or endeavors to influence, obstruct, or impede the due and proper administration of the law under which any pending proceeding is being had before any department or agency of the United States, or the due and proper exercise of the power of inquiry under which any inquiry or investigation is being had by either House, or any committee of either House or any joint committee of the Congress —

Shall be fined under this title or imprisoned not more than five years, or both.

§1510. Obstruction of Criminal Investigations

(a) Whoever willfully endeavors by means of bribery to obstruct, delay, or prevent the communication of information relating to a violation of any criminal statute of the United States by any person to a criminal investigator shall be fined under this title, or imprisoned not more than five years, or both. . . .

§1512. Tampering with a Witness, Victim or an Informant

Editors' Note. Section 1512(c) was added by the Sarbanes-Oxley Act of 2002, Pub. L. No. 107-204, which was signed into law by President Bush on July 30, 2002.

(a)(1) Whoever kills or attempts to kill another person, with intent to —

(A) prevent the attendance or testimony of any person in an official proceeding;

(B) prevent the production of a record, document, or other object, in an official proceeding; or

(C) prevent the communication by any person to a law enforcement officer or judge of the United States of information relating to the commission or possible commission of a Federal offense or a violation of conditions of probation, parole, or release pending judicial proceedings;

shall be punished as provided in paragraph (2).

(2) The punishment for an offense under this subsection is —

(A) in the case of murder (as defined in section 1111), the death penalty or imprisonment for life, and in the case of any other killing, the punishment provided in section 1112; and

(B) in the case of an attempt, imprisonment for not more than twenty years.

(b) Whoever knowingly uses intimidation or physical force, threatens, or corruptly persuades another person, or attempts to do so, or engages in misleading conduct toward another person, with intent to —

(1) influence, delay, or prevent the testimony of any person in an official proceeding;

(2) cause or induce any person to-

(A) withhold testimony, or withhold a record, document, or other object, from an official proceeding;

(B) alter, destroy, mutilate, or conceal an object with intent to impair the object's integrity or availability for use in an official proceeding;

(C) evade legal process summoning that person to appear as a witness, or to produce a record, document, or other object, in an official proceeding; or

(D) be absent from an official proceeding to which such person has been summoned by legal process; or

(3) hinder, delay, or prevent the communication to a law enforcement officer or judge of the United States of information relating to the commission or possible commission of a Federal offense or a violation of conditions of probation, parole, or release pending judicial proceedings; shall be fined under this title or imprisoned not more than ten years, or both.

(c) Whoever corruptly —

(1) alters, destroys, mutilates, or conceals a record, document, or other object, or attempts to do so, with the intent to impair the object's integrity or availability for use in an official proceeding; or

(2) otherwise obstructs, influences, or impedes any official proceeding, or attempts to do so, shall be fined under this title or imprisoned not more than 20 years, or both.

(d) Whoever intentionally harasses another person and thereby hinders, delays, prevents, or dissuades any person from —

(1) attending or testifying in an official proceeding;

(2) reporting to a law enforcement officer or judge of the United States the commission or possible commission of a Federal offense or a violation of conditions of probation, parole, or release pending judicial proceedings;

(3) arresting or seeking the arrest of another person in connection with a Federal offense; or

(4) causing a criminal prosecution, or a parole or probation revocation proceeding, to be sought or instituted, or assisting in such prosecution or proceeding; or attempts to do so, shall be fined under this title or imprisoned not more than one year, or both.

(e) In a prosecution for an offense under this section, it is an affirmative defense, as to which the defendant has the burden of proof by a preponderance of the evidence, that the conduct consisted solely of lawful conduct and that the defendant's sole intention was to encourage, induce, or cause the other person to testify truthfully.

(f) For the purposes of this section —

(1) an official proceeding need not be pending or about to be instituted at the time of the offense; and

(2) the testimony, or the record, document, or other object need not be admissible in evidence or free of a claim of privilege. . . .

(j) If the offense under this section occurs in connection with a trial of a criminal case, the maximum term of imprisonment which may be imposed for the offense shall be the higher of that otherwise provided by law or the maximum term that could have been imposed for any offense charged in such case.

§1515. Definitions for Certain Provisions; General Provisions

(a) As used in sections 1512 and 1513 of this title and in this section —

(1) the term "official proceeding" means —

(A) a proceeding before a judge or court of the United States, a United States magistrate judge, a bankruptcy judge, a judge of the United States Tax Court, a special trial judge of the Tax Court, a judge of the United States Claims Court [United States Court of Federal Claims], or a Federal grand jury;

(B) a proceeding before the Congress;

(C) a proceeding before a Federal Government agency which is authorized by law; or

(D) a proceeding involving the business of insurance whose activities affect interstate commerce before any insurance regulatory official or agency or any agent or examiner appointed by such official or agency to examine the affairs of any person engaged in the business of insurance whose activities affect interstate commerce;

(2) the term "physical force" means physical action against another, and includes confinement;

(3) the term "misleading conduct" means —

(A) knowingly making a false statement;

(B) intentionally omitting information from a statement and thereby causing a portion of such statement to be misleading, or intentionally concealing a material fact, and thereby creating a false impression by such statement;

(C) with intent to mislead, knowingly submitting or inviting reliance on a writing or recording that is false, forged, altered, or otherwise lacking in authenticity;

(D) with intent to mislead, knowingly submitting or inviting reliance on a sample, specimen, map, photograph, boundary mark, or other object that is misleading in a material respect; or

(E) knowingly using a trick, scheme, or device with intent to mislead;

(4) the term "law enforcement officer" means an officer or employee of the Federal Government, or a person authorized to act for or on behalf of the Federal Government or serving the Federal Government as an advisor or consultant —

(A) authorized under law to engage in or supervise the prevention, detection, investigation, or prosecution of an offense; or

(B) serving as a probation or pretrial services officer under this title;

(5) the term "bodily injury" means —

(A) a cut, abrasion, bruise, burn, or disfigurement;

(B) physical pain;

(C) illness;

(D) impairment of the function of a bodily member, organ, or mental faculty; or

(E) any other injury to the body, no matter how temporary; and

(6) the term "corruptly persuades" does not include conduct which would be misleading conduct but for a lack of a state of mind.

(b) As used in section 1505, the term "corruptly" means acting with an improper purpose, personally or by influencing another, including making a false or misleading statement, or withholding, concealing, altering, or destroying a document or other information.

(c) This chapter does not prohibit or punish the providing of lawful, bona fide, legal representation services in connection with or anticipation of an official proceeding.

§1519. Destruction, Alteration, or Falsification of Records in Federal Investigations and Bankruptcy

Editors' Note. Section 1519 was added by the Sarbanes-Oxley Act of 2002, Pub. L. No. 107-204, which was signed into law by President Bush on July 30, 2002.

Whoever knowingly alters, destroys, mutilates, conceals, covers up, falsifies, or makes a false entry in any record, document, or tangible object with the intent to impede, obstruct, or influence the investigation or proper administration of any matter within the jurisdiction of any department or agency of the United States or any case filed under title 11, or in relation to or contemplation of any such matter or case, shall be fined under this title, imprisoned not more than 20 years, or both.

§1621. Perjury Generally

Whoever —

(1) having taken an oath before a competent tribunal, officer, or person, in any case in which a law of the United States authorizes an oath to be administered, that he will testify, declare, depose, or certify truly, or that any written testimony, declaration, deposition, or certificate by him subscribed, is true, willfully and contrary to such oath states or subscribes any material matter which he does not believe to be true; or

(2) in any declaration, certificate, verification, or statement under penalty of perjury as permitted under section 1746 of title 28, United States Code, willfully subscribes as true any material matter which he does not believe to be true;

is guilty of perjury and shall, except as otherwise expressly provided by law, be fined under this title or imprisoned not more than five years, or both. This section is applicable whether the statement or subscription is made within or without the United States.

Editors' Note. 28 U.S.C. §1746, which is mentioned in §§1621, 1622, and 1623, provides, in essence, that whenever federal law permits or requires a person to support any matter with an affidavit or other sworn declaration, then "such matter may, with like force and effect, be supported . . . by the unsworn declaration . . . in writing of such person which is subscribed by him, as true under penalty of perjury . . . in substantially the following form: . . . 'I declare . . . under penalty of perjury under the laws of the United States of America that the foregoing is true and correct.' "

§1622. Subornation of Perjury

Whoever procures another to commit any perjury is guilty of subornation of perjury, and shall be fined under this title or imprisoned not more than five years, or both.

§1623. False Declarations before Grand Jury or Court

(a) Whoever under oath (or in any declaration, certificate, verification, or statement under penalty of perjury as permitted under section 1746 of title 28, United States Code) in any proceeding before or ancillary to any court or grand jury of the United States knowingly makes any false material declaration or makes or uses any other information, including any book, paper, document, record, recording, or other material, knowing the same to contain any false material declaration, shall be fined under this title or imprisoned not more than five years, or both.

(b) This section is applicable whether the conduct occurred within or without the United States.

§1905. Disclosure of Confidential Information Generally

Whoever, being an officer or employee of the United States or of any department or agency thereof, any person acting on behalf of the

Office of Federal Housing Enterprise Oversight, or agent of the Department of Justice as defined in the Antitrust Civil Process Act (15 U.S.C. 1311-1314), publishes, divulges, discloses, or makes known in any manner or to any extent not authorized by law any information coming to him in the course of his employment or official duties or by reason of any examination or investigation made by, or return, report or record made to or filed with, such department or agency or officer or employee thereof, which information concerns or relates to the trade secrets, processes, operations, style of work, or apparatus, or to the identity, confidential statistical data, amount or source of any income, profits, losses, or expenditures of any person, firm, partnership, corporation, or association; or permits any income return or copy thereof or any book containing any abstract or particulars thereof to be seen or examined by any person except as provided by law; shall be fined under this title, or imprisoned not more than one year, or both; and shall be removed from office or employment.

§3500. Demands for Production of Statements and Reports of Witnesses ["Jencks Act"]

(a) In any criminal prosecution brought by the United States, no statement or report in the possession of the United States which was made by a Government witness or prospective Government witness (other than the defendant) shall be the subject of subpoena, discovery, or inspection until said witness has testified on direct examination in the trial of the case.

(b) After a witness called by the United States has testified on direct examination, the court shall, on motion of the defendant, order the United States to produce any statement (as hereinafter defined) of the witness in the possession of the United States which relates to the subject matter as to which the witness has testified. If the entire contents of any such statement relate to the subject matter of the testimony of the witness, the court shall order it to be delivered directly to the defendant for his examination and use.

(c) If the United States claims that any statement ordered to be produced under this section contains matter which does not relate to the subject matter of the testimony of the witness, the court shall order the United States to deliver such statement for the inspection of the court in camera. Upon such delivery the court shall excise the portions of such statement which do not relate to the subject matter of the testimony of the witness. With such material excised, the court shall then direct delivery of such statement to the defendant for his use. . . .

(d) If the United States elects not to comply with an order of the court under subsection (b) or (c) hereof to deliver to the defendant any such statement, or such portion thereof as the court may direct, the court shall strike from the record the testimony of the witness, and the trial shall proceed unless the court in its discretion shall determine that the interests of justice require that a mistrial be declared.

(e) The term "statement", as used in subsections (b), (c), and (d) of this section in relation to any witness called by the United States, means —

(1) a written statement made by said witness and signed or otherwise adopted or approved by him;

(2) a stenographic, mechanical, electrical, or other recording, or a transcription thereof, which is a substantially verbatim recital of an oral statement made by said witness and recorded contemporaneously with the making of such oral statement; or

(3) a statement, however taken or recorded, or a transcription thereof, if any, made by said witness to a grand jury.

SELECTED PROVISIONS FROM 28 U.S.C.

§530B. Ethical Standards for Attorneys for the Government

(a) An attorney for the Government shall be subject to State laws and rules, and local Federal court rules, governing attorneys in each State where such attorney engages in that attorney's duties, to the same extent and in the same manner as other attorneys in that State.

(b) The Attorney General shall make and amend rules of the Department of Justice to assure compliance with this section.

(c) As used in this section, the term "attorney for the Government" includes any attorney described in section 77.2(a) of part 77 of title 28 of the Code of Federal Regulations and also includes any independent counsel, or employee of such a counsel, appointed under chapter 40.

§535. Investigation of Crimes Involving Government Officers and Employees; Limitations

. . . (b) Any information, allegation, or complaint received in a department or agency of the executive branch of the Government relating to violations of Title 18 involving Government officers and employees shall be expeditiously reported to the Attorney General by the head of the department or agency, unless —

(1) the responsibility to perform an investigation with respect thereto is specifically assigned otherwise by another provision of law; or

(2) as to any department or agency of the Government, the Attorney General directs otherwise with respect to a specified class of information, allegation, or complaint. . . .

SELECTED PROVISIONS FROM 28 C.F.R.

Editors' Note. Under 28 C.F.R. §45.1, Department of Justice employees are subject to most of the same provisions of the Code of Federal Regulations that govern other Executive Department employees. These are set out at 5 C.F.R. Part 2635. These are supplemented by some specific Department of Justice regulations set out at 5 C.F.R. Part 3801. (A series of regulations numbered §45.735-4 through §45.735-12 formerly applied to Department of Justice employees — see our 1997 edition — but they were repealed effective May 2, 1997.) Executive branch employees, including Department of Justice employees, are also subject to financial disclosure regulations set out at 5 C.F.R. Part 2634, and to regulations governing general responsibilities and conduct set out at 5 C.F.R. Part 735.

In addition, Department of Justice employees must abide by various guidelines set out in 50 C.F.R. Part 50. We reprint here 50 C.F.R. §50.2, which establishes guidelines regarding extrajudicial statements and the release of information to the press, and 50 C.F.R. §50.19, which establishes procedures that government attorneys must follow before moving to disqualify a judge or magistrate.

28 C.F.R. §50.2. Release of Information by Personnel of the Department of Justice Relating to Criminal and Civil Proceedings

(a) *General.* (1) The availability to news media of information in criminal and civil cases is a matter which has become increasingly a subject of concern in the administration of justice. The purpose of this statement is to formulate specific guidelines for the release of such information by personnel of the Department of Justice.

(2) While the release of information for the purpose of influencing a trial is, of course, always improper, there are valid reasons for making available to the public information about the administration of the law. The task of striking a fair balance between the protection of individuals accused of crime or involved in civil proceedings with the Government and public understandings of the problems of controlling crime and administering government depends largely on the exercise of sound judgment by those responsible for administering the law and by representatives of the press and other media.

(3) Inasmuch as the Department of Justice has generally fulfilled its responsibilities with awareness and understanding of the competing needs in this area, this statement, to a considerable extent, reflects and formalizes the standards to which representatives of the Department have adhered in the past. Nonetheless, it will be helpful in ensuring uniformity of practice to set forth the following guidelines for all personnel of the Department of Justice.

(4) Because of the difficulty and importance of the questions they raise, it is felt that some portions of the matters covered by this statement, such as the authorization to make available Federal conviction records and a description of items seized at the time of arrest, should be the subject of continuing review and consideration by the Department on the basis of experience and suggestions from those within and outside the Department.

(b) *Guidelines to criminal actions.* (1) These guidelines shall apply to the release of information to news media from the time a person is the subject of a criminal investigation until any proceeding resulting from such an investigation has been terminated by trial or otherwise.

(2) At no time shall personnel of the Department of Justice furnish any statement or information for the purpose of influencing the outcome of a defendant's trial, nor shall personnel of the Department furnish any statement or information, which could reasonably be expected to be disseminated by means of public communication, if such a statement or information may reasonably be expected to influence the outcome of a pending or future trial.

(3) Personnel of the Department of Justice, subject to specific limitations imposed by law or court rule or order, may make public the following information:

(i) The defendant's name, age, residence, employment, marital status, and similar background information.

(ii) The substance or text of the charge, such as a complaint, indictment, or information.

(iii) The identity of the investigating and/or arresting agency and the length or scope of an investigation.

(iv) The circumstances immediately surrounding an arrest, resistance, pursuit, possession and use of weapons, and a description of physical items seized at the time of arrest.

Disclosures should include only incontrovertible, factual matters, and should not include subjective observations. In addition, where background information or information relating to the circumstances of an arrest or investigation would be highly prejudicial or where the release thereof would serve no law enforcement function, such information should not be made public.

(4) Personnel of the Department shall not disseminate any information concerning a defendant's prior criminal record.

(5) Because of the particular danger of prejudice resulting from statements in the period approaching and during trial, they ought strenuously to be avoided during that period. Any such statement or release shall be made only on the infrequent occasion when circumstances absolutely demand a disclosure of information and shall include only information which is clearly not prejudicial.

(6) The release of certain types of information generally tends to create dangers of prejudice without serving a significant law enforce-

ment function. Therefore, personnel of the Department should refrain from making available the following:

(i) Observations about a defendant's character.

(ii) Statements, admissions, confessions, or alibis attributable to a defendant, or the refusal or failure of the accused to make a statement.

(iii) Reference to investigative procedures such as fingerprints, polygraph examinations, ballistic tests, or laboratory tests, or to the refusal by the defendant to submit to such tests or examinations.

(iv) Statements concerning the identity, testimony, or credibility of prospective witnesses.

(v) Statements concerning evidence or argument in the case, whether or not it is anticipated that such evidence or argument will be used at trial.

(vi) Any opinion as to the accused's guilt, or the possibility of a plea of guilty to the offense charged, or the possibility of a plea to a lesser offense.

(7) Personnel of the Department of Justice should take no action to encourage or assist news media in photographing or televising a defendant or accused person being held or transported in Federal custody. Departmental representatives should not make available photographs of a defendant unless a law enforcement function is served thereby.

(8) This statement of policy is not intended to restrict the release of information concerning a defendant who is a fugitive from justice.

(9) Since the purpose of this statement is to set forth generally applicable guidelines, there will, of course, be situations in which it will limit the release of information which would not be prejudicial under the particular circumstances. If a representative of the Department believes that in the interest of the fair administration of justice and the law enforcement process information beyond these guidelines should be released, in a particular case, he shall request the permission of the Attorney General or the Deputy Attorney General to do so.

(c) *Guidelines to civil actions.* Personnel of the Department of Justice associated with a civil action shall not during its investigation or litigation make or participate in making an extrajudicial statement, other than a quotation from or reference to public records, which a reasonable person would expect to be disseminated by means of public communication if there is a reasonable likelihood that such dissemination will interfere with a fair trial and which relates to:

(1) Evidence regarding the occurrence or transaction involved.

(2) The character, credibility, or criminal records of a party, witness, or prospective witness.

(3) The performance or results of any examinations or tests or the refusal or failure of a party to submit to such.

(4) An opinion as to the merits of the claims or defenses of a party, except as required by law or administrative rule.

(5) Any other matter reasonably likely to interfere with a fair trial of the action.

§50.19. Procedures to Be Followed by Government Attorneys Prior to Filing Recusal or Disqualification Motions

The determination to seek for any reason the disqualification or recusal of a justice, judge, or magistrate is a most significant and sensitive decision. This is particularly true for government attorneys, who should be guided by uniform procedures in obtaining the requisite authorization for such a motion. This statement is designed to establish a uniform procedure.

(a) No motion to recuse or disqualify a justice, judge, or magistrate (see, e.g., 28 U.S.C. 144, 455) shall be made or supported by any Department of Justice attorney, U.S. Attorney (including Assistant U.S. Attorneys) or agency counsel conducting litigation pursuant to agreement with or authority delegated by the Attorney General, without the prior written approval of the Assistant Attorney General having ultimate supervisory power over the action in which recusal or disqualification is being considered.

(b) Prior to seeking such approval, Justice Department lawyer(s) handling the litigation shall timely seek the recommendations of the U.S. Attorney for the district in which the matter is pending, and the views of the client agencies, if any. Similarly, if agency attorneys are primarily handling any such suit, they shall seek the recommendations of the U.S. Attorney and provide them to the Department of Justice with the request for approval. In actions where the United States Attorneys are primarily handling the litigation in question, they shall seek the recommendation of the client agencies, if any, for submission to the Assistant Attorney General.

(c) In the event that the conduct and pace of the litigation does not allow sufficient time to seek the prior written approval by the Assistant Attorney General, prior oral authorization shall be sought and a written record fully reflecting that authorization shall be subsequently prepared and submitted to the Assistant Attorney General.

(d) Assistant Attorneys General may delegate the authority to approve or deny requests made pursuant to this section, but only to Deputy Assistant Attorneys General or an equivalent position.

(e) This policy statement does not create or enlarge any legal obligations upon the Department of Justice in civil or criminal litigation, and it is not intended to create any private rights enforceable by private parties in litigation with the United States.

Statutes on Disqualification and Discipline of Federal Judges

Editors' Introduction. The Code of Judicial Conduct prohibits judges from presiding over cases in which they have conflicts of interest or in which they are biased. However, the Code of Judicial Conduct does not by itself give parties the right to disqualify judges who fail to heed those prohibitions. In federal court, the right to disqualify judges derives from two federal statutes, 28 U.S.C. §§144 and 455, which we reprint below.

Federal judges appointed under Article III of the Constitution enjoy life tenure and can only be removed from office through impeachment by Congress. Provisions for discipline short of removal are contained in 28 U.S.C. §372(c), which follows the disqualification statutes below.

Contents

28 U.S.C. §144. Bias or Prejudice of Judges
28 U.S.C. §455. Disqualification of Justice, Judge, or Magistrate
28 U.S.C. §372(c). Retirement for Disability; Substitute Judge on Failure to Retire; Judicial Discipline

28 U.S.C. §144. Bias or Prejudice of Judges

Whenever a party to any proceeding in a district court makes and files a timely and sufficient affidavit that the judge before whom the matter is pending has a personal bias or prejudice either against him or in favor of any adverse party, such judge shall proceed no further therein, but another judge shall be assigned to hear such proceeding.

The affidavit shall state the facts and the reasons for the belief that bias or prejudice exists, and shall be filed not less than ten days before the beginning of the term at which the proceeding is to be heard, or good cause shall be shown for failure to file it within such time. A party

may file only one such affidavit in any case. It shall be accompanied by a certificate of counsel of record stating that it is made in good faith.

28 U.S.C. §455. Disqualification of Justice, Judge, or Magistrate

(a) Any justice, judge, or magistrate of the United States shall disqualify himself in any proceeding in which his impartiality might reasonably be questioned.

(b) He shall also disqualify himself in the following circumstances:

(1) Where he has a personal bias or prejudice concerning a party, or personal knowledge of disputed evidentiary facts concerning the proceeding;

(2) Where in private practice he served as lawyer in the matter in controversy, or a lawyer with whom he previously practiced law served during such association as a lawyer concerning the matter, or the judge or such lawyer has been a material witness concerning it;

(3) Where he has served in governmental employment and in such capacity participated as counsel, adviser or material witness concerning the proceeding or expressed an opinion concerning the merits of the particular case in controversy;

(4) He knows that he, individually or as a fiduciary, or his spouse or minor child residing in his household, has a financial interest in the subject matter in controversy or in a party to the proceeding, or any other interest that could be substantially affected by the outcome of the proceeding;

(5) He or his spouse, or a person within the third degree of relationship to either of them, or the spouse of such a person:

(i) Is a party to the proceeding, or an officer, director, or trustee of a party;

(ii) Is acting as a lawyer in the proceeding;

(iii) Is known by the judge to have an interest that could be substantially affected by the outcome of the proceeding;

(iv) Is to the judge's knowledge likely to be a material witness in the proceeding.

(c) A judge should inform himself about his personal and fiduciary financial interests, and make a reasonable effort to inform himself about the personal financial interests of his spouse and minor children residing in his household.

(d) For the purposes of this section the following words or phrases shall have the meaning indicated:

(1) "proceeding" includes pretrial, trial, appellate review, or other stages of litigation;

(2) the degree of relationship is calculated according to the civil law system;

(3) "fiduciary" includes such relationships as executor, administrator, trustee, and guardian;

(4) "financial interest" means ownership of a legal or equitable interest, however small, or a relationship as director, adviser, or other active participant in the affairs of a party, except that:

(i) Ownership in a mutual or common investment fund that holds securities is not a "financial interest" in such securities unless the judge participates in the management of the fund;

(ii) An office in an educational, religious, charitable, fraternal, or civic organization is not a "financial interest" in securities held by the organization;

(iii) The proprietary interest of a policyholder in a mutual insurance company, of a depositor in a mutual savings association, or a similar proprietary interest, is a "financial interest" in the organization only if the outcome of the proceeding could substantially affect the value of the interest;

(iv) Ownership of governmental securities is a "financial interest" in the issuer only if the outcome of the proceeding could substantially affect the value of the securities.

(e) No justice, judge, or magistrate shall accept from the parties to the proceeding a waiver of any ground for disqualification enumerated in subsection (b). Where the ground for disqualification arises only under subsection (a), waiver may be accepted provided it is preceded by a full disclosure on the record of the basis for disqualification.

(f) Notwithstanding the preceding provisions of this section, if any justice, judge, magistrate, or bankruptcy judge to whom a matter has been assigned would be disqualified, after substantial judicial time has been devoted to the matter, because of the appearance or discovery, after the matter was assigned to him or her, that he or she individually or as a fiduciary, or his or her spouse or minor child residing in his or her household, has a financial interest in a party (other than an interest that could be substantially affected by the outcome), disqualification is not required if the justice, judge, magistrate, bankruptcy judge, spouse or minor child, as the case may be, divests himself or herself of the interest that provides the grounds for the disqualification.

Editors' Note. Subsection (f) of §455 was added by Congress in Public Law 100-702, effective November 19, 1988.

28 U.S.C. §372(c). Retirement for Disability; Substitute Judge on Failure to Retire; Judicial Discipline

. . . (c)(1) Any person alleging that a circuit, district, or bankruptcy judge, or a magistrate, has engaged in conduct prejudicial to the effective and expeditious administration of the business of the courts, or alleging that such a judge or magistrate is unable to discharge all the duties of office by reason of mental or physical disability, may file with the clerk of the court of appeals for the circuit a written complaint containing a brief statement of the facts constituting such conduct. In the interests of the effective and expeditious administration of the business of the courts and on the basis of information available to the chief judge of the circuit, the chief judge may, by written order stating reasons therefor, identify a complaint for purposes of this subsection and thereby dispense with filing of a written complaint.

(2) Upon receipt of a complaint filed under paragraph (1) of this subsection, the clerk shall promptly transmit such complaint to the chief judge of the circuit, or, if the conduct complained of is that of the chief judge, to that circuit judge in regular active service next senior in date of commission (hereafter, for purposes of this subsection only, included in the term "chief judge"). The clerk shall simultaneously transmit a copy of the complaint to the judge or magistrate whose conduct is the subject of the complaint.

(3) After expeditiously reviewing a complaint, the chief judge, by written order stating his reasons, may —

(A) dismiss the complaint, if he finds it to be (i) not in conformity with paragraph (1) of this subsection, (ii) directly related to the merits of a decision or procedural ruling, or (iii) frivolous; or

(B) conclude the proceeding if he finds that appropriate corrective action has been taken or that action on the complaint is no longer necessary because of intervening events.

The chief judge shall transmit copies of his written order to the complainant and to the judge or magistrate whose conduct is the subject of the complaint.

(4) If the chief judge does not enter an order under paragraph (3) of this subsection, such judge shall promptly —

(A) appoint himself and equal numbers of circuit and district judges of the circuit to a special committee to investigate the facts and allegations contained in the complaint;

(B) certify the complaint and any other documents pertaining thereto to each member of such committee; and

(C) provide written notice to the complainant and the judge or magistrate whose conduct is the subject of the complaint of the action taken under this paragraph.

A judge appointed to a special committee under this paragraph may continue to serve on that committee after becoming a senior judge or, in the case of the chief judge of the circuit, after his or her term as chief judge terminates under subsection (a)(3) or (c) of section 45 of this title. If a judge appointed to a committee under this paragraph dies, or retires from office under section 371(a) of this title, while serving on the committee, the chief judge of the circuit may appoint another circuit or district judge, as the case may be, to the committee.

(5) Each committee appointed under paragraph (4) of this subsection shall conduct an investigation as extensive as it considers necessary, and shall expeditiously file a comprehensive written report thereon with the judicial council of the circuit. Such report shall present both the findings of the investigation and the committee's recommendations for necessary and appropriate action by the judicial council of the circuit.

(6) Upon receipt of a report filed under paragraph (5) of this subsection, the judicial council —

(A) may conduct any additional investigation which it considers to be necessary;

(B) shall take such action as is appropriate to assure the effective and expeditious administration of the business of the courts within the circuit, including, but not limited to, any of the following actions:

(i) directing the chief judge of the district of the magistrate whose conduct is the subject of the complaint to take such action as the judicial council considers appropriate;

(ii) certifying disability of a judge appointed to hold office during good behavior whose conduct is the subject of the complaint, pursuant to the procedures and standards provided under subsection (b) of this section;

(iii) requesting that any such judge appointed to hold office during good behavior voluntarily retire, with the provision that the length of service requirements under section 371 of this title shall not apply;

(iv) ordering that, on a temporary basis for a time certain, no further cases be assigned to any judge or magistrate whose conduct is the subject of a complaint;

(v) censuring or reprimanding such judge or magistrate by means of private communication;

(vi) censuring or reprimanding such judge or magistrate by means of public announcement; or

(vii) ordering such other action as it considers appropriate under the circumstances, except that (I) in no circumstances may the council order removal from office of any judge appointed to hold office during good behavior, and (II) any removal of a magistrate shall be in accordance with section 631 of this title and any removal of a bankruptcy judge shall be in accordance with section 152 of this title;

(C) may dismiss the complaint; and

(D) shall immediately provide written notice to the complainant and to such judge or magistrate of the action taken under this paragraph.

(7)(A) In addition to the authority granted under paragraph (6) of this subsection, the judicial council may, in its discretion, refer any complaint under this subsection, together with the record of any associated proceedings and its recommendations for appropriate action, to the Judicial Conference of the United States.

(B) In any case in which the judicial council determines, on the basis of a complaint and an investigation under this subsection, or on the basis of information otherwise available to the council, that a judge appointed to hold office during good behavior may have engaged in conduct —

(i) which might constitute one or more grounds for impeachment under article II of the Constitution; or

(ii) which, in the interest of justice, is not amenable to resolution by the judicial council,

the judicial council shall promptly certify such determination, together with any complaint and a record of any associated proceedings, to the Judicial Conference of the United States.

(C) A judicial council acting under authority of this paragraph shall, unless contrary to the interests of justice, immediately submit written notice to the complainant and to the judge or magistrate whose conduct is the subject of the action taken under this paragraph.

(8)(A) Upon referral or certification of any matter under paragraph (7) of this subsection, the Judicial Conference, after consideration of the prior proceedings and such additional investigation as it considers appropriate, shall by majority vote take such action, as described in paragraph (6)(B) of this subsection, as it considers appropriate. If the Judicial Conference concurs in the determination of the council, or makes its own determination, that consideration of impeachment may be warranted, it shall so certify and transmit the determination and the record of proceedings to the House of Representatives for whatever action the House of Representatives considers to be necessary. Upon receipt of the determination and record of proceedings in the House of Representatives, the Clerk of the House of Representatives shall make available to the public the determination and any reasons for the determination.

(B) If a judge or magistrate has been convicted of a felony and has exhausted all means of obtaining direct review of the conviction, or the time for seeking further direct review of the conviction has passed and no such review has been sought, the Judicial Conference may, by majority vote and without referral or certification under paragraph (7), transmit to the House of Representatives a determination that consideration of impeachment may be warranted, together with appropriate court records, for whatever action the House of Representatives considers to be necessary.

(9)(A) In conducting any investigation under this subsection, the judicial council, or a special committee appointed under paragraph (4) of this subsection, shall have full subpoena powers as provided in section 332(d) of this title.

(B) In conducting any investigation under this subsection, the Judicial Conference, or a standing committee appointed by the Chief Justice under section 331 of this title, shall have full subpoena powers as provided in that section.

(10) A complainant, judge, or magistrate aggrieved by a final order of the chief judge under paragraph (3) of this subsection may petition the judicial council for review thereof. A complainant, judge, or magistrate aggrieved by an action of the judicial council under paragraph (6) of this subsection may petition the Judical Conference of the United States for review thereof. The Judicial Conference, or the standing committee established under section 331 of this title, may grant a petition filed by a complainant, judge, or magistrate under this paragraph. Except as expressly provided in this paragraph, all orders and determinations, including denials of petitions for review, shall be final and conclusive and shall not be judicially reviewable on appeal or otherwise.

(11) Each judicial council and the Judicial Conference may prescribe such rules for the conduct of proceedings under this subsection, including the processing of petitions for review, as each considers to be appropriate. Such rules shall contain provisions requiring that —

(A) adequate prior notice of any investigation be given in writing to the judge or magistrate whose conduct is the subject of the complaint;

(B) the judge or magistrate whose conduct is the subject of the complaint be afforded an opportunity to appear (in person or by counsel) at proceedings conducted by the investigating panel, to present oral and documentary evidence, to compel the attendance of witnesses or the production of documents, to cross-examine witnesses, and to present argument orally or in writing; and

(C) the complainant be afforded an opportunity to appear at proceedings conducted by the investigating panel, if the panel concludes that the complainant could offer substantial information.

Any such rule shall be made or amended only after giving appropriate public notice and an opportunity for comment. Any rule promulgated under this subsection shall be a matter of public record, and any such rule promulgated by a judicial council may be modified by the Judicial Conference. No rule promulgated under this subsection may limit the period of time within which a person may file a complaint under this subsection.

(12) No judge or magistrate whose conduct is the subject of an investigation under this subsection shall serve upon a special committee appointed under paragraph (4) of this subsection, upon a judicial council, upon the Judicial Conference, or upon the standing committee established under section 331 of this title, until all related proceedings under this subsection have been finally terminated.

(13) No person shall be granted the right to intervene or to appear as amicus curiae in any proceeding before a judical council or the Judicial Conference under this subsection.

(14) Except as provided in paragraph (8), all papers, documents, and records of proceedings related to investigations conducted under this subsection shall be confidential and shall not be disclosed by any person in any proceeding except to the extent that —

(A) the judicial council of the circuit in its discretion releases a copy of a report of a special investigative committee under paragraph (5) to the complainant whose complaint initiated the investigation by that special committee and to the judge or magistrate whose conduct is the subject of the complaint;

(B) the judicial council of the circuit, the Judicial Conference of the United States, or the Senate or the House of Representatives by resolution, releases any such material which is believed necessary to an impeachment investigation or trial of a judge under article I of the Constitution; or

(C) such disclosure is authorized in writing by the judge or magistrate who is the subject to the complaint and by the chief judge of the circuit, the Chief Justice, or the chairman of the standing committee established under section 331 of this title.

(15) Each written order to implement any action under paragraph (6)(B) of this subsection, which is issued by a judicial council, the Judicial Conference, or the standing committee established under section 331 of this title, shall be made available to the public through the appropriate clerk's office of the court of appeals for the circuit. Unless contrary to the interests of justice, each such order issued under this paragraph shall be accompanied by written reasons therefor.

(16) Upon the request of a judge or magistrate whose conduct is the subject of a complaint under this subsection, the judicial council may, if the complaint has been finally dismissed under paragraph (6)(C), recommend that the Director of the Administrative Office of the United States Courts award reimbursement, from funds appropriated to the Federal judiciary, for those reasonable expenses, including attorneys' fees, incurred by that judge or magistrate during the investigation which would not have been incurred but for the requirements of this subsection.

(17) Except as expressly provided in this subsection, nothing in this subsection shall be construed to affect any other provision of this title, the Federal Rules of Civil Procedure, the Federal Rules of Criminal Procedure, the Federal Rules of Appellate Procedure, or the Federal Rules of Evidence.

(18) The United States Claims Court, the Court of International Trade, and the Court of Appeals for the Federal Circuit shall each

prescribe rules, consistent with the foregoing provisions of this subsection, establishing procedures for the filing of complaints with respect to the conduct of any judge of such court and for the investigation and resolution of such complaints. In investigating and taking action with respect to any such complaint, each such court shall have the powers granted to a judicial council under this subsection.

California Materials

California Rules of Professional Conduct

Editors' Introduction. The California Rules of Professional Conduct are unique. They are not directly based on either the ABA Model Rules of Professional Conduct or the old ABA Model Code of Professional Responsibility, and they use a numbering system exclusive to California. For some rules (but not all), the California Supreme Court has adopted a short official Discussion to explain particular parts of the rule.

Perhaps the most unusual feature of California's Rules of Professional Conduct is that they do not contain any rule governing confidentiality (i.e., they have no rule comparable to ABA Model Rule 1.6). Rather, the duty of confidentiality is stated in §6068(e) of California's Business and Professions Code, which says simply: "It is the duty of an attorney to . . . maintain inviolate the confidence, and at every peril to himself or herself to preserve the secrets, of his or her client." The statutory provision has no exceptions.

Since our last edition, the California Rules of Professional Conduct have not changed in any way. However, several important developments suggest that changes may be coming soon. First, on June 28, 2002, the California State Bar forwarded to the California Supreme Court a proposed new paragraph to the Discussion following Rule 3-310 of the California Rules of Professional Conduct, which is California's main provision governing conflicts of interest. (The proposed amendment would not change the text of Rule 3-310.) The proposal marks another step in responding to the decision in State Farm Mutual Insurance Company v. Federal Insurance Company, 72 Cal. App. 4th 1422 (5th Dist. 1999). In *State Farm,* a law firm simultaneously (a) represented State Farm in a coverage action filed directly *against* Federal Insurance, and (b) represented a driver *insured* by Federal Insurance in an unrelated case. Federal Insurance moved to disqualify the law firm from opposing it in the *State Farm* case, arguing that the law firm had an attorney-client relationship with Federal Insurance by virtue of representing its insured in the unrelated case. The trial court denied the motion, but the appellate court reversed, holding that "for purposes of disqualification, the attorney representing an insured is also representing the insurance company." In 2001, the California Legislature passed a law

(Business & Professions Code §6068.11) ordering the California State Bar to study the professional responsibility issues posed by *State Farm*. The Bar then identified the "key issue" as whether *State Farm* could be expanded to disqualify an attorney from opposing a particular insurance company's insured in one case while representing a different insured of the same insurance company in a separate, unrelated matter. To discourage this expansion, the Bar proposes adding the following new paragraph to the Discussion following Rule 3-310:

> In *State Farm* . . . the court held that subparagraph (C)(3) [of Rule 3-310] was violated when a member, retained by an insurer to defend one suit, and while that suit was still pending, filed a direct action against the same insurer in an unrelated action without securing the insurer's consent. Notwithstanding *State Farm*, subparagraph (C)(3) is not intended to apply with respect to the relationship between an insurer and a member when, in each matter, the insurer's interest is only as an indemnity provider and not as a direct party to the action.

The proposal was still pending before the California Supreme Court when this book went to press in September 2002.

In another major development, the California Supreme Court rejected proposed amendments to Rule 3-600 (Organization as Client) that would have clarified the circumstances under which public agency attorneys may disclose client confidences to report corruption or wrongdoing by government officials. The issue gained public attention in 1999 when an attorney at California's Department of Insurance went to the legislature to report wrongdoing by the insurance commissioner. A legislative oversight committee granted the whistle-blowing attorney immunity from criminal prosecution for giving the committee the information it needed to investigate the charges (which eventually led to the insurance commissioner's resignation), but the State Bar nevertheless began a disciplinary investigation against the attorney regarding possible violations of the duty of confidentiality. (California has a statute protecting whistleblowers, but in May 2001, California's attorney general ruled that the whistleblower protection statute excused an attorney's breach of the statutory duty of confidentiality.) The California Legislature therefore began exploring ways of clarifying the rights of government attorneys to divulge confidential information for the purpose of exposing public corruption. The legislator spearheading the effort, Assemblyman Darrell Steinberg, introduced a bill (A.B. 363) titled the "Public Agency Attorney Accountability Act" but soon decided that the State Bar was the appropriate body to develop and recommend a rule governing lawyers. Mr. Steinberg then worked with the State Bar and its Committee on Professional Responsibility and Conduct, as well as representatives of local public agency attorneys, the Department of Justice, the Judicial Council, and others, to develop proposed amendments to Rule 3-600. The proposed amendments, which roughly parallel Rule 1.13 of the ABA Model Rules of Professional Conduct, set forth the steps an attorney representing a public agency must follow if he or she wishes to reveal improper governmental activity without violating his or her duty of confidentiality. The proposed amendments provided as follows:

> (C) If, in the course of representing a governmental organization, a member learns that an act or refusal to act of an actual or apparent agent of the organization (i) is or may be a violation of law reasonably imputable to the orga-

nization, (ii) is likely to result in substantial injury to the organization, (iii) constitutes the use of the organization's official authority or influence by the agent to commit a crime, fraud or other violation of law, (iv) involves the agent's willful misuse of public funds or willful breach of fiduciary duty, or (v) involves the agent's willful omission to perform his or her official duty, then the member shall not violate his or her duty of protecting all confidential information as provided in Business and Professions Code section 6068, subdivision (e). Subject to Business and Professions Code section 6068, subdivision (e), the member may take such actions as appear to the member to be in the best lawful interest of the organization. Such actions may include among others:

(1) Urging reconsideration of the matter while explaining its likely consequences to the organization; and

(2) Referring the matter to the next higher authority in the organization, including, if warranted by the seriousness of the matter, referral to the highest internal authority that can act on behalf of the organization.

(D) Provided the member has taken action as described in subparagraphs (C)(1) and (2) without the matter being resolved, or, if the highest internal authority that can act on behalf of the organization is an agent whose conduct is described in paragraph (C), then the member would act consistently with his or her duty of protecting any confidential information as provided in Business and Professions Code section 6068, subdivision (e) by referring the matter to the law enforcement agency or official charged with overseeing or regulating the matter, if:

(1) the referral is warranted by the seriousness of the circumstances and not otherwise prohibited by law; and

(2) the agent's act or refusal to act constitutes the use of the organization's official authority or influence to commit a crime or fraud, or a willful misuse of public funds or a willful breach of fiduciary duty.

A member representing a governmental organization shall not be subject to discipline under these rules for making a referral under this paragraph if the member has acted in good faith to determine the propriety of making a referral and to identify the appropriate governmental agency or official as described in this paragraph.

On May 10, 2002, in a one-line opinion, the California Supreme Court rejected these proposed amendments. The Court did not criticize the substance of the proposed amendments but stated that the proposed rule conflicted with the statutory confidentiality provisions in §6068(e) of California's State Bar Act. After the Supreme Court rejected the proposed amendments, Assemblyman Steinberg reintroduced A.B. 363. On August 28, 2002, the California Legislature enacted a new §6068.1 of the Business and Professions Code that largely paralleled the language in rejected Rule 3-600. On September 30, 2002, however, Governor Davis vetoed the bill. We discuss the bill in more detail in our Editors' Introduction to the Selected California Statutes below, and we reprint the full text of the bill together with some explanatory material.

In another important development, in February 2002 the State Bar of California reactivated its Commission for the Revision of the Rules of Professional Conduct and directed the commission to review the California Rules of Professional Conduct comprehensively and recommend amendments. The Commission will consider judicial and statutory developments, the Final Report and Recommendations of the ABA Ethics 2000 Commission, the Restatement (Third) of the Law Governing Lawyers, and other authorities. The Commission is specifically directed to consider local, state, and national work relevant to "Multi-Disciplinary Practice,

Multi-Jurisdictional Practice, court facilitated *propria persona* assistance, discrete task representation and to other subjects that have a substantial impact upon the development of professional responsibility standards." The commission has been expressly instructed to "[e]liminate and avoid unnecessary differences between California and other states, fostering the evolution of a national standard with respect to professional responsibility issues." The review project is expected to continue for perhaps four or five years. During that time, proposed amendments to the existing Rules of Professional Conduct are likely to be funneled through the Commission for the Revision of the Rules of Professional Conduct rather than through the usual channel, the State Bar's Committee on Professional Responsibility and Conduct (COPRAC).

In addition, California continues to study both the multidisciplinary practice of law and the multijurisdictional practice of law, both of which were the subject of lengthy reports issued in California since our last edition. (The California Legislature also plays a major role in the regulation of lawyers. Legislative developments are discussed in the Editors' Introduction to our chapter on Selected California Statutes below.)

Finally, California's Board of Legal Specialization has recommended three major substantive changes to the rules governing California's Legal Specialization program: (1) reinstating an alternative to the certification exam, which would allow certification applicants the option of satisfying additional task and experience requirements instead of passing a written exam; (2) increasing from three years to five years the number of years during which the "percentage of practice" requirement applies; and (3) adding criteria relating to discipline and professional negligence that may be used in evaluating an applicant's proficiency and ethics, and imposing on the applicant of a duty to disclose information satisfying the new criteria within a given time frame. Public comments were due on June 13, 2002. The proposals were still pending when we went to press in September of 2002.

For updated information on developments relating to the California Rules of Professional Conduct, visit the web site at www.calbar.ca.gov. The site is complicated, but the best starting point is usually to click on the right-hand menu on the word "Ethics."

Contents

Chapter 1. Professional Integrity in General

Rule 1-100. Rules of Professional Conduct, in General
Rule 1-110. Disciplinary Authority of the State Bar
Rule 1-120. Assisting, Soliciting, or Inducing Violations
Rule 1-200. False Statement Regarding Admission to the State Bar
Rule 1-300. Unauthorized Practice of Law
Rule 1-310. Forming a Partnership with a Non-Lawyer
Rule 1-311. Employment of Disbarred, Suspended, Resigned, or Involuntarily Inactive Member

Rule 1-320. Financial Arrangements with Non-Lawyers
Rule 1-400. Advertising and Solicitation
Rule 1-500. Agreements Restricting a Member's Practice
Rule 1-600. Legal Service Programs
Rule 1-700. Member as Candidate for Judicial Office
Rule 1-710. Member as Temporary Judge, Referee, or Court Appointed Arbitrator

Chapter 2. Relationship Among Members

Rule 2-100. Communication with a Represented Party
Rule 2-200. Financial Arrangements Among Lawyers
Rule 2-300. Sale or Purchase of a Law Practice of a Member, Living or Deceased
Rule 2-400. Prohibited Discriminatory Conduct in a Law Practice

Chapter 3. Professional Relationship with Clients

Rule 3-110. Failing to Act Competently
Rule 3-120. Sexual Relations with Client
Rule 3-200. Prohibited Objectives of Employment
Rule 3-210. Advising the Violation of Law
Rule 3-300. Avoiding Interests Adverse to a Client
Rule 3-310. Avoiding the Representation of Adverse Interests
Rule 3-320. Relationship with Other Party's Lawyer
Rule 3-400. Limiting Liability to Client
Rule 3-500. Communication
Rule 3-510. Communication of Settlement Offer
Rule 3-600. Organization as Client
Rule 3-700. Termination of Employment

Chapter 4. Financial Relationship with Clients

Rule 4-100. Preserving Identity of Funds and Property of a Client
Rule 4-200. Fees for Legal Services
Rule 4-210. Payment of Personal or Business Expenses Incurred by or for a Client
Rule 4-300. Purchasing Property at a Foreclosure or a Sale Subject to Judicial Review
Rule 4-400. Gifts from Client

Chapter 5. Advocacy and Representation

Rule 5 100. Threatening Criminal, Administrative, or Disciplinary Charges
Rule 5-110. Performing the Duty of Member in Government Service

Rule 5-120. Trial Publicity
Rule 5-200. Trial Conduct
Rule 5-210. Member as Witness
Rule 5-220. Suppression of Evidence
Rule 5-300. Contact with Officials
Rule 5-310. Prohibited Contact with Witnesses
Rule 5-320. Contact with Jurors

CHAPTER 1. PROFESSIONAL INTEGRITY IN GENERAL

Rule 1-100. Rules of Professional Conduct, in General

(A) ***Purpose and Function.***

The following rules are intended to regulate professional conduct of members of the State Bar through discipline. They have been adopted by the Board of Governors of the State Bar of California and approved by the Supreme Court of California pursuant to Business and Professions Code sections 6076 and 6077 to protect the public and to promote respect and confidence in the legal profession. These rules together with any standards adopted by the Board of Governors pursuant to these rules shall be binding upon all members of the State Bar.

For a willful breach of any of these rules, the Board of Governors has the power to discipline members as provided by law.

The prohibition of certain conduct in these rules is not exclusive. Members are also bound by applicable law including the State Bar Act (Bus. & Prof. Code, §6000 et seq.) and opinions of California courts. Although not binding, opinions of ethics committees in California should be consulted by members for guidance on proper professional conduct. Ethics opinions and rules and standards promulgated by other jurisdictions and bar associations may also be considered.

These rules are not intended to create new civil causes of action. Nothing in these rules shall be deemed to create, augment, diminish, or eliminate any substantive legal duty of lawyers or the non-disciplinary consequences of violating such a duty.

(B) ***Definitions.***

(1) "Law Firm" means:

(a) two or more lawyers whose activities constitute the practice of law, and who share its profits, expenses, and liabilities; or

(b) a law corporation which employs more than one lawyer; or

(c) a division, department, office, or group within a business entity, which includes more than one lawyer who performs legal services for the business entity; or

(d) a publicly funded entity which employs more than one lawyer to perform legal services.

(2) "Member" means a member of the State Bar of California.

(3) "Lawyer" means a member of the State Bar of California or a person who is admitted in good standing of and eligible to practice before the bar of any United States court or the highest court of the District of Columbia or any state, territory, or insular possession of the United States, or is licensed to practice law in, or is admitted in good standing and eligible to practice before the bar of the highest court of, a foreign country or any political subdivision thereof.

(4) "Associate" means an employee or fellow employee who is employed as a lawyer.

(5) "Shareholder" means a shareholder in a professional corporation pursuant to Business and Professions Code section 6160 et seq.

(C) *Purpose of Discussions.*

Because it is a practical impossibility to convey in black letter form all of the nuances of these disciplinary rules, the comments contained in the Discussions of the rules, while they do not add independent basis for imposing discipline, are intended to provide guidance for interpreting the rules and practicing in compliance with them.

(D) *Geographic Scope of Rules.*

(1) As to members: These rules shall govern the activities of members in and outside this state, except as members lawfully practicing outside this state may be specifically required by a jurisdiction in which they are practicing to follow rules of professional conduct different from these rules.

(2) As to lawyers from other jurisdictions: These rules shall also govern the activities of lawyers while engaged in the performance of lawyer functions in this state; but nothing contained in these rules shall be deemed to authorize the performance of such functions by such persons in this state except as otherwise permitted by law.

(E) These rules may be cited and referred to as "Rules of Professional Conduct of the State Bar of California."

DISCUSSION

The Rules of Professional Conduct are intended to establish the standards for members for purposes of discipline. (See Ames v. State Bar (1973) 8 Cal. 3d 910 [106 Cal. Rptr. 489].) The fact that a member has engaged in conduct that may be contrary to these rules does not automatically give rise to a civil cause of action. (See Noble v. Sears, Roebuck & Co. (1973) 33 Cal.

App. 3d 654 [109 Cal. Rptr. 269]; Wilhelm v. Pray, Price, Williams & Russell (1986) 186 Cal. App. 3d 1324 [231 Cal. Rptr. 355].) These rules are not intended to supercede existing law relating to members in non-disciplinary contexts. (See, e.g., Klemm v. Superior Court (1977) 75 Cal. App. 3d 893 [142 Cal. Rptr. 509] (motion for disqualification of counsel due to a conflict of interest); Academy of California Optometrists, Inc. v. Superior Court (1975) 51 Cal. App. 3d 999 [124 Cal. Rptr. 668] (duty to return client files); Chronometrics, Inc. v. Sysgen, Inc. (1980) 110 Cal. App. 3d 597 [168 Cal. Rptr. 196] (disqualification of member appropriate remedy for improper communication with adverse party).)

Law firm, as defined by subparagraph (B)(1), is not intended to include an association of lawyers who do not share profits, expenses, and liabilities. The subparagraph is not intended to imply that a law firm may include a person who is not a member in violation of the law governing the unauthorized practice of law.

Rule 1-110. Disciplinary Authority of the State Bar

A member shall comply with conditions attached to public or private reprovals or other discipline administered by the State Bar pursuant to Business and Professions Code sections 6077 and 6078 and rule 956, California Rules of Court.

Rule 1-120. Assisting, Soliciting, or Inducing Violations

A member shall not knowingly assist in, solicit, or induce any violation of these rules or the State Bar Act.

Rule 1-200. False Statement Regarding Admission to the State Bar

(A) A member shall not knowingly make a false statement regarding a material fact or knowingly fail to disclose a material fact in connection with an application for admission to the State Bar.

(B) A member shall not further an application for admission to the State Bar of a person whom the member knows to be unqualified in respect to character, education, or other relevant attributes.

(C) This rule shall not prevent a member from serving as counsel of record for an applicant for admission to practice in proceedings related to such admission.

DISCUSSION

For purposes of rule 1-200 "admission" includes readmission.

Rule 1-300. Unauthorized Practice of Law

(A) A member shall not aid any person or entity in the unauthorized practice of law.

(B) A member shall not practice law in a jurisdiction where to do so would be in violation of regulations of the profession in that jurisdiction.

Rule 1-310. Forming a Partnership with a Non-Lawyer

A member shall not form a partnership with a person who is not a lawyer if any of the activities of that partnership consist of the practice of law.

DISCUSSION

Rule 1-310 is not intended to govern members' activities which cannot be considered to constitute the practice of law. It is intended solely to preclude a member from being involved in the practice of law with a person who is not a lawyer.

Rule 1-311. Employment of Disbarred, Suspended, Resigned, or Involuntarily Inactive Member

(A) For purposes of this rule:

(1) "Employ" means to engage the services of another, including employees, agents, independent contractors and consultants, regardless of whether any compensation is paid;

(2) "Involuntarily inactive member" means a member who is ineligible to practice law as a result of action taken pursuant to Business and Professions Code sections 6007, 6203(c), or California Rule of Court 958(d); and

(3) "Resigned member" means a member who has resigned from the State Bar while disciplinary charges are pending.

(B) A member shall not employ, associate professionally with, or aid a person the member knows or reasonably should know is a

disbarred, suspended, resigned, or involuntarily inactive member to perform the following on behalf of the member's client:

(1) Render legal consultation or advice to the client;

(2) Appear on behalf of a client in any hearing or proceeding or before any judicial officer, arbitrator, mediator, court, public agency, referee, magistrate, commissioner, or hearing officer;

(3) Appear as a representative of the client at a deposition or other discovery matter;

(4) Negotiate or transact any matter for or on behalf of the client with third parties;

(5) Receive, disburse or otherwise handle the client's funds; or

(6) Engage in activities which constitute the practice of law.

(C) A member may employ, associate professionally with, or aid a disbarred, suspended, resigned, or involuntarily inactive member to perform research, drafting or clerical activities, including but not limited to:

(1) Legal work of a preparatory nature, such as legal research, the assemblage of data and other necessary information, drafting of pleadings, briefs, and other similar documents;

(2) Direct communication with the client or third parties regarding matters such as scheduling, billing, updates, confirmation of receipt or sending of correspondence and messages; or

(3) Accompanying an active member in attending a deposition or other discovery matter for the limited purpose of providing clerical assistance to the active member who will appear as the representative of the client.

(D) Prior to or at the time of employing a person the member knows or reasonably should know is a disbarred, suspended, resigned, or involuntarily inactive member, the member shall serve upon the State Bar written notice of the employment, including a full description of such person's current bar status. The written notice shall also list the activities prohibited in paragraph (B) and state that the disbarred, suspended, resigned, or involuntarily inactive member will not perform such activities. The member shall serve similar written notice upon each client on whose specific matter such person will work, prior to or at the time of employing such person to work on the client's specific matter. The member shall obtain proof of service of the client's written notice and shall retain such proof and a true and correct copy of the client's written notice for two years following termination of the member's employment with the client.

(E) A member may, without client or State Bar notification, employ a disbarred, suspended, resigned, or involuntarily inactive member whose sole function is to perform office physical plant or equipment maintenance, courier or delivery services, catering, reception, typing or transcription, or other similar support activities.

(F) Upon termination of the disbarred, suspended, resigned, or involuntarily inactive member, the member shall promptly serve upon the State Bar written notice of the termination.

DISCUSSION

For discussion of the activities that constitute the practice of law, see Farnham v. State Bar (1976) 17 Cal.3d 605 [131 Cal. Rptr. 611]; Bluestein v. State Bar (1974) 13 Cal. 3d 162 [118 Cal. Rptr. 175]; Baron v. City of Los Angeles (1970) 2 Cal. 3d 535 [86 Cal. Rptr. 673]; Crawford v. State Bar (1960) 54 Cal. 2d 659 [7 Cal. Rptr. 746]; People v. Merchants Protective Corporation (1922) 189 Cal. 531, 535 [209 P. 363]; People v. Landlords Professional Services (1989) 215 Cal. App. 3d 1599 [264 Cal. Rptr. 548]; and People v. Sipper (1943) 61 Cal. App. 2d Supp. 844 [142 P. 2d 960].

Paragraph (D) is not intended to prevent or discourage a member from fully discussing with the client the activities that will be performed by the disbarred, suspended, resigned, or involuntarily inactive member on the client's matter. If a member's client is an organization, then the written notice required by paragraph (D) shall be served upon the highest authorized officer, employee, or constituent overseeing the particular engagement. (See rule 3-600.)

Nothing in rule 1-311 shall be deemed to limit or preclude any activity engaged in pursuant to rules 983, 983.1, 983.2, and 988 of the California Rules of Court, or any local rule of a federal district court concerning admission pro hac vice.

Rule 1-320. Financial Arrangements with Non-Lawyers

(A) Neither a member nor a law firm shall directly or indirectly share legal fees with a person who is not a lawyer, except that:

(1) An agreement between a member and a law firm, partner, or associate may provide for the payment of money after the member's death to the member's estate or to one or more specified persons over a reasonable period of time; or

(2) A member or law firm undertaking to complete unfinished legal business of a deceased member may pay to the estate of the deceased member or other person legally entitled thereto that proportion of the total compensation which fairly represents the services rendered by the deceased member;

(3) A member or law firm may include non-member employees in a compensation, profit-sharing, or retirement plan even though the plan is based in whole or in part on a profit-sharing arrangement, if such plan does not circumvent these rules or Business and Professions Code section 6000 et seq.; or

(4) A member may pay a prescribed registration, referral, or participation fee to a lawyer referral service established, sponsored, and operated in accordance with the State Bar of California's Minimum Standards for a Lawyer Referral Service in California.

(B) A member shall not compensate, give, or promise anything of value to any person or entity for the purpose of recommending or securing employment of the member or the member's law firm by a client, or as a reward for having made a recommendation resulting in employment of the member or the member's law firm by a client. A member's offering of or giving a gift or gratuity to any person or entity having made a recommendation resulting in the employment of the member or the member's law firm shall not of itself violate this rule, provided that the gift or gratuity was not offered or given in consideration of any promise, agreement, or understanding that such a gift or gratuity would be forthcoming or that referrals would be made or encouraged in the future.

(C) A member shall not compensate, give, or promise anything of value to any representative of the press, radio, television, or other communication medium in anticipation of or in return for publicity of the member, the law firm, or any other member as such in a news item, but the incidental provision of food or beverage shall not of itself violate this rule.

DISCUSSION

Rule 1-320(C) is not intended to preclude compensation to the communications media in exchange for advertising the member's or law firm's availability for professional employment.

Rule 1-400. Advertising and Solicitation

Editors' Note. In 1997, the California Supreme Court added a new Rule 1-400(D)(6) to govern any lawyer claiming to be a "certified specialist." The new rule replaced a similar rule repealed by the California Supreme Court in 1992.

In a related development, in 1997 the State Bar Board of Governors substantially amended the Rules Governing the State Bar of California Program for Certifying Legal Specialists. These rules are lengthy and we do not reprint them. For more information about specialization in California, visit the California State Bar's web page at www.calbar.org (then look under "Organization of the Bar" and click on "Legal Specialization").

(A) For purposes of this rule, "communication" means any message or offer made by or on behalf of a member concerning the availability for professional employment of a member or a law firm directed to any former, present, or prospective client, including but not limited to the following:

(1) Any use of firm name, trade name, fictitious name, or other professional designation of such member or law firm; or

(2) Any stationery, letterhead, business card, sign, brochure, or other comparable written material describing such member, law firm, or lawyers; or

(3) Any advertisement (regardless of medium) of such member or law firm directed to the general public or any substantial portion thereof; or

(4) Any unsolicited correspondence from a member or law firm directed to any person or entity.

(B) For purposes of this rule, a "solicitation" means any communication:

(1) Concerning the availability for professional employment of a member or a law firm in which a significant motive is pecuniary gain; and

(2) Which is:

(a) delivered in person or by telephone, or

(b) directed by any means to a person known to the sender to be represented by counsel in a matter which is a subject of the communication.

(C) A solicitation shall not be made by or on behalf of a member or law firm to a prospective client with whom the member or law firm has no family or prior professional relationship, unless the solicitation is protected from abridgment by the Constitution of the United States or by the Constitution of the State of California. A solicitation to a former or present client in the discharge of a member's or law firm's professional duties is not prohibited.

(D) A communication or a solicitation (as defined herein) shall not:

(1) Contain any untrue statement; or

(2) Contain any matter, or present or arrange any matter in a manner or format which is false, deceptive, or which tends to confuse, deceive, or mislead the public; or

(3) Omit to state any fact necessary to make the statements made, in the light of circumstances under which they are made, not misleading to the public; or

(4) Fail to indicate clearly, expressly, or by context, that it is a communication or solicitation, as the case may be; or

(5) Be transmitted in any manner which involves intrusion, coercion, duress, compulsion, intimidation, threats, or vexatious or harassing conduct.

(6) State that a member is a "certified specialist" unless the member holds a current certificate as a specialist issued by the Board of Legal Specialization, or any other entity accredited by the State Bar to designate specialists pursuant to standards adopted by the Board of Governors, and states the complete name of the entity which granted certification.

(E) The Board of Governors of the State Bar shall formulate and adopt standards as to communications which will be presumed to violate this rule 1-400. The standards shall only be used as presumptions affecting the burden of proof in disciplinary proceedings involving alleged violations of these rules. "Presumption affecting the burden of proof" means that presumption defined in Evidence Code sections 605 and 606. Such standards formulated and adopted by the Board, as from time to time amended, shall be effective and binding on all members.

(F) A member shall retain for two years a true and correct copy or recording of any communication made by written or electronic media. Upon written request, the member shall make any such copy or recording available to the State Bar, and, if requested, shall provide to the State Bar evidence to support any factual or objective claim contained in the communication.

STANDARDS

Pursuant to rule 1-400(E) the Board of Governors of the State Bar has adopted the following standards, effective May 27, 1989 as forms of "communication" defined in rule 1-400(A) which are presumed to be in violation of rule 1-400:

(1) A "communication" which contains guarantees, warranties, or predictions regarding the result of the representation.

(2) A "communication" which contains testimonials about or endorsements of a member unless such communication also contains an express disclaimer such as "this testimonial or endorsement does not constitute a guarantee, warranty, or prediction regarding the outcome of your legal matter."

(3) A "communication" which is delivered to a potential client whom the member knows or should reasonably know is in such a physical, emotional, or mental state that he or she would not be expected to exercise reasonable judgment as to the retention of counsel.

(4) A "communication" which is transmitted at the scene of an accident or at or en route to a hospital, emergency care center, or other health care facility.

(5) A "communication," except professional announcements, seeking professional employment for pecuniary gain which is transmitted by mail or equivalent means which does not bear the words "Advertisement," "Newsletter" or words of similar import in 12 point print on the first page. If such communication, including firm brochures, newsletters, recent legal developments advisories, and similar materials, is transmitted in an envelope, the envelope shall bear the word "Advertisement," "Newsletter" or words of similar import on the outside thereof.

(6) A "communication" in the form of a firm name, trade name, fictitious name, or other professional designation which states or implies a relationship between any member in private practice and a government agency or instrumentality or a public or non-profit legal services organization.

(7) A "communication" in the form of a firm name, trade name, fictitious name, or other professional designation which states or implies that a member has a relationship to any other lawyer or a law firm as a partner or associate, or officer or shareholder pursuant to Business and Professions Code sections 6160-6172 unless such relationship in fact exists.

(8) A "communication" which states or implies that a member or law firm is "of counsel" to another lawyer or a law firm unless the former has a relationship with the latter (other than as a partner or associate, or officer or shareholder pursuant to Business and Professions Code sections 6160-6172) which is close, personal, continuous, and regular.

(9) A "communication" in the form of a firm name, trade name, fictitious name, or other professional designation used by a member or law firm in private practice which differs materially from any other such designation used by such member or law firm at the same time in the same community.

(10) A "communication" which implies that the member or law firm is participating in a lawyer referral service which has been certified by the State Bar of California or as having satisfied the Minimum Standards for Lawyer Referral Services in California, when that is not the case.

(11) [Repealed in 1997.]

(12) A "communication," except professional announcements, in the form of an advertisement primarily directed to seeking professional employment primarily for pecuniary gain transmitted to the general public or any substantial portion thereof by mail or equivalent means or by means of television, radio, newspaper, magazine or other form of commercial mass media which does not state the name of the member responsible for the communication. When the communication is made on behalf of a law firm, the communication shall state the name of at least one member responsible for it.

(13) A "communication" which contains a dramatization unless such communication contains a disclaimer which states "this is a dramatization" or words of similar import.

(14) A "communication" which states or implies "no fee without recovery" unless such communication also expressly discloses whether or not the client will be liable for costs.

(15) A "communication" which states or implies that a member is able to provide legal services in a language other that English unless the member can actually provide legal services in such language or the communication also states in the language of the communication (a) the employment title of the person who speaks such language and (b) that the person is not a member of the State Bar of California, if that is the case.

(16) An unsolicited "communication" transmitted to the general public or any substantial portion thereof primarily directed to seeking

professional employment primarily for pecuniary gain which sets forth a specific fee or range of fees for a particular service where, in fact, the member charges a greater fee than advertised in such communication within a period of 90 days following dissemination of such communication, unless such communication expressly specifies a shorter period of time regarding the advertised fee. Where the communication is published in the classified or "yellow pages" section of telephone, business or legal directories or in other media not published more frequently than once a year, the member shall conform to the advertised fee for a period of one year from initial publication, unless such communication expressly specifies a shorter period of time regarding the advertised fee.

Rule 1-500. Agreements Restricting a Member's Practice

(A) A member shall not be a party to or participate in offering or making an agreement, whether in connection with the settlement of a lawsuit or otherwise, if the agreement restricts the right of a member to practice law, except that this rule shall not prohibit such an agreement which:

(1) Is a part of an employment, shareholders', or partnership agreement among members provided the restrictive agreement does not survive the termination of the employment, shareholder, or partnership relationship; or

(2) Requires payments to a member upon the member's retirement from the practice of law; or

(3) Is authorized by Business & Professions Code sections 6092.5(i) or 6093.

(B) A member shall not be a party to or participate in offering or making an agreement which precludes the reporting of a violation of these rules.

DISCUSSION

Paragraph (A) makes it clear that the practice, in connection with settlement agreements, of proposing that a member refrain from representing other clients in similar litigation, is prohibited. Neither counsel may demand or suggest such provisions nor may opposing counsel accede or agree to such provisions.

Paragraph (A) permits a restrictive covenant in a law corporation, partnership, or employment agreement. The law corporation shareholder, partner, or associate may agree not to have a separate practice during the existence of the relationship; however, upon termination of the relationship (whether voluntary or involuntary), the member is free to practice law without any contractual restriction except in the case of retirement from the active practice of law.

Rule 1-600. Legal Service Programs

(A) A member shall not participate in a nongovernmental program, activity, or organization furnishing, recommending, or paying for legal services, which allows any third person or organization to interfere with the member's independence of professional judgment, or with the client-lawyer relationship, or allows unlicensed persons to practice law, or allows any third person or organization to receive directly or indirectly any part of the consideration paid to the member except as permitted by these rules, or otherwise violates the State Bar Act or these rules.

(B) The Board of Governors of the State Bar shall formulate and adopt Minimum Standards for Lawyer Referral Services, which, as from time to time amended, shall be binding on members.

DISCUSSION

The participation of a member in a lawyer referral service established, sponsored, supervised, and operated in conformity with the Minimum Standards for a Lawyer Referral Service in California is encouraged and is not, of itself, a violation of these rules.

Rule 1-600 is not intended to override any contractual agreement or relationship between insurers and insureds regarding the provision of legal services.

Rule 1-600 is not intended to apply to the activities of a public agency responsible for providing legal services to a government or to the public.

For purposes of paragraph (A), "a nongovernmental program, activity, or organization" includes, but is not limited to group, prepaid, and voluntary legal service programs, activities, or organizations.

> **Editors' Note.** Rule 1-600(b) refers to "Minimum Standards for Lawyer Referral Services." These Minimum Standards were originally adopted by the California Supreme Court in 1989 and were amended most recently in 1997, when they were clarified and renamed "Rules and Regulations of the State Bar of California Pertaining to Lawyer Referral Services." They are too lengthy to reprint here, but can be found in California statute books following §6155 of the Business and Professions Code.

Rule 1-700. Member as Candidate for Judicial Office

(A) A member who is a candidate for judicial office in California shall comply with Canon 5 of the Code of Judicial Ethics.

(B) For purposes of this rule, "candidate for judicial office" means a member seeking judicial office by election. The determination of when a member is a candidate for judicial office is defined in the terminology section of the California Code of Judicial Ethics. A member's duty to comply with paragraph (A) shall end when the member announces withdrawal of the member's candidacy or when the results of the election are final, whichever occurs first.

DISCUSSION

Nothing in rule 1-700 shall be deemed to limit the applicability of any other rule or law.

Rule 1-710. Member as Temporary Judge, Referee, or Court Appointed Arbitrator

A member who is serving as a temporary judge, referee, or court-appointed arbitrator, and is subject to under the Code of Judicial Ethics to Canon 6D, shall comply with the terms of that canon.

DISCUSSION

This rule is intended to permit the State Bar to discipline members who violate applicable portions of the Code of Judicial Ethics while acting in a judicial capacity pursuant to an order or appointment by a court.

Nothing in Rule 1-710 shall be deemed to limit the applicability of any other rule or law.

CHAPTER 2. RELATIONSHIP AMONG MEMBERS

Rule 2-100. Communication with a Represented Party

(A) While representing a client, a member shall not communicate directly or indirectly about the subject of the representation with a party the member knows to be represented by another lawyer in the matter, unless the member has the consent of the other lawyer.

(B) For purposes of this rule, a "party" includes:

(1) An officer, director, or managing agent of a corporation or association, and a partner or managing agent of a partnership; or

(2) An association member or an employee of an association, corporation, or partnership, if the subject of the communication is any

act or omission of such person in connection with the matter which may be binding upon or imputed to the organization for purposes of civil or criminal liability or whose statement may constitute an admission on the part of the organization.

(C) This rule shall not prohibit:

(1) Communications with a public officer, board, committee, or body;

(2) Communications initiated by a party seeking advice or representation from an independent lawyer of the party's choice; or

(3) Communications otherwise authorized by law.

DISCUSSION

Rule 2-100 is intended to control communications between a member and persons the member knows to be represented by counsel unless a statutory scheme or case law will override the rule. There are a number of express statutory schemes which authorize communications between a member and person who would otherwise be subject to this rule. These statutes protect a variety of other rights such as the right of employees to organize and to engage in collective bargaining, employee health and safety, or equal employment opportunity. Other applicable law also includes the authority of government prosecutors and investigators to conduct criminal investigations, as limited by the relevant decisional law.

Rule 2-100 is not intended to prevent the parties themselves from communicating with respect to the subject matter of the representation, and nothing in the rule prevents a member from advising the client that such communication can be made. Moreover, the rule does not prohibit a member who is also a party to a legal matter from directly or indirectly communicating on his or her own behalf with a represented party. Such a member has independent rights as a party which should not be abrogated because of his or her professional status. To prevent any possible abuse in such situations, the counsel for the opposing party may advise that party (1) about the risks and benefits of communications with a lawyer-party, and (2) not to accept or engage in communications with the lawyer-party.

Rule 2-100 also addresses the situation in which member A is contacted by an opposing party who is represented and, because of dissatisfaction with that party's counsel, seeks A's independent advice. Since A is employed by the opposition, the member cannot give independent advice.

As used in paragraph (A), "the subject of the representation," "matter," and "party" are not limited to a litigation context.

Paragraph (B) is intended to apply only to persons employed at the time of the communication.

Subparagraph (C)(2) is intended to permit a member to communicate with a party seeking to hire new counsel or to obtain a second opinion. A member contacted by such a party continues to be bound by other Rules of Professional Conduct. (See, e.g., rules 1-400 and 3-310.)

Editors' Note. During 1993, the California State Bar considered a proposed amendment to the Discussion following Rule 2-100. The proposed amendment would have clarified that Rule 2-100 does not apply to government prosecutors during the investigative phase of a criminal, disciplinary, or civil law enforcement proceeding. In August 1993, however, after considering public comments, the State Bar Board Committee on Admissions and Competence (which has oversight over rule production) determined "to take no further action on the matter."

Rule 2-200. Financial Arrangements Among Lawyers

(A) A member shall not divide a fee for legal services with a lawyer who is not a partner of, associate of, or shareholder with the member unless:

(1) The client has consented in writing thereto after a full disclosure has been made in writing that a division of fees will be made and the terms of such division; and

(2) The total fee charged by all lawyers is not increased solely by reason of the provision for division of fees and is not unconscionable as that term is defined in rule 4-200.

(B) Except as permitted in paragraph (A) of this rule or rule 2-300, a member shall not compensate, give, or promise anything of value to any lawyer for the purpose of recommending or securing employment of the member or the member's law firm by a client, or as a reward for having made a recommendation resulting in employment of the member or the member's law firm by a client. A member's offering of or giving a gift or gratuity to any lawyer who has made a recommendation resulting in the employment of the member or the member's law firm shall not of itself violate this rule, provided that the gift or gratuity was not offered in consideration of any promise, agreement, or understanding that such a gift or gratuity would be forthcoming or that referrals would be made or encouraged in the future.

Rule 2-300. Sale or Purchase of a Law Practice of a Member, Living or Deceased

All or substantially all of the law practice of a member, living or deceased, including goodwill, may be sold to another member or law firm subject to all the following conditions:

(A) Fees charged to clients shall not be increased solely by reason of such sale.

(B) If the sale contemplates the transfer of responsibility for work not yet completed or responsibility for client files or information protected by Business and Professions Code section 6068, subdivision (e), then;

(1) if the seller is deceased, or has a conservator or other person acting in a representative capacity, and no member has been appointed to act for the seller pursuant to Business and Professions Code section 6180.5, then prior to the transfer:

(a) the purchaser shall cause a written notice to be given to the client stating that the interest in the law practice is being transferred to the purchaser; that the client has the right to retain other counsel; that the client may take possession of any client papers and property, as required by rule 3-700(D); and that if no response is received to the notification within 90 days of the sending of such notice, or in the event the client's rights would be prejudiced by a failure to act during that time, the purchaser may act on behalf of the client until otherwise notified by the client. Such notice shall comply with the requirements as set forth in rule 1-400(D) and any provisions relating to attorney-client fee arrangements, and

(b) the purchaser shall obtain the written consent of the client provided that such consent shall be presumed until otherwise notified by the client if no response is received to the notification specified in subparagraph (a) within 90 days of the date of the sending of such notification to the client's last address as shown on the records of the seller, or the client's rights would be prejudiced by a failure to act during such 90-day period.

(2) in all other circumstances, not less than 90 days prior to the transfer:

(a) the seller, or the member appointed to act for the seller pursuant to Business and Professions code section 6180.5, shall cause a written notice to be given to the client stating that the interest in the law practice is being transferred to the purchaser; that the client has the right to retain other counsel; that the client may take possession of any client papers and property, as required by rule 3-700(D); and that if no response is received to the notification within 90 days of the sending of such notice, the purchaser may act on behalf of the client until otherwise notified by the client. Such notice shall comply with the requirements as set forth in rule 1-400(D) and any provisions relating to attorney-client fee arrangements, and

(b) the seller, or the member appointed to act for the seller pursuant to Business and Professions Code section 6180.5, shall obtain the written consent of the client prior to the transfer

provided that such consent shall be presumed until otherwise notified by the client if no response is received to the notification specified in subparagraph (a) within 90 days of the date of the sending of such notification to the client's last address as shown on the records of the seller.

(C) If substitution is required by the rules of a tribunal in which a matter is pending, all steps necessary to substitute a member shall be taken.

(D) All activity of a purchaser or potential purchaser under this rule shall be subject to compliance with rules 3-300 and 3-310 where applicable.

(E) Confidential information shall not be disclosed to a non-member in connection with a sale under this rule.

(F) Admission to or retirement from a law partnership or law corporation, retirement plans and similar arrangements, or sale of tangible assets of a law practice shall not be deemed a sale or purchase under this rule.

DISCUSSION

Paragraph (A) is intended to prohibit the purchaser from charging the former clients of the seller a higher fee than the purchaser is charging his or her existing clients.

"All or substantially all of the law practice of a member" means, for purposes of rule 2-300, that, for example, a member may retain one or two clients who have such a longstanding personal and professional relationship with the member that transfer of those clients' files is not feasible. Conversely, rule 2-300 is not intended to authorize the sale of a law practice in a piecemeal fashion except as may be required by subparagraph (B)(1)(a) or paragraph (D).

Transfer of individual client matters, where permitted, is governed by rule 2-200. Payment of a fee to a non-lawyer broker for arranging the sale or purchase of a law practice is governed by rule 1-320.

Rule 2-400. Prohibited Discriminatory Conduct in a Law Practice

Editors' Note. Rule 2-400, which prohibits unlawful discrimination in the operation or management of a law practice, was adopted by the California Supreme Court in 1994. It is narrower in scope than similar rules in most other states because no disciplinary investigation or proceeding may be initiated under the rule "unless and until a tribunal of competent jurisdiction, other than a disciplinary tribunal, shall have first adjudicated a complaint of alleged discrimination and found that unlawful conduct occurred."

(A) For purposes of this rule:

(1) "law practice" includes sole practices, law partnerships, law corporations, corporate and governmental legal departments, and other entities which employ members to practice law;

(2) "knowingly permit" means a failure to advocate corrective action where the member knows of a discriminatory policy or practice which results in the unlawful discrimination prohibited in paragraph (B); and

(3) "unlawfully" and "unlawful" shall be determined by reference to applicable state or federal statutes or decisions making unlawful discrimination in employment and in offering goods and services to the public.

(B) In the management or operation of a law practice, a member shall not unlawfully discriminate or knowingly permit unlawful discrimination on the basis of race, national origin, sex, sexual orientation, religion, age or disability in:

(1) hiring, promoting, discharging or otherwise determining the conditions of employment of any person; or

(2) accepting or terminating representation of any client.

(C) No disciplinary investigation or proceeding may be initiated by the State Bar against a member under this rule unless and until a tribunal of competent jurisdiction, other than a disciplinary tribunal, shall have first adjudicated a complaint of alleged discrimination and found that unlawful conduct occurred. Upon such adjudication, the tribunal finding or verdict shall then be admissible evidence of the occurrence or non-occurrence of the alleged discrimination in any disciplinary proceeding initiated under this rule. In order for discipline to be imposed under this rule, however, the finding of unlawfulness must be upheld and final after appeal, the time for filing an appeal must have expired, or the appeal must have been dismissed.

DISCUSSION

In order for discriminatory conduct to be actionable under this rule, it must first be found to be unlawful by an appropriate civil administrative or judicial tribunal under applicable state or federal law. Until there is a finding of civil unlawfulness, there is no basis for disciplinary action under this rule.

A complaint of misconduct based on this rule may be filed with the State Bar following a finding of unlawfulness in the first instance even though that finding is therafter appealed.

A disciplinary investigation or proceeding for conduct coming within this rule may be initiated and maintained, however, if such conduct warrants discipline under California Business and Professions Code sections 6106 and 6068, the California Supreme Court's inherent authority to impose discipline, or other disciplinary standard.

CHAPTER 3. PROFESSIONAL RELATIONSHIP WITH CLIENTS

Editors' Note on Confidentiality. California is the only American jurisdiction without a rule on confidentiality in its Rules of Professional Conduct. This remains true despite the California State Bar's repeated efforts to gain the California Supreme Court's approval of a rule on confidentiality. In 1993 the California Supreme Court rejected a proposed new Rule 3-100 that would have added a duty of confidentiality to California's ethics rules for the first time. California's confidentiality obligation is now solely statutory; it is found in §6068(e) of the California Business and Professions Code, which has no exceptions allowing disclosure. (Section 6068(e) is reprinted in the next chapter.) The rejected Rule 3-100 would have allowed disclosure of information necessary to prevent a client from committing a life-threatening crime.

In 1996, the State Bar circulated a new draft of proposed Rule 3-100 for public comment. The new proposal closely tracked Rule 1.6 of the ABA Model Rules of Professional Conduct. In light of the public comments, the proposal was slightly redrafted in 1997, and in 1998, the State Bar's Board of Governors forwarded the redrafted proposal to the California Supreme Court. On September 2, 1998, however, the California Supreme Court issued a one-sentence order stating that the State Bar's request for approval of proposed Rule 3-100 was denied. The court gave no reason for rejecting the rule.

Rule 3-110. Failing to Act Competently

(A) A member shall not intentionally, recklessly, or repeatedly fail to perform legal services with competence.

(B) For purposes of this rule, "competence" in any legal service shall mean to apply the 1) diligence, 2) learning and skill, and 3) mental, emotional, and physical ability reasonably necessary for the performance of such service.

(C) If a member does not have sufficient learning and skill when the legal service is undertaken, the member may nonetheless perform such services competently by 1) associating with or, where appropriate, professionally consulting another lawyer reasonably believed to be competent, or 2) by acquiring sufficient learning and skill before performance is required.

DISCUSSION

The duties set forth in rule 3-110 include the duty to supervise the work of subordinate attorney and non-attorney employees or agents. (See, e.g., Waysman v. State Bar (1986) 41 Cal. 3d 452; Trousil v. State Bar (1985) 38 Cal. 3d 337, 342 [211 Cal. Rptr. 525]; Palomo v. State Bar (1984)

36 Cal. 3d 785 [205 Cal. Rptr. 834]; Crane v. State Bar (1981) 30 Cal. 3d 117, 122; Black v. State Bar (1972) 7 Cal. 3d 676, 692 [103 Cal. Rptr. 288; 499 P.2d 968]; Vaughn v. State Bar (1972) 6 Cal. 3d 847, 857 858 [100 Cal. Rptr. 713; 494 P.2d 1257]; Moore v. State Bar (1964) 62 Cal. 2d 74, 81 [41 Cal. Rptr. 161; 396 P.2d 577].)

In an emergency a lawyer may give advice or assistance in a matter in which the lawyer does not have the skill ordinarily required where referral to or consultation with another lawyer would be impractical. Even in an emergency, however, assistance should be limited to that reasonably necessary in the circumstances.

Rule 3-120. Sexual Relations with Client

Editors' Note. The following rule is a direct outgrowth of California Business and Professions Code §6106.8 (reprinted in the following chapter), enacted by the California legislature in 1989. That statute found there was "no rule that governs the propriety of sexual relationships between lawyers and clients," and commanded the Bar to submit an appropriate rule to the California Supreme Court. In 1992, the California Supreme Court adopted the rule almost as proposed, but deleted the following proposed subparagraph E:

> (E) A member who engages in sexual relations with his or her client will be presumed to violate rule 3-120, paragraph (B)(3). This presumption shall only be used as a presumption affecting the burden of proof in disciplinary proceedings involving alleged violations of these rules. "Presumption affecting the burden of proof" means that presumption defined in Evidence Code sections 605 and 606.

Thus, violation of Rule 3-120 does not carry a presumption of incompetence in providing legal services.

California was the first state to adopt a rule of legal ethics expressly addressing sexual relationships with clients. For a parallel state statute signed into law in September 1992, see §6106.9 of the California Business and Professions Code below.

(A) For purposes of this rule, "sexual relations" means sexual intercourse or the touching of an intimate part of another person for the purpose of sexual arousal, gratification, or abuse.

(B) A member shall not:

(1) Require or demand sexual relations with a client incident to or as a condition of any professional representation; or

(2) Employ coercion, intimidation, or undue influence in entering into sexual relations with a client; or

(3) Continue representation of a client with whom the member has sexual relations if such sexual relations cause the member to perform legal services incompetently in violation of rule 3-110.

(C) Paragraph (B) shall not apply to sexual relations between members and their spouses or to ongoing consensual lawyer-client sexual relations which predate the initiation of the lawyer-client relationship.

(D) Where a lawyer in a firm has sexual relations with a client but does not participate in the representation of that client, the lawyers in the firm shall not be subject to discipline under this rule solely because of the occurrence of such sexual relations.

DISCUSSION

Rule 3-120 is intended to prohibit sexual exploitation by a lawyer in the course of a professional representation. Often, based upon the nature of the underlying representation, a client exhibits great emotional vulnerability and dependence upon the advice and guidance of counsel. Attorneys owe the utmost duty of good faith and fidelity to clients. (See, e.g., Greenbaum v. State Bar (1976) 15 Cal. 3d 893, 903 [126 Cal. Rptr. 785]; Alkow v. State Bar (1971) 3 Cal. 3d 924, 935 [92 Cal. Rptr. 278]; Cutler v. State Bar (1969) 71 Cal. 2d 241, 251 [78 Cal. Rptr. 172]; Clancy v. State Bar (1969) 71 Cal. 2d 140, 146 [77 Cal. Rptr. 657].) The relationship between an attorney and client is a fiduciary relationship of the very highest character and all dealings between an attorney and client that are beneficial to the attorney will be closely scrutinized with the utmost strictness for unfairness. (See, e.g., Giovanazzi v. State Bar (1980) 28 Cal. 3d 465, 472 [169 Cal. Rptr. 581]; Benson v. State Bar (1975) 13 Cal. 3d 581, 586 [119 Cal. Rptr. 297]; Lee v. State Bar (1970) 2 Cal. 3d 927, 939 [88 Cal. Rptr. 361]; Clancy v. State Bar (1969) 71 Cal. 2d 140, 146 [77 Cal. Rptr. 657].) Where attorneys exercise undue influence over clients or take unfair advantage of clients, discipline is appropriate. (See, e.g., Magee v. State Bar (1962) 58 Cal. 2d 423 [24 Cal. Rptr. 839]; Lantz v. State Bar (1931) 212 Cal. 213 [298 P. 497].) In all client matters, a member is advised to keep clients' interests paramount in the course of the member's representation.

For purposes of this rule, if the client is an organization, any individual overseeing the representation shall be deemed to be the client. (See rule 3-600.)

Although paragraph (C) excludes representation of certain clients from the scope of rule 3-120, such exclusion is not intended to preclude the applicability of other Rules of Professional Conduct, including rule 3-110.

Rule 3-200. Prohibited Objectives of Employment

A member shall not seek, accept, or continue employment if the member knows or should know that the objective of such employment is:

(A) To bring an action, conduct a defense, assert a position in litigation, or take an appeal, without probable cause and for the purpose of harassing or maliciously injuring any person; or

(B) To present a claim or defense in litigation that is not warranted under existing law, unless it can be supported by a good faith argument for an extension, modification, or reversal of such existing law.

Rule 3-210. Advising the Violation of Law

A member shall not advise the violation of any law, rule, or ruling of a tribunal unless the member believes in good faith that such law, rule, or ruling is invalid. A member may take appropriate steps in good faith to test the validity of any law, rule, or ruling of a tribunal.

DISCUSSION

Rule 3-210 is intended to apply not only to the prospective conduct of a client but also to the interaction between the member and client and to the specific legal service sought by the client from the member. An example of the former is the handling of physical evidence of a crime in the possession of the client and offered to the member. (See People v. Meredith (1981) 29 Cal. 3d 682 [175 Cal. Rptr. 612].) An example of the latter is a request that the member negotiate the return of stolen property in exchange for the owner's agreement not to report the theft to the police or prosecutorial authorities. (See People v. Pic'l (1982) 31 Cal. 3d 731 [183 Cal. Rptr. 685].)

Rule 3-300. Avoiding Interests Adverse to a Client

A member shall not enter into a business transaction with a client; or knowingly acquire an ownership, possessory, security, or other pecuniary interest adverse to a client, unless each of the following requirements has been satisfied:

(A) The transaction or acquisition and its terms are fair and reasonable to the client and are fully disclosed and transmitted in writing to the client in a manner which should reasonably have been understood by the client; and

(B) The client is advised in writing that the client may seek the advice of an independent lawyer of the client's choice and is given a reasonable opportunity to seek that advice; and

(C) The client thereafter consents in writing to the terms of the transaction or the terms of the acquisition.

DISCUSSION

Rule 3-300 is not intended to apply to the agreement by which the member is retained by the client, unless the agreement confers on the member an ownership, possessory, security, or other pecuniary interest adverse to the client. Such an agreement is governed, in part, by rule 4-200.

Rule 3-300 is not intended to apply where the member and client each make an investment on terms offered to the general public or a significant portion thereof. For example, rule 3-300 is not intended to apply where A, a member, invests in a limited partnership syndicated by a third party. B, A's client, makes the same investment. Although A and B are each investing in the same business, A did not enter into the transaction "with" B for the purposes of the rule.

Rule 3-300 is intended to apply where the member wishes to obtain an interest in client's property in order to secure the amount of the member's past due or future fees.

Rule 3-310. Avoiding the Representation of Adverse Interests

Editors' Note. On June 28, 2002, the State Bar of California forwarded to the California Supreme Court a proposed new paragraph to the Discussion after Rule 3-310. (The proposal did not recommend any changes to the text of the rule.) We reprint the proposed new Discussion paragraph, but put it in brackets to indicate that the Supreme Court had not yet adopted it when this book went to press in September of 2002. For more information about the proposal, see the Editors' Introduction at the beginning of these Rules.

(A) For purposes of this rule:

(1) "Disclosure" means informing the client or former client of the relevant circumstances and of the actual and reasonably foreseeable adverse consequences to the client or former client;

(2) "Informed written consent" means the client's or former client's written agreement to the representation following written disclosure;

(3) "Written" means any writing as defined in Evidence Code section 250.

(B) A member shall not accept or continue representation of a client without providing written disclosure to the client where:

(1) The member has a legal, business, financial, professional, or personal relationship with a party or witness in the same matter; or

(2) The member knows or reasonably should know that:

(a) the member previously had a legal, business, financial, professional, or personal relationship with a party or witness in the same matter; and

(b) the previous relationship would substantially affect the member's representation; or

(3) The member has or had a legal, business, financial, professional, or personal relationship with another person or entity the member knows or reasonably should know would be affected substantially by resolution of the matter; or

(4) The member has or had a legal, business, financial, or professional interest in the subject matter of the representation.

(C) A member shall not, without the informed written consent of each client:

(1) Accept representation of more than one client in a matter in which the interests of the clients potentially conflict; or

(2) Accept or continue representation of more than one client in a matter in which the interests of the clients actually conflict; or

(3) Represent a client in a matter and at the same time in a separate matter accept as a client a person or entity whose interest in the first matter is adverse to the client in the first matter.

(D) A member who represents two or more clients shall not enter into an aggregate settlement of the claims of or against the clients, without the informed written consent of each client.

(E) A member shall not, without the informed written consent of the client or former client, accept employment adverse to the client or former client where, by reason of the representation of the client or former client, the member has obtained confidential information material to the employment.

(F) A member shall not accept compensation for representing a client from one other than the client unless:

(1) There is no interference with the member's independence of professional judgment or with the client-lawyer relationship; and

(2) Information relating to representation of the client is protected as required by Business and Professions Code section 6068, subdivision (e); and

(3) The member obtains the client's informed written consent, provided that no disclosure or consent is required if:

(a) such nondisclosure is otherwise authorized by law; or

(b) the member is rendering legal services on behalf of any public agency which provides legal services to other public agencies or the public.

DISCUSSION

Rule 3-310 is not intended to prohibit a member from representing parties having antagonistic positions on the same legal question that has arisen in different cases, unless representation of either client would be adversely affected.

Other rules and laws may preclude making adequate disclosure under this rule. If such disclosure is precluded, informed written consent is likewise precluded. (See, e.g., Business and Professions Code section 6068, subsection (e).)

Paragraph (B) is not intended to apply to the relationship of a member to another party's lawyer. Such relationships are governed by rule 3-320.

Paragraph (B) is not intended to require either the disclosure of the new engagement to a former client or the consent of the former client to the new engagement. However, such disclosure or consent is required if paragraph (E) applies.

While paragraph (B) deals with the issues of adequate disclosure to the present client or clients of the member's present or past relationships to other parties or witnesses or present interest in the subject matter of the representation, paragraph (E) is intended to protect the confidences of another present or former client. These two paragraphs are to apply as complementary provisions.

Paragraph (B) is intended to apply only to a member's own relationships or interests, unless the member knows that a partner or associate in the same firm as the member has or had a relationship with another party or witness or has or had an interest in the subject matter of the representation.

Subparagraphs (C)(1) and (C)(2) are intended to apply to all types of legal employment, including the concurrent representation of multiple parties in litigation or in a single transaction or in some other common enterprise or legal relationship. Examples of the latter include the formation of a partnership for several partners or a corporation for several shareholders, the preparation of an ante-nuptial agreement, or joint or reciprocal wills for a husband and wife, or the resolution of an "uncontested" marital dissolution. In such situations, for the sake of convenience or economy, the parties may well prefer to employ a single counsel, but a member must disclose the potential adverse aspects of such multiple representation (e.g., Evid. Code, §962) and must obtain the informed written consent of the clients thereto pursuant to subparagraph (C)(1). Moreover, if the potential adversity should become actual, the member must obtain the further informed written consent of the clients pursuant to subparagraph (C)(2).

Subparagraph (C)(3) is intended to apply to representations of clients in both litigation and transactional matters.

[In State Farm Mutual Automobile Ins. Co. v. Federal Ins. Co. (1999), 72 Cal. App. 4th 1422, 86 Cal. Rptr. 2d 20, the court held that subparagraph (C)(3) was violated when a member, retained by an insurer to defend one suit, and while that suit was still pending, filed a direct action against the same insurer in an unrelated action without securing the insurer's consent. Notwithstanding *State Farm*, subparagraph (C)(3) is not intended to apply with respect to the relationship between an insurer and a member when in each matter the insurer's interest is only as an indemnity provider and not as a direct party to the action.]

There are some matters in which the conflicts are such that written consent may not suffice for non-disciplinary purposes. (See Woods v. Superior Court (1983) 149 Cal. App. 3d 931 [197 Cal. Rptr. 185]; Klemm v. Superior Court (1977) 75 Cal. App. 3d 893 [142 Cal. Rptr. 509]; Ishmael v. Millington (1966) 241 Cal. App. 2d 520 [50 Cal. Rptr. 592].)

Paragraph (D) is not intended to apply to class action settlements subject to court approval.

Paragraph (F) is not intended to abrogate existing relationships between insurers and insureds whereby the insurer has the contractual right to unilaterally select counsel for the insured, where there is no conflict of interest. (See San Diego Navy Federal Credit Union v. Cumis Insurance Society (1984) 162 Cal. App. 3d 358 [208 Cal. Rptr. 494].)

Rule 3-320. Relationship with Other Party's Lawyer

A member shall not represent a client in a matter in which another party's lawyer is a spouse, parent, child, or sibling of the member, lives with the member, is a client of the member, or has an intimate personal relationship with the member, unless the member informs the client in writing of the relationship.

DISCUSSION

Rule 3-320 is not intended to apply to circumstances in which a member fails to advise the client of a relationship with another lawyer who is merely a partner or associate in the same law firm as the adverse party's counsel, and who has no direct involvement in the matter.

Rule 3-400. Limiting Liability to Client

A member shall not:

(A) Contract with a client prospectively limiting the member's liability to the client for the member's professional malpractice; or

(B) Settle a claim or potential claim for the member's liability to the client for the member's professional malpractice unless the client is informed in writing that the client may seek the advice of an independent lawyer of the client's choice regarding the settlement and is given a reasonable opportunity to seek that advice.

DISCUSSION

Rule 3-400 is not intended to apply to customary qualifications and limitations in legal opinions and memoranda, nor is it intended to prevent a member from reasonably limiting the scope of the member's employment or representation.

Rule 3-500. Communication

Editors' Note. In 1997, the California Supreme Court amended Rule 3-500. The main change was to add the phrase "and copies of significant documents when necessary to keep the client so informed." The court also added the second and third paragraphs to the Discussion following the rule. The amendments capped a decade of debate about the scope of a lawyer's duty to provide documents to clients. In 1988, the California Legislature enacted Business and Professions Code §6068(n), which requires lawyers to "provide copies to the client of certain documents under time limits and as prescribed in a rule of professional conduct which the board shall adopt." Five years later, in 1993, the State Bar's Board of Governors forwarded to the California Supreme Court a proposed new Rule 3-520 that would have required lawyers to provide certain documents to clients within a specified time, but the court remanded and ultimately rejected that proposal out of fear that it would burden public coffers by requiring the state to provide free transcripts to indigent criminal defendants. As adopted in 1997, Rule 3-500 does not specify particular documents or time periods.

A member shall keep a client reasonably informed about significant developments relating to the employment or representation, including promptly complying with reasonable requests for information and copies of significant documents when necessary to keep the client so informed.

DISCUSSION

Rule 3-500 is not intended to change a member's duties to his or her clients. It is intended to make clear that, while a client must be informed of significant developments in the matter, a member will not be disciplined for failing to communicate insignificant or irrelevant information. (See Bus. & Prof. Code, §6068, subd. (m).)

A member may contract with the client in their employment agreement that the client assumes responsibility for the cost of copying significant documents. This rule is not intended to prohibit a claim for the recovery of the member's expense in any subsequent legal proceeding.

Rule 3-500 is not intended to create, augment, diminish, or eliminate any application of the work product rule. The obligation of the member to provide work product to the client shall be governed by relevant statutory and decisional law. Additionally, this rule is not intended to apply to any document or correspondence that is subject to a protective order or non-disclosure agreement, or to override applicable statutory or decisional law requiring that certain information not be provided to criminal defendants who are clients of the member.

Rule 3-510. Communication of Settlement Offer

(A) A member shall promptly communicate to the member's client:

(1) All terms and conditions of any offer made to the client in a criminal matter; and

(2) All amounts, terms, and conditions of any written offer of settlement made to the client in all other matters.

(B) As used in this rule, "client" includes a person who possesses the authority to accept an offer of settlement or plea, or, in a class action, all the named representatives of the class.

DISCUSSION

Rule 3-510 is intended to require that counsel in a criminal matter convey all offers, whether written or oral, to the client, as give and take negotiations are less common in criminal matters, and, even were they to occur, such negotiations should require the participation of the accused.

Any oral offers of settlement made to the client in a civil matter should also be communicated if they are "significant" for the purposes of rule 3-500.

Rule 3-600. Organization as Client

(A) In representing an organization, a member shall conform his or her representation to the concept that the client is the organization itself, acting through its highest authorized officer, employee, body, or constituent overseeing the particular engagement.

(B) If a member acting on behalf of an organization knows that an actual or apparent agent of the organization acts or intends or refuses to act in a manner that is or may be a violation of law reasonably imputable to the organization, or in a manner which is likely to result in substantial injury to the organization, the member shall not violate his or her duty of protecting all confidential information as provided in Business and Professions Code section 6068, subdivision (e). Subject to Business and Professions Code section 6068, subdivision (e), the member may take such actions as appear to the member to be in the best lawful interest of the organization. Such actions may include among others:

(1) Urging reconsideration of the matter while explaining its likely consequences to the organization; or

(2) Referring the matter to the next higher authority in the organization, including, if warranted by the seriousness of the matter, referral to the highest internal authority that can act on behalf of the organization.

(C) If, despite the member's actions in accordance with paragraph (B), the highest authority that can act on behalf of the organization insists upon action or a refusal to act that is a violation of law and is likely to result in substantial injury to the organization, the member's response is limited to the member's right, and, where appropriate, duty to resign in accordance with rule 3-700.

(D) In dealing with an organization's directors, officers, employees, members, shareholders, or other constituents, a member shall explain the identity of the client for whom the member acts, whenever it is or becomes apparent that the organization's interests are or may become adverse to those of the constituent(s) with whom the member is dealing. The member shall not mislead such a constituent into believing that the constituent may communicate confidential information to the member in a way that will not be used in the organization's interest if that is or becomes adverse to the constituent.

(E) A member representing an organization may also represent any of its directors, officers, employees, members, shareholders, or other constituents, subject to the provisions of rule 3-310. If the organization's consent to the dual representation is required by rule 3-310, the consent shall be given by an appropriate constituent of the organization other than the individual or constituent who is to be represented, or by the shareholder(s) or organization members.

DISCUSSION

Rule 3-600 is not intended to enmesh members in the intricacies of the entity and aggregate theories of partnership.

Rule 3-600 is not intended to prohibit members from representing both an organization and other parties connected with it, as for instance (as simply one example) in establishing employee benefit packages for closely held corporations or professional partnerships.

Rule 3-600 is not intended to create or to validate artificial distinctions between entities and their officers, employees, or members, nor is it the purpose of the rule to deny the existence or importance of such formal distinctions. In dealing with a close corporation or small association, members commonly perform professional engagements for both the organization and its major constituents. When a change in control occurs or is threatened, members are faced with complex decisions involving personal and institutional relationships and loyalties and have frequently had difficulty in perceiving their correct duty. (See People ex rel. Deukmejianv. Brown (1981) 29 Cal. 3d 150 [172 Cal. Rptr. 478]; Goldstein v. Lees (1975) 46 Cal. App. 3d 614 [120 Cal. Rptr. 253]; Woods

v. Superior Court (1983) 149 Cal. App. 3d 931 [197 Cal. Rptr. 185]; In re Banks (1978) 283 Ore. 459 [584 P.2d 284]; 1 A.L.R.4th 1105.) In resolving such multiple relationships, members must rely on case law.

Rule 3-700. Termination of Employment

(A) ***In General.***

(1) If permission for termination of employment is required by the rules of a tribunal, a member shall not withdraw from employment in a proceeding before that tribunal without its permission.

(2) A member shall not withdraw from employment until the member has taken reasonable steps to avoid reasonably foreseeable prejudice to the rights of the client, including giving due notice to the client, allowing time for employment of other counsel, complying with rule 3-700(D), and complying with applicable laws and rules.

(B) ***Mandatory Withdrawal.***

A member representing a client before a tribunal shall withdraw from employment with the permission of the tribunal, if required by its rules, and a member representing a client in other matters shall withdraw from employment, if:

(1) The member knows or should know that the client is bringing an action, conducting a defense, asserting a position in litigation, or taking an appeal, without probable cause and for the purpose of harassing or maliciously injuring any person; or

(2) The member knows or should know that continued employment will result in violation of these rules or of the State Bar Act; or

(3) The member's mental or physical condition renders it unreasonably difficult to carry out the employment effectively.

(C) ***Permissive Withdrawal.***

If rule 3-700(B) is not applicable, a member may not request permission to withdraw in matters pending before a tribunal, and may not withdraw in other matters, unless such request or such withdrawal is because:

(1) The client

(a) insists upon presenting a claim or defense that is not warranted under existing law and cannot be supported by good faith argument for an extension, modification, or reversal of existing law, or

(b) seeks to pursue an illegal course of conduct, or

(c) insists that the member pursue a course of conduct that is illegal or that is prohibited under these rules or the State Bar Act, or

(d) by other conduct renders it unreasonably difficult for the member to carry out the employment effectively, or

(e) insists, in a matter not pending before a tribunal, that the member engage in conduct that is contrary to the judgment and advice of the member but not prohibited under these rules or the State Bar Act, or

(f) breaches an agreement or obligation to the member as to expenses or fees.

(2) The continued employment is likely to result in a violation of these rules or of the State Bar Act; or

(3) The inability to work with co-counsel indicates that the best interests of the client likely will be served by withdrawal; or

(4) The member's mental or physical condition renders it difficult for the member to carry out the employment effectively; or

(5) The client knowingly and freely assents to termination of the employment; or

(6) The member believes in good faith, in a proceeding pending before a tribunal, that the tribunal will find the existence of other good cause for withdrawal.

(D) *Papers, Property, and Fees.*

A member whose employment has terminated shall:

(1) Subject to any protective order or non-disclosure agreement, promptly release to the client, at the request of the client, all the client papers and property. "Client papers and property" includes correspondence, pleadings, deposition transcripts, exhibits, physical evidence, expert's reports, and other items reasonably necessary to the client's representation, whether the client has paid for them or not; and

(2) Promptly refund any part of a fee paid in advance that has not been earned. This provision is not applicable to a true retainer fee which is paid solely for the purpose of ensuring the availability of the member for the matter.

DISCUSSION

Subparagraph (A)(2) provides that "a member shall not withdraw from employment until the member has taken reasonable steps to avoid reasonably foreseeable prejudice to the rights of the clients." What such steps would include, of course, will vary according to the circumstances. Absent special circumstances, "reasonable steps" do not include providing additional services to the client once the successor counsel has been employed and rule 3-700(D) has been satisfied.

Paragraph (D) makes clear the member's duties in the recurring situation in which new counsel seeks to obtain client files from a member discharged by the client. It codifies existing case law. (See Academy of California Optometrists v. Superior Court (1975) 51 Cal. App. 3d 999 [124 Cal. Rptr. 668]; Weiss v. Marcus (1975) 51 Cal. App. 3d 590 [124 Cal. Rptr. 297].)

Subparagraph (D)(2) requires that the member "promptly" return unearned fees paid in advance. If such fees have been placed in a trust account pursuant to rule 4-100, the member shall comply with the provisions of rule 4-100(A)(2), should the client dispute the amount to be returned. If the written fee agreement expressly provided that the fee paid in advance was nonrefundable and the engagement is not completed, the member may repay the client from the member's own funds. In any event all advances for costs and expenses must be placed in a trust account. (See Stevens v. State Bar (1990) 51 Cal. 3d 283 [272 Cal. Rptr. 167].)

Paragraph (D) is not intended to prohibit a member from making, at the member's own expense, and retaining copies of papers released to the client, nor to prohibit a claim for the recovery of the member's expense in any subsequent legal proceeding.

CHAPTER 4. FINANCIAL RELATIONSHIP WITH CLIENTS

Rule 4-100. Preserving Identity of Funds and Property of a Client

(A) All funds received or held for the benefit of clients by a member or law firm, including advances for costs and expenses, shall be deposited in one or more identifiable bank accounts labelled "Trust Account," "Client's Funds Account" or words of similar import, maintained in the State of California, or, with written consent of the client, in any other jurisdiction where there is a substantial relationship between the client or the client's business and the other jurisdiction. No funds belonging to the member or the law firm shall be deposited therein or otherwise commingled therewith except as follows:

(1) Funds reasonably sufficient to pay bank charges.

(2) In the case of funds belonging in part to a client and in part presently or potentially to the member or the law firm, the portion belonging to the member or law firm must be withdrawn at the earliest reasonable time after the member's interest in that portion becomes fixed. However, when the right of the member or law firm to receive a portion of trust funds is disputed by the client, the disputed portion shall not be withdrawn until the dispute is finally resolved.

(B) A member shall:

(1) Promptly notify a client of the receipt of the client's funds, securities, or other properties.

(2) Identify and label securities and properties of a client promptly upon receipt and place them in a safe deposit box or other place of safekeeping as soon as practicable.

(3) Maintain complete records of all funds, securities, and other properties of a client coming into the possession of the member or law firm and render appropriate accounts to the client regarding them; preserve such records for a period of no less than five years after final appropriate distribution of such funds or properties; and

comply with any order for an audit of such records issued pursuant to the Rules of Procedure of the State Bar.

(4) Promptly pay or deliver, as requested by the client, any funds, securities, or other properties in the possession of the member which the client is entitled to receive.

(C) The Board of Governors of the State Bar shall have the authority to formulate and adopt standards as to what "records" shall be maintained by members and law firms in accordance with subparagraph (B)(3). The standards formulated and adopted by the Board, as from time to time amended, shall be effective and binding on all members.

TRUST ACCOUNT RECORD KEEPING STANDARDS AS ADOPTED BY THE BOARD OF GOVERNORS

Pursuant to rule 4-100(C) the Board of Governors of the State Bar has adopted the following standards, effective January 1, 1993, as to what "records" shall be maintained by members and law firms in accordance with subparagraph (B)(3).

(1) A member shall, from the date of receipt of client funds through the period ending five years from the date of appropriate disbursement of such funds, maintain:

(a) a written ledger for each client on whose behalf funds are held that sets forth:

(i) the name of such client,

(ii) the date, amount and source of all funds received on behalf of such client,

(iii) the date, amount, payee and purpose of each disbursement made on behalf of such client, and

(iv) the current balance for such client;

(b) a written journal for each bank account that sets forth

(i) the name of such account,

(ii) the date, amount and client affected by each debit and credit, and

(iii) the current balance in such account;

(c) all bank statements and cancelled checks for each bank account; and

(d) each monthly reconciliation (balancing) of (a), (b), and (c).

(2) A member shall, from the date of receipt of all securities and other properties held for the benefit of client through the period ending five years from the date of appropriate disbursement of such securities and other properties, maintain a written journal that specifies:

(a) each item of security and property held;
(b) the person on whose behalf the security or property is held;
(c) the date of receipt of the security or property;
(d) the date of distribution of the security or property; and
(e) person to whom the security or property was distributed.

Rule 4-200. Fees for Legal Services

(A) A member shall not enter into an agreement for, charge, or collect an illegal or unconscionable fee.

(B) Unconscionability of a fee shall be determined on the basis of all the facts and circumstances existing at the time the agreement is entered into except where the parties contemplate that the fee will be affected by later events. Among the factors to be considered, where appropriate, in determining the conscionability of a fee are the following:

(1) The amount of the fee in proportion to the value of the services performed.

(2) The relative sophistication of the member and the client.

(3) The novelty and difficulty of the questions involved and the skill requisite to perform the legal service properly.

(4) The likelihood, if apparent to the client, that the acceptance of the particular employment will preclude other employment by the member.

(5) The amount involved and the results obtained.

(6) The time limitations imposed by the client or by the circumstances.

(7) The nature and length of the professional relationship with the client.

(8) The experience, reputation, and ability of the member or members performing the services.

(9) Whether the fee is fixed or contingent.

(10) The time and labor required.

(11) The informed consent of the client to the fee.

Rule 4-210. Payment of Personal or Business Expenses Incurred by or for a Client

(A) A member shall not directly or indirectly pay or agree to pay, guarantee, represent, or sanction a representation that the member or member's law firm will pay the personal or business expenses of a

prospective or existing client, except that this rule shall not prohibit a member:

(1) With the consent of the client, from paying or agreeing to pay such expenses to third persons from funds collected or to be collected for the client as a result of the representation; or

(2) After employment, from lending money to the client upon the client's promise in writing to repay such loan; or

(3) From advancing the costs of prosecuting or defending a claim or action or otherwise protecting or promoting the client's interests, the repayment of which may be contingent on the outcome of the matter. Such costs within the meaning of this subparagraph (3) shall be limited to all reasonable expenses of litigation or reasonable expenses in preparation for litigation or in providing any legal services to the client.

(B) Nothing in rule 4-210 shall be deemed to limit rules 3-300, 3-310, and 4-300.

Rule 4-300. Purchasing Property at a Foreclosure or a Sale Subject to Judicial Review

(A) A member shall not directly or indirectly purchase property at a probate, foreclosure, receiver's, trustee's, or judicial sale in an action or proceeding in which such member or any lawyer affiliated by reason of personal, business, or professional relationship with that member or with that member's law firm is acting as a lawyer for a party or as executor, receiver, trustee, administrator, guardian, or conservator.

(B) A member shall not represent the seller at a probate, foreclosure, receiver, trustee, or judicial sale in an action or proceeding in which the purchaser is a spouse or relative of the member or of another lawyer in the member's law firm or is an employee of the member or the member's law firm.

Rule 4-400. Gifts from Client

A member shall not induce a client to make a substantial gift, including a testamentary gift, to the member or to the member's parent, child, sibling, or spouse, except where the client is related to the member.

DISCUSSION

A member may accept a gift from a member's client, subject to general standards of fairness and absence of undue influence. The member who participates in the preparation of an instrument memorializing a gift which is otherwise permissible ought not to be subject to professional discipline. On the other hand, where impermissible influence occurred, discipline is appropriate. (See Magee v. State Bar (1962) 58 Cal. 2d 423 [24 Cal. Rptr. 839].)

Editors' Note. On February 23, 1995, the California Supreme Court rejected a proposed amendment to Rule 4-400. The amendment would have prohibited a lawyer from inducing a client to make "any" gift to the lawyer or the lawyer's relatives, not just a "substantial" gift as in the present version of Rule 4-400. The amended rule would also have prohibited a lawyer from preparing an instrument providing for "any" gift to the lawyer or the lawyer's relatives, except where the client is related to the lawyer or transferee. In its order rejecting the proposed amendment, the Court said the amendment appeared to conflict with §§21350 and 21351 of the California Probate Code.

CHAPTER 5. ADVOCACY AND REPRESENTATION

Rule 5-100. Threatening Criminal, Administrative, or Disciplinary Charges

(A) A member shall not threaten to present criminal, administrative, or disciplinary charges to obtain an advantage in a civil dispute.

(B) As used in paragraph (A) of this rule, the term "administrative charges" means the filing or lodging of a complaint with a federal, state, or local governmental entity which may order or recommend the loss or suspension of a license, or may impose or recommend the imposition of a fine, pecuniary sanction, or other sanction of a quasi-criminal nature but does not include filing charges with an administrative entity required by law as a condition precedent to maintaining a civil action.

(C) As used in paragraph (A) of this rule, the term "civil dispute" means a controversy or potential controversy over the rights and duties of two or more parties under civil law, whether or not an action has been commenced, and includes an administrative proceeding of a quasi-civil nature pending before a federal, state, or local governmental entity.

DISCUSSION

Rule 5-100 is not intended to apply to a member's threatening to initiate contempt proceedings against a party for a failure to comply with a court order.

Paragraph (B) is intended to exempt the threat of filing an administrative charge which is a prerequisite to filing a civil complaint on the same transaction or occurrence.

For purposes of paragraph (C), the definition of "civil dispute" makes clear that the rule is applicable prior to the formal filing of a civil action.

Rule 5-110. Performing the Duty of Member in Government Service

A member in government service shall not institute or cause to be instituted criminal charges when the member knows or should know that the charges are not supported by probable cause. If, after the institution of criminal charges, the member in government service having responsibility for prosecuting the charges becomes aware that those charges are not supported by probable cause, the member shall promptly so advise the court in which the criminal matter is pending.

Rule 5-120. Trial Publicity

Editors' Note. On September 14, 1995, the California Supreme Court approved a new Rule 5-120, which took effect on October 1, 1995. Up to that point, California was the only state in the country without a rule restricting extrajudicial statements by lawyers. The history of the rule is unique. The public statements by lawyers involved in the O. J. Simpson murder case, which began with Simpson's arrest in June 1994, spurred the California legislature to pass a statute commanding the State Bar to submit to the Supreme Court, no later than March 1, 1995, "a rule of professional conduct governing trial publicity and extrajudicial statements made by attorneys concerning adjudicative proceedings." Governor Wilson signed this law on September 26, 1994, the first day of jury selection in the Simpson trial. (The full text of the statute, §6103.7 of the California Business and Professions Code, is reprinted in our California statutory materials.)

The State Bar dutifully drafted and submitted a proposal to the Court in February 1995 but, in an unusual move, did so "without recommendation." The proposal largely tracked ABA Model Rule 3.6 as amended in August 1994, but — unlike the ABA rule — would have applied only to jury trials and would have applied only to extrajudicial statements that posed a "clear and present danger" to trial proceedings. On March 29, 1995, the Court wrote to the State Bar suggesting that the Bar either propose a trial publicity rule that it recommended "or particularly explain the reasons why it does not recommend approval of the rule already submitted." On June 1, 1995, the State Bar President, Donald Fischbach, sent the Court a detailed five-page letter saying the State Bar opposed the proposed rule because: (1) there is no evidence that out-of-court remarks by attorneys have prejudiced anyone's right to a fair trial; (2) judges already have remedies such as gag orders to control out-of-court publicity; (3) the proposed rule would be ineffective because it would not apply to non-lawyers; (4) any trial publicity rule would be extremely difficult to enforce; (5) a trial publicity rule could "become a sword used by litigants seeking strategic advantage over one another"; and (6) the rule would "impair attorneys' duty to represent their clients zealously."

On September 14, 1995, the Supreme Court nevertheless adopted a trial publicity rule, but it tracks ABA Model Rule 3.6 rather than the State Bar proposal. The only significant differences between the ABA Rule and the new California rule are that California has dropped Rule 3.6(d), which provides that "[n]o lawyer associated in a firm or government agency with a lawyer subject to paragraph (a) shall make a statement prohibited by paragraph (a)," and the official Discussion following the California rule bears no resemblance to the Comment following Model Rule 3.6.

(A) A member who is participating or has participated in the investigation or litigation of a matter shall not make an extrajudicial statement that a reasonable person would expect to be disseminated by means of public communication if the member knows or reasonably should know that it will have a substantial likelihood of materially prejudicing an adjudicative proceeding in the matter.

(B) Notwithstanding paragraph (A), a member may state:

(1) the claim, offense or defense involved and, except when prohibited by law, the identity of the persons involved;

(2) the information contained in a public record;

(3) that an investigation of the matter is in progress;

(4) the scheduling or result of any step in litigation;

(5) a request for assistance in obtaining evidence and information necessary thereto;

(6) a warning of danger concerning the behavior of a person involved, when there is reason to believe that there exists the likelihood of substantial harm to an individual or to the public interest; and

(7) in a criminal case, in addition to subparagraphs (1) through (6):

(a) the identity, residence, occupation, and family status of the accused;

(b) if the accused has not been apprehended, information necessary to aid in apprehension of that person;

(c) the fact, time, and place of arrest; and

(d) the identity of investigating and arresting officers or agencies and the length of the investigation.

(C) Notwithstanding paragraph (A), a member may make a statement that a reasonable member would believe is required to protect a client from the substantial undue prejudicial effect of recent publicity not initiated by the member or the member's client. A statement made pursuant to this paragraph shall be limited to such information as is necessary to mitigate the recent adverse publicity.

DISCUSSION

Rule 5-120 is intended to apply equally to prosecutors and criminal defense counsel. Whether an extrajudicial statement violates rule 5-120 depends on many factors, including:

(1) whether the extrajudicial statement presents information clearly inadmissible as evidence in the matter for the purpose of proving or disproving a material fact in issue;

(2) whether the extrajudicial statement presents information the member knows is false, deceptive, or the use of which would violate Business and Professions Code section 6068(d);

(3) whether the extrajudicial statement violates a lawful "gag" order, or protective order, statute, rule of court, or special rule of confidentiality (for example, in juvenile, domestic, mental disability, and certain criminal proceedings); and

(4) the timing of the statement.

Paragraph (A) is intended to apply to statements made by or on behalf of the member. Subparagraph (B)(6) is not intended to create, augment, diminish, or eliminate any application of the lawyer-client privilege or of Business and Professions Code section 6068(e) regarding the member's duty to maintain client confidence and secrets.

Rule 5-200. Trial Conduct

In presenting a matter to a tribunal, a member:

(A) Shall employ, for the purpose of maintaining the causes confided to the member such means only as are consistent with truth;

(B) Shall not seek to mislead the judge, judicial officer, or jury by an artifice or false statement of fact or law;

(C) Shall not intentionally misquote to a tribunal the language of a book, statute, or decision;

(D) Shall not, knowing its invalidity, cite as authority a decision that has been overruled or a statute that has been repealed or declared unconstitutional; and

(E) Shall not assert personal knowledge of the facts at issue, except when testifying as a witness.

Rule 5-210. Member as Witness

A member shall not act as an advocate before a jury which will hear testimony from the member unless:

(A) The testimony relates to an uncontested matter; or

(B) The testimony relates to the nature and value of legal services rendered in the case; or

(C) The member has the informed, written consent of the client. If the member represents the People or a governmental entity, the consent shall be obtained from the head of the office or a designee of the head of the office by which the member is employed and shall be consistent with principles of recusal.

DISCUSSION

Rule 5-210 is intended to apply to situations in which the member knows or should know that he or she ought to be called as a witness in litigation in which there is a jury. This rule is not intended to encompass situations in which the member is representing the client in an adversarial proceeding and is testifying before a judge. In non-adversarial proceedings, as where the member testifies on behalf of the client in a hearing before a legislative body, rule 5-210 is not applicable.

Rule 5-210 is not intended to apply to circumstances in which a lawyer in an advocate's firm will be a witness.

Rule 5-220. Suppression of Evidence

A member shall not suppress any evidence that the member or the member's client has a legal obligation to reveal or to produce.

Rule 5-300. Contact with Officials

(A) A member shall not directly or indirectly give or lend anything of value to a judge, official, or employee of a tribunal unless the personal or family relationship between the member and the judge, official, or employee is such that gifts are customarily given and exchanged. Nothing contained in this rule shall prohibit a member from contributing to the campaign fund of a judge running for election or confirmation pursuant to applicable law pertaining to such contributions.

(B) A member shall not directly or indirectly communicate with or argue to a judge or judicial officer upon the merits of a contested matter pending before such judge or judicial officer, except:

(1) In open court; or

(2) With the consent of all other counsel in such matter; or

(3) In the presence of all other counsel in such matter; or

(4) In writing with a copy thereof furnished to such other counsel; or

(5) In ex parte matters.

(C) As used in this rule, "judge" and "judicial officer" shall include law clerks, research attorneys, or other court personnel who participate in the decision-making process.

Rule 5-310. Prohibited Contact with Witnesses

A member shall not:

(A) Advise or directly or indirectly cause a person to secrete himself or herself or to leave the jurisdiction of a tribunal for the purpose of making that person unavailable as a witness therein.

(B) Directly or indirectly pay, offer to pay, or acquiesce in the payment of compensation to a witness contingent upon the content of the witness's testimony or the outcome of the case. Except where prohibited by law, a member may advance, guarantee, or acquiesce in the payment of:

(1) Expenses reasonably incurred by a witness in attending or testifying.

(2) Reasonable compensation to a witness for loss of time in attending or testifying.

(3) A reasonable fee for the professional services of an expert witness.

Rule 5-320. Contact with Jurors

(A) A member connected with a case shall not communicate directly or indirectly with anyone the member knows to be a member of the venire from which the jury will be selected for trial of that case.

(B) During trial a member connected with the case shall not communicate directly or indirectly with any juror.

(C) During trial a member who is not connected with the case shall not communicate directly or indirectly concerning the case with anyone the member knows is a juror in the case.

(D) After discharge of the jury from further consideration of a case a member shall not ask questions of or make comments to a member of that jury that are intended to harass or embarrass the juror or to influence the juror's actions in future jury service.

(E) A member shall not directly or indirectly conduct an out of court investigation of a person who is either a member or the venire or a juror in a manner likely to influence the state of mind of such person in connection with present or future jury service.

(F) All restrictions imposed by this rule also apply to communications with, or investigations of, members of the family of a person who is either a member of the venire or a juror.

(G) A member shall reveal promptly to the court improper conduct by a person who is either a member of a venire or a juror, or by another toward a person who is either a member of a venire or a juror or a member of his or her family, of which the member has knowledge.

(H) This rule does not prohibit a member from communicating with persons who are members of a venire or jurors as a part of the official proceedings.

(I) For purposes of this rule, "juror" means any empaneled, discharged, or excused juror.

Selected California Statutes

Editors' Introduction. Perhaps more than any other state, California governs the conduct of lawyers by statute. California's provision on confidentiality, for example, is found in Business and Professions Code §6068, which lists the duties of an attorney. In addition, California addresses by statute the issue of conflict of interest when an insurance company provides a lawyer for the defense of an insured. The Business and Professions Code also contains provisions governing fee agreements, settlement offers, attorney discipline, and many other matters.

We have included here the statutory materials that parallel issues usually covered in law school courses on professional responsibility. We have omitted statutes on such things as state bar administration, state bar committees, and bar dues. We have also omitted lengthy procedural rules concerning bar admission and discipline. What remains is a representative collection of the major statutes governing California lawyers.

Since the last edition of this book went to press in September 2001, the California Legislature has considered many bills relating to lawyers. Some bills were passed and signed into law by Governor Gray Davis. One bill was passed but Governor Davis vetoed it. Other bills were defeated, stalled in committee, or deferred for another year. Here is a summary of what happened during the 2001-2002 legislative session:

Bills signed into law:

- *AB 830 (Cohn),* titled "Senior Legal Services," instructs the California Department of Aging to establish a task force to study and recommend innovative measures to improve the delivery of legal services to California's senior citizens, including statewide hotlines for senior legal services. Signed October 10, 2001; codified at §9320 of the Welfare and Institutions Code; operative on January 1, 2002. (Not reprinted in this volume.)
- *AB 913 (Steinberg),* titled "Attorneys: Pro Bono Services," requires a contract with the state for legal services exceeding $50,000 to certify that the contracting law firm agrees to make a good faith effort to provide thirty (30) hours of pro bono legal services during each year of the contract. ("Pro bono" is defined in the bill.) Failure

to make a good faith effort, as determined by considering specified factors, could constitute cause for nonrenewal of a contract and could be taken into account when awarding future contracts. The pro bono requirements do not apply to certain specified contracts. Signed October 14, 2001; effective January 1, 2003; codified at §6072 of the Business and Professions Code (reprinted below).

- *AB 935 (Hertzberg),* titled "Public Interest Attorney Loan Repayment Program," establishes a Public Interest Attorney Loan Repayment Program for licensed attorneys who practice or agree to practice in public interest areas of the law and who meet other designated criteria. The program would be administered by the Student Aid Commission, which could make up to 3,000 awards of loan assumption annually. The bill also creates the Public Interest Attorney Loan Repayment Endowment Account in the state treasury, which will consist both of funds appropriated by the Legislature and private contributions to the program. Signed October 14, 2001; effective January 1, 2002; codified at §69740 of the California Education Code. (Not reprinted in this volume.)
- *AB 1083 (Bates),* titled "Paralegals," amends existing statutes defining the term "paralegal" and restricting the activities that a paralegal may lawfully perform if the person is not employed by a lawyer or law firm and working under the direction and supervision of a member of the State Bar. The amendments specifically exempt qualified legal services programs from certain restrictions contained in the predecessor legislation, which took effect in 2000. Signed September 19, 2001; effective January 1, 2002; codified at Business and Professions Code §§6450 and 6451 (reprinted below).
- *SB 1194 (Romero),* titled "Legal Services: Attorneys and Immigration Consultants," a measure sponsored by the California Attorney General, will allow victims of the unauthorized practice of law to recover damages and equitable relief in an enforcement action brought in the name of the people of the State of California by the Attorney General, by a district attorney, or by a city attorney acting as a public prosecutor. Signed September 19, 2001; effective January 1, 2002; codified at Business and Professions Code §6126.5 (reprinted below).
- *SB 1459 (Romero),* titled "Practice of Law," amends §6126 of the Business and Professions Code by increasing the penalties for laypeople and for suspended, disbarred, or involuntarily inactive lawyers who engage in the unauthorized practice law. Signed September 19, 2002; effective January 1, 2003. (We reprint the amendments below.)

Bills vetoed by the Governor:

- *AB 363 (Steinberg):* On August 28, 2002, the California Legislature enacted a new §6068.1 of the Business and Professions Code to guide and protect governmental attorneys who want to disclose client wrongdoing. The bill gained support in the legislature after the California Supreme Court earlier in 2002 refused to adopt a new

Rule of Professional Conduct to cover the same situation. (We discuss the rejected proposal for a new Rule 3-600 at length in our Editors' Introduction to the California Rules of Professional Conduct above.) The bill would have authorized an attorney who learned of improper government activity in the course of representing a governmental organization to urge reconsideration of the matter and to refer it to a higher authority within the governmental organization. In specified circumstances, the bill would also have authorized the attorney to refer the matter to law enforcement agents or to another governmental agency, and would have exempted the attorney from disciplinary action for making such a referral. On September 30, 2002, however, Govenor Davis vetoed the bill. We reprint the full text of the bill and some explanatory materials below following §6068.

- *AB 698 (Wesson),* titled "Attorney General: Office of Immigrant Assistance." This bill would have created the Office of Immigrant Assistance in the office of the attorney general to provide education and outreach services to California's resident immigrant community. The bill would also have required that information developed for education and outreach purposes be printed or broadcast in any language deemed necessary to reach immigrant communities. Governor Davis's veto message said these things had already been done.

Bills defeated or never pursued: A number of bills were defeated or never pursued. *AB 752 (Briggs)* would have required advertisements by lawyers seeking to provide legal services relating to home construction defects to disclose specified information, including expenses charged to a client, legal obligations imposed on homeowners upon a finding that their home has or may have a construction defect, and potential financial impacts that may result if a homeowner does not rectify a discovered home construction defect in his or her home. A violation of these provisions would have been cause for discipline by the State Bar. *AB 1504 (Robert Pacheco)* would have required all contingency fee agreements for legal services to include, in writing, the actual hourly rate the contracting attorney charges for his or her services. *SB 139 (Haynes)* would have repealed the current IOLTA law requiring interest on attorney trust accounts for unsegregated client funds to be paid to the State Bar for distribution to legal services programs, and would instead have required attorneys to pay this interest to clients on a *pro rata* basis.

Bills stalled in the Legislature: At least two important bills never reached a vote. *AB 36 (Steinberg)* would limit the use of secrecy agreements and protective orders in defective products and environmental hazard cases in order to allow the public to learn about potentially deadly harms. A similar bill, *SB 11 (Escutia),* would generally prohibit secret settlements in a broad range of cases, including actions based upon defective products, unlawful energy price manipulation, unfair insurance claims practices, or environmental hazards, and would make void and unenforceable any provision in a settlement agreement that restricts the ability of a party to disclose information that is evidence of one of the specified public hazards to a government agency with enforcement authority over that public hazard unless the information is a trade secret or is otherwise privileged under the law.

Bills pending on our press date: The most significant law practice bill pending when this book went to press was *AB 982 (Firebaugh),* which would encourage the State Bar to develop accreditation standards for online law schools and to study California's so-called Baby Bar (a bar exam required after a student's first year at a non-accredited law school) to determine whether certain students should be exempted from the exam based on education, experience, or test scores. The author agreed to place the bill on hold after the Committee of Bar Examiners initiated a review of current accreditation standards and their applicability to online legal education.

For detailed updates and additional information regarding California legislative activities, visit the California State Bar's web site at www.calbar.ca.gov (click on the right-hand menu on "Legislative News").

Contents

CALIFORNIA BUSINESS AND PROFESSIONS CODE

CHAPTER 4. ATTORNEYS

Article 1. General Provisions
- §6000. Short Title

Article 4. Admission to the State Bar
- §6067. Oath
- §6068. Duties of Attorney
- §6068.1. [Untitled] [vetoed by Governor]

Article 5. Disciplinary Authority of the Board of Governors
- §6079.4. Exercise by Attorney of Constitutional or Statutory Privileges Not Deemed Failure to Cooperate
- §6086.7. Court Actions, Judgments and Sanctions Against Attorneys; Notification to State Bar
- §6086.8. Judgments for Actions Committed in a Professional Capacity; Claims or Actions for Damages; Reports to State Bar

Article 5.5. Miscellaneous Disciplinary Provisions
- §6090.5. Settlements: Prohibited Agreements
- §6091. Trust Funds; Investigation and Audit of Complaint Alleging Mishandling; Statement of Attorney at Client's Request
- §6094. Privileged Communications; Immunity

Article 6. Disciplinary Authority of the Courts
- §6103.5. Written Offers of Settlement; Required Communication to Client; Discovery
- §6103.7. [Trial Publicity and Extrajudicial Statements]
- §6106. Moral Turpitude, Dishonesty or Corruption Irrespective of Criminal Conviction
- §6106.1. Advocacy of Overthrow of Government
- §6106.5. Insurance Claims; Fraud
- §6106.8. Sexual Involvement Between Lawyers and Clients; Rule of Professional Conduct

§6106.9. Sexual Relations Between Attorney and Client; Cause for Discipline; Complaints to State Bar
Article 7. Unlawful Practice of Law
§6125. Necessity of Active Membership in State Bar
§6126. [Unauthorized Practice, Advertising or Holding Out; Penalties]
§6126.5. [Increased Penalties for Unauthorized Practice of Law]
§6128. Deceit, Collusion, Delay of Suit and Improper Receipt of Money as Misdemeanor
§6133. Resigned, Suspended or Disbarred Attorneys; Supervision of Activities by Firms
Article 8.5. Fee Agreements
§6146. Limitations; Periodic Payments
§6147. Contingency Fee Contracts; Duplicate Copy; Contents; Effect of Noncompliance; Recovery of Workers' Compensation Benefits
§6147.5. Contingency Fee Contracts; Recovery of Claims Between Merchants
§6148. Contracts for Services in Cases Not Coming Within §6147; Bills Rendered by Attorney; Contents; Failure to Comply
§6149. Written Fee Contract as Confidential Communication
§6149.5. Third-Party Liability Claim; Settlement by Insurer; Notice to Claimant; Effect on Action or Defense
Article 9. Unlawful Solicitation
§6151. Definitions
§6152. Prohibition of Solicitation
Article 9.5. Legal Advertising
§6157. Definitions
§6157.1. False, Misleading or Deceptive Statements; Prohibition
§6157.2. Prohibited Statements Regarding Outcome; Dramatizations; Contingent Fee Basis Representations
§6157.3. Advertisements Made on Behalf of Member; Required Representations
§6157.4. Lawyer Referral Service Advertising
§6158. Electronic Media Advertising; False, Misleading or Deceptive Message; Factual Substantiation
§6158.1. False, Misleading or Deceptive Messages; Rebuttable Presumption
§6158.3. Electronic Media Advertising; Required Disclosures
Article 10.5. Provision of Financial Services by Lawyers
§6175. Definitions
§6175.3. Selling Financial Products to Clients — Disclosure Requirements
§6175.4. Remedies for Damages
§6175.5. Violation — Cause for Discipline
§6175.6. Court Reporting Requirements for Violations
§6177. State Bar Report to the Legislature — Complaints Filed; Disciplinary Action Taken

CHAPTER 5.5. LEGAL DOCUMENT ASSISTANTS AND UNLAWFUL DETAINER ASSISTANTS

§6400. Definitions
§6401.6. Legal Document Assistant; Limitation on Service; Services of Attorney
§6402. Registration Requirement; Registration of Disbarred and Suspended Lawyers Prohibited
§6402.1. Registration Eligibility
§6411. Unlawful Acts

CHAPTER 5.6. PARALEGALS

§6450. [Paralegals]
§6451. [Restrictions on Paralegal Activities]

CALIFORNIA CIVIL CODE

§51.9. Sexual Harassment; Business, Service and Professional Relationships
§1714.10. Attorney-Client Civil Conspiracy; Proof and Pre-Pleading Court Determination; Defense; Limitations; Appeal
§2860. Conflict of Interest; Duty to Provide Independent Counsel; Waiver; Qualifications of Independent Counsel; Fees; Disclosure of Information

CALIFORNIA CIVIL PROCEDURE CODE

§128.5. Frivolous Actions or Delaying Tactics, Award of Expenses, Including Attorney's Fees on Motion
§128.6. Bad Faith Actions or Tactics, Award of Expenses, Including Attorney's Fees on Motion
§177.5. Judicial Officers, Sanctions
§206. Criminal Actions — Discussions with Jury After Discharge
§283. Authority to Bind Client
§284. Substitution, Consent or Order
§285. Notice to Adversary
§285.1. Withdrawal in Domestic Relations Matters
§285.2. Withdrawal When Public Funding Reduced
§286. Death or Disability, Appearance
§340.6. Attorneys; Wrongful Professional Act or Omission; Tolling Period
§907. Appeal Frivolous or Taken Solely for Delay
§1209. Acts and Omissions Constituting Contempt
§1282.4. Representation by Counsel

CALIFORNIA FAMILY CODE

§8800. Unethical for Attorney to Represent Both Prospective Adopting Parents and Natural Parents — Conflict of Interest

CALIFORNIA INSURANCE CODE

§750. Unlawful to Receive Consideration for Referral of Clients

§750.5. Permissible Acts for Attorneys and Law Firms under Section 750
§1871.7. Unlawful Solicitation of Business
§1872.83. Reporting Incidents of Fraud to Appropriate Disciplinary Body
§1872.95. Medical & Chiropractic Boards and State Bar; Investigation of Motor Vehicle or Disability Insurance Fraud by Licensees

CALIFORNIA PENAL CODE

§118. Perjury Defined; Proof
§118a. False Affidavit as to Perjurious Testimony; Subsequent Testimony
§126. Punishment
§127. Subornation of Perjury — Definition, Punishment
§132. Offering False Evidence
§133. Deceiving a Witness
§134. Preparing False Evidence
§135. Destroying or Concealing Documentary Evidence
§3215. Referral of Clients or Patients for Compensation; Penalty

CALIFORNIA PROBATE CODE

§710. Preservation of Documents Transferred to Attorney
§713. No Duty as to Content of Document; Provision of Legal Services Arising from Document Retention

CALIFORNIA BUSINESS AND PROFESSIONS CODE

CHAPTER 4. ATTORNEYS

ARTICLE 1. GENERAL PROVISIONS

§6000. Short Title

This chapter of the Business and Professions Code constitutes the chapter on attorneys. It may be cited as the State Bar Act.

ARTICLE 4. ADMISSION TO THE STATE BAR

§6067. Oath

Every person on his admission shall take an oath to support the Constitution of the United States and the Constitution of the State of California, and faithfully to discharge the duties of any attorney at law to the best of his knowledge and ability. A certificate of the oath shall be indorsed upon his license.

§6068. Duties of Attorney

It is the duty of an attorney to do all of the following:

(a) To support the Constitution and laws of the United States and of this state.

(b) To maintain the respect due to the courts of justice and judicial officers.

(c) To counsel or maintain such actions, proceedings, or defenses only as appear to him or her legal or just, except the defense of a person charged with a public offense.

(d) To employ, for the purpose of maintaining the causes confided to him or her such means only as are consistent with truth, and never to seek to mislead the judge or any judicial officer by an artifice or false statement of fact or law.

(e) To maintain inviolate the confidence, and at every peril to himself or herself to preserve the secrets, of his or her client.

(f) To abstain from all offensive personality, and to advance no fact prejudicial to the honor or reputation of a party or witness, unless required by the justice of the cause with which he or she is charged.

(g) Not to encourage either the commencement or the continuance of an action or proceeding from any corrupt motive of passion or interest.

(h) Never to reject, for any consideration personal to himself or herself, the cause of the defenseless or the oppressed.

(i) To cooperate and participate in any disciplinary investigation or other regulatory or disciplinary proceeding pending against the attorney. However, this subdivision shall not be construed to deprive an attorney of any privilege guaranteed by the Fifth Amendment to the Constitution of the United States or any other constitutional or statutory privileges.

(j) To comply with the requirements of Section 6002.1.

(k) To comply with all conditions attached to any disciplinary probation, including a probation imposed with the concurrence of the attorney.

(l) To keep all agreements made in lieu of disciplinary prosecution with the agency charged with attorney discipline.

(m) To respond promptly to reasonable status inquiries of clients and to keep clients reasonably informed of significant developments in matters with regard to which the attorney has agreed to provide legal services.

(n) To provide copies to the client of certain documents under time limits and as prescribed in a rule of professional conduct which the board shall adopt.

(o) To report to the agency charged with attorney discipline, in writing, within 30 days of the time the attorney has knowledge of any of the following:

(1) The filing of three or more lawsuits in a 12-month period against the attorney for malpractice or other wrongful conduct committed in a professional capacity.

(2) The entry of judgment against the attorney in any civil action for fraud, misrepresentation, breach of fiduciary duty, or gross negligence committed in a professional capacity.

(3) The imposition of any judicial sanctions against the attorney, except for sanctions for failure to make discovery or monetary sanctions of less than one thousand dollars ($1,000).

(4) The bringing of an indictment or information charging a felony against the attorney.

(5) The conviction of the attorney, including any verdict of guilty, or plea of guilty or no contest, of any felony, or any misdemeanor committed in the course of the practice of law, or in any manner such that a client of the attorney was the victim, or a necessary element of which, as determined by the statutory or common law definition of the misdemeanor, involves improper conduct of an attorney, including dishonesty or other moral turpitude, or an attempt or a conspiracy or solicitation of another to commit a felony or any such misdemeanor.

(6) The imposition of discipline against the attorney by any professional or occupational disciplinary agency or licensing board, whether in California or elsewhere.

(7) Reversal of judgment in a proceeding based in whole or in part upon misconduct, grossly incompetent representation, or willful misrepresentation by an attorney.

(8) As used in this subdivision, "against the attorney" includes claims and proceedings against any firm of attorneys for the practice of law in which the attorney was a partner at the time of the conduct complained of and any law corporation in which the attorney was a shareholder at the time of the conduct complained of unless the matter has to the attorney's knowledge already been reported by the law firm or corporation.

(9) The State Bar may develop a prescribed form for the making of reports required by this section, usage of which it may require by rule or regulation.

(10) This subdivision is only intended to provide that the failure to report as required herein may serve as a basis of discipline.

Editors' Note. On August 28, 2002, the California Legislature enacted a new §6068.1 of the Business and Professions Code. On September 30, 2002, Governor Davis vetoed the bill. The Legislature's explanation of the bill provided as follows:

> (a) The Legislature hereby finds and declares the following:
>
> (1) The California Rules of Professional Conduct appropriately underscore the importance in our justice system of protecting attorney-client

confidential information. However, in the representation of governmental organizations, circumstances may arise where the interests of the public may justify an attorney reporting client information that is otherwise confidential. . . .

(2) Current law and the California Rules of Professional Conduct do not provide adequate guidance and clarity for attorneys representing governmental organizations to determine the circumstances under which they may properly seek to protect the public interest by reporting improper governmental activity to appropriate enforcement, regulatory, and oversight bodies.

(3) Generally, the governmental organization itself is the client of the attorney and not any official or entity within the organization, notwithstanding the ability of the official or entity to exercise exclusive power over any given subject on behalf of the organization.

(b) The California Supreme Court did not approve amendments to the California Rules of Professional Conduct proposed by the State Bar, stating that the proposed modifications conflict with subdivision (e) of Section 6068 of the Business and Professions Code. Accordingly, the Legislature hereby finds and declares that statutory changes are necessary to address this issue.

In his veto message, Governor Davis stated, in part:

> While this bill is well intended, it chips away at the attorney-client relationship which is intended to foster candor between an attorney and client. It is critical that clients know they can disclose in confidence so they can receive appropriate advice from counsel.

The effective operation of our legal system depends on the fundamental duty of confidentiality owed by lawyers to their clients.

§6068.1. [Untitled] [vetoed by Governor]

(a) If in the course of representing a governmental organization, an attorney learns of improper governmental activity, the attorney may take one or both of the following actions:

(1) Urge reconsideration of the matter while explaining its likely consequences to the organization.

(2) Refer the matter to a higher authority in the organization, including, if warranted by the seriousness of the matter, referral to the highest internal authority that can act on behalf of the organizaiton.

(b) Notwithstanding subdivision (e) of Section 6068, if the attorney has taken both actions as described in paragraphs (1) and (2) of subdivision (a) without the matter being resolved, or if the attorney reasonably believes that the highest internal authority that can act on behalf of the organization has directly or indirectly participated in the improper governmental activity, or if the attorney reasonably believes that taking the actions described in subdivision (a) are futile, the attorney may refer the matter to the law enforcement agency charged with responsibility over the matter or to any other governmental agency or official charged with overseeing or regulating the matter if all of the following exist:

(1) The referral is warranted by the seriousness of the circumstances and is not otherwise prohibited by law.

(2) The improper governmental activity constitutes the use of the organization's official authority or influence to commit a crime or to perpetrate fraud.

(3) Further action is required in order to prevent or rectify substantial harm to the public interest or to the governmental organization resulting from the improper governmental activity.

(c) An attorney's conduct in making a referral under subdivision (b) shall not be a cause for disbarment, suspension, or other discipline if the attorney has acted reasonably and in good faith to determine the propriety of making a referral and to identify the appropriate governmental agency or official as described in subdivision (b) and to cooperate with the agency or official in the execution of the oversight or regulatory responsibilities of the agency or official regarding the referral. However, once an attorney has made the referral, this subdivision shall not apply to any further affirmative conduct outside of the scope of subdivision (b) or this subdivision that is initiated by the attorney to address the improper governmental activity.

(d) An attorney may, but has no affirmative duty to, take action pursuant to this section.

(e) As used in this section, "improper governmental activity" means conduct by the governmental organization or by its agent that comes within one or more of the following:

(1) Constitutes the use of the organization's official authority or influence by the agent to commit a crime, fraud, or other serious and willful violation of law.

(2) Involves the agent's willful misuse of public funds, willful breach of fiduciary duty, or willful or corrupt misconduct in office.

(3) Involves the agent's willful omission to perform his or her official duty.

(f) This section shall not be construed to require that the improper governmental activity subject to its provisions be related, directly or indirectly, to the matter for which the attorney was engaged as outside counsel by the governmental organization.

ARTICLE 5. DISCIPLINARY AUTHORITY OF THE BOARD OF GOVERNORS

§6079.4. Exercise by Attorney of Constitutional or Statutory Privileges Not Deemed Failure to Cooperate

The exercise by an attorney of his or her privilege under the Fifth Amendment to the Constitution of the United States, or of any other

constitutional or statutory privileges shall not be deemed a failure to cooperate within the meaning of subdivision (i) of Section 6068.

§6086.7. Court Actions, Judgments and Sanctions Against Attorneys; Notification to State Bar

A court shall notify the State Bar of any of the following:

(a) A final order of contempt imposed against an attorney that may involve grounds warranting discipline under this chapter. The court entering the final order shall transmit to the State Bar a copy of the relevant minutes, final order, and transcript, if one exists.

(b) Whenever a modification or reversal of a judgment in a judicial proceeding is based in whole or in part on the misconduct, incompetent representation, or willful misrepresentation of an attorney.

(c) The imposition of any judicial sanctions against an attorney, except sanctions for failure to make discovery or monetary sanctions of less than one thousand dollars ($1,000).

In the event of a notification made under subdivision (a), (b), or (c), the court shall also notify the attorney involved that the matter has been referred to the State Bar.

The State Bar shall investigate any matter reported under this section as to the appropriateness of initiating disciplinary action against the attorney.

§6086.8. Judgments for Actions Committed in a Professional Capacity; Claims or Actions for Damages; Reports to State Bar

(a) Within 20 days after a judgment by a court of this state that a member of the State Bar of California is liable for any damages resulting in a judgment against the attorney in any civil action for fraud, misrepresentation, breach of fiduciary duty, or gross negligence committed in a professional capacity, the court which rendered the judgment shall report that fact in writing to the State Bar of California.

(b) Every claim or action of damages against a member of the State Bar of California for fraud, misrepresentation, breach of fiduciary duty, or negligence committed in a professional capacity shall be reported to the State Bar of California within 30 days of receipt by the admitted insurer or licensed surplus brokers providing professional liability insurance to that member of the State Bar.

(c) An attorney who does not possess professional liability insurance shall send a complete written report to the State Bar as to any settlement, judgment, or arbitration award described in subdivision (b), in the manner specified in that subdivision.

ARTICLE 5.5. MISCELLANEOUS DISCIPLINARY PROVISIONS

§6090.5. Settlements; Prohibited Agreements

(a) It is a cause for suspension, disbarment, or other discipline for any member whether as a party or as an attorney for a party, to agree or seek agreement, that

(1) The professional misconduct or the terms of a settlement of a claim for professional misconduct shall not be reported to the disciplinary agency.

(2) The plaintiff shall withdraw a disciplinary complaint or shall not cooperate with the investigation or prosecution conducted by the disciplinary agency.

(3) The record of any civil action for professional misconduct shall be sealed from review by the disciplinary agency.

(b) This section applies to all settlements, whether made before or after the commencement of a civil action.

§6091. Trust Funds; Investigation and Audit of Complaint Alleging Mishandling; Statement of Attorney at Client's Request

If a client files a complaint with the State Bar alleging that his or her trust fund is being mishandled, the State Bar shall investigate and may require an audit if it determines that circumstances warrant. . . .

§6094. Privileged Communications; Immunity

(a) Communications to the disciplinary agency relating to lawyer misconduct or disability or competence, or any communication related to an investigation or proceeding and testimony given in the proceeding are privileged, and no lawsuit predicated thereon may be instituted against any person. . . .

(b) Upon application by the disciplinary agency and notice to the appropriate prosecuting authority, the superior court may grant immunity from criminal prosecution to a witness in any disciplinary agency proceeding.

ARTICLE 6. DISCIPLINARY AUTHORITY OF THE COURTS

§6103.5. Written Offers of Settlement; Required Communication to Client; Discovery

(a) A member of the State Bar shall promptly communicate to the member's client all amounts, terms, and conditions of any written offer of settlement made by or on behalf of an opposing party. As used in this section, "client" includes any person employing the member of the State Bar who possesses the authority to accept an offer of settlement, or in a class action, who is a representative of the class.

(b) Any written offer of settlement or any required communication of a settlement offer, as described in subdivision (a), shall be discoverable by either party in any action in which the existence or communication of the offer of settlement is an issue before the trier of fact.

§6103.7. [Trial Publicity and Extrajudicial Statements]

Editors' Note. In 1994, Governor Wilson signed a new law commanding the State Bar to submit to the California Supreme Court, no later than March 1, 1995, "a rule of professional conduct governing trial publicity and extrajudical statements made by attorneys concerning adjudicative proceedings." The new law was prompted by publicity and extrajudicial statements surrounding the O. J. Simpson murder charges. The original bill would have codified a version of ABA Model Rule 3.6 as a California statute. Ultimately, however, the legislature decided to let the State Bar draft a rule. The California Supreme Court approved a new Rule 5-120 on September 14, 1995. For details, see our Editors' Note to Rule 5-120 in the California Rules of Professional Conduct above.

Sec. 1. No later than March 1, 1995, the State Bar of California shall submit to the Supreme Court for approval a rule of professional conduct governing trial publicity and extrajudicial statements made by attorneys concerning adjudicative proceedings.

Sec. 2. The Legislature finds and declares the following:

(1) Recent legal proceedings have generated extraordinary media coverage and raised serious questions regarding the potentially prejudicial and otherwise harmful effect of some media coverage. Important constitutional issues of free speech, the right to a fair trial, and related questions are implicated and require thorough review by the State Bar.

(2) In light of the fact that the American Bar Association has now reformed its rule on this subject, it is appropriate to require the State

Bar to commence and complete its rulemaking process no later than March 1, 1995.

(3) During the rulemaking process, the State Bar shall, among other materials, review and consider the American Bar Association's Model Rule 3.6, as modified.

Sec. 3. It is the intent of the Legislature in enacting this act to memorialize the Supreme Court expeditiously to review and, as appropriate, approve the rule adopted by the State Bar pursuant to this section.

§6106. Moral Turpitude, Dishonesty or Corruption Irrespective of Criminal Conviction

The commission of any act involving moral turpitude, dishonesty or corruption, whether the act is committed in the course of his relations as an attorney or otherwise, and whether the act is a felony or misdemeanor or not, constitutes a cause of disbarment or suspension.

If the act constitutes a felony or misdemeanor, conviction thereof in a criminal proceeding is not a condition precedent to disbarment or suspension from practice therefor.

§6106.1. Advocacy of Overthrow of Government

Advocating the overthrow of the Government of the United States or of this State by force, violence, or other unconstitutional means, constitutes a cause for disbarment or suspension.

§6106.5. Insurance Claims; Fraud

It shall constitute cause for disbarment or suspension for an attorney to engage in any conduct prohibited under Section . . . 1871.4 of the Insurance Code.

Editors' Note. Section 1871.4 of the California Insurance Code was enacted in 1991. Violation of the statute is punishable by a fine, imprisonment, or both. It provides, in pertinent part, as follows:

§1871.4. Unlawful Conduct; Penalties

(a) It is unlawful to do any of the following:

(1) Make or cause to be made any knowingly false or fraudulent material statement or material representation for the purpose of obtaining or denying any compensation, as defined in Section 3207 of the Labor Code.

(2) Present or cause to be presented any knowingly false or fraudulent written or oral material statement in support of, or in opposition to, any claim for compensation for the purpose of obtaining or denying any compensation. . . .

(3) Knowingly assist, abet, solicit, or conspire with any person who engages in an unlawful act under this section. . . .

§6106.8. Sexual Involvement Between Lawyers and Clients; Rule of Professional Conduct

Editors' Note. In May 1991, a few months after the deadline set forth in §6106.8(c), the California State Bar submitted a proposed rule (Rule 3-120) to the California Supreme Court to govern sexual relations with clients. On August 13, 1992, the California Supreme Court adopted the proposed rule with modifications. The rule is reprinted above in the California Rules of Professional Conduct.

(a) The Legislature hereby finds and declares that there is no rule that governs propriety of sexual relationships between lawyers and clients. The Legislature further finds and declares that it is difficult to separate sound judgment from emotion or bias which may result from sexual involvement between a lawyer and his or her client during the period that an attorney client relationship exists, and that emotional detachment is essential to the lawyer's ability to render competent legal services. Therefore, in order to ensure that a lawyer acts in the best interest of his or her client, a rule of professional conduct governing sexual relations between attorneys and their clients shall be adopted.

(b) With the approval of the Supreme Court, the State Bar shall adopt a rule of professional conduct governing sexual relations between attorneys and their clients in cases involving, but not limited to, probate matters and domestic relations, including dissolution proceedings, child custody cases, and settlement proceedings.

(c) The State Bar shall submit the proposed rule to the Supreme Court for approval no later than January 1, 1991.

(d) Intentional violation of this rule shall constitute a cause for suspension or disbarment.

§6106.9. Sexual Relations Between Attorney and Client; Cause for Discipline; Complaints to State Bar

(a) It shall constitute cause for the imposition of discipline of an attorney within the meaning of this chapter for an attorney to do any of the following:

(1) Expressly or impliedly condition the performance of legal services for a current or prospective client upon the client's willingness to engage in sexual relations with the attorney.

(2) Employ coercion, intimidation, or undue influence in entering into sexual relations with a client.

(3) Continue representation of a client with whom the attorney has sexual relations if the sexual relations cause the attorney to perform legal services incompetently in violation of Rule 3-110 of the Rules of Professional Conduct of the State Bar of California, or if the sexual relations would, or would be likely to, damage or prejudice the client's case.

(b) Subdivision (a) shall not apply to sexual relations between attorneys and their spouses or persons in an equivalent domestic relationship or to ongoing consensual sexual relationships that predate the initiation of the attorney-client relationship.

(c) Where an attorney in a firm has sexual relations with a client but does not participate in the representation of that client, the attorneys in the firm shall not be subject to discipline under this section solely because of the occurrence of those sexual relations.

(d) For the purposes of this section, "sexual relations" means sexual intercourse or the touching of an intimate part of another person for the purpose of sexual arousal, gratification, or abuse.

(e) Any complaint made to the State Bar alleging a violation of subdivision (a) shall be verified under oath by the person making the complaint.

Sec. 2. Commencing January 1, 1993, the State Bar shall maintain statistical data regarding the number of complaints presented and the disposition or discipline imposed pursuant to Section 6106.9 of the Business and Professions Code. The State Bar shall submit a report to the Legislature regarding the statistical compilation on or before January 1, 1996.

The State Bar shall also develop and implement uniform standards for the implementation of Section 6106.9 of the Business and Professions Code and policies and procedures to ensure that complaints will be handled in a responsive and sensitive manner. The State Bar shall also provide appropriate training to staff on the standards, policies, and practices.

ARTICLE 7. UNLAWFUL PRACTICE OF LAW

§6125. Necessity of Active Membership in State Bar

No person shall practice law in California unless the person is an active member of the State Bar.

§6126. Unauthorized Practice, Advertising or Holding Out; Penalties

Editors' Note. In August 2002, the California Legislature amended §6126 by significantly increasing the penalties for the unauthorized practice of law. Governor Davis signed the bill into law on September 19, 2002.

(a) Any person advertising or holding himself or herself out as practicing or entitled to practice law or otherwise practicing law who is not an active member of the State Bar, or otherwise authorized pursuant to statute or court rule to practice law in this state at the time of doing so, is guilty of a misdemeanor punishable by up to one year in a county jail or by a fine of up to one thousand dollars ($1,000), or by both that fine and imprisonment. Upon a second or subsequent conviction, the person shall be confined in a county jail for not less than 90 days, except in an unusual case where the interests of justice would be served by imposition of a lesser sentence or a fine. If the court imposes only a fine or a sentence of less than 90 days for a second or subsequent conviction under this subdivision, the court shall state the reasons for its sentencing choice on the record.

(b) Any person who has been involuntarily enrolled as an inactive member of the State Bar, or has been suspended from membership from the State Bar, or has been disbarred, or has resigned from the State Bar with charges pending, and thereafter practices or attempts to practice law, advertises or holds himself or herself out as practicing or otherwise entitled to practice law, is guilty of a crime punishable by imprisonment in the state prison or county jail. However, any person who has been involuntarily enrolled as an inactive member of the State Bar pursuant to paragraph (1) of subdivision (e) of Section 6007 and who knowingly thereafter practices or attempts to practice law, or advertises or holds himself or herself out as practicing or otherwise entitled to practice law, is guilty of a crime punishable by imprisonment in the state prison or county jail.

(c) The willful failure of a member of the State Bar, or one who has resigned or been disbarred, to comply with an order of the Supreme Court to comply with Rule 955, constitutes a crime punishable by imprisonment in the state prison or county jail.

(d) The penalties provided in this section are cumulative to each other and to any other remedies or penalties provided by law. . . .

§6126.5. [Increased Penalties for Unauthorized Practice of Law]

(a) In addition to any remedies and penalties available in any enforcement action brought in the name of the people of the State of

California by the Attorney General, a district attorney, or a city attorney, acting as a public prosecutor, the court shall award relief in the enforcement action for any person who obtained services offered or provided in violation of Section 6125 or 6126 or who purchased any goods, services, or real or personal property in connection with services offered or provided in violation of Section 6125 or 6126 against the person who violated Section 6125 or 6126, or who sold goods, services, or property in connection with that violation. The court shall consider the following relief:

(1) Actual damages.

(2) Restitution of all amounts paid.

(3) The amount of penalties and tax liabilities incurred in connection with the sale or transfer of assets to pay for any goods, services, or property.

(4) Reasonable attorney's fees and costs expended to rectify errors made in the unlawful practice of law.

(5) Prejudgment interest at the legal rate from the date of loss to the date of judgment.

(6) Appropriate equitable relief, including the rescission of sales made in connection with a violation of law.

(b) The relief awarded under paragraphs (1) to (6), inclusive, of subdivision (a) shall be distributed to, or on behalf of, the person for whom it was awarded or, if it is impracticable to do so, shall be distributed as may be directed by the court pursuant to its equitable powers.

(c) The court shall also award the Attorney General, district attorney, or city attorney reasonable attorney's fees and costs and, in the court's discretion, exemplary damages as provided in Section 3294 of the Civil Code.

(d) This section shall not be construed to create, abrogate, or otherwise affect claims, rights, or remedies, if any, that may be held by a person or entity other than those law enforcement agencies described in subdivision (a). The remedies provided in this section are cumulative to each other and to the remedies and penalties provided under other laws.

§6128. Deceit, Collusion, Delay of Suit and Improper Receipt of Money as Misdemeanor

Every attorney is guilty of a misdemeanor who either:

(a) Is guilty of any deceit or collusion, or consents to any deceit or collusion, with intent to deceive the court or any party.

(b) Willfully delays his client's suit with a view to his own gain.

(c) Willfully receives any money or allowance for or on account of any money which he has not laid out or become answerable for.

Any violation of the provisions of this section is punishable by imprisonment in the county jail not exceeding six months, or by a fine not exceeding two thousand five hundred dollars ($2,500), or by both.

§6133. Resigned, Suspended or Disbarred Attorneys; Supervision of Activities by Firms

Any attorney or any law firm, partnership, corporation, or association employing an attorney who has resigned, or who is under actual suspension from the practice of law, or is disbarred, shall not permit that attorney to practice law or so advertise or hold himself or herself out as practicing law and shall supervise him or her in any other assigned duties. A willful violation of this section constitutes a cause for discipline.

ARTICLE 8.5. FEE AGREEMENTS

§6146. Limitations; Periodic Payments

(a) An attorney shall not contract for or collect a contingency fee for representing any person seeking damages in connection with an action for injury or damage against a health care provider based upon such person's alleged professional negligence in excess of the following limits:

(1) Forty percent of the first fifty thousand dollars ($50,000) recovered.

(2) Thirty-three and one-third percent of the next fifty thousand dollars ($50,000) recovered.

(3) Twenty-five percent of the next five hundred thousand dollars ($500,000) recovered.

(4) Fifteen percent of any amount on which the recovery exceeds six hundred thousand dollars ($600,000).

The limitations shall apply regardless of whether the recovery is by settlement, arbitration, or judgment, or whether the person for whom the recovery is made is a responsible adult, an infant, or a person of unsound mind. . . .

§6147. Contingency Fee Contracts; Duplicate Copy; Contents; Effect of Noncompliance; Recovery of Workers' Compensation Benefits

(a) An attorney who contracts to represent a client on a contingency fee basis shall, at the time the contract is entered into, provide a duplicate copy of the contract, signed by both the attorney and the client, or the client's guardian or representative, to the plaintiff, or to the client's guardian or representative. The contract shall be in writing and shall include, but is not limited to, all of the following:

(1) A statement of the contingency fee rate that the client and attorney have agreed upon.

(2) A statement as to how disbursements and costs incurred in connection with the prosecution or settlement of the claim will affect the contingency fee and the client's recovery.

(3) A statement as to what extent, if any, the client could be required to pay any compensation to the attorney for related matters that arise out of their relationship not covered by their contingency fee contract. This may include any amounts collected for the plaintiff by the attorney.

(4) Unless the claim is subject to the provisions of Section 6146, a statement that the fee is not set by law but is negotiable between attorney and client.

(5) If the claim is subject to the provisions of Section 6146, a statement that the rates set forth in that section are the maximum limits for the contingency fee agreement, and that the attorney and client may negotiate a lower rate.

(b) Failure to comply with any provision of this section renders the agreement voidable at the option of the client, and the attorney shall thereupon be entitled to collect a reasonable fee.

(c) This section shall not apply to contingency fee contracts for the recovery of workers' compensation benefits.

(d) This section shall become operative on January 1, 2000.

§6147.5. Contingency Fee Contracts; Recovery of Claims Between Merchants

(a) Sections 6147 and 6148 shall not apply to contingency fee contracts for the recovery of claims between merchants as defined in Section 2104 of the Commercial Code, arising from the sale or lease of goods or services rendered, or money loaned for use, in the conduct of a business or profession if the merchant contracting for legal services employs 10 or more individuals.

(b)(1) In the instances in which no written contract for legal services exists as permitted by subdivision (a), an attorney shall not contract for or collect a contingency fee in excess of the following limits:

(A) Twenty percent of the first three hundred dollars ($300) collected.

(B) Eighteen percent of the next one thousand seven hundred dollars ($1,700) collected.

(C) Thirteen percent of sums collected in excess of two thousand dollars ($2,000).

(2) However, the following minimum charges may be charged and collected:

(A) Twenty-five dollars ($25) in collections of seventy-five dollars ($75) to one hundred twenty-five dollars ($125).

(B) Thirty-three and one-third percent of collections less than seventy-five dollars ($75).

§6148. Contracts for Services in Cases Not Coming Within §6147; Bills Rendered by Attorney; Contents; Failure to Comply

(a) In any case not coming within Section 6147 in which it is reasonably foreseeable that total expense to a client, including attorney fees, will exceed one thousand dollars ($1,000), the contract for services in the case shall be in writing. At the time the contract is entered into, the attorney shall provide a duplicate copy of the contract signed by both the attorney and the client, or the client's guardian or representative, to the client or to the client's guardian or representative. The written contract shall contain all of the following:

(1) Any basis of compensation including, but not limited to, hourly rates, statutory fees or flat fees, and other standard rates, fees, and charges applicable to the case.

(2) The general nature of the legal services to be provided to the client.

(3) The respective responsibilities of the attorney and the client as to the performance of the contract.

(b) All bills rendered by an attorney to a client shall clearly state the basis thereof. Bills for the fee portion of the bill shall include the amount, rate, basis for calculation, or other method of determination of the attorney's fees and costs. Bills for the cost and expense portion of the bill shall clearly identify the costs and expenses incurred and the amount of the costs and expenses. Upon request by the client, the attorney shall provide a bill to the client no later than 10 days following the request. . . .

(c) Failure to comply with any provision of this section renders the agreement voidable at the option of the client, and the attorney shall, upon the agreement being voided, be entitled to collect a reasonable fee.

(d) This section shall not apply to any of the following:

(1) Services rendered in an emergency to avoid foreseeable prejudice to the rights or interests of the client or where a writing is otherwise impractical.

(2) An arrangement as to the fee implied by the fact that the attorney's services are of the same general kind as previously rendered to and paid for by the client.

(3) If the client knowingly states in writing, after full disclosure of this section, that a writing concerning fees is not required.

(4) If the client is a corporation.

(e) This section applies prospectively only to fee agreements following its operative date.

(f) This section shall become operative on January 1, 2000.

§6149. Written Fee Contract as Confidential Communication

A written fee contract shall be deemed to be a confidential communication within the meaning of subdivision (e) of Section 6068 and of Section 952 of the Evidence Code.

Editors' Note. Section 6068(e) of the Business and Professions Code is reprinted above in this chapter. Section 952 of the Evidence Code is reprinted above in the chapter on the attorney-client privilege and work product.

§6149.5. Third-Party Liability Claim; Settlement by Insurer; Notice to Claimant; Effect on Action or Defense

(a) Upon the payment of one hundred dollars ($100) or more in settlement of any third-party liability claim the insurer shall provide written notice to the claimant if both of the following apply:

(1) The claimant is a natural person.

(2) The payment is delivered to the claimant's lawyer or other representative by draft, check, or otherwise.

(b) For purposes of this section, "written notice" includes providing to the claimant a copy of the cover letter sent to the claimant's attorney or other representative that accompanied the settlement payment.

(c) This section shall not create any cause of action for any person against the insurer based upon the insurer's failure to provide the notice to a claimant required by this section. This section shall not create a defense for any party to any cause of action based upon the insurer's failure to provide this notice.

ARTICLE 9. UNLAWFUL SOLICITATION

§6151. Definitions

As used in this article:

(a) A runner or capper is any person, firm, association or corporation acting for consideration in any manner or in any capacity as an agent for an attorney at law or law firm, whether the attorney or any member of the law firm is admitted in California or any other jurisdiction, in the solicitation or procurement of business for the attorney at law or law firm as provided in this article.

(b) An agent is one who represents another in dealings with one or more third persons.

§6152. Prohibition of Solicitation

(a) It is unlawful for:

(1) Any person, in his individual capacity or in his capacity as a public or private employee, or for any firm, corporation, partnership or association to act as a runner or capper for any such attorneys or to solicit any business for any such attorneys in and about the state prisons, county jails, city jails, city prisons, or other places of detention of persons, city receiving hospitals, city and county receiving hospitals, county hospitals, justice courts, municipal courts, superior courts, or in any public institution or in any public place or upon any public street or highway or in and about private hospitals, sanitariums or in and about any private institution or upon private property of any character whatsoever.

(2) Any person to solicit another person to commit or join in the commission of a violation of subdivision (a). . . .

(d) Nothing in this section shall be construed to mean that a public defender or assigned counsel may not make known his or her services as a criminal defense attorney to persons unable to afford legal counsel whether such persons are in custody or otherwise.

ARTICLE 9.5. LEGAL ADVERTISING

§6157. Definitions

As used in this article, the following definitions apply: . . .

(d) "Electronic medium" means television, radio, or computer networks.

§6157.1. False, Misleading or Deceptive Statements; Prohibition

No advertisement shall contain any false, misleading, or deceptive statement or omit to state any fact necessary to make the statements made, in light of circumstances under which they are made, not false, misleading, or deceptive.

§6157.2. Prohibited Statements Regarding Outcome; Dramatizations; Contingent Fee Basis Representations

No advertisement shall contain or refer to any of the following:

(a) Any guarantee or warranty regarding the outcome of a legal matter as a result of representation by the member.

(b) Statements or symbols stating that the member featured in the advertisement can generally obtain immediate cash or quick settlements.

(c)(1) An impersonation of the name, voice, photograph, or electronic image of any person other than the lawyer, directly or implicitly purporting to be that of a lawyer.

(2) An impersonation of the name, voice, photograph, or electronic image of any person, directly or implicitly purporting to be a client of the member featured in the advertisement, or a dramatization of events, unless disclosure of the impersonation or dramatization is made in the advertisement.

(3) A spokesperson, including a celebrity spokesperson, unless there is disclosure of the spokesperson's title.

(d) A statement that a member offers representation on a contingent basis unless the statement also advises whether a client will be held responsible for any costs advanced by the member when no recovery is obtained on behalf of the client. If the client will not be held responsible for costs, no disclosure is required.

§6157.3. Advertisements Made on Behalf of Member; Required Representations

Any advertisement made on behalf of a member, which is not paid for by the member, shall disclose any business relationship, past or present, between the member and the person paying for the advertisement.

§6157.4. Lawyer Referral Service Advertising

Any advertisement that is created or disseminated by a lawyer referral service shall disclose whether the attorneys on the organization's referral list, panel, or system, paid any consideration, other than a proportional share of actual cost, to be included on that list, panel, or system.

§6158. Electronic Media Advertising; False, Misleading or Deceptive Message; Factual Substantiation

In advertising by electronic media, to comply with Sections 6157.1 and 6157.2, the message as a whole may not be false, misleading, or deceptive, and the message as a whole must be factually substantiated. The message means the effect in combination of the spoken word, sound, background, action, symbols, visual image, or any other technique employed to create the message. Factually substantiated means capable of verification by a credible source.

§6158.1. False, Misleading or Deceptive Messages; Rebuttable Presumption

There shall be a rebuttable presumption affecting the burden of producing evidence that the following messages are false, misleading, or deceptive within the meaning of Section 6158:

(a) A message as to the ultimate result of a specific case or cases presented out of context without adequately providing information as to the facts or law giving rise to the result.

(b) The depiction of an event through methods such as the use of displays of injuries, accident scenes, or portrayals of other injurious events which may or may not be accompanied by sound effects and which may give rise to a claim for compensation.

(c) A message referring to or implying money received by or for a client in a particular case or cases, or to potential monetary recovery for a prospective client. A reference to money or monetary recovery includes, but is not limited to, a specific dollar amount, characterization of a sum of money, monetary symbols, or the implication of wealth.

§6158.3. Electronic Media Advertising; Required Disclosures

In addition to any disclosure required by Section 6157.2, Section 6157.3, and the Rules of Professional Conduct, the following disclosure shall appear in advertising by electronic media. Use of the following disclosure alone may not rebut any presumption created in Section 6158.1. If an advertisement in the electronic media conveys a message portraying a result in a particular case or cases, the advertisement must state, in either an oral or printed communication, either of the following disclosures: The advertisement must adequately disclose the factual and legal circumstances that justify the result portrayed in the message, including the basis for liability and the nature of injury or damage sustained, or the advertisement must state that the result portrayed in the advertisement was dependent on the facts of that case, and that the results will differ if based on different facts.

ARTICLE 10.5. PROVISION OF FINANCIAL SERVICES BY LAWYERS

§6175. Definitions

As used in this article, the following definitions apply: . . .

(b) "Client" means a person who has, within the three years preceding the sale of financial products by a lawyer to that person, employed that lawyer for legal services. The settlor and trustee of a trust shall be considered one person.

(c) "Elder" and "dependent elder" shall have the meaning as defined in Chapter 11 (commencing with Section 15600) of Part 3 of Division 9 of the Welfare and Institutions Code.

(d) "Financial products" means long-term care insurance, life insurance, and annuities governed by the Insurance Code, or its successors.

(e) "Sell" means to act as a broker for a commission.

§6175.3. Selling Financial Products to Clients — Disclosure Requirements

A lawyer, while acting as a fiduciary, may sell financial products to a client who is an elder or dependent adult with whom the lawyer has or has had, within the preceding three years, an attorney-client relationship, if the transaction or acquisition and its terms are fair and reasonable to the client, and if the lawyer provides that client with a disclosure that satisfies all of the following conditions:

(a) The disclosure is in writing and is clear and conspicuous. The disclosure shall be a separate document, appropriately entitled, in 12-point print with one inch of space on all borders.

(b) The disclosure, in a manner that should reasonably have been understood by that client, is signed by the client, or the client's conservator, guardian, or agent under a valid durable power of attorney.

(c) The disclosure states that the lawyer shall receive a commission and sets forth the amount of the commission and the actual percentage rate of the commission, if any. If the actual amount of the commission cannot be ascertained at the outset of the transaction, the disclosure shall include the actual percentage rate of the commission or the alternate basis upon which the commission will be computed, including an example of how the commission would be calculated.

(d) The disclosure identifies the source of the commission and the relationship between the source of the commission and the person receiving the commission.

(e) The disclosure is presented to the client at or prior to the time the recommendation of the financial product is made.

(f) The disclosure advises the client that he or she may obtain independent advice regarding the purchase of the financial product and will be given a reasonable opportunity to seek that advice.

(g) The disclosure contains a statement that the financial product may be returned to the issuing company within 30 days of receipt by the client for a refund as set forth in Section 10127.10 of the Insurance Code.

(h) The disclosure contains a statement that if the purchase of the financial product is for the purposes of Medi-Cal planning, the client has been advised of other appropriate alternatives, including spend-down strategies, and of the possibility of obtaining a fair hearing or obtaining a court order.

§6175.4. Remedies for Damages

(a) A client who suffers any damage as the result of a violation of this article by any lawyer may bring an action against that person to recover or obtain one or more of the following remedies:

(1) Actual damages, but in no case shall the total award of damages in a class action be less than five thousand dollars ($5,000).

(2) An order enjoining the violation.

(3) Restitution of property.

(4) Punitive damages.

(5) Any other relief that the court deems proper.

(b) A client may seek and be awarded, in addition to the remedies specified in subdivision (a), an amount not to exceed ten thousand dollars ($10,000) where the trier of fact (1) finds that the client has suffered substantial physical, emotional, or economic damage resulting from the defendant's conduct, (2) makes an affirmative finding in regard to one or more of the factors set forth in subdivision (b) of Section 3345 of the Civil Code, and (3) finds that an additional award is appropriate. Judgment in a class action may award each class member the additional award where the trier of fact has made the foregoing findings.

§6175.5. Violation — Cause for Discipline

A violation of this article by a member shall be cause for discipline by the State Bar.

§6175.6. Court Reporting Requirements for Violations

The court shall report the name, address, and professional license number of any person found in violation of this article to the appropri-

ate professional licensing agencies for review and possible disciplinary action.

§6177. State Bar Report to the Legislature — Complaints Filed; Disciplinary Action Taken

The State Bar by December 31 of each year shall report to the Legislature on the number of complaints filed against California attorneys alleging a violation of this article. The report shall also include the type of charges made in each complaint, the number of resulting investigations initiated, and the number and nature of any disciplinary actions taken by the State Bar for violations of this article.

CHAPTER 5.5. LEGAL DOCUMENT ASSISTANTS AND UNLAWFUL DETAINER ASSISTANTS

Editors' Note. Sections 6400 through 6416 of California's Business and Professions Code authorize non-lawyers to perform limited services related to legal proceedings. The purpose of the law was stated by the Legislature as follows when its predecessor was enacted in 1993:

> The Legislature finds and declares that there currently exist numerous unscrupulous individuals and associations of individuals who purport to offer protection to tenants from eviction. These unscrupulous individuals and associations represent themselves as legitimate tenants' rights associations, legal consultants, professional legal assistants, paralegals, attorneys, or typing services. In fact, these individuals and associations act to defraud tenants of both their funds and their rights under the law. While allegedly acting to assist unsuspecting tenants, these individuals have filed thousands of frivolous or fraudulent legal pleadings in both state and federal courts. In most instances, the nature of the legal pleadings filed or the very fact of their filing has not been disclosed to the tenant. The acts of these unscrupulous individuals and associations are particularly despicable in that they target low-income and non-English-speaking Californians as victims for their fraudulent practices.
>
> In several counties . . . the problem has reached epidemic proportions resulting in the defrauding of thousands of tenants, severe economic losses to landlords, and the clogging of both state and federal courts with frivolous or fraudulent proceedings. . . .
>
> Law enforcement officials have been frustrated in their attempts to prosecute these unscrupulous individuals due to the transient nature of their operations. Frequently, these individuals and associations literally disappear overnight making prosecution impossible. A registration requirement for unlawful detainer consultants and the printing of a registration number on all advertisements and prepared pleadings will assist law enforcement in locating and prosecuting unscrupulous individuals and associations. Further, the requirement of the posting of a bond will make funds available to those tenants who have been defrauded. . . .

In 1994, the law was expanded to include a new category called "Legal Document Assistants." Some sections of the law were amended in 1999, and certain sections of the law do not take effect until January 1, 2003. A violation of the law is a misdemeanor punishable by a fine of between $1,000 and $2,000 as to each client with respect to whom a violation occurs, or imprisonment for not more than one year, or by both fine and imprisonment. A court may also order restitution. We reprint only a few sections of the law.

§6400. Definitions . . .

(c) "Legal document assistant" means:

(1) Any person who . . . provides . . . for compensation, any self-help service to a member of the public who is representing himself or herself in a legal matter. . . . This paragraph shall not apply to any individual whose assistance consists merely of secretarial or receptionist services. . . .

(d) "Self-help service" means all of the following:

(1) Completing legal documents in a ministerial manner, selected by a person who is representing himself or herself in a legal matter, by typing or otherwise completing the documents at the person's specific direction.

(2) Providing general published factual information that has been written or approved by an attorney, pertaining to legal procedures, rights or obligations to a person who is representing himself or herself in a legal matter, to assist the person in representing himself or herself. This service in and of itself, shall not require registration as a legal document assistant.

(3) Making published legal documents available to a person who is representing himself or herself in a legal matter.

(4) Filing and serving legal forms and documents at the specific direction of a person who is representing himself or herself in a legal matter.

. . .

(g) A legal document assistant shall not provide any kind of advice, explanation, opinion, or recommendation to a consumer about possible legal rights, remedies, defenses, options, selection of forms, or strategies. . . .

§6401.6. Legal Document Assistant; Limitation on Service; Services of Attorney

A legal document assistant shall not provide service to a client who requires assistance that exceeds the definition of self-help service in subdivision (b) of Section 6400, and shall inform the client that the client requires the services of an attorney.

§6402. Registration Requirement; Registration of Disbarred and Suspended Lawyers Prohibited

An unlawful detainer assistant shall be registered pursuant to this chapter by the county clerk in the county in which his or her principal place of business is located (deemed primary registration), and in any other county in which he or she performs acts for which registration is required (deemed secondary registration). Any registration in a county other than the county of the person's place of business shall state the person's principal place of business and provide proof that the registrant has satisfied the bonding requirement of Section 6405. No person who has been disbarred or suspended from the practice of law pursuant to Article 6 (commencing with Section 6100) of Chapter 4 shall, during the period of any disbarment or suspension, register as an unlawful detainer assistant.

This section shall become operative January 1, 2003, or the date the director suspends the requirements of this chapter applicable to legal document assistants pursuant to Section 6416, whichever first occurs.

§6402.1. Registration Eligibility

To be eligible to apply for registration under this chapter as a legal document assistant, the applicant shall possess at least one of the following:

(a) A high school diploma or general equivalency diploma, and either a minimum of two years of law-related experience under the supervision of a licensed attorney, or a minimum of two years experience, prior to January 1, 1999, providing self-help service.

(b) A baccalaureate degree in any field and either a minimum of one year of law-related experience under the supervision of a licensed attorney, or a minimum of one year of experience, prior to January 1, 1999, providing self-help service.

(c) A certificate of completion from a paralegal program that is institutionally accredited but not approved by the American Bar Association, that requires successful completion of a minimum of 24 semester units, or the equivalent, in legal specialization courses.

(d) A certificate of completion from a paralegal program approved by the American Bar Association. . . .

§6411. Unlawful Acts

It is unlawful for any person engaged in the business or acting in the capacity of a legal document assistant or unlawful detainer assistant to do any of the following: . . .

(d) Provide assistance or advice which constitutes the unlawful practice of law pursuant to Sections 6125, 6126, or 6127.

(e) Engage in the unauthorized practice of law, including, but not limited to, giving any kind of advice, explanation, opinion, or recommendation to a consumer about possible legal rights, remedies, defenses, options, selection of forms, or strategies. . . .

CHAPTER 5.6. PARALEGALS

Editors' Note. Chapter 5.6, one of the only statutes in the nation directly regulating paralegals, was originally enacted in 2000 and consisted only of §6450. In September of 2001, Governor Gray Davis signed a bill (AB 1083) that slightly amended §6450 and added a wholly new §6451. The amendment to §6450 amplifies the existing definition of a "paralegal" by adding that a paralegal is also "a person who holds himself or herself out to be a paralegal, [and] who is qualified by education, training, or work experience. . . ." New §6451 generally makes it unlawful for a paralegal to serve consumers except under the supervision of an attorney. The 2001 legislation also enacted a version of §6450 that will become operative on January 1, 2004. It is identical to the 2001 version of §6450 except that it eliminates existing paragraph (f) and changes the operative date in existing paragraph (g).

§6450. [Paralegals]

(a) "Paralegal" means a person who holds himself or herself out to be a paralegal, who is qualified by education, training, or work experience, and who either contracts with or is employed by an attorney, law firm, corporation, governmental agency, or other entity, and who performs substantial legal work under the direction and supervision of an active member of the State Bar of California, as defined in Section 6060, or an attorney practicing law in the federal courts of this state, that has been specifically delegated by the attorney to him or her. Tasks performed by a paralegal may include, but are not limited to, case planning, development, and management; legal research; interviewing clients; fact gathering and retrieving information; drafting and analyzing legal documents; collecting, compiling, and utilizing technical information to make an independent decision and recommendation to the supervising attorney; and representing clients before a state or federal administrative agency if that representation is permitted by statute, court rule, or administrative rule or regulation.

(b) Notwithstanding subdivision (a), a paralegal shall not do any of the following:

(1) Provide legal advice.

(2) Represent a client in court.

(3) Select, explain, draft, or recommend the use of any legal document to or for any person other than the attorney who directs and supervises the paralegal.

(4) Act as a runner or capper, as defined in Sections 6151 and 6152.

(5) Engage in conduct that constitutes the unlawful practice of law.

(6) Contract with, or be employed by, a natural person other than an attorney to perform paralegal services.

(7) In connection with providing paralegal services, induce a person to make an investment, purchase a financial product or service, or enter a transaction from which income or profit, or both, purportedly may be derived.

(8) Establish the fees to charge a client for the services the paralegal performs, which shall be established by the attorney who supervises the paralegal's work. This paragraph does not apply to fees charged by a paralegal in a contract to provide paralegal services to an attorney, law firm, corporation, governmental agency, or other entity as provided in subdivision (a).

(c) A paralegal shall possess at least one of the following:

(1) A certificate of completion of a paralegal program approved by the American Bar Association.

(2) A certificate of completion of a paralegal program at, or a degree from, a postsecondary institution that requires the successful completion of a minimum of 24 semester, or equivalent, units in law-related courses and that has been accredited by a national or regional accrediting organization or approved by the Bureau for Private Postsecondary and Vocational Education.

(3) A baccalaureate degree or an advanced degree in any subject, a minimum of one year of law-related experience under the supervision of an attorney who has been an active member of the State Bar of California for at least the preceding three years or who has practiced in the federal courts of this state for at least the preceding three years, and a written declaration from this attorney stating that the person is qualified to perform paralegal tasks.

(4) A high school diploma or general equivalency diploma, a minimum of three years of law-related experience under the supervision of an attorney who has been an active member of the State Bar of California for at least the preceding three years or who has practiced in the federal courts of this state for at least the preceding three years, and a written declaration from this attorney stating that the person is qualified to perform paralegal tasks. This experience and training shall be completed no later than December 31, 2003.

(d) All paralegals shall be required to certify completion every three years of four hours of mandatory continuing legal education in legal ethics. All continuing legal education courses shall meet the requirements of Section 6070. Every two years, all paralegals shall be required to certify completion of four hours of mandatory continuing education in either general law or in a specialized area of law. Certification of these continuing education requirements shall be made with the paralegal's supervising attorney. The paralegal shall be responsible for keeping a record of the paralegal's certifications.

(e) A paralegal does not include a nonlawyer who provides legal services directly to members of the public or a legal document assistant or unlawful detainer assistant as defined in Section 6400.

(f) If a legal document assistant, as defined in subdivision (c) of Section 6400, has registered, on or before January 1, 2001, as required by law, a business name that includes the word "paralegal," that person may continue to use that business name until he or she is required to renew registration.

(g) This section shall remain in effect only until January 1, 2004, and as of that date is repealed, unless a later enacted statute, which is enacted before January 1, 2004, deletes or extends that date.

§6451. [Restrictions on Paralegal Activities]

It is unlawful for a paralegal to perform any services for a consumer except as performed under the direction and supervision of the attorney, law firm, corporation, government agency, or other entity that employs or contracts with the paralegal. Nothing in this chapter shall prohibit a paralegal who is employed by an attorney, law firm, governmental agency, or other entity from providing services to a consumer served by one of these entities if those services are specifically allowed by statute, case law, court rule, or federal or state administrative rule or regulation. "Consumer" means a natural person, firm, association, organization, partnership, business trust, corporation, or public entity.

CALIFORNIA CIVIL CODE

§51.9. Sexual Harassment; Business, Service and Professional Relationships

> **Editors' Note.** Section 51.9 of the California Civil Code, which gives clients a right to sue their lawyers for sexual harassment, took effect on January 1, 1995. The law complements §12940 of the California Government Code, which prohibits a wide range of employers, including lawyers, from sexually harassing their employees.

(a) A person is liable in a cause of action for sexual harassment when the plaintiff proves all of the following elements:

(1) There is a business, service, or professional relationship between the plaintiff and defendant. Such a relationship includes any of the following:

(A) Physician, psychotherapist, or dentist-patient.

(B) Attorney, marriage, family or child counselor, licensed clinical social worker, master of social work, real estate agent, real estate appraiser, accountant, banker, trust officer, financial planner, loan officer, collection service, contractor, or escrow loan officer-client.

(C) Executor, trustee, or administrator beneficiary.

(D) Landlord or property manager-tenant.

(E) Teacher-student.

(F) A relationship that is substantially similar to any of the above.

(2) The defendant has made sexual advances, solicitations, sexual requests, or demands for sexual compliance by the plaintiff that were unwelcome and persistent or severe, continuing after a request by the plaintiff to stop.

(3) There is an inability by the plaintiff to easily terminate the relationship without tangible hardship.

(4) The plaintiff has suffered or will suffer economic loss or disadvantage or personal injury as a result of the conduct described in paragraph (2). . . .

§1714.10. Attorney-Client Civil Conspiracy; Proof and Pre-Pleading Court Determination; Defense; Limitations; Appeal

(a) No cause of action against an attorney for a civil conspiracy with his or her client arising from any attempt to contest or compromise a claim or dispute, and which is based upon the attorney's representation of the client, shall be included in a complaint or other pleading unless the court enters an order allowing the pleading that includes the claim for civil conspiracy to be filed after the court determines that the party seeking to file the pleading has established that there is a reasonable probability that the party will prevail in the action. The court may allow the filing of a pleading claiming liability based upon such a civil conspiracy following the filing of a verified petition therefor accompanied by the proposed pleading and supporting affidavits stating the facts upon which the liability is based. The court shall order service of the petition upon the party against whom the action is proposed to be filed and permit that party to submit opposing affidavits prior to making its determination. The filing of the petition, proposed pleading, and accompanying affidavits shall toll the running of any applicable statute of limitations until the final determination of the matter, which ruling, if favorable to the petitioning party, shall permit the proposed pleading to be filed.

(b) Failure to obtain a court order where required by subdivision (a) shall be a defense to any action for civil conspiracy filed in violation thereof. The defense shall be raised by the attorney charged with civil conspiracy upon that attorney's first appearance by demurrer, motion to strike, or such other motion or application as may be appropriate. Failure to timely raise the defense shall constitute a waiver thereof.

(c) This section shall not apply to a cause of action against an attorney for a civil conspiracy with his or her client, where (1) the attorney has an independent legal duty to the plaintiff, or (2) the attorney's acts go beyond the performance of a professional duty to serve the client and involve a conspiracy to violate a legal duty in furtherance of the attorney's financial gain.

(d) This section establishes a special proceeding of a civil nature. Any order made under subdivision (a), (b), or (c) which determines the rights of a petitioner or an attorney against whom a pleading has been or is proposed to be filed, shall be appealable as a final judgment in a civil action.

(e) Subdivision (d) does not constitute a change in, but is declaratory of, the existing law.

§2860. Conflict of Interest; Duty to Provide Independent Counsel; Waiver; Qualifications of Independent Counsel; Fees; Disclosure of Information

(a) If the provisions of a policy of insurance impose a duty to defend upon an insurer and a conflict of interest arises which creates a duty on the part of the insurer to provide independent counsel to the insured, the insurer shall provide independent counsel to represent the insured unless, at the time the insured is informed that a possible conflict may arise or does exist, the insured expressly waives, in writing, the right to independent counsel. An insurance contract may contain a provision which sets forth the method of selecting that counsel consistent with this section.

(b) For purposes of this section, a conflict of interest does not exist as to allegations or facts in the litigation for which the insurer denies coverage; however, when an insurer reserves its rights on a given issue and the outcome of that coverage issue can be controlled by counsel first retained by the insurer for the defense of the claim, a conflict of interest may exist. No conflict of interest shall be deemed to exist as to allegations of punitive damages or be deemed to exist solely because an insured is sued for an amount in excess of the insurance policy limits.

(c) When the insured has selected independent counsel to represent him or her, the insurer may exercise its right to require that the counsel selected by the insured possess certain minimum qualifications which may include that the selected counsel have (1) at least five years of civil litigation practice which includes substantial defense experience in the subject at issue in the litigation, and (2) errors and omissions coverage. The insurer's obligation to pay fees to the independent counsel selected by the insured is limited to the rates which are actually paid by the insurer to attorneys retained by it in the ordinary course of business in the defense of similar actions in the community where the claim arose or is being defended. This subdivision does not invalidate other different or additional policy provisions pertaining to attorney's fees or providing for methods of settlement of disputes concerning those fees. Any dispute concerning attorney's fees not resolved by these methods shall be resolved by final and binding arbitration by a single neutral arbitrator selected by the parties to the dispute.

(d) When independent counsel has been selected by the insured, it shall be the duty of that counsel and the insured to disclose to the insurer all information concerning the action except privileged materials relevant to coverage disputes, and timely to inform and consult with the insurer on all matters relating to the action. Any claim of privilege asserted is subject to in camera review in the appropriate law and motion department of the superior court. Any information disclosed by the insured or by independent counsel is not a waiver of the privilege as to any other party.

(e) The insured may waive its right to select independent counsel by signing the following statement: "I have been advised and informed of my right to select independent counsel to represent me in this lawsuit. I have considered this matter fully and freely waive my right to select independent counsel at this time. I authorize my insurer to select a defense attorney to represent me in this lawsuit."

(f) Where the insured selects independent counsel pursuant to the provisions of this section, both the counsel provided by the insurer and independent counsel selected by the insured shall be allowed to participate in all aspects of the litigation. Counsel shall cooperate fully in the exchange of information that is consistent with each counsel's ethical and legal obligation to the insured. Nothing in this section shall relieve the insured of his or her duty to cooperate with the insurer under the terms of the insurance contract.

CALIFORNIA CODE OF CIVIL PROCEDURE

§128.5. Frivolous Actions or Delaying Tactics, Award of Expenses, Including Attorney's Fees on Motion

(a) Every trial court may order a party, the party's attorney, or both to pay any reasonable expenses, including attorney's fees, incurred by another party as a result of bad-faith actions or tactics that are frivolous or solely intended to cause unnecessary delay. This section also applies to judicial arbitration proceedings under Chapter 2.5 (commencing with Section 1141.10) of Title 3 of Part 3.

(b) For purposes of this section:

(1) "Actions or tactics" include, but are not limited to, the making or opposing of motions or the filing and service of a complaint or cross-complaint only if the actions or tactics arise from a complaint filed, or a proceeding initiated, on or before December 31, 1994. The mere filing of a complaint without service thereof on an opposing party does not constitute "actions or tactics" for purposes of this section.

(2) "Frivolous" means (A) totally and completely without merit or (B) for the sole purpose of harassing an opposing party.

(c) Expenses pursuant to this section shall not be imposed except on notice contained in a party's moving or responding papers; or the court's own motion, after notice and opportunity to be heard. An order imposing expenses shall be in writing and shall recite in detail the conduct or circumstances justifying the order.

(d) In addition to any award pursuant to this section for conduct described in subdivision (a), the court may assess punitive damages against the plaintiff upon a determination by the court that the plaintiff's action was an action maintained by a person convicted of a felony against the person's victim, or the victim's heirs, relatives, estate, or personal representative, for injuries arising from the acts for which the person was convicted of a felony, and that the plaintiff is guilty of fraud, oppression, or malice in maintaining the action.

(e) The liability imposed by this section is in addition to any other liability imposed by law for acts or omissions within the purview of this section.

§128.6. Bad Faith Actions or Tactics, Award of Expenses, Including Attorney's Fees on Motion

(a) Every trial court may order a party, the party's attorney, or both to pay any reasonable expenses, including attorney's fees, incurred by another party as a result of bad-faith actions or tactics that are frivolous or solely intended to cause unnecessary delay. This section also applies to judicial arbitration proceedings under Chapter 2.5 (commencing with Section 1141.10) of Title 3 of Part 3.

(b) For purposes of this section:

(1) "Actions or tactics" include, but are not limited to, the making or opposing of motions or the filing and service of a complaint or cross-complaint. The mere filing of a complaint without service thereof on an opposing party does not constitute "actions or tactics" for purposes of this section.

(2) "Frivolous" means

(A) totally and completely without merit or

(B) for the sole purpose of harassing an opposing party.

(c) Expenses pursuant to this section shall not be imposed except on notice contained in a party's moving or responding papers; or the court's own motion, after notice and opportunity to be heard. An order imposing expenses shall be in writing and shall recite in detail the conduct or circumstances justifying the order.

(d) In addition to any award pursuant to this section for conduct described in subdivision (a), the court may assess punitive damages against the plaintiff upon a determination by the court that the plaintiff's action was an action maintained by a person convicted of a felony against the person's victim, or the victim's heirs, relatives, estate, or personal representative, for injuries arising from the acts for which the person was convicted of a felony, and that the plaintiff is guilty of fraud, oppression, or malice in maintaining the action.

(e) The liability imposed by this section is in addition to any other liability imposed by law for acts or omissions within the purview of this section.

(f) This section shall become operative on January 1, 2003, unless a statute that becomes effective on or before this date extends or deletes the repeal date of Section 128.7.

§177.5. Judicial Officers, Sanctions

A judicial officer shall have the power to impose reasonable money sanctions, not to exceed fifteen hundred dollars ($1,500), notwithstanding any other provision of law, payable to the county in which the judicial officer is located, for any violation of a lawful court order by a person, done without good cause or substantial justification. This power shall not apply to advocacy of counsel before the court. For the purposes of this section, the term "person" includes a witness, a party, a party's attorney, or both.

Sanctions pursuant to this section shall not be imposed except on notice contained in a party's moving or responding papers; or on the court's own motion, after notice and opportunity to be heard. An order imposing sanctions shall be in writing and shall recite in detail the conduct or circumstances justifying the order.

§206. Criminal Actions — Discussions with Jury After Discharge

(a) Prior to discharging the jury from the case, the judge in a criminal action shall inform the jurors that they have an absolute right to discuss or not to discuss the deliberation or verdict with anyone. The judge shall also inform the jurors of the provisions set forth in subdivisions (b), (d), and (e).

(b) Following the discharge of the jury in a criminal case, the defendant, or his or her attorney or representative, or the prosecutor, or his or her representative, may discuss the jury deliberation or verdict with a member of the jury, provided that the juror consents to the discussion and that the discussion takes place at a reasonable time and place.

(c) If a discussion of the jury deliberation or verdict with a member of the jury pursuant to subdivision (b) occurs at any time more than 24 hours after the verdict, prior to discussing the jury deliberation or verdict with a member of a jury pursuant to subdivision (b), the defendant or his or her attorney or representative, or the prosecutor or his or her representative, shall inform the juror of the identity of the case, the party in that case which the person represents, the subject of the interview, the absolute right of the juror to discuss or not discuss the deliberations or verdict in the case with the person, and the juror's right to review and have a copy of any declaration filed with the court.

(d) Any unreasonable contact with a juror by the defendant, or his or her attorney or representative, or by the prosecutor, or his or her representative, without the juror's consent shall be immediately reported to the trial judge.

(e) Any violation of this section shall be considered a violation of a lawful court order and shall be subject to reasonable monetary sanctions in accordance with Section 177.5 of the Code of Civil Procedure.

(f) Nothing in the section shall prohibit a peace officer from investigating an allegation of criminal conduct.

(g) Pursuant to Section 237, a defendant or defendant's counsel may, following the recording of a jury's verdict in a criminal proceeding, petition the court for access to personal juror identifying information within the court's records necessary for the defendant to communicate with jurors for the purpose of developing a motion for new trial or any other lawful purpose. This information consists of jurors' names, addresses, and telephone numbers. The court shall consider all requests for personal juror identifying information pursuant to Section 237.

§283. Authority to Bind Client

An attorney and counselor shall have authority:

(1) To bind his client in any of the steps of an action or proceeding by his agreement filed with the clerk, or entered upon the minutes of the court, and not otherwise;

(2) To receive money claimed by his client in an action or proceeding during the pendency thereof, or after judgment, unless a revocation of his authority is filed, and upon the payment thereof, and not otherwise, to discharge the claim or acknowledge satisfaction of the judgment.

§284. Substitution, Consent or Order

The attorney in an action or special proceeding may be changed at any time before or after judgment or final determination, as follows:

(1) Upon the consent of both client and attorney, filed with the clerk, or entered upon the minutes.

(2) Upon the order of the court, upon the application of either client or attorney, after notice from one to the other.

§285. Notice to Adversary

When an attorney is changed, as provided in the last section, written notice of the change and of the substitution of a new attorney, or of the appearance of the party in person, must be given to the adverse party. Until then he must recognize the former attorney.

§285.1. Withdrawal in Domestic Relations Matters

An attorney of record for any party in any civil action or proceeding for dissolution of marriage, legal separation, or for a declaration of void or voidable marriage, or for the support, maintenance or custody of minor children may withdraw at any time subsequent to the time when any judgment in such action or proceeding, other than an interlocutory judgment, becomes final, and prior to service upon him of pleadings or motion papers in any proceeding then pending in said cause, by filing a notice of withdrawal. Such notice shall state (a) date of entry of final decree or judgment, (b) the last known address of such party, (c) that such attorney withdraws as attorney for such party. A copy of such notice shall be mailed to such party at his last known address and shall be served upon the adverse party.

§285.2. Withdrawal When Public Funding Reduced

If a reduction in public funding for legal service materially impairs a legal service agency attorney's ability to represent an indigent client, the court, on its own motion or on the motion of either the client or attorney, shall permit the withdrawal of such attorney upon a showing that all of the following apply:

(a) There are not adequate public funds to continue the effective representation of the indigent client.

(b) A good faith effort was made to find alternate representation for such client.

(c) All reasonable steps to reduce the legal prejudice to the client have been taken.

A showing of indigency of the client, in and of itself, will not be deemed sufficient cause to deny the application for withdrawal.

§286. Death or Disability, Appearance

When an attorney dies, or is removed or suspended, or ceases to act as such, a party to an action, for whom he was acting as attorney, must, before any further proceedings are had against him, be required by the adverse party, by written notice, to appoint another attorney, or to appear in person.

§340.6(a). Attorneys; Wrongful Professional Act or Omission; Tolling of Period

An action against an attorney for a wrongful act or omission, other than for actual fraud, arising in the performance of professional services shall be commenced within one year after the plaintiff discovers, or through the use of reasonable diligence should have discovered, the facts constituting the wrongful act or omission, or four years from the date of the wrongful act or omission, whichever occurs first. In no event shall the time for commencement of legal action exceed four years except that the period shall be tolled during the time that any of the following exist:

(1) The plaintiff has not sustained actual injury;

(2) The attorney continues to represent the plaintiff regarding the specific subject matter in which the alleged wrongful act or omission occurred;

(3) The attorney willfully conceals the facts constituting the wrongful act or omission when such facts are known to the attorney, except that this subdivision shall toll only the four-year limitation; and

(4) The plaintiff is under a legal or physical disability which restricts the plaintiff's ability to commence legal action.

§907. Appeal Frivolous or Taken Solely for Delay

When it appears to the reviewing court that the appeal was frivolous or taken solely for delay, it may add to the costs on appeal such damages as may be just.

§1209. Acts and Omissions Constituting Contempt

(a) The following acts or omissions in respect to a court of justice, or proceedings therein, are contempt of the authority of the court:

(1) Disorderly, contemptuous, or insolent behavior toward the judge while holding the court, tending to interrupt the due course of a trial or other judicial proceeding;

(2) A breach of the peace, boisterous conduct, or violent disturbance, tending to interrupt the due course of a trial or other judicial proceeding;

(3) Misbehavior in office, or other willful neglect or violation of duty by an attorney, counsel, clerk, sheriff, coroner, or other person, appointed or elected to perform a judicial or ministerial service;

(4) Abuse of the process or proceedings of the court, or falsely pretending to act under authority of an order or process of the court;

(5) Disobedience of any lawful judgment, order, or process of the court; . . .

(7) Unlawfully detaining a witness, or party to an action while going to, remaining at, or returning from the court where the action is on the calendar for trial;

(8) Any other unlawful interference with the process or proceedings of a court;

(9) Disobedience of a subpoena duly served, or refusing to be sworn or answer as a witness; . . .

(b) No speech or publication reflecting upon or concerning any court or any officer thereof shall be treated or punished as a contempt of such court unless made in the immediate presence of such court while in session and in such a manner as to actually interfere with its proceedings.

§1282.4. Representation by Counsel

Editors' Note. In January of 1998, the California Supreme Court decided Birbrower, Montalbano, Condon & Frank v. Superior Court, 17 Cal. 4th 643a (1998), partially affirming summary judgment against a New York law firm that had sought legal fees for services performed in preparation for a California arbitration proceeding. The basis for the decision was that the New York law firm and its lawyers were not licensed to practice law in California as required by §6125 of the California Business and Professions Code. In response to *Birbrower,* the California Legislature amended §1282.4 of the California Civil Procedure Code. The statute countermands *Birbrower* by permitting out-of-state attorneys who meet certain conditions to appear in arbitration proceedings conducted in California. However, the statute will remain operative only until January 1, 2006. On that date, the entire statute except paragraph (a) will be automatically repealed.

In a related development, on July 1, 1999, the California Supreme Court adopted a new Rule 983.4 of the California Rules of Court, which reinforces and amplifies §1282.4. We reprint the new rule below in an Editors' Note immediately after §1282.4.

(a) A party to the arbitration has the right to be represented by an attorney at any proceeding or hearing in arbitration under this title. A waiver of this right may be revoked; but if a party revokes such waiver, the other party is entitled to a reasonable continuance for the purpose of procuring an attorney.

(b) Notwithstanding any other provision of law, including Section 6125 of the Business and Professions Code, an attorney admitted to the bar of any other state may represent the parties in the course of, or in connection with, an arbitration proceeding in this state, provided that the attorney, if not admitted to the State Bar of California, timely files the certificate described in subdivision (c) and the attorney's appearance is approved by the arbitrator, the arbitrators, or the arbitral form.

(c) Prior to the first scheduled hearing in an arbitration, the attorney described in subdivision (b) shall serve a certificate on the arbitrator or arbitrators, the State Bar of California, and all other parties and counsel in the arbitration whose addresses are known to the attorney. In the event that the attorney is retained after the first hearing has commenced, then the certificate shall be served prior to the first hearing at which the attorney appears. The certificate shall state all of the following:

(1) The attorney's residence and office address.

(2) The courts before which the attorney has been admitted to practice and the dates of admission.

(3) That the attorney is currently a member in good standing of, and eligible to practice law before, the bar of those courts.

(4) That the attorney is not currently on suspension or disbarred from the practice of law before the bar of any court.

(5) That the attorney is not a resident of the State of California.

(6) That the attorney is not regularly employed in the State of California.

(7) That the attorney is not regularly engaged in substantial business, professional, or other activities in the State of California.

(8) That the attorney agrees to be subject to the jurisdiction of the courts of this state with respect to the law of this state governing the conduct of attorneys to the same extent as a member of the State Bar of California.

(9) The title of the court and the cause in which the attorney has filed an application to appear as counsel pro hac vice in this state or filed a certificate pursuant to this section in the preceding two years, the date of each application, and whether or not it was granted.

(10) The name, address, and telephone number of the active member of the State Bar of California who is the attorney of record.

(d) Failure to timely file the certificate described in subdivision (c) or, absent special circumstances, repeated appearances shall be grounds for disqualification from serving as the attorney of record in the arbitration in which the certificate was filed.

(e) An attorney who files a certificate containing false information or who otherwise fails to comply with the standards of professional conduct required of members of the State Bar of California shall be subject to the disciplinary jurisdiction of the State Bar with respect to any of his or her acts occurring in the course of the arbitration.

(f) Notwithstanding any other provision of law, including Section 6125 of the Business and Professions Code, an attorney who is a member in good standing of the bar of any state may represent the parties in connection with rendering legal services in this state in the course of and in connection with an arbitration pending in another state.

(g) Notwithstanding any other provision of law, including Section 6125 of the Business and Professions Code, any party to an arbitration arising under collective bargaining agreements in industries and provisions subject to either state or federal law may be represented in the course of, and in connection with, those proceedings by any person, regardless of whether that person is licensed to practice law in this state.

(h) Nothing in this section shall apply to Division 4 (commencing with Section 3201) of the Labor Code.

(i)(1) In enacting the amendments to this section made by Assembly Bill 2086 of the 1997-98 Regular Session, it is the intent of the Legislature to respond to the holding in Birbrower v. Superior Court (1998) 17 Cal. 4th 119, as modified at 17 Cal.4th 543a (hereafter Birbrower), to provide a procedure for nonresident attorneys who are not licensed in this state to appear in California arbitration proceedings.

(2) In enacting subdivision (g), it is the intent of the Legislature to make clear that any party to an arbitration arising under a collective bargaining agreement governed by the laws of this state may be represented in the course of and in connection with those proceedings by any person regardless of whether that person is licensed to practice law in this state.

(3) Except as otherwise specifically provided in this section, in enacting the amendments to this section made by Assembly Bill 2086 of the 1997-98 Regular Session, it is the Legislature's intent that nothing in this section is intended to expand or restrict the ability of a party prior to the decision in Birbrower to elect to be represented by any person in a nonjudicial arbitration proceeding to the extent those rights or abilities existed prior to that decision. To the extent that Birbrower is interpreted to expand or restrict that right or ability pursuant to the laws of this state, it is hereby abrogated except as specifically provided in this section.

(4) In enacting subdivision (h), it is the intent of the Legislature to make clear that nothing in this section shall affect those provisions of law governing the right of injured workers to elect to be represented by any person, regardless of whether that person is licensed to practice law in this state, as set forth in Division 4 (commencing with Section 3200) of the Labor Code.

(j) This section shall be operative until January 1, 2006, and on that date shall be repealed.

Editors' Note. On July 1, 1999, to reinforce and clarify §1282.4, the California Supreme Court promulgated the following new Rule 983.4 of the California Rules of Court:

Rule 983.4 Out-of-State Attorney Arbitration Counsel

(a) *[Definition]*

(1) An "Out-of-State Attorney Arbitration Counsel" is an attorney who is not a member of the State Bar of California but who is a member in good standing of and eligible to practice before the bar of any United States court or the highest court in any state, territory or insular possession of the United States, and who has been retained to appear in the course of, or in connection with, an arbitration proceeding in this state; and

(2) has served a certificate in accordance with the requirements of Code of Civil Procedure section 1282.4 upon the arbitrator, the arbitrators, or the arbitral forum, the State Bar of California, and all other parties and counsel in the arbitration whose addresses are known to the attorney; and

(3) whose appearance has been approved by the arbitrator, the arbitrators or the arbitral forum.

(b) *[The State Bar Out-of-State Attorney Arbitration Counsel Program]* The State Bar of California shall establish and administer a program to implement the State Bar of California's responsibilities under Code of Civil Procedure section 1282.4. The State Bar of California's program shall be operative only as long as the applicable provisions of Code of Civil Procedure section 1282.4 remain in effect.

(c) *[Eligibility to appear as an Out-of-State Attorney Arbitration Counsel]* To be eligible to appear as an Out-of-State Attorney Arbitration Counsel, an attorney must comply with all of the applicable provisions of Code of Civil Procedure section 1282.4 and the requirements of this rule and the rules and regulations adopted by the State Bar of California pursuant to this rule.

(d) *[Discipline]* An attorney who files a certificate containing false information or who otherwise fails to comply with the standards of professional conduct required of members of the State Bar of California shall be subject to the disciplinary jurisdiction of the State Bar with respect to any of his or her acts occurring in the course of the arbitration.

(e) *[Disqualification]* Failure to timely file a certificate or, absent special circumstances, appearances in multiple separate arbitration matters shall be grounds for disqualification from serving in the arbitration in which the certificate was filed.

(f) *[Fee]* Out-of-State Attorney Arbitration Counsel shall pay a reasonable fee not exceeding $50 to the State Bar of California with the copy of the certificate that is served upon the State Bar.

(g) *[Inherent power of Supreme Court]* Nothing in these rules shall be constructed as affecting the power of the Supreme Court to exercise its inherent jurisdiction over the practice of law in California.

CALIFORNIA FAMILY CODE

§8800. Unethical for Attorney to Represent Both Prospective Adopting Parents and Natural Parents — Conflict of Interest

(a) The Legislature finds and declares that an attorney's ability to effectively represent his or her client may be seriously impaired when conflict of interest deprives the client of the attorney's undivided loyalty and effort. The Legislature further finds and declares that the relation between attorney and client is a fiduciary relation of the very highest character, and binds the attorney to the most conscientious fidelity.

(b) The Legislature finds that Rule 2-111(A)(2) of the State Bar Rules of Professional Conduct provides that an attorney shall not withdraw from employment until the attorney has taken reasonable steps to avoid foreseeable prejudice to the rights of the client, including giving due notice to the client, allowing time for employment of other counsel, delivering to the client all papers and property to which the client is entitled, and complying with applicable laws and rules.

(c) The Legislature declares that in an independent adoption proceeding, whether or not written consent is obtained, multiple representation by an attorney should be avoided whenever a birth parent displays the slightest reason for the attorney to believe any controversy might arise. The Legislature finds and declares that it is the duty of the attorney when a conflict of interest occurs to withdraw promptly from any case, advise the parties to retain independent counsel, refrain from taking positions in opposition to any of these former clients, and thereafter maintain an impartial, fair, and open attitude toward the new attorneys.

(d) Notwithstanding any other law, it is unethical for an attorney to undertake the representation of both the prospective adoptive parents and the birth parents of a child in any negotiations or proceedings in connection with an adoption unless a written consent is obtained from both parties. The written consent shall include all of the following:

(1) A notice to the birth parents, in the form specified in this section, of their right to have an independent attorney advise and represent them in the adoption proceeding and that the prospective adoptive parents may be required to pay the reasonable attorney's fees up to a maximum of five hundred dollars ($500) for that representation, unless a higher fee is agreed to by the parties.

(2) A notice to the birth parents that they may waive their right to an independent attorney and may be represented by the attorney representing the prospective adoptive parents.

(3) A waiver by the birth parents of representation by an independent attorney.

(4) An agreement that the attorney representing the prospective adoptive parents shall represent the birth parents.

(e) Upon the petition or motion of any party, or upon motion of the court, the court may appoint an attorney to represent a child's birth parent or parents in negotiations or proceedings in connection with the child's adoption.

(f) The birth parent or parents may have an attorney, other than the attorney representing the interests of the prospective adoptive parents, to advise them fully of the adoption procedures and of their legal rights. The birth parent or parents also may retain an attorney to represent them in negotiations or proceedings in connection with the child's adoption. The court may award attorney's fees and costs for just cause and based upon the ability of the parties to pay those fees and costs.

(g) In the initial communication between the attorney retained by or representing the prospective adoptive parents and the birth parents, or as soon thereafter as reasonable, but before any written consent for dual representation, the attorney shall advise the birth parents of their rights regarding an independent attorney and that it is possible to waive the independent attorney.

(h) The attorney retained by or representing the prospective adoptive parents shall inform the prospective adoptive parents in writing that the birth parent or parents can revoke consent to the adoption pursuant to Section 8814.5 and that any moneys expended in negotiations or proceedings in connection with the child's adoption are non-reimbursable. The prospective adoptive parents shall sign a statement to indicate their understanding of this information.

(i) Any written consent to dual representation shall be filed with the court before the filing of the birth parent's consent to adoption.

CALIFORNIA INSURANCE CODE

§750. Unlawful to Receive Consideration for Referral of Clients

(a) Except as provided in Section 750.5, any person acting individually or through his or her employees or agents, who engages in the practice of processing, presenting, or negotiating claims, including claims under policies of insurance, and who offers, delivers, receives, or accepts any rebate, refund, commission, or other consideration, whether in the form of money or otherwise, as compensation or inducement to or from any person for the referral or procurement of clients, cases, patients, or customers, is guilty of a crime.

§750.5. Permissible Acts for Attorneys and Law Firms under Section 750

Nothing in Section 750 of the Insurance Code, Section 549 of the Penal Code, or Section 3215 of the Labor Code shall be construed to prevent an attorney or law firm from the following:

(a) Dividing fees for legal services with a lawyer under circumstances expressly permitted by Rule 2-200 of the Rules of Professional Conduct of the State Bar.

(b) Offering or giving an incidental nonmonetary gift or gratuity to a person who has made a recommendation resulting in the employment of the attorney or law firm, provided that the gift or gratuity was not offered in consideration of any promise, agreement, or understanding that the gift or gratuity would be forthcoming or that referrals would be made or encouraged in the future.

(c) Offering or giving a bonus to an employee who has made a referral or recommendation resulting in the employment of the attorney or law firm, provided that the bonus was not offered in consideration of any promise, agreement, or understanding that the bonus would be forthcoming or that referrals or recommendations would be made or encouraged in the future.

§1871.7. Unlawful Solicitation of Business

(a) It is unlawful to knowingly employ runners, cappers, steerers, or other persons to procure clients or patients to perform or obtain services or benefits pursuant to [California's Workers' Compensation laws] or to procure clients or patients to perform or obtain services or benefits under a contract of insurance or that will be the basis for a claim against an insured individual or his or her insurer. . . .

§1872.83. Reporting Incidents of Fraud to Appropriate Disciplinary Body

(a) The commissioner shall ensure that the Bureau of Fraudulent Claims aggressively pursues all reported incidents of probable workers' compensation fraud . . . and forwards to the appropriate disciplinary body the names, along with all supporting evidence, of any individuals licensed under the Business and Professions Code who are suspected of actively engaging in fraudulent activity. . . .

§1872.95. Medical & Chiropractic Boards and State Bar; Investigation of Motor Vehicle or Disability Insurance Fraud by Licensees

(a) Within existing resources, the Medical Board of California, the Board of Chiropractic Examiners, and the State Bar shall each designate employees to investigate and report on possible fraudulent activities relating to workers' compensation, motor vehicle insurance, or disability insurance by licensees of the board or the bar. Those employees shall actively cooperate with the bureau in the investigation of those activities.

(b) The Medical Board of California, the Board of Chiropractic Examiners, and the State Bar shall each report annually, on or before March 1, to the committees of the Senate and Assembly having jurisdiction over insurance on their activities established pursuant to subdivision (a) for the previous year. That report shall specify, at a minimum, the number of cases investigated, the number of cases forwarded to the bureau or other law enforcement agencies, the outcome of all cases listed in the report, and any other relevant information concerning those cases or general activities conducted under subdivision (a) for the previous year. The report shall include information regarding activities conducted in connection with cases of suspected automobile insurance fraud.

CALIFORNIA PENAL CODE

§118. Perjury Defined; Proof

(a) Every person who, having taken an oath that he or she will testify, declare, depose, or certify truly before any competent tribunal, officer, or person, in any of the cases in which the oath may by law of the State of California be administered, willfully and contrary to the oath, states as true any material matter which he or she knows to be false, and every person who testifies, declares, deposes, or certifies under penalty of perjury in any of the cases in which the testimony, declarations, depositions, or certification is permitted by law of the State of California under penalty of perjury and willfully states as true any material matter which he or she knows to be false, is guilty of perjury.

This subdivision is applicable whether the statement, or the testimony, declaration, deposition, or certification is made or subscribed within or without the State of California.

(b) No person shall be convicted of perjury where proof of falsity rests solely upon contradiction by testimony of a single person other than the defendant. Proof of falsity may be established by direct or indirect evidence.

§118a. False Affidavit as to Perjurious Testimony; Subsequent Testimony

Any person who, in any affidavit taken before any person authorized to administer oaths, swears, affirms, declares, deposes, or certifies that he will testify, declare, depose, or certify before any competent tribunal, officer, or person, in any case then pending or thereafter to be instituted, in any particular manner, or to any particular fact, and in such affidavit willfully and contrary to such oath states as true any material matter which he knows to be false, is guilty of perjury. In any prosecution under this section, the subsequent testimony of such person, in any action involving the matters in such affidavit contained, which is contrary to any of the matters in such affidavit contained, shall be prima facie evidence that the matters in such affidavit were false.

§126. Punishment

Perjury is punishable by imprisonment in the state prison for two, three or four years.

§127. Subornation of Perjury — Definition, Punishment

Every person who willfully procures another person to commit perjury is guilty of subornation of perjury, and is punishable in the same manner as he would be if personally guilty of the perjury so procured.

§132. Offering False Evidence

Every person who upon any trial, proceeding, inquiry, or investigation whatever, authorized or permitted by law, offers in evidence, as genuine or true, any book, paper, document, record, or other instrument in writing, knowing the same to have been forged or fraudulently altered or ante-dated, is guilty of felony.

§133. Deceiving a Witness

Every person who practices any fraud or deceit, or knowingly makes or exhibits any false statement, representation, token, or writing, to any witness or person about to be called as a witness upon any trial, proceeding, inquiry, or investigation whatever, authorized by law, with intent to affect the testimony of such witness, is guilty of a misdemeanor.

§134. Preparing False Evidence

Every person guilty of preparing any false or ante-dated book, paper, record, instrument in writing, or other matter or thing, with intent to produce it, or allow it to be produced for any fraudulent or deceitful purpose, as genuine or true, upon any trial, proceeding, or inquiry whatever, authorized by law, is guilty of felony.

§135. Destroying or Concealing Documentary Evidence

Destroying Evidence. Every person who, knowing that any book, paper, record, instrument in writing, or other matter or thing, is about to be produced in evidence upon any trial, inquiry, or investigation whatever, authorized by law, willfully destroys or conceals the same, with intent thereby to prevent it from being produced, is guilty of a misdemeanor.

§3215. Referral of Clients or Patients for Compensation; Penalty

Except as otherwise permitted by law, any person acting individually or through his or her employees or agents, who offers, delivers, receives, or accepts any rebate, refund, commission, preference, patronage, dividend, discount or other consideration, whether in the form of money or otherwise, as compensation or inducement for referring clients or patients to perform or obtain services or benefits pursuant to this division, is guilty of a crime.

CALIFORNIA PROBATE CODE

§710. Preservation of Documents Transferred to Attorney

If a document is deposited with an attorney, the attorney, and a successor attorney that accepts transfer of the document, shall use ordinary care for preservation of the document on and after July 1, 1994, whether or not consideration is given, and shall hold the document in a safe, vault, safe deposit box, or other secure place where it will be reasonably protected against loss or destruction.

§713. No Duty as to Content of Document; Provision of Legal Services Arising from Document Retention

The acceptance by an attorney of a document for deposit imposes no duty on the attorney to do either of the following:

(a) Inquire into the content, validity, invalidity, or completeness of the document, or the correctness of any information in the document.

(b) Provide continuing legal services to the depositor or to any beneficiary under the document. This subdivision does not affect the duty, if any, of the drafter of the document to provide continuing legal services to any person.

District of Columbia Materials

District of Columbia Rules of Professional Conduct

Editors' Introduction. The current version of the District of Columbia Rules of Professional Conduct was adopted by the D.C. Court of Appeals effective November 1, 1996, and has been amended several times since then. The District of Columbia's rules are closely modeled on the ABA Model Rules of Professional Conduct, but the D.C. rules differ from the ABA Model Rules in many significant ways. For example, both the text and comments of the District of Columbia's provisions governing such core issues as confidentiality, conflicts of interest, and candor to the court are lengthier and more detailed than their counterparts in the ABA Model Rules. At the same time, D.C.'s provisions governing advertising are far less detailed than their ABA counterparts — D.C. has no equivalent of ABA Model Rules 7.2, 7.3, or 7.4. (In our Selected State Variations following each ABA Model Rules of Professional Conduct, we identify the D.C. rules that differ significantly from the corresponding ABA Model Rules.) Our version of the D.C. rules is current as of our press deadline in September 2002.

Since our last edition went to press in September of 2001, the District of Columbia has not amended its Rules of Professional Conduct in any way. However, at its May 14, 2002, meeting, the District of Columbia Bar Board of Governors voted to forward to the D.C. Court of Appeals (the District's highest court) the final report and recommendations of the D.C. Bar's Special Committee on Multidisciplinary Practice. That report, dated October 23, 2001, addresses the circumstances under which lawyers and nonlawyers should be permitted to work together and share fees in the delivery of professional services. The report recommends significant amendments to Rule 1.7 (Conflict of Interest: General Rule) and to Rule 5.4 (Professional Independence of a Lawyer) to permit lawyers to enter partnerships with nonlawyers and to share legal fees with nonlawyers under certain conditions. The amended version of Rule 1.7(b)(4) would provide as follows:

> (b) Except as permitted by paragraph (c) below, a lawyer shall not represent a client with respect to a matter if: . . .
>
> (4) The lawyer's professional judgment on behalf of the client will be or reasonably may be adversely affected by the lawyer's responsibilities or interests in a third party or the lawyer's own financial, business, property, or personal interests, including, without limitation, the lawyer's interest in non-legal business of the lawyer's organization or firm or non-legal business of an organization affiliated with the lawyer or his or her firm.

The amended version of Rule 5.4(c), which would move further toward integrated multidisciplinary practice than the rules in any other jurisdiction, would provide as follows:

> (c) A lawyer may practice law in a partnership or other form of organization in which a financial interest is held or managerial authority is exercised by one or more nonlawyers who perform professional services on behalf of the organization or its clients, but only if:
>
> (1) Lawyers who perform legal services on behalf of the organization assume responsibility for nonlawyer participants engaged in legal representations as provided under Rule 5.3, and such lawyers make reasonable efforts to ensure that the organizations in which they practice do not intentionally or inadvertently lead their clients or customers receiving nonlegal services to believe that those services are subject to the professional conduct standards and confidentiality protections applicable to legal services.
>
> (2) At the outset of a legal representation on behalf of a new client for legal services, a lawyer practicing law in such an organization makes full disclosure to the prospective client of information sufficient to permit the prospective client to make an informed decision whether to retain the lawyer to provide legal services, including (i) the nature of the lawyer's interest in other services provided by the organization; (ii) that some of the services provided by the organization are not legal services and are not governed by the standards and confidentiality protections applicable to legal services; (iii) that nonlawyer participants in the organization may undertake to provide nonlegal services to the client or to adversaries of the client; (iv) that actual or potential conflicts of interest may arise from the lawyer's interest in services provided by nonlawyer participants in the organization; (v) that the form of partnership or organization may create risks with respect to the attorney-client privilege and of precautions necessary or appropriate to protect confidences and secrets of the client; and (vi) that legal services are available from sources that do not present the same risks.
>
> (3) In considering the acceptance or retention of a legal representation, the lawyer complies with Rule 1.7 with respect to conflicts of interest and, where required, obtains from legal services clients such informed consent as may be required by Rule 1.7(c) to permit the acceptance or continuation of such a representation.

The proposed amendments were accompanied by extensive amendments to the Comment to Rule 5.4 (but no amendments were proposed to the Comment to Rule 1.7). The proposed amendments were still pending before the District of Columbia Court of Appeals when we went to press in September of 2002, and the court had not set any deadline for considering them.

For updates on the District of Columbia Rules of Professional Conduct, visit the District's excellent web site at www.dcbar.org (click on "Legal Ethics" or use the search engine).

SCOPE

The Rules of Professional Conduct are rules of reason. They should be interpreted with reference to the purposes of legal representation and of the law itself. Some of the Rules are imperatives, cast in the terms "shall" or "shall not." These define proper conduct for purposes of professional discipline. Others, generally cast in the term "may," are permissive and define areas under the Rules in which the lawyer has professional discretion. No disciplinary action should be taken when the lawyer chooses not to act or acts within the bounds of such discretion. Other Rules define the nature of relationships between the lawyer and others. The Rules are thus partly obliga-tory and disciplinary and partly constitutive and descriptive in that they define a lawyer's professional role. Many of the Comments use the term "should." Comments do not add obligations to the Rules but provide guidance for interpreting the Rules and practicing in compliance with them.

The Rules presuppose a larger legal context shaping the lawyer's role. That context includes court rules and statutes relating to matters of licensure, laws defining specific obligations of lawyers, and substantive and procedural law in general. Compliance with the Rules, as with all law in an open society, depends primarily upon understanding and voluntary compliance, secondarily upon reinforcement by peer and public opinion, and finally, when necessary, upon enforcement through disciplinary proceedings. The Rules do not, however, exhaust the moral and ethical considerations that should inform a lawyer, for no worthwhile human activity can be completely defined by legal rules. The Rules simply provide a framework for the ethical practice of law.

Failure to comply with an obligation or prohibition imposed by a Rule is a basis for invoking the disciplinary process. The Rules presuppose that disciplinary assessment of a lawyer's conduct will be made on the basis of the facts and circumstances as they existed at the time of the conduct in question and in recognition of the fact that a lawyer often has to act upon uncertain or incomplete evidence of the situation. Moreover, the Rules presuppose that whether or not discipline should be imposed for a violation, and the severity of a sanction, depend on all the circumstances, such as the willfulness and seriousness of the violation, extenuating factors and whether there have been previous violations.

Nothing in these Rules, the Comments associated with them, or this Scope section is intended to enlarge or restrict existing law regarding the liability of lawyers to others or the requirements that the testimony of expert witnesses or other modes of proof must be employed in determining the scope of a lawyer's duty to others. Moreover, nothing in the Rules or associated Comments or this Scope section is intended to confer rights on an adversary of a lawyer to enforce the Rules in a proceeding other than a disciplinary proceeding. A tribunal presented with claims that the conduct of a lawyer appearing before that tribunal requires, for example, disqualification of the lawyer and/or the lawyer's firm may take such action as seems appropriate in the circumstances, which may or may not involve disqualification.

In interpreting these Rules, the specific shall control the general in the sense that any rule that specifically addresses conduct shall control the disposition of matters and the outcome of such matters shall not turn upon the application of a more general rule that arguably also applies to the conduct in question. In a number of instances, there are specific rules that address specific types of conduct. The rule of interpretation expressed here is meant to make it clear that the general rule does not supplant, amend, enlarge, or extend the specific rule. So, for instance, the general terms of Rule 1.3 are not intended to govern conflicts of interest, which are particularly discussed in Rules 1.7, 1.8, and 1.9. Thus, conduct that is proper under the specific conflicts rules is not improper under the more general rule of Rule 1.3. Except where the principle of priority stated here is applicable, however, compliance with one rule does not generally excuse compliance with other rules. Accordingly, once a lawyer has analyzed the ethical considerations under a given rule, the lawyer must generally extend the analysis to ensure compliance with all other applicable rules.

The Comment accompanying each Rule explains and illustrates the meaning and purpose of the Rule. This note on Scope provides general orientation and general rules of interpretation. The Comments are intended as guides to interpretation, but the text of each Rule is controlling.

TERMINOLOGY

"Belief" or "believes" denotes that the person involved actually supposed the fact in question to be true. A person's belief may be inferred from circumstances.

"Consent" denotes a client's uncoerced assent to a proposed course of action, following consultation with the lawyer regarding the matter in question.

"Consult" or "consultation" denotes communication of information reasonably sufficient to permit the client to appreciate the significance of the matter in question.

"Firm" or "law firm" denotes a lawyer or lawyers in a private firm, lawyers employed in the legal department of a corporation or other organization, and lawyers employed in a legal services organization. See Comment, Rule 1.10.

"Fraud" or "fraudulent" denotes conduct having a purpose to deceive and not merely negligent misrepresentation or failure to apprise another of relevant information.

"Knowingly," "known," or "knows" denotes actual knowledge of the fact in question. A person's knowledge may be inferred from circumstances.

"Law clerk" denotes a person, typically a recent law school graduate, who acts, typically for a limited period, as confidential assistant to a judge or judges of a court; to an administrative law judge or a similar administrative hearing officer; or to the head of a governmental agency or to a member of a governmental commission, either of which has authority to adjudicate or to promulgate rules or regulations of general application.

"Matter" means any litigation, administrative proceeding, lobbying activity, application, claim, investigation, arrest, charge or accusation, the drafting of a contract, a negotiation, estate or family relations practice issue, or any other representation, except as expressly limited in a particular Rule.

"Partner" denotes a member of a partnership and a shareholder in a law firm organized as a professional corporation.

"Reasonable" or "reasonably" when used in relation to conduct by a lawyer denotes the conduct of a reasonably prudent and competent lawyer.

"Reasonably should know" when used in reference to a lawyer denotes that a lawyer of reasonable prudence and competence would ascertain the matter in question.

"Substantial" when used in reference to degree or extent denotes a material matter of clear and weighty importance.

"Tribunal" denotes a court, regulatory agency, commission, and any other body or individual authorized by law to render decisions of a judicial or quasi-judicial nature, based on information presented before it, regardless of the degree of formality or informality of the proceedings.

CLIENT-LAWYER RELATIONSHIP

Rule 1.1. Competence

(a) A lawyer shall provide competent representation to a client. Competent representation requires the legal knowledge, skill, thoroughness, and preparation reasonably necessary for the representation.

(b) A lawyer shall serve a client with skill and care commensurate with that generally afforded to clients by other lawyers in similar matters.

COMMENT

Legal Knowledge and Skill

[1] In determining whether a lawyer employs the requisite knowledge and skill in a particular matter, relevant factors include the relative complexity and specialized nature of the matter, the lawyer's general experience, the lawyer's training and experience in the field in question, the preparation and study the lawyer is able to give the matter, and whether it is feasible to refer the matter to, or associate or consult with, a lawyer of established competence in the field in question. In many instances, the required proficiency is that of a general practitioner. Expertise in a particular field of law may be required in some circumstances. One such circumstance would be where the lawyer, by representations made to the client, has led the client reasonably to expect a special level of expertise in the matter undertaken by the lawyer.

[2] A lawyer need not necessarily have special training or prior experience to handle legal problems of a type with which the lawyer is unfamiliar. A newly admitted lawyer can be as competent as a practitioner with long experience. Some important legal skills, such as the analysis of precedent, the evaluation of evidence and legal drafting, are required in all legal problems. Perhaps the most fundamental legal skill consists of determining what kind of legal problems a situation may involve, a skill that necessarily transcends any particular specialized knowledge. A lawyer can provide adequate representation in a wholly novel field through necessary study. Competent representation can also be provided through the association of a lawyer of established competence in the field in question.

[3] In an emergency a lawyer may give advice or assistance in a matter in which the lawyer does not have the skill ordinarily required where referral to or consultation or association with another lawyer would be impractical. Even in an emergency, however, assistance should be limited to that reasonably necessary in the circumstances, for ill-considered action under emergency conditions can jeopardize the client's interest.

[4] A lawyer may accept representation where the requisite level of competence can be achieved by reasonable preparation. This applies as well to a lawyer who is appointed as counsel for an unrepresented person. See also Rule 6.2.

Thoroughness and Preparation

[5] Competent handling of a particular matter includes inquiry into and analysis of the factual and legal elements of the problem, and use of

methods and procedures meeting the standards of competent practitioners. It also includes adequate preparation, and continuing attention to the needs of the representation to assure that there is no neglect of such needs. The required attention and preparation are determined in part by what is at stake; major litigation and complex transactions ordinarily require more elaborate treatment than matters of lesser consequence.

Maintaining Competence

[6] To maintain the requisite knowledge and skill, a lawyer should engage in such continuing study and education as may be necessary to maintain competence, taking into account that the learning acquired through a lawyer's practical experience in actual representations may reduce or eliminate the need for special continuing study or education. If a system of peer review has been established, the lawyer should consider making use of it in appropriate circumstances.

Rule 1.2. Scope of Representation

(a) A lawyer shall abide by a client's decisions concerning the objectives of representation, subject to paragraphs (c), (d), and (e), and shall consult with the client as to the means by which they are to be pursued. A lawyer shall abide by a client's decision whether to accept an offer of settlement of a matter. In a criminal case, the lawyer shall abide by the client's decision, after consultation with the lawyer, as to a plea to be entered, whether to waive jury trial, and whether the client will testify.

(b) A lawyer's representation of a client, including representation by appointment, does not constitute an endorsement of the client's political, economic, social, or moral views or activities.

(c) A lawyer may limit the objectives of the representation if the client consents after consultation.

(d) A government lawyer's authority and control over decisions concerning the representation may, by statute or regulation, be expanded beyond the limits imposed by paragraphs (a) and (c).

(e) A lawyer shall not counsel a client to engage, or assist a client, in conduct that the lawyer knows is criminal or fraudulent, but a lawyer may discuss the legal consequences of any proposed course of conduct with a client and may counsel or assist a client to make a good faith effort to determine the validity, scope, meaning, or application of the law.

(f) When a lawyer knows that a client expects assistance not permitted by the rules of professional conduct or other law, the lawyer shall consult with the client regarding the relevant limitations on the lawyer's conduct.

COMMENT

Scope of Representation

[1] Both lawyer and client have authority and responsibility in the objectives and means of representation. The client has ultimate authority to determine the purposes to be served by legal representation, within the limits imposed by law and the lawyer's professional obligations. Within these limits, a client also has a right to consult with the lawyer about the means to be used in pursuing those objectives. At the same time, a lawyer is not required to pursue objectives or employ means simply because a client may wish that the lawyer do so. A clear distinction between objectives and means sometimes cannot be drawn, and in many cases the client-lawyer relationship partakes of a joint undertaking. In questions of means, the lawyer should assume responsibility for technical and legal tactical issues, but should defer to the client regarding such questions as the expense to be incurred and concern for third persons who might be adversely affected. Law defining the lawyer's scope of authority in litigation varies among jurisdictions.

[2] In a case in which the client appears to be suffering mental disability, the lawyer's duty to abide by the client's decisions is to be guided by reference to Rule 1.14.

Independence From Client's Views or Activities

[3] Legal representation should not be denied to people who are unable to afford legal services, or whose cause is controversial or the subject of popular disapproval. By the same token, representing a client does not constitute approval of the client's views or activities.

Services Limited in Objectives or Means

[4] The objectives or scope of services provided by the lawyer may be limited by agreement with the client or by terms under which the lawyer's services are made available to the client. For example, a retainer may be for a specifically defined purpose. Representation provided through a legal aid agency may be subject to limitations on the types of cases the agency handles. When a lawyer has been retained by an insurer to represent an insured, the representation may be limited to matters related to the insurance coverage. The terms upon which representation is undertaken may exclude specific objectives or means. Such limitations may exclude objectives or means that the lawyer regards as repugnant or imprudent.

[5] An agreement concerning the scope of representation must accord with the Rules of Professional Conduct and other law. Thus, the client may

not be asked to agree to representation so limited in scope as to violate Rule 1.1, or to surrender the right to terminate the lawyer's services or the right to settle litigation that the lawyer might wish to continue.

Criminal, Fraudulent, and Prohibited Transactions

[6] A lawyer is required to give an honest opinion about the actual consequences that appear likely to result from a client's conduct. The fact that a client uses advice in a course of action that is criminal or fraudulent does not, of itself, make a lawyer a party to the course of action. However, a lawyer may not knowingly assist a client in criminal or fraudulent conduct. There is a critical distinction between presenting an analysis of legal aspects of questionable conduct and recommending the means by which a crime or fraud might be committed with impunity.

[7] When the client's course of action has already begun and is continuing, the lawyer's responsibility is especially delicate. The lawyer is not permitted to reveal the client's wrongdoing, except where permitted by Rule 1.6. However, the lawyer is required to avoid furthering the purpose, for example, by suggesting how it might be concealed. A lawyer may not continue assisting a client in conduct that the lawyer originally supposes is legally proper but then discovers is criminal or fraudulent. Withdrawal from the representation, therefore, may be required.

[8] Where the client is a fiduciary, the lawyer may be charged with special obligations in dealings with a beneficiary.

[9] Paragraph (d) applies whether or not the defrauded party is a party to the transaction. Hence, a lawyer should not participate in a sham transaction; for example, a transaction to effectuate criminal or fraudulent escape of tax liability. Paragraph (d) does not preclude undertaking a criminal defense incident to a general retainer for legal services to a lawful enterprise. The last clause of paragraph (d) recognizes that determining the validity or interpretation of a statute or regulation may require a course of action involving disobedience of the statute or regulation or of the interpretation placed upon it by governmental authorities.

Rule 1.3. Diligence and Zeal

(a) A lawyer shall represent a client zealously and diligently within the bounds of the law.

(b) A lawyer shall not intentionally:

(1) Fail to seek the lawful objectives of a client through reasonably available means permitted by law and the disciplinary rules; or

(2) Prejudice or damage a client during the course of the professional relationship.

(c) A lawyer shall act with reasonable promptness in representing a client.

COMMENT

[1] The duty of a lawyer, both to the client and to the legal system, is to represent the client zealously within the bounds of the law, including the Rules of Professional Conduct and other enforceable professional regulations, such as agency regulations applicable to lawyers practicing before the agency. This duty requires the lawyer to pursue a matter on behalf of a client despite opposition, obstruction, or personal inconvenience to the lawyer, and to take whatever lawful and ethical measures are required to vindicate a client's cause or endeavor. A lawyer should act with commitment and dedication to the interests of the client. However, a lawyer is not bound to press for every advantage that might be realized for a client. A lawyer has professional discretion in determining the means by which a matter should be pursued. See Rule 1.2. A lawyer's work load should be controlled so that each matter can be handled adequately.

[2] This duty derives from the lawyer's membership in a profession that has the duty of assisting members of the public to secure and protect available legal rights and benefits. In our government of laws and not of individuals, each member of our society is entitled to have such member's conduct judged and regulated in accordance with the law; to seek any lawful objective through legally permissible means; and to present for adjudication any lawful claim, issue, or defense.

[3] The bounds of the law in a given case are often difficult to ascertain. The language of legislative enactments and judicial opinions may be uncertain as applied to varying factual situations. The limits and specific meaning of apparently relevant law may be made doubtful by changing or developing constitutional interpretations, ambiguous statutes, or judicial opinions, and changing public and judicial attitudes.

[4] Where the bounds of law are uncertain, the action of a lawyer may depend on whether the lawyer is serving as advocate or adviser. A lawyer may serve simultaneously as both advocate and adviser, but the two roles are essentially different. In asserting a position on behalf of a client, an advocate for the most part deals with past conduct and must take the facts as the advocate finds them. By contrast, a lawyer serving as adviser primarily assists the client in determining the course of future conduct and relationships. While serving as advocate, a lawyer should resolve in favor of the client doubts as to the bounds of the law but even when acting as an advocate, a lawyer may not institute or defend a proceeding unless the positions taken are not frivolous. See Rule 3.1. In serving a client as adviser, a lawyer, in appropriate circumstances, should give a lawyer's professional opinion as to what the ultimate decisions of the courts would likely be as to the applicable law.

[5] In the exercise of professional judgment, a lawyer should always act in a manner consistent with the best interests of the client. However, when an action in the best interests of the client seems to be unjust, a lawyer may ask the client for permission to forgo such action. If the lawyer knows that the client expects assistance that is not in accord with the Rules of Professional Conduct or other law, the lawyer must inform the client of the pertinent limitations on the lawyer's conduct. See Rule 1.2(e) and (f). Similarly, the lawyer's obligation not to prejudice the interests of the client is subject to the duty of candor toward the tribunal under Rule 3.3 and the duty to expedite litigation under Rule 3.2.

[6] The duty of a lawyer to represent the client with zeal does not militate against the concurrent obligation to treat with consideration all persons involved in the legal process and to avoid the infliction of needless harm. Thus, the lawyer's duty to pursue a client's lawful objectives zealously does not prevent the lawyer from acceding to reasonable requests of opposing counsel that do not prejudice the client's rights, being punctual in fulfilling all professional commitments, avoiding offensive tactics, or treating all persons involved in the legal process with courtesy and consideration.

[7] Perhaps no professional shortcoming is more widely resented by clients than procrastination. A client's interests often can be adversely affected by the passage of time or the change of conditions; in extreme instances, as when a lawyer overlooks a statute of limitations, the client's legal position may be destroyed. Even when the client's interests are not affected in substance, however, unreasonable delay can cause a client needless anxiety and undermine confidence in the lawyer's trustworthiness. Neglect of client matters is a serious violation of the obligation of diligence.

[8] Unless the relationship is terminated as provided in Rule 1.16, a lawyer should carry through to conclusion all matters undertaken for a client. If a lawyer's employment is limited to a specific matter, the relationship terminates when the matter has been resolved. If a lawyer has served a client over a substantial period in a variety of matters, the client sometimes may assume that the lawyer will continue to serve on a continuing basis unless the lawyer gives notice of withdrawal. Doubt about whether a client-lawyer relationship still exists should be eliminated by the lawyer, preferably in writing, so that the client will not mistakenly suppose the lawyer is looking after the client's affairs when the lawyer has ceased to do so. For example, if a lawyer has handled a judicial or administrative proceeding that produced a result adverse to the client but has not been specifically instructed concerning pursuit of an appeal, the lawyer should advise the client of the possibility of appeal before relinquishing responsibility for the matter.

[9] Rule 1.3 is a rule of general applicability, and it is not meant to enlarge or restrict any specific rule. In particular, Rule 1.3 is not meant to govern conflicts of interest, which are addressed by Rules 1.7, 1.8, and 1.9.

Rule 1.4. Communication

(a) A lawyer shall keep a client reasonably informed about the status of a matter and promptly comply with reasonable requests for information.

(b) A lawyer shall explain a matter to the extent reasonably necessary to permit the client to make informed decisions regarding the representation.

(c) A lawyer who receives an offer of settlement in a civil case or a proffered plea bargain in a criminal case shall inform the client promptly of the substance of the communication.

COMMENT

[1] The client should have sufficient information to participate intelligently in decisions concerning the objectives of the representation and the means by which they are to be pursued, to the extent the client is willing and able to do so. For example, a lawyer negotiating on behalf of a client should provide the client with facts relevant to the matter, inform the client of communications from another party, and take other reasonable steps that permit the client to make a decision regarding a serious offer from another party. A lawyer who receives from opposing counsel an offer of settlement in a civil controversy or a proffered plea bargain in a criminal case is required to inform the client promptly of its substance. See Rule 1.2(a). Even when a client delegates authority to the lawyer, the client should be kept advised of the status of the matter.

[2] A client is entitled to whatever information the client wishes about all aspects of the subject matter of the representation unless the client expressly consents not to have certain information passed on. The lawyer must be particularly careful to ensure that decisions of the client are made only after the client has been informed of all relevant considerations. The lawyer must initiate and maintain the consultative and decision-making process if the client does not do so and must ensure that the ongoing process is thorough and complete.

[3] Adequacy of communication depends in part on the kind of advice or assistance involved. The guiding principle is that the lawyer should fulfill reasonable client expectations for information consistent with (1) the duty to act in the client's best interests, and (2) the client's overall requirements and objectives as to the character of representation.

[4] Ordinarily, the information to be provided is that appropriate for a client who is a comprehending and responsible adult. However, fully informing the client according to this standard may be impracticable, for example, where the client is a child or suffers from mental disability. See Rule 1.14. When the client is an organization or group, it is often impossible or inappropriate to inform every one of its members about its legal affairs; ordi-

narily, the lawyer should address communications to the appropriate officials of the organization. See Rule 1.13. Where many routine matters are involved, a system of limited or occasional reporting may be arranged with the client. Practical exigency may also require a lawyer to act for a client without prior consultation. When the lawyer is conducting a trial, it is often not possible for the lawyer to consult with the client and obtain the client's acquiescence in tactical matters arising during the course of trial. It is sufficient if the lawyer consults with the client in advance of trial on significant issues that can be anticipated as arising during the course of the trial, and consults during trial to the extent practical, given the nature of the trial process.

Withholding Information

[5] In rare circumstances, a lawyer may be justified in delaying transmission of information when the client would be likely to react imprudently to an immediate communication. Thus, a lawyer might withhold a psychiatric diagnosis of a client when the examining psychiatrist indicates that disclosure would harm the client. Similarly, a lawyer may be justified, for humanitarian reasons, in not conveying certain information, for example, where the information would merely be upsetting to a terminally ill client. A lawyer may not withhold information to serve the lawyer's own interest or convenience. Rules or court orders governing litigation (such as a protective order limiting access to certain types of discovery material to counsel only) may provide that information supplied to a lawyer may not be disclosed to the client. Rule 3.4(c) directs compliance with such rules or orders.

Rule 1.5. Fees

(a) A lawyer's fee shall be reasonable. The factors to be considered in determining the reasonableness of a fee include the following:

(1) The time and labor required, the novelty and difficulty of the questions involved, and the skill requisite to perform the legal service properly;

(2) The likelihood, if apparent to the client, that the acceptance of the particular employment will preclude other employment by the lawyer;

(3) The fee customarily charged in the locality for similar legal services;

(4) The amount involved and the results obtained;

(5) The time limitations imposed by the client or by the circumstances;

(6) The nature and length of the professional relationship with the client;

(7) The experience, reputation, and ability of the lawyer or lawyers performing the services; and

(8) Whether the fee is fixed or contingent.

(b) When the lawyer has not regularly represented the client, the basis or rate of the fee shall be communicated to the client, in writing, before or within a reasonable time after commencing the representation.

(c) A fee may be contingent on the outcome of the matter for which the service is rendered, except in a matter in which a contingent fee is prohibited by paragraph (d) or other law. A contingent fee agreement shall be in writing and shall state the method by which the fee is to be determined, including the percentage or percentages that shall accrue to the lawyer in the event of settlement, trial or appeal, litigation, and other expenses to be deducted from the recovery, and whether such expenses are to be deducted before or after the contingent fee is calculated. Upon conclusion of a contingent fee matter, the lawyer shall provide the client with a written statement stating the outcome of the matter and, if there is a recovery, showing the remittance to the client and the method of its determination.

(d) A lawyer shall not enter into an arrangement for, charge, or collect a contingent fee for representing a defendant in a criminal case.

(e) A division of a fee between lawyers who are not in the same firm may be made only if:

(1) The division is in proportion to the services performed by each lawyer or each lawyer assumes joint responsibility for the representation;

(2) The client is advised, in writing, of the identity of the lawyers who will participate in the representation, of the contemplated division of responsibility, and of the effect of the association of lawyers outside the firm on the fee to be charged;

(3) The client consents to the arrangement; and

(4) The total fee is reasonable.

(f) Any fee that is prohibited by paragraph (d) above or by law is per se unreasonable.

COMMENT

Basis or Rate of Fee

[1] When the lawyer has regularly represented a client, they ordinarily will have evolved an understanding concerning the basis or rate of the fee. In a new client-lawyer relationship, however, an understanding as to the fee should be promptly established. It is not necessary to recite all the factors that underlie the basis of the fee, but only those that are directly involved in its computation. It is sufficient, for example, to state that the basic rate is an hourly charge or a fixed amount or an estimated amount, or to identify the factors that may be taken into account in finally fixing the fee. When de-

velopments occur during the representation that render an earlier estimate substantially inaccurate, a revised estimate should be provided to the client.

[2] A written statement concerning the fee, required to be furnished in advance in most cases by paragraph (b), reduces the possibility of misunderstanding. In circumstances in which paragraph (b) requires that the basis for the lawyer's fee be in writing, an individualized writing specific to the particular client and representation is generally not required. Unless there are unique aspects of the fee arrangement, the lawyer may utilize a standardized letter, memorandum, or pamphlet explaining the lawyer's fee practices, and indicating those practices applicable to the specific representation. Such publications would, for example, explain applicable hourly billing rates, if billing on an hourly rate basis is contemplated, and indicate what charges (such as filing fees, transcript costs, duplicating costs, long-distance telephone charges) are imposed in addition to hourly rate charges.

[3] Where the services to be rendered are covered by a fixed fee schedule that adequately informs the client of the charges to be imposed, a copy of such schedule may be utilized to satisfy the requirement for a writing. Such services as routine real estate transactions, uncontested divorces, or preparation of simple wills, for example, may be suitable for description in such a fixed-fee schedule.

Terms of Payment

[4] A lawyer may require advance payment of a fee, but is obliged to return any unearned portion. See Rule 1.16(d). A lawyer may accept property in payment for services, such as an ownership interest in an enterprise. However, a fee paid in property instead of money may be subject to special scrutiny because it involves questions concerning both the value of the services and the lawyer's special knowledge of the value of the property.

[5] An agreement may not be made whose terms might induce the lawyer improperly to curtail services for the client or perform them in a way contrary to the client's interest. For example, a lawyer should not enter into an agreement whereby services are to be provided only up to a stated amount when it is foreseeable that more extensive services probably will be required, unless the situation is adequately explained to the client. Otherwise, the client might have to bargain for further assistance in the midst of a proceeding or transaction. However, it is proper to define the extent of services in light of the client's ability to pay. A lawyer should not exploit a fee arrangement based primarily on hourly charges by using wasteful procedures.

Contingent Fees

[6] Generally, contingent fees are permissible in all civil cases. However, paragraph (d) continues the prohibition, imposed under the

previous Code of Professional Responsibility, against the use of a contingent fee arrangement by a lawyer representing a defendant in a criminal case. Applicable law may impose other limitations on contingent fees, such as a ceiling on the percentage. And in any case, if there is doubt whether a contingent fee is consistent with the client's best interests, the lawyer should explain any existing payment alternatives and their implications.

[7] Contingent fees in domestic relations cases, while rarely justified, are not prohibited by Rule 1.5. Contingent fees in such cases are permitted in order that lawyers may provide representation to clients who might not otherwise be able to afford to contract for the payment of fees on a noncontingent basis.

[8] Paragraph (c) requires that the contingent fee arrangement be in writing. This writing must explain the method by which the fee is to be computed. The lawyer must also provide the client with a written statement at the conclusion of a contingent fee matter, stating the outcome of the matter and explaining the computation of any remittance made to the client.

Division of Fee

[9] A division of fee is a single billing to a client covering the fee of two or more lawyers who are not in the same firm. A division of fee facilitates association of more than one lawyer in a matter in which neither alone could serve the client as well, and most often is used when the fee is contingent and the division is between a referring lawyer and a trial specialist.

[10] Paragraph (e) permits the lawyers to divide a fee either on the basis of the proportion of services they render or by agreement between the participating lawyers if all assume responsibility for the representation as a whole. Joint responsibility for the representation entails the obligations stated in Rule 5.1 for purposes of the matter involved. Permitting a division on the basis of joint responsibility, rather than on the basis of services performed, represents a change from the basis for fee divisions allowed under the prior Code of Professional Responsibility. The change is intended to encourage lawyers to affiliate other counsel, who are better equipped by reason of experience or specialized background to serve the client's needs, rather than to retain sole responsibility for the representation in order to avoid losing the right to a fee.

[11] The concept of joint responsibility is not, however, merely a technicality or incantation. The lawyer who refers the client to another lawyer, or affiliates another lawyer in the representation, remains fully responsible to the client, and is accountable to the client for deficiencies in the discharge of the representation by the lawyer who has been brought into the representation. If a lawyer wishes to avoid such responsibility for the potential deficiencies of another lawyer, the matter must be referred

to the other lawyer without retaining a right to participate in fees beyond those fees justified by services actually rendered.

[12] The concept of joint responsibility does not require the referring lawyer to perform any minimum portion of the total legal services rendered. The referring lawyer may agree that the lawyer to whom the referral is made will perform substantially all of the services to be rendered in connection with the representation, without review by the referring lawyer. Thus, the referring lawyer is not required to review pleadings or other documents, attend hearings or depositions, or otherwise participate in a significant and continuing manner. The referring lawyer does not, however, escape the implications of joint responsibility, see Comment [11], by avoiding direct participation.

[13] When fee divisions are based on assumed joint responsibility, the requirement of paragraph (a) that the fee be reasonable applies to the total fee charged for the representation by all participating lawyers.

[14] Paragraph (e) requires that the client be advised, in writing, of the fee division and states that the client must affirmatively consent to the proposed fee arrangement. The Rule does not require disclosure to the client of the share that each lawyer is to receive but does require that the client be informed of the identity of the lawyers sharing the fee, their respective responsibilities in the representation, and the effect of the association of lawyers outside the firm on the fee charged.

Disputes Over Fees

[15] If a procedure has been established for resolution of fee disputes, such as an arbitration or mediation procedure established by the Bar, the lawyer should conscientiously consider submitting to it. Law may prescribe a procedure for determining a lawyer's fee, for example, in representation of an executor or administrator, a class, or a person entitled to a reasonable fee as part of the measure of damages. The lawyer entitled to such a fee and a lawyer representing another party concerned with the fee should comply with the prescribed procedure.

Rule 1.6. Confidentiality of Information

(a) Except when permitted under paragraph (c) or (d), a lawyer shall not knowingly:

(1) Reveal a confidence or secret of the lawyer's client;

(2) Use a confidence or secret of the lawyer's client to the disadvantage of the client;

(3) Use a confidence or secret of the lawyer's client for the advantage of the lawyer or of a third person.

(b) "Confidence" refers to information protected by the attorney-client privilege under applicable law, and "secret" refers to other information gained in the professional relationship that the client has requested be held inviolate, or the disclosure of which would be embarrassing, or would be likely to be detrimental, to the client.

(c) A lawyer may reveal client confidences and secrets, to the extent reasonably necessary:

(1) To prevent a criminal act that the lawyer reasonably believes is likely to result in death or substantial bodily harm absent disclosure of the client's secrets or confidences by the lawyer; or

(2) To prevent the bribery or intimidation of witnesses, jurors, court officials, or other persons who are involved in proceedings before a tribunal if the lawyer reasonably believes that such acts are likely to result absent disclosure of the client's confidences or secrets by the lawyer.

(d) A lawyer may use or reveal client confidences or secrets:

(1) With the consent of the client affected, but only after full disclosure to the client;

(2)(A) When permitted by these Rules or required by law or court order; and

(B) If a government lawyer, when permitted or authorized by law;

(3) To the extent reasonably necessary to establish a defense to a criminal charge, disciplinary charge, or civil claim, formally instituted against the lawyer, based upon conduct in which the client was involved, or to the extent reasonably necessary to respond to specific allegations by the client concerning the lawyer's representation of the client;

(4) When the lawyer has reasonable grounds for believing that a client has impliedly authorized disclosure of a confidence or secret in order to carry out the representation; or

(5) To the minimum extent necessary in an action instituted by the lawyer to establish or collect the lawyer's fee.

(e) A lawyer shall exercise reasonable care to prevent the lawyer's employees, associates, and others whose services are utilized by the lawyer from disclosing or using confidences or secrets of a client, except that such persons may reveal information permitted to be disclosed by paragraphs (c) or (d).

(f) The lawyer's obligation to preserve the client's confidences and secrets continues after termination of the lawyer's employment.

(g) The obligation of a lawyer under paragraph (a) also applies to confidences and secrets learned prior to becoming a lawyer in the course of providing assistance to another lawyer.

(h) For purposes of this rule, a lawyer who serves as a member of the D.C. Bar Lawyer Counseling Committee, or as a trained intervenor for that Committee, shall be deemed to have a lawyer-client relationship

with respect to any lawyer-counselee being counseled under programs conducted by or on behalf of the Committee. Information obtained from another lawyer being counseled under the auspices of the Committee, or in the course of and associated with such counseling, shall be treated as a confidence or secret within the terms of paragraph (b). Such information may be disclosed only to the extent permitted by this Rule.

(i) For purposes of this rule, a lawyer who serves as a member of the D.C. Bar Lawyer Practice Assistance Committee, or a staff assistant, mentor, monitor or other consultant for that Committee, shall be deemed to have a lawyer-client relationship with respect to any lawyer-counselee being counseled under programs conducted by or on behalf of the Committee. Communications between the counselor and the lawyer being counseled under the auspices of the Committee, or made in the course of and associated with such counseling, shall be treated as a confidence or secret within the terms of paragraph (b). Such information may be disclosed only to the extent permitted by this rule. However, during the period in which the lawyer-counselee is subject to a probationary or monitoring order of the Court of Appeals or the Board of Professional Responsibility in a disciplinary case instituted pursuant to Rule XI of the Rules of the Court of Appeals Governing the Bar, such information shall be subject to disclosure in accordance with the order.

(j) The client of the government lawyer is the agency that employs the lawyer unless expressly provided to the contrary by appropriate law, regulation, or order.

COMMENT

[1] The lawyer is part of a judicial system charged with upholding the law. One of the lawyer's functions is to advise clients so that they avoid any violation of the law in the proper exercise of their rights.

[2] The observance of the ethical obligation of a lawyer to hold inviolate confidential information of the client not only facilitates the full development of facts essential to proper representation of the client but also encourages people to seek early legal assistance.

[3] Almost without exception, clients come to lawyers in order to determine what their rights are and what is, in the maze of laws and regulations, deemed to be legal and correct. The common law recognizes that the client's confidences must be protected from disclosure. Based upon experience, lawyers know that almost all clients follow the advice given, and the law is upheld.

[4] A fundamental principle in the client-lawyer relationship is that the lawyer holds inviolate the client's secrets and confidences. The client is thereby encouraged to communicate fully and frankly with the lawyer even as to embarrassing or legally damaging subject matter.

Relationship Between Rule 1.6 and Attorney-Client Evidentiary Privilege and Work Product Doctrine

[5] The principle of confidentiality is given effect in two related bodies of law: the attorney-client privilege and the work product doctrine in the law of evidence and the rule of confidentiality established in professional ethics. The attorney-client privilege and the work product doctrine apply in judicial and other proceedings in which a lawyer may be called as a witness or otherwise required to produce evidence concerning a client. This Rule is not intended to govern or affect judicial application of the attorney-client privilege or work product doctrine. The privilege and doctrine were developed to promote compliance with law and fairness in litigation. In reliance on the attorney-client privilege, clients are entitled to expect that communications within the scope of the privilege will be protected against compelled disclosure. The attorney-client privilege is that of the client and not of the lawyer. The fact that in exceptional situations the lawyer under this Rule has limited discretion to disclose a client confidence does not vitiate the proposition that, as a general matter, the client has a reasonable expectation that information relating to the client will not be voluntarily disclosed and that disclosure of such information may be judicially compelled only in accordance with recognized exceptions to the attorney-client privilege and work product doctrine.

[6] The rule of client-lawyer confidentiality applies in situations other than those where evidence is sought from the lawyer through compulsion of law; furthermore, it applies not merely to matters communicated in confidence by the client (i.e., confidences) but also to all information gained in the course of the professional relationship that the client has requested be held inviolate, or the disclosure of which would be embarrassing or would be likely to be detrimental to the client (i.e., secrets). This ethical precept, unlike the evidentiary privilege, exists without regard to the nature or source of the information or the fact that others share the knowledge. It reflects not only the principles underlying the attorney-client privilege, but the lawyer's duty of loyalty to the client.

The Commencement of the Client-Lawyer Relationship

[7] Principles of substantive law external to these Rules determine whether a client-lawyer relationship exists. Although most of the duties flowing from the client-lawyer relationship attach only after the client has requested the lawyer to render legal services and the lawyer has agreed to do so, the duty of confidentiality imposed by this Rule attaches when the lawyer agrees to consider whether a client-lawyer relationship shall be established. Thus, a lawyer may be subject to a duty of confidentiality with

respect to information disclosed by a client to enable the lawyer to determine whether representation of the potential client would involve a prohibited conflict of interest under Rule 1.7, 1.8, or 1.9.

Exploitation of Confidences and Secrets

[8] In addition to prohibiting the disclosure of a client's confidences and secrets, subparagraph (a)(2) provides that a lawyer may not use the client's confidences and secrets to the disadvantage of the client. For example, a lawyer who has learned that the client is investing in specific real estate may not seek to acquire nearby property where doing so would adversely affect the client's plan for investment. Similarly, information acquired by the lawyer in the course of representing a client may not be used to the disadvantage of that client even after the termination of the lawyer's representation of the client. However, the fact that a lawyer has once served a client does not preclude the lawyer from using generally known information about the former client when later representing another client. Under subparagraphs (a)(3) and (d)(1) a lawyer may use a client's confidences and secrets for the lawyer's own benefit or that of a third party only after the lawyer has made full disclosure to the client regarding the proposed use of the information and obtained the client's affirmative consent to the use in question.

Authorized Disclosure

[9] A lawyer is impliedly authorized to make disclosures about a client when appropriate in carrying out the representation, except to the extent that the client's instructions or special circumstances limit that authority. In litigation, for example, a lawyer may disclose information by admitting a fact that cannot properly be disputed, or in negotiation by making a disclosure that facilitates a satisfactory conclusion.

[10] The obligation to protect confidences and secrets obviously does not preclude a lawyer from revealing information when the client consents after full disclosure, when necessary to perform the professional employment, when permitted by these Rules, or when required by law. Unless the client otherwise directs, a lawyer may disclose the affairs of the client to partners or associates of the lawyer's firm. It is a matter of common knowledge that the normal operation of a law office exposes confidential professional information to nonlawyer employees of the office, particularly secretaries and those having access to the files; and this obligates a lawyer to exercise care in selecting and training employees so that the sanctity of all confidences and secrets of clients may be preserved. If the obligation extends to two or more clients as to the same information, a lawyer should obtain the permission of all before revealing the

information. A lawyer must always be sensitive to the rights and wishes of the client and act scrupulously in the making of decisions that may involve the disclosure of information obtained in the course of the professional relationship. Thus, in the absence of consent of the client after full disclosure, a lawyer should not associate another lawyer in the handling of a matter; nor should the lawyer, in the absence of consent, seek counsel from another lawyer if there is a reasonable possibility that the identity of the client or the client's confidences or secrets would be revealed to such lawyer. Proper concern for professional duty should cause a lawyer to shun indiscreet conversations concerning clients.

[11] Unless the client otherwise directs, it is not improper for a lawyer to give limited information from client files to an outside agency necessary for statistical, bookkeeping, accounting, data processing, banking, printing, or other legitimate purposes, provided the lawyer exercises due care in the selection of the agency and warns the agency that the information must be kept confidential.

Disclosure Adverse to Client

[12] The confidentiality rule is subject to limited exceptions. In becoming privy to information about a client, a lawyer may foresee that the client intends serious harm to another person. However, to the extent a lawyer is required or permitted to disclose a client's purposes, the client will be inhibited from revealing facts that would enable the lawyer to counsel against a wrongful course of action. The public is better protected if full and open communication by the client is encouraged than if it is inhibited. Nevertheless, when the client's confidences or secrets are such that the lawyer knows or reasonably should know that the client or any other person is likely to kill or do substantial bodily injury to another unless the lawyer discloses client confidences or secrets, the lawyer may reveal the client's confidences and secrets if necessary to prevent harm to the third party.

[13] Several situations must be distinguished.

[14] First, the lawyer may not counsel or assist a client to engage in conduct that is criminal or fraudulent. See Rule 1.2(e). Similarly, a lawyer has a duty not to use false evidence of a non-client and may permit introduction of the false evidence of a client only in extremely limited circumstances in criminal cases when the witness is the defendant client. See Rule 3.3(a)(4) and (b). This Rule is essentially a special instance of the duty prescribed in Rule 1.2(e) to avoid assisting a client in criminal or fraudulent conduct.

[15] Second, the lawyer may have been innocently involved in past conduct by the client that was criminal or fraudulent. In such a situation the lawyer has not violated Rule 1.2(e), because to "counsel or assist" criminal or fraudulent conduct requires knowing that the conduct is of that character.

[16] Third, the lawyer may learn that a client intends prospective conduct that is criminal and likely to result in death or substantial bodily harm unless disclosure of the client's intentions is made by the lawyer. As stated in paragraph (c), the lawyer has professional discretion to reveal information in order to prevent such consequences. The lawyer may make a disclosure in order to prevent homicide or serious bodily injury which the lawyer reasonably believes is intended by a client. The "reasonably believes" standard is applied because it is very difficult for a lawyer to "know" when such a heinous purpose will actually be carried out, for the client may have a change of mind.

[17] The lawyer's exercise of discretion in determining whether to make disclosures that are reasonably likely to prevent the death or substantial bodily injury of another requires consideration of such factors as the client's tendency to commit violent acts or, conversely, to make idle threats. In any case, a disclosure adverse to the client's interest should be no greater than the lawyer reasonably believes necessary to the purpose. A lawyer's decision not to take preventive action permitted by subparagraph (c)(1) does not violate this Rule.

Withdrawal

[18] If the lawyer's services will be used by the client in materially furthering a course of criminal or fraudulent conduct, the lawyer must withdraw, as stated in Rule 1.16(a)(1). If the client persists in a course of action involving the lawyer's services that the lawyer reasonably believes is criminal or fraudulent, or if the client has used the lawyer's services to perpetrate a crime or a fraud, the lawyer may (but is not required to) withdraw, as stated in Rule 1.16(b)(1) and (2).

[19] After withdrawal under either Rule 1.16(a)(1) or Rule 1.16(b)(1) or (2), the lawyer is required to refrain from making disclosure of the client's confidences, except as otherwise provided in Rule 1.6. Giving notice of withdrawal, without elaboration, is not a disclosure of a client's confidences and is not proscribed by this Rule or by Rule 1.16(d). Furthermore, a lawyer's statement to a court that withdrawal is based upon "irreconcilable differences between the lawyer and the client," as provided under paragraph [3] of the Comment to Rule 1.16, is not elaboration. Similarly, after withdrawal under either Rule 1.16(a)(1) or Rule 1.16(b)(1) or (2), the lawyer may retract or disaffirm any opinion, document, affirmation, or the like that contains a material misrepresentation by the lawyer that the lawyer reasonably believes will be relied upon by others to their detriment.

[20] Where the client is an organization, the lawyer may be in doubt whether contemplated conduct will actually be carried out by the organization. Where necessary to guide conduct in connection with this Rule, the lawyer may make inquiry within the organization. See Comment to Rule 1.13.

Dispute Concerning Lawyer's Conduct

[21] Where a legal claim or disciplinary charge alleges complicity of the lawyer in a client's conduct or other misconduct of the lawyer involving representation of the client, the lawyer may respond to the extent the lawyer reasonably believes necessary to establish a defense. The same is true with respect to a claim involving the conduct or representation of a former client. Charges, in defense of which a lawyer may disclose client confidences and secrets, can arise in a civil, criminal, or professional disciplinary proceeding, and can be based on a wrong allegedly committed by the lawyer against the client, or on a wrong alleged by a third person; for example, a person claiming to have been defrauded by the lawyer and client acting together.

[22] The lawyer may not disclose a client's confidences or secrets to defend against informal allegations made by third parties; the Rule allows disclosure only if a third party has formally instituted a civil, criminal, or disciplinary action against the lawyer. Even if the third party has formally instituted such a proceeding, the lawyer should advise the client of the third party's action and request that the client respond appropriately, if this is practicable and would not be prejudicial to the lawyer's ability to establish a defense.

[23] If a lawyer's client, or former client, has made specific allegations against the lawyer, the lawyer may disclose that client's confidences and secrets in establishing a defense, without waiting for formal proceedings to be commenced. The requirement of subparagraph (d)(3) that there be "specific" charges of misconduct by the client precludes the lawyer from disclosing confidences or secrets in response to general criticism by a client; an example of such a general criticism would be an assertion by the client that the lawyer "did a poor job" of representing the client. But in this situation, as well as in the defense of formally instituted third-party proceedings, disclosure should be no greater than the lawyer reasonably believes is necessary to vindicate innocence, the disclosure should be made in a manner that limits access to the information to the tribunal or other persons having a need to know it, and appropriate protective orders or other arrangements should be sought by the lawyer to the fullest extent practicable.

Fee Collection Actions

[24] Subparagraph (d)(5) permits a lawyer to reveal a client's confidences or secrets if this is necessary in an action to collect fees from the client. This aspect of the Rule expresses the principle that the beneficiary of a fiduciary relationship may not exploit it to the detriment of the fiduciary. Subparagraph (d)(5) should be construed narrowly; it does not authorize broad, indiscriminate disclosure of secrets or confidences. The lawyer should evaluate the necessity for disclosure of information at each

stage of the action. For example, in drafting the complaint in a fee collection suit, it would be necessary to reveal the "secrets" that the lawyer was retained by the client, that fees are due, and that the client has failed to pay those fees. Further disclosure of the client's secrets and confidences would be impermissible at the complaint stage. If possible, the lawyer should prevent even the disclosure of the client's identity through the use of John Doe pleadings.

[25] If the client's response to the lawyer's complaint raised issues implicating confidences or secrets, the lawyer would be permitted to disclose confidential or secret information pertinent to the client's claims or defenses. Even then, the Rule would require that the lawyer's response be narrowly tailored to meet the client's specific allegations, with the minimum degree of disclosure sufficient to respond effectively. In addition, the lawyer should continue, throughout the action, to make every effort to avoid unnecessary disclosure of the client's confidences and secrets and to limit the disclosure to those having the need to know it. To this end the lawyer should seek appropriate protective orders and make any other arrangements which would minimize the risk of disclosure of the confidential information in question, including the utilization of in camera proceedings.

Disclosures Otherwise Required or Authorized

[26] The attorney-client privilege is differently defined in various jurisdictions. If a lawyer is called as a witness to give testimony concerning a client, absent waiver by the client, subparagraph (d)(2) requires the lawyer to invoke the privilege when it is applicable. The lawyer may comply with the final orders of a court or other tribunal of competent jurisdiction requiring the lawyer to give information about the client. But a lawyer ordered by a court to disclose client confidences or secrets should not comply with the order until the lawyer has personally made every reasonable effort to appeal the order or has notified the client of the order and given the client the opportunity to challenge it.

[27] The Rules of Professional Conduct in various circumstances permit or require a lawyer to disclose information relating to the representation. See Rules 2.2, 2.3, 3.3, and 4.1. In addition to these provisions, a lawyer may be obligated or permitted by other provisions of law to give information about a client. Whether another provision of law supersedes Rule 1.6 is a matter of interpretation beyond the scope of these Rules, but a presumption exists against such a supersession.

Former Client

[28] The duty of confidentiality continues after the client-lawyer relationship has terminated.

Services Rendered in Assisting Another Lawyer Before Becoming a Member of the Bar

[29] There are circumstances in which a person who ultimately becomes a lawyer provides assistance to a lawyer while serving in a nonlawyer capacity. The typical situation is that of the law clerk or summer associate in a law firm or government agency. Paragraph (g) addresses the confidentiality obligations of such a person after becoming a member of the Bar; the same confidentiality obligations are imposed as would apply if the person had been a member of the Bar at the time confidences or secrets were received. This resolution of the confidentiality obligation is consistent with the reasoning employed in D.C. Bar Legal Ethics Committee Opinion 84 (1980). For a related provision dealing with the imputation of disqualifications arising from prior participation as a law clerk, summer associate, or in a similar position, see Rule 1.10(b).

Bar Sponsored Counseling Programs

[30] Paragraph (h) adds a provision dealing specifically with the disclosure obligations of lawyers who are assisting in the counseling programs of the D.C. Bar's Lawyer Counseling Committee. Members of that committee, and lawyer-intervenors who assist the committee in counseling, may obtain information from lawyer-counselees who have sought assistance from the counseling programs offered by the committee. It is in the interests of the public to encourage lawyers who have alcohol or other substance abuse problems to seek counseling as a first step toward rehabilitation. Some lawyers who seek such assistance may have violated provisions of the Rules of Professional Conduct, or other provisions of law, including criminal statutes such as those dealing with embezzlement. In order for those who are providing counseling services to evaluate properly the lawyer-counselee's problems and enhance the prospects for rehabilitation, it is necessary for the counselors to receive completely candid information from the lawyer-counselee. Such candor is not likely if the counselor, for example, would be compelled by Rule 8.3 to report the lawyer-counselee's conduct to Bar Counsel, or if the lawyer-counselee feared that the counselor could be compelled by prosecutors or others to disclose information.

[31] It is similarly in the interest of the public to encourage lawyers to seek the assistance of the D.C. Bar's Lawyer Practice Assistance Committee to address management problems in their practices. In order for those who are providing counseling services through the Lawyer Practice Assistance Committee to evaluate properly the lawyer-counselee's problems and enhance the prospects for self-improvement by the counselee, paragraph (i) adds a provision addressing the confidentiality obligations of lawyers who are assisting in the counseling programs of the Lawyer Practice Assistance Committee.

[32] These considerations make it appropriate to treat the lawyer-counselee relationship as a lawyer-client relationship, and to create an additional limited class of information treated as secrets or confidences subject to the protection of Rule 1.6. The scope of that information is set forth in paragraphs (h) and (i). The lawyer-client relationship is deemed to exist only with respect to the obligation of confidentiality created under Rule 1.6, and not to obligations created elsewhere in these Rules, including the obligation of zealous representation under Rule 1.3 and the obligation to avoid conflicts of interest set forth in Rules 1.7 and 1.9. The obligation of confidentiality extends to non-lawyer assistants of lawyers serving the committee. See Rule 5.1.

[33] Notwithstanding the obligation of confidentiality under paragraph (i), during the period in which a lawyer-counselee is subject to a probationary or monitoring order of the Court of Appeals or the Board of Professional Responsibility in a disciplinary case instituted pursuant to Rule XI of the Rules of the Court of Appeals Governing the Bar, communications between the counselor and the lawyer being counseled under the auspices of the Lawyer Practice Assistance Committee shall be subject to disclosure in accordance with an order of the Court or the Board, since the participation of the lawyer-counselee in the programs of the committee in such circumstances is not voluntary.

[34] Ethical rules established by the District of Columbia Court of Appeals with respect to the kinds of information protected from compelled disclosure may not be accepted by other forums or jurisdictions. Therefore, the protections afforded by paragraphs (h) and (i) may not be available to preclude disclosure in all circumstances. Furthermore, lawyers who are members of the bar of other jurisdictions may not be entitled, under the ethics rules applicable to members of the bar in such other jurisdictions, to forgo reporting violations to disciplinary authorities pursuant to the other jurisdictions' counterparts to Rule 8.3.

Government Lawyers

[35] Subparagraph (d)(2) was revised, and paragraph (i) was added, to address the unique circumstances raised by attorney-client relationships within the government.

[36] Subparagraph (d)(2)(A) applies to both private and government attorney-client relationships. Subparagraph (d)(2)(B) applies to government lawyers only. It is designed to permit disclosures that are not required by law or court order under Rule 1.6(d)(2)(A), but which the government authorizes its attorneys to make in connection with their professional services to the government. Such disclosures may be authorized or required by statute, executive order, or regulation, depending on the constitutional or statutory powers of the authorizing entity. If so authorized or required, subparagraph (d)(2)(B) governs.

[37] The term "agency" in paragraph (i) includes, inter alia, executive and independent departments and agencies, special commissions, committees of the legislature, agencies of the legislative branch such as the General Accounting Office, and the courts to the extent that they employ lawyers (e.g., staff counsel) to counsel them. The employing agency has been designated the client under this Rule to provide a commonly understood and easily determinable point for identifying the government client.

[38] Government lawyers may also be assigned to provide an individual with counsel or representation in circumstances that make clear that an obligation of confidentiality runs directly to that individual and that subparagraph (d)(2)(A), not (d)(2)(B) applies. It is, of course, acceptable in this circumstance for a government lawyer to make disclosures about the individual representation to supervisors or others within the employing governmental agency so long as such disclosures are made in the context of, and consistent with, the agency's representation program. See, e.g., 28 C.F.R. §§50.15 and 50.16. The relevant circumstances, including the agreement to represent the individual, may also indicate the extent to which the individual client to whom the government lawyer is assigned will be deemed to have granted or denied consent to disclosures to the lawyer's employing agency. Examples of such representation include representation by a public defender, a government lawyer representing a defendant sued for damages arising out of the performance of the defendant's government employment, and a military lawyer representing a court-martial defendant.

Rule 1.7. Conflict of Interest: General Rule

(a) A lawyer shall not advance two or more adverse positions in the same matter.

(b) Except as permitted by paragraph (c) below, a lawyer shall not represent a client with respect to a matter if:

(1) That matter involves a specific party or parties, and a position to be taken by that client in that matter is adverse to a position taken or to be taken by another client in the same matter, even though that client is unrepresented or represented by a different lawyer;

(2) Such representation will be or is likely to be adversely affected by representation of another client;

(3) Representation of another client will be or is likely to be adversely affected by such representation; or

(4) The lawyer's professional judgment on behalf of the client will be or reasonably may be adversely affected by the lawyer's responsibilities to or interests in a third party or the lawyer's own financial, business, property, or personal interests.

(c) A lawyer may represent a client with respect to a matter in the circumstances described in paragraph (b) above if each potentially

affected client provides consent to such representation after full disclosure of the existence and nature of the possible conflict and the possible adverse consequences of such representation.

(d) If a conflict not reasonably foreseeable at the outset of a representation arises under paragraph (b)(1) after the representation commences, and is not waived under paragraph (c), a lawyer need not withdraw from any representation unless the conflict also arises under paragraphs (b)(2), (b)(3), or (b)(4).

COMMENT

[1] Rule 1.7 is intended to provide clear notice of circumstances that may constitute a conflict of interest. Rule 1.7(a) sets out the limited circumstances in which representation of conflicting interests is absolutely prohibited even with the consent of all involved clients. Rule 1.7(b) sets out those circumstances in which representation is barred in the absence of informed client consent. The difference between Rule 1.7(a) and Rule 1.7(b) is that in the former, the lawyer is representing multiple interests in the same matter, while in the latter the lawyer is representing a single interest, but a client of the lawyer who is represented by different counsel has an interest adverse to that advanced by the lawyer. The application of Rules 1.7(a) and 1.7(b) to specific facts must also take into consideration the principles of imputed disqualification described in Rule 1.10. Rule 1.7(c) states the procedure that must be used to obtain client consent if representation is to commence or continue in the circumstances described in Rule 1.7(b). Rule 1.7(d) governs withdrawal in cases arising under Rule 1.7(b)(1).

Representation Absolutely Prohibited — Rule 1.7(a)

[2] Institutional interests in preserving confidence in the adversary process and in the administration of justice preclude permitting a lawyer to represent adverse positions in the same matter. For that reason, paragraph (a) prohibits such conflicting representations, with or without client consent.

[3] The same lawyer (or law firm, see Rule 1.10) should not espouse adverse positions in the same matter during the course of any type of representation, whether such adverse positions are taken on behalf of clients or on behalf of the lawyer or an association of which the lawyer is a member. On the other hand, for purposes of Rule 1.7(a), an "adverse" position does not include inconsistent or alternative positions advanced by counsel on behalf of a single client. Rule 1.7(a) is intended to codify the result reached in D.C. Bar Legal Ethics Committee Opinion 204, including the

conclusion that a rulemaking whose result will be applied retroactively in pending adjudications is the same matter as the adjudications, even though treated as separate proceedings by an agency. However, if the adverse positions to be taken relate to different matters, the absolute prohibition of paragraph (a) is inapplicable, even though paragraphs (b) and (c) may apply.

[4] The absolute prohibition of paragraph (a) applies only to situations in which a lawyer would be called upon to espouse adverse positions for different clients in the same matter. It is for this reason that paragraph (a) refers to adversity with respect to a "position taken or to be taken" in a matter rather than adversity with respect to the matter or the entire representation. This approach is intended to reduce the costs of litigation in other representations where parties have common, nonadverse interests on certain issues, but have adverse (or contingently or possibly adverse) positions with respect to other issues. If, for example, a lawyer would not be required to take adverse positions in providing joint representation of two clients in the liability phase of a case, it would be permissible to undertake such a limited representation. Then, after completion of the liability phase, and upon satisfying the requirements of paragraph (c) of this Rule, and of any other applicable Rules, the lawyer could represent either one of those parties as to the damages phase of the case, even though the other, represented by separate counsel as to damages, might have an adverse position as to that phase of the case. Insofar as the absolute prohibition of paragraph (a) is concerned, a lawyer may represent two parties that may be adverse to each other as to some aspects of the case so long as the same lawyer does not represent both parties with respect to those positions. Such a representation comes within paragraph (b), rather than paragraph (a), and is therefore subject to the consent provisions of paragraph (c).

[5] The ability to represent two parties who have adverse interests as to portions of a case may be limited because the lawyer obtains confidences or secrets relating to a party while jointly representing both parties in one phase of the case. In some circumstances, such confidences or secrets might be useful, against the interests of the party to whom they relate, in a subsequent part of the case. Absent the consent of the party whose confidences or secrets are implicated, the subsequent adverse representation is governed by the substantial relationship test, which is set forth in Rule 1.9.

[6] The prohibition of paragraph (a) relates only to actual conflicts of positions, not to mere formalities. For example, a lawyer is not absolutely forbidden to provide joint or simultaneous representation if the clients' positions are only nominally but not actually adverse. Joint representation is commonly provided to incorporators of a business, to parties to a contract, in formulating estate plans for family members, and in other circumstances where the clients might be nominally adverse in some respect but have retained a lawyer to accomplish a common purpose. If no actual

conflict of positions exists with respect to a matter, the absolute prohibition of paragraph (a) does not come into play. Thus, in the limited circumstances set forth in Opinion 143 of the D.C. Bar Legal Ethics Committee, this prohibition would not preclude the representation of both parties in an uncontested divorce proceeding, there being no actual conflict of positions based on the facts presented in Opinion 143.

Representation Conditionally Prohibited — Rule 1.7(b)

[7] Paragraphs (b) and (c) are based upon two principles: (1) that a client is entitled to wholehearted and zealous representation of its interests, and (2) that the client as well as the lawyer must have the opportunity to judge and be satisfied that such representation can be provided. Consistent with these principles, paragraph (b) provides a general description of the types of circumstances in which representation is improper in the absence of informed consent. The underlying premise is that disclosure and consent are required before assuming a representation if there is any reason to doubt the lawyer's ability to provide wholehearted and zealous representation of a client or if a client might reasonably consider the representation of its interest to be adversely affected by the lawyer's assumption of the other representation in question. Although the lawyer must be satisfied that the representation can be wholeheartedly and zealously undertaken, if an objective observer would have any reasonable doubt on that issue, the client has a right to disclosure of all relevant considerations and the opportunity to be the judge of its own interests.

[8] A client may, on occasion, adopt unreasonable positions with respect to having the lawyer who is representing that client also represent other parties. Such an unreasonable position may be based on an aversion to the other parties being represented by a lawyer, or on some philosophical or ideological ground having no foundation in the rules regarding representation of conflicting interests. Whatever difficulties may be presented for the lawyer in such circumstances as a matter of client relations, the unreasonable position taken by a client do not fall within the circumstances requiring notification and consent. Clients have broad discretion to terminate their representation by a lawyer and that discretion may generally be exercised on unreasonable as well as reasonable grounds.

[9] If the lawyer determines or can foresee that an issue with respect to the application of paragraph (b) exists, the only prudent course is for the lawyer to make disclosure, pursuant to paragraph (c), to each affected client and enable each to determine whether in its judgment the representation at issue is likely to affect its interests adversely.

[10] Paragraph (b) does not purport to state a uniform rule applicable to cases in which two clients may be adverse to each other in a matter

in which neither is represented by the lawyer or in a situation in which two or more clients may be direct business competitors. The matter in which two clients are adverse may be so unrelated or insignificant as to have no possible effect upon a lawyer's ability to represent both in other matters. The fact that two clients are business competitors, standing alone, is usually not a bar to simultaneous representation. Thus, in a matter involving a specific party or parties, paragraphs (b)(1) and (c) require notice and consent if the lawyer will take a position on behalf of one client adverse to another client even though the lawyer represents the latter client only on an unrelated position or in an unrelated matter. Paragraphs (b)(2), (3), (4), and (c) require disclosure and consent in any situation in which the lawyer's representation of a client may be adversely affected by representation of another client or by any of the factors specified in paragraph (b)(4).

Lawyer's Duty to Make Inquiries to Determine Potential Conflicts

[11] The scope of and parties to a "matter" are typically apparent in on-the-record adversary proceedings or other proceedings in which a written record of the identity and the position of the parties exists. In Rule 1.7(b)(1), the phrase "matter involving a specific party or parties" refers to such situations. In other situations, however, it may not be clear to a lawyer whether the representation of one client is adverse to the interests of another client. For example, a lawyer may represent a client only with respect to one or a few of the client's areas of interest. Other lawyers, or non-lawyers (such as lobbyists), or employees of the client (such as government relations personnel) may be representing that client on many issues whose scope and content are unknown to the lawyer. Clients often have many representatives acting for them, including multiple law firms, nonlawyer lobbyists, and client employees. A lawyer retained for a limited purpose may not be aware of the full range of a client's other interests or positions on issues. Except in matters involving a specific party or parties, a lawyer is not required to inquire of a client concerning the full range of that clients interests in issues, unless it is clear to the lawyer that there is a potential for adversity between the interests of clients of the lawyer. Where lawyers are associated in a firm within the meaning of Rule 1.10(a), the rule stated in the preceding sentence must be applied to all lawyers and all clients in the firm. Unless a lawyer is aware that representing one client involves seeking a result to which another client is opposed, Rule 1.7 is not violated by a representation that eventuates in the lawyer's unwittingly taking a position for one client adverse to the interests of another client. The test to be applied here is one of reasonableness and may turn on whether the lawyer has an effective conflict checking system in place.

Situations That Frequently Arise

[12] A number of types of situations frequently arise in which disclosure and informed consent are usually required. These include joint representation of parties to criminal and civil litigation, joint representation of incorporators of a business, joint representation of a business or government agency and its employees, representation of family members seeking estate planning or the drafting of wills, joint representation of an insurer and an insured, representation in circumstances in which the personal or financial interests of the lawyer, or the lawyer's family, might be affected by the representation, and other similar situations in which experience indicates that conflicts are likely to exist or arise. For example, a lawyer might not be able to represent a client vigorously if the client's adversary is a person with whom the lawyer has longstanding personal or social ties. The client is entitled to be informed of such circumstances so that an informed decision can be made concerning the advisability of retaining the lawyer who has such ties to the adversary. The principles of disclosure and consent are equally applicable to all such circumstances, except that if the positions to be taken by two clients in a matter as to which the lawyer represents both are actually adverse, then, as provided in paragraph (a), the lawyer may not undertake or continue the representation with respect to those issues even if disclosure has been made and consent obtained.

Organization Clients

[13] As is provided in Rule 1.13, the lawyer who represents a corporation, partnership, trade association or other organization-type client is deemed to represent that specific entity, and not its shareholders, owners, partners, members or "other constituents." Thus, for purposes of interpreting this Rule, the specific entity represented by the lawyer is the "client." Ordinarily that client's affiliates (parents and subsidiaries), other stockholders and owners, partners, members, etc., are not considered to be clients of the lawyer. Generally, the lawyer for a corporation is not prohibited by legal ethics principles from representing the corporation in a matter in which the corporation's stockholders or other constituents are adverse to the corporation. See D.C. Bar Legal Ethics Committee Opinion No. 216. A fortiori, and consistent with the principle reflected in Rule 1.13, the lawyer for an organization normally should not be precluded from representing an unrelated client whose interests are adverse to the interests of an affiliate (e.g., parent or subsidiary), stockholders and owners, partners, members, etc., of that organization in a matter that is separate from and not substantially related to the matter on which the lawyer represents the organization.

[14] However, there may be cases in which a lawyer is deemed to represent a constituent of an organization client. Such de facto representation has been found where a lawyer has received confidences from a

constituent during the course of representing an organization client in circumstances in which the constituent reasonably believed that the lawyer was acting as the constituent's lawyer as well as the lawyer for the organization client. See generally ABA Formal Opinion 92-365. In general, representation may be implied where on the facts there is a reasonable belief by the constituent that there is individual as well as collective representation. Id. The propriety of representation adverse to an affiliate or constituent of the organization client, therefore, must first be tested by determining whether a constituent is in fact a client of the lawyer. If it is, representation adverse to the constituent requires compliance with Rule 1.7. See ABA Opinion 92-365, supra. The propriety of representation must also be tested by reference to the lawyer's obligation under Rule 1.6 to preserve confidences and secrets and to the obligations imposed by paragraphs (b)(2) through (b)(4) of this Rule. Thus, absent consent under Rule 1.7(c), such adverse representation ordinarily would be improper if:

(a) the adverse matter is the same as, or substantially related to, the matter on which the lawyer represents the organization client,

(b) during the course of representation of the organization client the lawyer has in fact acquired confidences or secrets (as defined in Rule 1.6(b)) of the organization client or an affiliate or constituent that could be used to the disadvantage of any of the organization client or its affiliate or constituents, or

(c) such representation seeks a result that is likely to have a material adverse effect on the financial condition of the organization client.

[15] In addition, the propriety of representation adverse to an affiliate or constituent of the organization client must be tested by attempting to determine whether the adverse party is in substance the "alter ego" of the organization client. The alter ego case is one in which there is likely to be a reasonable expectation by the constituents or affiliates of an organization that each has an individual as well as a collective client-lawyer relationship with the lawyer, a likelihood that a result adverse to the constituent would also be adverse to the existing organization client, and a risk that both the new and the old representation would be so adversely affected that the conflict would not be "consentable." Although the alter ego criterion necessarily involves some imprecision, it may be usefully applied in a parent-subsidiary context, for example, by analyzing the following relevant factors: whether (i) the parent directly or indirectly owns all or substantially all of the voting stock of the subsidiary, (ii) the two companies have common directors, officers, office premises, or business activities, or (iii) a single legal department retains, supervises and pays outside lawyers for both the parent and the subsidiary. If all or most of those factors are present, for conflict of interest purposes those two entities normally would be considered alter egos of one another and the lawyer for one of them should refrain from engaging in representation adverse to the other, even on a matter where clauses (a), (b) and (c) of the preceding paragraph [14] are not applicable. Similarly, if the organization client is a corporation that is wholly owned by

a single individual, in most cases for purposes of applying this Rule, that client should be deemed to be the alter ego of its sole stockholder. Therefore, the corporation's lawyer should refrain from engaging in representation adverse to the sole stockholder, even on a matter where clauses (a), (b) and (c) of the preceding paragraph [14] are not applicable.

[16] If representation otherwise appropriate under the preceding paragraphs seeks a result that is likely ultimately to have a material adverse effect on the financial condition of the organization client, such representation is prohibited by Rule 1.7(b)(3). If the likely adverse effect on the financial condition of the organization client is not material, such representation is not prohibited by Rule 1.7(b)(3). Obviously, however, a lawyer should exercise restraint and sensitivity in determining whether to undertake such representation in a case of that type, particularly if the organization client does not realistically have the option to discharge the lawyer as counsel to the organization client.

[17] The provisions of paragraphs [13] through [16] are subject to any contrary agreement or other understanding between the client and the lawyer. In particular, the client has the right by means of the original engagement letter or otherwise to restrict the lawyer from engaging in representations otherwise permissible under the foregoing guidelines. If the lawyer agrees to such restrictions in order to obtain or keep the client's business, any such agreement between client and lawyer will take precedence over these guidelines. Conversely, an organization client, in order to obtain the lawyer's services, may in the original engagement letter or otherwise give consent to the lawyer in advance to engage in representations adverse to an affiliate, owner or other constituent of the client not otherwise permissible under the foregoing guidelines so long as the requirements of Rule 1.7(c) can be met.

[18] In any event, in all cases referred to above, the lawyer must carefully consider whether Rule 1.7(b)(2) or Rule 1.7(b)(4) requires consent from the second client whom the lawyer proposes to represent adverse to an affiliate, owner or other constituent of the first client.

Disclosure and Consent

[19] Disclosure and consent are not mere formalities. Adequate disclosure requires such disclosure of the parties and their interests and positions as to enable each potential client to make a fully informed decision as to whether to proceed with the contemplated representation. If a lawyer's obligation to one or another client or to others or some other consideration precludes making such full disclosure to all affected parties, that fact alone precludes undertaking the representation at issue. Full disclosure also requires that clients be made aware of the possible extra expense, inconvenience, and other disadvantages that may arise if an actual conflict of position should later arise and the lawyer be required to terminate the representation.

[20] The Rule does not require that disclosure be in writing or in any other particular form in all cases. Nevertheless, it should be recognized that the form of disclosure sufficient for more sophisticated business clients may not be sufficient to permit less sophisticated clients to provide fully informed consent. Moreover, under District of Columbia substantive law, the lawyer bears the burden of proof to demonstrate the existence of consent. For those reasons, it would be prudent for the lawyer to provide potential joint clients with at least a written summary of the considerations disclosed and to request and receive a written consent.

[21] The term "consent" is defined in the Terminology section of these Rules. As indicated there, a client's consent must not be coerced either by the lawyer or by any other person. In particular, the lawyer should not use the client's investment in previous representation by the lawyer as leverage to obtain or maintain representation that may be contrary to the client's best interests. If a lawyer has reason to believe that undue influence has been used by anyone to obtain agreement to the representation, the lawyer should not undertake the representation.

Withdrawal

[22] It is preferred that a representation that is likely to lead to a conflict be avoided before the representation begins, and a lawyer should bear this fact in mind in considering whether disclosure should be made and consent obtained at the outset. If, however, a conflict arises after a representation has been undertaken, and the conflict falls within paragraph (a), or if a conflict arises under paragraph (b) and informed and uncoerced consent is not or cannot be obtained pursuant to paragraph (c), then the lawyer should withdraw from the representation, complying with Rule 1.16. Where a conflict is not foreseeable at the outset of representation and arises only under Rule 1.7(b)(1), a lawyer should seek consent to the conflict at the time that the conflict becomes evident, but if such consent is not given by the opposing party in the matter, the lawyer need not withdraw. In determining whether a conflict is reasonably foreseeable, the test is an objective one. In determining the reasonableness of a lawyer's con-duct, such factors as whether the lawyer (or lawyer's firm) has an adequate conflict-checking system in place, must be considered. Where more than one client is involved and the lawyer must withdraw because a conflict arises after representation has been undertaken, the question whether the lawyer may continue to represent any of the clients is determined by Rule 1.9.

Imputed Disqualification

[23] All of the references in Rule 1.7 and its accompanying Comment to the limitation upon a "lawyer" must be read in light of the imputed dis-

qualification provisions of Rule 1.10, which affect lawyers practicing in a firm.

[24] In the government lawyer context, Rule 1.7(b) is not intended to apply to conflicts between agencies or components of government (federal, state, or local) where the resolution of such conflicts has been entrusted by law, order, or regulation to a specific individual or entity.

Businesses Affiliated with a Lawyer or Firm

[25] Lawyers, either alone or through firms, may have interests in enterprises that do not practice law but that, in some or all of their work, become involved with lawyers or their clients either by assisting the lawyer in providing legal services or by providing related services to the client. Examples of such enterprises are accounting firms, consultants, real estate brokerages, and the like. The existence of such interests raises several questions under this Rule. First, a lawyer's recommendation, as part of legal advice, that the client obtain the services of an enterprise in which the lawyer has an interest implicates paragraph 1.7(b)(4). The lawyer should not make such a recommendation unless able to conclude that the lawyer's professional judgment on behalf of the client will not be adversely affected. Even then, the lawyer should not make such a recommendation without full disclosure to the client so that the client can make a fully informed choice. Such disclosure should include the nature and substance of the lawyer's or the firm's interest in the related enterprise, alternative sources for the non-legal services in question, and sufficient information so that the client understands that the related enterprise's services are not legal services and that the client's relationship to the related enterprise will not be that of client to attorney. Second, such a related enterprise may refer a potential client to the lawyer; the lawyer should take steps to assure that the related enterprise will inform the lawyer of all such referrals. The lawyer should not accept such a referral without full disclosure of the nature and substance of the lawyer's interest in the related enterprise. See also Rule 7.1(b). Third, the lawyer should be aware that the relationship of a related enterprise to its own customer may create a significant interest in the lawyer in the continuation of that relationship. The substantiality of such an interest may be enough to require the lawyer to decline a proffered client representation that would conflict with that interest; at least Rule 1.7(b)(4) and (c) may require the prospective client to be informed and to consent before the representation could be undertaken. Fourth, a lawyer's interest in a related enterprise that may also serve the lawyer's clients creates a situation in which the lawyer must take unusual care to fashion the relationship among lawyer, client, and related enterprise to assure that confidences and secrets are properly preserved pursuant to Rule 1.6 to the maximum extent possible. See Rule 5.3.

Rule 1.8. Conflict of Interest: Prohibited Transactions

(a) A lawyer shall not enter into a business transaction with a client or knowingly acquire an ownership, possessory, security or other pecuniary interest adverse to a client unless:

(1) The transaction and terms on which the lawyer acquires the interest are fair and reasonable to the client and are fully disclosed and transmitted in writing to the client in a manner which can be reasonably understood by the client;

(2) The client is given a reasonable opportunity to seek the advice of independent counsel in the transaction; and

(3) The client consents in writing thereto.

(b) A lawyer shall not prepare an instrument giving the lawyer or a person related to the lawyer as parent, child, sibling, or spouse any substantial gift from a client, including a testamentary gift, except where the client is related to the donee.

(c) Prior to the conclusion of representation of a client, a lawyer shall not make or negotiate an agreement giving the lawyer literary or media rights to a portrayal or account based in substantial part on information relating to the representation.

(d) While representing a client in connection with contemplated or pending litigation or administrative proceedings, a lawyer shall not advance or guarantee financial assistance to the client, except that a lawyer may pay or otherwise provide:

(1) The expenses of litigation or administrative proceedings, including court costs, expenses of investigation, expenses of medical examination, costs of obtaining and presenting evidence; and

(2) Other financial assistance which is reasonably necessary to permit the client to institute or maintain the litigation or administrative proceeding.

(e) A lawyer shall not accept compensation for representing a client from one other than the client unless:

(1) The client consents after consultation;

(2) There is no interference with the lawyer's independence of professional judgment or with the client-lawyer relationship; and

(3) Information relating to representation of a client is protected as required by Rule 1.6.

(f) A lawyer who represents two or more clients shall not participate in making an aggregate settlement of the claims of or against the clients, or in a criminal case an aggregated agreement as to guilty or nolo contendere pleas, unless each client consents after consultation, including disclosure of the existence and nature of all the claims or pleas involved and of the participation of each person in the settlement.

(g) A lawyer shall not:

(1) Make an agreement prospectively limiting the lawyer's liability to a client for malpractice; or

(2) Settle a claim for such liability with an unrepresented client or former client without first advising that person in writing that independent representation is appropriate in connection therewith.

(h) A lawyer related to another lawyer as parent, child, sibling, or spouse shall not represent a client in a representation directly adverse to a person who the lawyer knows is represented by the other lawyer except upon consent by the client after consultation regarding the relationship.

(i) A lawyer may acquire and enforce a lien granted by law to secure the lawyer's fees or expenses, but a lawyer shall not impose a lien upon any part of a client's files, except upon the lawyer's own work product, and then only to the extent that the work product has not been paid for. This work product exception shall not apply when the client has become unable to pay, or when withholding the lawyer's work product would present a significant risk to the client of irreparable harm.

COMMENT

Transactions Between Client and Lawyer

[1] As a general principle, all transactions between client and lawyer should be fair and reasonable to the client. In such transactions a review by independent counsel on behalf of the client is often advisable. Paragraph (a) does not, however, apply to standard commercial transactions between the lawyer and the client for products or services that the client generally markets to others; for example, banking or brokerage services, medical services, products manufactured or distributed by the client, and utility services. In such transactions, the lawyer has no advantage in dealing with the client, and the restrictions in paragraph (a) are unnecessary and impracticable.

[2] A lawyer may accept a gift from a client, if the transaction meets general standards of fairness. For example, a simple gift such as a present given at a holiday or as a token of appreciation is permitted. If effectuation of a substantial gift requires preparing a legal instrument such as a will or conveyance, however, the client should be advised by the lawyer to obtain the detached advice that another lawyer can provide. Paragraph (b) recognizes an exception where the client is a relative of the donee or the gift is not substantial.

[3] This Rule does not prevent a lawyer from entering into a contingent fee arrangement with a client in a civil case, if the arrangement satisfies all the requirements of Rule 1.5(c).

Literary Rights

[4] An agreement by which a lawyer acquires literary or media rights concerning the conduct of the representation creates a conflict between

the interests of the client and the personal interests of the lawyer. Measures that might otherwise be taken in the representation of the client may detract from the publication value of an account of the representation. Paragraph (c) does not prohibit a lawyer representing a client in a transaction concerning literary property from agreeing that the lawyer's fee shall consist of a share in ownership in the property, if the arrangement conforms to Rule 1.5.

Paying Certain Litigation Costs and Client Expenses

[5] Historically, under the Code of Professional Responsibility, lawyers could only advance the costs of litigation. The client remained ultimately responsible, and was required to pay such costs even if the client lost the case. That rule was modified by this Court in 1980 in an amendment to DR 5-103(B) that eliminated the requirement that the client remain ultimately liable for costs of litigation, even if the litigation was unsuccessful. The provisions of Rule 1.8(d) embrace the result of the 1980 modification, but go further by providing that a lawyer may also pay certain expenses of a client that are not litigation expenses. Thus, under Rule 1.8(d), a lawyer may pay medical or living expenses of a client to the extent necessary to permit the client to continue the litigation. The payment of these additional expenses is limited to those strictly necessary to sustain the client during the litigation, such as medical expenses and minimum living expenses. The purpose of permitting such payments is to avoid situations in which a client is compelled by exigent financial circumstances to settle a claim on unfavorable terms in order to receive the immediate proceeds of settlement. This provision does not permit lawyers to "bid" for clients by offering financial payments beyond those minimum payments necessary to sustain the client until the litigation is completed. Regardless of the types of payments involved, assuming such payments are proper under Rule 1.8(d), client reimbursement of the lawyer is not required. However, no lawyer is required to pay litigation or other costs to a client. The Rule merely permits such payments to be made without requiring reimbursement by the client.

Person Paying for Lawyer's Services

[6] Paragraph (e) requires disclosure of the fact that the lawyer's services are being paid for by a third party. Such an arrangement must also conform to the requirements of Rule 1.6 concerning confidentiality and Rule 1.7 concerning conflict of interest. Where the client is a class, consent may be obtained on behalf of the class by court-supervised procedure.

Family Relationships Between Lawyers

[7] Paragraph (h) applies to related lawyers who are in different firms. Related lawyers in the same firm are governed by Rules 1.7, 1.9 and 1.10. Pursuant to the provisions of Rule 1.10, the disqualification stated in paragraph (h) is personal and is not imputed to members of firms with whom the lawyers are associated. Since each of the related lawyers is subject to paragraph (h), the effect is to require the consent of all materially affected clients.

Lawyer's Liens

[8] The substantive law of the District of Columbia has long permitted lawyers to assert and enforce liens against the property of clients. See, e.g., Redevelopment Land Agency v. Dowdey, 618 A.2d 153, 159-60 (D.C. 1992), and cases cited therein. Whether a lawyer has a lien on money or property belonging to a client is generally a matter of substantive law as to which the ethics rules take no position. Exceptions to what the common law might otherwise permit are made with respect to contingent fees and retaining liens. See, respectively, Rule 1.5(c) and Rule 1.8(i).

[9] Rule 1.16(d) requires a lawyer to surrender papers and property to which the client is entitled when representation of the client terminates. Paragraph (i) of this Rule states a narrow exception to Rule 1.16(d): a lawyer may retain anything the law permits — including property except for files. As to files, a lawyer may retain only the lawyer's own work product, and then only if the client has not paid for the work. However, if the client has paid for the work product, the client is entitled to receive it, even if the client has not previously seen or received a copy of the work product. Furthermore, the lawyer may not retain the work product for which the client has not paid, if the client has become unable to pay or if withholding the work product might irreparably harm the client's interest.

[10] Under Rule 1.16(d), for example, a lawyer would be required to return all papers received from a client, such as birth certificates, wills, tax returns, or "green cards." Rule 1.8(i) does not permit retention of such papers to secure payment of any fee due. Only the lawyer's own work product — results of factual investigations, legal research and analysis, and similar materials generated by the lawyer's own effort — could be retained. (The term "work product" as used in paragraph (i) is limited to materials falling within the "work product doctrine," but includes any material generated by the lawyer that would be protected under that doctrine whether or not created in connection with pending or anticipated litigation.) And a lawyer could not withhold all of the work product merely because a portion of the lawyer's fees had not been paid.

[11] There are situations in which withholding the work product would not be permissible because of irreparable harm to the client. The possibility of involuntary incarceration or criminal conviction constitutes one category of irreparable harm. The realistic possibility that a client might irretrievably lose a significant right or become subject to a significant liability because of the withholding of the work product constitutes another category of irreparable harm. On the other hand, the mere fact that the client might have to pay another lawyer to replicate the work product does not, standing alone, constitute irreparable harm. These examples are merely indicative of the meaning of the term "irreparable harm," and are not exhaustive.

Rule 1.9. Conflict of Interest: Former Client

A lawyer who has formerly represented a client in a matter shall not thereafter represent another person in the same or a substantially related matter in which that person's interests are materially adverse to the interests of the former client unless the former client consents after consultation.

COMMENT

[1] After termination of a client-lawyer relationship, a lawyer may not represent another client except in conformity with the Rule. The principles in Rule 1.7 determine whether the interests of the present and former client are adverse. Thus, a lawyer could not properly seek to rescind on behalf of a new client a contract drafted on behalf of the former client. So also a lawyer who has prosecuted an accused person could not properly represent the accused in a subsequent civil action against the government concerning the same transaction.

[2] The scope of a "matter" for purposes of this Rule may depend on the facts of a particular situation or transaction. The lawyer's involvement in a matter can also be a question of degree. When a lawyer has been directly involved in a specific transaction, subsequent representation of other clients with materially adverse interests clearly is prohibited. On the other hand, a lawyer who recurrently handled a type of problem for a former client is not precluded from later representing another client in a wholly distinct problem of that type even though the subsequent representation involves a position adverse to the prior client. Similar considerations can apply to the reassignment of military lawyers between defense and prosecution functions within the same military jurisdiction. The underlying question is whether the lawyer was so involved in the matter that the subsequent representation can be justly regarded as a changing of sides in the matter in question. Rule 1.9 is intended to incorporate federal case law defining the "substantial

relationship" test. See, e.g., T.C. Theatre Corp. v. Warner Bros. Pictures, 113 F. Supp. 265 (S.D.N.Y. 1953), and its progeny; see also Conflicts of Interest in the Legal Profession, 94 Harv. L. Rev. 1244, 1315-1334 (1981).

[3] Disqualification from subsequent representation is for the protection of clients and can be waived by them. A waiver is effective only if there is disclosure of the circumstances, including the lawyer's intended role in behalf of the new client. The question of whether a lawyer is personally disqualified from representation in any matter on account of successive government and private employment is governed by Rule 1.11 rather than by Rule 1.9.

[4] With regard to an opposing party's raising a question of conflict of interest, see Comment to Rule 1.7. With regard to disqualification of a firm with which a lawyer is associated, see Rules 1.10 and 1.11.

Rule 1.10. Imputed Disqualification: General Rule

(a) While lawyers are associated in a firm, none of them shall knowingly represent a client when any one of them practicing alone would be prohibited from doing so by Rules 1.7, 1.8(b), 1.9, or 2.2; provided, however, that this paragraph shall not apply if an individual lawyer's disqualification results solely from the fact that the lawyer consulted with a potential client for the purpose of enabling that potential client and the firm to determine whether they desired to form a client-lawyer relationship, but no such relationship was ever formed.

(b) When a lawyer becomes associated with a firm, the firm may not knowingly represent a person in a matter which is the same as, or substantially related to, a matter with respect to which the lawyer had previously represented a client whose interests are materially adverse to that person and about whom the lawyer has in fact acquired information protected by Rule 1.6 that is material to the matter. The firm is not disqualified if the lawyer participated in a previous representation or acquired information under the circumstances covered by the proviso to paragraph (a) of this Rule or by Rule 1.6(g).

(c) When a lawyer has terminated an association with a firm, the firm is not prohibited from thereafter representing a person with interests materially adverse to those of a client represented by the formerly associated lawyer during the association unless the matter is the same or substantially related to that in which the formerly associated lawyer represented the client during such former association.

(d) A disqualification prescribed by this Rule may be waived by the affected client under the conditions stated in Rule 1.7.

(e) A lawyer who, while affiliated with a firm, is made available to assist the Office of Corporation Counsel or the District of Columbia Financial Responsibility and Management Assistance Authority in

providing legal services to that agency is not considered to be associated in a firm for purposes of paragraph (a), provided, however, that no such lawyer shall represent the Office of Corporation Counsel or the District of Columbia Financial Responsibility and Management Assistance Authority with respect to a matter in which the lawyer's firm appears on behalf of an adversary.

COMMENT

Definition of "Firm"

[1] For purposes of the Rules of Professional Conduct, the term "firm" includes lawyers in a private firm, and lawyers employed in the legal department of a corporation or other organization, or in a legal services organization, but does not include a government agency or other government entity. Whether two or more lawyers constitute a firm within this definition can depend on the specific facts. For example, two practitioners who share office space and occasionally consult or assist each other ordinarily would not be regarded as constituting a firm. However, if they present themselves to the public in a way suggesting that they are a firm or conduct themselves as a firm, they should be regarded as a firm for purposes of the Rules. The terms of any formal agreement between associated lawyers are relevant in determining whether they are a firm, as is the fact that they have mutual access to confidential information concerning the clients they serve. Furthermore, it is relevant in doubtful cases to consider the underlying purpose of the rule that is involved. A group of lawyers could be regarded as a firm for purposes of the rule that the same lawyer should not represent opposing parties in litigation, while it might not be so regarded for purposes of the rule that information acquired by one lawyer is attributed to another.

[2] With respect to the law department of an organization, there is ordinarily no question that the members of the department constitute a firm within the meaning of the Rules of Professional Conduct. However, there can be uncertainty as to the identity of the client. For example, it may not be clear whether the law department of a corporation represents a subsidiary or an affiliated corporation, as well as the corporation by which the members of the department are directly employed. A similar question can arise concerning an unincorporated association and its local affiliates.

[3] Similar questions can also arise with respect to lawyers in legal aid organizations. Lawyers employed in the same unit of a legal service organization constitute a firm, but not necessarily those employed in separate units. As in the case of independent practitioners, whether the lawyers should be treated as associated with each other can depend on the particular rule that is involved, and on the specific facts of the situation.

[4] Where a lawyer has joined a private firm after having represented the government, the situation is governed by Rule 1.11. The individual lawyer involved is bound by the Rules generally, including Rules 1.6, 1.7, and 1.9.

[5] Different provisions are thus made for movement of a lawyer from one private firm to another and for movement of a lawyer from the government to a private firm. The government is entitled to protection of its client confidences, and therefore to the protections provided in Rules 1.6 and 1.11. However, if the more extensive disqualification in Rule 1.10 were applied to former government lawyers, the potential effect on the government would be unduly burdensome. The government deals with all private citizens and organizations, and thus has a much wider circle of adverse legal interests than does any private law firm. In these circumstances, the government's recruitment of lawyers would be seriously impaired if Rule 1.10 were applied to the government. On balance, therefore, the government is better served in the long run by the protections stated in Rule 1.11.

Principles of Imputed Disqualification

[6] The rule of imputed disqualification stated in paragraph (a) gives effect to the principle of loyalty to the client as it applies to lawyers who practice in a law firm. Such situations can be considered from the premise that a firm of lawyers is essentially one lawyer for purposes of the rules governing loyalty to the client, or from the premise that each lawyer is vicariously bound by the obligation of loyalty owed by each lawyer with whom the lawyer is associated. Paragraph (a) operates only among the lawyers currently associated in a firm. When a lawyer moves from one firm to another, the situation is governed by paragraph (b) or (c).

Exception in the Case of a Prospective New Client

[7] As indicated by the proviso in paragraph (a) of this Rule, the principle of loyalty diminishes in importance if the sole reason for an individual lawyer's disqualification is the lawyer's initial consultation with a prospective new client with whom no client-lawyer relationship was ever formed, either because the lawyer detected a conflict of interest as a result of the initial consultation, or for some other reason (e.g., the prospective client decided not to retain the law firm). As provided by Rule 1.6(a), and Comment [7] thereunder, the individual lawyer involved in any such initial consultation is required to maintain in strict confidence all information obtained from the prospective client even if a client-lawyer relationship was never formed. That obligation may in turn cause the individual

lawyer to be disqualified pursuant to Rule 1.7(b)(4) from representing a current or future client of the firm adverse to the prospective client because that lawyer's inability to use or disclose information obtained from the prospective client may adversely affect that lawyer's professional judgment on behalf of the current or future client of the firm whose interests are adverse to the interests of the prospective client.

[8] The individual lawyer of the firm who obtains information from a prospective client under the circumstances described in the proviso to paragraph (a) of this Rule is permitted by Rule 1.6(a) to disclose that information to other persons in the lawyer's firm only to the minimum extent necessary to enable the firm to determine whether it may ethically accept the proposed representation, and if so, whether it desires to do so. For the reasons stated in paragraph [7], any such dissemination may necessarily cause additional individual lawyers of the firm to be personally disqualified from representing a current or future client of the firm adverse to the potential client. Nevertheless, as provided in Rule 1.10(a), the personal disqualification of individual lawyers is not imputed to the firm as a whole. Accordingly, any other lawyer in the firm who is not personally disqualified vis-a-vis the prospective client may represent a current or future client of the firm adverse to the prospective client.

[9] When a firm relies on the proviso in paragraph (a) to this Rule to avoid imputed disqualification of the firm as a whole, that firm must take affirmative steps — as soon as an actual or potential conflict is suspected — to prevent the personally disqualified lawyers from disseminating any information about the potential client that is protected by Rule 1.6, except as necessary to investigate potential conflicts of interest, to any other person in the firm, including non-lawyer staff. Conversely, the personally disqualified lawyers should not receive any confidences or secrets of the firm's clients in the conflicted matter.

Lawyers Moving Between Firms

[10] When lawyers move between firms or when lawyers have been associated in a firm but then end their association, the fiction that the law firm is the same as a single lawyer is no longer wholly realistic. There are several competing considerations. First, the client previously represented must be reasonably assured that the principle of loyalty to the client is not compromised. Second, the rule of disqualification should not be so broadly cast as to preclude other persons from having reasonable choice of legal counsel. Third, the rule of disqualification should not unreasonably hamper lawyers from forming new associations and taking on new clients after having left a previous association. In this connection, it should be recognized that today many lawyers practice in firms, that many to some degree limit their practice to one field or another, and that many move from one association to another several times in their careers. If the concept of imputed disqualifica-

tion were defined with unqualified rigor, the result would be radical curtailment of the opportunity of lawyers to move from one practice setting to another and of the opportunity of clients to change counsel.

[11] Reconciliation of these competing principles in the past has been attempted under two rubrics. One approach has been to seek per se rules of disqualification. For example, it has been held that a partner in a law firm is conclusively presumed to have access to all confidences concerning all clients of the firm. Under this analysis, if a lawyer has been a partner in one law firm and then becomes a partner in another law firm, there is a presumption that all confidences known by a partner in the first firm are known to all partners in the second firm. This presumption might properly be applied in some circumstances, especially where the client has been extensively represented, but may be unrealistic where the client was represented only for limited purposes. Furthermore, such a rigid rule exaggerates the difference between a partner and an associate in modern law firms.

[12] The other rubric formerly used for dealing with vicarious disqualification is the appearance of impropriety proscribed in Canon 9 of the Code of Professional Responsibility. Applying this rubric presents two problems. First, the appearance of impropriety can be taken to include any new client-lawyer relationship that might make a former client feel anxious. If that meaning were adopted, disqualification would become little more than a question of subjective judgment by the former client. Second, since "impropriety" is undefined, the term "appearance of impropriety" is question-begging. It therefore has to be recognized that the problem of imputed disqualification cannot be properly resolved either by simple analogy to a lawyer practicing alone or by the very general concept of appearance of impropriety.

[13] A rule based on a functional analysis is more appropriate for determining the question of vicarious disqualification. Two functions are involved: preserving confidentiality and avoiding positions adverse to a client.

Confidentiality

[14] Preserving confidentiality is a question of access to information. Access to information, in turn, is essentially a question of fact in particular circumstances, aided by inferences, deductions, or working presumptions that reasonably may be made about the way in which lawyers work together. A lawyer may have general access to files of all clients of a law firm and may regularly participate in discussions of their affairs; it should be inferred that such a lawyer in fact is privy to all information about all the firm's clients. In contrast, another lawyer may have access to the files of only a limited number of clients and participate in discussion of the affairs of no other clients; in the absence of information to the contrary, it should be inferred that such a lawyer in fact is privy to information about the clients actually served but not those of other clients.

[15] Application of paragraph (b) depends on a situation's particular facts. In any such inquiry, the burden of proof should rest upon the firm whose disqualification is sought.

[16] The provisions of paragraph (b) which refer to possession of protected information operate to disqualify the firm only when the lawyer involved has actual knowledge of information protected by Rule 1.6. Thus, if a lawyer while with one firm acquired no knowledge of information relating to a particular client of the firm, and that lawyer later joined another firm, neither the lawyer individually nor the second firm is disqualified from representing another client in the same or a substantially related matter even though the interests of the two clients conflict.

[17] Independent of the question of disqualification of a firm, a lawyer changing professional association has a continuing duty to preserve confidentiality of information about a client formerly represented. See Rule 1.6.

Adverse Positions

[18] The second aspect of loyalty to a client is the lawyer's obligation to decline subsequent representations involving positions adverse to a former client arising in substantially related matters. This obligation requires abstention from adverse representations by the individual lawyer involved, and may also entail abstention of other lawyers through imputed disqualification. Hence, this aspect of the problem is governed by the principles of Rule 1.9. Thus, under paragraph (b), if a lawyer left one firm for another, the new affiliation would preclude the lawyer's new firm from continuing to represent clients with interests materially adverse to those of the lawyer's former clients in the same or substantially related matters. In this respect paragraph (b) is at odds with — and thus must be understood to reject — the dicta expressed in the "second" hypothetical in the second paragraph of footnote 5 of Brown v. District of Columbia Board of Zoning Adjustment, 486 A.2d 37, 42 n.5 (D.C. 1984) (en banc), premised on LaSalle National Bank v. County of Lake, 703 F.2d 252, 257-59 (7th Cir. 1983).

[19] The concept of "former client" as used in paragraph (b) extends only to actual representation of the client by the newly affiliated lawyer while that lawyer was employed by the former firm. Thus, not all of the clients of the former firm during the newly affiliated lawyer's practice there are necessarily deemed former clients of the newly affiliated lawyer. Only those clients with whom the newly affiliated lawyer in fact personally had a lawyer-client relationship are former clients within the terms of paragraph (b).

[20] Conversely, when a lawyer terminates an association with a firm, paragraph (c) provides that the old firm may not thereafter represent clients whose interests are materially adverse to those of the formerly as-

sociated lawyer's client in respect to a matter that is the same or substantially related to a matter with respect to which the formerly associated lawyer represented the client during the former association. For example, if a lawyer who represented a client in a litigation while with Firm A departs the firm, taking to the lawyer's new firm the litigation, Firm A may not, despite the departure of the lawyer, who takes the matter and the client to the new firm, undertake a representation adverse to the former client in that same litigation. See Rule 1.9 and the Comment thereto for the definition of "substantially related matter."

[21] The last sentence of paragraph (b) limits the imputation rule in certain limited circumstances. Those circumstances involve situations in which any secrets or confidences obtained were received before the lawyer had become a member of the Bar, but during a time when such person was providing assistance to another lawyer. The typical situation is that of the part-time or summer law clerk, or so-called summer associate. Other types of assistance to a lawyer, such as working as a paralegal or legal assistant, could also fall within the scope of this sentence. The limitation on the imputation rule is similar to the provision dealing with judicial law clerks under Rule 1.11(b). Not applying the imputation rule reflects a policy choice that imputation in such circumstances could unduly impair the mobility of persons employed in such nonlawyer positions once they become members of the Bar. The personal disqualification of the former nonlawyer is not affected, and the lawyer who previously held the nonlegal job may not be involved in any representation with respect to which the firm would have been disqualified but for the last sentence of paragraph (b). Rule 1.6(g) provides that the former nonlawyer is subject to the requirements of Rule 1.6 (regarding protection of client confidences and secrets) just as if the person had been a member of the Bar when employed in the prior position.

Lawyers Assisting the Office of Corporation Counsel and the District of Columbia Financial Responsibility and Management Assistance Authority

[22] The Office of Corporation Counsel and the District of Columbia Financial Responsibility and Management Assistance Authority may experience periods of peak need for legal services which cannot be met by normal hiring programs, or may experience problems in dealing with a large backlog of matters requiring legal services. In such circumstances, the public interest is served by permitting private firms to provide the services of lawyers affiliated with such private firms on a temporary basis to assist the Office of Corporation Counsel and the District of Columbia Financial Responsibility and Management Assistance Authority. Such arrangements do not fit within the classical pattern of situations involving the general imputation rule of paragraph (a). Provided that safeguards

are in place which preclude the improper disclosure of client confidences or secrets, and the improper use of one client's confidences or secrets on behalf of another client, the public interest benefits of such arrangements justify an exception to the general imputation rule, just as comment [1] excludes from the definition of "firm" lawyers employed by a government agency or other government entity. Lawyers assigned to assist the Office of Corporation Counsel or the District of Columbia Financial Responsibility and Management Assistance Authority pursuant to such temporary programs are, by virtue of paragraph (e), treated as if they were employed as government employees and as if their affiliation with the private firm did not exist during the period of temporary service with the Office of Corporation Counsel or the District of Columbia Financial Responsibility and Management Assistance Authority. See Rule 1.11(h) with respect to the procedures to be followed by lawyers participating in such temporary programs and by the firms with which such lawyers are affiliated after the participating lawyers have ended their participation in such temporary programs. (Amended Nov. 7, 1995.)

[23] The term "made available to assist the Office of the Corporation Counsel or the District of Columbia Financial Responsibility and Management Assistance Authority in providing legal services" in paragraph (e) contemplates the temporary cessation of practice with the firm during the period legal services are being made available to the Office of Corporation Counsel or the District of Columbia Financial Responsibility and Management Assistance Authority, so that during that period the lawyer's activities which involve the practice of law are devoted fully to assisting the Office of Corporation Counsel or the District of Columbia Financial Responsibility and Management Assistance Authority. (Amended Nov. 7, 1995.)

[24] Rule 1.10(e) prohibits a lawyer who is assisting the Office of Corporation Counsel or the District of Columbia Financial Responsibility and Management Assistance Authority from representing that office in any matter in which the lawyer's firm represents an adversary. Rule 1.10(e) does not, however, by its terms, prohibit lawyers assisting the Office of Corporation Counsel or the District of Columbia Financial Responsibility and Management Assistance Authority from participating in every matter in which the Corporation Counsel or the District of Columbia Financial Responsibility and Management Assistance Authority is taking a position adverse to that of a current client of the firm with which the participating lawyer was affiliated prior to joining the program of assistance to the Office of Corporation Counsel or the District of Columbia Financial Responsibility and Management Assistance Authority. Such an unequivocal prohibition would be overly broad, difficult to administer in practice, and inconsistent with the purpose of Rule 1.10(e). (Amended Nov. 7, 1995.)

[25] The absence of such a per se prohibition in Rule 1.10(e) does not diminish the importance of a thoughtful and restrained approach to

defining those matters in which it is appropriate for a participating lawyer to be involved. An appearance of impropriety in programs of this kind can undermine the public's acceptance of the program and embarrass the Office of Corporation Counsel or the District of Columbia Financial Responsibility and Management Assistance Authority, the participating lawyer, that lawyer's law firm and clients of that firm. For example, it would not be appropriate for a participant lawyer to engage in a representation adverse to a party who is known to be a major client of the participating lawyer's firm, even though the subject matter of the representation of the Office of Corporation Counsel or the District of Columbia Financial Responsibility and Management Assistance Authority bears no substantial relationship to any representation of that party by the participating lawyer's firm. Similarly, it would be inappropriate for a participating lawyer to be involved in a representation adverse to a party that the participating lawyer has been personally involved in representing while at the firm, even if the client is not a major client of the firm. The appropriate test is that of conservative good judgment; if any reasonable doubts concerning the unrestrained vigor of the participating lawyer's representation on behalf of the Office of Corporation Counsel or the District of Columbia Financial Responsibility and Management Assistance Authority, the lawyer should advise the appropriate officials of the Office of Corporation Counsel or the District of Columbia Responsibility and Management Assistance Authority, and decline to participate. Similarly, if participation on behalf of the Office of Corporation Counsel or the District of Columbia Financial Responsibility and Management Assistance Authority might reasonably give rise to a concern on the part of a participating lawyer's firm or a client of the firm that its secrets or confidences (as defined by Rule 1.6) might be comprised, participation should be declined. It is not anticipated that situations suggesting the appropriateness of the refusal to participate will occur so frequently as to significantly impair the usefulness of the program of participation by lawyers from private firms. (Amended Nov. 7, 1995.)

[26] The primary responsibility for identifying situations in which representation by the participating lawyer might raise reasonable doubts as to the lawyer's zealous representation on behalf of the Office of Corporation Counsel or the District of Columbia Financial Responsibility and Management Assistance Authority must rest on the participating lawyer, who will generally be privy to nonpublic information bearing on the appropriateness of the lawyer's participation in a matter on behalf of the Office of Corporation Counsel or the District of Columbia Financial Responsibility and Management Assistance Authority. Recognizing that many representations by law firms are nonpublic matters the existence and nature of which may not be disclosed consistent with Rule 1.6, it is not anticipated that law firms from whom participating lawyers have been drawn would be asked to perform formal "conflicts checks" with respect to matters in which participating lawyers may be involved. However, consultations between participating

lawyers and their law firms to identify potential areas of concern, provided that such consultations honor the requirements of Rule 1.6, are appropriate to protect the interests of all involved — the Office of Corporation Counsel, the District of Columbia Financial Responsibility and Management Assistance Authority, the participating lawyer, that lawyer's law firm and any clients whose interests are potentially implicated.

Rule 1.11. Successive Government and Private Employment

(a) A lawyer shall not accept other employment in connection with a matter which is the same as, or substantially related to, a matter in which the lawyer participated personally and substantially as a public officer or employee. Such participation includes acting on the merits of a matter in a judicial or other adjudicative capacity.

(b) If a lawyer is required to decline or to withdraw from employment under paragraph (a) on account of personal and substantial participation in a matter, no partner or associate of that lawyer, or lawyer with an of counsel relationship to that lawyer, may accept or continue such employment except as provided in paragraphs (c) and (d) below. The disqualification of such other lawyers does not apply if the sole form of participation was as a judicial law clerk.

(c) The prohibition stated in paragraph (b) shall not apply if the personally disqualified lawyer is screened from any form of participation in the matter or representation as the case may be, and from sharing in any fees resulting therefrom, and if the requirements of paragraphs (d) and (e) are satisfied.

(d) Except as provided in paragraph (e), when any of counsel, lawyer, partner, or associate of a lawyer personally disqualified under paragraph (a) accepts employment in connection with a matter giving rise to the personal disqualification, the following notifications shall be required:

(1) The personally disqualified lawyer shall submit to the public department or agency by which the lawyer was formerly employed and serve on each other party to any pertinent proceeding a signed document attesting that during the period of disqualification the personally disqualified lawyer will not participate in any manner in the matter or the representation, will not discuss the matter or the representation with any partner, associate, or of counsel lawyer, and will not share in any fees for the matter or the representation.

(2) At least one affiliated lawyer shall submit to the same department or agency and serve on the same parties a signed document attesting that all affiliated lawyers are aware of the requirement that the personally disqualified lawyer be screened from participating in or discussing the matter or the representation and describing the procedures being taken to screen the personally disqualified lawyer.

(e) If a client requests in writing that the fact and subject matter of a representation subject to paragraph (d) not be disclosed by submitting the signed statements referred to in paragraph (d), such statements shall be prepared concurrently with undertaking the representation and filed with bar counsel under seal. If at any time thereafter the fact and subject matter of the representation are disclosed to the public or become a part of the public record, the signed statements previously prepared shall be promptly submitted as required by paragraph (d).

(f) Signed documents filed pursuant to paragraph (d) shall be available to the public, except to the extent that a lawyer submitting a signed document demonstrates to the satisfaction of the public department or agency upon which such documents are served that public disclosure is inconsistent with Rule 1.6 or provisions of law.

(g) This Rule applies to any matter involving a specific party or parties.

(h) A lawyer who participates in a program of temporary service to the Office of Corporation Counsel or the District of Columbia Financial Responsibility and Management Assistance Authority of the kind described in Rule 1.10(e) shall be treated as having served as a public officer or employee for purposes of paragraph (a), and the provisions of paragraphs (b)-(e) shall apply to the lawyer and to lawyers affiliated with the lawyer.

COMMENT

[1] This Rule deals with lawyers who leave public office and enter other employment. It applies to judges and their law clerks as well as to lawyers who act in other public capacities. It is a counterpart of Rule 1.10(b), which applies to lawyers moving from one firm to another.

[2] A lawyer representing a government agency, whether employed or specially retained by the government, is subject to the Rules of Professional Conduct, including the prohibition against representing adverse interests stated in Rule 1.7 and the protections afforded former clients in Rule 1.9. In addition, such a lawyer is subject to this Rule 1.11 and to statutes and government regulations concerning conflict of interest. In the District of Columbia, where there are so many lawyers for the federal and D.C. governments and their agencies, a number of whom are constantly leaving government and accepting other employment, particular heed must be paid to the federal conflict-of-interest statutes. See, e.g., 18 U.S.C. Chapter 11 and regulations and opinions thereunder.

[3] Rule 1.11, in paragraph (a), flatly forbids a lawyer to accept other employment in a matter in which the lawyer participated personally and substantially as a public officer or employee; participation specifically includes acting on a matter in a judicial capacity. There is no provision for waiver of the individual lawyer's disqualification. "Matter" is defined in

paragraph (g) so as to encompass only matters that are particular to a specific party or parties. The making of rules of general applicability and the establishment of general policy will ordinarily not be a "matter" within the meaning of Rule 1.11. When a lawyer is forbidden by paragraph (a) to accept private employment in a matter, the partners and associates of that lawyer are likewise forbidden, by paragraph (b), to accept the employment unless the screening and disclosure procedures described in paragraphs (c) through (f) are followed.

[4] The Rule forbids lawyers to accept other employment in connection with matters that are the same as or "substantially related" to matters in which they participated personally and substantially while serving as public officers or employees. The leading case defining "substantially related" matters in the context of former government employment is Brown v. District of Columbia Board of Zoning Adjustment, 486 A.2d 37 (D.C. 1984) (en banc). There the D.C. Court of Appeals, en banc, held that in the "revolving door" context, a showing that a reasonable person could infer that, through participation in one matter as a public officer or employee, the former government lawyer "may have had access to information legally relevant to, or otherwise useful in" a subsequent representation, is prima facie evidence that the two matters are substantially related. If this prima facie showing is made, the former government lawyer must disprove any ethical impropriety by showing that the lawyer "could not have gained access to information during the first representation that might be useful in the later representation." Id. at 49-50. In *Brown,* the Court of Appeals announced the "substantially related" test after concluding that, under former DR 9-101(B), see "Revolving Door," 445 A.2d 615 (D.C. 1982) (en banc) (per curiam), the term "matter" was intended to embrace all matters "substantially related" to one another — a test that originated in "side-switching" litigation between private parties. See Rule 1.9, Comment [2]; *Brown,* 486 A.2d at 39-40 n.1, 41-42 and n.4. Accordingly, the words "or substantially related to" in paragraph (a) are an express statement of the judicial gloss in *Brown* interpreting "matter."

[5] Paragraph (a)'s absolute disqualification of a lawyer from matters in which the lawyer participated personally and substantially carries forward a policy of avoiding both actual impropriety and the appearance of impropriety that is expressed in the federal conflict-of-interest statutes and was expressed in the former Code of Professional Responsibility. Paragraph (c) requires the screening of a disqualified lawyer from such a matter as a condition to allowing any lawyers in the disqualified lawyer's firm to participate in it. This procedure is permitted in order to avoid imposing a serious deterrent to lawyers' entering public service. Governments have found that they benefit from having in their service both younger and more experienced lawyers who do not intend to devote their entire careers to public service. Some lawyers might not enter into short-term public service if they thought that, as a result of their active governmental practice, a firm would

hesitate to hire them because of a concern that the entire firm would be disqualified from matters as a result.

[6] There is no imputed disqualification and consequently no screening requirement in the case of a judicial law clerk. But such clerks are subject to a personal obligation not to participate in matters falling within paragraph (a), since participation by a law clerk is within the term "judicial or other adjudicative capacity."

[7] Paragraph (d) imposes a further requirement that must be met before lawyers affiliated with a disqualified lawyer may participate in the representation. Except to the extent that the exception in paragraph (e) is satisfied, both the personally disqualified lawyer and at least one affiliated lawyer must submit to the agency signed documents basically stating that the personally disqualified lawyer will be screened from participation in the matter. The personally disqualified lawyer must also state that the lawyer will not share in any fees paid for the representation in question. And the affiliated lawyer must describe the procedures to be followed to ensure that the personally disqualified lawyer is effectively screened.

[8] Paragraph (e) makes it clear that the lawyer's duty, under Rule 1.6, to maintain client confidences and secrets may preclude the submission of any notice required by paragraph (d). If the client requests in writing that the fact and subject matter of the representation not be disclosed, the lawyer must comply with that request. If the client makes such a request, the lawyer must abide by the client's wishes until such time as the fact and subject matter of the representation become public through some other means, such as a public filing. Filing a pleading or making an appearance in a proceeding before a tribunal constitutes a public filing. Once information concerning the representation is public, the notifications called for must be made promptly, and the lawyers involved may not honor a client request not to make the notifications. If a government agency has adopted rules governing practice before the agency by former government employees, members of the District of Columbia Bar are not exempted by Rule 1.11(e) from any additional or more restrictive notice requirements that the agency may impose. Thus the agency may require filing of notifications whether or not a client consents. While the lawyer cannot file a notification that the client has directed the lawyer not to file, the failure to file in accordance with agency rules may preclude the lawyer's representation of the client before the agency. Such issues are governed by the agency's rules, and Rule 1.11(e) is not intended to displace such agency requirements.

[9] Although paragraph (e) prohibits the lawyer from disclosing the fact and subject matter of the representation when the client has requested in writing that the information be kept confidential, it requires the lawyer to prepare the documents described in paragraph (d) as soon as the representation commences and to preserve the documents for possible submission to the agency and parties to any pertinent proceeding if and when the client does consent to their submission or the information becomes public.

[10] "Other employment," as used in paragraph (a) of this Rule, includes the representation of a governmental body other than an agency of the government by which the lawyer was employed as a public officer or employee, but in the case of a move from one government agency to another the prohibition provided in paragraph (a) may be waived by the government agency with which the lawyer was previously employed. As used in paragraph (a), it would not be "other employment" for a lawyer who has left the employment of a particular government agency and taken employment with another government agency (e.g., the Department of Justice) or with a private law firm to continue or accept representation of the same government agency with which the lawyer was previously employed.

[11] Paragraph (c) does not prohibit a lawyer from receiving a salary or partnership share established by prior independent agreement. It prohibits directly relating the attorney's compensation in any way to the fee in the matter in which the lawyer is disqualified.

[12] Rule 1.10(e) provides an exception to the general imputation imposed by Rule 1.10(a) for lawyers assisting the Office of Corporation Counsel or the District of Columbia Financial Responsibility and Management Assistance Authority on a temporary basis. Rule 1.10(e) provides that lawyers providing such temporary assistance are not considered to be affiliated with their law firm during such periods of temporary assistance. However, lawyers participating in such temporary assistance programs have a potential for conflicts of interest or the abuse of information obtained while participating in such programs. It is appropriate to subject lawyers participating in temporary assistance programs to the same rules which paragraphs (a)-(g) impose on former government employees. Paragraph (h) effects this result.

[13] In addition to ethical concerns, provisions of conflict of interest statutes or regulations may impose limitations on the conduct of lawyers while they are providing assistance to the Office of Corporation Counsel or the District of Columbia Financial Responsibility and Management Assistance Authority, or after they return from such assignments. See, e.g., 18 U.S.C. §§207, 208. Compliance with the Rules of Professional Conduct does not necessarily constitute compliance with all of the obligations imposed by conflict of interest statutes or regulations.

Rule 1.12. Former Arbitrator

(a) Except as stated in paragraph (b), a lawyer shall not represent anyone in connection with a matter in which the lawyer participated personally and substantially as an arbitrator, unless all parties to the proceeding consent after disclosure.

(b) An arbitrator selected as a partisan of a party in a multimember arbitration panel is not prohibited from subsequently representing that party.

COMMENT

[1] This Rule extends the basic requirements of Rule 1.11(a) to privately employed arbitrators. Paragraph (a) is substantially similar to Rule 1.11(a), except that it allows an arbitrator to represent someone in connection with a matter with which the lawyer was substantially involved while serving as an arbitrator if the parties to the arbitration consent. Paragraph (b) makes it clear that the prohibition set forth in paragraph (a) does not apply to partisan arbitrators serving on a multimember arbitration panel.

Rule 1.13. Organization as Client

(a) A lawyer employed or retained by an organization represents the organization acting through its duly authorized constituents.

(b) In dealing with an organization's directors, officers, employees, members, shareholders, or other constituents, a lawyer shall explain the identity of the client when it is apparent that the organization's interests may be adverse to those of the constituents with whom the lawyer is dealing.

(c) A lawyer representing an organization may also represent any of its directors, officers, employees, members, shareholders, or other constituents, subject to the provisions of Rule 1.7. If the organization's consent to the dual representation is required by Rule 1.7, the consent shall be given by an appropriate official of the organization other than the individual who is to be represented, or by the shareholders.

COMMENT

The Entity as the Client

[1] An organizational client is a legal entity, but it cannot act except through its officers, directors, employees, shareholders, and other constituents.

[2] Officers, directors, employees, and shareholders are the constituents of the corporate organizational client. The duties defined in this Comment apply equally to unincorporated associations. "Other constituents" as used in this Comment means the positions equivalent to officers, directors, employees, and shareholders held by persons acting for organizational clients that are not corporations.

[3] When one of the constituents of an organizational client communicates with the organization's lawyer in that person's organizational capacity, the communication is protected by Rule 1.6. Thus, by way of example, if an organizational client requests its lawyer to investigate allegations

of wrongdoing, interviews made in the course of that investigation between the lawyer and the client's employees or other constituents are covered by Rule 1.6. This does not mean, however, that constituents of an organizational client are the clients of the lawyer. The lawyer may not disclose to such constituents information relating to the representation except for disclosures explicitly or impliedly authorized by the organizational client in order to carry out the representation or as otherwise permitted by Rule 1.6.

[4] When constituents of the organization make decisions for it, the decisions ordinarily must be accepted by the lawyer even if their utility or prudence is doubtful. Decisions concerning policy and operations, including ones entailing serious risk, are not as such in the lawyer's province. However, different considerations arise when the lawyer knows that the organization may be substantially injured by tortious or illegal conduct by a constituent member of an organization that reasonably might be imputed to the organization or that might result in substantial injury to the organization. In such a circumstance, it may be reasonably necessary for the lawyer to ask the constituent to reconsider the matter. If that fails, or if the matter is of sufficient seriousness and importance to the organization, it may be reasonably necessary for the lawyer to take steps to have the matter reviewed by a higher authority in the organization. Clear justification should exist for seeking review over the head of the constituent normally responsible for it. The stated policy of the organization may define circumstances and prescribe channels for such review, and a lawyer should encourage the formulation of such a policy. Even in the absence of organization policy, however, the lawyer may have an obligation to refer a matter to a higher authority, depending on the seriousness of the matter and whether the constituent in question has apparent motives to act at variance with the organization's interest. Review by the chief executive officer or by the board of directors may be required when the matter is of importance commensurate with their authority. At some point it may be useful or essential to obtain an independent legal opinion.

[5] In an extreme case, it may be reasonably necessary for the lawyer to refer the matter to the organization's highest authority. Ordinarily, that is the board of directors or similar governing body. However, applicable law may prescribe that under certain conditions highest authority reposes elsewhere; for example, in the independent directors of a corporation.

Relation to Other Rules

[6] This Rule does not limit or expand the lawyer's responsibility under Rules 1.6, 1.8, 1.16, 3.3, and 4.1. If the lawyer's services are being used by an organization to further a crime or fraud by the organization, Rule 1.2(e) can be applicable.

Government Agency

[7] Because the government agency that employs the government lawyer is the lawyer's client, the lawyer represents the agency acting through its duly authorized constituents. Any application of Rule 1.13 to government lawyers must, however, take into account the differences between government agencies and other organizations.

Clarifying the Lawyer's Role

[8] There are times when the organization's interest may be or become adverse to those of one or more of its constituents. In such circumstances the lawyer should advise any constituent, whose interest the lawyer finds adverse to that of the organization, of the conflict or potential conflict of interest, that the lawyer cannot represent such constituent, and that such person may wish to obtain independent representation. Care must be taken to assure that the individual understands that, when there is such adversity of interest, the lawyer for the organization cannot provide legal representation for that constituent individual, and that discussions between the lawyer for the organization and the individual may not be privileged.

[9] Whether such a warning should be given by the lawyer for the organization to any constituent individual may turn on the facts of each case.

Dual Representation

[10] Paragraph (c) recognizes that a lawyer for an organization may also represent a principal officer or major shareholder.

Derivative Actions

[11] Under generally prevailing law, the shareholders or members of a corporation may bring suit to compel the directors to perform their legal obligations in the supervision of the organization. Members of unincorporated associations have essentially the same right. Such an action may be brought nominally by the organization, but usually is, in fact, a legal controversy over management of the organization.

[12] The question can arise whether counsel for the organization may defend such an action. The proposition that the organization is the lawyer's client does not alone resolve the issue. Most derivative actions are a normal incident of an organization's affairs, to be defended by the organization's lawyer like any other suit. However, if the claim involves

serious charges of wrongdoing by those in control of the organization, a conflict may arise between the lawyer's duty to the organization and the lawyer's relationship with the board. In those circumstances, Rule 1.7 governs whether lawyers who normally serve as counsel to the corporation can properly represent both the directors and the organization.

Rule 1.14. Client Under a Disability

(a) When a client's ability to make adequately considered decisions in connection with the representation is impaired, whether because of minority, mental disability, or for some other reason, the lawyer shall, as far as reasonably possible, maintain a normal client-lawyer relationship with the client.

(b) A lawyer may seek the appointment of a guardian or take other protective action with respect to a client, only when the lawyer reasonably believes that the client cannot adequately act in the client's own interest.

COMMENT

[1] The normal client-lawyer relationship is based on the assumption that the client, when properly advised and assisted, is capable of making decisions about important matters. When the client is a minor or suffers from a mental disorder or disability, however, maintaining the ordinary client-lawyer relationship may not be possible in all respects. In particular, an incapacitated person may have no power to make legally binding decisions. Nevertheless, a client lacking legal competence often has the ability to understand, deliberate upon, and reach conclusions about matters affecting the client's own well-being. Furthermore, to an increasing extent the law recognizes intermediate degrees of competence. For example, children as young as five or six years of age, and certainly those of ten or twelve, are regarded as having opinions that are entitled to weight in legal proceedings concerning their custody. So also, it is recognized that some persons of advanced age can be quite capable of handling routine financial matters while needing special legal protection concerning major transactions.

[2] The fact that a client suffers a disability does not diminish the lawyer's obligation to treat the client with attention and respect. If the person has no guardian or legal representative, the lawyer often must act as de facto guardian. Even if the person does have a legal representative, the lawyer should as far as possible accord the represented person the status of client, particularly in maintaining communication.

[3] If a legal representative has already been appointed for the client, the lawyer should ordinarily look to the representative for deci-

sions on behalf of the client. If a legal representative has not been appointed, the lawyer should see to such an appointment where it would serve the client's best interests. Thus, if a disabled client has substantial property that should be sold for the client's benefit, effective completion of the transaction ordinarily requires appointment of a legal representative. In many circumstances, however, appointment of a legal representative may be expensive or traumatic for the client. Evaluation of these considerations is a matter of professional judgment on the lawyer's part.

Disclosure of the Client's Condition

[4] Rules of procedure in litigation generally provide that minors or persons suffering mental disability shall be represented by a guardian or next friend if they do not have a general guardian. However, disclosure of the client's disability can adversely affect the client's interests. For example, raising the question of disability could, in some circumstances, lead to proceedings for involuntary commitment. The lawyer's position in such cases is an unavoidably difficult one. The lawyer may seek guidance from an appropriate diagnostician.

Rule 1.15. Safekeeping Property

(a) A lawyer shall hold property of clients or third persons that is in the lawyer's possession in connection with a representation separate from the lawyer's own property. Funds shall be kept in a separate account maintained in a financial institution which is authorized by federal, District of Columbia, or state law to do business in the jurisdiction where the account is maintained and which is a member of the Federal Deposit Insurance Corporation, or the Federal Savings and Loan Insurance Corporation, or successor agencies. Other property shall be identified as such and appropriately safeguarded; provided, however, that funds need not be held in an account in a financial institution if such funds (1) are permitted to be held elsewhere or in a different manner by law or court order, or (2) are held by a lawyer under an escrow or similar agreement in connection with a commercial transaction. Complete records of such account funds and other property shall be kept by the lawyer and shall be preserved for a period of five years after termination of the representation.

(b) Upon receiving funds or other property in which a client or third person has an interest, a lawyer shall promptly notify the client or third person. Except as stated in this Rule or otherwise permitted by law or by agreement with the client, a lawyer shall promptly deliver to the client or third person any funds or other property that the client or third person is entitled to receive and, upon request by the client or

third person, shall promptly render a full accounting regarding such property, subject to Rule 1.6.

(c) When in the course of representation a lawyer is in possession of property in which interests are claimed by the lawyer and another person, or by two or more persons to each of whom the lawyer may have an obligation, the property shall be kept separate by the lawyer until there is an accounting and severance of interests in the property. If a dispute arises concerning the respective interests among persons claiming an interest in such property, the undisputed portion shall be distributed and the portion in dispute shall be kept separate by the lawyer until the dispute is resolved. Any funds in dispute shall be deposited in a separate account meeting the requirements of paragraph (a).

(d) Advances of unearned fees and unincurred costs shall be treated as property of the client pursuant to paragraph (a) until earned or incurred unless the client consents to a different arrangement. Regardless of whether such consent is provided, Rule 1.16(d) applies to require the return to the client of any unearned portion of advanced legal fees and unincurred costs at the termination of the lawyer's services.

> **Editors' Note.** In mid-1999, the District of Columbia Court of Appeals amended Rule 1.15(d) effective January 1, 2000. The amended rule is explained by a new Comment [2] to Rule 1.15. The Court of Appeals order amending Rule 1.15(d) explained that "the amendment shall be applied prospectively only, but shall apply to new advances made by existing clients as well as new clients."

(e) Nothing in this Rule shall prohibit a lawyer or law firm from placing clients' funds which are nominal in amount or to be held for a short period of time in one or more interest-bearing accounts for the benefit of the charitable purposes of a court-approved "Interest on Lawyers Trust Account (IOLTA)" program.

(f) Nothing in this Rule shall prohibit a lawyer from placing a small amount of the lawyer's funds into a trust account for the sole purpose of defraying bank charges that may be made against that account.

COMMENT

[1] A lawyer should hold property of others with the care required of a professional fiduciary. Securities should be kept in a safe deposit box, except when some other form of safekeeping is warranted by special circumstances.

All property that is the property of clients or third persons should be kept separate from the lawyer's business and personal property and, if monies, in one or more trust accounts maintained with financial institutions meeting the requirements of paragraph (a). Separate trust accounts may be warranted when administering estate monies or acting in similar fiduciary capacities.

[2] Paragraph (d) of Rule 1.15 permits advances against unearned fees and unincurred costs to be treated as either the property of the client or the property of the lawyer, but absent consent by the client to a different arrangement, the Rule's default position is that such advances be treated as the property of the client, subject to the restrictions provided in paragraph (a). In any case, at the termination of an engagement, advances against fees that have not been incurred must be returned to the client as provided in Rule 1.16(d).

Editors' Note. Comment [2] was added to Rule 1.15 effective January 1, 2000 to explain the amended version of Rule 1.15(d), which also took effect on January 1, 2000. The remaining paragraphs of the Comment to Rule 1.15 were renumbered to make room for the new Comment [2].

[3] The District of Columbia Court of Appeals has promulgated specific rules allowing lawyers to place clients' funds that are nominal in amount, or that are to be held for a short period of time, into interest-bearing accounts for the benefit of the charitable purposes of a court-approved "Interest on Lawyers Trust Account (IOLTA)" program. On February 22, 1985, the court added to DR 9-103 a new paragraph (C) that expressly permitted IOLTA accounts meeting the requirements of Appendix B to Rule X of the court's Rules Governing the Bar of the District of Columbia. Appendix B sets forth detailed rules to be followed in establishing and administering IOLTA accounts. Paragraph (e) of this Rule is substantially identical to DR 9-103(C). The rules contained in Appendix B to Rule X are hereby incorporated and must be followed in setting up IOLTA programs pursuant to paragraph (e).

[4] Lawyers often receive funds from third parties from which the lawyer's fee will be paid. If there is risk that the client may divert the funds without paying the fee, the lawyer is not required to remit the portion from which the fee is to be paid. However, a lawyer may not hold funds to coerce a client into accepting the lawyer's contention. The disputed portion of the funds should be kept in trust and the lawyer should suggest means for prompt resolution of the dispute, such as arbitration. The undisputed portion of the funds should be promptly distributed.

[5] Third parties, such as a client's creditors, may have just claims against funds or other property in a lawyer's custody. A lawyer may have a duty under applicable law to protect such third-party claims against wrongful interference by the client, and accordingly may refuse to surrender the

property to the client. However, a lawyer should not unilaterally assume to arbitrate a dispute between the client and the third party.

[6] The obligations of a lawyer under this Rule are independent of those arising from activity other than rendering legal services. For example, a lawyer who serves as an escrow agent is governed by the applicable law relating to fiduciaries even though the lawyer does not render legal services in the transaction.

[7] A "clients' security fund" provides a means through the collective efforts of the Bar to reimburse persons who have lost money or property as a result of dishonest conduct of a lawyer. Where such a fund has been established, a lawyer should participate.

[8] With respect to property that constitutes evidence, such as the instruments or proceeds of crime, see Rule 3.4(a).

Rule 1.16. Declining or Terminating Representation

(a) Except as stated in paragraph (c), a lawyer shall not represent a client or, where representation has commenced, shall withdraw from the representation of a client if:

(1) The representation will result in violation of the Rules of Professional Conduct or other law;

(2) The lawyer's physical or mental condition materially impairs the lawyer's ability to represent the client; or

(3) The lawyer is discharged.

(b) Except as stated in paragraph (c), a lawyer may withdraw from representing a client if withdrawal can be accomplished without material adverse effect on the interests of the client; or if:

(1) The client persists in a course of action involving the lawyer's services that the lawyer reasonably believes is criminal or fraudulent;

(2) The client has used the lawyer's services to perpetrate a crime or fraud;

(3) The client fails substantially to fulfill an obligation to the lawyer regarding the lawyer's services and has been given reasonable warning that the lawyer will withdraw unless the obligation is fulfilled;

(4) The representation will result in an unreasonable financial burden on the lawyer or obdurate or vexatious conduct on the part of the client has rendered the representation unreasonably difficult;

(5) The lawyer believes in good faith, in a proceeding before a tribunal, that the tribunal will find the existence of other good cause for withdrawal.

(c) When ordered to do so by a tribunal, a lawyer shall continue representation notwithstanding good cause for terminating the representation.

(d) In connection with any termination of representation, a lawyer shall take timely steps to the extent reasonably practicable to protect a

client's interests, such as giving reasonable notice to the client, allowing time for employment of other counsel, surrendering papers and property to which the client is entitled, and refunding any advance payment of fee that has not been earned. The lawyer may retain papers relating to the client to the extent permitted by Rule 1.8(i).

COMMENT

[1] A lawyer should not accept representation in a matter unless it can be performed competently, promptly, without improper conflict of interest, and to completion.

Mandatory Withdrawal

[2] A lawyer ordinarily must decline or withdraw from representation if the client demands that the lawyer engage in conduct that is illegal or violates the Rules of Professional Conduct or other law. The lawyer is not obliged to decline or withdraw simply because the client suggests such a course of conduct; a client may make such a suggestion in the hope that a lawyer will not be constrained by a professional obligation.

[3] When a lawyer has been appointed to represent a client, withdrawal ordinarily requires approval of the appointing authority. See also Rule 6.2. Difficulty may be encountered if withdrawal is based on the client's demand that the lawyer engage in unprofessional conduct. The court may wish an explanation for the withdrawal, while the lawyer may be bound to keep confidential the facts that would constitute such an explanation. The lawyer's statement that irreconcilable differences between the lawyer and client require termination of the representation ordinarily should be accepted as sufficient.

Discharge

[4] A client has a right to discharge a lawyer at any time, with or without cause, subject to liability for payment for the lawyer's services. Where future dispute about the withdrawal may be anticipated, it may be advisable to prepare a written statement reciting the circumstances.

[5] Whether a client can discharge appointed counsel may depend on applicable law. A client seeking to do so should be given a full explanation of the consequences. These consequences may include a decision by the appointing authority that appointment of successor counsel is unjustified, thus requiring the client to proceed pro se.

[6] If the client is mentally incompetent, the client may lack the legal capacity to discharge the lawyer, and in any event the discharge may be

seriously adverse to the client's interests. The lawyer should make a special effort to help the client consider the consequences and, in an extreme case, may initiate proceedings for a conservatorship or similar protection of the client. See Rule 1.14.

Optional Withdrawal

[7] A lawyer may withdraw from representation in some circumstances. The lawyer has the option to withdraw if the withdrawal can be accomplished without material adverse effect on the client's interests. Withdrawal is also justified if the client persists in a course of action that the lawyer reasonably believes is criminal or fraudulent, for a lawyer is not required to be associated with such conduct even if the lawyer does not further it. Withdrawal is also permitted if the lawyer's services were misused in the past even if that would materially prejudice the client.

[8] A lawyer may withdraw if the client refuses to abide by the terms of an agreement relating to the representation, such as an agreement concerning the timely payment of the lawyer's fees, court costs or other out-of-pocket expenses of the representation, or an agreement limiting the objectives of the representation.

[9] If the matter is not pending in court, a lawyer will not have "other good cause for withdrawal" unless the lawyer is acting in good faith and the circumstances are exceptional enough to outweigh the material adverse effect on the interests of the client that withdrawal will cause.

Assisting the Client Upon Withdrawal

[10] Even if the lawyer has been unfairly discharged by the client, a lawyer must take all reasonable steps to mitigate the consequences to the client. The lawyer may retain papers as security for a fee only to the extent permitted by Rule 1.8(i).

Compliance with Requirements of a Tribunal

[11] Paragraph (c) reflects the possibility that a lawyer may, by appearing before a tribunal, become subject to the tribunal's power in some circumstances to prevent a withdrawal that would otherwise be proper. Paragraph (c) requires the lawyer who is ordered to continue a representation before a tribunal to do so. However, paragraph (c) is not intended to prevent the lawyer from challenging the tribunal's order as beyond its jurisdiction, arbitrary, or otherwise improper, while, in the interim, continuing the representation.

Return of Client's Property or Money

[12] Paragraph (d) requires a lawyer to make timely return to the client of any property or money "to which the client is entitled." Where a lawyer holds property or money of a client at the termination of a representation and there is a dispute concerning the distribution of such property or money — whether such dispute is between the lawyer and a client, the lawyer and another lawyer who is owed a fee in the matter, or between either the lawyer or the client and a third party — the lawyer must segregate the disputed portion of such property or money, hold that property or money in trust as required by Rule 1.15, and promptly distribute any undisputed amounts. See Rule 1.15 and Comment [3] thereto. Notwithstanding the foregoing, where a lawyer has a valid lien covering undisputed amounts of property or money, the lawyer may continue to hold such property or money to the extent permitted by the substantive law governing the lien asserted. See generally Rules 1.8, l.15(b).

Rule 1.17. Trust Account Overdraft Notification

(a) Funds coming into the possession of a lawyer that are required by these Rules to be segregated from the lawyer's own funds (such segregated funds hereinafter being referred to as "trust funds") shall be deposited in one or more specially designated accounts at a financial institution. The title of each such account shall contain the words "Trust Account" or "Escrow Account," as well as the lawyer's or the lawyer's law firm's identity.

(b) The accounts required pursuant to paragraph (a) shall be maintained only in institutions that are listed as "D.C. Bar Approved Depositories" on a list maintained for this purpose by the Board on Professional Responsibility, unless (1) the account is permitted to be held elsewhere or in a different manner by law or court order, or (2) a lawyer holds trust funds under an escrow or similar agreement in connection with a commercial transaction. If a lawyer is a member of the District of Columbia Bar and practices law outside the District of Columbia, D.C. Bar Approved Depositories shall be used for deposit of any: (1) trust funds received by the lawyer in the District of Columbia; (2) trust funds received by the lawyer from, or for the benefit of, parties or persons located in the District of Columbia; and/or (3) trust funds received by the lawyer that arise from transactions negotiated or consummated in the District of Columbia.

To be listed as an Approved Depository, a financial institution shall file an undertaking with the Board on Professional Responsibility, on a form to be provided by the Board's Office, agreeing promptly to report to the Office of Bar Counsel each instance in which an instrument that would properly be payable if sufficient funds were available has been presented

against a lawyer's or law firm's specially designated account at such institution at a time when such account contained insufficient funds to pay such instrument, whether or not the instrument was honored and irrespective of any overdraft privileges that may attach to such account. In addition to undertaking to make the above-specified reports, Approved Depositories, wherever they are located, shall also undertake to respond promptly and fully to subpoenas from the Office of Bar Counsel that seek a lawyer's or law firm's specially designated account records, notwithstanding any objections that might be raised based upon the territorial limits on the effectiveness of such subpoenas or upon the jurisdiction of the District of Columbia Court of Appeals to enforce them. Such undertaking shall apply to all branches of the financial institution and shall not be cancelled by the institution except upon thirty (30) days written notice to the Office of Bar Counsel. The failure of an Approved Depository to comply with its undertaking hereunder shall be grounds for immediate removal of such institution from the list of D.C. Bar Approved Depositories.

(c) Reports to Bar Counsel by Approved Depositories pursuant to paragraph (b) above shall contain the following information:

(1) In the case of a dishonored instrument, the report shall be identical to the overdraft notice customarily forwarded to the institution's other regular account holders.

(2) In the case of an instrument that was presented against insufficient funds but was honored, the report shall identify the depository, the lawyer or law firm maintaining the account, the account number, the date of presentation for payment and the payment date of the instrument, as well as the amount of overdraft created thereby.

The report to the Office of Bar Counsel shall be made simultaneously with, and within the time period, if any, provided by law for notice of dishonor. If an instrument presented against insufficient funds was honored, the institution's report shall be mailed to Bar Counsel within five (5) business days of payment of the instrument.

(d) The establishment of a specially designated account at an Approved Depository shall be conclusively deemed to be consent by the lawyer or law firm maintaining such account to that institution's furnishing to the Office of Bar Counsel all reports and information required hereunder. No Approved Depository shall incur any liability by virtue of its compliance with the requirements of this Rule, except as might otherwise arise from bad faith, intentional misconduct, or any other acts by the Approved Depository or its employees which, unrelated to this rule, would create liability.

(e) The designation of a financial institution as an Approved Depository pursuant to this Rule shall not be deemed to be a warranty, representation, or guaranty by the District of Columbia Court of Appeals, the District of Columbia Bar, the Board on Professional Responsibility, or the Office of Bar Counsel as to the financial soundness, business practices, or other attributes of such institution. Approval

of an institution under this rule means only that the institution has undertaken to meet the reporting requirements enumerated above.

(f) Nothing in this rule shall preclude a financial institution from charging a lawyer or law firm for the reasonable cost of producing the reports and records required by this rule.

(g) Definitions:

"Law Firm" — includes a partnership of lawyers, a professional or non-profit corporation of lawyers, and a combination thereof engaged in the practice of law.

"Financial Institution" — includes banks, savings and loan associations, credit unions, savings banks and any other business that accepts for deposit funds held in trust by lawyers which is authorized by Federal, District of Columbia, or state law to do business in the District of Columbia or the state in which the financial institution is situated and that maintains accounts which are insured by an agency or instrumentality of the United States.

COUNSELOR

Rule 2.1. Advisor

In representing a client, a lawyer shall exercise independent professional judgment and render candid advice. In rendering advice, a lawyer may refer not only to law but to other considerations such as moral, economic, social, and political factors, that may be relevant to the client's situation.

COMMENT

Scope of Advice

[1] A client is entitled to straightforward advice expressing the lawyer's honest assessment. Legal advice often involves unpleasant facts and alternatives that a client may be disinclined to confront. In presenting advice, a lawyer endeavors to sustain the client's morale and may put advice in as acceptable a form as honesty permits. However, a lawyer should not be deterred from giving candid advice by the prospect that the advice will be unpalatable to the client.

[2] Advice couched in narrowly legal terms may be of little value to a client, especially where practical considerations, such as cost or effects on other people, are predominant. Purely technical legal advice, therefore, can sometimes be inadequate. It is proper for a lawyer to refer to relevant moral and ethical considerations in giving advice. Although a lawyer is not a moral advisor as such, moral and ethical considerations impinge upon

most legal questions and may decisively influence how the law will be applied.

[3] A client may expressly or impliedly ask the lawyer for purely technical advice. When such a request is made by a client experienced in legal matters, the lawyer may accept it at face value. When such a request is made by a client inexperienced in legal matters, however, the lawyer's responsibility as advisor may include indicating that more may be involved than strictly legal considerations.

[4] Matters that go beyond strictly legal questions may also be in the domain of another profession. Family matters can involve problems within the professional competence of psychiatry, clinical psychology, or social work; business matters can involve problems within the competence of the accounting profession or of financial specialists. Where consultation with a professional in another field is itself something a competent lawyer would recommend, the lawyer should make such a recommendation. At the same time, a lawyer's advice at its best often consists of recommending a course of action in the face of conflicting recommendations of experts.

Offering Advice

[5] In general, a lawyer is not expected to give advice until asked by the client. However, when a lawyer knows that a client proposes a course of action that is likely to result in substantial adverse legal consequences to the client, duty to the client under Rule 1.4 may require that the lawyer act if the client's course of action is related to the representation. A lawyer ordinarily has no duty to initiate investigation of a client's affairs or to give advice that the client has indicated is unwanted, but a lawyer may initiate advice to a client when doing so appears to be in the client's interest.

Rule 2.2. Intermediary

(a) A lawyer may act as intermediary between clients if:

(1) The lawyer consults with each client concerning the implications of the common representation, including the advantages and risks involved, and the effect on the attorney-client privileges, and obtains each client's consent to the common representation;

(2) The lawyer reasonably believes that the matter can be resolved on terms compatible with the clients' best interests, that each client will be able to make adequately informed decisions in the matter, and that there is little risk of material prejudice to the interests of any of the clients if the contemplated resolution is unsuccessful; and

(3) The lawyer reasonably believes that the common representation can be undertaken impartially and without improper effect on other responsibilities the lawyer has to any of the clients.

(b) A lawyer should, except in unusual circumstances that may make it infeasible, provide both clients with an explanation in writing of the risks involved in the common representation and of the circumstances that may cause separate representation later to be necessary or desirable. The consent of the clients shall also be in writing.

(c) While acting as intermediary, the lawyer shall consult with each client concerning the decisions to be made and the considerations relevant in making them, so that each client can make adequately informed decisions.

(d) A lawyer shall withdraw as intermediary if any of the clients so request, or if any of the conditions stated in paragraph (a) are no longer satisfied. Upon withdrawal, the lawyer shall not continue to represent any of the clients in the matter that was the subject of the intermediation.

COMMENT

[1] A lawyer acts as intermediary under this Rule when the lawyer represents two or more parties with potentially conflicting interests. A key factor in defining the relationship is whether the parties share responsibility for the lawyer's fee, but the common representation may be inferred from other circumstances. Because confusion can arise as to the lawyer's role where each party is not separately represented, it is important that the lawyer make clear the relationship.

[2] Because the potential for confusion is so great, paragraph (b) imposes the requirement that an explanation of the risks of the common representation be furnished in writing, except in unusual circumstances. The process of preparing the writing causes the lawyer involved to focus specifically on those risks, a process that may suggest to the lawyer that the particular situation is not suited to the use of the lawyer as an intermediary. In any event, the writing performs a valuable role in educating the client to such risks as may exist — risks that many clients may not otherwise comprehend. Mere agreement by a client to waive the requirement for a written analysis of the risks does not constitute the "unusual circumstances" that justify omitting the writing. The "unusual circumstances" requirement may be met in rare situations where an assessment of risks is not feasible at the beginning of the intermediary role. In such circumstances, the writing should be provided as soon as it becomes feasible to assess the risks with reasonable clarity. The consent required by paragraph (b) should refer to the disclosure upon which it is based.

[3] The Rule does not apply to a lawyer acting as arbitrator or mediator between or among parties who are not clients of the lawyer, even where the lawyer has been appointed with the concurrence of the parties. In performing such a role the lawyer may be subject to applicable codes of ethics, such as the Code of Ethics for Arbitration in Commercial Disputes prepared by a Joint Committee of the American Bar Association and the American Arbitration Association.

[4] A lawyer acts as intermediary in seeking to establish or adjust a relationship between clients on an amicable and mutually advantageous basis; for example, in helping to organize a business in which two or more clients are entrepreneurs, working out the financial reorganization of an enterprise in which two or more clients have an interest, arranging a property distribution in settlement of an estate, or mediating a dispute between clients. The lawyer seeks to resolve potentially conflicting interests by developing the parties' mutual interests. The alternative can be that each party may have to obtain separate representation, with the possibility in some situations of incurring additional cost, complication, or even litigation. Given these and other relevant factors, all the clients may prefer that the lawyer act as intermediary.

[5] In considering whether to act as intermediary between clients, a lawyer should be mindful that if the intermediation fails the result can be additional cost, embarrassment, and recrimination. In some situations the risk of failure is so great that intermediation is plainly impossible. For example, a lawyer cannot undertake common representation of clients between whom contentious litigation is imminent or who contemplate contentious negotiations. More generally, if the relationship between the parties has already assumed definite antagonism, the possibility that the clients' interests can be adjusted by intermediation ordinarily is not very good.

[6] The appropriateness of intermediation can depend on its form. Forms of intermediation range from informal arbitration where each client's case is presented by the respective client and the lawyer decides the outcome, to mediation, to common representation where the clients' interests are substantially though not entirely compatible. One form may be appropriate in circumstances where another would not. Other relevant factors are whether the lawyer subsequently will represent both parties on a continuing basis and whether the situation involves creating a relationship between the parties or terminating one.

[7] Since the lawyer is required to be impartial between commonly represented clients, intermediation is improper when that impartiality cannot be maintained. For example, a lawyer who has represented one of the clients for a long period of time and in a variety of matters could have difficulty being impartial between that client and one to whom the lawyer has only recently been introduced.

Confidentiality and Privilege

[8] A particularly important factor in determining the appropriateness of intermediation is the effect on client-lawyer confidentiality and the attorney-client privilege. In a common representation, the lawyer is still required both to keep each client adequately informed and to maintain confidentiality of information relating to the representation. See Rules 1.4 and 1.6. Complying with both requirements while acting as intermediary requires a delicate balance. If the balance cannot be maintained, the com-

mon representation is improper. With regard to the attorney-client privilege, the prevailing rule is that as between commonly represented clients the privilege does not attach. Hence, it must be assumed that if litigation eventuates between the clients, the privilege will not protect any such communications, and the clients should be so advised.

Consultation

[9] In acting as intermediary between clients, the lawyer is required to consult with the clients on the implications of doing so, and proceed only upon consent based on such a consultation. The consultation should make clear that the lawyer's role is not that of partisanship normally expected in other circumstances.

[10] Paragraph (c) is an application of the principle expressed in Rule 1.4. Where the lawyer is intermediary, the clients ordinarily must assume greater responsibility for decisions than when each client is independently represented.

Withdrawal

[11] Common representation does not diminish the rights of each client in the client-lawyer relationship. Each has the right to loyal and diligent representation, the right to discharge the lawyer as stated in Rule 1.16, and the protection of Rule 1.9 concerning obligations to a former client.

Rule 2.3. Evaluation for Use by Third Persons

(a) A lawyer may undertake an evaluation of a matter affecting a client for the use of someone other than the client if:

(1) The lawyer reasonably believes that making the evaluation is compatible with other aspects of the lawyer's relationship with the client; and

(2) The client consents after consultation.

(b) Except as disclosure is required in connection with a report of an evaluation, information relating to the evaluation is otherwise protected by Rule 1.6.

COMMENT

Definition

[1] An evaluation may be performed at the client's direction but for the primary purpose of establishing information for the benefit of third

parties; for example, an opinion concerning the title of property rendered at the behest of a vendor for the information of a prospective purchaser, or at the behest of a borrower for the information of a prospective lender. In some situations, the evaluation may be required by a government agency; for example, an opinion concerning the legality of the securities registered for sale under the securities laws. In other instances, the evaluation may be required by a third person, such as a purchaser of a business.

[2] A legal evaluation should be distinguished from an investigation of a person with whom the lawyer does not have a client-lawyer relationship. For example, a lawyer retained by a purchaser to analyze a vendor's title to property does not have a client-lawyer relationship with the vendor. So also, an investigation into a person's affairs by a government lawyer, or by special counsel employed by the government, is not an evaluation as that term is used in this Rule. The question is whether the lawyer is retained by the person whose affairs are being examined. When the lawyer is retained by that person, the general Rules concerning loyalty to client and preservation of confidences apply, which is not the case if the lawyer is retained by someone else. For this reason, it is essential to identify the person by whom the lawyer is retained. This should be made clear not only to the person under examination, but also to others to whom the results are to be made available.

Duty to Third Person

[3] When the evaluation is intended for the information or use of a third person, a legal duty to that person may or may not arise. That legal question is beyond the scope of this Rule. However, since such an evaluation involves a departure from the normal client-lawyer relationship, careful analysis of the situation is required. The lawyer must be satisfied as a matter of professional judgment that making the evaluation is compatible with other functions undertaken in behalf of the client. For example, if the lawyer is acting as advocate in defending the client against charges of fraud, it would normally be incompatible with that responsibility for the lawyer to perform an evaluation for others concerning the same or a related transaction. Assuming no such impediment is apparent, however, the lawyer should advise the client of the implications of the evaluation, particularly the lawyer's responsibilities to third persons and the duty to disseminate the findings.

Access to and Disclosure of Information

[4] The quality of an evaluation depends on the freedom and extent of the investigation upon which it is based. Ordinarily a lawyer should have whatever latitude of investigation seems necessary as a matter of professional judgment. Under some circumstances, however, the terms of the evaluation may be limited. For example, certain issues or sources may be categorically

excluded, or the scope of search may be limited by time constraints or the noncooperation of persons having relevant information. Any such limitations that are material to the evaluation should be described in the report. If after a lawyer has commenced an evaluation, the client refuses to comply with the terms upon which it was understood the evaluation was to have been made, the lawyer's obligations are determined by law, having reference to the terms of the client's agreement and the surrounding circumstances.

Financial Auditors' Requests for Information

[5] When a question concerning the legal situation of a client arises at the insistence of the client's financial auditor and the question is referred to the lawyer, the lawyer's response may be made in accordance with procedures recognized in the legal profession. Such a procedure is set forth in the American Bar Association Statement of Policy Regarding Lawyers' Responses to Auditors' Requests for Information, adopted in 1975.

ADVOCATE

Rule 3.1. Meritorious Claims and Contentions

A lawyer shall not bring or defend a proceeding, or assert or controvert an issue therein, unless there is a basis for doing so that is not frivolous, which includes a good-faith argument for an extension, modification, or reversal of existing law. A lawyer for the defendant in a criminal proceeding, or for the respondent in a proceeding that could result in involuntary institutionalization, shall, if the client elects to go to trial or to a contested fact-finding hearing, nevertheless so defend the proceeding as to require that the government carry its burden of proof.

COMMENT

[1] The advocate has a duty to use legal procedure for the fullest benefit of the client's cause, but also a duty not to abuse legal procedure. The law, both procedural and substantive, establishes the limits within which an advocate may proceed. However, the law is not always clear and never is static. Accordingly, in determining the proper scope of advocacy, account must be taken of the law's ambiguities and potential for change.

[2] The filing of an action or defense or similar action taken for a client is not frivolous merely because the facts have not first been fully substantiated or because the lawyer expects to develop vital evidence only by discovery. Such action is not frivolous even though the lawyer believes that the client's position ultimately will not prevail. The action is frivolous

if the lawyer is unable either to make a good-faith argument on the merits of the action taken or to support the action taken by a good-faith argument for an extension, modification, or reversal of existing law.

[3] In criminal cases or proceedings in which the respondent can be involuntarily institutionalized, such as juvenile delinquency and civil commitment cases, the lawyer is not only permitted, but is indeed required, to put the government to its proof whenever the client elects to contest adjudication.

Rule 3.2. Expediting Litigation

(a) In representing a client, a lawyer shall not delay a proceeding when the lawyer knows or when it is obvious that such action would serve solely to harass or maliciously injure another.

(b) A lawyer shall make reasonable efforts to expedite litigation consistent with the interests of the client.

COMMENT

[1] Dilatory practices bring the administration of justice into disrepute. Delay should not be indulged merely for the convenience of the advocates, or for the purpose of frustrating an opposing party's attempt to obtain rightful redress or repose. It is not a justification that similar conduct is often tolerated by the bench and bar. The question is whether a competent lawyer acting in good faith would regard the course of action as having some substantial purpose other than delay. Realizing financial or other benefit from otherwise improper delay in litigation is not a legitimate interest of the client.

Rule 3.3. Candor Toward the Tribunal

(a) A lawyer shall not knowingly:

(1) Make a false statement of material fact or law to a tribunal;

(2) Counsel or assist a client to engage in conduct that the lawyer knows is criminal or fraudulent, but a lawyer may discuss the legal consequences of any proposed course of conduct with a client and may counsel or assist a client to make a good-faith effort to determine the validity, scope, meaning, or application of the law;

(3) Fail to disclose to the tribunal legal authority in the controlling jurisdiction not disclosed by opposing counsel and known to the lawyer to be dispositive of a question at issue and directly adverse to the position of the client; or

(4) Offer evidence that the lawyer knows to be false, except as provided in paragraph (b).

(b) When the witness who intends to give evidence that the lawyer knows to be false is the lawyer's client and is the accused in a criminal case, the lawyer shall first make a good-faith effort to dissuade the client from presenting the false evidence; if the lawyer is unable to dissuade the client, the lawyer shall seek leave of the tribunal to withdraw. If the lawyer is unable to dissuade the client or to withdraw without seriously harming the client, the lawyer may put the client on the stand to testify in a narrative fashion, but the lawyer shall not examine the client in such manner as to elicit testimony which the lawyer knows to be false, and shall not argue the probative value of the client's testimony in closing argument.

(c) The duties stated in paragraph (a) continue to the conclusion of the proceeding.

(d) A lawyer who receives information clearly establishing that a fraud has been perpetrated upon the tribunal shall promptly reveal the fraud to the tribunal unless compliance with this duty would require disclosure of information otherwise protected by Rule 1.6, in which case the lawyer shall promptly call upon the client to rectify the fraud.

COMMENT

[1] This Rule defines the duty of candor to the tribunal. In dealing with a tribunal the lawyer is also required to comply with the general requirements of Rule 1.2(d) and (e). However, an advocate does not vouch for the evidence submitted in a cause; the tribunal is responsible for assessing its probative value.

Representations by a Lawyer

[2] An assertion purported to be made by the lawyer, as in an affidavit by the lawyer or in a statement in open court, may properly be made only when the lawyer knows the assertion is true or believes it to be true on the basis of a reasonably diligent inquiry. There may be circumstances where failure to make a disclosure is the equivalent of an affirmative misrepresentation. The obligation prescribed in Rule 1.2(e) not to counsel a client to commit or assist the client in committing a fraud applies in litigation but is subject to Rule 3.3(b) and (d). Regarding compliance with Rule 1.2(e), see the Comment to that Rule. See also Comment to Rule 8.4(b).

Misleading Legal Argument

[3] Legal argument based on a knowingly false representation of law constitutes dishonesty toward the tribunal. A lawyer is not required to

make a disinterested exposition of the law, but must recognize the existence of pertinent legal authorities. Furthermore, as stated in subparagraph (a)(3), an advocate has a duty to disclose directly adverse authority in the controlling jurisdiction that has not been disclosed by the opposing party and that is dispositive of a question at issue. The underlying concept is that legal argument is a discussion seeking to determine the legal premises properly applicable to the case.

False Evidence

[4] When evidence that a lawyer knows to be false is provided by a person who is not the client, the lawyer must refuse to offer it regardless of the client's wishes.

[5] When false evidence is offered by the client, however, a conflict may arise between the lawyer's duty to keep the client's revelations confidential and the duty of candor to the court. Upon ascertaining that material evidence is false, the lawyer should seek to persuade the client that the evidence should not be offered or, if it has been offered, that its false character should immediately be disclosed.

[6] Paragraph (d) provides that if a lawyer learns that a fraud has been perpetrated on the tribunal, the lawyer must reveal the fraud to the tribunal. However, if the notification of the tribunal would require disclosure of information protected by Rule 1.6, the lawyer may not inform the tribunal of the fraud; the lawyer's only duty in such an instance is to call upon the client to rectify the fraud. In other cases, the lawyer may learn of the client's intention to present false evidence before the client has had a chance to do so. In this situation, paragraphs (a)(4) and (b) forbid the lawyer to present the false evidence, except in rare instances where the witness is the accused in a criminal case, the lawyer is unsuccessful in dissuading the client from going forward, and the lawyer is unable to withdraw without causing serious harm to the client. The terms "criminal case" and "criminal defendant" as used in Rule 3.3 and its Comment include juvenile delinquency proceedings and the person who is the subject of such proceedings.

Perjury by a Criminal Defendant

[7] Paragraph (b) allows the lawyer to permit a client who is the accused in a criminal case to present false testimony in very narrowly circumscribed circumstances and in a very limited manner. Even in a criminal case the lawyer must seek to persuade the defendant-client to refrain from perjurious testimony. There has been dispute concerning the lawyer's duty when that persuasion fails. Paragraph (b) requires the lawyer to withdraw rather than offer the client's false testimony, if this can be done without seriously harming the client.

[8] Serious harm to the client sufficient to prevent the lawyer's withdrawal entails more than the usual inconveniences that necessarily result from withdrawal, such as delay in concluding the client's case or an increase in the costs of concluding the case. The term should be construed narrowly to preclude withdrawal only where the special circumstances of the case are such that the client would be significantly prejudiced, such as by express or implied divulgence of information otherwise protected by Rule 1.6. If the confrontation with the client occurs before trial, the lawyer ordinarily can withdraw. Withdrawal before trial may not be possible, however, either because trial is imminent, or because the confrontation with the client does not take place until the trial itself, or because no other counsel is available. In those rare circumstances in which withdrawal without such serious harm to the client is impossible, the lawyer may go forward with examination of the client and closing argument subject to the limitations of paragraph (b).

Refusing to Offer Proof of a Nonclient Known to Be False

[9] Generally speaking, a lawyer may not offer testimony or other proof, through a nonclient, that the lawyer knows to be false. Furthermore, a lawyer may not offer evidence of a client if the evidence is known by the lawyer to be false, except to the extent permitted by paragraph (b) where the client is a defendant in a criminal case.

Rule 3.4. Fairness to Opposing Party and Counsel

A lawyer shall not:

(a) Obstruct another party's access to evidence or alter, destroy, or conceal evidence, or counsel or assist another person to do so, if the lawyer reasonably should know that the evidence is or may be the subject of discovery or subpoena in any pending or imminent proceeding. Unless prohibited by law, a lawyer may receive physical evidence of any kind from the client or from another person. If the evidence received by the lawyer belongs to anyone other than the client, the lawyer shall make a good-faith effort to preserve it and to return it to the owner, subject to Rule 1.6;

(b) Falsify evidence, counsel or assist a witness to testify falsely, or offer an inducement to a witness that is prohibited by law;

(c) Knowingly disobey an obligation under the rules of a tribunal except for an open refusal based on an assertion that no valid obligation exists;

(d) In pretrial procedure, make a frivolous discovery request or fail to make reasonably diligent effort to comply with a legally proper discovery request by an opposing party;

(e) In trial, allude to any matter that the lawyer does not reasonably believe is relevant or that will not be supported by admissible evidence, assert personal knowledge of facts in issue except when testifying as a witness, or state a personal opinion as to the justness of a cause, the credibility of a witness, the culpability of a civil litigant, or the guilt or innocence of an accused; or

(f) Request a person other than a client to refrain from voluntarily giving relevant information to another party unless:

(1) The person is a relative or an employee or other agent of a client; and

(2) The lawyer reasonably believes that the person's interests will not be adversely affected by refraining from giving such information.

COMMENT

[1] The procedure of the adversary system contemplates that the evidence in a case is to be marshaled competitively by the contending parties. Fair competition in the adversary system is secured by prohibitions against destruction or concealment of evidence, improperly influencing witnesses, obstructive tactics in discovery procedure, and the like.

[2] Documents and other items of evidence are often essential to establish a claim or defense. Subject to evidentiary privileges, the right of an opposing party, including the government, to obtain evidence through discovery or subpoena is an important procedural right. The exercise of that right can be frustrated if relevant material is altered, concealed, or destroyed. To the extent clients are involved in the effort to comply with discovery requests, the lawyer's obligations are to pursue reasonable efforts to assure that documents and other information subject to proper discovery requests are produced. Applicable law in many jurisdictions makes it an offense to destroy material for purpose of impairing its availability in a pending proceeding or a proceeding whose commencement can be foreseen. Falsifying evidence is also generally a criminal offense. Paragraph (a) applies to evidentiary material generally, including computerized information.

[3] Paragraph (a) permits, but does not require, the lawyer to accept physical evidence (including the instruments or proceeds of crime) from the client or any other person. Such receipt is, as stated in paragraph (a), subject to other provisions of law and the limitations imposed by paragraph (a) with respect to obstruction of access, alteration, destruction, or concealment, and subject also to the requirements of paragraph (a) with respect to return of property to its rightful owner, and to the obligation to comply with subpoenas and discovery requests. The term "evidence" includes any document or physical object that the lawyer reasonably should know may be the subject of discovery or subpoena in any pending or im-

minent litigation. See D.C. Bar Legal Ethics Committee Opinion No. 119 (March 15, 1983) (test is whether destruction of document is directed at concrete litigation that is either pending or almost certain to be filed).

[4] A lawyer should ascertain that the lawyer's handling of documents or other physical objects does not violate any other law. Federal criminal law may forbid the destruction of documents or other physical objects in circumstances not covered by the ethical rules set forth in paragraph (a). See, e.g., 18 U.S.C. §1503 (obstruction of justice); 18 U.S.C. §1505 (obstruction of proceedings before departments, agencies, and committees); 18 U.S.C. §1510 (obstruction of criminal investigations). And it is a crime in the District of Columbia for one who knows or has reason to know that an official proceeding has begun or is likely to be instituted to alter, destroy, or conceal a document with intent to impair its integrity or availability for use in the proceeding. D.C. Code §22-723 (1981). Finally, some discovery rules having the force of law may prohibit the destruction of documents and other material even if litigation is not pending or imminent. This Rule does not set forth the scope of a lawyer's responsibilities under all applicable laws. It merely imposes on the lawyer an ethical duty to make reasonable efforts to comply fully with those laws. The provisions of paragraph (a) prohibit a lawyer from obstructing another party's access to evidence, and from altering, destroying, or concealing evidence. These prohibitions may overlap with criminal obstruction provisions and civil discovery rules, but they apply whether or not the prohibited conduct violates criminal provisions or court rules. Thus, the alteration of evidence by a lawyer, whether or not such conduct violates criminal law or court rules, constitutes a violation of paragraph (a).

[5] Because of the duty of confidentiality under Rule 1.6, the lawyer is generally forbidden to volunteer information about physical evidence received from a client without the client's consent after consultation. In some cases, the Office of Bar Counsel will accept physical evidence from a lawyer and then turn it over to the appropriate persons; in those cases this procedure is usually the best means of delivering evidence to the proper authorities without disclosing the client's confidences. However, Bar Counsel may refuse to accept evidence; thus lawyers should keep the following in mind before accepting evidence from a client, and should discuss with Bar Counsel's office the procedures that may be employed in particular circumstances.

[6] First, if the evidence received from the client is subpoenaed or otherwise requested through the discovery process while held by the lawyer, the lawyer will be obligated to deliver the evidence directly to the appropriate persons, unless there is a basis for objecting to the discovery request or moving to quash the subpoena. A lawyer should therefore advise the client of the risk that evidence may be subject to subpoena or discovery, and of the lawyer's duty to turn the evidence over in that event, before accepting it from the client.

[7] Second, if the lawyer has received physical evidence belonging to the client, for purposes of examination or testing, the lawyer may later return the property to the client pursuant to Rule 1.15, provided that the evidence has not been subpoenaed. The lawyer may not be justified in returning to a client physical evidence the possession of which by the client would be per se illegal, such as certain drugs and weapons. And if it is reasonably apparent that the evidence is not the client's property, the lawyer may not retain the evidence or return it to the client. Instead, the lawyer must, under paragraph (a), make a good-faith effort to return the evidence to its owner.

[8] With regard to paragraph (b), it is not improper to pay a witness's expenses or to compensate a witness for loss of time in preparing to testify, in attending, or in testifying. A fee for the services of a witness who will be proffered as an expert may be made contingent on the outcome of the litigation, provided, however, that the fee, while conditioned on recovery, shall not be a percentage of the recovery.

[9] Paragraph (f) permits a lawyer to advise employees of a client to refrain from giving information to another party, for the employees may identify their interests with those of the client. See also Rule 4.2.

Rule 3.5. Impartiality and Decorum of the Tribunal

A lawyer shall not:

(a) Seek to influence a judge, juror, prospective juror, or other official by means prohibited by law;

(b) Communicate ex parte with such a person except as permitted by law; or

(c) Engage in conduct intended to disrupt a tribunal.

COMMENT

[1] Many forms of improper influence upon a tribunal are proscribed by criminal law. Others are specified in the ABA Model Code of Judicial Conduct, with which an advocate should be familiar. A lawyer is required to avoid contributing to a violation of such provisions.

[2] The advocate's function is to present evidence and argument so that the cause may be decided according to law. Refraining from abusive or obstreperous conduct is a corollary of the advocate's right to speak on behalf of litigants. A lawyer may stand firm against abuse by a judge but should avoid reciprocation; the judge's default is not justification for similar dereliction by an advocate. An advocate can present the cause, protect the record for subsequent review, and preserve professional integrity by patient firmness no less effectively than by belligerence or theatrics.

Rule 3.6. Trial Publicity

A lawyer engaged in a case being tried to a judge or jury shall not make an extrajudicial statement that a reasonable person would expect to be disseminated by means of mass public communication if the lawyer knows or reasonably should know that the statement will create a serious and imminent threat to the impartiality of the judge or jury.

COMMENT

[1] It is difficult to strike a proper balance between protecting the right to a fair trial and safeguarding the right of free expression, which are both guaranteed by the Constitution. On one hand, publicity should not be allowed to influence the fair administration of justice. On the other hand, litigants have a right to present their side of a dispute to the public, and the public has an interest in receiving information about matters that are in litigation. Often a lawyer involved in the litigation is in the best position to assist in furthering these legitimate objectives. No body of rules can simultaneously satisfy all interests of fair trial and all those of free expression.

[2] The special obligations of prosecutors to limit comment on criminal matters involve considerations in addition to those implicated in this Rule, and are dealt with in Rule 3.8. Furthermore, this Rule is not intended to abrogate special court rules of confidentiality in juvenile or other cases. Lawyers are bound by Rule 3.4(c) to adhere to any such rules that have not been found invalid.

[3] Because administrative agencies should have the prerogative to determine the ethical rules for prehearing publicity, this Rule does not purport to apply to matters before administrative agencies.

Rule 3.7. Lawyer as Witness

(a) A lawyer shall not act as advocate at a trial in which the lawyer is likely to be a necessary witness except where:

(1) The testimony relates to an uncontested issue;

(2) The testimony relates to the nature and value of legal services rendered in the case; or

(3) Disqualification of the lawyer would work substantial hardship on the client.

(b) A lawyer may not act as advocate in a trial in which another lawyer in the lawyer's firm is likely to be called as a witness if the other lawyer would be precluded from acting as advocate in the trial by Rule 1.7 or Rule 1.9. The provisions of this paragraph (b) do not apply if the lawyer who is appearing as an advocate is employed by, and appears on behalf of, a government agency.

COMMENT

[1] Combining the roles of advocate and witness can prejudice the opposing party and can involve a conflict of interest between the lawyer and client.

[2] The opposing party has proper objection where the combination of roles may prejudice that party's rights in the litigation. A witness is required to testify on the basis of personal knowledge, while an advocate is expected to explain and comment on evidence given by others. It may not be clear whether a statement by an advocate-witness should be taken as proof or as an analysis of the proof.

[3] Subparagraph (a)(1) recognizes that if the testimony will be uncontested, the ambiguities in the dual role are purely theoretical. Subparagraph (a)(2) recognizes that where the testimony concerns the extent and value of legal services rendered in the action in which the testimony is offered, permitting the lawyers to testify avoids the need for a second trial with new counsel to resolve that issue. Moreover, in such a situation the judge has first-hand knowledge of the matter in issue; hence, there is less dependence on the adversary process to test the credibility of the testimony.

[4] Apart from these two exceptions, subparagraph (a)(3) recognizes that a balancing is required between the interests of the client and those of the opposing party. Whether the opposing party is likely to suffer prejudice depends on the nature of the case, the importance and probable tenor of the lawyer's testimony, and the probability that the lawyer's testimony will conflict with that of other witnesses. Even if there is risk of such prejudice, in determining whether the lawyer should be disqualified due regard must be given to the effect of disqualification on the lawyer's client. It is relevant that one or both parties could reasonably foresee that the lawyer would probably be a witness.

[5] If the only reason for not permitting a lawyer to combine the roles of advocate and witness is possible prejudice to the opposing party, there is no reason to disqualify other lawyers in the testifying lawyer's firm from acting as advocates in that trial. In short, there is no general rule of imputed disqualification applicable to Rule 3.7. However, the combination of roles of advocate and witness may involve an improper conflict of interest between the lawyer and the client in addition to or apart from possible prejudice to the opposing party. Whether there is such a client conflict is determined by Rule 1.7 or 1.9. For example, if there is likely to be a significant conflict between the testimony of the client and that of the lawyer, the representation is improper by the standard of Rule 1.7(b) without regard to Rule 3.7(a). The problem can arise whether the lawyer is called as a witness on behalf of the client or is called by the opposing party. Determining whether such a conflict exists is, in the first instance, the responsibility of the lawyer involved. See Comment to Rule 1.7. Rule 3.7(b) states that other lawyers in the testifying lawyer's firm are disqualified only when there is such a client conflict and the testifying lawyer

therefore could not represent the client under Rule 1.7 or 1.9. The principles of client consent, embodied in Rules 1.7 and 1.9, also apply to paragraph (b). Thus, the reference to Rules 1.7 and 1.9 incorporates the client consent aspects of those Rules. Paragraph (b) is designed to provide protection for the client, not rights of disqualification to the adversary. Subject to the disclosure and consultation requirements of Rules 1.7 and 1.9, the client may consent to the firm's continuing representation, despite the potential problems created by the nature of the testimony to be provided by a lawyer in the firm.

[6] Even though a lawyer's testimony does not involve a conflict with the client's interests under Rule 1.7 or 1.9 and would not be precluded under Rule 3.7, the client's interests might nevertheless be harmed by the appearance as a witness of a lawyer in the firm that represents the client. For example, the lawyer's testimony would be vulnerable to impeachment on the grounds that the lawyer-witness is testifying to support the position of the lawyer's own firm. Similarly, a lawyer whose firm colleague is testifying in the case should recognize the possibility that the lawyer might not scrutinize the testimony of the colleague carefully enough and that this could prejudice the client's interests, whether the colleague is testifying for or against the client. In such instances, the lawyer should inform the client of any possible adverse effects on the client's interests which might result from the lawyer's relationship with the colleague-witness, so that the client may make a meaningful choice whether to retain the lawyer for the representation in question.

Rule 3.8. Special Responsibilities of a Prosecutor

The prosecutor in a criminal case shall not:

(a) In exercising discretion to investigate or to prosecute, improperly favor or invidiously discriminate against any person;

(b) File in court or maintain a charge that the prosecutor knows is not supported by probable cause;

(c) Prosecute to trial a charge that the prosecutor knows is not supported by evidence sufficient to establish a prima facie showing of guilt;

(d) Intentionally avoid pursuit of evidence or information because it may damage the prosecution's case or aid the defense;

(e) Intentionally fail to disclose to the defense, upon request and at a time when use by the defense is reasonably feasible, any evidence or information that the prosecutor knows or reasonably should know tends to negate the guilt of the accused or to mitigate the offense, or, in connection with sentencing, intentionally fail to disclose to the defense upon request any unprivileged mitigating information known to the prosecutor and not reasonably available to the defense, except when the prosecutor is relieved of this responsibility by a protective order of the tribunal;

(f) Except for statements which are necessary to inform the public of the nature and extent of the prosecutor's action and which serve a legitimate law enforcement purpose, make extrajudicial comments which serve to heighten condemnation of the accused;

(g) In presenting a case to a grand jury, intentionally interfere with the independence of the grand jury, preempt a function of the grand jury, abuse the processes of the grand jury, or fail to bring to the attention of the grand jury material facts tending substantially to negate the existence of probable cause; or

(h) Peremptorily strike jurors on grounds of race, religion, national or ethnic background, or sex.

COMMENT

[1] A prosecutor has the responsibility of a minister of justice and not simply that of an advocate. This responsibility carries with it specific obligations to see that the defendant is accorded procedural justice and that guilt is decided upon the basis of sufficient evidence. Precisely how far the prosecutor is required to go in this direction is a matter of debate and varies in different jurisdictions. Many jurisdictions have adopted the ABA Standards of Criminal Justice Relating to Prosecution Function, which in turn are the product of prolonged and careful deliberation by lawyers experienced in both criminal prosecution and defense. This Rule is intended to be a distillation of some, but not all, of the professional obligations imposed on prosecutors by applicable law. The Rule, however, is not intended either to restrict or to expand the obligations of prosecutors derived from the United States Constitution, federal or District of Columbia statutes, and court rules of procedure.

[2] Apart from the special responsibilities of a prosecutor under this Rule, prosecutors are subject to the same obligations imposed upon all lawyers by these Rules of Professional Conduct, including Rule 5.3, relating to responsibilities regarding nonlawyers who work for or in association with the lawyer's office. Indeed, because of the power and visibility of a prosecutor, the prosecutor's compliance with these Rules, and recognition of the need to refrain even from some actions technically allowed to other lawyers under the Rules, may, in certain instances, be of special importance. For example, Rule 3.6 prohibits extrajudicial statements that will have a substantial likelihood of destroying the impartiality of the judge or jury. In the context of a criminal prosecution, pretrial publicity can present the further problem of giving the public the incorrect impression that the accused is guilty before having been proven guilty through the due process of the law. It is unavoidable, of course, that the publication of an indictment may itself have severe consequences for an accused. What is avoidable, however, is extrajudicial comment by a prosecutor that serves unnecessarily to heighten public condemnation of the

accused without a legitimate law enforcement purpose before the criminal process has taken its course. When that occurs, even if the ultimate trial is not prejudiced, the accused may be subjected to unfair and unnecessary condemnation before the trial takes place. Accordingly, a prosecutor should use special care to avoid publicity, such as through televised press conferences, which would unnecessarily heighten condemnation of the accused.

[3] Nothing in this Comment, however, is intended to suggest that a prosecutor may not inform the public of such matters as whether an official investigation has ended or is continuing, or who participated in it, and the prosecutor may respond to press inquiries to clarify such things as technicalities of the indictment, the status of the matter, or the legal procedures that will follow. Also, a prosecutor should be free to respond, insofar as necessary, to any extrajudicial allegations by the defense of unprofessional or unlawful conduct on the part of the prosecutor's office.

Rule 3.9. Advocate in Nonadjudicative Proceedings

A lawyer representing a client before a legislative or administrative body in a nonadjudicative proceeding shall disclose that the appearance is in a representative capacity and shall conform to the provisions of Rules 3.3, 3.4(a) through (c), and 3.5.

COMMENT

[1] In representation before bodies such as legislatures, municipal councils, and executive and administrative agencies acting in a rule-making or policy-making capacity, lawyers present facts, formulate issues, and advance argument in the matters under consideration. The decision-making body, like a court, should be able to rely on the integrity of the submissions made to it. A lawyer appearing before such a body should deal with it honestly and in conformity with applicable rules of procedure.

[2] Lawyers have no exclusive right to appear before nonadjudicative bodies, as they do before a court. The requirements of this Rule therefore may subject lawyers to regulations inapplicable to advocates, such as non-lawyer lobbyists, who are not lawyers. However, legislatures and administrative agencies have a right to expect lawyers to deal with them as they deal with courts.

[3] This Rule does not apply to representation of a client in a negotiation or other bilateral transaction with a government agency; representation in such a transaction is governed by Rules 4.1 through 4.4.

[4] This Rule is closely related to Rules 3.3 through 3.5, which deal with conduct regarding tribunals. The term "tribunal," as defined in the

Terminology section of these Rules, refers to adjudicative or quasi-adjudicative bodies.

TRANSACTIONS WITH PERSONS OTHER THAN CLIENTS

Rule 4.1. Truthfulness in Statements to Others

In the course of representing a client, a lawyer shall not knowingly:

(a) Make a false statement of material fact or law to a third person; or

(b) Fail to disclose a material fact to a third person when disclosure is necessary to avoid assisting a criminal or fraudulent act by a client, unless disclosure is prohibited by Rule 1.6.

COMMENT

Misrepresentation

[1] A lawyer is required to be truthful when dealing with others on a client's behalf, but generally has no affirmative duty to inform an opposing party of relevant facts. A misrepresentation can occur if the lawyer incorporates or affirms a statement of another person that the lawyer knows is false. Misrepresentations can also occur by failure to act. The term "third person" as used in paragraphs (a) and (b) refers to any person or entity other than the lawyer's client.

Statements of Fact

[2] This Rule refers to material statements of fact. Whether a particular statement should be regarded as material, and as one of fact, can depend on the circumstances. Under generally accepted conventions in negotiation, certain types of statements ordinarily are not taken as statements of material fact. Estimates of price or value placed on the subject of a transaction and a party's intentions as to an acceptable settlement of a claim are in this category, and so is the existence of an undisclosed principal except where nondisclosure of the principal would constitute fraud. There may be other analogous situations.

Fraud by Client

[3] Paragraph (b) recognizes that substantive law may require a lawyer to disclose certain information to avoid being deemed to have assisted the

client's crime or fraud. The requirement of disclosure created by this paragraph is, however, subject to the obligations created by Rule 1.6.

Rule 4.2. Communication Between Lawyer and Opposing Parties

(a) During the course of representing a client, a lawyer shall not communicate or cause another to communicate about the subject of the representation with a party known to be represented by another lawyer in the matter, unless the lawyer has the prior consent of the lawyer representing such other party or is authorized by law to do so.

(b) During the course of representing a client, a lawyer may communicate about the subject of the representation with a nonparty employee of the opposing party without obtaining the consent of that party's lawyer. However, prior to communicating with any such nonparty employee, a lawyer must disclose to such employee both the lawyer's identity and the fact that the lawyer represents a party with a claim against the employee's employer.

(c) For purposes of this Rule, the term "party" includes any person, including an employee of a party organization, who has the authority to bind a party organization as to the representation to which the communication relates.

(d) This Rule does not prohibit communication by a lawyer with government officials who have the authority to redress the grievances of the lawyer's client, whether or not those grievances or the lawyer's communications relate to matters that are the subject of the representation, provided that in the event of such communications the disclosures specified in (b) are made to the government official to whom the communication is made.

COMMENT

[1] This Rule does not prohibit communication with a party, or an employee or agent of a party, concerning matters outside the representation. For example, the existence of a controversy between two organizations does not prohibit a lawyer for either from communicating with nonlawyer representatives of the other regarding a separate matter. Also, parties to a matter may communicate directly with each other and a lawyer having independent justification for communicating with the other party is permitted to do so.

[2] In the case of an organization, this Rule prohibits communication by a lawyer for one party concerning the matter in representation with persons having the power to bind the organization as to the particular representation to which the communication relates. If an agent or employee of the organization with authority to make binding decisions

regarding the representation is represented in the matter by separate counsel, the consent by that agent's or employee's counsel to a communication will be sufficient for purposes of this Rule.

[3] The Rule does not prohibit a lawyer from communicating with employees of an organization who have the authority to bind the organization with respect to the matters underlying the representation if they do not also have authority to make binding decisions regarding the representation itself. A lawyer may therefore communicate with such persons without first notifying the organization's lawyer. See D.C. Bar Legal Ethics Committee Opinion No. 129 (1983). But before communicating with such a "nonparty employee," the lawyer must disclose to the employee the lawyer's identity and the fact that the lawyer represents a party with a claim against the employer. It is preferable that this disclosure be made in writing. The notification requirements of Rule 4.2(b) apply to contacts with government employees who do not have the authority to make binding decisions regarding the representation.

[4] This Rule also covers any person, whether or not a party to a formal proceeding, who is represented by counsel concerning the matter in question.

[5] This Rule does not apply to the situation in which a lawyer contacts employees of an organization for the purpose of obtaining information generally available to the public, or obtainable under the Freedom of Information Act, even if the information in question is related to the representation. For example, a lawyer for a plaintiff who has filed suit against an organization represented by a lawyer may telephone the organization to request a copy of a press release regarding the representation, without disclosing the lawyer's identity, obtaining the consent of the organization's lawyer, or otherwise acting as paragraphs (a) and (b) of this Rule require.

[6] Paragraph (d) recognizes that special considerations come into play when a lawyer is seeking to redress grievances involving the government. It permits communications with those in government having the authority to redress such grievances (but not with any other government personnel) without the prior consent of the lawyer representing the government in such cases. However, a lawyer making such a communication without the prior consent of the lawyer representing the government must make the kinds of disclosures that are required by paragraph (b) in the case of communications with nonparty employees.

[7] Paragraph (d) does not permit a lawyer to bypass counsel representing the government on every issue that may arise in the course of disputes with the government. It is intended to provide lawyers access to decision makers in government with respect to genuine grievances, such as to present the view that the government's basic policy position with respect to a dispute is faulty, or that government personnel are conducting themselves improperly with respect to aspects of the dispute. It is not intended to provide direct access on routine disputes such as ordinary dis-

covery disputes, extensions of time or other scheduling matters, or similar routine aspects of the resolution of disputes.

[8] This Rule is not intended to enlarge or restrict the law enforcement activities of the United States or the District of Columbia which are authorized and permissible under the Constitution and law of the United States or the District of Columbia. The "authorized by law" proviso to Rule 4.2(a) is intended to permit government conduct that is valid under this law. The proviso is not intended to freeze any particular substantive law, but is meant to accommodate substantive law as it may develop over time.

Rule 4.3. Dealing with Unrepresented Person

In dealing on behalf of a client with a person who is not represented by counsel, a lawyer shall not:

(a) Give advice to the unrepresented person other than the advice to secure counsel, if the interests of such person are or have a reasonable possibility of being in conflict with the interests of the lawyer's client;

(b) State or imply to unrepresented persons whose interests are not in conflict with the interests of the lawyer's client that the lawyer is disinterested. When the lawyer knows or reasonably should know that the unrepresented person misunderstands the lawyer's role in the matter, the lawyer shall make reasonable efforts to correct the misunderstanding.

COMMENT

[1] An unrepresented person, particularly one not experienced in dealing with legal matters, might assume that a lawyer will provide disinterested advice concerning the law even when the lawyer represents a client. In dealing personally with any unrepresented third party on behalf of the lawyer's client, a lawyer must take great care not to exploit these assumptions.

[2] The Rule distinguishes between situations involving unrepresented third parties whose interests may be adverse to those of the lawyer's client and those in which the third party's interests are not in conflict with the client's. In the former situation, the possibility of the lawyer's compromising the unrepresented person's interests is so great that the Rule prohibits the giving of any advice, apart from the advice that the unrepresented person obtain counsel. A lawyer is free to give advice to unrepresented persons whose interests are not in conflict with those of the lawyer's client, but only if it is made clear that the lawyer is acting in the interests of the client. Thus the lawyer should not represent to such

persons, either expressly or implicitly, that the lawyer is disinterested. Furthermore, if it becomes apparent that the unrepresented person misunderstands the lawyer's role in the matter, the lawyer must take whatever reasonable, affirmative steps are necessary to correct the misunderstanding.

[3] This Rule is not intended to restrict in any way law enforcement efforts by government lawyers that are consistent with constitutional requirements and applicable federal law.

Rule 4.4. Respect for Rights of Third Persons

In representing a client, a lawyer shall not use means that have no substantial purpose other than to embarrass, delay, or burden a third person, or use methods of obtaining evidence that violate the legal rights of such a person.

COMMENT

[1] Responsibility to a client requires a lawyer to subordinate the interests of others to those of the client, but that responsibility does not imply that a lawyer may disregard the rights of third persons. It is impractical to catalogue all such rights, but they include legal restrictions on methods of obtaining evidence from third persons.

LAW FIRMS AND ASSOCIATIONS

Rule 5.1. Responsibilities of a Partner or Supervisory Lawyer

(a) A partner in a law firm shall make reasonable efforts to ensure that the firm has in effect measures giving reasonable assurance that all lawyers in the firm conform to the Rules of Professional Conduct.

(b) A lawyer having direct supervisory authority over another lawyer shall make reasonable efforts to ensure that the other lawyer conforms to the Rules of Professional Conduct.

(c) A lawyer shall be responsible for another lawyer's violation of the Rules of Professional Conduct if:

(1) The lawyer orders or, with knowledge of the specific conduct, ratifies the conduct involved; or

(2) The lawyer has direct supervisory authority over the other lawyer or is a partner in the law firm in which the other lawyer practices, and knows or reasonably should know of the conduct at a time when its consequences can be avoided or mitigated but fails to take reasonable remedial action.

COMMENT

[1] Paragraphs (a) and (b) refer to lawyers who have supervisory authority over the professional work of a firm or legal department of a government agency. This includes members of a partnership and the shareholders in a law firm organized as a professional corporation; lawyers having supervisory authority in the law department of an enterprise or government agency; and lawyers who have intermediate managerial responsibilities in a firm.

[2] The measures required to fulfill the responsibility prescribed in paragraphs (a) and (b) can depend on the firm's structure and the nature of its practice. In a small firm, informal supervision and occasional admonition ordinarily might be sufficient. In a large firm, or in practice situations in which intensely difficult ethical problems frequently arise, more elaborate procedures may be necessary. Some firms, for example, have a procedure whereby junior lawyers can make confidential referral of ethical problems directly to a designated senior partner or special committee. See Rule 5.2. Firms, whether large or small, may also rely on continuing legal education in professional ethics. In any event, the ethical atmosphere of a firm can influence the conduct of all its members and a lawyer having authority over the work of another may not assume that the subordinate lawyer will inevitably conform to the Rules.

[3] Paragraph (c) sets forth general principles of imputed responsibility for the misconduct of others. Subparagraph (c)(1) makes any lawyer who orders or, with knowledge, ratifies misconduct responsible for that misconduct. See also Rule 8.4(a). Subparagraph (c)(2) extends that responsibility to any lawyer who is a partner in the firm in which the misconduct takes place, or who has direct supervisory authority over the lawyer who engages in misconduct, when the lawyer knows or should reasonably know of the conduct and could intervene to ameliorate its consequences. Whether a lawyer has such supervisory authority in particular circumstances is a question of fact. A lawyer with direct supervisory authority is a lawyer who has an actual supervisory role with respect to directing the conduct of other lawyers in a particular representation. A lawyer who is technically a "supervisor" in organizational terms, but is not involved in directing the effort of other lawyers in a particular representation, is not a supervising lawyer with respect to that representation.

[4] The existence of actual knowledge is also a question of fact; whether a lawyer should reasonably have known of misconduct by another lawyer in the same firm is an objective standard based on evaluation of all the facts, including the size and organizational structure of the firm, the lawyer's position and responsibilities within the firm, the type and frequency of contacts between the various lawyers involved, the nature of the misconduct at issue, and the nature of the supervision or other direct responsibility (if any) actually exercised. The mere fact of partnership or a position as a principal in a firm is not sufficient, without more, to satisfy

this standard. Similarly, the fact that a lawyer holds a position on the management committee of a firm, or heads a department of the firm, is not sufficient, standing alone, to satisfy this standard.

[5] Appropriate remedial action would depend on the immediacy of the involvement and the seriousness of the misconduct. The supervisor is required to intervene to prevent avoidable consequences of misconduct if the supervisor knows that the misconduct occurred. Thus, if a supervising lawyer knows that a subordinate misrepresented a matter to an opposing party in a negotiation, the supervisor as well as the subordinate has a duty to correct the resulting misapprehension.

[6] Professional misconduct by a lawyer under supervision could reveal a violation of paragraph (b) on the part of the supervisory lawyer even though it does not entail a violation of paragraph (c) because there was no direction, ratification, or knowledge of the violation.

[7] Apart from this Rule and Rule 8.4(a), a lawyer does not have disciplinary liability for the conduct of a partner, associate, or subordinate. Whether a lawyer may be liable civilly or criminally for another lawyer's conduct is a question of law beyond the scope of these Rules.

Rule 5.2. Responsibilities of a Subordinate Lawyer

(a) A lawyer is bound by the Rules of Professional Conduct notwithstanding that the lawyer acted at the direction of another person.

(b) A subordinate lawyer does not violate the Rules of Professional Conduct if that lawyer acts in accordance with a supervisory lawyer's reasonable resolution of an arguable question of professional duty.

COMMENT

[1] Although a lawyer is not relieved of responsibility for a violation by the fact that the lawyer acted at the direction of a supervisor, that fact may be relevant in determining whether a lawyer had the knowledge required to render conduct a violation of the Rules. For example, if a subordinate filed a frivolous pleading at the direction of a supervisor, the subordinate would not be guilty of a professional violation unless the subordinate knew of the document's frivolous character.

[2] When lawyers in a supervisor-subordinate relationship encounter a matter involving professional judgment as to ethical duty, the supervisor may assume responsibility for making the judgment. Otherwise a consistent course of action or position could not be taken. If the question can reasonably be answered only one way, the duty of both lawyers is clear and they are equally responsible for fulfilling it. However, if the question is reasonably arguable, someone has to decide upon the course of action.

That authority ordinarily reposes in the supervisor, and a subordinate may be guided accordingly. For example, if a question arises whether the interests of two clients conflict under Rule 1.7, the supervisor's reasonable resolution of the question should protect the subordinate professionally if the resolution is subsequently challenged.

Rule 5.3. Responsibilities Regarding Nonlawyer Assistants

With respect to a nonlawyer employed or retained by or associated with a lawyer:

(a) A partner in a law firm shall make reasonable efforts to ensure that the firm has in effect measures giving reasonable assurance that the person's conduct is compatible with the professional obligations of the lawyer;

(b) A lawyer having direct supervisory authority over the nonlawyer shall make reasonable efforts to ensure that the person's conduct is compatible with the professional obligations of the lawyer; and

(c) A lawyer shall be responsible for conduct of such a person that would be a violation of the Rules of Professional Conduct if engaged in by a lawyer if:

(1) The lawyer requests or, with the knowledge of the specific conduct, ratifies the conduct involved; or

(2) The lawyer has direct supervisory authority over the person, or is a partner in the law firm in which the person is employed, and knows of the conduct at a time when its consequences can be avoided or mitigated but fails to take reasonable remedial action.

COMMENT

[1] Lawyers generally employ assistants in their practice, including secretaries, investigators, law student interns, and paraprofessionals. Such assistants, whether employees or independent contractors, act for the lawyer in rendition of the lawyer's professional services. A lawyer should give such assistants appropriate instruction and supervision concerning the ethical aspects of their employment, particularly regarding the obligation not to disclose information relating to representation of the client, and should be responsible for their work product. The measures employed in supervising nonlawyers should take account of the fact that they do not have legal training and are not subject to professional discipline.

[2] Just as lawyers in private practice may direct the conduct of investigators who may be independent contractors, prosecutors and other government lawyers may effectively direct the conduct of police or other governmental investigative personnel, even though they may not have,

strictly speaking, formal authority to order actions by such personnel, who report to the chief of police or the head of another enforcement agency. Such prosecutors or other government lawyers have a responsibility with respect to police or investigative personnel, whose conduct they effectively direct, equivalent to that of private lawyers with respect to investigators whom they retain. See also Comments [3], [4], and [5] to Rule 5.1, in particular, the concept of what constitutes direct supervisory authority, and the significance of holding certain positions in a firm. Comments [3], [4], and [5] of Rule 5.1 apply as well to Rule 5.3.

Rule 5.4. Professional Independence of a Lawyer

(a) A lawyer or law firm shall not share legal fees with a nonlawyer, except that:

(1) An agreement by a lawyer with the lawyer's firm, partner, or associate may provide for the payment of money, over a reasonable period of time after the lawyer's death, to the lawyer's estate or to one or more specified persons;

(2) A lawyer who undertakes to complete unfinished legal business of a deceased lawyer may pay to the estate of the deceased lawyer that proportion of the total compensation which fairly represents the services rendered by the deceased lawyer;

(3) A lawyer or law firm may include nonlawyer employees in a compensation or retirement plan, even though the plan is based in whole or in part on a profit-sharing arrangement; and

(4) Sharing of fees is permitted in a partnership or other form of organization which meets the requirements of paragraph (b).

(b) A lawyer may practice law in a partnership or other form of organization in which a financial interest is held or managerial authority is exercised by an individual nonlawyer who performs professional services which assist the organization in providing legal services to clients, but only if:

(1) The partnership or organization has as its sole purpose providing legal services to clients;

(2) All persons having such managerial authority or holding a financial interest undertake to abide by these Rules of Professional Conduct;

(3) The lawyers who have a financial interest or managerial authority in the partnership or organization undertake to be responsible for the nonlawyer participants to the same extent as if nonlawyer participants were lawyers under Rule 5.1;

(4) The foregoing conditions are set forth in writing.

(c) A lawyer shall not permit a person who recommends, employs, or pays the lawyer to render legal services for another to direct or regulate the lawyer's professional judgment in rendering such legal services.

COMMENT

[1] The provisions of this Rule express traditional limitations on sharing fees with nonlawyers. (On sharing fees among lawyers not in the same firm, see Rule 1.5(e).) These limitations are to protect the lawyer's professional independence of judgment. Where someone other than the client pays the lawyer's fee or salary, or recommends employment of the lawyer, that arrangement does not modify the lawyer's obligation to the client. As stated in paragraph (c), such arrangements should not interfere with the lawyer's professional judgment.

[2] Traditionally, the canons of legal ethics and disciplinary rules prohibited lawyers from practicing law in a partnership that includes nonlawyers or in any other organization where a nonlawyer is a shareholder, director, or officer. Notwithstanding these strictures, the profession implicitly recognized exceptions for lawyers who work for corporate law departments, insurance companies, and legal service organizations.

[3] As the demand increased for a broad range of professional services from a single source, lawyers employed professionals from other disciplines to work for them. So long as the nonlawyers remained employees of the lawyers, these relationships did not violate the disciplinary rules. However, when lawyers and nonlawyers considered forming partnerships and professional corporations to provide a combination of legal and other services to the public, they faced serious obstacles under the former rules.

[4] This Rule rejects an absolute prohibition against lawyers and nonlawyers joining together to provide collaborative services, but continues to impose traditional ethical requirements with respect to the organization thus created. Thus, a lawyer may practice law in an organization where nonlawyers hold a financial interest or exercise managerial authority, but only if the conditions set forth in subparagraphs (b)(1), (b)(2), and (b)(3) are satisfied, and pursuant to subparagraph (b)(4), satisfaction of these conditions is set forth in a written instrument. The requirement of a writing helps ensure that these important conditions are not overlooked in establishing the organizational structure of entities in which nonlawyers enjoy an ownership or managerial role equivalent to that of a partner in a traditional law firm.

[5] Nonlawyer participants under Rule 5.4 ought not be confused with nonlawyer assistants under Rule 5.3. Nonlawyer participants are persons having managerial authority or financial interests in organizations that provide legal services. Within such organizations, lawyers with financial interests or managerial authority are held responsible for ethical misconduct by nonlawyer participants about which the lawyers know or reasonably should know. This is the same standard of liability contemplated by Rule 5.1, regarding the responsibilities of lawyers with direct supervisory authority over other lawyers.

[6] Nonlawyer assistants under Rule 5.3 do not have managerial authority or financial interests in the organization. Lawyers having direct

supervisory authority over nonlawyer assistants are held responsible only for ethical misconduct by assistants about which the lawyers actually know.

[7] As the introductory portion of paragraph (b) makes clear, the purpose of liberalizing the rules regarding the possession of a financial interest or the exercise of management authority by a nonlawyer is to permit nonlawyer professionals to work with lawyers in the delivery of legal services without being relegated to the role of an employee. For example, the Rule permits economists to work in a firm with antitrust or public utility practitioners, psychologists or psychiatric social workers to work with family law practitioners to assist in counseling clients, nonlawyer lobbyists to work with lawyers who perform legislative services, certified public accountants to work in conjunction with tax lawyers or others who use accountants' services in performing legal services, and professional managers to serve as office managers, executive directors, or in similar positions. In all of these situations, the professionals may be given financial interests or managerial responsibility, so long as all of the requirements of paragraph (c) are met.

[8] Paragraph (b) does not permit an individual or entity to acquire all or any part of the ownership of a law partnership or other form of law practice organization for investment or other purposes. It thus does not permit a corporation, an investment banking firm, an investor, or any other person or entity to entitle itself to all or any portion of the income or profits of a law firm or other similar organization. Since such an investor would not be an individual performing professional services within the law firm or other organization, the requirements of paragraph (b) would not be met.

[9] The term "individual" in subparagraph (b) is not intended to preclude the participation in a law firm or other organization by an individual professional corporation in the same manner as lawyers who have incorporated as a professional corporation currently participate in partnerships that include professional corporations.

[10] Some sharing of fees is likely to occur in the kinds of organizations permitted by paragraph (b). Subparagraph (a)(4) makes it clear that such fee sharing is not prohibited.

Rule 5.5. Unauthorized Practice of Law

A lawyer shall not:

(a) Practice law in a jurisdiction where doing so violates the regulation of the legal profession in that jurisdiction; or

(b) Assist a person who is not a member of the bar in the performance of activity that constitutes the unauthorized practice of law.

COMMENT

[1] The definition of the practice of law is established by law and varies from one jurisdiction to another. Whatever the definition, limiting

the practice of law to members of the bar protects the public against rendition of legal services by unqualified persons. Paragraph (b) does not prohibit a lawyer from employing the services of paraprofessionals and delegating functions to them, so long as the lawyer supervises the delegated work and retains responsibility for their work. See Rule 5.3. Likewise, it does not prohibit lawyers from providing professional advice and instruction to nonlawyers whose employment requires knowledge of law; for example, claims adjusters, employees of financial or commercial institutions, social workers, accountants and persons employed in government agencies. In addition, a lawyer may counsel nonlawyers who wish to proceed pro se.

Rule 5.6. Restrictions on Right to Practice

A lawyer shall not participate in offering or making:

(a) A partnership or employment agreement that restricts the rights of a lawyer to practice after termination of the relationship, except an agreement concerning benefits upon retirement; or

(b) An agreement in which a restriction on the lawyer's right to practice is part of the settlement of a controversy between parties.

COMMENT

[1] An agreement restricting the right of partners or associates to practice after leaving a firm not only limits their professional autonomy but also limits the freedom of clients to choose a lawyer. Paragraph (a) prohibits such agreements except for restrictions incident to provisions concerning retirement benefits for service with the firm.

[2] Paragraph (b) prohibits a lawyer from agreeing not to represent other persons in connection with settling a claim on behalf of a client.

PUBLIC SERVICE

Rule 6.1. Pro Bono Publico Service

Editors' Note. Effective July 1, 1999, Comment [5] to Rule 6.1 was amended to increase the guidelines to which D.C. lawyers should aspire regarding the number of hours of pro bono service or the amount of a financial contribution to a legal assistance organization.

A lawyer should participate in serving those persons, or groups of persons, who are unable to pay all or a portion of reasonable attorneys'

fees or who are otherwise unable to obtain counsel. A lawyer may discharge this responsibility by providing professional services at no fee, or at a substantially reduced fee, to persons and groups who are unable to afford or obtain counsel, or by active participation in the work of organizations that provide legal services to them. When personal representation is not feasible, a lawyer may discharge this responsibility by providing financial support for organizations that provide legal representation to those unable to obtain counsel.

COMMENT

[1] This Rule reflects the long-standing ethical principle underlying Canon 2 of the previous Code of Professional Responsibility that "A lawyer should assist the legal profession in fulfilling its duty to make legal counsel available." The Rule incorporates the legal profession's historical commitment to the principle that all persons in our society should be able to obtain necessary legal services. The Rule also recognizes that the rights and responsibilities of individuals and groups in the United States are increasingly defined in legal terms and that, as a consequence, legal assistance in coping with the web of statutes, rules, and regulations is imperative for persons of modest and limited means, as well as for the relatively well-to-do. The Rule also recognizes that a lawyer's pro bono services are sometimes needed to assert or defend public rights belonging to the public generally where no individual or group can afford to pay for the services.

[2] This Rule carries forward the ethical precepts set forth in the Code. Specifically, the Rule recognizes that the basic responsibility for providing legal services for those unable to pay ultimately rests upon the individual lawyer, and that every lawyer, regardless of professional prominence or professional workload, should find time to participate in or otherwise support the provision of legal services to the disadvantaged.

[3] The Rule also acknowledges that while the provision of free legal services to those unable to pay reasonable fees continues to be an obligation of each lawyer as well as the profession generally, the efforts of individual lawyers are often not enough to meet the need. Thus, it has been necessary for the profession and government to institute additional programs to provide legal services. Accordingly, legal aid offices, lawyer referral services, and other related programs have been developed, and others will be developed by the profession and government. Every lawyer should support all proper efforts to meet this need for legal services. A lawyer also should not refuse a request from a court or bar association to undertake representation of a person unable to obtain counsel except for compelling reasons such as those listed in Rule 6.2.

[4] This Rule expresses the profession's traditional commitment to make legal counsel available, but it is not intended that the Rule be en-

forced through disciplinary process. Neither is it intended to place any obligation on a government lawyer that is inconsistent with laws such as 18 U.S.C. §§203 and 205 limiting the scope of permissible employment or representational activities.

[5] In determining their responsibilities under this Rule, lawyers admitted to practice in the District of Columbia should be guided by the Resolutions on Pro Bono Services passed by the Judicial Conferences of the District of Columbia and the D.C. Circuit as amended from time to time. Those Resolutions as adopted in 1997 and 1998, respectively, call on members of the D.C. Bar, at a minimum, each year to (1) accept one court appointment, or (2) provide 50 hours of pro bono legal service, or (3) when personal representation is not feasible, contribute the lesser of $400 or 1 percent of earned income to a legal assistance organization which services the community's economically disadvantaged, including pro bono referral and appointment offices sponsored by the Bar and the courts.

Editors' Note. Comment [5] to Rule 6.1 was amended effective July 1, 1999. The main effect of the amendment is to increase the aspirational guideline for pro bono services from 40 to 50 hours per year, and to increase the alternative financial contribution from a minimum of $200 to $400 per year.

Rule 6.2. Accepting Appointments

A lawyer shall not seek to avoid appointment by a tribunal to represent a person except for good cause, such as:

(a) Representing the client is likely to result in violation of the Rules of Professional Conduct or other law;

(b) Representing the client is likely to result in a substantial and unreasonable burden on the lawyer; or

(c) The client or the cause is so repugnant to the lawyer as to be likely to impair the client-lawyer relationship or the lawyer's ability to represent the client.

COMMENT

[1] A lawyer ordinarily is not obliged to accept a client whose character or cause the lawyer regards as repugnant. The lawyer's freedom to select clients is, however, qualified. All lawyers have a responsibility to assist in providing pro bono publico service. See Rule 6.1. An individual lawyer fulfills this responsibility by accepting a fair share of unpopular matters or indigent or unpopular clients. A lawyer may also be subject to appointment by a court to serve unpopular clients or persons unable to afford legal services.

Appointed Counsel

[2] For good cause a lawyer may seek to decline an appointment to represent a person who cannot afford to retain counsel or whose cause is unpopular. Good cause exists if the lawyer could not handle the matter competently, see Rule 1.1, or if undertaking the representation would result in an improper conflict of interest; for example, when the client or the cause is so repugnant to the lawyer as to be likely to impair the client-lawyer relationship or the lawyer's ability to represent the client. A lawyer may also seek to decline an appointment if acceptance would be substantially and unreasonably burdensome, such as when it would impose a financial sacrifice so great as to be unjust.

[3] An appointed lawyer has the same obligations to the client as retained counsel, including the obligations of loyalty and confidentiality, and is subject to the same limitations on the client-lawyer relationship, such as the obligation to refrain from assisting the client in violation of the Rules.

Rule 6.3. Membership in Legal Services Organization

A lawyer may serve as a director, officer, or member of a legal services organization, apart from the law firm in which the lawyer practices, notwithstanding that the organization serves persons having interests adverse to a client of the lawyer. The lawyer shall not knowingly participate in a decision or action of the organization:

(a) If participating in the decision would be incompatible with the lawyer's obligations to a client under Rule 1.7; or

(b) Where the decision could have a material adverse effect on the representation of a client of the organization whose interests are adverse to a client of the lawyer.

COMMENT

[1] Lawyers should be encouraged to support and participate in legal service organizations. A lawyer who is an officer or a member of such an organization does not thereby have a client-lawyer relationship with persons served by the organization. However, there is potential conflict between the interests of such persons and the interests of the lawyer's clients. If the possibility of such conflict disqualified a lawyer from serving on the board of a legal services organization, the profession's involvement in such organizations would be severely curtailed.

[2] It may be necessary in appropriate cases to reassure a client of the organization that the representation will not be affected by conflicting loy-

alties of a member of the board. Established, written policies in this respect can enhance the credibility of such assurances.

Rule 6.4. Law Reform Activities

(a) A lawyer should assist in improving the administration of justice. A lawyer may discharge this requirement by rendering services in activities for improving the law, the legal system, or the legal profession.

(b) A lawyer may serve as a director, officer, or member of an organization involved in reform of the law or its administration notwithstanding that the reform may affect the interests of a client of the lawyer. When the lawyer knows that the interests of a client may be materially benefited by a decision in which the lawyer participates, the lawyer shall disclose that fact but need not identify the client.

COMMENT

[1] Changes in human affairs and imperfections in human institutions make necessary constant efforts to maintain and improve our legal system. This system should function in a manner that commands public respect and fosters the use of legal remedies to achieve redress of grievances. By reason of education and experience, lawyers are especially qualified to recognize deficiencies in the legal system and to initiate corrective measures therein. Thus, they should participate in proposing and supporting legislation and programs to improve the system, without regard to the general interests or desires of clients or former clients. Rules of law are deficient if they are not just, understandable, and responsive to the needs of society. If a lawyer believes that the existence or absence of a rule of law, substantive or procedural, causes or contributes to an unjust result, the lawyer should endeavor by lawful means to obtain appropriate changes in the law. This Rule expresses the policy underlying Canon 8 of the previous Code of Professional Responsibility that "A lawyer should assist in improving the legal system," but it is not intended that it be enforced through disciplinary process.

[2] Lawyers involved in organizations seeking law reform generally do not have a client-lawyer relationship with the organization. Otherwise, it might follow that a lawyer could not be involved in a bar association law reform program that might indirectly affect a client. See also Rule 1.2(b). For example, a lawyer specializing in antitrust litigation might be regarded as disqualified from participating in drafting revisions of rules governing that subject. In determining the nature and scope of participation in such activities, a lawyer should be mindful of obligations to clients under other Rules, particularly Rule 1.7. A lawyer is professionally obligated to protect the integrity of the program by making an appropriate

disclosure within the organization when the lawyer knows a private client might be materially benefited.

INFORMATION ABOUT LEGAL SERVICES

Rule 7.1. Communications Concerning a Lawyer's Services

(a) A lawyer shall not make a false or misleading communication about the lawyer or the lawyer's services. A communication is false or misleading if it:

(1) Contains a material misrepresentation of fact or law, or omits a fact necessary to make the statement considered as a whole not materially misleading; or

(2) Contains an assertion about the lawyer or the lawyer's services that cannot be substantiated.

(b) A lawyer shall not seek by in-person contact, or through an intermediary, employment (or employment of a partner or associate) by a nonlawyer who has not sought the lawyer's advice regarding employment of a lawyer, if:

(1) The solicitation involves use of a statement or claim that is false or misleading, within the meaning of paragraph (a);

(2) The solicitation involves the use of undue influence;

(3) The potential client is apparently in a physical or mental condition which would make it unlikely that the potential client could exercise reasonable, considered judgment as to the selection of a lawyer;

(4) The solicitation involves use of an intermediary and the lawyer knows or could reasonably ascertain that such conduct violates the intermediary's contractual or other legal obligations; or

(5) The solicitation involves the use of an intermediary and the lawyer has not taken all reasonable steps to ensure that the potential client is informed of (a) the consideration, if any, paid or to be paid by the lawyer to the intermediary, and (b) the effect, if any, of the payment to the intermediary on the total fee to be charged.

(c) A lawyer shall not knowingly assist an organization that furnishes or pays for legal services to others to promote the use of the lawyer's services or those of the lawyer's partner or associate, or any other lawyer affiliated with the lawyer or the lawyer's firm, as a private practitioner, if the promotional activity involves the use of coercion, duress, compulsion, intimidation, threats, or vexatious or harassing conduct.

(d) No lawyer or any person acting on behalf of a lawyer shall solicit or invite or seek to solicit any person for purposes of representing that person for a fee paid by or on behalf of a client or under the Criminal Justice Act, D.C. Code Ann. §11-2601 et seq., in any present or future case in the District of Columbia Courthouse, on the sidewalks on

the north, south, and west sides of the Courthouse, or within 50 feet of the building on the east side.

COMMENT

[1] This Rule governs all communications about a lawyer's services, including advertising. It is especially important that statements about a lawyer or the lawyer's services be accurate, since many members of the public lack detailed knowledge of legal matters. Certain advertisements such as those that describe the amount of a damage award, the lawyer's record in obtaining favorable verdicts, or those containing client endorsements, unless suitably qualified, have a capacity to mislead by creating an unjustified expectation that similar results can be obtained for others. Advertisements comparing the lawyer's services with those of other lawyers are false or misleading if the claims made cannot be substantiated.

Advertising

[2] To assist the public in obtaining legal services, lawyers should be allowed to make known their services not only through reputation but also through organized information campaigns in the form of advertising. Advertising involves an active quest for clients, contrary to the tradition that a lawyer should not seek clientele. However, the public's need to know about legal services can be fulfilled in part through advertising. This need is particularly acute in the case of persons of moderate means who have not made extensive use of legal services. The interest in expanding public information about legal services ought to prevail over considerations of tradition.

[3] This Rule permits public dissemination of information concerning a lawyer's name or firm name, address, and telephone number; the kinds of services the lawyer will undertake; the basis on which the lawyer's fees are determined, including prices for specific services and payment and credit arrangements; a lawyer's foreign language ability; names of references and, with their consent, names of clients regularly represented; and other information that might invite the attention of those seeking legal assistance.

[4] Questions of effectiveness and taste in advertising are matters of speculation and subjective judgment. Some jurisdictions have had extensive prohibitions against television advertising, against advertising going beyond specific facts about a lawyer, or against "undignified" advertising. Television is now one of the most powerful media for getting information to the public, particularly persons of low and moderate income; prohibiting television advertising, therefore, would impede the flow of information

about legal services to many sectors of the public. Limiting the information that may be advertised has a similar effect and assumes that the Bar can accurately forecast the kind of information that the public would regard as relevant.

[5] There is no significant distinction between disseminating information and soliciting clients through mass media or through individual personal contact. In-person solicitation can, however, create additional problems because of the particular circumstances in which the solicitation takes place. This Rule prohibits in-person solicitation in circumstances or through means that are not conducive to intelligent, rational decisions.

Paying Others to Recommend a Lawyer

[6] A lawyer is allowed to pay for advertising permitted by this Rule. This Rule also permits a lawyer to pay another person for channeling professional work to the lawyer. Thus, an organization or person other than the lawyer may advertise or recommend the lawyer's services. Likewise, a lawyer may participate in lawyer referral programs and pay the usual fees charged by such programs. However, special concerns arise when a lawyer is making payments to intermediaries to recommend the lawyer's services to others. These concerns are particularly significant when the payments are not being made to a recognized or established agency or organization, such as an organized lawyer referral program. In employing intermediaries, the lawyer is bound by all of the provisions of this Rule. However, subparagraphs (b)(4) and (b)(5) contain provisions specifically relating to the use of intermediaries.

[7] Subparagraph (b)(4) forbids a lawyer to solicit clients through another person when the lawyer knows or could reasonably ascertain that such conduct violates a contractual or other legal obligation of that other person. For example, a lawyer may not solicit clients through hospital or court employees if solicitation by such employees is prohibited by their employment contracts or rules established by their employment. This prohibition applies whether or not the intermediary is being paid.

[8] Subparagraph (b)(5) imposes specific obligations on the lawyer who employs an intermediary to ensure that the potential client who is the target of the solicitation is informed of the consideration paid or to be paid by the lawyer to the intermediary, and any effect of the payment of such consideration on the total fee to be charged. The concept of payment, as incorporated in subparagraph (b)(5), includes giving anything of value to the recipient and is not limited to payments of money alone. For example, if an intermediary were provided the free use of an automobile in return for soliciting clients on behalf of the lawyer, the obligations imposed by subparagraph (b)(5) would apply and impose the specified disclosure requirements.

Solicitations in the Vicinity of the District of Columbia Courthouse

[9] Paragraph (d) is designed to prohibit unseemly solicitations of prospective clients in and around the District of Columbia Courthouse. The words "for a fee paid by or on behalf of a client or under the Criminal Justice Act" have been added to paragraph (d) as it was originally promulgated by the District of Columbia Court of Appeals in 1982. The purpose of the addition is to permit solicitation in the District of Columbia Courthouse for the purposes of pro bono representation. For the purposes of this Rule, pro bono representation, whether by individual lawyers or nonprofit organizations, is representation undertaken primarily for purposes other than a fee. That representation includes providing services free of charge for individuals who may be in need of legal assistance and may lack the financial means and sophistication necessary to have alternative sources of aid. Cases where fees are awarded under the Criminal Justice Act do not constitute pro bono representation for the purposes of this Rule. However, the possibility that fees may be awarded under the Equal Access to Justice Act and Civil Rights Attorneys' Fees Awards Act of 1976, as amended, or other statutory attorney fee statutes, does not prevent representation from constituting pro bono representation.

Rule 7.5. Firm Names and Letterheads

(a) A lawyer shall not use a firm name, letterhead, or other professional designation that violates Rule 7.1. A trade name may be used by a lawyer in private practice if it does not imply a connection with a government agency or with a public or charitable legal services organization and is not otherwise in violation of Rule 7.1.

(b) A law firm with offices in more than one jurisdiction may use the same name in each jurisdiction, but identification of the lawyers in an office of the firm shall indicate the jurisdictional limitations on those not licensed to practice in the jurisdiction where the office is located.

(c) The name of a lawyer holding a public office shall not be used in the name of a law firm, or in communications on its behalf, during any substantial period in which the lawyer is not actively and regularly practicing with the firm.

(d) Lawyers may state or imply that they practice in a partnership or other organization only when that is the fact.

COMMENT

[1] A firm may be designated by the names of all or some of its members, by the names of deceased members where there has been a continuing

succession in the firm's identity, or by a trade name such as the ABC Legal Clinic. Although the United States Supreme Court has held that legislation may prohibit the use of trade names in professional practice, use of such names in law practice is acceptable so long as it is not misleading. If a private firm uses a trade name that includes a geographical name such as Springfield Legal Clinic, an express disclaimer that it is a public legal aid agency may be required to avoid a misleading implication. It may be observed that any firm name including the name of a deceased partner is, strictly speaking, a trade name. The use of such names to designate law firms has proven a useful means of identification. However, it is misleading to use the name of a lawyer not associated with the firm or a predecessor of the firm.

[2] With regard to paragraph (d), lawyers sharing office facilities, but who are not in fact partners, may not denominate themselves as, for example, Smith and Jones, for that title suggests partnership in the practice of law.

MAINTAINING THE INTEGRITY OF THE PROFESSION

Rule 8.1. Bar Admission and Disciplinary Matters

An applicant for admission to the Bar, or a lawyer in connection with a Bar admission application or in connection with a disciplinary matter, shall not:

(a) Knowingly make a false statement of material fact; or

(b) Fail to disclose a fact necessary to correct a misapprehension known by the lawyer or applicant to have arisen in the matter, or knowingly fail to respond reasonably to a lawful demand for information from an admissions or disciplinary authority, except that this Rule does not require disclosure of information otherwise protected by Rule 1.6.

COMMENT

[1] The duty imposed by this Rule extends to persons seeking admission to the Bar as well as to lawyers. Hence, if a person makes a material false statement in connection with an application for admission, it may be the basis for subsequent disciplinary action if the person is admitted, and in any event may be relevant in a subsequent admission application. The duty imposed by this Rule applies to a lawyer's own admission or discipline as well as that of others. Thus, it is a separate professional offense for a lawyer knowingly to make a misrepresentation or omission in con-

nection with a disciplinary investigation of the lawyer's own conduct. This Rule also requires affirmative clarification of any misunderstanding on the part of the admissions or disciplinary authority of which the person involved becomes aware.

[2] This Rule is subject to the provisions of the Fifth Amendment of the United States Constitution and corresponding provisions of state constitutions. A person relying on such a provision in response to a question, however, should do so openly and not use the right of nondisclosure as a justification for failure to comply with this Rule.

[3] A lawyer representing an applicant for admission to the Bar, or representing a lawyer who is the subject of a disciplinary inquiry or proceeding, is governed by the Rules applicable to the client-lawyer relationship. For example, Rule 1.6 may prohibit disclosures, which would otherwise be required, by a lawyer serving in such representative capacity.

Rule 8.3. Reporting Professional Misconduct

(a) A lawyer having knowledge that another lawyer has committed a violation of the Rules of Professional Conduct that raises a substantial question as to that lawyer's honesty, trustworthiness, or fitness as a lawyer in other respects, shall inform the appropriate professional authority.

(b) A lawyer having knowledge that a judge has committed a violation of applicable rules of judicial conduct that raises a substantial question as to the judge's fitness for office shall inform the appropriate authority.

(c) This Rule does not require disclosure of information otherwise protected by Rule 1.6.

COMMENT

[1] Self-regulation of the legal profession requires that members of the profession initiate disciplinary investigation when they know of a violation of the Rules of Professional Conduct. Lawyers have a similar obligation with respect to judicial misconduct. An apparently isolated violation may indicate a pattern of misconduct that only a disciplinary investigation can uncover. Reporting a violation is especially important where the victim is unlikely to discover the offense.

[2] A report about misconduct is not required where it would involve violation of Rule 1.6. However, a lawyer should encourage a client to consent to disclosure where prosecution would not substantially prejudice the client's interests.

[3] If a lawyer were obliged to report every violation of the Rules, the failure to report any violation would itself be a professional offense. Such a requirement existed in many jurisdictions but proved to be

unenforceable. This Rule limits the reporting obligation to those offenses that a self-regulating profession must vigorously endeavor to prevent. A measure of judgment is, therefore, required in complying with the provisions of this Rule. The term "substantial" refers to the seriousness of the possible offense and not the quantum of evidence of which the lawyer is aware. A report should be made to the Office of Bar Counsel. A lawyer who believes that another lawyer has a significant problem of alcohol or other substance abuse which does not require reporting to Bar Counsel under this Rule, may nonetheless wish to report the perceived situation to the Lawyer Counseling Committee, operated by the D.C. Bar, which assists lawyers having such problems.

[4] The duty to report professional misconduct does not apply to a lawyer retained to represent a lawyer whose professional conduct is in question. Such a situation is governed by the Rules applicable to the client-lawyer relationship.

[5] Rule 1.6(h) brings within the protections of Rule 1.6 certain types of information gained by lawyers participating in lawyer counseling programs of the D.C. Bar Lawyer Counseling Committee. To the extent information concerning violations of the Rules of Professional Conduct fall within the scope of Rule 1.6(h), a lawyer-counselor would not be required or permitted to inform the "appropriate professional authority" referred to in Rule 8.3. Where disclosure is permissive under Rule 1.6 (see paragraph 1.6(c) for cases of permitted disclosures), discretion to disclose to the "appropriate professional authority" would also exist pursuant to paragraph 8.3(c). See also Comment to Rule 1.6, paragraphs [29], [30], and [31].

Rule 8.4. Misconduct

It is professional misconduct for a lawyer to:

(a) Violate or attempt to violate the Rules of Professional Conduct, knowingly assist or induce another to do so, or do so through the acts of another;

(b) Commit a criminal act that reflects adversely on the lawyer's honesty, trustworthiness, or fitness as a lawyer in other respects;

(c) Engage in conduct involving dishonesty, fraud, deceit, or misrepresentation;

(d) Engage in conduct that seriously interferes with the administration of justice;

(e) State or imply an ability to influence improperly a government agency or official;

(f) Knowingly assist a judge or judicial officer in conduct that is a violation of applicable rules of judicial conduct or other law; or

(g) Seek or threaten to seek criminal charges or disciplinary charges solely to obtain an advantage in a civil matter.

COMMENT

[1] Many kinds of illegal conduct reflect adversely on fitness to practice law, such as offenses involving fraud and the offense of willful failure to file an income tax return. However, some kinds of offenses carry no such implication. Traditionally, the distinction was drawn in terms of offenses involving "moral turpitude." That concept can be construed to include offenses concerning some matters of personal morality, such as adultery and comparable offenses, that have no specific connection to fitness for the practice of law. Although a lawyer is personally answerable to the entire criminal law, a lawyer should be professionally answerable only for offenses that indicate lack of those characteristics relevant to law practice. Offenses involving violence, dishonesty, breach of trust, or serious interference with the administration of justice are in that category. A pattern of repeated offenses, even ones of minor significance when considered separately, can indicate indifference to legal obligation.

[2] Paragraph (d)'s prohibition of conduct that "seriously interferes with the administration of justice" includes conduct proscribed by the previous Code of Professional Responsibility under DR 1-102(A)(5) as "prejudicial to the administration of justice." The extensive case law on that standard, as set forth below, is hereby incorporated into this Rule.

[3] The majority of these cases involve a lawyer's failure to cooperate with Bar Counsel. A lawyer's failure to respond to Bar Counsel's inquiries or subpoenas may constitute misconduct, see In re Cope, 455 A.2d 1357 (D.C. 1983); In re Haupt, 444 A.2d 317 (D.C. 1982); In re Lieber, 442 A.2d 153 (D.C. 1982); In re Whitlock, 441 A.2d 989 (D.C. 1982); In re Spencer, No. M-112-82 (D.C. June 4, 1982); In re L. Smith, No. M-91-82 (D.C. App. Mar. 9, 1982); In re Walsh, No. 70 (81) (D.C. Sept. 25, 1981) en banc; In re Schattman, No. M-63-81 (D.C. June 2, 1981); In re Russell, 424 A.2d 1087 (D.C. 1980); In re Willcher, 404 A.2d 185 (D.C. 1979); In re Carter, No. D-31-79 (D.C. Oct. 28, 1979); In re Tucker, No. M-13-75/S-56-78 (D.C. Nov. 15, 1978); In re Bush (Bush II), No. S-58-79 (D.C. Oct. 1, 1979), as may the failure to abide by agreements made with Bar Counsel; In re Harmon, M-79-81 (D.C. Dec. 14, 1981) (breaking promise to Bar Counsel to offer complainant refund of fee or vigorous representation constitutes conduct prejudicial to the administration of justice).

[4] A lawyer's failure to appear in court for a scheduled hearing is another common form of conduct deemed prejudicial to the administration of justice. See In re Evans, No. M-126-82 (D.C. Dec. 18, 1982); In re Doud, Bar Docket No. 442-80 (Sept. 23, 1982); In re Bush (Bush III), No. S-58-79/D/39/80 (D.C. App. Apr. 30, 1980); In re Molovinsky, No. M-31-79 (D.C. Aug. 23, 1979). Similarly, failure to obey court orders may constitute misconduct under paragraph (d). Whitlock, 441 A.2d at 989-91; In re Brown, Bar Docket No. 222-78 (Aug. 4, 1978); In re Bush (Bush I), No. DP-22-75 (D.C. July 26, 1977).

[5] While the above categories — failure to cooperate with Bar Counsel and failure to obey Court orders — encompass the major forms of misconduct proscribed by paragraph (d), that provision is to be interpreted flexibly and includes any improper behavior of an analogous nature. For example, the failure to turn over the assets of a conservatorship to the court or to the successor conservator has been held to be conduct "prejudicial to the administration of justice." In re Burka, 423 A.2d 181 (D.C. 1980). In Russell, supra, the court found that failure to keep the Bar advised of respondent's changes of address, after being warned to do so, was also misconduct under that standard. And in Schattman, supra, the court found that failure to keep the Bar advised of respondent's changes of address, after being warned to do so, was also misconduct under that standard. And in Schattman, supra, it was held that a lawyer's giving a worthless check in settlement of a claim against the lawyer by a client was improper.

Rule 8.5. Disciplinary Authority; Choice of Law

(a) *Disciplinary Authority.* A lawyer admitted to practice in this jurisdiction is subject to the disciplinary authority of this jurisdiction, regardless of where the lawyer's conduct occurs. A lawyer may be subject to the disciplinary authority of both this jurisdiction and another jurisdiction where the lawyer is admitted for the same conduct.

(b) *Choice of Law.* In any exercise of the disciplinary authority of this jurisdiction, the Rules of Professional Conduct to be applied shall be as follows:

(1) For conduct in connection with a proceeding in a court before which a lawyer has been admitted to practice (either generally or for purposes of that proceeding), the rules to be applied shall be the rules of the jurisdiction in which the court sits, unless the rules of the court provide otherwise; and

(2) for any other conduct,

(i) if the lawyer is licensed to practice only in this jurisdiction, the rules to be applied shall be the rules of this jurisdiction, and

(ii) if the lawyer is licensed to practice in this and another jurisdiction, the rules to be applied shall be the rules of the admitting jurisdiction in which the lawyer principally practices; provided, however, that if particular conduct clearly has its predominant effect in another jurisdiction in which the lawyer is licensed to practice, the rules of that jurisdiction shall be applied to that conduct.

COMMENT

Disciplinary Authority

[1] Paragraph (a) restates long-standing law.

Choice of Law

[2] A lawyer may be potentially subject to more than one set of rules of professional conduct which impose different obligations. The lawyer may be licensed to practice in more than one jurisdiction with differing rules, or may be admitted to practice before a particular court with rules that differ from those of the jurisdiction or jurisdictions in which the lawyer is licensed to practice. In the past, decisions have not developed clear or consistent guidance as to which rules apply in such circumstances.

[3] Paragraph (b) seeks to resolve such potential conflicts. Its premise is that minimizing conflicts between rules, as well as uncertainty about which rules are applicable, is in the best interest of both clients and the profession (as well as the bodies having authority to regulate the profession). Accordingly, it takes the approach of (i) providing that any particular conduct of an attorney shall be subject to only one set of rules of professional conduct, and (ii) making the determination of which set of rules applies to particular conduct as straightforward as possible, consistent with recognition of appropriate regulatory interests of relevant jurisdictions.

[4] Paragraph (b) provides that as to a lawyer's conduct relating to a proceeding in a court before which the lawyer is admitted to practice (either generally or pro hac vice), the lawyer shall be subject only to the rules of professional conduct of that court. As to all other conduct, paragraph (b) provides that a lawyer licensed to practice only in this jurisdiction shall be subject to the rules of professional conduct of this jurisdiction, and that a lawyer licensed in multiple jurisdictions shall be subject only to the rules of the jurisdiction where he or she (as an individual, not his or her firm) principally practices, but with one exception: if particular conduct clearly has its predominant effect in another admitting jurisdiction, then only the rules of that jurisdiction shall apply. The intention is for the latter exception to be a narrow one. It would be appropriately applied, for example, to a situation in which a lawyer admitted in, and principally practicing in, State A, but also admitted in State B, handled an acquisition by a company whose headquarters and operations were in State B of another, similar such company. The exception would not appropriately be applied, on the other hand, if the lawyer handled an acquisition by a company whose headquarters and operations were in State A of a company whose headquarters and main operations were in State A, but which also had some operations in State B.

[5] If two admitting jurisdictions were to proceed against a lawyer for the same conduct, they should, applying this rule, identify the same governing ethics rules. They should take all appropriate steps to see that they do apply the same rule to the same conduct, and in all events should avoid proceeding against a lawyer on the basis of two inconsistent rules.

[6] The choice of law provision is not intended to apply to transnational practice. Choice of law in this context should be the subject of agreements between jurisdictions or of appropriate international law.

NONDISCRIMINATION BY MEMBERS OF THE BAR

Rule 9.1. Discrimination in Employment

A lawyer shall not discriminate against any individual in conditions of employment because of the individual's race, color, religion, national origin, sex, age, marital status, sexual orientation, family responsibility, or physical handicap.

COMMENT

[1] This provision is modeled after the D.C. Human Rights Act, D.C. Code §1-2512 (1981), though in some respects more limited in scope. There are also provisions of federal law that contain certain prohibitions on discrimination in employment. The rule is not intended to create ethical obligations that exceed those imposed on a lawyer by applicable law.

[2] A similar rule has been adopted by the highest court in Vermont. A similar rule is also under consideration for adoption by the courts in New York based on the recommendations of the New York State Bar Association.

[3] The investigation and adjudication of discrimination claims may involve particular expertise of the kind found within the D.C. Office of Human Rights and the federal Equal Employment Opportunity Commission. Such experience may involve, among other things, methods of analysis of statistical data regarding discrimination claims. These agencies also have, in appropriate circumstances, the power to award remedies to the victims of discrimination, such as reinstatement or back pay, which extend beyond the remedies that are available through the disciplinary process. Remedies available through the disciplinary process include such sanctions as disbarment, suspension, censure, and admonition, but do not extend to monetary awards or other remedies that could alter the employment status to take into account the impact of prior acts of discrimination.

[4] If proceedings are pending before other organizations, such as the D.C. Office of Human Rights or the Equal Employment Opportunity Commission, the processing of complaints by Bar Counsel may be deferred or abated where there is substantial similarity between the complaint filed with Bar Counsel and material allegations involved in such other proceedings. See §19(d) of Rule XI of the Rules Governing the Bar of the District of Columbia.

New York Materials

New York Code of Professional Responsibility

Editors' Introduction. New York has not adopted the ABA Model Rules of Professional Conduct but has instead retained a version of the ABA Model Code of Professional Responsibility. The New York Code, which is codified in the joint rules of the Appellate Divisions at 22 N.Y.C.R.R. Part 1200, has always varied somewhat from the ABA Model Code. Furthermore, in a series of amendments since 1990, the Appellate Divisions have added many provisions to the New York Code that had no counterpart in the ABA Model Code. The New York State Bar Association has then amended the Code to reflect the changes adopted by the courts. Most of these amendments track the language of the Model Rules or otherwise draw heavily upon positions in them.

The Appellate Divisions have not adopted the Ethical Considerations of the Code as rules governing the behavior of lawyers, but the New York State Bar Association has adopted them, as modified to conform to the Code amendments adopted by the Appellate Divisions. The State Bar has also adopted the ABA Model Code's Preamble and Preliminary Statement, but these too have not been adopted by the Appellate Divisions.

Since our last edition went to press in September of 2001, New York has amended only one provision in its Code of Professional Responsibility. In December of 2001, the Appellate Divisions announced minor amendments to DR 1-107 (Contractual Relationships Between Lawyers and Nonlegal Professionals), which had just taken effect on November 1, 2001. We reprint the amended rule in legislative style, underscoring the added language and striking through deleted language.

More significant developments occurred in the court rules outside the Code of Professional Responsibility. Effective March 4, 2002, the New York courts adopted a new court rule, 22 N.Y.C.R.R. Part 1215, which requires lawyers to provide their clients with written letters of engagement in all matters not expressly exempted by the rule. (Last year, we reprinted the proposed rule on letters of engagement, which was then circulating for public comment.) The new rule, which was amended effective April 3, 2002 to clarify a few ambiguities, provides as follows:

Part 1215. Written Letter of Engagement

§1215.1. Requirements

(a) Effective March 4, 2002, an attorney who undertakes to represent a client and enters into an arrangement for, charges or collects any fee from a client shall provide to the client a written letter of engagement before commencing the representation, or within a reasonable time thereafter (i) if otherwise impracticable or (ii) if the scope of services to be provided cannot be determined at the time of the commencement of representation. For purposes of this rule, where an entity (such as an insurance carrier) engages an attorney to represent a third party, the term "client" shall mean the entity that engages the attorney. Where there is a significant change in the scope of services or the fee to be charged, an updated letter of engagement shall be provided to the client.

(b) The letter of engagement shall address the following matters:

(1) Explanation of the scope of the legal services to be provided;

(2) Explanation of attorney's fees to be charged, expenses and billing practices; and, where applicable, shall provide that the client may have a right to arbitrate fee disputes under Part 137 of the Rules of the Chief Administrator.

(c) Instead of providing the client with a written letter of engagement, an attorney may comply with the provisions of subdivision (a) by entering into a signed written retainer agreement with the client, before or within a reasonable time after commencing the representation, provided that the agreement addresses the matters set forth in subdivision (b).

§1215.2. Exceptions

This section shall not apply to

(1) representation of a client where the fee to be charged is expected to be less than $3000,
(2) representation where the attorney's services are of the same general kind as previously rendered to and paid for by the client, or
(3) representation in domestic relations matters subject to Part 1400 of the Joint Rules of the Appellate Division (22 NYCRR), or
(4) representation where the attorney is admitted to practice in another jurisdiction and maintains no office in the State of New York, or where no material portion of the services are to be rendered in New York.

Another new court rule, 22 N.Y.C.R.R. Part 137 (Fee Dispute Resolution Program), took effect as scheduled on January 1, 2002. The rule requires a lawyer to notify a client about the right to arbitrate a fee dispute, and requires a lawyer to participate in the arbitration process if the client chooses arbitration.

When we went to press in September of 2002, neither the New York State Bar Association nor the courts were formally considering any amendments to the New York Code of Professional Responsibility. However, the State Bar's Committee on Standards of Attorney Conduct (COSAC) was in the preliminary stages of considering whether New York should adopt the format of the ABA Model Rules of Professional Conduct (i.e., black letter rules followed by official Comments) to replace the three-part format of the existing Code of Professional Responsibility (i.e., Canons, Ethical

Considerations, and Disciplinary Rules), and perhaps adopt some of the substance of the ABA Model Rules as amended in February of 2002. Even if the Committee recommends the change and the State Bar approves, however, several years of study and debate are likely to follow before New York changes over to a Model Rules format.

We reprint below the full text of the New York Code of Professional Responsibility as amended through our press deadline in September of 2002. For Disciplinary Rules, we use both the "DR" numbering system adopted by the State Bar and the "Part 1200" numbering system officially adopted by the courts.

For updated information about the New York Code of Professional Responsibility and related regulations, visit the New York State Bar Association's recently redesigned web site at www.nysba.org. (For the full text of the New York Code of Professional Responsibility, click at the right on "Attorney Resources," then scroll down to "Lawyer's Code of Professional Responsibility.") For updated information about court rules, visit the official web site of the New York courts at www.courts.state.ny.us.

Contents

Preamble
Preliminary Statement
Definitions

Canon 1. A Lawyer Should Assist in Maintaining the Integrity and Competence of the Legal Profession

DR 1-101. Maintaining Integrity and Competence of the Legal Profession
DR 1-102. Misconduct
DR 1-103. Disclosure of Information to Authorities
DR 1-104. Responsibilities of a Partner or Supervisory Lawyer and Subordinate Lawyers
DR 1-105. Disciplinary Authority and Choice of Law
DR 1-106. Responsibilities Regarding Nonlegal Services
DR 1-107. Contractual Relationships Between Lawyers and Nonlegal Professionals

Canon 2. A Lawyer Should Assist the Legal Profession in Fulfilling Its Duty to Make Legal Counsel Available

DR 2-101. Publicity and Advertising
DR 2-102. Professional Notices, Letterheads, and Signs
DR 2-103. Solicitation and Recommendation of Professional Employment
DR 2-104. Suggestion of Need of Legal Services
DR 2-105. Identification of Practice and Specialty
DR 2-106. Fee for Legal Services

DR 2-107. Division of Fees Among Lawyers
DR 2-108. Agreements Restricting the Practice of a Lawyer
DR 2-109. Obligation to Decline Employment
DR 2-110. Withdrawal from Employment
DR 2-111. Sale of Law Practice

Canon 3. A Lawyer Should Assist in Preventing the Unauthorized Practice of Law

DR 3-101. Aiding Unauthorized Practice of Law
DR 3-102. Dividing Legal Fees with a Non-Lawyer
DR 3-103. Forming a Partnership with a Non-Lawyer

Canon 4. A Lawyer Should Preserve the Confidences and Secrets of a Client

DR 4-101. Preservation of Confidences and Secrets of a Client

Canon 5. A Lawyer Should Exercise Independent Professional Judgment on Behalf of a Client

DR 5-101. Conflicts of Interest — Lawyer's Own Interests
DR 5-102. Lawyers as Witnesses
DR 5-103. Avoiding Acquisition of Interest in Litigation
DR 5-104. Transactions Between Lawyer and Client
DR 5-105. Conflict of Interest — Simultaneous Representation
DR 5-106. Settling Similar Claims of Clients
DR 5-107. Avoiding Influence by Others Than the Client
DR 5-108. Conflict of Interest — Former Client
DR 5-109. Organization as Client
DR 5-110. Membership in Legal Services Organization
DR 5-111. Sexual Relations with Clients

Canon 6. A Lawyer Should Represent a Client Competently

DR 6-101. Failing to Act Competently
DR 6-102. Limiting Liability to Client

Canon 7. A Lawyer Should Represent a Client Zealously Within the Bounds of the Law

DR 7-101. Representing a Client Zealously
DR 7-102. Representing a Client within the Bounds of the Law
DR 7-103. Performing the Duty of Public Prosecutor or Other Government Lawyer
DR 7-104. Communicating with Represented and Unrepresented Parties

DR 7-105. Threatening Criminal Prosecution
DR 7-106. Trial Conduct
DR 7-107. Trial Publicity
DR 7-108. Communication with or Investigation of Jurors
DR 7-109. Contact with Witnesses
DR 7-110. Contact with Officials

Canon 8. A Lawyer Should Assist in Improving the Legal System

DR 8-101. Action as a Public Official
DR 8-102. Statements Concerning Judges and Other Adjudicatory Officers
DR 8-103. Lawyer Candidate for Judicial Office

Canon 9. A Lawyer Should Avoid Even the Appearance of Professional Impropriety

DR 9 101. Avoiding Even the Appearance of Impropriety
DR 9-102. Preserving Identity of Funds and Property of Others; Fiduciary Responsibility; Commingling and Misappropriation of Client Funds or Property; Maintenance of Bank Accounts; Recordkeeping; Examination of Records

PREAMBLE

The continued existence of a free and democratic society depends upon recognition of the concept that justice is based upon the rule of law grounded in respect for the dignity of the individual and the capacity of the individual through reason for enlightened self-government. Law so grounded makes justice possible, for only through such law does the dignity of the individual attain respect and protection. Without it, individual rights become subject to unrestrained power, respect for law is destroyed, and rational self-government is impossible.

Lawyers, as guardians of the law, play a vital role in the preservation of society. The fulfillment of this role requires an understanding by lawyers of their relationship with and function in our legal system. A consequent obligation of lawyers is to maintain the highest standards of ethical conduct.

In fulfilling professional responsibilities, a lawyer necessarily assumes various roles that require the performance of many difficult tasks. Not every situation which the lawyer may encounter can be foreseen, but fundamental ethical principles are always present for guidance. Within the framework of these principles, a lawyer must with courage and foresight be able and ready to shape the body of the law to the ever-changing relationships of society.

The Code of Professional Responsibility points the way to the aspiring and provides standards by which to judge the transgressor. Each lawyer's own conscience must provide the touchstone against which to test the extent to which the lawyer's actions should rise above minimum standards. But in the last analysis it is the desire for the respect and confidence of the members of the professional and of the society which the lawyer serves that should provide to a lawyer the incentive for the highest possible degree of ethical conduct. So long as its practitioners are guided by these principles, the law will continue to be a noble profession. This is its greatness and its strength, which permit of no compromise.

PRELIMINARY STATEMENT

The Code of Professional Responsibility consists of three separate but interrelated parts: Canons, Ethical Considerations, and Disciplinary Rules. The Code is designed to be both an inspirational guide to the members of the profession and a basis for disciplinary action when the conduct of a lawyer falls below the required minimum standards stated in the Disciplinary Rules.

Obviously the Canons, Ethical Considerations, and Disciplinary Rules cannot apply to non-lawyers; however, they do define the type of ethical conduct that the public has a right to expect not only of lawyers but also of their non-professional employees and associates in all matters pertaining to professional employment. A lawyer should ultimately be responsible for the conduct of the lawyer's employees and associates in the course of the professional representation of the client.

The Canons are statements of axiomatic norms, expressing in general terms the standards of professional conduct expected of lawyers in their relationships with the public, with the legal system, and with the legal professional. They embody the general concepts from which the Ethical Considerations and the Disciplinary Rules are derived.

The Ethical Considerations are aspirational in character and represent the objectives toward which every member of the profession should strive. They constitute a body of principles upon which the lawyer can rely for guidance in many specific situations.

The Disciplinary Rules, unlike the Ethical Considerations, are mandatory in character. The Disciplinary Rules state the minimum level of conduct below which no lawyer can fall without being subject to disciplinary action. The Disciplinary Rules should be uniformly applied to all lawyers, regardless of the nature of their professional activities. The Code makes no attempt to prescribe either disciplinary procedures or penalties for violation of a Disciplinary Rule, nor does it undertake to define standards for civil liability of lawyers for professional conduct. The severity of judgment against one found guilty of violating a Disciplinary Rule should be determined by the character of the offense and the attendant circumstances. An enforcing agency, in applying the Disciplinary Rules, may find interpretive guidance in the basic principles embodied in the Canons and in the objectives reflected in the Ethical Considerations.

No codification of principles can expressly cover all situations that may arise. Accordingly, conduct that does not appear to violate the express terms of any Disciplinary Rule nevertheless may be found by an enforcing agency to be the subject of discipline on the basis of a general principle illustrated by a Disciplinary Rule or on the basis of an accepted common law principle applicable to lawyers.

[§1200.01] Definitions*

(a) "Differing interests" include every interest that will adversely affect either the judgment or the loyalty of a lawyer to a client, whether it be a conflicting, inconsistent, diverse, or other interest.

(b) "Law firm" includes, but is not limited to, a professional legal corporation, a limited liability company or partnership engaged in the practice of law, the legal department of a corporation or other organization and a qualified legal assistance organization.

(c) "Person" includes a corporation, an association, a trust, a partnership, and any other organization or legal entity.

(d) "Professional legal corporation" means a corporation, or an association treated as a corporation, authorized by law to practice law for profit.

(e) "State" includes the District of Columbia, Puerto Rico, and other federal territories and possessions.

(f) "Tribunal" includes all courts, arbitrators and other adjudicatory bodies.

(g) (Repealed.)

(h) "Qualified legal assistance organization" means an office or organization of one of the four types listed in DR 2-103(d)(1) through (4) inclusive, that meets all the requirements thereof.

(i) "Fraud" does not include conduct, although characterized as fraudulent by statute or administrative rule, which lacks an element of scienter, deceit, intent to mislead, or knowing failure to correct misrepresentations which can be reasonably expected to induce detrimental reliance by another.

(j) "Domestic relations matters" means representation of a client in a claim, action or proceeding, or preliminary to the filing of a claim, action or proceeding, in either Supreme Court or Family

*"Confidence" and "Secret" are defined in DR 4-101(a). "Sexual relations" is defined in DR 5-111(a). "Copy" is defined in DR 9-102(d)(10).

Court, or in any court of appellate jurisdiction, for divorce, separation, annulment, custody, visitation, maintenance, child support, or alimony, or to enforce or modify a judgment or order in connection with any such claims, actions or proceedings.

CANON 1. A LAWYER SHOULD ASSIST IN MAINTAINING THE INTEGRITY AND COMPETENCE OF THE LEGAL PROFESSION

EC 1-1 A basic tenet of the professional responsibility of lawyers is that every person in our society should have ready access to the independent professional services of a lawyer of integrity and competence. Maintaining the integrity and improving the competence of the bar to meet the highest standards is the ethical responsibility of every lawyer.

EC 1-2 The public should be protected from those who are not qualified to be lawyers by reason of deficiency in education or moral standards or of other relevant factors but who nevertheless seek to practice law. To assure the maintenance of high moral and educational standards of the legal profession, lawyers should affirmatively assist courts and other appropriate bodies in promulgating, enforcing, and improving requirements for admission to the bar. In like manner, the bar has a positive obligation to aid in the continued improvement of all phases of pre-admission and post-admission legal education.

EC 1-3 Before recommending an applicant for admission, a lawyer should be satisfied that the applicant is of good moral character. Although a lawyer should not become a self-appointed investigator or judge of applicants for admission, the lawyer should report to proper officials all unfavorable information the lawyer possesses relating to the character or other qualifications of an applicant.

EC 1-4 The integrity of the profession can be maintained only if conduct of lawyers in violation of the Disciplinary Rules is brought to the attention of the proper officials. A lawyer should reveal voluntarily to those officials all knowledge, other than knowledge protected as a confidence or secret, of conduct of another lawyer which the lawyer believes clearly to be a violation of the Disciplinary Rules that raises a substantial question as to the other lawyer's honesty, trustworthiness or fitness in other respects as a lawyer. A lawyer should, upon request, serve on and assist committees and boards having responsibility for the administration of the Disciplinary Rules.

EC 1-5 A lawyer should maintain high standards of professional conduct and should encourage other lawyers to do likewise. A lawyer should be temperate and dignified, and should refrain from all illegal and morally reprehensible conduct. Because of the lawyer's position in society, even minor violations of law by a lawyer may tend to lessen public confidence in the legal profession. Obedience to law exemplifies respect for law. To lawyers especially, respect for the law should be more than a platitude.

EC 1-6 An applicant for admission to the bar or a lawyer may be unqualified, temporarily or permanently, for other than moral and educational reasons, such as mental or emotional instability. Lawyers should be diligent in taking steps to see that during a period of disqualification such person is not granted a license or, if licensed, is not permitted to practice. In like manner, when the disqualification has terminated, members of the bar should assist such person in being licensed, or, if licensed, in being restored to the full right to practice.

EC 1-7 A lawyer should avoid bias and condescension toward, and treat with dignity and respect, all parties, witnesses, lawyers, court employees, and other persons involved in the legal process.

EC 1-8 A law firm should adopt measures giving reasonable assurance that all lawyers in the firm conform to the Disciplinary Rules and that the conduct of non-lawyers employed by the firm is compatible with the professional obligations of the lawyers in the firm. Such measures may include informal supervision and occasional admonition, a procedure whereby junior lawyers can make confidential referral of ethical problems directly to a designated senior lawyer or special committee, and continuing legal education in professional ethics.

Editors' Note. In November of 2000, when the New York State Bar Association voted to formally propose new DR's 1-106 and 1-107 to the courts, the State Bar also voted to conditionally approve ten new Ethical Considerations, EC's 1-9 through 1-18, to explain the proposed rules. If the courts had approved DR's 1-106 and 1-107 exactly as proposed, the proposed EC's would have taken effect automatically. However, because the versions of DR's 1-106 and 1-107 adopted by the courts differed somewhat from the State Bar's proposals, the State Bar had to review the proposed EC's to determine whether to make any changes. In September of 2001, the State Bar released final versions of the new EC's, which took effect on November 1, 2001.

Provision of Nonlegal Services

EC 1-9 For many years, lawyers have provided nonlegal services to their clients. By participating in the delivery of these services, lawyers can serve a broad range of economic and other interests of clients. Whenever a lawyer directly provides nonlegal services, the lawyer must avoid confusion on the part of the client as to the nature of the lawyer's role, so that the person for whom the nonlegal services are performed understands that the services may not carry with them the legal and ethical protections that ordinarily accompany an attorney-client relationship. The recipient of the nonlegal services may expect, for example, that the protection of client confidences and secrets, prohibitions against representation of persons with conflicting interests, and obligations of a lawyer to maintain professional independence apply to the provision of nonlegal services, when that may not be the case. The risk of confusion is especially acute when the lawyer renders both legal and nonlegal services with respect to the same matter. Under some circumstances, the legal and nonlegal services may be so closely entwined that they cannot be distinguished from each other. In this situation, the recipient is likely to be confused as to whether and when the relationship is protected as an attorney-client relationship. Therefore, where the legal and nonlegal services are not distinct, DR 1-106(a)(1) requires that the lawyer providing nonlegal services adhere to all of the requirements of the Code of Professional Responsibility with respect to the nonlegal services. DR 1-106(a)(1) applies to the provision of nonlegal services by a law firm if the person for whom the nonlegal services are being performed is also receiving legal services from the firm that are not distinct from the nonlegal services.

EC 1-10 Even when the lawyer believes that the provision of nonlegal services is distinct from any legal services being provided, there is still a risk that the recipient of the nonlegal services might reasonably believe that the recipient is receiving the protection of an attorney-client relationship. Therefore, DR 1-106(a)(2) requires that the lawyer providing the nonlegal services adhere to the Disciplinary Rules, unless exempted. Nonlegal services also may be provided through an entity with which a lawyer is affiliated, for example, as owner, controlling party or agent. In this situation, there is still a risk that the recipient of the nonlegal services might reasonably believe that the recipient is receiving the protection of an attorney-client relationship. Therefore, DR 1-106(a)(3) requires that the lawyer involved with the entity providing nonlegal services adhere to all the Disciplinary Rules with respect to the nonlegal services, unless exempted.

EC 1-11 The Disciplinary Rules will be presumed to apply to a lawyer who directly provides or is otherwise involved in the provision of nonlegal services unless the lawyer complies with DR 1-106(a)(4) by communicating in writing to the person receiving the nonlegal services that the services are not legal services and that the protection of an attorney-client relationship does not exist with respect to the nonlegal services. Such a communication should be made before entering into an agreement for the provision of nonlegal services, in a manner sufficient to assure that the person understands the significance of the communication. In certain circumstances, however, additional steps may be required to communicate the desired understanding. For example, while the written disclaimer set forth in DR 1-106(a)(4) will be adequate for a sophisticated user of legal and nonlegal services, a more detailed explanation may be required for someone unaccustomed to making distinctions between legal services and nonlegal services. The lawyer or law firm will not be required to comply with these requirements if its interest in the entity providing the nonlegal services is so small as to be de minimis.

EC 1-12 Although a lawyer may be exempt from the application of Disciplinary Rules with respect to nonlegal services on the face of DR 1-106(a), the scope of the exemption is not absolute. A lawyer who provides or who is involved in the provision of nonlegal services may be excused from compliance with only those Disciplinary Rules that are dependent upon the existence of a representation or attorney-client relationship. Other rules, such as those prohibiting lawyers from engaging in illegal, dishonest, fraudulent or deceptive conduct (DR 1-102), requiring lawyers to report certain attorney misconduct (DR 1-103), and prohibiting lawyers from misusing the confidences or secrets of a former client (DR 4-101(b)), apply to a lawyer irrespective of the existence of a representation, and thus govern a lawyer otherwise exempt under DR 1-106(a). A lawyer or law firm is always subject to these Disciplinary Rules with respect to the rendering of legal services.

Contractual Relationships Between Lawyers and Nonlegal Professionals

EC 1-13 DR 1-107 permits lawyers to enter into interprofessional contractual relationships for the systematic and continuing provision of legal and nonlegal professional services provided the nonlegal professional or nonlegal professional service firm with which the lawyer or law firm is affiliated does not own, control, supervise or manage, directly or indirectly, in whole or in part, the practice of law by the lawyer or law firm. The nonlegal professional or nonlegal professional service firm may not play a role in, for example, the decision whether to accept or terminate an engagement to provide legal services in a particular matter or to a particular client, determining the manner in which lawyers are hired or trained, the assignment of lawyers to handle particular matters or to provide legal services to particular clients, decisions relating to the undertaking of pro bono publico and other public-interest legal work, financial and budgetary decisions relating to the legal practice, and determining the compensation and advancement of lawyers and of persons assisting law-yers on legal matters.

EC 1-14 The contractual relationship permitted by DR 1-107 may provide for the sharing of premises, general overhead, or administrative costs and services on an arm's length basis. Such financial arrangements, in the context of an agreement between lawyers and other professionals to provide legal and other professional services on a systematic and continuing basis, are permitted subject to the requirements of DR 2-103(b)(1) and DR 1-107(d). Similarly, lawyers participating in such arrangements remain subject to general ethical principles in addition to those set forth in DR 1-107 including, at a minimum, DR 2-102(b), DR 5-105(a), DR 5-105(b), DR 5-107(b), DR 5-107(c), and DR 5-108(a). Thus, the lawyer or law firm may not, for example, include in its firm name the name of the nonlegal professional service firm or any individual nonlegal professional, or enter into formal partnerships with nonlawyers, or practice in an organization authorized to practice law for a profit in which nonlawyers own any interest. Moreover, a lawyer or law firm may not enter into an agreement or arrangement for the use of a name in respect of which a nonlegal professional or nonlegal professional service firm has or exercises a proprietary interest if, under or pursuant to the agreement or arrangement, that nonlegal professional or firm acts or is entitled to act in a manner inconsistent with DR 1-107(a)(2) or EC 1-13. More generally, although the existence of a contractual relationship permitted by DR 1-107 does not by itself create a conflict of interest violating DR 5-101(a) whenever a law firm represents a client in a matter in which the nonlegal professional service firm's client is also involved, the law firm's interest in maintaining an advantageous relationship with a nonlegal professional service firm might, in certain circumstances, adversely affect the independent professional judgment of the law firm, creating a conflict of interest.

EC 1-15 Each lawyer and law firm having a contractual relationship under DR 1-107 has an ethical duty to observe these Disciplinary Rules with respect to its own conduct in the context of the contractual relationship. For example, the lawyer or law firm cannot permit its obligation to maintain client confidences as required by DR 4-101 to be compromised by the contractual relationship or by its implementation by or on behalf of nonlawyers involved in the relationship. In addition, the prohibition in DR 1-102(a)(2) against a lawyer or law firm circumventing a Disciplinary Rule through actions of another applies generally to the lawyer or law firm in the contractual relationship.

EC 1-16 The contractual relationship permitted by DR 1-107 may provide for the reciprocal referral of clients by and between the lawyer or law firm and the nonlegal professional or nonlegal professional service firm. When in the context of such a contractual relationship a lawyer or law firm refers a client to the nonlegal professional or nonlegal professional service firm, the lawyer or law firm shall observe the ethical standards of the legal profession in verifying the competence of the nonlegal professional or nonlegal professional services firm to handle the relevant affairs and interests of the client. Referrals should only be made when requested by the client or deemed to be reasonably necessary to serve the client. Thus, even if otherwise permitted by DR 1-107, a contractual relationship may not require referrals on an exclusive basis.

EC 1-17 To assure that only appropriate professional services are involved, a contractual relationship for the provision of services is permitted under DR 1-107 only if the nonlegal party thereto is a professional or professional service firm meeting appropriate standards as regards ethics, education, training, and licensing. The Appellate Divisions maintain a public list of eligible professions. A member of the nonlegal profession or professional service firm may apply for the inclusion of particular professions on the list, or professions may be added to the list by the Appellate Divisions sua sponte. A lawyer or law firm not wishing to affiliate with a nonlawyer on a systematic and continuing basis, but only to engage a nonlawyer on an ad hoc basis to assist in a specific matter, is not governed by DR 1-107 when so dealing with the nonlawyer. Thus, a lawyer advising a client in connection with a discharge of chemical wastes may engage the services of and consult with an environmental engineer on that matter without the need to comply with DR 1-107. Likewise, the requirements of DR 1-107 need not be met when a lawyer retains an expert witness in a particular litigation.

EC 1-18 Depending upon the extent and nature of the relationship between the lawyer or law firm, on the one hand, and the nonlegal professional or nonlegal professional service firm, on the other hand, it may be appropriate to treat the parties to a contractual relationship permitted by DR 1-107 as a single law firm for purposes of these Disciplinary Rules, as would be the case if the nonlegal professional or nonlegal professional service firm were in an "of counsel" relationship with the lawyer or law firm. If the parties to the relationship are treated as a single law firm, the principal effects would be that conflicts of interest are imputed as between them pursuant to DR 5-105(d), and that the law firm would be required to maintain systems for determining whether such conflicts exist pursuant to DR 5-105(e). To the extent that the rules of ethics of the nonlegal profession conflict with these Disciplinary Rules, the rules of the legal profession will still govern the conduct of the lawyers and the law firm participants in the relationship. A lawyer or law firm may also be subject to legal obligations arising from a relationship with nonlawyer professionals who are themselves subject to regulation.

[§1200.2] DR 1-101 Maintaining Integrity and Competence of the Legal Profession

(a) A lawyer is subject to discipline if the lawyer has made a materially false statement in, or has deliberately failed to disclose a material

fact requested in connection with, the lawyer's application for admission to the bar.

(b) A lawyer shall not further the application for admission to the bar of another person that the lawyer knows to be unqualified in respect to character, education, or other relevant attribute.

[§1200.3] DR 1-102 Misconduct

(a) A lawyer or law firm shall not:

(1) Violate a Disciplinary Rule.

(2) Circumvent a Disciplinary Rule through actions of another.

(3) Engage in illegal conduct that adversely reflects on the lawyer's honesty, trustworthiness or fitness as a lawyer.

(4) Engage in conduct involving dishonesty, fraud, deceit, or misrepresentation.

(5) Engage in conduct that is prejudicial to the administration of justice.

(6) Unlawfully discriminate in the practice of law, including in hiring, promoting or otherwise determining conditions of employment, on the basis of age, race, creed, color, national origin, sex, disability, marital status, or sexual orientation. Where there is a tribunal with jurisdiction to hear a complaint, if timely brought, other than a Departmental Disciplinary Committee, a complaint based on unlawful discrimination shall be brought before such tribunal in the first instance. A certified copy of a determination by such a tribunal, which has become final and enforceable, and as to which the right to judicial or appellate review has been exhausted, finding that the lawyer has engaged in an unlawful discriminatory practice shall constitute *prima facie* evidence of professional misconduct in a disciplinary proceeding.

(7) Engage in any other conduct that adversely reflects on the lawyer's fitness as a lawyer.

[§1200.4] DR 1-103 Disclosure of Information to Authorities

(a) A lawyer possessing knowledge, (1) not protected as a confidence or secret, or (2) not gained in the lawyer's capacity as a member of a bona fide lawyer assistance or similar program or committee, of a violation of DR 1-102 that raises a substantial question as to another lawyer's honesty, trustworthiness or fitness in other respects as a lawyer shall report such knowledge to a tribunal or other authority empowered to investigate or act upon such violation.

(b) A lawyer possessing knowledge or evidence, not protected as a confidence or secret, concerning another lawyer or a judge shall reveal fully such knowledge or evidence upon proper request of a tribunal or other authority empowered to investigate or act upon the conduct of lawyers or judges.

[§1200.5] DR 1-104 Responsibilities of a Partner or Supervisory Lawyer and Subordinate Lawyers

(a) A law firm shall make reasonable efforts to ensure that all lawyers in the firm conform to the disciplinary rules.

(b) A lawyer with management responsibility in the law firm or direct supervisory authority over another lawyer shall make reasonable efforts to ensure that the other lawyer conforms to the disciplinary rules.

(c) A law firm shall adequately supervise, as appropriate, the work of partners, associates and non-lawyers who work at the firm. The degree of supervision required is that which is reasonable under the circumstances, taking into account factors such as the experience of the person whose work is being supervised, the amount of work involved in a particular matter, and the likelihood that ethical problems might arise in the course of working on the matter.

(d) A lawyer shall be responsible for a violation of the Disciplinary Rules by another lawyer or for conduct of a non-lawyer employed or retained by or associated with the lawyer that would be a violation of the Disciplinary Rules if engaged in by a lawyer if:

(1) The lawyer orders, or directs the specific conduct, or, with knowledge of the specific conduct, ratifies it; or

(2) The lawyer is a partner in the law firm in which the other lawyer practices or the non-lawyer is employed, or has supervisory authority over the other lawyer or the non-lawyer, and knows of such conduct, or in the exercise of reasonable management or supervisory authority should have known of the conduct so that reasonable remedial action could be or could have been taken at a time when its consequences could be or could have been avoided or mitigated.

(e) A lawyer shall comply with these Disciplinary Rules notwithstanding that the lawyer acted at the direction of another person.

(f) A subordinate lawyer does not violate these Disciplinary Rules if that lawyer acts in accordance with a supervisory lawyer's reasonable resolution of an arguable question of professional duty.

[§1200.5-a] DR 1-105 Disciplinary Authority and Choice of Law

(a) A lawyer admitted to practice in this state is subject to the disciplinary authority of this state, regardless of where the lawyer's conduct occurs. A lawyer may be subject to the disciplinary authority of both this state and another jurisdiction where the lawyer is admitted for the same conduct.

(b) In any exercise of the disciplinary authority of this state, the rules of professional conduct to be applied shall be as follows:

(1) For conduct in connection with a proceeding in a court before which a lawyer has been admitted to practice (either generally or for purposes of that proceeding), the rules to be applied shall be the rules of the jurisdiction in which the court sits, unless the rules of the court provide otherwise; and

(2) For any other conduct:

(i) If the lawyer is licensed to practice only in this state, the rules to be applied shall be the rules of this state, and

(ii) If the lawyer is licensed to practice in this state and another jurisdiction, the rules to be applied shall be the rules of the admitting jurisdiction in which the lawyer principally practices; provided, however, that if particular conduct clearly has its predominant effect in another jurisdiction in which the lawyer is licensed to practice, the rules of that jurisdiction shall be applied to that conduct.

[§1200.5-b] DR 1-106 Responsibilities Regarding Nonlegal Services

Editors' Note. On July 23, 2001, the New York courts issued an order adopting new DR's 1-106 and 1-107 and amending existing DR's 2-101, 2-102, and 2-103. The amendments took effect on November 1, 2001 (though DR 1-107 was slightly amended in December 2001).

(a) With respect to lawyers or law firms providing nonlegal services to clients or other persons:

(1) A lawyer or law firm that provides nonlegal services to a person that are not distinct from legal services being provided to that person by the lawyer or law firm is subject to these Disciplinary Rules with respect to the provision of both legal and nonlegal services.

(2) A lawyer or law firm that provides nonlegal services to a person that are distinct from legal services being provided to that person by the lawyer or law firm is subject to these Disciplinary Rules with respect to the nonlegal services if the person receiving the services could reasonably believe that the nonlegal services are the subject of an attorney-client relationship.

(3) A lawyer or law firm that is an owner, controlling party or agent of, or that is otherwise affiliated with, an entity that the lawyer or law firm knows to be providing nonlegal services to a person is subject to these Disciplinary Rules with respect to the nonlegal services if the person receiving the services could reasonably believe that the nonlegal services are the subject of an attorney-client relationship.

(4) For purposes of DR 1-106(a)(2) and (a)(3), it will be presumed that the person receiving nonlegal services believes the ser-

vices to be the subject of an attorney-client relationship unless the lawyer or law firm has advised the person receiving the services in writing that the services are not legal services and that the protection of an attorney-client relationship does not exist with respect to the nonlegal services, or if the interest of the lawyer or law firm in the entity providing nonlegal services is de minimis.

(b) Notwithstanding the provisions of DR 1-106(a), a lawyer or law firm that is an owner, controlling party, agent, or is otherwise affiliated with an entity that the lawyer or law firm knows is providing nonlegal services to a person shall not permit any nonlawyer providing such services or affiliated with that entity to direct or regulate the professional judgment of the lawyer or law firm in rendering legal services to any person, or to cause the lawyer or law firm to compromise its duty under DR 4-101(b) and (d) with respect to the confidences and secrets of a client receiving legal services.

(c) For purposes of DR 1-106, "nonlegal services" shall mean those services that lawyers may lawfully provide and that are not prohibited as an unauthorized practice of law when provided by a nonlawyer.

[§1200.5-c] DR 1-107 Contractual Relationships Between Lawyers and Nonlegal Professionals

Editors' Note. DR 1-107 took effect on November 1, 2002, together with a new DR 1-106, related amendments to DR's 2-101, 2-102, and 2-103, new EC's 1-9 through 1-18, and an amended EC 2-10. In December of 2001, less than two months after it took effect, DR 1-107 was amended in relatively minor ways. We reprint DR 1-107 in legislative style to show the December 2001 amendments, underscoring new language and striking through deleted language.

(a) The practice of law has an essential tradition of complete independence and uncompromised loyalty to those it services. Recognizing this tradition, clients of lawyers practicing in New York State are guaranteed "independent professional judgment and undivided loyalty uncompromised by conflicts of interest."[1] Indeed, these guarantees represent the very foundation of the profession and allow and foster its continued role as a protector of the system of law. Therefore, a lawyer must remain completely responsible for

[1]"Statement of Client's Rights," 22 NYCRR Part 1210. [Footnote by the Courts. — Eds.]

his or her own independent professional judgment, maintain the confidences and secrets of clients, preserve funds of clients and third parties in his or her control, and otherwise comply with the legal and ethical principles governing lawyers in New York State.

Multi-disciplinary practice between lawyers and non-lawyers is incompatible with the core values of the legal profession and, therefore, a strict division between services provided by lawyers and those provided by non-lawyers is essential to protect those values. However, a lawyer or law firm may enter into and maintain a contractual relationship with a non-legal professional or non-legal professional service firm for the purpose of offering to the public, on a systematic and continuing basis, legal services performed by the lawyer or law firm, as well as other non-legal professional services, notwithstanding the provisions of DR 5-101(a), provided that:

(1) The profession of the non-legal professional or non-legal professional service firm is included in a list jointly established and maintained by the Appellate Divisions pursuant to section 1205.3 of the Joint Appellate Division Rules;

(2) The lawyer or law firm neither grants to the non-legal professional or non-legal professional service firm, nor permits such person or firm to obtain, hold or exercise, directly or indirectly, any ownership or investment interest in, or managerial or supervisory right, power or position in connection with the practice of law by the lawyer or law firm nor, as provided in DR 2-103(b)(1), shares legal fees with a non-lawyer or receives or gives any monetary or other tangible benefit for giving or receiving a referral; and

(3) The fact that the contractual relationship exists is disclosed by the lawyer or law firm to any client of the lawyer or law firm before the client is referred to the non-legal professional service firm, or to any client of the non-legal professional service firm before that client receives legal services from the lawyer or law firm; and the client has given informed written consent and has been provided with a copy of the "Statement of Client's Rights In Cooperative Business Arrangements" pursuant to section 1205.4 of the Joint Appellate Division Rules.

(b) For purposes of DR 1-107(a):

(1) Each profession on the list maintained pursuant to a joint rule of the Appellate Divisions shall have been designated sua sponte, or approved by the Appellate Divisions upon application of a member of a non-legal profession or non-legal professional service firm, upon a determination that the profession is composed of individuals who, with respect to their profession:

(A) have been awarded a Bachelor's Degree or its equivalent from an accredited college or university, or have attained an

equivalent combination of educational credit from such a college or university and work experience;

(B) are licensed to practice the profession by an agency of the State of New York or the United States Government; and

(C) are required under penalty of suspension or revocation of license to adhere to a code of ethical conduct that is reasonably comparable to that of the legal profession.

(2) The term "ownership or investment interest" shall mean any such interest in any form of debt or equity, and shall include any interest commonly considered to be an interest accruing to or enjoyed by an owner or investor.

(c) DR 1-107(a)~~(1)~~ shall not apply to relationships consisting solely of non-exclusive reciprocal referral agreements or understandings between a lawyer or law firm and a non-legal professional or non-legal professional service firm.

(d) Notwithstanding DR 3-102(a), a lawyer or law firm may allocate costs and expenses with a non-legal professional or non-legal professional service firm pursuant to a contractual relationship permitted by DR 1-107(a), provided the allocation reasonably reflects the costs and expenses incurred or expected to be incurred by each.

Editors' Note. New DR 1-107(a) refers twice to 22 N.Y.C.R.R. Part 1205, which was added to New York's court rules by the same order that adopted DR 1-107. Part 1205 is designed to supplement and reinforce DR 1-107. Because Part 1205 is an integral part of the changes effected by DR 1-107 and the related amendments, we reprint Part 1205 below in its entirety.

Part 1205. Cooperative Business Arrangements between Lawyers and Nonlegal Professionals

§1205.1. Application

This Part shall apply to all lawyers who, pursuant to a cooperative business arrangement, (1) undertake to provide legal services to a client referred by a nonlegal service provider or (2) refer an existing client to a nonlegal service provider.

§1205.2. Definition

A cooperative business arrangement is a contractual relationship between a lawyer or law firm and a nonlegal professional or nonlegal professional service firm for the purpose of offering to the public, on a systematic and continuing basis, legal services performed by the lawyer or law firm, as well as other nonlegal professional services, as authorized by §1200.5-c [DR 1-107] of the Disciplinary Rules of the Code of Professional Responsibility.

§1205.3. List of Professions

(a) The Appellate Divisions jointly shall establish and maintain a list of professions, designated by the Appellate Divisions sua sponte or approved by them upon application of a member of a nonlegal profession or nonlegal professional service firm, with whose members a lawyer may enter into a cooperative business arrangement to perform legal and nonlegal services as authorized by §1200.5-c [DR 1-107] of the Disciplinary Rules.

(b) A profession shall be eligible for inclusion in the list if the profession is composed of individuals who, with respect to their profession, meet the requirements set forth in §1200.5-c(b)(1) [DR 1-107(b)(1)] of the Disciplinary Rules.

§1205.4. Statement of Client's Rights in Cooperative Business Arrangements

In the furtherance of a cooperative business arrangement, (a) prior to the commencement of legal representation of a client referred by a nonlegal service provider or (b) prior to the referral of an existing client to a nonlegal service provider, a lawyer shall provide the client with a statement of client's rights. That statement shall include a consent to the referral to be signed by the client and shall contain the following:

Statement of Client's Rights in Cooperative Business Arrangements

Your lawyer is providing you with this document to explain how your rights may be affected by the referral of your particular matter by your lawyer to a nonlegal service provider, or by the referral of your particular matter by a nonlegal service provider to your lawyer.

To help avoid any misunderstanding between you and your lawyer please read this document carefully. If you have any questions about these rights, do not hesitate to ask your lawyer.

Your lawyer has entered into a contractual relationship with a nonlegal professional or professional service firm, in the form of a cooperative business arrangement which may include sharing of costs and expenses, to provide legal and nonlegal services. Such an arrangement may substantially affect your rights in a number of respects. Specifically, you are advised:

(1) A lawyer's clients are guaranteed the independent professional judgment and undivided loyalty of the lawyer, uncompromised by conflicts of interest. The lawyer's business arrangement with a provider of nonlegal services may not diminish these rights.

(2) Confidences and secrets imparted by a client to a lawyer are protected by the attorney/client privilege and may not be disclosed by the lawyer as part of a referral to a nonlegal service provider without the separate written consent of the client.

(3) The protections afforded to a client by the attorney/client privilege may not carry over to dealings between the client and a nonlegal service provider. Information that would be protected as a confidence or secret, if imparted by the client to a lawyer, may not be so protected when disclosed by the client to a nonlegal service provider. Under some circumstances, the nonlegal service provider may be required by statute or a code of ethics to make disclosure to a government agency.

(4) Even where a lawyer refers a client to a nonlegal service provider for assistance in financial matters, the lawyer's obligation to preserve and safeguard client funds in his or her possession continues.

You have the right to consult with an independent lawyer or other third party before signing this agreement.

Client's Consent:

I have read the above Statement of Client's Rights in Cooperative Business Arrangements and I consent to the referral of my particular matter in accordance with that Statement.

____

Client's Signature: Date

CANON 2. A LAWYER SHOULD ASSIST THE LEGAL PROFESSION IN FULFILLING ITS DUTY TO MAKE LEGAL COUNSEL AVAILABLE

EC 2-1 The need of members of the public for legal services is met only if they recognize their legal problems, appreciate the importance of seeking assistance, and are able to obtain the services of acceptable legal counsel. Hence, important functions of the legal profession are to educate people to recognize their problems, to facilitate the process of intelligent selection of lawyers, and to assist in making legal services fully available.

Recognition of Legal Problems

EC 2-2 The legal professional should help the public to recognize legal problems because such problems may not be self-revealing and often are not timely noticed. Therefore, lawyers should encourage and participate in educational and public relations programs concerning our legal system with particular reference to legal problems that frequently arise.

EC 2-3 Whether a lawyer acts properly in volunteering in-person advice to a non-lawyer to seek legal services depends upon the circumstances. The giving of advice that one should take legal action could well be in fulfillment of the duty of the legal profession to assist the public in recognizing legal problems.

EC 2-4 [Repealed]

EC 2-5 A lawyer who writes or speaks for the purpose of educating members of the public to recognize their legal problems should carefully refrain from giving or appearing to give a general solution applicable to all apparently similar individual problems since slight changes in fact situations may require a material variance in the applicable advice; otherwise, the public may be misled and misadvised. Talks and writings by lawyers for non-lawyers should caution them not to attempt to solve individual problems upon the basis of the information contained therein.

Selection of a Lawyer

EC 2-6 Formerly a potential client usually knew the reputations of local lawyers for competence and integrity and therefore could select a practitioner in whom he or she had confidence. This traditional selection process worked well because it was initiated by the client and the choice was an informed one.

EC 2-7 Changed conditions, however, have seriously restricted the effectiveness of the traditional selection process. Often the reputations of lawyers are not sufficiently known to enable potential users of legal services to make intelligent choices. The law has become increasingly complex and specialized. Few lawyers are willing and competent to deal with every kind of legal matter, and many people have difficulty in determining the competence of lawyers to render different types of legal services. The selection of legal counsel is particularly difficult for transients, persons moving into new areas, persons of limited education or means, and others who have little or no contact with lawyers. Lack of information about the availability of lawyers, the qualifications of particular lawyers, the areas of law in which lawyers accept representation and the cost of legal services impedes the intelligent selection of lawyers.

EC 2-8 Selection of a lawyer should be made on an informed basis. Disclosure of truthful and relevant information about lawyers and their areas of practice should assist in the making of an informed selection. Disinterested and informed advice and recommendation of third parties — relatives, friends, acquaintances, business associates, or other lawyers — may also be helpful.

Lawyer Advertising

EC 2-9 The attorney client relationship is personal and unique and should not be established as a result of pressures and deceptions.

Editors' Note. The following amended version of EC 2-10 was approved by the New York State Bar Association effective November 1, 2001, the same date that new DR's 1-106 and 1-107 and related amendments to the advertising rules took effect.

EC 2-10 A lawyer should ensure that the information contained in any advertising which the lawyer publishes, broadcasts or causes to be published or broadcast is relevant, is disseminated in an objective and understandable fashion, and would facilitate the prospective client's ability to select a lawyer. A lawyer should strive to communicate such information without undue emphasis upon style and advertising stratagems which serve to hinder rather than to facilitate intelligent selection of counsel. Although communications involving puffery and claims that cannot be measured or verified are not specifically referred to in DR 2-101, such communications would be prohibited to the extent that they are false, deceptive or misleading. Special care should be taken to avoid the use of any statement or claim which is false, fraudulent, misleading, deceptive or unfair, or which is violative of any statute or rule of court, in ~~In~~ disclosing information, by advertisements or otherwise, relating to a lawyer's legal or nonlegal education, experience or professional qualifications, the nature or extent of any nonlegal services provided by the lawyer or by an entity owned and controlled by the lawyer, or the existence of contractual relationships between the lawyer or law firm and a nonlegal professional or nonlegal professional service firm, to the extent permitted by DR 1-107, and the nature and extent of services available through those contractual relationships. A lawyer who advertises in a state other than New York should comply with the advertising rules or regulations applicable to lawyers in that state.

EC 2-11 The name under which a lawyer practices may be a factor in the selection process. The use of a trade name or an assumed name could mislead non-lawyers concerning the identity, responsibility, and status of those practicing thereunder. For many years some law firms have used a firm name retaining one or more names of deceased or retired partners and such practice is not improper if the firm is a bona fide successor of a firm in which the deceased or retired person was a member, if the use of the name is authorized by law or by contract, and if the public is not misled thereby. However, the name of a partner who withdraws from a firm but continues to practice law should be omitted from the firm name in order to avoid misleading the public.

EC 2-12 A lawyer occupying a judicial, legislative, or public executive or administrative position who has the right to practice law concurrently may allow his or her name to remain in the name of the firm if the lawyer actively continues to practice law as a member thereof. If the lawyer does not have the right to practice law concurrently, the lawyer's name should be removed from the firm name, and the lawyer should not be identified as a past or present member of the firm; and the lawyer should not hold himself or herself out as being a practicing lawyer.

EC 2-13 In order to avoid the possibility of misleading persons with whom a lawyer deals, a lawyer should be scrupulous in the representation of professional status. A lawyer should not hold himself or herself out as being a partner or associate of a law firm if not one in fact, and thus should not hold himself or herself out as being a partner or associate if the lawyer only shares offices with another lawyer.

EC 2-14 The following, if used in public communications or communications to a prospective client, are likely to be false, deceptive or misleading: (1) a communication that promises the outcome of any legal matter; (2) a communication that states or implies that the lawyer has the ability to influence improperly a court, court officer, governmental agency or government official; (3) a letter or other written communication made to appear as a legal document; (4) the inclusion of names, addresses and telephone numbers as required by DR 2-101(k) in a manner that is too small or too fast for an average viewer to receive the information in a meaningful fashion; (5) the use of dollar signs, the terms "most cash" or "maximum dollars," or like terms that suggest the outcome of the legal matter; (6) the use of an actor to portray the lawyer or another representative of the lawyer's firm; or (7) any other use of an actor or use of a dramatization without meaningful disclosure thereof.

EC 2-15 The legal profession has developed lawyer referral systems designed to aid individuals who are able to pay fees but need assistance in locating lawyers competent to handle their particular problems. Use of a lawyer referral system enables an individual to avoid an uninformed selection of a lawyer because such a system makes possible the employment of competent lawyers who have indicated an interest in the subject matter involved. Lawyers should support the principle of lawyer referral systems and should encourage the evolution of other ethical plans which aid in the selection of qualified counsel.

EC 2-16 Persons unable to pay all or a portion of a reasonable fee should be able to obtain necessary legal services, and lawyers should support and participate in appropriate activities designed to achieve that objective.

Financial Ability to Employ Counsel: Persons Able to Pay Reasonable Fees

EC 2-17 The determination of a proper fee requires consideration of the interests of both client and lawyer. A lawyer should not charge more than a reasonable fee, for excessive cost of legal service would deter nonlawyers from using the legal system to protect their rights and to minimize and resolve disputes. Furthermore, an excessive charge abuses the professional relationship between lawyer and client.

EC 2-18 The determination of the reasonableness of a fee requires consideration of all relevant circumstances, including those stated in the Disciplinary Rules. The fees of a lawyer will vary according to many factors, including the time required, the lawyer's experience, ability, and reputation, the nature of the employment, the responsibility involved and the results obtained. It is a commendable and long-standing tradition of the bar that special consideration is given in the fixing of any fee for services rendered another lawyer or a member of the lawyer's immediate family.

EC 2-19 As soon as feasible after a lawyer has been employed, it is desirable that a clear agreement be reached with the client as to the basis of the fee charges to be made. Such a course will not only prevent later misunderstanding but will also work for good relations between the lawyer and the client. It is usually beneficial to reduce to writing the understanding of the parties regarding the fee, particularly when it is contingent. A lawyer should be mindful that many persons who desire to employ a lawyer may have had little or no experience with fee charges of lawyers, and for this reason lawyers should explain fully to such persons the reasons for the particular fee arrangement proposed.

EC 2-20 Contingent fee arrangements in civil cases have long been commonly accepted in the United States in proceedings to enforce claims. The historical bases of their acceptance are that (1) they often, and in a variety of circumstances, provide the only practical means by which one having a claim against another can economically afford, finance, and obtain the services of a competent lawyer to prosecute a claim, and (2) a successful prosecution of the claim produces a fund out of which the fee can be paid. Although a lawyer generally should decline to accept employment on a contingent fee basis by one who is able to pay a reasonable fixed fee, it is not necessarily improper for a lawyer, where justified by the particular circumstances of a case, to enter into a contingent fee contract in a civil case with any client who, after being fully informed of all relevant factors, desires that arrangement. Because of the human relationships involved and the unique character of the proceedings, contingent fee arrangements in domestic relations matters are rarely justified. In administrative agency proceedings, contingent fee contracts should be governed by the same considerations as in other civil cases. Public policy properly condemns contingent fee arrangements in criminal cases, largely on the ground that legal services in criminal cases do not produce a fund out of which the fee can be paid.

EC 2-21 A lawyer should not accept compensation or anything of value incident to the lawyer's employment or services from one other than the client without the knowledge and consent of the client after full disclosure.

EC 2-22 Without the consent of the client, a lawyer should not associate in a particular matter another lawyer outside the lawyer's firm. A fee may properly be divided between lawyers properly associated if the division is in proportion to the services performed by each lawyer or, by a writing given to the client, each lawyer assumes joint responsibility for the representation and if the total fee is reasonable.

EC 2-23 A lawyer should be zealous in efforts to avoid controversies over fees with clients and should attempt to resolve amicably any differences on the subject. A lawyer should not sue a client for a fee unless necessary to prevent fraud or gross imposition by the client.

Financial Ability to Employ Counsel: Persons Unable to Pay Reasonable Fees

EC 2-24 A person whose financial ability is not sufficient to permit payment of any fee cannot obtain legal services, other than in cases where a contingent fee is appropriate, unless the services are otherwise provided. Even a person of means may be unable to pay a reasonable fee, which is large because of the complexity, novelty, or difficulty of the problem or similar factors.

EC 2-25 A lawyer has an obligation to render public interest and pro bono legal service. A lawyer may fulfill this responsibility by providing professional services at no fee or at a reduced fee to individuals of limited financial means or to public service or charitable groups or organizations, or by participation in programs and organizations specifically designed to increase the availability of legal services. In addition, lawyers or law firms are encouraged to supplement this responsibility through the financial and other support of organizations that provide legal services to persons of limited means.

Acceptance and Retention of Employment

EC 2-26 A lawyer is under no obligation to act as advisor or advocate for every person who may wish to become a client; but in furtherance of the objective of the bar to make legal services fully available, a lawyer should not lightly decline proffered employment. The fulfillment of this objective requires acceptance by a lawyer of a fair share of tendered employment which may be unattractive both to the lawyer and the bar generally.

EC 2-27 History is replete with instances of distinguished sacrificial services by lawyers who have represented unpopular clients and causes. Regardless of personal feelings, a lawyer should not decline representation because a client or a cause is unpopular or community reaction is adverse. A lawyer's representation of a client, including representation by appointment, does not constitute an endorsement of the client's political, economic, social or moral views or activities.

EC 2-28 The personal preference of a lawyer to avoid adversary alignment against judges, other lawyers, public officials or influential members of the community does not justify rejection of tendered employment.

EC 2-29 When a lawyer is appointed by a court or requested by a bar association to undertake representation of a person unable to obtain counsel, whether for financial or other reasons, the lawyer should not seek to be excused from undertaking the representation except for compelling reasons. Compelling reasons do not include such factors as the repugnance of the subject matter of the proceeding, the identity or position of a person involved in the case, the belief of the lawyer that the defendant in a criminal proceeding is guilty, or the belief of the lawyer regarding the merits of the civil case.

EC 2-30 Employment should not be accepted by a lawyer who is unable to render competent service or who knows or it is obvious that the person seeking to employ the lawyer desires to institute or maintain an action merely for the purpose of harassing or maliciously injuring another. Likewise, a lawyer should decline employment if the intensity of personal feelings, as distinguished from a community attitude, may impair effective representation of a prospective client. If a lawyer knows that a client has previously obtained counsel, the lawyer should not accept employment in the matter unless the other counsel approves or withdraws, or the client terminates the prior employment.

EC 2-31 Full availability of legal counsel requires both that persons be able to obtain counsel and that lawyers who undertake representation complete the work involved. Trial counsel for a convicted defendant should continue to represent the client by advising whether to take an appeal and, if the appeal is prosecuted, by representing the client through the appeal unless new counsel is substituted or withdrawal is permitted by the appropriate court.

EC 2-32 A decision by a lawyer to withdraw should be made only on the basis of compelling circumstances and, in a matter pending before a tribunal, the lawyer must comply with the rules of the tribunal regarding withdrawal. A lawyer should not withdraw without considering carefully and endeavoring to minimize the possible adverse effect on the rights of the client and the possibility of prejudice to the client as a result of the withdrawal. Even when withdrawal is justifiable, a lawyer should protect the welfare of the client by giving due notice of the withdrawal, suggesting employment of other counsel, delivering to the client all papers and property to which the client is entitled, cooperating with counsel subsequently employed, and otherwise endeavoring to minimize the possibility of harm. Further, the lawyer should refund to the client any compensation not earned during the employment.

EC 2-33 As part of the legal profession's commitment to the principle that high quality legal services should be available to all, lawyers are encouraged to cooperate with qualified legal assistance organizations providing prepaid legal services. Such participation should at all times be in accordance with the basic tenets of the profession: independence, integrity, competence and devotion to the interests of individual clients. A lawyer so participating should make certain that the relationship with a qualified legal assistance organization in no way interferes with independent, professional representation of the interests of the individual client. A lawyer should avoid situations in which officials of the organization who are not lawyers attempt to direct lawyers concerning the manner in which legal services are performed for individual members and should also avoid situations in which considerations of economy are given undue weight in determining the lawyers employed by an organization or the legal services to be performed for the member or beneficiary, rather than competence and quality of service. A lawyer interested in maintaining the historic traditions of the profession and preserving the function of a lawyer as a trusted and independent advisor to individual members of society should carefully assess such factors when accepting employment by, or otherwise participating in a particular, qualified legal assistance organization and, while so participating, should adhere to the highest professional standards of effort and competence.

Sale of Law Practice

EC 2-34 Lawyers and law firms, particularly sole practitioners, should have the ability to sell law practices, including goodwill, provided certain conditions, designed primarily to protect clients, are satisfied. Where a lawyer is deceased, disabled, or missing, the sale may be effected by the lawyer's personal representative. Although the sale of a law practice should ideally result in the entire practice being transferred to a single buyer, there is no single-buyer requirement.

EC 2-35 Notice to clients of the sale of the practice should be timely provided, preferably as soon as possible after an agreement has been reached by the seller and the buyer, and in any event no later than as soon as practicable after the day of closing. The sale of litigated matters does not relieve the seller of his or her obligation under DR 2-110 regarding withdrawal. To the extent that conflicts of interest preclude the buyer from undertaking the representation of any particular clients of the seller, the seller shall, to the extent reasonably practicable, assist such clients in securing successor counsel. If the client declines to engage successor counsel, and if the seller cannot properly withdraw from the representation under DR 2-110, the seller shall retain responsibility for the representation.

EC 2-36 Information concerning client confidences and secrets should not be disclosed to prospective buyers except to the extent permitted by DR 2-111. To the extent disclosures are made, extreme care should be taken to ensure that client confidences and secrets are protected by all lawyers who become privy to such information in the course of examining the seller's practice for possible purchase. Sellers should consider requiring prospective buyers to execute written confidentiality agreements prior to affording them access to any information concerning client matters.

Improper Political Contributions

EC 2-37 Campaign contributions by lawyers to government officials or candidates for public office who are, or may be, in a position to influence the award of a legal engagement may threaten government integrity by subjecting the recipient to a conflict of interest. Correspondingly, when a lawyer makes a significant contribution to a public official or an election campaign for a candidate for public office and is later engaged by the official to perform legal services for the official's agency, it may appear that the official has been improperly influenced in selecting the lawyer, whether or not this is so. This appearance of influence reflects poorly on the integrity of the legal profession and government as a whole. For these reasons, just as the Code prohibits a lawyer from compensating or giving anything of value to a person or organization to recommend or obtain employment by a client, the Code prohibits a lawyer from making or soliciting a political contribution to any candidate for government office, government official, political campaign committee or political party, if a disinterested person would conclude that the contribution is being made or solicited for the purpose of obtaining or being considered eligible to obtain a government legal engagement. This would be true even in the absence of an understanding between the lawyer and any government official or candidate that special consideration will be given in return for the political contribution or solicitation.

EC 2-38 In determining whether a disinterested person would conclude that a contribution to a candidate for government office, government official, political campaign committee or political party is or has been made for the purpose of obtaining or being considered eligible to obtain a government legal engagement, the factors to be considered include (a) whether legal work awarded to the contributor or solicitor, if any, was awarded pursuant to a process that was insulated from political influence, such as a "Request for Proposal" process, (b) the amount of the contribution or the contributions resulting from a solicitation, (c) whether the contributor or any law firm with which the lawyer is associated has sought or plans to seek government legal work from the official or candidate, (d) whether the contribution or solicitation was made because of an existing personal, family or non-client professional relationship with the government official or candidate, (e) whether prior to the contribution or solicitation in question, the contributor or solicitor had made comparable contributions or had engaged in comparable solicitations on behalf of governmental officials or candidates for public office for which the lawyer or any law firm with which the lawyer is associated did not perform or seek to perform legal work, (f) whether the contributor has made a contribution to the government official's or candidate's opponent(s) during the same campaign period and, if so, the amounts thereof and (g) whether the contributor is eligible to vote in the jurisdiction of the government official or candidate, and if not, whether other factors indicate that the contribution or solicitation was nonetheless made to further a genuinely held political, social or economic belief or interest rather than to obtain a legal engagement.

Editors' Note. When the New York courts approved new DR's 1-106 and 1-107 on July 23, 2001 (effective November 1, 2001), the courts simultaneously amended DR's 2-101, 2-102, and 2-103 to reflect the impact of the two new Disciplinary Rules.

[§1200.6] DR 2-101 Publicity and Advertising

(a) A lawyer on behalf of himself or herself or partners or associates, shall not use or disseminate or participate in the preparation or dissemination of any public communication or communication to a prospective client containing statements or claims that are false, deceptive, or misleading.

(b) (Repealed.)

(c) It is proper to include information, provided its dissemination does not violate the provisions of DR 2-101(a), as to:

(1) legal and nonlegal education, degrees and other scholastic distinctions; dates of admission to any bar; areas of the law in which the lawyer or law firm practices, as authorized by the code of professional responsibility; public offices and teaching positions held; memberships in bar associations or other professional societies or organizations, including offices and committee assignments therein; foreign language fluency;

(2) names of clients regularly represented, provided that the client has given prior written consent;

(3) bank references; credit arrangements accepted; prepaid or group legal services programs in which the attorney or firm participates; nonlegal services provided by the lawyer or by an entity owned and controlled by the lawyer; the existence of contractual relationships between the lawyer or law firm and a nonlegal professional or nonlegal professional service firm, to the extent permitted by DR 1-107 and the nature and extent of services available through those contractual relationships; and

(4) ~~legal~~ fees for initial consultation; contingent fee rates in civil matters when accompanied by a statement disclosing the information required by DR 2-101(l); range of fees for legal and nonlegal services, provided that there be available to the public free of charge a written statement clearly describing the scope of each advertised service; hourly rates; and fixed fees for specified legal and nonlegal services.

(d) Advertising and publicity shall be designed to educate the public to an awareness of legal needs and to provide information relevant to the selection of the most appropriate counsel. Information other than that specifically authorized in DR 2-101(c) that is consistent with these purposes may be disseminated providing that it does not violate any other provisions of this Rule.

(e) A lawyer or law firm advertising any fixed fee for specified legal services shall, at the time of fee publication, have available to the public a written statement clearly describing the scope of each advertised service, which statement shall be delivered to the client at the time of retainer for any such service. Such legal services shall include all those services which are recognized as reasonable and necessary under local custom in the area of practice in the community where the services are performed.

(f) If the advertisement is broadcast, it shall be prerecorded or taped and approved for broadcast by the lawyer, and a recording or videotape of the actual transmission shall be retained by the lawyer for a period of not less than one year following such transmission. All advertisements of legal services that are mailed, or are distributed other than by radio, television, directory, newspaper, magazine or other periodical, by a lawyer or law firm that practices law in this state, shall also be subject to the following provisions:

(1) a copy of each advertisement shall at the time of its initial mailing or distribution be filed with the Departmental Disciplinary Committee of the appropriate judicial department.

(2) Such advertisement shall contain no reference to the fact of filing.

(3) If such advertisement is directed to a predetermined address, a list, containing the names and addresses of all persons to whom the advertisement is being or will thereafter be mailed or distributed, shall

be retained by the lawyer or law firm for a period of not less than one year following the last date of mailing of distribution.

(4) The advertisement filed pursuant to this subdivision shall be open to public inspection.

(5) The requirements of this subdivision shall not apply to such professional cards or other announcements the distribution of which is authorized by DR 2-102(a).

(g) If a lawyer or law firm advertises a range of fees or an hourly rate for services, the lawyer or law firm may not charge more than the fee advertised for such services. If a lawyer or law firm advertises a fixed fee for specified legal services, or perform services described in a fee schedule, the lawyer or law firm may not charge more than the fixed fee for such stated legal service as set forth in the advertisement or fee schedule, unless the client agrees in writing that the services performed or to be performed were not legal services referred to or implied in the advertisement or in the fee schedule and, further, that a different fee arrangement shall apply to the transaction.

(h) Unless otherwise specified in the advertisement, if a lawyer publishes any fee information authorized under this Disciplinary Rule in a publication which is published more frequently than once per month, the lawyer shall be bound by any representation made therein for a period of not less than 30 days after such publication. If a lawyer publishes any fee information authorized under this Rule in a publication which is published once per month or less frequently, the lawyer shall be bound by any representation made therein until the publication of the succeeding issue. If a lawyer publishes any fee information authorized under this Rule in a publication which has no fixed date for publication of a succeeding issue, the lawyer shall be bound by any representation made therein for a reasonable period of time after publication, but in no event less than 90 days.

(i) Unless otherwise specified, if a lawyer broadcasts any fee information authorized under this Rule, the lawyer shall be bound by any representation made therein for a period of not less than 30 days after such broadcast.

(j) A lawyer shall not compensate or give any thing of value to representatives of the press, radio, television or other communication medium in anticipation of or in return for professional publicity in a news item.

(k) All advertisements of legal services shall include the name, office address and telephone number of the attorney or law firm whose services are being offered.

(l) A lawyer or law firm advertising any contingent fee rates shall, at the time of the fee publication, disclose:

(1) Whether percentages are computed before or after deduction of costs, disbursements and other expenses of litigation;

(2) That, in the event there is no recovery, the client shall remain liable for the expenses of litigation, including court costs and disbursements.

[§1200.7] DR 2-102 Professional Notices, Letterheads, and Signs

(a) A lawyer or law firm may use professional cards, professional announcement cards, office signs, letterheads or similar professional notices or devices, provided the same do not violate any statute or court rule, and are in accordance with DR 2-101, including the following:

(1) A professional card of a lawyer identifying the lawyer by name and as a lawyer, and giving addresses, telephone numbers, the name of the law firm, and any information permitted under DR 2-101(c), DR 2-101(d), or DR 2-105. A professional card of a law firm may also give the names of members and associates.

(2) A professional announcement card stating new or changed associations or addresses, change of firm name, or similar matters pertaining to the professional offices of a lawyer or law firm or of any nonlegal business conducted by the lawyer or law firm pursuant to DR 1-106. It may state biographical data, the names of members of the firm and associates and the names and dates of predecessor firms in a continuing line of succession. It may state the nature of the legal practice if permitted under DR 2-105 of this Part.

(3) A sign in or near the office and in the building directory identifying the law office and any nonlegal business conducted by the lawyer or law firm pursuant to DR 1-106. The sign may state the nature of the legal practice if permitted under DR 2-105 of this Part.

(4) The letterhead identifying the lawyer by name and as a lawyer, and giving addresses, telephone numbers, the name of the law firm, associates and any information permitted under DR 2-101(c), DR 2-101(d), or DR 2-105 of this Part. A letterhead of a law firm may also give the names of members and associates, and names and dates relating to deceased and retired members. A lawyer or law firm may be designated "Of Counsel" on a letterhead if there is a continuing relationship with a lawyer or law firm, other than as a partner or associate. A lawyer or law firm may be designated as "General Counsel" or by similar professional reference on stationery of a client if the lawyer or the firm denotes a substantial amount of professional time in the representation of that client. The letterhead of a law firm may give the names and dates of predecessor firms in a continuing line of succession.

(b) A lawyer in private practice shall not practice under a trade name, a name that is misleading as to the identity of the lawyer or lawyers practicing under such name, or a firm name containing names other than those of one or more of the lawyers in the firm, except that the name of a professional corporation shall contain "P.C." or such symbols permitted by law, the name of a limited liability company or partnership shall contain "L.L.C.," "L.L.P." or such symbols permitted by law, and, if otherwise lawful, a firm may use as, or continue to include in its name the name or names of one or more deceased or retired members of the firm or of a predecessor firm in a continuing line of succession. Such terms as "legal clinic," "legal aid," "legal service office," "legal assistance office," "defender office" and the like, may be used only by qualified legal assistance organizations, except that the term legal clinic may be used by any lawyer or law firm provided the name or a participating lawyer or firm is incorporated therein. A lawyer or law firm may not include the name of a nonlawyer in its firm name, nor may a lawyer or law firm that has a contractual relationship with a nonlegal professional or nonlegal professional service firm pursuant to DR 1-107 to provide legal and other professional services on a systematic and continuing basis include in its firm name the name of the nonlegal professional service firm or any individual nonlegal professional affiliated therewith. A lawyer who assumes a judicial, legislative or public executive or administrative post or office shall not permit his or her name to remain in the name of a law firm or to be used in professional notices of the firm during any significant period in which the lawyer is not actively and regularly practicing law as a member of the firm and, during such period, other members of the firm shall not use the lawyer's name in the firm name or in professional notices of the firm.

(c) A lawyer shall not hold himself or herself out as having a partnership with one or more other lawyers unless they are in fact partners.

(d) A partnership shall not be formed or continued between or among lawyers licensed in different jurisdictions unless all enumerations of the members and associates of the firm on its letterhead and in other permissible listings make clear the jurisdictional limitations on those members and associates of the firm not licensed to practice in all listed jurisdictions; however, the same firm name may be used in each jurisdiction.

[§1200.8] DR 2-103 Solicitation and Recommendation of Professional Employment

(a) A lawyer shall not solicit professional employment from a prospective client:

(1) By in-person or telephone contact, except that a lawyer may solicit professional employment from a close friend, relative, former client or current client:

(2) By written or recorded communication if:

(i) The communication or contact violates DR 2-101(a);

(ii) The prospective client has made known to the lawyer a desire not to be solicited by the lawyer;

(iii) The solicitation involves coercion, duress or harassment;

(iv) The lawyer knows or reasonably should know that the age or the physical, emotional or mental state of the recipient make it unlikely that the recipient will be able to exercise reasonable judgment in retaining an attorney; or

(v) The lawyer intends or expects, but does not disclose, that the legal services necessary to handle the matter competently will be performed primarily by another lawyer who is not affiliated with the soliciting lawyer as a partner, associate or of counsel.

(b) A lawyer shall not compensate or give anything of value to a person or organization to recommend or obtain employment by a client, or as a reward for having made a recommendation resulting in employment by a client, except that:

(1) A lawyer or law firm may refer clients to a nonlegal professional or nonlegal professional service firm pursuant to a contractual relationship with such nonlegal professional or nonlegal professional service firm to provide legal and other professional services on a systematic and continuing basis as permitted by DR 1-107, provided however that such referral shall not otherwise include any monetary or other tangible consideration or reward for such, or the sharing of legal fees; or

(2) A lawyer may pay the usual and reasonable fees or dues charged by a qualified legal assistance organization or referral fees to another lawyer as permitted by DR 2-107 of this Part.

(c) No written solicitation shall be sent by a method that requires that recipient to travel to a location other than that at which the recipient ordinarily receives business or personal mail.

(d) A lawyer or the lawyer's partner or associate or any other affiliated lawyer may be recommended, employed or paid by, or may cooperate with one of the following offices or organizations which promote the use of the lawyer's services or those of a partner or associate or any other affiliated lawyer, or request one of the following offices or organizations to recommend or promote the use of the lawyer's services or those of the lawyer's partner or associate, or any other affiliated lawyer as a private practitioner, if there is no interference with the exercise of independent professional judgment on behalf of the client.

(1) A legal aid office or public defender office:

(i) Operated or sponsored by a duly accredited law school;

(ii) Operated or sponsored by a bona fide, non-profit community organization;

(iii) Operated or sponsored by a governmental agency; or

(iv) Operated, sponsored, or approved by a bar association;

(2) A military legal assistance office;

(3) A lawyer referral service operated, sponsored or approved by a bar association or authorized by law or court rule;

(4) Any bona fide organization which recommends, furnishes or pays for legal services to its members or beneficiaries provided the following conditions are satisfied:

(i) Neither the lawyer, [nor] the lawyer's partner, nor associate, nor any other affiliated lawyer nor any non-lawyer, shall have initiated or promoted such organization for the primary purpose of providing financial or other benefit to such lawyer, partner, associate or affiliated lawyer.

(ii) Such organization is not operated for the purpose of procuring legal work or financial benefit for any lawyer as a private practitioner outside of the legal service program of the organization.

(iii) The member or beneficiary to whom the legal services are furnished, and not such organization, is recognized as the client of the lawyer in the matter.

(iv) The legal service plan of such organization provides appropriate relief for any member or beneficiary who asserts a claim that representation by counsel furnished, selected or approved by the organization for the particular matter involved would be unethical, improper or inadequate under the circumstances of the matter involved; and the plan provides an appropriate procedure for seeking such relief.

(v) The lawyer does not know or have cause to know that such organization is in violation of applicable laws, rules of court or other legal requirements that govern its legal service operations.

(vi) Such organization has filed with the appropriate disciplinary authority, to the extent required by such authority, at least annually a report with respect to its legal service plan, if any, showing its terms, its schedule of benefits, its subscription charges, agreements with counsel and financial results of its legal service activities or, if it has failed to do so, the lawyer does not know or have cause to know of such failure.

(e) A lawyer shall not accept employment when the lawyer knows or it is obvious that the person who seeks services does so as a result of conduct prohibited under this Disciplinary Rule.

(f) Advertising not proscribed under DR 2-101 shall not be deemed in violation of any provision of this Disciplinary Rule.

[§1200.9] DR 2-104 Suggestion of Need of Legal Services

(a) (Repealed.)

(b) (Repealed.)

(c) A lawyer may accept employment which results from participation in activities designed to educate the public to recognize legal problems, to make intelligent selection of counsel or to utilize available legal services.

(d) A lawyer who is recommended, furnished or paid by a qualified legal assistance organization may represent a member or beneficiary thereof, to the extent and under the conditions prescribed therein.

(e) Without affecting the right to accept employment, a lawyer may speak publicly or write for publication on legal topics so long as the lawyer does not undertake to give individual advice.

(f) If success in asserting rights or defenses of a client in litigation in the nature of a class action is dependent upon the joinder of others, a lawyer may accept employment from those contacted for the purpose of obtaining their joinder, provided such acceptance does not violate any statute or court rule in the judicial department in which the lawyer practices.

[§1200.10] DR 2-105 Identification of Practice and Specialty

(a) A lawyer or law firm may publicly identify one or more areas of law in which the lawyer or the law firm practices, or may state that the practice of the lawyer or law firm is limited to one or more areas of law, provided that the lawyer or law firm shall not state that the lawyer or law firm is a specialist or specializes in a particular field of law, except as provided in DR 2-105(b) or (c).

(b) A lawyer admitted to engage in patent practice before the United States Patent and Trademark Office may use the designation "Patent Attorney" or a substantially similar designation.

(c) A lawyer may state that the lawyer has been recognized or certified as a specialist only as follows:

(1) A lawyer who is certified as a specialist in a particular area of law or law practice by a private organization approved for that purpose by the American Bar Association may state the fact of certification if, in conjunction therewith, the certifying organization is identified and the following statement is prominently made: "The [name of the private certifying organization] is not affiliated with any governmental authority. Certification is not a requirement for the practice of law in the State of New York and does not necessarily indicate greater competence than other attorneys experienced in this field of law."

(2) A lawyer who is certified as a specialist in a particular area of law or law practice by the authority having jurisdiction over specialization under the laws of another state or territory may state the fact of certification if, in conjunction therewith, the certifying state or territory is identified and the following statement is prominently made: "Certification granted by the [identify state or territory] is not recognized by any governmental authority within the State of New York.

Certification is not a requirement for the practice of law in the State of New York and does not necessarily indicate greater competence than other attorneys experienced in this field of law."

[§1200.11] DR 2-106 Fee for Legal Services

(a) A lawyer shall not enter into an agreement for, charge or collect an illegal or excessive fee.

(b) A fee is excessive when, after a review of the facts, a lawyer of ordinary prudence would be left with a definite and firm conviction that the fee is in excess of a reasonable fee. Factors to be considered as guides in determining the reasonableness of a fee may include the following:

(1) The time and labor required, the novelty and difficulty of the questions involved and the skill requisite to perform the legal service properly.

(2) The likelihood, if apparent or made known to the client, that the acceptance of the particular employment will preclude other employment by the lawyer.

(3) The fee customarily charged in the locality for similar legal services.

(4) The amount involved and the results obtained.

(5) The time limitations imposed by the client or by circumstances.

(6) The nature and length of the professional relationship with the client.

(7) The experience, reputation and ability of the lawyer or lawyers performing the services.

(8) Whether the fee is fixed or contingent.

(c) A lawyer shall not enter into an arrangement for, charge or collect:

(1) A contingent fee for representing a defendant in a criminal case.

(2) Any fee in a domestic relations matter:

(i) The payment or amount of which is contingent upon the securing of a divorce or in any way determined by reference to the amount of maintenance, support, equitable distribution, or property settlement;

(ii) Unless a written retainer agreement is signed by the lawyer and client setting forth in plain language the nature of the relationship and the details of the fee arrangement. A lawyer shall not include in the written retainer agreement a nonrefundable fee clause; or

(iii) Based on a security interest, confession of judgment or other lien, without prior notice to the client in a signed retainer agreement and approval from a tribunal after notice to the adversary. A lawyer shall not foreclose on a mortgage placed on the marital residence while the spouse who consents to the mortgage remains the titleholder and the residence remains the spouse's primary residence.

(3) A fee proscribed by law or rule of court.

(d) Promptly after a lawyer has been employed in a contingent fee matter, the lawyer shall provide the client with a writing stating the method by which the fee is to be determined, including the percentage or percentages that shall accrue to the lawyer in the event of settlement, trial or appeal, litigation and other expenses to be deducted from the recovery and whether such expenses are to be deducted before or, if not prohibited by statute or court rule, after the contingent fee is calculated. Upon conclusion of a contingent fee matter, the lawyer shall provide the client with a written statement stating the outcome of the matter, and if there is a recovery, showing the remittance to the client and the method of its determination.

(e) Where representation is in a civil matter, a lawyer shall resolve fee disputes by arbitration at the election of the client pursuant to a fee arbitration program established by the Chief Administrator of the Courts and approved by the justices of the Appellate Divisions.

(f) In domestic relation matters, a lawyer shall provide a prospective client with a statement of client's rights and responsibilities at the initial conference and prior to the signing of a written retainer agreement.

[§1200.12] DR 2-107 Division of Fees Among Lawyers

(a) A lawyer shall not divide a fee for legal services with another lawyer who is not a partner in or associate of the lawyer's law firm unless:

(1) The client consents to employment of the other lawyer after a full disclosure that a division of fees will be made.

(2) The division is in proportion to the services performed by each lawyer or, by a writing given the client, each lawyer assumes joint responsibility for the representation.

(3) The total fee of the lawyers does not exceed reasonable compensation for all legal services they rendered the client.

(b) This Disciplinary Rule does not prohibit payment to a former partner or associate pursuant to a separation or retirement agreement.

[§1200.13] DR 2-108 Agreements Restricting the Practice of a Lawyer

(a) A lawyer shall not be a party to or participate in a partnership or employment agreement with another lawyer that restricts the right of a lawyer to practice law after the termination of a relationship created by the agreement, except as a condition to payment of retirement benefits.

(b) In connection with the settlement of a controversy or suit, a lawyer shall not enter into an agreement that restricts the right of a lawyer to practice law.

[§1200.14] DR 2-109 Obligation to Decline Employment

(a) A lawyer shall not accept employment on behalf of a person if the lawyer knows or it is obvious that such person wishes to:

(1) Bring a legal action, conduct a defense, or assert a position in litigation, or otherwise have steps taken for such person, merely for the purpose of harassing or maliciously injuring any person.

(2) Present a claim or defense in litigation that is not warranted under existing law, unless it can be supported by a good faith argument for an extension, modification, or reversal of existing law.

[§1200.15] DR 2-110 Withdrawal from Employment

(a) *In general.*

(1) If permission for withdrawal from employment is required by the rules of a tribunal, a lawyer shall not withdraw from employment in a proceeding before that tribunal without its permission.

(2) Even when withdrawal is otherwise permitted or required under DR 2-110 (a)(1), (b) or (c), a lawyer shall not withdraw from employment until the lawyer has taken steps to the extent reasonably practicable to avoid foreseeable prejudice to the rights of the client, including giving due notice to the client, allowing time for employment of other counsel, delivering to the client all papers and property to which the client is entitled and complying with applicable laws and rules.

(3) A lawyer who withdraws from employment shall refund promptly any part of a fee paid in advance that has not been earned.

(b) *Mandatory withdrawal.* A lawyer representing a client before a tribunal, with its permission if required by its rules, shall withdraw from employment, and a lawyer representing a client in other matters shall withdraw from employment, if:

(1) The lawyer knows or it is obvious that the client is bringing the legal action, conducting the defense, or asserting a position in the litigation, or is otherwise having steps taken, merely for the purpose of harassing or maliciously injuring any person.

(2) The lawyer knows or it is obvious that continued employment will result in violation of a Disciplinary Rule.

(3) The lawyer's mental or physical condition renders it unreasonably difficult to carry out the employment effectively.

(4) The lawyer is discharged by his or her client.

(c) *Permissive withdrawal.* Except as stated in DR 2-110(a), a lawyer may withdraw from representing a client if withdrawal can be accomplished without material adverse effect on the interests of the client, or if:

(1) The client:

(i) Insists upon presenting a claim or defense that is not warranted under existing law and cannot be supported by good faith argument for an extension, modification, or reversal of existing law.

(ii) Persists in a course of action involving the lawyer's services that the lawyer reasonably believes is criminal or fraudulent.

(iii) Insists that the lawyer pursue a course of conduct which is illegal or prohibited under the Disciplinary Rules.

(iv) By other conduct renders it unreasonably difficult for the lawyer to carry out employment effectively.

(v) Insists, in a matter not pending before a tribunal, that the lawyer engage in conduct which is contrary to the judgment and advice of the lawyer but not prohibited under the Disciplinary Rules.

(vi) Deliberately disregards an agreement or obligation to the lawyer as to expenses or fees.

(vii) Has used the lawyer's services to perpetrate a crime or fraud.

(2) The lawyer's continued employment is likely to result in a violation of a Disciplinary Rule.

(3) The lawyer's inability to work with co-counsel indicates that the best interests of the client likely will be served by withdrawal.

(4) The lawyer's mental or physical condition renders it difficult for the lawyer to carry out the employment effectively.

(5) The lawyer's client knowingly and freely assents to termination of the employment.

(6) The lawyer believes in good faith, in a proceeding pending before a tribunal, that the tribunal will find the existence of other good cause for withdrawal.

[§1200.15-a] DR 2-111 Sale of Law Practice

(a) A lawyer retiring from a private practice of law, a law firm one or more members of which are retiring from the private practice of law with the firm, or the personal representative of a deceased, disabled or missing lawyer, may sell a law practice, including goodwill, to one or more lawyers or law firms, who may purchase the practice. The seller and the buyer may agree on reasonable restrictions on the seller's private practice of law, notwithstanding any other provision of this Code. Retirement shall include the cessation of the private practice of law in the geographic area, that is, the county and city and any county or city contiguous thereto, in which the practice to be sold has been conducted.

(b) *Confidences and Secrets.*

(1) With respect to each matter subject to the contemplated sale, the seller may provide prospective buyers with any information not protected as a confidence or secret under DR 4-101.

(2) Notwithstanding DR 4-101 the seller may provide the prospective buyer with information as to individual clients:

(i) concerning the identity of the client, except as provided in DR 2-111(b)(6);

(ii) concerning the status and general nature of the matter;

(iii) available in public court files; and

(iv) concerning the financial terms of the attorney-client relationship and the payment status of the client's account.

(3) Prior to making any disclosure of confidences or secrets that may be permitted under DR 2-111(b)(2) the seller shall provide the prospective buyer with information regarding the matters involved in the proposed sale sufficient to enable the prospective buyer to determine whether any conflicts of interest exist. Where sufficient information cannot be disclosed without revealing client confidences or secrets, the seller may make the disclosures necessary for the prospective buyer to determine whether any conflict of interest exists, subject to DR 2-111(b)(6). If the prospective buyer determines that conflicts of interest exist prior to reviewing the information, or determines during the course of review that a conflict of interest exists, the prospective buyer shall not review or continue to review the information unless seller shall have obtained the consent of the client in accordance with DR 4-101(c)(1).

(4) Prospective buyers shall maintain the confidentiality of and shall not use any client information received in connection with the proposed sale in the same manner and to the same extent as if the prospective buyers represented the client.

(5) Absent the consent of the client after full disclosure, a seller shall not provide a prospective buyer with information if doing so would cause a violation of the attorney-client privilege.

(6) If the seller has reason to believe that the identity of the client or the fact of the representation itself constitutes a confidence or secret in the circumstances, the seller may not provide such information to a prospective buyer without first advising the client of the identity of the prospective buyer and obtaining the client's consent to the proposed disclosure.

(c) Written notice of the sale shall be given jointly by the seller and the buyer to each of the seller's clients and shall include information regarding:

(1) The client's right to retain other counsel or to take possession of the file;

(2) The fact that the client's consent to the transfer of the client's file or matter to the buyer will be presumed if the client does not take any action or otherwise object within 90 days of the sending of the notice, subject to any court rule or statute requiring express approval by the client or a court;

(3) The fact that agreements between the seller and the seller's clients as to fees will be honored by the buyer;

(4) Proposed fee increases, if any, permitted under DR 2-111(e) and

(5) The identity and background of the buyer or buyers, including principal office address, bar admissions, number of years in practice in the state, whether the buyer has ever been disciplined for professional misconduct or convicted of a crime, and whether the buyer currently intends to re-sell the practice.

(d) When the buyer's representation of a client of the seller would give rise to a waivable conflict of interest, the buyer shall not undertake such representation unless the necessary waiver or waivers have been obtained in writing.

(e) The fee charged a client by the buyer shall not be increased by reason of the sale, unless permitted by a retainer agreement with the client or otherwise specifically agreed to by the client.

CANON 3. A LAWYER SHOULD ASSIST IN PREVENTING THE UNAUTHORIZED PRACTICE OF LAW

EC 3-1 The prohibition against the practice of law by a non-lawyer is grounded in the need of the public for integrity and competence of those who undertake to render legal services. Because of the fiduciary and personal character of the lawyer-client relationship and the inherently complex nature of our legal system, the public can better be assured of the requisite responsibility and competence if the practice of law is confined to those who are subject to the requirements and regulations imposed upon members of the legal profession.

EC 3-2 The sensitive variations in the considerations that bear on legal determinations often make it difficult even for a lawyer to exercise appropriate professional judgment, and it is therefore essential that the personal nature of the relationship of client and lawyer be preserved. Competent professional judgment is the product of a trained familiarity with law and legal processes, a disciplined, analytical approach to legal problems, and a firm ethical commitment.

EC 3-3 A non-lawyer who undertakes to handle legal matter is not governed as to integrity or legal competence by the same rules that govern the conduct of a lawyer. A lawyer is not only subject to that regulation but also is committed to high standards of ethical conduct. The public interest is best served in legal matters by a regulated profession committed to such standards. The Disciplinary Rules protect the public in that they prohibit a lawyer from seeking employment by improper overtures, from acting in cases of divided loyalties, and from submitting to the control of others in the exercise of judgment. Moreover, a person who entrusts legal matters to a lawyer is protected by the attorney-client privilege and by the duty of the lawyer to hold inviolate the confidences and secrets of the client.

EC 3-4 A person who seeks legal services often is not in a position to judge whether he or she will receive proper professional attention. The entrustment of a legal matter may well involve the confidences, the reputation, the property, the freedom, or even the life of the client. Proper protection of members of the public demands that no person be permitted to act in the confidential and demanding capacity of a lawyer without being subject to the regulations of the legal profession.

EC 3-5 It is neither necessary nor desirable to attempt the formulation of a single, specific definition of what constitutes the practice of law. Functionally, the practice of law relates to the rendition of services for others that call for the professional judgment of a lawyer. The essence of the professional judgment of the lawyer is the educated ability to relate the general body and philosophy of law to a specific legal problem of a client; and thus, the public interest will be better served if only lawyers are permitted to act in matters involving professional judgment. Where this professional judgment is not involved, non-lawyers, such as court clerks, police officers, abstracters, and many governmental employees, may engage in occupations that require special knowledge of law in certain areas. But the services of a lawyer are essential in the public interest whenever the exercise of professional legal judgment is required.

EC 3-6 A lawyer often delegates tasks to clerks, secretaries, and other lay persons. Such delegation is proper if the lawyer maintains a direct relationship with the client, supervises the delegated work, and has complete professional responsibility for the work product. This delegation enables a lawyer to render legal service more economically and efficiently.

EC 3-7 The prohibition against a non-lawyer practicing law does not prevent a non-lawyer from representing himself or herself, for then only that person is ordinarily exposed to possible injury. The purpose of the legal profession is to make educated legal representation available to the public; but anyone who does not wish to take advantage of such representation is not required to do so. Even so, the legal professional should help members of the public to recognize legal problems and to understand why it may be unwise for them to act for themselves in matters having legal consequences.

EC 3-8 Since a lawyer should not aid or encourage a non-lawyer to practice law, the lawyer should not practice law in association with a non-lawyer or otherwise share legal fees with a non-lawyer. This does not mean, however, that the pecuniary value of the interest of a deceased lawyer in a firm or practice may not be paid to the lawyer's estate or specified persons such as the lawyer's spouse or heirs. In like manner, profit-sharing compensation or retirement plans of a lawyer or law firm which include non-lawyer office employees are not improper. These limited exceptions to the rule against sharing legal fees with non-lawyers are permissible since they do not aid or encourage non-lawyers to practice law.

EC 3-9 Regulation of the practice of law is accomplished principally by the respective states. Authority to engage in the practice of law conferred in any jurisdiction is not per se a grant of the right to practice elsewhere, and it is improper for a lawyer to engage in practice where not permitted by law or by court order to do so. However, the demands of business and the mobility of our society pose distinct problems in the regulation of the practice of law by the states. In furtherance of the public interest, the legal profession should discourage regulation that unreasonably imposes territorial limitations upon the right of a lawyer to handle the legal affairs of a client or upon the opportunity of a client to obtain the services of a lawyer of the client's choice in all matters including the presentation of a contested matter in a tribunal before which the lawyer is not permanently admitted to practice.

[§1200.16] DR 3-101 Aiding Unauthorized Practice of Law

(a) A lawyer shall not aid a non-lawyer in the unauthorized practice of law.

(b) A lawyer shall not practice law in a jurisdiction where to do so would be in violation of regulations of the profession in that jurisdiction.

[§1200.17] DR 3-102 Dividing Legal Fees with a Non-lawyer

(a) A lawyer or law firm shall not share legal fees with a non-lawyer, except that:

(1) An agreement by a lawyer with his or her firm, partner, or associate may provide for the payment of money, over a reasonable period of time after the lawyer's death, to the lawyer's estate or to one or more specified persons.

(2) A lawyer who undertakes to complete unfinished legal business of a deceased lawyer may pay to the estate of the deceased lawyer that proportion of the total compensation which fairly represents the services rendered by the deceased lawyer.

(3) A lawyer or law firm may compensate a non-lawyer employee, or include a non-lawyer employee in a retirement plan, based in whole or in part on a profit-sharing arrangement.

[§1200.18] DR 3-103 Forming a Partnership with a Non-lawyer

(a) A lawyer shall not form a partnership with a non-lawyer if any of the activities of the partnership consist of the practice of law.

CANON 4. A LAWYER SHOULD PRESERVE THE CONFIDENCES AND SECRETS OF A CLIENT

EC 4-1 Both the fiduciary relationship existing between lawyer and client and the proper function of the legal system require the preservation by the lawyer of confidences and secrets of one who has employed or sought to employ the lawyer. A client must feel free to discuss anything with his or her lawyer and a lawyer must be equally free to obtain information beyond that volunteered by the client. A lawyer should be fully informed of all the facts of the matter being handled in order for the client to obtain the full advantage of our legal system. It is for the lawyer in the exercise of the independent professional judgment to separate the relevant and important from the irrelevant and unimportant. The observance of the ethical obligation of a lawyer to hold inviolate the confidences and secrets of a client not only facilitates the full development of facts essential to proper representation of the client but also encourages non-lawyers to seek early legal assistance.

EC 4-2 The obligation to protect confidences and secrets obviously does not preclude a lawyer from revealing information when the client consents after full disclosure, when necessary to perform the lawyer's professional employment, when permitted by a Disciplinary Rule, or when required by law. Unless the client otherwise directs, a lawyer may disclose the affairs of the client to partners or associates of his or her firm. It is a matter of common knowledge that the normal operation of a law office exposes confidential professional information to non-lawyer employees of the office, particularly secretaries and those having access to the files; and this obligates a lawyer to exercise care in selecting and training employees so that the sanctity of all confidences and secrets of clients may be preserved. If the obligation extends to two or more clients as to the same information, a lawyer should obtain the permission of all before revealing the information. A lawyer must always be sensitive to the rights and wishes of the client and act scrupulously in the making of decisions which may involve the disclosure of information obtained in the professional relationship. Thus, in the absence of consent of the client after full disclosure, a lawyer should not associate another lawyer in the handling of a matter, nor should the lawyer, in the absence of consent, seek counsel from another lawyer if there is a reasonable possibility that the identity of the client or the client's confidences or secrets would be revealed to such lawyer. Both social amenities and professional duty should cause a lawyer to shun indiscreet conversations concerning clients.

EC 4-3 Unless the client otherwise directs, it is not improper for a lawyer to give limited information to an outside agency necessary for statistical, bookkeeping, accounting, data processing, banking, printing, or other legitimate purposes, provided the lawyer exercises due care in the selection of the agency and warns the agency that the information must be kept confidential.

EC 4-4 The attorney-client privilege is more limited than the ethical obligation of a lawyer to guard the confidences and secrets of the client. This ethical precept, unlike the evidentiary privilege, exists without regard to the nature or source of information or the fact that others share the knowledge. A lawyer should endeavor to act in a manner which preserves the evidentiary privilege; for example, the lawyer should avoid professional discussions in the presence of a person to whom the privilege does not extend. A lawyer owes an obligation to advise the client of the attorney-client privilege and timely to assert the privilege unless it is waived by the client.

EC 4-5 A lawyer should not use information acquired in the course of the representation of a client to the disadvantage of the client and a lawyer should not use, except with the consent of the client after full disclosure, such information for the lawyer's own purposes. Likewise, a lawyer should be diligent in his or her efforts to prevent the misuse of such information by employees and associates. Care should be exercised by a lawyer to prevent the disclosure of the confidences and secrets of one client to another, and no employment should be accepted that might require such disclosure.

EC 4-6 The obligation to protect confidences and secrets of a client continues after the termination of employment. For example, a lawyer might provide for the personal papers of the client to be returned to the client and for the papers of the lawyer to be delivered to another lawyer or to be destroyed. In determining the method of disposition, the instructions and wishes of the client should be a dominant consideration. DR 2-111 sets forth the procedures for protecting confidences and secrets of clients in connection with the sale of a law practice.

EC 4-7 The lawyer's exercise of discretion to disclose confidences and secrets requires consideration of a wide range of factors and should not be subject to reexamination. A lawyer is afforded the professional discretion to reveal the intention of a client to commit a crime and the information necessary to prevent the crime and cannot be subjected to discipline either for revealing or not revealing such intention or information. In exercising this discretion, however, the lawyer should consider such factors as the seriousness of the potential injury to others if the prospective crime is committed, the likelihood that it will be committed and its imminence, the apparent absence of any other feasible way in which the potential injury can be prevented, the extent to which the client may have attempted to involve the lawyer in the prospective crime, the circumstances under which the lawyer acquired the information of the client's intent, and any other possibly aggravating or extenuating circumstances. In any case, a disclosure adverse to the client's interest should be no greater than the lawyer reasonably believes necessary to the purpose.

[§1200.19] DR 4-101 Preservation of Confidences and Secrets of a Client

(a) "Confidence" refers to information protected by the attorney-client privilege under applicable law, and "secret" refers to other information gained in the professional relationship that the client has requested be held inviolate or the disclosure of which would be embarrassing or would be likely to be detrimental to the client.

(b) Except when permitted under DR 4-101(c) a lawyer shall not knowingly:

(1) Reveal a confidence or secret of a client.

(2) Use a confidence or secret of a client to the disadvantage of the client.

(3) Use a confidence or secret of a client for the advantage of the lawyer or of a third person, unless the client consents after full disclosure.

(c) A lawyer may reveal:

(1) Confidences or secrets with the consent of the client or clients affected, but only after a full disclosure to them.

(2) Confidences or secrets when permitted under Disciplinary Rules or required by law or court order.

(3) The intention of a client to commit a crime and the information necessary to prevent the crime.

(4) Confidences or secrets necessary to establish or collect the lawyer's fee or to defend the lawyer or his or her employees or associates against an accusation of wrongful conduct.

(5) Confidences or secrets to the extent implicit in withdrawing a written or oral opinion or representation previously given by the lawyer and believed by the lawyer still to be relied upon by a third person where the lawyer has discovered that the opinion or representation was based on materially inaccurate information or is being used to further a crime or fraud.

(d) A lawyer shall exercise reasonable care to prevent his or her employees, associates, and others whose services are utilized by the lawyer from disclosing or using confidences or secrets of a client, except that a lawyer may reveal the information allowed by subdivision (c) of this section through an employee.

CANON 5. A LAWYER SHOULD EXERCISE INDEPENDENT PROFESSIONAL JUDGMENT ON BEHALF OF A CLIENT

EC 5-1 The professional judgment of a lawyer should be exercised, within the bounds of the law, solely for the benefit of the client and free of compromising influences and loyalties. Neither the lawyer's personal interests, the interests of other clients, nor the desires of third persons should be permitted to dilute the lawyer's loyalty to the client.

Interests of a Lawyer That May Affect the Lawyer's Judgment

EC 5-2 A lawyer should not accept proffered employment if the lawyer's personal interests or desires will, or there is reasonable probability that they will, affect adversely the advice to be given or services to be rendered the prospective client. After accepting employment, a lawyer carefully should refrain from acquiring a property right or assuming a position that would tend to make his or her judgment less protective of the interests of the client.

EC 5-3 The self-interest of a lawyer resulting from ownership of property in which the client also has an interest or which may affect property of the client may interfere with the exercise of free judgment on behalf of the client. If such interference would occur with respect to a prospective client, a lawyer should decline proffered employment. After accepting employment, a lawyer should not acquire property rights that would adversely affect the lawyer's professional judgment in the representation of the client. Even if the property interests of a lawyer do not presently interfere with the exercise of independent judgment, but the likelihood of interference can be reasonably foreseen by the lawyer, the lawyer should explain the situation to the client and should decline employment or withdraw unless after full disclosure the client consents, preferably in writing, to the continuance of the relationship. A lawyer should not seek to persuade a client to permit the lawyer to invest in an undertaking of the client nor make improper use of a professional relationship to influence the client to invest in an enterprise in which the lawyer is interested.

EC 5-4 As a general principle, all transactions between client and lawyer should be fair and reasonable to the client. In such transactions, a review by independent counsel on behalf of the client is often advisable. Furthermore, a lawyer may not exploit information relating to the representation to the client's disadvantage. For example, a lawyer who has learned that the client is investing in specific real estate may not, without the client's consent, seek to acquire nearby property where doing so would adversely affect the client's plan for investment. A lawyer may, however, enter into standard commercial transactions with a client for products and services that the client generally markets to others, for example, banking or brokerage services, medical services, products manufactured or distributed by the client, and utilities services. In such transactions, the lawyer has no advantage in dealing with the client and restrictions are unnecessary and impracticable.

If, in the course of the representation of a client, a lawyer is permitted to receive from the client a beneficial ownership in literary or media rights relating to the subject matter of the employment, the lawyer may be tempted to subordinate the interests of the client to the lawyer's own anticipated pecuniary gain. For example, a lawyer in a criminal case who obtains from the client television, radio, motion picture, newspaper, magazine, book, or other literary or media rights with respect to the case may be influenced, consciously or unconsciously, to a course of conduct that will enhance the value of the literary or media rights to the prejudice of the client. To prevent these potentially differing interests, such arrangements should be scrupulously avoided prior to the termination of all aspects of the matter giving rise to the employment, even though the employment has previously ended. Likewise, arrangements with third parties, such as book, newspaper or magazine publishers or television, radio or motion picture producers, pursuant to which the lawyer conveys whatever literary or media rights the lawyer may have, should not be entered into prior to the conclusion of the matter.

EC 5-5 A lawyer should not suggest to the client that a gift be made to the lawyer or for the lawyer's benefit. If a lawyer accepts a gift from the client, the lawyer is peculiarly susceptible to the charge that he or she unduly influenced or overreached the client. If a client voluntarily offers to make a gift to the lawyer, the lawyer may accept the gift, but before doing so, should urge that the client secure disinterested advice from an independent, competent person who is cognizant of all the circumstances. Other than in exceptional circumstances, a lawyer should insist that an instrument in which the client desires to name the lawyer beneficially be prepared by another lawyer selected by the client.

EC 5-6 A lawyer should not consciously influence a client to name the lawyer as executor, trustee, or lawyer in an instrument. In those cases where a client wishes to name the lawyer as such, care should be taken by the lawyer to avoid even the appearance of impropriety.

EC 5-7 The possibility of an adverse effect upon the exercise of free judgment by the lawyer on behalf of the client during litigation generally makes it undesirable for the lawyer to acquire a proprietary interest in the cause of the client or otherwise to become financially interested in the outcome of the litigation. However, it is not improper for a lawyer to protect the right to collect a fee for his or her services by the assertion of legally permissible liens, even though by doing so the lawyer may acquire an interest in the outcome of litigation. Although a contingent fee arrangement gives a lawyer a financial interest in the outcome of litigation, a reasonable contingent fee is permissible in civil cases because it may be the only means by which a non-lawyer can obtain the services of a lawyer of his or her choice. But a lawyer, who is in a better position to evaluate a cause of action, should enter into a contingent fee arrangement only in those instances where the arrangement will be beneficial to the client.

EC 5-8 A financial interest in the outcome of litigation also results if monetary advances are made by the lawyer to the client. Although this assistance generally is not encouraged, there are instances when it is not improper to make loans to a client. For example, the advancing or guaranteeing of payment of the costs and expenses of litigation by a lawyer may be the only way a client can enforce a cause of action, but the ultimate liability for such costs and expenses must be that of the client except, where not prohibited by law or court rule, in the case of an indigent client represented on a pro bono basis.

EC 5-9 Occasionally a lawyer is called upon to decide in a particular case whether the lawyer will be a witness or an advocate. If a lawyer is both counsel and witness on a significant issue, the lawyer becomes more easily impeachable for interest and thus may be a less effective witness. Conversely, the opposing counsel may be handicapped in challenging the credibility of the lawyer when the lawyer also appears as an advocate on issues of fact in the case. An advocate who becomes a witness is in the unseemly and ineffective position of arguing his or her own credibility. The roles of an advocate on issues of fact and of a witness are inconsistent; the function of an advocate is to advance or argue the cause of another, while that of a witness is to state facts objectively.

EC 5-10 Problems incident to the lawyer witness relationship arise at different stages; they relate either to whether a lawyer should accept employment or should withdraw from employment. Regardless of when the problem arises, the lawyer's decision is to be governed by the same basic considerations. It is not objectionable for a lawyer who is a potential witness to be an advocate on issues of fact if it is unlikely that he or she will be called as a witness because the testimony would be merely cumulative or if the testimony will relate only to an uncontested issue. In the exceptional situation where it will be manifestly unfair to the client for the lawyer to refuse employment or to withdraw when the lawyer will likely be a witness on a contested issue, the lawyer may serve as advocate on issues of fact even though he or she may be a witness. In making such decision, the lawyer should determine the personal or financial sacrifice of the client that may result from the lawyer's refusal of employment or withdrawal therefrom, the materiality of the lawyer's testimony, and the effectiveness of the lawyer's representation in view of his or her personal involvement. In weighing these factors, it should be clear that refusal or withdrawal will impose an unreasonable hardship upon the client before the lawyer accepts or continues the employment. Where the question arises, doubts should be resolved in favor of the lawyer testifying and against the lawyer's becoming or continuing as an advocate on issues of fact.

EC 5-11 A lawyer should not permit personal interests to influence the lawyer's advice relative to a suggestion by the client that additional counsel be employed. In like manner, the lawyer's personal interests should not deter the lawyer from suggesting that additional counsel be employed; on the contrary, the lawyer should be alert to the desirability of recommending additional counsel when, in his or her judgment, the proper representation of the client requires it.

EC 5-12 Inability of co-counsel to agree on a matter vital to the representation of their client requires that their disagreement be submitted by them jointly to their client for resolution by the client, and the decision of the client shall control the action to be taken.

EC 5-13 A lawyer should not maintain membership in or be influenced by any organization of employees that undertakes to prescribe, direct, or suggest when or how to fulfill his or her professional obligations to a person or organization that employs the lawyer. Although it is not necessarily improper for a lawyer employed by a corporation or similar entity to be a member of an organization of employees, the lawyer should be vigilant to safeguard his or her fidelity as a lawyer to the employer, free from outside influences.

Interests of Multiple Clients

EC 5-14 Maintaining the independence of professional judgment required of a lawyer precludes acceptance or continuation of employment that will adversely affect the lawyer's judgment on behalf of or dilute the lawyer's loyalty to a client. This problem arises whenever a lawyer is asked to represent two or more clients who may have differing interests, whether such interests be conflicting, inconsistent, diverse, or otherwise discordant.

EC 5-15 If a lawyer is requested to undertake or to continue representation of multiple clients having potentially differing interests, the lawyer must weigh carefully the possibility that the lawyer's judgment may be impaired or loyalty divided if the lawyer accepts or continues the employment. The lawyer should resolve all doubts against the propriety of the representation. A lawyer should never represent in litigation multiple clients with differing interests; and there are few situations in which the lawyer would be justified in representing in litigation multiple clients with potentially differing interests. If a lawyer accepted such employment and the interests did become actually differing, the lawyer would have to withdraw from employment with likelihood of resulting hardship on the clients; and for this reason it is preferable that the lawyer refuse the employment initially. On the other hand, there are many instances in which a lawyer may properly serve multiple clients having potentially differing interests in matters not involving litigation. If the interests vary only slightly, it is generally likely that the lawyer will not be subjected to an adverse influence and that the lawyer can retain his or her independent judgment on behalf of each client; and if the interests become differing, withdrawal is less likely to have a disruptive effect upon the causes of the clients. Simultaneous representation in unrelated matters of clients whose interests are only generally diverse, such as competing economic enterprises, does not by itself require consent of the respective clients. Likewise, a lawyer may generally represent parties having antagonistic positions on a legal question that has arisen in different cases, unless representation of either client would be adversely affected. Thus, it is ordinarily not improper to assert such positions in cases pending in different trial courts.

EC 5-16 In those instances in which a lawyer is justified in representing two or more clients having differing interests, it is nevertheless essential that each client be given the opportunity to evaluate the need for representation free of any potential conflict and to obtain other counsel if the client so desires. Thus before a lawyer may represent multiple clients, the lawyer should explain fully to each client the implications of the common representation and otherwise provide to each client information reasonably sufficient, giving due regard to the sophistication of the client, to permit the client to appreciate the significance of the potential conflict, and should accept or continue employment only if each client consents, preferably in writing. If there are present other circumstances that might cause any of the multiple clients to question the undivided loyalty of the lawyer, the lawyer should also advise all of the clients of those circumstances.

If a disinterested lawyer would conclude that any of the affected clients should not agree to the representation under the circumstances, the lawyer involved should not ask for such agreement or provide representation on the basis of the client's consent. In addition, there may be circumstances in which it is impossible to make the disclosure necessary to obtain consent, such as when the lawyer represents different clients in related matters and one of the clients refuses to consent to the disclosure necessary to permit the other client to make an informed decision. In all cases in which the fact, validity or propriety of client consent is called into question, the lawyer must bear the burden of establishing that consent was properly obtained and relied upon by the lawyer.

EC 5-17 Typically recurring situations involving potentially differing interests are those in which a lawyer is asked to represent co-defendants in a criminal case, co-plaintiffs or co-defendants in a personal injury case, an insured and insurer, and beneficiaries of the estate of a decedent. Whether a lawyer can fairly and adequately protect the interests of multiple clients in these and similar situations depends upon an analysis of each case. In certain circumstances, there may exist little chance of the judgment of the lawyer being adversely affected by the slight possibility that the interests will become actually differing; in other circumstances, the chance of adverse effect upon the lawyer's judgment is not unlikely.

EC 5-18 A lawyer employed or retained by a corporation or similar entity owes allegiance to the entity and not to a shareholder, director, officer, employee, representative, or other person connected with the entity. In advising the entity, a lawyer should keep paramount its interests and the lawyer's professional judgment should not be influenced by the personal desires of any person or organization. Occasionally a lawyer for an entity is requested to represent a shareholder, director, officer, employee, representative, or other person connected with the entity in an individual capacity; in such case the lawyer may serve the individual only if the lawyer is convinced that differing interests are not present. Representation of a corporation or similar entity does not necessarily constitute representation of all of its affiliates. A number of factors should be considered before undertaking a representation adverse to the affiliate of a client including, without limitation, the nature and extent of the relationship between the entities, the nature and extent of the relationship between the matters, and the reasonable understanding of the organizational client as to whether its affiliates fall within the scope of the representation.

Occasionally, the lawyer may learn that an officer, employee or other person associated with the entity is engaged in action, refuses to act, or intends to act or to refrain from acting in a matter related to the representation that is a violation of a legal obligation to the entity, or a violation of law which reasonably might be imputed to the entity, and is likely to result in substantial injury to the entity. In such event, the lawyer must proceed as is reasonably necessary in the best interest of the entity. In determining how to proceed, the lawyer should give due consideration to the seriousness of the violation and its consequences, the scope and nature of the lawyer's representation, the responsibility in the entity and the apparent motivation of the person involved, the policies of the entity concerning such matters and any other relevant considerations. Any measures taken should be designed to minimize disruption of the entity and the risk of revealing confidences and secrets of the entity. Such measures may include among others: asking reconsideration of the matter, advising that a separate legal opinion on the matter be sought for presentation to appropriate authority in the entity, and referring the matter to higher authority in the entity not involved in the wrongdoing, including, if warranted by the seriousness of the matter, referral to the highest authority that can act in behalf of the entity as determined by applicable law.

A lawyer for a corporation or other organization who is asked to become a member of its board of directors should determine whether the responsibilities of the two roles may conflict. The lawyer may be called on to advise the corporation in matters involving actions of the directors. Consideration should be given to the frequency with which such situations may arise, the potential intensity of the conflict, the effect of the lawyer's resignation from the board and the possibility of the corporation's obtaining legal advice from another lawyer in such situations. If there is a material risk that the dual role will compromise the lawyer's independent professional judgment on behalf of the corporation, the lawyer should not serve as a director.

EC 5-19 A lawyer may in a single matter represent several clients whose interests are not actually or potentially differing. Nevertheless, the lawyer should explain any circumstances that might cause a client to question the lawyer's undivided loyalty. Regardless of the belief of a lawyer that he or she may properly represent multiple clients, the lawyer must defer to a client who holds the contrary belief and withdraw from representation of that client.

EC 5-20 A lawyer is often asked to serve as an impartial arbitrator or mediator in matters which involve present or former clients. The lawyer may serve in either capacity after disclosing such present or former relationships. A lawyer who has undertaken to act as an impartial arbitrator or mediator should not thereafter represent in the dispute any of the parties involved.

Desires of Third Persons

EC 5-21 The obligation of a lawyer to exercise professional judgment solely on behalf of the client requires disregarding the desires of others that might impair the lawyer's free judgment. The desires of a third person will seldom adversely affect a lawyer unless that person is in a position to exert strong economic, political, or social pressures upon the lawyer. These influences are often subtle, and a lawyer must be alert to their existence. A lawyer subjected to outside pressures should make full disclosure of them to the client; and if the lawyer or the client believes that the effectiveness of the representation has been or will be impaired thereby, the lawyer should take proper steps to withdraw from representation of the client.

EC 5-22 Economic, political or social pressures by third persons are less likely to impinge upon the independent judgment of a lawyer in a matter in which the lawyer is compensated directly by the client and the professional work is exclusively with the client. On the other hand, if a lawyer is compensated from a source other than the client, the lawyer may feel a sense of responsibility to someone other than the client.

EC 5-23 A person or organization that pays or furnishes lawyers to represent others possesses a potential power to exert strong pressures against the independent judgment of those lawyers. Some employers may be interested in furthering their own economic, political, or social goals without regard to the professional responsibility of the lawyer to an individual client. Others may be far more concerned with establishment or extension of legal principles than in the immediate protection of the rights of the lawyer's individual client. On some occasions, decisions on priority of work may be made by the employer rather than the lawyer with the result that prosecution of work already undertaken for clients is postponed to their detriment. Similarly, an employer may seek, consciously or unconsciously, to further its own economic interests through the actions of the lawyers employed by it. Since a lawyer must always be free to exercise professional judgment without regard to the interests or motives of a third person, the lawyer who is employed by one to represent another must constantly guard against erosion of professional freedom.

EC 5-24 To assist a lawyer in preserving professional independence, a number of courses are available. For example, a lawyer should not practice with or in the form of a professional legal corporation, even though the corporate form is permitted by law, if any of its directors, officers, or shareholders is a non-lawyer. Although a lawyer may be employed by a business corporation with non-lawyers serving as directors or officers, and they necessarily have the right to make decisions of business policy, a lawyer must decline to accept direction of his or her professional judgment from any non-lawyer. Various types of legal aid offices are administered by boards of directors composed of lawyers and non-lawyers. A lawyer should not accept employment from such an organization unless the board sets only broad policies and there is no interference in the relationship of the lawyer and his or her individual client. Where a lawyer is employed by an organization, a written agreement that defines the relationship between the lawyer and the organization and provides for the lawyer's independence is desirable since it may serve to prevent misunderstanding as to their respective roles. Although other innovations in the means of supplying legal counsel may develop, the responsibility of the lawyer to maintain professional independence remains constant, and the legal profession must insure that changing circumstances do not result in loss of the professional independence of the lawyer.

[§1200.20] DR 5-101 Conflicts of Interest — Lawyer's Own Interests

(a) A lawyer shall not accept or continue employment if the exercise of professional judgment on behalf of the client will be or reasonably may be affected by the lawyer's own financial, business, property, or personal interests, unless a disinterested lawyer would believe that the representation of the client will not be adversely affected thereby and the client consents to the representation after full disclosure of the implications of the lawyer's interest.

[§1200.21] DR 5-102 Lawyers as Witnesses

(a) A lawyer shall not act, or accept employment that contemplates the lawyer's acting, as an advocate on issues of fact before any tribunal if the lawyer knows or it is obvious that the lawyer ought to be called as a witness on a significant issue on behalf of the client, except that the lawyer may act as an advocate and also testify:

(1) If the testimony will relate solely to an uncontested issue.

(2) If the testimony will relate solely to a matter of formality and there is no reason to believe that substantial evidence will be offered in opposition to the testimony.

(3) If the testimony will relate solely to the nature and value of

legal services rendered in the case by the lawyer or the lawyer's firm to the client.

(4) As to any matter, if disqualification as an advocate would work a substantial hardship on the client because of the distinctive value of the lawyer as counsel in the particular case.

(b) Neither a lawyer nor the lawyer's firm shall accept employment in contemplated or pending litigation if the lawyer knows or it is obvious that the lawyer or another lawyer in the lawyer's firm may be called as a witness on a significant issue other than on behalf of the client, and it is apparent that the testimony would or might be prejudicial to the client.

(c) If, after undertaking employment in contemplated or pending litigation, a lawyer learns or it is obvious that the lawyer ought to be called as a witness on a significant issue on behalf of the client, the lawyer shall not serve as an advocate on issues of fact before the tribunal, except that the lawyer may continue as an advocate on issues of fact and may testify in the circumstances enumerated in DR 5-102(a)(1) through (4).

(d) If, after undertaking employment in contemplated or pending litigation, a lawyer learns or it is obvious that the lawyer or a lawyer in his or her firm may be called as a witness on a significant issue other than on behalf of the client, the lawyer may continue the representation until it is apparent that the testimony is or may be prejudicial to the client at which point the lawyer and the firm must withdraw from acting as an advocate before the tribunal.

[§1200.22] DR 5-103 Avoiding Acquisition of Interest in Litigation

(a) A lawyer shall not acquire a proprietary interest in the cause of action or subject matter of litigation he or she is conducting for a client, except that the lawyer may:

(1) Acquire a lien granted by law to secure the lawyer's fee or expenses.

(2) Except as provided in DR 2-106(c)(2) or (3), contract with a client for a reasonable contingent fee in a civil case.

(b) While representing a client in connection with contemplated or pending litigation, a lawyer shall not advance or guarantee financial assistance to the client, except that:

(1) A lawyer may advance or guarantee the expenses of litigation, including court costs, expenses of investigation, expenses of medical examination, and costs of obtaining and presenting evidence, provided the client remains ultimately liable for such expenses.

(2) Unless prohibited by law or rule of court, a lawyer representing an indigent client on a pro bono basis may pay court costs and reasonable expenses of litigation on behalf of the client.

[§1200.23] DR 5-104 Transactions Between Lawyer and Client

(a) A lawyer shall not enter into a business transaction with a client if they have differing interests therein and if the client expects the lawyer to exercise professional judgment therein for the protection of the client, unless:

(1) The transaction and terms on which the lawyer acquires the interest are fair and reasonable to the client and are fully disclosed and transmitted in writing to the client in a manner that can be reasonably understood by the client;

(2) The lawyer advises the client to seek the advice of independent counsel in the transaction; and

(3) The client consents in writing, after full disclosure, to the terms of the transaction and to the lawyer's inherent conflict of interest in the transaction.

(b) Prior to conclusion of all aspects of the matter giving rise to employment, a lawyer shall not negotiate or enter into any arrangement or understanding:

(1) With a client or a prospective client by which the lawyer acquires an interest in literary or media rights with respect to the subject matter of the employment or proposed employment.

(2) With any person by which the lawyer transfers or assigns any interest in literary or media rights with respect to the subject matter of employment by a client or prospective client.

[§1200.24] DR 5-105 Conflict of Interest; Simultaneous Representation

(a) A lawyer shall decline proffered employment if the exercise of independent professional judgment in behalf of a client will be or is likely to be adversely affected by the acceptance of the proffered employment, or if it would be likely to involve the lawyer in representing differing interests, except to the extent permitted under subdivision (c) of this section.

(b) A lawyer shall not continue multiple employment if the exercise of independent professional judgment in behalf of a client will be or is likely to be adversely affected by the lawyer's representation of another client, or if it would be likely to involve the lawyer in representing differing interests, except to the extent permitted under subdivision (c) of this section.

(c) In the situations covered by subdivisions (a) and (b) of this section, a lawyer may represent multiple clients if a disinterested lawyer would believe that the lawyer can competently represent the interest of each and if each consents to the representation after full disclosure of the implications of the simultaneous representation and the advantages and risks involved.

(d) While lawyers are associated in a law firm, none of them shall knowingly accept or continue employment when any one of them practicing alone would be prohibited from doing so under DR 5-101(a), DR 5-105(a) or (b), DR 5-108(a) or (b), or DR 9-101(b) except as otherwise provided therein.

(e) A law firm shall keep records of prior engagements, which records shall be made at or near the time of such engagements and shall have a policy implementing a system by which proposed engagements are checked against current and previous engagements, so as to render effective assistance to lawyers within the firm in complying with DR 5-105(d). Failure to keep records or to have a policy which complies with this subdivision, whether or not a violation of DR 5-105(d) occurs, shall be a violation by the firm. In cases in which a violation of this subdivision by the firm is a substantial factor in causing a violation of DR 5-105(d) by a lawyer, the firm, as well as the individual lawyer, shall also be responsible for the violation of DR 5-105(d).

[§1200.25] DR 5-106 Settling Similar Claims of Clients

(a) A lawyer who represents two or more clients shall not make or participate in the making of an aggregate settlement of the claims of or against the clients, unless each client has consented after full disclosure of the implications of the aggregate settlement and the advantages and risks involved, including the existence and nature of all the claims involved and the participation of each person in the settlement.

[§1200.26] DR 5-107 Avoiding Influence by Others Than the Client

(a) Except with the consent of the client after full disclosure a lawyer shall not:

(1) Accept compensation for legal services from one other than the client.

(2) Accept from one other than the client anything of value related to his or her representation of or employment by the client.

(b) Unless authorized by law, a lawyer shall not permit a person who recommends, employs, or pays the lawyer to render legal service for another to direct or regulate his or her professional judgment in rendering such legal services, or to cause the lawyer to compromise the lawyer's duty to maintain the confidences and secrets of the client under DR 4-101(b).

(c) A lawyer shall not practice with or in the form of a limited liability company, limited liability partnership or professional corporation authorized to practice law for a profit, if:

(1) A non-lawyer owns any interest therein, except that a fiduciary representative of the estate of a lawyer may hold the stock or interest of the lawyer for a reasonable time during administration;

(2) A non-lawyer is a member, corporate director or officer thereof; or

(3) A non-lawyer has the right to direct or control the professional judgment of a lawyer.

[§1200.27] DR 5-108 Conflict of Interest; Former Client

(a) Except as provided in DR 9-101(b) with respect to current or former government lawyers, a lawyer who has represented a client in a matter shall not, without the consent of the former client after full disclosure:

(1) Thereafter represent another person in the same or a substantially related matter in which that person's interests are materially adverse to the interests of the former client.

(2) Use any confidences or secrets of the former client except as permitted by DR 4-101(b) or when the confidence or secret has become generally known.

(b) Except with the consent of the affected client after full disclosure, a lawyer shall not knowingly represent a person in the same or a substantially related matter in which a firm with which the lawyer formerly was associated had previously represented a client:

(1) Whose interests are materially adverse to that person; and

(2) About whom the lawyer had acquired information protected by DR 4-101(b) that is material to the matter.

(c) Notwithstanding the provisions of DR 5-105(d), when a lawyer has terminated an association with a firm, the firm is prohibited from thereafter representing a person with interests that are materially adverse to those of a client represented by the formerly associated lawyer and not currently represented by the firm only if the law firm or any lawyer remaining in the firm has information protected by DR 4-101(b) that is material to the matter, unless the affected client consents after full disclosure.

[§1200.28] DR 5-109 Organization as Client

(a) When a lawyer employed or retained by an organization is dealing with the organization's directors, officers, employees, members, shareholders or other constituents, and it appears that the organization's interests may differ from those of the constituents with whom the lawyer is dealing, the lawyer shall explain that the lawyer is the lawyer for the organization and not for any of the constituents.

(b) If a lawyer for an organization knows that an officer, employee or other person associated with the organization is engaged in action, intends to act or refuses to act in a matter related to the representation that is a violation of a legal obligation to the organization, or a violation of law that reasonably might be imputed to the organization, and is likely to result in substantial injury to the organization, the lawyer shall proceed as is reasonably necessary in the best interest of the organization. In determining how to proceed, the lawyer shall give due consideration to the seriousness of the violation and its consequences, the scope and nature of the lawyer's representation, the responsibility in the organization and the apparent motivation of the person involved, the policies of the organization concerning such matters and any other relevant considerations. Any measures taken shall be designed to minimize disruption of the organization and the risk of revealing information relating to the representation to persons outside the organization. Such measures may include, among others:

(1) Asking reconsideration of the matter;

(2) Advising that a separate legal opinion on the matter be sought for presentation to appropriate authority in the organization; and

(3) Referring the matter to higher authority in the organization, including, if warranted by the seriousness of the matter, referral to the highest authority that can act in behalf of the organization as determined by applicable law.

(c) If, despite the lawyer's efforts in accordance with DR 5-109(b), the highest authority that can act on behalf of the organization insists upon action, or a refusal to act, that is clearly a violation of law and is likely to result in a substantial injury to the organization, the lawyer may resign in accordance with DR 2-110.

[§1200.29] DR 5-110 Membership in Legal Service Organization

(a) A lawyer may serve as a director, officer or member of a not-for-profit legal services organization, apart from the law firm in which the lawyer practices, notwithstanding that the organization serves persons having interests that differ from those of a client of the lawyer or the lawyer's firm, provided that the lawyer shall not knowingly participate in a decision or action of the organization:

(1) If participating in the decision or action would be incompatible with the lawyer's duty of loyalty to a client under DR 5-101 through DR 5-110; or

(2) Where the decision or action could have a material adverse effect on the representation of a client of the organization whose interests differ from those of a client of the lawyer or the lawyer's firm.

[§1200.29-a] DR 5-111 Sexual Relations with Clients

(a) "Sexual relations" means sexual intercourse or the touching of an intimate part of another person for the purpose of sexual arousal, sexual gratification, or sexual abuse.

(b) A lawyer shall not:

(1) Require or demand sexual relations with a client or third party incident to or as a condition of any professional representation.

(2) Employ coercion, intimidation, or undue influence in entering into sexual relations with a client.

(3) In domestic relations matters, enter into sexual relations with a client during the course of the lawyer's representation of the client.

(c) Section DR 5-111(b) shall not apply to sexual relations between lawyers and their spouses or to ongoing consensual sexual relationships that predate the initiation of the lawyer-client relationship.

(d) Where a lawyer in a firm has sexual relations with a client but does not participate in the representation of that client, the lawyers in the firm shall not be subject to discipline under this rule solely because of the occurrence of such sexual relations.

CANON 6. A LAWYER SHOULD REPRESENT A CLIENT COMPETENTLY

EC 6-1 Because of the lawyer's vital role in the legal process, the lawyer should act with competence and proper care in representing clients. The lawyer should strive to become and remain proficient in his or her practice and should accept employment only in matters which he or she is or intends to become competent to handle.

EC 6-2 A lawyer is aided in attaining and maintaining competence by keeping abreast of current legal literature and developments, participating in continuing legal education programs, concentrating in particular areas of the law, and by utilizing other available means. The lawyer has the additional ethical obligation to assist in improving the legal profession, and should do so by participating in bar activities intended to advance the quality and standards of members of the profession. Of particular importance is the careful training of younger associates and the giving of sound guidance to all lawyers who consult the lawyer. In short, a lawyer should strive at all levels to aid the legal profession in advancing the highest possible standards of integrity and competence and personally to meet those standards.

EC 6-3 While the licensing of a lawyer is evidence of meeting the standards then prevailing for admission to the bar, a lawyer generally should not accept employment in any area of the law in which he or she is not qualified. However, the lawyer may accept such employment if in good faith the lawyer expects to become qualified through study and investigation, as long as such preparation would not result in unreasonable delay or expense to the client. Proper preparation and representation may require the association by the lawyer of professionals in other disciplines. A lawyer offered employment in a matter in which the lawyer is not and does not expect to become so qualified should either decline the employment or, with the consent of the client, accept the employment and associate a lawyer who is competent in the matter.

EC 6-4 Having undertaken representation, a lawyer should use proper care to safeguard the interests of the client. If a lawyer has accepted employment in a matter beyond the lawyer's competence but in which the lawyer expected to become competent, the lawyer should diligently undertake the work and study necessary to be qualified. In addition to being qualified to handle a particular matter, the lawyer's obligation to the client requires adequate preparation for and appropriate attention to the legal work, as well as promptly responding to inquiries from the client.

EC 6-5 A lawyer should have pride in his or her professional endeavors. The obligation to act competently calls for higher motivation than that arising from fear of civil liability or disciplinary penalty.

EC 6-6 A lawyer should not seek, by contract or other means, to limit prospectively the lawyer's individual liability to the client for malpractice nor shall a lawyer settle a claim for malpractice with an otherwise unrepresented client without first advising the client that independent representation is appropriate. A lawyer who handles the affairs of the client properly has no need to attempt to limit liability for professional activities and one who does not handle the affairs of the client properly should not be permitted to do so. A lawyer who is a shareholder in or is associated with a professional legal corporation, a member of a limited liability company or a partner in a limited liability partnership engaged in the practice of law may, however, limit the lawyer's liability for malpractice to the extent permitted by law.

[§1200.30] DR 6-101 Failing to Act Competently

(a) A lawyer shall not:

(1) Handle a legal matter which the lawyer knows or should know that he or she is not competent to handle, without associating with a lawyer who is competent to handle it.

(2) Handle a legal matter without preparation adequate in the circumstances.

(3) Neglect a legal matter entrusted to the lawyer.

[§1200.31] DR 6-102 Limting Liability to Client

(a) A lawyer shall not seek, by contract or other means, to limit prospectively the lawyer's individual liability to a client for malpractice, or, without first advising that person that independent representation is appropriate in connection therewith, to settle a claim for such liability with an unrepresented client or former client.

CANON 7. A LAWYER SHOULD REPRESENT A CLIENT ZEALOUSLY

EC 7-1 The duty of a lawyer, both to the client and to the legal system, is to represent the client zealously within the bounds of the law, which includes Disciplinary Rules and enforceable professional regulations. The professional responsibility of a lawyer derives from membership in a profession which has the duty of assisting members of the public to secure and protect available legal rights and benefits. In our government of laws and not of individuals, each member of our society is entitled to have his or her conduct judged and regulated in accordance with the law; to seek any lawful objective through legally permissible means; and to present for adjudication any lawful claim, issue, or defense.

EC 7-2 The bounds of the law in a given case are often difficult to ascertain. The language of legislative enactments and judicial opinions may be uncertain as applied to varying factual situations. The limits and specific meaning of apparently relevant law may be made doubtful by changing or developing constitutional interpretations, inadequately expressed statutes or judicial opinions, and changing public and judicial attitudes. Certainty of law ranges from well settled rules through areas of conflicting authority to areas without precedent.

EC 7-3 Where the bounds of law are uncertain, the action of a lawyer may depend on whether the lawyer is serving as advocate or adviser. A lawyer may serve simultaneously as both advocate and adviser, but the two roles are essentially different. In asserting a position on behalf of the client, an advocate for the most part deals with past conduct and must take the facts as they are. By contrast, a lawyer serving as adviser primarily assists the client in determining the course of future conduct and relationships. While serving as advocate, a lawyer should resolve in favor of the client doubts as to the bounds of the law. In serving a client as adviser, a lawyer in appropriate circumstances should give his or her professional opinion as to what the ultimate decisions of the courts would likely be as to the applicable law.

Duty of the Lawyer to a Client

EC 7-4 The advocate may urge any permissible construction of the law favorable to the client, without regard to the lawyer's professional opinion as to the likelihood that the construction will ultimately prevail. The lawyer's conduct is within the bounds of the law, and therefore permissible, if the position taken is supported by the law or is supportable by a good faith argument for an extension, modification, or reversal of the law. However, a lawyer is not justified in asserting a position in litigation that is frivolous.

EC 7-5 A lawyer as adviser furthers the interest of the client by giving a professional opinion as to what he or she believes would likely be the ultimate decision of the courts on the matter at hand and by informing the client of the practical effect of such decision. The lawyer may continue in the representation of the client even though the client has elected to pursue a course of conduct contrary to the advice of the lawyer so long as the lawyer does not thereby knowingly assist the client to engage in illegal conduct or to take a frivolous legal position. A lawyer should never encourage or aid the client to commit criminal acts or counsel the client on how to violate the law and avoid punishment therefor.

EC 7-6 Whether the proposed action of a lawyer is within the bounds of the law may be a perplexing question when the client is contemplating a course of conduct having legal consequences that vary according to the client's intent, motive, or desires at the time of the action. Often a lawyer is asked to assist the client in developing evidence relevant to the state of mind of the client at a particular time. The lawyer may properly assist the client in the development and preservation of evidence of existing motive, intent, or desire; obviously, the lawyer may not do anything furthering the creation or preservation of false evidence. In many cases a lawyer may not be certain as to the state of mind of the client, and in those situations the lawyer should resolve reasonable doubts in favor of the client.

EC 7-7 In certain areas of legal representation not affecting the merits of the cause or substantially prejudicing the rights of a client, a lawyer is entitled to make decisions. But otherwise the authority to make decisions is exclusively that of the client and, if made within the framework of the law, such decisions are binding on the lawyer. As typical examples in civil cases, it is for the client to decide whether to accept a settlement offer or whether to waive the right to plead an affirmative defense. A defense lawyer in a criminal case has the duty to advise the client fully on whether a particular plea to a charge appears to be desirable and as to the prospects of success on appeal, but it is for the client to decide what plea should be entered and whether an appeal should be taken.

EC 7-8 A lawyer should exert best efforts to ensure that decisions of the client are made only after the client has been informed of relevant considerations. A lawyer ought to initiate this decision-making process if the client does not do so. Advice of a lawyer to the client need not be confined to purely legal considerations. A lawyer should advise the client of the possible effect of each legal alternative. A lawyer should bring to bear upon this decision-making process the fullness of his or her experience as well as the lawyer's objective viewpoint. In assisting the client to reach a proper decision, it is often desirable for a lawyer to point out those factors which may lead to a decision that is morally just as well as legally permissible. The lawyer may emphasize the possibility of harsh consequences that might result from assertion of legally permissible positions. In the final analysis, however, the lawyer should always remember that the decision whether to forego legally available objectives or methods because of non-legal factors is ultimately for the client and not for the lawyer. In the event that the client in a non-adjudicatory matter insists upon a course of conduct that is contrary to the judgment and advice of the lawyer but not prohibited by Disciplinary Rules, the lawyer may withdraw from the employment.

EC 7-9 In the exercise of the lawyer's professional judgment on those decisions which are for the lawyer's determination in the handling of a legal matter, a lawyer should always act in a manner consistent with the best interests of the client. However, when an action in the best interest of the client seems to the lawyer to be unjust, the lawyer may ask the client for permission to forego such action.

EC 7-10 The duty of a lawyer to represent the client with zeal does not militate against the concurrent obligations to treat with consideration all persons involved in the legal process and to avoid the infliction of needless harm.

EC 7-11 The responsibilities of a lawyer may vary according to the intelligence, experience, mental condition or age of a client, the obligation of a public officer, or the nature of a particular proceeding. Examples include the representation of an illiterate or an incompetent, service as a public prosecutor or other government lawyer, and appearances before administrative and legislative bodies.

EC 7-12 Any mental or physical condition that renders a client incapable of making a considered judgment on his or her own behalf casts additional responsibilities upon the lawyer. Where an incompetent is acting through a guardian or other legal representative, a lawyer must look to such representative for those decisions which are normally the prerogative of the client to make. If a client under disability has no legal representative, the lawyer may be compelled in court proceedings to make decisions on behalf of the client. If the client is capable of understanding the matter in question or of contributing to the advancement of his or her interests, regardless of whether the client is legally disqualified from performing certain acts, the lawyer should obtain from the client all possible aid. If the disability of a client and the lack of a legal representative compel the lawyer to make decisions for the client, the lawyer should consider all circumstances then prevailing and act with care to safeguard and advance the interests of the client. But obviously a lawyer cannot perform any act or make any decision which the law requires the client to perform or make, either acting alone if competent, or by a duly constituted representative if legally incompetent.

EC 7-13 The responsibility of a public prosecutor differs from that of the usual advocate; it is to seek justice, not merely to convict. This special duty exists because: (1) the prosecutor represents the sovereign and therefore should use restraint in the discretionary exercise of governmental powers, such as in the selection of cases to prosecute; (2) during trial the prosecutor is not only an advocate but also may make decisions normally made by an individual client, and those affecting the public interest should be fair to all; and (3) in our system of criminal justice the accused is to be given the benefit of all reasonable doubts. With respect to evidence and witnesses, the prosecutor has responsibilities different from those of a lawyer in private practice; the prosecutor should make timely disclosure to the defense of available evidence, known to the prosecutor, that tends to negate the guilt of the accused, mitigate the degree of the offense, or reduce the punishment. Further, a prosecutor should not intentionally avoid pursuit of evidence merely because he or she believes it will damage the prosecutor's case or aid the accused.

EC 7-14 A government lawyer who has discretionary power relative to litigation should refrain from instituting or continuing litigation that is obviously unfair. A government lawyer not having such discretionary power who believes there is lack of merit in a controversy submitted to the lawyer should so advise his or her superiors and recommend the avoidance of unfair litigation. A government lawyer in a civil action or administrative proceeding has the responsibility to seek justice and to develop a full and fair record, and should not use his or her position or the economic power of the government to harass parties or to bring about unjust settlements or results. The responsibilities of government lawyers with respect to the compulsion of testimony and other information are generally the same as those of public prosecutors.

EC 7-15 The nature and purpose of proceedings before administrative agencies vary widely. The proceedings may be legislative or quasi-judicial, or a combination of both. They may be ex parte in character, in which event they may originate either at the instance of the agency or upon motion of an interested party. The scope of an inquiry may be purely investigative or it may be truly adversary looking toward the adjudication of specific rights of a party or of classes of parties. The foregoing are but examples of some of the types of proceedings conducted by administrative agencies. A lawyer appearing before an administrative agency, regardless of the nature of the proceeding it is conducting, has the continuing duty to advance the cause of the client within the bounds of the law. Where the applicable rules of the agency impose specific obligations upon a lawyer, it is the lawyer's duty to comply therewith, unless the lawyer has a legitimate basis for challenging the validity thereof. In all appearances before administrative agencies, a lawyer should identify the lawyer, the client, if identity of the client is not privileged, and the representative nature of the lawyer's appearance. It is not improper, however, for a lawyer to seek from an agency information available to the public without identifying the client.

EC 7-16 The primary business of a legislative body is to enact laws rather than to adjudicate controversies, although on occasion the activities of a legislative body may take on the characteristics of an adversary proceeding, particularly in investigative and impeachment matters. The role of a lawyer supporting or opposing proposed legislation normally is quite different from the lawyer's role in representing a person under investigation or on trial by a legislative body. When a lawyer appears in connection with proposed legislation, it is to affect the lawmaking process, but when the lawyer appears on behalf of a client in investigatory or impeachment proceedings, it is to protect the rights of the client. In either event, the lawyer should identify the lawyer and the client, if identity of the client is not privileged, and should comply with applicable laws and legislative rules.

EC 7-17 The obligation of loyalty to the client applies only to a lawyer in the discharge of professional duties and implies no obligation to adopt a personal viewpoint favorable to the interests or desires of the client. While a lawyer must act always with circumspection in order that the lawyer's conduct will not adversely affect the right of a client in a matter the lawyer is then handling, the lawyer may take positions on public issues and espouse legal reforms favored by the lawyer without regard to the individual views of any client.

EC 7-18 The legal system in its broadest sense functions best when persons in need of legal advice or assistance are represented by their own counsel. For this reason a lawyer should not communicate on the subject matter of the representation of the client with a person the lawyer knows to be represented in the matter by a lawyer, unless pursuant to law or rule of court or unless the lawyer has the consent of the lawyer for that person. However, a lawyer may properly advise a client to communicate directly with a represented person, if that person is legally competent, without obtaining consent from the represented person's counsel, and may advise a client with respect to those communications (including by drafting papers for the client to present to the represented person), provided the lawyer gives reasonable advance notice to the represented person's counsel that such communications will be taking place. "Reasonable advance notice" means notice provided sufficiently in advance of the direct client-to-client communications, and of sufficient content, so that the represented person's lawyer has an opportunity to advise his or her own client with respect to the client-to-client communications before they take place. A lawyer who advises a client with respect to communications with a represented person should also advise the client against engaging in abusive, harassing or unfair conduct. A lawyer who is a party or who is otherwise personally involved in a legal matter or transaction, whether appearing pro se or represented by counsel, may communicate with a represented person on the subject matter of the representation pursuant to the provisions of DR 7-104(a) and (b). If one is not represented by counsel, a lawyer representing another may have to deal directly with the unrepresented person; in such an instance a lawyer should not undertake to give advice to the person who is not represented by a lawyer, except to advise the person to obtain a lawyer.

Duty of the Lawyer to the Adversary System of Justice

EC 7-19 Our legal system provides for the adjudication of disputes governed by the rules of substantive, evidentiary, and procedural law. An adversary presentation counters the natural human tendency to judge too swiftly in terms of the familiar that which is not yet fully known; the advocate, by zealous preparation and presentation of facts and law, enables the tribunal to come to the hearing with an open and neutral mind and to render impartial judgments. The duty of a lawyer to a client and the lawyer's duty to the legal system are the same: to represent the client zealously within the bounds of the law.

EC 7-20 In order to function properly, our adjudicative process requires an informed, impartial tribunal capable of administering justice promptly and efficiently according to procedures that command public confidence and respect. Not only must there be competent, adverse presentation of evidence and issues, but a tribunal must be aided by rules appropriate to an effective and dignified process. The procedures under which tribunals operate in our adversary system have been prescribed largely by legislative enactments, court rules and decisions, and administrative rules. Through the years certain concepts of proper professional conduct have become rules of law applicable to the adversary adjudicative process. Many of these concepts are the bases for standards of professional conduct set forth in the Disciplinary Rules.

EC 7-21 The civil adjudicative process is primarily designed for the settlement of disputes between parties, while the criminal process is designed for the protection of society as a whole. Threatening to use, or using, the criminal process to coerce the adjustment of private civil claims or controversies is a subversion of that process; further, the person against whom the criminal process is so misused may be deterred from asserting legal rights and thus the usefulness of the civil process in settling private disputes is impaired. As in all cases of abuse of judicial process, the improper use of criminal process tends to diminish public confidence in our legal system.

EC 7-22 Respect for judicial rulings is essential to the proper administration of justice; however, a litigant or lawyer may, in good faith and within the framework of the law, take steps to test the correctness of a ruling of a tribunal.

EC 7-23 The complexity of law often makes it difficult for a tribunal to be fully informed unless the pertinent law is presented by the lawyers in the cause. A tribunal that is fully informed on the applicable law is better able to make a fair and accurate determination of the matter before it. The adversary system contemplates that each lawyer will present and argue the existing law in the light most favorable to the client. Where a lawyer knows of controlling legal authority directly adverse to the position of the client, the lawyer should inform the tribunal of its existence unless the adversary has done so; but, having made such disclosure, the lawyer may challenge its soundness in whole or in part.

EC 7-24 In order to bring about just and informed decisions, evidentiary and procedural rules have been established by tribunals to permit the inclusion of relevant evidence and argument and the exclusion of all other considerations. The expression by a lawyer of a personal opinion as to the justness of a cause, as to the credibility of a witness, as to the culpability of a civil litigant, or as to the guilt or innocence of an accused is not a proper subject for argument to the trier of the fact. It is improper as to factual matters because admissible evidence possessed by a lawyer should be presented only as sworn testimony. It is improper as to all other matters because, were the rule otherwise, the silence of a lawyer on a given occasion could be construed unfavorably to the client. However, a lawyer may argue, based on the lawyer's analysis of the evidence, for any position or conclusion with respect to any of the foregoing matters.

EC 7-25 Rules of evidence and procedure are designed to lead to just decisions and are part of the framework of the law. Thus while a lawyer may take steps in good faith and within the framework of the law to test the validity of rules, the lawyer is not justified in consciously violating such rules and should be diligent in his or her efforts to guard against unintentional violation of them. As examples, a lawyer should subscribe to or verify only those pleadings that the lawyer believes are in compliance with applicable law and rules; a lawyer should not make any prefatory statement before a tribunal in regard to the purported facts of the case on trial unless the lawyer believes that the statement will be supported by admissible evidence; a lawyer should not ask a witness a question solely for the purpose of harassment or embarrassment; and a lawyer should not by subterfuge put before a jury matters which it cannot properly consider.

EC 7-26 The law and Disciplinary Rules prohibit the use of fraudulent, false, or perjured testimony or evidence. A lawyer who knowingly participates in introduction of such testimony or evidence is subject to discipline. A lawyer should, however, present any admissible evidence the client desires to have presented unless the lawyer knows, or from facts within the lawyer's knowledge should know, that such testimony or evidence is false, fraudulent, or perjured.

EC 7-27 Because it interferes with the proper administration of justice, a lawyer should not suppress evidence that the lawyer or the client has a legal obligation to reveal or produce. In like manner, a lawyer should not advise or cause a person to hide or to leave the jurisdiction of a tribunal for the purpose of being unavailable as witness therein.

EC 7-28 Witnesses should always testify truthfully and should be free from any financial inducements that might tempt them to do otherwise. A lawyer should not pay or agree to pay a non-expert witness an amount in excess of reimbursement for expenses and financial loss incident to being a witness; however, a lawyer may pay or agree to pay an expert witness a reasonable fee for services as an expert. But in no event should a lawyer pay or agree to pay a contingent fee to any witness. A lawyer should exercise reasonable diligence to see that the client and lay associates conform to these standards.

EC 7-29 To safeguard the impartiality that is essential to the judicial process, members of the venire and jurors should be protected against extraneous influences. When impartiality is present, public confidence in the judicial system is enhanced. There should be no extra judicial communication with members of the venire prior to trial or with jurors during trial or on behalf of a lawyer connected with the case. Furthermore, a lawyer who is not connected with the case should not communicate with or cause another to communicate with a member of the venire or a juror about the case. After the trial, communication by a lawyer with jurors is permitted so long as the lawyer refrains from asking questions or making comments that tend to harass or embarrass the juror or to influence actions of the juror in future cases. Were a lawyer to be prohibited from communicating after trial with a juror, the lawyer could not ascertain if the verdict might be subject to legal challenge, in which event the invalidity of a verdict might go undetected. When an extrajudicial communication by a lawyer with a juror is permitted by law, it should be made considerately and with deference to the personal feelings of the juror.

EC 7-30 Vexatious or harassing investigations of members of the venire or jurors seriously impair the effectiveness of our jury system. For this reason, a lawyer or anyone on the lawyer's behalf who conducts an investigation of members of the venire or jurors should act with circumspection and restraint.

EC 7-31 Communications with or investigation of members or families of members of the venire or jurors by a lawyer or by anyone on the lawyer's behalf are subject to the restrictions imposed upon the lawyer with respect to communications with or investigations of members of the venire and jurors.

EC 7-32 Because of the duty to aid in preserving the integrity of the jury system, a lawyer who learns of improper conduct by or towards a member of the venire, a juror, or a member of the family of either should make a prompt report to the court regarding such conduct.

EC 7-33 A goal of our legal system is that each party shall have his or her case, criminal or civil, adjudicated by an impartial tribunal. The attainment of this goal may be defeated by dissemination of news or comments which tend to influence judge or jury. Such news or comments may prevent prospective jurors from being impartial at the outset of the trial and may also interfere with the obligation of jurors to base their verdict solely upon the evidence admitted in the trial. The release by a lawyer of out-of-court statements regarding an anticipated or pending trial may improperly affect the impartiality of the tribunal. For these reasons, standards for permissible and prohibited conduct of a lawyer with respect to trial publicity have been established.

EC 7-34 The impartiality of a public servant in our legal system may be impaired by the receipt of gifts or loans. A lawyer, therefore, is never justified in making a gift or a loan to a judge, a hearing officer, or an officer or employee of a tribunal except as permitted by the Code of Judicial Conduct, but a lawyer may make a contribution to the campaign fund of a candidate for judicial office in conformity with the Code of Judicial Conduct.

EC 7-35 All litigants and lawyers should have access to tribunals on an equal basis. Generally, in adversary proceedings a lawyer should not communicate with a judge relative to a matter pending before, or which is to be brought before, a tribunal over which the judge presides in circumstances which might have the effect or give the appearance of granting undue advantage to one party. For example, a lawyer should not communicate with a tribunal by a writing unless a copy thereof is promptly delivered to opposing counsel or to the adverse party if such party is not represented by a lawyer. Ordinarily an oral communication by a lawyer with a judge or hearing officer should be made only upon adequate notice to opposing counsel, or if there is none, to the opposing party. A lawyer should not condone or participate in private importunities by another with a judge or hearing officer on behalf of the lawyer or the client.

EC 7-36 Judicial hearings ought to be conducted through dignified and orderly procedures designed to protect the rights of all parties. Although a lawyer has the duty to represent the client zealously, the lawyer should not engage in any conduct that offends the dignity and decorum of proceedings. While maintaining independence, a lawyer should be respectful, courteous, and above-board in relations with a judge or hearing officer before whom the lawyer appears. The lawyer should avoid undue solicitude for the comfort or convenience of judge or jury and should avoid any other conduct calculated to gain special consideration.

EC 7-37 In adversary proceedings, clients are litigants and though ill feeling may exist between clients, such ill feeling should not influence a lawyer's conduct, attitude, and demeanor toward opposing lawyers. A lawyer should not make unfair or derogatory personal reference to opposing counsel. Haranguing and offensive tactics by lawyers interfere with the orderly administration of justice and have no proper place in our legal system.

EC 7-38 A lawyer should be courteous to opposing counsel and should accede to reasonable requests regarding court proceedings, settings, continuances, waiver of procedural formalities, and similar matters which do not prejudice the rights of the client. A lawyer should follow local customs of courtesy or practice, unless he or she gives timely notice to opposing counsel of the intention not to do so. A lawyer should be punctual in fulfilling all professional commitments.

EC 7-39 In the final analysis, proper functioning of the adversary system depends upon cooperation between lawyers and tribunals in utilizing procedures which will preserve the impartiality of tribunals and make their decisional processes prompt and just, without impinging upon the obligation of lawyers to represent their clients zealously within the framework of the law.

[§1200.32] DR 7-101 Representing a Client Zealously

(a) A lawyer shall not intentionally:

(1) Fail to seek the lawful objectives of the client through reasonably available means permitted by law and the Disciplinary Rules, except as provided by subdivision (b) of this section. A lawyer does not violate this Disciplinary Rule, however, by acceding to reasonable requests of opposing counsel which do not prejudice the rights of the client, by being punctual in fulfilling all professional commitments, by avoiding offensive tactics, or by treating with courtesy and consideration all persons involved in the legal process.

(2) Fail to carry out a contract of employment entered into with a client for professional services, but the lawyer may withdraw as permitted under DR 2-110, DR 5-102 and DR 5-105.

(3) Prejudice or damage the client during the course of the professional relationship, except as required under DR 7-102(b) or as authorized by DR 2-110.

(b) In the representation of a client, a lawyer may:

(1) Where permissible, exercise professional judgment to waive or fail to assert a right or position of the client.

(2) Refuse to aid or participate in conduct that the lawyer believes to be unlawful, even though there is some support for an argument that the conduct is legal.

[§1200.33] DR 7-102 Representing a Client within the Bounds of the Law

(a) In the representation of a client, a lawyer shall not:

(1) File a suit, assert a position, conduct a defense, delay a trial, or take other action on behalf of the client when the lawyer knows or when it is obvious that such action would serve merely to harass or maliciously injure another.

(2) Knowingly advance a claim or defense that is unwarranted under existing law, except that the lawyer may advance such claim or defense if it can be supported by good faith argument for an extension, modification, or reversal of existing law.

(3) Conceal or knowingly fail to disclose that which the lawyer is required by law to reveal.

(4) Knowingly use perjured testimony or false evidence.

(5) Knowingly make a false statement of law or fact.

(6) Participate in the creation or preservation of evidence when the lawyer knows or it is obvious that the evidence is false.

(7) Counsel or assist the client in conduct that the lawyer knows to be illegal or fraudulent.

(8) Knowingly engage in other illegal conduct or conduct contrary to a Disciplinary Rule.

(b) A lawyer who receives information clearly establishing that:

(1) The client has, in the course of the representation, perpetrated a fraud upon a person or tribunal shall promptly call upon the client to rectify the same, and if the client refuses or is unable to do so, the lawyer shall reveal the fraud to the affected person or tribunal, except when the information is protected as a confidence or secret.

(2) A person other than the client has perpetrated a fraud upon a tribunal shall reveal the fraud to the tribunal.

[§1200.34] DR 7-103 Performing the Duty of Public Prosecutor or Other Government Lawyer

(a) A public prosecutor or other government lawyer shall not institute or cause to be instituted criminal charges when he or she knows or it is obvious that the charges are not supported by probable cause.

(b) A public prosecutor or other government lawyer in criminal litigation shall make timely disclosure to counsel for the defendant, or to a defendant who has no counsel, of the existence of evidence, known to the prosecutor or other government lawyer, that tends to negate the guilt of the accused, mitigate the degree of the offense or reduce the punishment.

[§1200.35] DR 7-104 Communicating with Represented and Unrepresented Persons Parties

(a) During the course of the representation of a client a lawyer shall not:

(1) Communicate or cause another to communicate on the subject of the representation with a party the lawyer knows to be repre-

sented by a lawyer in that matter unless the lawyer has the prior consent of the lawyer representing such other party or is authorized by law to do so.

(2) Give advice to a person party who is not represented by a lawyer, other than the advice to secure counsel, if the interests of such person party are or have a reasonable possibility of being in conflict with the interests of the lawyer's client.

(b) Notwithstanding the prohibitions of section 1200.35(a) of this Part, and unless prohibited by law, a lawyer may cause a client to communicate with a represented person party if that person party is legally competent, and counsel the client with respect to those communications, provided the lawyer gives reasonable advance notice to the represented person's party's counsel that such communications will be taking place.

[§1200.36] DR 7-105 Threatening Criminal Prosecution

(a) A lawyer shall not present, participate in presenting, or threaten to present criminal charges solely to obtain an advantage in a civil matter.

[§1200.37] DR 7-106 Trial Conduct

(a) A lawyer shall not disregard or advise the client to disregard a standing rule of a tribunal or a ruling of a tribunal made in the course of a proceeding, but the lawyer may take appropriate steps in good faith to test the validity of such rule or ruling.

(b) In presenting a matter to a tribunal, a lawyer shall disclose:

(1) Controlling legal authority known to the lawyer to be directly adverse to the position of the client and which is not disclosed by opposing counsel.

(2) Unless privileged or irrelevant, the identities of the clients the lawyer represents and of the persons who employed the lawyer.

(c) In appearing as a lawyer before a tribunal, a lawyer shall not:

(1) State or allude to any matter that he or she has no reasonable basis to believe is relevant to the case or that will not be supported by admissible evidence.

(2) Ask any question that he or she has no reasonable basis to believe is relevant to the case and that is intended to degrade a witness or other person.

(3) Assert personal knowledge of the facts in issue, except when testifying as a witness.

(4) Assert a personal opinion as to the justness of a cause, as to the credibility of a witness, as to the culpability of a civil litigant, or as to the guilt or innocence of an accused; but the lawyer may argue,

upon analysis of the evidence, for any position or conclusion with respect to the matters stated herein.

(5) Fail to comply with known local customs of courtesy or practice of the bar or a particular tribunal without giving to opposing counsel timely notice of the intent not to comply.

(6) Engage in undignified or discourteous conduct which is degrading to a tribunal.

(7) Intentionally or habitually violate any established rule of procedure or of evidence.

[§1200.38] DR 7-107 Trial Publicity

(a) A lawyer participating in or associated with a criminal or civil matter, or associated in a law firm or government agency with a lawyer participating in or associated with a criminal or civil matter, shall not make an extrajudicial statement that a reasonable person would expect to be disseminated by means of public communication if the lawyer knows or reasonably should know that it will have a substantial likelihood of materially prejudicing an adjudicative proceeding in that matter. Notwithstanding the foregoing, a lawyer may make a statement that a reasonable lawyer would believe is required to protect a client from the substantial prejudicial effect of recent publicity not initiated by the lawyer or the lawyer's client. A statement so made shall be limited to such information as is necessary to mitigate the recent adverse publicity.

(b) A statement ordinarily is likely to prejudice materially an adjudicative proceeding when it refers to a civil matter triable to a jury, a criminal matter, or any other proceeding that could result in incarceration, and the statement relates to:

(1) The character, credibility, reputation or criminal record of a party, suspect in a criminal investigation or witness, or the identity of a witness, or the expected testimony of a party or witness.

(2) In a criminal case or proceeding that could result in incarceration, the possibility of a plea of guilty to the offense or the existence or contents of any confession, admission, or statement given by a defendant or suspect or that person's refusal or failure to make a statement.

(3) The performance or results of any examination or test or the refusal or failure of a person to submit to an examination or test, or the identity or nature of physical evidence expected to be presented.

(4) Any opinion as to the guilt or innocence of a defendant or suspect in a criminal case or proceeding that could result in incarceration.

(5) Information the lawyer knows or reasonably should know is likely to be inadmissible as evidence in a trial and would if disclosed create a substantial risk of prejudicing an impartial trial.

(6) The fact that a defendant has been charged with a crime, unless there is included therein a statement explaining that the charge

is merely an accusation and that the defendant is presumed innocent until and unless proven guilty.

(c) Provided that the statement complies with DR 7-107(a), a lawyer involved with the investigation or litigation of a matter may state the following without elaboration:

(1) The general nature of the claim or defense.

(2) The information contained in a public record.

(3) That an investigation of the matter is in progress.

(4) The scheduling or result of any step in litigation.

(5) A request for assistance in obtaining evidence and information necessary thereto.

(6) A warning of danger concerning the behavior of a person involved, when there is reason to believe that there exists the likelihood of substantial harm to an individual or to the public interest.

(7) In a criminal case:

(i) The identity, age, residence, occupation and family status of the accused.

(ii) If the accused has not been apprehended, information necessary to aid in apprehension of that person.

(iii) The fact, time and place of arrest, resistance, pursuit, use of weapons, and a description of physical evidence seized, other than as contained only in a confession, admission, or statement.

(iv) The identity of investigating and arresting officers or agencies and the length of the investigation.

[§1200.39] DR 7-108 Communication with or Investigation of Jurors

(a) Before the trial of a case a lawyer connected therewith shall not communicate with or cause another to communicate with anyone the lawyer knows to be a member of the venire from which the jury will be selected for the trial of the case.

(b) During the trial of a case:

(1) A lawyer connected therewith shall not communicate with or cause another to communicate with any member of the jury.

(2) A lawyer who is not connected therewith shall not communicate with or cause another to communicate with a juror concerning the case.

(c) Subdivisions (a) and (b) of this section do not prohibit a lawyer from communicating with members of the venire or jurors in the course of official proceedings.

(d) After discharge of the jury from further consideration of a case with which the lawyer was connected, the lawyer shall not ask questions of or make comments to a member of that jury that are calculated merely to harass or embarrass the juror or to influence the juror's actions in future jury service.

(e) A lawyer shall not conduct or cause, by financial support or otherwise, another to conduct a vexatious or harassing investigation of either a member of the venire or a juror.

(f) All restrictions imposed by this section upon a lawyer also apply to communications with or investigations of members of a family of a member of the venire or a juror.

(g) A lawyer shall reveal promptly to the court improper conduct by a member of the venire or a juror, or by another toward a member of the venire or a juror or a member of his or her family of which the lawyer has knowledge.

[§1200.40] DR 7-109 Contact with Witnesses

(a) A lawyer shall not suppress any evidence that the lawyer or the client has a legal obligation to reveal or produce.

(b) A lawyer shall not advise or cause a person to hide or to leave the jurisdiction of a tribunal for the purpose of making the person unavailable as a witness therein.

(c) A lawyer shall not pay, offer to pay, or acquiesce in the payment of compensation to a witness contingent upon the content of his or her testimony or the outcome of the case. But a lawyer may advance, guarantee, or acquiesce in the payment of:

(1) Expenses reasonably incurred by a witness in attending or testifying.

(2) Reasonable compensation to a witness for the loss of time in attending, testifying, preparing to testify or otherwise assisting counsel.

(3) A reasonable fee for the professional services of an expert witness.

[§1200.41] DR 7-110 Contact with Officials

(a) A lawyer shall not give or lend anything of value to a judge, official, or employee of a tribunal except is permitted by the Code of Judicial Conduct, but a lawyer may make a contribution to the campaign fund of a candidate for judicial office in conformity with the Code of Judicial Conduct.

(b) In an adversary proceeding, a lawyer shall not communicate, or cause another to communicate, as to the merits of the cause with a judge or an official before whom the proceeding is pending, except:

(1) In the course of official proceedings in the cause.

(2) In writing if the lawyer promptly delivers a copy of the writing to opposing counsel or to an adverse party who is not represented by a lawyer.

(3) Orally upon adequate notice to opposing counsel or to an adverse party who is not represented by a lawyer.

(4) As otherwise authorized by law, or by the Code of Judicial Conduct.

CANON 8. A LAWYER SHOULD ASSIST IN IMPROVING THE LEGAL SYSTEM

EC 8-1 Changes in human affairs and imperfections in human institutions make necessary constant efforts to maintain and improve our legal system. This system should function in a manner that commands public respect and fosters the use of legal remedies to achieve redress of grievances. By reason of education and experience, lawyers are especially qualified to recognize deficiencies in the legal system and to initiate corrective measures therein. Thus they should participate in proposing and supporting legislation and programs to improve the system, without regard to the general interests or desires of clients or former clients.

EC 8-2 Rules of law are deficient if they are not just, understandable, and responsive to the needs of society. If a lawyer believes that the existence or absence of a rule of law, substantive or procedural, causes or contributes to an unjust result, the lawyer should endeavor by lawful means to obtain appropriate changes in the law. The lawyer should encourage the simplification of laws and the repeal or amendment of laws that are outmoded. Likewise, legal procedures should be improved whenever experience indicates a change is needed.

EC 8-3 The fair administration of justice requires the availability of competent lawyers. Members of the public should be educated to recognize the existence of legal problems and the resultant need for legal services, and should be provided methods for intelligent selection of counsel. Those persons unable to pay for legal services should be provided needed services. Clients and lawyers should not be penalized by undue geographical restraints upon representation in legal matters, and the bar should address itself to improvements in licensing, reciprocity, and admission procedures consistent with the needs of modern commerce.

EC 8-4 Whenever a lawyer seeks legislative or administrative changes, the lawyer should identify the capacity in which he or she appears, whether on behalf of the lawyer, a client, or the public. A lawyer may advocate such changes on behalf of a client even though the lawyer does not agree with them. But when a lawyer purports to act on behalf of the public, the lawyer should espouse only those changes which the lawyer conscientiously believes to be in the public interest. Lawyers involved in organizations seeking law reform generally do not have a lawyer-client relationship with the organization. In determining the nature and scope of participation in law reform activities, a lawyer should be mindful of obligations under Canon 5, particularly DR 5-101 through DR 5-110. A lawyer is professionally obligated to protect the integrity of the organization by making an appropriate disclosure within the organization when the lawyer knows a private client might be materially affected.

EC 8-5 Fraudulent, deceptive, or otherwise illegal conduct by a participant in a proceeding before a tribunal or legislative body is inconsistent with fair administration of justice, and it should never be participated in or condoned by lawyers. Unless constrained by the obligation to preserve the confidences and secrets of the client, a lawyer should reveal to appropriate authorities any knowledge the lawyer may have of such improper conduct.

EC 8-6 Judges and administrative officials having adjudicatory powers ought to be persons of integrity, competence, and suitable temperament. Generally, lawyers are qualified, by personal observation or investigation, to evaluate the qualifications of persons seeking or being considered for such public offices, and for this reason they have a special responsibility to aid in the selection of only those who are qualified. It is the duty of lawyers to endeavor to prevent political considerations from outweighing judicial fitness in the selection of judges. Lawyers should protest earnestly against the appointment or election of those who are unsuited for the bench and should strive to have elected or appointed thereto only those who are willing to forego pursuits, whether of a business, political, or other nature, that may interfere with the free and fair consideration of questions presented for adjudication. Adjudicatory officials, not being wholly free to defend themselves, are entitled to receive the support of the bar against unjust criticism. While a lawyer as a citizen has a right to criticize such officials publicly, the lawyer should be certain of the merit of the complaint, use appropriate language, and avoid petty criticisms, for unrestrained and intemperate statements tend to lessen public confidence in our legal system. Criticisms motivated by reasons other than a desire to improve the legal system are not justified.

EC 8-7 Since lawyers are a vital part of the legal system, they should be persons of integrity, of professional skill, and of dedication to the improvement of the system. Thus a lawyer should aid in establishing, as well as enforcing, standards of conduct adequate to protect the public by insuring that those who practice law are qualified to do so.

EC 8-8 Lawyers often serve as legislators or as holders of other public offices. This is highly desirable, as lawyers are uniquely qualified to make significant contributions to the improvement of the legal system. A lawyer who is a public officer, whether full or part-time, should not engage in activities in which the lawyer's personal or professional interests are or foreseeably may be in conflict with the lawyer's official duties.

EC 8-9 The advancement of our legal system is of vital importance in maintaining the rule of law and in facilitating orderly changes; therefore, lawyers should encourage, and should aid in making, needed changes and improvements.

[§1200.42] DR 8-101 Action as a Public Official

(a) A lawyer who holds public office shall not:

(1) Use the public position to obtain, or attempt to obtain, a special advantage in legislative matters for the lawyer or for a client under circumstances where the lawyer knows or it is obvious that such action is not in the public interest.

(2) Use the public position to influence, or attempt to influence, a tribunal to act in favor of the lawyer or of a client.

(3) Accept anything of value from any person when the lawyer knows or it is obvious that the offer is for the purpose of influencing the lawyer's action as a public official.

[§1200.43] DR 8-102 Statements Concerning Judges and Other Adjudicatory Officers

(a) A lawyer shall not knowingly make false statements of fact concerning the qualifications of a candidate for election or appointment to a judicial office.

(b) A lawyer shall not knowingly make false accusations against a judge or other adjudicatory officer.

[§1200.44] DR 8-103 Lawyer Candidate for Judicial Office

Editors' Note. On March 14, 2001, effective immediately, the Appellate Divisions amended DR 8-103 to specify the particular provisions of the New York Code of Judicial Conduct that apply to lawyers who run for judicial office.

(a) A lawyer who is a candidate for judicial office shall comply with §100.5 of the Chief Administrator's Rules Governing Judicial Conduct (22 NYCRR) and Canon 5 of the Code of Judicial Conduct.

CANON 9. A LAWYER SHOULD AVOID EVEN THE APPEARANCE OF PROFESSIONAL IMPROPRIETY

EC 9-1 Continuation of the American concept that we are to be governed by rules of law requires that the people have faith that justice can be obtained through our legal system. A lawyer should promote public confidence in our system and in the legal profession.

EC 9-2 Public confidence in law and lawyers may be eroded by irresponsible or improper conduct of a lawyer. On occasion, ethical conduct of a lawyer may appear to non-lawyers to be unethical. In order to avoid misunderstandings and hence to maintain confidence, a lawyer should fully and promptly inform the client of material developments in the matters being handled for the client. While a lawyer should guard against otherwise proper conduct that has a tendency to diminish public confidence in the legal system or in the legal profession, the lawyer's duty to clients or to the public should never be subordinate merely because the full discharge of the lawyer's obligation may be misunderstood or may tend to subject the lawyer or the legal profession to criticism. When explicit ethical guidance does not exist a lawyer should determine prospective conduct by acting in a manner that promotes public confidence in the integrity and efficiency of the legal system and the legal profession.

EC 9-3 A lawyer who leaves judicial office or other public employment should not thereafter accept employment in connection with any matter in which the lawyer had substantial responsibility prior to leaving, since to accept employment would give the appearance of impropriety even if none exists.

EC 9-4 Because the very essence of the legal system is to provide procedures by which matters can be presented in an impartial manner so that they may be decided solely upon the merits, any statement or suggestion by a lawyer that the lawyer can or would attempt to circumvent those procedures is detrimental to the legal system and tends to undermine public confidence in it.

EC 9-5 Separation of the funds of a client from those of the lawyer not only serves to protect the client but also avoids even the appearance of impropriety, and therefore commingling of such funds should be avoided.

EC 9-6 Every lawyer owes a solemn duty to uphold the integrity and honor of the profession; to encourage respect for the law and for the courts and the judges thereof; to observe the Code of Professional Responsibility; to act as a member of a learned profession, one dedicated to public service; to cooperate with other lawyers in supporting the organized bar through devoting time, efforts, and financial support as the lawyer's professional standing and ability reasonably permit; to act so as to reflect credit on the legal profession and to inspire the confidence, respect, and trust of clients and of the public; and to strive to avoid not only professional impropriety but also the appearance of impropriety.

[§1200.45] [DR 9-101] Avoiding Even the Appearance of Impropriety

(a) A lawyer shall not accept private employment in a matter upon the merits of which the lawyer has acted in a judicial capacity.

(b) Except as law may otherwise expressly permit:

(1) A lawyer shall not represent a private client in connection with a matter in which the lawyer participated personally and substantially as a public officer or employee, and no lawyer in a firm with which that lawyer is associated may knowingly undertake or continue representation in such a matter unless:

(i) The disqualified lawyer is effectively screened from any participation, direct or indirect, including discussion, in the matter and is apportioned no part of the fee therefrom; and

(ii) There are no other circumstances in the particular representation that create an appearance of impropriety.

(2) A lawyer having information that the lawyer knows is confidential government information about a person, acquired when the lawyer was a public officer or employee, may not represent a private client whose interests are adverse to that person in a matter in which the information could be used to the material disadvantage of that person. A firm with which that lawyer is associated may knowingly undertake or continue representation in the matter only if the disqualified lawyer is effectively screened from any participation, direct or indirect, including discussion, in the matter and is apportioned no part of the fee therefrom.

(3) A lawyer serving as a public officer or employee shall not:

(i) Participate in a matter in which the lawyer participated personally and substantially while in private practice or nongovernmental employment, unless under applicable law no one is, or by lawful delegation may be, authorized to act in the lawyer's stead in the matter; or

(ii) Negotiate for private employment with any person who is

involved as a party or as attorney for a party in a matter in which the lawyer is participating personally and substantially.

(c) A lawyer shall not state or imply that the lawyer is able to influence improperly or upon irrelevant grounds any tribunal, legislative body, or public official.

(d) A lawyer related to another lawyer as parent, child, sibling or spouse shall not represent in any matter a client whose interests differ from those of another party to the matter who the lawyer client consents to the representation after full disclosure and the lawyer concludes that the lawyer can adequately represent the interests of the client.

[§1200.46] DR 9-102 Preserving Identity of Funds and Property of Others; Fiduciary Responsibility; Commingling and Misappropriation of Client Funds or Property; Maintenance of Bank Accounts; Record Keeping; Examination of Records

(a) *Prohibition Against Commingling and Misappropriation of Client Funds or Property.*

A lawyer in possession of any funds or other property belonging to another person, where such possession is incident to his or her practice of law, is a fiduciary, and must not misappropriate such funds or property or commingle such funds or property with his or her own.

(b) *Separate Accounts.*

(1) A lawyer who is in possession of funds belonging to another person incident to the lawyer's practice of law, shall maintain such funds in a banking institution within the State of New York which agrees to provide dishonored check reports in accordance with the provisions of Part 1300 of the joint rules of the Appellate Divisions. "Banking institution" means a state or national bank, trust company, savings bank, savings and loan association or credit union. Such funds shall be maintained, in the lawyer's own name, or in the name of a firm of lawyers of which he or she is a member, or in the name of the lawyer or firm of lawyers by whom he or she is employed, in a special account or accounts, separate from any business or personal accounts of the lawyer or lawyer's firm, and separate from any accounts which the lawyer may maintain as executor, guardian, trustee or receiver, or in any other fiduciary capacity, into which special account or accounts all funds held in escrow or otherwise entrusted to the lawyer or firm shall be deposited; provided, however, that such funds may be maintained in a banking institution located outside the State of New York if such banking institution complies with such Part

1300, and the lawyer has obtained the prior written approval of the person to whom such funds belong which specifies the name and address of the office or branch of the banking institution where such funds are to be maintained.

(2) A lawyer or the lawyer's firm shall identify the special bank account or accounts required by DR 9-102(b)(1) as an "Attorney Special Account," or "Attorney Trust Account," or "Attorney Escrow Account," and shall obtain checks and deposit slips that bear such title. Such title may be accompanied by such other descriptive language as the lawyer may deem appropriate provided that such additional language distinguishes such special account or accounts from other bank accounts that are maintained by the lawyer or lawyer's firm.

(3) Funds reasonably sufficient to maintain the account or to pay account charges may be deposited therein.

(4) Funds belonging in part to a client or third person and in part presently or potentially to the lawyer or law firm shall be kept in such special account or accounts, but the portion belonging to the lawyer or law firm may be withdrawn when due unless the right of the lawyer or law firm to receive it is disputed by the client or third person, in which event the disputed portion shall not be withdrawn until the dispute is finally resolved.

(c) *Notification of Receipt of Property; Safekeeping; Rendering Accounts; Payment or Delivery of Property.*

A lawyer shall:

(1) Promptly notify a client or third person of the receipt of funds, securities, or other properties in which the client or third person has an interest.

(2) Identify and label securities and properties of a client or third person promptly upon receipt and place them in a safe deposit box or other place of safekeeping as soon as practicable.

(3) Maintain complete records of all funds, securities, and other properties of a client or third person coming into the possession of the lawyer and render appropriate accounts to the client or third person regarding them.

(4) Promptly pay or deliver to the client or third person as requested by the client or third person the funds, securities, or other properties in the possession of the lawyer which the client or third person is entitled to receive.

(d) *Required Bookkeeping Records.* A lawyer shall maintain for seven years after the events which they record:

(1) The records of all deposits in and withdrawals from the accounts specified in DR 9-102(b) and of any other bank account which concerns or affect the lawyer's practice of law. These records shall specifically identify the date, source and description of each item deposited, as well as the date, payee and purpose of each withdrawal or disbursement.

(2) A record for special accounts, showing the source of all funds deposited in such accounts, the names of all persons for whom the funds are or were held, the amount of such funds, the description and amounts, and the names of all persons to whom such funds were disbursed.

(3) Copies of all retainer and compensation agreements with clients.

(4) Copies of all statements to clients or other persons showing the disbursement of funds to them or on their behalf.

(5) Copies of all bills rendered to clients.

(6) Copies of all records showing payments to lawyers, investigators or other persons, not in the lawyer's regular employ, for services rendered or performed.

(7) Copies of all retainer and closing statements filed with the Office of Court Administration.

(8) All checkbooks and check stubs, bank statements, prenumbered canceled checks and duplicate deposit slips.

(9) Lawyers shall make accurate entries of all financial transactions in their records of receipts and disbursements, in their special accounts, in their ledger books or similar records, and in any other books of account kept by them in the regular course of their practice, which entries shall be made at or near the time of the act, condition or event recorded.

(10) For purposes of DR 9-102(d), a lawyer may satisfy the requirements of maintaining "copies" by maintaining any of the following items: original records, photocopies, microfilm, optical imaging, and any other medium that preserves an image of the document that cannot be altered without detection.

(e) *Authorized Signatories.* All special account withdrawals shall be made only to a named payee and not to cash. Such withdrawals shall be made by check or, with the prior written approval of the party entitled to the proceeds, by bank transfer. Only an attorney admitted to practice law in New York State shall be an authorized signatory of a special account.

(f) *Missing Clients.* Whenever any sum of money is payable to a client and the lawyer is unable to locate the client, the lawyer shall apply to the court in which the action was brought if in the unified court system, or, if no action was commenced in the unified court system, to the Supreme Court in the county in which the lawyer maintains an office for the practice of law, for an order directing payment to the lawyer of any fees and disbursements that are owed by the client and the balance, if any, to the Lawyers' Fund for Client Protection for safeguarding and disbursement to persons who are entitled thereto.

(g) *Designation of Successor Signatories.*

(1) Upon the death of a lawyer who was the sole signatory on an attorney trust, escrow or special account, an application may be made to the Supreme Court for an order designating a successor signatory for such trust, escrow or special account who shall be a member of the bar in good standing and admitted to the practice of law in New York State.

(2) An application to designate a successor signatory shall be made to the Supreme Court in the judicial district in which the deceased lawyer maintained an office for the practice of law. The application may be made by the legal representative of the deceased lawyer's estate; a lawyer who was affiliated with the deceased lawyer in the practice of law; any person who has a beneficial interest in such trust, escrow or special account; an officer of a city or county bar association; or counsel for an attorney disciplinary committee. No lawyer may charge a legal fee for assisting with an application to designate a successor signatory pursuant to this rule.

(3) The Supreme Court may designate a successor signatory and may direct the safeguarding of funds from such trust, escrow or special account, and the disbursement of such funds to persons who are entitled thereto, and may order that funds in such account be deposited with the Lawyer's Fund for Client Protection for safeguarding and disbursement to persons who are entitled thereto.

(h) *Dissolution of a Firm.* Upon the dissolution of any firm of lawyers, the former partners or members shall make appropriate arrangements for the maintenance by one of them or by a successor firm of the records specified in DR 9-101(d).

(i) *Availability of Bookkeeping Records: Records Subject to Production in Disciplinary Investigations and Proceedings.* The financial records required by this Disciplinary Rule shall be located, or made available, at the principal New York State office of the lawyers subject hereto and any such records shall be produced in response to a notice or subpoena duces tecum issued in connection with a complaint before or any investigation by the appropriate grievance or departmental disciplinary committee, or shall be produced at the direction of the appropriate Appellate Division before any person designated by it. All books and produced pursuant to this subdivision shall be kept confidential, except for the purpose of the particular proceeding, and their contents shall not be disclosed by anyone in violation of the lawyer-client privilege.

(j) *Disciplinary Action.* A lawyer who does not maintain and keep the accounts and records as specified and required by this Disciplinary Rule, or who does not produce any such records pursuant to this Rule, shall be deemed in violation of these Rules and shall be subject to disciplinary proceedings.

Selected Provisions of the New York Judiciary Law

Editors' Introduction. The practice of law and admission to the bar in New York are heavily governed by statute, especially by New York's Judiciary Law. We reprint the sections of the Judiciary Law most relevant to law students studying professional responsibility.

Since our last edition went to press in September of 2001, the New York Legislature has not amended any of the statutes reprinted below. However, on August 20, 2002, Governor Pataki signed into law an amendment to §4503 of the CPLR to narrow and clarify the common law "fiduciary exception" to the attorney-client privilege. We reprint the amended version of §4503 above in our chapter on Attorney-Client Privilege and Work Product provisions.

In addition, in May of 2002, Governor Pataki signed a new law, 2002 N.Y. Laws ch. 71, §§1-2, prohibiting a matrimonial attorney from foreclosing on "the primary residence of a litigant in a matrimonial action pursuant to a mortgage or security interest given by such litigant to his or her attorney to secure payment of legal fees in connection with such matrimonial action." The new law does not prohibit an attorney from taking a mortgage or other security interest on a litigant's primary residence; it only prohibits an attorney from foreclosing on such an interest. (The same subject is also regulated by 22 N.Y.C.R.R. §1400.5, which is a court rule.) In July 2002, an attorney who held a mortgage on a client's home filed a suit to challenge the retroactive application of the new law on due process grounds. We do not reprint this law, which had not been codified at the time we went to press in September 2002.

For updates on New York legislation, visit the New York State Bar Association's web site at www.nysba.org (click at the right on "Attorney Resources," then click at the left on "Governmental Relations") — or visit the official web site of the New York Legislature at http://assembly.state.ny.us, which permits searches of Assembly and Senate bills either by keyword or by bill number.

Contents

§90. Admission to and Removal from Practice by Appellate Division; Character Committees

§460. Examination and Admission of Attorneys
§460-a. Disclosure with Respect to Loans Made or Guaranteed by the New York State Higher Education Services Corporation
§466. Attorney's Oath of Office
§470. Attorneys Having Offices in This State May Reside in Adjoining State
§474-a. Contingent Fees for Attorneys in Claims or Actions for Medical, Dental or Podiatric Malpractice
§475. Attorney's Lien in Action, Special or Other Proceeding
§477. Settlement of Actions for Personal Injury
§478. Practicing or Appearing as Attorney-at-Law Without Being Admitted and Registered
§479. Soliciting Business on Behalf of an Attorney
§480. Entering Hospital to Negotiate Settlement or Obtain Release or Statement
§481. Aiding, Assisting or Abetting the Solicitation of Persons or the Procurement of a Retainer for or on Behalf of an Attorney
§482. Employment by Attorney of Person to Aid, Assist or Abet in the Solicitation of Business or the Procurement Through Solicitation of a Retainer to Perform Legal Services
§484. None but Attorneys to Practice in the State
§485. Violation of Certain Preceding Sections a Misdemeanor
§487. Misconduct by Attorneys
§491. Sharing of Compensation by Attorneys Prohibited
§495. Corporations and Voluntary Associations Not to Practice Law
§496. [Prepaid Legal Services Plans; Registration Statement]
§498. Professional Referrals
§499. Lawyer Assistance Committees

---

§90. Admission to and Removal from Practice by Appellate Division; Character Committees

(1)(a) Upon the state board of law examiners certifying that a person has passed the required examination, or that the examination has been dispensed with, the appellate division of the supreme court in the department to which such person shall have been certified by the state board of law examiners, if it shall be satisfied that such person possesses the character and general fitness requisite for an attorney and counsellor-at-law, shall admit him to practice as such attorney and counsellor-at-law in all the courts of this state, provided that he has in all respects complied with the rules of the court of appeals and the rules of the appellate divisions relating to the admission of attorneys.

(b) Upon the application, pursuant to the rules of the court of appeals, of any person who has been admitted to practice law in another

state or territory or the District of Columbia of the United States or in a foreign country, to be admitted to practice as an attorney and counsellor-at-law in the courts of this state without taking the regular bar examination, the appellate division of the supreme court, if it shall be satisfied that such person is currently admitted to the bar in such other jurisdiction or jurisdictions, that at least one such jurisdiction in which he is so admitted would similarly admit an attorney or counsellor-at-law admitted to practice in New York state to its bar without examination and that such person possesses the character and general fitness requisite for an attorney and counsellor-at-law, and has satisfied the requirements of section 3-503 of the general obligations law,* shall admit him to practice as such attorney and counsellor-at-law in all the courts of this state, provided, that he has in all respects complied with the rules of the court of appeals and the rules of the appellate divisions relating to the admission of attorneys. Such application, which shall conform to the requirements of section 3-503 of the general obligations law, shall be submitted to the appellate division of the supreme court in the department specified in the rules of the court of appeals.

(c) The members of the committee appointed by the appellate division in each department to investigate the character and fitness of applicants for admission to the bar, shall be entitled to their necessary traveling, hotel and other expenses, incurred in the performance of their duties, payable by the state out of moneys appropriated therefor, upon certificate of the presiding justice of the appellate division by which such committee is appointed. . . .

(2) The supreme court shall have power and control over attorneys and counsellors-at-law and all persons practicing or assuming to practice law, and the appellate division of the supreme court in each department is authorized to censure, suspend from practice or remove from office any attorney and counsellor-at-law admitted to practice who is guilty of professional misconduct, malpractice, fraud, deceit, crime or misdemeanor, or any conduct prejudicial to the administration of justice; and the appellate division of the supreme court is hereby authorized to revoke such admission for any misrepresentation or suppression of any information in connection with the application for admission to practice.

It shall be the duty of the appellate division to insert in each order of suspension or removal hereafter rendered a provision which shall command the attorney and counsellor-at-law thereafter to desist and refrain from the practice of law in any form, either as principal or as agent, clerk or employee of another. In addition it shall forbid the performance of any of the following acts, to wit:

(a) The appearance as an attorney or counsellor-at-law before any court, judge, justice, board, commission or other public authority.

*General Obligations Law §3-503 addresses fulfillment of child support obligations and is described following this section.

(b) The giving to another of an opinion as to the law or its application, or of any advice in relation thereto.

In case of suspension only, the order may limit the command to the period of time within which such suspension shall continue, and if justice so requires may further limit the scope thereof.

If an attorney and counsellor-at-law has been heretofore removed from office, the appellate division shall upon application of any attorney and counsellor-at-law, or of any incorporated bar association, and upon such notice to the respondent as may be required, amend the order of removal by adding thereto as a part thereof, provisions similar to those required to be inserted in orders hereafter made.

If a certified copy of such order or of such amended order, be served upon the attorney and counsellor-at-law suspended or removed from office, a violation thereof may be punished as a contempt of court.

(2-a)(a) The provisions of this subdivision shall apply in all cases of an attorney licensed, registered or admitted to practice in this state who is in arrears in payment of child support or combined child and spousal support which matter shall be referred to the appropriate appellate division by a court pursuant to the requirements of section two hundred forty-four-c of the domestic relations law or pursuant to section four hundred fifty-eight-b of the family court act.

(b) Upon receipt of an order from the court pursuant to one of the foregoing provisions of law, the appropriate appellate division within thirty days of receipt of such order, if it finds such person to be so licensed, registered or admitted, shall provide notice to such attorney of, and initiate, a hearing which shall be held by it at least twenty days and no more than thirty days after the sending of such notice to the attorney. The hearing shall be held solely for the purpose of determining whether there exists as of the date of the hearing proof that full payment of all arrears of support established by the order of the court to be due from the licensed, registered or admitted attorney have been paid. Proof of such payment shall be a certified check showing full payment of established arrears or a notice issued by the court or the support collection unit, where the order is payable to the support collection unit designated by the appropriate social services district. Such notice shall state that full payment of all arrears of support established by the order of the court to be due have been paid. The licensed attorney shall be given full opportunity to present such proof of payment at the hearing in person or by counsel. The only issue to be determined as a result of the hearing is whether the arrears have been paid. No evidence with respect to the appropriateness of the court order or ability of the respondent party in arrears to comply with such order shall be received or considered by the disciplinary committee.

(c) Notwithstanding any inconsistent provision of this section or of any other provision of law to the contrary, the license to practice law in this state of an attorney admitted to practice shall be suspended by the appellate division if, at the hearing provided for by paragraph b of this subdivision, the licensed attorney fails to present proof of payments as required by such subdivision. Such suspension shall not be lifted unless the original court or the support collection unit, where the court order is payable to the support collection unit designated by the appropriate social services district, issues notice to the appellate division that full payment of all arrears of support established by the order of the original court to be due have been paid.

(d) The appellate division shall inform the original court of all actions taken hereunder.

(e) This subdivision two-a applies to support obligations paid pursuant to any order of child support or child and spousal support issued under provisions of article three-A or section two hundred thirty-six or two hundred forty of the domestic relations law, or article four, five, or five-A of the family court act.

(f) Notwithstanding any inconsistent provision of this section or of any other provision of law to the contrary, the provisions of this subdivision two-a shall apply to the exclusion of any other requirements of this section and to the exclusion of any other requirement of law to the contrary.

(3) The suspension or removal of an attorney or counsellor-at-law, by the appellate division of the supreme court, operates as a suspension or removal in every court of the state.

(4)(a) Any person being an attorney and counsellor-at-law who shall be convicted of a felony as defined in paragraph e of this subdivision shall upon such conviction, cease to be an attorney and counsellor-at-law, or to be competent to practice law as such.

(b) Whenever any attorney and counsellor-at-law shall be convicted of a felony as defined in paragraph e of this subdivision, there may be presented to the appellate division of the supreme court a certified or exemplified copy of the judgment of such conviction, and thereupon the name of the person so convicted shall, by order of the court, be struck from the roll of attorneys.

(c) Whenever an attorney shall be convicted of a crime in a court of record of the United States or of any state, territory or district, including this state, whether by a plea of guilty or nolo contendere or from a verdict after trial or otherwise, the attorney shall file, within thirty days thereafter, with the appellate division of the supreme court, the record of such conviction.

The failure of the attorney to so file shall be deemed professional misconduct provided, however, that the appellate division may upon application of the attorney, grant an extension upon good cause shown.

(d) For purposes of this subdivision, the term serious crime shall mean any criminal offense denominated a felony under the laws of any state, district or territory or of the United States which does not constitute a felony under the laws of this state, and any other crime a necessary element of which, as determined by statutory or common law definition of such crime, includes interference with the administration of justice, false swearing, misrepresentation, fraud, willful failure to file income tax returns, deceit, bribery, extortion, misappropriation, theft, or an attempt or conspiracy or solicitation of another to commit a serious crime.

(e) For purposes of this subdivision, the term felony shall mean any criminal offense classified as a felony under the laws of this state or any criminal offense committed in any other state, district, or territory of the United States and classified as a felony therein which if committed within this state, would constitute a felony in this state.

(f) Any attorney and counsellor-at-law convicted of a serious crime, as defined in paragraph d of this subdivision, whether by plea of guilty or nolo contendere or from a verdict after trial or otherwise, shall be suspended upon the receipt by the appellate division of the supreme court of the record of such conviction until a final order is made pursuant to paragraph (g) of this subdivision.

Upon good cause shown the appellate division of the supreme court may, upon application of the attorney or on its own motion, set aside such suspension when it appears consistent with the maintenance of the integrity and honor of the profession, the protection of the public and the interest of justice.

(g) Upon a judgment of conviction against an attorney becoming final the appellate division of the supreme court shall order the attorney to show cause why a final order of suspension, censure or removal from office should not be made.

(h) If the attorney requests a hearing, the appellate division of the supreme court shall refer the proceeding to a referee, justice or judge appointed by the appellate division for hearing, report and recommendation.

After said hearing, the appellate division may impose such discipline as it deems proper under the facts and circumstances.

(5)(a) If such removal or debarment was based upon conviction for a serious crime or upon a felony conviction as defined in subdivision four of this section, and such felony conviction was subsequently reversed or pardoned by the president of the United States, or governor of this or another state of the United States, the appellate division shall have power to vacate or modify such order or debarment, provided, however, that if such attorney or counsellor-at-law has been removed from practice in another jurisdiction, a pardon in said jurisdiction shall not be a basis for application for re-admission in this jurisdiction unless he shall have been readmitted in the jurisdiction where pardoned.

(b) If such removal or debarment was based upon conviction for a felony as defined in subdivision four of this section, the appellate division shall have power to vacate or modify such order or debarment after a period of seven years provided that such person has not been convicted of a crime during such seven-year period.

(c) An attorney and counsellor-at-law who has been convicted of a felony without the state and whose name has been struck from the roll of attorneys prior to July thirteenth, nineteen hundred seventy-nine by virtue of the provisions of subdivision four of this section may, if he alleges that such felony committed without the state would not constitute a felony if committed within the state, petition the appellate division to vacate or modify such debarment. If the appellate division finds that the felony of which the attorney and counsellor-at-law has been convicted without the state would not constitute a felony if committed within the state, it shall grant a hearing and may retroactively vacate or modify such debarment and impose such discipline as it deems just and proper under the facts and circumstances.

The attorney and counsellor-at-law shall petition for reinstatement by filing in the appellate division a copy of the order of removal together with a request for a hearing pursuant to the provisions of this paragraph. Upon such application, the order of removal shall be deemed an order of suspension for the purposes of a proceeding pursuant to this paragraph.

(6) Before an attorney or counsellor-at-law is suspended or removed as prescribed in this section, a copy of the charges against him must be delivered to him personally within or without the state or, in case it is established to the satisfaction of the presiding justice of the appellate division of the supreme court to which the charges have been presented, that he cannot with due diligence be served personally, the same may be served upon him by mail, publication or otherwise as the said presiding justice may direct, and he must be allowed an opportunity of being heard in his defense. In all cases where the charges are served in any manner other than personally, and the attorney and counsellor-at-law so served does not appear, an application may be made by such attorney or in his behalf to the presiding justice of the appellate division of the supreme court to whom the charges were presented at any time within one year after the rendition of the judgment, or final order of suspension or removal, and upon good cause shown and upon such terms as may be deemed just by such presiding justice, such attorney and counsellor-at-law must be allowed to defend himself against such charges.

The justices of the appellate division in any judicial department, or a majority of them, may make an order directing the expenses of any disciplinary proceedings, and the necessary costs and disbursements of the petitioner in prosecuting such charges, including the expense of any preliminary investigation in relation to professional conduct of an attorney and counsellor-at-law, to be paid out of funds appropriated to the office of court administration for that purpose.

(a) Where the appellate division of supreme court orders the censure, suspension from practice or removal from office of an attorney or counsellor-at-law following disciplinary proceedings at which it found, based upon a preponderance of the legally admissible evidence, that such attorney or counsellor-at-law wilfully misappropriated or misapplied money or property in the practice of law, its order may require him or her to make monetary restitution in accordance with this subdivision. Its order also may require that he or she reimburse the lawyers' fund for client protection of the state of New York for awards made to the person whose money or property was wilfully misappropriated or misapplied.

(b) Monetary restitution, as authorized hereunder, shall be made to the person whose money or property was wilfully misappropriated or misapplied and shall be for the amount or value of such money or property, as found in the disciplinary proceedings. In the event that such person dies prior to completion of such restitution, any amount remaining to be paid shall be paid to the estate of the deceased.

(c) Any payment made as restitution pursuant to this subdivision shall not limit, preclude or impair any liability for damages in any civil action or proceeding for an amount in excess of such payment; nor shall any order of the appellate division made hereunder deprive a criminal court of any authority pursuant to article sixty of the penal law.

(d) An order issued pursuant to this subdivision may be entered as a civil judgment. Such judgment shall be enforceable as a money judgment in any court of competent jurisdiction by any person to whom payments are due thereunder, or by the lawyers' fund for client protection where it has been subrogated to the rights of such person.

(e) Where an attorney or counsellor-at-law is permitted to resign from office, the appellate division may, if appropriate, issue an order as provided herein requiring him or her to make payments specified by this subdivision.

(f) Notwithstanding any other provision of this subdivision, no order may be issued hereunder unless the person required to make payments under such order first is given an opportunity to be heard in opposition thereto.

(7) In addition to the duties prescribed by section seven hundred of the county law, it shall be the duty of any district attorney within a department, when so designated by the justices of the appellate division of the supreme court in such department, or a majority of them, to prosecute all proceedings for the removal or suspension of attorneys and counsellors-at-law or the said justices, or a majority of them, may appoint any attorney and counsellor-at-law to conduct a preliminary investigation and to prosecute any disciplinary proceedings and, during or upon the termination of the investigation or proceedings, may fix the compensation to be paid to such attorney and counsellor-at-law for

the services rendered, which compensation shall be a charge against the county specified in his certificate and shall be paid thereon.

(8) Any petitioner or respondent in a disciplinary proceeding against an attorney or counsellor-at-law under this section, including a bar association or any other corporation or association, shall have the right to appeal to the court of appeals from a final order of any appellate division in such proceeding upon questions of law involved therein, subject to the limitations prescribed by article six, section seven, of the constitution of this state. [Now Const. Art. 6, §3.]

(9) No objection shall be taken to the appointment of any member of the bar to act as referee or judge in a disciplinary proceeding under this section on the ground that he is a member of a bar association or other corporation or association which is the petitioner therein.

(10) Any statute or rule to the contrary notwithstanding, all papers, records and documents upon the application or examination of any person for admission as an attorney and counsellor-at-law and upon any complaint, inquiry, investigation or proceeding relating to the conduct or discipline of an attorney or attorneys, shall be sealed and be deemed private and confidential. However, upon good cause being shown, the justices of the appellate division having jurisdiction are empowered, in their discretion, by written order, to permit to be divulged all or any part of such papers, records and documents. In the discretion of the presiding or acting presiding justice of said appellate division, such order may be made either without notice to the persons or attorneys to be affected thereby or upon such notice to them as he may direct. In furtherance of the purpose of this subdivision, said justices are also empowered, in their discretion, from time to time to make such rules as they may deem necessary. Without regard to the foregoing, in the event that charges are sustained by the justices of the appellate division having jurisdiction in any complaint, investigation or proceeding relating to the conduct or discipline of any attorney, the records and documents in relation thereto shall be deemed public records.

Editors' Note. Section 3-503 of New York General Obligations Law, added in 1995, requires every applicant for a license or the renewal of a license to certify under oath that "he or she is (or is not) under an obligation to pay child support and that if he or she is under such an obligation, that he or she does (or does not) meet one of the following requirements. . . ." These requirements are intended to reveal whether the applicant is in violation of any child support obligation. If the applicant is in violation as defined in the statute, a license may issue but must expire within six months unless the applicant certifies under oath within that time that the violation has been corrected. Thereafter, any licensees who are "four months or more in arrears in child support may be subject to suspension of their business, professional and/or driver's license." "License" is defined to include "any . . . profession."

§460. Examination and Admission of Attorneys

An applicant for admission to practice as an attorney or counsellor in this state, must be examined and licensed to practice as prescribed in this chapter and in the rules of the court of appeals. Race, creed, color, national origin, alienage or sex shall constitute no cause for refusing any person examination or admission to practice.

§460-a. Disclosure with Respect to Loans Made or Guaranteed by the New York State Higher Education Services Corporation

Every application for admission to practice as an attorney or counsellor in the courts in this state issued pursuant to the provisions of this chapter shall contain a question inquiring whether the applicant has any loans made or guaranteed by the New York state higher education services corporation currently outstanding, and if so, whether such applicant is presently in default on any such loan. The name and address of any applicant who answers either or both of such questions in the affirmative shall be transmitted to such corporation by the appellate division prior to the date on which such license is issued.

§466. Attorney's Oath of Office

Each person, admitted as prescribed in this chapter must, upon his admission, take the constitutional oath of office in open court, and subscribe the same in a roll or book, to be kept in the office of the clerk of the appellate division of the supreme court for that purpose. . . .

Editors' Note. The "constitutional oath of office" referred to in §466 is found in the New York State Constitution at Article 13, §1, which provides, in relevant part, as follows:

> Members of the legislature, and all officers, executive and judicial, except such inferior officers as shall be by law exempted, shall, before they enter on the duties of their respective offices, take and subscribe the following oath or affirmation: "I do solemnly swear (or affirm) that I will support the constitution of the United States, and the constitution of the State of New York, and that I will faithfully discharge the duties of the office of . . . . , according to the best of my ability"; and no other oath, declaration or test shall be required as a qualification for any office of public trust. . . .

§470. Attorneys Having Offices in This State May Reside in Adjoining State

A person, regularly admitted to practice as an attorney and counsellor, in the courts of record of this state, whose office for the transaction of law business is within the state, may practice as such attorney or counsellor, although he resides in an adjoining state.

§474-a. Contingent Fees for Attorneys in Claims or Actions for Medical, Dental or Podiatric Malpractice

> **Editors' Note.** During the 2000 legislative session, the Assembly and the Senate voted to repeal §474-a, but Governor Pataki vetoed the bill. However, the governor said that he might sign a similar bill in the future if it were part of a more comprehensive package of tort reform, such as limits on pain and suffering awards, the abolition of joint and several liability, and the adoption of a statute of repose.

1. For the purpose of this section, the term "contingent fee" shall mean any attorney's fee in any claim or action for medical, dental or podiatric malpractice, whether determined by judgment or settlement, which is dependent in whole or in part upon the success of the prosecution by the attorney of such claim or action, or which is to consist of a percentage of any recovery, or a sum equal to a percentage of any recovery, in such claim or action.

2. Notwithstanding any inconsistent judicial rule, a contingent fee in a medical, dental or podiatric malpractice action shall not exceed the amount of compensation provided for in the following schedule:

30 percent of the first $250,000 of the sum recovered;
25 percent of the next $250,000 of the sum recovered;
20 percent of the next $500,000 of the sum recovered;
15 percent of the next $250,000 of the sum recovered;
10 percent of any amount over $1,250,000 of the sum recovered.

3. Such percentages shall be computed on the net sum recovered after deducting from the amount recovered expenses and disbursements for expert testimony and investigative or other services properly chargeable to the enforcement of the claim or prosecution of the action. In computing the fee, the costs as taxed, including interest upon a judgment, shall be deemed part of the amount recovered. For the following or similar items there shall be no deduction in computing such percentages: liens, assignments or claims in favor of hospitals, for medical care, dental care,

podiatric care and treatment by doctors and nurses, or of self-insurers or insurance carriers.

4. In the event that claimant's or plaintiff's attorney believes in good faith that the fee schedule set forth in subdivision two of this section, because of extraordinary circumstances, will not give him adequate compensation, application for greater compensation may be made upon affidavit with written notice and an opportunity to be heard to the claimant or plaintiff and other persons holding liens or assignments on the recovery. . . .

5. Any contingent fee in a claim or action for medical, dental or podiatric malpractice brought on behalf of an infant shall continue to be subject to the provisions of section four hundred seventy-four of this chapter.

§475. Attorney's Lien in Action, Special or Other Proceeding

From the commencement of an action, special or other proceeding in any court or before any state, municipal or federal department, except a department of labor, or the service of an answer containing a counterclaim, the attorney who appears for a party has a lien upon his client's cause of action, claim or counterclaim, which attaches to a verdict, report, determination, decision, judgment or final order in his client's favor, and the proceeds thereof in whatever hands they may come; and the lien cannot be affected by any settlement between the parties before or after judgment, final order or determination. The court upon the petition of the client or attorney may determine and enforce the lien.

§477. Settlement of Actions for Personal Injury

If, in an action commenced to recover damages for a personal injury or for death as the result of a personal injury, an attorney having or claiming to have a lien for services performed or to be performed who shall have appeared for the person or persons having or claiming to have a right of action for such injury or death, no settlement or adjustment of such action shall be valid, unless consented to in writing by such attorney and by the person or persons for whom he shall have appeared, or approved by an order of the court in which such action is brought.

§478. Practicing or Appearing as Attorney-at-Law Without Being Admitted and Registered

It shall be unlawful for any natural person to practice or appear as an attorney-at-law or as an attorney and counselor-at-law for a person other than himself in a court of record in this state, or to furnish attorneys or counsel or an attorney and counsel to render legal services, or to hold himself out to the public as being entitled to practice law as aforesaid, or in any other manner, or to assume to be an attorney or counselor-at-law, or to assume, use, or advertise the title of lawyer, or attorney and counselor-at-law, or attorney-at-law or counselor-at-law, or attorney, or counselor, or attorney and counselor, or equivalent terms in any language, in such manner as to convey the impression that he is a legal practitioner of law or in any manner to advertise that he either alone or together with any other persons or person has, owns, conducts or maintains a law office or law and collection office, or office of any kind for the practice of law, without having first been duly and regularly licensed and admitted to practice law in the courts of record of this state, and without having taken the constitutional oath. . . .

§479. Soliciting Business on Behalf of an Attorney

It shall be unlawful for any person or his agent, employee or any person acting on his behalf, to solicit or procure through solicitation either directly or indirectly legal business, or to solicit or procure through solicitation a retainer, written or oral, or any agreement authorizing an attorney to perform or render legal services, or to make it a business so to solicit or procure such business, retainers or agreements.

§480. Entering Hospital to Negotiate Settlement or Obtain Release or Statement

It shall be unlawful for any person to enter a hospital for the purpose of negotiating a settlement or obtaining a general release or statement, written or oral, from any person confined in said hospital or sanitarium as a patient, with reference to any personal injuries for which said person is confined in said hospital or sanitarium within fifteen days after the injuries were sustained, unless at least five days prior to the obtaining or procuring of such general release or statement such injured party has signified in writing his willingness that such general release or statement be given. This section shall not apply to a person entering a hospital for the purpose of visiting a person therein confined, as his attorney or on behalf of his attorney.

§481. Aiding, Assisting or Abetting the Solicitation of Persons or the Procurement of a Retainer for or on Behalf of an Attorney

It shall be unlawful for any person in the employ of or in any capacity attached to any hospital, sanitarium, police department, prison or court, or for a person authorized to furnish bail bonds, to communicate directly or indirectly with any attorney or person acting on his behalf for the purpose of aiding, assisting or abetting such attorney in the solicitation of legal business or the procurement through solicitation of a retainer, written or oral, or any agreement authorizing the attorney to perform or render legal services.

§482. Employment by Attorney of Person to Aid, Assist or Abet in the Solicitation of Business or the Procurement Through Solicitation of a Retainer to Perform Legal Services

It shall be unlawful for an attorney to employ any person for the purpose of soliciting or aiding, assisting or abetting in the solicitation of legal business or the procurement through solicitation either directly or indirectly of a retainer, written or oral, or of any agreement authorizing the attorney to perform or render legal services.

§484. None but Attorneys to Practice in the State

No natural person shall ask or receive, directly or indirectly, compensation for appearing for a person other than himself as attorney in any court or before any magistrate, or for preparing deeds, mortgages, assignments, discharges, leases or any other instruments affecting real estate, wills, codicils, or any other instrument affecting the disposition of property after death, or decedents' estates, or pleadings of any kind in any action brought before any court of record in this state, or make it a business to practice for another as an attorney in any court or before any magistrate unless he has been regularly admitted to practice, as an attorney or counselor, in the courts of record in the state; but nothing in this section shall apply (1) to officers of societies for the prevention of cruelty to animals, duly appointed, when exercising the special powers conferred upon such corporations under section fourteen hundred three of the not-for-profit corporation law; or (2) to law students who have completed at least two semesters of law school or persons who have graduated from a law school, who have taken the examination for admittance to practice law in the courts of record in the state immediately available after graduation from law school, or the examination immediately available after being notified by the board of law examiners that they failed to pass said exam, and who have not been notified by the board of law examiners that they have failed to pass two such examinations, acting under the supervision of a legal aid organization, when such students and persons are acting under a program approved by the appellate division of the supreme court of the department in which the principal office of such organization is located and specifying the extent to which such students and persons may engage in activities prohibited by this statute; or (3) to persons who have graduated from a law school approved pursuant to the rules of the court of appeals for the admission of attorneys and counsellors-at-law and who have taken the examination for admission to practice as an attorney and counsellor-at-law immediately available after graduation from law school or the examination immediately available after being notified by the board of law examiners that they failed to pass said exam, and who have not been notified by the board of law examiners that they have failed to pass two such examinations, when such persons are acting under the supervision of the state or a subdivision thereof or of any officer or agency of the state or a subdivision thereof, pursuant to a program approved by the appellate division of the supreme court of the department within which such activities are taking place and specifying the extent to which they may engage in activities otherwise prohibited by this statute and those powers of the supervising governmental entity or officer in connection with which they may engage in such activities.

§485. Violation of Certain Preceding Sections a Misdemeanor

Any person violating the provisions of sections four hundred seventy-eight, four hundred seventy-nine, four hundred eighty, four hundred eighty-one, four hundred eighty-two, four hundred eighty-three or four hundred eighty-four, shall be guilty of a misdemeanor.

§487. Misconduct by Attorneys

An attorney or counsellor who:

(1) Is guilty of any deceit or collusion, or consents to any deceit or collusion, with intent to deceive the court or any party; or,

(2) Wilfully delays his client's suit with a view to his own gain; or, wilfully receives any money or allowance for or on account of any money which he has not laid out, or becomes answerable for,

Is guilty of a misdemeanor, and in addition to the punishment prescribed therefor by the penal law, he forfeits to the party injured treble damages, to be recovered in a civil action.

§491. Sharing of Compensation by Attorneys Prohibited

(1) It shall be unlawful for any person, partnership, corporation, or association to divide with or receive from, or to agree to divide with or receive from, any attorney-at-law or group of attorneys-at-law, whether practicing in this state or elsewhere, either before or after action brought, any portion of any fee or compensation, charged or received by such attorney-at-law or any valuable consideration or reward, as an inducement for placing, or in consideration of having placed, in the hands of such attorney-at-law, or in the hands of another person, a claim or demand of any kind for the purpose of collecting such claim, or bringing an action thereon, or of representing claimant in the pursuit of any civil remedy for the recovery thereof. But this section does not apply to an agreement between attorneys and counsellors-at-law to divide between themselves the compensation to be received.

(2) Any person violating any of the provisions of this section is guilty of a misdemeanor.

§495. Corporations and Voluntary Associations Not to Practice Law

(1) No corporation or voluntary association shall

(a) practice or appear as an attorney-at-law for any person in any court in this state or before any judicial body, nor

(b) make it a business to practice as an attorney-at-law, for any person, in any of said courts, nor

(c) hold itself out to the public as being entitled to practice law, or to render legal services or advice, nor

(d) furnish attorneys or counsel, nor

(e) render legal services of any kind in actions or proceedings of any nature or in any other way or manner, nor

(f) assume in any other manner to be entitled to practice law, nor

(g) assume, use or advertise the title of lawyer or attorney, attorney-at-law, or equivalent terms in any language in such manner as to convey the impression that it is entitled to practice law or to furnish legal advice, services or counsel, nor

(h) advertise that either alone or together with or by or through any person whether or not a duly and regularly admitted attorney-at-law, it has, owns, conducts or maintains a law office or an office for the practice of law, or for furnishing legal advice, services or counsel. . . .

(7) This section does not apply to organizations which offer prepaid legal services; to non-profit organizations whether incorporated or unincorporated, organized and operating primarily for a purpose other than the provision of legal services and which furnish legal services as

an incidental activity in furtherance of their primary purpose; or to organizations which have as their primary purpose the furnishing of legal services to indigent persons.

§496. [Prepaid Legal Services Plans; Registration Statement]

An organization described in subdivision seven of section four hundred ninety-five of this article shall file with the appellate division department in which its principal office is located a statement describing the nature and purposes of the organization, the composition of its governing body, the type of legal services being made available, and the names and addresses of any attorneys and counselors-at law employed by the organization or with whom commitments have been made. An updating of this information shall be furnished the appropriate appellate division on or before July first of each year and the names and addresses of attorneys and counsellors-at-law who rendered legal services during that year shall be included.

§498. Professional Referrals

(1) There shall be no cause of action for damages arising against any association or society of attorneys and counsellors at law authorized to practice in the state of New York for referring any person or persons to a member of the profession for the purpose of obtaining legal services, provided that such referral was made without charge and as a public service by said association or society, and without malice, and in the reasonable belief that such referral was warranted, based upon the facts disclosed.

(2) For the purposes of this section, "association or society of attorneys or counsellors at law" shall mean any such organization, whether incorporated or unincorporated, which offers professional referrals as an incidental service in the normal course of business, but which business does not include the providing of legal services.

§499. Lawyer Assistance Committees

(1) *Confidential information privileged.* The confidential relations and communications between a member or authorized agent of a lawyer assistance committee sponsored by a state or local bar association and any person, firm or corporation communicating with such committee, its members or authorized agents shall be deemed to be privileged on the same basis as those provided by law between attorney and client.

Such privilege may be waived only by the person, firm or corporation which has furnished information to the committee.

(2) *Immunity from liability.* Any person, firm or corporation in good faith providing information to, or in any other way participating in the affairs of, any of the committees referred to in subdivision one of this section shall be immune from civil liability that might otherwise result by reason of such conduct. For the purpose of any proceeding, the good faith of any such person, firm or corporation shall be presumed.

Special Section: Some Legal Ethics Issues in the Enron Investigation

Special Section: Some Legal Ethics Issues in the Enron Investigation

Editors' Introduction. This special section contains original documents, a factual background, and questions that raise legal ethics and lawyering issues in connection with the collapse of Enron and the prosecution and conviction of its auditors, Arthur Andersen LLP, which until recently was one of five major United States accounting firms. We include excerpts from a class action complaint, the indictment of Arthur Andersen, testimony before the Senate Judiciary Committee by Professor Susan Koniak, internal Andersen memos, and extensive note material including a time line of events at Andersen beginning in the fall of 2001.

Enron, which filed for bankruptcy in December of 2001, evolved in the 1990s from a regional trader in natural gas to an international energy company. Until Enron's bankruptcy, Andersen was its auditor and Enron was among Andersen's largest clients. By the summer of 2001, after suspicions arose about Enron's financial practices, attention focused on Andersen and the performance of its auditing functions. In this time, memos and discussions at Andersen turned to its document retention and destruction policies. Large quantities of documents were shredded, leading to the indictment and conviction of the firm for obstruction of justice, as discussed below. In the summer of 2002, various investigations of Enron and others were still underway. In addition to SEC and Justice Department investigations and prosecutions, civil actions are pending against Enron, Arthur Andersen, and two law firms — Vinson & Elkins and Kirkland & Ellis.

The principal players in our ensuing discussion include, in addition to Enron, Arthur Andersen, and the two law firms, the following. Additional persons or entities are identified in the course of the narrative.

- David Duncan, a former partner at Andersen who pled guilty to violation of 18 U.S.C. §1512(b)(2), which is further discussed below, and testified for the government at Andersen's trial;
- Nancy Temple, an in-house lawyer at Andersen, formerly a litigation partner at Sidley & Austin; and
- The New York law firm of Davis, Polk & Wardwell.

The Class Action Complaint

The 499-page class action civil complaint filed against various defendants who worked for or provided services to Enron, including Vinson & Elkins and Kirkland & Ellis, alleges as follows:

- "Each of the defendants sued for fraud engaged or participated in the implementation of manipulative devices to inflate Enron's reported profits and financial condition, made or participated in the making of false and misleading statements, **and** participated in a scheme to defraud **or** a course of business that operated as a fraud or a deceit on purchasers of Enron's publicly traded securities between 10/10/98 and 11/27/01. . . .
- "This fraudulent scheme and course of business enabled defendants to pocket **billions of dollars** of legal accounting, auditing, and consulting fees, underwriting commissions, interest in credit facility payments, cash bonuses based on Enron's reported earnings and its stock performance, and illegal insider trading proceeds, such that each defendant was significantly enriched. . . .
- "This fraud was accomplished, in part, through clandestinely controlled partnerships and so-called special purpose entities ('SPEs') that the defendants created, structured, financed and used to do transactions with Enron to inflate its profits and hide its debt and thus perpetuate the fraud by violating Generally Accepted Accounting Principles ('GAAP') and the principles of 'fair presentation' of financial results."

In re Enron Corporation Securities Litigation, Civil Action No. H-01-3624, United States District Court, Southern District of Texas, Houston Division (boldface in original). The full complaint is posted on the web site of Milberg Weiss, the law firm representing the Regents of the University of California, the lead named plaintiff in the class action litigation. See www.Milbergweiss.com. Although the Milberg Weiss complaint claims copyright protection (can you copyright a complaint?), we have reproduced several pages of it below for a flavor of the allegations against Vinson & Elkins and Kirkland & Ellis. See paragraphs 801, 803, and 859-861.

Special Section: Some Legal Ethics Issues in the Enron Investigation

UNITED STATES DISTRICT COURT
SOUTHERN DISTRICT OF TEXAS
HOUSTON DIVISION

In re ENRON CORPORATON SECURITIES LITIGATION	§ Civil Action No. H-01-3624 § **(Consolidated)** §
This Document Relates To:	§ CLASS ACTION §
MARK NEWBY, et al., Individually and On Behalf of All Others Similarly Situated, Plaintiffs, vs. ENRON CORP., et al., Defendants.	§ § CONSOLIDATED COMPLAINT FOR § VIOLATION OF THE SECURITIES § LAWS § § § § § § § §
THE REGENTS OF THE UNIVERSITY OF CALIFORNIA, et al., Individually and On Behalf of All Others Similarly Situated, Plaintiffs, vs. KENNETH L. LAY, JEFFREY K. SKILLING, ANDREW S. FASTOW, RICHARD A. CAUSEY, JAMES V. DERRICK, JR.,	§ § § § § § § § § § §

[Caption continued on following page.]

801. Vinson & Elkins was general corporate counsel to Enron for many years and throughout the Class Period. Enron was Vinson & Elkin's largest client. Vinson & Elkins participated in the negotiations for, prepared the transaction documents for, and structured Enron's LJM and Chewco/JEDI partnerships and virtually all of the related SPE entities and transactions — manipulative devices which falsified Enron's reported profits and financial condition. These manipulations resulted in Enron's massive restatement in 11/01 and collapse into bankruptcy shortly thereafter. Vinson & Elkins knew that these partnership entities and SPE entities were ***not*** independent of Enron and were ***not*** valid SPEs, but rather, were manipulative contrivances being utilized to artificially inflate Enron's reported financial results. Nevertheless, Vinson & Elkins repeatedly gave "true sale" and other opinions that were false — but were indispensable for those deals to "close," i.e., take place, and the fraudulent scheme to continue. Vinson & Elkins also drafted and/or approved the adequacy of Enron's press releases, shareholder reports and SEC filings (including 10Ks and Registration Statements alleged in this Complaint which Vinson & Elkins knew were false and misleading). Vinson & Elkins also wrote the disclosures regarding the related party transactions, which Vinson & Elkins knew were misleading and concealed material facts concerning those transactions. Finally, during the Summer and Fall of 01, Vinson & Elkins also engaged and participated in covering up the fraudulent scheme and wrongful course of business by conducting a whitewash investigation of what it knew were correct allegations of fraudulent misconduct — which Vinson & Elkins had itself been involved in. . . .

803. A prime example of the depth of Vinson & Elkin's knowledge of, and participation in the fraudulent scheme was the hiding of billions of dollars of debt that should have been on Enron's balance sheet via the Mahonia phony commodities trades — a contrivance involving JP Morgan. Vinson & Elkins issued opinions to Enron, Mahonia and JP Morgan representing that billions of dollars in forward sales contracts of natural gas and oil by Enron were legitimate commodities trades when, in fact, as Vinson & Elkins knew, the trades were bogus — manipulative devices to disguise loans from JP Morgan to Enron so those loans would not have to be shown as debt on Enron's balance sheet. No physical delivery of product was required or contemplated. Rather, the transactions were disguised loans through Mahonia, an entity set up by and controlled by JP Morgan. Mahonia and the bogus trades were an artifice to allow Enron to keep some $3.9 billion in debt off its balance sheet.

(1) Kirkland & Ellis's Role in the SPEs

859. Kirkland & Ellis's ostensibly separate legal representation was utilized to provide the appearance of independence of these SPE's. In fact, Kirkland & Ellis was selected by Fastow because of Kirkland & Ellis's

willingness to take direction from Fastow and Enron and was an active participant in the scheme. Kirkland & Ellis's participation in the scheme was essential as it provided some of the expertise necessary for creating SPE transactions that would appear to be arm's-length transactions with independent entities. Working with Andersen, Vinson & Elkins and Enron's banks, Kirkland & Ellis structured the manipulative devices that formed the core of the scheme, including the partnerships and SPE's known as LJM1, LJM2, Chewco and the Raptors, which were used to artificially inflate Enron's reported financial condition and results.

860. Kirkland & Ellis engaged and participated in the scheme by: (i) structuring the SPE's utilized to perpetrate the scheme; (ii) participating in the monetization of assets to facilitate the falsification of Enron's financial statements and results; (iii) preparing partnership and loan agreements for Chewco, LJM1 and LJM2; (iv) participating in the offering and sale of partnership interests in LJM2 via the LJM2 private placement memoranda; and (v) issuing of dozens of legal opinions concerning the structure, legality and *bona fides* of SPE's used to perpetuate the scheme.

861. Kirkland & Ellis knew of the defects in and lack of *bona fides* of the SPEs it created and that these transactions were not arm's length from Enron but, in fact, were manipulative contrivances designed to artificially boost Enron's reported financial results. Kirkland & Ellis also knew that because these entities were not independent of Enron, ***it was not representing independent entities nor was it providing independent representation to those entities but, in fact, it was working with, under the control of and at the direction of Fastow, Kopper, Skilling, Lay and other Enron insiders,*** to paper transactions and close deals as they directed ***without regard to the legal or economic interests or rights of the entities Kirkland & Ellis purportedly represented.***

Federal Obstruction of Justice Law

Enron's auditor was Arthur Andersen LLP. Andersen admitted that employees had destroyed Enron-related documents at a time when some Arthur Andersen personnel were aware of an impending SEC investigation. But Arthur Andersen denied that these documents were destroyed with criminal intent. At this point, it is useful to identify various federal statutes governing obstruction of justice. Following are brief descriptions of 18 U.S.C. §§1503, 1505, 1512, and 1515. The full text of these can be found in the chapter on Federal Provisions on Conflicts, Confidentiality and Crimes. Notice these differences.

1. The so-called "omnibus clause" in §1503 makes it a crime if a person "corruptly . . . influences, obstructs, or impedes, or endeavors to influence, obstruct, or impede, the due administration of justice. . . ." For this provision to be violated, the administration of

justice must then be occurring, which means there must be a pending court or agency proceeding or a sitting grand jury. United States v. Neal, 951 F.2d 630 (5th Cir. 1992).

2. 18 U.S.C. §1505 penalizes the same conduct where the act is aimed at the "proper administration of the law under which any pending proceeding is being had before any department or agency of the United States, or the due and proper exercise of the power of inquiry under which any inquiry or investigation is being had" in Congress. For this section to be violated, there must be a then-pending congressional or agency investigation or proceeding.
3. By contrast, 18 U.S.C. §1512, particularly paragraph (b)(2)(B), makes it a crime if a person "*corruptly persuades* another person, or attempts to do so, or engages in misleading conduct toward another person, with intent to . . . cause or induce any person to . . . alter, destroy, mutilate, or conceal an object with intent to impair the object's integrity or availability for use in an official proceeding." (Emphasis added.) No proceeding need then be impending or in progress and the destroyed item need not even be admissible in evidence. §1512(e). This is the section to which Andersen partner David Duncan entered a guilty plea and under which Arthur Andersen was prosecuted. The government attempted to prove that certain persons at Andersen were "corrupt persuaders" who tried to get other Andersen employees to destroy documents relevant to an *impending* SEC investigation. In United States v. Frankhauser, 80 F.3d 641 (1st Cir. 1996), the court affirmed a conviction under §1512 where the evidence showed that the defendant "expected a grand jury investigation and/or a trial in the foreseeable future, and that his intent was to make the items unavailable for use in such a proceeding," although no proceeding was then pending.
4. Finally, 18 U.S.C. §1515 provides certain definitions. Note in particular §1515(c), which provides a "safe harbor" defense exclusively for lawyers who are providing "lawful, bona fide, legal representation services." In United States v. Kloess, 251 F.3d 941 (11th Cir. 2001), the court held that once a lawyer produces evidence that could support a reasonable doubt with regard to the elements of this defense, the government has the burden of disproving it beyond a reasonable doubt.*

*In the summer of 2002, in response to Andersen, Enron, and other corporate scandals, Congress passed and President Bush signed the "Sarbanes-Oxley Act of 2002." The Act does many things to encourage trust in corporate governance and accuracy in corporate accounting. For our immediate purpose, the Act adds two sections to the obstruction statutes. A new section, §1512(c), duplicates other sections aimed at destruction of real evidence, but it increases the penalty for these acts to twenty years. New §1519 provides for a twenty-year punishment for destruction, alteration, concealment, or mutilation of evidence and for making a false entry in any document with the intent to obstruct a federal investigation or bankruptcy case. We reprint these amendments above in our selection of Federal Provisions on Conflicts, Confidentiality, and Crimes.

Special Section: Some Legal Ethics Issues in the Enron Investigation

An Enron/Andersen Timeline

Following is a timeline of some events leading to the indictment of Arthur Andersen, followed by the indictment itself. Items in **bold** are printed following the timeline.

Timeline of Reported Events Surrounding Andersen Document Destruction

9/28-10/12/01 Nancy Temple, Andersen in-house lawyer, has meetings with Andersen officers including David Duncan re document retention (source: Hearings, 1/24/02, before House Energy and Commerce Subcommittee).

10/9/01 Temple notes on conversation with her boss say "highly probable some SEC inquiry" re Enron (source: Wall Street Journal 6/4/02).

10/9/01 Andersen hires Davis Polk with the understanding that it would start work on October 16 (source: Hearings on 1/24/02 before House Energy and Commerce Subcommittee and Andersen indictment).

10/10/01 Michael Odom, Andersen's practice director in Houston, tells accountants: "If documents are destroyed and litigation is filed the next day, that's great. We've followed our own policy, and whatever there was that might have been of interest to somebody is gone and irretrievable" (source: New York Times 3/18/02). This statement was videotaped with the videotape played at Andersen's criminal trial.

10/12/01 **Temple e-mails Andersen's document retention and destruction policy to Mike Odom to "remind" the Enron engagement team of the policy and that it would be "helpful" to ensure compliance. Odom forwards a copy to Duncan immediately.**

Before House Energy and Commerce Subcommittee, 1/24/02:

Rep. Markey: Is it your legal opinion that Andersen is free to shred documents relating to its work for Enron until such time as it actually receives a subpoena from the SEC, or is formally named as a defendant in a class action lawsuit by Enron's employees or other investors?

Ms. Temple: I have not reached that legal opinion.
Rep. Markey: Was that your view at that time?
Ms. Temple: I was not asked . . . to reach a legal opinion at any particular time, and I was unaware of any shredding activity.

10/14-10/16/01 **David Duncan prepares drafts of a file memorandum describing his conversations with Rick Causey, Enron's Chief Accounting Officer, in which he warned that the word "non-recurring" in a forthcoming Enron press release could be misinterpreted. Duncan sends the draft file memorandum to various Andersen personnel, including Nancy Temple.**

Editors' Note. The following e-mail responds to a different draft of the Duncan e-mail than the one summarized above and printed below. The draft to which Temple replies could not be found but it does not appear to differ significantly from the draft we obtained and the differences that exist are readily apparent from the text of Temple's e-mail, also printed below.

10/16/01 **Temple responds by e-mail with "a few suggested comments for consideration," including deletion of reference to her and the "legal group" from the file memorandum and "deleting some language that might suggest we have concluded the release is misleading." Temple also says that she will consult with the "legal group" as to whether the use of the word "non-recurring" in the Enron press release requires Andersen to "do anything more to protect ourselves from potential §10A issues."**

10/16/01 Davis Polk commences work (source: Hearings, 1/24/02, before House Energy and Commerce Subcommittee).

Before House Energy and Commerce Subcommittee, 1/24/02:

Rep. Greenwood: When was the first time that Davis Polk gave the company any advice whatsoever or counsel whatsoever with regard to document retention and destruction?

	Ms. Temple:	I believe in my conversation on October 16th I discussed the documentation and retention issues that had arisen as of that date with Davis Polk.
10/19/01	Temple sends the Andersen document retention and destruction policy to two Andersen partners in the Chicago office professional standards group, who have been consulting on the Enron engagement.	
10/19 to 10/20/01	Duncan first learns of SEC informal inquiry (source: Hearings, 1/24/02, before House Energy and Commerce Subcommittee).	
10/22/01	Enron publicly announces SEC informal inquiry.	
10/23/01	Wholesale destruction of documents at Andersen's office in Houston begins. Instructions given to destroy Enron documents in other Andersen offices (source: Andersen indictment). On 5/14/02, at Andersen's criminal trial, Duncan testified that Temple's 10/12 e-mail played a role in his decision to order the destruction of documents and at meetings with partners on 10/23 everyone understood that his direction to get in compliance with the firm's document policy meant destroying documents. Duncan testified: "I thought this was all entirely appropriate until I received a subpoena" from the SEC. Until a subpoena was received, he testified, no one at Andersen told him not to destroy documents (source: Wall Street Journal, 5/15/02).	
10/24-10/26/01	Andersen destroys more than 3,500 pounds of documents in a three-day period compared with an average of 70-90 pounds a day during 2001 (source: Prosecution summation in Andersen trial, Wall Street Journal 6/6/02).	
11/9/01	Temple sends Duncan a voice mail directing him to preserve all Enron-related documents due to receipt of SEC subpoena.	

11/9/01	Duncan's assistant sends an e-mail to others on the Enron engagement stating, "no more shredding."
11/10/01	Temple sends an e-mail regarding document preservation to individuals on the Enron engagement, including Duncan. Temple testifies that the text was written by Davis Polk.
3/7/02	**Andersen indicted under 18 U.S.C. §1512(b)(2).**
4/9/02	David Duncan pleads guilty to obstruction of justice.

Following are the documents identified in **bold** in this timeline.

To: David B. Duncan@ANDERSEN WO
CC:
BCC:
Date: 10/12/2001 08:56 AM
From: Michael C. Odom
Subject: Document retention policy
Attachments:

More help.

_______________ Forwarded by Michael C. Odom on 10/12/2001 10:55 AM

____

To: Michael C. Odom@ANDERSEN WO
cc:
Date: 10/12/2001 10:53 AM
From: Nancy A. Temple, Chicago 33 W. Monroe, 50 / 11234
Subject: Document retention policy

Mike-
It might be useful to consider reminding the engagement team of our documentation and retention policy. It will be helpful to make sure that we have complied with the policy. Let me know if you have any questions.

Nancy

http://www.intranet.andersen.com/onefirm.nsf/content/ResourcesFirmwide PolicicsPolicy-ClientInformationOrganization!Open Document

Memo

ANDERSEN

Draft

To The Files

From David B. Duncan

Date October 15, 2001

Subject Enron Press Release Discussions

On Friday evening, October 12, 2001, I received a draft of Enron's anticipated press release regarding third quarter 2001 results which indicated Enron's intentions to record numerous charges against income for the quarter totaling approximately $1 billion on an after-tax basis. The charges were described as "non-recurring" in the draft.

Enron had sometimes used this description in past press releases. In such cases, we had always informed management that, although we understood that press releases were the Company's responsibility, we did not advise the use of "non-recurring" as a description and were concerned it could potentially be misunderstood by investors. We pointed out that such items are, more often than not, included in normal operating earnings in the GAAP financial statements. We also insisted that the Company not use such a description in public filings with which we may have some association (i.e., in 10-Q and 10-K MD&A information). Whether because of our views or otherwise, management has generally described these or similar items as "Items Impacting Comparability in such public filings".

Because of the magnitude of the anticipated third quarter 2001 charges and because they were being described as "non-recurring" in the draft release, I shared excerpts of the draft with Mike Odom, Rich Corgel and Gary Goolsby of our practice risk management group.

After discussion with the above individuals, on Sunday, October 14, I spoke with Rick Causey, Enron's Chief Accounting Officer, about the company's presentation approach. I told Rick that, while we recognized that press releases are solely the Company's responsibility, we had strong concerns that the presentation of the charges as non-recurring could be misconstrued or misunderstood by investors. Our advice was that the Company should consider changing the presentation or should otherwise undertake whatever procedures they might deem necessary, including the involvement of counsel. Rick acknowledged my advice.

On Monday, October 15, 2001, the night before the release, I inquired of Rick what procedures may have been performed. He responded that he had raised the issue internally and that the press release had gone through "normal legal review".

The release was issued early Tuesday, October 16, 2001, with essentially the original presentation.

cc: Mike Odom
Rich Corgel
Gary Goolsby

To:	David B. Duncan
CC:	Michael C. Odom@ANDERSEN WO; Richard Corgel@ANDERSEN WO; Gary B. Goolsby@ANDERSEN WO
BCC:	
Date:	10/16/2001 08:39 PM
From:	Nancy A. Temple
Subject:	Re: Press Release draft
Attachments:	ATT8ICIQ; 3rd qtr press release memo.doc

Dave – Here are a few suggested comments for consideration.

–I recommend deleting reference to consultation with the legal group and deleting my name on the memo. Reference to the legal group consultation arguably is a waiver of attorney-client privileged advice and if my name is mentioned it increases the chances that I might be a witness, which I prefer to avoid.

–I suggested deleting some language that might suggest we have concluded the release is misleading.

–In light of the "non-recurring" characterization, the lack of any suggestion that this characterization is not in accordance with GAAP, and the lack of income statements in accordance with GAAP, I will consult further within the legal group as to whether we should do anything more to protect ourselves from potential Section 10A issues.

Nancy

CLERK U.S. DISTRICT COURT
SOUTHERN DISTRICT OF TEXAS
FILED
3/7/02

MICHAEL N. MILBY, CLERK

UNITED STATES DISTRICT COURT
SOUTHERN DISTRICT OF TEXAS

---------------------------X

UNITED STATES OF AMERICA,

–against–

ARTHUR ANDERSEN, LLP,

Defendant.

---------------------------X

CR H–02–121

I N D I C T M E N T

Cr. No. ______________
(T. 18, U.S.C., §§1512(b)(2) and 3551 et seq.)

THE GRAND JURY CHARGES:

I. ANDERSEN AND ENRON

1. ARTHUR ANDERSEN, LLP ("ANDERSEN"), is a partnership that performs, among other things, accounting and consulting services for clients that operate businesses throughout the United States and the world. ANDERSEN is one of the so-called "Big Five" accounting firms in the United States. ANDERSEN has its headquarters in Chicago, Illinois, and maintains offices throughout the world, including in Houston, Texas.

2. Enron Corp. ("Enron") was an Oregon corporation with its principal place of business in Houston, Texas. For most of 2001, Enron was considered the seventh largest corporation in the United States based on its reported revenues. In the previous ten years, Enron had evolved from a regional natural gas provider to, among other things, a trader of natural gas, electricity and other commodities, with retail operations in energy and other products.

3. For the past 16 years, up until it filed for bankruptcy in December 2001, Enron retained ANDERSEN to be its auditor. Enron was one of ANDERSEN's largest clients worldwide, and became ANDERSEN's largest client in ANDERSEN's Gulf Coast region. ANDERSEN earned tens of millions of dollars from Enron in annual auditing and other fees.

4. ANDERSEN performed both internal and external auditing work for Enron mainly in Houston, Texas. ANDERSEN established within Enron's offices in Houston a work space for the ANDERSEN team that had primary responsibility for performing audit work for Enron. In addition to Houston, ANDERSEN personnel performed work for Enron in, among other locations, Chicago, Illinois, Portland, Oregon, and London, England.

II. THE ANTICIPATION OF LITIGATION AGAINST ENRON AND ANDERSEN

5. In the summer and fall of 2001, a series of significant developments led to ANDERSEN's foreseeing imminent civil litigation against, and government investigations of, Enron and ANDERSEN.

6. On or about October 16, 2001, Enron issued a press release announcing a $618 million net loss for the third quarter of 2001. That same day, but not as part of the press release, Enron announced to analysts that it would reduce shareholder equity by approximately $1.2 billion. The market reacted immediately and the stock price of Enron shares plummeted.

7. The Securities and Exchange Commission ("SEC"), which investigates possible violations of the federal securities laws, opened an inquiry into Enron the very next day, requesting in writing information from Enron.

8. In addition to the negative financial information disclosed by Enron to the public and to analysts on October 16, 2001, ANDERSEN was aware by this time of additional significant facts unknown to the public.

- The approximately $1.2 billion reduction in shareholder equity disclosed to analysts on October 16, 2001, was necessitated by ANDERSEN and Enron having previously improperly categorized hundreds of millions of dollars as an *increase*, rather than a decrease, to Enron shareholder equity.
- The Enron October 16, 2001, press release characterized numerous charges against income for the third quarter as "non-recurring" even though ANDERSEN believed the company did not have a basis for concluding that the charges would in fact be non-recurring. Indeed, ANDERSEN advised Enron against using that term, and documented its objections internally in the event of litigation, but did not report its objections or otherwise take steps to cure the public statement.
- ANDERSEN was put on direct notice of the allegations of Sherron Watkins, a current Enron employee and former ANDERSEN employee, regarding possible fraud and other improprieties at Enron, and in particular, Enron's use of off-balance-sheet "special purpose entities" that enabled the company to camouflage the true financial condition of the company. Watkins had reported her concerns to a partner at ANDERSEN, who thereafter disseminated them within ANDERSEN, including to the team working on the Enron audit. In addition, the team had received warnings about possible undisclosed side-agreements at Enron.
- The ANDERSEN team handling the Enron audit directly contravened the accounting methodology approved by ANDERSEN's own specialists working it its Professional Standards Group. In opposition to the views of its own experts, the ANDERSEN auditors had advised Enron in the spring of 2001 that it could use a favorable accounting method for its "special purpose entities."
- In 2000, an internal review conducted by senior management within ANDERSEN evaluated the ANDERSEN team assigned to audit Enron and rated the team as only a "2" on a scale of one to five, with five being the highest rating.
- On or about October 9, 2001, correctly anticipating litigation and government investigations, ANDERSEN, which had an internal department of lawyers for routine legal matters, retained an experienced New York law firm to handle future Enron-related litigation.

III. <u>THE WHOLESALE DESTRUCTION OF DOCUMENTS BY ANDERSEN</u>

9. By Friday, October 19, 2001, Enron alerted the ANDERSEN audit team that the SEC had begun an inquiry regarding the Enron "special purpose

entities" and the involvement of Enron's Chief Financial Officer. The next morning, an emergency conference call among high-level ANDERSEN management was convened to address the SEC inquiry. During the call, it was decided that documentation that could assist Enron in responding to the SEC was to be assembled by the ANDERSEN auditors.

10. After spending Monday, October 22, 2001 at Enron, ANDERSEN partners assigned to the Enron engagement team launched on October 23, 2001, a wholesale destruction of documents at ANDERSEN's offices in Houston, Texas. ANDERSEN personnel were called to urgent and mandatory meetings. Instead of being advised to preserve documentation so as to assist Enron and the SEC, ANDERSEN employees on the Enron engagement team were instructed by ANDERSEN partners and others to destroy immediately documentation relating to Enron, and told to work overtime if necessary to accomplish the destruction. During the next few weeks, an unparalleled initiative was undertaken to shred physical documentation and delete computer files. Tons of paper relating to the Enron audit were promptly shredded as part of the orchestrated document destruction. The shredder at the ANDERSEN office at the Enron building was used virtually constantly and, to handle the overload, dozens of large trunks filled with Enron documents were sent to ANDERSEN's main Houston office to be shredded. A systematic effort was also undertaken and carried out to purge the computer hard-drives and e-mail system of Enron-related files.

11. In addition to shredding and deleting documents in Houston, Texas, instructions were given to ANDERSEN personnel working on Enron audit matters in Portland, Oregon, Chicago, Illinois, and London, England, to make sure that Enron documents were destroyed there as well. Indeed, in London, a coordinated effort by ANDERSEN partners and others, similar to the initiative undertaken in Houston, was put into place to destroy Enron-related documents within days of notice of the SEC inquiry. Enron-related documents also were destroyed by ANDERSEN partners in Chicago.

12. On or about November 8, 2001, the SEC served ANDERSEN with the anticipated subpoena relating to its work for Enron. In response, members of the ANDERSEN team on the Enron audit were alerted finally that there could be "no more shredding" because the firm had been "officially served" for documents.

THE CHARGE: OBSTRUCTION OF JUSTICE

13. On or about and between October 10, 2001, and November 9, 2001, within the Southern District of Texas and elsewhere, including Chicago, Illinois, Portland, Oregon, and London, England, ANDERSEN, through its partners and others, did knowingly, intentionally and corruptly persuade and attempt to persuade other persons, to wit: ANDERSEN employees, with intent to cause and induce such persons to (a) withhold records, documents and other objects from official proceedings, namely: regulatory and criminal proceedings and investigations, and (b) alter, destroy, mutilate and conceal objects with intent to impair the objects' integrity and availability for use in such official proceedings.

(Title 18, United States Code, Sections 1512(b)(2) and 3551 et seq.)

A TRUE BILL

____

FOREPERSON

JOSHUA R. HOCHBERG
ACTING UNITED STATES ATTORNEY
SOUTHERN DISTRICT OF TEXAS

LESLIE R. CALDWELL
DIRECTOR, ENRON TASK FORCE

By: ______________________

Samuel W. Buell
Andrew Weissmann
Special Attorneys
Department of Justice

The Koniak Testimony

On February 6, 2002, three months before the beginning of the Arthur Andersen criminal trial, Professor Susan P. Koniak of the Boston University School of Law and a nationally prominent academic expert in the field of lawyer regulation, testified by invitation before the Senate Judiciary Committee. Professor Koniak titled her testimony "Where Were the Lawyers? Behind the Curtain Wearing Their Magic Caps." Much of her prepared testimony criticized Vinson & Elkins, but she also had harsh things to say about Nancy Temple, the in-house lawyer at Andersen, and about Davis, Polk & Wardwell. We focus here on the latter two. Recall that Davis Polk was retained by Andersen in connection with the Enron matter on October 9, 2001, with the understanding that it would begin work October 16, 2001. Except for Temple's testimony before the House Energy & Commerce Subcommittee, some of which is summarized in the timeline, she has declined to provide further testimony, including at the Andersen criminal trial, citing her Fifth Amendment rights. News reports have suggested that she may be at risk of indictment in connection with the Enron/Andersen investigation. *Wall Street Journal,* June 17, 2002. Do you agree with Professor Koniak's criticism of Ms. Temple and Davis Polk?

TESTIMONY OF SUSAN P. KONIAK, PROFESSOR OF LAW BOSTON UNIVERSITY SCHOOL OF LAW

Before the
Senate Judiciary Committee
February 6, 2002

Hearing on Accountability Issues: Lessons Learned from Enron's Fall . . .

Some group of people at Arthur Andersen shredded some substantial number of Enron documents. The shredding not only left Andersen's reputation in ruins, it put Andersen into serious legal jeopardy under civil and criminal law. What were Andersen's lawyers doing while Andersen's accountants and staff were doing that shredding? The facts disclosed thus far suggest three possibilities; none of them good. Andersen's lawyers were either (1) encouraging this destruction through none-too-subtle hints; (2) recklessly ignoring the strong likelihood that documents were headed for the shredder; or (3) acting carelessly in relation to whether the Enron files were preserved or not.

What should they have done to prevent the wholesale shredding that apparently began on or about October 23rd and continued for some considerable time thereafter? What they did way too late: Issue unequivocal legal advice that all Enron documents were to be preserved and suggest procedures to Andersen's management that would have helped ensure that the documents were actually preserved.

Instead, on October 12th Nancy Temple, a member of Andersen's in-house legal staff, wrote the now infamously ambiguous retention/destruction memo that David Duncan, the Andersen partner in charge of Enron's account, has told congressional investigators he read as authorizing him to begin the shredding. I have read that memo and the policy that it says might be "helpful" and thus suggests should be followed. As I read those documents, it seems like Attorney Temple's memo was an effort to encourage others to destroy Enron documents, while preserving for its author the ability to deny that she meant any such thing. (Indeed, Andersen's retention/destruction policy seems designed to achieve that same result and was probably written by a lawyer too.)

Perhaps, Attorney Temple did not mean the memo that way. She has testified that she did not. She says that she meant the partner in charge, Mr. Duncan, to read the policy and interpret what it meant for himself. Why? Was she unsure of what the policy demanded? If so, was it sensible to believe an accountant would have an easier time deciphering it, this document that resembles a legal regulation much more than an accounting rule? And what of the law's demands? Did she have no information to give Mr. Duncan and the other accountants on that either?

But this is not a tale of one poorly-intentioned or careless lawyer, writing a reckless or slip-shod memo on one particular day. The story gets much worse. Attorney Temple wrote her incredibly unhelpful memo on October 12th. A few days earlier, Arthur Andersen hired the well respected firm of Davis, Polk & Wardwell to advise it on Enron-related matters. Now, according to the testimony of Mr. Andrews, a senior partner at Arthur Andersen, while Davis Polk was retained before the October 12th memo was written, it did not begin its work for Andersen until October 16th. No matter. Attorney Temple has testified that on Davis Polk's first day on the job, October 16th, she consulted with Davis Polk lawyers on "document retention and destruction." Thus, before the major shredding party at Andersen began, which was on or around October 23rd, Davis Polk was consulted on the steps Andersen was taking or not taking to see to it that documents were preserved.

Did Davis Polk advise Temple or anyone else at Arthur Andersen to clarify Temple's October 12th memo when she talked to Davis Polk lawyers on October 16th?

Davis Polk was on the job about a week before the shredding extravaganza began. Why didn't it take steps to see to it that Andersen's notes, drafts and e-mails on Enron were preserved? We don't know what, if anything, Davis Polk did advise because Arthur Andersen seems to be relying on attorney-client privilege when it comes to what Davis Polk said, but we do know that the Temple memo was not withdrawn and the Andersen retention/destruction policy was not clarified in the first week of Davis Polk's involvement in this case or the second week or the third.

Before October 22nd, Arthur Andersen's lawyers should have done something to make it clear to Andersen partners and staff that the Enron files were to be preserved. The preservation of those Enron documents was necessary to protect Andersen's legal interests as well as its future viability as a respected accounting firm. First, how is Andersen to demonstrate its innocence, assuming it is innocent, when its files are not intact. Second, assuming someone at Andersen did something wrong on the Enron account, how is Andersen to convince people that it has gotten to the bottom of the problem and made all necessary changes when its files are incomplete? Third, if your client destroys documents when it is reasonably foreseeable that it will be sued and the documents will be relevant to that suit, a judge can instruct the jury to assume that the destroyed evidence would have shown your client's guilt. And that is the least of the legal troubles that the destruction of these documents might bring.

On October 22nd, Enron disclosed that the SEC had opened an inquiry into the company's financial dealings, particularly the strange partnership transactions and Enron's fuzzy disclosures on those deals. As with most legal matters, there is some uncertainty on precisely how formal an investigation by a government agency must be before destroying documents might qualify as obstruction of justice. But there is precedent that holds that some, if not all, preliminary inquiries by the SEC qualify. Even more ominous, another section of the obstruction statute, 18 U.S.C. Section 1512, provides, a person may be fined or imprisoned for "knowingly . . . engaging in misleading conduct toward another person, with intent to cause or induce any person to (A) . . . withhold a record, document, or other object, from an official proceeding; (or) (B) alter, destroy, mutilate, or conceal an object with intent to impair the object's integrity or availability for use in an official proceeding." Under section 1512, the proceeding need not be pending at the time of the offense, so some of the questions presented by section 1505 do not arise.

Presumably, Arthur Andersen had no interest in being accused of obstructing justice, even if it could ultimately establish its innocence because the government could not quite prove that it had the requisite corrupt intent, because some court held that the SEC's inquiry of Enron was not formal enough to constitute "a proceeding" under the obstruction statute, or because the elements of 18 U.S.C. Section 1512 were not precisely met. Given that Andersen's very survival might be threatened, if it managed to convey that as Enron started coming apart, Andersen was busy flirting with violations of the criminal code, Andersen's lawyers should have done everything possible to clarify the Temple memo and Andersen's poorly written policy — at the latest — immediately after they became aware that an informal SEC inquiry of Enron was underway. They didn't.

On October 25, Enron, getting good legal advice — at least at this point — sent e-mails to its employees worldwide and to its auditors at Andersen, directing everyone to preserve all Enron documents. Andersen's lawyers take no action to rescind the Temple memo or to clarify the policy to which the memo refers. A few more days go by, and on October 31, Enron announces that the SEC investigation has been upgraded to "formal." Now any doubt about the potential applicability of Section 1505 should have been removed. Still Andersen's lawyers did nothing. Even assuming that they somehow imagined that Temple's memo and Andersen's nonrobust, poorly written retention policy were adequate to convey the "don't destroy documents" advice that they should have been giving, why weren't Andersen's lawyers checking to see what procedures Andersen was following to ensure that Temple's supposed directive was being followed by Andersen's Enron team?

Finally, Andersen receives its own subpoena from the SEC. That happened, I believe, on November 8th. The next day Attorney Temple calls Duncan, the head of Andersen's Enron team, and leaves him a message to preserve all documents. Apparently, that message managed to convey what Temple's October 12th e-mail and Andersen's woefully inadequate retention/destruction policy could not. Duncan's assistant now sends out an e-mail to those shredding Enron documents and tells them to stop. That e-mail went out the same day Temple left her voice message for Duncan with its clear legal advice. The following day, November 10th,

Attorney Temple sends an e-mail memo to the personnel at Andersen, which said in part, according to press reports:

> One of the first things we must do in preparing to respond to this subpoena and the lawsuits is to take all necessary steps to preserve all the documents and other materials that we may have relating to the claims that are being filed. . . .
>
> To do this we must first insure (sic) that all documents and materials already in existence are preserved and that nothing is done to destroy or discard any documents or materials now in your possession.

What took her so long? And why didn't Davis Polk, Andersen's outside counsel, do any better than Attorney Temple and the rest of Andersen's in-house legal team managed to do?

Most troubling, how is it possible that Davis Polk has agreed to conduct an investigation for Arthur Andersen to discover how so much shredding could have gone on at Arthur Andersen between October 23rd and November 9th? That shredding occurred on Davis Polk's watch. Who is going to find out why Arthur Andersen's outside counsel, Davis Polk, did not properly protect its client and Enron's documents? Davis Polk? One of the first questions Andersen needs to ask in its internal investigation is: where were the lawyers? The lawyers who were out to lunch at the critical time should not be the ones Andersen or the rest of us should be depending on to explain what went wrong. It's that simple. . . .

The Verdict

On June 15, 2002, on the tenth day of deliberation, and after having told the judge that it was deadlocked, the jury in the Andersen criminal trial convicted it of obstruction of justice. In a special verdict, the jury identified Nancy Temple as the only "corrupt persuader" at Andersen. Recall that under §1512(b)(2), it is a crime to "corruptly" persuade another to destroy or alter documents to keep them from a foreseeable official proceeding. But it wasn't, as the government claimed, the Temple e-mail of October 12, 2001, that four jurors later cited as the basis for the jury's conclusion. Rather, it was a different e-mail, which had received almost no attention from the trial lawyers or the press. In her e-mail of October 16, 2001, set out in the timeline above, Temple "suggested" that David Duncan delete "some language" from a draft of a file memorandum. Duncan had shown Temple and others the memorandum "for your comments." In the draft, Duncan recounted a conversation he had had with an Enron officer with regard to a planned Enron press release. Temple suggested deleting language "that might suggest we have concluded the release is misleading." Despite Temple's suggestion, Duncan kept a copy of the original of the memorandum, which Andersen later gave to the government in an effort to cooperate in the investigation.

The *Wall Street Journal* on June 17, 2002 reported:

> The Upshot: What began as an indictment for massive illegal document destruction by [Enron's] accountants ended with a finding [four jurors said] of a lone instance of attempted illegal document alteration by a newly hired Andersen lawyer. The jurors unanimously agreed Ms. Temple had acted as a corrupt persuader.

And one juror told the *New York Times* (June 17, 2002):

> "Nancy Temple was found guilty of altering one document. . . . One person did one thing and tore the whole company down."

Questions

1. Pause for a moment to appreciate the irony of this narrative. Nancy Temple gave her client Arthur Andersen (via partner David Duncan) legal advice in reply to Duncan's request. The advice may have been good advice or bad advice, but the jury found that by virtue of giving that advice she was attempting "corruptly" to persuade Duncan to destroy a document relevant to a forthcoming SEC investigation, namely his draft memo. As a result, the client, the recipient of the advice, has now been found guilty of obstruction of justice because it is vicariously responsible for the conduct of its lawyer-employee Nancy Temple. Reread §1515(c), which applies to §1512. It creates a "safe harbor" for lawyers giving "bona fide" legal advice. Why didn't Temple and her client enjoy this protection? Of course, in order to get the benefit of the "safe harbor," defense counsel would have had to raise the issue, but the burden of disproving the defense beyond a reasonable doubt would then have fallen to the government. See United States v. Kloess, 251 F.3d 941 (11th Cir. 2001). We can only guess why §1515(c) was not a centerpiece at trial, at least to the extent that Temple was alleged to be a "corrupt persuader." Whether four juror's post-trial revelations of Temple's e-mail of October 16 as the sole basis for its verdict can help Andersen win a new trial or appeal is yet to be seen, as of this writing.
2. Temple's October 16, 2001, e-mail to Duncan did not only recommend deleting "some language that might suggest we have concluded the release is misleading." It also recommended deleting reference to consultation with the legal group and "deleting my name on the memo." Temple said that reference to the legal group could operate as "a waiver of attorney-client privileged advice and if my name is mentioned it increases the chances that

I might be a witness, which I prefer to avoid." So, literally, here is a second way in which Temple advised Duncan to alter a document. Temple's stated reasons for removing her name and any mention of the legal group are perfectly plausible, aren't they? It's her job to protect the privilege and lawyers generally wish to avoid finding themselves in the role of witness, especially as that may limit their work as lawyers. See Rule 3.7. In her congressional testimony, Temple responded to a question about deletion of her name as follows: "It is our standard practice in the legal group to advise the engagement team not to write down and discuss in their memos legal advice that the legal group might give, because it might be a waiver down the road of attorney-client privilege." Could it be, however, that these otherwise sensible recommendations turned Temple into a "corrupt persuader" and vicariously incriminated her client?

3. Would Andersen, Temple's client, have been vicariously responsible for Temple's conduct if she were an outside lawyer and not a member of its in-house legal department? It would seem that Andersen's vicarious liability depended on Temple's status as an employee. What effect, if any, might this have on a corporate client's decision about whom to retain in particular circumstances?
4. What about Professor Koniak's criticism of Davis Polk? Documents were destroyed on its "watch," she told the Senate Committee. Is her criticism valid? Should Davis Polk have taken steps as soon as it began work on October 16 to warn its client not to destroy documents and to make certain that word went out giving that clear instruction to all Andersen personnel? How do we know — how does Professor Koniak know — it didn't? Confidentiality rules prevent the law firm from responding to Professor Koniak's criticism. In other words, it cannot defend itself. Under those circumstances, was Professor Koniak's testimony fair? A generally favorable profile of Professor Koniak in the *Wall Street Journal* reported on a subsequent phone conversation she had with Michael Carroll, a Davis Polk partner. Ms. Koniak had called Mr. Carroll to discuss a law review article she planned to write based on her testimony.

> Mr. Carroll told her that her comments were "reckless," that she didn't know what had actually happened, and that she was "clearly in the pocket of the plaintiffs' bar," Ms. Koniak recalls. . . . "During our conversation, Ms. Koniak admitted that she didn't have the facts and that she doesn't think that other law firms would have acted any differently," says Mr. Carroll, who added that the conversation ended cordially. Ms. Koniak says she has enough facts about Davis Polk "to draw the conclusion I have drawn and which I stand by."

Michael Orey, *Launching Broadsides at the Bar, Wall Street Journal,* May 8, 2002. What "facts" does Ms. Koniak have, and do they justify her public accusation?

5. Reread Nancy Temple's colloquy with Representative Markey (at 10/21/01 on the timeline). Did Ms. Temple have to wait to be "asked" her opinion on document shredding or should she have volunteered it when she sent her e-mail of October 12 to "remind" Andersen personnel of the firm's document retention policy?
6. How should a lawyer instruct a corporate client when the lawyer can anticipate a *possible* official proceeding some way off, but which may never come? Meanwhile, the client, for legitimate business reasons, wishes to continue an otherwise unobjectionable document destruction policy. How foreseeable does the proceeding have to be for §1512 to apply? Since we know that a criminal indictment, even one the client may beat, can be devastating (Andersen would not likely have recovered even if it had been acquitted), a cautious lawyer is going to be inclined to advise suspension of a document destruction policy if an investigation into possible wrongdoing is even distantly possible. Is this sound policy?